Classical Music
A CHRONOLOGY

Classical Music
A CHRONOLOGY

Jon Paxman

with contributions by
Terry Barfoot • Katy Hamilton
Thomas Lydon • Robert Rawson

OVERLOOK OMNIBUS

This edition published by Omnibus Press and distributed in the United States and Canada by The Overlook Press, Peter Mayer Publishers Inc, 141 Wooster Street, New York, NY 10012.

For bulk and special sales requests, please contact sales@overlookny.com or write to us at the above address.

Copyright © 2015 Omnibus Press (A Division of Music Sales Limited) 14/15 Berners Street, London, W1T 3LJ, UK.

Cover and book designed by Chloë Alexander Design. Project managed and edited by Sam Lung. Copy edited by Andrew Paxman and Ann Barkway. Indexed by Paula Clerk & Peter Nickol. Picture research by Jon Paxman and Sarah Datblygu.

ISBN 978-1-4683-1272-0.

Every effort has been made to trace the copyright holders of the photographs in this book but one or two were unreachable. We would be grateful if the photographers concerned would contact us.

Printed in China.

A catalogue record for this book is available from the British Library.

Cataloguing-in-Publication data is available from the Library of Congress.

Visit Omnibus Press on the web at www.omnibuspress.com

Page 2
Guitar and Violin
Pablo Picasso *c.*1912
© Succession Picasso/DACS, London 2013.

Picture agencies and lenders
For full list see page 704

Anatoly Sapronenkovp
Archives Charmet
Alfredo Dagli Orti/Art Resource, NY
Adoc-photos/Art Resource, NY
Bridgeman-Giraudon/Art Resource, NY
Digital Image © The Museum of
    Modern Art/Licensed by Scala/
    Art Resource, NY
Erich Lessing/Art Resource, NY
The Pierpont Morgan Library/Art Resource, NY
RMN-Grand Palais/Art Resource, NY
Nicolas Sapieha/Art Resource, NY
Scala/Art Resource, NY
Scala/White Images/Art Resource, NY
Snark/Art Resource, NY
Tate, London/Art Resource, NY
The Trustees of the British Museum/
    Art Resource, NY
VEGAP/Art Resource, NY
The Bridgeman Art Library
Private Collection/The Bridgeman
    Art Library
British Library Board
Gaudenzio Ferrari
Corbis
Alfredo Dagli Orti/The Art Archive/Corbis
Bettmann/Corbis
Burstein Collection/Corbis
The Gallery Collection/Corbis
Hulton-Deutsch Collection/Corbis
Margaretta Mitchell
Columbia University Computer Music
    Centre
Royal Swedish Opera
Getty Images
AFP/Getty Images
De Agostini/Getty Images
Hulton Collection/Getty Images
Popperfoto/Getty Images
Roger Viollet/Getty Images
Time & Life Pictures/Getty Images
Imagno
Jon Paxman Collection
© Kristy Komuso
Lebrecht Music & Arts
Lebrecht Music & Arts Photo Library
Lebrecht Authors
Lebrecht/ColouriserAL
Lebrecht
A. Koch Interfoto/Lebrecht Music & Arts
Alinari/Lebrecht
Andrea Felvégi/Lebrecht Music & Arts
Artcolor Interfoto/Lebrecht Music & Arts
Arthur Reynolds Collection/
    Lebrecht Music & Arts
B. Rafferty/Lebrecht Music & Arts
Betty Freeman/Lebrecht Music & Arts
Bildarchiv Hansmann Interfoto/
    Lebrecht Music & Arts
Brian Morris/Lebrecht Music & Arts
Costa Leemage/Lebrecht Music & Arts
culture-images/Lebrecht

culture-images/ua/Lebrecht
D. Bayes/Lebrecht Music & Arts
© Decca/Lebrecht
Derek Bayes/Lebrecht Music & Arts
Electa/Leemage/Lebrecht
EM Rydberg/Lebrecht Music & Arts
Guy Vivien/Lebrecht Music & Arts
Haga Library/Lebrecht Music & Arts
Horst Tappe/Lebrecht Music & Arts
IMAGNO/Lebrecht
Interfoto/Lebrecht Music & Arts JazzSign/
    Lebrecht
Kaplan Foundation Collection/NY/
    Lebrecht
Kurt Weill Foundation/Lebrecht Music
    & Arts
Laurie Lewis/Lebrecht Music & Arts
L. Birnbaum/Lebrecht Music & Arts
Lebrecht Authors Leemage/Lebrecht
Leemage/Lebrecht Music & Arts
Mirrorpix/Lebrecht Authors
MP Leemage/Lebrecht Music & Arts
Neil Libbert/Lebrecht Music & Arts
Photofest/Lebrecht Music & Arts
Private Collection/Lebrecht Music & Arts
RA/Lebrecht
RA/Lebrecht Music & Arts
Ravenna Leemage/Lebrecht Music & Arts
RIA Novosti/Lebrecht Music & Arts
Richard H. Smith/Lebrecht Music & Arts
Richard Haughton/Lebrecht Music & Arts
Royal Academy of Music/Lebrecht Music
    & Arts
Royal Academy of Music Coll/Lebrecht
Sueddeutsche Zeitung Photo/Lebrecht
Suzie Maeder/Lebrecht Music & Arts
TAL RA/Lebrecht Music & Arts
Tallandier RA/Lebrecht Music & Arts
www.lebrecht.co.uk
Mary Evans Picture Library
Mary Evans Picture Library/
    Alexander Meledin
Mary Evans/Iberfoto
Mary Evans Picture Library/Imagno
Mary Evans/Interfoto
Mary Evans Picture Library/
    Interfoto Agentur
Interfoto/Sammlung Rauch/
    Mary Evans
Modena, Biblioteca Estense, CGA2,
    Carta del Cantino
National Portrait Gallery, London
Public Domain
Redferns
Henry Salazar, LA County
Schott Music GmbH & Co. KG
Scott E. Barbour
© Sikorski Musikverlage
© Steve Morgan
SuperStock
© Universal
© Weonki Kim

Author's acknowledgements

There are many individuals who contributed in some way to the creation of this book, but particular thanks go to members of my family for their enduring support, especially to my brother, Dr Andrew Paxman, for his textual amendments and advice on style. Also my immense gratitude goes to those who have given crucial guidance over the content of this book, notably Terry Barfoot, Dr H. Lynn Raley and Dr Paul Archbold. And huge thanks are also due to my learned collaborators: Terry Barfoot, Dr Katy Hamilton, Thomas Lydon and Dr Robert Rawson.

Thanks are also due to the libraries, venues and publishers that have supplied material to assist with this book's musical chronology, and above all to the immensely helpful staff at Westminster Music Library. The world events timeline included in this book owes a debt to David Lambert, Maurice Chandler and Bernard Moore, whose entries for *The Book of Key Facts* have been reproduced here in abridged form. Thanks also go to Eleonore Paxman and Emmanuel Souvairan for their assistance in preparing the updated timeline. And finally, special thanks go to my late mother, Mrs Jo Pratt, who more than anyone encouraged my love of classical music.

Contributing authors

Dr Robert Rawson	Chapter 3
Terry Barfoot	Chapter 4; Chapter 5 with Jon Paxman
Dr Katy Hamilton	Chapter 6 with Jon Paxman
Thomas Lydon	Chapter 7 with Jon Paxman

Contributed material edited by Jon Paxman and Terry Barfoot.

I hope the contributors will not be displeased with the editorial changes that have been made to their chapters for purposes of consistency. The reader should assume any mistakes therein to be of my own error.

Jon Paxman

Contents

Chapter 1

1600–1649 47

Period including Byrd, G. Caccini, G. Gabrielli, Philips, Peri, Sweelinck, Bull, Dowland, Hassler, Lobo, Monteverdi, S. Rossi, Praetorius, Wilbye, Romero, Weelkes, Frescobaldi, Gibbons, Schütz, Schein, Grandi, F. Caccini, Scheidt, L. Rossi, Chambonnières, Marini, Cavalli, Carissimi

Chapter 2

1650–1699 105

Period including Schütz, Cavalli, Carissimi, Mont, Hammerschmidt, Froberger, Strozzi, Schmelzer, Locke, Cesti, L. Couperin, Legrenzi, Pallavicino, Lully, Nivers, Buxtehude, Stradella, Charpentier, Biber, Blow, Corelli, Muffat, Pachelbel, Marais, Torelli, Purcell, Kuhnau, A. Scarlatti, Campra

Chapter 3
1700–1749

Period including Corelli, Torelli, Fux, Kuhnau, A. Scarlatti, Campra, F. Couperin, Bononcini, Albinoni, Keiser, Vivaldi, Zelenka, Telemann, Rameau, Handel, J. S. Bach, D. Scarlatti, Tartini, Vinci, Quantz, Hasse, Sammartini, Leclair, Graun, Galuppi, Pergolesi, Stanley, C. P. E. Bach, Stamitz

Chapter 4
1750–1799

Period including Rameau, Hasse, Sammartini, Galuppi, Boyce, Stanley, Rousseau, C. P. E. Bach, Jommelli, Gluck, Wagenseil, Stamitz, Piccinni, Soler, Haydn, Cannabich, Gossec, J. C. Bach, Paisiello, Grétry, Boccherini, Cimarosa, Salieri, Clementi, Mozart, Dussek, Cherubini, Beethoven

Contents

Chapter 7

1900–1949 ₄₉₃

Period including Janáček, Elgar, Puccini, Mahler, Debussy, R. Strauss, Nielsen, Sibelius, Satie, Vaughan Williams, Rachmaninov, Ives, Schoenberg, Ravel, Falla, Bartók, Stravinsky, Webern, Varèse, Berg, Villa-Lobos, Prokofiev, Hindemith, Gershwin, Poulenc, Copland, Shostakovich, Messiaen, Britten

Chapter 8

1950–2000 ₅₉₅

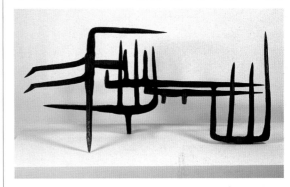

Period including Tippett, Shostakovich, Messiaen, Menotti, Cage, Lutosławski, Britten, Ginastera, Bernstein, Xenakis, Ligeti, Nono, Berio, Boulez, Henze, Stockhausen, Takemitsu, Gubaidulina, Penderecki, Maxwell Davies, Schnittke, Pärt, Reich, Glass, Zwilich, Tavener, Adams, Rihm, Saariaho

Preface

THIS REFERENCE book charts four centuries of Western classical music in two complementary formats. The chapters, extending from the Baroque era through to the end of the 20th century, examine musical developments mainly from the viewpoints of style, genre and location. The chronology, 1600–2000, summarises information relating to composers, patrons, publishers, impresarios, conductors and performers. Births, deaths, compositions, performances and many biographical highs and lows are included to give the reader a varied summary of what happened when. The primary emphasis is on new music and those involved in its first performance.

Names in the chronology cited in bold indicate musical figures and librettists alive at the time. Other references to such persons, as well as references to other creative artists and historical figures, are cited in normal type. Unfortunately restrictions of space have not allowed mention of some very worthy musical figures and compositions. Further, there is a bias towards the older, more established composers of recent times, since few are now able to make a profound impression on the international scene early on in their career, for a variety of cultural reasons.

If there is an unconventional aspect to this book, it is the chapter-by-chapter presentation of music in 50-year periods. This is not to suggest that cultural movements take cue points from round numbers. The various stylistic epochs are of course examined—Baroque, Classical, Romantic, and the multi-faceted 20th century—but the format serves to set music in its own time and place. This assists historical cross-referencing (tying in with the chronology) and emphasises the fact that composers themselves operate first and foremost in the day-to-day of their artistic, social, economic and political environment.

There is much within the following pages to appeal to the music student; but while the chapters occasionally explore technical aspects of music, this book is intended to appeal to the non-specialist, from the classical music newcomer to the lifelong enthusiast.

Jon Paxman

◀ *The Lute Player*
by Caravaggio

...NUSSTANSINMONTESION ETCUEOCENTUT QUATTUOR MILIA HABE...
CITHARAS

HISECUNTUR AGNU...

Medieval and Renaissance music

WE KNOW that Europeans were blowing into bone flutes 35,000 years ago, that Egyptians plucked harps 5,000 years ago, and that ensembles performed biblical psalms 3,000 years ago, but we can only imagine how this music sounded. Those were the days when music was either memorised or improvised, and so it essentially remained throughout the first millennium A.D. The subsequent development of notation transformed the West's approach to music. Committing notes to paper enabled composers to unlock music's structural, polyphonic and rhythmic potential, stimulating innovation and diverse creativity in response to cultural change.

◀ *The Lamb of Mt Zion and the Chaste* (Spain *c.*950), from the *Commentary on the Apocalypse* by Beatus de Liébana. The featured instrument is a type of lute, a close relation of the Middle Eastern *oud*.

Medieval era

In its broadest definition, the term 'medieval', from the Latin expression for 'middle-age', refers to a period that begins with the decline of the Roman Empire in the fifth century and ends with the rise of humanism in the 14th and 15th centuries. During the first millennium A.D., south-eastern Europe remained largely under Byzantine rule. Goths, Moors and Vikings fought for new dominions, but it was the Franks who made the greatest territorial gains, spreading out from north German lands to occupy most of central and western Europe. Charlemagne brought increased unity to the Frankish empire by forging close political ties with Rome. Crowned Emperor of the Romans in the year 800, he paved the way for the Holy Roman Empire, established in 962.

Religious differences brought about the Great Schism of 1054, with the subsequent formation of the Roman Catholic and Eastern Orthodox churches. Some 40 years later the West launched the First Crusade, beginning two centuries of sporadic and often brutal military campaigns in the Middle East. Shameful episodes in the history of Christianity, they nonetheless opened up trade routes and opportunities for scientific learning from which Europe profited enormously. During the 14th century, power struggles between contenders for the French and English thrones ignited the 'Hundred Years' War', terminating three centuries of close political ties between the two countries. The Black Death, rampant during the years 1348–50, took tens of millions of lives.

▼ Charlemagne, or Charles the Great. He was crowned Holy Roman Emperor by Pope Leo III in A.D. 800.

The high medieval era was not all terror and torment. In Western Europe it witnessed the demise of the feudal system and the rise of a social group of artisans and tradesmen, the beginnings of a 'middle class', who formed guilds to protect their business interests. One such group, the stonemasons, were the decisive workforce behind the magnificent Gothic cathedrals that began to dominate city skylines at this time. Centres of learning gradually shifted from monasteries to universities (formed by scholastic guilds), with Bologna, Salamanca, Paris, Oxford and Cambridge among the first established. Foundation texts of Western literature appeared: *The Song of Roland* (France, 1100s), *The Poem of the Cid* (Spain, *c.*1200), Dante's *Divine Comedy* (Italy, early 1300s) and Chaucer's *Canterbury Tales* (England, late 1300s). And it is during this remarkable cultural epoch that we find the earliest documented foundations of Western classical music. Notation and polyphony count as the most significant musical inventions of all time. Major compositional forms evolved, including the polyphonic mass, motet and *chanson*, and the professional composer was born.

Christian chant: from monody to polyphony

Christian chant is Europe's earliest well-documented musical tradition, but its origins are obscure. There is no reference to chant as such in the New Testament, but we know from St Paul's letter to the Ephesians that first-century Christians sang 'psalms, hymns and spiritual songs'. Most likely evolving from earlier Jewish practices, chant became central to Christian worship as a method of declaiming sacred text, such as biblical passages, the mass liturgy and prayers. It was monophonic, consisting of just one melodic part, and was flowing in movement and unmeasured in rhythm. As Christianity spread far and wide over the early centuries A.D., liturgical practice and chant styles diversified. Emperor Charlemagne (*c.*742–814) attempted to bring unity to the Church and centralise its power by enforcing the Roman liturgy and with it a common form of chant attributed to, but probably not authored by, the venerated Pope Gregory I (540–604). Throughout Charlemagne's vast Frankish empire, 'Gregorian' chant, known also as 'plainsong', gradually supplanted all other forms of liturgical melody. Even Christian territories outside the empire, such as England and Spain, eventually succumbed to these influences.

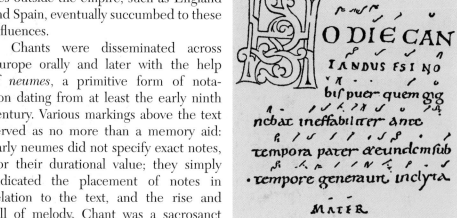

Chants were disseminated across Europe orally and later with the help of *neumes*, a primitive form of notation dating from at least the early ninth century. Various markings above the text served as no more than a memory aid: early neumes did not specify exact notes, nor their durational value; they simply indicated the placement of notes in relation to the text, and the rise and fall of melody. Chant was a sacrosanct

Neumes

▶ The neumatic notation of *Hodie Cantandus*, by the composer and monk Tutilo of St Gall (d.915).

tradition that was supposed to be accurately observed, but oral transmission and the limitations of early notation inevitably resulted in chant variants. Moreover, new chants emerged to meet increasing liturgical demands, be they additional portions of the mass, ceremonial practices like 'sequences', or new holy days and festivals.

German abbess, visionary, composer, writer and poet Hildegard of Bingen, inspired by the Holy Spirit. The monk depicted is Volmar, her spiritual advisor and secretary. Hildegard was widely respected and sought for her scholarship, wisdom and insight.

Pitch-accurate forms of notation using letters date back to the Roman philosopher Boethius (*c.*475–*c.*524), but the only place where one might find examples was in a musical treatise. Pitch-line notation appeared much later. One type was developed during the 11th century by the Italian monk Guido of Arezzo (*c.*991– after 1033), who codified a four-line staff with lines set at intervals of a third. Still employing neumatic notation, Guido colour-coded his staff lines to make his manuscripts easy to decipher. He also

Guido of Arezzo

invented solmisation for teaching and sight-singing purposes. His six-note (hexachord) sequence from C to A—ut, re, mi, fa, sol, la—was derived from the words of an old hymn to St John, *Ut queant laxis*. In a setting of this hymn (probably Guido's own), each line of text begins on the next note in the ascending scale, using the Latin words ut, resonare, mira, famuli, solve, labi. A seventh note, *si* (or *ti*), was added much later, inspired by the name 'Sancte Iohannes' (Saint John).

Guido's staff notation, matured over centuries, was to prove invaluable to the development of classical music, although his methods still lacked indications for note values and rhythms. Most music of his time was monophonic. This was still the case more than a century later when the German abbess Hildegard of Bingen (1098–1179) was writing her serene, mystical chants. Hildegard departed from the Gregorian tradition in setting her own vision-inspired verse. Wide in vocal range but narrow in melodic form, some 70 chants are found in her compilation *Symphonia armonie celestium revelationum* (Symphony of the harmony of heavenly revelations). Hildegard is also remembered for writing the earliest surviving 'morality play' with music, *Ordo virtutum* (The Play of the Virtues), a type of liturgical drama in which the Devil battles with the Virtues to possess a female soul.

Hildegard of Bingen

Harmonised chant may have originated in France, with some of the earliest evidence provided by the ninth-century *Musica enchiriadis* (Music Manual). Termed *organum*, the method was first restricted to parallel harmonies beneath the chant, either in fourths or fifths, or in some improvised combination of the two, and incorporating doublings at the octave and unison. Notated music of two independent parts began to appear around the 11th century. The music of the *Winchester*

Organum

Prologue

Troper (*c*.1050) is difficult to decipher accurately, but it gives evidence of some of the earliest two-part *polyphonic* writing, with parts variously moving in parallel, oblique and contrary motion.

St Martial Another major early source of harmonised chant appears in a collection of 12th-century Aquitanian manuscripts, originally assembled at St Martial in Limoges. The music is transcribed in advanced neumatic notation and includes Gregorian chant and new liturgical melodies, as well as note-against-note, or 'discant', organum. Of special interest is the appearance of a florid style of organum, although the practice itself may have been long established. Here the original chant is sung in long note values by the *tenor* (from the Latin *tenere*, to hold), while an added upper voice sings long sequences of notes, or *melismas*, against it. The chant is therefore employed as a *cantus firmus*, a fixed melody around which faster moving parts may be added. The chant text would often be obscured within this process.

The music of St Martial highlights the long-running tension between sacred text and music: is it right to sacrifice textual clarity for musical enrichment, or should music always be the servant of the text? Long before the invention of polyphony, Saint Augustine (354–430) was wary of the diverting pleasures of music in church. He will have known well the Psalmist's exhortation 'Make a joyful noise unto God', and he considered music useful because 'by the delights of the ear the weaker minds may be stimulated into a devotional mood'. But, he admitted: 'when I happen to be more moved by the singing than by what is sung, I confess myself to have sinned criminally.' These issues were to preoccupy the Church for centuries.

The modes

Medieval chant was, by and large, composed using any one of eight modes. The modes were divided into two categories: four 'authentic' modes and four related 'plagal' modes. Example 1 shows Mode I, representing the authentic Dorian mode, beginning on the note of D; Mode II is its plagal version, the Hypodorian, which begins a fourth below, on A. In both of these scales the common root, the *finalis* (the concluding note), is D.

▶ **Example 1**

In theory (if not always in practice), authentic modes used pitches mainly above the *finalis*, while the plagal modes concentrated their range below as well as above the *finalis*. But modes were primarily distinguished by their unique sequence of tones and semitones. The various modes may be easily appreciated in correspondence to the white notes of the keyboard, ascending stepwise from D (Dorian), E (Phrygian), F (Lydian) and G (Mixolydian), with their plagals (*hypo-*) beginning a fourth below.

One more defining feature of the mode was its *tenor*, a recurrent tone that featured in the recitation of prayers and scripture. In the authentic modes this was the dominant note (A in the Dorian), while in the plagal modes it was the third above the *finalis* (F in the Hypodorian).

The Notre Dame School

From the middle of the 12th century the polyphonic style experienced major developments in France. This activity was centred on Paris, the cultural capital of Europe, and owed much of its success to two of the earliest known church composers: Léonin, working during the latter half of the 1100s, and his successor, Pérotin. Their music is associated with the cathedral of Notre Dame, which remained under construction during their lifetimes. The building's vast acoustic space was conducive to the emergent polyphonic forms. While it was difficult to project the spoken word clearly, texts intoned and chanted resonated between the stone walls and up to the high vaulted ceilings, mingling with incense to the glory of God and edifying the spirits of the entire congregation. (This was a time, after all, when music was considered interconnected with the harmony of the spheres, *musica mundana*, and the harmony of body and soul, *musica humana*.) Such conditions seem to have encouraged composers to search out ever more elaborate ways to sing God's praises.

How much music Léonin wrote for the cathedral itself is not known, but at some point of his ecclesiastical career he may have become a canon there. His vital contribution was the collection *Magnus Liber Organi*, which reveals a new style of responsorial chant for the entire church year. These are constructed with monophonic choral sections and two-part polyphonic sections for soloists. The soloists retain the choral chant line in the tenor, while the upper part, the *duplum*, typically features florid, textless organum. Pérotin revised the *Magnus Liber*, and since no original manuscripts survive, the exact extent of Léonin's work is unclear. It seems that Pérotin rewrote much of Léonin's organa in discant, note-against-note, a favourite style of

his time. But there are more important trends that emerge though the work of Pérotin and his contemporaries. The first is a preoccupation with *conductus*, a non-liturgical, processional piece sung in discant style, featuring a newly-composed tenor and typically structured in strophic verse form (with the same music to each verse). A second, crucial development was the expansion of two-part polyphony to three parts, and very occasionally four, as in Pérotin's lavish gradual *Viderunt omnes*. And for the first time, music was being written with a limited but clear indication of rhythm. Composers recognised six 'rhythmic modes', derived from the rhythms of poetic feet, the *iamb*, the *trochee*, and so on.

Léonin, Pérotin

Magnus Liber Organi

Conductus

◀ Franconian notation from a 14th-century Antiphonary.

Prologue

On the page these rhythms were indicated by note groupings called *ligatures*. At first there were just two note types: a long note, 'Long', and a short note, 'Breve'. Composers could employ different rhythmic modes in succession, and allocate different modes to separate melodic lines to add greater variety to the polyphonic texture.

Motet

From the Notre Dame School emerged the motet, which in time supplanted the conductus and evolved into one of the most important genres of Medieval and Renaissance music. The early polyphonic motet probably derived from the *clausula*, an interpolated polyphonic section in a setting of organum. The clausula featured a tenor *cantus firmus* and wordless upper parts. The motet introduced the radical idea of adding different texts to the upper parts—the *duplum* and the *triplum*. Thus the 'motet', from the French 'mot', meaning 'word', was conceived as a polytextual genre, even mixing sacred and secular texts in Latin and French. The compositional aim was to combine texts that would in some way complement one another. An added vernacular text, for example, may serve as a 'gloss' on the Latin text, elucidating something of its meaning. The end result was probably appreciated more by the performers than the listeners. The polytextual motet became largely secularised by the end of the 13th century, and was to remain popular in this form until the mid-15th century.

Franco of Cologne

The processes of motet composition presented new challenges for notation. With such differentiated parts, the motet required a rhythmic order that was beyond the limitations of the rhythmic modes. This problem was solved in part around the mid-13th century by the theorist Franco of Cologne. Building on the practice of rhythmic modes and ligature grouping, he assigned relative durations to different note shapes, inventing within this process a shorter note value than the 'breve', a diamond-shaped 'semibreve'. This new *mensural* notation, possibly developed in Paris, represented a giant leap for Western music. Franco codified the system in his *Ars cantus mensurabilis* (*c*.1280) and so laid the foundations of 'measured music'.

Secular music

Written forms of music were nearly all sacred until the 13th century, so our knowledge of earlier secular music derives largely from pictorial, historical and literary references. Secular vocal music prior to 1200 was essentially monophonic in style and performed by voice(s) alone, or with one or more instruments doubling the melody. Instrumental drones were used occasionally, while percussive accompaniment was common.

There were several categories of secular musician during the later Medieval period. Lowest ranking were the *jongleurs*, male and female street entertainers and strolling players who were equally adept at dancing and performing tricks as performing music.

▶ Heinrich von Meissen (d.1318), better known as 'Frauenlob' (praise of women), one of the last German *Minnesingers*. Deferential musicians perform with drum, cornett, shawm, fiddles, psaltery and bagpipe. Frauenlob is thought to have launched the era of the middle-class *Meistersingers* (Master singers), establishing the first guild in Mainz in 1311.

Some made music their speciality, as did the *minstrels*, who often found employment as house or court musicians. The jongleurs and minstrels sang in the vernacular, whereas the educated *goliards* sang in Latin. Goliards were mostly itinerant scholars and lower-order clerics, whose songs ranged from moral themes to satire, romance and bawdy subjects such as drinking and gambling. The bardic poet-singers probably represent another class altogether, since they championed epic poetry like the *chansons de geste*, dealing with heroic and historical subject matter. The musical element in these chansons seems to have been very simple and repetitive, purely an aid for drawing attention to dramatic points in the poems.

Jongleurs, minstrels, goliards

An elite class of poet-composer emerged in France around the 11th century: in the south, the *troubadours*, and not long after in the north, the slightly less refined *trouvères*. The German equivalent was the *Minnesinger*, appearing a century later. Troubadours sang of courtly love, whether fulfilled or unrequited, sometimes with satire and humour. Some troubadours were of noble birth, such as Guillaume IX, Duke of Aquitaine (1071–1126); but all, regardless of social rank, sang in the vernacular *langue d'oc*, or Provençal. Among the greatest of the troubadours was Bernart de Ventadorn (*c.*1130–*c.*1190), a musician of humble birth who served Eleanor of Aquitaine, later the wife of Henry II of England. Eighteen poems by Bernart survive with accompanying melodies. These include his Dorian-mode *Quan vei la lauzeta mover* (When I see the lark beat its wings), one of the most famous medieval melodies. A song of unrequited love, it is eight stanzas long, strophic in musical form, and corresponds to 6/8 metre, typical of (non-chant) music from this time. Performances will probably have varied widely in respect of tempo—as modern renditions do today—since that aspect was open to interpretation.

Troubadours, trouvères

Bernart de Ventadorn: *Quan vei la lauzeta mover*

The most historically important trouvère was Adam de la Halle, active during the second half of the 13th century. Besides monophonic chansons, he wrote several three-voice motets and *rondeaux*, some of the very first polyphonic secular music. In around 1283 Adam produced a pastoral play with music, *Le Jeu de Robin et de Marion*—those characters being a shepherd and shepherdess, not Robin Hood and Maid Marian of English folklore. Plays with music were commonly based on religious subjects and performed in chant styles in churches, in Latin, or in secular venues, in the vernacular. *Robin et Marion* contains 16 dance-songs and duets; it is a rare phènomenon, as no other secular drama from the period survives with anything like this amount of music intact. However, scholars consider much of the music to be traditional, rather than the work of Adam.

Adam de la Halle

While troubadours often sang unaccompanied, most trouvères, and certainly jongleurs and minstrels, seem to have accompanied themselves with harps and fiddles. Five-string fiddles and smaller three-string *rebecs* derived from Byzantine and Arabic instruments and were commonly played against the shoulder or chest, or held vertically. From the East also came the lute, directly related to the Arabic *oud*, and the double-reed *shawm*, a woodwind instrument of Greek-Arabic origin and a precursor of the oboe. Medieval instruments became categorised either as *haut* ('high' in volume), or *bas* ('low' in volume). In the first category were instruments such as

Medieval instruments

Prologue

drums, nasal winds and slide trumpets, popular for outdoor functions and festive music; in the second, recorders, and bowed and plucked strings.

Popular for their note-against-drone capabilities were the bagpipe and hurdy-gurdy, the latter even used in sacred music, functioning as a kind of organ. Until the 13th century the hurdy-gurdy was called an *organistrum* and was sufficiently large to require two performers to operate it. The pipe organ, Greek in origin and dating back to around the third century B.C., became associated with sacred ritual during the tenth century. Both small 'portative' organs and the larger 'positive' organs remained in secular use, though by around the 13th century the large organ had become exclusively a church instrument.

The Ars Nova

The 14th century was a tumultuous time for Europe. The Great Famine of 1315–17, caused by heavy rains and cold weather, blighted northern states and decimated communities. The 1340s saw the start of the Hundred Years' War between England and France, and 1348–50 brought the height of the Black Death. This calamitous sequence of events annihilated as much as half of Europe's population, and in turn fomented peasant unrest, with excessive taxation igniting mass uprisings. Many regarded society's woes as God's judgment on corruption within the Roman Church. A succession of French popes occupied a new papal seat in Avignon (south-eastern France) during the 14th century. In 1378 an unresolved contest for papal authority resulted in the simultaneous reign of popes, one in Rome, the other in Avignon. Confidence in the Church dropped to an all time low.

And yet this was a remarkable century for the arts. Dante, Petrarch, Boccaccio and Chaucer were all writing at this time. Giotto was creating some of the early Renaissance masterpieces, such as the frescos that adorn the Scrovegni Chapel in Padua. In the realm of music, the 14th century ushered in the *Ars Nova* (New Art), a term deriving from a treatise of the same name (*c.*1323) by the French composer, theorist, poet and bishop Philippe de Vitry (1291–1361). The Ars Nova represented a departure from the old musical art (*Ars Antiqua*) of the 13th century, since recent developments in notation, expounded in Vitry's treatise, had rapidly widened the scope of music. There were two key innovations: first, the creation of a smaller note value than the semibreve, the minim; second, the introduction of duple time. Previously, virtually all written music had corresponded to compound triple metres. Now with a wider array of note values and metrical rhythms, the substance of music changed dramatically.

Philippe de Vitry

Most of Vitry's music is lost or beyond positive identification. However, a manuscript *c.*1317 of the *Roman de Fauvel*, an allegorical, moralising poem by Gervès de Bus, includes as many as five polyphonic motets by Vitry among its 169 interpolated (mostly monophonic) pieces of music. These polytextual secular motets demonstrate the popular technique of *isorhythm*, a term meaning 'the same rhythm'. Isorhythmic motets featured repetitions of a rhythmic phrase, the *talea*, interlocking with a fixed series of melodic intervals, the *color*. By shifting the relative positions of rhythmic and melodic patterns, a composer could create unity and variety simultaneously. The technique was first applied to the tenor part, but then to the upper voices also. Various types of elaboration of this method (often based on strict mathematical proportions) resulted in polyphonic music of great complexity. The growing sophistication of the motet encouraged a similar trend in sacred music also, and it was not long before isorhythmic techniques could be found in movements of the mass.

The Church was troubled: was the composer-cleric the slave of his own ingenuity and vanity, rather than the servant of God? To writers such as Petrarch (Francesco Petrarca, 1304–74), there was no contradiction. A great admirer of Vitry, Petrarch encouraged manifestations of faith and secular learning, regarding their marriage as crucial to the betterment of man. Pope John XXII (r.1316–34), the second pope to reside at Avignon, was largely hostile to polyphony and attempted to restrict its use in church services. As a result, the most gifted composers of the age looked increasingly to secular opportunities. This state of affairs contributed to the dominance of secular music over sacred music in the 14th century.

Machaut to Dunstable

The French Ars Nova produced the most sophisticated music in Europe. It found its highest expression through Guillaume de Machaut (1300–77), a composer who in his own day was equally famed for his poetry. Machaut spent the early part of his career in the employ of Jean de Luxembourg, King of Bohemia, but he also took holy orders and eventually became a canon at Reims Cathedral. Machaut's church output is not extensive, but it includes the most renowned sacred work of the century, the *Messe de Notre Dame* (1360s), the earliest known polyphonic Mass Ordinary written by a single composer. Masses of this time were normally assembled with sections written by different, often anonymous, authors. Machaut enhanced the unity of the music of the mass by giving his movements greater consistency of mood and texture, and by incorporating isorhythmic techniques throughout. Cast in four parts, Machaut's *cantus firmus* mass is more expansive than the typical three-part settings of the period. It is perfectly possible that instruments may have doubled or even at times replaced some of the vocal parts.

Machaut's surviving music includes 23 motets and well over 100 chansons composed in the prevailing forms, namely the multiple-stanza *lai*, and three *formes fixes* (fixed-form refrain poetry): the *ballade, rondeau* and *virelai*. While the majority of his 19 *lais* and 33 *virelais* are monophonic (Machaut is regarded as the last great trouvère), his 42 ballades

Isorhythm

Fixed forms

Prologue

▶ Guillaume de Machaut, poet and leading composer of the Ars Nova.

and 22 rondeaux are mainly polyphonic. These display remarkably forward-looking construction, with a vocal melody supported by fully independent textless parts that can be rendered either by voices or instruments. His songs are preoccupied with courtly love and chivalry (typical themes of the age), but the text of his most famous rondeau, *Ma fin est mon commencement* (My end is my beginning), is simply designed to show off his own talent. Its music features an upper part (*triplum*) that corresponds to the middle part (*cantus*) in reverse, and a lower part whose second half corresponds to its first half read backwards. On one level the piece reflects the late medieval fascination with mathematical order, but it also brings to mind the later notion of the composer as an individual, creative artist.

The Ars Nova was slow to make its impact on Italy, where until the 14th century only monophony and improvised polyphony had been practised. Italian music, like French music of the 1300s, was predominantly secular. Francesco Landini (*c*.1325–97), composer, organist, singer, instrument builder and poet, was the towering figure of Italian music during the so-called 'Trecento' (14th century). He was also blind, having lost his sight in childhood as a result of smallpox. At the heart of his entirely secular surviving output are around 130 *ballatas*, written for either two or three voices. The genre derives from a monophonic dance-song (*ballare*, 'to dance'), which Landini transformed into an extremely mellifluous polyphonic refrain song. His two-voice *Abbonda di virtù* and *Ecco la primavera*, and the three-voice *Che cosa è questa, Amor* are just three among many delightful examples of the 14th-century ballata. Landini also wrote two- and three-part madrigals, which resemble the 16th-century variety only in their pastoral and amatory subject matter. Landini's ballatas and madrigals often follow the contemporary French chanson practice of including a textless part, suiting them to either vocal or vocal-instrumental combinations. We do not know for certain the extent of instrumental participation, but at this time and for many centuries to come, the voice was considered the supreme instrument. Standing out among Landini's successors, Johannes Ciconia (*c*.1370–1412) served as cantor at Padua Cathedral. He was a leading composer of sacred music and the first of many important Franco-Flemish émigrés to enrich musical life in Italy.

England boasted a strong and individual musical tradition, although there were no English composers of international standing before the 15th century. It is an intriguing fact, therefore, that the most well known piece of medieval music is both anonymous and English: the canon, or

Francesco Landini

'round', *Sumer is icumen in*, dating from around 1250. Remarkably, this is a secular piece of polyphonic music written for as many as six voices: two providing a repeated musical pattern (*pes*) alternating fifths and thirds, while four other voices each enter in turn, canonically. *Sumer* is unprecedented and no other six-part music appears for another two centuries. The harmonies and *pes* patterns of the piece are nonetheless characteristic of late medieval English music. The free use of thirds and sixths throughout is striking. Whereas French composers usually steered clear of consecutive thirds and sixths, considering them dissonances, the English clearly delighted in them.

Sumer is icumen in

The English fondness of triadic harmony is well illustrated by the music of the late-13th century 'Worcester fragments' and the early-15th century Old Hall manuscripts. To modern ears the recurrent sonorities of thirds and sixths give England's medieval music a particular warmth and strong tonal emphasis. These qualities merged with Ars Nova techniques in the music of the two leading English composers: Leonel Power (*c.*1380–1445) and John Dunstable (*c.*1390–1453).

John Dunstable

In the service of John of Lancaster, Duke of Bedford (1389–1435), Dunstable became known internationally. He very probably followed his employer to France in 1422 when the Duke, as Regent, presided over the English occupation during the Hundred Years' War. This would explain why more than half of Dunstable's surviving works derive from continental manuscripts. Dunstable was praised for his smooth part-writing, controlled and sparing use of dissonance, and sumptuous, full-bodied harmonies. His most famous piece is *Quam pulchra es* (How beautiful thou art), a three-part setting of text from the Song of Songs. It is a motet, but quite different from the French type, using only one text, delivered by the voices together in an expressive, homorhythmic, declamatory style.

Both Dunstable and Power were pioneers of the 'cyclic mass', their first examples appearing around the 1430s. The cyclic mass was unified through a single tenor cantus firmus, which provided the backbone of all movements of the Mass Ordinary. This formal device could appear in exact or modified form from one movement to the next. Some of the earliest cyclic masses have been attributed to both Dunstable and Power, since their authorship is uncertain. Power takes the credit for the earliest author-identified cyclic mass: *Alma redemptoris mater*. Dunstable, more than Power, was keen to combine the idioms of the Ars Nova with the English style, as demonstrated by a number of his isorhythmic, polytextual motets. So while England and France were in the throes of tearing apart their political union, a happy marriage of Anglo-French styles was beginning to shape Europe's musical future. It was from Dunstable that Guillaume Dufay (1397–1474) and Gilles Binchois (*c.*1400–60), the leading lights of the Burgundian School, took direct inspiration. And it is above all in the work of Dufay that Europe saw the musical dawn of the Renaissance era.

Cyclic mass

Prologue

The Renaissance

In the musical world the Renaissance began in the mid-15th century and persisted in various parts of Europe well into the 17th century. As a cultural movement characterised by the 'rebirth' of classical values, the Renaissance had its principal origins in the humanist convictions of Italian thinkers of the 14th century. The outstanding figure was the Tuscan scholar and poet Petrarch. Commonly referred to as 'the father of humanism', Petrarch believed that the study of antiquity and the Christian absorption of Greco-Roman ideals—such as secular wisdom, individualism and earthly ambition—would expedite cultural progress. His ideas gathered influential support at a time when confidence in the Roman Church was at a low ebb. It was also a time when commercial dealings with the near and far East were greatly profiting the fabric of European society.

A combination of humanistic zeal and favourable economic conditions seemed to unlock the medieval fetters binding man's potential. The Renaissance witnessed the Age of Exploration (1400s–1600s), the invention of perspective in art (*c.*1425), Gutenberg's printing press (*c.*1440), and the classically-inspired architecture of Filippo Brunelleschi and Michelangelo. It also ushered in the scientific age, with the empirical enquiry of Leonardo da Vinci and Copernicus following its course through Tycho Brahe, Galileo and Kepler. The Renaissance also brought the 'perfection' of the polyphonic technique and a strengthening union of words and music.

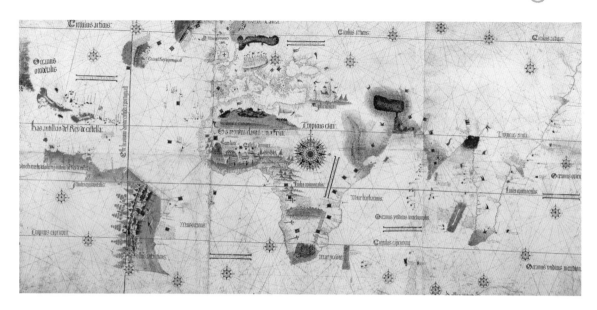

Franco-Flemish composers

'Although it seems beyond belief, there does not exist a single piece of music not composed within the last 40 years that is regarded by the learned as worth hearing.'

So wrote the Franco-Flemish composer-theorist Johannes Tinctoris (1430s–1511) in 1477. To his mind, good music began with John Dunstable (and the English School) and the Burgundian composers influenced by him, notably Dufay and Binchois. Tinctoris may have overstated the case, but a new era of music had certainly begun.

During the 15th century the court of Burgundy became the musical centre of Europe. The Burgundian lands at this time comprised territories from central-eastern France northwards to present-day Luxembourg, Belgium and Holland. Successive dukes of the House of Valois (1363–1482) patronised and fostered the gamut of artistic endeavour, their lavish pursuits financed by shrewd political manoeuvres, alliances and marriages. It was Philip the Good (r.1419–67) who handed Joan of Arc over to the English (specifically, the Duke of Bedford, patron of John Dunstable) for a massive ransom of 10,000 gold crowns in 1430. An alliance with Charles VII of France then brought more financial reward and territorial security. Philip the Good anticipated Italy's Lorenzo de Medici in his passionate enthusiasm for the arts. He commissioned portraits from Rogier van der Weyden and appointed Jan van Eyck as his official court painter. Early on in his reign he employed Gilles Binchois to enrich the court's religious and secular musical life, a role the composer fulfilled with mass movements and psalm settings, motets and graceful chansons. Binchois devoted nearly three decades of his professional life to the court—from the late 1420s to the early 1450s—creating a style characterised by melodious three-part settings with upper-voice dominance. His chief fame rests on an output of courtly love

Court of Burgundy

Binchois, Dufay

Prologue

▶ The Franco-Flemish composers Guillaume Dufay (left) and Gilles Binchois; the organ and harp identify them respectively as masters of sacred and secular music.

songs (set mainly in rondeau form), whose elegance and balance proved an inspiration to the next generation of Flemish composers.

Dufay, a canon at the cathedral of Cambrai, had intermittent affiliation with the Burgundian court. His education and career took him to southern France and northern Italy, with stints in the service of the duke of Savoy and as a member of the pope's chapel in Rome, Florence and Bologna. History grants Dufay the status of the leading composer of the age, since his musical expertise, progressivism and influence was so far-reaching. Dufay popularised the cyclic mass (Binchois wrote none), while at the same time promoting four-part harmony, a rarity in medieval music. He was also one of the first to employ a secular melody as the basis of a cantus firmus mass. His earliest example is the *Missa Se la face ay pale* (*c.*1450s), which draws its tenor line from one of his own *ballades*. This cantus firmus is quoted in various ways throughout the mass: in its original form, in longer or shorter note values, or in portions (using similar techniques to isorhythm). Dufay's most famous mass is *L'homme armé* (The Armed Man), if only because it was the first of many masses based on what was one of the most popular tunes of the day. His four-part masses display smooth polyphonic textures modelled on the rich, triadic part-writing of Dunstable, combined with Italianate melodic clarity. We also see in Dufay's masses a greater equality among the vocal parts, and just the first hints of imitative part writing, a predominant feature of 16th-century music.

The French composer Antoine Busnois (*c.*1430–92) followed Binchois in service to the Burgundian court during the reign of Charles the Bold, the last duke of Burgundy. Remembered chiefly for his chansons, Busnois may well have been a pupil of the Franco-Flemish composer Johannes Ockeghem (*c.*1420–97), who opted to spend most of his career in the service of French kings. Ockeghem's surviving oeuvre consists of some 40 compositions in the forms of the mass, motet and chanson. The mass had by now surpassed the motet as the most elevated, sophisticated genre, as we can see by the composer's *Missa prolationum*, which employs complex double canons throughout each of its movements. Renowned as a musical puzzle-master, Ockeghem wrote the earliest surviving polyphonic Requiem, as well as his own *Missa L'homme armé*. His vocal textures are more full-bodied than that of earlier music due to their widened range, with the bass voice descending as much as a fifth below the medieval standard of bass-clef C (the octave below middle C).

Continuing the imposing line of Franco-Flemish composers were Alexander Agricola (*c.*1445–1506), Henricus Isaac (1450s–1517) and Jacob

Johannes Ockeghem

Obrecht (*c.*1457–1505), the latter a leading composer of the cyclic mass. Both Agricola and Isaac worked for some time in Italy, as Dufay had done before them, taking full advantage of the region's dearth of home-grown musical giants. In Florence, Isaac wrote Italian songs for Lorenzo de' Medici (1449–92), whose circle included some of the supreme artists of the Renaissance, notably Botticelli, Leonardo da Vinci and the young Michelangelo. Later in the employ of Holy Roman Emperor Maximilian I, Isaac also wrote German *lieder*, French chansons, more than 30 masses, as well as 99 settings for the Proper of the Mass (Introit, Gradual, Alleluia, etc.), posthumously compiled in *Choralis Constantinus*.

Isaac at one time competed for a post at the Este court of Ferrara, but he was eclipsed by the formidable talent of Josquin des Prez (*c.*1450–1521). Born near Saint Quentin in the north-east of France, Josquin spent considerable time in Italy: in service to Cardinal Ascanio Sforza during the 1480s, then a six-year stint from 1489 as a member of the Papal choir in Rome, and a brief spell from 1503 as master of the chapel choir at the Ferrarese ducal court. He cut his incumbency short to flee an outbreak of plague, in 1504. (He was succeeded by Jacob Obrecht, who died of the plague the following year.) While recent scholarship has cast doubts on the extent of Josquin's legacy, he has retained his status as the most important and influential composer of his time. In an output dominated by four-part masses, sacred motets in two to six parts, and chansons, his genius is manifest in consummate part-writing and varied compositional techniques, but above all in the unprecedented expressive depth he achieves through a close correspondence of music and text.

Josquin brought together the most imaginative and progressive aspects of his craft in the sacred motet. An outstanding example is *Ave Maria … Virgo serena* (*c.*1480s), an early motet that in no small way inspired the compositional manners of the High Renaissance. Based on a plainchant tune, the music unfolds through an eloquent process of imitative part writing, with the original melody paraphrased and embellished with melismas. At certain points the texture switches to homophonic declamation in two or four parts. The first instance of such four-part declamation is harmonically static, emphasising the word 'solemn' in the phrase 'full of solemn joy'; when the stanza concludes 'fills all things in heaven and earth with renewed gladness', the music becomes syncopated and finally breaks into ornate melismas. Similar attention to textual detail prevails throughout the motet. This intimate union of poetry and music was an ancient, therefore humanist ideal. Josquin was not just developing the communicative, rhetorical power of music, he was reaching towards the kind of naturalistic expression governing the style of contemporary artists like Leonardo and Raphael.

When Josquin left Ferrara in 1504 he settled in Condé-sur-Escaut (a town on today's France-Belgium border), yet his stature in Italy only increased. Three years earlier in Venice, Ottaviano Petrucci had set up the world's first music printing business, which he launched with pieces by the most distinguished living composers. The very first masses out of Petrucci's shop were by Josquin, and the composer's *Ave Maria … Virgo serena* was placed as the opening work in the first publication of motets, issued in 1502.

Josquin des Prez

Ave Maria … Virgo serena

Prologue

Chansons and madrigals

Music printing expanded rapidly in the 1500s, aided by a marked growth in middle-class wealth and leisure time. Secular music, vocal and instrumental, profited enormously. Domestic music making became all the more popular as musical ability suggested superior breeding and a sound education. Song remained the most highly valued medium of secular music. William Byrd enforced this view in his *Psalmes, Sonets and Songs* of 1588: 'There is not any Musicke of instruments whatsoever, comparable to that which is made of the voyces of Men'.

With French widely spoken in western Europe, the chanson tradition remained fashionable and influential. During the early 1500s the genre was popularised in a four-part, through-composed form. It therefore abandoned the medieval fixed forms—the *ballade*, *rondeau* and *virelai*—which typically employed a lot of repetition in their musical schemes. While Josquin wrote in these older forms, most of his chansons are through-composed and based on popular tunes of the day. His borrowed material is paraphrased and embellished in a variety of ways (sometimes treated canonically), with free movement between imitation and chordal declamation, as appropriate to the text, much in the manner of his motets. Heart-rending themes of love are common, as in *La belle se siet*, where a fair maiden cries for her imprisoned and condemned beloved, and the five-part *Incessament mon povre cueur lamente*, in which a forlorn lover languishes close to death.

Franco-Flemish composers of the next generation, such as Nicolas Gombert (*c*.1495–*c*.1560) and Thomas Crecquillon (*c*.1510–57), continued the polyphonic chanson tradition, often favouring fairly dense, imitative textures. In Paris the chanson blossomed as a lighter, more rhythmic and homophonic genre. Rising urban prosperity and the appearance of Pierre Attaingnant's music printing business in the 1520s led to a 'Parisian chanson' boom. The leading composers in this field were Clément Janequin (*c*.1485–*c*.1560) and Claudin de Sermisy (*c*.1490–1562), and their favourite texts, by contemporary poets like Clément Marot, concerned love in all its serious and comical aspects. Sermisy was the most represented composer in Attaingnant's first songbook, the *Chansons nouvelles* of 1528. *Tant que vivray*, probably his most famous song, is characteristically short, simple and lyrical, while also being potently homorhythmic. Other songs, such as *Si j'ay eu du mal* and *Joyeulx adieu*, display more variation in their four-part textures, mixing homophony and polyphony, enlivened by melismatic flourishes. Janequin, author of more than 250 chansons, made his greatest impression with animated onomatopoeic works. Among these are *Le chant des oiseaux*, in which singers imitate bird calls, and the astonishing *La guerre*, featuring battle-sound vocal effects.

Josquin

Clément Janequin, Claudin de Sermisy

Prologue

During the second half of the 16th century diverse influences came to bear on the chanson, encouraging textural and rhythmic variety, increased part-writing and a far greater range of expression. These new aesthetic concerns owed much to the Italian madrigal style (see below and *Prelude*) as championed by the great Franco-Flemish composer Orlande de Lassus (*c.*1532–94), whose own chansons were published in Paris during the 1570s and 80s. Concurrently, and in contrast to the 'madrigalian' chanson, a new form of French verse based on the rules of ancient prosody encouraged syllabic and homorhythmic musical settings. This *musique mesurée* was intimately allied to poetic structures, though it was limited in expressive detail. Lassus contributed to the repertory, as did the French composer Claude Le Jeune (*c.*1528–1600), who set such poetry in the form of (predominantly) homophonic *airs*. Le Jeune also wrote polyphonic chansons, Italian *canzonettas* and *chansons spirituelles*, the latter a Protestant sub-species stimulated by France's Wars of Religion.

The 16th-century madrigal, as noted earlier, was effectively unrelated to the 14th-century strophic variety. With the first examples appearing during the 1520s, the madrigal supplanted the Italian *frottola*, whose soprano-dominated chordal style was unsuited to 'serious' poetry. The 14th-century verse of Petrarch had experienced a revival, and modern poets like Pietro Bembo (1470–1547) were now creating new verse inspired by the *Trecento* style. This weightier, more expressive medium invited a wide-ranging compositional manner, resulting in a frottola-chanson crossbreed that gained in complexity through increased part-writing, textural variety and chromaticism. The equal-voice madrigal became the pinnacle genre of Renaissance secular music. Often recounting the misfortunes of love, it was an entertainment enjoyed primarily by aristocracy and intellectuals.

The madrigal was advanced mainly by northern émigrés, since few Italian composers of the time could match their compositional depth and versatility. So while locals such as Costanzo Festa (*c.*1485–1545) and Bernado Pisano (1490–1548) are counted among the early madrigalists, the outstanding pioneers were the Frenchman Philippe Verdelot (*c.*1480–1552), the Netherlander Adrian Willaert (1490–1562) and the French-Netherlander Jacques Arcadelt (*c.*1507–68). The earliest madrigals were set syllabically in a homophonic, four-part texture, but the 1530s and 40s witnessed elevated musico-poetic expressivity, helped by homophonic and polyphonic exchanges, and part-writing in five and six voices. The 25 madrigals within Willaert's *Musica Nova* (*c.*1540s, published 1559), almost all Petrarch sonnet settings, demonstrate this sophistication with close attention paid to poetic description, syntax and sonority.

The Flemish composer Cipriano de Rore (*c.*1516–65) was a pupil of Willaert and his successor as organist at St Mark's Cathedral in Venice. Like his teacher, he wrote texturally diverse madrigals under the spell of the Petrarchan movement, consolidating a 'Venetian' madrigal style. Applying chromaticism more liberally, Rore was able to intensify the emotional message of the poetry. This is conspicuous in such pieces as *Chi non sa, come amor* and the markedly homophonic *Se ben il duol*, both published in 1557. His chromaticism pulled the music out of a conventional modal framework

Italian madrigal

Cipriano de Rore

into one more tonal in orientation. Rore set a path for the expressionism of late madrigalists like Marenzio, Monteverdi and Gesualdo, whose vividly expressive style, shaped by Greco-Roman musical ideals, is considered in the *Prelude*.

Instrumental music and intermedi

Most Renaissance instrumental music was vocal in origin. Madrigals and chansons were sometimes transcribed for instrumental performance: popular madrigals by Verdelot and Arcadelt, for example, were published in lute transcription in Venice from the mid 1500s. Multi-part songs could also be performed by mixed ensembles, or more homogeneous groups, such as a consort of recorders or viols. If instrumentalists were not performing directly from vocal parts, then they might be playing music inspired by a vocal form, such as the *canzona*, the instrumental equivalent of the chanson.

While the instrumental performance of vocal music dates from medieval times, we can see more visible changes to instrumental practices during the 1500s. These include the appearance of eminent composer-instrumentalists who nurtured idiomatic compositional styles for the solo repertory. One was the Spaniard Luis Milán (*c.*1500–*c.*1560), a composer-performer of music for the *vihuela*, an instrument related to the lute. His *Libro de música de vihuela* (1536) is the earliest publication of its kind and consists of *fantasias*, pieces of an improvisatory style that served as song preludes. Perfectly suited to solo performance and song accompaniment, the lute became the most popular instrument in 16th-century Europe and reached its zenith in the music of England's John Dowland (see *Chapter 1*).

Keyboard

Music for keyboard, both the organ and harpsichord family, was also gaining in prominence. The organ tradition was particularly strong in Germany, where Arnolt Schlick (1460–1521) helped establish an idiomatic style. Spain's Antonio de Cabezón (*c.*1510–66), who like Schlick was blind, and Italy's Claudio Merulo (1533–1604) were similarly leaders in this field, as well as being pivotal composers of harpsichord music. Merulo championed the *toccata*, with its contrasting sections of counterpoint and brilliant passagework, as well as the *ricercare* (meaning 'to seek out'), a form suited to both solo instrument and ensemble, imitative in texture and stylistically related to the motet.

Dance music

The proliferation of dance music brought another significant change to the instrumental medium. During Renaissance times dancing was an indispensable part of any grand social occasion. More than a popular pastime, it again (like musical performance) evoked good breeding: all the cultivated people knew how to dance. Little dance music before 1500 has survived, suggesting that it was a largely memorised and improvised tradition, but with the advent of music printing, collections began to appear. The dances could be presented as slow–fast variation pairs: the stately duple-metre *pavane* was commonly followed by a vigorous triple-metre *galliard* featuring much hopping and jumping, while the leisurely duple-metre *passamezzo* might be twinned with a bounding triple-metre *saltarello*. There was plenty of opportunity for the women to display elegance and charm, while the

men demonstrated physical strength and dexterity. Other popular dances included the *balletto*, commonly danced by no more than two or three couples, and the *branle*, a line or circle dance for large groups. Stylised dances, to be enjoyed simply as music, were written for both lute and keyboard, and gained early popularity in Elizabethan England.

The place of dance and instruments in theatrical entertainment is well documented, even if hardly any of the music survives. Dances featured in banquet pantomimes, while dance and instrumental interludes were common to the *intermedio*, a form of music-theatre inserted between the acts of a play. The *intermedi* became hugely popular, often a greater attraction than the play itself. The spectacular entertainment provided for the wedding of Ferdinando Medici and Christine of Lorraine at Florence in 1589 is a case in point. Girolamo Bargagli's five-act comic play *La pellegrina* had to compete with six allegorical *intermedi* boasting elaborate stage machinery (animating clouds, seas and dragons), inventive lighting effects, sumptuous costumes, and some of the most lavish music ever conceived, performed by as many as 60 singers and 24 instrumentalists. Cristofano Malvezzi (1547–99) composed most of the music, which included instrumental sinfonias, solos, madrigals, choruses and dances. Luca Marenzio, one of the foremost madrigalists of the day, provided music for the second and third *intermedi*. There were other influential figures among the collaborators: Emilio de' Cavalieri (musical producer, additional music), the scholar-poet Count Giovanni de' Bardi (scenario, co-librettist, additional music), and members of Bardi's close academic circle, notably Jacopo Peri (singer, additional music), Giulio Caccini (additional music) and Ottavio Rinuccini (principal librettist). These poets and composers were to shortly make their mark as the pioneers of opera.

Intermedio

Prologue

The Reformation

Long-running dissent brought about the dramatic schism of the Western Church. As far back as the 14th century the English theologian John Wycliff had criticised the Catholic Church's abuse of power and wealth. Wycliff influenced the Czech reformer Jan Hus, founder of the Hussite Church, who in the early 15th century fulminated against the sale of indulgences. At the start of the 16th century the Dutch priest and scholar Desiderius Erasmus gave influential voice to the Renaissance humanistic spirit, stressing reason and the free will of man, rather than blind obedience to the Church. His new edition of the Greek New Testament

(1516) encouraged others to translate the Bible into living languages. Although Erasmus remained a Catholic, his activities hastened the Reformation movement.

Martin Luther

In 1517 Martin Luther launched a renewed offensive against Church corruption by nailing up his 95 Theses to the door of the Schlosskirche at Wittenberg. He roundly attacked the sale of indulgences and the Church's power mongering, and he advocated a closer observance of Biblical doctrine. Emphasising man's personal relationship with God, he encouraged worship in the vernacular and the principle of salvation by God's grace through faith alone. While his drive for reformation was initially peaceful, his message was soon appropriated by malcontents and belligerents, from peasants to princes, and became a catalyst for violent political opposition.

In the realm of church music, Luther was perfectly content to retain the use of the Latin liturgy, albeit with modifications, and its associated polyphonic style. He was, after all, a lover of music and a devotee of Josquin. But his introduction of German-language congregational worship represented an important departure. Lutheran church songs, or *chorales*, were set strophically with a single melody, sung in unison without accompaniment. The tunes themselves were both freely composed or 'borrowed', either from other sacred pieces or from secular music. Luther himself wrote many chorales, both texts and music. Ludwig Senfl (1486–1543) and Johann Walter (1496–1570) contributed to the early polyphonic chorale, written specifically for the choir. Homophonic chorale arrangements intended for congregational participation, with or without organ accompaniment, were to become popular during the 17th century.

The English Reformation

The disgruntled King Henry VIII (r.1509–47) initiated England's Reformation, primarily because he rejected the Church's teaching on divorce and remarriage. He declared himself the supreme head of the Church of England in 1534 but retained Catholic doctrine. It was only following the accession of the child king Edward VI that the country experienced some of its first Protestant vernacular liturgy and church music. Thomas Tallis (*c*.1505–85), England's leading composer of the mid-century, provided service music and anthems for the new Anglican Church, even though he remained a Catholic at heart. He was an expert polyphonist, as evidenced by his sumptuous 40-part motet *Spem in alium*, but his Anglican music was often restricted to a simple syllabic style so to allow better comprehension of the sung word. Similar musical compromises were being discussed by Counter-Reformationists around this very time in Italy (see below and *Prelude*).

While Mary Tudor (r.1553–58) briefly returned England to Catholicism, her Protestant successor, Elizabeth I, attempted to foster a more ecumenical fellowship with the Religious Settlement of 1559. Instated as Supreme Governor of the Church of England, Elizabeth naturally avowed independence from Rome. William Byrd (*c*.1540–1623) followed Tallis, his teacher, as England's foremost composer. Byrd maintained his Catholic faith, and most of the time enjoyed enough religious freedom to write music for both Protestant and private Catholic worship (see *Chapter 1*).

Counter Reformation

A new Catholic era was launched by the Papal licensing of the Jesuit order under Ignatius Loyola in 1540, along with the meetings of the Council of Trent, held between 1545 and 1563. The Church tackled various abuses of clerical privilege and reassessed and redefined its principal doctrines. Unfortunately, the politico-religious enmity now rife in Europe was not calmed by these internal reforms.

Council of Trent

The Council of Trent found time to make significant proclamations on the place of music in church. One complaint targeted the *parody mass* (or *imitation mass*), where a pre-existing polyphonic piece, sacred or secular, would provide the basis for the entire polyphonic fabric of a Mass Ordinary. Many popular madrigals and chansons were used for this purpose. The Council decried the practice since the music would likely remind the performers and listeners of the original secular text. Some composers in Italy, in Rome especially, responded to the Church's complaint with due respect, while others, like the prolific Orlande de Lassus, carried on regardless. Lassus's most inflammatory example is surely the mass *Entre vous filles* (1581), based on a crude chanson about nubile 15-year-old girls by the Flemish composer Jacobus Clemens non Papa (*c*.1510–*c*.1556).

Parody mass

The Council also declared that sacred music should be written 'in such a way that the words be clearly understood by all'. The Church's objec-

Textual clarity

◀ Ecclesiastical dignitaries convene for the Council of Trent (1545–63). Instigated by Pope Paul III, the meetings gave critical direction to the Counter Reformation.

Prologue

tion to elaborate polyphony that obscured the audibility of sacred text was centuries old. Some popes had tried to ban it. The Flemish composer Jacobus de Kerle (*c.*1532–91) demonstrated to the Council a favourable compromise in his settings of prayers, sung at the meetings, which afforded textual transparency through measured polyphony and a judicious use of homophony. This devotional 'Roman' style became expressed most perfectly in the music of Giovanni Pierluigi da Palestrina (*c.*1525–94).

Giovanni da Palestrina

Palestrina spent his entire career moving between posts in Rome, eventually becoming choirmaster of the Cappella Giulia at St Peter's. He wrote around 100 secular madrigals, but his 104 masses, together with some 250 motets and 50 spiritual madrigals, make clear his deep commitment to sacred music. Around half of his masses adopt the polyphonic parody method, with most of these based on sacred motets. Palestrina's characteristic style, marked by plainsong tunes, stepwise movement of the melodic line, clear textures and careful control of dissonance, was at once conservative, serene and unsurpassed in structural beauty. Such quality is vividly displayed in his most famous creation, the *Pope Marcellus Mass*, probably written in memory of, rather than for, Pope Marcellus, who held office for just three weeks before his death in 1555 (see also *Prelude*). The second most important composer of the Roman school was Tomás Luis de Victoria (1548–1611), a Spaniard who spent the early part of his career in the papal city (see also *Chapter 1*). Masses, Magnificats, hymns, and some particularly expressive motets dominate Victoria's output. So devoted was he to sacred music that he left not one secular composition.

Towards the end of an era

The *Prelude* and *Chapter 1* take account of the late Renaissance musical style in conjunction with the emergent Baroque era, since old and new styles coexisted for some time. The dating of cultural epochs always presents problems, especially for music, given that it is traditionally slow to respond to cultural change, lagging behind literature and painting. If Renaissance music reached its stylistic climax during the late 16th century, then it was about half a century behind the climax of Renaissance painting and sculpture. Leonardo's *Last Supper* and *Mona Lisa*, Raphael's *The Sistine Madonna* and *The School of Athens*, Michelangelo's sculpture of *David* and his paintings on the Sistine Chapel ceiling—these monumental works all date from 1495–1520, coinciding with the career of Josquin.

It was not the passing of Leonardo and Raphael (in 1519 and 1520 respectively) that signalled the end of an era, but a sequence of events that directly challenged Renaissance values. The first was the War of the League of Cognac (1526–30), which saw the immensely powerful Holy Roman Emperor, Charles V of Spain, victorious against Pope Clement VII and his French and Italian allies. It is often claimed that the sacking of Rome by Charles's mutinous troops in 1527 sounded the death-knell for the Renaissance: this was not only the literal desecration of a key centre of Renaissance scholarship and art, it was also the symbolic destruction of the belief that man's moral improvement could emanate from the pursuit of classical ideals.

The quarrels and conflicts between Protestants and Catholics, begun during the 1520s, also posed challenges to Renaissance values, even if the disagreements themselves had been partly motivated by humanist convictions. The bloody battles of France's 'Wars of Religion' (c. 1562–98) hardly testified to a Petrarchan notion of moral improvement. Another powerful Holy Roman Emperor, Philip II of Spain, took the Catholic cause into the international arena, though he failed to reclaim England for the Catholic faith.

Inhumanity was discharged from all sides, and in the process classical values appeared irrelevant. A rejection of Renaissance ideals may be seen in the mid to late century Mannerist style of painters like Jacopo Tintoretto and El Greco. Naturalism and balanced proportion give way to exaggerated forms and unexpected contrasts, which serve to heighten dramatic intensity. Figures themselves may be given dynamic expression with pained faces and twisted poses. Mannerism was to influence the dramatic *chiaroscuro* (light and dark) technique of Caravaggio and was even to find correspondence in musical style before the century was over (see *Prelude*).

Still, aspects of the Renaissance spirit persisted in Europe throughout the late 1500s and beyond. Scholarship in Greek and Roman antiquity remained strong. Pastoral traditions lingered in the Italian plays of Torquato Tasso and Battista Guarini and in the poetry of France's Pierre de Ronsard and England's Edmund Spenser. Classical themes and allusions pervaded Shakespeare's plays, which themselves espoused self-knowledge and the understanding of man's nature as imperative to human wisdom. In architecture, Renaissance classicism blended with Baroque exuberance in many parts of Europe, conspicuous in such splendid buildings as St Peter's Basilica in Rome, Spain's Royal Palace of Aranjuez, the Louvre in Paris, and London's St Paul's Cathedral, rebuilt 1675–1710 on designs by Christopher Wren.

◀ Rejecting classical (natural) form: the distorted, surreal style of El Greco in *The Repentant Magdalen*, c.1577.

Towards the Baroque style

WHILE THE French were embroiled in the Wars of Religion (1562–98) and while England was fending off invasion during the Anglo-Spanish War (1585–1604), a musical revolution was taking place on Italian soil. It was driven by an aesthetic ideal governing the all-important vocal genres, in which music was 'commanded' as the servant of the word. Consistent with Renaissance humanism, this attitude was expressed by Church and secular academies alike. The Church required music that could allow for the clear expression of sacred text, not render it unintelligible through complex part-writing; the secular academies, inspired by their research into the music-dramas of antiquity, desired music that could move freely with the emotions of the word, heighten its meaning, and stimulate the very 'states' of the listener's soul. Secular activities were to prove supremely influential in creating a radically new musical style, but both movements threatened the pervasive vernacular of Renaissance music: polyphony.

◀ The composer Giovanni da Palestrina presenting a mass to Pope Julius III, 1554.

Sacred music

Polyphony was the pinnacle of the Renaissance composer's craft. A texture comprising separate layers of melodic lines was far more difficult to manipulate and control than homophonic part-writing, where most or all of the parts sound together. Polyphonic music tended to be rhythmically and dynamically restrained, but it could be sophisticated, multi-dimensional, and wide-ranging in texture and structure. The Church, however, had long voiced concerns over elaborate polyphonic music that stifled sacred text. To distinguish a sung word spun out over a period of several seconds was difficult enough, but virtually impossible if other words were being sung at the same time. Such were the objections raised by the Council of Trent (see *Prologue*). Indeed, there were both Catholic and Protestant leaders who felt that too many composers had become self-indulgent, wholly preoccupied with musical ingenuity—a transgression, no doubt, born of humanistic zeal.

Palestrina's *Pope Marcellus Mass*, written sometime between 1555 and 1562, was a model response to the criticisms voiced by the Catholic Council. Masterly in part-writing and fluid in harmonic movement, the mass was singled out for its eloquent and lucid text setting. In this piece Palestrina generally employs polyphony in sections where the text is short and simple, as in the Kyrie or Agnus Dei, constructing short periods between the vocal entries to give the words transparency. Where a section consists of several lines of text, as in the Gloria or Credo, the style is largely

Palestrina: *Pope Marcellus Mass*

Prelude

▲ Example 2
Homophonic
opening of Gloria
from Palestrina's
*Missa Papae
Marcelli (c.1562)*

homophonic, with the simultaneous movement of vocal parts, as in the Gloria extract of Example 2. By way of contrast, Example 3 shows the polyphonic opening bars of a Gloria written some 25 years earlier by the great Flemish composer Adrian Willaert, who spent most of his working life in Italy.

In later years it was romantically suggested that Palestrina saved sacred polyphony from the papal pyre. He remained a true Renaissance composer, steadfast in his equal-voiced harmony, and never wrote what we would term Baroque music. The most learned musicians of the early Baroque were to maintain a healthy reverence for the polyphonic style, whilst giving due consideration to the Church's preference for homophonic clarity. Polyphonic mastery was still the mark of the great composer, but polyphony itself had lost much of its sacred ground.

Secular music

The influence of ancient Greece

While the Church was making new demands for sacred music, Italian scholars and composers were carrying out detailed research into ancient Greek musical customs. As the great era of antiquity was widely regarded as superior, it followed that their music must have been better. And so it seemed. Aristotle (384–322 B.C.) maintained that music, or specifically the Greek 'modes', embodied qualities that could affect the emotions and

▲ Example 3
Polyphonic opening
of the Gloria from
Willaert's *Missa
Quaeramus cum
Pastoribus* (*c.*1536).
Staggered vocal
entries result in
different words
sounding together.

morals of man, for good or ill. States of the soul, such as sorrow, joy, anger, fear and hope, could be encouraged and even instigated by music. (Baroque-era theorists described this concept as the 'doctrine of the affections'.) Coupled with this, the role of music, argued by Plato (*c.*429–347 B.C.) in his third book of *The Republic*, was to intensify the meaning of the text; thus music should be the *servant* of the word. Further evidence suggested that the ancient Greeks incorporated music much more extensively into their dramas than was the practice in Renaissance Italy.

The Florentine Camerata

In around 1570 an influential group of musicians, scholars and poets began academic meetings at the Florentine palace of Count Giovanni de Bardi (1534–1612). Inspired by their studies of antiquity, members of the so-called *Camerata* were particularly interested in heightening musical expression in drama. Count Bardi and the composer-theorist Vincenzo Galilei (d.1591)—father of the astronomer Galileo—carried out detailed research in correspondence with another Florentine, Girolamo Mei (1519–94). Having worked and lived in Rome for a number of years,

▲ *Fête des hommages*, Piazza della Signoria in Florence (anonymous, late 16th century). Florence was the birthplace of opera and a leading centre in the development of the baroque musical style.

Mei had been able to study all the available sources on music in Greek drama. He and his colleagues concluded (perhaps incorrectly) that classical Greek tragedy had been sung throughout and facilitated to this end by monody: the use of a single, unencumbered melodic line that permitted the clear and free declamation of text.

The polyphonic style was incompatible with the gestures and free rhythms of speech. And even though monodic forms were not unknown, no musico-dramatic genre of the Renaissance incorporated scored dialogue. In an Italian *intermedio* or *entr'acte*, a French *ballet de cour* or an English *masque*, monologue or conversational exchanges were either absent or unaccompanied. So the Camerata engineered a new monodic style of music, comprising a solo melodic line supported by an independent bass part. The inner harmonies were supplied by *continuo* players who improvised from numbers written in the bass part (the 'figured bass'), which gave indications of inversions and dissonances. The new texture of *basso-continuo* emancipated the vocal line, enabling wide-ranging declamation and quick changes of mood and expression. Thus *recitative*—sung monologue or dialogue—was born, and with it the beginnings of opera: a dramatic genre in which there was no need to stop the music to allow the

characters to interact, argue, seduce, implore or fight.

Early 17th-century operas were commonly called *favola in musica* (a story in music) or *dramma per musica* (drama in music); the term *opera* did not appear until Pietro Cavalli used it in 1639 in reference to *Le nozze di Teti e Peleo*, his so-called *opera-scenica*. Using the term retrospectively, 'opera' was launched with *Dafne* (1598), scored by Jacopo Peri (1561–1633) and Jacopo Corsi (1561–1602) to a libretto by Ottavio Rinuccini. It was performed several times, but while the text survives, the music is lost. The earliest surviving opera is *Euridice*, co-composed by Jacopo Peri and Giulio Caccini (1551–1618) and given its first performance in 1600 at the Medici's Palazzo Pitti in Florence. The style is very simple and heavily focused on recitative (see also *Chapter 1*). In Rome that same year Emilio de' Cavalieri (*c.*1550–1602) produced an early experiment in oratorio form: *La rappresentatione di anima e di corpo* (The Representation of Soul and Body). It predates *Euridice* by eight months and stands as the earliest surviving dramatic work with music throughout. Rinuccini, Peri, Corsi, Cavalieri and Caccini were all affiliates of the Camerata, and their early dramatic productions, if not masterpieces, were monumentally influential.

> ◀ Singer and composer Jacopo Peri (in costume as Arion, 1589), one of the pioneers of opera.

The birth of opera

The progressive madrigal style
Basso continuo was undoubtedly the single most radical musical invention of the time, yet the *fin de siècle* revolution was energised by gifted madrigalists who were, like the Camerata, inspired by the ideas of the ancient Greeks. Seeking a language of the 'affections', they created multi-voiced (predominantly five-part) unaccompanied madrigals of increasing expressivity and virtuosity, reaching a climax of style towards the end of the century.

Unlike the Camerata, even the most progressive madrigalists were keen to study and build on the compositional techniques of the respected masters. There were many composers who contributed to the development of the late madrigal, with Cipriano de Rore, Andrea Gabrieli and Orlando Lassus among the most important. The Flemish émigré Giaches de Wert (1535–96), *maestro di cappella* at the Gonzaga court of Mantua from 1565,

Giaches de Wert

was a particularly influential madrigalist of the late century. He champi-oned a chordal, declamatory style in his madrigals of the 1560s and 70s, setting texts of staple Renaissance poets like the revered Petrarch and the more recent Pietro Bembo (1470–1547). In the 1580s and 90s he turned to the dramatic texts of contemporary poets, notably Torquato Tasso's epic poem *Gerusalemme liberata* (Jerusalem Delivered) and Giovanni Battista Guarini's pastoral play *Il pastor fido* (The Faithful Shepherd). Wert's late madrigals promoted dramatic musical gestures and textural diversity, juxtaposing imitative polyphony, declamatory homophony, and upper voice-dominated part-writing.

Luca Marenzio: word-painting

Among the younger progressives was Luca Marenzio (*c*.1553–99), who began publishing madrigal collections in the 1580s while serving Cardinal Luigi d'Este in Rome. Marenzio's songs exemplify the period's infatuation with word-painting: birds sing cheerful florid passages; the wind murmurs in arpeggiated patterns; the long, curling hair of the beloved descends in beautiful melodic waves; and so on. Although such procedures were typical of the time, Marenzio would sometimes design his notation on the page to resemble the content of the text. In *Occhi sereni* (1581), eyes are depicted by pairs of semibreves, while in *Cedan l'antiche* (1584), grand classical arches are suggested by rising and falling quavers. In his Sixth to Ninth books of madrigals (1594–99), Marenzio abandoned much of this so-called 'eye music', though he maintained expressive word-painting techniques; he also adopted a freer use of dissonance and chromaticism to illustrate what was altogether more serious and pessimistic verse. The severe, emotionally-charged aspects of Marenzio's music come to the fore in pieces such as *Crudele acerba inesorabil' morte* (Cruel, bitter, inexorable death), a setting of Petrarch, from Book Nine.

Luzzaschi, Monteverdi

The renowned keyboard composer Luzzasco Luzzaschi (*c*.1545–1607), organist at the Este court of Ferrara, was also influen-tial in the five-part madrigal style. In the preface of his *Sesto libro de' madrigali* (1596) he stated, 'Music … does not dare to move its foot where its superior [poetry] has not proceeded'. His settings, like Marenzio's, follow closely the emotional and pictorial contours of the text, with chromaticism and abrupt dissonance employed

▶ The composer Carlo Gesualdo, Prince of Venosa (kneeling), with his uncle, Carlo Borromeo.

for special textual emphasis. Claudio Monteverdi (1567–1643) adopted a similar approach, taking inspiration directly from Wert when he became musician to the Mantuan court in around 1590. In his Third Book of Madrigals (1592) he came under the spell of Tasso and Guarini, setting their texts of nature and desolation with sensuous harmonies and progressive, yet measured, dissonance. The virtual mini-drama *Vattene pur crudel* (Go then, cruel man) demonstrates both the extremes and flexibility of Monteverdi's musical idiom. It describes an abandoned lover left paralysed in a state of grief, anger and despair, and uses a dramatic mix of recitative and declamation, angular vocal leaps and anguished chromaticism.

Monteverdi was later reproached by conservatives for his harmonic perversions (see *Chapter 1*). It was, however, the infamous Prince Carlo Gesualdo (*c*.1561–1613)—murderer of his first wife and her lover in 1590—who gave the five-part madrigal its most avant-garde harmonic expression. His fourth to sixth books of madrigals respect the 'old school' in their attention to polyphonic textures, and yet they wallow in dissonance, chromaticism and astringent tonal shifts. Gesualdo issued his first four books of madrigals in the mid 1590s in Ferrara, not long after his (second) marriage to Leonora d'Este, niece of Duke Alfonso II. A number of madrigals published in his fifth and sixth books (1611) were quite possibly also composed in Ferrara

Claudio Monteverdi

Prince Carlo Gesualdo

▼ *Procession from the cross on the Piazza San Marco*, by Gentile Bellini. In the background stands the splendid St Mark's Basilica.

at the end of the 90s. Therein, and common to all of the intense madrigals of the period, the most audacious applications of dissonance correspond to emotional torment, as demonstrated by the opening contortions and clashes of *But you, the cause of that atrocious pain* (Part Two) from Book Five. It is easy to imagine that Gesualdo's favoured, angst-ridden texts resonated with his guilt-ridden state of mind.

The philosophy of these progressive madrigalists was similar to that of the Camerata: to create music that engaged and stirred the passions. If this meant breaking away from the time-honoured 'rules' of composition, so be it. Their expressionistic, five-part madrigal style (sometimes labelled 'mannerist') was superseded in the early 17th century by monody and basso continuo, but its legacy was enormously significant. Firstly, more than any other mature musical genre of the Renaissance, the late madrigal established the concept that the text was sovereign: music, as noted earlier in Plato's ideal, was serving to heighten the meaning of the word. Secondly, it promoted the doctrine of the affections, which became a guiding aesthetic of the Baroque era. And thirdly, the style's harmonically rich musical language shaped that of leading composers of the next generation, including Girolamo Frescobaldi (1583–1643) and, abroad, Heinrich Schütz (1585–1672).

The Venetian Style

An appraisal of the momentous changes in music during this period has also to recognise the powerful influence of the late 16th-century Venetian style. Venice itself had become a major centre of musical excellence during the Renaissance. Ottaviano Petrucci, the 'father' of music printing, set up shop there in 1501 (see *Prologue*), and the locale itself boasted some 200 churches, most of which demanded the skills of performers and composers. Representing the spiritual and musical heart of the republic was the magnificent St Mark's Basilica, a vast Byzantine-Gothic building that converged epochs, cultures and continents (see picture p.43).

Adrian Willaert: cori spezzati

The Flemish composer Adrian Willaert became *maestro di capella* of St Mark's in 1527; by the time of his death, in 1562, he had promoted the church as one of the most important musical institutions in Europe. Taking full advantage of its resonant acoustics and opposing choir lofts, Willaert popularised the use of *cori spezzati*—'divided choirs'. Separating choral groups within a church was not itself unusual; the radical feature of *cori spezzati* was the structuring of musical material into distinct units. Each choir was assigned a unique set of parts, sung in alternation, in echo arrangement, or fully combined. This antiphonal polychoral idiom was continued by successive composers employed at St Mark's, reaching new heights of splendour in the hands of the organist-composers Andrea and Giovanni Gabrieli.

Andrea Gabrieli

Andrea Gabrieli (*c.*1532–85) probably absorbed the polychoral style from his teacher, the eminent Franco-Flemish composer Orlande de Lassus, and this positioned him favourably at St Mark's in his duty to provide music for ceremonial occasions. By the 1580s his compositions were combining the *cori spezzati* technique with alternating polyphonic and chordal styles.

These he further elaborated with striking contrasts between small and large vocal forces (sometimes doubled with instruments), and rhythmic variety, with shifts from duple to triple metre. The residential musical force numbered around 30 singers and instrumentalists, but on grand occasions, such as the welcoming of a visiting monarch or a battle victory celebration, numbers could be swelled two- or three-fold by recruiting from other churches.

Giovanni Gabrieli (*c.*1555–1612) succeeded his uncle as composer of ceremonial music in 1585. In his *Sacrae symphoniae* of 1597 and the posthumously published *Sacrae symphoniae* of 1615, there is an even greater emphasis on contrast, both textural and dynamic. The *Sonata pian' e forte* for two instrumental 'choirs' is the most famous piece of the 1597 publication, owing to its innovative use of specified dynamics and designated instrumentation (one group comprising a cornetto and three sackbuts, the other, a viola and three sackbuts). The earlier collection even sees the polychoral idiom expanded to four four-part choirs in the spectacular motet *Omnes gentes*. In the 1615 publication, vocal and instrumental forces—cornetts, sackbuts, strings and continuo—combine and alternate in a great variety of permutations. Gabrieli's church style was sumptuous, magnificent and powerful, more so than any heard before it. At the same time his music was not simply about grand effects— it had poignancy and depth, as we can hear in the solo sections of the polychoral piece *In ecclesiis*, which offer heartfelt devotions in praise to the Almighty.

The Venetian school thus pioneered what became known as the *concertato* style—the distinct grouping of instruments and voices in contrasting combinations. And by specifying the make-up of instrumental groups, foundations were being laid for the development of the orchestra. These innovations were noted by the Englishman Thomas Coryat, who visited Venice in 1608:

Sometimes there sung sixteene or twenty men together, having their master or moderator to keepe them in order; and when they sung, the instrumentall musitians played also. Sometimes sixteene played together upon their instruments, ten Sagbuts, foure Cornets, and two

Giovanni
Gabrieli
*Sacrae
symphoniae*

Concertato
style

Prelude

Violdegambaes ... sometimes tenne, sixe Sagbuts and foure Cornets;
sometimes two, a Cornet and a treble violl...

His account continues with further details of performer permutations, such
was the novelty of this music. The impact of the Venetian style was actually
limited in Italy, even though it was to shape the music of Monteverdi prior
to his move to Venice in 1613. By contrast, its affect on German Baroque
music in the early 17th century was profound (see *Chapter 1*).

The etymology of 'Baroque'

Among the terms used to designate major periods of artistic style, 'Baroque'
is the most confusing. No composers of what we now call the Baroque period
ever thought of their work as 'baroque'—or rather if they did, they would
have burned it. To them the word will have denoted something imperfect:
specifically, a rough or irregular-shaped pearl. The pejorative label seems
to have been first applied to music in 1734 by an anonymous writer of
the *Mercure de France*, who criticised Rameau's opera *Hippolyte et
Aricie* (1733) for its 'baroque' style, noting stilted melody, awkward
dissonances and compositional extravagance. The philosopher-composer
Jean Jacques Rousseau, in his *Dictionnaire de musique* (1768), defined
'baroque music' as: 'harmonically confused, excessive in modulation
and dissonance, melodically harsh and unnatural, difficult to intone
and constrained in movement'. By the end of the 19th century the term had
found currency among art historians, particularly regarding architecture of
the 17th and 18th centuries, although it was not yet fully expunged of its
negative connotations. Music historians en masse finally adopted the term
towards the mid 20th century to refer to a post-Renaissance period covering
approximately 1600 to 1750. Or, to delineate the period in another popular
manner, Baroque music begins with the birth of opera and culminates
with Bach and Handel.

1600—1649

1600–1649

T HE EARLY Baroque period saw the rise of royal absolutism, a monarchical form of government already known to Spain, introduced to England by James I and to France by Louis XIII. The belief in the 'divine right of kings' contributed to an escalation of state-sponsored art, whose prime function was to promote the magnificence and supremacy of the monarchy. Great art reflected great power. The royal courts of Europe were vying with the Church as the leading arts patrons, with painters, sculptors, architects and composers little more than servants to their interests.

Under the eye of less powerful patrons, composers in Italy established the new musical epoch with the cultivation of opera, the oratorio and trio sonata, as well as new song forms, such as the solo madrigal and cantata. Their activities amounted to a localised concentration of musical innovation unparalleled in Western history, before or since. German-speaking lands fused the Lutheran Chorale tradition with Italian idioms, while experiencing crippling hardships during the Thirty Years' War (1618–48). Elsewhere the Renaissance–Baroque transition was very gradual, especially in countries with strong musical traditions: England rode the wave of its Elizabethan golden age, while France developed its love affair with the *ballet de cour*.

◄ *The Concert* by the French painter Nicolas Tournier, *c.*1630 (Louvre, Paris).

The musical language of the early Baroque

Prima prattica, seconda prattica

At the outset of the 17th century there existed two fundamental approaches to vocal music. The 'old style' represented the polyphonic tradition, epitomised in the works of Palestrina, Lassus and the leading Spanish composer, Tomás Luis de Victoria. The 'modern style' stood for a musical language of dramatic sensitivity, often favouring chordal textures and monody, and unafraid of breaking musical 'rules' for dramatic effect. Claudio Monteverdi termed the old style *prima prattica*, the 'first practice', where the text is set into polyphonic structures, therefore limited in its expressive capacity. In the modern style, *seconda prattica*, music becomes the servant of the text, supporting, enhancing, but not overpowering.

While the 'second practice' found its way into sacred music, it was most radically expressed through secular genres. Such modernism met with opposition from conservatives like the composer-theorist Giovanni Artusi (*c*.1540–1613), who in 1600 complained in print:

> *It pleases me, at my age, to see a new method of composing, though it would please me much more if I saw that these passages were founded upon some reason which could satisfy the intellect … Such composers … corrupt, spoil and ruin the good traditional rules handed down in former times by so many theorists and most excellent musicians.*

Artusi took particular exception to any kind of unprepared or unresolved dissonance, which to his mind compromised balance, order and aesthetic beauty. Monteverdi found himself at the heart of Artusi's attacks: his expressive madrigal *Cruda Amarilli* (Cruel Amaryllis; *c*.1590s) was one of the pieces cited for its compositional perversions. It was published in his Fifth Book of Madrigals (1605), and in the preface to that volume Monteverdi wrote a defence of his methods, making reference for the first time to the 'second practice'. His brother, Giulio Cesare, then published an expanded defence in Monteverdi's *Scherzi musicali* (1607). Distinguished composers such as Cipriano de Rore, Giaches de Wert, Marenzio, Luzzaschi, Gesualdo and members of the Florentine 'Camerata' (see *Prelude*) were cited as key exponents of the *seconda prattica*. Monteverdi was keen to stress the continuing relevance of the noble 'first practice', knowing well that it could produce music of remarkable elegance and beauty. He also insisted that the expressive language of the 'second practice' was built on traditional foundations; the old and new styles could therefore co-exist in the same works.

Basso continuo

The modern style became epitomised by the revolutionary three-part texture afforded by *basso continuo* (see *Prelude*). While the polyphonic style had emphasised a certain equality between the parts, music featuring basso continuo was texturally hierarchical: melody, followed by bass-line, followed by inner harmonies. The contrast between what was often a florid melody over a slower moving bass was central to the new style. Notes in between the melody and bass were not fully written out, so in order to convey inversions of chords and chromatic alterations, the composer would insert numbers and accidentals in the bass part to indicate the harmony required. The harmonies of the so-called *figured bass* were realised by the *continuo* player(s)—usually employing keyboard, viol or lute-family instruments—who would also improvise appropriate embellishments.

▶ Opening page of Caccini's solo madrigal 'Movetevi a pietà' from *Le nuove musiche* (1601/02), notated with figured bass.

◀ *The Martyrdom
of Saint Matthew*,
Caravaggio (1600).
The preoccupation
with contrast in
Italianate music
of this period has
a parallel with
the tenebrist
(or *chiaroscuro*)
technique
in painting.
Championed by
Caravaggio, the
tenebrist style
exploits light and
shade to exaggerate
human features,
heighten drama
and bring diversity
to form.

The concertato style

In Renaissance times the role of instruments in vocal music was generally confined to the replacement or doubling of vocal parts. Now a
greater desire for contrast, expression and grandeur was encouraging a
concerted approach to music, which gave independent roles to voices and
instruments. A *concerto* in the first half of the 17th century was typically a vocal work incorporating an independent instrumental part (the
purely instrumental concerto would not appear until the 1680s). Pieces in
concertato style not only featured this kind of writing but also emphasised
colourful contrasts of sonorities and dynamics, particularly by juxtaposing
instrumental and vocal sections. The practice could be used within a
small ensemble, or to massive effect, as found in sections of Monteverdi's
Vespers (1610), Giovanni Gabrieli's posthumously published *Symphoniae
sacrae* (1615) and Michael Praetorius's *Polyhymnia caduceatrix* (1619).
This revolutionary approach widened the composer's sound-world
dramatically, encouraging a more considered treatment of timbre and
instrumental idiom.

Tonality

From Medieval times musical language had been based on eight modes (see
Prologue). Theorists in the 16th century identified four 'new' modes: the
Aeolian (on 'A') and Ionian (on 'C'), and their corresponding plagal modes,

Hypoaeolian and Hypoionian. To modern ears the Aeolian and Ionian modes sound tonal, as they effectively represent minor and major scales. In practice, composers had been using such scales for some time by incorporating a flattened B in the minor-sounding Dorian mode, beginning on D, and in the major-sounding Lydian mode, beginning on F. The 13th-century English 'round' *Sumer is icumen in* (see *Prologue*) is a famous early example of major-scale music.

There were several factors that gave tonal vocabulary increasing popularity during the 16th century. By making subtle changes to the Pythagorean tuning system, composers were able to appreciate thirds and sixths as consonant harmonies, rather than dissonances that required resolution into bare fifths or octaves. A measured preference for homophony over polyphony, especially for purposes of textual clarity, was also critical, as it emphasised the role of 'triadic' harmony. Such music became thought of less as a linear texture and more as a vertical compound, which gave emphasis to chords as harmonic units. Excursions into closely-related key areas, and passages concluding with cadences formed around dominant and tonic, similarly encouraged the tonal approach.

While a great deal of music of the late 16th and early 17th century embodies a strong sense of tonality, composers were still thinking and talking about music in terms of modes. The modal–tonal transition was in fact very gradual, and vestiges of modality would still be present in music even at the turn of the 18th century.

The development of opera

Opera became the most important and highly regarded of all Baroque genres. Embracing acting, poetry, music, costume, scenery and, more often than not, elaborate effects and machinery, it drew together disparate art forms and disciplines that together epitomised the splendour and ingenuity of the new Baroque age. Opera was first cultivated at court, commissioned to add appropriate spectacle to weddings, coronations, state visits and other formal or festive occasions. Operatic narratives, like those of the English *masque* and the French *ballet de cour*, were sometimes chosen to allegorise royal wisdom, power and virtue. From the outset, opera drew on stories from Greek myth, a natural choice for a genre that was itself inspired by ancient Greek drama (see *Prelude*).

It is often the case that the pioneers of a genre are not its most gifted exponents, and so it was with opera (see also 'Florentine Camerata', *Prelude*). Jacopo Peri's *Euridice* of 1600 was beyond question an important and influential work, but it contains little formal variety. There are a handful of (strophic) arias, a chorus to end each *scena*, and an instrumental *ritornello*; the opera is otherwise heavily preoccupied with free-form recitative. Caccini, who contributed to Peri's score, followed with his very own production of *Euridice* in 1602, but in these early Florentine dramas music was not intended to take centre-stage. It was therefore not until Monteverdi's *Orfeo*, performed as Carnival entertainment at Mantua in 1607, that opera began to realise its dramatic potential.

Jacopo Peri: *Euridice*

Monteverdi: *Orfeo*

Maestro di cappella to Duke Vincenzo Gonzaga, Monteverdi was 40 years old when he produced opera's first repertory standard. As a modernist he assimilated the Camerata's monodic innovations, but unlike the Florentines he also drew on the respected forms and techniques of the previous century. His *Orfeo*, a so-called *favola in musica* (story in music), opens with a resplendent fanfare-style brass toccata, followed immediately by an exquisite *ritornello* prologue within which the personification of music extols her own virtues. It will have been instantly clear to the select Mantuan audience that they were in for a feast of music. Set in five acts to a libretto by Alessandro Striggio, the work was substantially larger in scale than the Camerata operas. And whereas previous Florentine productions demanded only a small instrumental group, mainly continuo, Monteverdi drew together an impressive 40-strong orchestral prototype, comprising recorder, cornets, trumpets, sackbuts (trombones), a string section of viols and violins, and continuo instruments. It is important to emphasise that this extravagant assembly of musicians did not initiate an immediate trend. Further, at no point did the whole ensemble play together and nor was it orchestrated throughout. Nevertheless, the range of instrumentation allowed for a wide variety of contrast and colour, reflected also in the work's formal diversity: instrumental sinfonias and ritornellos, choruses, recitative, solos, duets, and ensembles in madrigal style. Monteverdi built on the success of *Orfeo* a year later with his second opera, *L'Arianna*. Unfortunately, apart from a small portion of the score, 'Ariadne's lament', the music has not survived.

As the early century progressed, opera in both Florence and Mantua struggled to gain pride of place, contending still with other theatrical entertainments. However in Rome the genre was supported with the enthusiastic patronage of the powerful, papal Barberini family. Roman opera established itself during the 1620s, asserting a more spectacular approach than that of the early Florentine and Mantuan models. The instrumental ensembles seem to have been kept relatively small (nothing to match Monteverdi's *Orfeo*), but visual exuberance, a hallmark of Baroque art, increasingly infused opera in effects, elaborate machinery and set design.

Roman opera: 1620s–40s

Roman opera gave more emphasis to the chorus and proved influential in its treatment of recitative and the aria. Domenico Mazzocchi (1592–1665) desired to 'break the tedium of recitative' by reducing its role and placing greater emphasis on lyricism, both in the form of the aria and shorter *mezz'arie*, or *arioso* passages. He adopted and defended this approach in his one opera, *La catena d'Adone* (1626), and much Roman opera of the 1630s and 40s followed suit. Dramatic continuity was enhanced by a smooth flow from recitative into lyrical arioso and aria, and then back again, in close correspondence with the text.

Barberini Theatre

In 1632 Rome opened its first opera house, the Barberini Theatre, built on designs by the great Gian Lorenzo Bernini. The private venue could accommodate an audience of 3,000 and was equipped to house and hide sophisticated stage machinery. Here one could witness stormy seas in motion, gods descending on clouds, chariots drawn by dragons and a hero riding a hippogriff. Stefano Landi (1587–1639) supplied the music for the inaugurating production, *Il Sant'Alessio*. The opera ventured into new territory with religious history and provided a dazzling spectacle of angels flying across the stage. The text was by Rome's leading librettist, Giulio Rospigliosi (1600–69).

Rospigliosi, who was to become Pope Clement IX (1667–69), later collaborated with the composer Virgilio Mazzocchi (1597–1646) on *Chi soffre speri* (1637/9). This landmark production prefigured *opera buffa*, since it was the first opera to include dialect-speaking comic characters while at the same time excluding the chorus. Possibly most gifted among the Roman composers was Luigi Rossi (*c.*1597–1653), whose operas are represented by the extravagant seven-hour *Il palazzo incantato* (The Enchanted Palace, 1642) and *Orfeo* (1647). After the death of Pope Urban VIII in 1644, Roman opera experienced a downturn. The new Pope, Innocent X, had negligible interest in the arts, and he saw fit to charge prominent members of the Barberini family with the embezzlement of public funds. The Barberinis fled to France and remained in exile for ten years.

Venetian opera: 1630s & 40s

Even before the end of the Barberini era, Venice was challenging Rome as the leading centre of opera. The city opened the very first public opera house in 1637—the Teatro San Cassiano—and here, unlike in Rome, women were allowed to appear on the stage. Venetian opera could thereby achieve

▶ Giacomo Torelli's set design for Francesco Sacrati's opera *Venere gelosa* (Jealous Venus). The imposing statue of Helios stands at the Port of Rhodes. On the water are the figures of Fortune and Thetis. Premièred at the Teatro Novissimo, Venice, 1643.

a much greater sense of realism and, without Papal censorship, happily embrace themes of depravity. Public productions, while often receiving some sort of state or aristocratic support, had to be cost-effective, and could rarely match the grandeur of court-sponsored opera. Monteverdi wrote four operas for Venice, though only two have survived: *Il ritorno d'Ulisse in patria* (1640) and *L'incoronazione di Poppea* (1643). They were conceived as public productions, so Monteverdi employed just a small instrumental ensemble of strings and continuo, and gave only a minor role to the chorus.

Poppea is Monteverdi's operatic masterpiece, although it is accepted that not all of the music is of his hand. Rome would have never countenanced this opera about the immoral Emperor Nero and power-hungry Poppea, but Roman trends are apparent in the lyrical style, faster-paced recitative and comic moments. The opera was groundbreaking for its historical, non-religious subject matter, even if the librettist, Giovanni Busenello, deemed it necessary to mix in mythological ingredients. More importantly, *Poppea* raised the bar for dramatic intensity, introducing protagonists of unprecedented emotional depth. Monteverdi's gift for characterisation owed much to his commanding compositional technique, giving powerful expression to emotions of insecurity, despair, fury, erotic love and lust. *Poppea* is a controversial opera, one that seems to glorify immorality, though perhaps with irony. Scholars still debate the matter, but not one contests the work's milestone significance. It is one of the few 17th-century operas to hold a popular place in the modern repertory.

Italy lost its greatest composer in 1643, but Venetian opera more than survived Monteverdi's passing. Important figures at this time included Benedetto Ferrari (*c.*1603–81), who very possibly contributed music to *Poppea*, Francesco Manelli (*c.*1595–1667) and Francesco Sacrati (1605–50). Monteverdi's most esteemed successor, however, was one of his subordinates at St Mark's Cathedral, the organist-composer Francesco (Pietro) Cavalli (1602–76). The opera *L'Egisto*, premièred at the Teatro San Cassiano in 1643, was an early career milestone for Cavalli and consolidated his partnership with the librettist Giovanni Faustini. Cavalli and Faustini shared many other successes during the 1640s with historical or pseudo-historical subject matter. But it was with *Giasone*, a one-off collaboration with the librettist Giacinto Cicognini in 1649, that Cavalli landed his greatest triumph. Back firmly in the land of myth, the fast-paced tale of Jason, leader of the Argonauts, captured the public's imagination and became the most frequently performed opera of the century.

Margin notes:
Monteverdi: *L'incoronazione di Poppea*

Francesco Cavalli

Italian secular song

The madrigal tradition, having reached its height by the end of the 16th century, persisted only for a short time in Italy. The genre had become increasingly elitist: only gifted, trained singers could manage most of these songs, and the leading composers of the era were frequently writing for the pleasure of courts and wealthy families.

Among the most important late Italian madrigal collections are Benedetto Pallavicino's posthumously published Seventh and Eighth books

(1604, 1612), and Gesualdo's harmonically progressive Fifth and Sixth books (1611; see *Prelude*). Monteverdi's Fourth and Fifth books of Madrigals were issued in 1603 and 1605 respectively, the latter featuring some of his first songs with continuo accompaniment. His Sixth Book (1614) followed a similar format, and yet included two of his finest traditional examples: 'Ariadne's lament', reset in five parts from the original operatic recitative, and the lengthy 'Lagrimae d'amante al sepolcro dell'amata' (The lover's tears at the tomb of the beloved).

By the second decade the popularity of the multi-voice madrigal was giving way to the fresh genres of the solo madrigal and solo aria. The solo madrigal generally kept to the free-form organisation of the polyphonic madrigal, while the solo aria was structured in strophic form, with each verse set to the same music. Both monodic song forms accommodated vocal clarity and flexibility, including improvised embellishment, by means of chordal instrumental accompaniment.

The Florentine monodists championed both the solo madrigal and solo aria. Caccini published some of the earliest examples in his influential *Le nuove musiche* (1602), containing 12 madrigals and ten arias. Its literary sources match those of the multi-voice madrigals, favouring contemporary poets like Guarini and Ottavio Rinuccini with their heart-rending themes of unrequited love. Songs such as *Dovro dunque morire* (Must I then die?) and *Sfogava con le stelle* (One who was lovesick) offer the sort of drifting, freely expressive declamation that was utterly beyond the reach of the polyphonic madrigal.

The Florentines were not the only pioneers of such monodic song forms. In Ferrara, Luzzasco Luzzaschi was composing accompanied solo madrigals some time before he published them in his *Madrigali per cantare et sonare*, in 1601. Indeed, the originality of accompanied monody should not be overstressed. Italy's pre-madrigal *frottola*, a song form popular in the early 1500s, had occasionally anticipated the 17th-century monodic style, with virtual melody-harmony-bass organisation. Other monodic styles were found in various parts of Europe during the early 1600s, as in France with its *voix de ville*, featuring solo voice with chordal accompaniment.

A number of highly-skilled, forward-thinking composers embraced monody while hedging their bets with the older madrigal tradition. Sigismondo d'India (*c.*1582–1629) published his earliest essays in the monodic style in 1609 with a first book of *Musiche*, yet continued issuing sets of polyphonic madrigals well into the 1620s. Monteverdi, as already noted, was reluctant to abandon the polyphonic song, even though he had readily employed monody in his operas and the ballet *Tirsi e Clori* (1616).

A marked change came with his Seventh Book of Madrigals, published with the title *Concerto* in 1619. The major part of the collection concentrates on the chamber duet and pieces in *concertato* style, pitting solo and duet against choral and instrumental ensemble. Two of the monodic songs are composed in *genere rapresentativo*—to be sung and partially acted—and the collection concludes with the *Ballo: Tirsi e Clori*. All the pieces of the Seventh Book are scored with continuo.

In his astoundingly diverse Eighth Book of Madrigals (1638),

Monteverdi published a number of previously composed works under the title *Madrigali guerrieri et amorosi* (Madrigals of War and Love). The expressive power of the early Baroque is superbly illustrated in solos, duets and trio settings, five- and six-voice madrigals, as well as other expansive *concertato* works for soloists, chorus and larger instrumental ensembles. The most famous piece is the 'little theatrical work' *Combattimento di Tancredi e Clorinda* (1624), set for three singers, strings and continuo, with text drawn from Tasso's epic poem *Gerusalemme liberata* (Jerusalem Delivered). In this dramatic madrigal Monteverdi introduced his *stile concitato* (agitated or excited style), with fast repetitions of single notes representing the rage and adrenaline rush of battling Crusader knight and Saracen warrior. A narrator relates much of the action, and quick changes of melody,

ALEXANDRO GRANDI MVSIC·PRÆF·EXCELL·
PATRI MORVM PIETATE ÆSTIMABILI

▲ Alessandro Grandi, deputy to Monteverdi at St Marks Venice (1620–27), then maestro for three years at Santa Maria Maggiore, Bergamo. His life was cut short by the plague.

rhythm, pace and meter, vividly reflect the physical and emotional conflict. The story itself is tragic: at the end of the fight Tancredi lifts his opponent's visor, only to discover that he has slain the woman he loves.

By the end of the 1630s the (secular) cantata was achieving popularity. Alessandro Grandi (*c.*1586–1630), a leading composer of concertato-style motets and secular solo songs, was one of the first to use the term 'cantata', in his *Cantade et arie* of 1620. His examples for solo voice feature strophic variations over a bass *ostinato* (a repeated pattern). Giovanni Sances (*c.*1600–79), active in northern Italy and Vienna, was another early exponent of the cantata, and with his two-part *Cantade* (1633) he began to expand the genre's compositional scope by combining recitative and aria styles. The early cantata emerged accordingly as a multi-sectional piece, bringing together recitative and aria styles (strophic or through-composed), and typically scored for one or two voices with continuo. The cantata texts largely maintained the established fashions of other song forms, with pastoral and amatory themes predominant. The genre found its most committed advocates in Rome, promoted by such figures as Luigi Rossi, Marco Marazzoli (*c.*1602–62) and Giacomo Carissimi (1605–74, see *Chapter 2*).

Cantata

Sacred music and the birth of the oratorio

Both the polyphonic mass and motet, the principal sacred genres of the Renaissance, retained a time-honoured place in the early Baroque, though with diminished importance. Alongside the legacies of tradition, revolutionary stylistic inventions were quick to infect the Church. As early as 1602 Lodovico da Viadana incorporated basso continuo into his first volume of concertato motets, *Cento concerti ecclesiastici* (One Hundred Church Concertos), and in a second volume of 1607 he introduced liturgical monody for the first time. Monteverdi's monumental Vespers of 1610 combined both modern and traditional methods: Venetian polychoral writing, solos and duets, dramatic recitative, concertato settings, but also *cantus firmus* and imitative polyphonic techniques—there is barely any form, old or new, not represented. Particularly striking is the inclusion of adapted music from his opera *Orfeo*, creating a spectacular effect in the opening versicle and response *Deus in adjutorium*. This uncommissioned magnum opus will have surely helped secure Monteverdi's position as *maestro di capella* at St Mark's, Venice, in 1613.

The oratorio was another Italian genre to lay down roots in the early Baroque period. Its primary antecedent was the *laude*, a spiritual song based on a dramatic biblical text, which became the genre of choice for Rome's Congregazione dell'Oratorio, a religious order established by Filippo Neri (1515–95). For this order the composer Emilio de' Cavalieri wrote the allegorical religious work *La rappresentatione di anima e di corpo* (The Representation of the Soul and the Body), which had its first performance at the Oratorio de Santa Maria, in Vallicella, Rome, in 1600. It was scored throughout with recitative, song forms and choruses—all of which sits happily with what we now call oratorio. On the other hand, it was partially acted out with scenery and costumes, and so in this respect *La rappresentatione* resembles sacred opera.

Other precursors of the oratorio followed, such as *Eccone al gran Damasco*, a theatrical madrigal based on the conversion of St Paul by Giovanni Anerio (*c.*1567–1630). Forming part of his collection *Teatro armonico spirituale di madrigali* (1619), the work lasts around 20 minutes and comprises sung narration, soloists (representing Saul/Paul, Ananias and God), double choir (soldiers and angels), and ensemble instruments. In 1640, Pietro della Valle (1586–1652) apparently used the term 'oratorio' for the first time, though for a composition that lasts just 12 minutes. The oratorio, in the sense of a sung religious drama, unstaged, composed throughout and incorporating recitative, aria and chorus, was to establish itself decisively in the hands of Carissimi, the leading Roman composer of the mid century.

Influenced by Roman opera, Carissimi's *Jephte* (1648) is one of the early masterpieces of the oratorio genre. The story, conveyed in Latin, concerns the eponymous 'mighty warrior', who makes an unprompted and reckless vow to God that if he grants him victory over the Ammonites, he will sacrifice the first thing that comes out of his house to meet him on his return. Jephthah enjoys a resounding victory, but as he approaches home he is met by his daughter, his only child. Devastated, he relates to her his vow. She insists that he should remain steadfast to his promise, but asks to be granted two months to roam the hills and weep with her friends. *Jephte* is introduced by the *historicus* (narrator), who sets the scene from Judges chapter 11, starting at verse 28. The following ten verses are related in the form of recitative, ariettas, duets and choruses, with further narration taken up by the chorus, in declamatory style, and other smaller vocal groups.

Additional text is interpolated at various points to help dramatise the story. The most effective instance of this is found in the final chorus, 'Weep, O children of Israel', a poignant lament on the fate of Jephthah's daughter.

Since the Catholic Church demanded the closure of theatres during Lent, the oratorio flourished during that time of year as a kind of unstaged sacred opera. Only some were composed specifically for performance in an oratory (a place of prayer). The Church encouraged both public and private productions, since they could serve a useful didactic purpose in relaying biblical stories, usually drawn from the Old Testament. Like Roman opera, the instrumental forces involved were small, sometimes nothing more than a continuo ensemble (see also *Chapter 2*).

Instrumental music: new paths

The growth of instrumental music during the 16th century, as noted in the *Prologue*, owed much to the burgeoning music printing industry and an expanding middle class. It is difficult to ascertain how much instrumental music was written, even printed, and many documents of untexted music do not obviously suggest instrumental idioms. But lute and keyboard pieces were popular, as were ensemble dances, and vocal pieces will have been occasionally performed in instrumental form. While the voice reigned supreme during the Renaissance, the Baroque era saw a levelling of the musical field with a marked rise in instrumental composition.

By the end of the 16th century the pairing of ensemble dances through thematic variation had become common; for example, the *pavane-galliard* in France and England, or the *passamezzo-saltarello* in Italy. These were still primarily functional dances, devised for social occasions such as weddings and banquets. During the early 17th century there was a progressive tendency to issue collections of dances in different styles. This practice was to establish the dance suite: a group of contrasting, stylised dances composed with little regard for practical dancing, rather to be enjoyed by both performer and listener simply as music. The term 'suite' was at this time confined to a sequence of mixed *branles*; not until the second half of the century was the term applied to sets of contrasting dances. Thus suites in all but name, collections were often issued with titles specifying the contained

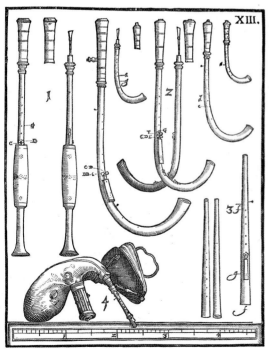

1. Baſſett: Nicolo. 2. Krumbhorner. 3. Cornetti muti: ſtille Zincken.
4. Sackpfeiff mit dem Blaßbalg.
B iii

Early dance suite

◀ A selection of wind instruments from *Theatrum instrumentorum* (pub. 1620), a pictorial supplement to Book II (De organographia) of Praetorius's Syntagma Musicum.
1. Shawms;
2. Crumbhorns;
3. Cornetts;
4. Bagpipe.

XXI

▶ Stringed instruments from the *Theatrum instrumentorum*. The represented violin family ranges from the three-stringed rebec (1) to the 'Bas-Geig de bracio', essentially a five-string cello (6); also 7. Trumpet marine; 8. Scheitholt, ancestor of the modern zither.

ɪ. ꝫ. Kleine Poſchen / Geigen ein Octav höher. ꝫ. Diſcant-Geig ein Quart höher. 4. Rechte Diſcant-Geig. 5. Tenor-Geig. 6 Bas-Geig de bracio. 7. Trumſcheit. 8. Scheidtholtz.

sequence of dances: *Newe Padouan, Intrada, Däntz und Galliarda* (1611), by the German composer Paul Peuerl, is one of the early examples. Both Peuerl and his compatriot Johann Schein commonly used melodic variation to provide unity to dance collections. The 20 suites of Schein's *Banchetto musicale* (Musical Banquet, 1617) adhere to either variation form or freer methods of composition, though each one comprises a pavane, galliarde, courante and allemande-*tripla* (a duple-metre allemande ending with a triple-metre variation). The Germans were the leading pioneers of the Baroque suite.

Other instrumental genres

A number of Renaissance instrumental genres maintained popularity in the early Baroque. They included the vocally inspired *canzona* and the pseudo-improvisatory *fantasia*, which were both contrapuntal in style and served the repertories of the solo instrument and ensemble. Girolamo Frescobaldi's keyboard canzonas and John Dowland's lute fantasias represent Italian and English exemplars of each. The more restrained, contrapuntal (often fugal) *ricercare* was another favourite, increasingly a genre for the keyboard. Contrasting to that style was the keyboard *toccata*, typically fast and flashy, featuring swift passage-work against held chords, alternating with periods of counterpoint. Frescobaldi, again, was the leading early 17th-century composer of both ricercares and toccatas. The revered German composers Hans Hassler and Johann Froberger contributed to each of the above named genres, while the English were largely happy to restrict their solo music to fantasias and stylised dances.

Instrumental pieces often acquired their form through procedures like fugue or variation technique. More rigid formal structures were also common, such as the time-honoured repeated harmonic sequence, along with its modern 'ground-bass' variant, featuring melodic variations over a repeated bass pattern. Binary form was popular in dance music. At the outset of the century the form typically consisted of two repeated sections, each of which would adhere closely to the tonic key. A more sophisticated binary form, as found in various ensemble dances of William Lawes's (later named) 'Fantasia Suites' (1630s), was built around two principal key centres. In this type, the first section of the piece introduces material that drives tonal progression from the tonic to the dominant key centre; the second section, of equal or greater length, begins in the dominant key and steers back towards the tonic, sometimes via other keys. In a minor key work, the second key centre may be that of the relative major or the dominant.

Binary form

These structural techniques helped bring focus to a widening instrumental repertory, and with it came a new emphasis on idiom. In lute and keyboard music, embellished transcriptions of vocal music were in decline. Keyboard music itself started to become written specifically for organ or harpsichord, not so interchangeable as it had been in the previous century. Composers were beginning to consider instrumental sonority and idiomatic expression as central to the conception of their work.

The Italian innovators

Girolamo Frescobaldi (1583–1643) was Italy's outstanding keyboard composer of the early 17th century. A renowned virtuoso, he was elected to the post of organist at St Peter's in Rome in 1608, and financial security was assured a few years later when he gained an additional position with Cardinal Aldobrandini, patron of the poet Tasso. Apart from a six-year period in Florence (1628–34), Frescobaldi centred his career on Rome. His published keyboard compositions explore the emotionally-charged harmonic language of his teacher, Luzzaschi, and other modernists of the *seconda prattica* school. Often virtuosic, the music is wide-ranging, full of spontaneity and expressive freedom. The *Ricercari et canzoni* (1615), two books of keyboard toccatas (1615, 1627) and the liturgical organ collection *Fiori musicali* (Musical Flowers, 1635) are among his highest achievements. The latter was particularly influential: J. S. Bach made his own manuscript copy some 80 years later, and Johann Fux, greatly impressed by Frescobaldi's strict counterpoint, included various pieces in his lauded composition treatise *Gradus ad Parnassum* (1725).

For all his forward thinking and harmonic daring, Frescobaldi did not advance new Italianate idioms in the vein of Monteverdi or Alessandro Grandi. In the realm of instrumental ensemble music he was a comparative latecomer to *basso continuo*, succumbing to the style in his first book of *Canzoni*, published in 1628. Lesser Italian composers were much quicker to employ basso continuo, using the texture to emancipate the solo instrument, as it had the solo voice. Their industry resulted in the development of the

Girolamo Frescobaldi

◄ Girolamo Frescobaldi, one of the most influential keyboard composers of the early Baroque. He nurtured many younger talents, among them the German virtuoso Johann J. Froberger.

61

instrumental sonata, a genre that asserted the metrical unit while allowing the soloist(s) unprecedented melodic and rhythmic freedom.

The term 'sonata', from the Italian *suonare* (to sound), had initially a rather vague usage. Giovanni Gabrieli seems to have claimed it first for his instrumental *Sonata pian' e forte* of 1597 (see *Prelude*), a piece modelled on vocal textures and one that other composers might have called a 'sinfonia' or 'canzone'. The trio sonata, emerging in the early years of the 17th century, brought greater idiomatic and virtuosic expression to instrumental ensemble music. Comprising two lead instruments and continuo, the trio sonata emphasised the relationship of upper melodic parts to an independent bass line (the 'trio' designation thus relating to the parts, not the performers, who are typically four in number). The Jewish Italian composer Salomone Rossi (1570–c.1630) was one of the first to bring definition to this new ensemble style in his *Sinfonie e gagliarde* (Books I and II), published 1607/8, followed by Giovanni Cima (1570–1630) in his *Concerti ecclesiastici* (of 1610). Cima's collection also introduced the first

sonata for violin and continuo, a combination that Biagio Marini (1594–1663) promoted with great flair in the extensive *Affetti musicali* (Musical Affections, 1617).

Born in Brescia, Marini was working under Monteverdi as a violinist at St Mark's, Venice, when he brought out his *Affetti musicali*. Desiring to impress the right people, he named the 26 pieces of the collection after prominent Venetians. Nearly a third of them are inspired by dances, while others (generally more serious in sentiment) are classed as sinfonias, canzonas or sonatas. There is not much to distinguish his sinfonias from his sonatas, except that the sinfonia may be very short and more cohesive in mood. Marini's resourceful and idiomatic approach comes to the fore in the two sinfonias for solo violin and continuo, *La Orlandina* and *La Gardana*, which are in places quasi-improvisatory and technically demanding. The remarkable *La Foscarina* for two violins and continuo is a substantial, multisectional sonata, one of the first to include tremolo effects and phrasing directions. The composer's Op. 8 collection of 1629 is also striking, especially for its triple-stopping and scordatura—tuning the strings to alternative pitches to create colouristic and harmonic diversity.

Carlo Farina (c.1604–39) went even further than Marini in demonstrating the violin's expressive potential: his playful *Capriccio stravagante* (1627) utilises the techniques of tremolo, pizzicato, glissando and *col legno* (with the wood of the bow) to mimic the sounds of other musical instruments and even animals. Farina was a key figure in the transmission of the new Italian instrumental style, since he served the Elector of Saxony, Johann Georg I, in Dresden for several years (under Heinrich Schütz) and published his music there. He too promoted the solo sonata, as did Giovanni Battista Fontana (c.1589–c.1630) and Giovanni Battista Buonamente (d.1642). The violin was favoured above other instruments in such music due to its expressive, vocal-like qualities, penetrating sonority and unrivalled agility. It was to become the instrument of the professional, relegating the fretted treble viol mainly to domestic music-making.

Europe and the dissemination of the Italian style

German lands

The German states suffered miserably during the Thirty Years' War (1618–48). The brutal conflicts caused bloodshed on an unprecedented scale as Protestant powers fought to protect or snatch new territories from the Holy Roman Empire. The conflict became Europe-wide as the Protestant lands of Denmark, Sweden and Holland, joined by Catholic France, sought to curtail the power of the Habsburgs. Matters of religion became almost irrelevant. An unstable conclusion was reached with the Peace of Westphalia in 1648, leaving many German states in economic ruin.

German musical life had been comparatively unruffled during much of the previous century. The period had witnessed the flourishing of the Lutheran chorale: a vernacular, strophic form that was commonly sung in unison without accompaniment. Luther had ensured its place as an integral part of the church service, enabling the congregation to actively proclaim their personal relationship with God. The tradition of four-part chorale harmonisation, begun during the 16th century, gathered pace during the early Baroque.

Close geographical proximity and established trade routes encouraged the speedy dissemination of the Baroque style into German-speaking lands. Whilst there were few incentives to attract Italian composers into the unstable territories of central Europe (beyond the Habsburg capital of Vienna at least), a number of German composers visited Italy and brought back the new forms. One of the first important composers to do so was

▼ General Albrecht von Wallenstein's army besieges Protestant-held Leipzig, 1632, during the Thirty Years' War (1618–48).

▲ Michael Praetorius, a leading exponent of the Lutheran church style and author of the famous musical treatise *Syntagma musicum*.

Hans Leo Hassler (1564–1612). Having studied and worked for a brief period in Venice (1584/5), he occupied posts at Augsburg, Nuremberg and Dresden, where he promoted the Italian madrigal and the polychoral style.

Unlike Hassler, Michael Praetorius (1571–1621) never studied or worked in Italy, but he absorbed the Italian style from others. First as an organist, then as *Kapellmeister*, he spent 18 years in service to Duke Heinrich Julius of Brunswick at Wolfenbüttel. After the duke's death in 1613, he became virtually itinerant and much in demand at courts throughout Northern Germany. Praetorius was devoted to the Lutheran chorale tradition, publishing more than 1,000 settings for small to large vocal groups in his nine-volume *Musae Sioniae* (1605–10). His first Italianisms appeared in the *Polyhymnia caduceatrix* (1619), a lavish fusion of the Venetian polychoral style and Lutheran chorale, scored for soloists, multiple choirs, brass and continuo. Reminiscent of Monteverdi's Vespers, the collection indulges grand concertato settings, as in 'Wachet auf' (Sleepers, awake) and 'In dulci jubilo' (In sweet jubilation). The traditional tune of the latter is familiar to the English-speaking world in the form of the 19th-century carol 'Good Christian men, rejoice'.

Praetorius's one surviving secular collection is the *Terpsichore* (1612), containing 312 four- to six-part settings of French dances, some freely invented, others arrangements of existing pieces. The composer gained a reputation as one of the most important music scholars of the age with the ambitious *Syntagma musicum*. Examining compositional forms and practice, instruments and notation, the treatise was published in three large volumes between 1615 and 1619, with a pictorial supplement, *Theatrum instrumentorum* (Theatre of Instruments), appearing in 1620.

Heinrich Schütz

It was probably Heinrich Schütz (1585–1672) who fired Praetorius's enthusiasm for the Italian manner when the pair met at Dresden. Having studied for several years with Giovanni Gabrieli in Venice, Schütz gained employment at the Dresden court in 1615 and remained there most of his professional life. He was an outstanding emissary of the Italian style and unlike other important German composers of his era, he barely took notice of the Lutheran chorale. Nonetheless, he was inspired by the Protestant liturgy and Lutheran ideal of vernacular worship. His first major sacred

Psalms of David

publication was the imposing *Psalms of David* (1619), a collection that brings together German polyphonic traditions, solo instruments, basso-continuo and the Venetian polychoral idiom. Amongst the most spectacular pieces is 'Alleluja! Lobet den Herren in seinem Heiligtum', an appropriately opulent interpretation of Psalm 150. Set in concertato style, it alternates vocal-instrumental duets and sumptuous choruses with the mighty force of four choirs and a varied ensemble of recorder, violin, pairs of bassoons, cornetts and trombones, and continuo.

Schütz turned to a more intimate manner with his *Resurrection History*, an important forerunner of the German oratorio. Sometimes referred to as his *Easter Oratorio*, it incorporates a liturgical recitative style (chant with continuo), as well as solos, duets, choruses and independent instrumental parts. The work's completion, in 1623, coincided with a desperate period of war-time hardship at the Dresden court; Schütz and other court musicians has to endure unpaid salaries for close on two years.

It was not always easy for Schütz to publish his music in Dresden. His first collection of *Symphoniae sacrae* dates from his second trip to Venice, 1628–9, and we might assume that during this time he met Monteverdi. This outstanding collection comprises emotionally wide-ranging motets for one to three voices, *obbligato* instruments and continuo. Its very title reflects the influence of Schütz's teacher, Gabrieli, whose two principal collections of sacred music—published 1597 and 1615—bear the same designation. But the work also derives inspiration from Monteverdi, particularly with its pervasive concertato-madrigal style. Extended instrumental preludes and interludes add structural and colouristic diversity to a number of the motets.

Symphoniae sacrae

Schütz is generally considered the author of the first German opera, *Daphne* (1627), based on Rinnuccini's libretto of 1597. The music is lost, so it is impossible to verify the fact. Five years after composing the work, Schütz wrote about his experiences of opera in Italy, noting 'how a comedy of diverse voices can be translated into declamatory style and be brought to the stage and enacted in song'. He also recorded that to his knowledge the method was 'completely unknown in Germany'. It seems that Schütz learned about operatic recitative only after he wrote *Daphne*. He had created recitative of sorts in the *Resurrection History*, though the style lacks the expressive freedom of operatic recitative, and clearly Schütz thought as much. The earliest surviving German opera is the Singspiel *Seelewig* (1644) by the Nuremberg-based Sigmund Staden (1607–55).

Other pieces by Schütz from this period include the *Musikalische Exequien* (1636) and a second volume of *Symphoniae sacrae* (1647). His oratorio-style *Seven Last Words* may also date from the late 1640s. In keeping with a number of works composed during the crippling war years, its scoring is utilitarian: five singers, five unspecified solo instruments (that is, whatever is available) and continuo. Schütz was Germany's first composer to gain international renown and he remained active well into old age (see also *Chapter 2*).

Johann Schein (1586–1630) was another composer who melded German and Italian styles. Aged 30 he took up as *Thomaskantor* at Leipzig, the post that J. S. Bach would occupy over a century later. He employed continuo for the first time in his chorale-based *Opella nova* (Part I: 1618), a progressive collection but one more modest in scope than Praetorius's *Polyhymnia caduceatrix*. Schein was pioneering in secular music also; his *Banchetto musicale* (metioned earlier) represents an early example of the variation dance suite, while in *Hirten Lust* (Pastoral Delights, 1624) he produced the first collection of German continuo madrigals.

Johann Schein

German
keyboard
composers

The German keyboard tradition advanced significantly at this time. Samuel Scheidt (1587–1654) and Heinrich Scheidemann (*c.*1595–1663), both pupils of the Dutch composer Jan Sweelinck, established the central and north German organ schools respectively. Scheidt's three-volume *Tabulatura nova* (1624) contains both secular and sacred organ music; eight sets within the collection are based on Lutheran chorales and rank alongside the finest instrumental church music of the age. Towards the middle of the century Johann Froberger (1616–67) became the region's leading harpsichordist. A pupil of Frescobaldi, he served intermittently in Vienna as court organist, but was otherwise busy as an itinerant composer-performer. His chief importance lies in his transmission of the keyboard suite (see *Chapter 2*).

Andreas
Hammerschmidt

The Bohemian-born Andreas Hammerschmidt (*c.*1612–75) was also a gifted keyboardist and a leading composer of sacred music. From 1639 he served as organist to the Johanniskirche in Zittau, where he produced church concertos, sacred madrigals and motets in several sets of *Musikalische Andachten* (Musical Devotions, 1639–46). He was additionally the author of 'sacred dialogues', including the concertato-style collection *Gespräche zwischen Gott und einer gläubigen Seelen* (Conversations Between God and a Believer, 1645), scored for two to four voices and continuo.

German composers were heavily preoccupied with sacred music during the early century, far more so than their counterparts in Italy, France or England. The Thirty Years' War, with its uncertainties and privations, together with regular out-breaks of plague, undoubtedly stimulated heavenwards perspectives. The melding of the Lutheran chorale, basso continuo and concertato styles resulted in a strong, progressive sacred musical tradition that would inspire an impressive succession of German composers, culminating in the genius of Bach.

The low countries

Comprising modern-day Holland, Belgium and Luxembourg, the Low Countries were embroiled in the Eighty Years' War with Spain from 1568 to 1648. Struggling for independence, many Dutch people in the northern provinces embraced Reformation teaching, converting to Calvinism either out of religious conviction or in defiance of Spanish rule. The Southern Netherlands (Luxembourg and most of Belgium) remained Catholic and subject to Spain until 1713. War and economic adversity took its toll on musical life, while strict Calvinist teaching in the north severely limited the role of music in church. These factors go some way towards explaining why the region that had spawned some of the greatest Renaissance composers— Du Fay, Josquin des Prez, Willaert and Lassus among them—was to lose its reputation for musical excellence.

Jan
Pieterszoon
Sweelinck

The Dutch composer Jan Pieterszoon Sweelinck (1562–1621), lifelong organist at the Oude Kerke in Amsterdam, brought to an end the impressive musical heritage of the Low Countries. In sacred music he is chiefly remembered for polyphonic psalm settings built around *cantus firmi*, based on the melodies of the Genevan Psalter. Published in four volumes between 1604 and 1621, his collections set the Marot and Bèze French texts and were probably intended for private use by Calvinist Bourgeoisie. Sweelinck seems to have been sympathetic to Catholicism given his inclusion of a Marian antiphon in the motet collection *Cantiones sacrae* (1619), although Calvinist and Lutheran liturgies take priority.

Sweelinck was markedly eclectic in his secular music, both vocal and instrumental. His four-volume *Rimes françoises et italiennes* of 1612 contains French chansons and Italian madrigals, essentially maintaining a 16th-century tradition. The (posthumously published) keyboard music consists of variations, toccatas and fantasias, and draws inspiration from the music of Italy, Spain and England. The English connection is linked to Peter Philips (*c.*1560–1628) and John Bull (*c.*1562–1628), both Catholic composers who sought refuge in Belgium. Bull's situation was ignominious, with a swift exit from England following a charge of adultery in 1613; he managed to plead sufficient innocence to secure the post of organist of Antwerp Cathedral in 1617.

▲ Dutch composer Jan Pieterszoon Sweelinck

Sweelinck barely ventured into the Baroque style. Of those that followed him, the diplomat Constantijn Huygens is conspicuous as the first Dutch composer of the vocal monodic style. He issued monodies in his *Pathodia sacra et profana* in Paris in 1647, the collection apparently the earliest French print of music with continuo. The amateur composer produced a famous son, Christiaan Huygens—mathematician, astronomer, physicist and inventor of the pendulum clock.

France

France's 'Wars of Religion' were officially ended in 1598 by the Edict of Nantes, which granted Protestants civil rights and freedom of worship. However, religious and political life was far from settled. Cardinal Richelieu, chief minister of France from 1624 to 1642, sought to diminish the political power of both Protestants and nobles who opposed absolute monarchy. The increasing centralisation of authority and control naturally affected the arts, which became ever more concentrated around the royal court in Paris.

The French court was at this time nurturing the *ballet de cour* (court ballet), a hybrid genre of musical theatre derived in part from the Burgundian pantomime (*entremet*) and Italian *intermedio*. The first examples, appearing in the 1570s, were theme-based dramas with rather diffuse narratives. But with *Circé, ou le Balet comique de la Royne*

Ballet de cour

(1581) the genre achieved considerable unity, with all the constituent elements of text, music, courtly dance, set design and costume working together in a manner that pre-empted Italian opera. Possibly due to court fashions, no subsequent productions came close to the unity of *Circé* for many years.

The *ballet de cour* was a medium of royal propaganda: its narratives celebrated the power and influence of the king and often bestowed on him god-like status. Unfortunately for Henry IV, this noble art form did little to discourage his assassin, Francois Ravaillac, in 1610. Following the succession of his son, the eight-year-old Louis XIII (r. 1610–43), the genre matured with a renewed vision of dramatic unity. The typical *ballet de cour* engaged sung commentaries (solo *récits*), dances and choruses (*entrées*), rhymed verse (*vers*), and a concluding *grand ballet*. Pierre Guédron (c. 1564–c. 1620) and Antoine Boësset (1586–1643) were two of the leading court ballet composers, and both created songs of lasting popularity. Their typical courtly *air* was a strophic verse-setting, arranged either polyphonically for several voices or as a solo song with lute accompaniment. The *air de cour* remained the leading French song form throughout the early 17th century.

24 Violons du Roi

The '24 Violons du Roi' was another important feature of the French court. Established around 1614, the ensemble was chiefly engaged for the performance of ballets and dance suites. Smaller string-orientated ensembles were not unknown elsewhere, but the French model was of particular significance for its configuration: *dessus* (violins), *haute contres* (small violas), *tailles* (medium size violas), *quintes* (large violas) and *basses de violon* (bass violins). The French were accordingly the leading pioneers of the five-part orchestral string texture, soon to become a convention throughout Europe.

Imported opera

For some time France cheerfully ignored Italian opera. But in 1643, while the infant King Louis XIV was still trying to formulate complete sentences, let alone foreign policy, the Italian-born chief minister, Cardinal Jules Mazarin, set about importing Italian musical culture. He lured to Paris the composer Marazzoli, who stayed for two years writing music for the court of the Queen Regent, Anne of Austria. By 1645 Mazarin had succeeded in funding a production of Francesco Sacrati's *La finta pazza*, followed by Cavalli's *L'Egisto* in 1646; both operas were performed in Italian, by Italians. The composer Luigi Rossi arrived in Paris around this same time and immediately gained support from the exiled Cardinal Antonio Barberini, his former patron. Barberini joined forces with Mazarin to mount a lavish staging of Rossi's *Orfeo* in 1647. With sets and machine-operated effects by Giacomo Torelli, the opera was repeated seven times but criticised outside royal circles for its exorbitant expense. Mazarin took scant notice of public and political criticism; he was in any case intent on strengthening monarchical rule. When the pro-*parlement* Fronde movement took to the streets in 1648 to challenge his power-mongering strategies, they pursued and punished those guilty by association. Rossi escaped Paris, but Torelli was imprisoned. Fronde unrest persisted until 1653.

Despite the committed and continuing efforts of Mazarin, Italian opera in mid-century France was to prove something of a non-starter. It is therefore ironic that French music theatre would soon be transformed by another Italian émigré: Giovanni Battista Lulli.

Spain

Tomás Luis de Victoria (1548–1611) was the towering composer of the Spanish Renaissance and one of the greatest polyphonists of the age. Exclusively devoted to religious music, he rose to prominence in Rome where he trained, held several appointments, and entered the priesthood. In the 1580s he returned to Spain to become chaplain and choirmaster to Empress Maria of Austria, sister of King Philip II. Victoria wrote around 20 masses, mainly using the 'parody' technique, but his chief fame rests on expressive motets—such arresting pieces as *O quam gloriosum est regnum* (1572) and the exquisite *Trahe me, post te* (1583). During his own lifetime he enjoyed an international reputation, his music performed throughout much of southen and central Europe, even as far afield as Mexico and Columbia.

Victoria crowned his output with the *Officium defunctorum*, a self-described swan-song written in 1603 for the funeral of Empress Maria. The magnificent six-voice Requiem Mass from the *Officium* betrays a clear debt to the Roman polyphonic style, though Victoria's spiritual vigour inspires a more modernistic harmonic language, a characteristic feature that sets his music apart from the polished style of Palestrina. For its passion and intensity, his craft has been compared to the expressionistic paintings of his compatriot El Greco. Victoria was the last in an influential line of Spanish Renaissance composers, his country's hall of fame including Cristóbal de Morales (*c.*1500–53), Luís Milán (*c.*1500–*c.*1561), Antonio de Cabezón (*c.*1510–66) and Francisco Guerrero (1528–99).

The early years of the 17th century saw no pronounced changes of musical style in Spain. The same was true of neighbouring Portugal, a country politically unified with Spain, where Filipe de Magalhães (*c.*1563–1652) and Duarte Lobo (1564?–1646) continued the Renaissance sacred music tradition. However, as in Italy, there was a lessening interest in the polyphonic mass and motet. A colourful addition to church music came from the otherwise secular and rustic *villancico*, which served as a sacred or devotional vocal piece in the vernacular. Typically syncopated and triple-metered, it employed a refrain-stanza-refrain form that was also common to secular text settings.

Following Victoria, Spain's most prominent composer was Mateo Romero (*c.*1575–1647). Of Flemish birth, Romero served the royal court as *maestro de capilla* for 35 years until his retirement in 1633. He is largely

Tomás Luis de Victoria

Officium defunctorum

Mateo Romero

credited for steering Spanish music into the Baroque era, incorporating basso continuo in such pieces as his antiphonal *Missa bonae voluntatis* and the eight-voice motet *In devotione*. In secular songs he employed accented dissonances and chromaticisms that would have tickled the ears of the Italian *moderno* school. In the 1640s Juan Hidalgo (1614–1685) began to make his indelible impression on Spanish musical culture, establishing his reputation with *villancicos* and secular songs.

Spain's one early attempt at opera was *La selva sin amor* (The Forest Without Love, 1627), with libretto by the acclaimed poet Lope de Vega. While not unappreciated, it failed to inspire any immediate progeny. The Spanish may have considered the pastoral fable rather dull. Moreover, the Italian composers involved—Filippo Piccinini and Bernardo Monanni—possessed little expertise in opera.

England

A golden age of poetry, drama and music that had begun in late Elizabethan England continued well into the reign of the first Stuart King, James I (r. 1603–25). This was the era of William Shakespeare, John Donne, Ben Jonson and Francis Bacon, with composers such as William Byrd, John Dowland, John Bull, Thomas Weelkes and Orlando Gibbons all leading

▼ A view of London from the engraving *Londinum Florentissima Britanniae Urbs* (1616). St Pauls dominates the north side of the Thames; the Bear Garden Theatre and Globe Theatre can be seen on the south side.

figures in English musical life. While not innovators like the Italians, the English school blazed in artistic excellence.

The light, pastoral Italian madrigal style made its deepest impression on the English when translated examples began to appear towards the end of the 16th century. The success of the collections *Musica Transalpina* (1588) and *Italian Madrigals Englished* (1590) encouraged native composers to naturalise the genre. They sometimes set translated Italian texts, but the English on balance preferred new bespoke verse and some composers even wrote their own. Thomas Morley (*c.*1557–1602) was first at the helm of the English madrigal style, writing both light and sombre pieces in his *First Book of Madrigals for Four Voices*, published 1594. Owning a royal license to print music and music paper, he supervised the publication of *The Triumphes of Oriana* (1601), an anthology of 25 pastoral madrigals by 23 English composers, written in honour of Queen Elizabeth.

English madrigal

Incorporated in *The Triumphes* were pieces by Thomas Weelkes (1576–1623) and John Wilbye (1574–1638), two outstanding composers who enriched the vintage of the madrigalian era. Weelkes published several sets of songs, the finest of which are found in his *Madrigals of 5 & 6 Parts* (1600). Wilbye produced just two madrigal sets, in 1598 and 1609, the second arguably the crowning collection of the English madrigal style. In this there is some joyous music, but the composer's sensitivity and skill come to the fore in songs of deep melancholy—a perfect example being 'Weep, weep mine eyes'—as well as in songs of wide-ranging emotions, such as 'All pleasure is of this condition'.

Thomas Weelkes, John Wilbye

Orlando Gibbons (1583–1625) issued his *First Set of Madrigals and Mottets* in 1612, and with it the short but exquisite 'The Silver Swanne'. In style this famous piece veers toward the *ayre*, giving major prominence to its uppermost part. Gibbons was never a strict madrigalist; a sign of the times, since the equal-voiced madrigal was by now pushing its sell-by date and losing ground to the lute song (or lute *ayre*), as championed by the itinerant musician John Dowland (1563–1626).

Dowland was one of Europe's foremost lutenists and benefited from several well paid years (1598–1606) in service to King Christian IV of Denmark. The international circulation of his compositions for solo lute (an instrument enormously popular throughout the 16th and early 17th centuries) further bolstered his reputation, though in England he struggled to gain the recognition he deserved. In vocal music he was intensely expressive and unmatched among the English composers in his appetite for melancholy. Impassioned solo songs such as 'I saw my lady weep', 'Mourn, mourn, day is with darkness fled', together with his renowned 'Flow, my teares', appear in his *Second Booke of Songs or Ayres* (1600) and reflect the kind of despair and pessimism common to many Italian songs of the same period. A similar mood pervades the seven stunning Lachrimae pavans of his consort anthology *Lachrimae, or Seaven Teares* (1604). The opening motif of the song 'Flow, my teares' provides the starting point of each contrapuntal pavan, scored for viols in five parts with lute accompaniment. Light relief is afforded by other dances of the 21-piece collection, such as 'The Earle of Essex Galliard' and 'Mistresse Nichols Almand'.

John Dowland and the lute song

▲ William Byrd, whose heart and finest music were rooted in the Catholic tradition.

Dowland may have met members of the Camerata when he visited Florence in 1595, but he never adopted their monodic style. His expressive airs for solo voice with lute accompaniment and bass part remained predominantly contrapuntal, even if his final song collection, A *Pilgrime's Solace* (1612), accommodated a more declamatory, chordal style. While his music was in some ways conservative, his powerfully expressionistic text settings adhered to the principles of Monteverdi's *seconda prattica*. Typical is the affecting song 'In darkness let me dwell' (1610), in which lute accompaniment and vocal melody share in the anguish of the text, generating abrupt dissonances, false relations and angular turns of phrase.

Virginalists

Key to England's importance and influence as a musical centre was its burgeoning school of virginalists. In no other European country was the development of keyboard style and technique more significant. Leading the way was William Byrd (*c.*1540–1623), the country's greatest composer of the period, together with John Bull and Orlando Gibbons. They were the sole contributors to the first printed collection of keyboard works in England, the *Parthenia* (1613), comprising dances, preludes and fantasias. Among Byrd's pieces is the often-played *Pavan: the Earl of Salisbury*, composed in memory of the politician and music patron Robert Cecil (1563–1612). A second important and much larger collection followed with the (now so-called) *Fitzwilliam Virginal Book*, possibly compiled by the recusant Francis Tregian while serving time in London's Fleet prison. Completed in 1619, it contains nearly 300 pieces by predominantly English composers from Thomas Tallis to the present. The opening work is one of Bull's masterpieces, 30 variations on the song *Walsingham*. Byrd, Peter Philips and Giles Farnaby (*c.*1563–1640) are also featured composers.

William Byrd: sacred music

Byrd's genius had been recognised at an early age. As a 20-year-old he became organist and choirmaster at Lincoln Cathedral, and in 1572 he was appointed organist of the Chapel Royal, sharing the post with his teacher, Thomas Tallis (*c.*1505–85). Byrd mastered every genre he touched, as his *Psalms, Songs and Sonnets* (1611) confirms in part with its various anthems, polyphonic songs, consort songs and consort fantasias. He excelled above all in sacred music and is widely considered to be the greatest English church composer who ever lived. As a Catholic he enjoyed a certain degree of religious freedom under Queen Elizabeth, his own forbearance (and loyalty to the crown) apparent from some 60 Anglican anthems and other music he supplied for the Protestant liturgy. His finest sacred compositions, however, were conceived for the Roman rite. These are represented by Latin motets, most of them published in three sets of *Cantiones* (1575–91), and three commanding masses dating from the 1590s. Such pieces will have been composed for illegal use in the private chapels of wealthy Catholics.

More unaccompanied liturgical music—Mass propers and Office music—appeared in two volumes of *Gradualia*. In the first, issued in 1605, Byrd wrote about his mystical approach to scriptural text setting:

I have found there is a certain hidden power in the thoughts behind the words, so that as one meditates upon the scared texts, continually and deeply considering them, the right melodies, in some mysterious way, freely suggest themselves.

Byrd was neither the first nor the last composer to sense a guiding hand in the creative process. Yet the timing of the *Gradualia* could hardly have been worse: just months later the Gunpowder Plot was uncovered, resulting in a new era of Catholic persecution. The publication was immediately withdrawn. Nevertheless, the situation for Byrd was not so bad to prevent the London publication of his second volume in 1607, and the republication of both in 1610. Designed for private worship and possibly with a foreign market in mind, the two *Gradualia* were Byrd's last published works of Latin Church music.

Other important contributors to English sacred music included Weelkes, Gibbons, Thomas Tomkins (1572–1656) and William Lawes (1602–45), each of whom wrote anthems in some quantity. The English anthem, comparable to the Latin motet, took two forms at this time. The 'full' anthem was a polyphonic choral setting; Tomkins's *When David heard*, published in his *Songs of 3. 4. 5. & 6. parts* (1622), and Gibbons's jubilant *O clap your hands*, are marvellous examples of the form. The newer 'verse' anthem featured soloists with instrumental accompaniment (usually organ), in alternation with the chorus, as in Weelkes's 'Give ear, O Lord'. The more expressive verse anthem became increasingly popular during the course of the early century.

Anthem

Many leading composers of the day had little to do with the burgeoning theatrical form of the *masque*. The Stuart masque was to the English what the *ballet de cour* was to the French: a vehicle for the celebration of royalty, asserting its power, authority and wisdom. It would typically include songs, dances and instrumental interludes, and yet the composer's role was lower in pecking order to that of every other artistic contributor—a state of affairs confirmed by the absence of any surviving masque score. Still, with the carrot of royal patronage, the masque attracted the talents of a few notable composers including Alfonso Ferrabosco II (*c.*1575–1628) and the poet-composer Thomas Campion (1567–1620). The dramatist and poet Ben Johnson, in collaboration with the set designer (and architect) Inigo Jones, provided the English court with many productions in the early century. However it is John Milton's *Comus* (1634), with music by Henry Lawes (1596–1662), that history remembers above all others.

Masque

Baroque
idioms

▼ The Puritans
sought to purge
churches of all
'idolatrous' imagery,
so to bring the focus
of worship upon
God rather than the
image itself. Organs
were abolished
(and polyphonic
music in general)
because harmony
was regarded as
inappropriately
sensual. The Puritan
assault on stage
plays led to the
destruction of the
Globe Theatre, in
1644.

Considering the importance of the masque to courtly life, as well as the healthy state of music in early Stuart England, it is not surprising that opera, and Italian Baroque idioms generally, were slow to make their mark. Nicholas Lanier (1588–1666) was one of the very few English composers to travel to Italy during the first quarter century. His first-hand experiences induced him to introduce Italian-style recitative to the English stage in Ben Jonson's masque *Lovers Made Men* in 1617. A lesser composer, Walter Porter (d.1659), may have studied with Monteverdi in the 1620s. His *Madrigales and Ayres* (1632) include one of the first English examples of the concertato style, and additionally contains continuo parts and recitative. The 1630s and 40s witnessed more Italian influences in English music, particularly the declamatory monodic style that was well suited to the English *air*. The first experiments in full opera would not occur until the second half of the century.

By the end of the first Stuart reign in 1625, England's musical golden age was over. Virtually all of her major composers—Morley, Dowland, Campion, Byrd, Gibbons, Weelkes, Wilbye, and the exiled Philips and Bull—were dead or in frail old age. Yet Charles I's England was by no means devoid of musical talent. Thomas Tomkins lived on, while the talented Lawes brothers found gainful employment at the Royal Court. Whereas Henry excelled in

song forms, his brother William was more versatile, a composer of secular songs and sacred pieces, though chiefly renowned for his ensemble and theatre music. W. Lawes's instrumental music, including the famous dance collection *The Royall Consort* (probably mid 1630s), embodied England's most explicit allegiances to the modern Italian manner. Counterpoint prevails, but angular melodies, notated continuo parts, venturesome harmonies and trio-sonata textures are all common to his style. He was one of the earliest English composers to explore the potential of the violin, following the example of his teacher, John Coprario (d. 1626).

Henry & William Lawes

John Jenkins (1592–1678) rivalled Lawes as master of the viol fantasia, the principal form of 17th-century English chamber music. He built on the rich legacy of Byrd and Gibbons, producing many five-part fantasias in contrasting forms for viols and (doubling) organ. During the 1640s he began to compose three-part fantasias for two viols and bass viol, clearly influenced by the Italian trio sonata. More than 800 instrumental pieces by Jenkins survive.

John Jenkins

Not surprisingly, most leading composers supported or even fought for the royalist cause during the English Civil War (1642–51). Among them was William Lawes, who as a non-combatant was killed in crossfire at the battle of Chester in 1645. Cultural life around this time took a mighty battering: royal patronage collapsed, the Puritans smashed or dismantled every church organ in England, instruments were banned from worship, and theatres shut down. The situation for the professional English musician could hardly have been worse.

Chronology
1600–1649

Italian theorist and composer **Giovanni Maria Artusi** publishes *Delle imperfettioni della moderna musica* (On the Imperfections of Modern Music). He takes particular exception to the liberal use of dissonance, criticising progressive composers— **Claudio Monteverdi** especially—for corrupting traditional musical rules and practices.

John Dowland's *Second Booke of Songs or Ayres* is published. Included in the collection is the affecting 'Flow my teares' (or 'Lachrimae').

Salomone Rossi publishes his first book of five-part madrigals. It contains the earliest printed example of chitarrone accompaniment in tablature.

Thomas Luis de Victoria publishes a large collection of sacred works in his *Missae, Magnificat, Motecta, Psalmi*, in Madrid. His polychoral masses prove very popular.

February *La rappresentatione di anima e di corpo* (The Representation of Soul and Body) by **Emilio de' Cavalieri** is first performed in the church of Santa Maria in Vallicella, Rome. The staged work includes solos, instrumental sections and recitative, and incorporates a figured bass in the score—the earliest example of such in printed music. Sitting somewhere between sacred opera and oratorio, *La rappresentatione* is the first surviving drama with music scored throughout.

September **Claude Le Jeune**, prolific French Huguenot composer remembered above all for his *chansons*, dies in Paris, aged about 70.

6 October **Jacopo Peri** sings the part of Orpheus in his own pastoral opera *Euridice*, premièred at the wedding of Henri IV of France and Maria de Medici, in Florence. With text by **Ottavio Rinuccini** and various parts composed by fellow *Camerata* member **Giulio Caccini**, *Euridice* is the earliest surviving opera. Peri's music to an earlier opera, *Dafne* (1597), is lost.

9 October **Caccini**'s pastoral opera *Il Rapimento di Cefalo* is presented for the continuing wedding celebrations of Henri IV and Maria de Medici. Virtually all of the music is now lost.

10 November **Cavalieri** argues in a letter that recitative 'was invented by me, and everyone knows it as I have already stated this in print' (i.e. in the published preface to *La Rappresentatione*, dated 3 September 1600). **Peri** later acknowledges Cavalieri as the originator of the style, but **Caccini** maintains that he has been using it for the past 15 years.

December The competitive **Caccini** completes his own version of *Euridice* and will beat **Peri** to the publisher by six weeks.

The marriage of Henri IV of France and Maria de Medici, in Florence

Influential French harpsichordist and composer **Jacques Champion de Chambonnières** is born around this time in Paris.

Hans Hassler composes his influential *Lustgarten neuer teuscher Gesäng* (Pleasure Garden of New German Song). A number of later German composers will incorporate passages and melodies from the collection into their own works, notably J. S. Bach in his *St Matthew Passion*.

Luzzasco Luzzaschi composes *Madrigali per cantare et sonare* for the renowned 'three singing ladies' of Ferrara. Published in Rome, the collection (for one to three voices) is one of the first publications to feature a full keyboard accompaniment.

Thomas Morley arranges the publication of *The Triumphes of Oriana*, an anthology of 25 madrigals by 23 composers honouring Elizabeth I. Contributors include himself, **Thomas Weelkes**, **John Wilbye**, **Thomas Tomkins** and **Michael East**. Each madrigal ends with the words 'Long live fair Oriana', the name applied to Queen Elizabeth in much poetry of the time.

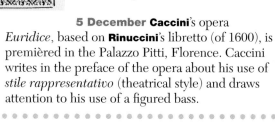

February Peri's score to *Euridice* is published in Florence.

26 November Benedetto Pallavicino dies in Mantua. **Monteverdi** succeeds him as *maestro di cappella* to the Gonzaga court.

Caccini's influential *Le nuove musiche* for solo voice and basso continuo is published in Florence. Featuring madrigals and strophic arias, the collection incorporates a treatise on the new monodic style of composition, which Caccini claims to have invented.

Cesare Negri publishes his dance treatise *Le gratie d'amore*, detailing contemporary practices of social and theatrical dance music.

Progressive Italian-Jewish composer **Salamone Rossi** publishes his second book of madrigals, with basso continuo.

Lodovico da Viadana publishes the first instalment of his *Cento concerti ecclesiastici* in Venice. Written for one to four voices, it is the first publication of sacred works to incorporate basso continuo.

14 February Pietro Caletti-Bruni, who will later change his name to **Cavalli** in honour of his patron, Federico Cavalli, is born in Crema.

11 March Composer and Camerata affiliate **Emilio de' Cavalieri** dies in Rome, aged about 52.

1 May English composer **William Lawes**, brother of composer **Henry Lawes** (b. 1596), is baptised in Salisbury.

October Influential English madrigalist **Thomas Morley** dies in London, aged about 44.

5 December Caccini's opera *Euridice*, based on **Rinuccini**'s libretto (of 1600), is premièred in the Palazzo Pitti, Florence. Caccini writes in the preface of the opera about his use of *stile rappresentativo* (theatrical style) and draws attention to his use of a figured bass.

1601 The Earl of Essex (Eng) attempts rebellion against Elizabeth I and is executed for treason • Astronomer Tycho Brahe dies; Johann Kepler takes charge at Prague observatory • New Poor Law in England makes parishes responsible for providing for the needy • Caravaggio (It) paints *The Conversion of St Paul*

1602 Persia declares war on the Ottoman Empire • Victory by English governor Lord Mountjoy over Spanish-Irish force around Kinsale virtually ends Irish rebellion • Caravaggio (It) paints *The Taking of Christ* • Shakespeare (Eng): *All's Well that Ends Well*, *Troilus and Cressida* and *Hamlet* • Bodleian Library, Oxford, opens

1603

Dowland publishes his *Third and Last Booke of Songs or Aires*, in London.

German composer **Melchior Franck** is appointed *Kapellmeister* to the Duke of Saxe-Coburg, in whose service he will remain for the rest of his life.

Monteverdi publishes his *Fourth Book of Madrigals*, in Venice.

English composer and Catholic refugee **Peter Philips** publishes his *Second Book of Madrigals*, in Antwerp.

Victoria composes his stunning *Officium defunctorum* for the funeral of Empress Maria of Austria. The Spanish composer calls it his 'swan song'.

Thomas Weelkes, aged about 26, gains his Bachelor of Arts degree in music from New College, Oxford.

17 February *Maestro di cappella* of St Mark's since 1590, **Baldassare Donato** dies in Venice, aged about 73. **Giovanni Croce** succeeds him, having served as *vicemaestro* for the last ten years.

All nature itself … is nothing but a perfect music that the creator causes to resound in the ears of man, to give him pleasure and to draw him gently to Himself.

30 March Jan Pieterszoon Sweelinck writes to the Burgomasters and Aldermen of Amsterdam.

4 July Philippe de Monte (left), Flemish composer of masses, motets, and more than 1,000 madrigals, dies in Prague, aged about 81.

1604

Dowland publishes his most famous instrumental collection, *Lachrimae, or Seaven teares*, containing 21 pieces for five viols and lute. Included in the set are seven contrapuntal pavans, each a variation on the descending 'flow my tears' motif of Dowland's song *Lachrimae* (1600).

Michael East brings out his first collection of Madrigales apt for Viols and Voices, in London.

Alfonso Ferrabosco, London-born composer of Italian descent, becomes viol teacher to Prince Henry of Wales.

Girolamo Frescobaldi, aged about 21, is appointed organist at the Accademia di Santa Cecilia in Rome.

Orlande de Lassus's *Magnum opus musicum*, containing 516 motets, is published ten years after the composer's death, in Munich.

Michael Praetorius is promoted from organist to *Kapellmeister* at the court of Duke Heinrich Julius of Brunswick in Wolfenbüttel.

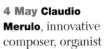

Leading Dutch composer **Jan P. Sweelinck** (left) publishes the first of his polyphonic Psalter settings, *50 pseaumes de David*, in Amsterdam.

4 May Claudio Merulo, innovative composer, organist and publisher, dies in the service of the ducal chapel at Parma, aged 71.

28 June Composer **Heinrich Albert**, cousin of **Heinrich Schütz**, is born in Voigtland, Saxony.

1603 Elizabeth I (Eng) dies; is succeeded by her distant cousin James VI of Scotland as James I of England • Sir Walter Raleigh implicated in a plot to dethrone King James; is imprisoned in Tower of London • Tokugawa Ieyasu appointed shogun of Japan • Gerommo Fabrizio (It) publishes first accurate description of valves in the veins

1604 James I (Eng) proposes full union of England and Scotland • Peace is restored between England and Spain • Shakespeare (Eng) writes *Measure for Measure* and *Othello* • Astronomer Johann Kepler (Ger), in *Astronomiae Pars Optica*, defines light rays and nature of vision • Lope de Vega (Sp): first volumes of *Comedias*

William Byrd, aged about 65, publishes his first volume of *Gradualia* for Catholic worship. After the Gunpowder Plot of this year, strict measures against Catholicism result in the work being withdrawn.

Orlando Gibbons becomes organist of the Chapel Royal.

Incorporating six pieces scored with basso continuo, **Monteverdi**'s Fifth Book of Madrigals is published in Venice. In its preface Monteverdi defends his expressive modernist style in response to criticisms published by the composer-theorist **Artusi** (see also 1607). The collection includes *Cruda Amarilli*, one of the madrigals Artusi had singled out for its compositional degeneracy.

William Byrd

6 January Ben Jonson's *The Masque of Blackness* is presented for King James, with stage design by Inigo Jones and music by English court composer **Alfonso Ferrabosco**. Queen Anne, who has commissioned the masque, performs in a leading role. The production is the first of many masque collaborations between Jonson and Jones.

19 February Orazio Vecchi, innovative madrigalist and *maestro di capella* to the Duke of Moderna, dies aged 54.

4 April Michael Praetorius courageously defends his patron, Duke Heinrich Julius, against an ambush in Brunswick. Years later he is rewarded with a plot of land and a gift of 2,000 thaler.

18 April Composer **Giacomo Carissimi** is baptised in Marino, near Rome.

German theorist and composer **Joachim Burmeister** defines 26 musical-rhetorical figures in *Musica poetica*, published in Rostock.

Orlando Gibbons receives a Bachelor of Music degree from Cambridge University.

A decree issued by Duke Vincenzo Gonzaga spares the composer **Salamone Rossi** the indignity of wearing a yellow badge required of Jews in Mantua.

January Court musician **Alfonso Ferrabosco (II)** provides music for **Ben Jonson**'s *The Masque of Hymen*. Later this year he composes music for Jonson's play *Volpone*, staged at the Globe Theatre, London.

February Students of the Jesuit Seminario Romano introduce **Agostino Agazzari**'s dramatic pastorale-cum-sacred opera *Eumelio* during Carnival. Stylistically similar to Cavalieri's *Rappresentatione* (1600), *Eumelio* depicts conflict between earthly and heavenly powers.

The Globe Theatre, London

February Paolo Quagliati's celebratory work *Il carro di fedeltà d'amore*, comprising solos, duets and a concluding five-part concerted madrigal, is first performed around this time on a decorated cart in Rome during Carnival.

February After irregular attendance and a series of salary advances, **John Dowland** is dismissed from his position as lutenist to the Court of Denmark. He returns to London.

19 May Composer **Edmund Hooper**, aged about 53, becomes the first official organist of Westminster Abbey.

1605 'Gunpowder plot' to blow up English Houses of Parliament is discovered: conspirator Guy Fawkes is arrested in vaults of Houses of Parliament • Tsar Boris Godunov (Russ) dies; 'Time of Troubles' continues • English colonists land in Barbados • Shakespeare (Eng): *Macbeth* • Miguel de Cervantes (Sp): first half of *Don Quixote*

1606 In England, Guy Fawkes and other 'Gunpowder Plotters' are executed • Basil Shuisky (Russ) assassinates 'False Dmitri' and becomes tsar in his place • Dutch fleet routs Portuguese-Spanish fleet in East Indies • Shakespeare (Eng): *King Lear* • Ben Jonson (Eng): *Volpone* • Joseph Scaliger (Fr): *Thesaurus Temporum*, a chronology of ancient times

Agazzari produces his influential treatise *Del sonare sopra il basso*, expounding the principles of basso continuo and the realisation of a figured bass. He also specifies the roles of 'foundation' and 'ornament' instruments. In the first group, providing harmonic support, are the organ, harpsichord and, where voices are few in number, lute, theorbo and harp. The second type serve to decorate melodic lines and again include the lute, theorbo and harp; also instruments such as the lirone (similar to the fretted tenor viol), cittern, spinet and violin.

Hassler publishes his *Psalmen und Christliche Gesäng*, comprising 52 four-part settings of Lutheran tunes in imitative style.

Monteverdi presents three-voice madrigals and arias in *Scherzi musicali*, published in Venice. In a postscript to this work, **Giulio Cesare Monteverdi** elaborates his brother's approach to traditional and modern styles of composition (explaining the terminology *prima prattica* and *seconda prattica*) in response to **Artusi**'s published criticisms (of 1600, 1603).

Salamone Rossi produces *Il primo libro delle sinfonie e gagliarde*. This book and a second the following year provide some of the earliest examples of the trio sonata, with music divided into three parts (based on the texture of basso continuo) for three to five instruments.

Viadana issues the second volume of his *Concerti ecclesiastici*. Included within the anthology is the *Missa dominicalis*, containing the earliest example of liturgical monody.

February Byrd supports private Catholic worship in England with his second book of *Gradualia*, published with some of the withdrawn pieces of the ill-fated 1605 volume. Both sets of *Gradualia* are reissued three years later.

The Lute Player by Caravaggio. Popular with both men and women, the lute is described by Agostino Agazzari as 'the noblest instrument of them all'.

24 February and **1 March Monteverdi** presents the first operatic masterpiece, *Orfeo*, commissioned by Prince Francesco Gonzaga and twice performed during Carnival in Mantua. With libretto by **Alessandro Striggio**, the five-act opera owes much to **Peri** and **Rinuccini**'s *Euridice* (1600), though it employs a far greater diversity of musical styles and forms.

26 February Francesca Caccini, daughter of Giulio, produces her first opus, *La stiava*, a *balletto* for Carnival entertainment at Pisa. Later this year she takes an official position as singer, teacher and composer to the Medici family.

11 March Giovanni Maria Nanino, a leading composer of the Roman school, dies in Rome, aged about 63.

10 September Progressive Italian composer **Luzzasco Luzzaschi** dies in Ferrara, aged about 62.

10 September Monteverdi's wife, Claudia, dies, leaving him with three young children.

1607 Jamestown Colony (Va), first permanent English settlement on the American mainland, is founded • 'Flight of the Earls': leading Ulster nobles flee to Spain, leaving the way clear for colonisation of Northern Ireland • English parliament rejects King's proposal for a united Scotland and England • Navigator Pedro Fernandez de Quires (Sp) reaches islands to the east of Tahiti, goes on to cross Pacific Ocean to America • Explorer Henry Hudson (Eng) attempts to find the Northeast Passage, but is confounded by thick ice • Table forks come into use in France and England, having originated in Italy • Caravaggio paints *Davide/Galea* • Shakespeare (Eng): *Timon of Athens*

French royal printer Pierre Ballard issues his company's first volume of solo *airs* in *Airs de différents autheurs mis en tablature de luth*.

Cesario Gussago publishes a collection of *Sonate*, adopting the 'instrumental choir' approach championed by **Giovanni Gabrieli**.

Hassler (left) becomes organist at the Electoral Chapel in Dresden, where he will remain until his death. His hymn collection *Kirchengesänge* is published in Nuremburg.

Heinrich Schütz enrols at the University of Margburg to prepare for a career in law.

Thomas Weelkes composes *Ayeres or Phantasticke Spirites for Three Voices*. The composer-organist is currently in post at Chichester Cathedral, where he has become infamous for once urinating on the Dean from the organ loft during Evensong—probably while drunk.

February Marco da Gagliano's opera *Dafne* is premièred in Mantua with a revised version of **Rinuccini**'s libretto (previously set by Peri and Corsi). This year the composer becomes *maestro di capella* at San Lorenzo, Florence.

28 May Monteverdi's opera *L'Arianna*, on a libretto by **Rinuccini**, is first performed in celebration of the marriage of Francesco Gonzaga to Margherita of Savoy in Mantua. It is a resounding success, though in time all the music will be lost apart from the emotional recitative of Ariadne's lament.

4 June Monteverdi's dramatic ballet *Il ballo delle ingrate* (The Ballet of the Ungrateful Women) is premièred during the ongoing wedding festivities of Francesco Gonzaga and Margherita of Savoy. The text, by **Rinuccini**, is set in opera-style recitative.

21 July Girolamo Frescobaldi is appointed organist of St Peter's Rome. This year the 25-year-old composer brings out his first major publications: 12 keyboard pieces in *Il Primo libro delle fantasie a quattro*, and his first book of five-part madrigals.

16 August The Scuola di San Rocco, Venice, celebrate the Feast Day of their Patron Saint with a lavish three-hour ceremony. The English visitor Thomas Coryat later writes of the event:

'Sometimes there sung sixteene or twenty men together, having their master or moderator to keepe them in order; and when they sung, the instrumentall musitians played also … ten Sagbuts, foure Cornets, and two Violdegambaes … every time that every severall musicke played, the Organs, whereof there are seven faire paire in that room, standing al in a rowe together, plaied with them.'

December Recuperating in Cremona, the exhausted **Monteverdi** receives a summons back to the Court of Mantua. He replies by letter, complaining of headaches and itching all over his body: *'My father attributes my bad head to overwork and the itching to the air of Mantua which, he suspects, will soon be the death of me.'* Monteverdi tends his resignation, but very early the following year he is back in service with a pay rise and promised pension.

1608 Religious dissension in Germany leads to the formation of Protestant Union by German states, led by Elector Frederick IV of the Palatinate • Emperor Rudolf II, weak and mentally ill, loses control of the Holy Roman Empire • Explorer Samuel de Champlain (Fr), on second voyage to North America, founds Quebec settlement • Dutch East India Company begins import of China tea to Europe • Spectacle maker Hans Lippershey (Neth) builds one of the earliest telescopes • El Greco (Gk/Sp) paints *St Luke the Painter* • Thomas Middleton (Eng): *A Mad World, My Masters* and *A Trick to Catch the Old One* published

Itinerant English composer and viol player **William Brade** contributes to the evolution of the dance suite with his *Newe ausserlesene Paduanen, Galliarden, Cantzonen, Allmand und Coranten*, published in Hamburg.

> ' … the English doe carroll; the French sing; the Spaniards weepe; the Italians, which dwell about the coasts of Ianua, caper with their voyces; the others barke; but the Germanes (which I am ashamed to utter) doe howle like wolves.'

John Dowland translates Ornithoparcus's *Musicae active micrologus* (1515), published as *The Art of Singing*.

Thomas Ravenscroft assembles and publishes *Pammelia*, the first English collection of popular song arrangements, rounds and catches, including the children's hit *Three Blind Mice*.

Samuel Scheidt becomes court organist to Margrave Christian Wilhelm of Brandenburg.

German composer **Heinrich Schütz**, aged 23, travels to Venice to study with **Gabrieli**.

Francis Tregian, serving time in London's Fleet prison (most likely for religious dissension or unpaid debt), begins to copy and compile what will become known as the *Fitzwilliam Virginal Book*. (See also 1619.)

John Wilbye publishes his emotionally extensive *Second Set of Madrigals* (in three to six parts), his crowning achievement.

2 February Ferrabosco provides music for **Ben Jonson**'s *The Masque of Queens*.

15 May Giovanni Croce, a leading composer of the Venetian school, dies in Venice, aged about 52.

Giovanni Paolo Cima publishes his *Concerti ecclesiastici*. This stylistically wide-ranging collection includes an early example of the trio sonata (the charming *Sonata per violino, cornetto e violone*) and what may be considered as the earliest sonata for violin and continuo.

Robert Dowland, son of **John**, issues the musical anthologies *A Musicall Banquet* and *Varietie of Lute-Lessons*, containing music of England and the continent. Included in the *Banquet* is John Dowland's lauded song 'In darknesse let me dwell'.

French composer **Michel Lambert** is born around this time in Champigny-sur-Veudes.

Monteverdi combines old and modern compositional styles (*prima prattica* and *seconda prattica*) in his sacred masterpiece *Vespers of the Blessed Virgin*. Serving the court of Mantua, Monteverdi is at this time the most famous Italian composer of secular music. The *Vespers*, published in Venice, promote him as a leading composer of religious music.

Michael Praetorius (right) completes the final volume of his *Musae Sioniae*, begun in 1605. The nine-part collection comprises over 1,200 hymns and psalm settings.

Viadana issues his one and only instrumental collection, the festive *Sinfonie musicali à 8*, in Venice. Each piece is named after an Italian city.

1609 Catholic League is formed in Germany, headed by Maximilian, Duke of Bavaria • Sigismund III of Poland makes war on Russia to claim the Russian throne • Johann Kepler (Ger) publishes *Astronomia Nova*, stating that planets move in elliptical orbits around Sun • Galileo Galilei (It) makes an improved telescope • Shakespeare (Eng): *Coriolanus*

1610 Henry IV (Fr) assassinated; is succeeded by his infant son Louis XIII; his widow, Marie de Médicis, is appointed regent • Russian nobles depose Tsar Basil Shuisky • Tea is introduced to Europe • Galileo Galilei (It) publishes the first observations of Moon mountains and craters • El Greco (Gk/Sp) paints *Lacoonte*

'A song that is well and artificially made cannot be well perceived nor understood at the first hearing, but the oftner you shall heare it, the better cause for liking you will discover.'

Byrd, aged 70, issues his *Psalmes, Songs and Sonnets* in London.

Prince Gesualdo publishes his fifth and sixth books of madrigals, containing some of the most harmonically progressive music of the era. He also composes the sacred work *Responsoria*, to be performed at his castle for his single pleasure.

German-Italian composer **Giovanni Kapsberger** brings out his *Libro I d'intavolatura di lauto*, his one surviving collection of lute pieces.

English lutenist and composer **John Maynard** publishes 12 songs in his *XII Wonders of the World* for 'Violl de Gambo, the Lute and the Voyce'.

German composer **Paul Peuerl** pioneers the variation suite in his *Newe Padouan, Intrada, Däntz und Galliarda*.

Michael Praetorius completes a series of liturgical works with *Missodia Sionia, Hymnodia Sionia, Eulogodia Sionia* and *Megalynodia Sionia*.

Lucia Quinciani's *Udite lagrimosi spirti d'Averno, udite* (Listen, tearful spirit of Averno, listen) is published in **Marc'Antonio Negri**'s anthology *Affetti amorosi* in Venice. It is the earliest known work of solo monody by a female composer.

Heinrich Schütz's *Primo libro de madrigali* is published in Venice.

20 August Tomás Luis de Victoria, Spain's pre-eminent composer of exclusively religious works, dies in Madrid, aged 62.

Gibbons publishes *The First Set of Madrigals and Mottets*, for voices and viols. It contains the majority of his secular vocal pieces, including the delightful five-part madrigal 'The Silver Swanne'.

Peter Phillips publishes his *Cantiones sacrae* for 5 voices, in Antwerp. A devout Catholic, the English exile writes that these pieces are for 'the consolation and salvation of the Christian people, the confirmation and amplification of the Catholic, Apostolic and Roman faith, and the extirpation and confusion of heresy and heretics'.

Michael Praetorius organises the publication of *Terpsichore* (The Muse of Dancing), an anthology of 312 French dances for instrumental ensembles.

Sweelinck brings out his *Rimes françoises et italiennes*, containing French chansons and Italian madrigals.

18 February The death of Duke Vincenzo Gonzaga marks the end of **Monteverdi**'s favour at the Mantuan Court. The new duke, Francesco Gonzaga (who commissioned *Orfeo*), will dismiss the composer during the summer as part of his downsizing procedures.

8 June Leading German composer and organist **Hans Leo Hassler** dies from tuberculosis in Frankfurt, aged 47.

August Influential Italian composer **Giovanni Gabrieli** dies from kidney stone complications aged about 55, in Venice.

September Florentine Camerata host, patron and composer **Count Giovanni de' Bardi** dies in Rome, aged 78.

28 October John Dowland becomes one of the King's Lutes (to James I), receiving a salary of 20d a day. This year has seen the publication of *A Pilgrime's Solace*, his final collection of sacred and secular lute songs.

1611 'Plantation of Ulster': Scottish and English Protestants settle in Northern Ireland • Explorer Henry Hudson (Eng) dies in St James Bay, Canada, when his crew mutiny and cast him adrift • Peter Paul Rubens (Flem) paints *Massacre of the Innocents* • Shakespeare (Eng): *The Tempest* • King James Bible (Authorised Version) is published in England

1612 Holy Roman Emperor Rudolf II dies; is succeeded by his aging and ailing brother, Matthias • Last recorded executions for heresy in England • Russian national militia drives Poles away from besieging Moscow • Trigonometrical tables published in Germany employ decimal point • El Greco (Gk) paints *Baptism of Christ*

21 keyboard pieces by **Byrd** (8), **Bull** (7) and **Gibbons** (6) are issued in the *Parthenia*, subtitled *The Maydenhead of the first musicke that ever was printed for the Virginalls*. The landmark collection is published in London in celebration of the marriage between the 15-year-old daughter of James I, Princess Elizabeth, and Frederick V, Elector Palatine of Heidelberg.

Priest and musician **Pietro Cerone** publishes his 1,160-page music theory and history tome *El melopeo y maestro*, in Naples.

Schütz returns to Kassel after the death of his teacher, Giovanni Gabrieli, the previous year in Venice. He takes up the position of second court organist to the Landgrave of Moritz.

Sweelinck brings out his second book of *Pseaumes de David*, in Amsterdam.

14 February *The Lords' Maske* is staged in London for the marriage of Frederick V (Elector Palatine) and Princess Elizabeth Stuart. The songs are supplied by **Thomas Campion**, with instrumental music possibly by **Robert Johnson**.

1 August Monteverdi applies for the position of *maestro di capella* at St Mark's, Venice, by providing music for a mass.

August Facing charges of adultery, **John Bull** leaves England, never to return. The Archbishop of Canterbury, George Abbott, declares in a letter that Bull 'hath more music than honesty and is as famous for marring of virginity as he is for fingering of organs and virginals'.

18 August Remembered more for his anti-modernist polemics than his music, **Giovanni Artusi** dies in Bologna, aged about 73.

PARTHENIA or THE MAYDENHEAD of the first musicke that ever was printed for the VIRGINALLS COMPOSED By three famous Masters William Byrd D: John Bull & Orlando Gibbons. Gentilmen of his Ma:ties most Illustrious Chappell. Ingrauen by William Hole.

19 August Monteverdi is appointed *maestro di capella* at St Mark's, Venice, with a handsome annual salary of 300 ducats.

8 September Carlo Gesualdo, prince, avant-garde composer and double-murderer (of his wife and her lover in 1590), dies in Gesualdo, Avellino, aged about 52. He is buried at the *Gesù Nuovo* church in Naples.

October Travelling to Venice, **Monteverdi** and his maidservant are robbed at gunpoint by highwaymen. They complete their journey penniless.

Highwayman; 17th century etching.

1613 Russian national assembly elects Tsar Mikhail Romanov, first of Romanov dynasty, which lasts until 1917; end of Russia's 'Time of Troubles' • Denmark and Sweden end War of Kolmar with Peace of Knarod • German Protestant Union forms alliance with Netherlands • Elizabeth, daughter of James I (Eng), marries Elector Frederick V of the Palatinate (Ger) • English trading stations are established at Hirado, Japan, and Surat, India • Fire destroys Globe Theatre, London • Galileo Galilei (It) publishes his acceptance of the Copernican theory that the Earth goes round the Sun • Guido Reni (It) paints *Aurora and the Hours*

The French court of Louis XIII establishes the *24 violons du Roi*.

Caccini publishes a second collection of songs with some points on musical theory in *Nuove musiche e nuova maniera di scriverle* (New Music and New Methods of Notation).

In prison for unpaid debt, **Sir William Leighton** organises the publication of *The Teares or Lamentations of a Sorrowfull Soule*. The collection contains 55 settings of his poetry, with some consort songs by Leighton himself. **Wilbye** and **Byrd** are among the 21 English composers who contribute to the volume.

Monteverdi begins to revitalise the musical establishment at St Mark's, Venice, employing new musicians and expanding the music library with part-books by Lassus, Palestrina and others. This same year he completes his *Sixth Book of Madrigals*, which includes a beautiful re-setting of 'Lamento d'Arianna' from the opera *L'Arianna* (1608), and several other five-part madrigals with continuo accompaniment.

Heinrich Pfendner publishes *Delli motetti* in Graz, one of the first motet collections with continuo by a German composer.

Sweelinck brings out his third book of *Pseaumes de David* in Amsterdam.

German composer **Franz Tunder** is born in Bannesdorf, near Burg.

Late September Former composer to the papal choir, **Felice Anerio** dies in Rome, aged about 54.

Frescobaldi completes two sets of keyboard works: his first book of *Toccate*, and *Recercari et canzoni*. Both collections are published in Rome.

A collection of works by the late Giovanni Gabrieli and Hans Hassler (both d. 1612) is published in Venice under the title *Reliquae sacrorum concentum*. Gabrieli's second book of *Symphoniae sacrae* and his *Canzoni e sonate* are also published at this time.

Michael Praetorius publishes the first book of his three-volume *Syntagma musicum* in Wittenberg. It becomes a major document of musical life in the early 17th century, detailing musical history, notation, instruments and compositional practice.

Johann Schein publishes his first collection of motets, *Cymbalum Sionium*, based on Latin and German biblical texts. This year he becomes *Kapellmeister* at the court of Duke Johann in Weimar.

19 July King James I rewards **Orlando Gibbons** with £150 worth of grants for 'good and faithful service'.

August Composer **Christopher Gibbons**, eldest surviving son of **Orlando**, is born in London.

August Schütz begins his employment at the Electoral chapel in Saxony. He serves unofficially in the capacity of *Kapellmeister*.

1 December Carpet-weaver, court jester and violinist, **Hans Bach** (left) dies while in service to the court of Nürtingen, aged about 60. He was the first of the professional Bach musicians.

1614 Gustavus II Adolphus of Sweden captures Novgorod (Russ) • Pocahontas, daughter of an American Indian chief, becomes a Christian and marries John Rolfe, an English settler • Explorer Sir Walter Raleigh (Eng) is imprisoned in the Tower of London for treason • Mathematician John Napier (Scot) announces his development of natural logarithms

1615 Forces of shogun Tokugawa Ieyasu gain decisive victory at battle of Osaka • Navigator William Baffin (Eng) discovers Baffin Island and Baffin's Bay, Canada • White settlers in Latin America begin learning about the use of rubber from American Indians • Miguel de Cervantes (Sp) publishes Part II of *Don Quixote*

Bartholomaeus Praetorius publishes his dance collection *Newe liebliche Paduanen und Galliarden* in Berlin.

Johann Staden issues his first important work, *Harmoniae sacrae*, which includes some of the earliest German sacred concertos.

Italian composer-poet **Giovanni Valentini** publishes his *Secondo libro di madrigali*, scored for voices and instruments.

January Monteverdi entertains the Ducal Palace in Mantua with his enchanting dialogue ballet *Tirsi e Clori*. The short pastoral work is set in two parts: the first a madrigal for two singers with string accompaniment, the second a *ballo* in five parts for voices and instruments.

19 May Keyboard maestro **Johann Jacob Froberger** is born in Stuttgart.

24 August *Maestro di cappella* at St Mark's, Venice, **Monteverdi** receives a salary increase to 400 ducats, making him one of the highest paid composers in Europe. Accounts for this year show that he presides over one assistant *maestro*, two *maestri de concerti*, a 24-strong choir, two organists and 16 instrumentalists.

Autumn Schein becomes *Kantor* of the Thomaskirche in Leipzig.

22 October Tarquinio Merula, aged about 21, is engaged with a three-year contract as organist of Santa Maria Incoronata, Lodi.

Thomas Campion brings out his Third and Forth Booke of Ayres, in London

Violinist at St Mark's, Venice, **Biagio Marini** issues his *Affetti musicali* (Op. 1), scored for one to two soloists and continuo. The diverse collection of 'musical affections'—comprising sinfonias, sonatas, canzonas and dances—represents a significant development for both violin music and the Baroque trio sonata.

Schein composes his instrumental variation suite *Il Banchetto musicale* (The Musical Banquet), containing pavanes, galliards, courantes and allemandes. The set is one of the earliest examples of the variation suite (together with Peuerl's of 1611), although it is written without continuo, essentially in a 16th-century manner.

January Schütz, aged 31, is appointed musical director of the Electoral Court in Dresden.

22 February Nicholas Lanier (right), supplying music for **Ben Jonson**'s masque *Lovers Made Men*, makes his mark as the first English author of Italian-style recitative.

18 December Francesco Bruni (later **Cavalli**), aged 14, joins the choir at St Mark's, Venice.

29 December Bull is promoted to organist of Antwerp Cathedral. He gains the post having persuaded the town mayor that his exile from England was due to Catholic persecution, not for any alleged adultery (see 1613).

1616 Roman Catholic Church forbids Galileo Galilei (It) to defend theory that the Earth revolves around the Sun, but permits him to discuss it as a mathematical supposition • Navigator Willem Schouten (Neth) rounds perilous Cape Horn • Explorer Sir Walter Raleigh (Eng) is released from prison to go in search of El Dorado

1617 Treaty of Stolbovo ends war between Sweden and Russia • War breaks out between Sweden and Poland • Ferdinand II is elected King of Bohemia • Shogun Hidetada (Jap) makes determined effort to stamp out Christianity; begins executing missionaries and Japanese converts • Peter Paul Rubens (Neth) paints *The Last Judgment*

Francesca Caccini, daughter of **Giulio** (see below), completes *Il Primo Libro delle musiche*, a collection of 36 monodic songs (32 for solo voice, four for soprano and bass), both secular and sacred, written in various forms including madrigal, sonnet, aria, motet and hymn.

22-year-old French philosopher and mathematician **René Descartes** completes his *Compendium musicae*, a treatise on the nature of music, the perception of music, and the effect of music upon the listener. It is not published until 1650.

Charles Racquet, aged 21, is appointed organist at Notre Dame, Paris.

Michael Praetorius discusses the instruments of the day in the second book of his *Syntagma musicum*, entitled *De organographia* and published in German, in Wolfenbüttel. A pictorial supplement to this volume is issued two years later.

Schein publishes his *Opella nova* (Part I) containing some of the earliest examples of the German sacred concerto with continuo. Influenced by Viadana's *Cento concerti ecclesiastici* of 1602, the settings are mainly based on Lutheran chorales.

December Giulio Caccini, one of the pioneering composers of opera and the monodic style, dies in Florence, aged 67. In later life he had turned to gardening for extra income.

Giovanni Anerio publishes *Teatro armonico spirituale*. Mainly a collection of sacred madrigals, it includes the first Roman examples of obbligato instrumental writing and some short precursors to the mid-century oratorio.

Rome-based composer **Stefano Landi**, currently at Padua, writes his opera *La morte d'Orfeo*.

Monteverdi abjures tradition in his *Seventh Book of Madrigals*, scored for voices and instruments and published under the title *Concerto*. He dedicates the assorted and innovative collection to Catherine de' Medici, hoping for a pension in return. He is rewarded only with a necklace.

Michael Praetorius completes his *Polyhymnia caduceatrix*. Reminiscent of **Monteverdi**'s Vespers (1610), the work melds the Venetian style with the Lutheran chorale, producing a grand set of polychoral sacred concertos with brilliant instrumental passages. This year the composer issues his third book of *Syntagma musicum*.

Schütz introduces Italian-style monody to German music with his first collection of *Psalmen Davids* (Psalms of David), scored for multiple choirs, soloists and *concertato* instruments. This year the 33-year-old composer marries the 18-year-old Magdalene Wildeck.

Composer and singer **Barbara Strozzi** is born in Venice.

Sweelinck publishes a collection of 37 motets for the Catholic liturgy in his *Cantiones sacrae*.

Containing 297 (predominantly English) keyboard works, the *Fitzwilliam Virginal Book* is completed in London, two years after the death of its principal compiler, Francis Tregian.

1618 Thirty Years' War begins with 'Defenestration of Prague' • Philosopher and lawyer Francis Bacon is appointed Lord Chancellor of England • Sir Walter Raleigh (Eng) is beheaded following his failure to find El Dorado • Astronomer Johann Kepler (Ger) outlines third law of planetary motion • James I (Eng): *Book of Sports*

1619 America's first elected assembly meets in Virginia • Ferdinand II becomes Holy Roman Emperor; briefly deposed as King of Bohemia and replaced by Frederick V • First black slaves arrive in Virginia • Kepler (Ger) publishes *Harmonices Mundi*, further supporting the theory that the Earth revolves around the Sun

In Lisbon **Manuel Coelho** issues his *Flores de Musica* (Flowers of Music), Portugal's earliest surviving printed keyboard music.

Monteverdi's opera *Andromeda* is completed and performed around this time in Mantua. The music is now lost.

Michael Praetorius publishes *Polyhymnia exercitatrix*, a collection of Latin psalm settings. He also issues a pictorial supplement to his second volume of *Syntagma musicum*, entitled *Theatrum instrumentorum* (Theatre of Instruments).

Scheidt is promoted to *Kapellmeister* at the court of Margrave Christian Wilhelm of Brandenburg. This year marks his first publication, *Cantiones sacrae*, a collection of mainly double-choir motets for eight voices.

February Filippo Vitali's opera *L'Aretusa* is premièred at the house of Ottavio Corsini in Rome. Influenced by the examples of Peri and Caccini, it is Rome's first secular opera.

1 March Thomas Campion, composer, poet and physician, dies in London, aged 53. He is remembered exclusively for his lute songs.

17 November Alessandro Grandi is promoted from singer to second *maestro di capella* (deputy to **Monteverdi**) at St Mark's, Venice. This year has seen the publication of his *Cantade et arie* for solo voice and continuo, featuring some of the earliest (secular) cantatas.

Two hundred copies of **Duarte Lobo**'s *Liber missarum* are printed in Antwerp. The widely-circulated collection features eight masses and two motets, including the angelic *Audivi vocem de caelo* (I heard a voice from heaven). Lobo, Portugal's leading composer, is currently *maestro de capilla* at Lisbon Cathedral.

Tarquinio Merula becomes court organist to Sigismund III, King of Poland.

Taking inspiration from the Italian pastorale, **Schein** produces the first of his three-part *Musica boscareccia* (or *Wald-Liederlein*). The secular songs are written for two sopranos and one bass with continuo.

Francesco Turini includes some early examples of the trio sonata in his *First Book of Madrigals*, published in Venice.

Giovanni Valentini issues the unprecedented *Messa, Magnificat et Jubilate Deo*, indulgently scored for seven choirs. His adventurous spirit is also apparent in *Musiche a doi voci*, which incorporates verses in 5/4 time.

15 February Influential German composer **Michael Praetorius** dies in Wolfenbüttel, aged 50. He leaves most of his sizeable fortune to the setting up of a charity for the poor.

Summer English composer **Thomas Tomkins** becomes an organist of the Chapel Royal.

16 October The great tradition of Dutch Renaissance composers breathes its last as **Jan Pieterszoon Sweelinck** dies in Amsterdam, aged 59. The fourth and final book of the composer's *Pseaumes de David* is published soon afterwards.

1620 Battle of White Mountain: troops of Holy Roman Emperor crush Protestant forces of Frederick V of Bohemia • Voyage of the Mayflower: Pilgrim Fathers (English settlers) arrive at Cape Cod and form Plymouth settlement • Terms 'cosine' and 'cotangent' introduced into trigonometrical terminology • Rubens (Flem) paints *The Battle of the Amazons*

1621 Spain and Netherlands renew hostilities after 12-year truce • Johann Kepler (Ger) completes publication of *Epitome Astronomiae Copernicanae*, on theory that Earth revolves around the Sun; Roman Catholic Church bans the work • Pope Paul V dies; is succeeded by Gregory XV • G. L. Bernini (It) begins sculpture of *The Rape of Proserpine*

John Attey's optimistically titled *The First Booke of Ayres* becomes the last published book exclusively devoted to ayres for voices and lute, just 25 years since John Dowland began this type of publication.

English composer **Matthew Locke** is born around this time.

'The Physitians will tell you that the exercise of Musicke is a great lengthener of life, by stirring and reviving the Spirits, holding a secret sympathy with them.'

Author and musician
Henry Peacham
in *The Compleat Gentleman*.

Salamone Rossi publishes his *Fifth Book of Madrigals* and composes *Hashirim asher lish'lomo* (The Songs of Solomon), featuring polyphonic settings of synagogue songs, and Hebrew psalms and hymns. The title of the work appears to be a pun on Rossi's first name, as there are no actual text settings from *The Songs of Solomon*. In the preface of the collection the publisher (and Rossi's pupil) Rabbi Leo da Modena attempts to justify the use of polyphony in Jewish worship by referencing the Talmud and rabbinical texts.

Scheidt brings out his *Concertus sacri*, a collection of sacred vocal concertos with instrumental obbligato parts and sinfonias.

Tomkins issues sacred and secular pieces in *Songs of 3. 4. 5. & 6. parts*. The collection includes his poignant five-part anthem *When David heard*.

15 January French playwright, actor and librettist **Jean-Baptiste Poquelin** (later **Molière**) is born in Paris.

Orlando Gibbons and **Thomas Day** share the responsibilities of choirmaster and organist at Westminster Abbey.

Schein (left) publishes *Fontana d'Israel* (Fountain of Israel), composed after the classic Italian madrigal style with texts mainly set for five voices with continuo.

Schütz composes his oratorio-style *Resurrection History* (Op. 3) in Dresden. The work features liturgical recitative (not as freely expressive as operatic recitative), as well as solos, duets, choruses and independent instrumental parts.

France's foremost composer-organist **Jehan Titelouze** publishes his *Hymnes de l'Eglise*, a collection of organ pieces based on plainsong.

27 March Filipe de Magalhães becomes *mestre de capela* at the royal court in Portugal.

4 July William Byrd, England's leading composer, dies in Stondon Massey, Essex, aged about 83.

6 July Italian composer **Jacopo Melani** is born in Pistoia.

5 August Italian composer and singer **Antonio Cesti** is baptised in Arezzo.

30 November Infamous in later life for drunkenness, foul language and blasphemy, English composer **Thomas Weelkes** dies at the house of a friend, Henry Drinkwater, in the parish of St Brides, London, aged 47. He is remembered chiefly for his madrigals and anthems.

1622 James I (Eng) dissolves Parliament, imprisoning three members who oppose him • French statesman Armand Jean de Richelieu is made a cardinal • Jamestown Massacre: Indians slaughter 347 English Settlers; survivors take revenge • William Oughtred (Eng) invents slide-rule • *London Weekly Newes* begins publication in England

1623 Dutch massacre English and Japanese merchants at Amboina (now Ambon, Indonesia) • Pope Gregory XV dies; is succeeded by Urban VIII • First European settlements in New Hampshire • Wilhelm Schickard (Ger) invents a mechanical calculator ('Calculating Clock') • 'First Folio' edition of works of William Shakespeare (Eng) published

Giacomo Carissimi is appointed organist at Tivoli Cathedral, where he had previously been a chorister.

Frescobaldi publishes his first book of keyboard *Capricci*, in Rome.

Monteverdi's enthralling *Combattimento di Tancredi et Clorinda*, depicting a fight between a Christian crusader and a female Saracen warrior, premières at the Venetian palace of Girolamo Mozzenigo. Scored for two costumed singers, a narrator, string ensemble and continuo, this dramatic dialogue features the composer's *stile concitato* (excited style), by which the music corresponds to the battle action in a strikingly descriptive manner.

Scheidt publishes his three-volume *Tabulatura nova*, an instructive collection of sacred and secular works for organ.

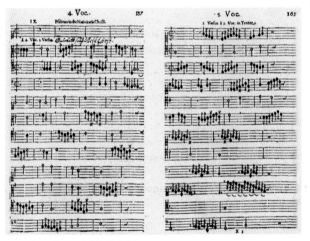

Pages from Scheidt's *Tabulatura nova*

Schein publishes the earliest collection of German continuo madrigals in *Diletti pastorali* or *Hirten Lust* (Pastoral Delights). It represents a secular counterpart to the composer's sacred *Fontana d'Israel* of the previous year.

John Coprario (probably born John Cooper) is appointed Composer-in-Ordinary to the court of the new King of England, Charles I.

Paul Peuerl brings out *Gantz neue Padouanen* in Nuremberg. He becomes the first German to publish a work with the Italianate combination of two lead instruments with continuo.

Scheidt's position as *Kapellmeister* to Christian Wilhelm in Halle becomes unsaleried as the Margrave leaves to support the Protestant King of Denmark in the Thirty Years' War.

Schütz composes *Cantiones sacrae*, a collection of motets including both polyphonic and concertato settings.

3 February Francesca Caccini (right) has her opera *La liberazione di Ruggiero* presented in honour of the visiting Prince Władisław of Poland, in Florence. Caccini, daughter of Giulio (d. 1618), is the first female opera composer and currently the highest paid musician of the Medici court.

June Suffering the vicissitudes of war, **Schütz** and musicians of the Dresden court write a joint letter to Johann Georg I, complaining that they have not received salaries for nearly two years.

5 June Composer **Orlando Gibbons** dies from a brain haemorrhage in Canterbury, aged 42.

6 September Schütz, aged 39, loses his beloved wife, Magdalena, to smallpox. Daunted by single parenthood, he places his two young daughters in the care of Magdalena's mother. Schütz never remarries.

1624 Cardinal Richelieu becomes chief minister to Louis XIII, and the real master of France • Chemist Jan Baptist van Helmont (Flem) coins the word 'gas' (corruption of 'chaos') • Bernini (It) completes sculpture of *David* and works on *Apollo and Daphne* • Thomas Middleton (Eng): satirical play *A Game of Chesse*

1625 James I (Eng; VI of Scot) dies; succeeded by his son Charles I • Charles I marries Princess Henrietta Maria of France • French priest St Vincent de Paul founds order of Sisters of Mercy in Paris • London plague forces parliament to move to Oxford • Francis Bacon (Eng): *Essays* (final form) • Rubens (Flem) paints *The Landing of the Medicis*

Giovanni Battista Buonamente has his *Il quarto libro de varie sonate* published in Venice. The composer-violinist is at this time *musicista da camera* to Emperor Ferdinand II in Vienna.

French composer and keyboardist **Louis Couperin** is born around this time in Chaumes-en-Brie.

Schein publishes the second part of his *Opella nova* in Leipzig. Composed for voices, obbligato instruments and basso continuo, the collection incorporates colourful settings of biblical texts and Lutheran chorales.

In Paris **Titelouze** publishes *Le Magnificat*, containing eight cycles of fugal *versets* for organ.

12 February Domenico Mazzocchi's opera *La catena d'Adone* is premièred in Rome. It heralds the advent of a more lyrical style of opera, with the prominent use of the *mezz'arie*, or *arioso* passages. Mazzocchi asserts that he desires to 'break the tedium of recitative'.

20 February John Dowland is buried at St Ann Blackfriars in London, aged 63. (His actual day of death is unknown.) **Robert Dowland** has by this time already assumed his father's position as one of the court lutenists.

July Upon the death of **John Coprario**, **Ferrabosco** takes up his position as Composer-in-Ordinary to Charles I of England.

11 July Nicholas Lanier becomes England's first Master of the King's Music, at an annual salary of £200. He will hold the position until King Charles loses his head in 1649.

12 August Italian composer **Giovanni Legrenzi** is born in Clusone, near Bergamo.

Carlo Farina publishes his innovative *Capriccio stravagante* for violin and continuo. Effects such as tremolo, glissando, pizzicato, strumming, *sul ponticello* and even *spiccato col legno* (hitting the strings with the back of the bow) are employed to mimic the sounds of a dog, cat, hen, clarion, military drum and guitar. Superficial but entertaining episodes sit alongside sections of high musical substance.

Alessandro Grandi becomes *maestro di capella* at Santa Maria Maggiore, Bergamo.

Schein edits the *Cantional* in Leipzig. He adds his own hymns to the collection, complete with figured-bass parts for continuo instruments.

January Frescobaldi (left), Italy's leading keyboard composer, brings out his second book of *Toccate*, this time with pieces for both harpsichord and organ. The collection also features liturgical plainchant variations and stylised dances, including the earliest keyboard chaconne.

April Schütz's *Dafne*—possibly the first German opera—is staged at Torgau for the wedding celebrations of Princess Sophie of Saxony, eldest daughter of the composer's employer. The music is now lost.

2 May Composer **Lodovico Viadana** dies in Gualtieri, near Parma, aged about 67.

21 August Jacques Mauduit, French composer and music director, dies in Paris, aged 69.

18 December Italians **Filippo Piccinini** and **Bernardo Monanni** introduce opera to the Spanish royal court, setting **Lope de Vega**'s *La selva sin amor* (The Forest Without Love). No further operatic productions occur in Spain until the second half of the century.

1626 Thirty Years' War continues: Holy Roman Emperor Ferdinand II's general Albrecht von Wallenstein defeats Protestant army under Ernst von Mansfeld at Bridge of Dessau • Dutch buy Manhattan Island from Amerindians and establish New Amsterdam (later New York) • French establish settlements in Senegal and Madagascar

1627 Huguenots besieged at La Rochelle by armies of King Louis XIII • England goes to war with France; Duke of Buckingham fails to relieve La Rochelle • Holy Roman Emperor Ferdinand II's armies conquer Schleswig and Holstein • Kepler (Ger) gives the positions of more than 1,000 stars in *Rudolphine Tables* • Francis Bacon (Eng): *The New Atlantis*

Carissimi is appointed *maestro di cappella* at the cathedral of Assisi.

Tarquinio Merula brings out his *Libro secondo de concerti spirituali con alcune sonate*.

Once imprisoned in The Hague, falsely accused of plotting to murder Queen Elizabeth I, English Catholic exile **Peter Philips** dies in Brussels, aged about 67.

February Scheidt takes up the post of musical director of the Marktkirche in Halle.

11 March English composer **Alfonso Ferrabosco** dies in London, aged about 53.

13 March English émigré composer **John Bull** dies in Antwerp, aged about 65.

8 July Monteverdi writes to the diplomat and librettist **Alessandro Striggio** to gain his intervention on behalf of his son, Massimiliano, who has been arrested on the charge of possessing a book outlawed by the Church. Facing a prison term or the Inquisitor's torture rack, Massimiliano is later acquitted.

11 August Schütz embarks on another visit to Italy, where he learns more about recitative, possibly from **Monteverdi**. This year sees the publication of his partsong collection *Der Psalter nach Cornelius Becker*.

14 October Marco da Gagliano's final opera, *La Flora*, is presented for the wedding celebrations of Margherita de' Medici and Duke Odoardo Farnese. **Jacopo Peri** has assisted the composition and performs in a lead role.

November Frescobaldi becomes organist to the 18-year-old Ferdinando II de' Medici, Grand Duke of Tuscany, in Florence. He dedicates to his new patron his *Primo libro delle canzoni*, a collection of 40 instrumental canzonas.

Biagio Marini publishes a large collection of ensemble pieces in his Op. 8, including trio sonatas and sonatas for solo violin and continuo. The pioneering Italian composer exploits the resources of the violin by using triple-stopping and *scordatura* (detuning).

Virgilio Mazzocchi becomes *maestro di cappella* at St Peter's, Rome (below).

Schütz issues his first book of *Symphoniae sacrae* (Op. 6) in Venice during his second visit to the city. Influenced by **Monteverdi**, the collection features arias and modern madrigal forms, as well as polychoral and concertato styles. Pieces range from the dark sorrow of *Fili mi, Absalon* for bass voice, trombones and continuo to the beautiful and airy *Exultavit cor meum in Domino* (My heart rejoices in the Lord) for soprano, two violins (or cornets) and continuo.

27 January Remembered chiefly for his Venetian-style polychoral motets, North German composer and organist **Hieronymus Praetorius** dies in Hamburg, aged 68.

April Sigismondo d'India, renowned Italian composer of secular vocal music, dies in Modena, aged about 47.

December Carissimi, aged 24, becomes *maestro di capella* at the Jesuit Collegio Germanico in Rome. He will hold the post for the rest of his life

1628 End of Huguenots as an important political force • English troops capture Quebec City from France • Holy Roman Emperor's armies capture much of the Pomeranian coast on the Baltic Sea • Duke of Buckingham (Eng) is assassinated • William Harvey (Eng) publishes his treaty on the circulation of the blood, *Exercitatio Anatomica*

1629 Peace of Alais gives Huguenots freedom of worship • Holy Roman Emperor Ferdinand II and King Christian IV of Denmark sign Treaty of Lübeck: Christian abandons his allies and receives in return all land lost during Thirty Years' War • Giovanni Branca (It) designs a turbine-boiler with spout to direct steam against wooden blades of a wheel

Frescobaldi publishes *Arie musicali*, a collection of 44 songs for one to three voices and continuo.

Martin Peerson publishes the first English examples of a figured bass in his *Mottects or Grave Chamber Musique*.

Around this time Italian-Jewish composer **Salamone Rossi** dies in Mantua, aged about 60.

7 January Francesco Bruni (**Cavalli**), aged 27, weds a wealthy widow, Maria Sozomeno.

April Monteverdi's opera *Proserpina rapita* (The Abduction of Proserpine) is first performed at the Palazzo Mocenigo, Venice, during the wedding celebrations of Giustiniana Mocenigo and Lorenzo Giustiniani. Apart from one trio, the music is lost.

8 June Nobleman **Alessandro Striggio** (**II**), musician and librettist, dies of the plague while on diplomatic business in Venice, aged about 57.

Summer Alessandro Grandi (below), one of Italy's foremost composers, dies from the plague

in Bergamo, aged about 44. Plague rages across northern Italy at this time; some towns and cities lose as much as half their population.

ALEXANDRO GRANDI MVSIC·PRÆF·EXCELL·PATRI MORVM PIETATE ÆSTIMABILI

19 November Johann Schein, aged 44, dies from chronic ill-health in Leipzig. **Schütz**, his friend and compatriot, fulfils his death-bed request by composing a setting of 1 Timothy 1:15–17, the motet *Das ist je gewisslich wahr* (That is surely true).

Juan Hidalgo, aged 16, begins his professional career as harpist to the Spanish Royal Chapel.

Scheidt issues the first of four books of *Geistliche Concerten* (Spiritual Concertos).

Pier Francesco Valentini publishes his *Canone nel modo Salomonis* for 96 voices. He advises that additional voices to the *canone* (canon) may be applied as required, up to 144,000—the 'sealed' number from the 12 tribes of Israel in Revelation, chapter 7.

22 February Dramatist **Ben Jonson** and designer Inigo Jones present the English court masque *Chloridia*, their final collaboration. Jonson regards the masque as an opportunity for high art; Jones sees it simply as a *pièce d'occasion*. Their artistic differences and bickering result in Jonson being excluded from

subsequent royal masque commissions. Shown (right) is Jones's revealing costume design for 'Spring', from *Chloridia*.

12 April Merula is appointed *maestro di capella* of Santa Maria Maggiore in Bergamo.

21 November Monteverdi provides a *Solemn Mass for the Feast of Sancta Maria* (*Mass of Thanksgiving*) at St Mark's to celebrate the end of a devastating period of plague in Venice (the Gloria appears in his *Selva morale* of 1641). Around a third of the city's population have died from an outbreak that began the previous year.

- -

1630 England makes peace with France and Spain • Charles I (Eng) begins 11-year rule without parliament • About 1,000 English settlers arrive in Massachusetts; Boston founded • Diego Velazquez (Sp) paints *The Forge of Vulcan* • Galilei (It) completes his *Dialogue on The Two Chief Systems of the World* (Ptolemaic and Copernican)

1631 Sweden gains powerful allies—France, the Netherlands, Saxony, Brandenburg and Hesse—against Holy Roman Emperor Ferdinand II • First French newspaper, *La Gazette*, is published • Earthquake in Naples and first serious eruption of volcano Vesuvius since 1068: 3,000 killed • Scientist Pierre Vernier (Fr) invents the secondary scale (vernier)

Stefano Landi presents the ascetic life of Saint Alexis in his opera *Il Sant'Alessio* (1631), staged for the inauguration of Rome's first opera house, the Teatro Barberini. The libretto, by **Giulio Rospigliosi** (the future Pope Clement IX), is notable for its departure from Greek myth and pastoral fable. Landi contributes to the evolution of the overture, introducing the opera with an instrumental prelude in three sections.

Composer, singer and lutenist **Walter Porter** issues his *Madrigales and Ayres* for two to five voices, in London. The collection features continuo parts, recitative and one of the earliest English examples of the concertato style.

18 February Composer and cellist **Giovanni Vitali** is born in Bologna.

16 April Monteverdi is ordained as a priest. This year also marks the publication of a second book of *Scherzi musicali*. In addition to songs for solo voice and continuo, the collection includes his evocative *Zefiro torna* (Zephyr Returns) for two tenors and continuo.

29 November Composer **Giovanni Battista Lulli** (later Jean-Baptiste Lully) is born into a milling family, in Florence.

29 December Merula is sacked from his position as *maestro di cappella* of Santa Maria Maggiore in Bergamo for alleged acts of indecency towards various pupils. He contests his loss of salary, but later backs down and writes an official statement of apology to avoid criminal proceedings.

Widowed for the second time, **Francesca Caccini** returns to Florence to resume her musical services to the Medici family.

Luigi Rossi is appointed organist at San Luigi dei Francesi in Rome, a position he will hold for the rest of his life. The church's sumptuous Baroque interior is home to Caravaggio's famous triptych on the life of St Matthew, including *The Inspiration of St Matthew* (left).

Giovanni Sances brings out his *Cantade … libro secondo*, the first publication to incorporate both strophic and through-composed cantatas.

In disarray from the continuing Thirty Years' War, the Dresden Court Chapel grants **Schütz** leave to become *Kapellmeister* to the royal court in Copenhagen.

30 January Michelangelo Rossi's opera *Erminia sul Giordano* (Herminia on the Jordan) is first staged at the Palazzo Barberini in Rome. The libretto, by **Rospigliosi**, is based upon Tasso's epic *Gerusalemme liberata*.

12 August Jacopo Peri, singer and one of the pioneering composers of opera, dies in Florence, aged 71. For much of his life he was in musical service to the Medici court.

24 October Renowned organist and composer **Jehan Titelouze** dies in Rouen, aged about 70. A musical conservative, he is considered by many as the founding father of the French organ school.

1632 Gustavus Adolphus of Sweden dies at the Battle of Lutzen; his infant daughter Christina succeeds him • Galileo Galilei publishes *Dialogue on the Two Chief Systems of the World*, but Church allows him only to hypothesise that the Earth revolves around Sun • Rembrandt van Rijn (Neth) paints *The Anatomy Lesson of Dr Nicolaes Tulp*

1633 Thirty Years' War continues: Protestant Duke Bernhard of Saxe-Weimar invades Franconia, seizes Barnberg and Höchstädt from the Bavarians, and occupies much of the Palatinate • Roman Catholic Church places Galileo Galilei under house arrest for life for insinuating as fact that the Earth revolves around the Sun

1634

Composer and theorist **Adriano Banchieri** dies in Bologna, aged about 66.

Austrian composer **Antonio Draghi** is born around this time.

Frescobaldi returns to Rome, resuming duties as organist at St Peter's. He now gains the patronage of the influential Barberini family.

Scheidt issues the second book of his *Geistliche Concerte*, small-scale sacred works for voices and continuo. He indicates that many of the pieces are reductions of much works, and 'Whoever would like to publish and print them, to the glory of God, can obtain them from me at any time'.

3 February James Shirley's lavish masque *The Triumph of Peace*, with music by **William Lawes** and **Simon Ives**, together with scenery and costumes by Inigo Jones, is staged in the Banqueting House in Whitehall for King Charles I. The total cost of the spectacle is estimated at £21,000 (the modern-day equivalent of around £2.5m).

29 September The masque *Comus*, a collaboration between **Henry Lawes** and **John Milton**, is staged at Ludlow Castle (below) in honour of the Earl of Bridgewater, Lord President of Wales.

Mid November German composer and organist **Johann Staden** dies in Nuremberg, aged 53.

1635

Angelo Cecchini sets to music **Ottaviano Castelli**'s *Primavera urbana*. Performed in Rome during Carnival, the musical drama steers towards *opera buffa* with the inclusion of dialect-speaking comic characters.

Frescobaldi publishes his influential *Fiori musicali* (Musical Flowers) in Venice. His most famous work presents a sizeable and diverse collection of organ pieces for use in the Mass, including toccatas, canzonas, ricercares and capriccios. It is later studied by J. S. Bach and J. Fux.

William Lawes takes up a court position as one of the King's Lutes.

Scheidt publishes 12 concertos for two voices and continuo in *Liebliche Krafft-Blümlein*, mostly comprising settings of Old Testament texts.

15 March Part-time composer **Louis XIII** (above) presents *The Ballet de la Merlaison* at Chantilly, France. The music, words and choreography are all by the king himself.

May Schütz leaves Copenhagen and returns to Dresden to resume duties as *Kapellmeister*. The economic hardships of the Thirty Years' War continue to afflict the court.

1634 Holy Roman Emperor Ferdinand II dismisses Albrecht von Wallenstein from supreme army command; Wallenstein is murdered at the emperor's instigation • Ferdinand II's son, Ferdinand of Hungary, becomes Imperial commander-in-chief • Scientist Thomas Moffett (Eng), father of 'Little Miss Muffet', compiles *Theatrum Insectorum*, work on entomology

1635 In Thirty Years' War, Treaty of Prague: Ferdinand II makes peace with Saxony • France declares war on Spain • King Charles I opens Hyde Park to the public; he also establishes the Royal Mail service • Rembrandt (Neth) paints *Belshazzar's Feast* • William Davenant (Eng): play *The Platonick Lovers*

Buonamente has his *Sixth Book of Sonatas*, scored for two to six instruments with continuo, published in Venice. The composer-violinist is now *maestro di cappella* at the Basilica di S Francesco in Assisi.

Melchior Franck publishes his stunning *Paradisus musicus*.

French musical theorist **Marin Mersenne** issues the first volume of his four-part *Harmonie universelle* (Universal Harmony). The treatise offers descriptions and classifications of the musical instruments of the time, and a thorough appraisal of the French musical style. Mersenne also presents groundbreaking observations on acoustics, exploring the relationship between pitch and vibration, and the process of sound wave transmittance through the air to the listener's ear.

HARMONIE VNIVERSELLE.

Laudate eum in Psalterio & Cithara. Omnis spiritus laudet Dominum. Pseaume 150.

Schütz publishes his *Kleiner geistlichen Concerten* (Little Sacred Concertos) in Leipzig, scored predominantly for one to five voices and continuo. He explains in the dedication of the work that he has not included *obbligato* instruments due to the economic constraints of the time.

Scheidt loses his four children during an outbreak of plague in Halle.

4 February Schütz's heartfelt *Musikalische Exequien*, scored for six soloists, choir and continuo, is first performed at the funeral of Prince Heinrich Posthumus von Reuss in Gera. The final part of the memorial features spatially-separated choral groups singing two different texts simultaneously.

23 February William Davenant's masque *The Triumphs of the Prince d'Amour*, with music by brothers **William** and **Henry Lawes**, is introduced at Middle Temple in London.

Buonamente's seventh and final book of sonatas and sinfonias is published in Venice. The publisher dedicates each piece to a famous Venetian, mostly noblemen but including the composers **Monteverdi** and **Giovanni Rovetta**.

Dietrich Buxtehude, composer and organist of German ancestry but possibly Danish birth, is born around this time.

Jakob Froberger is appointed court organist in Vienna on the accession of Ferdinand III. He soon obtains leave to study with **Frescobaldi** in Rome.

The Teatro San Cassiano in Venice becomes the world's first public opera house (with boxes reserved for the nobility), opening with *L'Andromeda* by **Francesco Manelli** and **Benedetto Ferrari**. Manelli's wife, **Maddalena**, takes one of the female roles, becoming one of the first women of opera.

Merula's *Canzoni overo sonate concertate per chiesa e camera* is published in Venice. It is one of the earliest printed collections to specify church and chamber instrumental styles.

12 February Virgilio Mazzocchi supplies music to the first comic opera, *L'Egisto* or *Il Falcone* (The Falcon), staged at the Palazzo Barberini, Rome. With libretto by **Rospigliosi**, the opera is revived two years later as *Chi soffre speri* (see 1639).

August Schütz again secures leave from war-torn Dresden. He returns to the Danish court at Copenhagen and stays until the following year.

6 August English dramatist, poet and (masque) librettist **Ben Jonson** dies in London, aged about 64.

7 December Bernardo Pasquini is born in Pistoia, Tuscany.

1636 In the Thirty Years' War, Spain launches attack on France from the north, but repelled in Picardy • General Court of the Massachusetts Bay Colony establishes three militia regiments, the first of America's National Guard; they also establish Harvard College, N America's first institute of higher education • Justus Sustermans (Flem) paints *Galileo Galilei*

1637 Holy Roman Emperor Ferdinand II dies; is succeeded by his son Ferdinand III • Pierre Fermat (Fr, founder of modern number theory) and Rene Descartes (Fr) independently develop analytic geometry; Descartes introduces his philosophy in *Discours de la Méthode* • Claude Lorrain (Fr) paints *Port Scene with the Villa Medici*

Organist at the cathedral in Königsberg, **Heinrich Albert** issues his first book of sacred and secular songs in *Arien* (Arias), scored with continuo. In this and his second book (1640), Albert provides useful notes on continuo performance, including the essential advice that it should not sound like 'hacking a cabbage'.

Gregorio Allegri (right) composes his strikingly beautiful *Miserere* around this time for the papal choir of the Sistine Chapel. A singer and devout priest, he is respected for his deep concern for the poor and imprisoned.

Caspar Kittel, pupil of **Schütz**, publishes his only known musical collection, *Cantade und Arien*, and in so doing introduces the Italian cantata into the German musical tradition.

Domenico Mazzocchi publishes *Madrigali a cinque voci* in Rome. Featuring both unaccompanied and concerted madrigals, the collection contains some of the earliest instructions of crescendo and diminuendo. In addition to the part books, Mazzocchi issues the madrigals in full score, 'so that if ears are not granted the occasion to hear them, neither the eye nor intellect will be deprived of delighting in their better moments'.

Monteverdi publishes his *Madrigali guerrieri et amorosi* (Madrigals of War and Love), otherwise known as his *Eighth Book of Madrigals*. Included in the collection is a revised version of *Il ballo delle ingrate* (1608) and the first print of *Combattimento di Tancredi e Clorinda* (see 1624).

Autumn John Wilbye, one of England's leading madrigalists, dies in Colchester, aged 64.

Andreas Hammerschmidt, aged about 27, brings out the first volume of his *Musicalische Andachten* (Musical Devotions). The five-part collection, published at various stages over the next 14 years, contains over 150 sacred pieces for one to 12 voices. This year the composer begins a life-long position as organist of the Johanniskirche in Zittau.

Schütz brings out a second book of *Kleine geistliche Concerten* (Op. 9), in Dresden.

Loreto Vittori composes his pastoral opera *Galatea*, most likely first performed at the Barberini Palace this year.

23 January Francesco Cavalli secures the post of second organist at St Mark's, Venice. The next day his first opera, *Le nozze di Teti e Peleo*, is premièred at the Teatro San Cassiano. It is the earliest surviving Venetian opera.

27 February Virgilio Mazzocchi's *Chi soffre speri* (He Who Suffers May Hope), a revised version of his comic opera *L'Egisto* (1637), is performed with scenic effects by Gian Lorenzo Bernini at the Barberini Theatre in Rome. The production features added *intermedi* by **Marco Marazzoli**.

3 April Italian composer **Alessandro Stradella** is born outside Viterbo.

1 June Prolific German composer **Melchior Franck** whose output includes secular songs, psalm-settings and over 600 motets, dies in Coburg, aged about 60.

July Inventive violinist-composer **Carlo Farina** dies of the plague, in Venice.

28 October Stefano Landi, one of the pioneering composers of Roman opera (see 1632), dies in Rome, aged 52.

1638 General assembly in Scotland abolishes episcopacy (rule by bishops) in Scottish Church • Shogunate forces effectively wipe out Christianity in Japan • Galileo Galilei (It) publishes *Dialogues Concerning Two New Sciences*, describing laws of motion for falling bodies and projectiles • Rembrandt (Neth) paints *Stormy Landscape*

1639 First Bishops' War: Scottish Covenanters (Presbyterians), protesting against Episcopalianism, capture Edinburgh Castle • Sakoku now enforced in Japan: no foreigners allowed into the country and no Japanese allowed to leave; penalty of torture or death • Francis Day (Eng) founds Madras as a fort for the English East India Company

The Whole Booke of Psalmes (otherwise known as *The Bay Psalm Book*) is published in Cambridge, Massachusetts. It is the first English language book printed in America.

Cavalli's second opera, *Gli amori d'Apollo e di Dafne*, opens in Venice.

Monteverdi (left) sets Homer in his first opera for Venice, *Il ritorno d'Ulisse in patria* (Ulysses' Homecoming), which manages a healthy run of ten performances at the Teatro SS Giovanni e Paolo. This same year the septuagenarian composer issues a retrospective sacred music collection, *Selva morale e spirituale*.

Monteverdi's opera *L'Arianna* (1608) inaugurates the Teatro San Moisè in Venice. Soon afterwards the venue plays host to **Benedetto Ferrari**'s new opera *Il pastor regio*.

German composer **Paul Siefert**, organist at the Marienkirche in Danzig, publishes his *Psalmen Davids*, chorale motet settings of the Calvinist Reformed Church Psalter. He is later criticised in print by his rival, the composer-theorist **Marco Scacchi**, for corrupt technique and distasteful examples of sacred music.

In a letter to musical theorist Giovanni Doni, **Pietro della Valle** refers to his *Oratorio della Purificatione*, which is to be performed at the oratory of the Chiesa Nuova. This is the first documented use of the term *oratorio* in application to a musical genre, although the work itself only lasts around 12 minutes.

The building of the Palais Royal (below) is completed in Paris. In the second half of the century the venue becomes home to the Académie Royale de Musique.

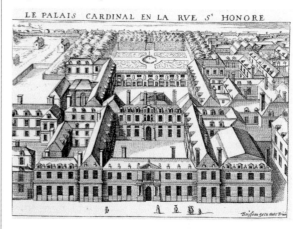

LE PALAIS CARDINAL EN LA RVE St HONORE

Neapolitan composer **Gioanpietro Del Buono** publishes the earliest known sonatas for harpsichord, in Palermo.

Cavalli's opera *La Didone* (Dido) is introduced at the Teatro San Cassiano in Venice. Adapting the story from Virgil's *Aeneid* to contemporary tastes, librettist **Giovanni Busenello** avoids Queen Dido's suicide and instead marries her off to King Iarbas of the Gaetuli.

Monteverdi's opera *Le nozze d'Enea con Lavinia* (The Marriage of Aeneas and Lavinia) has its première at the Teatro SS Giovanni e Paolo. No music survives.

January Francesco Sacrati and librettist **Giulio Strozzi** enjoy a resounding triumph with their opera *La finta pazza* (The Pretended Madwoman), which inaugurates the Teatro Novissimo in Venice. (See also 1645.)

September Franz Tunder, aged 27, becomes organist of the Marienkirche in Lübeck, where he later begins the renowned *Abendmusiken* concerts.

1640 Scots wage Second Bishops' War against Charles I; to raise money for the war, Charles summons the so-called Long Parliament (1640–60), which opposes him and moves to impeach his advisers • Portuguese revolt and overthrow their Spanish rulers: Duke João of Bragança becomes King João IV • Rubens (Flem) paints *The Village Wedding*

1641 Thousands of Protestants are massacred in Ulster rebellion • English parliament's 'Grand Remonstrance' lists grievances against King Charles I; royal advisor Earl of Strafford executed • Rene Descartes (Fr) publishes *Meditationes de Prima Philosophia* • England's House of Commons authorises destruction of altars and images

With the onset of the English Civil War, musical life in London is restricted as the Puritans close the theatres and outlaw acting. King Charles flees London and sets up court in Oxford.

German composer and theorist **Johann Andreas Herbst** publishes *Musica practica*, the first independent singing tutorial with practical exercises.

Monteverdi begins work on *L'incoronazione di Poppea* (The Coronation of Poppea) in collaboration with the librettist **Giovanni Busenello**. Based on the licentious life of Nero, the opera sets new standards for characterisation and breaks fresh ground with its focus on non-religious historical subject matter. (See also 1643.)

22 February Musician to Cardinal Antonio Barberini, **Luigi Rossi** sees his first opera, *Il palazzo incantato* (The Enchanted Palace) premièred at the Barberini Theatre in Rome. With text by **Rospigliosi**, the seven-hour epic includes performances by the leading castrati of the day—**Loreto Vittori** and **Marc'Antonio Pasqualini**.

29 August Giovanni Battista Buonamente, renowned for his pioneering violin music, dies in Assisi, probably aged in his late 40s. For the last nine years he had served as *maestro di cappella* at the Basilica of San Francesco.

Autumn Unsalaried in Dresden due to the ongoing war, **Schütz** secures further leave and returns to Copenhagen as *Hofkapellmeister* to the court of King Christian IV (right). He remains there for just over two years.

The French printer Ballard issues the final collection of solo *airs de cour*.

Cavalli's richly lyrical *L'Egisto*, on a libretto by **Giovanni Faustini**, triumphs at the Teatro San Cassiano in Venice. A tale of love lost and found, the opera is soon performed in many major Italian cities.

Composer **Marc-Antoine Charpentier** is born in Paris.

Herbst publishes his *Musica poetica*, the first German language compositional treatise. In this and **Marco Scacchi**'s *Cribrum musicum* (also published this year) are some of the earliest printed criticisms of parallel fifths and octaves.

Thomas Selle, kantor at Hamburg's Johanneum (grammar school), composes his *St John Passion*. Notable for its inclusion of instrumental interludes, the work begins the history of the German oratorio Passion.

28 January Sacrati's opera *Venere gelosa* (Jealous Venus), with sets by Torelli, opens to great acclaim at the Teatro Novissimo, Venice.

1 March Girolamo Frescobaldi, one of the foremost keyboard composers of the era, dies in Rome, aged 59.

Autumn Love, even of an immoral kind, seems to conquer all in **Monteverdi**'s final and finest opera, *L'incoronazione di Poppea*, premièred at the Teatro SS Giovanni e Paolo in Venice. Some of the music is thought to be by **Ferrari** and **Cavalli**. (See also 1642.)

29 November Monteverdi, the most famous and revered composer in Europe, dies in Venice, aged 76. He is buried in the Church of the Frari, Venice.

- -

1642 English Civil War begins between Royalists (Cavaliers) and Parliamentarians (Roundheads); in Battle of Edgehill both sides claim victory, but Royalists then fail to take London at Battle of Turnham Green • Isaac Newton (Eng) born • Astronomer and physicist Galileo Galilei (It) dies • Rembrandt (Neth) paints *The Militia Company*

1643 King Charles I holds most of England except the south east as the English Civil War continues • Louis XIII (Fr) dies; is succeeded by his son Louis XIV, aged five • Physicist Evangelista Torricelli (It) makes the first mercury barometer • Navigator Abel Tasman (Neth) discovers Tonga and Fiji after unknowingly circumnavigating Australia

As the English Civil War continues, the Puritan parliamentarians step up their nationwide campaign to purge all churches of organs, stained glass windows and 'superstitious' images. The *Book of Common Prayer* is abolished and replaced with the *Directory for the Publique Worship of God*, advocating only the unaccompanied singing of metrical psalms.

Pope Urban VIII (born Maffeo Barberini) dies. His successor, Innocent X, charges members of the Barberini family with embezzlement of public funds. The prominent arts patrons leave Rome the following year and seek refuge in Paris, where they remain for nine years.

Cavalli and the librettist **G. Faustini** present to the public their third operatic collaboration, *Ormindo*, at the Teatro San Cassiano, Venice. Highlights include the tender prison scene duet of Act 3, as Erisbe and Ormindo, believing themselves poisoned, prepare to die.

Composer **Giovanni Rovetta** is appointed successor to Monteverdi as *maestro di capella* of St Mark's, Venice. He remains in the post until his death in 1668.

Scheidt, *Kapellmeister* to Duke August of Saxony in Halle, publishes his *LXX Symphonien*—short instrumental pieces in trio style to be performed as introductions or ritornellos within vocal concertos.

Sigmund Staden, aged 36, composes the pastoral Singspiel *Das geistliche Waldgedicht oder Freudenspiel genant Seelewig* (The Sacred Forest Poem or Play of Rejoicing called Seelewig), a Christian morality play scored for soprano, bass, a supporting cast of six and a small ensemble of strings and winds. Performed this year at court in Nuremburg, *Seelewig* explores the conflicts between body and soul. It is the earliest surviving German opera.

Instrument maker **Antonio Stradivari** is born around this time in Cremona.

Singer and composer **Barbara Strozzi**—adopted (perhaps natural) daughter of the librettist **Giulio Strozzi**—publishes her first opus, *Il primo libro de madrigali*. Her first of eight volumes of vocal music contains madrigals for two to five voices on texts by her father. The music is deeply expressive and frequently virtuosic.

12 August Austrian violinist and composer **Heinrich Ignaz Franz Biber** is born in Wartenberg, Bohemia.

December Schütz, having left Copenhagen earlier this year, presents *Theatralische neue Vorstellung von der Maria Magdalena* at the Wolfenbüttel court. Some of the music may be by his pupil, **Sophie Elisabeth**, Duchess of Brunswick-Lüneburg.

Oliver Cromwell winning a decisive victory at Marston Moor (English Civil War), 2 July.

1644 In English Civil War, Scots invade England; parliamentary cavalry general Oliver Cromwell defeats Royalists under Prince Rupert at Marston Moor • In Thirty Years' War, French army under Vicomte de Turenne and Duc d'Enghien invades the Rhineland • China, Manchu Ch'ing Dynasty replaces Ming Dynasty • China's new Manchu rulers order the Chinese to have shaven heads with queues ('pigtails') • Aged 18, Queen Christina (Swe) comes of age and is crowned • René Descartes (Fr) describes various phenomena mechanistically in *Principia philosophiae* • John Milton (Eng) writes the tract *Areopagitica* to defend press freedom • Pierre Corneille (Fr) publishes tragedy *Pompée*

1645

In Venice **Giovanni Antonio Bertoli** publishes his *Compositioni musicali*, containing the earliest-known collection of bassoon sonatas.

Hammerschmidt publishes his *Gespräche zwischen Gott und einer gläubigen Seelen* (Conversations Between God and a Believer), comprising 22 concertos for two to four voices and continuo. A second, shorter set of dialogues, scored principally for one to two voices, is also published this year.

Around this time **Juan Hidalgo** is promoted as court composer of chamber songs, villancicos and theatre music at the Spanish court. He also becomes director of the court's chamber musicians.

Johann Rosenmüller, aged about 26, brings out his first instrumental collection, *Paduanen, Alemanden, Couranten, Balletten, Sarabanden*, with some of the dances presented in suite form.

Schütz, 60 this year, returns to Dresden eager to retire. The elector grants him only semi-retirement: the composer has to continue working for six months each year for the next ten years.

February The guardianship of Francesca Caccini's teenage son passes to the boy's uncle, Girolamo Raffaelli, indicating the possible recent death of the composer and singer. She is remembered above all as the first female opera composer.

30 July **Giovanni Legrenzi** takes up the post of organist at Santa Maria Maggiore, Bergamo.

24 September **William Lawes**, aged 43, is killed in crossfire at the battle of Rowton Heath (near Chester) during the English Civil War. The Royalist poet Thomas Jordan writes an epitaph:

Concord is conquer'd;
in this urn there lies
The Master of
great Musick's mysteries;
And in it is a riddle like the cause
Will Lawes was slain
by such whose will were laws.

14 December **Sacrati**'s opera *La finta pazza* (first performed at Venice, 1641) is presented in the hall of Le Petit Bourbon, Paris. Instigated largely by Cardinal Mazarin, the occasion appears to mark the first staging of an Italian opera in Paris.

A scene from Francesco Sacrati's opera *La finta pazza* (The Pretended Madwoman). The French production owed much of its success to the impressive sets and machinery of Giacomo Torelli.

1645 In English Civil War, Marquis of Montrose arouses Scottish clans to fight for Charles I, but is defeated by parliamentary army; Archbishop Laud, former advisor to Charles, is executed; Generals Fairfax and Cromwell lead parliament's 'New Model Army' which defeats Charles conclusively at Naseby, Northamptonshire • In Thirty Years' War, Swedish troops beat forces of Holy Roman Emperor Ferdinand III in Bohemia and take Moravia; Sweden and Demark make peace • Turks start a long war with Venice • Presbyterianism becomes the official religion in England • François Mansart (Fr) promotes Baroque architecture in France with his designs for Val-de-Grâce Church, Paris • Pascal (Fr) invents the *Pascaline* mechanical calculator calculator • Claude Lorrain paints *Mercury Stealing Apollo's Oxen*

The 14-year-old **Giovanni Battista Lulli** leaves Italy for Paris, where he takes up an appointment of Italian tutor to Anne-Marie-Louise d'Orléans

(left), the 19-year-old niece of the Chevalier de Guise. He continues his musical training in violin, harpsichord and composition.

Luigi Rossi arrives in Paris at the invitation of Cardinal Mazarin who has granted protection to Rossi's exiled patron, Cardinal Antonio Barberini. He begins to write his opera *Orfeo*.

Around this time **Schütz** writes his exceptional Passion oratorio *Die sieben Worte Jesu Christi am Kreuz* (also known in translation as *Seven Last Words*).

Franz Tunder begins his series of *Abendspielen* (Evening Performances) in Lübeck. The origin of these free public concerts is thought to have been the composer's weekly organ recitals, given to entertain local businessmen awaiting the midday opening of the stock exchange. Assisted by the patronage of wealthy townspeople, the concerts will later evolve into the famous tradition of *Abendmusiken* under Tunder's son-in-law, **Buxtehude**.

February Cavalli's *L'Egisto* (1643) receives its French première at the Palais-Royal, Paris.

24 September Composer **Duarte Lobo**, leading Portuguese exponent of the polyphonic style, dies in Lisbon, aged about 80.

3 October Italian composer **Virgilio Mazzocchi** dies in Civita Castellana, aged 49.

7 October Orazio Benevoli is appointed successor to V. Mazzocchi as *maestro di cappella* of the Cappella Giulia at St Peter's, Rome.

Johannes Crüger publishes his influential *Praxis pietatis melica* (The Practice of Piety in Song), a large compilation of chorales, including arrangements and compositions of his own. A number of his settings will remain in use for centuries to come, including *Now thank we all our God* and *Jesu, joy and treasure*.

English composer **Pelham Humfrey** is born around this time.

Dutch diplomat, amateur poet and composer **Constantijn Huygens** publishes his *Pathodia sacra et profana*, a collection of motets and airs, in Paris. It is the first work printed in France to incorporate basso continuo.

Leading Czech composer **Adam Václav Michna** brings out his *Česká mariánská muzika* (Czech Marian Music).

Constantijn Huygens, father of the scientist Christian Huygens.

Schütz publishes his second collection of *Symphoniae sacrae* for solo voices, obbligato instruments and continuo.

2 March Luigi Rossi's opera *Orfeo*, commissioned by Cardinal Mazarin, is premièred at the Palais-Royal in Paris. Performed in Italian with impressive stage machinery by Giacomo Torelli, the opera is well received, although some of Mazarin's dissenters criticise the vast extravagance of the production.

10 May Leading Spanish composer **Mateo Romero** dies in Madrid, aged about 72. He was a long-serving *maestro de capilla* at the Spanish court and largely responsible for introducing the modern Italian manner to Spain.

- -

1646 First English Civil War ends with the Royalist surrender of Oxford; King Charles I escapes to the Scots at Newcastle; negotiations between king and parliament collapse when Charles rejects Presbyterianism as England's national religion • In Thirty Years' War, Swedes and French invade Bavaria; Swedish forces enter Prague • Velázquez (Sp) paints *The Thread Spinners*

1647 Scottish army hands over King Charles I to English parliament • Cornet Joyce kidnaps Charles for the English army; parliament recaptures Charles I, but Scots secretly offer to reinstate him if he abolishes episcopacy (rule of Church by bishops) • England's parliament passes further ordinances against the theatre: performers to be whipped and audiences fined

Around this time **Carissimi** composes his most famous oratorio: *Jephte*. Based on the story from the Book of Judges, the work is introduced by a *historicus* (narrator) and features recitatives, ariettas, duets and choruses. Like most 17th-century oratorios, *Jephte* demands only chamber-size forces.

German composer **Wolfgang Ebner** produces a set of 36 variations for harpsichord on a theme by Emperor Ferdinand III.

Henry Lawes publishes a collection of 60 psalm settings in *Choice Psalmes*, dedicated to his brother, William, who died three years previously at the siege of Chester. The collection comprises an equal amount of pieces by the two brothers.

French civilians and members of parliament, uniting as the Fronde, attempt to limit the power

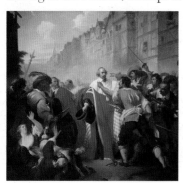

of the monarchy and with it that of the chief royal advisor, Cardinal Mazarin (left). Political pamphleteering also targets those patronised by Marazin, including the composer **Luigi Rossi** and the set designer Giacomo Torelli. During the ensuing armed conflicts, Rossi manages to flee Paris, but Torelli is imprisoned.

Schütz publishes his *Geistliche Chor-Musik* (Sacred Choral Music), an important collection of German motets for five to seven voices, conceived primarily for *a cappella* worship.

1 September French philosopher, mathematician and music theorist **Marin Mersenne** dies in Paris, aged 59.

John Blow is born around this time in Newark, Nottinghamshire.

Les Passions de l'âme by **Descartes** (right) is published in Amsterdam. The treatise proves influential for its advancement of the philosophy of musical 'affections'.

Johann Jakob Froberger completes his second book of keyboard pieces (first book lost), including some of the earliest keyboard suites.

Hammerschmidt publishes his third book of secular songs in *Weltliche Oden* (books I and II published 1642/3) and also 20 sacred concertos in his *Motettae* for one to two voices and basso continuo.

5 January **Cavalli**'s *Giasone*, accounting the amorous machinations of Jason, leader of the Argonauts, enjoys a triumphant première at the Teatro San Cassiano in Venice. It becomes the most often performed opera of the 17th century, thanks in part to **Giacinto Cicognini**'s accomplished libretto, which provides a faster-paced narrative than that of previous opera.

27 February German composer **Johann Philipp Krieger** is baptised in Nuremberg.

29/30 April Italian composer **Giovanni Valentini** dies in Vienna, aged about 66. **Antonio Bertali** succeeds him as *Kapellmeister* to the imperial court in Vienna.

1 October Virtuoso **Johann Heinrich Schmelzer** is appointed court violinist in Vienna.

1648 Second English Civil War: Scots invade England on behalf of Charles I, but are defeated at Preston, Lancashire, by Cromwell's parliamentary army • Presbyterian members are expelled from England's parliament; remainder of parliament becomes known as 'The Rump' • Treaty of Westphalia ends The Thirty Years' War • Fronde (literally 'sling') rebellions begin in Paris

1649 Second English Civil War ends with execution of King Charles I • A republican Commonwealth replaces England's monarchy (until 1660), under the 'Rump' parliament; actual power rests with Oliver Cromwell • Charles's son is proclaimed as King Charles II in Scotland • Third English Civil War: royalist revolts in Scotland and Ireland • Velázquez (Sp) paints *Pope Innocent X*

1650—1699

1650–1699

B RUISED AND battered, the German and Habsburg lands sought social and political order following the bloody upheavals of the Thirty Years' War. France became the major power of Europe, and King Louis XIV exploited to the full the prerogatives of royal absolutism. He allowed Lully to become a musical dictator, and in the process the Italian émigré cultivated a truly national style of opera. In England the Commonwealth proved unsustainable following the death of Cromwell. The Restoration witnessed renewed artistic endeavour: semi-opera flourished, and Henry Purcell emerged as the most significant English-born composer of the Baroque.

Italian opera became more indulgent as a public entertainment and soon spread into German lands. Both Italians and Germans championed old and new genres: Carissimi and Stradella the oratorio, Corelli the trio sonata and concerto grosso, Froberger the keyboard suite and Buxtehude the sacred cantata. At the very end of the century Alessandro Scarlatti brought clear definition to the secular cantata and set new standards for serious opera.

◀ *A Lady Seated at a Virginal*, Jan Vermeer *c.*1672. To the left rests a six-string bass viol (viola da gamba).

Opera and related genres

Italian opera

Venice may have long lost its status as Europe's most important trading post, but it remained a vibrant and exciting mercantile republic that offered some of the most lavish parties and festivals in Europe. Music was ingrained in its culture and public opera was now on the rise. Venice held on to its prestige as Italy's leading operatic centre, even while embroiled in long, unstable periods of war against the Ottomans.

Venetian opera relied on aristocratic support, but it was an increasingly commercial concern that pandered to public taste. Impresarios were expected to provide a degree of spectacle, while of course keeping a close eye on profits. Productions nearly always incorporated scenes in godly realms, temples, dungeons and palaces, so sets and stage machinery could be reused. Reduced casts saved yet more money: the chorus was dropped and just a small instrumental ensemble retained, usually continuo and a few strings. Because privately-funded Roman opera had set a more spectacular precedent, composers and librettists in Venice compensated by squeezing into their operas an ever greater number of arias. The aria was easier on the ear than recitative, but more importantly it allowed ample room for the singers—the castrati especially—to display their dazzling vocal technique.

Operatic style

▲ A performance of Cesti's extravagant *Il pomo d'oro* at the Hoftheater auf der Cortina, Vienna, 1668. Royal opera productions were more orderly than those for the public: the opera house was usually a chaotic place, with much chatting and coming and going. The greater the staging, effects, arias and castrati, the more likely an opera was going to succeed. Subtlety was rarely an option.

Francesco Cavalli, Antonio Cesti

The subject matter of opera at mid-century was turning from classic Greek myth towards heroic stories of antiquity and the Roman Empire. The narratives were formulaic: elements of the supernatural, lovers separated by trials or obstacles, comic situations involving minor characters, scenes involving madness, lament and slumber, were all common. Familiar characters included the gods of the prologue, two pairs of lovers, a devoted or ill-mannered servant, a shrewd ruler, a devious conspirator, and a nurse played by a man, for added comedy. (Venice, unlike Rome, allowed women on stage.)

Francesco Cavalli and Antonio Cesti (1623–69) were Italy's leading opera composers at the mid-century. Cavalli, organist at St Mark's, Venice, continued to cultivate his heroic brand of opera, following up his triumphs of the 1640s (see *Chapter 1*) with successes like *L'Orimonte* (1650) and *Xerse* (1654). The semi-comical Greek myth *La Calisto*, now Cavalli's best-known opera, failed to impress at its première in 1651.

In 1659 the French first minister, Cardinal Mazarin, invited Cavalli to Paris to bolster French interest in Italian opera. Cavalli agreed somewhat reluctantly, and then witnessed his six-hour *Ercole amante* (Hercules in Love, 1662) struggle to fill the acoustic space of the grand Salle des Machines in the Tuileries. It effectively crowned the failure of Italian opera in France. Cavalli returned to Venice and despite success with his next opera, *Scipione affricano* (1664), he was unable to match his achievements of the 1640s and 50s. However, his career blossomed in other ways, and he rose to the position of *maestro di capella* at St Mark's in 1668.

Cesti was a renowned singer and the only opera composer to challenge Cavalli's pre-eminence. He was also a monk, and his celebrity and worldly attitudes distressed his Franciscan superiors. Cesti achieved outstanding success at the court of Innsbruck where he produced two of the most popular operas of the century: *L'Orontea* (1656) and *La Dori* (1657). Historically his chief fame rests on the colossal *Il pomo d'oro* (The Golden Apple, 1668), a collaboration with the librettist Francesco Sbarra. The eight-hour mythological spectacle was commissioned by Emperor Leopold I and performed in two parts at the newly-built Hoftheater auf der Cortina in the Habsburg capital of Vienna. It featured 23 sets, machine-operated dragons and battle effects, and a massive cast with 50 sung parts. Its excesses were far beyond those common to late 17th-century opera.

The composers Antonio Sartorio (1630–80) and Giovanni Legrenzi (1626–90) worked in Venice and upheld the heroic style of Cavalli. They also brought greater distinction to the aria, a form they exploited to the full. The aria itself had undergone changes: previously, the favoured structure was a sequence of verses sung to more or less the same music, but now alternative forms that emphasised contrast became common. This led to the classic *da capo* aria (*da capo* meaning 'from the head'), characterised by a tripartite structure of A section, contrasting B section, A section repeat. On paper the composer would simply write 'da capo' after the B section, but in practice the singer was expected to embellish the repeated A section. Composers desiring more control over their arias might create ABB[1] or ABA[1] structures, writing out repeated sections with specific modifications. Arias of this period were short and fairly straightforward in harmonic design. During the 1670s and 80s, enthusiasm for the aria was at its height: Legrenzi's *Il Giustino* (1683), one of the composer's finest operas, is a representative work containing over 70 arias. The division between recitative and aria was now clear, not deliberately blurred for the sake of dramatic continuity, as characteristic of earlier opera.

The evolving aria

By the 1690s Naples was drawing considerable attention for its court-sponsored opera. Having hosted Venetian exports for several decades, it was now commissioning its own operas from the Sicilian-born composer Alessandro Scarlatti (1660–1725). *Maestro di cappella* from 1684, he achieved an international reputation by his thirties with tuneful operas like *Gli equivoci* (1690) and *Pirro e Demetrio* (1694). He did much to popularise the *da capo* aria and, with the runaway success of *La caduta de' Decemviri* (The Downfall of the Ten Judges, 1697), established the Italian overture with its fast–slow–fast sections. He was in the process of defining quintessential Italian heroic opera, the genre commonly known as *opera seria*.

Naples: Alessandro Scarlatti

Lully and the birth of French opera

All the misfortunes of man, all the disasters recorded in history—the blunders of statesmen, the breaches of generals—they all occurred for lack of knowledge of how to dance.

Molière: *Le bourgeois gentilhomme* (1670)

For opera to take root in France it needed to embrace two things: the dance and the French language. The French court and public had scant interest in the Italian language, and even less in Italian sung in recitative.

▲ Louis XIV as Apollo in the *Ballet de la Nuit* (1653). His portrayal of (and fascination with) Apollo, the sun god, led to his epithet 'The Sun King'.

Molière

Pierre Perrin & Robert Cambert: first French opera

Even so, Cardinal Mazarin, the Italian-born first minister, worked stubbornly to establish a vogue for Italian opera (see also *Chapter 1*). His last great commission was Cavalli's ill-fated *Ercole amante*, whose production in 1662 he did not live to witness. In an attempt to appease the Parisian audience, a ballet with the French title *Hercule amoureux* was inserted in between the acts of the opera. Surprisingly, the composer of the ballet was not a Frenchman, but the Italian-born Jean-Baptiste Lully. At this moment in time, Lully considered the fortunes of Italian opera in France dead and buried with Mazarin.

Lully was actually well placed to remould opera to French taste. Born Giovanni Battista Lulli in Florence, 1632, he arrived in Paris aged 13 to become a valet and Italian teacher to the king's cousin, Mlle de Montpensier. Lully meanwhile continued his own education, advancing his knowledge of music and dance. By the age of 20 he was tutoring the 14-year-old Louis XIV in ballet, dancing alongside him in such productions as *La ballet de la nuit*, performed in 1653. That same year Lully was appointed 'court composer of instrumental music', in which role he supplied overtures, *récits*, airs and dances to *ballets de cour* in collaboration with the poet Isaac de Benserade (1613–91). Lully's natural flair for music-theatre then led to a seven-year association with the dramatist and actor Jean-Baptiste Poquelin (1622–73), better known as Molière.

Molière had already invented the comédie-ballet with *Les fâcheux* (The Bores, 1661). He asked Lully to supply music for this new sub-genre, beginning with *Le Mariage forcé* (1664) and including the famous social class satire *Le bourgeois gentilhomme* (1670). The comédie-ballet consisted of a spoken play with airs and dance interludes. Dance and music were more integrated than previously, gearing up the comedy and dramatic action, and providing greater cohesion to the whole. Conceived for royal pleasure, comédies-ballets would normally transfer from court to Molière's theatre company at the Palais Royal in Paris, for a run before a paying public.

While Lully was busy with court ballets, the poet Pierre Perrin (*c.*1620–75) and composer Robert Cambert (*c.*1628–77) were attempting to devise the French answer to Italian opera. In 1659 they produced the *Pastorale d'Issy*, an intimate work containing songs and continuous music, although lacking plot. Their real breakthrough came eight years later,

when Perrin managed to establish the *Académie de Musique* with royal endorsement. Perrin and Cambert staged their first full-blown French opera in 1671 with the Greek comedy *Pomone*. Still designated a *pastorale*, it observed an overture, prologue and five-act structure, and incorporated ballets and recitative. There were also magical elements and the sort of exciting stage effects that were now the staple of Italian opera. The production was extremely successful, but things suddenly went wrong for Perrin—he was bamboozled out of the profits of *Pomone* by financiers and ended up in debtors' prison. Lully, now realising the potential of homegrown opera, bought the *Académie* licence from Perrin and immediately pursued a dictatorial monopoly over all music-theatre in France.

Lully fell out with Molière, so he turned to the librettist Philippe Quinault to help him define a path for French opera. Molière meanwhile paired up with the considerable talent of Marc-Antoine Charpentier (1643–1704). The Molière-Charpentier union was short: during a production of their comédie-ballet *Le malade imaginaire* at the Palais Royal in 1673, Molière, performing the role of a hypochondriac, suffered a seizure on stage and died soon afterwards. No doubt relishing the enormous irony, and with the blessing of Louis XIV, Lully commandeered the theatre and ejected Molière's production company, hammering the final nail in his adversary's coffin.

▲ 'The Palace of Time', prologue decor of Lully's *Atys*, 1676. The prologue begins with lavish praise for a 'glorious hero', one unmistakably recognised as Louis XIV.

Marc-Antoine Charpentier

111

Lully:
*tragédie
lyrique*

For their first production Lully and Quinault set the ancient Greek tale of *Cadmus et Hermione* (1673) as a *tragédie en musique*, a genre also known as *tragédie lyrique*. The five-act opera accommodated the standard prologue to flatter the Sun King—an essential component inherited from the *ballet de cour*—ballet *divertissements*, minor comic parts and supernatural elements. Emphasising action above character development, it was designed as an accessible work with high entertainment value. With *Alceste*, staged the following year, Lully incurred criticism for integrating comedy, a popular ingredient of Italian opera. He was accordingly forced towards a more serious approach that reflected the refined traditions of the French stage, exemplified in the tragedies of Corneille and Racine. Lully's subsequent *tragédies* still demanded impressive stage machinery, but their simplified plots provided greater scope for human emotion and psychology. Representative works of his mature style include the Ovid-inspired *Atys* (1676) and *Phaëton* (1683), and the chivalric tales *Amadis* (1684) and *Armide* (1686).

Armide

Armide, based on Tasso's famous epic poem *Gerusalemme liberata*, is Lully's greatest opera. His expressive recitative is superbly illustrated in the monologue 'Enfin il est en ma puissance' from Act II, where Armide approaches the sleeping Renaud with murderous intent, but rage and revenge dissipate as she is overcome by love. The recitative here is powerful and natural, yet Lully's craft was born through difficult labour. It had taken many years for the Italian composer to make the transition from Italian to French text setting, not least because French verse abounds in irregular rhythms and sung French uses alternative pronunciations to help it flow musically. (Consider the traditional French nursery song *Frère Jacques*: the two syllables 'Frère Jacques' are each split to render the more rhythmical 'Frè - re Jac - ques'.) Lully used varying time signatures in conjunction with a more lyrical, arioso-style of recitative to cope with these idiosyncrasies. In the aria, he rejected the florid Italian manner, favouring instead *airs* of noble simplicity. This appealed to French audiences, who were able to sing along to their favourite tunes, often drowning out the on-stage performer.

French
overture

Lully is intimately linked with the evolution of the French overture, a structure comprising repeated slow–fast sections and ending with a shorter slow section. The slow sections are distinguished by stately dotted rhythms, whereas the fast section is lighter and imitative or fully fugal in texture. He may not have invented the form, but he certainly standardised its inclusion in ballet (from the late 1650s) and in opera. Another innovation was his orchestrally-accompanied recitative, used as an alternative to 'secco' recitative with its minimal continuo support. Lully first employed the accompanied style in *Triomphe de l'amour* (1681), a ballet-opera that also engaged the first professional female dancers. The practice was commonly saved for moments of high drama, as in the scenes featuring Armide and Hatred in Act III of *Armide*.

Lully's
monopoly

Holding the *Académie* licence, Lully controlled French opera with an iron fist. He restricted the number of performers a company could employ so that no-one was able to match the grandeur of his own productions. He even banned rival companies from using dancers. It was therefore impossible for other composers to break into commercial French opera; only private productions, such as Charpentier's *La descente d'Orphée aux enfers* (*c.*1686), remained beyond Lully's control. No doubt in 1687, after Lully was unfortunate enough to stab his foot with a conductor's staff, contract gangrene and die, many composers breathed a huge sigh of relief. Not least Charpentier, who created his most important public opera with *Médée* in 1693. Even so, the reverence afforded to Lully's legacy was considerable and his operas remained in the French repertory well into the 18th century. This was a remarkable feat, as opera throughout Europe was customarily the privilege of living composers.

English music-theatre: Locke, Blow, Purcell

English opera attempted to launch itself with *The Siege of Rhodes* (1656) during the censorial period of Cromwell's Commonwealth. The work combined the music of no fewer than five composers, including Henry Lawes and Matthew Locke (*c.*1622–77). William Davenant, in the role of librettist and impresario, advertised it as 'Representation by the art of perspective in scenes, and the story sung in recitative music'. Its designation was crucial, as spoken plays were outlawed at the time, so its conception had more to do with existing laws than with a genuine desire to establish opera on English shores. Not long into the Restoration, *The Siege of Rhodes* was mounted as straight theatre. The music does not survive.

The masque *Cupid and Death* by the playwright James Shirley is another historically important work from the 1650s. Christopher Gibbons (1615–76) and Locke contributed music (since lost) to the first production in 1653. Six years later Locke revised the score and adapted much of the original dialogue into recitative, quite possibly to appease the Puritans. The new version accordingly teetered on opera, combining spoken dialogue, recitative, songs, choruses and ballet.

With the advent of the Restoration in 1660, England's theatres reopened. The English were proud of their theatrical tradition and content with the masque, so they were little inclined to produce through-composed opera. Even so, there was artistic interest in creating a genre in which music and drama attained a greater degree of integration—much in the vein of France's comédie-ballet—and it was from this impulse that English semi-opera was born. One of the first major semi-operas was a lavish version of Shakespeare's *The Tempest* staged in 1674, with text adapted by Thomas Shadwell and music by various composers, including Locke. The following year Shadwell and Locke collaborated on *Psyche*, a version of Molière's *tragédie-ballet* of 1671. Incorporating spoken lines, songs, choruses, recitative and incidental music, the production was described by Locke as an 'English Opera'. As far as Shadwell and Locke were concerned, the idea of conventional opera, with its incessant music, was intrinsically un-English because it went against the grain of the country's beloved theatrical traditions. *Psyche* was as close to opera as the English were going to accept, so why not call it English opera?

Their assessment almost proved right: only two through-composed operatic works were produced in England in the last quarter century. John Blow (1649–1708) created the first with a work he designated a masque, *Venus and Adonis*, in effect a tragic opera structured in a prologue and three

Through-composed opera

John Blow

acts. Probably first performed at court in 1682, it features prominent dances, almost ignores the aria, and at just under one hour falls some way short of full-length opera.

Purcell: *Dido and Aeneas*

Purcell followed with the similarly brief *Dido and Aeneas*, the only Baroque opera composed by an Englishman to hold a firm place in the modern repertory. The first known performance took place in 1689 at Josias Priest's boarding school for girls in Chelsea. The outline of the story is simple: Dido, Queen of Carthage, confesses her love for the Trojan prince Aeneas, who, duty bound, is soon compelled to leave Carthage. Grief stricken, Dido commits suicide. Purcell modelled his work on Blow's *Venus*, so the operas shared common traits; for example the prologue and three-act format (Purcell's original prologue is lost), lyrical recitative, choruses and dances. Both are tragedies that find room for light comedy. But Purcell sought deeper dramatic unity; his recitative is more sensitive and the aria serves a critical role for Dido's poignant outpourings. The best example of this occurs during the spellbinding climax of the opera, as Dido comes to terms with her fate and welcomes the release of death. In her final lament she segues from pained recitative into the celebrated aria 'When I am laid in earth'. A chromatically descending *ground bass* (a repeated pattern) compounds the grief and sinking finality of Dido's last words, and a chorus concludes in mourning.

► Henry Purcell, after John Closterman, 1695.

Purcell: 1690s

Purcell was England's pre-eminent composer, producing works for domestic music making, court and church. The balance of his activities swung after 1689 since the new monarchy of William and Mary demanded little music at court. He now responded all the more readily to opportunities in public theatre, including semi-opera: *The Prophetess, or The History of Dioclesian* (1690), *King Arthur* (1691), *The Fairy Queen* (1692) and *The Indian Queen* (1695). Only the Dryden-Purcell collaboration of *King Arthur* was conceived as music-theatre, all the other semi-operas being musical adaptations of plays. Though they do not match the musical unity of *Dido*, the dramas reveal some of Purcell's finest music. *Dioclesian* contains the descriptive 'Dance of the Furies' (Act 2) and the musical extravaganza 'Masque of the Triumph of Love' of Act 5. More powerful still are the Frost Scene in Act 3 of *King Arthur* (the aria 'What power art thou' especially) and Titania's sleep scene in Act 2 of *The Fairy Queen*. Purcell's incidental music for some 40 plays includes his now most widely recognised piece, the Rondeau from *Abdelzar*, composed in the year of his death, 1695, and popularised by Benjamin Britten 250 years later in *The Young Person's Guide to the Orchestra*.

Opera in German lands and Spain

Italian opera, as noted earlier in the activities of Cesti, made significant headway into the German-speaking region of Lower Austria. Cities further north also embraced the genre: Munich established an opera house in the 1650s, and venues in Dresden, Darmstadt and Hanover soon followed. Agostino Steffani (1654–1728) was the most influential Italian working in Germany, writing and directing opera in Munich and then Hanover, with teams of Italian singers at his disposal. Among his greatest successes were *Servio Tullio* (Munich, 1686) and *Henrico Leone*, which inaugurated the new opera house at Hanover in 1689.

◀ Pedro Calderón de la Barca, Spanish dramatist and pioneer of the *zarzuela*.

Vernacular opera was virtually non-existent in Germany, despite the earlier efforts of Schütz (*Daphne*, 1627) and Sigmund Staden (*Seelewig*, 1644). Signs of change appeared in 1678 when the townspeople of Hamburg founded the Theatre am Gänsemarkt, hoping to advance a distinctively German brand of opera. The 'Goose-market' opera house was opened by Johann Theile's *Adam und Eva*, which set a local fashion for operas on biblical subject matter. In around 1696 the young but not inexperienced Reinhard Keiser (1674–1739) took charge of the institution, beginning a prolific career as the guiding light of German opera.

Hamburg: Theatre am Gänsemarkt

Spain's attitude towards Italian opera was much the same as England's. It too boasted a sacrosanct theatrical tradition, crowned by the plays of Lope de Vega and Pedro Calderón de la Barca, and there were music-theatre alternatives on offer. Calderón was a pivotal figure, creating mythological plays that incorporated songs and recitative, and devising the pastoral *zarzuela* with its spoken and sung dialogue, songs, choruses and dances. There are only two Spanish operas documented in the latter half of the century; both date from 1660 and feature texts by Calderón. Just one survives: *Celos aun del aire matan* (Even Groundless Jealousy Can Kill), with music by Spain's leading composer of theatrical music, Juan Hidalgo.

Pedro Calderón de la Barca

Trends in sacred music

The maturing of the Italian oratorio

Nurtured in the early 1600s, the Italian oratorio now came of age. Two forms of the un-staged sacred musical drama existed: the Latin-set *oratorio latino* and the Italian-set *oratorio volgare*. The *oratorio latino* was usually set in one part, the *volgare* in two, and their subject matter, commonly drawn from the Old Testament, was intended to be morally and spiritually instructive, much in the manner of Church-commissioned religious painting.

▲ *Jonah Leaving the Whale* by Gaspard Dughet (1615–75). Setting dramatic Biblical stories like Jonah, oratorios were able to compete with opera in musical range and expression.

The oratorio adopted the forms and styles of contemporary opera, with recitative, arioso passages and arias, accompanied by a modest ensemble mainly comprising continuo instruments. Apart from the mode of its presentation, the mid-century oratorio departed from an operatic idiom by giving prominence to the chorus, which was used to represent groups of characters or crowds within the drama. Another defining attribute was the role of the narrator, commonly identified as *testo* or *historicus*. The narration would sometimes pass to the chorus, who would deliver it in a declamatory, homophonic style. When a two-part oratorio was performed in a prayer hall (oratory), it was intersected by a sermon. Since oratorios could be performed during Lent—a time when the theatres were closed— they also became an opera substitute, presented largely for entertainment in secular venues such as academies and royal palaces.

Giacomo Carissimi

Giacomo Carissimi wrote the first masterpieces of the Latin oratorio. As a Rome-based composer he was much in demand, serving as *maestro di cappella* at the Collegio Germanico, while also composing for other churches and private patrons. He wrote his oratorios for a religious brotherhood (the 'Arciconfraternita del SS Crocifisso') and directed their performance at the Oratorio di San Marcello. His commissions included *Jepthe* (c.1648; see *Chapter 1*), *Jonas* and *Abraham et Isaac* (dates unknown), and *Judicium Salomonis* (c.1669). Carissimi's approach to text setting corresponded to trends in opera, with fluid movement between recitative, arioso and aria to aid the natural flow of the biblical drama.

Giovanni Legrenzi, Alessandro Stradella (1639–82) and Alessandro Scarlatti were prominent composers of the more popular *oratorio volgare*. In their hands the oratorio gravitated even closer to opera, with a diminished role for the chorus and the occasional absence of the narrator. We see this in Stradella's *San Giovanni Battista* (St John the Baptist, 1675), one of his most outstanding oratorios. It anticipates the 18th-century archetype with the inclusion of orchestral arias and *concerto grosso* style instrumentation, comprising small (*concertino*) and large (*ripieno*) instrumental groups. The narrated *La Susanna* of 1681, probably Stradella's last oratorio, is highly regarded for its exquisite melodies and contrapuntal flair. Its message of moral decency contrasts with what is known about Stradella's own life; renowned for his sexual recklessness, the composer was stabbed to death at the age of 42, possibly a revenge killing over an affair with a married noblewoman.

Alessandro Stradella

France and the Grand Motet

Louis XIV was not enamoured with the polyphonic mass, a genre still prevalent in 17th-century France and much of Europe. Instead he encouraged the development of the *grand motet*, which he had performed at Low Mass in the Chapelle Royale. Full of pomp and grandeur, *grands motets* were often created as much to impress and glorify the king, as God Himself. The poet Pierre Perrin, writing of the motet in the late 1660s, articulates this sycophancy:

As you are the greatest king, I have desired on my part to contribute … beautiful texts for these incomparable musicians … We will see in the person of Your Majesty a new Gallic Hercules, who, by the charms of his music … will bind our hearts and ears in golden chains.

Henry Du Mont (*c.*1610–84) led the way in transforming the motet. During the 1650s he became one of the first to bring the Baroque style to French sacred music, employing basso continuo in his *petits motets* for one to three voices. Shortly afterwards he began writing *grands motets*, typically a psalm setting for solo voice, five-part chorus (divided into a *grand* and *petit choeur*) and five-part orchestra. The best known motets of the period, however, belong to Lully, even though he devoted little time to sacred music. These include his *Miserere* (1664),

Henry Du Mont

◀ The Italian-born Jean-Baptiste Lully, the leading figure of 17th century French music. Renowned as a stage composer, he made an important (if modest) contribution to the Chapelle Royale.

117

with text drawn from Psalm 51, and the Te Deum (1677). His style is characteristically homophonic—more so than that of his contemporaries—and full of contrasts, both in vocal and instrumental textures, and in the wide range of emotion he explores. The *Miserere*, with its inherent sorrow and penitence, is a wonderfully expressive work, appropriately subtle and restrained, though not without sudden bursts of excitement. It is the earliest-known *grand motet* to be introduced by a five-part string *symphonie*. The larger Te Deum expresses exactly the sort of pomp that will have set the king's pulse racing. The opening Symphonie, emboldened with trumpets and drums, conjures imagery of a regal procession and prepares the way for a magnificent chorus in praise of God. 'All the earth doth worship thee' exclaims the multitude; one can only imagine what was going on in the mind of the Sun King.

Marc-
Antoine
Charpentier

Marc-Antoine Charpentier, who never held a major court post, was the most important church composer in France. He wrote both *petits* and *grands motets* in some quantity for the Dauphin's chapel and the magnificent Sainte-Chapelle, and created the French answer to the Latin oratorio with dramatic motets like *Judith* (*c.*1675) and *Filius prodigus* (The Prodigal Son, 1680). Charpentier's sacred music output is vast—nearly 500 works survive—and impressively wide-ranging, encompassing polyphonic masses, motets, Tenebrae lessons and responsories, hymns, psalms settings and antiphons for churches and convents. He set the Te Deum several times, his *chef d'oeuvre* being the sumptuously-scored example in D major (H.146; *c.*1690). Its infectiously sunny prelude, now a regular feature of weddings and festive events worldwide, is probably the most famous piece of French Baroque music.

Towards the end of the century, court composer Michel-Richard de Lalande (1657–1726) continued the supply of *grands motets* to the Chapelle Royale. Inspired by the examples of Lully, he carried the genre over into the 18th century and, towards the end of his life, introduced it to the public with great success at the *Concert Spirituel*.

Germany and the Sacred Cantata

There was considerable diversity in German church music during the second half of the 17th century. Within the Lutheran tradition, Orthodoxy embraced all the latest trends and styles in sacred music, Italian influences included, whereas Pietism (like Puritanism and Calvinism) sought modesty in worship, encouraging personal expressions of devotion through simple musical settings. Added to this was the divide between the Protestant north and the predominantly Catholic south, together with the variety of tastes and resources found at parish churches and court chapels across the German-speaking states.

Social and economic stability returned only slowly following the Thirty Years' War. Andreas Hammerschmidt, prolific in church music, remained active as musical director at Zittau, while the composer and organist Johann Rosenmüller (1619–84) started a new life for himself at Venice in 1658, partly to escape charges of homosexual activity in Leipzig.

Schütz

Schütz, entering old age, had to continue in part-time service for several

years because his Dresden employer refused him a proper pension. The war years had left the Dresden court finances in disarray and its musicians often went unpaid. In a letter of 1651, Schütz with heartfelt concern drew his employer's attention to one of the court singers who 'lives like a sow in a pigsty, has no bedding, lies on straw and has pawned his coat and jerkin'. Schütz himself felt 'deprived of sustenance and courage'.

Amid such dreary conditions Schütz published (in his 66th year) a third and final set of sacred concertos in the *Symphoniae sacrae* (1650), which includes among its 21 pieces the dramatic *Saul, Saul, why do you persecute me?* In full retirement he became an honorary *Kapellmeister* and composed his *Christmas Story* (1660), an oratorio replete with all the modern trimmings now associated with the genre. Even as a deaf 80-year-old his genius continued undimmed with three unaccompanied modal Passions, according to St Luke, St John and St Matthew, composed 1665–66. Schütz remained musically active up to his final year. By the time he died aged 87 in 1672, Dieterich Buxtehude (*c.*1637–1707) had already established himself as one of Germany's leading composers.

Buxtehude followed Franz Tunder (1614–67) as organist to the exalted Marienkirche at Lübeck in 1668. There he developed his predecessor's church concerts into the renowned *Abendmusiken*, an evening series around Advent time that hosted the majority of his (now lost) oratorios. Buxtehude was particularly important to the development of the German church cantata. During the late seventeenth century the church cantata was not so called, nor necessarily regarded as a genre. Derived from the sacred concerto, cantatas were simply designated *Kirchenmusik* or *Kirchenstück* (Church music or Church piece), and operated as the principal music of the Lutheran service. They were set for a few voices only, sometimes just one, and variously brought together the instrumental sonata, vocal concerto, chorale and concerted strophic aria. The text settings were of mixed provenance: scripture, chorale or devotional poetry. Because the cantata was not formalised as a genre, structures differed enormously, even in a composer's own output. Buxtehude's examples range from the simple strophic setting of *Klag-Lied* (Elegy) for solo voice and continuo instruments, to the jubilant, concerto-aria *Gott fähret auf mit Jauchzen* (God has gone up with a shout), an Ascension cantata for three voices,

Dieterich Buxtehude

Jubilate Domino

brass, strings and continuo. One of his best-known cantatas is the elaborate *Jubilate Domino*, scored for alto solo, viola da gamba and continuo. Introduced by an instrumental sinfonia, it presents florid vocal work set in a rich formal structure that engages instrumental responses, ritornellos, and even a contemplative fantasia-like section. Other major contributors to the early cantata repertory included Tunder, Johann Philipp Krieger (1649–1725) and Philipp Heinrich Erlebach (1657–1714).

The English Symphony Anthem

During Cromwell's Commonwealth the Puritans deemed only the unaccompanied singing of metrical psalms suitable for the church. They had, after all, dismantled or demolished every church organ in England in order to enforce decorum in worship. With the Restoration (from 1660), organ builders joyfully returned to their workshops, and 'services' and anthems were brought back as the main forms of Anglican church music. The service music consisted of canticle settings for Matins and Evensong, various parts of the Ordinary of Holy Communion, and sentences from the Burial Service. Of greater musical significance was the anthem, the English-language equivalent of the Latin motet. The traditional anthem was a polyphonic vocal setting of scriptural text, usually taken from the Psalms. During the early 17th century, the 'full' choral anthem was popular: most of William Lawes's anthems adhered to this category. But its predominance was challenged by the 'verse' anthem, featuring verses sung by soloists (with instrumental accompaniment) in alternation with choral sections, as in Thomas Tomkins's widely performed *O Lord, let me know mine end*.

▼ Westminster Abbey at the time of Purcell's incumbency as organist.

With the Restoration, the verse anthem became more homophonic and the role of the chorus was reduced. The most decisive transformation

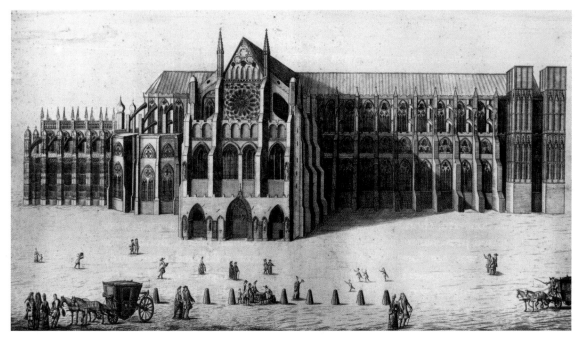

of the genre was brought by the symphony anthem, a royal form favoured by Charles II that engaged musicians drawn from the 'King's Violins'. Symphony anthems were written in verse and 'full-with-verse' forms, the second alternating solo groups (rather than single soloist) and choral sections. The emboldened instrumental forces encouraged orchestral preludes and ritornellos, making the symphony anthem the English answer to the French *grand motet*. This was tremendously pleasing to the king, who had been impressed by the French manner during his years of exile.

Symphony anthem

Pelham Humfrey (1647/8–1674) and Matthew Locke were influential composers of the Restoration anthem, but it was Blow and Purcell who produced the most enduring examples. Organist of Westminster Abbey, Blow wrote his anthems while in multiple service to the Chapel Royal— as Master of the Children, a composer-in-ordinary, and one of the Chapel organists. He excelled in the symphony anthem with works such as *I said in the cutting off of my days* (mid 1670s) and the coronation anthem *God spake sometime in visions*, composed for King James II in 1685. Blow was prolific, writing well over 100 anthems in both polyphonic and modern concerted styles.

John Blow

Purcell followed Blow as organist of Westminster Abbey in 1679, and three years later he too became one of the affiliated organists to the Chapel Royal. Like Blow, he composed anthems in every known style. One of his most popular symphony anthems is *Rejoice in the Lord alway* (*c.*1684), otherwise known as the *Bell Anthem* because of the descending step-wise string parts of its instrumental prelude, reminiscent of pealing church bells. Other famous examples include the coronation anthem *My Heart is Inditing* (1685) and *Praise the Lord, O Jerusalem* (1689; possibly also a coronation anthem). All three works fall into the 'verse' category—Purcell's favourite anthem form—and enlist solo voices, choir, strings and continuo. When composing full-with-verse anthems Purcell usually scored continuo accompaniment only, as in *O God, thou art my God* and *O Lord God of hosts* (both *c.*1682).

Purcell

Secular vocal music

Cantata

The cantata was evolving in style to closely resemble a self-contained scene from an opera. Normally set for one or two voices, it increasingly drew on operatic idioms, and amatory themes (unrequited love, especially), remained common to its poetry.

The cantata was gaining ground throughout Italy. In 1651 the composer and singer Barbara Strozzi (1619–77), the adopted daughter of the poet Giulio Strozzi, began issuing cantatas in Venice, starting with *Cantate, ariette e duetti* for one to two voices and continuo. In 1655 she published *Sacri musicali affetti* and became one of the first Italian authors of the spiritual cantata.

Barbara Strozzi

◄ Italian composer and singer Barbara Strozzi, whose output comprises madrigals, motets, ariettas, arias and cantatas.

Legrenzi, also in Venice, and Agostino Steffani, active mainly in northern Germany, made significant contributions to the genre later in the century. But it was in Rome that the cantata flourished most of all, its style matured by the illustrious line of Carissimi, Stradella and Alessandro Scarlatti.

Carissimi: Piangete ohimè piangete

Carissimi wrote nearly 150 cantatas, many of them for the exiled Queen Christina of Sweden, his principal secular patron. His cantata *Piangete ohimè piangete* (Weep, alas, weep) for soprano and continuo is a rich example of the strophic cantata, popular at the mid-century. A minor-key lament on the pains of love, its two bipartite stanzas are set with the same music, conflating aria and meandering arioso in a multi-sectional structure. Each stanza is brought to a close in tears, beautifully tone-painted by a sliding chromatic descent in the vocal part. Carissimi's later cantatas favoured a mixture of strophe and free verse, resulting in varied musical sections of recitative and arioso, mixed with binary-form arias.

Alessandro Scarlatti

In the hands of Stradella the cantata moved ever more towards a series of clearly defined sections, in keeping with developing operatic trends. The role of the continuo increased, providing introductions and ritornellos, often augmented by violins to supply a more substantial accompaniment. The genre's most prolific exponent was Alessandro Scarlatti, who scored the majority of his 600 cantatas for continuo and solo voice. His interest in the cantata developed during his early years in Rome, from around 1680, when he became *maestro di cappella* to Queen Christina. After his move to Naples (1684) he made his historic imprint on the cantata by standardising its structure as recitative–aria–recitative–aria. His recitatives are based on lines of prose consisting of seven or eleven syllables ('versi sciolti'), while the arias tend to follow *da capo* (ABA) construction. The cantatas *Del' Tirreno à le sponde* (1697) and *Giù di Vulcan* (1698) demonstrate this classic form. Scarlatti carried the cantata into the 18th century, where it remained the principal genre of Italian vocal chamber music until the end of the Baroque era.

Purcell's English Odes

The English court ode arose as a secular offspring of the symphony anthem. Essentially an extended secular cantata, the ode celebrated events relating to royal personages: birthdays, marriages, coronations, funerals, or the welcoming of a monarch returning to London. Such pieces were also commissioned for the New Year, St Cecilia's Day (22 November), banquets and military victories. As a royal genre, odes were commonly performed by members of the Chapel Royal and the King's Violins. Blow wrote several for the kings' birthdays (although none for James II) and many for New Year, while Purcell presided over the welcome songs and the birthday of Queen Mary II. Purcell also composed four odes for the feast day of St Cecilia, the patron saint of music.

Since ode texts were of negligible literary worth, it is not surprising that only a handful of odes remain well known. They are all by Purcell, including *Welcome to All the Pleasures* (1683), his first St Cecilia's day ode; *The Yorkshire Feast Song* (1690), the first English work to employ the full Baroque orchestra; his last birthday ode for Queen Mary (1692); and *Come*

Ye Sons of Art Away (1694). His greatest and most popular ode is *Hail! Bright Cecilia* (1692), a 50-minute work extravagantly scored for six soloists, chorus, woodwind, trumpets, strings and timpani. The ode's structure conforms to the established pattern of an overture followed by various solos, duets, trios and choruses. Purcell emphasises the instrumental contribution from the outset, expanding the standard bipartite French overture into a rich multi-sectional format. Instrumental passages add appropriate colour, from the delicate trio sonata of recorders and continuo that introduces 'Thou tun'st this world', to the bellicose timpani and trumpet salvos heard in 'The fife and the harmony of war'. At various points Purcell foreshadows Handel, most conspicuously in the fast second section of the overture, whose textures and motifs anticipate the *Water Music*, and in the magnificent choruses.

Ensemble music

The trio and solo sonata

In Italy two forms of the trio sonata emerged: the *sonata da camera* and the *sonata da chiesa*. The standard instrumentation involved two violins and basso continuo (the 'trio' sonata implying three parts, not three instruments), and rhythmic and textural contrast between movements was important. There were otherwise divergent characteristics. The *sonata da camera* (chamber sonata) represented music for home entertainment. Most comprise three to five movements, usually beginning with a prelude, followed by dances in binary form—much in the manner of a dance suite. The *sonata da chiesa* (church sonata) was usually cast in four movements and scored with additional organ continuo. It embodied a more serious tone, inherited from sacred vocal genres. Pieces alluding to dance styles were sometimes employed, but given titles such as *Adagio* or *Allegro*, so as not to suggest anything so profane as dancing in church. However, the *sonata da chiesa* was also performed for private entertainment, which resulted in ever more cross-fertilisation between the *camera* and *chiesa* styles. By the end of the century the *camera* and *chiesa* distinctions carried much less relevance.

Maurizio Cazzati (1616–78) and Giovanni Legrenzi were busy with the new trio sonata forms around the mid-century. Their increasing emphasis on tonal design, with harmonic sequences and modulations, mobilised the genre towards the high Baroque style. Giovanni-Battista Vitali (1632–92), a pupil of Cazzati, also wrote trio sonatas of fine quality, though it was the composer and violinist Arcangelo Corelli (1653–1713) who gave the genre its greatest expression.

Corelli was unusual among the major composers of his time since his international fame rested on a modest output of purely instrumental music. One of the most gracious and equable musicians of the period, he based himself in Rome, securing patronage from the exiled Queen Christina of Sweden and later from two arts-loving clerics, Cardinal Benedetto Pamphili and Cardinal Pietro Ottoboni. Corelli's published oeuvre consists of two sets of church trio sonatas (Op. 1, 1681 and Op. 3, 1689), two sets of chamber trio sonatas (Op. 2, 1685 and Op. 4, 1694), 12 duo sonatas (Op. 5, 1700), and 12 *concerti grossi* (Op. 6, published posthumously in 1714). The quality of the

Arcangelo Corelli

music more than makes up for the quantity, a fact confirmed by the international circulation of multiple editions of each set in Corelli's own lifetime. In the Op. 1 and Op. 3 he established the formal church sonata archetype by giving prominence to the four movement slow–fast–slow–fast plan, the third and fourth movements typically alluding to dance styles. Many of his chamber sonatas emulate a similar structure, opening with a slow prelude and continuing with dance movements such as a fast *allemanda*, slow *sarabanda* and fast *giga*. Whilst Corelli's dances are 'stylised', there is little reason to doubt that many will have pleasured the feet, not just the ear.

The movements of Corelli's chamber and church sonatas are very short, most lasting between one and two minutes. In a typical four-movement scheme, three would be set in the same key and one in the relative major or minor. Thematic links between movements appear only occasionally, as in Op. 2 No. 8. Imitative counterpoint, including fugue, is a prominent feature and serves both expressive adagios and fast movements. Corelli was especially fond of lush suspension sequences, a device he exploited to arouse the emotions and provide important harmonic momentum.

Corelli:
Op. 5 duo
sonatas

Corelli conceived his Op. 5 violin sonatas as duo sonatas for violin and violone, with the option of replacing the violone (bass violin or violoncello) with a harpsichord. This set was reprinted around 50 times during the 1700s, and in the second half of the century the historian Charles Burney declared that on these examples 'all good schools for the violin have been founded'. The sonatas were popular for their tunefulness, exquisite craftsmanship and player accessibility—Corelli may well have had pedagogical concerns in writing them. Mostly cast in five movements, they adopt church and chamber styles in equal proportion, but with a great deal of convergence between the two. We find a church sonata ending with a *giga* (No. 5), and a chamber sonata with only its final movement described as a dance (No. 11). The exception is *La follia*, a concluding set of variations on a well-known 15th-century tune; it is also atypical in that it accommodates a degree of bravura. Corelli's string music, though in places technically demanding, generally avoids virtuosic display, a judicious constraint that undoubtedly contributed to its commercial success.

Johann
Heinrich
Schmelzer &
Heinrich
Biber

The Austrian composer-virtuosos Johann Heinrich Schmelzer (*c.*1620–80) and Heinrich Biber (1644–1704) wrote violin sonatas for the professional. Schmelzer came into contact with the Italian style while serving as a violinist to the Habsburg court in Vienna. His six *Sonatae unarum fidium* of 1664 are concentrated on variation form and appear to be the first printed German solo sonatas with continuo. Biber, who may have been taught by Schmelzer, is most famous for his 16 Mystery Sonatas (*c.*1676). The set in fact constitutes 15 *Rosary* sonatas and one unaccompanied, meditative *Passacaglia* that prefigures Bach's illustrious *Chaconne*. The *Rosary* sonatas are scored for violin and bass only (like Corelli's Op. 5) and use concentrated variation form and *ostinato* bass lines. More flamboyant than Schmelzer's sonatas, they reflect the composer's preoccupation with *scordatura*—the retuning of strings to different pitches in order to obtain a wider palette of sonorities.

The trumpet sonata also began to flourish at this time. Both Schmelzer and Biber wrote for the instrument, as did the Bolognese composer Maurizio Cazzati and the distinguished violin virtuoso Giuseppe Torelli (1658–1709). Born in Verona, Torelli began writing for the trumpet in the 1680s while occupying church posts at Bologna. Variously termed sonatas, sinfonias or concertos, his trumpet compositions are predominantly festive in style—some may have been performed during festival celebrations in the Basilica of San Petronio. Torelli rarely explored the cantabile capabilities of the instrument; he wrote his slower movements exclusively for strings, demanding intricate filigree well beyond the reach of the natural trumpet. The first keyed trumpet, after all, was still a century away.

Giuseppe Torelli

The trio sonata exported

In England the young Purcell first chose the (antiquated) viol fantasia to prove his contrapuntal gift in instrumental form, producing some crown jewels of the genre in around 1680. He then turned his attention to the trio sonata, his first collection appearing in 1683 and the second, containing works probably contemporaneous with the first, posthumously in 1697. In the preface to the first set he wrote that he had 'faithfully endeavour'd a just imitation of the fam'd Italian masters'. Three-part continuo textures and lively motivic figurations impart an Italian manner, though French and English influences are apparent in some of the weighty contrapuntal slow movements. These qualities are well illustrated in the most famous of the set, No. 9 in F (*The Golden*), which remained popular long into the 18th century.

The German composers Buxtehude, Georg Muffat (1653–1704) and Johann Jakob Walther (*c.*1650–1717) also took up the trio sonata in the final quarter of the century. The first to do so was Walther, whose *Scherzi* for solo violin and continuo appeared in 1676 and promoted his reputation as one of Europe's leading virtuosos. The French interest came a little later, with the earliest trio sonatas by François Couperin (1668–1733) probably dating from the 1690s, and examples by Marin Marais (1656–1728) appearing in his *Pièces en trio* of 1692.

The *concerto grosso*

Originating in Rome, the *concerto grosso* gained rapid popularity as a genre that flaunted contrasts of volume and instrumental colour. It was characterised by alternating instrumental groups: a small *concertino*— essentially a trio sonata group—and the full ensemble (absorbing the

▶ *The Concert* by Antonio D Gabbiani *c.*1690. The seven musicians are thought to be from the Modena or Medici court.

concertino), termed *ripieno*, or *tutti*, meaning 'all'. While large ensembles— or 'orchestras'—of 20 or more players were not unknown at this time, the norm was one player per part and instrumental pieces were generally written to suit minimal forces. Early *concerti grossi* were set in either four or five independent parts; a proficient ensemble of seven players could produce a very satisfying result, although, with the presence of a keyboard, just four musicians could manage a performance of sorts.

Alessandro Stradella

Alessandro Stradella, influential in the oratorio and cantata, was a notable pioneer of the concerto grosso. His serenata *Vola, vola in altri petti* (1674) contains the earliest dated concerto-grosso designation, while his *Sonata di viole*, composed soon afterwards, introduced the concertino–ripieno scoring for an exclusively instrumental composition. Stradella resided in Rome for a number of years (until 1677) and will have surely influenced Corelli. Some of the pieces of Corelli's posthumously published Op. 6 collection of 1714 were probably conceived around 1680—there are certainly contemporary references to his concertos at that time. Like his Op. 5 solo sonatas, the Op. 6 concertos are grouped in church and chamber styles, eight *da chiesa* and four *da camera*, but with some mixing of the two approaches. The majority of the concertos employ a six-movement scheme. Most popular is No. 8 in G minor, the last of the church-style works, also known as the *Christmas Concerto* as it was 'made for Christmas Eve' (*fatto per la notte di natale*). Corelli's inspiration pours out in exquisite melodies and exciting fugal allegros. His sublime aria-style third movement, written in the sub-mediant key of E flat, revealed how overarching tonal design could be used to add breadth to the concerto as a whole, generating an extended harmonic journey.

Corelli's Op. 6

Muffat & Torelli

Among the early exponents of the concerto, Georg Muffat composed concerto-grosso style sonatas in *Armonico tributo* (1682) after hearing Corelli's concertos in Rome. Giuseppe Torelli was more influential. His six *concerti a quattro* Op. 5 (1692) are the first printed examples of instrumental concertos, while two of his 12 *Concerti musicali* Op. 6 (Nos. 6 & 12, 1698) incorporate solo violin passages, preparing the way for the 18th-century solo concerto.

Solo keyboard music

Suites and sonatas

The stylised dance had long been popular in keyboard music, but no-one appears to have combined contrasting dances into a unified keyboard set before the late 1640s. This is surprising considering that such collections already existed in lute and ensemble repertories. One of the first to do so was the German composer Johann Jakob Froberger (1616–67), who did more than any other to establish the classic form of the keyboard suite. A Frescobaldi-trained virtuoso, Froberger spent two extended periods in service to the Viennese Imperial Court (1634–45, 1653–68) but otherwise toured widely, teaching and performing. His fame was international: he was honoured with a concert in Paris and drew a royal audience in the Spanish Netherlands. Pirates in the English Channel showed him a little less respect—they robbed him blind and he turned up in Dover wearing sailors' clothes. He reflected on this unhappy incident in one of his keyboard movements: *Plainte faite à Londres pour passer la mélancholie* (from Suite No. 30).

Froberger's influence was far-reaching, even though he was barely printed in his own lifetime. His first surviving collection dates from 1649 and presents some of the earliest keyboard suites, although they were not so called. Most follow a three-movement plan of allemande, courante and sarabande; one (No. 2) admits a fourth-movement gigue. His second surviving collection, from 1656, promotes the four-movement suite in the order of allemande, gigue, courante and sarabande. Almost certainly inspired by French lute music, a number of Froberger's movements—

▼ *Lament on the Death of King Ferdinand IV by the German composer Johann J. Froberger. Ferdinand IV, King of Bohemia from 1646 and King of the Romans from 1653, died from smallpox, aged 20, in 1654.*

allemandes especially—mix arpeggiated chords with explorative, expressive melody, while others favour contrapuntal textures. The 'Lament' was also important to Froberger, not only appearing in his suites (such as No. 14), but also as a semi-programmatic composition. One such piece, *Tombeau fait à Paris sur la mort de Monsieur Blancrocher* (1652), was stimulated by the death of a celebrated lutenist who fell from a ladder and apparently died in Froberger's arms.

Froberger's output includes toccatas, ricercares, capriccios and canzonas, and represents a cosmopolitan fusion of Italian, French and German styles. Less eclectic but still innovative was Johann Kuhnau (1660–1722), who followed Froberger in the keyboard suite with his two sets of *Neue Clavier-Übung* (1689, 1692). Kuhnau is famous for being J. S. Bach's predecessor as Thomskantor at Leipzig, but more importantly he was a pioneer of the multi-movement keyboard sonata. His first printed sonata appeared in 1692; seven sonatas followed in *Frische Clavier Früchte* (Fresh Keyboard Fruit, 1696) and six in the *Biblische Historien*, published in 1700. The second set stands out for the programmatic nature of its sonatas, featuring titles such as *The Fight Between David and Goliath* and *Saul Cured by David Through Music*. These pieces seem to be influenced by the structures of the trio sonata, inasmuch as they incorporate fugal forms, lyrical slow movements and often finish with a dance-like movement. The *Biblische Historien* represents a significant milestone in the development of programmatic music.

Organ composers and repertory

The church pipe organ was one of man's most sophisticated mechanisms and its communal importance was unmatched by any other instrument. For many composers, organ music—performance, improvisation and composition—was vocational bread and butter. However, only a few composers achieved international reputations as organists. One such composer was the Spaniard Juan Cabanilles (1644–1712), some of whose vast output was known in southern Italy and France. By contrast, Henry Purcell, an organist of the Chapel Royal and principal organist of Westminster Abbey, appears to have committed very little organ music to manuscript at all. In terms of legacy, the French and German organ traditions were the most significant of the period.

French keyboard music as a whole was prospering. Jacques de Chambonnières (c.1601–72) had brought an idiomatic style to harpsichord music, while Louis Couperin (c.1626–61) and Guillaume Nivers (c.1632–1714) were building on the legacy of Jehan Titelouze (c.1562–1633) to establish a French organ school. Nivers was organist at St Sulpice in Paris for over half a century, while also holding posts elsewhere. His three influential publications of *Livre d'orgue*, issued between 1665 and 1675, created a point of reference for later organ collections of the French school. They comprise in excess of 200 liturgical versets, extending from lightly ornamented chant melodies and fugues to *récits*, 'duos' and 'dialogues', some subtly influenced by song and dance styles. In Book II is the *organ mass*, a characteristic genre of the French school featuring versets to be played in between sung parts of the Ordinary ('Kyrie', 'Gloria',

Johann Kuhnau

France

etc.) or Proper ('Introit', 'Gradual', etc.). In such settings the choir would normally sing in plainsong, so by alternating organ versets and plainsong the organ mass achieved both musical interest and textual clarity. This was the genre through which Louis Couperin's nephew, François Couperin (1668–1733), announced his genius. At the age of 21 he wrote the two organ masses of his *Pièces d'orgue* (1690), producing works that rank alongside the finest French organ music of the century. Couperin will have known Nivers first by reputation and then through personal contact, since they both occupied organist posts at the royal chapel. Couperin and Nicolas de Grigny (1672–1703) joined Nivers in consolidating the French organ tradition.

◄ The Marienkirche at Lübeck. Dieterich Buxtehude secured the post of organist in 1668, following the death of Franz Tunder. The same year he married his predecessor's youngest daughter, possibly a stipulation of his employment.

In Germany the dominant composers of organ music were Buxtehude and Pachelbel. Buxtehude's organ playing was legendary, so much so that the 20-year-old Bach, in 1705, was to walk well over 200 miles to Lübeck to hear it. Central to his organ music are the *praeludia*, multi-sectional pieces that combine formal fugues with freer improvisatory styles. Also important are the organ chorales, appearing in three forms: chorale variations, chorale fantasias and chorale preludes. The chorale prelude traditionally served as an introduction to a congregational hymn, but Buxtehude and his contemporaries developed the form as an independent composition. The chorale tune would serve as a *cantus firmus* within an often elaborate four-part contrapuntal setting.

German lands: Buxtehude

Johann Pachelbel (1653–1706) held successive organ posts at Vienna, Eisenach, Erfurt, Württemberg, Gotha and Nuremberg. He also found time to compose ensemble suites, sacred concertos, masses and motets, and a wide range of keyboard music. As a jobbing organist, liturgical organ pieces were high on his agenda and it is these, above all the chorales and nearly 100 Magnificat fugues, which take pride of place. Little of Pachelbel's music was printed during his lifetime, but among the published chorales are those of *Musikalische Sterbens-Gedancken* (Musical Meditation On Death), a collection probably stimulated by the loss of his wife and child to plague in 1683.

Johann Pachelbel

Pachelbel's extensive organ music output also includes a number of non-liturgical genres such as the toccata, fugue, prelude, fantasia and *chaconne*. His highest achievement in this sphere is *Hexachordum Apollinis* (Apollo's Hexachord, 1699), a work suitable for organ or harpsichord that comprises six arias with variations, each set in a different key. Pachelbel is remembered above all for one very tuneful *Canon in D*, originally scored for three violins and continuo. Not published until around 1920, it has become the most famous instrumental piece from the entire 17th century.

Chronology
1650–1699

Heinrich Albert completes his eighth and final book of *Arien*, featuring sacred and secular songs.

Charles Dassoucy provides music for **Pierre Corneille**'s *Andromède*, staged at the Petit Bourbon in Paris during Carnival. Torelli, recently out of prison (see 1648), provides stage machinery, largely recycled from Rossi's *Orfeo* (1647). Dassoucy publishes two choral works from the production (in his *Airs à 4 Parties*) three years later; the rest of the music is lost.

Around this time **John Jenkins**, England's leading composer of music for viols, completes his collection of 21 fantasias for two trebles and a bass.

Eaves dropping (above) and bird song (top right), from Kircher's *Musurgia universalis*

In Rome, German music theorist and historian **Athanasius Kircher** publishes *Musurgia universalis*, a significant treatise containing musical theories and a discussion of Italian and German compositional practices. Kircher quotes various musical examples by Morales, Gesualdo, **Giovanni Kapsberger** and **Carissimi**. The compendium also includes a fantasia by **J. J. Froberger**, his first printed work.

Monteverdi's *Messa et salmi* is published posthumously in Venice.

Scheidt brings out his *Görlitzer Tabulatur-Buch*, containing 100 four-part chorale settings for organ.

German composer and violinist **Johann Jacob Walther** is born around this time in Witterda, Thuringia.

11 February René Descartes dies in Stockholm, aged 53. His musical treatise *Compendium musicae*, written 32 years previously, is published in Utrecht this same year. It presents one of the earliest discources on the relationship between the scientific and psychological phenomena in music.

20 February Cavalli's opera *L'Orimonte*, on a libretto by **Faustini**, opens at the Teatro San Cassiano in Venice.

20 May Italian opera composer **Francesco Sacrati** dies (possibly in Modena) aged 44.

Summer Cesti's lifestyle outside his duties as a monk causes concern within his Franciscan order, with suspicions of unchaste conduct. Later this year he is accused by a superior-general of bringing dishonour to his monastery through his celebrity as an opera singer.

December Schütz (left) publishes his third and final set of *Symphoniae sacrae*. The 65-year-old *Hofkapellmeister* is still unable to fully retire due to lack of funds at the Dresden court.

1650 Royalist Marquis of Montrose leads rebellion in Scotland: is defeated and executed • Prince Charles (eldest son of Charles I) lands in Scotland and is again proclaimed king; parliamentary general Oliver Cromwell defeats Scots at Battle of Dunbar • Anglican clergyman James Ussher (Ire) uses Biblical 'proofs' to put the date of creation at 4004 BC

• England's Puritan rulers make adultery punishable by death • World population reaches 500 million • Anne Bradstreet (Eng/N Amer): poems *The Tenth Muse, Lately Sprung Up in America* • Rembrandt (Neth) paints the *Jewish Merchant* • Nicolas Poussin (Fr) paints *Self Portrait* and his second *Arcadian Shepherds*

The 13-year-old Louis XIV dances the role of the Sun in **Benserade**'s *Ballet de Cassandre* at the Palais Royal. With further *ballet de cour* appearances as Apollo, he gains the epithet *The Sun King*.

Giovanni Legrenzi is ordained a priest. The 25-year-old composer is subsequently elected as resident chaplain at the church of Santa Maria Maggiore, Bergamo, where he also serves as organist.

John Playford publishes 100 traditional folk tunes in *The English Dancing Master*, a collection that will enjoy repeated editions well into the next century. He also publishes *A Musicall Banquet*, comprising rounds, catches, pieces for viols and two-part consort music. Playford soon becomes England's leading music publisher.

The English Dancing Master:
OR,
Plaine and easie Rules for the Dancing of Country Dances, with the Tune to each Dance.

march 19th
LONDON,
Printed by *Thomas Harper*, and are to be fold by *John Playford*, at his Shop in the Inner Temple neere the Church doore. 1651 1650

Strozzi publishes her first cantatas in *Cantate, ariette e duetti*, for one to two voices and continuo, in Venice.

June Monteverdi's *Ninth Book of Madrigals* is published posthumously in Venice.

6 October German composer and poet **Heinrich Albert** dies aged 47 in Königsberg (now Kaliningrad), where he had served as cathedral organist for the last 20 years.

28 November Cavalli's racy mythological opera *La Calisto*, after Ovid's *Metamorphoses*, struggles to please at the Teatro San Apollinare, Venice. The libretto is by the composer's close collaborator **Giovanni Faustini**, who dies the following month, aged 36.

Robert Cambert is appointed organist at the church of St Honoré, Paris.

The Parisian printer Ballard issues **Henry Du Mont**'s *Cantica sacra*, a stunning collection of *petits motets* for voices, viols or violins, and basso continuo. Scored in two to four parts, it is the first printed work by a French composer to incorporate continuo accompaniment.

English composer **John Hilton** issues the popular song book *Catch That Catch Can*, in London.

17 January Cavalli's opera *Eritrea* opens at the Teatro San Apollinare, in Venice.

17 February Composer, singer and priest **Gregorio Allegri** dies in Rome, aged about 70.

September Froberger performs in Paris, and is also honoured with a concert at the Convent of the Jacobins. Two months later, in the same city, he witnesses the death of a lutenist, who dies in his arms after a fall from a ladder. The experience inspires his moving keyboard elegy *Tombeau de M. Blancrocher*.

November Queen Christina of Sweden (right) engages an Italian opera troupe for her court in Stockholm. Within two years she will abdicate her throne and settle in Rome as a Catholic convert and a major arts patron.

December Cesti is appointed director of the *Kammermusiker* at the Innsbruck court of Archduke Ferdinand Karl. With an ensemble of Italian musicians, he has to provide and direct vocal chamber music and opera.

1651 Prince Charles, son of Charles I (Eng) is crowned King of the Scots at Scone; his Scottish army invades England but parliamentary army under Oliver Cromwell routs it at Worcester; Charles escapes to France • *Leviathan* by philosopher Thomas Hobbes (Eng) acknowledges the sovereign's absolute power, provided he makes proper use of it

1652 First Anglo-Dutch War begins with an English naval victory off Dover • End of Fronde rule in Paris; Royal authority restored in Paris, but Fronde revolt continues • King Felipe IV (Sp) crushes a Catalan revolt after besieging Barcelona for more than a year • Dutch settlers establish Cape Town in South Africa

Around this time **Froberger** makes a trip to London. Midway between France and England, pirates attack and ransack his ship; he arrives in Dover penniless and wearing sailor's clothes. The composer later alludes to the incident in the first movement of his keyboard Suite No. 30: 'Plainte faite à Londres pour passer la melancholie'.

In service to Archduke Ferdinand Karl at Innsbruck, **William Young** becomes the first English composer to publish a set of works entitled *sonatas*. His collection, also incorporating dances, is scored for two to four violins and continuo.

17 February Italian composer **Arcangelo Corelli** is born in Fusignano.

20 February Luigi Rossi, opera composer and prolific writer of canzonettas and cantatas, dies in Rome, aged about 55.

23 February Louis XIV and **Lully** both dance in **Lambert**'s *Ballet Royal de la Nuit*. The following month Lully is appointed *Compositeur de la musique instrumentale* to the French royal court.

26 March James Shirley's masque *Cupid and Death*, with music by **Christopher Gibbons** (and possibly **Matthew Locke**), is first performed in London for the principal pleasure of the Portuguese ambassador.

1 June German composer and organist **Georg Muffat** is baptised in Mégève, Savoy.

1 September German composer and organist **Johann Pachelbel** is baptised in Nuremberg.

Outgunned: a pirates' schooner (right) at the mercy of a frigate.

Legrenzi issues his first opus, *Concerti musicali per uso di chiesa*, in Venice.

Playford publishes *A Breefe Introduction to the Skill of Musick*, in London.

4 January Cesti's new opera *Cleopatra* inaugurates Archduke Ferdinand's Komödienhaus at Innsbruck. The purpose-built opera house is the first of its kind in a German-speaking country.

12 January Cavalli's opera *Xerse* premières and triumphs at the Teatro San Giovanni e Paolo, Venice. The libretto, by **Nicolò Minato**, will be later used by Handel.

12 February The comic opera *Dal male il bene* (Good Comes from Bad), jointly composed by **Antonio Abbatini** and **Marco Marazzoli**, premières in Rome during the wedding festivities of Maffeo Barberini and Olimpia Giustiniani.

24 March German composer and organist **Samuel Scheidt**, court *Kapellmeister* at Halle, dies aged 66. He is remembered for his church music, particularly his many organ chorale preludes.

April–May Carlo Caproli's opera *Le nozze di Peleo e di Teti* (The Marriage of Peleus and Thetis), commissioned by Cardinal Mazarin, receives nine performances at the Petit Bourbon, Paris. Accommodating the Italian genre to French taste, ballets form *entrées* between the scenes of the opera and local musicians are included among the performers. The 15-year-old Louis XIV, who dances several roles in the ballets, invites the public to attend the final two performances.

1653 Oliver Cromwell becomes Lord Protector of the Commonwealth of England, Scotland and Ireland • Fronde rebellions end in France; Fronde leader Prince de Condé (formerly Duc d'Enghien) invades France with Spanish troops, but is repulsed • N. Poussin (Fr) paints *The Holy Family* • The Taj Mahal is completed in India

1654 Treaty of Westminster ends first Anglo-Dutch War • Louis XIV is crowned at Rheims • Portuguese drive Dutch from Brazil • Poland and Russia fight for the Ukraine • Sweden's Queen Christina abdicates and secretly converts to Catholicism • Carel Fabritius (Neth) paints *The Goldfinch*; he is killed soon after by an exploding powder magazine

Legrenzi publishes his touching *Harmonia d'affetti devoti* (Music of Devotional Moods), his first book of motets and psalm settings. This year also sees the publication of his first book of instrumental sonatas, *Sonate a due, e tre*, Op. 2.

Marini issues his final instrumental collection, *Diversi generi di sonate*, comprising both *da camera* and *da chiesa* sonatas. He also publishes his final sacred work, *Lagrime di David* (Tears of David) for voices, strings and organ.

Composer and organist **Johann Rosenmüller**, currently teaching at Leipzig's Thomasschule, is imprisoned along with some of his pupils on suspicion of homosexual activity. Escaping both jail and Leipzig, he resettles in Venice three years later, finding employment at St Mark's as a trombonist.

Barbara Strozzi (right) brings out her luminous *Sacri musicali affetti*, featuring some of the earliest spiritual cantatas, in Venice. In her dedication to Archduchess Anne of Innsbruck, Strozzi highlights her place as a female composer in a man's world. She concludes with sycophancy characteristic of the age: 'on the lightest leaves I fly in devotion to bow down before you'.

22 January **Michel de La Guerre**'s *Le Triomphe de l'Amour* (The Triumph of Love) is first performed at the Louvre in Paris. With music throughout (now lost), the work stands as the earliest known French *pastorale*.

4 May Piano inventor **Bartolomeo Cristofori** is born in Padua.

4 November **Cesti**'s opera *L'Argia* is premièred at the Hoftheater in Innsbruck for the pleasure of the visiting Queen Christina of Sweden, who has recently abdicated her throne.

8 November The annual music festival for The Corporation of the Sons of the Clergy is begun

by a group of London merchants, themselves all vicars' sons. The charity is founded during the Commonwealth period due to Cromwell's widespread persecution of clergy who remain loyal to the Crown. For centuries to come, it provides funds for clergy families in financial need.

December Queen Christina of Sweden takes up residence in Rome in the Palazzo Farnese. She immediately establishes regular artistic and scholastic meetings which in time give rise to the Accademia Reale.

30 December **Cavalli**'s opera *Erismena* is first staged at the Teatro San Apollinare in Venice. An English language version is later prepared and may have been performed in London in the 1670s.

1655 Dissension in England persuades Lord Protector Oliver Cromwell to dissolve parliament; Cromwell organises England into 12 military districts • England captures Jamaica from Spain • Sweden, under King Charles X (Gustav), begins the first Northern War against Poland to win Baltic lands • England's Anglican clergy are forbidden to preach; Roman Catholic priests are expelled • Pope Innocent X dies; is succeeded by Alexander VII • Waldensians, a Protestant minority, are brutally massacred by Catholic soldiers in Piedmont (north-west Italy) • Work begins on Church of St Sulpice, Paris (Fr) • Rembrandt (Neth) paints *Woman Bathing in a Stream* • Molière (Fr): *L'Etourdi*

The Teatro della Pergola opens in Florence. It remains one of the oldest surviving theatres in Italy.

Cavalli publishes *Musiche sacre*, a collection of sacred works that includes his *Messa concertata*, a lavish Venetian-style festive mass for double choir and instrumental ensemble.

Froberger completes his fourth book of keyboard pieces (third book lost). Included in the anthology are four-movement suites in the order of allemande, gigue, courante and sarabande. Froberger is a leading exponent of the early keyboard suite.

Legrenzi becomes *maestro di cappella* of the Accademia dello Spirito Santo, Ferrara. This year also sees the publication of his *Sonate da chiesa e da camera* (Op. 4) in Venice.

31 January The opera *La vita humana*, with music by **Marazzoli** and text by **Rospigliosi**, premières at the Barberini theatre in Rome. It celebrates both Carnival and the new Roman citizenship of Queen Christina of Sweeden.

3 February Lully's first full work, the ballet *La galanterie du temps*, is introduced at the Louvre. Taking part is the newly-created 'Petits Violons', an ensemble that under Lully's direction soon eclipses the King's prestigious '24 Violons' in musical excellence.

19 February Cesti's romantic comedy *Orontea*, based on Cicognini's libretto of 1649, delights the archducal court at Innsbruck. Concerning mortal characters, the narrative develops more quickly than that of much opera of the period, following in the manner of Cavalli's celebrated *Giasone* (1649, libretto also by Cicognini). Featuring such delights as the love song 'Intorno all'idol mío' (Around my idol), *Orontea* becomes one of the most popular operas of the 17th century.

18 May Filipe de Cruz becomes *mestre* of the Portuguese royal chapel.

31 May French composer and viol player **Marin Marais** is born in Paris.

18 July Queen Christina of Sweden employs **Carissimi** as *maestro di cappella del concerto di camera* at her new residence, the Palazzo Farnese, in Rome.

September Composers **Henry Lawes**, **Matthew Locke**, **Henry Cooke**, **George Hudson** and **Charles Coleman** collaborate with librettist **William Davenant** on *The Siege of Rhodes*, staged in a small theatre at Davenant's London home, Rutland House. Often referred to as the first English opera, the music is now lost. Diarist John Evelyn

Backdrop design for *The Siege of Rhodes*

is certainly none too impressed with the work, writing that it is 'in recitative music and scenes much inferior to the Italian composure and magnificence'.

8 October Schütz's Dresden employer of over 40 years, Elector Johann Georg, dies after several months of illness.

1656 War breaks out between England and Spain; English seize Spanish treasure ships off Cádiz • Lord Protector Oliver Cromwell (Eng) calls second parliament; he again excludes hostile members • João IV of Portugal dies; is succeeded by his son, the mentally unstable Afonso VI, aged 13 • Armies of Sweden and Brandenburg invade Poland • Muhammad Kiuprili becomes chief minister of Turkey and bolsters the sagging Ottoman Empire • Jewish authorities denounce Jewish philosopher Baruch Spinoza (Neth) for heresy • Giovanni Bernini (It) designs colonnade flanking the square of St Peter's, Rome • Velázquez (Sp) paints *Las Meninas*

Maurizio Cazzati becomes *maestro di cappella* at San Petronio, Bologna.

Cesti's semi-comical opera *La Dori*, with libretto by **Giovanni Apolloni**, premières at Innsbruck. Spinning an intricate web of betrothal and tangled love, mixed with pirates, slavery, gender swapping and the supernatural, *La Dori* repeats the success of *Orontea* (1656) and becomes one of the most popular operas of the 17th century.

Froberger writes the keyboard piece 'Lamentation on the Death of Emperor Ferdinand III'.

Adam Krieger, organist of the Nicolaikirche in Leipzig, publishes his secular *Arien*, a collection of 50 songs scored for one to three voices, strings and continuo.

Under the new elector Johann Georg II in Dresden, **Schütz** is now able to fully retire with a proper pension.

February *Kapellmeister* **Johann Kaspar Kerll** presents the opera *L'Oronte* to inaugurate Munich's Residenz Theater.

5 February **Jacopo Melani**'s opera *Il potestà di Colognole* (or *La Tancia*) inaugurates the Teatro della Pergola of the Florentine Immobili academy. This year the composer is promoted to *maestro di cappella* of Pistoia Cathedral.

25 July German composer **Philipp Heinrich Erlebach** is baptised in Esens, East Friesland.

15 December Composer **Michel-Richard de Lalande** is born in Paris.

Dietrich Buxtehude, aged 20, is appointed organist of St Maria Kyrka, Helsingborg. His father had previously held the post.

French composer **Robert Cambert** experiments with operatic forms in *La muette ingrate* (The Ungrateful Mute), an Italianesque comedy scored for three voices in recitative style with instrumental interludes.

The affluent **Carissimi**, composer to the exiled Queen Christina of Sweden, begins a sideline financial enterprise by offering to buy up debts of individuals and institutions in return for repayments at competitive rates of interest.

London publisher Playford issues **Henry Lawes**'s *Ayres and Dialogues for One, Two and Three Voyces* (Book III).

17 January *Ballet d'Alcidiane*, a musical collaboration between **Lully**, **Louis de Mollier** and **Antoine de Boësset**, is presented for Carnival entertainment at the Louvre in Paris. The ballet contains an early example of the

French overture, a form characterised by a stately opening section in dotted rhythm, followed by a fast, lighter second section, imitative or fugal in texture. Lully will do much to popularise and disseminate the form.

22 April Italian composer and violinist **Giuseppe Torelli** is born in Verona.

12 June **Cavalli**'s opera *Hipermestra* is first performed at the theatre of the Immobili Academy, Florence.

Costume design for a 'Fury' in the Ballet of Furies, from *Hipermestra*.

1657 France's chief minister Cardinal Mazarin agrees with Cromwell on Anglo-French treaty against Spain • War begins between Dutch and Portuguese • Holy Roman Emperor Ferdinand III dies • Thomas Middleton (Eng): *Women Beware Women* published posthumously • Accademia del Cimento in Florence (It) becomes the first organised scientific academy

1658 The Spanish are defeated in Battle of the Dunes and England takes Dunkirk • Lord Protector Oliver Cromwell (Eng) dies; he is succeeded by his son, Richard • Swedes invade Denmark • Leopold I, son of Ferdinand III, is elected Holy Roman Emperor • Edward Phillips (Eng): philological dictionary *A New World of Words*

Robert Cambert collaborates with librettist **Pierre Perrin** on *La pastorale d'Issy*. An early example of the French *pastorale* (a precursor of French opera), the modest five-act work proves popular, managing around eight repeat performances. No music survives from this or the subsequent Cambert-Perrin collaboration, *Ariane, ou Le mariage de Bacchus*.

In Bologna composer **Maurizio Cazzati** publishes early examples of the spiritual cantata with his *Cantate morali e spirituali*.

Matthew Locke undertakes a revival of **James Shirley**'s masque *Cupid and Death* (1653), adding to, and in places revising or replacing, the music of **Christopher Gibbons**. Locke resets much of the original dialogue as recitative, steering the work towards opera.

Henry Purcell, the greatest native English composer of the Baroque era, is born in London.

Composer, theorist and viol payer **Christopher Simpson** publishes *The Division-Violist* (left) in London. Extremely popular in its day, the instruction manual becomes a valuable historical source of 17th-century musical practice.

19 February Lully's *Ballet de la raillerie*, with text by **Benserade**, is presented at the Louvre in Paris. The work features comical exchanges between French and Italian singers, who mock each other's vocal style. In this and other ballets around this time Lully popularises the graceful, triple-metre 'minuet'.

With the Restoration, musicians of the court, theatre and church return to their former activities. King Charles II enlarges the court string ensemble to 24, inspired by France's *24 Violons du Roi* and to satisfy his penchant for the French instrumental style.

At the invitation of Cardinal Mazarin, **Cavalli** adapts his opera *Xerse* (1654) to French taste for the wedding celebrations of Louis XIV and Princess Maria Teresa of Spain. Performed at the Louvre, Paris, the new production includes an inserted ballet (of six *entrées*) by **Lully**.

Maurizio Cazzati issues his charming *Trattenimento per camera d'arie, correnti, e balletti* (Op. 22) for two violins and continuo.

Johann Joseph Fux, Austrian composer and theorist, is born in Hirtenfeld, Styria.

Schütz, aged around 75 and in retirement, composes his oratorio *Historia der Geburt Jesu Christi* (Christmas Story) for Elector Johann Geoge II of Saxony.

1 January Samuel Pepys begins his diaries, containing many observations on musical life in London.

6 April German composer **Johann Kuhnau** is born in Geising, Erzgebirge.

2 May Italian composer **Alessandro Scarlatti** is born in Palermo.

4 December French composer **André Campra** is baptised in Aix-en-Provence.

5 December **Juan Hidalgo** and dramatist **Caldéron de la Barca** produce the earliest surviving Spanish opera, *Celos aun del aire matan* (Even Groundless Jealousy Can Kill), in Madrid. The work has been commissioned to celebrate the marriage between Princess Maria Teresa of Spain and Louis XIV.

1659 Richard Cromwell (Eng) forced to resign as Lord Protector; the 'Rump Parliament' is briefly reconvened • General John Lambert stages a military coup; General George Monk prepares to march on London • Treaty of the Pyrenees ends the Franco-Spanish War • Danes repel Swedish assault on Copenhagen (Den)

1660 Convention Parliament proclaims Charles II king, and the English monarchy is restored • Treaties of Oliva and Copenhagen hand Polish and Danish lands to Sweden, and confirm German state of Brandenburg's claim to East Prussia • The Royal Society is established in London • Caesar van Everdingen (Neth) paints *Bacchus en Ariadne*

Louis XIV installs the Académie Royale de Danse.

J. Blow, aged 12, joins the choir of Chapel Royal.

Composer and keyboardist **Louis Couperin** dies in Paris aged about 35. A key influence on the French keyboard tradition and pioneer of the 'unmeasured' keyboard prelude (written with no rhythmic indications), Couperin leaves all of his music unpublished.

Matthew Locke becomes Composer to the King's Private Music. He composes *Music for His Majesty's Sagbutts and Cornetts* for Charles II's coronation celebrations.

Lully and **Benserade** collaborate on two ballets: *L'impatience*, performed at the Louvre, and *Les saisons*, performed at Fontainebleu. While both ballets feature texts mainly in Italian (Lully's native language), over the next few years the composer will incorporate an increasing amount of French settings into his productions for wider audience appreciation.

9 March Cardinal Mazarin, French First Minister, Royal advisor, and high-profile patron of Italian opera, dies in Paris. His death heralds the demise of Italian opera in France, and the gradual development of home-grown French opera.

23 April **Henry Lawes**'s anthem *Zadok the Priest* is first performed at the coronation of King Charles II.

16 May **Lully** succeeds the late Jean de Cambefort as superintendent of music to Louis XIV, the highest musical position at court. At the end of the year he becomes a naturalised Frenchman.

6 June Italian composer **Giacomo Antonio Perti** is born in Bologna.

1 July **Domenico Anglesi** provides music to the horse ballet *Il mondo festeggiante*, presented in the amphitheatre of the Boboli gardens, Florence. The spectacle contributes to the wedding celebrations of Prince Cosimo III de' Medici and Princess Marguérite Louise d'Orléans.

8 July **Jacopo Melani**'s opera *Ercole in Tebe* is premièred during the ongoing matrimonial festivities of Prince Cosimo III (later the Grand Duke of Tuscany) and Princess Marguérite, in Florence.

17 August The dramatist **Molière** launches *comédie-ballet* in collaboration with the composer-choreographer **Pierre Beauchamp**, presenting *Les fâcheux* (The Bores) at the inauguration of Nicolas Fouquet's spectacular Chateau de Vaux-le-Vicomte (below) in Maincy. Fouquet, finance minister to Louis XIV, also

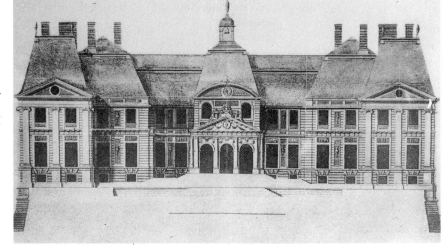

provides a sumptuous feast for the king and thousands of guests. The spendthrift is later charged with embezzlement of the Crown's money and imprisoned for life.

1661 Pro-Royalist 'Cavalier' parliament meets in England • General John Lambert (Eng) is executed for treason • France's chief minister Cardinal Mazarin (Fr) dies; King Louis XIV rules as absolute monarch • Sweden and Russia agree the Peace of Kardis • Dutch and Portuguese settle colonial disputes • Arabs raid Portuguese settlement in Mombasa (now in Kenya) • Repressive laws (Clarendon Code) re-establish Anglicanism in England • Stockholm's Banco (Swe) issues world's first banknote • Anatomist Marcello Malpighi (It) describes lung structure • Johannes Vermeer (Neth) paints *View of Delft* • Molière (Fr): comedy *L'École des maris*

John Banister becomes leader of King Charles II's '24 Violins'. (See also below.)

Robert Cambert is appointed *maître de musique* to the Queen Mother (of Marie-Thérèse), Anne of Austria.

Legrenzi's first opera, *Nino il giusto*, is introduced in Ferrara.

26 January Marco Marazzoli, celebrated above all for his cantatas, dies in Rome, aged in his late 50s.

7 February Cavalli's opera *Ercole amante* (Hercules in Love) is premièred at the Tuileries Palace in Paris. Commissioned by the opera-loving Cardinal Mazarin (d.1661) for the wedding of Louis XIV (1660), the production is slanted toward French tastes with its inclusion of a ballet by **Lully** and **Benserade**: *Hercule amoureux*. The opera is not a success, and the fortunes of Italian opera in France come to a swift end.

24 July Lully marries Madeleine Lambert, daughter of the composer **Michel Lambert**. Louis XIV and Queen Marie-Thérèse both sign his marriage contract.

21 October Composer **Henry Lawes** dies in London, aged 66. He is buried in Westminster Abbey.

… instead of the antient and solemn wind musique accompanying the organ was introduced a Consort of 24 Violins betweene every pause, after the French fantastical light way, better suiting a Tavern or Playhouse than a Church.

21 December Diarist John Evelyn bemoans the music of the Chapel Royal.

Legrenzi's opera *L'Achille in Sciro* is produced in Ferrara. This year also marks the publication of his third book of chamber sonatas (Op. 8), in Venice.

Lully and his father-in-law, **Michel Lambert**, jointly compose the music to **Benserade**'s *Ballet des arts*, first performed at the Palais Royal, Paris.

Lully and the playwright **Molière** begin their collaborative partnership with the one act comedy *L'impromptu de Versailles*. It is performed before the king in the royal hunting-lodge at Versailles.

Biagio Marini, innovative Italian composer-violinist, dies in Venice, aged about 69.

Louis XIV appoints four *sous-maîtres de la chapelle royale* (vice-directors of the Royal Chapel): **Henry Du Mont**, **Pierre Robert**, **Thomas Gobert** and, the following year, **Gabriel Expilly**. Each composer holds the post for three months of the year.

Georg Muffat, aged ten, arrives in Paris to further his musical education. He will stay for six years, studying with several teachers including **Lully**.

2 July German composer **Thomas Selle**, remembered chiefly for his sacred music, dies in Hamburg, aged 64.

26 September Heinrich Scheidemann (right), one of the leading lights of the north German organ school, dies from the plague in Hamburg, aged about 68.

IN VERAM EFFIGIEM MUSICI ET OR-GANICI LONGE PRÆSTANTISSIMI CELEBER-RIMQVE HENRICI SCHEIDEMANNI.

1664

Emperor Leopold I ennobles the German composer-keyboardist **Johann Caspar Kerll**.

Lully composes his most famous grand motet, the commanding *Miserere*, scored for soloists, double choir and orchestra.

On the death of Henry Purcell (the elder), his brother, Thomas Purcell, takes up guardianship of the younger **Henry Purcell**, who turns five this year.

Johann Schmelzer (right) issues his *Sonatae unarum fidium*, the earliest known German print of sonatas for violin and continuo. The six pieces of the collection are rich in contrast, offering languid heartfelt sections and exciting passagework in equal measure.

29 January Lully and **Molière** collaborate on their first *comédie-ballet*, *Le Mariage forcé* (The Forced Marriage), presented at the Louvre in Paris. Molière's recently invented genre of *comédie-ballet* presents spoken satire/comedy with airs and dances. Music and dance play a much more integrated dramatic role than in previous court ballets.

9 February Cavalli's opera *Scipione affricano* is staged for the first time, at the Teatro SS Giovanni e Paolo, Venice.

13 February Lully, in collaboration with **Benserade** and **Octave de Périgny**, introduces *Ballet des amours déguisés*, at the Palais Royal, Paris. Possessing little talent for dance, Queen Marie-Thérèse takes a cameo role as Proserpine, appearing for the first and last time in a ballet.

8 May Lully and **Molière**, presenting a three-day festival at Versailles, introduce their *comédie-ballet* *La princesse d'Élide*.

1665

Cazzati publishes his Op. 35 sonatas in Bologna. The collection is formed of twelve pieces for two to five instruments and basso continuo, and includes three of the earliest knownsonatas for trumpet and strings.

French composer **Guillaume Nivers**, organist at St Sulpice, Paris, publishes 100 keyboard pieces in his first *Livre d'orgue*.

Schütz composes his *St Luke* and *St John Passion* for unaccompanied choir, thus adhering to the liturgical requirements for Holy Week. The 80-year-old composer writes his *St Matthew Passion* in the same manner the following year.

Christopher Simpson, England's leading authority on music, publishes *The Principles of Practical Musick*, later revised as *A Compendium of Practical Musick* (1667).

January Cavalli is officially appointed principal organist at St Mark's, Venice, though in practice he has been the highest paid organist there for many years.

28 January Lully and **Benserade**'s *Ballet de la naissance de Vénus*, a tribute to Henrietta of England, premières at the Palais Royal, Paris.

17 March Composer and keyboardist **Elisabeth Jacquet** (later, **Elisabeth Jacquet de la Guerre**) is baptised in Paris.

14 September *L'amore médecin* (The Love Doctor), a *comédie-ballet* by **Lully** and **Molière**, is introduced at Versailles.

10 December Tarquinio Merula, progressive Italian composer and Knight of the Golden Spur, dies in Cremona, aged about 70.

1664 England seizes New Netherlands, which is handed to James, Duke of York; City of New Amsterdam is renamed New York • Austrians and French defeat Turks south east of Vienna; Turks sue for peace • *Le Monde*, by philosopher René Descartes (Fr), is published posthumously • Jean Baptiste Racine (Fr): first tragedy, *La Thébaïde*

1665 In the Second Anglo-Dutch War, English fleet defeats Dutch off Lowestoft (Eng) • Felipe IV of Spain dies; succeeded by his four-year-old son Carlos II • Mathematician Isaac Newton (Eng) develops differential calculus; begins research into light and gravitation • Outbreak of bubonic plague in London; 68,596 people die • Molière (Fr): *Don Juan*

Italian composer **Antonio Lotti** is born in Hanover, where his father, Matteo, is serving as *Kapellmeister*.

Lully's *Ballet des muses* débuts at the palace of St Germain-en-Laye. The work anticipates the solo concerto texture with its introduction to the exquisite 'Trop indiscret Amour', where solo violin sections, representing Orpheus, alternate with ensemble tutti. Lully himself performs the violin part.

Carlo Pallavicino becomes *Vice-Kapellmeister* to Elector Johann Georg II in Dresden, where **Schütz** (81 this year) is principal *Kapellmeister* in name.

Antonio Stradivari makes his earliest surviving dated violin, in Cremona.

12 July Cesti's *Nettuno e Flora*, with text by **Francesco Sbarra**, premières at the Hofburg in Vienna. The opera sets an allegorical tale about Margarita Teresa's journey from Spain to Vienna to marry her uncle, Leopold I (in costume, left). The Holy Roman Emperor, who weds his 15-year-old niece in December this year, contributes an aria to the production, while additional ballet music is provided by **Schmelzer**.

14 August Matthew Locke's polychoral anthem *Be Thou Exalted Lord* is first performed at the Chapel Royal in celebration of the Duke of Albemarle's naval victory against the Dutch.

Johann Christoph Pepusch is born in Berlin.

Rosenmüller, now a trombonist and composer at St Mark's, Venice (see 1655), publishes his *Sonate da camera a 5 stromenti*.

Giovanni Battista Vitali publishes his first *Sonate*, for two violins and continuo, in Bologna.

January/February Lully produces two *comédies-ballets* for Louis XIV: *La pastorale comique* and *Le Sicilien*, both staged at St Germain-en-Laye.

19 February Cesti's opera *Le disgrazie d'Amore* (The Misfortunes of Love) is first performed at the Hofburg in Vienna.

6/7 May Leading German keyboard-composer **Johann Froberger** dies from a stroke in Héricourt, France, aged 50. He has requested for all his manuscripts to be destroyed after his death, in fear that his music will be incorrectly performed. Thankfully for posterity, his wish is ignored.

5 November German composer **Franz Tunder** dies in Lübeck, aged about 53.

15 November The prodigious **Pelham Humfrey**, recently appointed a Gentleman of the Chapel Royal, joins Samuel Pepys (left) for dinner. While impressed with Humfrey's musical talent, Pepys finds the 20-year-old composer odious and arrogant, afterwards writing that he is 'full of form and confidence and vanity, and disparages everything and everyone's skill but his own'.

15 December Composer **Michel-Richard de Lalande** is born in Paris.

1666 French join Dutch in war against England • Dutch tighten their hold on East Indies by taking Celebes (Sulawesi, Indonesia) from Portugal • Five-day fire destroys much of London, including Old St Paul's Cathedral • Vermeer (Neth) paints *Die Malkunst* • Gottfried von Leibniz (Ger): first major philosophical work, *Dissertatio de Arte Combinatoria*

1667 Dutch, French, English and Danes conclude the Treaty of Breda • King Louis XIV (Fr) tries to seize Flanders from Spain • Portugal's king Alfonso VI is exiled • Russia gets eastern Ukraine from Poland in the Treaty of Andrussovo • Pope Alexander VII dies; is succeeded by Clement IX • John Milton (Eng): *Paradise Lost*

Bénigne de Bacilly publishes his treatise *Remarques curieuses sur l'art de bien chanter*, one of the most valuable sources on 17th-century French vocal practice.

Violin virtuoso and composer **Heinrich von Biber** is appointed musician and *valet de chambre* to the Bishop of Olmütz, Kroměríz Castle, Moravia.

Blow (aged about 20) is appointed organist of Westminster Abbey in London. The following year he secures an additional court post as musician for the virginals.

Cavalli is appointed *maestro di capella* at St Mark's, Venice.

Italian-born composer **Antonio Draghi** becomes assistant *Kapellmeister* to the dowager Empress Eleonora in Vienna. He is promoted as her chief *Kapellmeister* the following year.

Henry Du Mont brings out his *Motets à deux voix avec la basse continue*.

Lully composes his motet *Plaude Laetare*.

4 February Jacopo Melani's opera *Il Girello*, a satirical critique of absolutism, is first performed at the Palazzo Colonna in Rome. Incorporating a prologue composed by **Stradella**, it becomes one of the most successful operas of the century.

11 April The 31-year-old **Buxtehude** secures the position of organist at the Lübeck Marienkirche. Four months later he marries his predecessor's youngest daughter, Anna Margarethe Tunder, very possibly a condition of his employment.

Late April Lully collaborates with **Philippe Quinault** (later his prized opera librettist) on the court ballet *La grotte de Versailles*, introduced around this time at Versailles.

Just one of the 23 set designs for Cesti's *Il pomo d'oro*

12/14 July Cesti's *Il pomo d'oro* (The Golden Apple), based on the Judgement of Paris myth, is premièred in two parts at the Hoftheater auf der Cortina in Vienna. The opera is Cesti's most famous creation, if only because of its vast scale, lasting eight hours and incorporating 50 sung parts, imaginative scenic effects and 23 stage sets. Presented for the birthday celebrations of Leopold's wife (his niece, Margarita Teresa), it is by all accounts the most lavish musical stagework of the 17th century.

18 July A man marries above his station in *George Dandin*, a comedie-ballet by **Molière** with music by **Lully**, introduced at Versailles.

10 November Composer and keyboardist **François Couperin** (*le Grand*), nephew of Louis Couperin (d. 1661), is born in Paris.

1668 England, Netherlands and Sweden form Triple Alliance to counter encroachment by France into the Spanish Netherlands • Holy Roman Emperor Leopold I joins War of Devolution against France • France seizes Burgundy, but by Treaty of Aix-la-Chapelle, Spain regains it; France keeps Spanish Netherlands border towns • Spain recognises Portugal's independence • Quaker lawyer William Penn (Eng) is imprisoned in the Tower of London for questioning the doctrine of the Trinity in his book *Sandy Foundation Shaken* • Vermeer (Neth) paints *The Astronomer* • Jean Baptiste Racine (Fr): play *Les Plaideurs* • Molière (Fr): play *L'Avare* (The Miser)

Henry Du Mont and **Pierre Robert** are appointed to share the duties of *compositeur de la musique de la chapelle et de la chambre* to the court of Louis XIV.

Christopher Simpson, one of England's leading instrumental composers, dies in London, aged in his mid-60s.

Vitali, in Bologna, publishes his *Sonate* Op. 5, twelve pieces for two to five instruments and basso continuo.

13 February Lully and **Benserade**'s *Ballet de Flore* is performed at the Tuileries Palace, Paris. Later this year Lully collaborates with **Molière** on the comedy-ballet *Monsieur de Pourceaugnac*, performed at Chambord.

17 February Alessandro Melani's *L'empio punito*, the first opera on the subject of Don Juan, is premièred in the Palazzo Colonna, Rome.

16 April Antonio Bertali, *Kapellmeister* to imperial court in Vienna, dies aged 64. **Giovanni Sances** succeeds him, having served 20 years as assistant *Kapellmeister*. This same year Sances is ennobled by Leopold I.

June Librettist **Pierre Perrin** and Jean Baptiste Colbert, minister to Louis XIV, establish the Académie d'Opéra (also known as the Académie de Musique, or Paris Opéra) to promote a French form of opera.

14 October Antonio Cesti, fêted Italian composer of some of the century's most famous operas, dies in Florence, aged 46. A rumour will later escalate that he was poisoned by rivals.

9 December The librettist **Giulio Rospigliosi**, for the last two years Pope Clement IX, dies in Rome, aged 69.

Italian composer **Antonio Caldara** is born around this time in Venice.

Founder of the French harpsichord school, **Jacques Champion Chambonnières** publishes 60 keyboard works in two anthologies entitled *Pièces de clavessin*.

Corelli, aged 17, enrols at the recently created Accademia Filarmonica of Bologna.

Legrenzi issues his beautiful sacred motet collection *Acclamationi Divote* (Book I) for solo voice, Op. 10. This year the composer becomes choirmaster at the *Ospedale dei Derelitti* (Hospital for the Abandoned) in Venice.

Johann Pachelbel enters the Gymnasium Poeticum at Regensburg as a scholarship student. Outside the Gymnasium he studies music with Kaspar Prentz.

4 February Louis XIV dances his last role, performing in *Les amants magnifiques* by **Lully** and **Molière**, staged at St Germain-en-Laye.

23 April Loreto Vittori, Italian composer and one of the earliest operatic castratos, dies in Rome, aged 69.

18 July Italian composer **Giovanni Bononcini** is born in Modena.

14 October Lully and **Molière** produce *Le bourgeois gentilhomme* (The Commoner Gentleman), their most famous collaboration, at Chambord. Repeated several times, the *comédie-ballet* transfers to the Palais-Royal in Paris where it sustains a lengthy run before a paying public.

All the political upheavals, all that goes wrong in the world, occur only from a failure to learn music.

Molière, *Le bourgeois gentilhomme*

1669 James, Duke of York, brother and heir of King Charles II (Eng), is suspected to have rejected Anglicanism for Roman Catholicism • Venice loses Mediterranean island of Crete to Ottoman Empire • India's Muslim Mogul rulers ban Hinduism and smash Hindu temples • Pope Clement IX dies • Nicolaus Steno (Den) explains the true nature of fossils

1670 King Charles II (Eng) signs Treaty of Dover with King Louis XIV (Fr) promising to help France against Spain and the Dutch Republic • James, Duke of York, heir to Charles II, declares his Roman Catholicism • Clement X is elected Pope • Philosopher Blaise Pascal (Fr) defends Christianity against sceptics in his book *Pensées*

Cazatti resigns from his post as musical director at San Petronio, Bologna (possibly due to in-fighting). He finds employment in Mantua as director of chamber music to Duchess Isabella Gonzaga.

Schütz, 86 years old, completes his *Schwanengesang*. His final musical collection comprises 13 motets for double choir with continuo: Psalm 119 (in 11 motets), Psalm 100, and a Magnificat Canticle.

January Exiled Queen Christina of Sweden opens Rome's first public opera house, the Teatro Tor di Nona. **Cavalli**'s *Scipione africano* (1664) is the inaugurating opera, furnished with a new prologue by **Stradella**.

17 January Lully collaborates with **Molière**, **Quinault** and **Pierre Corneille** to produce *Psyché*, a *tragédie-ballet*, at the Tuileries Palace. Unique of its kind, the work will serve as a model for Lully's first operatic collaboration with Quinault two years later.

3 March Robert Cambert and librettist **Pierre Perrin** stage *Pomone* with the newly created Académie Royale de Musique, in Paris. The production is spectacularly successful, achieving around 140 performances. *Pomone* is generally regarded as the first true French opera.

June Perrin's business partners pilfer the proceeds from *Pomone* (see above) and land the librettist in jail for unpaid debt. **Cambert**, out of pocket, looks for a new collaborator.

8 June Italian composer and violinist **Tommaso Albinoni** is born in Venice.

3 November Dresden-based Italian composers **Giovanni Bontempi** and **Marco Peranda** produce the German opera *Daphne*, based on the translation of Rinuccini's *Dafne* by Martin Opitz.

Jacques Champion Chambonnières dies in Paris, aged about 71.

Having fallen out with **Lully**, **Molière** begins a collaborative partnership with the composer **Marc-Antoine Charpentier**. They quickly produce new versions of Molière's *comédies-ballets*, including *Le mariage forcé*.

English violinist and composer **John Banister** (below) begins a series of fee-paying public concerts—possibly the first of their kind—at his house in Whitefriars. Advertising them in the *London Gazette*, the concerts are held daily at 4pm with tickets priced at one shilling.

February Antonio Sartorio's opera *L'Adelaide* opens at the Teatro San Salvatore in Venice.

March Lully buys the privilège (licence) of the Paris Opéra from **Pierre Perrin**, who is at this time in debtors' prison. Now with a monopoly over the staging of opera in France, Lully swiftly closes down **Cambert**'s second opera, *Les peines et les plaisirs de l'amour*, currently playing at the Jeu de Paume de la Bouteille (a converted tennis court) in Paris.

6 November Heinrich Schütz, the most significant German composer of the 17th century, dies in Dresden, aged 87. **Carlo Pallavicino** replaces him as *Kapellmeister* to the Elector of Saxony.

22 December Hidalgo and **Juan Vélez de Guevara** present *Los celos hacen estrellas* (Jealousy Produces Stars), one of the earliest surviving *zarzuelas*, at the Alcázar Palace in Madrid.

1671 English buccaneer Henry Morgan destroys Panama City • King Louis XIV (Fr) acts to isolate his Dutch opponents, signing treaties with German states of Brunswick, Hanover, Lüneburg and Osnabruck • Astronomer Giovanni Cassini (It) discovers satellites of the planet Saturn • Milton (Eng): *Paradise Regained*

1672 England and France are at war with Dutch Republic • France forms secret alliance with Sweden • French invade southern Holland • Dutch defeat an Anglo-French fleet in Sole Bay, off Suffolk coast (Eng) • Turks invade Poland • Thomas Shadwell (Eng): play *Epsom Wells* • Molière (Fr): comedy *Les Femmes savantes*

Buxtehude establishes the Advent concert series of *Abendmusiken* (Evening Music) at Lübeck, following the tradition of *Abendspielen* by his predecessor, Franz Tunder.

Locke publishes *Melothesia*, a treatise on music theory containing many examples of his own keyboard pieces, presented as suites. Also included are the earliest surviving printed rules for thoroughbass in English.

The 20-year-old **Pachelbel** arrives in Vienna and becomes deputy organist at the Stephansdom (St Stephen's Cathedral).

February *Le malade imaginaire* (The Imaginary Invalid), a *comédie-ballet* by **Charpentier** and **Molière**, opens at the Palais Royal, Paris. Molière (right) takes the title role of a hypochondriac, but during the fourth performance, in an unfortunate moment of irony, collapses on stage and dies a few hours later.

27 April Lully and **Philippe Quinault** present in a prologue and five acts *Cadmus et Hermione*, their first *tragédie lyrique*, at the Jeu de Paume de Béquet (Bel-Air tennis court), Paris. Thereafter Louis XIV authorises Lully to transfer his productions to the Palais Royal, ousting Molière's former company. Lully secures his public stage music monopoly in France by restricting rival opera companies to six instrumentalists and two singers, and banning them from employing dancers.

June His voice now broken, the 13-year-old **Henry Purcell** leaves the Chapel Royal and becomes an assistant to the organist and composer **John Hingeston**, repairer and tuner of the king's wind and keyboard instruments.

The Theatre Royal in London's Drury Lane opens.

English composer **Jeremiah Clarke** is born around this time.

The poet **Thomas Shadwell** produces a musical version of Shakespeare's *The Tempest* based on an adaptation by Davenant and Dryden. Staged at London's Dorset Garden Theatre, the semi-opera (containing spoken words) incorporates music by six composers including **Pelham Humfrey, Matthew Locke, Giovanni Draghi** and **John Banister**.

12 January Opera composer **Reinhard Keiser** is baptised near Weissenfels, Germany.

12 January Giacomo Carissimi, leading Italian composer of sacred music, dies in Rome, aged 68.

19 January Lully's five-act *Alceste* is premièred by the Paris Opéra at the Palais Royal, with the printed libretto available for purchase at the door. While successful, the production is criticised by a highly vocal minority, angry at the composer's dictatorial monopoly over French opera (see April 1673).

14 July English composer **Pelham Humfrey** dies in Windsor, aged 26, after several months of weakening health.

August Stradella's serenata *Vola, vola in altri petti* is performed in Rome before Christina of Sweden. The work is one of the earliest to incorporate *concerto grosso* instrumentation.

1673 Dutch fleet defeats English and French fleets at Schooneveld Banks, in mouth of Scheldt River • English seize St Helena from Dutch; Dutch capture New York City from English • Brandenburg makes separate peace with France • Test Act makes it virtually impossible for Roman Catholics and Nonconformists to hold public office in England

1674 Treaty of Westminster ends Third Anglo-Dutch War; Dutch return New York City to English • Holy Roman Empire and Spain declare war on France • Anatomist Thomas Willis (Eng) publishes *Pharmaceutice Rationalis* • Philosopher Nicolas Malebranche (Fr): *De la recherché de la vérité* (Search After Truth) • Racine (Fr) writes tragedy *Iphigénie*

Having settled in Venice, **Legrenzi** produces his first operas for the city: *La divisione del mondo* and *Eteocle e Polinice*. Both works are introduced at the Teatro San Salvatore.

Locke and **Giovanni Draghi** collaborate on the music for **Shadwell**'s *Psyche*, lavishly staged at the Dorset Garden Theatre (left) in London. The semi-opera, based on Molière's *Psyché* of 1671, manages a run of around eight performances.

Saint-Sulpice organist **Guillaume Nivers** issues his *Troisième livre d'orgue des huit tons de l'église*.

11 January Lully presents *Thésée* (Theseus) at the palace of St Germain-en-Laye. With libretto by **Quinault**, the opera enjoys revivals well into the following century.

March Marc-Antoine Charpentier provides incidental music for Thomas Corneille's play *Circé* at the Hôtel de Guénégaud, Paris. The production proves extremely popular and aids the fortunes of Molière's old theatre company, Le Troupe du Roy (recently ejected from the Palais Royal by **Lully**).

31 March Stradella's celebrated oratorio *San Giovanni Battista* (Saint John the Baptist) premières in Rome. In this dramatic work the composer continues to pioneer *concerto grosso* scoring, with contrasts between small (*concertino*) and large (*concerto grosso*) instrumental groups.

29 October Andreas Hammerschmidt, prominent German composer and organist, dies in Zittau, aged about 63.

Heinrich Biber (below) composes his *Mystery Sonatas* for violin and bass, corresponding to the 15 meditations on the life of Christ as reflected in the Mysteries of the Rosary. Most of the sonatas

require *scordatura* (the retuning of violin strings to different sets of notes), which heightens the contrast of moods within the work.

Thomas Mace publishes *Musick's Monument*, a significant commentary on musical activity in mid-17th-century England.

Johann Jakob Walther publishes his *Scherzi da violino solo con il basso continuo*, a collection of virtuosic violin pieces that explore the instrument's expressive capabilities (without *scordatura*). Walther ranks alongside **Biber** as one of the foremost composer-violinists of the day.

10 January Lully and the librettist **Quinault** present a story of unrequited love in their mythological opera *Atys*, introduced with great success at St Germain-en-Laye.

14 January Francesco Cavalli, one of the most performed opera composers of the century, dies in Venice, aged 73.

18 August Comic opera composer **Jacopo Melani** dies in Pistoia, aged 53.

20 October Composer **Christopher Gibbons** dies in Westminster, aged 61.

· ·

1675 In the Dutch War against France, army of German state of Brandenburg defeats the Swedes at Battle of Fehrbellin; German troops defeat French at Sasbach, Baden • King Christian V (Den) makes war on Sweden and regains Scania • Greenwich Royal Observatory is founded in England • Benedict de Spinoza (Neth) finishes *Ethics*

1676 Denmark, at war with Sweden, joins Dutch in successful attack on Götland; Swedes defeat Danes at Lund • In Spain, Don Juan takes over the government • Treaty of Zuravna ends war between Poles and Turks • Astronomer Edmund Halley (Eng) catalogues the southern stars • Pope Clement X dies; Innocent XI succeeds

Alessandro Poglietti, court organist at Vienna, publishes his most famous work, *Rossignolo*, a large and varied collection of pieces for harpsichord, some of which are lightly programmatic.

Antonio Sartorio, one of the leading Venetian composers of the day, presents two new operas at the San Salvatore Theatre in Venice: *Antonino e Pompejano* and *L'Anacreonte tiranno*.

5 January Lully's opera *Isis* is premièred at St Germain-en-Laye. The opera causes controversy, as the character of Juno is seen to be an unflattering representation of the king's mistress, Mme de Montespan (right). Lully's librettist, **Quinault**, becomes the scapegoat, sidelined from operatic productions for the next two years.

March Robert Cambert, co-founder of French opera, dies in London, aged about 49.

August Composer **Matthew Locke** dies in London, aged in his mid-50s. **Purcell**, who turns 18 this year, succeeds him as Composer to the King's Violins.

9 September Lully's Te Deum is first performed at Fontainebleau. Ten years from now the work will play a part in the composer's death.

10 October Stradella marries his pupil, Agnese Van Uffele, mistress of a Venetian senator, Alvise Contarini. In retaliation, Contarini hires two henchmen who attack Stradella and leave him severely beaten. Stradella recovers, but apparently soon parts from his wife.

11 November Barbara Strozzi, Italian composer and singer, dies in Padua, aged about 58.

Georg Muffat is appointed organist at Salzburg Cathedral and chamber musician to Archbishop Max Gandol.

Pallavicino composes his opera *Vespasiano* for the inauguration of the Teatro San Giovanni Grisostomo, the most exclusive opera house in Venice.

2 January Johann Theile's opera *Adam und Eva* inaugurates Hamburg's Gänsemarkt Theater, the first public opera house outside of Venice.

4 March Composer **Antonio Lucio Vivaldi** is born the same day an earthquake rocks Venice. Possibly because of this, or due to worrying respiratory problems, the midwife performs an improvised baptism.

12 April Alessandro Scarlatti, aged 17, marries Antonia Anzaloni. Later this year he becomes *maestro di cappella* at the church of San Giacomo degli Incurabili in Rome.

16 April Lully stages *Psyché*, adapted for the Paris Opéra, in collaboration with **Thomas Corneille** and **Bernard le Bovier de Fontenelle**.

Summer Pachelbel, aged 24, becomes organist at the Predigerkirche in Erfurt.

28 September Pioneering composer **Maurizio Cazzati** dies in Mantua, aged 62.

27 October Composer **John Jenkins** dies in Kimberley, Norfolk, aged about 86. **Purcell** possibly writes his graceful Pavan in G minor, for three violins and bass, in commemoration.

10 November Stradella's opera *La forza dell'amor paterno* premières in Genoa.

- -

1677 Mary, daughter of James, Duke of York—brother and heir of Charles II (Eng)—marries Willem III of Orange, Stadtholder (head of state) of the Netherlands • Turkey and Russia at war following Cossack raids on Turkish territory • Pieter de Hooch (Neth) paints *Musical Party in a Courtyard* • Jean Baptiste Racine (Fr): *Phèdre*

1678 Titus Oates begins making allegations of the *Popish Plot*, a Catholic conspiracy to assassinate King Charles II of England • Treaties of Nijmegen ends wars between Netherlands and France, and Spain and France: Netherlands keeps its territories intact and France gains lands in Flanders from Spain • John Bunyan (Eng): *The Pilgrim's Progress* (part I)

Biber is appointed assistant *Kapellmeister* to the Archbishop of Salzburg.

Corelli becomes a chamber musician and composer to the exiled Queen Christina of Sweden in Rome.

Charles Couperin, organist at the church of St Gervais, dies, leaving his ten-year-old son, **François**, in the care of his mother. Court organist **Jacques Thomelin** becomes musical tutor to François, and the church council arranges for the boy to inherit his father's old post at the age of 18. In the meantime the church engages the services of **Michel-Richard de Lalande**.

Marin Marais, aged 23, becomes an *Ordinaire de musique de la chambre du roi*.

Pallavicino's opera *Le amazzoni nell'isole fortunate* (The Amazons in the Fortunate Isles) inaugurates the Teatro Contarini in Piazzola sul Brenta, outside Venice.

The 20-year-old **Purcell** becomes organist at Westminster Abbey following the resignation of **John Blow**.

31 January Lully's opera *Bellérophon* is introduced at the Paris Opéra.

5 February Alessandro Scarlatti's first staged opera, *Gli equivoci nel sembiante* (Mistaken Identities), is presented in Rome at the private theatre of Giambattista Contini, to great acclaim. The 18-year-old composer catches the attention of the exiled Queen Christina of Sweden.

1 October Schmelzer is appointed *Kapellmeister* at the Viennese court, replacing the ailing **Giovanni Sances**, who dies the following month.

16 October Czech composer **Jan Dismas Zelenka** is baptised in Louňovice, Bohemia.

Buxtehude creates what is generally considered to be the first Lutheran Oratorio, *Membra Jesu Nostri*, consisting of seven cantatas.

Benedetto Ferrari's oratorio *Il Sansone* (Samson) is first performed for the Este court in Modena.

Cristóbal Galán is appointed *maestro de capilla* to the Spanish royal court.

Purcell, aged 21, marries Frances Peters. Compositions this year very likely include his Fantasias for Viols in three to five parts. Although the viol fantasia is now unfashionable (and detested by King Charles II), these works represent some of the finest of the repertory.

Antonio Stradivari sets up a workshop in Cremona and makes his earliest known cello.

3 February A. Scarlatti's second opera, *L'honestà negli amori* (Honesty in Love Affairs), commissioned by Queen Christina of Sweden, premières at the Bernini palace in Rome. The work is remembered solely for its uplifting aria 'Già il sole dal Gange' (The sun form the Orient). Scarlatti, aged 19, married and a father, is now Queen Christina's *maestro di cappella*.

3 February Lully, back in collaboration with the librettist **Quinault**, introduces his opera *Proserpine* at St Germain-en-Laye.

March Having escaped to Prague with the Imperial Court to avoid a plague epidemic in Vienna, *Kapellmeister* **Johann Schmelzer** dies from the disease, aged in his late 50s. The Austrian composer and violin virtuoso was one of the first non-Italians to promote the solo violin sonata.

September Purcell's song *Welcome, Vicegerent of the Mighty King*, scored for voices, strings and continuo, is first performed for Charles II.

1679 King Charles II (Eng) dissolves parliament • James, Duke of York, Charles's Roman Catholic brother and heir, leaves England for exile abroad • Rebellion of Scottish Covenanters (Presbyterians) ruthlessly crushed by Duke of Monmouth troops • War between Sweden and state of Brandenburg continues

1680 King Charles II (Eng) calls his fourth parliament but it is again dissolved • King Louis XIV (Fr) establishes Chambers of Reunion (special courts) to decide what lands France should possess; he annexes Luxembourg and Saarbrucken to France • The last dodo is hunted and killed, in Mauritius

Biber publishes his *Sonatae violino solo*, a collection of eight virtuosic sonatas for violin and basso continuo.

Corelli publishes his Op. 1: 12 four-movement *da chiesa* trio sonatas, dedicated to the exiled Queen Christina of Sweden. It appears that around this time Corelli may have left Italy for a short period of service to the electoral prince of Bavaria.

5 January Legrenzi is appointed *vice maestro di cappella* at St Mark's, Venice.

21 January The history of the ballerina begins with the first professional female dancers (led by Mlle de Lafontaine) taking the stage in **Lully**'s ballet-opera *Le triomphe de l'amour*. Male dancers continue to dominate the scenes, enjoying greater flexibility than the female dancers who have to cope with floor-length skirts. The work also includes the first examples of Lully's orchestrally-accompanied recitative.

14 March German composer **Georg Philipp Telemann** is born in Magdeburg.

Spring A condemnation of lust and deceit, **Stradella**'s oratorio *La Susanna* receives its first performance, in Modena. Expressive arias combine with contrapuntal elegance in one of the finest sacred works of the period. This same year Stradella pens the joyful serenata *Il barcheggio* for the wedding festivities of Carlo Spinola and Paola Brignole.

28 September German composer, theorist and critic **Johann Mattheson** is born in Hamburg.

VIOLINO PRIMO.
SONATE
A trè, doi Violini, e Violone, ò Arcileuto, col Basso per l'Organo.
CONSECRATE
ALLA SACRA REAL MAESTÀ DI
CRISTINA ALESSANDRA
REGINA DI SVEZIA, &c.
DA ARCANGELO CORELLI DA FVSIGNANO, detto il Bolognese,
OPERA PRIMA.

In ROMA Nella Stamperia di Gio. Angelo Mutij 1681 Con licenza de' Super.

Scored in 53 parts for six spatially-separated choirs and ensembles, with additional brass and timpani, the *Missa Salisburgensis* (Salzburg Festival Mass) is performed to mark the 1100th anniversary of the Archbishopric of Salzburg. The musical colossus is possibly the work of **Biber**.

Johann Kusser brings out the first German suites to incorporate French-style overtures in his *Composition de musique suivant la methode françoise*, published in Stuttgart.

Georg Muffat publishes his *Armonico tributo*, comprising five multi-movement sonatas for strings and continuo. Published in Salzburg, the sonatas reveal progressive *concerto grosso* scoring, a style Muffat adopted having heard **Corelli**'s (unpublished) concertos in Rome.

Purcell acquires one of the three posts of organist at the Chapel Royal.

French guitarist and lutenist **Robert de Visée**, court musician to Louis XIV, issues his first publication, *Livre de guitare dédié au roy*.

January Antonio Draghi becomes *Kapellmeister* to the imperial court in Vienna. This year he composes the oratorio *Il terremoto*.

25 February Alessandro Stradella, aged 42, is stabbed to death in Genoa. Infamous for his sexual indiscretions, the composer and singer may have been murdered at the behest of a jealous mistress or rival. Another theory suggests reprisals for an affair with a married member of the powerful Lomellini family.

18 April Lully's opera *Persée*, on a libretto by **Quinault**, premières at the Paris Opéra.

1681 King Charles II calls his fifth parliament; Whigs reintroduce the Exclusion Bill to bar James, Duke of York from succession to the crown; Charles dissolves parliament • Turks sign Treaty of Radzin with Russia • Oil lamps are used to light streets in London • Luca Giordano (It) paints frescoes for the Palazzo Medici Riccardi, Florence

1682 Spain and Holy Roman Empire make pact against French aggression • King Louis XIV (Fr) calls Church assembly at St Germain: it decides that Popes have no temporal rights over kings and are inferior to French church councils • Astronomer Edmund Halley (Eng) observes what is called Halley's Comet and tries to calculate its orbit

1683

Blow composes his opera *Venus and Adonis* around this time. Designated a masque, the work is scored throughout and will later serve as the model for Purcell's opera *Dido and Aeneas*.

André Campra becomes *Maître de musique* at the Cathedral of St Étienne, Toulouse.

Charpentier composes an early example of the French cantata with his *Orphée descendant aux Enfers* (Orpheus Descending to the Underworld). Scored for three male voices, the cantata features an expressive instrumental sinfonia followed by the Italianate alternation of arias and recitatives.

Innocent XI stops pension payments to **Corelli**'s patron, the exiled Queen Christina of Sweden. With his income reduced, Corelli seeks additional patronage the following year from Cardinal Benedetto Pamphili.

Michel-Richard de Lalande and **Charpentier** compete with 33 other composers for one of the four posts of *sous-maître* to the French royal chapel. Lalande is successful, but Charpentier has to retire from the contest due to ill health. (Louis XIV later grants him a pension anyway.) **Pascal Collasse**, **Nicolas Coupillet** and **Guillaume Minoret** secure the other positions.

Pachelbel loses both his wife and baby son to plague. In memory he writes his *Musicalische Sterbens-Gedancken* (Musical Meditation on Death), a collection of chorale variations for keyboard.

6 January Lully (right) presents *Phaëton* at Versailles (now the permanent residence of the royal court). Three months later the opera enjoys a sensational public première at the Paris Opéra, aided by elaborate scenery and stage machinery. This year also marks the composer's penitential sacred work *De profundis* (From the depths).

13 January German composer **Christoph Graupner** is born in Kirchberg, Saxony.

25 January Scarlatti's opera *Il Pompeo* (Pompey) premières at the Teatro Colonna, Rome. Around this time the composer also stages his opera *La guerriera costante* at the Roman palace of the Duchess of Bracciano. Few operas are publicly performed in the city due to severe restrictions imposed by Pope Innocent XI.

12 February Legrenzi's most successful opera, *Guistino* (Justinian), is introduced at the Teatro San Salvatore, Venice.

17 April German composer and theorist **Johann Heinichen** is born in Krössuln, near Weissenfels.

25 September French composer **Jean Philipe Rameau** is baptised in Dijon.

Mid December Following the death of John Hingeston, the 24-year-old **Purcell** is appointed instrument keeper to the king. This year marks Purcell's first ode for St Cecilia's Day, *Welcome to All the Pleasures*, and the publication of his *Sonnata's of III Parts* (for two violins, viol and continuo), which he claims to be 'a just imitation of the most fam'd Italian Masters'.

1683 The Rye House Plot to assassinate Charles II of England is discovered, coinciding with a lawful attempt by statesmen to curb his powers; the statesmen concerned suffer severe treatment: Lord William Russell and Algernon Sidney are executed, the Earl of Essex is driven to suicide, the Duke of Monmouth (Charles's bastard son) is exiled • James, Duke of York, brother of Charles II, is reinstated in office • Spain and France are at war; France invades Spanish Netherlands • Turks lay siege to Vienna; a German-Polish army relieves the city • Anton van Leeuwenhoek (Neth) records the first observation of bacteria under a microscope

1684

Biber is promoted to *Kapellmeister* at the archducal court of Salzburg.

English writer and preacher **John Bunyan**, currently serving a 12-year jail sentence for preaching without a licence, pens the second part of his *Pilgrim's Progress*, and in it the hymn 'He Who Would Valiant Be'.

Charpentier becomes *maître de musique* of the Jesuit church of St Louis, Paris.

18 January Abandoning ancient mythology, **Lully** and **Quinault** present a medieval tale of love and chivalry with in *Amadis*, first performed at the Paris Opéra. The milestone opera is remembered above all for its beautiful air *Bois épais* (Sombre Woods) from Act 2.

February Scarlatti becomes *maestro di cappella* of the Neapolitan royal chapel and director of the Teatro San Bartolomeo. He will remain in Naples for 18 years.

8 May Franco-Belgian composer **Henry Du Mont**, one of the first composers to bring the Baroque style to the French Chapelle Royale, dies in Paris, aged about 74.

8 July Composer and director **Pierre Gautier** receives permission from **Lully** to open an opera house in Marseilles. Gautier has to pay a fee to Lully, who continues to hold a tight monopoly on all music drama in France.

24 August Pachelbel marries Judith Drommer, his second wife, having lost his first wife and son to plague the previous year.

September Giuseppe Torelli, aged 26, moves to Bologna to take up a post of violinist with the *Accademia Filarmonica*.

October Johann Kuhnau becomes organist at the Thomaskirche in Leipzig.

1684 In the Franco-Spanish War, French seize city of Trier and duchy of Luxembourg from Holy Roman Empire (Spain's ally) and invade the Spanish Netherlands • Louis XIV begins campaign against heretics: Huguenots (Protestants) in southern France revolt • Venice joins Austria and Poland in Holy League against the Turks, backed by Pope Innocent XII

1685

Corelli publishes his Op. 2 Trio Sonatas (*sonate da camera*) in Rome.

Giacomo Perti's *Oreste in Argo* is first performed in Modena. The opera presents one of the earliest examples of the three-movement Italian overture, in fast-slow-fast sections.

Purcell draws on Psalm 107 in his vocally-challenging anthem *They That Go Down to the Sea in Ships*.

8 January Lully's opera *Roland* enjoys success at Versailles. This year marks the composer's final ballet, *Le temple de la paix*, and also final *comédie-ballet*, *Idylle sur la paix*, to verses by **Jean Racine**. In the midst of his productivity, the bisexual composer suffers the displeasure of Louis XIV due to scandalous misconduct with his page.

23 February George Frideric Handel is born in Halle to a barber-surgeon.

21 March Johann Sebastian Bach is born in Eisenach, Thuringia, to court musician **Johann Ambrosius Bach**.

31 March Spanish composer **Juan Hidalgo** dies in Madrid, aged 70.

16 April Legrenzi is elected *maestro di cappella* at St Mark's, Venice. This year he writes his final opera, *Ifianassa e Melampo*, after which he devotes himself to sacred works.

23 April Purcell's lavish and dramatic anthem *My Heart is Inditing* is first performed for the coronation celebrations of James II.

June Playwright, poet and librettist **John Gay** is born in Barnstaple, England.

26 October Domenico Scarlatti is born in Naples. His 25-year-old father, **Alessandro**, has already become one of Italy's leading opera composers.

1685 Charles II (Eng) dies; is succeeded by his Roman Catholic brother, James II • Duke of Monmouth proclaims himself king; Duke of Argyll lands with an army; both are captured and executed • Louis XIV (Fr) revokes Edict of Nantes, which gave religious freedom to Huguenots • Isaac Newton (Eng) formulates law of gravitation

1686

Blow provides incidental music to Aphra Behn's *The Lucky Chance*. Behn (below) is a leading playwright of the Restoration and one of England's first professional female writers.

Renowned viol virtuoso **Marin Marais** publishes his first collection of works, *Pièces de violes* (Book I).

Giuseppe Torelli publishes ten trio sonatas in his *Sonate a 3*, Op. 1, and 12 dance pieces in his *Concerti da camera*, Op. 2.

1 January Blow announces the New Year with his regal ode *Hail Monarch, Sprung of Race Divine*. **Purcell** takes particular interest in the piece, copying its style (and even some of its material) in his royal 'welcome song' *Ye Tuneful Muses*, performed later this year.

February Pallavicino's tuneful love story *L'Amazone corsara* (The Amazon Pirate) opens at Venice's Teatro SS Giovanni e Paolo.

15 February Lully and librettist **Quinault** look to Tasso's *Gerusalemme liberata* in their greatest collaboration, *Armide* (right), introduced at the Paris Opéra. The tragedy is hugely successful but does not enjoy a royal audience, as the king continues to distance himself from Lully following the composer's sexual indiscretions of the previous year (see 1685).

11 June Antonio Draghi's opera *Il nodo gordiano* (The Gordian knot) opens in Vienna. Part-time composer Emperor Leopold I contributes music (as he does to many other stageworks by Draghi), one of his happy diversions from the ongoing war with the Turks (1683–99).

July Italian composer and writer **Benedetto Marcello** (brother of **Alessandro** b.1669), is born around this time in Venice.

17 August Composer **Nicola Antonio Porpora** is born in Naples.

6 September Lully premières *Acis et Galatée*, a mythical *pastorale-héroïque*, for a hunting party hosted by the Duke of Vendôme at Anet.

12 October German lutenist-composer **Sylvius Leopold Weiss** is born in Breslau.

Winter The music publisher John Playford dies in London, aged about 63.

Lully's *Armide*. Only through magic can the sorceress Armide seduce the noble knight Renaud.

1686 James II (Eng) rejects Test Act and allows Catholics public office • Louis XIV (Fr) lays claims to lands of the Palatinate (Ger) following the death of its last Elector, Charles; as a result the League of Augsburg is formed against France by the Holy Roman Empire, the Palatinate, the Netherlands, Saxony, Spain and Sweden • The Holy League alliance captures Buda (Hung) from the Turks • French seize North American trading posts from Hudson's Bay Company • Sweden's first theatre opens in Stockholm • John Ray (Eng) begins classifying plants with the first instalment of his three-volume *Historia generalis plantarum* • Bernard Le Bovier de Fontenelle (Fr) publishes *Conversations on the Plurality of Worlds*

1687

G.B. Degli Antoni's Op. 1, *Ricercate*, is published in Bologna. The set features some of the earliest printed music for solo cello.

Elisabeth-Claude Jacquet de la Guerre becomes the first French woman to publish a set of harpsichord works with her *Pièces de clavecin*.

Dutch composer **Johann Reincken** issues a set of six sonatas and suites in *Hortus musicus* (Music Garden), for two violins, viol and continuo. With this accomplished and diverse collection, Reincken intends to cast an unforgiving light on inept composers and banish them from the 'sacred garden of music'.

4 January Pallavicino stages his last opera, *La Gerusalemme liberata*, in Venice.

22 March Composer **Jean-Baptiste Lully** dies from gangrene, aged 54, in Paris. He had fatally wounded himself several weeks earlier by striking his foot with a heavy conductor's staff while rehearsing his Te Deum.

July Corelli becomes musical director at the palace of Cardinal Pamphili, in Rome.

24 August Michael Wise, aged about 40, is 'knock'd on the head and kill'd downright by the Night Watch at Salisbury for giving stubborne and refractory language to them' (as recorded by his contemporary, Anthony Wood). It is thought that the English composer had been in a bad mood following an argument with his wife.

5 December Composer and violinist **Francesco Geminiani** (possibly born two days earlier) is baptised in Lucca.

1688

Kuhnau publishes his student dissertation *De juribus circa musicos ecclesiasticos* (On the Laws Governing Church Musicians). He begins to practise law, but continues as organist to the Thomaskirche in Leipzig.

Purcell provides incidental music for Thomas D'Urfey's comedy *A Fool's Preferment*.

Torelli publishes his *Concertino per camera* for violin and cello, dedicated to Francesco II, Duke of Modena.

J. J. Walther publishes his second surviving collection of violin music, the entertaining *Hortulus chelicus* (left, extract), in Mainz. As in his *Scherzi* of 1676, Walther explores the technical and expressive capabilities of the violin, including descriptive effects of other instruments such as timpani, trumpets and bagpipes, as well as a variety of birds. (Walther's effects are not unprecedented: see Carlo Farina, 1627.)

29 January Italian opera composer **Carlo Pallavicino** dies in Dresden, aged about 47.

28 February Charpentier's sacred opera *David et Jonathas* is first performed at the Collège de Louis-le-Grand, Paris, between the acts of Pierre Chamillart's spoken drama *Saül*.

26 November French dramatist and librettist **Philippe Quinault** dies in Paris, aged 53. Lully's loyal collaborator, he is remembered as a pioneering figure in the development of French opera.

- -

1687 King James II grants freedom of worship in England and Scotland • Venice completes its conquest of Morea (Greece) from Turks, and captures Athens • Turkish army leaders depose sultan Muhammad IV and install his brother Suleiman III • Newton (Eng): *Philosophiae Naturalis Principia Mathematica*, expounding laws of motion and gravity

1688 Birth of James II's first son raises fears of continuing Roman Catholic monarchy: nobility petition Willem III of Orange (Neth) to save England from 'Catholic tyranny' • Willem lands at Torbay, Devon, with 14,000 Dutch troops; James flees to France • French troops invade the Palatinate (Ger), beginning the War of the League of Augsburg

Court harpsichordist **Jean-Henri D'Anglebert** issues his elaborate *Pièces de clavecin*, containing some of the finest French keyboard music of the age. Beautifully engraved, the influential publication includes four suites, six organ pieces, and transcriptions of dances, airs and overtures from stageworks by Lully. Also supplied is a comprehensive table of ornaments, which becomes a valuable reference for both French and German composers, including **J. S. Bach.**

Corelli directs an orchestra of over 80 players (including 39 violins, ten violas, 17 cellos and ten basses) at the palace of Cardinal Pamphili in Rome, in honour of the visiting Cardinal Rinaldo d'Este. This year marks the publication of the composer's Op. 3, *12 sonate da chiesa*. The set is dedicated to Duke Francesco II d'Este, who rewards Corelli with 100 ounces of silver and a beautiful silver dish.

The visually impaired Jean-Henri D'Anglebert (1629–91), clavecinist to Louis XIV.

Kerll's *Missae sex* is published in Munich. The collection contains six *concertato* masses and one Requiem; the latter the composer hopes to have performed at his own funeral.

Kuhnau, organist at Leipzig's Thomaskirche, publishes seven keyboard suites in *Neuer Clavier-Übung erster Theil*, each in a different major key (C, D, E, F, G, A and B flat).

Legrenzi, declining in health, brings out his final book of sacred concertos for two to three voices (Book III, Op. 15), in Venice.

London publisher Playford issues *The Second Part of Musick's Handmaid*, including keyboard works by **Blow** and **Purcell**.

Vitali, *vicemaestro di cappella* to the Duke of Modena, publishes his instructive *Artifici musicali* (Musical Skills), comprising 60 pieces of increasing difficulty for a variety of instruments, with rules of counterpoint explained.

11 January Pascal Collasse's mythological *Thétis et Pélée* (Thetis and Peleus) premières with enormous success at the Paris Opéra.

30 January Steffani's opera *Henrico Leone* opens Hanover's Grosses Schlosstheater.

Spring Purcell and librettist **Nahum Tate** compress passion, excitement and heartbreak in their exquisite opera *Dido and Aeneas*, staged at Josias Priest's School for Young Ladies in Chelsea, London. Modelled on **Blow**'s *Venus and Adonis* (*c.*1683), the short three-act tragedy may have been performed previously at court. It is Purcell's only theatrical work scored throughout.

11 April Purcell boosts his income by charging spectators admittance into Westminster Abbey's organ loft to watch the coronation of King William and Queen Mary. The Dean of Westminster learns of the enterprise and orders Purcell to surrender all of his profits.

11 April Blow's delightful 'full with verse' anthem *The Lord God is a Sun and a Shield* is first performed for the coronation of King William and Queen Mary.

19 April Exiled Queen Christina of Sweden, champion of the arts, dies in Rome aged 62.

1689 William III of Orange and his wife Mary Stuart (daughter of runaway king James II) accede to the English throne • Declaration of Rights assures parliamentary supremacy • James II (Eng) lands in Ireland and besieges Londonderry • Scottish bishops are abolished • League of Augsburg makes war on France and is joined by England to form a Grand Alliance • Petr I (Russ) overthrows his sister Sophia as regent and takes sole command of government • English dissenters win the right not to attend Church of England services • Philosopher John Locke (Eng): *Essay Concerning Human Understanding* • Meindert Hobbema (Neth) paints *The Avenue at Middelharnis*

Emperor Leopold I ennobles **Biber**. The composer gains the title Biber von Bibern.

Aged 21, **François Couperin** publishes some of the finest French keyboard music of the period with the two organ masses of his *Pièces d'orgue*.

With his *VI Sonatas or Solo's*, the Moravian composer **Gottfried Finger** issues the earliest known English print of sonatas for solo instrument and continuo.

Muffat is appointed *Kapellmeister* to Johann Philipp von Lamberg, Bishop of Passau.

Wolfgang Printz publishes the first German history of music with his *Historische Beschreibung der edelen Sing- und Kling-Kunst*.

January Alexander the Great imprisons then marries his rival's daughter in the love and honour opera *La Statira*, with music by **A. Scarlatti**, premièred at the Teatro Tordinona in Rome. The libretto is by the 22-year-old **Cardinal Pietro Ottoboni**.

27 May Composer **Giovanni Legrenzi** dies in Venice, aged 63.

Late May The actor-director Thomas Betterton collaborates with **Purcell** on the semi-opera *Dioclesian* at the Dorset Garden Theatre, London.

6 August Antonio Lotti, aged 24, becomes second organist's assistant at St Mark's, Venice. He will eventually rise to *maestro di cappella*, but not for another 46 years.

September Pachelbel becomes organist to the Württemberg court in Stuttgart.

The Gartentheater (Garden Theatre) in Herrenhausen, Hanover, is completed. It remains the oldest surviving palace theatre in Germany.

Blow composes his Cecilian ode *The Glorious Day is Come*, scored for voices, woodwind, brass, strings and, for the first time in English notated music, kettledrum.

Legrenzi's *Balletti e Correnti*, a dance music collection for strings and continuo, is published posthumously in Venice.

Pachelbel composes *Musicalische Ergötzung* (Musical Delights), six suites for two *scordatura* violins and basso continuo.

Purcell's semi-opera *Dioclesian*, introduced the previous year, is published in London. It is the only theatrical work by the composer to be fully published during his lifetime.

22-year-old Italian poet and librettist **Apostolo Zeno** establishes the 'Accademia degli Animosi' to promote Arcadian values (pastoral life, naturalness, etc.) in the arts.

25 February Scarlatti's opera *L'humanità nelle fiere* opens at the Teatro di San Bartolomeo, Naples.

June Purcell collaborates with **John Dryden** (left) on the semi-opera *King Arthur, or The British Worthy*, performed for the first time at the Dorset Garden Theatre, London. This year Purcell also writes incidental music to Thomas Southerne's comedy *The Wives' Excuse*.

1692

Kuhnau publishes the second part of his *Neuer Clavier-Übung* (New Keyboard Music), containing seven suites, each set in a different minor key, and including a single sonata, the first German example of its kind.

Marais (left), viol virtuoso and royal chamber musician, produces the earliest published French collection of *pièces en trio*.

With the looming threat of a French invasion during the ongoing War of the League of Augsburg (1688–97), Pachelbel leaves Stuttgart and settles in Gotha, Thuringia, where he becomes town organist.

In Bologna Torelli publishes his Op. 5, comprising six *Sinfonie à tre* (trio sonatas) and six *Concerti à quattro*. The latter appear to be the first printed orchestral concertos.

8 April Italian composer and violinist Giuseppe Tartini is born in Pirano, Istria.

2 May Purcell's *The Fairy Queen* is staged at the Dorset Garden Theatre, London. With a libretto adapted (anonymously) from *A Midsummer Night's Dream*, it is the first semi-opera based on a Shakespeare play.

31 May Antonio Lotti becomes second organist at St Mark's, Venice.

12 October Composer Giovanni Battista Vitali dies in Bologna, aged 60.

22 November Purcell's finest ode, *Hail! Bright Cecilia*, is first performed for the St Cecilia's Day celebrations in London. Structured in 13 sections, it is sumptuously scored for solo voices, chorus, woodwinds, strings, brass, timpani and continuo.

1693

Antonio Caldara, currently a cellist at St Mark's, Venice, publishes his first instrumental pieces, *12 Suonate a 3* (trio sonatas).

John Lenton publishes the earliest known violin tutor, *The Gentleman's Diversion, or the Violin Explained*, in London.

Pachelbel publishes *Acht Choräle zum Praeambulieren* (Eight Chorale Preludes) in Nuremberg.

Nicolaus Strungk establishes an opera house in Leipzig and inaugurates it with his own *Alceste*.

Having just composed his first opera, *Sigismundus*, the 12-year-old Telemann has his instruments confiscated by his mother to discourage him from a career in music. Undeterred, he composes on the quiet and practises on borrowed instruments.

Antonio Vivaldi is tonsured (top of head shaved) and begins training for the priesthood.

13 February Johann K. Kerll, composer and keyboardist, dies in Munich, aged 65.

4 December Medea is a lover scorned in the crimes-of-passion opera *Médée*, by Charpentier (right), premièred at the Paris Opéra. With libretto by Thomas Corneille, the opera is royally endorsed and critically acclaimed, but suffers unfavourable reactions from those loyal to Lully (d. 1687).

26 December The 25-year-old François Couperin, already distinguished for his *Pièces d'orgue* (1690), takes up one of the posts of organist to the royal chapel of Louis XIV.

1692 War of the League of Augsburg continues: French fleet defeated at Cap La Hogue, ending French threat to invade England • Hanover (Ger) becomes an electorate of the Holy Roman Empire • Witch trials at Salem, Massachusetts: 19 people are hanged for witchcraft • Florent Dancourt (Fr): *Les Bourgeoises à la mode* • William Congreve (Eng): *Incognito*

1693 War of the League of Augsburg continues: French defeat the forces of William III (Eng) at Neerwinden (Neth) and the army of Savoy at Marsaglia (It) • English government borrows £1m in loans from the public at 10%, starting England's National Debt • William Penn (Eng): *An Essay on the Present and Future Peace of Europe*

Tomaso Albinoni, aged 22, produces his first opera, *Zenobia, regina de' Palmireni*, at the Teatro di SS Giovanni e Paolo. This year also sees the publication of his Op. 1 trio sonatas.

Philippe de Bourbon, Duke of Chartres (and future Regent of France), composes his first opera, *Philomèle*, with the help of **Charpentier**. It is performed at the Palais Royal, Paris.

Corelli publishes 12 chamber sonatas as his Op. 4, in Rome. The set is dedicated to the young Cardinal Pietro Ottoboni, who becomes Corelli's most supportive patron.

Frenchman **André Cardinal Destouches**, aged 22, leaves the second company of the King's Musketeers for a career in music.

Purcell supplies incidental music for Thomas D'Urfey's *The Comical History of Don Quixote*.

Telemann is sent to school in Zellerfeld where his mother hopes he will be steered from music into a financially rewarding profession. Telemann's tutor, Caspar Calvoer, recognises the boy's talent and instructs him in music theory.

28 January **Scarlatti**'s *Il Pirro e Demetrio* triumphs at the Teatro San Bartolomeo, Naples. The opera achieves international success.

15 March *Céphale et Procris*, by the 28-year-old **Elisabeth Jacquet de la Guerre** (below left), is introduced at the Paris Opéra. This *tragédie lyrique* is the first opera written by a French female composer.

30 April **Purcell**'s ode *Come Ye Sons of Art*, scored for solo voices, chorus and orchestra, is presented for the birthday celebrations of Queen Mary. The English queen (right), aged 32, dies from smallpox at the end of the year.

21 June **André Campra** is appointed *Maître de musique* at Notre Dame Cathedral, Paris.

26 October Swedish composer **Johan Helmich Roman** is born in Stockholm.

22 November In London **Purcell**'s indulgent Te Deum and Jubilate, for solo voices, choir and orchestra, is first performed at St Bride's, Fleet Street, during the St Cecilia's Day celebrations.

1694 War of the League of Augsburg continues: English naval attack on Brest fails • Queen Mary II (Eng) dies, leaving her husband, William III, as sole ruler and without a direct heir • Elector Johann Georg IV of Saxony dies: is succeeded by his brother, Frederick Augustus I • Press censorship in England ends with the expiration of the Licensing Act •

The Dalai Lama's 'Red Palace', part of the Potala Palace, is completed in Tibet • Sir Godfrey Kneller (Eng) paints *Hampton Court Beauties* • William Congreve (Eng): comedy of manners *The Double Dealer* • John Dryden (Eng): tragi-comedy *Love Triumphant* • Académie Française publishes its first official French dictionary

Castrato singer, composer and theorist **Giovanni Bontempi** publishes *Historia musica*, the first Italian history of music.

Georg Muffat publishes *Florilegium primum*, a collection of orchestral suites inspired by the French style of Lully.

Pachelbel becomes organist of St Sebaldus, one of Nuremberg's oldest and most important churches.

Henry Purcell composes his last semi-opera, *The Indian Queen*, based on the play by **John Dryden** and Robert Howard. **Daniel Purcell** contributes music to the fifth act—possibly completing the work after his brother's death.

Around this time **Jean-Féry Rebel** composes his *Recueil de 12 sonates* for violin and continuo.

20 February **Johann Ambrosius Bach** dies, having just remarried the previous year. **Johann Sebastian**, aged nine, and his brother Jacob are taken into the care of his eldest brother, **Johann Christoph**, organist at the town of Ohrdruf.

5 March **Purcell**'s *Music for the Funeral of Queen Mary* is performed during the queen's state funeral at Westminster Abbey.

April **Purcell** provides incidental music to Aphra Behn's tragedy *Abdelazar* (1676), including the *Rondeau* that Benjamin Britten will popularise 250 years later in the *Young Person's Guide to the Orchestra*.

3 September Violin maestro **Pietro Antonio Locatelli** is born in Bergamo.

October **Michel Pignolet de Montéclair**'s *Adieu de Tircis à Climène*, an early example of the French cantata, appears in Ballard's monthly *Recueil d'airs sérieux et à boire* (Collection of Serious Airs and Drinking Songs).

October **Collasse** presents his *Ballet des saisons* at the Paris Opéra.

21 November **Henry Purcell** dies (possibly from tuberculosis) in Westminster, London, aged 36. Buried in the Abbey five days later, his epitaph reads: 'Here lyes Henry Purcell Esqre, who left Lyfe and is gone to that Blessed Place where only his harmony can been exceeded.'

*Henry Purcell,
by or after
John Closterman*

End of year Following the death of Purcell, **Blow** returns to the vacant post of organist of Westminster Abbey (from which he had resigned in 1679). He also replaces Purcell as keeper and tuner of the King's instruments.

1695 War of the League of Augsburg: army of William III (Eng) recaptures city of Namur (now Belg) from French • Russia and Turkey are at war: Russia's army, led by Tsar Petr I (The Great), fails to capture Azov, gateway to the Black Sea • The Royal Bank of Scotland is established • Isaac Newton becomes Master of the Mint, supervising England's coinage • A £2 fine is imposed for swearing in England • Hyacinthe Rigaud (Fr) paints the portrait of his mother • Philosopher John Locke (Eng): Essay on *The Reasonableness of Christianity* • William Congreve (Eng): comedy *Love for Love*

Buxtehude publishes a second set of string sonatas, *VII suonate* (Op. 2), a first set having been published about two years earlier.

François Couperin buys ennoblement and his own coat of arms, having served the French royal court for three years. Louis XIV has enabled social climbing through an edict that allows those of means and dignified occupation to purchase a title.

Around this time **Reinhard Keiser**, in his early 20s, becomes director of the Hamburg Opera, succeeding **Johann Sigismund Kusser**.

Kuhnau publishes *Frische Clavier-Früchte, oder sieben Suonaten* (Fresh Keyboard Fruit, or Seven Sonatas) in Leipzig.

Wolfgang Printz publishes his influential musical treatise *Phrynis Mitilenaeus, oder Satyrischer Componist.*

Purcell's *A Choice Collection of Lessons for the Harpsichord or Spinnet* is published posthumously in London. It is the first English keyboard collection devoted exclusively to one composer.

27 June Composer **Michel Lambert** dies in Paris, aged about 86.

12 August Composer **Maurice Greene** is born in London.

27 December Giovanni Bononcini's opera *Il trionfo di Camilla* (The Triumph of Camilla) is premièred with resounding success at the Teatro San Bartolomeo, Naples. During the early 18th century this *opera seria* swings the tastes of the London public towards Italian opera.

Louis XIV closes the Théâtre de L'Hôtel de Bourgogne and expels the resident Italian comedy troupe from Paris for the immorality of their productions. The royal judgement has been hastened by the company's mocking of the king's wife, Mme de Maintenon, in a recent *scenario.*

Around this time the keyboard virtuoso **Bernardo Pasquini** pens his *Partite diversi di follia* variations.

30 January German composer, flute player and maker **Johann Joachim Quantz** is born in Oberscheden, Hanover.

10 May French composer and violinist **Jean-Marie Leclair** is born in Lyons.

24 October The earliest known *opéra-ballet, L'Europe galante* by **André Campra** (left) and librettist **Antoine Houdar de Lamotte**, is introduced at the Paris Opéra. Featuring spoken drama, dances and airs, the work presents four stories of love and intrigue, set in France, Spain, Italy and Turkey. While the genre of *opéra-ballet* is not as dramatic as opera, it reflects the spirit of the Enlightenment with true-to-life characters in modern-day settings.

15 December A. Scarlatti collaborates for the first time with librettist **Silvio Stampiglia**, enjoying great success with *La caduta de' Decemviri* (The Downfall of the Ten Judges) at the Teatro San Bartolomeo, Naples.

1696 France and Savoy (It) sign Peace Treaty of Turin, marking beginning of end of the War of the League of Augsburg; League powers cease all fighting in Italy • Tsar Petr I (Russ) seizes Azov from Turks • English parliament imposes the Window Tax, which continues until 1851

1697 Treaty of Ryswick ends War of the League of Augsburg between France and the Grand Alliance • Austrian general Prince Eugene of Savoy defeats Turkish armies at Battle of Zenta • King Karl XI of Sweden dies; succeeded by Karl XII, aged 15 • J Dryden (Eng): poem *Alexander's Feast*

Fux's music is criticised by the Italian contingent of Leopold I's Viennese court after they hear a mass by the Austrian composer. A second mass, presented as the work of an anonymous Italian composer, is received enthusiastically by the Italians. They suffer double dismay: not only finding out that the work is in fact by Fux, but also witnessing his subsequent appointment as court composer.

Muffat publishes a second volume of French-style music in his *Florilegium secundum*, consisting of eight orchestral suites together with instructions on bowing and ornamentation.

An anthology of songs by Henry Purcell is published posthumously in London, entitled *Orpheus Britannicus*.

Torelli, *maestro di concerto* to the Margrave of Brandenburg in Augsburg, publishes his lively *12 Concerti musicali a quattro* (Op. 6), set variously in three and four movements. Concertos Nos. 6, 10 and 12 introduce passages with solo violin, anticipating the high Baroque solo concerto.

3 January Italian poet and librettist **Pietro Metastasio** is born in Rome.

28 June Charpentier is appointed *maître de musique* of the Sainte Chapelle in the Palais de Justice, Paris.

Caldara becomes *maestro di cappella* to Duke Ferdinando Gonzaga of Mantua. This same year he issues a second collection of 12 trio sonatas, *Suonate da camera* (Op. 2), and 12 chamber cantatas for solo voice, *Cantate da camera* (Op. 3).

Charpentier completes his *Motet pour une longue offrande* (Motet for a long offertory), and composes his finest mass, the *Missa Assumpta est Maria*. Both works are scored for soloists, choir and orchestra, and performed at the Sainte-Chapelle in Paris.

Nicolas de Grigny's *Premier livre d'orgue* is published in Paris.

Muffat writes his *Regulae concentuum partiturae*, a treatise on continuo performance.

The 18-year-old **Johann Mattheson** composes his first opera, *Die Plejades*, in Hamburg.

Pachelbel publishes *Hexachordum Apollinis* (Apollo's Hexachord), his most significant collection of keyboard variations. He dedicates

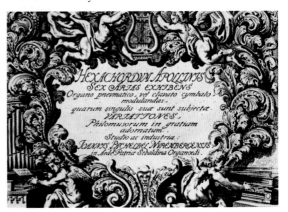

the volume to two compatriots: **F. T. Richter** and **Buxtehude**, representing the southern and northern German keyboard schools respectively.

25 March German composer **Johann Adolph Hasse** is baptised in Bergedorf, outside Hamburg.

- -

1698 First Treaty of Partition: France, England, Holy Roman Empire and Netherlands agree on how Spanish inheritance shall be divided when childless Carlos II (Sp) dies; Carlos (not consulted) makes Josef Ferdinand (Bavaria) his heir • Henry Winstanley's Eddystone Lighthouse, off Plymouth (Eng), completed • Tsar Petr I (Russ) imposes a tax on beards

1699 Death of Josef Ferdinand reopens Spanish succession question • Austria, Poland and Venice end war with Turks with Treaty of Karlowitz: Turks lose territories to all three opponents • Navigator William Dampier (Eng) begins a two-year voyage to East Indies, north-west Australia, New Guinea and Ascension Island

1700–1749

1700–1749

Two MAJOR conflicts raged in Europe at the outset of the 18th century: the Wars of the Spanish Succession (1702–13) and The Great Northern War (1700–21). Together they involved all the leading continental powers and many smaller ones besides. Yet despite the political turmoil, a transformation of social consciousness gave many in Europe a reason to be optimistic. The burgeoning middle class, who sold services in exchange for a wage, was beginning to undermine the age-old culture of a rigid social hierarchy. Moreover, scientific and philosophical endeavour was now broadly free from Church interference. The science- and reason-based Age of Enlightenment asserted individual freedom, legal equality and religious tolerance.

As the Baroque age approached its zenith, the emergent Enlightenment had a profound effect on musical style and form. Composers increasingly sought naturalness and clarity, and operatic narratives began promoting self-determination and the value of the individual. As with the start of the previous century, many popular stylistic changes hailed from Italy. This was especially apparent in the new concerto style, championed by Vivaldi, and in the development of *opera seria* and *opera buffa*. North of the Alps, Italianisms combined with existing traditions in a golden age of German music, spearheaded by the great J. S. Bach. France was deeply divided over the merits of the Italian style; Rameau took command of national opera, though even he could not entirely resist foreign influences. Britain struggled to produce a major composer following the death of Purcell, but then found its musical life transformed by the German émigré G. F. Handel.

◀ *Chamber concert at Ismaning Castle, Bavaria,* by Peter Jakob Horemans (1733).

▼ The prolific Italian composer Alessandro Scarlatti, founder of the Neapolitan school of opera.

The Italian style

Italy was the leading centre of musical innovation throughout the Baroque period. The latest developments in instrumental music and opera—the *concerto grosso* and *opera seria*—had occurred there shortly before the turn of the century (see *Chapter 2*). Corelli and Torelli continued to promote the concerto, while Alessandro Scarlatti and Giovanni Bononcini (1670–1747) were among the leading composers cultivating *opera seria*. Across

Europe the 'unity of affect' principle persisted, with sections of music tending to hold fast to common emotions. If divergent emotions were evoked, the musical structure would be divided accordingly, as in the *da capo* aria (ABA). *Basso continuo* remained fundamental to both ensemble and vocal music, with continuo players expected to realise their parts from a *figured bass*. The established genres of the ensemble sonata, suite, cantata (secular and sacred) and oratorio continued to flourish.

Texture and phrasing

The Italian style was increasingly characterised by clear textures, favouring melody with accompaniment over the kind of elaborate counterpoint maintaining popularity in German lands. Corelli and Torelli accommodated this lucid manner in their sonatas and concertos, even if they still found room for light counterpoint. Their successors included the Venetians Tomaso Albinoni (1671–1750/1) and Antonio Vivaldi (1678–1741), who went on to popularise balanced, or 'periodic', melodic phrasing—clearly structured melodies comprising an antecedent phrase (perhaps ending with a half cadence) and its answering partner, the consequent phrase. Such phrasing was to become a defining feature of the pre-Classical *galant* style.

Forms

A transparency of style encouraged changes to musical structure. Rather than form being driven by procedure, as in the *ricercare* or *fantasia*, more balanced structures became the norm. In stylised dances—usually contained within a suite or chamber sonata—binary form remained ubiquitous: AB, or with repeats AABB (see also *Chapter 1*). A departure from this was found in rounded binary form, AB|A, with a literal or varied repetition of the A section. Although it may look similar on paper, the ABA structure of ternary form features a B section of contrasting character (and often texture) to the A section. The third movement from Corelli's *Christmas Concerto* (published posthumously in 1714) demonstrates both clarity of texture and the contrasting sections of ternary form. The adagio 'A' sections are beautifully melodic and light in counterpoint; the allegro 'B' section is chordal (homophonic) and lively.

Also popular was *ritornello* form, found in many opening movements of Italian concertos. Its central feature is the opening melodic idea, or ritornello (meaning 'little return'), which returns throughout the movement, with statements separated by 'episodes' for the solo instrument(s). Each ritornello is usually presented in fragmented or altered form, and establishes the various key centres of the movement. Combined with periodic phrasing, ritornello design gave the high Baroque composer the perfect platform for a memorable tune. The famous opening Allegro from Vivaldi's 'Spring' (*The Four Seasons*, 1725) provides a classic example.

'Musical taste in Italy changes at least every ten years', noted the French writer Charles de Brosses in around 1739. The entrenched Italian craving for novelty certainly hastened the evolution of musical style. Among the most internationally famous Italian composers were Corelli, Vivaldi, Bononcini, Giuseppe Tartini (1692–1770) and Giovanni Battista Pergolesi (1710–36), and their predilection for structural and textural clarity was one that migrated to the rest of Europe. Soon nearly every important court or city was dominated by the modern Italian style, if not by Italian composers themselves.

Opera

Naples: *opera seria* and *opera buffa*

If Venice, with its numerous public festivals and at least half a dozen opera companies, remained a thriving centre of public opera, Naples was beginning to challenge its status as the hub of innovation and influence. Alessandro Scarlatti (see also *Chapter 2*) was a leading architect of *opera seria*, a 'serious' genre influenced by Classical Greek tragedy, favouring uncomplicated stories from antiquity with few or no supernatural elements included. Among Scarlatti's best works for Naples were the ill-fated *Il Mitridate Eupatore* (1707) and the acclaimed *Tigrane* (1715). Scarlatti consolidated the use and format of the Italian overture, with its fast–slow–fast structure, and observed great formality in the presentation of ideas. Characters would leave the stage with an 'exit aria', after which the scene would change; ensembles were few, and the chorus was used sparingly. Recitative, both *secco* ('dry', supported by continuo) and accompanied (supported by orchestra), followed clear syllabic contours, and the *da capo* aria became the standard medium for emotion, reflection and summary.

Alessandro Scarlatti

The great dramatist and librettist Pietro Metastasio (1698–1792) was of supreme importance to the maturation of opera seria. His career took off in Naples with *Didone abbandonata* (Dido Abandoned, 1724) in collaboration with the composer Domenico Sarro (1679–1744). His *Didone* libretto was then snapped up by Albinoni (Venice, 1725), Nicola Porpora (Reggio Emilia, 1725), Leonardo Vinci (Rome, 1726), and around 50 other composers during the 18th century. Metastasio sought to rid the theatre of artless indulgence and chaotic dramaturgy. He focused on historical figures

Pietro Metastasio

▼ *Il Palazzo Reale*, Naples, by Gaspare Vanvitelli (1653–1736).

and propagated the fashion for optimism and idealism. His central characters usually face some kind of serious moral dilemma, and via their choices and actions they emerge morally improved. Metastasio demanded music with clarity of vision. He once wrote: 'I know by daily experience that my own dramas are much more certain of success in Italy when declaimed by comedians than when sung by musicians.' This statement may not be corroborated by history, but it certainly attests to the poet's sensitivities over the function of music.

Leading composers

Leonardo Vinci (1696–1730)—not to be confused with the Renaissance polymath—was Alessandro Scarlatti's successor in Naples and one of Metastasio's closest collaborators. Renowned for his expressive and concise vocal writing, Vinci was the first to set *Siroe, re di Persia* (Venice, 1726), *Alessandro nell'Indie* and *Artaserse* (both Rome, 1730). Other dominant figures at this crucial time included Leonardo Leo (1694–1744), who also elevated comic opera on a par with opera seria; Nicola Porpora (1686–1768); the German composer Johann Adolf Hasse; and the tragically short-lived Giovanni Battista Pergolesi (1710–36). Despite advances in dramatic structure, coherence and flow, the harmonic language of most opera seria remained fairly simple. This partly reflected Italian tastes, but it was also a practical consideration since the singers had to memorise a great deal of music. Keys rarely ventured beyond three sharps or flats, and remote modulations were infrequent.

Pergolesi and the *intermezzo*

Pergolesi enjoyed success as a composer of church music and opera seria, but much of his fame rests on the comical intermezzo *La serva padrona* (The Maid as Mistress, Naples, 1733). *Intermezzi* were short dramas, usually set in two parts, and originally intended for performance between the acts of a spoken play or opera seria. Bringing light relief, they prioritised naturalness over artificiality. In *La serva padrona* a headstrong maid, eager to maintain rule of the house, manipulates her exasperated, ageing master into marrying her. With a cast of three (counting a silent role), this simple comedy enjoyed wide common appeal owing to its recognisable, run-of-the-mill characters. The music itself required chamber strings and continuo only and was progressively *galant*—direct, light and tuneful. Symptomatic of Enlightenment attitudes, the *intermezzo* eventually became an independent genre, though its forms and patterns remained familiar, each part typically consisting of *secco* recitative, two or three *da capo* arias, and duet finales.

Earlier types of opera sometimes contained comic elements, but come-

▶ Composer and theorist Jean-Philippe Rameau, the towering figure of French late Baroque opera.

dies on their own grew in earnest during the early 18th century. The comic intermezzo soon gave way to full-blown *opera buffa*, a vehicle for social satire that similarly sought dialect-speaking common characters in everyday settings. At first, due to the activities of Vinci and Leo, the home of Italian comic opera was Naples; by 1730 the city could boast three theatres devoted to opera buffa. As the genre spread to Rome and beyond (adopting designations such as *dramma giocoso* or *commedia per musica*) the dialect tradition disappeared. The Venetian composer Baldassare Galuppi (1706–85) was one of the first non-Neapolitans to take to buffa, composing *La forza d'amore* (The Power of Love) in 1745. By the mid-century, he and the librettist Carlo Goldoni (1707–93) were in regular collaboration and riding high the wave of buffa mania.

Early opera buffa

France: *tragédie lyrique* and other genres

The cult of Lully persisted in France throughout the early 18th century, with many of his theatrical works remaining in the repertory. Following in his footsteps was André Campra (1660–1744), whose five-act *tragédies* include *Tancrède* (1702) and *Idomenée* (1712). Campra's historical importance, however, owes more to his pioneering activity in the hybrid genre of *opéra-ballet*, which began in 1697 with colourful tales of courtship in *L'Europe galante*. Structured in a prologue and several entrées, this new style of dance-drama presented a collection of short stories based around a central theme. If not dramaturgically progressive, it reflected Enlightenment sensibilities in its casting of real-life characters in contemporary settings. André Cardinal Destouches (1672–1749) and Jean-Joseph Mouret (1682–1738) joined Campra as the most distinguished composers of both *tragédies* and *opéras-ballets* in the early decades of the century.

André Campra

Jean-Philippe Rameau (1683–1764) ultimately emerged as Lully's true heir. Taking up opera at the ripe age of 50, he triumphed with *Hippolyte et Aricie* (1733), a powerful *tragédie lyrique* that owes a debt to the Lullian model with its five acts and entertaining *divertissement*. Like Lully, Rameau sought natural declamation, placing a renewed emphasis on finely-crafted recitative. But seeking a closer integration of music and drama, he advanced well beyond his illustrious predecessor with colourful orchestration, vivid characterisation and a daring harmonic vocabulary. His highly-charged musical style (sometimes criticised for apparent Italianisms) was considered such a departure from the traditions of Lully that it split the opera-loving public into two factions: the defenders of tradition—the 'Lullists'—

Jean-Philippe Rameau

◀ A production of Rameau's (one and only) *comédie-ballet, La Princesse de Navarre*.

167

and the modernists who followed Rameau's lead. Among Rameau's many outstanding achievements are his dramatic choruses, such as the chorus of demons in Act 3 of *Castor et Pollux* (1737) and a similar scene in Act 5 of *Zoroastre* (1749).

Soon after Rameau turned to music-theatre he wrote the finest *opéra-ballet* of the period, *Les Indes galantes* (1735). Inspired by Campra's example of 1697, it too sets stories of love in different countries, only the locations are exotic: Turkey, Peru, Persia and North America. It is impossible to muscally identify one region from another, but Rameau extended the boundaries of *opéra-ballet* to bring unity to dances, airs and choruses of wide emotional range. Rameau was also attracted to the *pastorale-héroïque*, a sub-genre typically populated by mythical characters in fantasy worlds. His principal works here include *Zaïs* (1748), *Naïs* (1749), *Acante et Céphise* (1751) and *Daphnis et Eglé* (1753). As French opera entered the second half of the 18th century, the various genres of *opéra-ballet*, *tragédie lyrique* and *pastorale-héroïque* increasingly merged with one another.

England: serious opera and ballad opera

The first decade of the new century was a critical time for music on the English stage. The decline of semi-opera was clearly under way with the so-called 'Prize Musick' contest in 1701, where competitors set Congreve's masque *The Judgement of Paris*. Designed to discover the best opera composer in England, it was (and is widely believed to have been a stitch-up. The unknown John Weldon (1676–1736) took first prize, leaving the runners-up, the much more gifted John Eccles, Daniel Purcell and Gottfried Finger, with a growing distaste for such endeavours. Finger was so outraged by the result that he left the country in protest.

England, though historically receptive to foreign influences, was slow to yield to Italian opera. There had been just a handful of attempts at through-composed music-theatre in the previous century, the first in 1656, and not even Purcell's brief but masterly *Dido and Aeneas* (1689, see *Chapter 2*) had provoked much enthusiasm for the genre. Thomas Clayton (1673–1725) was the first English composer to attempt full opera, with *Arsinoe, Queen of Cyprus* (1705). Sung in English but based on an Italian libretto, it managed a successful two-season run in spite of a pounding by the critics. Clayton's next opera failed, but by that time the English appetite had been whetted by a translated version of Giovanni Bononcini's opera *Il trionfo di Camilla* (1696), which maintained a presence in London's theatres from 1706 until 1728. The composer Francesco Geminiani (1687–1762), a London resident from around 1714, noted that *Camilla* had 'astonished the musical world by its departure from the dry, flat melody to which their ears had until then been accustomed'. However, the place of Italian opera on the English stage was most convincingly secured not by an Italian but a German émigré, George Frideric Handel (1685–1759).

George Frideric Handel

Handel launched his opera-writing career aged 19 in Hamburg with *Almira* (1705) and spent some formative years in Italy, producing *Rodrigo* for Florence in 1707, and *Agrippina* for Venice in 1709. By the time he returned to Germany, in 1710, he was internationally famous. In June

◄ Portrait of
George Frideric
Handel by Philip
Mercier *c.*1735.

of that year he secured the post of *Kapellmeister* to the electoral court in Hanover, yet just months later he was given a year's leave to make his name in England. On arriving in London, he was commissioned to write the first major Italian opera specifically intended for the English stage. Premièred at the Haymarket Theatre in February 1711, *Rinaldo* created a minor sensation and paved the way for Handel's permanent residency in England.

Handel's involvement in opera was sporadic during his early London years, even if his five-act *Teseo*, introduced in 1713, proved that there was mileage in the heroic Italian format. *Amadigi di Gaula* saw productions in three consecutive years from 1715, but Handel otherwise abandoned opera composition for five years. A turning point came in 1719 as members of the nobility gained support from King George I—Handel's former patron at Hanover—to establish the Royal Academy of Music for the purpose of promoting Italian opera. To this end Handel was appointed 'Master of the Orchestra' and chief talent scout. His first production for the Academy, *Radamisto* (1720), achieved immediate success and indicated ripe conditions for *opera seria*.

Handel's fortunes were spectacularly mixed, but he still managed to compose the greatest operas of the age with such works as *Giulio Cesare* and *Tamerlano* (both 1724), *Rodelinda* (1725), *Ezio* (1732), *Orlando* (1733), *Ariodante* and *Alcina* (both 1735). All sung in Italian, Handel's operas follow similar formats: most begin with a French overture and proceed on a framework of recitatives—both 'dry' and 'accompanied'—and arias, primarily of the *da capo* variety; the chorus is used very sparingly. Handel observed other structural formalities, such as exit arias, but because English audiences were generally unfamiliar with the Italian language, he had to work hard to heighten the communicative power of his music. He therefore reduced *secco* recitative in favour of expanded, expressive arias, and developed opportunities for some wonderfully imaginative tone painting.

Giulio Cesare is a wonderful example of Handel's mature style. The expressive range of its accompanied recitatives and solo arias give Cleopatra, above all, a depth of characterisation rarely bettered in opera seria. She commands the opera's most poignant moments, as in her aria 'Se pietà di me non sento' ('If you feel no pity for me') from Act II. Her prayer for the protection of Caesar is conveyed first through accompanied recitative, and

Giulio Cesare

► Satirical scene from one of Handel's operas (*Giulio Cesare* or *Flavio*) showing castrati singers, left Senesino (born Francesco Bernardi) and right Berenstadt, with the soprano Francesca Cuzzoni centre.

then in ritornello-aria form as she pours out her anguish and fear. Handel intensifies Cleopatra's emotions by means of sensitive melodic exchanges between voice and strings. Elsewhere, independent instrumental parts are used to tone-paint images and situations. In the Act I aria 'Va tacito e nascosto', Caesar ruminates on Ptolemy's possible duplicity: 'The cunning hunter moves silently and stealthily'. The aria features a confident major key melody supported by a stalking, repetitive string accompaniment and, as if to labour the point, an independent part for solo horn, an instrument everyone at the time will have instantly associated with hunting.

Opera stars

During the height of opera-fever in 1720s London, it was not only the music that captured the public's imagination, but also the stars of the stage. There were a number of renowned castrati, such as Senesino and Gaetano Berenstadt (and later Carestini, Farinelli and Caffarelli), but none achieved as much notoriety as the rival sopranos Francesca Cuzzoni (1696–1778) and Faustina Bordoni (1697–1781). Their enmity even ignited an on-stage fracas (during a Bononcini opera), being reported in one pamphlet as a 'most horrid and bloody battle between Madam Faustina and Madam Cuzzoni' in which the two sopranos were seen fighting and pulling each other's hair.

London opera scene

Handel's impediments did not stop at diva trouble; there was a certain rivalry between himself and Bononcini, who had arrived in London in 1719 to join the ranks of the Royal Academy. Famous for his languid tunefulness, Bononcini enjoyed considerable success with several operas, even if everyone knew that Handel was the superior craftsman. The next obstacle arose in 1728 with the bankruptcy of the ill-managed Royal Academy, which had been paying its star divas and castrati as much as £2,000 a season. Handel then created the Second Academy with the impresario John Heidegger, but their successes were few and far between—not least due to the impact of *The Beggar's Opera* (below). The astounding *Orlando*, with the adored castrato Senesino in the lead role and a 'mad scene' of entrancing dramatic energy, managed only a modest run in 1733. The situation deteriorated further when the Prince of Wales established the 'Opera of the Nobility', later that same year. This rival company featured operas by Porpora and scheduled its performances to coincide with Handel's company, a state of affairs that probably played some part in the failure of Italian opera in London at this time. Handel gave up opera in 1741, a decision sealed by the public rejection of his romantic comedy *Deidamia*. His legacy, however, is one that places him alongside Monteverdi as the greatest opera composer of the Baroque era.

Comedies remained extremely popular in Britain throughout this period, and the demand for rustic and bawdy subjects that boomed after the Restoration only momentarily gave ground with the arrival of opera seria. English staged comedy often featured songs and even extended interludes, and genres in the masque tradition persisted. It was probably a combination of these influences and events that resulted in the appearance of the 'ballad opera' in 1728. The runaway success of that year, *The Beggar's Opera*, went on to become one of the most popular English stage works of all time. The play was written by the inventive poet and dramatist John Gay (1685–1732), while the music featured well-loved songs from the street and theatre, including airs by Bononcini and Handel. Johann Pepusch (1667–1752) supplied the arrangements with basso continuo and composed the overture. *The Beggar's Opera* was perfectly in step with Enlightenment ideals: instead of heroes from mythology or antiquity, the main characters are beggars, drunkards, prostitutes, schemers and other ne'er-do-wells, each given an apt and colourful name, such as Diana Trapes, Mrs Vixen, Sukey Tawdry and Molly Brazen. Featuring spoken dialogue rather than recitative, this antidote to Italian opera shattered all box-office records, starting with an uninterrupted run of 62 performances. A number of its songs, like 'Over the hills and far away', never fell from popularity. Other ballad operas followed and were soon to be found throughout the English-speaking world. Thomas Arne (1710–78) was one of the more famous exponents with works such as *The Blind Beggar of Bethnal Green* (1741) and *Miss Lucy in Town* (1742).

Comedy and The Beggar's Opera

German-speaking lands: imported and native opera

Court-sponsored opera at Vienna, Innsbruck, Munich, Hanover, Dresden and Darmstadt had taken root during the late 1600s. New opera houses had been built to indulge Italian opera, and in many German localities native composers found themselves competing with Italians for the best positions at court. The only venue attempting to promote an identifiably German operatic style was Hamburg's civic-run Theater am Gänsemarkt (Goose-market Theatre), established in 1678. Yet even here, in the new century, Italian influences proved irresistible.

Agostino Steffani (1654–1728), who had done more than anyone to promote Italian opera in Germany (see *Chapter 2*), effectively retired from composition after his tragedy *Tassilone* débuted at Düsseldorf in 1709. He

Italians abroad

instead chose to spend his final years working for the Catholic Church in North Germany. Of the Italians now based at German courts, Pietro Torri (*c.*1650–1737), working at Munich, was prolific and possibly the most renowned. Other Italians exerted their influence without relocating, such as the Venetian composer Antonio Lotti (1666–1740). His last four operas were all premièred at Dresden, where he witnessed in person the success of his *Teofane* and *Li quattro elementi* in 1719.

Germany's first major opera composer was Reinhard Keiser (1674–1739), who played a key role in making Hamburg, for a short time, one of the most important centres of opera in northern Europe. He composed well over 60 operas in both Italian and German, with a number of works, such as *Masaniello furioso* (1706), receiving successful revivals. Handel was directly influenced by Keiser, and even borrowed (pinched) some of his melodies. Georg Philipp Telemann (1681–1767) was also central to the rise of Hamburg's status in the opera world, especially with German-language comedies like *Der geduldige Socrates* (1721) and the semi-comical *Emma und Eginhard* (1728). His success, however, was modest in comparison to that of Johann Hasse (1699–1783), a Hamburg resident until 1721, who emerged as the leading German opera composer in continental Europe.

Hasse received formative training under both Porpora and Scarlatti at Naples, where he developed early brilliance in *opera seria* and the comic intermezzo. In 1730 he married the famous soprano Faustina Bordoni and afterwards began a 30-year association with the Dresden court. Hasse is remembered as Metastasio's most committed advocate; during his long career he set all but one of Metastasio's librettos, and several more than once. Their first joint venture was *Antigono*, introduced at Dresden in 1743. Praised for his languid melodies and dramatic sensitivity, Hasse was the leading German advocate of the *galant* style. *Cleofide* (1731), his first opera for Dresden, displays his progressive style with a homophonic overture of great vitality, exquisitely decorated vocal lines and elegant orchestral accompaniments. His opera seria enjoyed enormous popularity across Europe, from Naples to Warsaw. The composer's fame peaked around the mid-century, but then began to wane in the 1760s during the period of Gluck's operatic reforms.

Instrumental music

Vivaldi and the Italian Concerto

The concerto grosso was popular in Rome and Bologna before the end of the 17th century and spreading further afield via the works of Corelli, Torelli and Georg Muffat. Torelli was central to the evolution of the solo violin concerto, a form that reached virtual maturity in his Op. 8 collection, published in the year of his death, 1709. The Venetian composer Tomaso Albinoni was another early contributor to the concerto, beginning with the six concerti grossi contained within his *Sinfonie e concerti a cinque* Op. 2 of 1700. The most prolific and influential concerto composer of the Baroque also hailed from Venice, the flame-haired priest Antonio Vivaldi.

Ordained in 1703, Antonio Vivaldi spent much of his professional life in service to Venice's Pio Ospedale della Pietà (Devout Hospital of Mercy), an institution for orphaned and abandoned girls—one of four in the city, each of which offered a first-rate musical education. Vivaldi supplied many of his 500-plus concertos for the all-female orchestra at the Pietà, and the regular musical events held there became internationally famous. By 1716 Vivaldi had risen from violin tutor to *maestro de' concerti* and was additionally supplying sacred pieces, such as his one surviving oratorio, *Juditha triumphans* (1716), the Gloria in D major, RV589, and Magnificat in G minor, RV610 (dates uncertain). Indeed it was sacred music, oratorios in particular, that projected the musical soul of the ospedali, and sinfonias and concertos were often incorporated within this context as instrumental introductions and interludes.

Portrait thought to be of Antonio Vivaldi: composer, violin virtuoso and priest. Vivaldi centred his career on Venice, though he journeyed as far afield as Amsterdam and Prague. He died in Vienna, apparently in poverty, on 28 July 1741.

Vivaldi was largely responsible for making Venice the concerto capital of Italy. His 12 Op. 3 concertos *L'estro armonico* (Harmonic Inspiration), issued by the Amsterdam publisher Étienne Roger in 1711, marked a monumental breakthrough. The elegant use of ritornello and binary forms, together with inventive episodes for one, two and four solo violins, gave them instant success across Europe. German composers were particularly influenced by the collection, none more than J. S. Bach, who made from it a number of solo transcriptions for organ and harpsichord. *L'estro armonico* moved away from the more intricate counterpoint and delicate balance of earlier ensemble music toward periodic melodic structures, homophonic textures and driving rhythmic figurations. The collection also contributed to the popularity of the solo concerto, which was fast becoming the predominant concerto style.

L'estro armonico

By propagating the three-movement concerto layout (fast–slow–fast), Vivaldi largely negated 'church' and 'chamber' formats. At the same time he elevated the status of the slow movement: it became longer and more substantial in melodic material, in contrast to the often short, harmonically conceived adagios of earlier composers. In another departure from the Corellian model, Vivaldi placed greater emphasis on virtuosity and dramatic impact, although his tendency toward showmanship drew criticism. Nevertheless, this new type of Venetian concerto was widely imitated and integrated into existing regional styles.

Vivaldi wrote some 350 solo concertos, representing around two-thirds of his concerto output, and in these the violin reigns supreme. However, a considerable number of compositions give centre-stage to lower-register

▶ *Tartini's Dream*, a 19th-century illustration of the inspiration behind Tartini's Devil's Trill sonata.

instruments, as in 39 bassoon concertos and 30 cello concertos, while others showcase unconventional lead instruments, for instance the Concerto in D for lute and two violins (RV93; 1716) and the Concerto in G major for two mandolins (RV532). Elsewhere Vivaldi promoted instrumental diversity, and the expansion of the *concertino* into a colourful band of soloists was one way that he blurred the distinctions between the solo concerto and concerto grosso. One such example is the Concerto in C major for multiple instruments (RV555), scored for three violins, oboe, two recorders, two English violets, chalumeau, two cellos, two trombas marinas, two harpsichords, strings and continuo.

Il cimento dell'armonia e dell'inventione

Most famous of all are Vivaldi's Op. 8 solo violin concertos of 1725, *Il cimento dell'armonia e dell'inventione* ('The Contest between Harmony and Invention'), a collection dedicated to the private orchestra of Count Václav Morzin in Prague. The Czechs had established themselves as one of Europe's great musical nations and Vivaldi's imaginative concertos echoed their near obsession with programmatic works and imitations of nature—it is this set which contains his ever-popular *Four Seasons*. The distinguishing compositional features of the *Four Seasons*, as compared with Vivaldi's Op. 3, are found in the concentrated use of extended ritornello form, and in the increased emphasis on virtuosity and contrast. This is not simply dynamic and textural contrast, but also that provided by the polarity of tuneful ritornellos and quasi-improvisatory solo passages. The collection boasts some of the most melodious and exciting violin writing of the Baroque period.

When Vivaldi was not composing concertos faster than a copyist could write them down (as he apparently claimed), he was busy in other genres, such as the solo sonata, trio sonata and solo cantata. Vivaldi also wrote around 50 operas, most of which were produced for Venice—beginning with *Ottone in villa* in 1713—and other Italian centres including Mantua, Florence and Rome. Vivaldi's diverse productivity set him apart from two other celebrated violinist-composers of the late Baroque: Giuseppe Tartini (1692–1770) and Pietro Antonio Locatelli (1695–1764).

Tartini set out under the influence of Corelli, though he soon gravitated towards Vivaldi's Venetian style. Unlike Vivaldi, he avoided opportunities to write for the theatre (he considered Vivaldi's operas failures), though he did himself compose a handful of sacred works. While many of his concertos and solo sonatas are virtuosic pieces, they also display depth of feeling and great formal spontaneity. His most famous composition is the dream-inspired *Devil's Trill* Violin Sonata, a technically-demanding early career work that largely follows Corelli's four-movement design. Tartini was a theorist of limited significance, but his influence on violin technique was far-reaching. In around 1727 he established a violin school in Padua that attracted students from all over Europe; his institution thus gained the grand soubriquet 'The School of the Nations'.

Locatelli was active primarily in Italy and Amsterdam. The Dutch city was one of Europe's leading music-printing centres, and most of the composer's entirely instrumental output was issued there through the publishing house of Roger and Le Cène. Locatelli was the era's most progressive virtuoso and a specialist in the violin's high register. In the 12 concertos of his *L'arte del violino* (1733) he incorporated solo firework cadenzas in each of the outer movements—thus making 24 'caprices', foreshadowing the incredible virtuosity of Paganini by 70 years. His music, like Vivaldi's, was sometimes criticised for style over substance, but both his concertos and solo sonatas, especially the Op. 6 sonatas of 1737, remain distinctive and valuable contributions to the Baroque repertory.

Giuseppe Tartini

Pietro Antonio Locatelli

The concerto in Germany, England and France

The Italian concerto was an instant success in the German lands (facilitated by the dominance of Italian musicians at important courts) and it soon integrated local characteristics. While the Vivaldian three-movement layout became popular, composers like G. P. Telemann and Johann Fasch (1688–1758) often incorporated four or more movements, with some based on courtly or rustic dance forms. Not all composers of 'concertos' used the designation in a consistent way; the Dresden-based Czech composer Jan Zelenka (1679–1745), prominent in sacred music, wrote concerto-style pieces bearing titles like *capriccio* and *simphonie*.

Telemann

Telemann was inventive with his stunning variety of instrumental combinations. The impact of the Italian style on his music was profound, but one thing that helped keep him from joining the ranks of countless Vivaldi imitators was his openness to other influences, such as Polish and Czech folk music, which he combined with impeccable taste and balance with the German style. One of the most prolific composers who ever lived, Telemann produced some of his greatest instrumental works in the three anthologies of *Tafelmusik* (Table music), a veritable banqueting feast of music that brought together all the popular instrumental genres of the day: suites, concertos, and ensemble sonatas of various kinds.

Johann
Sebastian
Bach

The concerto reached its apotheosis—as did most genres of this time—in the hands of Johann Sebastian Bach (1685–1750), whose 'Brandenburg' concertos, harpsichord concertos and violin concertos are among the finest ever written. The Brandenburg concertos, completed in 1721, gained their appellation from a would-be patron, Margrave Christian Ludwig of Brandenburg, who did not even acknowledge their receipt. In organisation they are reminiscent of Vivaldi, mostly set in three movements with a heterogeneous assortment of solo groups. Concerto No. 1 (the only four-movement example) is colourfully diverse, featuring two horns, three oboes, bassoon and *violino piccolo*. The common use of ritornello-episode design is another Venetian feature, although in Bach the form is more interconnected and developed. Bach's imprint is most apparent in the musical language, which cheerfully extends into elaborate Germanic counterpoint. His melodies are frequently shaped by *fortspinnung* ('spinning out') techniques and polyphonic forms, and they are consequently not as symmetrical, or 'periodic', as Vivaldi's. Arguably the most remarkable Brandenburg piece is No. 5, whose dizzying cadenza for solo harpsichord and masterful expansion of Italian structural models make it one of the finest concertos of the century. Here we find the innovative spirit of Bach and the historical starting point of the keyboard concerto.

Bach pioneered the harpsichord concerto at Leipzig after he revived the concerts of the Collegium Musicum in 1729. Designed for his own talents as a performer, his seven solo works were essentially adaptations of existing compositions, notably the violin concertos he wrote ten years previously at Cöthen. Among the greatest of them is the Harpsichord Concerto in D minor (BWV1052), almost certainly a transcription of an earlier violin concerto, now lost. In fact, Bach had already recycled some of this material in his Leipzig cantatas: the opening Allegro and central Adagio of the

▼ Autograph first page of J. S. Bach's 'Brandenburg' concerto No. 5.

concerto relates to the sinfonia and chorus of the cantata *Wir müssen durch viel Trübsal* (Through bitter tribulation enter we into God's Kingdom, No.146, 1726), while the concerto's finale corresponds to the sinfonia of the cantata *Ich habe meine Zuversicht* (I have confidence in the Lord, No.188, 1728). Bach's habit of self-borrowing was especially marked at Leipzig, and this extends to his three double harpsichord concertos and two triples. The Double Concerto in C minor (BWV1062), for instance, is based on the glorious Double Violin Concerto in D minor (*c.*1731). Bach also produced a Concerto for Four Harpsichords (BWV1065, *c.*1730), a reworking of Vivaldi's Concerto for Four Violins, Op. 3, No. 10.

England

The Italian concerto had a favourable reception in England, since the country had a flourishing public-concert life and the demand for foreign music and musicians seemed insatiable. The Moravian composer Gottfried Finger (*c.*1655–1730) takes the credit for introducing the solo sonata to England, and he may well have introduced the solo concerto also. But it was the following generation of native and immigrant composers who popularised the concerto, figures such as William Babel (*c.*1690–1723), Robert Woodcock (1690–1728), Pepusch and eventually Handel.

Handel's *Concerti grossi*

Handel's priority was always vocal music, but his mature orchestral works are hardly less compelling. The six *Concerti grossi* (Op. 3) of 1734, and more importantly the 12 *Concerti grossi* (Op. 6) of 1739, are masterly examples of compositional technique and idiomatic string writing. Miraculously composed within the space of just one month, the Op. 6 represents the pinnacle of Baroque *concerto grosso* literature, alongside the essays of Bach. The set features concertos in four to six movements and draws on both Italian and French influences. Most begin with a slow introduction in a manner reminiscent of Corelli, although a few are firmly in the French overture mould: No. 5 in D major and No. 10 in D minor both begin with a stately dotted-rhythm 'overture' and proceed with fast fugal movements. A stronger contemporary influence comes in the form of Italianate periodic phrasing on clear ritornello structures, as in the fourth movement Allegro of No. 6 in G minor, a concerto of remarkable emotional breadth.

Handel broke new ground with his invention of the organ concerto. Dating from around 1735, these pieces were premièred in between the 'acts' of his oratorios and became enormously popular with the public. Handel produced 15 organ concertos in total, one of which was a transcription of the Harp Concerto in B flat major (1736). Other contributors to the concerto in England included the blind composer John Stanley (1712–86), who followed a Corelli-Handel model in his Six Concertos for Strings, Op. 2 (1742), and the Italian émigré Francesco Geminiani.

France

In the proud kingdom of France the reception of new Italian styles and genres was mixed. This was consistent with the prevailing attitudes of the previous century, which accounts for France's rejection of Italian opera and slow acceptance of the ensemble sonata. Joseph Bodin de Boismortier (1689–1755) advocated the Italian style by writing concerto-style pieces from the late 1720s, and adopting the fast–slow–fast structure in many of his instrumental works. Jean Marie Leclair (1697–1764) was also influential, creating a successful blend of French and Italian manners in his Op. 7 and

Op. 10 concertos (1737/45). Leclair is widely regarded as the founder of the French violin school, having brought violin playing up to date by incorporating multiple stopping and florid, Italianate melodic writing.

Couperin

Both François Couperin and Rameau chose to ignore the concerto, a fact that seems to betray a protective stance towards national idioms. Couperin, however, was most certainly a measured Italophile. He made clear his admiration for the Italian trio-sonata style in the programmatic *L'Apothéose de Corelli* (1724), even if he judiciously balanced this with a magnificent and more complex sister work: *L'Apothéose de Lulli* (1725). In spite of their titles, both collections represent a melding of Italian and French music: the Corellian trio sonata style on the one hand, and French dance and overture styles on the other. Couperin created a similar fusion in *Les nations* (1726), which features small ensemble pieces separated into church and chamber styles. Most typically French, yet still not without Italianisms, is his *Concerts royaux*, published in 1722. Composed by the end of Louis XIV's reign (that is, by 1715), they are effectively soloist-led dance suites for the king's chamber. The dance forms do not lend themselves to solo–tutti contrast and are therefore distinct in style from the concerto.

Solo keyboard music

Harpsichord and early pianoforte music

There was a rich diversity of style in the keyboard music of the early 1700s. While some composers continued to work with traditional forms like the prelude, fugue, ricercare and toccata, others built on the dance suite tradition, and the most progressive of them all turned to the (binary-form) sonata, a new keyboard genre well suited to textual clarity and periodic phrasing.

J. S. Bach

Bach's magnificent oeuvre dominates a golden age of Baroque keyboard music. Highlights include the two volumes of *Das Wohltemperierte Klavier* (The Well-Tempered Clavier, 1722, 1742), both sets containing 24 preludes and fugues in each key. The first collection, which Bach intended 'for the musical youth desirous of learning', was inspired by the German composer Johann C. F. Fischer (1656–1746), whose *Ariadne Musica* (1702) comprised 20 preludes and fugues in 18 different keys. Bach's title 'Well-tempered' indicates that the keyboard's intervals were altered from their pure tuning so that each and every key could sound relatively in tune. In the late 19th century the notion evolved that Bach intended the pieces as a demonstration of 'equal' temperament (with the octave divided into 12 equal intervals) but this has long since been dismissed. Exactly what kind of 'unequal' temperament Bach used is still a matter of debate.

Like the *Wohltemperierte Klavier*, the multi-part collections of the *Clavier-Übung* represent something of Bach's statement as both a composer and practical pedagogue. In total the series consists of four parts: Part I, the Partitas; Part II, the Italian Concerto and French Overture; Part III, various organ pieces making up the so-called 'German Organ Mass'; Part IV, the Aria with Diverse Variations (the so-called 'Goldberg Variations'). Of the last work, J. N. Forkel, Bach's first biographer, 'elaborated' anecdotes passed on to him by Bach's eldest two sons, bequeathing to history the charming story that Bach wrote the variations for J. G. Goldberg so that he could administer the musical diversion to the insomniac Russian ambassador Count Kaiserling.

One of Bach's final keyboard compositions was *The Art of Fugue*. Dating from the early 1740s, the collection comprises pieces of wide-ranging fugal complexity, each of which derives its music from the same thematic material. It is a monument of contrapuntal invention. Bach revised it in 1748/9, around the time that he completed the Mass in B minor. What may be said of the Mass may also be applied to *The Art of Fugue*: it was given no original title; it was assembled and completed at Bach's own pleasure; it testifies to his astonishing technical mastery and represents the very summit of his art.

The central figure of the Italian keyboard school was Domenico Scarlatti (1685–1757), whose 550 or so surviving sonatas are pillars of 18th-century invention and virtuosity. Italian by birth, education and early experience, he was the sixth child of the great Alessandro Scarlatti. He enjoyed little of his father's success as an opera composer, but his keyboard wizardry was acknowledged from an early age. Scarlatti and Handel apparently took part in keyboard 'duel' in Rome around 1709; it seems that the two young giants were evenly matched on the harpsichord, but Handel was a clear victor on the organ. Popular legend preserves that later in life Scarlatti would cross himself when mentioning Handel's genius. Scarlatti met yet another virtuoso in the Irish composer Thomas Roseingrave (1690/1–1766). The young Irishman heard Scarlatti perform in Venice and declared that the Italian gave the impression of 'ten-hundred devils' having been at the instrument. Roseingrave became a committed disciple of Scarlatti and did much to promote his reputation in London.

From 1719 Scarlatti served as *mestre* of the royal chapel at Lisbon. Ten years later he followed his pupil and new employer, Princess (later Queen) Maria Barbara, to Spain—first to Seville, then Madrid. Life in the Iberian peninsula brought colourful influences to bear on Scarlatti's keyboard style. Many of his pieces evoke the flavours of Spanish folk song and dance, particularly when combining accentuated rhythms, capricious harmonic shifts, and effects that suggest guitar techniques, clattering castanets, clapping and stamping. Scarlatti's personalised, single-movement sonatas first appeared in print in London with the 30 *Essercizi per gravicembalo* (1738). In this and later sets (mostly retro-

◀ The Italian keyboard virtuoso Domenico Scarlatti. Gambling debts may have prompted several volumes of sonatas, written out at the behest of Queen Maria Barbara and the affluent castrato Farinelli.

Domenico
Scarlatti

spective anthologies) he explored tremendous expressive variety within predominantly binary-form structures. A diverse selection could include the Sonata in A major, K. 24, flamboyant and bustling, featuring passages with hand-crossing; the Sonata in B minor, K. 87, a slow, searching piece of lucid counterpoint; the effervescent Sonata in D minor K. 141, toccata-style with trilling and strumming effects (and more hand-crossing); the measured Sonata in C major K. 308, appealing directly to the *galant* mindset; and the Sonata in D major K. 492, a cavorting pre-Classical triple-time dance with a guitaresque opening theme. Other instrumental idioms creep into his music also, as in the trumpet-like fanfare that opens the Sonata in D major, K. 436. It was the combination of melodic and textural spontaneity, virtuosity, popular Spanish idioms and Italianate clarity that gave Scarlatti's music a character so unlike any other of the period.

François Couperin

The French harpsichord school reached its peak with the music of François Couperin. Known as 'Le Grand', to distinguish him from many less talented musical relations, Couperin combined French and Italian influences to develop a fluid, richly ornamented style that eschewed contrapuntal and structural complexity. Between 1713 and 1730 he issued, in four volumes, more than 200 harpsichord pieces, grouped in *ordres* (or suites), the majority based on or inspired by binary-form dances. Much captivating music comes in the form of descriptive compositions whose appellations avouch vivid tone-painting, as in the fluttering ornaments of *Le moucheron* (The midge, Vol. II), and the gauche, hobbling gestures of *Le drôle de corps* (The funny-looking fellow, Vol. III). In other pieces Couperin painted musical portraits of friends and acquaintances, such as *Mlle de Charolais*, one of his pupils, and *La superbe, ou La Forqueray*, after the famous viol player Antoine Forqueray. These whimsical and playful miniatures, typically lasting between one and three minutes, were designed for the amateur's pleasure. Couperin added to his renown as the leading keyboard teacher in Paris with *L'arte de toucher* (1716), a celebrated treatise that provides modern scholars with valuable performance instructions on the style and other subtleties (such as fingerings) of the French school.

Rameau

When Couperin died in 1733 his mantle passed to Jean-Philippe Rameau, the greatest all-round French composer of the 18th century. By this time Rameau had in fact written and published most of his solo keyboard music, represented by the dance suite of his *Premier livre* (1706) and two collections of fashionable character pieces, the *Pieces de clavessin* (1724) and the *Nouvelles suites* (c.1730). Rameau penned some historic treatises too, first the 450-page *Traité de l'harmonie* (1722) in which he investigated all aspects of the tonal system, analysing harmonic ratios, triads, chordal inversions, modulation and the defining role of the bass. This and his *Nouveau système de musique théorique* (1726) were so influential that for some time many contemporaries considered Rameau first and foremost a theorist.

During this rich period of harpsichord music, experiments were under way to create a keyboard instrument capable of playing loud and soft, depending on the touch of the performer. The Italian keyboard manufacturer Bartolomeo Cristofori (1655–1732) had already developed

Pianoforte

a functional *pianoforte* with hammer mechanism by around 1700, but his invention was very slow to catch on. Lodovico Giustini (1685–1743) was one of the early advocates with his 12 sonatas *da cimbalo di piano, e forte, detto volgarmente di martelletti*, published in 1732, yet the piano had to wait several more decades to become the virtuoso's first choice. Nevertheless, the seeds were sewn and there is good evidence that some of Scarlatti's later works in Madrid were conceived for the pianoforte. In 1752 the German composer and flautist Johann Quantz (1697–1773) praised the instrument for its dynamic shading and considered it ideal for accompanying recitative. The early piano, like the harpsichord, used thin strings set in strong wooden frames, so the sound was bright and clear, though not terribly loud.

Bach and the organ repertory

The most important influence in Bach's life was God, whom he served as a committed Lutheran. It is therefore hardly surprising that alongside church cantatas (see below), organ pieces comprise the largest portion of his output. Bach acquired early mastery at the instrument having devoured the music of Buxtehude, Kuhnau and Pachelbel. The influence of the organist-composers Johann Reincken (1643–1722) and Georg Böhm (1661–1733) also ran deep, shaping Bach's musical style and playing technique. By the time he was 30, Bach had gained a reputation throughout the German lands as an organist and improviser of genius. He travelled widely, appraising organs by renowned builders like Tobias Tost and the Silbermann brothers, and advising others on organ construction.

There was considerable diversity among the organs of Bach's day. The finest mechanical church organs gave each manual (usually two keyboards) and the pedal section independent ranks of pipes in order to maximise volume and create varied sonorities. In a typical three-manual instrument, each department would require more than 40 pipes, all needing individual tuning. Performances would involve an organ blower, and sometimes an assistant to draw and retire dozens of stops that controlled timbre and effects.

Dominating the repertory of the instrument, Bach's organ music falls into four main types: Chorale Preludes, larger-scale works such as Preludes and Fugues, then Trios and Duets, with or without pedals, and transcriptions of music by other composers, such as Vivaldi. Whilst Bach composed for the organ throughout his career, the majority of his pieces date from the years

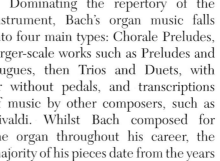

◀ Johann G. Walther's *Musicalisches Lexicon* frontispiece. The figure depicted at the organ may represent J. S. Bach.

at Weimar, 1708–17. The chorale preludes are most numerous. Serving as an introduction to the congregational hymn, they were typically short: many pieces of Bach's *Orgel-Büchlein* (*c*.1715), the first of six such collections, last only a minute or two. His intention was to employ hymn tunes in a variety of contexts, 'wherein an inexperienced organist is given guidance in treating a chorale'. Bach's Leipzig chorales, written some 20 years later, expand the dimensions of the Weimar pieces; for example, 'Komm, Gott Schöpfer, heiliger Geist' (BWV667) more than triples the size of the original *Orgel-Büchlein* version (BWV631). Bach's chorale preludes transcended mere harmonisations and became major compositions in their own right. Robert Schumann proclaimed the Leipzig chorale 'Schmüke dich, o liebe Seele' (BWV654) 'as priceless and profound a piece of music as ever sprang from an artist's imagination'.

Bach often linked preludes, fantasias and toccatas with an associated fugue. He never grouped these pieces into sets, and only the Prelude and Fugue in E flat, BWV552, known in the English-speaking world as 'St Anne', appeared in print during his lifetime—in Part III of the *Clavier-Übung*. Bach made his toccatas weightier and more closely motivic as the years passed. One of the finest examples from the Weimar years is the 'Dorian' Toccata and Fugue in D minor, BWV538, which integrates bravura dexterity and intellectual weight, while employing the pedal part in a typically thematic role. The hugely famous Toccata and Fugue in D minor, BWV565, with its suspenseful introduction and scalic principal theme, is the people's favourite, although some eminent scholars doubt that the piece is by Bach at all.

England

In central Germany, Italy and then England, Handel created for himself a performer's reputation that transcended all others save Bach. History remembers his organ concertos with string ensemble above the solo church pieces. Of greater significance to the English solo repertory was John Stanley, who produced three renowned sets of organ voluntaries, published between 1748 and 1754. Stanley, who lost his sight at the age of two, possessed one of the most remarkable memories of any musician who ever lived. It is said that he was able to memorise the organ continuo part to an entire oratorio after listening to it played just once. With this phenomenal gift he was able to direct some of Handel's oratorios during the 1750s, after which he collaborated with Handel's amanuensis, John Christopher Smith (1712–95), on the organisation of London's Lenten oratorio seasons.

France

The French organ tradition was brought into the new century by Guillaume Nivers and François Couperin (see *Chapter 2*), both of whom served Louis XIV as *organistes du roi*. Among the leading organists of the next generation were Louis Marchand (1669–1732) and Louis-Nicolas Clérambault (1676–1749). Marchand was successor to Nivers at the royal chapel (1708) and a formidable virtuoso, though he recognised that he was probably not the best player in Europe. He was in Dresden in 1717 when he got word that the court was planning a keyboard duel between himself and the visiting J. S. Bach, 16 years his junior. Marchand apparently fled the city in haste.

Performing

Concert life

During the 17th century the primary venue for professional music-making was the church, but the rise of public concerts in the 18th century resulted in the appearance of concert societies and purpose-built venues across Europe. The earliest known public concert series was held in London. The violinist and composer John Banister (*c.*1624–79) began holding regular concerts in a Whitefriars tavern in 1672, and soon his events became so popular that he had to relocate to larger premises. Another pioneer was Thomas Britton, the musical 'small coal' man, who held concerts from 1679 to 1714 in the loft above his Clerkenwell coal shop in London. Despite the cramped quarters, only accessible via a ladder on the outside of the house, it was a prestigious venue, with Handel and Pepusch among the regulars in the last years. The Swedish composer Johann Helmich Roman (1694–1758), a pupil of both Handel and Pepusch, may also have participated, and upon returning to Stockholm he duly pioneered his own country's first public concerts.

By the early 18th century there were several concert series in London, making the English capital the centre of concert life in Europe. The first purpose-built venue for public concerts, however, appeared in Oxford: the Holywell Music Room (1748), a rare survivor of later renovations. This

▼ Preparations for the Royal Fireworks display in London's Green Park, 1749, celebrating the end of the War of the Austrian Succession (1740–48).

venue was designed to hold around 250 audience members, its wooden construction ideally suited to the smaller-sized ensembles that were typical of the time.

On the continent one could enjoy the relative intimacy of Leipzig's Collegium Musicum concerts at Zimmerman's coffeehouse, or in the same proprietor's coffee garden during the summer months. Founded by Telemann and continued by Bach, the society drew most of its performers from the city's university. Similar *collegia* could be found in other European cities at this time. But by far the most esteemed concert organisation was Paris's *Concert Spirituel*, founded in 1725 by the composer Anne Danican-Philidor (1681–1728). Mounting concerts in the Tuileries Palace until 1784, the society itself ran until 1790, promoting both instrumental and sacred music with a natural bias towards French composers.

Concerts held in theatres and open-air venues—private grounds, public gardens, parks, town squares and the like—became a common feature of European musical life. Handel exploited all manner of locations, introducing his oratorios and many concertos in the theatre, and his two most famous orchestral suites outdoors. The ever-popular *Water Music* Suite (1717) was premièred on a large Thames barge for the pleasure of King George I, as he made his way up river from Whitehall to Chelsea. The occasion seems to have marked the first use of horns in English orchestral music. The *Music for the Royal Fireworks* was introduced as part of a grand public celebration of the Peace of Aix-la-Chapelle (1748). Held in London's Green Park in 1749, the event began well but ended with malfunctioning fireworks setting fire to one section of a giant purpose-built ceremonial building. Contemporary accounts of the event were so preoccupied with the highs and lows of the fireworks, no comment was ever made about the music.

Instruments and the orchestra

As audiences and venues grew in numbers and size, ensembles followed suit. What might resemble the classical orchestra began to take shape in these early decades. Although most music was still performed with one player per part, some composers specified doublings in concertos, overtures, sinfonias and the like. Musical centres including Venice, Mannheim, Dreseden, Paris and London witnessed expanding orchestras, and instruments themselves were evolving.

By the start of the 18th century the viola da gamba was found less often in its old role as a bass instrument and more usually in the tenor and alto range. Most mature viol works by the French composer Marin Marais (1656–1728) were published between 1701 and 1725 (books II–V), and music of the solo viol reached a high point in the fiendishly difficult and masterful suites of Antoine Forqueray (1672–1745) and his son Jean-Baptiste (1699–1782). Yet despite the triumphs of the viola da gamba in France, its use was declining in the rest of Europe.

The late 17th century had seen a fundamental change in how bass instruments were built, employed and played. Up until this time most string bass parts were played by some type of bass violin, typically tuned a whole-tone lower than the modern cello, therefore, B flat–F–C–G.

Coinciding with the development of the newer sonata and concerto types, the bass violin was scaled down so that it might better suit solo playing. This transformation left the bass without enough weight in certain situations, and so in *tutti* passages the double bass (common as a three-string instrument) was employed to support the continuo part. By the start of the 18th century the *violoncello* (abbreviated to cello) had nearly rendered the bass violin obsolete. The standard size of the cello was established by Antonio Stradivari (1644–1737) just after 1700, and within a few years the new instrument had attracted some of Europe's leading composers. Vivaldi's cello sonatas and cello concertos represent the finest Italian examples of their kind, while Bach's six suites for solo cello (1717–23) retain their place amongst the greatest works ever composed for the instrument.

The standard layout of four-part strings (sometimes with double bass) and continuo was now augmented by a pair of wind instruments, usually oboes or flutes. Until the 1730s the word 'flute' almost always indicated the recorder, but the *flauto traverso* (or 'German flute', in England) was rising in popularity. In Italy, Germany and France the *flauto traverso* became a regular concerto instrument, with notable appearances in Bach's Brandenburg concertos (especially Nos. 4 & 5), Vivaldi's Flute Concerto No. 2 in G minor 'La Notte', and in the solo concertos of Quantz.

The clarinet first appeared in the early 1700s but was not fully appreciated until the second half of the century. Vivaldi may have used the clarinet as early as 1716 in his oratorio *Juditha triumphans*; he certainly employed it in several later concertos. The orchestral use of the 'hunting' horn also took hold during the early 1700s, above all in vocal music. The natural trumpet, used to magnificent *tutti* effect in many grand ceremonial and sacred pieces of the 17th century, enjoyed its hey-day during the late Baroque and early Classical periods. Its golden-age repertory extends from Torelli's solo sonatas through to the concertos of Bach, Telemann and early Classical composers such as Franz Xaver Richter (1709–89) and Leopold Mozart (1719–87). The orchestra itself continued to be directed from within the ensemble, that is, by one or more of the performers. The éra of the professional conductor would not arise until the 19th century.

▲ Early 18th century ensemble (left to right): flute, harpsichord, bassoon, recorder, singer, hautbois (oboe), viola da gamba and violin. From the book *The Modern Musick-Master* or *The Universal Musician*, Peter (Pierre) Prelleur, London 1731.

Vocal music

Cantata

In Italy and most of Catholic Europe, the cantata appeared chiefly as a secular genre. By 1700 Alessandro Scarlatti had more or less standardised its structure, with pairs of recitatives and arias (see also *Chapter 2*). There was now a marked rise in cantatas with *obbligato* (that is, required) instruments. While only a small portion of Scarlatti's 600-plus cantatas demanded *obbligato* instruments, they nevertheless set the bar for the genre, promoting it to a position not far behind opera. Scored for one or two voices, the cantata continued to revolve around themes of love, presented in a pastoral, historical or mythical context.

Inspired by the Italian model, Jean-Baptiste Morin (1677–1745) was one of the first to cultivate the French cantata. Typically sweet and graceful in character, the French examples favour the solo voice and avoid the virtuosic demands of their Italian cousins. Many expand the Italianate structure to three alternating pairs of recitatives and airs. A balanced synthesis of the French and Italian traditions can be found in the compositions of Louis-Nicolas Clérambault, whose dramatic cantata *Orphée* (1710) ranks alongside the greatest and most popular cantatas of the century. Other composers in this field included Elisabeth Jacquet de La Guerre (1665–1729), who also promoted the French sacred cantata, Michel Pignolet Montéclair (1667–1737) and André Cardinal Destouches.

In Protestant Europe, the German lands especially, the sacred cantata began to dominate vernacular church music. Pioneered by composers such as Buxtehude, Philipp Erlebach and Johann Krieger, the German variety rarely used the term 'cantata', and they differed significantly from their Italian predecessors in their more elaborate design (see *Chapter 2*, and *Bach's Cantatas*, p.190). Contributing to the early 18th-century cantata were Friedrich Zachow (1663–1712), Johann Kuhnau and Telemann. With around 1,700 to his credit, Telemann was by far the most prolific cantata composer. Many of his works adopt a structure of aria–recitative–aria, a necessary formal simplification, since in his earlier years at Hamburg (from 1721) he was required to supply two church cantatas every week.

▶ *Charles VI, Holy Roman Emperor* c.1735, by Martin van Meytens the Younger. An extravagant patron of the arts, Charles appointed Fux as his *Hofkapellmeister* in 1715 and sought to make his court music among the most splendid in Europe.

He also produced many secular cantatas, composed for weddings, birthdays and ceremonies, and even one as a tribute to a deceased canary.

Oratorio

The oratorio, with its recitatives, arias, ensemble numbers, choruses and instrumental elements, had become common in Rome and other Italian cities during the second half of the 1600s (see *Chapter 2*). By 1700 it had spread to Lower Austria, France and Spain, and a number of German Protestant territories. Pioneered by Carissimi and Stradella, the oratorio had developed from an intimate genre, performable by less than a dozen musicians, into a musical spectacle that occasionally rivalled staged opera. Indeed, the reforms that improved opera librettos affected oratorio as well: many librettists wrote for both, such as Apostolo Zeno (1669–1750) and Metastasio. Owing to the close relationship between genres, many of the finest opera composers excelled in oratorio composition.

Oratorios were very rarely staged, but just a few, such as Handel's *La resurrezione* (Rome, Easter Sunday 1708), were presented with a painted backdrop and stage decorations. Handel based *La resurrezione*, his first true oratorio, on the larger models of Alessandro Scarlatti, who was himself producing the finest examples in Rome. Scarlatti's dramatic *Il Sedecia, rè di Gerusalemme* (1705) is representative for its concentration on expressive *da capo* arias and recitatives, and allowing just a small role for the chorus (reflecting trends in Italian opera). Enlisting oboes, trumpets, strings, timpani and continuo, it was one of the most lavishly-scored oratorios of the early century. After Scarlatti, the most significant Italian oratorio composer was Leonardo Leo, whose crowning achievements include *La morte d'Abele* (1738), with text by Metastasio. *(margin: Italian model)*

In Vienna the principal exponents of the oratorio were the successive *Kapellmeisters* to the imperial court, the most influential being Johann Joseph Fux (1660–1741) and his Italian deputy, Antonio Caldara (*c.*1671–1736). Their oratorios departed from the Italian model in that they were less concerned with operatic devices. They gave more prominence to the chorus, often employing it polyphonically rather than in a declamatory manner, resulting in a stronger church bias. Zeno and then Metastasio served Vienna as court poets, so texts were of particularly high quality. Caldara was the more prolific, producing over 40 oratorios during his lifetime, with *Il Batista* (with Zeno, 1727) and *La Passione di Gesù Cristo* (with Metastasio, 1730) among his finest examples for the Vienna Hofkapelle. Caldara and Fux were both renowned and fertile composers of masses, vespers and motets, and operas—Caldara wrote around 80. Fux's importance extends to music theory: his *Gradus ad Parnassum*, published in Latin in 1725, is indisputably one of the most influential harmony and composition manuals ever written. *(margin: Vienna)*

The German Protestant centre for oratorio was the same as that for opera, Hamburg, where Keiser, Telemann and Johann Mattheson (1681–1764) dominated the genre. Hasse wrote lyrical Italianate oratorios for Dresden. But the pinnacle of the oratorio tradition materialised elsewhere, thanks to the German-born, Italian-inspired immigrant to England: Handel.

Handel and the English Oratorio

Handel introduced the oratorio to England in 1718 with *Esther*, which he composed for a private performance at the Edgware home of his then patron, the Earl of Carnarvon. It was in this same year and for the same patron, James Brydges (later Duke of Chandos), that he wrote the masque *Acis and Galatea* and completed the 11 so-called *Chandos Anthems*.

Handel thereafter switched his attention to opera; but when he introduced *Esther* to the public with notable success in 1732, he began to consider the commercial potential of the oratorio. As with opera, Handel experienced mixed fortunes with the oratorio, variously owing to his own inspiration, the subject matter, the quality (and celebrity) of the singers, production costs and competing attractions. His second oratorio for London, *Deborah*, failed in 1733 largely because he misjudged his ticket prices. His oratorios for 1739, *Saul* and *Israel in Egypt*, were also financial failures, but *Messiah* (Dublin, 1742) and *Samson* (London, 1743) brought popular success. The most important oratorios to follow were *Joseph and his Brethren, Belshazzar, Judas Maccabaeus, Joshua* and *Alexander Balus* (performed 1744–48), then *Solomon, Susanna, Theodora* and *Jephtha* (performed 1749–52).

Handel's oratorio style

Handel's English oratorios are markedly dissimilar to their Italian cousins. Composed in three 'acts', as Handel called them, they were intended for concert performances in theatres and halls, not for church use. Handel was in fact criticised for presenting biblical subjects in the theatre, since such venues were associated with vulgar plays and hedonistic behaviour. The inclusion of concertos between the acts of the oratorio brought another secular dimension. But Handel can hardly be described as irreligious—he took his faith very seriously. After a London performance of *Messiah* he is recorded to have said 'I should be sorry if I only entertained them. I wished to make them better.'

Handel generally opened his oratorios with a French-style overture and proceeded with recitatives, arias and choruses, admitting the occasional sinfonia to set a scene. His powerful deployment of the chorus, departing from the Italian manner, derived from the English choral tradition. The choruses themselves provide the structural backbone of the oratorio, though they are diverse in function, style and form: witness the atmospheric narration of the plague chorus 'He sent a thick darkness' from *Israel in Egypt*, the rousing double fugue of 'Then shall they know' from *Samson*, and the spectacular pillars of sound in the climactic 'Hallelujah' chorus from *Messiah*. Handel occasionally tipped the balance too far; the original production of *Israel in Egypt* was so dominated by the chorus that the London public rejected it, resulting in a revision of the work with more Italian-style arias. Unfortunately the oratorio still failed to please.

The majority of Handel's oratorios dramatise Old Testament stories. *Israel in Egypt*, *Messiah* and the *Occasional Oratorio* (1746) are unusual for their non-dramatic librettos, while secular works such as *Semele* (1744) and *Hercules* (1745), though similar in form, were never designated as oratorios by Handel. A few oratorios were politically motivated, such as the heroic *Judas Maccabaeus* (1746), commissioned by the Prince of Wales in celebration of the English victory over the Jacobites at Culloden. The jubilant chorus in Act III, 'See, the conquering hero comes', was received with the utmost enthusiasm by contemporary English audiences.

Without question Handel's most successful oratorio was *Messiah*. The writer-librettist Charles Jennens (1700–73) arranged the text, faithfully drawing from both Old and New Testament sources to produce the three-part design. Despite its non-dramatic libretto and few recitatives, the oratorio is highly theatrical in style. *Part One* concerns the prophecy and the coming of the Lord. The French overture reflects the darkness of the world before Jesus Christ, while the ensuing *accompagnatos*, arias and choruses offer prophesies and warnings to mankind. The clouds are fully dispersed by the lively chorus announcing the Saviour's birth, 'For unto us a child is born', and a light pastoral mood ensues. In *Part Two* the tone becomes more serious. One of Handel's longest and most poignant arias, 'He was despised', leads on to a powerful treatment of the Passion story, culminating in the obstinately memorable 'Hallelujah' chorus. *Part Three* opens with one of Handel's most beautiful arias, 'I know that my Redeemer liveth' and draws to a rousing climax with the chorus *Worthy is the Lamb* and the closing *Amen*. Handel intended the work for around 30 voices with an orchestra to match. The popular tradition of using hundreds of voices was established by the 'Noblemen's Concert of Ancient Music' for the centenary celebration of Handel's birth, which by mistake they held one year early, in 1784.

Messiah

J. S. Bach and Lutheran Church Music

J. S. Bach was born into a family already boasting a century-old musical heritage. His father, Johann Ambrosius, was municipal director of music at Eisenach and a court musician, while various brothers, cousins and uncles worked in civic, church and court circles as performers, composers and musical directors. J. S. Bach lost both his parents by the age of ten, and for the next five years he was entrusted to the care of his older brother, Johann Christoph. Much of Bach's musical learning will have been gained though the family (Johann Christoph himself was an organist at Ohrdruf), although his compositional skill probably derived most from the copying out of works by distinguished German composers.

Following church positions at Arnstadt (1703) and Mühlhausen (1707–8), Bach took up an appointment to the Duke of Weimar, whom he served as chamber musician, organist, and later *Konzertmeister*. During this time he immersed himself in organ composition and fully absorbed the Italian style, making keyboard transcriptions of Vivaldi's *L'estro armonico* (Op. 3) and other concertos by prominent Italians.

Weimar

Bach and his first wife, his cousin Maria Barbara, had six children at Weimar, four of whom survived, including the composers Wilhelm Friedemann Bach (1710–84) and Carl Philipp Emanuel Bach (1714–88).

Bach's next move was to the post of *Kapellmeister* at the court of Prince Leopold Anhalt at Cöthen, in 1717. Due to Calvinist restrictions upon worship, Bach's church music activities were modest indeed. A number of secular cantatas date from this time, composed for days of celebration, such as New Year's Day and the Prince's birthday. This period is primarily associated with some of Bach's greatest instrumental masterpieces, including the works for unaccompanied violin, the suites for solo cello, the first volume of the *Well-Tempered Clavier* and the 'Brandenburg' concertos. Widowed in July 1720, Bach married his second wife, Anna Magdalena Wilcke, in late 1721, and she became the mother of composers Johann Christoph Friedrich Bach (1732–95) and Johann Christian Bach (1735–82). Bach had 20 children in all—seven from his first marriage, 13 from the second—though only half survived infancy.

Bach's move to Leipzig in 1723 is the subject of much speculation. The decision was seen as a professional step backward for the composer and the demands were much greater than at any previous post. The most convincing explanation is that the new church position suited his spiritual temperament (Cöthen having made more secular demands), and this is indeed where Bach fulfilled his ambitions to create 'well-ordered church music'. His duties not only involved composing and directing music for the Thomaskirche, but also teaching music and other subjects to the boys of the Thomasschule. He was additionally responsible for music at three other churches, the Nikolaikirche, Matthäeikirche (or Neukirche) and Petrikirche, and he even found time to write secular vocal and instrumental music. The rate of Bach's output matched the increase in demand and of course music for the liturgy was his first concern. As well as weekly cantatas he composed his finest vocal masterpieces, such as the Magnificat in D, the St John and St Matthew Passions and the (probably) unperformed B minor Mass. His Leipzig instrumental output incorporates the four orchestral suites, keyboard concertos, Concerto in D minor for two violins, and *The Art of Fugue*.

Bach's Cantatas

Bach never used the word 'cantata' to describe any of his compositions. He instead used the terms 'stück' or 'der musik' for the astonishing array of pieces we now define as 'church cantatas'. Johann Kuhnau and Telemann composed many more than Bach, but even so he probably wrote around 300. The term 'cantata' is in fact misleading, since Bach's works have little in common with the Italian type. His texts mix Biblical excerpts, chorales and poetic verses, and a variety of musical treatments occur, with recitatives, arias and a wide range of instrumental and vocal ensembles. In some respects they resemble miniature oratorios or passions. Cantatas were regularly performed at the principal Sunday morning service, or Hauptgottesdienst, prior to the sermon, and the text settings related to the Gospel reading.

Bach's cantatas are a veritable treasure-trove, since they contain so much that is wonderful and yet hardly known. Nearly 200 sacred cantatas have survived, spanning more than three decades, while there are 30 or so secular cantatas besides. His early mastery of the genre is evident in the well known *Gottes Zeit ist die allerbest Zeit* (God's time is the very best time, BWV106). Probably a funeral cantata dating from 1707, this intensely moving work follows a multi-sectional format, with opening sonatina, ariosos, arias and choruses, and features obbligato parts for recorders and viola da gamba.

Johann Sebastian Bach (1746) by Elias Gottlob Haussmann. Bach is probably the most universally revered composer of all time.

Owing to the heavy workload at Leipzig, Bach often reworked existing compositions. A good example is *Herz und Mund und Tat und Leben* (Heart and Mouth and Deed and Life, BWV147). Much of this cantata was written years before, at Weimar, where it was performed on the fourth Sunday of Advent in 1716. The earlier version lacked recitatives, but did incorporate the opening chorus and the four arias found in the later version. For Leipzig, Bach added three recitatives and the beloved chorale movement known in English as 'Jesu, joy of man's desiring', which concludes each of the two parts. The first Leipzig performance took place on the Feast of the Visitation (2 July) in 1723, just a few weeks after Bach had taken up his appointment.

Herz und Mund und Tat und Leben

The cantatas vary in scale and in character, since they cover every aspect of the church's year, and occasions both private and public. The cantata *Wir danken dir, Gott, danken dir* (We thank you, God, we thank you, BWV29) was composed to mark the installation of the new Leipzig town council on 27 August 1731. This festive occasion was celebrated with triumphant calls and hallelujahs accompanied by a sumptuous instrumental ensemble, including an obbligato role for the organ. The cantata begins with a sinfonia, a remarkable arrangement of the Prelude from the third unaccompanied Violin Partita in E major (BWV1006). The opening chorus is equally compelling, a motet in *stile antico*, the two clauses of its text (Psalm 75:1) corresponding with the two subjects treated in canon, first separately and then jointly, in the manner of a double fugue. This movement is famous for the two-fold use Bach made of it in the Mass in B minor, appearing in the 'Gratias' and the 'Dona nobis pacem'. Other well-known cantatas include *Christ lag in Todesbanden* (Christ lay in thrall of death, BWV4), an early Easter cantata comprising solos, duets and *cantus firmus* chorales, and *Ich habe genug* (I have enough, BWV82), which follows a more Italianate structure of alternating arias and recitatives.

Wir danken dir, Gott, danken dir

Bach's Passions and the Mass in B minor

According to his obituary, Bach composed five settings of the Passion story. The two surviving complete settings—John and Matthew—are among the finest works ever composed. As with his cantatas, Bach's Passion settings represented an apotheosis of established traditions. Passion settings had been sung since the medieval period, but Bach was particularly influenced by more recent Lutheran traditions that drew the congregation into active participation, joining in with the hymns or chorales. Following the earlier examples of Schütz and Kuhnau, the character at the centre of Bach's drama is really the Evangelist, who narrates the story in dramatic recitative.

Passion format   In the *St John Passion*, as in the *St Matthew*, the story of Christ's arrest, trial, crucifixion and entombment unfolds in four different ways, each equally significant to the whole: the narrative-dramatic, the lyrical, the devotional and the monumental. The narrative is conveyed through recitative, featuring Christ, the Evangelist and minor characters such as Peter and Pilate, as well as the short, lively 'turba' choruses, which evoke the responses of the people. This is therefore the central treatment of the Gospel text. The arias introduce the element of lyricism and contemplation, the personal response to the unfolding story. Bach's approach is the same as that found in the cantatas, with the aria itself preceded by recitative, and a distinctive, generally obbligato, instrumentation giving emphasis to the lyrical melodic line. The chorales, with their subtle harmonisations of existing hymn tunes, create the devotional mood, while the monumental aspect of the *Passion* is found in the large-scale contrapuntal choruses. The Biblical story is at once treated both historically and contemporaneously, since the responses to the text are those of Bach's day—or indeed our own. This central principle, along with the quality of Bach's musical invention, explains the enduring significance of both the *St Matthew* and the *St John Passion*.

Mass in B minor   Such is the stature of the Mass in B minor that it is seems appropriate to speak of it as the summit of Bach's art. But why should he, a Protestant composer working in Protestant Leipzig, want to compose a large-scale setting of the Latin Mass? As a starting point, the opening section, known as the

▶ The Gothic interior of Leipzig's famous Thomaskirche, one of four city churches under Bach's musical directorship. The composer's *St Matthew Passion* was premièred here on Good Friday, 1727.

Missa (comprising the Kyrie and Gloria), was probably intended for Catholic Dresden and completed in 1733. Bach sent a set of handsomely copied parts that year to the new Elector of Saxony, Friedrich August II, presumably in the hope of securing some kind of appointment. The next section of the Mass, known by the formal title *Symbolum Nicenum*, comprised the Credo and was added around 1745, along with the later movements, the Osanna, Benedictus and Agnus Dei. Much of this music was not new, however, since at every stage of his career Bach indulged in the healthy contemporary practice of parody, remoulding existing music in new contexts. Among these movements it seems that only the opening part of the Credo and the Et Incarnatus were actually new. The Sanctus originated in music composed for Christmas 1724, the year after Bach's arrival at Leipzig: Lutheran custom allowed performances using Latin texts on special 'feast days'. The deployment of the music of the Gratias to provide the conclusion for the final section, the Dona Nobis, shows that he certainly intended to develop the whole work as a unified composition.

Bach completed his Mass in B minor less than one year before his death in July 1750. He surely never envisaged a complete performance of the work, knowing that for liturgical and practical reasons it could not be performed as part of a Lutheran or Catholic service. It is not hard to imagine that as one of the most devout composers who ever lived, this was simply his swansong-offering to God Almighty: Himself the 'Creator of things seen and unseen'.

The *galant* style

In the early 18th century the term *galant* came to signify much that was in step with the Enlightenment, such as naturalness and accessibility. In music, the galant was represented by balanced phrasing, simple harmonic schemes and textural clarity, and the true-to-life character types popular in French *opéra-ballet*, and Italian *intermezzi* and *opera buffa*.

In France the galant had associations with courtly elegance and amatory themes. Both commoners and the privileged classes populate Campra's *L'Europe galante*, a modern-day satire of lover stereotypes, and even this early work—from 1697—affords the kind of simple melodies, lucid tonal design and homophonic textures that characterise much of the 18th-century galant aesthetic. Pergolesi's intermezzo *La serva padrona* (referred to earlier) goes further in naturalness, with its no-frills modern setting and common characters.

The melodic quality of galant music was partly enhanced by the avoidance of excessive dissonance. Harmonic movement tended to be slower, so rhythmic impetus from the accompanimental parts was essential. Early evidence of this is apparent in the so-called 'Alberti' figures in keyboard music by the likes of Baldassare Galuppi and of course from the composer who gave his name to the device, Domenico Alberti (1710–40). In galant orchestral music—concertos and symphonies—outer movements are typically driven with fast, staccato chords, while the slow movements are lightly contrapuntal at most, taking care to emphasise clear periodic phrasing.

The Early Symphony

The rising importance of the orchestra encouraged the expansion of instrumental genres. The modern symphony seems to have evolved primarily from the operatic sinfonia, which followed a three-movement structure of fast–slow–fast. However, the impact of the mature *concerto grosso*, as promoted by Vivaldi, Tartini and others, should not be dismissed. The symphony's most important pioneer was Giovanni Battista Sammartini (*c.*1700–75), who was producing three-movement examples by 1730. His early string symphonies, such as Symphony in C minor (JC. 9) and Symphony in D major (JC. 16), feature lively rhythms, clear homophonic textures, slow harmonic pacing and periodic phrasing, all quintessential attributes of the galant style. Also a composer of operas and concertos, Sammartini was influential in Italy and beyond. He made a profound impression on the great Classical opera reformer Christoph W. Gluck (1714–87), who even 'borrowed' some of Sammartini's music in his early theatrical works.

In 1740 the Austrian composer Matthias Monn (1717–50) introduced a four-movement symphony with a third movement minuet, though his example was not immediately emulated. The following year saw Antonio Brioschi's *XII Sonate*, Op. 1, the earliest known collection of symphonies. From this point both Italian and German composers, including

Giovanni Battista Sammartini

▼ *La Gamme d'Amour (The Scale of Love)* by Antoine Watteau, *c.*1717. The Frenchman pioneered the idealised 'fêtes galante' painting style, promoting simplicity, common pleasures, elegance, intimacy, romance, and harmony with nature.

Franz Xaver Richter (1709–89) and Johann Stamitz (1717–57), began to promote the symphony in Germany and France. By the mid-century the symphony had been widely disseminated, though it would remain subordinate to the more sophisticated and beloved concerto until the 1790s.

C. P. E. Bach and the *Empfindsamer Stil*

Distinctions such as Baroque and galant are broad and some composers succeeded without adhering to a single style. J. S. Bach's most gifted son, Carl Philipp Emanuel Bach, is a prime example with his high-Baroque background and contrapuntal skill, combined with the modern *empfindsamer stil*. This newer 'sensitive' or 'sentimental' style was in some ways similar to the galant manner, though it was less ornate and courtly, and melodically more spontaneous. The most striking aspect of the *empfindsamer stil* was its accommodation of forcefully contrasting emotions within a single movement, abjuring the Baroque ideal of 'unity of affect'. Carl Bach was much the ground-breaker in this respect. His solo keyboard music, for instance the *Prussian* and *Württemberg* sonatas (1742/44), offers the most compelling examples of the approach, but it is also skillfully handled in larger-scale works like the harpsichord concertos in G major (Wq. 9, *c.*1742) and D major (Wq. 27, 1750). In many ways Carl Bach represents an ideal musical character for the mid-18th century; a Janus-like figure who combines old learned techniques with the pre-Classical style, while at the same time relishing dynamic, impulsive methods that even presage the unbridled passion of Romanticism.

Chronology
1700–1749

In Venice **Albinoni** publishes his *Sinfonie e concerti a cinque* (Op. 2), comprising six *sinfonie* and six *concerti* for strings and continuo.

John Blow publishes an anthology of his solo and chamber vocal music, entitled *Amphion Anglicus*. This year he becomes Composer to the Chapel Royal, a post created specifically for him, and composes his final ode for St Cecilia's Day.

Around this time **Bartolomeo Cristofori**, keyboard builder to the Medicis in Florence, invents a *gravicembalo col piano e forte* (harpsichord with soft and loud) incorporating hammer-action and dampers to replace the plucked mechanism of the traditional harpsichord. Despite the instrument's dynamic flexibility, its volume does not exceed that of a large harpsichord. The pianoforte prototype fails to make any immediate impact.

Kuhnau publishes six programmatic keyboard sonatas on Old Testament stories (*Biblische Historien*), including his most popular work, *The Combat Between David and Goliath*. A veritable polymath—composer, music theorist, lawyer, linguist and translator—Kuhnau also publishes his satirical novel, *Der musicalische Quacksalber* (The Musical Charlatan), commenting on superficiality in contemporary music.

Telemann, aged 19, hears the prodigious musical talent of **Handel**, aged 15, as he passes through Halle on his way to study law at Leipzig.

1 January Corelli (right) dedicates his immensely influential 12 Sonatas Op. 5 to the arts patron Sofia Carlotta

of Brandenburg. Scored for violin and violone/harpsichord and published in Rome, the *duo* collection will be reprinted around 50 times during the course of the 18th century. This year Corelli becomes orchestral leader at the Congregazione di Santa Cecilia in Rome.

16 January Austrian composer **Antonio Draghi**, *Kapellmeister* to Emperor Leopold I in Vienna, dies aged 65.

March A contest is announced in London to determine the leading stage-music composer in England. Each applicant is required to set William Congreve's masque *The Judgment of Paris*. (See also 1701.)

April J. S. Bach, aged 15, becomes a member of the *Mettenchor* (Matins choir) at St Michael in Lüneburg. He continues his schooling at the affiliated Michaelisschule.

1 April Italian composer **Marc'Antonio Ziani** becomes deputy *Hofkapellmeister* at the imperial court in Vienna.

30 June John Eccles is appointed Master of the King's Music.

October The Theatre Royal in Covent Garden advertises in the *London Gazette* for the lost score of Purcell's *Fairy Queen*, concluding: '… whosoever brings the said score or a copy thereof, to Mr Zackary Baggs, Treasurer of the said Theatre, shall have 20 guineas'.

1700 Second Treaty of Partition fails to settle Spanish succession: King Carlos II names Philippe of Anjou, grandson of Louis XIV (Fr), his sole heir and dies six weeks later; Spain accepts Philippe as Felipe V • Russia ends war with Turkey • Start of Great Northern War: Russia, Poland and Denmark attack Sweden, in effort to break Swedish Baltic supremacy

• Mathematician Baron Gottfried von Leibnitz becomes first president of Prussian Academy of Science • Pope Innocent XII dies; is succeeded by Clement XI • American diarist and judge Samuel Sewall: *The Selling of Joseph*, first strong American protest against slavery

The 16-year-old **Bach**, hungry and virtually penniless, stops at an inn on his return to Lüneburg. A diner throws two heads of herring out of a window. Picking them up for a nibble, Bach finds a Danish ducat in the mouth of each fish, the equivalent of six months' stipend for a chorister.

Sébastien de Brossard publishes the first version of his *Dictionnaire de musique*, the earliest French language music dictionary.

Fux goes to print with his *Concentus musico-instrumentalis*, a varied collection of suites for forces ranging from chamber duet up to full orchestra

Twelve *concerti grossi* by **Muffat** are published in Passau.

Composer **Giovanni Battista Sammartini** is born around this time, probably in Milan.

Alessandro Scarlatti arranges for his 15-year-old son, **Domenico**, to take the position of organist and composer at the royal chapel in Naples.

April Kuhnau is made *Kantor* of the Thomaskirche in Leipzig.

March–May Four competition finalists present their settings of William Congreve's masque *The Judgment of Paris* at London's Dorset Garden Theatre (see also 1700). The little-known **John Weldon** wins the first prize of 100 guineas, followed (in order) by **John Eccles**, **Daniel Purcell** and the Moravian **Gottfried Finger**. Incredulous of the result, Finger leaves the country in protest.

Autumn Telemann arrives in Leipzig to study law, but very quickly becomes diverted into the city's musical life.

Bach wins the post of organist at the Jacobikirche, Sangerhausen, but to no avail. The Duke of Weissenfels overrules the church's decision, favouring instead a slightly older applicant, **J. A. Kobelius**.

French composer and flautist **Michel de La Barre** (left, turning page) publishes his Op. 4 suites for flute and continuo, the earliest known works of their kind.

Caldara flees with Duke Gonzaga's court during the War of the Spanish Succession as Habsburg forces advance on Mantua.

Johann C. F. Fischer publishes 20 preludes and fugues in 18 different keys in his *Ariadne musica*. Influenced by this work, **Bach** will later incorporate some of Fischer's themes into the *Well-Tempered Clavier* (1722).

In Leipzig **Telemann** establishes a student *collegium musicum* to provide both public and private concerts, and also church music. Regularly composing for the city's Thomaskirche and Nikolaikirche, Telemann also becomes musical director of the Leipzig Opera.

February/March Handel begins studying law at the University of Halle, and also takes the post of organist at the city's Calvinist Domkirche.

7 November Campra triumphs with *Tancrède* at the Théâtre du Palais-Royal in Paris. This *tragédie en musique* becomes one of his most frequently performed operas.

1701 English parliament passes Act of Settlement: sovereigns must be Protestants • Exiled ex-king James II dies • War of Spanish Succession begins • Elector Frederick III of Brandenburg adopts title of King Frederick I of Prussia • English agricultural reformer Jethro Tull devises a horse-drawn seed drill • Yale College established at New Haven

1702 William III dies; is succeeded in Britain and Ireland by his sister-in-law Anne, younger daughter of James II • In War of Spanish Succession, England declares war on France • Journalist Daniel Defoe (Eng): pamphlet *The Shortest Way with the Dissenters*, lampooning the absurdity of religious intolerance; it results in his imprisonment

German composer **Carl Heinrich Graun** is born in Wahrenbrück around this time.

Handel throws in the towel on his legal studies and moves to Hamburg, where he takes a position of violinist at the opera house. There he begins his friendship with **Johann Mattheson**.

German composer and organist **Georg Motz** publishes *The Defence of Church Music*, a strong counter-critique to Christian Gerber's disapproval of music in the Lutheran service.

January J. S. Bach becomes a court violinist to Duke Johann Ernst of Weimar, but soon leaves to take up the post of organist at the Neue Kirche in Arnstadt.

January In Rome **Alessandro Scarlatti** (below) becomes assistant *maestro di cappella* at the Oratorio di San Filippo Neri, Chiesa Nuova. At the end of this year he takes a second similar position at the church of Santa Maria Maggiore. Accepting opera commissions outside Rome from Ferdinando de' Medici (such as *Arminio*, this year) and composing numerous secular cantatas besides, Scarlatti frequently fails to deliver on all of his church duties.

23 March Vivaldi is ordained a priest.

31 March Johann Christoph Bach, composer, organist, first cousin once removed of **J. S. Bach** and up to this point the most renowned member of the family, dies in Eisenach, aged 60.

April Alessandro Scarlatti's oratorio *L'assunzione della Beata Vergine Maria*, with text by (Cardinal) **Pietro Ottoboni**, is first performed in Rome.

26 May Samuel Pepys, diarist and musical commentator, dies in London, aged 70.

August Handel accompanies **Mattheson** on a trip to Lübeck to assess the prospects for employment at the Marienkirche. The post of organist, currently held by the renowned but ageing **Buxtehude**, is an attractive one. Possibly less attractive is the requirement that the successful applicant should marry his predecessor's eldest available daughter. Suffice to note that Handel and Mattheson flee back to Hamburg.

September Vivaldi becomes *maestro di violino* at the *Ospedale della Pietà*, a school for orphaned and illegitimate girls, in Venice. The *Pietà* enjoys prominent status in Venice, with regular concerts and services attended by resident and visiting nobility.

14 October *Le Carnaval et la Folie*, a *comédie lyrique* by **André Cardinal Destouches**, premières with notable success at Fontainebleau.

30 November Nicolas de Grigny, distinguished French organist-composer, dies aged 31 in Reims, where he had been serving as cathedral organist.

November–December In Naples the 18-year-old **Domenico Scarlatti** (son of **Alessandro**) stages his first two operas, *L'Ottavia ristituita al trono* and *Il Giustino*, without much success.

1703 War Of Spanish Succession continues: John Churchill (now Duke of Marlborough) captures Bonn and Limburg; Archduke Karl, German claimant to Spanish throne, invades Catalonia and proclaims himself Carlos III of Spain; Savoy, France's ally, changes sides and joins the Grand Alliance headed by the Holy Roman Empire • Hungarians begin revolt against Austrian rule • In Great Northern War, Swedes defeat Saxons at Pultusk, Saxony • Tsar Petr I, the Great (Russ), founds the city of St Petersburg • A powerful earthquake rocks Tokyo, killing 100,000 people • Scientist Isaac Newton (Eng) becomes President of the Royal Society

François Duval publishes the earliest collection of French violin sonatas in *Sonates et autres pieces*.

Erlebach completes his *Gott geheiligte Sing-Stunde*, comprising 12 cantatas for voices and small ensemble.

23 February German composer **Georg Muffat** dies in Passau, aged 50.

24 February Leading French composer **Marc-Antoine Charpentier** dies in Paris, aged about 60.

May Jeremiah Clarke and **William Croft** take joint positions as organists of at the Chapel Royal.

3 May Heinrich von Biber, Austrian composer and the 17th century's foremost violin virtuoso, dies in Salzburg, aged 59.

5 December Mattheson takes the suicidal part of Mark Antony in his own opera *Cleopatra*, in Hamburg. On completing the role (in the third act) he exits the stage to replace his good friend **Handel** at the harpsichord, to further demonstrate his manifold talents. Handel refuses to budge and an almighty squabble breaks out. Goaded by audience members, the two composers leave the theatre to duel with swords. Mattheson lunges for the kill, only to see his weapon break on one of Handel's metal coat buttons. They immediately end their combat, reconcile and become, in Mattheson's words, 'better friends than ever'.

From an 18th-century manual on duelling.

Vivaldi publishes 12 trio sonatas as his Op. 1, in Venice.

8 January Handel's first opera *Almira* is introduced in Hamburg with great success, achieving 20 repeat performances. His second opera, *Nero*, staged the following month, survives just three performances.

16 January Thomas Clayton's *Arsinoe, Queen of Cyprus*, premièred at London's Drury Lane Theatre, becomes the first full-length, all-sung English opera in the Italian style. Despite its critics, the production runs for two seasons.

24 January Carlo Broschi (later the castrato **Farinelli**) is born in Andria, Apulia.

9 April Jakob Greber's pastoral *Gli amori d'Ergasto* (The Loves of Ergasto) inaugurates the Queen's Theatre in the Haymarket, London. It is the first Italian-sung opera performed in England.

June Telemann leaves Leipzig to become *Kapellmeister* to the Count of Promnitz in Sorau, Lower Lusatia.

August Bach, aged 20, is attacked by one of his students, Geyersbach, having called the younger man a 'nanny-goat bassoonist'. Bach draws a dagger to defend himself, while other students intervene to stop the fight. Bach and Geyersbach are admonished in court.

5 August Reinhard Keiser's opera *Octavia* premières in Hamburg.

October Bach walks some 260 miles to Lübeck to hear the organ playing of **Buxtehude**, having requested a month's leave from Arnstadt. To the annoyance of the church council, he does not return for nearly four months.

1704 In the war of the Spanish Succession, Austrians and English defeat French Bavarian force at Blenheim and knock Bavaria out of the war; English fleet captures Gibraltar from Spain • Isaac Newton (Eng) publishes *Opticks*, propounding the corpuscular theory of light and explaining his 'Method of Fluxions' (calculus)

1705 War of Spanish Succession continues; on behalf of Archduke Karl, a British force captures Barcelona; much of eastern Spain accepts Karl as King Carlos III; Austrians begin pushing French out of Savoy • An Ottoman officer, Hussein bin Ali, frees city of Tunis from Turkish rule and founds the Husseinite dynasty

John Eccles composes the music for Granville's semi-opera *The British Enchanters*. Despite some notable success, the genre of semi-opera (incorporating both sung and spoken roles) faces oblivion owing to a decree by the Lord Chamberlain that confines vocal music and spoken dialogue to separate theatres.

Michelangelo Faggioli, aged about 40, composes the music for *La Cilla*, the first comic opera in Neapolitan dialect.

Jean-Baptiste Morin promotes an emerging genre in his first book of *Cantates françoises* (French Cantatas).

Now in Paris, the 23-year-old **Rameau** publishes his *Premier livre de pieces de clavecin*. He also fills organ posts at the Jesuit Collège Louis-le-Grand and the Pères de la Merci.

Vivaldi gives up saying mass around this time, apparently due to his chronic respiratory problems. Some maintain that he cannot survive the duration of a mass without needing to jot down musical ideas.

February The Arnstadt Church council rebukes **Bach**, aged 20, for having overstayed his leave of absence by several months (see 1705). Shortly afterwards he is criticised over his complex chorale accompaniments. Yet more castigation follows concerning his inability to control his choirboys. By the end of this year he is looking elsewhere for employment.

February Telemann flees Sorau before the advancing army of King Charles XII of Sweden (Great Northern War, 1700–21). Finding refuge in Frankfurt an der Oder, the composer returns to Sorau five months later.

9 March Johann Pachelbel, one of Germany's leading composers and organists, is buried in Nuremburg, aged 52.

23 March A. Scarlatti's politically-charged oratorio *Il Sedecia, rè di Gerusalemme* (revised from 1705) presents the dramatic story of King Nebuchadnezzar at the Seminario Romano. The work comprises arias, recitatives and just one chorus.

30 March In London the vogue for Italian-style opera begins to take hold with an English version of **Bononcini**'s *Il trionfo di Camilla*, which receives the first of many performances at the Drury Lane Theatre (below). For the time being the internationally famous Italian composer resists enticements to visit England.

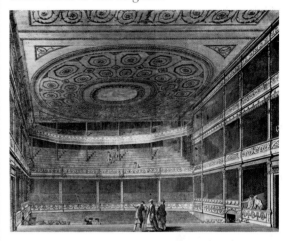

26 April Composers **Corelli**, **A. Scarlatti** and **Pasquini** are admitted to the Arcadian Academy in Rome.

Summer/Autumn Handel, aged 21, arrives in Florence at the invitation of Prince Gian Gastone de' Medici.

18 October Italian opera composer **Baldassare Galuppi** is born in Burano, outside Venice.

26 October German composer, organist and theorist **Andreas Werckmeister** dies in Halberstadt, aged 60.

- -

1706 In War of Spanish Succession, Portuguese invade Spain, capturing Madrid and holding it for four months before being driven out: Duke of Marlborough (Eng) defeats Duc de Villeroi's French force at Battle of Ramillies; Austrians defeat French at Turin • In Great Northern War, Swedes invade and defeat Saxony • Daniel Defoe (Eng): ghost story *True Relation of the Apparition of one Mrs Veal* • George Farquhar (Ire): comedy *The Recruiting Officer* • English deist Matthew Tindal publishes *Rights of the Christian Church Asserted*; it provokes a storm of protest

Isaac Watts publishes *Hymns and Spiritual Songs*, his collection including 'When I survey the wondrous cross'.

5 January Alessandro Scarlatti's opera *Il Mitridate Eupatore* premières at the Teatro San Giovanni Grisostomo, Venice, but fails to make an impression. Dismissed as too serious and musically complex, it is later recognised as one of Scarlatti's finest works.

April Bach plays the organ at St Blasius, Mühlhausen, impressing the church council who agree unanimously to offer him the post of organist. He leaves his job at Arnstadt during the summer.

May Handel, now in Rome, begins work on his first oratorio, *Il trionfo del Tempo e del Disinganno* (The Triumph of Time and Disenchantment), to a text by **Cardinal Pamphili**. While in Rome he meets **Corelli** and **Alessandro Scarlatti**.

9 May The renowned composer and organist **Dieterich Buxtehude** dies in Lübeck, aged about 70.

Autumn Handel, having returned to Florence, stages his Italian opera *Rodrigo*. Commissioned by Ferdinando de' Medici, the work is well received.

17 October Bach marries Maria Barbara Bach, his second cousin.

1 December English composer and organist **Jeremiah Clarke**, aged 33, shoots himself in a case of unrequited love for a beautiful woman of higher social standing. He is buried in the crypt of the nearly-complete St Paul's Cathedral.

Elisabeth Jacquet (**de la Guerre**) publishes her first book of French cantatas, all based on stories from the Old Testament.

Domenico Scarlatti and **Handel**, both aged 23, meet in Venice and become good friends. This year Scarlatti moves to Rome and takes up as *maestro di cappella* to the exiled Queen of Poland, Maria Casimira.

4 February Bach's Cantata No. 71 (*Gott ist mein König*) is performed to mark the inauguration of the new town council in Mühlhausen.

8 April (Easter Sunday): **Handel** displays his masterful flair for oratorio with *La resurrezione*, premièred at the Bonelli Palace in Rome. Inspired by the examples of Alessandro Scarlatti, the sacred work features backdrop scenery and a decorated stage to enhance the Easter drama. **Corelli** is enlisted to lead an orchestra of around 45 players.

Summer Duke Wilhelm Ernst hears the organ playing of **Bach** and offers him the post of court organist at Weimar. Bach resigns from Mühlhausen.

1 October John Blow (left) dies in Westminster, aged about 59. He is buried in the Abbey, close to Purcell. **William Croft** succeeds Blow as Master of the Children of the Chapel Royal and organist at the Abbey.

December Telemann is appointed *Konzertmeister* at the court of Duke Johann Wilhelm of Saxe-Eisenach.

29 December Bach baptises the first of his 20 children, Catharina Dorothea.

1707 England and Scotland are united under the name of Great Britain, with a single parliament and flag • War of Spanish Succession continues: Spaniards defeat Portuguese at Almanza; Austrians occupy Naples • Mogul emperor Aurangzeb, dies in India after 58 years' reign; his empire begins rapidly to disintegrate

1708 James Edward Stuart, 'Old Pretender', lands with an army in Scotland, but returns to France after defeat of a supporting French fleet by a British fleet • In Great Northern War, Karl XII (Swe), allied with Cossack leader Ivan Mazepa, advances in Russia • Herman Boerhaave (Neth): *Institutiones medicae*, a pioneering physiology textbook

Cardinal Ottoboni arranges a musical contest between **Handel** and **Domenico Scarlatti** at his palace in Rome. The two keyboard virtuosos are more or less equally matched on the harpsichord, although Scarlatti himself declares Handel hands-down winner on the organ.

Having left meagre-salaried positions in Rome, **Alessandro Scarlatti** resumes his old post as maestro di cappella at Naples.

Vivaldi publishes his Op. 2 violin sonatas. He loses his post at the Pietà this year, possibly due to financial cutbacks. He is reinstated two years later.

17 January **Agostino Steffani**'s opera *Tassilone* is staged in Düsseldorf. Later this year the Holy See appoints the composer and priest as vicar apostolic of North Germany.

8 February **Giuseppe Torelli** dies in Bologna, aged 50. His influential Op. 8 *concerti grossi* and solo violin concertos are published later this year. Including the popular *Christmas Eve Concerto* (No. 6), the collection promotes the three-movement fast–slow–fast plan, along with ritornello design and clear, uncomplicated textures.

August **Telemann** gains swift promotion to *Kapellmeister* at Eisenach. Required to manage a huge workload, he remains in post for three years.

22 November Bohemian composer and violinist **František (Franz) Benda** is born in Staré Benátky.

1 December German composer **Franz Xaver Richter** is born in Holleschau, Moravia.

26 December **Handel** triumphs in Venice with his greatest opera to date, the satirical *Agrippina*. With more than 20 repeat performances to audiences of Venetians, foreign visitors and dignitaries, his success gains him renown throughout Europe.

French composer and court organist **Louis-Nicolas Clérambault** publishes his first volume of *Cantates françoises*. The collection includes the dramatic cantata *Orphée*, one of the most celebrated cantatas of the 18th century.

Around this time **Keiser** composes *Der hochmütige, gestürzte und wieder erhabene Croesus* (The Proud, Overthrown and Again Exalted Croesus), one of his best-known operas, for Hamburg.

Giulio Taglietti publishes his *Concerti a cinque*, Op. 8, in Venice. Included in the set are the first concertos for four violins, predating Vivaldi's more famous examples by one year.

Sylvius Leopold Weiss, composer and lutenist, enters the service of Prince Alexander Sobiesky in Rome. The prince resides with his mother, the exiled Polish Queen, Maria Casimira.

4 January Composer **Giovanni Battista Pergolesi** is born in Jesi, Italy.

12 March Composer **Thomas Arne**, son of an upholsterer, is born in Covent Garden, London.

16 June Having returned to Germany from Italy, **Handel** is appointed *Kapellmeister* to the Elector of Hanover, George Leopold, future King of England. The composer is granted extended leave the following month to visit Düsseldorf and London.

17 June **Campra**'s *Les fêtes vénitiennes*, the first comic *opéra-ballet*, is performed in Paris.

22 November **Wilhelm Friedemann Bach**, first son of **J. S. Bach**, is born in Weimar.

22 November Italian composer and keyboard virtuoso **Bernardo Pasquini** dies in Rome, aged 72. Medallions bearing his portrait are struck in his honour.

1709 War of Spanish Succession continues • In Great Northern War, Russians crush Swedes at Poltava (Russ) and become the chief northern power • Russia, Saxony and Denmark form anti-Swedish coalition • Afghan state wins independence from Persia • Johann Farina (It) establishes his Eau de Cologne factory (in Cologne)

1710 In War of Spanish Succession, armies of the Grand Alliance capture Mons and Douai; French forces crush the alliance in Spain, Archduke Karl is expelled from Madrid, and Felipe V is re-established as king of Spain • British troops capture Port Royal from the French • Building of St Paul's Cathedral in London is completed

Around this time **Francesco Geminiani** suffers a humiliating demotion in Naples: he loses his position of leader of the opera orchestra and is forced into the viola section. Apparently he has trouble playing in time.

Michel Montéclair publishes the first French violin tutor, *Méthode facile pour apprendre à jouer du violon*.

24 February Handel and librettist **Giacomo Rossi** score an instant hit with the Italian-sung opera *Rinaldo*, premièred at the Queen's Theatre in London. Composed in just two weeks with a mixture of recycled material and new music, it is the earliest surviving Italian opera written specifically for the English stage.

As I was walking the streets about a fortnight ago, I saw an ordinary fellow carrying a cage full of little birds upon his shoulder; and as I was wondering with my self what use he would put them to, he was met very luckily by an acquaintance, who had the same curiosity. Upon his asking him what he had upon his shoulder, he told him that he had been buying sparrows for the opera. 'Sparrows for the opera', says his friend, licking his lips, 'what, are they to be roasted?' 'No, no,' says the other, 'they are to enter towards the end of the first act, and to fly about the stage.

6 March Joseph Addison (right) writing in the newly-founded *Spectator* about **Handel**'s opera *Rinaldo*.

1 May Manuel de Zumaya's opera *La Partenope* is given at the vice-regal palace in Mexico City. It is the earliest-known opera scored by a composer born in the Americas.

June Handel leaves England and returns (via Düsseldorf) to his post at the electoral court in Hanover.

September Vivaldi is reinstated to his post of violin master at the Pietà in Venice. This year sees the publication of his enormously influential *L'estro armonico* (Harmonic Inspiration, Op. 3), concertos for one, two and four violins. Printed in Amsterdam by Étienne Roger, the set is soon circulated throughout Europe, bringing the composer great fame and respect. Among Vivaldi's admirers is **Bach**, who transcribes a number of the pieces for the harpsichord and organ.

11 September Composer **William Boyce** is baptised in London.

17 September Austrian composer **Ignaz Holzbauer** is born in Vienna.

25 December French composer and violinist **Jean-Joseph Cassanéa de Mondonville** is baptised in Narbonne.

1711 Holy Roman Emperor Josef I dies; is succeeded by his brother, Karl VI • In Britain, the Duke of Marlborough's Tory enemies dismiss him and appoint the Duke of Ormonde commander-in-chief of the British army • The Grand Alliance ends: negotiations begin to end the War of Spanish Succession • Hungarian war of independence ends with Peace Of Szatmár • Turks surround the army of Petr I (Russ) forcing the Treaty of Pruth: the town of Azov is returned to Turkey • Queen Anne (UK) founds Ascot races • Alexander Pope (Eng): *An Essay on Criticism*

Around this time **Albinoni** publishes his *Trattenimenti armonici per camera* Op. 6, 12 trio sonatas for violin, bass (cello) and continuo.

Elector George of Hanover permits **Handel** to make a second trip to England, on condition that he will 'return within a reasonable time'. Handel never returns.

In Paris **Giovanni Piani** publishes his Op. 1 collection of violin and flute sonatas. He gives detailed instructions for the pieces, including tempo, bowing, and early examples of hairpin markings for *crescendo* and *diminuendo*.

1 January Ziani is promoted as *Hofkapellmeister* to the court of Emperor Charles VI in Vienna.

17 January Composer and organist **John Stanley** is born in London. He loses most of his sight at the age of two (see 1714).

26 January Giacomo Puccini, first of a succession of Puccini composers and great-great-grandfather of Giacomo Antonio Puccini, is baptised in Lucca.

18 March Having left Eisenach, **Telemann** arrives in Frankfurt to take up the position of musical director to the city and two of its main churches, the Barefoot Monks and St Catherine.

28 June Swiss philosopher and composer **Jean-Jacques Rousseau** is born in Geneva.

22 November Handel's *Il pastor fido* (The Faithful Shepherd), with libretto by **Giacomo Rossi**, opens at the Queen's Theatre in London. The composer's second opera for the English stage receives a lukewarm reception, lacking the heroism and spectacle of *Rinaldo* (1711).

24 December Caldara's commanding *Vaticini di pace* (Prophecies of Peace), a 'Christmas Cantata' for four voices, strings & continuo, is first performed at the Palazzo Bonelli in Rome.

Couperin publishes the first of four volumes of programmatic and descriptive harpsichord music in *Pièces de clavecin*.

The 18-year-old Earl of Burlington offers **Handel** residency at his house in Piccadilly, London. The composer will live there for three years.

Around this time **Giuseppe Tartini** composes his famous *Devil's Trill Sonata*, allegedly inspired by a dream in which the Devil performed on his violin with astonishing skill and elegance.

8 January Influential Italian composer **Arcangelo Corelli** dies in Rome, aged 59.

10 January Handel returns to heroism and spectacle in his opera *Teseo*, premièred at the Queen's Theatre, London. Following the second performance the theatre manager makes off with all the takings, escaping to Italy. With the cast unpaid, the impresario John Heidegger steps in and rescues the production. *Teseo* triumphs and restores Handel to his former glory.

May Vivaldi's earliest known opera, *Ottone in villa* (Otho in the Country), enjoys success in Vicenza. This year marks the completion of the composer's Op. 4 set of concertos, *La stravaganza* (The Extravagance).

7 July Handel's first English sacred works, a Te Deum and Jubilate, are introduced at St Paul's Cathedral in celebration the Peace of Utrecht. By this time Handel has been officially fired from his post in Hanover.

November Domenico Scarlatti is appointed assistant *maestro di cappella* at St Peter's, Rome.

28 December Queen Anne (right) grants **Handel** a lifetime yearly pension of £200.

1712 Felipe V (Sp), grandson of French king Louis XIV, is persuaded to renounce his claims to succeed to the French throne • St Petersburg becomes Russia's capital • Alexander Pope (Eng): poem *The Rape of the Lock* • Britain carries out last execution for witchcraft • Giuseppe Maria Crespi (It) paints the *Seven Sacraments*

1713 Treaty of Utrecht ends War of Spanish Succession; Felipe V acknowledged as king of Spain, provided French and Spanish crowns stay separate • In Great Northern War, Swedes invade Denmark • Russo-Turkish Peace of Adrianople is signed • Anthony Collins (Eng): *A Discourse of Free-Thinking* • Richard Steele (Ire) founds the periodical *The Guardian*

Corelli's Op. 6 collection of 12 *concerti grossi*, including the stunning *Christmas Concerto* (No. 8), is published in Amsterdam, a year after the composer's death. Some of the concertos may have been conceived over 30 years previously.

Arriving from Naples, the violinist-composer **Francesco Geminiani** begins a new life in London. He secures the lasting patronage of William Capel, 3rd Earl of Essex.

Mattheson issues some spirited keyboard music in his *Pièces de clavecin en deux volumes*.

John Stanley, aged two, stumbles holding a china basin that shatters in his face as he falls on a marble hearth. The accident leaves the future composer and organist clinically blind for life.

2 March Bach is promoted to the post of *Konzertmeister* to the Duke of Weimar. This year he begins to compose his first cycle of sacred cantatas. He is also at work on *Das Orgel-Büchlein* (The Little Organ Book), most of which is completed by the following year.

8 March J. S. Bach's second surviving son, **Carl Philipp Emanuel**, is born in Weimar. **Telemann** becomes his godfather.

17 April Philipp Erlebach, prolific German composer of church cantatas, dies in Rudolstadt, Thuringia, aged 56.

2 July Opera composer **Christoph Willibald Gluck** is born in Erasbach, Upper Austria.

28 August Three years after the death of his first wife, **Telemann**, aged 33, marries Maria Catharina

Textor, aged 16. The composer's second marriage produces nine children, but ultimately comes to a sorry end (see 1736).

10 September Composer **Niccolò Jommelli** is born in Aversa, near Naples.

26 September At St James's Palace, London (below), a Te Deum by **Handel** is performed in the presence of King George I—Handel's former employer at the electoral court of Hanover.

Procession of King George I to St James's Palace, 20 September

November Vivaldi's second opera, *Orlando finto pazzo* (Orlando Feigns Madness), struggles at the Teatro San Angelo, Venice.

December Domenico Scarlatti is promoted to *maestro di cappella* at St Peter's, Rome.

December Jean-Joseph Mouret's *Le mariage de Ragonde et de Colin*, the first *comédie lyrique*, premières at Sceaux, Paris.

1714 Queen Anne (UK) dies; is succeeded by the Elector Georg of Hanover, as George I • Treaties of Rastatt and Baden end remainder of War of Spanish Succession; Austria secures the Spanish Netherlands and keeps Milan, Naples and Sardinia • Venice and Turkey are at war • Russians defeat Swedes at Storkyro and gain control of Finland • Physicist Gabriel Fahrenheit (Ger) develops a mercury thermometer • English agricultural reformer Jethro Tull introduces a horse-drawn hoe • King Felipe V bans use of the Catalan language in Spain • Daniel Defoe (Eng): *A General History of Trade*

The annual Three Choirs Festival, held alternately in the cathedrals of Gloucester, Worcester and Hereford, is established around this time.

Virtuoso violinist **Geminiani** makes his court début before King George I, with **Handel** accompanying him on the harpsichord.

22 January On the death of **Marc'Antonio Ziani**, **Fux** is promoted to *Kapellmeister* at the court of Charles VI in Vienna.

29 January Composer **Georg Christoph Wagenseil** is born in Vienna.

16 February Alessandro Scarlatti presents *Il Tigrane*, one of his most respected operas, at the court theatre of San Bartolomeo, Naples.

21 April Bach's joyous cantata *Der Himmel lacht! Die Erde jubilieret* (Heaven laughs! The Earth rejoices) receives a festive Easter Day performance at Weimar.

May Giuseppe Orlandini's intermezzo *Bacocco e Serpilla* is first performed in Verona. Under this and alternative titles (with revisions by other composers), it becomes one of the most often performed musical dramas of the 18th century.

25 May Handel introduces his opera *Amadigi di Gaula* at the King's Theatre (formerly the Queen's Theatre) in London. Over the next five years he will write no new operas, concentrating instead on sacred and instrumental music.

June The Pietà governors reward **Vivaldi** with a bonus of 50 ducats for a steady stream of sacred works supplied over the last two years. He has compensated for the absence of the former choirmaster, **Francesco Gasparini**, who took leave in 1713 and never returned.

1 October Fux's one-act *Orfeo ed Euridice* celebrates the birthday of Charles VI, in Vienna.

Couperin publishes his *L'art de toucher le clavecin* (The Art of Playing the Harpsichord). This important keyboard treatise includes useful tips such as: 'One can correct facial grimaces by placing a mirror on the reading desk of the spinet or harpsichord.' It also offers historically intriguing insights into recommended performance manners:

… one should look at the audience, if there is any, as if one were occupied with nothing else.

Geminiani publishes his Corelli-influenced Op. 1 violin sonatas in London.

Johann Christoph Schmidt uproots from Ansbach to join **Handel** in London, where he becomes the composer's his life-long assistant.

The Amsterdam publisher Étienne Roger takes receipt of six sonatas and six concertos commissioned from **Vivaldi** (Op. 5 and Op. 6 respectively). Commissions by publishers are uncommon at this time, but Vivaldi's popularity makes it a safe venture.

March The Pietà governors fire **Vivaldi**, but then reinstate him two months later in the post of *maestro de' concerti*.

1 April Caldara takes up the post of *vice-Kapellmeister* at the court of Charles VI in Vienna.

August Johann Heinichen is appointed *Kapellmeister* to the Dresden Court.

November Vivaldi presents *Juditha triumphans* at the Ospedale della Pietà. Vivaldi's (one surviving) oratorio, composed for an all-female cast, contains allegorical references to the ongoing Venetian war against the Ottoman Turks.

14 November Carlo Pollarolo's *Ariodante* premières in Venice, providing **Faustina Bordoni** with her operatic début. The 19-year-old mezzo soprano gains the nickname *The New Siren*.

1715 Jacobite (Stuart) rising begins in Scotland; James Edward Stuart, the 'Old Pretender', arrives from France • Louis XIV (Fr) dies; is succeeded by his five-year-old great-grandson Louis XV • The Spanish Netherlands (Belgium) pass to Austria • Alain Lesage (Fr): *Gil Blas* (Vol. I) • Isaac Watts (Eng) completes the earliest English children's hymnal

1716 Jacobite rebellion in Scotland collapses; James Edward Stuart returns to France; leading rebels are executed • Austrians under Prince Eugene of Savoy defeat Turks at Peterwardein • Japan comes under rule of shogun Tokugawa Yoshimune • Chinese scholars produce K'ang Hsi dictionary • Giovanni Battista Tiepolo (It) paints *The Sacrifice of Isaac*

Bach completes his *Little Organ Book*: 'For the glory of the most high God alone, and for my neighbour to learn from.'

Couperin (right) becomes keyboard composer to the French royal court. By this time he has committed to print three *Leçons de ténèbres*, his finest sacred works, scored for one to two sopranos and continuo. This year sees the publication of his second book of *Pièces de clavecin*, featuring many character pieces.

Alessandro Marcello's melodious Oboe Concerto in D minor is published around this time in Amsterdam, forming part of an anthology of works by Italian composers.

21 February J. S. Bach's name appears in print for the first time, in **Mattheson**'s *Das beschützte Orchestre*. He is described as 'the famous Weimar organist'.

9 April Composer **Matthias Georg Monn** is born in Vienna.

19 June Composer **Jan Václav** (**Johann**) **Stamitz** is baptised in Německý Brod, Bohemia.

17 July (evening): **Handel**'s *Water Music* suite is first performed by around 50 musicians on a large barge on the Thames, accompanying King George and his entourage up river from Whitehall to Chelsea. The king enjoys the music so much that he orders two repeat performances, ending in the early hours of the morning. The event marks the first documented use of horns in English orchestral music.

Summer Handel moves to Cannons, Edgware (near London), home of Earl James Brydges of Carnarvon, future Duke of Chandos. As resident composer, Handel begins to concentrate on sacred works, including his (later named) *Chandos Anthems*.

5 August In Cöthen **Bach** is appointed *Kapellmeister* to the court of Prince Leopold, with the prospect of doubling his current salary. Bach's family move from Weimar, but Bach himself has to remain, unable to secure immediate release from his contract to Duke Wilhelm Ernst.

September Antonio Lotti moves to Dresden, having obtained leave from his post as first organist at St Mark's, Venice. He stages his opera *Giove in Argo* (Zeus in Argos) in the Redoutensaal the following month.

September The Dresden court invites **Bach** to undertake a keyboard duel with the virtuoso **Louis Marchand**, organist to King Louis XV of France. Daunted by the challenge, Marchand flees the city.

2 November Johann J. Walther, German composer and virtuoso violinist, dies in Mainz, aged about 67.

6 November Bach, still insistent that he should be released from service at Weimar, finally incurs the wrath of his employer, Duke Wilhelm Ernst. The composer spends the next month in jail for failure of duties and general impertinence. In December he is free to move to Cöthen to take up the post of *Kapellmeister*.

1717 Troops of Felipe V (Sp) seize island of Sardinia • Austrians under Prince Eugene capture Belgrade from Turks • Louis XV (Fr) grants charter for Louisiana territory to Scottish financier John Law and his Company of the West • Mongols seize city of Lhasa (Tibet) • German physicist Gabriel Fahrenheit announces his system for measuring temperature • East India Company (UK) gets trading concessions from India's Mogul emperor, Farrukh-Siar • Prussia becomes first country to introduce compulsory education • Antoine Watteau (Fr) paints *Pilgrimage to Cythera* • Alexander Pope (Eng): poem *Eloisa to Abelard*

Handel's *Esther*, the first English oratorio, is performed privately at the Edgware residence of the Earl of Carnarvon. The public will have to wait 14 years to hear it.

Composer-violinist **Francesco Manfredini** publishes his twelve *Concerti Grossi* Op. 3, for two violins and continuo, in Bologna.

Having left the Pietà in Venice, **Vivaldi** arrives in Mantua where he becomes chamber *maestro di cappella* to Prince Philip of Hesse-Darmstadt.

March Maurice Greene is appointed organist of St Paul's Cathedral, London.

12 April Fux presents his oratorio *Cristo nell'orto* (Christ in the Garden) for Holy Week at the Hofburgkapelle in Vienna.

Summer Handel's first English language stage-work, the masque *Acis and Galatea*, is performed at Cannons, Edgware. The libretto is co-written by **John Gay**, **Alexander Pope** and **John Hughes**.

22 June Vivaldi's opera *Scanderbeg* reopens the Teatro della Pergola in Florence. The story concerns the life of the eponymous 15th-century Albanian folk hero who battles against the Ottomans as they attempt to conquer Albania. Like his oratorio *Juditha triumphans* (1716), Vivaldi's opera patriotically allegorises the Venetian-Ottoman war (1714–18).

Autumn Nicola Porpora's opera *Temistocle* premières at the Hoftheater in Vienna. The libretto is by **Apostolo Zeno**, who has this year been appointed poet-laureate at the imperial court of Charles VI.

26 November Alessandro Scarlatti produces his first and last comic opera, *Il trionfo dell'onore*, at the Teatro dei Fiorentini, Naples. The opera is well received and performed 18 times during the winter season

In one of the famous musical non-events, **Bach** narrowly misses **Handel** in Halle, having travelled there from Cöthen to see him. The two composers will never meet.

Members of the nobility, with support from King George, establish The Royal Academy of Music for the promotion of Italian opera. **Handel** is authorised to headhunt high-quality singers from abroad.

Publisher Étienne Roger issues **Vivaldi**'s six Op. 6 concertos (received three years previously), in Amsterdam.

19 April Leonardo Vinci (of no relation to the Renaissance polymath) cements his opera-writing career with the Neapolitan dialect comedy *Lo cecato fauzo* (The Fake Blind Man), which creates a sensation at the Teatro Fiorentini in Naples.

Summer The Earl of Burlington, visiting Italy, invites **Bononcini** to become a composer for the Royal Academy of Music in London.

Summer Domenico Scarlatti resigns his position as *maestro di cappella* at St Peter's in Rome. He makes his way to Portugal (possibly via England) where he receives a significant increase in salary as *mestre* of the royal chapel in Lisbon.

13 September Lotti's opera *Teofane* premières in Dresden as part of the sumptuous festivities surrounding the marriage of Crown Prince Friedrich Augustus to Maria Josepha, Archduchess of Austria. The following month Lotti and his wife, the soprano **Santa Stella**, return to Venice, flush with a departing gift of carriage and horses.

14 November Composer and theorist **Leopold Mozart** is born in Augsburg.

30 November The Royal Academy appoints **Handel** as Master of the Orchestra. The composer is still abroad at this time (see above).

1718 Troops sent by Spanish king Felipe V seize the island of Sicily • Allied invasions of Sicily and northern Spain • Sweden attacks Norway; King Karl XII (Swe) is killed • Treaty of Passarowitz ends Austro-Turkish war • Building of Elysée Palace in Paris • Antoine Watteau (Fr) paints *La gamme d'amour* • Voltaire (Fr): tragedy *Oedipe*

1719 Spain sends an unsuccessful expedition to Scotland to help Jacobites (Stuart supporters) • Irish parliament passes Declaratory Act allowing British parliament to pass laws for Ireland • France is at war with Spain • Bubonic plague spreads from Russia to eastern-central Europe • Daniel Defoe (Eng): *Robinson Crusoe*

Bach composes his six Sonatas and Partitas for solo violin, and around this time the six Suites for solo cello. The solo string works are unprecedented in their compositional and emotional range. The crowning glory is (arguably) the Chaconne from the Partita No. 2 in D minor, with its grand opening statement and 31 imaginative variations.

Benedetto Marcello publishes *Il teatro alla moda* (The Theatre in Fashion), a much appreciated pamphlet satirising showy and commercial Italian opera. It remains in print across Europe throughout the 18th and 19th centuries.

Prince Philip of Hesse-Darmstadt makes **Vivaldi** his musical director in Mantua, but the composer continues his itinerancy, returning briefly to Venice, and then on to Rome. This year see the publication of his twelve *Concerti a 5 stromenti*, Op. 7, written about three years earlier.

January Bach presents the *Clavier-Büchlein* to his eldest son, **Wilhelm Friedemann**.

2 April Giovanni Porta's *Numitore* inaugurates the first opera season of the Royal Academy in London.

27 April Handel's opera *Radamisto*, the second production of the Royal Academy, is staged at the King's Theatre in London with great success. King George, to whom the opera is dedicated, attends the première with the Prince of Wales. The opera manages eleven performances on its opening run.

July Maria Barbara Bach dies and is buried in Cöthen while her husband is away in Carlsbad. As recounted by **C. P. E. Bach**, 'The news that she had been ill and died reached him only when he entered his own house'. **Bach** is left with four young children to parent alone.

October Porpora's serenata *Angelica e Medoro*, on a libretto by **Pietro Metastasio**, is introduced at court in Naples in celebration of Emperor Charles VI's birthday. The event marks the public début of the castrato **Carlo Broschi** (**Farinelli**), aged 15, who takes a minor role as the shepherd Tirsi. The libretto is Metastasio's first printed work.

November Handel publishes his first collection of keyboard music, *Suites des Pièces pour le Clavecin, Premier Volume*, containing works from the Hamburg period as well as new pieces composed in England.

19 November Bononcini revives his opera *Astarto* (1715) to open the second operatic season of the Royal Academy in London. The famous alto-castrato **Senesino** (left) heads up the cast and remains the Academy's leading performer over the next eight years.

December Bach is offered the position of organist at St Jacobi's in Hamburg. He turns the job down as it transpires that the new post-holder is required to present a significant gift of funds to the church. The position is eventually filled by the son of a rich merchant who donates 4,000 marks—around five times the annual wage of the post itself.

1720 Quadruple Alliance (Britain, France, Netherlands, Austria) and Spain agree Treaty of the Hague: Felipe V (Sp) gives up claims in Italy; Holy Roman Emperor Karl VI (Aus) abandons claims to Spain; Sicily goes to Austria; Savoy gets Sardinia • Chinese set up garrisons in Tibet • Treaties of Stockholm largely end the Great Northern War • Collapse of Scottish financier John Law's Mississippi scheme triggers financial panic in France and England leaving many people ruined • Giovanni Battista Tiepolo (It) paints *The Martyrdom of St Bartholomew* • Voltaire (Fr): tragedy *Artémise* • Alexander Pope (Eng) completes translation of Homer's *Iliad*

1721

Some say, compar'd to Buononcinny
That Mynheer Handel's
but a Ninny.
Others aver, that he to Handel
Is scarcely fit to hold a Candle:
Strange that this difference
there should be
Twixt Tweedle-dum
and Tweedle-dee!

John Byrom's epigram, written around this time, mocking the rivalry between London's opera giants, **Handel** and **Bononcini**. The last two lines of the verse have been attributed to both Pope and Swift.

Bononcini, Handel's elder by 15 years and arch-rival, was renowned for a sizeable ego. After refusing to play to Emperor Joseph of Austria, he remarked, 'there are many sovereign princes, but only one Bononcini.'

Pietro Antonio Locatelli's *XII Concerto grossi* Op. 1, is published in Amsterdam. The collection

follows the Corellian model of eight church concertos and four chamber concertos.

24 March Bach dedicates six concertos to the Margrave Christian Ludwig of Brandenburg (left) in the hope of gaining employment or patronage. The later named 'Brandenburg' concertos incorporate a rich variety of instrumental combinations and rank among the most innovative musical collections of the Baroque period. The Margrave takes little notice of them and no job offer is forthcoming.

15 April The opera *Muzio Scevola* by **Filippo Amadei**, **Bononcini** (above) and **Handel**—each of whom have set an act—is premièred at the King's Theatre in London. Beginning with Amadei and ending with Handel, the quality of the music increases during the course of the opera. The Royal Academy production fuels the rivalry between Bononcini and Handel.

Autumn In Hamburg **Telemann** begins his new appointment as music director of the city's five principal churches and *Kantor* of the Johanneum Lateinschule.

3 December 18 months after the death of his first wife, **Bach** marries the 20-year-old Anna Magdalena Wilken. The daughter of a court trumpeter, Anna is a skilled singer and harpsichordist. The composer's second marriage will produce 13 children, six of whom will survive into adulthood.

9 December Handel's one new dramatic work for the season, a *pasticcio* entitled *Floridante*, bores many at the King's Theatre, London.

1721 Whig statesman Sir Robert Walpole becomes Britain's First Lord of the Treasury and effectively the first-ever prime minister; he establishes Cabinet (committee) system of government • Spain joins Franco-British defensive alliance • Sweden and Russia agree the Peace of Nystadt: Russia gains much of eastern Baltic; Sweden is left as a minor nation • Pope Clement XI dies; is succeeded by Innocent XIII • Bubonic plague kills 9,000 people in the French cities of Marseille and Toulon • Norwegian pastor Hans Egede begins modern colonisation of Greenland • Nathan Bailey (Eng): *Universal Etymological Dictionary* • Charles de Montesquieu (Fr): *Lettres Persanes*

Albinoni's *12 Concerti a cinque*, Op. 9, is published in Amsterdam.

Bach completes the first volume of the *Well-Tempered Clavier* (right), containing 24 pairs of preludes and fugues in all major and minor keys. He will combine them with a second set 22 years later, making the renowned *Forty-eight Preludes and Fugues*. Inspired by **J. C. F. Fischer**'s *Ariadne musica* (1702), it becomes the most famous keyboard collection of the Baroque period. This year also marks the composition of the *Clavierbüchlein for Anna Magdalena*.

In Paris **Couperin** publishes his *Concerts royaux*, four works for harpsichord or (unspecified) instrumental ensemble. He also brings out the third volume of his *Pièces de clavecin*.

First page of the Fugue in C minor

In Hamburg **Mattheson** goes to press with *Critica musica*, the first periodical dedicated exclusively to musical events, composers, book reviews and discussions on music.

Rameau publishes his 450-page *Traité de l'harmonie* (Treatise on Harmony), in which he discusses chord inversions, key-centres and other aspects of tonality. It is soon recognised as a seminal publication on modern harmonic theory.

Czech composer **Jan Zelenka** issues his *Six Trio Sonatas* (ZWV181), scored mainly for two oboes, bassoon and continuo.

22 February Bononcini's opera *Griselda* consolidates a period of resounding success for both the composer and the Royal Academy of Music. Thanks to Bononcini the Academy achieves its first (but last) profitable season.

Late spring Telemann becomes musical director of the Gänsemarktoper, Hamburg (Hamburg Opera).

5 June Johann Kuhnau dies in Leipzig, aged 62. **Bach** and **Telemann** are among the applicants for the now vacant post of *Kantor*.

30 June Bohemian composer **Georg Benda** (brother of **Franz**) is born in Staré Benátky.

13 August Telemann is offered the post of *Kantor* of St Thomas's School in Leipzig. His current employers in Hamburg refuse to release him from his duties, but in compensation they grant him an increase of salary.

13 August Violin maestro **Francesco Veracini**, mentally disturbed, narrowly escapes serious injury as he jumps out of a third-story window, convinced that jealous rivals seek to kill him.

Autumn The Royal Academy decide not to engage **Bononcini** for the new opera season, possibly due to his association with Jacobite sympathisers.

24 November Dutch composer and organist **Johann Reincken**, co-founder of the Hamburg Opera (inaugurated 1678), dies in Hamburg, probably aged in his late 70s. He is buried two weeks later at St Catherine's Church in a grave he had purchased 15 years earlier.

1722 Prussia's government is centralised in a General Directory controlled by its king, Friedrich Wilhelm I • Mir Mahmud, ruler of Kandahar (India), leads an Afghan invasion of Persia and becomes Shah of Persia • Tsar Petr I, the Great (Russ), exploits Persian disunion to capture Persian city of Derbent • Dutch navigator Jacob Roggeveen discovers Easter Island and Samoa in the Pacific Ocean • Guy's Hospital, London, is founded with cash given by bookseller Thomas Guy • Daniel Defoe (Eng): novels *Moll Flanders* and *Colonel Jacque*; also *A Journal of the Plague Year* and *The History of Peter the Great*

Handel engages the angelic voice of 22-year-old **Francesca Cuzzoni** for £2,000 a season. During the first rehearsals they fall out, with the opera diva refusing to sing an aria according to Handel's instructions. Seizing Cuzzoni, Handel threatens to throw her out of the window. Cuzzoni decides to sing it Handel's way.

Leading French violinist **Jean-Marie Leclair** produces his *Premier livre de sonates* for violin and basso continuo.

Dresden-based **J. D. Zelenka** composes his Italianate Simphonie *a* 8 in A minor, possibly intended for the summer coronation celebrations of Charles VI in Prague.

January Unable to secure the services of **Telemann**, the Leipzig council elects **Christoph Graupner** above **Bach** as their new choice for *Kantor*. History repeats itself (see 1722): the Landgrave of Darmstadt refuses Graupner's resignation and compensates by giving him a payrise. (See also below.)

12 January Handel's first collaboration with librettist **Nicola Haym** produces one of his finest operas, *Ottone*, introduced at the King's Theatre, London. **Francesca Cuzzoni** gives a spectacular début performance as Teofane.

25 February Handel is granted an honorary appointment as Composer of Music for His Majesty's Chapel Royal.

April The Leipzig town council settles for what they consider to be 'mediocre' talent, appointing **Bach** to the post of *Kantor* of St Thomas's School

and musical director to the town's principal churches. Bach receives free lodging but a paltry yearly wage of 87 thaler. Additional commissions and engagements, together with endowments, give him an annual salary of around 700 thaler, roughly the same as a craftsman.

First Sunday after Trinity Bach begins the first of his five Leipzig cantata cycles. He supplies one cantata (up to around 20 minutes worth of music) each week for the three-hour Sunday service.

July The Pietà governors ask **Vivaldi** to supply two concertos a month for their orchestra and direct rehearsals on occasions while in Venice. Vivaldi accepts the arrangement and supplies 140 concertos over the following six years. He is paid one gold sequin for each concerto.

18 July Bach's unaccompanied motet *Jesu, meine Freude* is performed at the funeral of the wife of Leipzig's chief postmaster.

Vivaldi caricatured by Pier Leone Ghezzi

28 August Fux's opera *Costanza e Fortezza* (Constancy and Fortitude) is premièred with around 300 instrumentalists and singers during the coronation celebrations of Charles VI as King of Bohemia. Staged in a large open-air theatre in Prague, the event is directed by *vice maestro* **Caldera**, as Fux is incapacitated with chronic gout. The composer-instrumentalists **Zelenka**, **Graun**, **Weiss** and **Quantz** all perform in the orchestra.

Christmas Day Bach's Magnificat in E flat (BWV243a) is first performed at the Thomaskirche in Leipzig.

1723 Duc de Bourbon-Condé becomes first minister of France following the death of Duc d'Orléans; at 13, King Louis XV is deemed to be 'of age' • Abraham Davel (Switz) launches a doomed revolt in Vaud against rule by Bern • Hungarian parliament accepts Holy Roman Emperor Karl VI's Pragmatic Sanction, settling Habsburg succession on his daughter Maria Theresa • Russian forces take the city of Tiflis (modern Tbilisi) in the Caucasus, from disunited Persia • British traders claim the Gambia area for the African Company • Richard Steele (Ire): drama *The Conscious Lovers*

François Couperin blends French and Italian styles in *Les goûts-réünis*, a chamber music collection for unspecified instruments.

William Croft brings out his *Musica sacra*, a two-volume anthology of church music comprising 31 anthems and a *Burial Service*. The innovative publication is presented in score format, rather than in the standard parts. His *Burial Service* becomes regularly performed at state funerals.

In London **Geminiani** is appointed solo director and perpetual dictator of the Masonic society Philo Musicae et Architecturae Societas. The lodge functions to promote Italian music and architecture.

Benedetto Marcello (above) begins his influential *Estro poetico armonico*, containing 50 psalm settings together with a preface on musical style. He criticises complex (Baroque) polyphony and elaborate modulation, arguing instead for 'noble simplicity' in music. In so doing he becomes an important advocate of the galant style, steering musical thinking towards the Classical era.

Rameau publishes his second book of keyboard works in *Pièces de clavessin avec une méthode pour la méchanique des doigts*. Typical of French keyboard music of the time, most are based on dance forms and several feature intriguing character titles, such as *Les tricotets* (The Knitters), *Les sauvages* (The Savages) and *L'egiptienne* (The Egyptian Woman).

8 January The Neapolitan composer **Leonardo Vinci** secures major success in Rome with his opera *Farnace*, premièred at the Teatro delle Dame.

1 February **Domenico Sarro**'s opera *Didone abbandonata* opens with great success at the Teatro San Bartolomeo in Naples. **Pietro Metastasio** supplies the libretto and with it launches his own career.

20 February **Handel**'s masterful opera *Giulio Cesare*, to a text by **Haym**, premières at the King's Theatre, London. The success of the opera effectively finishes off the competition between Handel and **Bononcini**.

7 April **Bach** introduces his *St John Passion* during the Good Friday service at the church of St Nicholas, Leipzig. Performed in two sections before and after the sermon, it is his largest sacred work to date.

Autumn The 14-year-old mezzo soprano **Anna Girò** makes her Venice début in **Albinoni**'s opera *Laodice*. Around this time she becomes **Vivaldi**'s pupil and subsequently his prima-donna in more than 30 operatic productions.

31 October **Handel** introduces *Tamerlano* at the King's Theatre, London. Composed in around 20 days, the opera inaugurates the sixth season of the Royal Academy of Music.

1724 Spanish king Felipe V abdicates, but resumes throne after the death of his son Luis I • Russia and Turkey plot to carve up Persia, and Turks invade Kermanshah province and other parts of western Persia • In a fit of insanity, Mir Mahmud, ruler of Kandahar, massacres Persian nobles and others in Isfahan (Persia) • Pope Innocent XIII dies; is succeeded by Benedict VIII • Blenheim Palace in Woodstock, outside Oxford (Eng), is completed • La Bourse (stock exchange) is opened in Paris (Fr) • Cotton Mather (N Amer): *Curiosa Americana* • Daniel Defoe (Eng): *Tour Through the Whole Island of Great Britain* (first part)

Bach composes his second *Clavierbüchlein* for Anna Magdalena, and completes his second cycle of Leipzig cantatas.

The Court Theatre in Vienna engages the mezzo soprano **Faustina Bordoni** at a salary of 15,000 florins. Later this year the Royal Academy of Music, eager to inject new excitement into their opera season, invites Bordoni to London.

Fux publishes his *Gradus ad Parnassum* (Steps to Parnassus) in Vienna. Written in Latin, the compositional treatise is reprinted in German, Italian, English and French. It is one of the most important and influential music books ever written.

6 February Johann P. Krieger, composer of some 2,000 cantatas (very few of which survive), dies in Weissenfels aged 75.

13 February Handel's opera *Rodelinda* opens at the King's Theatre, London. Its success is only in part due to Handel's craftsmanship—women flock equally to see the brown silk dress with silver trimmings worn by the prima donna, **Cuzzoni**. Her dress sparks a new fashion across London.

18 March The inaugural concert of the *Concert Spirituel* takes place at the Tuileries Palace in Paris. Established by **Anne Danican Philidor**, the subscription concerts take place on religious holidays (when the theatres are closed) and offer public performances of instrumental and choral music.

GRADUS
AD
PARNASSUM,
Sive
MANUDUCTIO
AD
COMPOSITIONEM MUSICÆ
REGULAREM,
Methodo novâ, ac certâ, nondum antè
tam exacto ordine in lucem edita :

Elaborata à
JOANNE JOSEPHO FUX,
Sacræ Cæsareæ, ac Regiæ Catholicæ Majeſtatis CAROLI VI. Romanorum Imperatoris
SUPREMO CHORI PRÆFECTO.

VIENNÆ AUSTRIÆ,
Typis Joannis Petri Van Ghelen, Sac. Cæſ. Regiéque Catholicæ Majeſtatis Aulæ-Typographi. 1725.

September Johann Hasse displays galant sensitivities in the serenata *Antonio e Cleopatra*, first performed at the country estate of the royal advisor Carlo Carmignano in Naples. The 20-year-old **Farinelli**, rising castrato star, sings the role of Cleopatra, while the contralto **Vittoria Tesi**, complementing the gender swap, sings the part of Marc'Antonio.

27 September Telemann anticipates the Italian *buffa* style with his comic intermezzo *Pimpinone*, performed at the Theater am Gänsemarkt in Hamburg. This year also marks his publication of *Der harmonische Gottesdienst*, the first of a three-volume series of cantata cycles.

22 October Composer **Alessandro Scarlatti**, impoverished due to unpaid salary and expensive professional care of his sick daughter, dies in Naples aged 65.

December Vivaldi's *Il cimento dell'armonia e dell'invenzione* (The contest between Harmony and Invention, Op. 8) is published in Amsterdam. The collection includes a number of descriptive works including *The Four Seasons*, *The Storm at Sea* and *The Hunt*. Described by the 18th-century historian John Hawkins as 'wild and irregular', the concertos accentuate, more than ever before, dramatic contrasts between soloist and orchestra. The concertos of *The Four Seasons* (written perhaps ten years earlier) are issued with accompanying sonnets—probably Vivaldi's own—and represent milestone examples of programmatic orchestral music.

1725 On advice of his First Minister the Duc de Bourbon-Condé, Louis XV (Fr) cancels his plans to marry a Spanish princess • Spain and Austria sign the Treaty of Vienna; Britain, France, Prussia and Netherlands retaliate with the Treaty of Hanover • Louis XV marries Maria, daughter of former king of Poland Stanisław Leszczyński • Petr I, the Great (Russ), dies; is succeeded by second wife, Ekaterina (Catherine) I • The Imamate (Muslim country) of Futa Djallon (Guinea) is established • Antonio Canaletto (It) paints *View of the Grand Canal, Venice* • *Letters* by Marquise de Sévigné (Fr) published posthumously

Bach appears in print for the first time with his Partita No. 1 for keyboard, published at his own expense. He will combine this work with five others into his *Clavier-Übung* (Keyboard Practice), Op. 1.

In Paris **Couperin** publishes *Les nations*, comprising four trio sonata suites clearly influenced by Corelli.

Geminiani issues his concerto arrangements of the first six of Corelli's Op. 5 sonatas, backed by aristocratic subscription. This year he is involved with other prominent musicians including **Bononcini**, **Pepusch** and **William Croft** in the founding of The Academy of Vocal Music.

John Stanley, aged 14 and clinically blind, is appointed organist at St Andrew's, Holborn, 'in preference to a great number of candidates' (as later recounted by Charles Burney).

January Vinci and **Metastasio** begin their operatic collaborations with a new setting of *Didone* in Rome, and *Siroe, re di Persia* (Cyrus, King of Persia) the following month in Venice.

25 February Rameau, aged 42, marries Marie-Louise Mangot, aged 19. This year he follows up his *Traité de l'harmonie* (1722) with the publication of *Nouveau système de musique théorique* (New System of Music Theory), in Paris.

12 March Handel's opera *Scipione*, written in three weeks to a text by **Antonio Rolli**, is

£2000-a-season divas Faustina Bordoni (top) and Francesca Cuzzoni.

performed for the first time at the King's Theatre, London. A march from the largely forgotten opera is later adopted by the British Grenadier Guards as their *Regimental Slow March*.

12 April Music historian Charles Burney is born in Shrewsbury.

5 May Prima donnas **Francesca Cuzzoni** and **Faustina Bordoni** cross swords for the first time in Handel's opera *Alessandro*. The casting of rival sopranos as queens vying for the attention of Alexander is a deliberate ploy by the Royal Academy to spice up the opera season. Two camps of fans emerge and proclaim their loyalties by wearing either a Cuzzoni scarf or a Bordoni ribbon.

18 June Court composer **Michel-Richard de Lalande** dies in Versailles, aged 68.

Summer Bordoni and **Cuzzoni** go head to head at Newmarket. Such is the craze surrounding the two singers that even racehorses are named after them.

2 September Giovanni Ristori's *Calandro*, the first *opera buffa* to be written in Germany, is performed for the royal court in Dresden.

17 October François Francoeur and **François Rebel** present their opera *Pyrame et Thisbé* at the Paris Opéra. The work inaugurates a life-long collaborative partnership between the two composers.

1726 Britain is at war with Spain • France comes under the able administration of King Louis XV's tutor, Cardinal Fleury, who sends Duc de Bourbon-Condé, former First Minister, into exile • Persians defeat Turks marching on Isfahan, Persia's capital • An anti-Turkish alliance is formed by Russia and Austria • Prussia approves the Pragmatic Sanction by which Holy Roman Emperor Karl VI's daughter Maria Theresa is to inherit Habsburg lands • Giovanni Battista Tiepolo (It) paints ceiling frescoes in the archbishop's palace in Udine • Jonathan Swift (Ire): *Gulliver's Travels* • Chinese scholars complete a 5,020-volume encyclopaedia

Joseph Bodin de Boismortier publishes his quasi-concerto style *Six Concertos for Five Flutes*, Op. 15, in Paris.

Michele Mascitti brings out his Op. 7 collection of sonatas and concertos in Paris. The four string concertos included are the first of their kind to be published by a composer resident in France.

Swedish composer **Johan Helmich Roman**, director of the royal orchestra in Stockholm, makes a rare visit to the printing press with his *12 Flute Sonatas*. The pieces are in light *galant* style and aimed at competent amateurs.

Tartini sets up a violin school in Padua which soon attracts students from across Europe. It becomes known as 'The School of the Nations'.

Vivaldi's Op. 9 collection of solo violin concertos, *La cetra* (The Lyre), is published in Amsterdam.

31 January Handel's opera *Admeto* opens with huge success at the King's Theatre, London. With **Cuzzoni** and **Bordoni** again in leading roles, the behaviour of their loyal supporters becomes increasingly rowdy throughout the opera season. (See 6 June.)

20 February Handel (right), three days before his 42nd birthday, is granted British citizenship.

30 March Opera composer **Tommaso Traetta** is born in Bitonto, south-east Italy.

11 April (Good Friday): **Bach** directs the first version of his *St Matthew Passion* at St Thomas's Church, Leipzig. With libretto by the poet **Christian Henrici** (a.k.a. **Picander**), the setting calls for soloists, double choir, double orchestra and two organs—unusually large for the composer's Leipzig performances. The work fuses the sacred and dramatic into a monument of Christian devotion.

29 April Vivaldi's opera *Siroe, re di Persia* (text by **Metastasio**, first set by **Vinci** the previous year) is introduced at the Teatro Pubblico in Reggio Emilia. It is one of four operas Vivaldi produces this year.

6 June The rivalry between the prima donnas **Cuzzoni** and **Bordoni** erupts both on and off the stage during **Bononcini**'s opera *Astianatte*, at London's Haymarket. The two divas wrestle each other and fights break out in the audience between their loyal supporters. King George's daughter, Princess Amelia, looks on aghast, and the opera season draws to a swift close.

28 September André Cardinal Destouches becomes *maître de musique de la chambre* at the court at Versailles.

11 October Four anthems composed by **Handel** are sung at the coronation of George II at Westminster Abbey, including the spectacular *Zadok the Priest*. The royal favourite will be performed at each subsequent British coronation.

1727 King George I dies; is succeeded as ruler of Britain and Hanover by his son George II, who is influenced by his wife Caroline • Spain, at war with Britain and France, blockades Gibraltar • Russia's ruler Ekaterina I dies; is succeeded by Petr II, a grandson of Petr I, the Great • Turks are entrenched in western Transcaucasia • Persia and Turkey make peace; Turkey keeps conquered lands • China and Russia modify their Amur River boundary in the Treaty of Kiachta • Antonio Canaletto (It) paints *The Mole and the Ducal Palace* (Venice) • John Gay (Eng): *Fables* (1st series)

Johann Quantz becomes flute teacher to Crown Prince Frederick of Prussia.

Giovanni Battista Sammartini becomes *maestro di cappella* of Milan's Congregazione del SS Entierro.

Tartini's *Sei concerti à cinque e sei stromenti*, Op. 1/1, is published in Amsterdam.

Telemann publishes *Der getreue Musikmeister* (The True Music Master), a collection of works by himself and other composers including **Bach**, **Weiss** and **Zelenka**, geared particularly towards domestic music making.

16 January Opera composer **Niccolò Piccinni** is born in Bari, southern Italy.

29 January John Gay's *The Beggar's Opera* opens at John Rich's Lincoln's Inn Fields Theatre and gains an ecstatic response from the London public. Comprising spoken dialogue and popular tunes arranged by **Pepusch**, the ballad-opera includes music by Purcell, Jeremiah Clarke, **Handel**, **Bononcini** and **Eccles**. A variety of topical themes are satirised, such as hangings, the character of Prime Minister Walpole, Italian opera and the **Cuzzoni-Bordoni** rivalry. The first production runs for 62 performances making, in the words of the contemporary aphorism, 'Gay rich and Rich gay'.

17 February Handel, following **Vinci** (1726) and **Vivaldi** (1727), stages his own setting of **Metastasio**'s *Siroe, re di Persia* at the King's Theatre, London. The two divas **Cuzzoni** and **Bordoni** resume their work with a little more decorum than that displayed the previous year.

30 April Handel's final opera for the Royal Academy, *Tolomeo* (Ptolemy), opens at the King's Theatre, London.

15 May The 42-year-old **Domenico Scarlatti** marries the 16-year-old Maria Catalina Gentili, in Rome.

1 June The Royal Academy is declared bankrupt, having lost around £50,000 of shareholders' investment over its nine-year enterprise.

15 August Having withdrawn from public life many years earlier, the composer **Marin Marais** dies in Paris, aged 72.

September Vivaldi meets Emperor Charles VI of Austria and receives a substantial gift of money and a gold chain with medallion. Vivaldi dedicates to him his Op. 9 violin concertos.

December John Gay's virulent political satire *Polly*, sequel to *The Beggar's Opera*, is banned before it reaches the stage. Gay publishes over 10,000 copies of the text and makes a tidy profit. A production is finally staged in 1779.

25 December German composer **Johann Adam Hiller** is born in Wendisch-Ossig, near Görlitz.

The Beggar's Opera by William Hogarth

1728 Whig Prime Minister Sir Robert Walpole (UK) stays in office in the first parliament of George II • Anglo-Spanish war formally ends with the Convention of Prado • First Amish Mennonites arrive in America • Chartered Company of Guipuzcoa (Caracas) is formed in Spain to promote trade with South America • Astronomer James Bradley (Eng) calculates the speed of light to be around 301,000 km/s (actual speed, 299,792 km/s) • Voltaire (Fr): epic poem *La Henriade* on Henri IV of France • Alexander Pope (Eng): *The Dunciad* • Clergyman William Law (Eng): *A Serious Call to a Devout and Holy Life*, precursor of Methodism

Jean-Joseph Mouret brings out his *Suites de symphonies* in Paris. He is currently artistic director of the Concert Spirituel.

Princess Maria Barbara of Portugal marries the Crown Prince Ferdinando of Spain. **Domenico Scarlatti** leaves the royal court in Lisbon and follows his patron first to Seville, then Madrid in 1733.

The visually-impaired **John Stanley**, aged 17, becomes the youngest student to date to gain a Bachelor of Music degree at Oxford University.

The publisher Le Cène issues three sets of **Vivaldi** concertos, Opp. 10–12, in Amsterdam. With the Op. 10 collection Vivaldi introduces some of the earliest known flute concertos, including the celebrated six-movement 'La Notte' (No. 2).

1 January Bach brings in the New Year in Leipzig with his jubilant cantata *Gott, wie dein Name, so ist auch dein Ruhm* (God, as is Your name, so is Your renown).

18 January The directors of the bankrupt Royal Academy allow **Handel** and John Heidegger (left) to make use of the King's Theatre, together with costumes, stage machinery and scenery. With **Senesino**, **Bordoni** and **Cuzzoni** all having abandoned London, Handel leaves for the continent eight days later in the pursuit of new singers.

Spring Handel visits Venice where he secures the soprano **Anna Maria Strada del Pò** for his new opera company. After talent-scouting in Italy, Handel travels to Halle to visit his mother, whose health is failing rapidly. He misses an opportunity to visit Bach in Leipzig.

3 May Bohemian composer **Florian Leopold Gassmann** is born in Brüx (Cz., Most).

Mid May Bach takes up the directorship of Leipzig University's *collegium musicum* (founded by **Telemann** in 1702). Bach also gains the honorary title of court *Kapellmeister* from Duke Christian of Saxe-Weissenfels. A similar title from Cöthen had expired a year earlier with the death of Prince Leopold.

27 June Composer **Elisabeth-Claude Jacquet de la Guerre** dies in Paris, aged 64.

16 July Johann Heinichen dies from tuberculosis in Dresden, aged 46. The Czech composer **Jan Zelenka** takes over duties to the royal chapel, but he is denied the official post of court musical director because he does not write operas.

31 July Nicola Francesco Haym, Italian librettist of some of **Handel**'s finest operas (including *Giulio Cesare*, *Ottone*, *Tamerlano* and *Rodelinda*), dies in London, aged 51.

23 November Telemann introduces his serious opera *Flavius Bertaridus* at the Gänsemarkt in Hamburg.

26 November Vinci's serenata *La contesa dei Numi* (The Contest of the Gods), with libretto by **Metastasio**, is first performed at the palace of the French ambassador in Rome. The occasion celebrates the birth of the dauphin, son of Louis XV.

2 December With £20,000 of their own money invested, the **Handel**-Heidegger Second Academy opera season begins with the composer's *Lotario*. Introducing the soprano **Anna Strada**, the opera is only moderately successful, running for ten performances.

1729 Treaty of Seville ends war involving Spain, Britain, France and Netherlands: Britain keeps Gibraltar, but Britain and France recognise right for Carlos, third son of Spain's king Felipe V, to succession in Parma, Piacenza and Tuscany (It) • British government makes North and South Carolina Crown colonies because of the incompetence of their proprietors • Baltimore, Maryland, founded as 'tobacco port' • Scientist Stephen Gray (Eng) differentiates between electrical conductors and non-conductors • John Wesley (Eng) becomes head of the Oxford 'Methodist' society • Benjamin Franklin (N Amer) starts publishing *The Pennsylvania Gazette* • Jonathan Swift (Ire) attacks Irish poverty in satire *A Modest Proposal*

1730

Extract from the preface of **Couperin**'s *Pièces de clavecin* (Volume IV), published this year.

Around this time **Rameau** publishes *Nouvelles suites de pieces de clavecin* and *Cantates françoises à voix seule*.

January–February Vinci and the librettist **Metastasio** achieve great success with the operas *Alessandro nell'Indie* and *Artaserse*, premièred at the Teatro delle Dame, Rome.

February Johann Hasse sets his version of **Metastasio**'s *Artaserse*, first performed at the Teatro San Giovanni Grisostomo, Venice. Metastasio's libretto will be set by at least 70 different composers over the next 70 years.

16 February Marguerite-Antoinette Couperin inherits the court post of *ordinaire de la chambre pour le clavecin* from her father, **François**, whose health is failing. She becomes the first woman to hold the position.

24 February Handel stages his comedy *Partenope* at the King's Theatre, London. It manages only seven performances.

4 April Handel cobbles together the pasticcio *Ormisda*, incorporating music by **Vinci**, **Hasse** and others. With a run of 14 performances it is the most successful production of the season.

27 May Opera composer **Leonardo Vinci**, aged in his late 30s, dies suddenly in Naples. It is suspected that he had been poisoned due to an adulterous love affair.

June The Leipzig council vent their frustration at **Bach** for failing to carry out required duties at the Thomasschule. They accuse him of being stubborn and incorrigible, and failing to deliver quality choristers.

13 June The first **Handel**-Heidegger opera season limps to a close.

14 June Opera composer **Antonio Sacchini** is born in Florence.

July In one of the most successful celebrity pairings of 18th-century Europe, **Hasse** (left), now a major opera composer, marries the soprano **Faustina Bordoni**. Their union will last over 50 years.

August Bach sends Leipzig council a statement outlining proposals to better exploit the town's musical resources. Frustrated that his position of *Kantor* is being undermined, he ignores the bulk of criticisms levelled at him in June. The town council, in turn, ignores Bach's proposals.

28 October Bach writes to his friend Georg Erdmann in Danzig (Gdansk), enquiring of employment opportunities.

3 November A revival of *Scipione* opens the second **Handel**-Heidegger opera season, with the castrato **Senesino** back on the London stage.

1730 Mediterranean island of Corsica revolts against Genoese rule • Petr II (Russ) dies; is succeeded by Anna, daughter of Ivan V, who is dominated by her German lover, statesman Ernst Johann Biron • Persians under warrior Nadir Kuli drive Turks from Transcaucasia and end alien Afghan rule; Persian rule is restored under Shah Tahmasp II, with Nadir Kuli as the real power • Pope Benedict XIII dies; is succeeded by Clement XII • William Hogarth (Eng) paints *A Musical Party* • James Thomson (Scot): pastoral poem *The Seasons* • Physicist René-Antoine de Réaumur (Fr) devises a thermometer scale with 0° as the freezing point of water

Around this time **Bach** completes his Double Concerto in D minor for two violins. It will become the most famous work of its kind, hailed as one of the pinnacle instrumental works of the Baroque period. This year also sees the publication of his *Clavier-Übung I*, a collection of six previously published keyboard partitas.

Bononcini comes to blows with The Academy of Ancient Music (formerly The Academy of Vocal Music) having tried to pass off a madrigal by **Antonio Lotti** as his own. Although unacknowledged plagiarism is rife at this time (especially in opera), the Academy views the blatant deception with disgust. Bononcini leaves England for a while to avoid facing the negative publicity.

Having backed the wrong side in the **Bononcini** affair (above), composers **Maurice Greene** and **Michael Festing** leave The Academy of Ancient Music and establish the rival Apollo Academy at London's Devil Tavern, Fleet Street.

Mattheson publishes his manual on improvising from a given bass: *Grosse General-Bass-Schule*.

Inspired by his continental experiences, Swedish composer **J. H. Roman** launches Stockholm's first public concerts.

27 January Piano inventor **Bartolomeo Cristofori** (right) dies in Florence, aged 76. As yet, no major composer has demonstrated any real interest in Cristofori's hammer-action instrument. (See also **Lodovico Giustini**, 1732.)

2 February Handel scores a hit with his one new production of the season, *Poro, re dell'Indie* (Porus, King of India). Adapted from **Metastasio**'s *Alessandro nell'Indie*, the opera runs for 16 performances at London's King's Theatre.

Good Friday Bach directs his *St Mark Passion*, a parody work comprising pre-existing compositions, including chorales, the *Funeral Ode* cantata, and funeral music from Cöthen.

29 May Handel and Heidegger end the Second Academy's opera season in profit, thanks largely to some cost-effective revivals of old productions.

Summer Hasse takes up his new post of *Kapellmeister* to the King of Poland and the electoral court of Saxony.

13 September Hasse's opera *Cleofide* premières at the Hoftheater in Dresden. **Bach** and his eldest son, **Wilhelm Friedemann**, attend the performance.

1 October C. P. E. Bach, aged 17, begins studying law at Leipzig University.

25 November J. S. Bach's celebrated cantata *Wachet auf, ruft uns die Stimme* (commonly known in English as Sleepers Wake) is first performed at Leipzig.

11 December Giovanni Ristori's comic opera *Calandro* (1726) is revived for a performance in Moscow. It is the first Italian opera to be staged in Russia.

12 December Composer **Christian Cannabich** is baptised in Mannheim.

1731 Britain, Netherlands, Spain, Austria agree two treaties of Vienna • Felipe V (Sp) and maritime powers recognise Holy Roman Emperor Karl VI's Pragmatic Sanction, bequeathing Habsburg lands to his daughter Maria Theresa • Spanish troops kill rebel leader Jose de Antequera in Paraguay • A Spanish coastguard pillages a British ship and lops an ear from its captain, Robert Jenkins—an incident which later leads to war • William Hogarth (Eng) paints *The Conquest of Mexico* • Voltaire (Fr): *Histoire de Charles XII* (of Sweden) • L'Abbé Prévost (Fr): *Manon Lescaut* • George Lillo (Eng): prose tragedy *George Barnwell*

1732

Italian composer-keyboardist **Lodovico Giustini** issues his *12 Sonate da cimbalo di piano e forte* in Florence. These sonatas appear to be the only piano pieces published in the first half of the 18th century.

Leclair issues his *Sonates en trio* for two violins and continuo (Op. 4), in Paris.

Sammartini's first opera, *Memet*, is performed in Lodi. Movements from two of his (undated) symphonies serve as introductions to Acts 2 and 3.

> *The Opéra is nothing but a public gathering place, where we assemble on certain days without exactly knowing why.*
>
> **Voltaire**, writing to Pierre-Robert Le Cornier de Cideville.

Johann Walther publishes *Musicalisches Lexicon* in Leipzig. It is the first music dictionary to contain both musical terms and biographies of composers and theorists, past and present.

15 January Handel's first new opera of the season, *Ezio* (Aetius), fails miserably, surviving only five performances.

15 February Handel premières his opera *Sosarme, re di Media* at the King's Theatre, London. High-quality music lifts a shabby libretto, resulting in 11 performances.

23 February In celebration of **Handel**'s birthday, a staged version of *Esther* (1718) is performed privately at Crown and Anchor Tavern in the Strand, London. Handel devotee Princess Anne suggests that the oratorio be transferred to the King's Theatre in the Haymarket.

31 March Composer **Franz Joseph Haydn** is born to a village wheelwright in Rohrau, Lower Austria.

2 May Handel gives the first public performance of an English oratorio with his revised *Esther*, at the King's Theatre, London. (The Bishop of London has permitted an unstaged version only.) Members of the Royal Family attend and the work is repeated five times.

By His MAJESTY's COMMAND.
AT the KING's THEATRE in the Hay-Market, on Tuesday the 2d Day of May, will be performed,
The SACRED STORY of ESTHER:
AN
ORATORIO in ENGLISH.
Formerly composed by Mr. Handel, and now revised by him, with several Additions, and to be performed by a great Number of the best Voices and Instruments.
N. B. There will be no Action on the Stage, but the House will be fitted up in a decent Manner, for the Audience. The Musick to be disposed after the Manner of the Coronation Service.
Tickets will be delivered at the Office in the Opera house, at the usual Prices.
Never Perform'd in Publick before,
AT the Great Room in Villars-street York-Buildings, To-morrow, being Thursday the 20th of this Instant April, will be perform'd,
ESTHER an ORATORIO:
OR,
SACRED DRAMA.
As it was composed originally for the most noble James Duke of Chandos, the Words by Mr. Pope, and the Musick by Mr. Handel.
Tickets to be had at the Place of Performance at 5s. each.
To begin exactly at 7 o'Clock.

May–June The opera company of **John Lampe**, Thomas Arne (Snr) and **Henry Carey** purloins **Handel**'s *Acis and Galatea* for a run at the Little Theatre in the Haymarket. Adding insult to injury, they even employ Handel's cook, Waltz, in the production. Outraged, Handel hurries his own revised version at the King's Theatre, achieving moderate success thanks to the participation of his operatic stars, **Senesino** and **Anna Strada**.

27 September Giovanni Battista Pergolesi, aged 22, stages his first comic opera, *Lo frate 'nnamorato* (The Lovelorn Brother), at the Teatro dei Fiorentini in Naples.

4 December John Gay, inventor of the 'ballad opera', dies in London aged 47. Buried in Westminster Abbey, he has prepared his own epitaph:

> *Life is a jest
> and all things show it
> I thought so once
> and now I know it.*

7 December John Rich opens The Theatre Royal in Covent Garden, London, with profits from *The Beggar's Opera*.

1732 Persia and Russia agree Treaty of Resht: Russia abandons claims to Astrabad, Gilan and Mazandaran • All the Holy Roman Empire except Bavaria, the Palatinate and Saxony now at least nominally supports Pragmatic Sanction of Emperor Karl VI, leaving his Habsburg lands to his daughter Maria Theresa • British parliament bans imports of hats from colonies, to discourage colonists from competing with home manufacturers • Western Japan suffers a severe famine • Explorer Sieur de La Vérendrye (Fr) establishes Fort St Charles on the Lake of the Woods (now between Canada and USA) • Voltaire (Fr): *Zaïre*

1733

Pietro Locatelli issues his technically-progressive *L'arte del violino*, comprising 12 virtuoso violin concertos, each with a cadenza-like caprice for solo violin in the first and last movements.

Jean-Joseph Mondonville, aged 21, moves to Paris and publishes his *Sonates pour violon* Op. 1.

Telemann's *Musique de table* or *Tafelmusik* is published in three instalments in Hamburg. Each part begins with an orchestral suite, and continues (unusually) with concertos and chamber sonatas. With a publication subscription of 206 names, ranging from amateur and professional musicians to dukes and princes, it becomes Telemann's most famous instrumental collection.

27 January Handel produces his masterly *Orlando* at the King's Theatre, London. Containing some of his most expressive music and featuring **Senesino** in the leading role, the work manages a modest ten-performance run only, due to waning public interest in *opera seria*.

17 March Handel's oratorio *Deborah* premières before a royal audience at the King's Theatre, London. Handel is widely criticised for greediness, having significantly increased admission prices. The production fails.

15 June The Prince of Wales, eager to oppose the tastes of his father, King George II, conspires with the Duke of Marlborough to create the Opera of the Nobility. They engage the composer **Nicola Porpora** to spearhead the rivalry with Handel's opera company, itself in disarray having lost its £20,000 investment.

Summer Handel takes his opera company to Oxford, having lost many of his star singers to the Opera of the Nobility, including **Senesino**. He revives *Esther* and *Deborah*, and also presents a new oratorio, *Athalia*. Despite some xenophobic resentment, Handel reels in the audiences and makes a massive profit.

July Bach presents the *Kyrie* and *Gloria* of his future B minor Mass to the Elector of Saxony (Friedrich August II), in the hope of gaining an honorary position of *Kapellmeister*.

5 September Pergolesi introduces his comedy *La serva padrona* (The Maid as Mistress) between the acts of his serious opera *Il prigioniero superbo*

(The Proud Prisoner), in Naples. Staged with a cast of three, one of whom is mute, the *galant*-style intermezzo becomes an exemplar of Italian comic opera.

11 September François Couperin, one of France's foremost composers, dies in Paris, aged 64.

1 October The 50-year-old **Rameau** begins his opera-writing career with *Hippolyte et Aricie*, introduced at the Paris Opéra. The production features the inimitable ballerina Marie Anne Cupis de Camargo (left).

29 December The Opera of the Nobility launch their first season with **Porpora**'s *Arianna in Nasso* (Ariadne on Naxos) at the Lincoln's Inn Fields Theatre, London. The opera company deliberately schedules its performances on the same evenings as **Handel**'s Royal Academy.

1733 Augustus II of Poland dies: succession contested by ex-king Stanisław Leszczyński (backed by Poles, French and Spaniards) and Augustus's son Augustus of Saxony (backed by Russians and Austrians); France opens War of the Polish Succession against the Holy Roman Empire, occupying Lorraine and invading Lombardy; Russia invades Poland • Persians blockade Baghdad • James Oglethorpe founds Georgia colony in N. America • John Kay (Eng) patents the flying shuttle, a landmark in textile mass-production • Charles Fay (Fr) discovers that charges of static electricity may be resinous (positive) or vitreous (negative) • Alexander Pope (Eng): poem *Essay on Man*

1734

Bach writes his *Coffee Cantata* around this time, telling of a girl's secret passion for drinking coffee. The work has been composed for the students of Leipzig University's *collegium musicum*, who perform regularly at Zimmerman's Coffee House (left).

The London publisher John Walsh issues **Handel**'s Op. 3 *Concerti grossi*, probably without permission.

Keiser composes the Singspiel *Circe*, his final opera for Hamburg, furnishing it with German and Italian arias (including arias by **Hasse** and **Handel**) in equal measure.

Composer-violinist **Jean-Marie Leclair**, recently appointed *ordinaire de la musique du roi*, publishes his *Troisième livre de sonates*, dedicated to Louis XV.

In Paris **Mondonville** brings out his *Sonates en trio* Op. 2 and *Pièces de clavecin en sonates* Op. 3.

Tartini's Op. 1 collection of violin sonatas, including the folksy *Sonata pastorale*, is published in Amsterdam.

Telemann publishes *Six Concerts* and *Six Suites* in Hamburg. These cleverly-constructed ensemble pieces allow parts to be omitted in order to create trio and duo combinations.

17 January Composer **François-Joseph Gossec** is born in Vergnies, South Netherlands.

26 January Handel stages his opera *Arianna* with significant success against the competition of the Opera of the Nobility. The production sustains 16 performances at the King's Theatre, London.

July Despite a popular revival of *Il pastor fido*, **Handel** and Heidegger decide to terminate their business partnership as the opera season closes. Handel moves his productions to Covent Garden.

Autumn Heidegger hires out the King's Theatre to the Opera of the Nobility for its new season of Italian opera. In a further blow to **Handel**, the company also signs up the leading castrato of the day, **Farinelli**.

25 October Pergolesi's serious opera *Adriano in Siria*, starring the castrato **Caffarelli**, struggles at the Teatro San Bartolomeo, Naples. This year has seen the composer's appointment as deputy *maestro di cappella* under **Sarro**, in Naples.

4 November Caldara becomes the first of around 40 18th-century composers to set **Metastasio**'s *La clemenza di Tito*. The opera is premièred at Vienna's Hoftheater.

9 November Handel begins his first opera season at Covent Garden with a further revival of *Il pastor fido*. The opera features a new prologue, *Terpsichore*, in which the French ballerina Marie Sallé dances the part of the muse. Sallé and her dance company perform ballets in each of Handel's productions throughout the season.

Christmas Bach begins the direction of his *Christmas Oratorio* at the Thomaskirche in Leipzig. The six-part work, composed with a great deal of recycled music from his cantatas, is performed one part at a time over the festive period up to Epiphany (6 January).

26 December Sammartini's opera *L'ambizione superata dalla virtù* (Ambition Exceeded by Virtue) opens in Milan.

1734 In the War of the Polish Succession, Spanish troops defeat Austrians at Bitonto (It) and take Naples and Sicily; Russians take Danzig; Polish ex-king Stanisław Leszczyński flees to Prussia, and Augustus of Saxony becomes king as Augustus III • Russia and Britain agree a trade treaty • Jonathan Edwards revives Puritan intensity in New England's *Great Awakening* (1734–42) • Jean-Baptiste Chardin (Fr) paints *The House of Cards* • Voltaire (Fr) comes under political attack for his *Lettres sur les Anglais*, in which he advocates English-style representative rule • Philosopher Emanuel Swedenborg (Swe) publishes his mystical *Prodromus Philosophiae*

Albinoni's *Concerti a cinque* Op.10, for three violins, viola, cello and continuo, is published in Amsterdam.

Bach brings out his *Clavier-Übung II*. Included in the keyboard collection is the *Italian Concerto* (for unaccompanied clavier).

8 January Handel presents *Ariodante* at Covent Garden. The opera contains some of his finest music, but manages only a modest run of 11 performances.

8 January Pergolesi stages *L'Olimpiade* at the Teatro Tordinona, Rome. The opera meets with a cool reception, though gains acclaim in later years. Towards the end of this year the composer enjoys better success with the comedy *Il Flaminio*, in Naples.

12 January John Eccles dies at Hampton Wick, aged around 66. **Maurice Greene** is appointed his successor as Master of the King's Music.

1 February The renowned castrato **Farinelli** stars in **Porpora**'s opera *Polifemo*, introduced at the King's Theatre, London.

Spring During revivals of his oratorios *Esther*, *Deborah* and *Athalia*, **Handel** introduces the organ concerto to the English public. The works premièred will later appear as Nos. 2–5 of his Op. 4 collection (1738).

16 April Handel presents *Alcina* at Covent Garden. The opera proves popular, running for

Carlo Broschi, stage name Farinelli

18 performances to the end of the season. At that point Handel's castrato star, **Giovanni Carestini**, quits both the company and England. The ballerina Mlle Sallé also leaves England in the face of public opposition—primarily for being French.

August In Venice the Pietà governors reinstate **Vivaldi** as their *maestro di cappella*. They grant him an annual wage of 100 ducats, but demand that he curtails his travelling.

23 August Rameau's *Les Indes galantes* (The Gallant Indies), his finest *opéra-ballet*, is performed at the Opéra in Paris. Directly inspired by Campra's *L'Europe galante* (1697), the drama is set in four exotic locations: Turkey, Peru, Persia and North America. In a preface to the work Rameau attempts to pacify the 'Lullists' (those loyal to the style of Lully) by asserting his allegiance to French traditions.

5 September The last of **J. S. Bach**'s sons, **Johann Christian**, is born in Leipzig.

24 September Setting a revised version of **Metastasio**'s libretto *La clemenza di Tito*, **Hasse**'s opera *Tito Vespasiano* inaugurates the Teatro del Sole in Pesaro. The cast includes the composer's wife, **Faustina Bordoni**, and the castrato **Carestini**.

26 November Francesco Veracini's first opera, *Adriano in Siria*, is staged by the Opera of the Nobility at the King's Theatre, London. Famous as a violin virtuoso, Veracini leads the orchestra and enjoys a 20-performance run of his work.

1735 Statesman Sir Robert Walpole continues as Prime Minister of Britain in second parliament of George II • War of the Polish Succession ends: Augustus III confirmed as King of Poland; Austria recognises Carlos of Spain as Carlo IV of Naples and Sicily; Russia is now largely master of Polish affairs • Russia returns Baku and Derbent to Persia; Persians win Tiflis from Turks • Sugar production is established in Mauritius • Preacher John Wesley (Eng) visits America • William Hogarth (Eng) paints picture sequence *A Rake's Progress* • Canaletto (It) paints *Venice: A Regatta on the Grand Canal* • Alexander Pope (Eng): *Moral Essays* and *Epistle to Dr Arbuthnot*

The opera *Les génies*, with music by the 18-year-old **Mlle Duval**, is staged at the Paris Opéra. It is only the second opera by a female composer to be performed there (see also 1694). Duval's first name is unknown.

By this time **Telemann**'s second wife, Maria Catharina, has left him, having burdened the family with gambling debts.

3 February Austrian composer and teacher **Johann Georg Albrechtsberger** is born in Klosterneuburg, near Vienna.

19 February Handel directs the first performance of his Ode *Alexander's Feast* at Covent Garden. Composed in 20 days, the work showcases Handel's new rising star, the 19-year-old tenor **John Beard**. The evening's entertainments also include a cantata (*Cecilia volgi*) and three concertos, including the Harp Concerto in B flat major. With a full house and rapturous reception, Handel enjoys his best opening night for years.

16 March The 26-year-old **Giovanni Battista Pergolesi** (right), having just completed his *Stabat Mater* and *Salve regina*, dies in Pozzuoli, outside Naples. The likely cause of death is consumption.

30 March Bach directs a revised version of his *St Matthew Passion* at the Thomaskirche, Leipzig.

April William Boyce's sacred cantata *David's Lamentation over Saul and Jonathan* is introduced at the Apollo Academy in Fleet Street, London.

2 April After nearly half a century's near-constant service to St Mark's, Venice, **Lotti** finally secures the post of *maestro di cappella*. He receives a salary of 400 ducats and free lodging.

27 April Handel obediently directs his anthem *Sing unto God* at the wedding of his antagonist, Prince Frederick of Wales, and Princess Augusta of Saxe-Gotha.

4 May Porpora presents his serenata *La festa d'Imeneo* at the King's Theatre, London, for the ongoing wedding celebrations of his patron, the Prince of Wales. Realising that the Opera of the Nobility is on the verge of collapse, the Italian composer leaves England during the summer.

12 May Handel stages his opera *Atalanta*, dedicating it to the Prince of Wales in honour of his recent marriage. This, together with his wedding anthem of the previous month, begins a process of reconciliation between the two adversaries.

August Bach loses his authority to appoint choral prefects at the Thomasschule. He falls out with both the new rector, Johann August Ernesti, and the Leipzig town council, leading to strained relations over the next two years.

19 November Bach receives the title of court composer to Augustus III, Elector of Saxony and King of Poland.

28 December Renowned for his oratorios, cantatas and operas, Italian composer **Antonio Caldara** dies in Vienna, aged about 65.

1736 Riots in Edinburgh (Scot): mob seizes Captain John Porteous, who ordered guards to fire on crowd, and hangs him • Franz Stephen, Duke of Lorraine, marries Maria Theresa of Austria, heir to Holy Roman Emperor Karl VI • Ex-king Stanisław Leszczyński formally renounces Polish crown • Russia and Austria start war with Turks; Russia retakes Azov

• Nadir Shah fails to convert Persia from Shi'ite to Sunni Islam • British parliament repeals law punishing witchcraft with death • Swiss mathematician Leonhard Euler publishes first systematic mechanics textbook • Joseph Butler, Bishop of Durham (Eng) defends Christianity against Deism in *Analogy of Religion*

Christoph Willibald Gluck, aged 22, becomes a chamber musician to Prince Antonio Melzi in Milan. It is possible that around this time he also begins taking lessons from **Sammartini**.

Johann Franck takes **Josef Haydn** from his parental home in Rohrau to Hainburg. There the five year old continues his schooling and receives musical tuition.

P. Locatelli continues to push the boundaries of performance technique in his 12 *da camera* violin sonatas Op. 6, published in Amsterdam.

Jean-Féry Rebel (right) invents the tone-cluster for his final work, the ballet suite *Les élémens*. The first movement, *Cahos* (Chaos), opens with the orchestra playing every note of the D harmonic minor scale simultaneously. According to the septuagenarian composer this intense dissonance represents the 'confusion that reigned among the elements before the moment … they took their ordained places in the order of nature'.

January–May Handel fires off three operas in quick succession. *Arminio* is withdrawn after six performances, *Giustino* fairs slightly better with nine and *Berenice* collapses after only four. When his revival of the *Triumph of Time* also falls flat, the composer faces bankruptcy.

April Handel develops paralysis in his right arm, probably due to the stresses of the opera season. His mental health is also deteriorating.

12 April Veracini's version of *La clemenza di Tito*

is introduced by the Opera of the Nobility at the King's Theatre, London. It manages only four performances.

May Vivaldi's opera *Catone in Utica*, with libretto by **Metastasio**, is first performed in Verona.

11 June The Opera of the Nobility closes down with debts of £12,000. Their leading castrato, **Farinelli**, departs England for Spain a very wealthy man.

Autumn Handel convalesces in the sulphur baths of Aix-la-Chapelle. He returns to England in November having made a full recovery.

Autumn Telemann visits Paris where he secures a 20-year publishing privilege. He stays there until the following May.

24 October Rameau's greatest opera, the five-act mythical tragedy *Castor et Pollux*, premières with just modest success at the Paris Opéra. *Castor* later becomes a regular fixture at the Opéra and remains popular until the 1780s.

4 November Sarro's opera *Achille in Sciro*, on a libretto by **Metastasio**, inaugurates the San Carlo opera house in Naples.

17 December Handel's funeral anthem *The ways of Zion do mourn* is first performed with around 80 singers and a 100-piece orchestra for the funeral of Queen Caroline, at Westminster Abbey.

18 December Renowned violin-maker **Antonio Stradivari** dies in Cremona, aged about 90.

1737 Death of George II's wife Queen Caroline (UK) robs Prime Minister Sir Robert Walpole of important political support • Medici family's rule in Tuscany ends with death of Gian Gastone; Duke Franz Stephen of Lorraine becomes Grand Duke of Tuscany • Russians invade Turkish-held Moldavia and ravage Crimea, but Turks win upper band against Russians and Austrians • Forces of Nadir Shah (Persia) subdue cities of Balkh (now in Afghanistan) and Baluchistan (now in Pakistan) • Joshua Ward (Eng) produces sulfuric acid • Pierre Marivaux (Fr): comedy *Les Fausses confidences* • Theatre censorship by the Lord Chamberlain is introduced in Britain

Handel becomes one of the first contributors to The Fund for the Support of Decayed Musicians (later named the Royal Society of Musicians). This year sees the publication of six concertos for chamber organ and orchestra as the composer's Op. 4.

Mondonville's violin sonatas *Les sons harmoniques* are published in Paris and Lille. Eclectic and broad in style, they are the first printed violin works to contain notated harmonics.

Domenico Scarlatti (right) has his *Essercizi per gravicembalo* published in London. The set of 30 single-movement sonatas is dedicated to King João V of Spain, who this year ennobles Scarlatti as a Knight of the Order of Santiago.

Stanley, aged 26, marries Sarah Arlond, a captain's daughter, who brings with her a substantial dowry of £7,000. Sarah's sister Ann shortly becomes the blind composer's amanuensis.

Telemann publishes his *Nouveaux quatuors en 6 suites* in Paris.

3 January Handel's opera *Faramondo* premières at the King's Theatre. Back in collaboration with the impresario Heidegger, Handel shares the opera season with two other composers, **Veracini** and **Giovanni Pescetti**. Marking the London début of the castrato **Caffarelli**, the production achieves only eight performances.

7 January Vivaldi, special guest at the centenary celebrations of Amsterdam's Schouwburg Theatre, introduces his Violin Concerto in D major RV562a, composed for the occasion. His absence

from Venice results in the termination of his contract with the Pietà.

4 March Thomas A. Arne triumphs with his setting of Milton's masque *Comus* at London's Theatre Royal, Drury Lane.

28 March Handel stitches together some previously composed sacred works in a production advertised as *An Oratorio* at the King's Theatre. He reputedly makes £1,000 from the evening.

15 April Handel's opera *Serse* (Xerxes) begins a run of only five performances at the King's Theatre. The breathtaking song 'Ombre mai fu' (Never was a Shade) from Act 2 will later become Handel's most famous air, popularised by the instrumental transcription *Largo*.

May A marble statue of **Handel** by Louis Roubiliac is unveiled in Vauxhall Gardens, London. It is the first time a living composer has been honoured in this way.

May C. P. E. Bach takes up an unofficial post as court harpsichordist to Crown Prince Frederick of Prussia.

July Having heard that Heidegger is unable to raise funds for a new opera season, **Handel** embarks on the composition of an oratorio, *Saul*, in collaboration with the scholar **Charles Jennens**. Immediately following its completion, Handel writes the oratorio *Israel in Egypt*.

20 December Institutionalised for insanity, French composer **Jean-Joseph Mouret** dies in Charenton, aged 56.

1738 Austria formally abandons Naples, Sicily and Elba to Spain and gets Parma and Piacenza (It); ex-king Stanisław Leszczyński of Poland receives duchy of Lorraine and Bar • European powers seemingly agree Pragmatic Sanction, which secures Habsburg lands to Maria Theresa of Austria • Count Gyllenborg overthrows Arvid Horn as chief Swedish minister • Armies of Nadir Shah (Persia) overrun Afghanistan and invade India • Austria loses Orsova and Semindria to Turks • Pope Clement XII attacks Freemasonry in bull (proclamation) *In Eminenti* • Jean-Baptiste Chardin (Fr) paints *Scouring Maid* • John Gay (Eng): *Fables*, second series, published posthumously

Bach publishes his *Clavier-Übung III*. Comprising organ pieces based around the catechism and various hymns, it is the largest of his keyboard collections.

Geminiani publishes his *Sonate* Op. 4, 12 sonatas for violin and continuo, in London.

Mattheson (left), now severely deaf, brings out *Der vollkommene Capellmeister* (The Complete Music Master) in Hamburg. Chiefly a manual on music directing, the publication also discusses the doctrine of the 'affections'.

January Vivaldi learns that his revived opera *Siroe* (1727) has failed in Ferrara. He is currently banned from the town due to suspicions over his relationship with the prima-donna Anna Girò, and his refusal to say mass (which, he maintains, is due to respiratory problems). The composer's fortunes and favour, even in Venice, are at low ebb.

16 January Handel's oratorio *Saul*, composed the previous year, begins a run of six performances at the King's Theatre, London.

4 April Handel's second oratorio of the season, *Israel in Egypt*, fails to captivate audiences. Despite entertaining musical representations of flies, frogs, hail and other Egyptian plagues, together with some of Handel's most poignant musical symbolism, the work is withdrawn after just three performances.

1 May Handel stages his *pasticcio* opera *Giove in Argo* (Jupiter in Argos) at the King's Theatre. It manages only two performances. Handel is by now totally disillusioned—audiences seem to want neither his oratorios nor his operas.

12 May Composer **Johann Baptiste Vanhal** is born in Nechanice, Bohemia.

21 May Rameau's fourth opera, *Les fêtes d'Hébé*, enjoys spectacular success with a first run of 71 performances at the Paris Opéra.

24 July Benedetto Marcello dies in Brescia, aged 53. His tombstone inscription reads 'the Michelangelo of music'.

He is an old man with a prodigious passion for composing. I have heard him boast of composing a concerto in all its parts faster than a copyist could write it down.
29 August Charles de Brosses on **Vivaldi**.

12 September Pioneering German opera composer **Reinhard Keiser** dies in Hamburg, aged 65.

2 November Composer **Carl Ditters** (later, Ditters von Dittersdorf) is born in Vienna.

19 November Rameau's opera *Dardanus* achieves 26 performances at the Paris Opéra, despite criticisms of its nonsensical plot.

22 November As England enters into conflict with Spain (the so-called 'War of Jenkins' Ear'), **Handel** lifts public spirits with his *Ode for St Cecilia's Day*, performed at Lincoln's Inn Fields. Playing to packed houses, he also revives his Ode *Alexander's Feast* and *Acis and Galatea*, each for two performances.

1739 Britain starts War of Jenkins' Ear with Spain over mutilation of an English seaman in 1731; Admiral Edward Vernon storms Porto Bello, Darien • Russia and Turkey agree Treaty of Belgrade: Russia keeps Azov but is forbidden to build a Black Sea fleet • Forces of Nadir Shah (Persia) crush Mogul army and capture Delhi, India • Felipe, son of Felipe V (Sp), marries daughter of Louis XV (Fr) • Preacher George Whitefield (Eng) influences Great Awakening in North America • Philosopher David Hume (Scot) develops empiricist philosophy in *Treatise on Human Nature* • Dick Turpin, notorious English highwayman, is convicted of horse theft and executed

Mattheson lists his top 149 musicians, past and present, in his *Grundlage einer Ehren-Pforte* (Foundation for a Triumphal Arch).

Matthias Georg Monn composes the earliest known four-movement symphony with a third-movement minuet. It is unique among the composer's symphonies, all of which otherwise follow a three-movement plan.

Stanley's *Eight Solos for Flute and Continuo* are issued in London as the composer's Op. 1.

Telemann, around this time, issues his *Essercizii musici*, a marvellous collection of solo and trio sonatas for a variety of lead instruments (including oboe, viola da gamba and recorder) and two suites for harpsichord. The music itself probably dates from the 1720s.

5 January Composer **Antonio Lotti**, famous above all for his operas and sacred music, dies in Venice, aged about 73.

27 February **Handel**'s oratorio *L'Allegro, il Penseroso ed il Moderato*, with an adapted Milton text by **Jennens**, receives the first of six badly-attended performances at Lincoln's Inn Fields Theatre, London.

21 March **Vivaldi**'s Sinfonia in G major (RV149) and three concertos (RV540, 552, 558) are premièred at the Pietà in Venice, in honour of the visiting Crown Prince of Saxony. The prince praises the Concerto in A major, RV552, with its unusual scoring for violin, strings, and three echo violins positioned away from the ensemble. The concertos serve as entr'actes to the serenata *Il coro delle muse* by leading Venetian librettist **Carlo Goldoni** and composer **Gennaro d'Alessandro**.

Spring The eight-year-old **Josef Haydn** moves from Hainburg to Vienna to take up a place in the St Stephen's Cathedral choir.

April London publisher Walsh issues **Handel**'s *12 Grand Concertos* (Op. 6), masterpieces of the *concerti grossi* genre, written the previous year within the space of a month. Six members of the royal family are among the subscribers to the collection. A (second) set of Handel's organ concertos is published towards the end of this year, including *The Cuckoo and the Nightingale*.

9 May Italian opera composer **Giovanni Paisiello** is born at Roccaforzata, near Taranto.

12 May With **Vivaldi** about to leave Venice for Vienna, the Pietà governors decide to purchase 20 concertos from him at around three and a half ducats each.

31 May As Frederick the Great of Prussia takes to his throne, **C. P. E. Bach** is officially appointed Court Harpsichordist in Berlin at an annual salary of 300 thalers. Also in the king's musical retinue is **Quantz** (right), flute teacher and court composer engaged at 2,000 thalers a year, and **Carl Heinrich Graun**, who gains the same wage with his promotion to *Kapellmeister* the following year.

1 August **Thomas Arne**'s *Rule Britannia* is heard for the first time as part of the composer's masque *Alfred*, performed at a garden party of the Prince of Wales at Cliveden House, near Maidenhead.

22 November **Handel**'s opera *Imeneo*, begun two years previously but only completed the previous month, is introduced at Lincoln's Inn Fields. It survives just two performances, adding to Handel's catalogue of operatic failures.

1740 British colonists invade Spanish Florida • Bengal becomes independent of Delhi • Holy Roman Emperor Karl VI (Aus) dies; Europe's Great Powers refuse recognition of his daughter, Maria Theresa, as heir to Austria, despite earlier agreement to do so: Karl Albrecht of Bavaria, Felipe V of Spain and Augustus III of Saxony claim Austria, leading to War of the Austrian Succession • Prussians occupy Silesia in First Silesian War against Austria • Pope Clement XII dies; is succeeded by Benedict XIV • Antonio Canaletto (It) paints *The Square of St Mark's* • J-B Chardin (Fr) paints *Saying Grace* • Samuel Richardson (Eng): novel *Pamela*

1741

Albinoni composes the opera *Artamene* for the Teatro San Angelo in Venice. It is his last (and possibly 81st) stage work.

One of the earliest collections of symphonies, **Antonio Brioschi**'s *XII Sonate*, Op. 1 (composed in Milan), is published in Paris. Works of early symphonic form at this time are variously described as symphonies, concertos, sinfonias, overtures or sonatas.

Around this time **Johann Stamitz**, aged 24, is engaged as a string player at the electoral court in Mannheim.

Rameau publishes *Pièces de clavecin en concerts* for harpsichord, violin (or flute) and viola da gamba. Nine of the 19 pieces are named after friends, patrons and pupils.

January–February Handel's romantic comedy *Deidamia* fails after only three performances in London. Handel abandons opera for good.

8 February Composer **André-Ernest-Modeste Grétry** is born in Liège.

13 February Composer and theorist **Johann Fux** dies in Vienna, aged about 80.

28 July Having arrived in Vienna in search of new patronage, **Antonio Vivaldi** dies from an internal inflammation, aged 63. He receives a humble burial the same day.

22 August Handel begins composing the oratorio *Messiah* on

biblical text selected and arranged by **Charles Jennens**. Handel does not leave his house for three weeks and frequently goes without food.

Autumn Bach publishes *Aria with 30 Variations*—later known as the *Goldberg Variations*—as book IV of his *Clavier-Übung*. The set's more familiar name derives from Bach's pupil Johann Gottlieb Goldberg, who, as harpsichordist to Count Kaiserling in Dresden, is said to have regularly played the variations late at night to entertain his sleepless employer. Many scholars reject the story.

I did think I did see all Heaven before me and the great God Himself seated on His throne, with His Company of Angels.

Handel to his servant, on completing Part II of *Messiah*.

14 September Handel, in 23 days, completes the score of his *Messiah*.

November Handel arrives in Dublin (by invitation of the Lord-Lieutenant of Ireland) to participate in the winter concert season. The following month he revives his oratorio *L'Allegro* (1740). The work that failed to inspire London audiences is well appreciated.

26 December Gluck's first opera, *Artaserse*, to a libretto by **Metastasio**, premières in Milan.

Page of the 'Hallelujah Chorus', from Handel's *Messiah*.

1741 In War of the Austrian Succession, Prussians defeat Austrians at Mollwitz • Bavaria, France and Spain (later with Saxony and Prussia) conclude a secret anti-Austrian alliance • Franco-Bavarian troops invade Austria and Bohemia • Concordat curbs papal wealth and power in Naples • Military revolt overthrows Russian tsar Ivan VI and puts Elizaveta, youngest daughter of Petr I, the Great, on the throne • Burials outnumber baptisms by 2 to 1 in London at height of gin-drinking craze: 75 percent of children die before age five in England at this time • David Hume (Scot): *Essays Moral and Political*

C. P. E. Bach's six *Prussian Sonatas* for harpsichord are published in Nuremburg (see also 1744).

Stanley's *Six Concertos in Seven Parts* (Op. 2) are published in London.

2 March **Baldassare Galuppi**, promoting himself in London, presents his opera *Scipione in Cartagine* at the King's Theatre, Haymarket.

24 March **Handel** revives *Imeneo* for a concert performance in Dublin. As with *L'Allegro*, the London failure is hailed a triumph by the Irish.

13 April Great excitement surrounds the charity première of **Handel**'s *Messiah* in Dublin. A request is made for ladies not to wear hoop skirts and for gentlemen to leave their swords at home, in order to fit more people into the Fishamble Street Music Hall. 700 people attend the momentous occasion and nearly £400 is raised for charity.

14 April 'Words are wanting to express the exquisite delight it afforded to the admiring crowded audience.' Faulkner's Journal, reporting on **Handel**'s *Messiah*.

Fishamble Street, Dublin, venue for *Messiah*

2 May **Gluck**, again setting **Metastasio**, presents *Cleonice* (*Demetrio*), his second opera, in Venice.

13 August Having taken Dublin by storm, **Handel** returns to England.

7 December **Carl Graun**'s opera *Cleopatra e Cesare* inaugurates the new Berlin Opera House, built under the direction of Frederick the Great.

Johann Stamitz is promoted to first violinist at the Mannheim electoral court.

Composers **François Rebel** and **François Francoeur** are jointly appointed to the post of *inspecteur général* (musical director) at the Paris Opéra.

3 February **Sammartini** stages his last opera, *L'Agrippina, moglie di Tiberio*, at the Regio Ducal Teatro, Milan.

18 February **Handel**'s oratorio *Samson*, composed 1741, enjoys a victorious première at Covent Garden. The libretto, by **Newburgh Hamilton**, is largely an adaptation of Milton's dramatic poem *Samson Agonistes*.

19 February Italian composer and cellist **Luigi Boccherini** is born in Lucca.

23 March **Handel** directs the first London performance of *Messiah* at Covent Garden. During the *Hallelujah Chorus* King George II stands up, possibly greatly moved, or perhaps to relieve a stiff knee. The entire audience follows suit and so begins the long-running tradition. Unfortunately for Handel, many boycott his *Sacred Oratorio* for being performed in a playhouse; consequently it manages only two repeat performances.

April **Handel** suffers from another temporary 'paralytic disorder'.

27 November **Handel** directs his 'Dettingen' Te Deum and anthem *The King shall Rejoice* at the Chapel Royal, in celebration of George II's recent victory over the French at Dettingen, Bavaria.

1742 First Silesian War ends with Treaty of Breslau and Berlin: Austria cedes upper and lower Silesia to Prussia • War of the Austrian Succession, Austrians overrun Bavaria and Bohemia • Spanish forces attack Georgia from Florida • François Boucher (Fr) paints *Diana Resting* • Henry Fielding (Eng): *Joseph Andrews*

1743 Russo-Swedish Treaty of Abö cedes Finnish territory to Russia • Turkey and Persia are at war • In War of Jenkins' Ear Britain invades Florida • King George's War begins • France and Spain sign Treaty of Fontainebleau • Austria hands over Piacenza and Parma to Sardinia • French encyclopaedist Jean d'Alembert publishes *Treatise on Dynamics*

C. P. E. Bach publishes his *Württemberg Sonatas*, a collection of six harpsichord sonatas dedicated to his pupil Duke Carl Eugen of Württemberg. Together with the *Prussian Sonatas* (1742), the pieces demonstrate Carl Bach's mastery of contrapuntal techniques, as well as his innovative approach to harmonic organisation and thematic development. He is one of the first composers of the period to explore the transformation of emotion in a single movement, bucking the Baroque ideal of the unity of expression (or *affekt*).

Around this time **J. S. Bach** finishes a second volume of 24 preludes and fugues, completing the *Well-Tempered Clavier* (first volume 1722).

God Save the King appears in print for the first time. Published in a collection of songs under the title *Harmonia Anglicana*, the author is unknown. Henry Carey (d. 1743) has a popular vote, although it probably dates back to the early 17th century. The first of its kind, the anthem will in time ignite the trend for national anthems worldwide.

Locatelli's *X sonate* Op. 8, comprising solo and trio sonatas, is issued in Amsterdam and dedicated to Abraham Croock, a wealthy gunpowder merchant.

Franz Xaver Richter blends Baroque and pre-Classical styles in two sets of *6 grandes simphonies* (*à 4*), published in Paris.

10 February Handel's secular oratorio *Semele*, adapted from **William Congreve**'s opera libretto of the same name, begins a run of only four performances at Covent Garden. Some of the public condemn it for not being proper opera, others for sullying the sacred nature of the oratorio. His next oratorio, *Joseph*, follows three weeks later and although not a success, it is better received.

4 March Mondonville becomes *sous-maître* of the royal chapel in Paris.

29 June André Campra, a leading composer of the French stage and church, dies in Versailles, aged 83.

August Sweden's foremost composer, **Johan Roman**, produces his orchestral suite *Drottningholmsmusique* for the Stockholm wedding celebrations of Adolphus Frederik and Louisa Ulrika of Prussia.

23 October Handel completes his oratorio *Belshazzar*, with text by **Charles Jennens**.

3 November With Lord Middlesex's opera company unable to mount a new season at the King's Theatre (below), **Handel** moves in with his own oratorio subscription concerts. High-profile society members loyal to Middlesex boycott Handel's season, which, with a string of revivals, struggles from the outset.

1744 Armies of King Friedrich II, the Great, of Prussia invade Saxony and Bohemia, starting Second Silesian War (part of the War of the Austrian Succession) • France goes to war with Austria and Britain • French and Indians invade Nova Scotia, but have to withdraw • Lord George Anson (Eng) completes a four-year circumnavigation of the world, having explored islands north of Strait of Magellan • The London Club issues the earliest known version of the Laws of Cricket • Eliza Haywood (Eng) launches *The Female Spectator*, the first periodical written for women by a woman

Jommelli undertakes a short spell as musical director of the Ospedale degli Incurabili (Hospital for Incurables) in Venice. He leaves for Rome the following year.

Leclair, for the last five years in service to the Duke of Gramont, issues his Six Violin Concertos Op. 10, in Paris

Jean-Jacques Rousseau stages excerpts of his newly-composed opera *Les muses galantes* at the house of La Pouplinière in Paris. **Rameau**, invited to witness and comment, in no uncertain terms charges the philosopher-composer with plagiarism. He also asserts that the opera has been composed partly by a learned musician—the 19-year-old **F-A Philidor**—and partly 'by an ignoramus who does not understand the first thing about music'.

Johann Stamitz, aged 28, is appointed *Konzertmeister* at Mannheim. Over the ensuing years he will elevate the Mannheim orchestra to the most famous and respected ensemble in Europe, renowned for its precision playing and lively dynamic contrasts and crescendos.

Georg Wagenseil's first opera, *Ariodante*, is introduced in Venice.

Winter–spring Handel's oratorios *Hercules* and *Belshazzar*, both completed the previous year, are introduced at the King's Theatre with little success. The season of 24 planned subscription concerts peters out after 16 performances.

Jean-Philippe Rameau, France's leading composer of the late Baroque

January Thomas Arne attempts to write Italian-style comic opera with his inauspiciously entitled composition *The Temple of Dullness*. The opera quickly fails.

23 February Rameau's *La Princesse de Navarre*, a *comédie-ballet* with libretto by **Voltaire**, is first performed for the marital celebrations of the Dauphin and the Infanta Maria Theresa of Spain, at Versailles.

31 March Rameau's first *comédie lyrique*, *Platée*, is introduced at Versailles.

7 May Composer **Carl Stamitz**, son of **Johann**, is born in Mannheim.

Late summer Gluck arrives in London to take up the post of composer to the King's Theatre, having achieved several years of operatic success in Italy. The theatre is closed at this time, however, due to the Jacobite rebellion raging in Scotland and the north of England. Gluck stays for one year.

December In Dresden, King Frederick II is thrilled by a newly-revised version of **Hasse**'s opera *Arminio* (1730). Delighted also with the part played by Hasse's famous wife, **Faustina** (née **Bordoni**), the king requests the composer's attendance each evening at court to direct musical performances. Hasse is later rewarded with a diamond ring and 1,000 thalers to share out among members of the orchestra.

23 December Bohemian-born **Jan Zelenka**, long-serving church composer to the Dresden Court, dies aged 66.

1745 Charles Edward Stuart ('The Young Pretender') lands in Scotland from France and starts Jacobite rebellion; he wins battles of Prestonpans and Penrith • War of the Austrian Succession continues: Saxony and Netherlands join Britain and Austria against France and Bavaria • Holy Roman Emperor Karl VII dies; is succeeded by Franz I, husband of Maria Theresa • Naturalist Charles Bonnet (Switz) discovers instances of parthenogenesis (reproduction without mating) among insects • Physician Julien Offroy de La Mettrie (Fr) publishes *Natural History of the Soul* • William Hogarth (Eng) paints *Self Portrait* • Giovanni Battista Tiepolo (It) paints *Apollo and Daphne*

Bach publishes his six *Schübler Chorales* for organ, transcribed from earlier cantatas.

W. F. Bach resigns from his post at the Dresden Sophienkirche and takes up new employment as organist and musical director of the Liebfrauenkirche (Our Lady's Church) in Halle.

Neapolitan composer **Francesco Durante** writes his Requiem Mass in C minor.

Geminiani, aged 58, issues his final set of Sonatas (Op. 5), comprising six violin sontatas and six cello sonatas, and his final collection of *concerti grossi* (Op. 7).

7 January **Gluck** stages *La caduta de' giganti* (The Fall of the Giants), his first London production, at the King's Theatre. Incorporating much previously composed music, the opera panders to the London audience by allegorising the impending defeat of Bonnie Prince Charlie and the Jacobites.

14 February **Handel** directs the first performance of his *Occasional Oratorio*, composed with new and recycled music, in patriotic celebration of the Jacobites' retreat from England.

25 March A charity concert featuring works by both **Handel** and **Gluck** is given in London. Whether both composers attend is not recorded, although Handel's opinion of Gluck is (by Charles Burney): 'he knows no more of counterpoint than my cook, Waltz.'

End of March **Gluck** demonstrates his glass-harp skills, performing in two concerts (one of these possibly the charity event above) 'upon twenty-six drinking glasses, tuned with spring-water' (*General Advertiser*, 31 March).

July–August **Handel** composes his oratorio *Judas Maccabaeus*. Prince Frederick of Wales has commissioned the work in celebration of the victory (led by his brother, the Duke of

Cumberland) over the Jacobites at Culloden (above). Formerly antagonistic towards Handel, Prince Frederick now becomes an important royal patron.

27 August German composer **Johann C. F. Fischer** dies in Rastatt, aged 89.

14 October **Domenico Alberti** dies in Rome, aged 36. He is remembered chiefly for his use of arpeggiated bass patterns in his keyboard sonatas, hence the term 'Alberti bass'.

15 October **Wagenseil** stages his opera *La clemenza di Tito* in Vienna. At the end of the year he also premières *Demetrio*, in Florence.

1746 Jacobite rebellion quashed at Culloden; lasting around one hour, the battle is the last fought on British soil • Bonnie Prince Charlie flees to the Isle of Skye, then France • Harsh 'pacification' of Highland Scotland begins; wearing of tartans made illegal • In War of Austrian Succession, France defeats Austria and its allies at Raucoux, and conquers the Austrian Netherlands; Russia makes an alliance with Austria • French encyclopaedist Denis Diderot writes *Philosophical Thoughts* • Jean le Rond d'Alembert (Fr) develops theory of complex numbers • Antonio Canaletto (It) paints *Westminster Bridge* • Samuel Johnson (Eng) begins his *Dictionary of the English Language* (completed 1755)

Composer and virtuoso performer **Jean-Baptiste Forqueray** publishes *Pièces de viole avec la basse continue*, in Paris. Most of the 29 pieces are credited to his father, Antoine Forqueray (who died two years previously), with just three to himself. They are considered the most fiendishly difficult pieces of viol repertory.

Graupner indulges the timpanist in his courtly Sinfonia for two horns, timpani and strings. A blend of symphony and suite, it is one of over 100 works by the composer in the symphony or hybrid mould.

Monn, in Vienna, composes his fashionable Violin Concerto in B flat major. He appeals to the *galant* temperament with catchy tunes and harmonic clarity.

Tartini's Op. 4 and Op. 5, each containing six violin sonatas, are published in Paris.

2 January **Jean-Féry Rebel**, remembered mainly for his instrumental music, dies in Paris, aged 80.

28 January **Jommelli**'s serious opera *Didone abbandonata*, to a libretto by **Metastasio** (first set 1724), opens at the Teatro Argentina in Rome. Jommelli, recently arrived from Venice, is widely known in court circles throughout the Italian peninsula and continues to field commissions from Naples, his native city.

15 March *Les fêtes de l'Hymen et de l'Amour*, an *opéra-ballet* by **Rameau**, is first performed at Versailles for the wedding celebrations of the dauphin and his second wife, Maria-Josepha of Saxony. Around this time the composer also pens his virtuosic keyboard piece *La Dauphine*.

1 April **Handel** directs the première of *Judas Maccabaeus* at Covent Garden. Eager to witness the depiction of a heroic Jew on the London stage, a significant Jewish public bolsters attendance figures. The oratorio's anti-Jacobite allegory, devised by **Thomas Morell**, secures the work's immediate success.

May **J. S. Bach** visits his son **Carl** at the court of Frederick II (left) in Berlin. During his stay, Bach performs improvised fugues to the court, including a *ricercare* based on a theme by the king. Flattered by royal praise, Bach later composes a series of keyboard and chamber works all based on the royal theme. The resulting *Musikalisches Opfer* (Musical Offering) is dedicated to the king with servile propriety: ' … the most distinguished part of [the *Musikalisches Opfer*] is the work of your Majesty's own illustrious hand'.

Summer **Handel** composes the oratorios *Joshua* and *Alexander Balus*.

29 June The two-act serenata *Le nozze d'Ercole e d'Ebe* (The Marriage of Hercules and Hebe), with light Italianate music by **Gluck**, has its première at Pillnitz, near Dresden. Gluck furnishes the first movement of his overture with music poached from a **Sammartini** symphony.

9 July Italian opera composer **Giovanni Bononcini**, former London rival of Handel, dies in Vienna, aged 76.

26 December **Galuppi**'s opera *L'olimpiade* opens with great success at the Teatro Regio Ducal in Milan. **Metastasio**'s libretto, set several times previously (first by Caldara in 1733), inspires some 50 different operas during the 18th century.

1747 In the War of the Austrian Succession, British fleets defeat French fleets off Cape Finisterre, northwest Spain, and in the West Indies • The Dutch Republic appoints Willem IV of Orange as hereditary Stadtholder • In Persia, the assassination of Nadir Shah sparks off serious unrest, with three claimants to the throne; Ahmed Shah Durrani becomes ruler of an independent Afghanistan • The first clinic for venereal diseases is founded with the London Lock Hospital • James Lind (Scot) runs a pioneering clinical trial to establish that citrus fruits prevent scurvy • William Hogarth (Eng) draws *Industry and Idleness* • Charles Collé (Fr): comedy *Truth in Wine* • Voltaire (Fr): fictional philosophical tale *Zadig* • Samuel Richardson (Eng): *Clarissa, or The History of a Young Lady*

Oxford's Holywell Music Room opens its doors to the public. It is the first purpose-built concert hall in Europe.

Bach (right) revises *The Art of Fugue*. Composed in the early 1740s and comprising 12 fugues and two canons, the collection represents the apogee of Baroque fugal counterpoint. Bach continues the revision process into the following year, hampered by a debilitating eye disease.

In Holland **F-A Philidor** writes *L'analyze des échecs* (Analysis of Chess). The French composer, who turns 22 this year, is one of Europe's foremost chess players.

Rameau's nephew Jean-François insults the directors of the Paris Opéra and lands himself in jail. Rameau, lacking avuncular benevolence, advises the authorities to deport his nephew to the colonies. The Secretary of State politely dismisses the composer's request and releases the offender after three weeks.

Stanley publishes his first set of *Ten Voluntarys* (Op. 5) for organ.

Tartini's Op. 6 and Op. 7, each containing six violin sonatas, are published in Paris.

29 February A genie falls in love with a mortal shepherdess in **Rameau**'s *Zaïs*, a *pastorale-héroïque* boasting one of the composer's most inventive overtures, premièred at the Paris Opéra.

March Telemann presents his St Luke's Passion (TWV 5:33) at Hamburg's principal Lutheran churches during Lent. It is one of his most inspired choral works.

23 March German composer, organist and theorist **Johann G. Walther** dies in Weimar, aged 63.

April Porpora is appointed *Kapellmeister* at Dresden. He assumes control only for two years, when he is diplaced by his rival, the more popular composer **Hasse**.

Spring Handel's new oratorios *Joshua* and *Alexander Balus* fail to impress at Covent Garden. The composer writes the oratorios *Solomon* and *Susanna* over the summer.

14 May Gluck's opera *Semiramide riconosciuta* is first staged for the birthday celebrations of Empress Maria Theresa in Vienna. The opera, the composer's first for Vienna, simultaneously inaugurates the recently renovated Burgtheater. Gluck enjoys spectacular success.

27 August A sculptor falls in love with his own creation in *Pigmalion*, set as an *acte de ballet* (essentially a one-act opera) by **Rameau** and premièred with outstanding success at the Paris Opéra.

25 November Theologian **Isaac Watts**, considered the 'Father of English Hymnody', dies in Stoke Newington aged 74. Among his many classics are 'Joy to the world', 'When I survey the wondrous cross' and 'Our God, our help in ages past'.

13 December Graun presents *Ifigenie in Aulide* at the newly founded Berlin Opera. His employer, Frederick II, contributes to the libretto.

1748 The Treaty of Aix-la-Chapelle (Aachen) ends the War of Austrian Succession: Pragmatic Sanction in Austria (the succession of Empress Maria Theresa) and right of Hanoverian succession in Britain is agreed by all parties • In India, French forces repel a British naval attack on Pondicherry, but return Madras to Britain • British physician John Fothergill describes diphtheria • Excavation begins on the site of Pompeii (It) • Philosopher David Hume (Scot): *Enquiry Concerning Human Understanding* • French political philosopher Charles de Montesquieu publishes *The Spirit of Laws*, an entirely new approach to the study of social and political institutions • Tobias Smollett (Scot): novel *The Adventures of Roderick Random*

7 February Musketeer-turned-composer **André Cardinal Destouches** dies in Paris, aged 76.

17 March Handel's new oratorio *Solomon* (including the sinfonia *The Arrival of the Queen of Sheba*) encounters public apathy at Covent Garden. As with his previous oratorio season, Handel's purse is spared by successful revivals of earlier oratorios, including *Messiah*.

21 April Around 12,000 people attend the rehearsal of **Handel**'s *Music for the Royal Fireworks* at Vauxhall Gardens in London. The event causes one of the first recorded traffic jams in the city, with carriages held up on London Bridge for three hours.

27 April A huge celebration of the Peace of Aix-la-Chapelle (1748) takes place in Green Park, London. **Handel**'s *Music for the Royal Fireworks*, commissioned for the event, receives its official première. However, after a kingly salute of 101 brass cannons, the fireworks fail to perform as planned. A wing of the massive stage and set catches fire and, according to one source, two spectators are trampled to death in the ensuing panic.

27 May Handel directs his *Fireworks Music* and other pieces for the benefit of the Foundling Hospital. He will later be appointed to the governing body of the charity.

15 June German theorist and composer **Georg Vogler** is born in Würzburg.

25 August C. P. E. Bach completes his celebrated Magnificat.

Autumn Bach, virtually blind, has by now completed the amalgamation and revision of one of the crowning works of classical music: the Mass in B minor (BWV232). For liturgical and practical reasons, it cannot be performed during either Lutheran or Catholic worship; it seems Bach has simply created the mass as a devotional work to God. It is the summation of his art and his swansong.

Autumn Haydn resigns as chorister at St Stephen's (in Vienna) to avoid punishment following disorderly behaviour, having cut off another student's pigtail. The *Kapellmeister* accepts the 17-year-old's resignation, but decides to cane him anyway.

5 December Rameau stages the first version of his tragedy *Zoroastre* at the Paris Opéra.

17 December Italian composer **Domenico Cimarosa** is born in Aversa.

Disaster during the Royal Fireworks display at Green Park

1749 France and Britain manoeuvre for position in North America • The French send provincial governor Jean Baptiste de Bienville to take possession of the Ohio Valley, and meanwhile establish a fort on the site of modern Toronto • Spain and Britain sign a commercial treaty • Thomas Gainsborough (Eng) paints *Cornard Wood* • A sign language for deaf mutes is devised in Portugal • English philosopher and physician David Hartley publishes *Observations on Man, his Fame, Duty, and Expectations* • Henry Fielding (Eng): *Tom Jones* • Naturalist Georges de Buffon (Fr) publishes the first three volumes of his 44-volume *Natural History*

1750–1799

1750–1799

URING THE 1750s, Bach, Scarlatti and Handel took the glories of the Baroque style to their graves. A new approach had by this time evolved: the *galant* style, the musical counterpart to *rococo* in art and architecture, whose priorities were charming, light and graceful. A fusion of Italian, German and French manners, the galant had gained popularity in association with the Enlightenment, which recognised great value in the simplicity of nature and the importance of the common man. It found advocacy in the music and philosophical writings of Jean-Jacques Rousseau (1712–78), as well as in the works of other composers who straddled the mid-century, including Sammartini, Gluck, Johann Stamitz and C. P. E. Bach.

The Classical era witnessed seismic socio-political changes: America signed its Declaration of Independence in 1776, France's 500-year-old *Ancien Régime* was brought to an ignominious close by the Revolution of 1789, and a period of mechanisation in Britain launched the Industrial Revolution. A financially empowered middle class was on the rise and would soon become the composer's greatest ally. At this time two musical giants emerged, both Austrians. The first was good-natured and patronised by royalty, the second was too hot-headed to hold down a permanent court position: Joseph Haydn and Wolfgang Amadeus Mozart.

◀ *A Royal Banquet* (detail), by Martin van Meytens. The event celebrated the wedding of the future Emperor Joseph II of Austria and Isabella of Parma, Vienna 1760.

The evolving Classical style

It was around the mid-century that various composers and theorists first labelled earlier music as 'baroque', condemning it as harsh and unnatural. Excessive ornamentation, unstable harmonies, dense contrapuntal textures—such practices were out of touch with modern times and 'the truth of nature'. The proponents of the *galant* and *Empfindsamer* styles (see *Chapter 3*, final sections) sought to create music that spoke plainly and directly to the heart. Both on the stage and in instrumental form, their goal was to represent human emotion in its basic, natural state, and it was from this mindset that the Classical style evolved.

The Classical musical aesthetic was intimately attuned to the ancient Greco-Roman ideals of clarity, balance, proportion and naturalness. (This is distinct from the Renaissance style, when the 'rebirth' of ancient values promoted greater expressivity in text-setting, but only subtly influenced the structural substance of music itself.) Whilst Classical composers did not abandon counterpoint, they were now prioritising melodies formed of concisely balanced phrases and strong cadences, supported by chordal textures. Clear homophonic accompaniments were emboldened by an integrated bass part, which gave the music a pronounced rhythmic emphasis and added important impetus in fast movements. Basso continuo went into rapid decline, but retained a presence in sacred music and secco recitative for some time. Harmonic rhythm—the speed at which harmonies change—was reduced to enhance clarity and stability in melodic phrasing. To this end, tonic, subdominant and dominant chords were emphasised as the essential pillars of harmonic structure. At a wider organisational level, ternary rondo and sonata forms (referred to later on) provided secure, clear foundations for the processes of statement, contrast, variation and development.

In overview, the 1730s–60s represented a period of transition but also experimentation: the late Baroque masterpieces of Bach and Handel gave way to only a small handful of enduring pre-Classical works. Galant elegance was challenged in the 1760s and 70s by the *Sturm und Drang* (Storm and Stress) movement, which endeavoured to suffuse the arts with fervent subjectivism—the very approach that was to shape Romanticism. This storm abated, temporarily, and paved the way for the mature Classical style.

Classical opera

The Enlightened shift in cultural values brought about the decline of traditional *opera seria* in favour of more accessible *opera buffa*. Influenced by the *commedia dell'arte* and the galant *intermezzo*, the Italian buffa style offered not only comedy, but also the opportunity to develop a range of characterisation, sensitive to the realistic portrayal of ordinary people and their emotions. The audience members could in various ways identify with the characters on stage. Another strength of opera buffa was that its entertainment value relied less on vocal virtuosity. There were no castrato roles; instead, ensemble performance using a variety of voice types became one of its central ingredients.

Opera seria was in no immediate danger of evaporating since such works adorned formal state occasions. Classical opera seria continued the Baroque tradition of noble subject matter, usually based on stories from

ancient Greece or Rome, with the music itself largely reliant upon the virtuoso techniques of star singers, including castrati. The dramatic structure maintained a succession of arias linked by recitatives, all sung in Italian, the international language of opera. The prolific German composer Johann Hasse (see also *Chapter 3*) was the leading exponent of serious opera during the 1750s, creating popular extravaganzas at the Dresden Court by fusing spectacle with the homophonic galant manner, as in *Solimano* (1753). But courtly commissions aside, if serious opera was to survive alongside buffa, it was going to need a spring clean in the light of changing tastes.

▶ Johann Adolf Hasse, a leading figure in 18th century opera and the favoured composer of the renowned librettist Pietro Metastasio.

Gluck and the reform of opera seria

Christoph Willibald Gluck (1714–87) was the period's most influential reformer of opera, creating works that hold the stage to this day. By 1750 he had enjoyed success throughout Europe—Italy, London and Vienna especially—largely observing operatic convention. His subsequent interest in reform owed a good deal to his knowledge of French serious opera (*tragédie en musique*), in which, thanks to Jean-Philippe Rameau, music served the drama with little gratuitous vocal display.

The first of his so-called reform operas, *Orfeo ed Euridice*, had its Viennese première in 1762. The librettist was Raniero de Calzabigi, who then collaborated with Gluck on *Alceste* (1767) and *Paride ed Elena* (1770). *Orfeo* is the least adventurous of the three, though it does contain wonderfully distinctive music, with scenes rather than arias dominating the score. The melodies are direct and unadorned, as in the lament 'Che farò senza Euridice' and the beautiful flute tune of the 'Dance of the Blessed Spirits'. Gluck enriched his sensual style by scoring out his recitative with orchestral accompaniment, abandoning the *secco* style altogether.

Gluck: Orfeo

With *Alceste*, Gluck produced a preface explaining his theory of opera:

> *I have endeavoured to restrict music to its true purpose of serving poetry by expressing the emotions and situations of the story, without interrupting the action or impairing it with a superfluity of ornaments ... I have not deemed it appropriate to arrest an actor in the heat of dialogue so to make him wait out a tedious ritornello, or to stop him in mid-word over a favourable vowel, or to show off the agility of his fine voice with a lengthy passage, or to fill in time with the orchestra while he takes breath for a cadenza ...*

> *In short, I have sought to banish all those abuses against which good sense and reason have for so long cried out in vain.*

Gluck also believed that the overture 'ought to apprise the spectators on the nature of the action to be represented'. He applied this approach for the first time in *Alceste*, where the overture flows directly into the opening scene of the opera, asserting its direct relevance to the ensuing drama.

During the 1770s Gluck introduced the French to his modernised brand of serious opera. Following a successful French-language version of *Orfeo*, Paris premièred *Iphigénie en Aulide* (1774), *Armide* (1777) and *Iphigénie en Tauride* (1779). The latter ranks as one of the great

◀ Christoph Willibald Gluck. The chief operatic reformer of the 18th century, Gluck strove in his long and successful career to join music and drama more closely. He was hugely influential upon the masters of later generations, including Mozart and Berlioz.

Iphigénie en Tauride

243

Classical operas, achieving an intensification of an already noble style. The orchestral contribution offers considerable dramatic depth from the outset, and the entry of the heroine Iphigenia, as she takes over from the instrumental prelude, is a coup-de-théâtre. This music characterises the storm that rages in her mind, and similar emotional intensity is found throughout the whole score.

Traetta, Jommelli, Majo

Following Gluck's lead was Tommaso Traetta (1727–79) who trained at Naples but made his career elsewhere: at Parma from 1758, and later in London, Vienna and St Petersburg. With *Ifigenia in Tauride* (Vienna, 1763) he created his most successful *opera seria*, taking inspiration both from French operatic conventions and Gluck's *Orfeo*. Traetta was among the first to notate ornaments rather than leave them to the singer's discretion, enabling him to exercise greater control over the relationship between music and characterisation. Nicolò Jommelli (1714–74) also trained at Naples, and later fielded commissions throughout Italy. In 1753 he began a 16-year association with the Stuttgart court, where he wrote some 20 operas, employing a large orchestra of nearly 50 players. His operas are dominated by arias, though they also feature accompanied recitatives and dramatic finales, as in *Vologeso* (1766). With the tragic *Fetonte*, lavishly produced at Ludwigsburg in 1768, Jommelli intensified his expressive methods with descriptive orchestral writing, arioso intrusions into recitatives, declamation within arias, increased choruses and action ensembles. Gian Francesco Majo (1732–70) was yet another international composer who hailed from Naples. He wrote over 20 operas, adopting the orchestral approach to recitative and including ensembles and choruses. He anticipated Gluck in his own *Ifigenia in Tauride* (Mannheim, 1764), where material of the overture is recalled for the introductions to subsequent scenes.

▼ *Vienna, viewed from the Belvedere, Canaletto c.1761.*

Such reform was to influence Mozart's first major work of serious opera: *Idomeneo*. Wolfgang Amadeus Mozart (1756–91) launched his opera-writing career at the age of 12 with *La finta semplice* (The Feigned Madwoman, Salzburg, 1768), an opera buffa so mature and convincing that Mozart's father, Leopold, was accused of ghost-writing it. Mozart managed success in serious opera in his mid teens with *Mitridate* (1770) and *Lucio Silla* (1772), both traditional *serias* composed for the Royal Ducal Theatre in Milan. He was therefore a seasoned opera composer by the time he wrote *Idomeneo* (1780), a Greek version of the Biblical story of Jephtha, commissioned for the Munich court theatre. Combining dramatic flair and a consummate orchestral technique, Mozart drew on the models of Gluck and other reformers with a mix of *secco* and orchestrated recitative, arias, a few ensembles and powerful choruses. He pursued a seamless flow of recitatives and arias in the manner of Gluck, though he indulged Italianate lyricism to a much greater degree. *Idomeneo* was successfully premièred on 29 January 1781, two days after the composer's 25th birthday.

Wolfgang Amadeus Mozart

Idomeneo

Later that same year Mozart moved to Vienna, where he was to spend the rest of his short life. He wrote just one more opera seria, *La clemenza di Tito* (The Clemency of Titus), composed in the year of his death, 1791. Based on Metastasio's libretto, this two-act tale of intrigue and mercy was composed at a frenetic pace for the coronation of Emperor Leopold II as King of Bohemia. The prime attraction of the project was monetary, and Mozart even farmed out some of the material to his pupil Franz Süssmayr (1766–1803) to make his deadline. The opera was only moderately successful. But then serious opera had always held secondary appeal for Mozart; as a master of characterisation, his heart was in *buffa*.

La clemenza di Tito

Opera buffa

At the mid-century *opera buffa* was generating great commotion. In France, a revival of Pergolesi's intermezzo *La serva padrona* in 1752 inflamed the *Querelle des Bouffons* (Quarrel of the Buffoons), which raged over the respective merits of French and Italian opera. Rousseau joined in the squabble, promoting values of simplicity and rusticity in *Le Devin du village*, premièred that same year. In 1753 he published his 'Lettre sur la musique française', attacking the French operatic tradition, epitomised in the legacy of Lully and the contemporary output of Rameau. He complained,

The indolent quality of our French language makes it inflexible to our voices and a funeral tone continually reigns in our opera … French song is endless squealing, unbearable to the unbiased ear; French harmony is brutish, without expression.

While opera buffa was dividing Paris, in northern Italy it was going from strength to strength. The year 1750 saw the first production of *Il mondo della luna* (The World of the Moon), with music by Baldassare Galuppi (1706–85) and libretto by the Venetian Carlo Goldoni (1707–93). This was a busy time for Goldoni, who was working prolifically in collaboration with a number of composers to provide texts for the burgeoning buffa genre.

Italy

His *Il filosofo di campagna* (The Country Philosopher, Venice 1754), another collaboration with Galuppi, proved one of the operatic highlights of the decade.

Galuppi was chiefly renowned for his serious operas, though he never desired to be pigeonholed in either seria or buffa, since versatility was the order of the day. Similar in this respect was Niccolò Piccinni (1728–1800), who converted Goldini's libretto *La buona figliuola* (The Accomplished Maid, Rome 1760) into a Europe-wide buffa sensation. Ten years later he had one of the most prolific years in the history of opera: nine premières in one year, six of them buffa. He and Galuppi did much to establish the multi-section ensemble finale, anticipating trends in 19th-century opera.

The international influence of Italian composers was indeed extraordinary. Giovanni Paisiello (1740–1816) enjoyed an illustrious career during which he composed more than 80 operas.

His most famous work, *Il barbiere di Siviglia* (St Petersburg, 1782), inspired Mozart to write his *Marriage of Figaro*, using the next play in the trilogy by Pierre-Augustin Beaumarchais. Domenico Cimarosa (1749–1801) wrote both serious and comic operas, and his *Il matrimonio segreto* (Vienna, 1792) is both witty and masterly. Another Viennese favourite was Antonio Salieri (1750–1825), who worked many times with the court poet and librettist Lorenzo Da Ponte (1749–1838). It was however in Paris that Salieri scored what was probably his greatest triumph, *Tarare* (1787), in collaboration with Beaumarchais.

Virtually all the works mentioned here have since paled into insignificance in the unforgiving light of Mozart's buffa masterpieces. The first came in 1786 with *Le nozze di Figaro* (The Marriage of Figaro), a collaboration with Da Ponte, who with some careful editing managed to get the banned play approved by Emperor Joseph II. The plot takes place on the day of the valet Figaro's marriage to the maid Susanna, and revolves around Count Almaviva's desire to reinstate his 'droit du seigneur'—the lord's right to make love to his subject before her wedding. Mozart and Da Ponte created a range of colourful characters and took dramatic subtlety to a new level.

Mozart included solos and duets, but largely relied upon ensembles and finales. The librettist described finales as:

… the occasion for showing off the genius of the composer, the ability of the singers, and the most effective situation of the drama. Recitative is excluded, and every style of singing must find a place. All the singers should appear on the stage, even if there were three hundred of them.

The Act II finale, full of scheming, mocking, anger and confusion, fulfils these criteria: no other composer alive could match Mozart's formidable gift of complex emotional drama within ensemble settings. His melodic facility is also powerfully expressed throughout, most famously in Figaro's 'Non più andrai farfallone amoroso' (No more, you amorous butterfly) and Cherubino's 'Voi, che sapete che cosa è amor' (You ladies, who know what love is).

Mozart again collaborated with Da Ponte on *Don Giovanni* (Prague, 1787), another buffa ensemble opera, though the role of Donna Anna maintains the spirit of opera seria. The dark hues of the D minor overture immediately forewarn of the murky fate that awaits the lothario, but then the mood switches, with a playful D major allegro reflecting the carefree disposition of Don Giovanni himself. This argument—the moral consequences of loose living—is explored throughout with both comedy and tragedy, resulting in some of Mozart's most complex music. The ball scene in the finale of Act 1, for example, has an advanced musical language, with three on-stage ensembles playing different dance measures simultaneously, including a waltz, Vienna's latest fashion. The closing scene of the final act is suffused with rich harmonies; the drama Mozart wrenches from his orchestra reaches new heights of intensity, compounded with an off-stage chorus of demons as the ghost of the Commendatore drags Don Giovanni off to hell.

Don Giovanni

Mozart's third Da Ponte collaboration was *Così fan tutte* (All Women are the Same, 1790), in which the cynical Don Alfonso wagers with his two young friends, Ferrando and Guglielmo, that their lovers will not remain faithful in their absence. Whereas *Don Giovanni* strayed well beyond the boundaries of buffa, *Così* is firmly back in the comedic realm. Many find this Mozart's most accessible opera, with its straightforward intrigue and humour, heartache and affection. It is testament to the composer's genius that within outright farce he could produce inspired and subtle music that resonates with emotional authenticity.

Così fan tutte

Singspiel

Singspiel is a German opera with musical numbers separated by spoken dialogue. The French equivalent is the opéra-comique, the English the ballad opera. The Classical Singspiel tradition focused upon sentimentality, light comedy and folk ingredients. The Leipzig-based composer Johann Hiller (1728–1804) did much to popularise the style, gaining major success with *Die Jagd* (The Hunt, 1770), which remained in the repertory into the 19th century. From the 1780s, not least in Vienna, the melodic style

Die Entführung aus dem Serail

Die Zauberflöte

of Singspiel became increasingly bravura, while the plots introduced supernatural elements and aspects of comic farce rather like the English pantomime.

Mozart transcended the conventions of this formula in two mature Singspiels, dating date from his Vienna period. The first, *Die Entführung aus dem Serail* (The Abduction from the Harem, 1782), enjoyed resounding success and established Mozart's reputation throughout the German-speaking lands and beyond. Mixing seria and buffa elements, it represented a significant advance in Mozart's opera writing, since never before had he created such well drawn characters as the sensitive hero Belmonte, or the Pasha's uncouth, hot-tempered steward Osmin. The close correspondence between music and text was taken to a new level, with even complex ensembles advancing the action, anticipating the brilliance of Mozart's buffa masterpieces.

His second mature Singspiel was *Die Zauberflöte* (The Magic Flute), composed in 1791 for the suburban theatre of his Freemason friend Emmanuel Schikaneder. *The Magic Flute* has the widest range of musical styles that Mozart ever put into a single opera, and he employed a large orchestra, including trombones, to support the solemn, quasi-Masonic rites of Sarastro and his priests. As Freemasons, Mozart and Schikaneder filled the opera with Masonic symbols, apparently desiring to make a link between Freemasonry and Enlightenment principles. Mixing a broad range of roles, from the raging Queen of the Night (in stylised opera seria) to the comic bird catcher Papageno, the opera contains some of Mozart's most noble, charming and intriguing music.

The sonata principle

During the second half of the century the sonata became the dominant form within instrumental music. The term *sonata* designates a multi-movement composition, whereas *sonata form* defines the internal structure of a single movement. A sonata could feature any number of instruments. Pieces written for solo keyboard, or a solo instrument in partnership with keyboard, often used the term explicitly: keyboard sonata or violin sonata, for example. A sonata involving a larger group of instruments would be designated a trio, quartet or quintet, right up to a solo concerto or symphony.

Classical sonata form almost invariably applies in first movements and sometimes elsewhere. Broadly organised in three sections, a sonata form movement begins with an exposition that sets up tonal conflict between two opposing keys: this commonly accommodates two contrasting subjects (or themes), with the second subject presented in the dominant key or, in a minor key work, in the relative major key. A development section then heightens the harmonic tension with frequent modulation, adapting the material in different phrasing and harmonisation. The following recapitulation presents both subjects in the tonic key in order to resolve the tonal conflict set out at the beginning of the work. A coda may be employed to effect a rounded conclusion.

Variants of this structural procedure abound. There can be a slow introduction, and it is also possible for a movement to be monothematic, where the opening theme also announces the new key centre during the exposition. Haydn was fond of this approach right up to his final essays in the form, including his Symphony No. 104, *London*. However, the term monothematic is slightly misleading, as it does not preclude the incorporation of additional musical material elsewhere in the movement, even in the development section.

The classical sonata employs a sequence of three or four movements. In the second (slow) movement a ternary structure (ABA) often applies. An alternative might be a theme and variations, found in Haydn's Symphony No. 92. Minuets, predominating in third movements, are not necessarily dance-like, even if most are. That of Mozart's String Quintet in G minor, K. 516, for example, is laden with pathos. Finales are often rondos, deriving from Baroque *ritornello* movements, with a principal theme and contrasting episodes (ABACA etc.). The crucial difference between rondo and ritornello is that a rondo recalls its 'A' material in the same key, whereas the thematic repetitions in ritornello form occur in different keys. A variant on rondo form, sonata rondo form, was likewise used in final movements. Here a rondo-like structure, for example ABACABA, finds the final ABA sections all in the tonic key. The C section may be a new theme entirely, or some kind of development. Such formal characteristics of sonatas were pervasive and extended to the music of church and stage.

The Classical symphony

The year 1750 marked not just the death of Bach, but also that of a pioneer symphonist, the Austrian Matthias Georg Monn (1717–50). His symphonies derived from the Italian operatic sinfonia, with a structure of fast–slow–fast, but as early as 1740 he introduced the four-movement plan, complete with a third-movement minuet. Sammartini's early symphonies, dating from the 1730s, had nearly all employed a three-movement plan and were scored for strings alone (see also *Chapter 3*). Other composers created what they classed as symphonies, but were actually hybrids, lying somewhere between a dance suite and symphony. Such works may be found amongst the 170 (forgotten) symphonies of Johann Molter (1696–1765), an employee at the court of Karlsruhe and the period's most prolific symphonist. Symphonies

Mannheim

were usually composed under aristocratic patronage, but public concerts were on the rise, particularly in Paris and London. Testament to the changing times, the finest symphonies and concertos of the 1780s and 90s were nearly all written for the public arena.

Throughout the 1750s and 60s the symphony gained wide popularity. Composers advancing the genre included several based at Mannheim, led by Johann Stamitz (1717–57), who served as *Kapellmeister* from 1745. Stamitz established an orchestra of international renown, whose uniform bowing, atmospheric tremolandi and controlled crescendi were second to none. He matured the symphony by dispensing with the old continuo bass line, replacing it with written-out parts, and by promoting the four-movement plan. Two other prominent composers were already experienced symphonists before they joined the Mannheim court: Franz Xaver Richter (1709–87), who arrived in 1749, followed four years later by Ignaz Holzbauer (1717–83). Christian Cannabich (1731–98) took up the post of *Konzertmeister* shortly after Stamitz's death and later became full director of instrumental music, composing in the process around 70 symphonies for the court. Flush with leading players and composers, Mannheim was for many years the orchestral capital of Europe.

Working outside the Mannheim orbit, the Austrian composer Georg Christoph Wagenseil (1715–77) was particularly influential. Based in Vienna, he wrote some 60 symphonies for the Habsburg Court and was esteemed by Haydn and Mozart, since his music has clarity of thought, vitality and drama. Wagenseil and Stamitz were among the first composers to establish the combination of contrasting themes to delineate the tonic and dominant sections of a sonata exposition.

Joseph Haydn

The mild-mannered Joseph Haydn (1732–1809) was the leading figure in the development of the symphony. He wrote his first in around 1757 when he took up service to Count Morzin in Vienna, but it was during his employment at the Esterházy court, from 1761, that he enriched and expanded the scope of the genre with increasing creative independence. First at Eisenstadt in Austria, and then at the new Esterháza palace in western Hungary, Haydn had charge of an orchestra numbering around 20, but supplemented on special occasions. In total he composed more than 100 symphonies.

Haydn indulged his talents and could afford to be experimental. He even found himself in the enviable position of being able to summon his orchestra to try out ideas, later stating: 'Cut off from the world, I was compelled to become original.' In some of his early symphonies he ignored popular trends and began in 'church sonata' style (that is with a slow movement), as in No. 22, *The Philosopher* (1764), and No. 49, *La Passione* (1768). In response to the *Sturm und Drang* (Storm and Stress) literary movement he produced such works as Symphony No. 44 in E minor, *Trauer*, and Symphony No. 45 in F sharp minor, *Farewell*, both composed in 1772. Haydn's *Sturm und Drang* music is typical of the age, seeking emotional turbulence often through minor-key works that exploit powerful dynamic contrasts, sudden pauses, syncopation, tremolandos and fast scalic runs.

Major-key pieces that fit the mould include his Symphony No. 59 in A major, *Fire*, whose outer movements are bursting with volatile energy. The *Sturm und Drang* was by and large confined to Austro-Germany, but its influence was wide-reaching, contributing the decline of the *galant* and opening up new expressive possibilities for the Classical style.

While Haydn's career remained centred around the Esterházy court, his music became widely famous. During the 1780s this brought a prestigious commission from Le Concert de la Loge Olympique in Paris, resulting in his symphonies Nos. 82–87. They were his most ambitious and sophisticated to date, clearly a response to the

Paris Symphonies

challenge of writing for one of Europe's finest orchestras. The *Paris Symphonies* are brilliant and elegant, sometimes witty, but richly emotional. Symphony No. 83 in G minor, *La Poule*, opens with a fiery *Sturm und Drang* theme that contrasts humorously with a clucking, major-key second theme, supported by pecking dotted-rhythm motifs in the woodwind. The Symphony No. 86 in D, in contrast, opens with a short, restrained *adagio* that suddenly gives way to a bold and energetic *allegro spiritoso*, tightly unified by its monothematic design. The symphony's minuet and trio offers a good example of how Haydn enlivens a straightforward theme by extending or interrupting its melodic shape through unexpected phrasing and rhythm.

London Symphonies

After the death of Prince Nikolaus in 1790 Haydn was free to relocate to Vienna, a city he knew well. News of his availability spread, and the impresario Johann Peter Salomon travelled in person to invite him to London. He accepted, and between 1791 and 1795 he crowned his orchestral output with two sets of six symphonies, Nos. 93–104, which were presented to the London public in mixed programmes (shared with other composers) during Haydn's two English visits. The composer relished the large instrumental forces at his disposal, scoring for double woodwinds (pairs of flutes, oboes and bassoons, plus clarinets in the second set), pairs of horns and trumpets, timpani and strings. The orchestras he used ranged from 40 to 60 players, the largest made available for his final three symphonies under the direction of the composer-violinist Giovanni Battista Viotti (1755–1824).

All but one of these symphonies (No. 95 in C minor) is set in a major key and prefaced with a slow introduction. A number of first movements are broadly monothematic, employing the principal tonic-key theme (or one derived directly from it) to announce the dominant key centre of the exposition. But in spite of repeated formulas, Haydn displays great artistry

▲ Esterháza Palace and gardens in Haydn's time. Built as a summer retreat for Prince Nikolaus Esterházy in the mid-1760s.

and imagination. It is testament to his skill in organic monothematic development—such as we find in symphonies Nos. 96 and 101—that he manages to constantly beguile the ear, teasing thematic outgrowths, and enriching them through the subtlest of counter-subjects. The first movement of Symphony No. 96 also reveals one of his most inventive development sections, with its dramatic use of silence and false-start recapitulation. Indeed, Haydn liked to toy with structural conventions: we hear this in the *Military* Symphony, which offers what appears to be a mono-thematic first movement exposition, announcing the arrival of the dominant key with the principal subject, only to then introduce a second theme some 20 bars later.

Among the many fine inner movements of Haydn's last symphonies is that of No. 98, an Adagio that carries some deeply felt emotions, and the fascinating Minuet of No. 101, whose bucolic Trio sounds like it was inspired by intoxicated tavern musicians, complete with 'wrong notes'. Haydn's finales are varied in organisation and frequently infused with merriment and wit. That of Symphony No. 102 in B flat is a *presto* tour-de-force: a rondo dance tune, developed in a fugue-like manner, concluding with a jocular coda. His tuneful Symphony No. 104, *London*, arguably the greatest work of the set, displays similar high spirits in its folk-infused finale—a lasting impression for the English of Haydn's affable personality.

Mozart

The only other composer to match Haydn's symphonic skill was his revered friend Mozart. As a boy, Mozart had learnt much from J. C. Bach, whom he met in London whilst on a three-year European tour with his family. Suitably inspired, the eight-year-old set about writing his Symphony No. 1 in E flat, K. 16 (1764); by the time he returned to Salzburg, in 1766, he had penned six more symphonies. Technically precocious and remarkable though they are, the early symphonies tend to be formulaic and derivative.

In his late teens Mozart began to display his maturing genius, evidenced by the brilliant 'Storm and Stress' of Symphony No. 25 in G minor (1773) and the concentrated inspiration of Symphony No. 29 in A major (1774).

After moving to Vienna in 1781 Mozart switched his orchestral priorities to the piano concerto. He wrote just seven more symphonies, including No. 36 in C (*Linz*, 1783) and No. 38 in D (*Prague*, 1786). His last three, dating from 1788 and probably intended for subscription concerts, form the apotheosis of his achievement in the genre. Each has its own exquisite identity. No. 39 in E flat major has clarinets rather than oboes, with a warm expressiveness amid a powerful symphonic impetus, and a finale in tribute to Haydn. In No. 40 in G minor, scored for a smaller orchestra (without trumpets and drums), melancholy is pervasive. The famous first movement opens with its doleful lilting theme, and the tragic depth of the development is overwhelming. This mood continues in the major-key (E flat) slow movement; only the trio within the following minuet offers temporary respite with something resembling optimism. The surging final movement sets off as though it could find its way into the light, but instead it completes its course immersed in *Sturm und Drang*. No. 41 in C major is back to full orchestra, minus clarinets. Its brilliance encouraged the title *Jupiter*, though this was not Mozart's own. This is a finale-symphony, virtually without precedent, the last movement dominating the symphonic plan as a large sonata structure with fugal elements. In the climactic section, Baroque and Classical styles meet as themes are recalled one upon another, resulting in a display of dazzling musical prowess. With the symphonic balance shifted towards the closing phase, Mozart anticipated a later trend.

Symphonies Nos. 39–41

Chamber music: the rise of the string quartet

During the Baroque era the trio sonata had been the mainspring of chamber music; in the Classical era it was the string quartet. The new genre can be related to the earlier, since the late-Baroque trio sonata commonly comprised two violins plus a basso continuo of keyboard and cello. By replacing keyboard with viola, the ensemble becomes a string quartet. But the decline of the continuo was a symptom, not a cause. More important stimulus came from the early four-part string symphonies of Austrian and German composers—such as Monn, Holzbauer and Richter—which could be performed as chamber music with just one player per part.

During the late 1750s, Richter and Holzbauer were writing quartets for the Mannheim court, with the intention of entertaining the players as much as the listeners. This was typical of chamber trends elsewhere: in 1760 the English composer Charles Avison (1709–70) wrote in the preface to his Op. 7 Sonatas for harpsichord, two violins and cello: 'This kind of music is not calculated as much for public entertainment as for private amusements. It is rather like a conversation among friends.' Similarly, Luigi Boccherini (1743–1805) dedicated his first set of quartets (1765) to *veri dilettanti e conoscitori di musica*, indicating that the music was for both players and connoisseur listeners. This was as true for his quartets as his hundred-plus quintets (with extra cello), many of which were composed for his Spanish patron, Don Luis. Others were sent to the Prussian court after he was contracted as a non-resident composer to Friedrich Wilhelm II in 1786.

Haydn

Haydn was the central figure in the development of the string quartet—a true father of the genre, as opposed to his step-fathering of the symphony. Like other composers exploring the quartet's possibilities in the 1750s and 60s, his early examples are closely allied to *divertimenti*—a genre associated with background music, either indoors or outdoors—and indeed that is what he called his first examples, Opp. 1–3. Dating from around 1757 into the early 60s, they are simple five-movement works that often resort to two-part textures, with little sense of idiomatic instrumentation.

▶ The cellist and composer Luigi Boccherini, noted especially for his string quintets with second cello.

While in the employ of Prince Nicholas Esterházy (who succeeded his brother, Paul Anton, in 1762) Haydn was obliged to write numerous pieces for baryton trio. The baryton was an obsolete instrument, but the practice of writing string music in three independent parts—baryton, viola and cello—certainly refined Haydn's craft. He will have also advanced his understanding of the cello's expressive potential having written his first concerto for the instrument by around 1765. Matured through this experience, he produced the Op. 9 quartets in 1769, though again termed them *divertimenti*. The pieces boast several attributes that steer them towards a new genre, such as a four-movement scheme and the inclusion of contrapuntal textures. Most importantly, many of the first movements are cast in sonata form and themes undergo development, endowing the music with a level of complexity not typical of trifling entertainment. It is telling that towards the end of his life Haydn told Artaria, his Viennese publisher, that his published quartets should begin with the Op. 9 set.

Op. 9
Quartets

Op. 20
Quartets

Haydn's development of the string quartet continued in his Op. 17 (1771), but it was with the Op. 20 quartets (1772) that he brought new definition to the genre. Here the quartet, with its four increasingly equal parts, offers more variety of texture than the classical orchestra (in which instrumental roles are more firmly delineated) and the special characteristics of each instrument are explored in an intimate, idiomatic manner.

◄ The celebrated quartet party c.1784, at which Haydn and Mozart were joined by Vanhal and Dittersdorf. The figure observing in the background is Mozart's father, Leopold. Scene as imagined by German artist Julius Schmid.

Haydn's sophisticated structural organisation presents the foundations for heightened harmonic tension and rigorous thematic development. This is nowhere more apparent than in the Quartet in E flat, No. 1, which includes a soul-searching slow movement, marked *affetuoso e sostenuto*. The emotional gravity and underlying seriousness of these quartets no doubt owed something to the *Sturm und Drang* movement, even if alongside some of the composer's contemporaneous symphonies they seem politely *galant*.

In 1781 Haydn completed his Op. 33 quartets, written 'in a new and special way'. Although sales talk, Haydn's boast was justified by his music. Thematically there is an organic fluency about these pieces, with motivic counterpoint exploited within the most refined classical structures of the time. Generally of lighter tone than the Op. 20, they were conceived with even greater attention to idiomatic part writing. Haydn's other mature quartets include the *Prussian* Quartets (Op. 50, 1787) and the *Tost* Quartets (Opp. 54, 55 & 64, 1790), the second set composed for the Viennese merchant Johann Tost who had been a member of the Esterházy orchestra. The quartets of Opp. 71 & 74 were written in between his England visits, mostly in 1793. They reflect the popular London symphonies by employing slow introductions and in places suggesting symphonic textures. Haydn's final quartets appeared with his Op. 76 (1797) and Op. 77 (1799). The last set was commissioned by Prince Lobkowitz (an important future patron of Beethoven) and consists of just two marvellous pieces, which was all the aging composer could manage at the time.

Op. 33 Quartets

Mozart:
Haydn
Quartets

Mozart wrote string quartets while a teenager, but it was only after studying Haydn's Op. 33 that he produced his first masterpieces in the genre, the so-called *Haydn* Quartets (1782–85). The epithet comes from the dedication to Haydn, which appeared in the published collection of 1785. It was on hearing one or more of these pieces that Haydn famously remarked to Leopold Mozart: 'I tell you before God and as an honest man, your son is the greatest composer I know, either personally or by name.' What Mozart gleaned from Haydn's Op. 33 was four-part instrumental discourse, structural organisation and advanced methods of thematic development. At the same time, Mozart's collection is wider ranging in emotional scope. Thematic contrast is common and new ideas are freely interjected. Haydn, by comparison, handled his themes with remarkable economy. And what prompted Mozart to write the avant-garde, chromatic introduction to the C major Quartet (*Dissonance*), K. 465—the final quartet of the set—one can only wonder. This expressive *Sturm und Drang* gives way to a merry first subject, but the effect of contrast is serious, not humorous. Arguably, the prelude only makes sense within the context of the ensuing Andante, where Mozart plunges into profound reflection. It testifies to the status of the mature string quartet as music for the connoisseur.

String
Quintets
K. 515
& K. 516

Mozart maintained a similarly high standard in his last quartets, three of which he composed for the King of Prussia (K. 575, 589, 590) in 1789/90. However, his particular interest became the quintet with additional viola or, in one case, clarinet. Compared with his 23 string quartets, Mozart's quintets are few in number, with just six mature works composed during 1787–91. Their quality places them among his very best chamber offerings. Most adored is the Clarinet Quintet in A major (1789), owing to its stunning array of graceful and beguiling melodies. Also popular are the richly textured String Quintets No. 3 in C major and No. 4 in G minor (K. 515 and K. 516), which Mozart composed in 1787 possibly as a pair. These pieces occupy emotional extremes. The C major introduces itself with a bouncy, joyous melody and closes in light, vivacious spirits. The G minor opens with searching questions and is consumed by anxiety in its minuet; its third-movement lamentation seeps into the opening bars of the Allegro final movement, in which triple-time major-key merriment is tempered by despondency and hesitation. While composing this quintet Mozart knew his father, Leopold, was gravely ill; despite their sometimes volatile relationship, there is no denying their sincere familial bond. Was Mozart exploring his own confused emotions in the G minor? Leopold died on 28 May 1787, just days after the quintet's completion.

The emerging piano repertory

It took the best part of a century for Bartolomeo Cristofori's forte-piano invention (*c.*1700) to finally eclipse the harpsichord, but once its position became established, the new instrument changed music forever. The name 'fortepiano' signified the ability to project different levels of dynamic, unlike the harpsichord, whose volume was more or less fixed. With some 200 keyboard sonatas, Carl Bach was among the first to

C. P. E. Bach

◀ Carl Philipp Emanuel Bach, a leading figure in the transition from the Baroque to the Classical style.

explore the piano's expressive opportunities. He was associated with the *empfindsamer stil* (sensitive style, see *Chapter 3*), popular at a time when the harpsichord was still the instrument of choice. But with Bach's transition towards the piano his keyboard style became even more distinctive and individual, generating pieces of great intensity. Six sets of fortepiano pieces *für Kenner und Liebhaber* (for connoisseurs and amateurs), featuring rondos, sonatas and free fantasias, were published from 1779 until his penultimate year, 1787. Many of these display Bach's non-formulaic approach to musical construction and demand contrasts entirely dependent on the piano's dynamic range.

J. C. Bach

Johann Christian Bach (1735–82), younger brother of Carl, was another important advocate of the fortepiano. In 1762 he emigrated to England, secured noble and royal patronage, and became one of the most influential composers in London. The six pieces of his Op. 5 keyboard collection, published in 1766, were the first in London to be advertised as suitable for harpsichord or piano—even if the D major Sonata (No. 2), with its wide-ranging sonorities and dynamics, seems fully possible only on the newer instrument. Bach may have played some of these pieces in 1768 when, at the Thatched House Tavern in St James's Street, he apparently became the first person to give a public fortepiano performance in England.

Muzio Clementi

By this time the young Muzio Clementi (1752–1832) had been living in Dorset, England, for a year or two. He was residing with his guardian, Peter Beckford, who was sending regular amounts of money to Clementi's father in Italy for the privilege of nurturing and enjoying the boy's prodigious talent. Released from his contract with Beckford, Clementi made his successful London début at the harpsichord in 1775, though the fortepiano soon became his favoured instrument. His immensely popular Sonatas Op. 2 (1779) promoted both the piano and his own reputation as a composer. He gave regular performances in London over the next ten years (there were few better players in Europe) but he more or less retired from public concert-giving after 1790. His priorities became composition and teaching, and a little later, music publishing and piano manufacturing.

Haydn

Haydn's keyboard output was routinely focused on the harpsichord until 1780, when he brought out his *Sei Sonate per il Clavicembalo, o Forte Piano*. He wrote most of his piano music during the late 1780s and early 90s, with celebrated pieces including the F minor Variations HXVII/6 (1793) and three sonatas, HXVI/50–52, written around the time of his second London season, 1794–95. Also dating from the 1790s, and again with an

► Title page of Six Sonatas by Haydn, 1780, the first keyboard pieces the composer intended for either the harpsichord or the fortepiano.

SEI SONATE
Per il Clavicembalo, o Forte Piano.
Composte dal Celebre Sig.re
GIUSEPPE HAYDN.
Opera XXX.
Dedicate
Alle Ornatissime Signore
CATERINA e MARIANNA D'AUENBRUGGER
dalli umilissimi ed ossequiosissimi loro Servidori
Artaria e Compag.ᵃ

Jan Ladislav Dussek

English connection, were the early piano sonatas of Jan Ladislav Dussek (1760–1812). A virtuoso pianist, Dussek fled the French Revolution in 1789 and made his way to London, where he soon filled the gap Clementi left in public concert life. During his 11-year residency Dussek was probably the most progressive composer living in England. His Piano Sonata in C major for four hands Op. 32 (1796) and Piano Sonata in C minor, Op. 35, No. 3 (1797) are two outstanding pieces that display the kind of emotional breadth and harmonic colour associated with mature Beethoven and Schubert. Dussek had a significant influence on the English piano firm Broadwood, who expanded the range of their instruments from five to six octaves to meet his demands.

Mozart and the Classical piano concerto

Among the keyboard composers of his day, Mozart was supreme. A child prodigy as a performer and composer, he began writing keyboard works as a five year old with his Andante and Allegro K. 1a and 1b. The pre-Vienna compositions include some fine sonatas dating from his 1778 visit to Paris, notably the Sonata in A minor, K. 310, his first minor-key sonata.

In Vienna, Mozart gained wider appreciation for his keyboard variations than his piano sonatas. His easy-to-follow variations were particularly attractive to the publishers, since most were written on popular operatic tunes by the likes of Paisiello, Giuseppe Sarti (1729–1802), Salieri and Gluck. A number of Mozart's sonatas were also accessible home entertainment, although the (now) extremely famous Piano Sonata in C major, K. 545, designated 'for beginners', was not published in Mozart's lifetime. His solo piano music includes some wonderful single-movement

◀ *The Mozart family*, Painting by Johann Nepomuk della Croce, 1780. Wolfgang and Nannerl at the piano, with their father Leopold. Their mother, Anna Maria, is featured in a portrait since she had died in 1778 while in Paris with her son.

miniatures, such as the Rondo in A minor (K. 511) and the deeply expressive Adagio in B minor (K. 540).

The year 1784 was Mozart's *annus mirabilis* of piano music. As well as the hearty C minor Sonata, K. 457, he composed no fewer than six piano concertos, Nos. 14–19. The piano was taking pride of place in Mozart's concerto output. He had abandoned the violin concerto completely: his five popular essays all date from the Salzburg years, as does the *Sinfonia concertante* for violin and viola. The only other concertos of his Vienna years are the four smaller-scale horn concertos (1783–91) and the incomparable Clarinet Concerto in A major (1791). Mozart conceived the bulk of his piano concertos for his own gifts, enabling him to appear in the dual role of performer and composer at his Vienna subscription concerts. (Exceptions to this include No. 17 in G major, K. 453, composed for his pupil Barbara Ployer.) Given his personal investment in the genre, it is not surprising that the best of them stand alongside his greatest operas in artistic merit.

Mozart adopted a similar structural plan for his 21 original compositions for solo piano and orchestra. His first movements effectively consolidated the double-exposition sonata form structure that had already appeared in the concertos of his friend J. C. Bach. The first 'exposition', or more appropriately 'prelude', is for orchestra alone, during which the first and second subjects are introduced with little modulation beyond the home key. The piano entry, which very occasionally features a new theme, brings about the full sonata exposition, for only then does 'tonal drama' ensue with conclusive modulation to the dominant key or, alternatively, the relative major key (as in No. 24 in C minor, K. 491). At this point the piano introduces its second subject, often a new idea altogether. Formal modifications

Piano concerto structure

include orchestral ritornellos immediately before and after the development section. A solo cadenza in the recapitulation helps balance the movement's structure, and reasserts the importance of the solo instrument. A coda, for orchestra with or without piano, concludes the movement.

The slower middle movement is set in a contrasting key and adopts binary, ternary, variation or rondo form, while affording an opportunity for lyricism in contrast with the busier outer movements. The final movement typically follows a rondo or sonata-rondo pattern, but in two cases, No. 17 in G major, K. 453, and No. 24, there is a variation form. Mozart exercised great invention within these various formulas. He wrote what may be regarded as his first mature piano concerto in Salzburg at the age of 20, the Concerto No. 9 in E flat, K. 271, which is unusual for its brief piano entry in the opening orchestral prelude. The Vienna concertos begin with Nos. 11–13 (1782–83), but it was not until the prolific year of 1784 that Mozart made a significant attempt to widen the concerto's emotional scope. There is an operatic flavour to many of his great concertos, a relevant point since many were presented during Lent when the performance of opera was prohibited. A talented composer like Mozart could offer the Viennese an 'operatic experience' in instrumental form.

Piano
Concerto
No. 20
in D minor,
K. 466

The great Piano Concerto No. 20 in D minor, K. 466 (1785), illustrates this theatrical quality better than any other. The opening movement foreshadows *Don Giovanni*, with its disquieting atmosphere created by syncopated upper strings and a rising step-wise gesture in the cellos and basses. The music is oppressive and threatening until the piano makes its tender, lyrical entrance in vulnerable isolation. Any sense of hope arising in the movement is quickly obliterated. The slow movement, cast in B flat major, sets a plaintive lyrical melody into a rondo cycle that lulls the listener into a false sense of security. A violent *Sturm und Drang* section erupts to shake all foundations; but the fury eventually dissipates and innocence returns. The rondo-finale sets out in D minor with purposeful, bustling vigour. The orchestra makes some intimidating, ominous gestures, but Mozart steers the music, the piano part especially, with optimism and bravura, concluding his three-movement drama in the 'victorious' realm of the tonic major.

The Piano Concerto No. 25 in C major, K. 503 (1786), also exploits wide-ranging emotions and contrasts, extending from the celebratory first subject, majestically presented by full orchestra, to the graceful dominant-key subject. It does not strive for the same quasi-operatic stance of the D minor, but dramatic gestures and lyrical ideas are present in abundance. And this leads us to another aspect of Mozart's genius: his melodic prowess. Mozart had the ability to express the sublime with real economy of means, as in the beautiful Andante of Concerto No. 21 in C major, K. 467 (1785). Another superb example is found in the elegiac slow movement of Piano Concerto in A major, K. 488 (1786); set in the commonly avoided key of F sharp minor, it has a depth of feeling matching anything the composer ever created.

The A major Concerto's first movement exhibits detailed wind-section writing, a feature in Mozart's concertos from the time of his Concerto No. 15 of 1784. (Other composers of the period gave this group less attention in their piano concertos.) Mozart's winds can assume a prominent role in accompanying the piano, but they also supply thematic statements, answering phrases, and a connective tissue between themes, often as an isolated group.

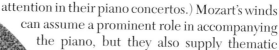

◀ The young Ludwig van Beethoven.

The arrival of Beethoven

Born in Bonn and part Flemish by ancestry, Ludwig van Beethoven (1770–1827) received musical tuition from his father, Johann Beethoven (a court singer), and the composer Christian Gottlob Neefe (1748–98). There are uncorroborated stories of Johann Beethoven pushing Ludwig to breaking point in an attempt to convert him into a second Mozart. Well documented, on the other hand, is the fact that Ludwig assumed headship of the family at the age of 18, because his father had turned to heavy drinking. This responsibility will have undoubtedly matured the young composer significantly. Beethoven was court organist and later violist in the employ of Elector Maximilian Franz (brother of Emperor Joseph II), but since musical opportunities in Bonn were limited, he moved to Vienna in 1792. There he honed his composition skills under Haydn, Johann Albrechtsberger (1736–1809) and Salieri. It was through Haydn that Beethoven made his most important contacts in Vienna, and within just a few years he had gained considerable attention as a pianist, improviser and composer—in that order.

Haydn's influence is conspicuous in Beethoven's early orchestral style, but it is the image of Mozart that predominates in the formal organisation of his first two piano concertos, both completed in 1795. The Piano Concerto No. 2 in B flat major was actually composed before No.1 in C major, but had a later publishing date. It is the most Classical of Beethoven's concertos and was begun during his Bonn years. The Concerto No. 1 is grander both in orchestration and scope, and in places presages his mature style. The noble prelude, for example, transforms into something heroic when it is emboldened by robust orchestration, emphasised by timpani. And in the development section he seems to be searching beyond the ordered structures of Mozart for a greater freedom of expression. Elsewhere influences are more apparent, as in the forceful theme of the third movement rondo-finale, whose enjoyably irregular contours were surely inspired by Haydn.

Piano Concerto No. 1

The year 1795 also saw Beethoven in print for the first time, with the set of Piano Trios, Op. 1. His most mature pieces of the 1790s were piano sonatas, the first appearing in 1796 as his Op. 2. An early masterpiece is found in the C minor *Sonate pathétique* Op. 13 (1798). Its organisation

Sonate pathétique

261

is inspired: the introductory Grave becomes a recurring agent of opposition in the rampaging Allegro that follows, reappearing at the start of the development section and again in the coda. The slow movement embodies a poignant lyrical lament, while the finale introduces a characterful theme related to the first movement's second subject. The mood is playful until the gravity of the opening movement returns in the closing bars. Beethoven's most personal and profound creation to date augured great things for the composer; he was, at this same time, just beginning to sense the deterioration of his 'noblest faculty': his hearing.

Sacred music

In the Classical era sacred music held less importance than previously, while secular choral music was rare. The greatest sacred works of the period were composed for the church rather than the concert hall, until Haydn's oratorios *The Creation* (1798) and *The Seasons* (1801) followed the Handelian precedent and were performed publicly. To some extent the enlightened Emperor Joseph II of Austria can be blamed for the dearth of outstanding sacred works during this period. In his Holy Roman Empire, public worship had to be a low-key affair; orchestras were not allowed in church because they encouraged pomp and ostentation. So just when the mature Classical style was taking hold, its cultural epicentre—Vienna—was witnessing a diminishing role for sacred music. Elsewhere and at other times, orchestral accompaniments in large churches were common (even if the Pope disapproved), with coloratura arias worthy of the opera house. Mozart's *Coronation Mass*, K. 317 (1779), a Salzburg creation, is a popular example.

As in opera, the Italian influence was widespread. Johann Hasse and Niccolo Jommelli wrote sacred music for Dresden and Stuttgart, alongside the operas that brought them fame. In Austria Haydn wrote some wonderful music for the church, since the Esterházy family gave him regular opportunities. His first oratorio, *Il ritorno di Tobia* (The Return of Tobias), dates from 1775. More than 20 years later the fruits of this were felt in *The Creation*. Although a devout Catholic, Haydn used a libretto from Protestant England, given to him in 1795 by the impresario Peter Salomon. In Vienna the Baroque enthusiast Gottfried van Swieten translated it into German, and the score was printed with the text in both languages. Haydn looked to the Handelian model in shaping *The Creation*, combining in a similar way narrative, description and glorification. He composed it on an extensive scale, scoring for the largest forces he ever used. 'Every day I fell to my knees and prayed to God to grant me the strength for a happy completion of the work,' Haydn told his biographer. His prayers were more than answered, beginning with the atmospheric orchestral 'Representation of Chaos' and the tutti fortissimo sunburst on 'There was light!', and onto the majestic choruses of praise, crowned by 'The Heavens are Telling'. Following a glorious private première at the Schwarzenberg Palace, Vienna, the oratorio went public and broke the city's box-office records. This popularity became international within a few years. Haydn, approaching 70, had experienced the greatest triumph of his career.

*Haydn:
The Creation*

◀ The Burgtheater in Vienna, one of the most significant musical venues of the Classical era. It was here that Gluck premièred *Orfeo ed Euridice* (1762), Mozart and Da Pont launched *The Marriage of Figaro* (1786), Beethoven made his Vienna début with the Piano Concerto in B flat major (1795), and Haydn gave the first public performance of *The Creation* (1799).

Haydn's brother Michael was, like Mozart, employed at the Salzburg court. He wrote several Masses, and in 1799 a lively Te Deum with a magnificent fugue. His Requiem (1792) is impressively powerful from the opening bar. The circumstances of its composition remain unknown; perhaps it was in tribute to his friend Mozart, who had died just months previously.

Mozart wrote 17 masses during the 1770s whilst in the service of Archbishop Colloredo in Salzburg, but none of them come close to the potency of his *Great Mass* in C minor, K. 427, of 1783. Although unfinished, this mass is an epic sacred composition that unleashes imposing force in the 'Kyrie' and menacing tension in 'Qui tollis', and beguiles with beautiful operatic lyricism in 'Laudamus te' and 'Et incarnatus est'. Its monumental grandeur recalls the masterworks of Bach and Handel, which Mozart had come to know thanks to van Swieten. These connections are conspicuous in 'In excelsis' at the beginning of the 'Gloria', which sounds remarkably like Handel's 'Hallelujah chorus'. In due course Mozart created a performing edition of *Messiah*, so the link is by no means fanciful. Although composed in Vienna, the so-called *Great Mass* was first performed in Salzburg (October, 1783), with Mozart's wife, Constanze, among the soloists.

During his final year, Mozart composed three choral masterpieces. The beautiful motet *Ave Verum Corpus*, K. 618, was written for Anton Stoll, parish priest at Baden, for the Feast of Corpus Christi. The Masonic cantata *Laut verkünde unser Freude* (Accordingly Announce Our Joy), K. 623, with text by Emmanuel Schikaneder, was written during Mozart's final illness. Employing male chorus and soloists, the resemblance to the priests' music in *The Magic Flute* is strong.

Count Franz von Walsegg-Stuppach anonymously commissioned Mozart's Requiem Mass in 1791, very likely in the hope that people might think it was his own work. The count had recently lost his wife and wanted to honour her memory. Mozart began the project enthusiastically, relishing an

Mozart:
Great Mass

Requiem
Mass in
D minor
K. 626

opportunity to write another mass, but during the autumn he fell gravely ill. Sensing his own end might be nigh, he entrusted the Requiem's completion to one of his pupils, Franz Süssmayr, giving instructions (no doubt of varying detail) as to how to go about the task. The later sections of the work probably owe much to Süssmayr, though they still embody the essence of Mozart. The orchestration favours the darker-hued instruments, abandoning flutes, oboes and horns, drawing instead upon basset horns, bassoons, trumpets and trombones. With its concentration of minor keys, contrapuntal textures and ceremonial homophony, this is a more solemn work than his *Great Mass*. (Some believe this reflects Mozart's anticipation of death, although much of what survives in Mozart's hand likely pre-dates his final illness.) There are again frequent Baroque references, asserted from the outset in the 'Requiem aeternam'—the only section of the mass that Mozart completed in full—and 'Kyrie'. The stormy episodes of the 'Confutatis' bring to mind the fate of Don Giovanni, while gentle major-key choral supplications are juxtaposed with spectacular effect. The Requiem is indeed a monumental meditation on death, but its trajectory is one of darkness through to light. The 'Sanctus' brings a major key exultation for double chorus that, while brief, offers radiant hope. 'Lux aeterna' closes the work by recalling the fugal music previously heard in the 'Kyrie', an appropriate decision and common practice, as found in Mozart's Salzburg Masses K. 220 and K. 317.

Centres of music: the options available to Mozart

When Mozart was considering his future beyond the artistic confines of Salzburg, there were several European capitals offering the potential of substantial rewards. St Petersburg, and more specifically the court of Catherine the Great, proved profitable for Italian composers such as Galuppi, Paisiello, Cimarosa and Sarti, and the Spaniard Martín y Soler (1754–1806), above all in the realm of opera. It was a centre that enjoyed close cultural connections with the rest of Europe, despite its geographical proximity. However, opportunities there were limited, with success largely dependent on royal invitation.

London   Alternatively, there was London, the largest and wealthiest metropolis in Europe. As a child Mozart had visited England and entertained royalty, but court-sponsored music was itself in decline, as it had been ever since the Restoration. In its place, however, the rising middle class had more than compensated. Entrepreneurship was now driving activities in the opera house and the newly-founded concert halls, as well as the printing presses.

Thomas Arne, William Boyce (1711–79) and John Stanley were the dominant native-born composers in England around the mid-century (see also *Chapter 3*). They had developed their careers in the shadow of Handel, but being of a younger generation, each of them turned to the pre-classical *galant* style: Boyce, for example, in the first four of his

Eight Symphonys (1760), Arne in his comic opera *Thomas and Sally* (1760). The passing of both Arne and Boyce at the end of the 1770s allowed non-native composers even greater dominance in a country that for years had favoured foreign talent. The émigrés included J. C. Bach, whose symphonies Mozart admired greatly, and Clementi, whose piano music Mozart disliked (his feelings coloured by his general resentment towards Italians). The possibilities in London for a composer of celebrity were considerable. Haydn, after his final concert there in 1795, noted 'I made 4,000 gulden on this evening; such a thing is possible only in England'. The operatic scene was dominated by everything Italian, giving Antonio Sacchini (1730–86) repeated success at the King's Theatre from the time of his arrival in 1772. Paisiello's operas were also performed frequently, and the composer himself paid a visit during the early 1790s.

Paris, Europe's second largest city, was better known to Mozart, and certainly up until the Revolution of 1789 it had much to offer. The French capital was home to the most renowned concert institution in Europe, the Concert Spirituel, as well as the Concert Italien and many private orchestras and ensembles. Johann Stamitz took time away from the court of Mannheim to direct the orchestra of Alexandre le Riche de la Pouplinière in 1754–55, and gave enormous impetus to the

Paris

◀ The attack on the Tuileries Palace, 10th August 1792, was one of the key events of the French Revolution, forcing the arrest and in due course the execution of King Louis XVI. The ideals of the French Revolution—Liberté, Égalité, Fraternité—were critical to the aesthetic of the next generation of composers, including Beethoven.

▲ Emperor Joseph II of Austria, the son of Empress Maria Theresa and the brother of Marie Antoinette. He ruled from Vienna during the 1780s, the decade of Mozart's residency.

cultivation of the French symphony. The young François-Joseph Gossec (1734–1829) followed Stamitz as director of La Pouplinière's orchestra and began producing his own symphonies from around 1756. The Concert Spirituel raised the profile of French and Austro-German symphonies substantially. Haydn's symphonies became a regular feature during the late 1770s, and Mozart's Symphony No. 31 *Paris* was premièred there in 1778. The subsequent founding of another important institution, Le Concert de la Loge Olympique, led to the commissioning of Haydn's famous *Paris Symphonies* in 1787.

During this period the Paris operatic scene was shaped by opposing traditions, as played out in the 'Querelle des Bouffons' in the early 1750s (see Opera buffa). Equally vociferous was the squabble between 'Gluckists' and 'Piccinnists' over *tragédie lyrique* in the late 1770s, which in effect saw French operatic heritage again threatened by the more melodic, florid Italian manner. The issue of national identity within the arts was deeply felt in Paris, and it was one that would occupy music, art and literature throughout Europe (and beyond) during the 19th and early 20th centuries.

Meanwhile composers such as François-André Danican Philidor (1726–95), Gossec and the Italian Egidio Duni (1708–75) were advancing the status of opéra comique. Incorporating spoken dialogue, the genre was close in spirit to Italian *opera buffa*, though it did not necessarily include comedy. André Grétry (1741–1813) emerged as the champion of this lighter form of opera, developing a plain and simple style with pleasing tunes and dance rhythms. His success was at its height prior to the Revolution, with works that included *Zemire et Azor* (1771)—studied by Mozart in preparation for *The Magic Flute*—and *Richard Cœur-de-lion* (1784). After 1789, Paris was awash with the inflated patriotic stage-works, hymns and marches of Gossec, Étienne Méhul (1763–1817) and Jean François Le Sueur (1760–1837). This period also saw the rise of Luigi Cherubini (1760–1842), whose opéra comique *Lodoïska* (1790) firmly established the fashion for 'rescue operas'. His arresting *Médée* (1797) was also conceived as an opéra comique and reveals how the genre was evolving to embrace more serious subject matter: the mythical tale ends with Medea's revengeful butchering of her own children.

Vienna

Shortly after arriving in the cosmopolitan hub of Vienna in the spring of 1781, Mozart wrote to his father: 'I assure you that this is a splendid place, and for my métier the best in the world.' By the summer he had been released from his duties to Archbishop Colloredo of Salzburg and was able to embark on a freelancing career. With a population of a quarter of a million, Vienna was an imperial capital and the largest city in the German-speaking world. It was an obvious choice for Mozart, but not without its challenges, since Italian composers had been favoured above Austrians and Germans for well over a century. The court and the nobility together dictated musical taste, and Italian opera buffa and French opéra comique were much in favour. Emperor Joseph II made a bold attempt to establish a German theatre in 1776 at the Burgtheater, ousting an opera buffa troupe in the process. He paved the way for Mozart's breakthrough opera *Die Entführung aus dem Serail* in 1782, but without the support of the nobility, the emperor's nationalistic endeavours came to nought.

The imperial court owned the city's principal theatres and counted the renowned poets Pietro Metastasio (from 1730) and his successor Lorenzo Da Ponte (from 1783) among its employees. Opera seria bored Joseph II intensely, so he installed a new opera buffa company at the Burgtheater in 1783, a decision that directly influenced the Mozart-Da Ponte collaborations *Le nozze di Figaro* and *Così fan tutte*. The emperor's influence on church music was quite different, however, as he actively discouraged the writing of lavish sacred works for public services. Joseph was a true disciple of the Enlightenment and keen to undermine the power of the Catholic Church in any way he could.

Instrumental music was in demand at court, but it was the wealthy aristocrats who shaped concert life, commissioning prolifically and providing vital support for subscription concerts. For a composer and virtuoso, opportunities for concert-giving were considerable. Mozart's own concert appearances regularly took place at the Burgtheater (during Lent) and at the Mehlgrube rooms, as well as at salons, private houses and palaces, and in open public spaces such as the Augarten recreation park.

Mozart had been fêted since childhood and his attitude was self-obsessed and often arrogant. He was never going to enjoy royal favour like the renowned court composer Salieri. Even so, the musically-minded emperor valued Mozart and secured his continued residency in Vienna by appointing him court chamber musician, with minimal official duties, in 1787. Mozart's popularity in 1780s Vienna may be gauged in part by his opera ranking: he achieves only eighth position for performances, behind the likes of Paisiello (who ranks first), Martín y Soler and Salieri. But Mozart's musical successes were many, and his income was healthy right up until his final year. That Mozart and his wife, Constanze, were often wanting for money had all to do with the pursuit of a lifestyle they could ill afford. Mozart's burial in a communal grave just outside Vienna in December 1791 was a low-key affair in accordance with Josephine reform. A week later in Prague, some 4,000 mourners gathered for Mozart's memorial service: a more fitting ceremony for the greatest composer of the age.

Chronology
1750–1799

Haydn, aged 17, begins the year jobless, penniless, and with no real expertise in composition or performance. He survives in Vienna largely on the generosity of others.

29 January Baldassare Galuppi and librettist **Carlo Goldoni** (right) present *Il mondo della luna* (The World on the Moon), a *dramma giocoso*, at Venice's Teatro San Moisè.

16 March Handel's new oratorio *Theodora*, with libretto by **Morell**, struggles to pull in the crowds at Covent Garden. A loyal supporter offers to buy up all the box seats to fund another performance, but Handel knows he is onto a loser, remarking 'The Jews will not come to it … because it is a Christian story, and the Ladies will not come because it is a virtuous one'. None of Handel's new oratorios since *Judas Maccabaeus* (1747) have achieved any success.

March–April Bach's eyes are twice operated on by the English oculist John Taylor, but with no success. His general health declines rapidly, possibly due to harmful medicines, perhaps also due to the advancing complications of diabetes.

1 May Handel directs a charity performance of *Messiah* for the Foundling Hospital (right). A thousand people flock to the concert given at the hospital chapel, and a similar number are turned away at the door. Handel compensates with a second performance two weeks later. From this time he presents *Messiah* once a year for the charity, raising over £500 with each event.

Summer Haydn finds lodging in a dark, dank garret under the Michaelerhaus in Vienna. Residents of the Michaelerhaus itself include the Dowager Princess Maria Octavia Esterházy and her sons, Paul Anton and Nicolaus (with whom Haydn will later gain historic employment), and the renowned poet and librettist **Metastasio**.

20 July Bach suffers a stroke. Two days later he takes his last communion at home.

28 July Johann Sebastian Bach dies in Leipzig, aged 65. His wife, Anna Magdalena, and nine children from two marriages survive him. His youngest son, **Johann Christian**, moves to Berlin a few months later to live with his half-brother **Carl**.

August Handel makes his final trip to Germany, visiting relatives and friends.

18 August Composer and teacher **Antonio Salieri** is born in Legnago.

3 October Matthias G. Monn, pioneering Austrian symphonist, dies in Vienna aged 33.

16 October Silvius Weiss, German composer and foremost lutenist of the late Baroque, dies in Dresden aged 64.

1750 King João V of Portugal dies; is succeeded by his son José; government passes into the hands of statesman Sebastião José Carvalho e Mello, a ruthless dictator who begins 27 years of absolute power by breaking the power of the Church and the nobility while promoting trade and agriculture • Britain joins Austria and Russia in a defensive alliance against Prussia • Britain gives up the Asiento, a monopoly of slave trade with the Spanish colonies • London's first Westminster Bridge is completed • François Boucher (Fr) paints *The Sleeping Shepherdess* • Thomas Gray (Eng): *Elegy in a Country Churchyard*

Johann Agricola is appointed court composer by Frederick the Great. This same year he marries a court singer, Benedetta Molteni, but thereby breaks a royal decree that forbids court singers to marry. The king punishes them both with a severe cut in wages.

J. S. Bach's final masterpiece *The Art of Fugue* is published posthumously.

Geminiani publishes his violin treatise *The Art of Playing on the Violin*, in London.

The poet **Metastasio** engages **Haydn** to give music lessons to one of his pupils, Fräulein Martinez (who will later become a respected composer). In exchange for the service, Haydn receives free lodging over the next three years.

French composer **F-A Philidor**, currently an English resident, embarks on a short chess tour. He plays before Frederick the Great in Potsdam and demonstrates his mental dexterity in Berlin, playing three simultaneous games blindfolded and winning them all.

January Handel composes his last orchestral work, the Organ Concerto in B flat (Op. 7 No. 3). This year he beings losing sight in his left eye.

17 January Tomaso Albinoni, prolific Italian composer who wrote in excess of 80 operas, 100 instrumental sonatas and 60 concertos, dies in Venice aged 79. He is best known for an Adagio that is barely by him at all (see 1945).

4 November Tommaso Traetta launches his opera-writing career with the success of *Il Farnace* at the Teatro San Carlo, Naples.

19 November *Acante et Céphise, ou La sympathie*, a three-act *pastorale héroïque* by **Rameau**, is first performed at the Paris Opéra. The work is remembered chiefly for its fireworks-filled overture.

Quantz publishes his widely-disseminated *Versuch einer Anweisung die Flöte traversiere zu spielen* (Essay on a Course for Playing the Transverse Flute).

D. Scarlatti oversees the compilation and copying of his *30 Keyboard Sonatas*, *Volume I* and *Volume II*. Both the castrato **Farinelli** and the Queen of Spain may have encouraged Scarlatti to produce the manuscripts, in exchange for paying off his gambling debts. Eleven more volumes, containing 30 sonatas each, follow over the next five years. Many of the single-movement pieces draw from Spanish folk music, simulating guitar techniques, stamping and clapping.

Stanley publishes a second set of *Ten Voluntarys* for organ, Op. 6. The collection includes the joyful Trumpet Voluntary in D Major (No. 5), now a wedding favourite.

23 January Composer and pianist **Muzio Clementi** is born in Rome.

26 February Handel directs a successful première of his oratorio *Jephtha* at Covent Garden. Blind in his left eye, sight in his right eye is now deteriorating.

1 August The revival of Pergolesi's *La serva padrona* causes great commotion in Paris, contributing to the escalating 'Querelle des Bouffons' (Quarrel of the Buffoons)—a bitter rivalry between the respective supporters of Italian *opera buffa* and traditional French opera.

18 October Rousseau achieves his first operatic success with *Le devin du village* (The Village Soothsayer), introduced at Fontainebleau before King Louis XV.

3 November The royal surgeon William Blomfield attempts to restore **Handel**'s sight at Guy's Hospital, London. The operation produces only temporary benefit.

1751 In India, a British force under Robert Clive seizes Arcot from the French • François Boucher (Fr) paints *The Toilet of Venus* • William Hogarth (Eng) paints *Gin Lane* • David Hume (Scot): *Enquiry Concerning the Principles of Morals* • French writers Diderot, Voltaire, Rousseau, Montesquieu and d'Alembert produce first volume of the *Encycolpédie*

1752 In India, British troops under Robert Clive capture Trichinopoly from the French • Britain changes from the Julian to the Gregorian Calendar, omitting 11 days from September to make the adjustment • American scientist Benjamin Franklin conducts his kite experiment, proving lightning flash and electric spark discharge to be the same

Handel is now blind. He relies on John Christopher Smith (his career-long friend and assistant) and Smith's son, also John Christopher, for dictation and copying services.

Metastasio introduces **Haydn** to **Nicola Porpora**, from whom he receives valuable musical tuition. Haydn will later reminisce: 'There was no lack of "ass", "blockhead", "rascal" and pokes in the ribs, but I willingly put up with it all, for I profited immensely from Porpora in singing, composition and Italian.'

C. P. E. Bach publishes the first volume of his *Versuch über die wahre Art das Clavier zu spielen* (Essay on the Proper Method of Playing the Clavier). Highly regarded in its time, the treatise is now one of the most important historical references for the interpretation of 18th-century keyboard music.

9 January Mondonville's opera *Titon et l'Aurore* is introduced with great success at the Paris Opéra. Together with **Rameau**'s revised *Castor et Pollux* of the following year, the work is singled out to champion the cause of French opera in the ongoing 'Quarrel of the Bufoons'.

5 February In Dresden **Hasse** enjoys the magnificent première of his opera *Solimano*, featuring camels, elephants, lavish costumes and dazzling stage effects.

1 March Rousseau witnesses the triumph of his one-act *Le Devin du village* (premièred 1752) at the Paris Opéra. Promoting simplicity, rusticity and the common man, the opera remains popular for well over half a century.

29 May Haydn's satirical singspiel *Der krumme Teufel* (The Crooked Devil) is performed with great success at the Kärntnertortheater in Vienna.

30 August Jommelli's opera *La clemenza di Tito* is first staged in Stuttgart for the birthday celebrations of Duchess Friederike of Württemberg. Jomelli is now famous throughout Europe and in much demand, having been offered posts at Mannheim, Stuttgart and Lisbon. He accepts the post of *Ober-Kapellmeister* to Duke Karl-Eugen of Württemberg, at Stuttgart, beginning official duties the following year.

November Rousseau (left) publishes his 'Lettre sur la musique française', fuelling the 'Querelle des Bouffons' by praising Italian music and attacking the French operatic style, epitomised in the works of **Rameau**. A few months later, orchestral players of the Paris Opéra burn an effigy of the philosopher-composer in protest.

… there is neither a clear beat nor a melody in French music because the French language is not inclined to either. French song is endless squealing, unbearable to the unbiased ear; French harmony is brutish and expressionless…

Rousseau, from his 'Lettre sur la musique française'

26 December The opera *Ciro in Armenia* by **Maria Teresa Agnesi Pinottini** premières in Milan.

1753 French troops are sent by Marquis Duquesne, governor of Quebec to occupy the British-held Ohio Valley; the colonial government of Virginia sends surveyor George Washington to demand that the French withdraw; the French decline, and build two forts • To increase trade between Portugal and Brazil, Portuguese dictator Sebastião Carvalho urges racial equality and the appointment of native Brazilians to key government posts • The British Museum is founded • Giovanni Battista Tiepolo (It) paints *Adoration of the Magi* • Tobias Smollett (Scot): novel *Ferdinand, Count Fathom* • Samuel Richardson (Eng): novel *Sir Charles Grandison* • Carlo Goldoni (It): play *La Locandiera*

Joseph Goupy caricatures **Handel** as a pig in 'The Charming Brute'(below), alleging the composer's remoteness and gluttony.

Niccolo Piccinni's *Le donne dispettose*, his first *opera buffa*, is introduced with success at the Teatro dei Fiorentini in Naples.

Rameau's opera *Castor et Pollux* (1737), revised and performed in Paris, is hailed an exemplar of French opera in the continuing 'Quarrel of the Buffoons'. Rameau also publishes a response to **Rousseau**'s damning 'Lettre' on French music of the previous year, with 'Observations sur notre instinct pour la musique' (Observations on our instinct for music).

The Figures odds, yet who would think: THE *Can Contrast such as this be found:*
Within the Tunn of Meat & Drink: Charming *Upon the Globes rotunno Round*
There dwells the Soul of soft Desires BRUTE. *There can you Hoglorad in his Seat*
And all that HARMONY inspires *His sole Devotion is — to Eat.*
Pub. according to the of Parliam. March 1754.

Summer Johann Stamitz arrives in Paris by invitation of Alexandre La Pouplinière, with whom he will stay until the following year. During his visit he directs orchestras at the Concert Spirituel and the Concert Italien.

24 September Gluck's opera *Le Cinesi* (The Chinese Women), to a libretto by **Metastasio**, premières before Vienna's imperial court. The emperor rewards the composer with a gold snuff-box filled with 100 ducats. Gluck shortly becomes musical director of Vienna's Burgtheater.

26 October Baldassare Galuppi and librettist **Carlo Goldoni** create a sensation with their comic opera *Il filosofo di campagna* (The Country Philosopher), first staged at the Teatro San Samuele in Venice.

20 January Hasse revives *Ezio* (1730, libretto by **Metastasio**) for a massive production in Dresden. The opera incorporates 400 soldiers, over 100 horses, eight mules and eight Bactrian camels. The closing ballet lasts over 40 minutes and involves 300 dancers. The considerable size and expense of the event highlights the importance and popularity of Hasse at this time.

26 March The passion oratorio *Der Tod Jesu*, by **C. H. Graun** (below), is premièred in Berlin. It becomes one of the composer's most popular works, widely regarded as an exemplar of sacred music: conservative and measured, commensurate with the ideals of the Enlightenment.

12 May Composer and violinist **Giovanni Battista Viotti** is born in Fontanetto da Po.

23 June Sammartini, aged 54, marries his second wife, Rosalinda Acquanio, aged 17.

30 September Francesco Durante, leading Neapolitan church composer and celebrated teacher (of Pergolesi, **Piccinni**, **Sacchini** and **Traetta**, to name a few), dies in Naples, aged 71.

1 December Maurice Greene dies in London, aged 59. **William Boyce** succeeds him as Master of the King's Music.

1754 A concordat between the Vatican and Spain makes Spanish Church largely independent of Rome • Representatives of American colonies discuss common defence plan at the Albany Convention; Benjamin Franklin's proposal of union rejected • France recalls governor-general, Marquis Dupleix, from India, leaving British influence unopposed

1755 The 'French and Indian Wars' begin in N. America • An earthquake devastates Lisbon (Port); 30,000 killed • Gainsborough (Eng) paints *Milkmaid and Woodcutter* • Voltaire (Fr): *The Maid of Orleans* • Rousseau (Fr): *Discourse on the Origin of Inequality* • Samuel Johnson (Eng) completes his *Dictionary of the English Language* (begun 1746)

The celebrated mezzo-soprano castrato **Caffarelli** retires from the stage at the age of 46, having amassed a substantial fortune.

François-Joseph Gossec publishes his first set of six symphonies (Op. 3) in Paris. Inspired by **J. Stamitz**, each symphony is written in three movements for strings alone. Three further sets of symphonies, Opp. 4–6, are published over the next six years.

Leopold Mozart composes the earliest known Trombone Concerto. This year also marks the publication of his famous violin treatise, *Versuch einer gründlichen Violinschule*.

Six symphonies by **Wagenseil** are published in Paris as his Op. 2.

27 January Johann Chrysostom Wolfgang Amadeus Mozart is born in Salzburg. He is the seventh but only second surviving child of **Leopold** and Maria Anna Mozart.

February Gluck is made a papal Knight of the Golden Spur.

16 February Hasse's opera *L'Olimpiade*, on a popular libretto by **Metastasio**, premieres at Dresden.

10 April Giacomo Antonio Perti dies in Bologna, aged 94. For the last 60 years he has served as *maestro di cappella* of San Petronio.

12 May With a heavy heart **Haydn** directs his own music during a ceremony in which the woman he loves, Therese Keller, takes the veil.

30 July In Naples **Niccolò Piccinni**, aged 28, marries his singing pupil Vincenza Sibilla, aged 14. The composer's first *opera seria* (following three comedies), *Zenobia*, opens at the Teatro San Carlo in December.

Around this time **Haydn** writes his *Divertimenti a Quattro*, representing some of the earliest string quartets. A number of the pieces are played at a musical gathering at Baron von Fürnberg's residence in Weinzierl, where the performers include Haydn and the 21-year-old **Johann Albrechtsberger** (both future teachers of Beethoven).

Around this time **Haydn** pens his Symphony No. 1 in D major, scored for two oboes, two horns and strings.

Jommelli sets **Metastasio**'s *Temistocle* (1736) for Naples.

11 March Handel's revised oratorio *The Triumph of Time and Truth* (1737) receives the first of four performances to a packed house at London's Covent Garden.

27 March Pioneering Czech composer and violinist **Johann W. A. Stamitz** dies in Mannheim, aged 39. This same month sees the publication of his six Op. 2 symphonies, demonstrating the four-movement plan that he has done much to establish in recent years (fast–slow–minuet and trio–fast finale).

15 May *Kapellmeister* **Graun** introduces his Te Deum at St Peter's Church in Berlin in celebration of the recent Prussian victory over the Austrians at the Battle of Prague (Seven Years' War), 6 May.

23 July Italian composer and keyboard virtuoso **Domenico Scarlatti** dies in Madrid, aged 71, having just overseen the compilation and copying of his 13th set of 30 keyboard sonatas.

26 July Egidio Duni and librettist **Louis Anseaume** launch their collaborative partnership with *Le peintre amoureux de son modèle* at the Foire St Laurent, Paris. The work immediately becomes a leading example of *opéra comique*.

1756 Seven Years' War started by colonial rivalry: Britain declares war on France; Friedrich II of Prussia attacks Saxony • In India, the Nawab of Bengal captures Calcutta and locks 146 British captives in a small room, the notorious 'Black Hole': many die • Voltaire (Fr): *Poem on the Lisbon Disaster*, attacking the idea of benign providence

1757 In the Seven Years' War a British force capitulates at Kloster-Zeven; French occupy Hanover • Russia and Sweden join the Austro-French alliance against Prussia and Britain • British army under Robert Clive defeats Nawab of Bengal; British rule established in India • David Hume (Scot): *The Natural History of Religion*

1758

The first English guitar manual is published in London.

Although blind, **Handel** presses on with a successful season of oratorio revivals, many of which include new arias composed with the assistance of John Christopher Smith (Jnr).

21 January Piccinni's first commission from Rome, the opera *Alessandro nelle Indie*, premières at the Teatro Argentina. This year the composer pens three more operas for Naples, as well as his oratorio *La morte di Abele* (The death of Abel).

14 March Mondonville's oratorio *Les Israëlites à la Montagne d'Horeb* is first performed at the Concert Spirituel in Paris.

Summer Handel endures another ineffectual eye operation, this time under the scalpel of John Taylor, the same oculist who unsuccessfully treated Bach.

Summer With the Seven Years' War (1756–63) raging, **C. P. E. Bach** leaves Berlin with his family to avoid the advancing Russian army. They stay with friends in Zerbst for several months. This year sees the completion of Bach's *Geistliche Oden und Lieder mit Melodien* (Spiritual odes and songs with melodies), based on poems by his renowned friend Christian Gellert.

20 November Leading Swedish composer **Johan Helmich Roman** dies near Kalmar, aged 68.

Frederick the Great leading his troops against the Russians at the bloody Battle of Zorndorf, 25 August, 1758

1759

In Philadelphia **Francis Hopkinson** pens his song *My Days have been so Wondrous Free*. It is the earliest surviving piece of American secular music.

6 simphonies by **F. X. Richter** are published as his Op. 2 in Amsterdam.

Quantz's *Sei duetti a due flauti traversi* (Six duets for transverse flute), Op. 2, is published in Berlin. The 62-year-old composer continues to teach flute to King Frederick of Prussia and direct concerts at court.

9 February The impresario G-B Locatelli brings comic opera to Moscow, with **Galuppi**'s recent hit *La calamità de' cuori* (The Calamity of Hearts, 1752).

6 April Handel directs his last concert, a triumphant performance of *Messiah* (1742), at Covent Garden. With failing health he is hereafter confined to his bed.

14 April George Frideric Handel dies in London, aged 74. Although impoverished at various stages of his life, he leaves a sizeable estate worth £20,000. Six days later he is buried in Westminster Abbey with some 3000 people in attendance.

7 July Arne receives a doctorate from Oxford University. Later this year he produces a revised and very successful version of Gay's *The Beggar's Opera* at Covent Garden.

8 August Composer **Carl Graun** dies in Berlin, aged about 55.

3 October Gluck's one-act opera *L'Arbre enchanté* is introduced at the Schönbrunn Schlosstheater in Vienna.

1758 Seven Years' War continues • Britain captures French Senegalese possessions • In India, Robert Clive (UK) becomes Governor of Bengal • François Boucher (Fr) paints *The Mill at Charenton* around this time • Denis Diderot (Fr): *The Father of the Family* • Claude Helvétius (Fr) in *De l'Esprit* claims enlightened self-interest is the mainspring of human conduct

1759 In the Seven Years' War, French are defeated at Minden (Ger); Russians and Austrians inflict a major defeat on Prussians at Kunersdorf (Pol) • British forces capture Quebec City from the French • Jesuits expelled from Portugal • G-B Tiepolo (It) paints *The Vision of St Anne* • Philosopher-economist Adam Smith (Scot): *Theory of Moral Sentiments*

J. C. Bach becomes second organist at Milan cathedral. He converts to Catholicism in order to increase his employment opportunities in Italy.

The 17-year-old **Boccherini**, already gaining fame as a virtuoso cellist, composes his first significant pieces, the Six String Trios Op. 1 (published 1767 as Op. 2).

Gossec composes his *Missa pro defunctis*, later published as *Messe des morts* (1780).

John Mainwaring's biography of Handel, *Memoirs of the Life of the Late George Frederic Handel*, is published anonymously in London. It is the first exclusive biography of a composer.

Composer **John Stanley** (right) and John Christopher Smith form a partnership to continue Handel's tradition of oratorio performances at London's Covent Garden. Clinically blind from the age of two, Stanley has developed a formidable musical memory: he is reputably able to perform the organ continuo part to an entire oratorio after just one hearing.

Wagenseil has *Six Symphonies* (Op. 3) published in Paris. A steady stream of his orchestral works are printed in the French capital, gaining the Vienna-based composer international standing.

6 February **Piccinni**'s comic opera *La buona figliuola* (The Accomplished Maid) goes down a storm at the Teatro delle Dame in Rome. Based on Samuel Richardson's *Pamela*, the work rapidly becomes a Europe-wide sensation.

12 February Czech composer and pianist **Jan Ladislav Dussek** is born in Čáslav.

22 February Anna Magdalena Bach, second wife of J. S. Bach (d. 1750), dies poverty stricken in Leipzig, with only her daughters having remained loyal to her.

10 May German composer **Christoph Graupner** dies in Darmstadt, aged 77. Extremely prolific, he is now best-known for his orchestral music and sacred cantatas.

July The armies of Frederick II blast Dresden and with it **Hasse**'s house, destroying many manuscripts ready for publication.

September Composer **Luigi Cherubini** is born in Florence, possibly on the 8th day of the month.

11 November **Boyce**'s anthem *The souls of the righteous* is first performed at the funeral of George II. This year has seen the publication of the composer's *Eight Symphonies*, Op. 2, whose music derives from overtures to earlier dramatic works.

26 November **Haydn** marries Maria Keller, the elder sister of his former love, Therese (see 1755). It is possible that the composer has entered into the marriage out of a sense of duty to Maria's father, who has shown him much kindness and generosity over recent years. The marriage will be a childless and unhappy one.

28 November **Arne** scores a hit with his Italian-style comic opera *Thomas and Sally* at Covent Garden. He is the first English-born composer to succeed with the genre. Set in a light *galant* style, the opera introduces the clarinet into English orchestral music.

25 December **Telemann**'s Christmas Cantata *Auf Zion!* is first performed in Hamburg.

1760 British king George II dies; is succeeded by his grandson, George III • In Seven Years' War, Prussians defeat Austrians at the Battle of Leignitz; Russians burn Berlin; a Prussian army defeats Austrians at the Battle of Torgau • In North America, British capture Montreal from the French, marking the virtual end of French power in Canada • In India, British troops defeat a combined French and Indian force at Wandiwash; Robert Clive returns to England and enters parliament • Scientist and statesman Benjamin Franklin (N Amer) invents bifocals • Thomas Gainsborough (Eng) paints *Mrs Philip Thicknesse* • Laurence Sterne (Ire): novel *Tristam Shandy*, first two volumes

C. P. E. Bach brings out his *Sechs Sonaten fürs Clavier* ('Fortsetzung' Sonatas, Wq. 51), in Berlin.

Boccherini composes his Six String Quartets Op. 2 (published 1767 as Op. 1).

Egidio Duni is appointed music director of the Comédie-ltalienne in Paris.

The five-year-old **Mozart** composes his first pieces: an Andante in C and Allegro in C for solo keyboard (K. 1a and 1b).

Start of year: Following four years' service as director of music to Count Morzin, **Haydn** is made redundant due to financial cutbacks.

1 May Haydn is officially instated as assistant *Kapellmeister* at the court of Prince Paul Anton Esterházy. His duties involve the composition and direction of secular works, for which he receives, unofficially, 600 gulden a year—200 more than the chief *Kapellmeister*, **Gregor Werner**. He has to present himself twice a day in full livery to 'inquire whether his Highness is pleased to order a performance of the orchestra'. Based at Eisenstadt, the Esterházy family are very accommodating employers, offering staff pensions and free medical care.

30 May Antonio Sacchini begins to set his path as a leading composer of *opera seria* with *Andromaca*, introduced at the Teatro San Carlo in Naples.

Summer Around this time **Haydn** composes his Symphonies Nos. 6–8, commonly known as *Le matin, Le midi, Le soir*. Each symphony begins with a slow introduction and follows a four-movement plan.

8 September Boyce's setting of the anthem *The King shall rejoice* is first performed for the wedding of George III and Princess Charlotte of Mecklenburg.

22 September Boyce (below) directs eight of his own anthems, including a double-choir setting of *My heart is inditing*, for the coronation of King George III. He has politely refused to reset *Zadok the Priest*, certain that he can not equal Handel's masterpiece.

17 October Gluck's pantomime ballet *Don Juan, ou Le festin de pierre* is premièred with great success at the Burgtheater in Vienna. The composer's *Le cadi dupé* (The Duped Judge), a one-act *opéra comique* pandering to the fashionable Turkish craze, is presented at the same venue in December.

3 November Telemann, aged 80, presents a concert performance of his one-act comic serenata *Don Quichotte* in Hamburg.

11 December Mozart completes his earliest dated piece of music, the Allegro in F for keyboard (K. 1c).

1761 Seven Years' War continues: Spain makes defensive pact with France against Britain • Portugal, refusing to close her ports to Britain, is invaded by Spanish and French troops • British secretary of state William Pitt (Whig), unable to persuade King George III to attack Spain, resigns; John Stuart, Earl of Bute (Tory), succeeds him • Prussia's fortunes decline as Austrians seize Schweidnitz (now Swidnica, Pol) and Russians occupy Kolberg (now Kolobrzeg, Pol) • British physician John Hill becomes the first to suggest link between tobacco and cancer • François Boucher (Fr) paints *Girl and Birdcatcher* • Jean Jacques Rousseau (Fr): *The New Héloïse*

1762

Arne introduces English language *opera seria* to the public with *Artaxerxes*. An instant hit, the opera will remain in the repertory for the next 70 years.

6 Simphonies à grand orquestre by **Christian Cannabich** are published in Paris. Currently *Konzertmeister* at the court of Mannheim, Cannabich composes in the four-movement symphonic plan established by his predecessor and former teacher, Johann Stamitz.

By this time **Haydn** has completed his Op. 2 String Quartets, designated *divertimenti* and cast in five movements.

January Mozart, around his sixth birthday, writes his Minuet in G major for keyboard, K. 1(e).

5 March Telemann's oratorio *Der Tag des Gerichts* (The Day of Judgement) is introduced in Hamburg.

18 March Prince Paul Anton Esterházy dies and is succeeded by his brother, Nicolaus. **Haydn** will serve his new employer for nearly three decades.

10 July Roubiliac's monument of Handel with the score of 'I know that my Redeemer liveth' (from *Messiah*) is unveiled in Westminster Abbey.

Summer J. C. Bach swaps Milan for London, where he has been invited to write Italian operas. He will have a major impact on English musical life.

4 August Galuppi is promoted to *maestro di coro* at St Mark's, Venice.

17 September Italian composer, violinist and theorist **Francesco Geminiani**, resident in Ireland for the last three years, dies in Dublin, aged 74.

5 October Gluck's opera *Orfeo ed Euridice*, with libretto by **Ranieri de' Calzabigi**, premières at the Burgtheater in Vienna. In his first real attempt to challenge the worn formulas of *opera seria*, Gluck avoids complicated plotlines and eliminates all spectacle and extravagance. The resulting opera of 'noble simplicity', performed before Emperor Francis I, meets with mixed reactions. It later becomes the composer's most famous and popular work.

13 October W. A. Mozart and his sister, **Nannerl**, perform before Emperor Francis I and Empress Maria Theresa at the Schönbrunn Palace in Vienna. Following his graceful performance the six-year-old Mozart falls flat on a polished floor. The Archduchess Maria Antonia (future Queen Marie-Antoinette of France), also six, helps him up. In return she receives the offer of marriage.

W. A. Mozart, aged 6; Maria Anna (Nannerl) Mozart, aged 11.

1762 Seven Years' War continues: Britain declares war on Spain, and seizes Cuba and Manila; Portugal repels Spanish invaders; a British fleet hits hard at the French West Indies, forcing the surrender of Grenada, Martinique and St Vincent • Prussians defeat Austrians at Battles of Burkersdorf and Freiburg • Tsarina Elizaveta of Russia dies; is succeeded by nephew Petr III, who makes peace with Prussia; Petr is assassinated and is succeeded by his widow, Catherine II (the Great) • France follows Portuguese example and expels Jesuits • Rousseau (Fr) publishes *The Social Contract*, arguing that the state is bound to guarantee the rights and liberties of the subject

In London **J. C. Bach** publishes Six Concertos for harpsichord and strings, Op. 1, dedicated to Queen Charlotte. The sixth concerto, presenting variations on 'God Save the King' in its finale, becomes one of the composer's most popular works.

Leopold Mozart is appointed *Vice-Kapellmeister* at the court of the Archbishop of Salzburg. **Michael Haydn** (younger brother of **Joseph**) also joins the staff as court *Konzertmeister*.

19 February J. C. Bach enjoys resounding success with his first London opera, *Orione*, premièred before King George III and Queen Charlotte at the King's Theatre. This year Bach is appointed music master to the Queen.

9 June The **Mozarts** begin a three-year European tour, with **Wolfgang** and **Nannerl** performing at court or in public concerts. This year includes appearances across Germany, followed by Brussels and Paris.

14 June German composer (**Johann**) **Simon Mayr** is born in Mendorf, Bavaria.

22 June French composer **Étienne-Nicolas Méhul** is born in Givet, Ardennes.

9 July Sacchini's opera *Olimpiade* is introduced in Padua with great success; further performances follow throughout Italy.

4 October Tommaso Traetta (right) presents *Ifigenia in Tauride*, influenced by **Gluck**'s 'reform' opera *Orfeo ed Euridice* (1762), at the Schönbrunn in Vienna.

Various **Haydn** symphonies are printed in Paris and become instant additions to the Concert Spirituel repertory. Haydn's new compositions this year include his popular Symphony No. 22 in E flat major, later nicknamed *The Philosopher*.

1 January Wolfgang and **Nannerl Mozart** perform before Louis XV. While in Paris, Mozart's first pieces are published—two sets of sonatas for keyboard and violin (K. 6–9).

7 January Gluck's last *opéra comique* for Vienna, *La rencontre imprévue* (The Unexpected Meeting), generates great excitement at the city's Burgtheater.

30 March Italian composer and violin maestro **Pietro Locatelli** dies in Amsterdam, aged 68.

17 April Johann Mattheson, composer, theorist and historian, dies in Hamburg, aged 82.

23 April The **Mozarts** arrive in England. Four days later **Wolfgang** and **Nannerl** play before King George III, and **Leopold** pockets 24 guineas for their efforts. The following month the Mozart children make a second royal appearance, on which occasion **J. C. Bach** and Wolfgang perform a sonata together. While in England the eight-year-old composes his Symphony No. 1 in E flat (K. 16).

12 September Jean-Philippe Rameau, France's leading composer, dies in Paris, aged 80.

22 October Jean-Marie Leclair, 67-year-old composer and founder of the French violin school, is stabbed to death on the doorstep of his house, in Paris. The chief suspect is his disgruntled nephew, the violinist Guillaume-François Vial.

1763 Seven Years' War is ended; France loses Canada, Grenada and Senegal to Britain and cedes Louisiana to Spain; Spain cedes Florida to Britain in return for the restoration of Cuba and Manila; France is left with few possessions in India beyond Pondichery and Chandernagor • Voltaire (Fr) attacks the Old Testament in *Saul*

1764 British parliament passes a Sugar Act to raise revenue from the American colonies • British East India Company takes over full control of Bengal • James Hargreaves (Eng) invents a multi-spool spinning wheel, the 'spinning jenny' • Voltaire: *Pocket Philosophical Dictionary* • Horace Walpole (Eng): *The Castle of Otranto*, the first gothic novel

C. P. E. Bach composes his oboe concertos in B flat major (Wq. 164) and E flat major (Wq. 165), around the same time that his elder brother, **W. F. Bach**, completes his 12 Keyboard Polonaises.

Haydn composes his Cello Concerto No. 1 for **Joseph Weigl**, principal cellist of the Esterházy orchestra. Quickly forgotten and lost, the work resurfaces in Prague in 1961.

12 January Composer of around 170 symphonies, **Johann Molter** dies in Karlsruhe, aged 69.

23 January Composers **J. C. Bach** and **Carl F. Abel** begin a series of concerts at Carlisle House in London's Soho Square. Possibly showcased this year are Bach's first six symphonies (Op. 3)—all three-movement, major-key *galant* compositions.

Summer Galuppi journeys to St Petersburg to provide operas for the court of Catherine the Great. Retaining his position as *maestro di coro* of St Mark's in Venice, the composer visits **C. P. E. Bach** and meets Casanova along the way.

Summer The **Mozart** family leave England for The Hague.

October *Kapellmeister* **Werner** at Eisenstadt writes an angry letter to Prince Esterházy complaining of **Haydn**'s apathy as assistant *Kapellmeister*, most of all his neglect of musical instruments and failure to reprimand disorderly musicians. The prince reproaches Haydn; at the same time he requests more baryton music and a first copy of all new compositions, written *neatly*.

The publishing house Artaria & Co., Founded in Mainz the previous year, relocate to Vienna.

J. C. Bach publishes his Op. 5 sonatas, specified as suitable for harpsichord or piano. As such they are England's first printed piano works.

Cannabich has *Six Symphonies* issued as his Op. 4, in Paris.

Peter Beckford returns to England from Rome accompanied by the 14-year-old **Muzio Clementi**. For the next seven years Beckford will act as guardian and musical patron to the boy. Clementi provides musical entertainment at Beckford's country estate, for which his Italian father receives quarterly payments in return.

Michael Haydn, at Salzburg, composes his Flute Concerto No. 1 in D major.

11 February Jommelli (below) presents his serious opera *Vologeso* at Ludwigsburg for the birthday celebrations of Duke Karl Eugen. This year he also produces two comic operas, *La critica* and *Il matrimonio per concorso*, as well as his Mass in D major.

Niclas Jomelli.

3 March Gregor Werner, *Kapellmeister* at the Court of Prince Esterházy, dies aged 73. **Haydn** is promoted to the vacant post, assuming charge of both sacred and secular music. Around this time he begins a thematic catalogue of his compositions.

29 November The **Mozarts** complete a three-year European tour, returning home to Salzburg.

1765 British parliament passes Stamp Act in North American colonies; riots follow in Boston, Mass; at New York Stamp Congress, delegates from nine colonies adopt a Declaration of Rights and Liberties • Jean Baptiste Greuze (Fr) paints *La Bonne mère* • Thomas Percy (Eng): *Reliques of Ancient English Poetry*

1766 Britain appeases its American colonies by repealing the hated Stamp Act, but antagonises them with the Declaratory Act • King Fredrik V of Denmark dies; he is succeeded by his mentally unstable son Christian VII • Britain's oldest surviving theatre, the Theatre Royal, Bristol, opens • Chemist Henry Cavendish (Eng) isolates hydrogen

1767

Arne's *Four New Overtures or Symphonies* are published in London. Probably adapted from theatre works, the three-movement *galant* symphonies suggest the influence of the resident **J. C. Bach** and also the Mannheim school.

C. P. E. Bach becomes honorary *Kapellmeister* to Princess Anna Amalia of Prussia.

Grétry sets up home in Paris, where he will establish himself as a leading composer of *opéra comique*.

Haydn composes his Symphonies Nos. 33–35 and the Stabat mater in G minor. He sends a copy of the liturgical work to **Hasse**, who responds with a letter of praise.

20 January Josef Mysliveček's opera *Il Bellerofonte* premières with great success at the Teatro San Carlo in Naples.

20 June Gossec enjoys a very favourable reception for his opera *Toinon et Toinette* at the Comédie-Italienne in Paris. Productions follow in Germany, Holland and Scandinavia.

25 June Probably the most prolific composer who ever lived, **Georg Philipp Telemann** dies in Hamburg, aged 86. His godson, **C. P. E. Bach**, secures the vacant post of *Kantor* of the Lateinschule and music director of Hamburg's five principal churches, but does not take office until the following year. **Georg Michael Telemann**, the composer's grandson,

fulfils duties as interim director of church music in Hamburg.

August Composer and harpsichordist **Johann Schobert**, together with his wife and child, a servant and three friends, die after a meal of poisonous fungi, which they thought to be mushrooms.

October Mozart, aged 11, contracts smallpox, but makes a good recovery the following month.

24 November F-A Philidor's *Ernelinde* is premièred at the Paris Opéra. Achieving 17 repeat performances, the opera is later revised under the title *Sandomir, prince de Dannemarck*.

26 December Gluck and librettist **Ranieri de' Calzabigi** introduce their opera *Alceste* at the Vienna Burgtheater (below). With the second of his 'reform operas' Gluck asserts a transparent unity between the overture and proceeding drama. He also discards operatic conventions that hinder dramatic continuity, such as perfunctory exit arias and showy coloratura passages. (See also 1769.)

1767 British Government suspends New York's colonial assembly for refusing to enforce the Quartering Act • Townshend Acts: British Chancellor of the Exchequer Charles Townshend persuades Parliament to tax lead, paint, paper and tea imported into the colonies; Boston (Mass) begins boycott of imports • Spain, Naples and Spanish colonies expel Jesuits • Methodism takes hold in the American colonies • G-B Tiepolo (It) paints *The Immaculate Conception* • Jean-Honoré Fragonard (Fr) paints *The Swing* • Clergyman-chemist Joseph Priestley (Eng): *History and Present State of Electricity*, suggests that inverse square law applies to electrical as well as to gravitational attraction

In the Thatched House Tavern in St James's Street, London, **J. C. Bach** gives what is possibly the first public piano performance in England. The German émigré plays on a small square piano made by Johannes Zumpe. This year Bach and his business partner, **C. F. Abel**, move their regular concert series to Almack's Great Room in King Street, St James's.

Around this time **Johann C. Friedrich Bach** completes his first three symphonies (in D minor, F major and B flat major).

Boyce, aged 56 and very deaf, resigns from his his post at St Michael's Cornhill following a complaint by wardens that 'the playing of the organ did not give the satisfaction to the Parish which they had a right to expect'.

Around this time **Carl Ditters** has his Six Symphonies Op. 1 published in Amsterdam.

Haydn composes his Symphony No. 49 in F minor, *La Passione*. This year he loses his home and many manuscripts in a fire that devastates Eisenstadt.

The 12-year-old **Mozart** composes the opera *La finta semplice* (The Feigned Madwoman) at the request of Emperor Joseph II. Incredulous at the result, the theatre director Giuseppe Afflisio accuses **Leopold Mozart** of ghost-writing the opera for his son. Plans for a performance this year are abandoned.

Josef Mysliveček publishes *Six sonates* for 2 violins and cello as his Op. 1, in Paris.

Richter's Six String Quartets Op. 5 are published in London. The date of composition may be as early as 1757.

Rousseau publishes his *Dictionnaire de musique* in Paris, containing musical terms and definitions as well as music history, theory, interpretation and aesthetics.

27 January Egido Duni's comic opera *Les moissonneurs*, to a libretto by **Charles-Simon Favart**, opens with great success at the Comédie-Italienne in Paris.

3 March Renowned Italian composer and teacher **Nicola Porpora** dies in Naples, aged 81. He has ended life in extreme poverty, largely due to the termination of his Dresden pension during the Seven Years' War (1756–63).

20 March Boccherini, aged 25, makes his Paris début at the Concert Spirituel, performing one of his cello sonatas.

Spring Leopold Mozart's wages from the Salzburg court are withheld until the end of the year due to his consistent absence. Meanwhile he continues to peddle his child prodigies, **Wolfgang** and **Nannerl**.

19 April C. P. E. Bach officially takes up his position as *Kantor* in Hamburg. He will have to supply music for nearly 200 events each year.

2 May Galuppi premières his opera *Ifigenia in Tauride* at the court of Catherine the Great in St Petersburg. This year the composer completes his three-year contract with the Russian court and returns to Venice.

20 August Grétry grabs attention with the success of *Huron*, an *opéra comique*, at the Comédie-Italienne in Paris.

September Haydn's three-act buffa opera *Lo speziale* (The Chemist) inaugurates the new opera house at Esterháza.

October Around this time **Mozart**'s one-act singspiel *Bastien und Bastienne* is premièred at the residence of Dr Anton Mesmer, founder of mesmerism.

8 November Sammartini, aged 67, is appointed *maestro di cappella* of the ducal court of Milan.

1768 Massachusetts assembly petitions King George III (UK) and contacts legislatures of other colonies calling on them for support; royal governor at Boston dissolves Massachusetts assembly; Boston refuses to quarter British troops • Genoa cedes Corsica to France • Poles fleeing into Turkish territory are pursued by Russians; Turkey declares war on Russia •

London Royal Academy founded • Laurence Sterne (Ire): *A Sentimental Journey* • Clergyman-chemist Joseph Priestley (Eng): *Essay on the First Principles of Government*, anticipating Jeremy Bentham's 'greatest happiness for greatest number' ideal • First weekly parts of the *Encyclopædia Britannica* are issued in Scotland

Johann Albrechtsberger veers from tradition in his Concerto for (Alto) Trombone and his Concerto for Jew's Harp and Mandora.

Boccherini, now in Spain, dedicates his Op. 8 string quartets to the Infante, Don Luis.

I have not deemed it appropriate to arrest an actor in the heat of dialogue so to make him wait out a tedious ritornello … or to show off the agility of his fine voice with a lengthy passage, or to fill in time with the orchestra while he takes breath for a cadenza …
I have sought to banish all those abuses against which good sense and reason have for so long cried out in vain.

Extract from **Gluck**'s opera manifesto, printed in the preface to the score of *Alceste* (1767), published this year.

Gossec establishes the Concert des Amateurs, which despite its name soon becomes one of Europe's leading orchestras. Gossec remains its director for the next four years, using the position to première his own symphonies. This year he issues his *Six simphonies à grande orchestre*, Op. 12.

Around this time **Haydn** composes his Op. 9 string quartets. Whilst these are termed *divertimenti a quattro*, Haydn's mature compositional style and idiomatic string writing creates advances on the Opp. 1 & 2 divertimento-style

quartets of the late 1750s. Henceforth, Haydn's quartets observe a four movement scheme.

Spring Bohemian composer **Johann Vanhal** leaves Vienna for a two-year career enhancement tour of Italy. Meanwhile his string quartet collections Opp. 1 and 2 are published in Paris.

24 April F. X. Richter becomes *maître de chapelle* of Strasbourg Cathedral.

1 May Mozart's *buffa* opera *La finta semplice* (The Pretended Simpleton) is very likely performed this day at the Archbishop's Palace in Salzburg.

27 October The 13-year-old **Mozart** is appointed third *Konzertmeister* to the Court Chapel in Salzburg.

1 November C. P. E. Bach's oratorio *Die Israeliten in der Wüste* (The Israelites in the Wilderness) is performed for the first time, in Hamburg.

13 December Leopold and **Wolfgang Mozart** set out for a 15-month tour of Italy. Travelling first to Verona, they will improvise their itinerary, stopping off at towns along the way to give public concerts or private performances to local nobility.

Instrument-makers' workshop, from Diderot's *Encyclopédie*

1769 British parliament urges application of 16th-century act to bring American colonists charged with treason to Britain for trial: Virginia assembly passes resolution of protest • Russians overrun Turkish provinces of Moldavia and Wallachia • King Friedrich II, the Great, of Prussia, plans to partition Poland as a means of keeping the peace •

Famine kills one third of the population of Bengal (India) • Pope Clement XIII dies; is succeeded by Pius VI • Jean Fragonard (Fr) paints *The Study* • George Stubbs (Eng) paints *Horse Attacked by a Lion* • Edmund Burke (Ire): *Observations on the Present State of the Nation*

Bostonian **William Billings** issues The New England Psalm-Singer, the first published collection of music by an American.

8 January Piccinni's opera *Didone abbandonata* is introduced at the Teatro Argentina in Rome. It is just one of nine operas by the composer premièred this year: two in Rome, three in Naples, three in Milan and one in Mannheim. The English historian Charles Burney, visiting Italy this year, regards Piccinni as 'ingenious and original'.

29 January Johann Hiller promotes the genre of the singspiel with *Die Jagd* (The Hunt), first performed in Weimar.

26 February Italian composer and violinist **Guiseppe Tartini** dies in Padua, aged 77.

Spring Mozart composes his String Quartet No. 1 in G major, K. 80, possibly inspired by a meeting with **Sammartini** in Milan. This year he also pens five symphonies, the opera *Mitridate* (see below) and the Miserere in A minor, K. 85.

11 April Mozart hears Allegri's *Miserere* in the Sistine Chapel, Rome. Desiring a copy of the music (which does not exist outside the Chapel itself), the 14-year-old writes out the entire piece from memory.

28 April Marie Anne Cupis de Camargo, one of the first great ballerinas, dies in Paris, aged 60.

May Rousseau collaborates with the composer **Horace Coignet** on *Pygmalion* at the Hôtel de Ville, Lyons. Soon popular throughout Europe, the work stands as the earliest *melodrama*, combining spoken drama with musical accompaniment.

5 July Pope Clemens XIV makes **Mozart** a Knight of the Golden Spur (below). Only one musician before Mozart—Orlando di Lasso (d. 1594)—has been awarded the same grade of honour. Although able to use the title of 'Cavaliere' (or 'Ritter'), Mozart will never use it.

3 September Gassmann's *La contessina*, his most popular opera, is first performed before Joseph II and Frederick the Great at Mährisch-Neustadt (now Uničov, Czech Republic).

3 November Gluck's third 'reform' opera, *Paride ed Elena* (Paris and Helen), divides its royal audience at Vienna's Burgtheater.

8 November Boccherini takes up his appointment of *compositore e virtuoso di camera* to the Infante Don Luis in Aranjuez, Spain.

6 December Grétry's *bouffon* opera *Les deux avares* (The Two Misers) is introduced at the Comédie-Italienne, Paris, during the wedding celebrations of the Dauphin and Marie Antoinette.

17 December Beethoven is baptised in Bonn, having most likely been born the previous day.

26 December Mozart directs the première of his opera *Mitridate* at the Teatro Regio Ducal, Milan. Lasting around six hours, the opera manages 21 repeat performances.

1770 'Boston Massacre': several citizens of Boston (Mass) are killed in a protest riot against presence of British troops • Townsend Acts of 1767 repealed, but tax on tea imported into N. America maintained • Russian fleet defeats Turkish fleet off the Anatolian coast • Spain disputes British possession of the Falkland Islands • British navigator James Cook discovers Botany Bay, Australia • Thomas Gainsborough (Eng) paints *The Blue Boy* • Jean Fragonard (Fr) paints *The Love Letter* • Poet Thomas Chatterton (Eng) commits suicide at age of 17 • German philosopher Immanuel Kant becomes professor of logic and metaphysics at Königsberg (Ger)

The theologian, philosopher and poet **Johann Herder** begins collaborating with **J. C. F. Bach** on a steady output of mainly sacred works at the court of Count Wilhelm of Schaumburg-Lippe.

Bohemian composer **Franz Benda** is appointed *Konzertmeister* to the court of Frederick the Great of Prussia.

Chamber composer to the Infante Don Luis in Aranjuez, **Boccherini** (right) completes his first collections of string quintets, Opp. 10 & 11, the latter containing his famous minuet, from Quintet No. 5. The works evolve from Boccherini's playing of an additional cello with the prince's quartet ensemble. This year he also completes his *Six symphonies* Op. 12 and the popular Cello Concerto in B flat major.

In Vienna **Florian Gassmann** establishes the Tonkünstler-Societät, a charity for musicians' widows and children.

Haydn composes his Op. 17 string quartets (maturing the genre yet further), the Salve Regina in G minor and one of his greatest keyboard works, the Piano Sonata No. 33 in C minor. Around this time he also completes his Symphony No. 44, nicknamed *Trauersinfonie* (Mourning Symphony).

Vanhal's *Sturm und Drang* style Symphony in G minor is published by Breitkopf & Härtel in Leipzig.

4 March Mozart is contracted to write *Lucio Silla*, his third opera for Milan.

28 March Leopold and **Wolfgang Mozart** arrive back in Salzburg after a 15-month tour of Italy. A second Italian trip, based in Milan, begins in the summer.

29 May Mondonville's last opera, *Les projets de l'Amour*, is introduced at Versailles.

2 June Salieri's first *opera seria*, the **Gluck**-influenced *Armida*, premières with great success in Vienna. The 20-year-old Salieri impresses Joseph II, who will do much to further the composer's career over the ensuing years.

16 October Hasse and **Metastasio** present the opera *Il Ruggiero* (their final collaboration) at the Regio Ducal Teatro, Milan. **Mozart**'s serenata *Ascanio in Alba* is staged there the next day. **Leopold Mozart** reports that his son's work has outshone that of Hasse. The 15-year-old Mozart, in awe of Hasse, has nothing but praise for him. For Hasse, one of the most famous opera composers of the century, the feeling is mutual—he remarks portentously, 'This boy will cause us all to be forgotten'.

I have seen four rascals hanged here in the Piazza del Duomo. They hang them just as they do in Lyon.

30 November Mozart writes to his mother and sister from Milan.

1771 Publication of British parliamentary speeches is permitted for the first time • French *parlements* are abolished in favour of a simpler system of courts • King Adolf Fredrik of Sweden dies, is succeeded by his son, Gustav III • Austria and Turkey make pact to force Russian withdrawal from Moldavia and Wallachia • Russians seize Crimea from Turks

• Benjamin West (N Amer) paints *The Death of Wolfe* • Louis-Antoine de Bougainville (Fr): *Voyage Around the World*, an account of his journey of 1766–69 • Henry Mackenzie (Scot): *The Man of Feeling* • First bound edition of *Encyclopædia Britannica* is published in Edinburgh

Dr Burney leaves England for the Low Countries and German-speaking lands where he will collect material for a new book on contemporary music. His personal encounters will include **Hasse**, **Gluck**, **C. P. E. Bach** and **Frederick the Great**.

Cimarosa, aged 22, gains international attention with the comedy *Le stravaganze del conte*, his first work for the stage.

The string quartet comes of age in **Haydn**'s Op. 20 (Nos. 23–28). The collection features idiomatic string writing and increased equality among the parts. Its expressive range is striking, from the reflective intimacy of Quartet No. 1 in E flat major through to the sunny temperament of No. 4 in D major. Quartet No. 5 in F minor—its 'Adagio' especially—offers a rare glimpse of Haydn in sombre mood.

Antonio Sacchini arrives in London where he will produce a string of successful *opera seria* for the King's Theatre. He remains in England for the next nine years.

2 January **Michael Haydn**'s *Requiem Pro Defuncto Archiepiscopo Sigismundo* is performed in memory of his former patron, Achbishop Sigismund von Schrattenbach, in Salzburg.

May **Mozart**, aged 16, presents his dramatic serenade *Il sogno di Scipione* (Scipio's Dream)

in honour of the new Archbishop of Salzburg, Hieronymus Colloredo.

13 May Composer **Anton Schweitzer** presents the first German melodrama, an adaptation of **Rousseau**'s *Pygmalion*, at the Hoftheater in Weimar.

Summer Prince Esterházy announces his intention to prolong his summer retreat at Esterháza (below) by several weeks. Members of his orchestra, eager to return to their wives in Eisenstadt, implore **Haydn** to intervene. The composer responds with a new symphony: No. 45. Quickly arranged for performance, the work ends with an Adagio during which musicians are in turn directed to pack up, snuff out their candles and leave. With the orchestra finally whittled down to Haydn and the principal violinist, the prince takes the hint: the next day he orders the departure from Esterháza. The symphony gains the nickname *Farewell*.

11 November **Traetta**'s finest opera, *Antigona*, is premièred at the Court of Catherine the Great in St Petersburg.

26 December Now on his third Italian tour, **Mozart** directs his opera *Lucio Silla* at the Teatro Regio Ducal in Milan. The *opera seria* is a huge success, achieving 25 further performances during Carnival season.

1772 Rhode Island colonists burn a British revenue boat • American statesman Samuel Adams forms Committees of Correspondence in Massachusetts, for action against the British • Gustav III of Sweden, fearing Austrian and Russian aggression, seizes absolute power by military *coup d'état* and begins a programme of social reform and religious tolerance • First Partition of Poland: 30 percent of its territory is taken by Russia, Austria and Prussia • Chemist Karl Wilhelm Scheele (Swe) isolates oxygen, but does not publish the fact • David Garrick (Eng): farce *The Irish Widow* • Gotthold Lessing (Ger): tragedy *Emilia Galotti*

C. P. E. Bach composes six string symphonies (Wq. 182) for Baron Gottfried van Swieten, the Austrian ambassador to Berlin.

How rarely do we meet with a proper amount of sympathy, knowledge, honesty and courage in a critic…

C. P. E. Bach (above), from his autobiography, completed this year.

Mozart composes his symphonies Nos. 22–27. Symphony No. 25 in G minor is conspicuous for its dramatic syncopations, arresting dynamic contrasts and agitated tremolando effects, all characteristic of the *Sturm und Drang* (Storm and Stress) style. It is his greatest symphony to date.

28 May Anton Schweitzer's five-act *Sturm und Drang* style singspiel *Alceste* is staged with great success at the Hoftheater in Weimar.

5 June Empress Maria Theresa ennobles Carl Ditters, making him **Carl Ditters von Dittersdorf**.

Summer During a four-month visit to Vienna, **Mozart** completes six string quartets (K. 168–73) and performs before Empress Maria Theresa.

12 July German composer and flautist **Johann Quantz** dies in Potsdam, aged 76.

26 July Haydn's rustic *L'infedeltà delusa* (Deceit outwitted) is first performed at Esterháza for the name day celebration of the Dowager Princess Maria Anna. Revived in the late 20th century, this light romantic farce has become Haydn's most popular opera.

Cannabich is appointed director of instrumental music at Mannheim.

The 22-year-old **Muzio Clementi** leaves the service of his Dorset-based English guardian, Peter Beckford, and settles in London.

Queen Marie Antoinette appoints **Grétry** as her musical director.

Haydn composes his symphonies Nos. 51, 52, 54–57 and 60. He also completes a three-hour oratorio, *Il ritorno di Tobia* (The Return of Tobias; see April 1775).

Mozart's compositions this year include his symphonies Nos. 28–30, and the Bassoon Concerto in B flat major, K. 191.

20 January Having recently suffered serious injury falling from his carriage, **Florian Gassmann** dies in Vienna, aged 44. **Salieri**, aged 24, succeeds him as director of the Italian opera in Vienna.

19 April Gluck's first opera for the French stage, *Iphigénie en Aulide*, premières with great success at the Paris Opéra. During the summer the composer (right) also triumphs with a French language version of *Orfeo ed Euridice*, but at the same time faces opposition from die-hard traditionalists who circulate anti-Gluck pamphlets.

25 August Prolific in opera and sacred music, **Niccolò Jommelli** dies in Naples, aged 69.

14 November Italian composer **Gaspare Spontini** is born in Maiolati, outside Iesi.

1773 'Boston Tea Party': colonists, in protest of tea duty, dump cargo of tea into Boston harbour (Mass) • King José I of Portugal becomes insane; his wife, Maria Anna, is made regent • Cossack Pugachev leads peasant uprising in south-east Russia • Captain Cook in HMS Resolution crosses Antarctic Circle • Oliver Goldsmith (Ire): *She Stoops to Conquer*

1774 British parliament passes 'Coercive Acts' against American colonies • First Continental Congress meets in Philadelphia to protest against the Acts • King Louis XV of France dies; is succeeded by his grandson, Louis XVI • Treaty of Kuchuk Kainarji ends Russo-Turkish War • Johann Wolfgang von Goethe (Ger): *The Sorrows of Young Werther*

Concert organisers **J. C. Bach** and **C. F. Abel**, in partnership with John Gallini, open the purpose-built Hanover Square Rooms in London. Audience members (generally of high social standing) are allowed to wander around and chat during performances.

Georg Benda establishes the musical archetype for German melodrama (spoken play accompanied by music) with his *Ariadne auf Naxos* and *Medea*, premièred in Thuringia and Leipzig respectively.

Cannabich has his Six Symphonies Op. 10 published in Mannheim.

Mozart composes the serenata *Il rè pastore* and his five violin concertos.

13 January Mozart's three-act *buffa* opera *La finta giardiniera* (The Pretend Garden-Girl) opens in Munich. The poet Christian Schubart writes in the *Deutsche Chronik*: 'Flashes of genius appear here and there … if Mozart is not a plant forced into the hothouse, he is bound to grow into one of the greatest composers who ever lived.'

15 January Giovanni Battista Sammartini, one of the pioneering composers of the Classical style, dies in Milan, aged 74.

2 April Haydn's oratorio *The Return of Tobias* premières with great success in Vienna at a concert organised by the Tonkünstler-Sozietät, a benevolent society for musicians. Around 200 musicians take part.

1 August Gluck's comic opera *Cythère assiégée* (Cythera Besieged, 1759) is revised as an *opéra-ballet* for the Opéra in Paris. At this time Gluck is back in Vienna, which is just as well as the work fails dismally.

16 December Composer **François-Adrien Boieldieu** is born in Rouen, France.

The Concert of Ancient Music is established in London to promote forgotten musical masterpieces from the Renaissance through to the era of Handel.

Dr Charles Burney's *General History of Music* (Vol. I) and Sir John Hawkins's *General History of the Science and Practice of Music* are both published in London.

C. P. E. Bach composes *Heilig* for double choir and orchestra. He writes: '… may [it] serve to ensure that I am not too quickly forgotten after my death.'

Mozart composes his March (K. 249) and the *Haffner* Serenade (K. 250) for the wedding of a family friend, Marie Elizabeth Haffner.

24 January German writer and composer **Ernst T. A. Hoffmann** is born in Königsberg (now Kaliningrad).

23 April Gluck's opera *Alceste* (1767), comprehensively revised for a French audience, struggles at the Paris Opéra.

May Thomas Gainsborough completes his portrait of **J. C. Bach** (below).

29 July Giovanni Paisiello leaves Naples to take up the appointment of *maestro di cappella* to Catherine II of Russia, in St Petersburg. He remains there for seven years.

16 November Piccinni leaves Naples to set up home in Paris.

1775 British fail to conciliate American colonists and Revolutionary War breaks out; American forces capture Crown Point and Fort Ticonderoga, NY • Second Continental Congress meets at Philadelphia; George Washington appointed commander-in-chief of its forces • Pierre de Beaumarchais (Fr): *The Barber of Seville* • Richard Sheridan (Ire): *The Rivals*

1776 In America, the Revolutionary War continues; British evacuate Boston, Mass, but drive American colonists from Canada • Continental Congress adopts a Declaration of Independence (4 July), drafted by Thomas Jefferson, Benjamin Franklin and John Adams • Adam Smith (Scot): *Inquiry into the Nature and Causes of the Wealth of Nations*

J. C. Bach's Six Concertos for harpsichord or pianoforte, Op. 13, are published in London.

Mozart composes the Piano Concerto in E flat, K. 271, his first mature work of the genre.

Josef Mysliveček, pre-disfigurement.

Mysliveček's nose is burnt off while receiving treatment for venereal disease, in Munich. On a happier note, the newly-revised version of his opera *Ezio* (1775) is a great success there.

Poet and musical theorist **Christian Schubart** begins a ten-year imprisonment for allegedly insulting the mistress of Duke Carl Eugen of Württemberg. During this time he will pen *Ideas on the Aesthetics of Music*, as well as his autobiography and various musical compositions.

Paris-based but itinerant composer **Carl Stamitz** visits London. There he publishes his six symphonies Op. 13.

5 January Ignaz Holzbauer's serious opera *Günther von Schwarzburg* is well received at the Hoftheater in Mannheim. Praised by Mozart, it is Holzbauer's finest stage work and the first German opera to be published in full score.

1 March Austrian composer **Georg Wagenseil**, a pioneer of the Classical style, dies in Vienna aged 62.

1 August Frustrated by limited opportunities in Salzburg, **Mozart** petitions Archbishop Colloredo (below) to dismiss him from his service. He argues that he should be free to improve the situation for himself and his family, because 'The Gospel teaches us to use our talents in this way'. Colloredo agrees to the request: 'Father and son granted permission to seek their fortune elsewhere, according to the Gospel.' The following month Mozart and his mother set off in search of a well-paid court position, though **Leopold** remains in Salzburg.

3 August Haydn's comic opera *Il mondo della luna* (The World of the Moon), setting **Goldoni**'s libretto, is premièred as part of the newly-established opera season at Eszterháza.

23 September Gluck's opera *Armide* is premièred at the Paris Opéra. It provokes a hostile response from French opera traditionalists.

'It was just as I expected; no money, but a fine gold watch ... I now have five watches. I am seriously thinking of having an additional watch pocket sewn on each of my trousers; then when I visit some great lord I can wear two watches (which is the fashion anyway) so he will not think to present me with another.'

13 November Mozart, writing to his father from Mannheim.

The **Mozarts**, mother and son, begin the year in Mannheim. The 22-year-old composer falls in love with Aloysia Weber, the daughter of his host, Fridolin Weber. While there he also strikes up friendships with the court composers **Cannabich** and **Holzbauer**.

27 January Piccinni presents his first French opera, *Roland*, at the Paris Opéra. **Gluck** attends the opening night and witnesses the work's enthusiastic reception. Subsequently two rival factions emerge: the 'Gluckists', who consider Gluck sympathetic to French operatic tradition, and the 'Piccinnists', who admire the more melodious Italian manner.

5 March Composer **Thomas Arne** dies in London, aged 67. He is buried in the churchyard of St Paul's in Covent Garden.

'Harmony and Sentiment', a caricature of Thomas Arne performing his most famous creation, Rule Britannia.

23 March Mozart and his mother arrive in Paris, having had no success in finding employment in Mannheim. One of the composer's first Paris commissions produces the Flute and Harp Concerto (K. 299) for the Duke of Guines and his daughter. Mozart receives no payment in return.

26 March Ludwig van Beethoven, aged seven, makes his concert début in Cologne. His father claims Ludwig to be six in order to exaggerate his son's prodigious talent. For many years Beethoven believes 1772 to be his year of birth.

18 June Following a shaky rehearsal, **Mozart**'s Symphony No. 31 *Paris* (K. 297) opens the Concert Spirituel season with great success in Paris. Commissioned by the institution's director, Joseph Legros, it is Mozart's most lavishly scored symphony to date, boasting a full compliment of double woodwinds along with horns, trumpets, timpani and strings.

19 June Soprano **Francesca Cuzzoni**, former £2,000-a-season attraction of Handel's London operas, dies an impoverished button-maker in Bologna.

2 July Swiss philosopher, composer and theorist **Jean-Jacques Rousseau** dies in Ermenonville, northern France, aged 66.

3 July Mozart's mother, Maria Anna, dies after two weeks of critical illness in Paris. Mozart writes to his father telling him of her illness, but not her death. A family friend, Abbé Bullinger, informs **Leopold** a few days later.

3 August Milan's La Scala opera house is inaugurated with **Salieri**'s *Europe riconosciuta* (Europe Rewarded), written for the occasion. For many years La Scala doubles up as a venue for gambling and business transactions, noisily undertaken even during performances.

26 September Mozart leaves Paris having secured no employment. He travels to Munich to stay with the relocated Weber family, hoping to rekindle his relationship with Aloysia. Unfortunately, she has completely lost interest in him.

14 November Composer and pianist **Johann Nepomuk Hummel** is born in Pressburg (now Bratislava).

27 December Salieri's *La scuola de' gelosi* (The School of Jealousy) premières in Venice. The opera triumphs and widens the composer's fame throughout Europe.

1778 France makes an alliance with the new United States of America, and war breaks out between France and Britain • The Marquis de Lafayette, already fighting in America, co-ordinates plans for a French expeditionary force to America; a former Prussian general, Baron von Steuben, becomes inspector-general of the American army, and issues the first US Army drill manual • Americans under George Washington win Battle of Monmouth, NJ • In India, British seize Pondicherry and Mahé from the French • War of the Bavarian Succession breaks out • Navigator James Cook (Br) discovers Hawaiian islands • Fanny Burney (Eng): first novel, *Evelina*

German poet and theologian **Johann G. Herder** publishes a compilation of *Volkslied* (Folksong), thus coining the term and establishing himself as a pioneer of ethnomusicology.

15 January Mozart takes up new employment under Archbishop Colloredo, becoming court organist in Salzburg. Compositions this year include symphonies Nos. 32 and 33, the *Coronation* Mass in C major (K. 317) and the *Posthorn* Serenade (K. 320). He also writes the singspiel *Zaide*, although it is not performed in public until 1866.

7 February Composer **William Boyce** dies in London, aged 67. **John Stanley** succeeds him as Master of the King's Music.

6 April Italian opera composer **Tommaso Traetta** dies in Venice, aged 52.

18 May Gluck and librettist **Nicolas-François Guillard** introduce *Iphigénie en Tauride* at the Paris Opéra. The embodiment of his sweeping operatic reforms, the composer's magnum opus delves deep into the emotions and psychologies of the ancient Greek characters, attaining a dramatic intensity unequalled by **Piccinni**'s rival production two years later.

24 September Recovering from a stroke, **Gluck** witnesses his new pastoral opera *Echo et Narcisse* struggle from the outset at the Paris Opéra. The following month he quits Paris and returns to Vienna.

18 November Fire destroys the Chinese ballroom at Esterháza and with it **Haydn**'s best harpsichord, several opera scores and many orchestral parts.

Four orchestral symphonies by **C. P. E. Bach**, Wq. 183, are published in Leipzig.

26 January Mysliveček's fortunes take a turn for the worst as his new opera, *Il Medonte*, fails in Rome. This comes just one month after the failure of his *Armida* in Milan.

February Muzio Clementi issues his Six Piano Sonatas Op. 4 in London. During the summer he leaves England to begin a tour of Europe.

Domenico Cimarosa
Nacque in Aversa nel 1754.
Morì in Padova nel 1801.

April Artaria & Co. begin publishing the music of **Haydn**, starting with six keyboard sonatas, Nos. 48–52 and 33 (HXVI: 35–39 and 20).

10 July Cimarosa (left) makes his La Scala début with a production of *L'italiana in Londra*, premièred with great success in Rome the previous year. This year sees four new operas by the composer for the Italian stage, including his serious opera *Caio Mario*.

6 November Mozart arrives in Munich to begin reheasals of his commissioned serious opera *Idomeneo*. He revises the work corresponding to the talents of the available singers. This year also sees the composition of his Symphony No. 34.

29 November Empress Maria Theresa of Austria dies. She is succeeded by her first son, Joseph II, a staunch advocate of Enlightenment beliefs and policies. Already a keen patron of opera, the new Holy Roman Emperor will do much to shape musical life in Vienna over the next decade.

1779 Spain joins France and America in war against Britain and begins siege of Gibraltar; the war causes a sharp increase in France's financial deficit • Treaty of Teschen ends the War of Bavarian Succession • Charles Willson Peale (US) paints portrait *George Washington* • David Hume's *Dialogues Concerning Natural Religion* published posthumously

1780 Netherlands joins Spain and France in the alliance against Britain • In America, the British take Charleston and overrun South Carolina, but are defeated at King's Mountain, NC • Emperor Josef II becomes sole ruler of Austria on the death of his mother, Maria Theresa • John Singleton Copley (US) paints *The Collapse of Chatham*

J. C. Bach's *Six Grand Overtures* (Op. 18), including three for double orchestra, are published in London. Throughout this year Bach's health declines significantly.

In Bonn the ten-year-old **Beethoven** begins music lessons with **Christian Gottlob Neefe**, his teacher for the next ten years.

Boccherini composes his *Stabat Mater* for solo soprano and strings. Modelled on Pergolesi's famous example, he will later revise the work for two sopranos and a tenor (1800).

Haydn completes his String Quartets Op. 33, composed in a 'new and special manner', according to his own marketing. Although not a significant advancement on his Op. 20 quartets (1772), the set proves influential in Vienna and inspires Mozart's 'Haydn' quartets, begun next year. Dedicated to Grand Duke Paul of Russia, the collection also becomes known as the *Six Russian Quartets*.

29 January Mozart directs *Idomeneo* at the court theatre in Munich. Despite a successful première, the opera receives only two repeat performances.

4 February Probably killed by advanced venereal disease, Czech composer **Josef Mysliveček** dies penniless in Rome, aged 43. His funeral is paid for by a former pupil.

12 March Mozart leaves Munich, having been summoned to Vienna by his employer, Archbishop Colloredo of Salzburg, who is there in residence for several months for the accession celebrations of Emperor Joseph II.

13 March William Herschel (below), composer, organist and amateur astronomer living in Bath, discovers Uranus. Herschel swaps his musical career for one in astronomy on receiving an annual stipend of £200 from King George III.

9 May Mozart, fed up with servitude to 'a presumptuous and conceited' employer, requests to be released from service. Archbishop Colloredo at first refuses, but a month later grants him his wish. Mozart reports to his father that he was dismissed 'with a kick on my arse', administered by the chief steward, Count Arco.

4 November Faustina Hasse (née **Bordoni**), one of the finest singers of the late Baroque, dies in Venice aged 84. Her husband, the celebrated opera composer **Johann Hasse**, will survive her by two years.

24 December While visiting Vienna, **Clementi** goes head to head with **Mozart** in a piano duel, organised by Emperor Joseph II. The contest includes performances of their own work, sight-reading and improvisation. The emperor is unable to pronounce a winner and so declares it a draw. Mozart reports back to his father that Clementi has great technical proficiency, but 'not a kreuzer's worth of taste or feeling'. Clementi, more generously, admires Mozart's 'spirit and grace'.

1781 United States begins peace negotiations with Britain, to the chagrin of its allies, France and Spain • Britain loses several of its West Indian possessions to France • Austria and Russia conclude a treaty designed to end Turkish power and divide the Balkans between them • Emperor Josef II issues the Edict of Tolerance, weakening Roman Catholic power in Austria; half the country's monasteries are closed within ten years • Henry Fuseli (Switz/UK) paints *The Nightmare* • Friedrich Schiller (Ger): play *The Robbers* • Jean Jacques Rousseau (Fr): *Confessions* published posthumously • Philosopher Immanuel Kant (Ger): *Critique of Pure Reason*

Beethoven's *Piano Variations on a March by Dressler* becomes his first publication. This year the 11-year-old begins to deputise as organist for his teacher, **Christian Neefe**, at the court chapel in Bonn.

Haydn composes his symphonies Nos. 76–78. Thanks to changes in his Esterházy contract allowing him to sell music abroad, they are Haydn's first symphonic works to be written with an international market in mind. The French publisher Boyer purchases them the following year.

Mozart composes his *Haffner* Symphony (K. 385) and the piano concertos Nos. 11 and 13 (K. 413 and K. 415). By the end of the year he has also composed his String Quartet in G major, K. 387, the first of his *Haydn Quartets*.

1 January Johann Christian Bach dies in London, aged 46. He leaves considerable debts, partly due to the failure of the Bach-Abel concerts, but also having been heavily defrauded by a servant. He is buried in St Pancras churchyard.

29 January French composer **Daniel-François-Esprit Auber** is born in Caen.

17 March Violin virtuoso **Giovanni Viotti** thrills Paris giving his début performance (possibly with his Violin Concerto No. 1 in C major) at the Concert Spirituel.

12 April Celebrated poet and librettist **Pietro Metastasio** dies in Vienna, aged 84.

16 July Mozart triumphs with his first opera for Vienna, *Die Entführung aus dem Serail* (The Abduction from the Harem), despite hissing from anti-Mozart cabals in the audience. Afterwards, Emperor Joseph (left) famously remarks, 'Very many notes, my dear Mozart', which gains the response 'Exactly the necessary number, your Majesty'.

26 July Composer and pianist **John Field** is born in Dublin.

4 August Mozart, aged 26, marries Constanze Weber, aged 20, at St Stephen's Cathedral in Vienna. Mozart's father, **Leopold**, harbours grave concerns about his son's ability to provide for a family, and at the same time establish his career in Vienna. His reluctant consent to the union arrives the next day.

14 September Italian composer **Giuseppe Sarti** launches one of the most popular comic operas of the late century with *Fra i due litiganti il terzo gode* (While Two Dispute, the Third Enjoys), staged at La Scala, Milan.

26 September Paisiello stages the first operatic version of Beaumarchais' *Le barbier de Séville* (The Barber of Seville). Premièred in St Petersburg, the opera achieves instant success, with many productions soon following across Europe.

27 October Composer and violinist **Nicolò Paganini** is born in Genoa.

1782 Treaty of Salbai brings to an end the war between Britain and Marathas • A British fleet under Admiral George Rodney defeats a French fleet commanded by Admiral François de Grasse at Battle of the Saints in West Indies • Britain and the United States sign a preliminary peace treaty in Paris: British lose Minorca to Spain, and Spain acquires Florida • Britain abandons its judicial and legislative supremacy over the Irish parliament • Bank of North America is established in Philadelphia • Montgolfier Brothers (Fr) build the first hot-air balloon • Fanny Burney (later Madame d'Arblay, Eng): novel *Cecilia*

1783

C. P. E. Bach's collection of sonatas, fantasias and rondos, Wq. 61, aimed at 'connoisseurs and amateurs', is printed in Leipzig.

English piano maker **John Broadwood** patents his invention of piano pedals.

Dittersdorf begins composing his *Twelve Symphonies on Ovid's 'Metamorphoses'*. Only six symphonies of the collection survive complete.

Haydn composes his graceful Cello Concerto (No. 2) in D major.

March Beethoven's teacher, **Christian Neefe**, publishes a notice in *Magazin der Musik*, declaring that Beethoven will 'certainly become a second Wolfgang Amadeus Mozart if he progresses as he has begun'.

23 March Mozart premières his 'Haffner' Symphony (No. 35) at a concert devoted to his own music at the Burgtheater in Vienna. Emperor Joseph II attends, as does **Gluck**, who enjoys Mozart's improvised variations on an aria from his own opera *La rencontre imprévue* (1764).

'Wolfgang Amadé Mozart takes pity on Leutgeb, ass, ox and simpleton...'

27 March Mozart displays mean-spirited humour with the dedication of the Horn Concerto K.417 to his friend **Joseph Leutgeb**, a virtuoso horn player.

7 April Austrian composer **Ignaz Holzbauer** dies in Mannheim, aged 71.

'Clementi is a charlatan, like all Italians.'

7 June Mozart exhibits his xenophobia as he writes to his sister, imploring her not to play too many sonatas by the Italian lest she ruin her touch.

Summer While visiting Salzburg, **Mozart** graciously helps his friend **Michael Haydn** who is too ill to fulfil a commission from Archbishop Colloredo. He composes two duets for violin and viola (K. 423 and K. 424) and submits the pieces as Haydn's work.

13 August Cimarosa conducts (from the harpsichord) his serious opera *Oreste*, which enjoys a successful première at the Teatro San Carlo in Naples.

26 October Constanze Mozart (left) leads the soloists in the first performance of **Mozart**'s (unfinished) Mass in C minor, in Salzburg. The breadth of emotion and quality of music is unprecedented in Mozart's sacred output, ranging from the grand solemnity of the Kyrie to the delectable operatic lyricism of Laudamus te. Mozart has composed the so-called *Great Mass* in gratitude to God for Constanze's recovery from ill health and their recent marriage.

4 November Composed 'at breakneck speed', **Mozart**'s Symphony No. 36 is premièred at Linz as Wolfgang and Constanze pass through on their return to Vienna.

16 December Johann Hasse, one of the most successful opera composers of the century, dies in Venice, aged 84.

1783 Britain, USA, France, and Spain sign the Peace of Versailles, recognising independence of the United States of America: British and French possessions in the West Indies are confirmed • William Pitt becomes British prime minister • Russia seizes Baku and assumes sovereignty over Georgia • British forces in India surrender to Tippoo Sahib, Sultan of Mysore • Pilatre de Rozier (Fr) makes the first manned hot-air balloon ascent in Paris, in a Montgolfier balloon • The first paddlewheel steamboat sails on the Saône River, France • William Blake (Eng): *Poetical Sketches* • Philosopher Moses Mendelssohn (Ger; grandfather of Felix): *Jerusalem*

Cherubini is appointed composer to the King's Theatre in London.

In Lyons **Clementi**, aged 33, attempts to elope with Mlle Imbert-Colomés, aged 18, only to have his plans thwarted by the girl's outraged father. To console himself the composer visits Berne and studies mathematics.

Haydn publishes his Piano Sonatas Nos. 40–42 and the Piano Concerto in D major.

The players were tolerable; not one of them excelled on the instrument he played, but there was a little science among them, which I dare say will be acknowledged when I name them: First violin: Haydn, Second violin: Baron Dittersdorf, Violoncello: Vanhal, Tenor [Viola]: Mozart.

A musical meeting this year, as later reminisced by the tenor **Michael Kelly**.

Mozart's solo and chamber compositions this year include the Piano Sonata in C minor, K. 457, and his String Quartet in B flat major, K. 458 (*The Hunt*), part of his collection of six *Haydn Quartets*.

February Mozart begins the *Verzeichnüss aller meiner Werke*, a thematic catalogue of his new works. The following month he performs at 13 private concerts and three subscription concerts.

9 February Mozart completes his Piano Concerto No. 14 in E flat major (K. 449). Five more piano concertos follow this year: No. 15 in B flat major (K. 450) through to No. 19 in F major (K. 459). Collectively, their

extended expressive range represents a watershed in Mozart's concerto writing.

5 April Versatile German maestro **Louis Spohr** is born in Brunswick.

26 April Salieri's *Les Danaïdes*, a five-act *tragédie lyrique* influenced by **Gluck**'s reforms, creates a sensation at the Paris Opéra. Management commission two further operas from the composer.

Summer Beethoven, aged 13, is appointed court organist to Elector Max Franz (youngest son of Maria Theresa) in Bonn. He receives a salary of 150 florins per year.

1 July Composer **W. F. Bach**, the eldest son of J. S. Bach, dies in Berlin aged 73. After many years of financial hardship, he leaves his wife and daughter struggling in poverty.

23 August Paisiello's comic opera *Il ré Teodoro in Venezia* (King Theodore in Venice) goes down a storm at the Vienna Burgtheater. **Mozart** attends the première but suffers 'a fearful attack of colic', ending in vomiting.

André-Ernest-Modeste Grétry

21 September The **Mozarts**' first surviving son, Karl Thomas, is born. By the end of the year Mozart has become an apprentice Freemason.

21 October Grétry's medieval *Richard Cœur-de-lion* opens in Paris. His *opéra comique* is a pioneering example of the 'rescue opera' and also notable for its use of a recurring *romance*, anticipating the *leitmotif*. The work remains in the French repertory throughout much of the 19th century.

1784 Russia annexes Crimea and Kuban • Holy Roman Emperor Josef II removes the Hungarian crown to Vienna and causes outcry; emperor is forced to restore the crown to Hungary • USA suffers economic depression • Serfdom is abolished in Denmark • Evangelist John Wesley (Eng) formalises the foundation of Methodism • Henry Cavendish (Eng) describes the composition of water • Joshua Reynolds (Eng) paints *Mrs Siddons as the Tragic Muse* • Jacques-Louis David (Fr) paints *Oath of the Horatii* • *The Marriage of Figaro* by Pierre Beaumarchais (Fr) is staged for the first time • Friedrich von Schiller (Ger): drama *Kabale und Liebe* (Intrigue and Love)

Beethoven, aged 14, completes his three Piano Quartets (clavecin, violin, viola and cello) WoO. 36, in Bonn.

Haydn begins composing his 'Paris' symphonies, commissioned by the French Freemason Count d'Ogny for the Concert de la Loge Olympique. (See also 1786.)

Vanhal's six Op. 33 string quartets are published in Vienna.

3 January Baldassare Galuppi, renowned above all for his *opera seria*, dies in Venice, aged 78.

12 January Paisiello premières his opera *Antigono* in Naples. It is the first of many operas he will compose under his new contract with the Neapolitan court. For the next five years he is unable to leave the kingdom without royal consent.

11 February Probably motivated by networking opportunities, **Haydn** becomes a full Freemason.

11 February Mozart (below) performs his brilliantly dramatic Piano Concerto No. 20 in D minor (K. 466) at the first of six subscription concerts at the Mehlgrube concert hall in Vienna. With the work completed just the previous day, the final movement has to be sight-read by the orchestra, as there has been no time to practise it.

12 February At a party thrown by **Mozart**, **Haydn** hears the younger composer's latest quartets (K. 458, K. 464 and K. 465—three of six quartets dedicated to Haydn later this year). Haydn remarks to **Leopold Mozart**, 'I tell you before God

and as an honest man that your son is the greatest composer I know, either in person or by name'.

10 March Mozart introduces his stunningly tuneful Piano Concerto No. 21 in C major (K. 467) at a benefit concert held in Vienna's Burgtheater. As with his Piano Concerto in D minor (February), it seems that he had completed the work only the previous day. A sumptuous, lyrical Allegro is followed by his best-known slow movement, the sublime Andante, and an elaborate sonata-rondo concludes with theatrical flamboyance.

14 April Samuel Wesley, aged 19, performs as soloist in the première of his Violin Concerto in B flat, in London.

August Thomas Attwood, aged 19, arrives in Vienna to continue his musical studies, financially supported by the Prince of Wales. He receives composition tuition from **Mozart**.

1 September Mozart's String Quartets Op. 10 (the *Haydn Quartets*) are published in Vienna. In the dedication, Mozart writes to Haydn: 'I send my six children to you, most celebrated and dear friend. They are indeed the fruit of long and laborious endeavour … From this moment I surrender to you all my rights over them.' Influenced by Haydn's Op. 33 quartets, Mozart has written them simply out of the need to create. They become his most celebrated works of the genre.

2 November Piccinni's tragic opera *Pénélope* fails to please the French court at Fontainebleau, although it soon finds favour with the public.

1785 US Land Ordinance establishes a survey system • Holy Roman Emperor Josef II attempts to exchange the Austrian Netherlands for Bavaria • Friedrich II, the Great, of Prussia creates a League of German Princes to combat Austrian expansion (under Joseph II) • Jean-Pierre Blanchard (Fr) and John Jeffries (US) make first aeronautical channel crossing (Dover to Calais) by hydrogen gas balloon • Philosopher Immanuel Kant (Ger) writes *Groundwork of the Metaphysics of Ethics* • Coal-dealer and printer John Walter (Eng) founds *The Daily Universal Register* (later *The Times*) newspaper • Anglican priest William Paley (Eng): *Principles of Moral and Political Philosophy*

Boccherini (in Spain) sends off four symphonies (Op. 37) to his new patron, Prince Wilhelm of Prussia.

Haydn completes his Paris Symphonies (Nos. 82–87), commissioned the previous year for the (Masonic) Concert de la Loge Olympique. This popular set includes *L'Ours* (The Bear), *La Poule* (The Hen) and *La Reine* (The Queen—so nicknamed as it becomes Marie Antoinette's favourite).

Mozart composes three remarkable piano concertos: No. 23 in A major (K. 488), No. 24 in C minor (K. 491) and No. 25 in C major (K. 503). Other works this year include the popular Horn Concerto No. 4 in E flat major (K. 495), the piano quartet in E flat major (K. 493), the *Hoffmeister* Quartet (K. 499) and the *Prague* symphony, No. 38 in D major (K. 504).

4 January Sacchini's opera *Oedipe à Colone* is premièred at Versailles. Introduced at the Paris Opéra the following year, this *tragédie lyrique* will become the composer's lasting legacy, with hundreds of performances over the next 40 years.

1 May Mozart directs the first performance of his operatic masterpiece *The Marriage of Figaro* at the Burgtheater in Vienna. Although the stage-play of Beaumarchais' *Figaro* has been banned, Emperor Joseph II has approved the production thanks to some judicious editing by the librettist **Lorenzo da Ponte** (right) of the overtly seditious sections. The popularity of opera increases on each subsequent performance, to the dismay of **Salieri** and other rivals of Mozart. (See also 17 November.)

19 May The blind composer **John Stanley** dies in London, aged 73.

July Cherubini, aged 26, arrives in Paris and shares an apartment with **Viotti**. He soon joins the Masonic Loge Olympique.

> *[The Marriage of Figaro] contains many beautiful things and a wealth of ideas that can only be drawn from the source of inherent genius.*
> **11 July** From the Vienna *Realzeitung*.

11 July Dittersdorf triumphs in Vienna with his comic singspiel *Doktor und Apotheker*. It becomes one of the few German-language operas of the Classical period to achieve success across Europe.

6 October Antonio Sacchini, one of the leading composers of *opera seria*, dies in Paris, aged 56.

17 November Vicente Martín y Soler's comic opera *Una cosa rara* (A Rare Thing), composed in collaboration with librettist **Lorenzo da Ponte**, takes Vienna by storm, completely eclipsing **Mozart**'s *Figaro*. The opera is one of the earliest to feature a waltz.

7 December Salieri's *Horace* opens at the Paris Opéra but fails to capture even a glimpse of the excitement surrounding *Les Danaïdes* (1784).

18 December German composer, conductor and pianist **Carl Maria Weber**, second cousin to **Constanze Mozart**, is born in Eutin, Schleswig-Holstein.

- -

1786 Friedrich II of Prussia dies; is succeeded by Friedrich Wilhelm II • Massachusetts farmers rebel against high taxes and are suppressed by state militia • Britain acquires the Malayan island of Penang • Willem V of Orange loses command of the Dutch army in conflict with the French-supported Patriot party • Jacques Balmat and Michel Paccard (Fr) make first assent of Mont Blanc • Count Alessandro Volta (It) invents a primitive electric battery • Chemist Martin Heinrich Klaproth (Ger) discovers uranium and zirconium • William Beckford (Eng) publishes Gothic novel *Vathek* • John Burgoyne (Eng): *The Heiress* • Philanthropist Thomas Clarkson (Eng): *Essay on Slavery*

Haydn completes *The Seven Last Words* for orchestra. New compositions this year include his celebrated Symphony No. 88 in G major and the six *Prussian Quartets*, Op. 50.

Mozart composes his C major and G minor String Quintets (K. 515 and K. 516), *A Musical Joke* for two horns and strings (K. 522), the Sonata in A major for piano and violin (K. 526) and the serenade *Eine Kleine Nachtmusik* (A Little Night Music) for chamber string ensemble.

11 January Mozart arrives in Prague where he will conduct his *Prague* Symphony (No. 38) and a performance of *The Marriage of Figaro*. For four weeks he revels in his immense popularity in the city, leaving the following month with a commission for a new opera (see below).

12 January Georg Vogler's French-style opera *Castore e Polluce* is introduced at the Munich Residenztheater.

April Beethoven, aged 16, is sent to Vienna to make contacts, display his talent and meet **Mozart**. The elder composer reputedly remarks, 'Keep your eyes on him; some day he will give the world something to talk about'. Beethoven's stay is cut short by news of his critically ill mother, who dies during the summer of tuberculosis.

A Canon by Mozart, dated 27 April; inscription written in English reads: 'Don't never forget your true and faithfull friend, Wolfgang Amadè Mozart.'

28 May Composer, violinist and theorist **Leopold Mozart** dies in Salzburg, aged 67.

4 June One week after the death of his father, **Mozart** buries Vogel Star—his pet starling. He and veiled mourners perform a funeral service for the bird. Mozart provides a eulogy and a headstone for the grave.

8 June Salieri wins back French favour (after the failure of *Horace*, 1786) with the hugely successful *Tarare*, in collaboration with **Pierre Beaumarchais**, at the Paris Opéra.

1 October Martín y Soler's third operatic collaboration with **Da Ponte**, *L'arbore di Diana*, premières sensationally at Vienna's Burgtheater. Da Ponte regards it as his best work.

29 October Mozart directs his opera *Don Giovanni* in Prague, having completed the overture only the previous night. With his second **Da Ponte** collaboration, Mozart mixes light *buffa* with profound *seria*, no doubt worrying the impresario Guardasoni who has commissioned the opera directly in response to the hit satirical comedy *Figaro* (1786). The opera is nonetheless a huge success.

15 November Opera reformer **Christoph Gluck** dies in Vienna aged 73, having suffered a severe stroke the previous day.

1 December Emperor Joseph II appoints **Mozart** to the position of court chamber musician in order to keep him in Vienna. His only duty is to supply dances for court balls.

3 December Cimarosa arrives in St Petersburg to take up his new appointment as *maestro di cappella* at the court of Catherine II.

1787 US Constitution is signed in Philadelphia; first states to ratify it are Delaware, Pennsylvania, New Jersey and Georgia • The Northwest Ordinance is enacted, providing for government of US north-west territories • Tsarina Catherine II of Russia forms a defensive alliance with Holy Roman Emperor Josef II • Josef makes the Netherlands an Austrian province • France moves towards revolution because of financial crisis • Willem V of Orange regains authority in Netherlands with Prussian help • Turkey declares war on Russia • Elisabeth Vigée-Lebrun (Fr) paints *Marie Antoinette and Her Children* • Schiller (Ger): *Iphigenie auf Tauris* • Methodist John Wesley (Eng): *Sermons*

Boccherini composes his Six String Quintets Op. 40, Two String Quartets Op. 41 and a Symphony in C minor, also Op. 41. At this time he holds the position of chamber music composer to Friedrich Wilhelm II of Prussia. He remains in Spain, however, sending the king a dozen instrumental works each year.

Haydn composes his String Quartets Op. 54 and Op. 55. He also receives two commissions, both for a set of three symphonies—the first from Prince Krafft Ernst von Oettingen-Wallerstein, the second from Count d'Ogny for the Concert de la Loge Olympique in Paris. He will submit the same three symphonies to both patrons: Nos. 90–92.

Méhul brings out his three Op. 2 Sonatas for harpsichord (or piano) and violin, in Paris.

In a year notable for **Mozart**'s symphonic triptych (see below), other compositions include the Piano Sonata No. 15 in C major (K. 545), the Adagio and Fugue in C minor for string quartet (K. 546) and the Violin Sonata in F major (K. 547).

8 January Salieri (left) and **Da Ponte** introduce their opera *Axur re d'Ormus* at the Burgtheater in Vienna. Both composer and librettist have recycled material from the Salieri-Beaumarchais collaboration *Tarare*, staged in Paris the previous year. *Axur* triumphs and becomes Joseph II's favourite opera.

11 January *Andromeda*, a three-act *opera seria* by Prussian court *Kapellmeister* **Johann Friedrich Reichardt**, receives a royal première in Berlin.

12 February Joseph II officially appoints **Salieri** to the post of *Hofkapellmeister* in Vienna. The composer will serve the court in this capacity for the next 36 years.

24 February Mozart completes his Piano Concerto No. 26 in D major (*Coronation*, K. 537).

29 March Charles Wesley (right), Methodist and writer of several thousand hymns (possibly as many as 8,000), dies in London, aged 80. His legacy includes 'And can it be that I should gain', 'Hark! The herald angels sing' and 'Love divine all loves excelling'.

7 May Mozart's *Don Giovanni* receives its Vienna première. The opera does not repeat its Prague success (1787), although it manages 14 repeat performances throughout the year.

June Mozart begins writing his last three symphonies—No. 39 in E flat major, No. 40 in G minor and No. 41 in C major—completing the uncommissioned works in around seven weeks. Nos. 40 and 41 crown his achievement in the genre. The English composer-publisher **J. B. Cramer** (b.1771) later gives No. 41 the moniker of *Jupiter*, no doubt inspired by the symphony's momentous finale.

Autumn Paisiello's comic opera *La molinara* (The Miller) opens in Naples. It quickly becomes a Europe-wide sensation.

14 December Carl P. E. Bach, the greatest composer of the Bach sons, dies in Hamburg, aged 74.

1788 Seven more states ratify the US Constitution (now totalling 11) • Seven-year trial of Warren Hastings (former Governor-General of India, accused of corruption) begins in Britain • Louis XVI summons French Estates-General (national assembly) for 1789 after demands by Paris *parlement* (local court) • British, Dutch and Prussians form Triple Alliance to preserve peace • Swedes invade Finland • Danes invade Sweden • Austria is at war with Turkey • Britain sends its first convicts to Port Jackson settlement in Australia • Britain founds Sierra Leone as a haven for former slaves • Philosopher Immanuel Kant (Ger): *Critique of Practical Reason*

J. C. F. Bach issues his *Drei leichte Sonaten fürs Klavier oder Piano Forte*.

Beethoven, aged 18, petitions the Elector of Bonn for half of his father's salary to be paid directly to himself for the education of his brothers, on account of their father being an incompetent alcoholic. The Elector agrees; Ludwig becomes head of the family and his father (a court singer) is suspended from service.

J. L. Dussek flees France's raging revolution. He finds refuge in London, his home for the next 11 years. He immediately settles into musical life, teaching piano and giving concerts.

Haydn completes his commission for three symphonies, Nos. 90–92, from two different patrons (see 1788). The last of the three symphonies—later nicknamed *Oxford*— becomes one of Haydn's best-loved works. Other compositions this year include the Piano Sonatas Nos. 43 and 44, and the Piano Trios Nos. 8–10.

Johann Friedrich Peter, German émigré, composes six quintets in Salem, Massachusetts. They are the earliest surviving chamber pieces composed in America.

April Mozart embarks on a two-month concert tour of Leipzig, Dresden and Berlin.

11 April George Bridgetower, ten-year-old violinist of West Indian and European parentage, makes his début at the Concert Spirituel in Paris.

17 June London's King's Theatre burns down.

14 July Mozart writes to his fellow freemason Baron Michael

von Puchberg, begging for financial assistance. Subscription concerts and commissions are in poor supply, publishing profits are down and pupils are few. Added to this, both Mozart and his wife are regularly experiencing bouts of ill health. The baron takes pity and lends him substantial funds, and not for the last time.

6 August Gossec's *Messe des morts* (1760) is performed in memory of those who died during the storming of the Bastille (below).

29 August Mozart's *The Marriage of Figaro* is revived with great success at the Burgtheater, Vienna. The production achieves 25 further performances this year.

12 September German composer **Franz X. Richter** dies in Strasbourg, aged 79. **Ignace Pleyel** (b.1757) succeeds him as *maître de chapelle* at Strasbourg Cathedral.

22 December Mozart's Clarinet Quintet in A major is premièred with the clarinettist **Anton Stadler** at a concert for the Tonkünstler-Societät (Musicians' Benevolent Society) in Vienna.

1789 French Revolution begins when Paris mob storms fortress-prison of the Bastille; French National Assembly adopts Declaration of the Rights of Man and prohibits its members from working for the king; for safety from the mob, Louis XVI is forced to move from Versailles to Paris • First US Congress meets in New York • George Washington becomes first US President • North Carolina ratifies the US Constitution and becomes 12th State • Judiciary Act establishes federal court system in USA • Belgium, encouraged by France, declares independence from Austria • William Blake (Eng): *Songs of Innocence* • Goethe (Ger): *Tasso*

Beethoven composes two cantatas, one to mark the death of Emperor Joseph II (WoO. 87) and the other for the new Emperor, Leopold II (WoO. 88). Neither cantata is published or performed during Beethoven's lifetime, but both serve as important calling cards for prospective patronage.

Clementi, in London, publishes his Six Piano Sonatas Op. 25, including the often-performed F sharp minor sonata, No. 5. This year the 38-year-old piano virtuoso decides to abandon his performing career and devote more time to composition.

Haydn completes his Six String Quartets Op. 64.

The 11-year-old **Johann Hummel** arrives in Edinburgh with his father. Hummel is taught English, and both father and son take music pupils.

The renowned Concert Spirituel, established in Paris by A. D. Philidor in 1725, closes down in the wake of the French Revolution.

26 January Mozart's third and final operatic collaboration with **Da Ponte**, *Così fan tutte* (All Women are the Same), opens at Vienna's Burgtheater. With an emphasis on ensembles, the colourful farce contains some of Mozart's best music, but manages only ten performances.

'Here I sit in my wilderness, forsaken, like a poor waif, almost without any human society; melancholy, full of the memories of past glorious days.'
9 February Haydn bemoans his life at Esterháza in a letter to Marianne von Genzinger. (He is, in fact, about to experience the most rewarding period of his career.)

14 July Gossec's Te Deum is performed by a 1,000-strong choir at the Fête de la Fédération in Paris to commemorate the storming of the Bastille. Later this year the composer writes his patriotic *Marche lugubre*.

4 September Étienne Méhul's first staged opera, the comedy *Euphrosine, ou Le tyran corrigé* (Euphrosine, or The Tyrant Reformed), opens with great success at the Théâtre Favart in Paris. The work will gain many admirers, including Berlioz.

28 September Haydn's employer, Prince Nicolaus Esterházy, dies, leaving the composer a yearly pension of 1,000 gulden in his will. His son, Anton, soon disbands the musical establishment at Esterháza, retaining Haydn as *Kapellmeister* in name and salary only. With no specific duties to perform, Haydn moves to Vienna.

Autumn The impresario Johann Peter Salomon (left) visits **Haydn** and declares in no uncertain terms that he has come to fetch him for London. He offers the composer a package deal of commissions and an advance on receipts to the tune of £1,200 (the modern-day equivalent of £100,000). Haydn will provide six symphonies, one opera, and a host of other works for concert appearances.

December Mozart composes his String Quintet in D, K. 593, 'for a Hungarian music-lover' (unnamed, but possibly the violinist **Johann Tost**).

14 December Salomon throws a farewell dinner for **Haydn** in Vienna, the day before their departure for England. Among the guests is **Mozart**, who at the end of the evening presciently remarks to Haydn, 'We are probably saying our last adieu in this life'.

1790 Rhode Island ratifies the US Constitution and becomes 13th State • French Revolution continues; political clubs, led by Robespierre and others, increase their authority; moderate leader Comte de Mirabeau tries to prevent overthrow of monarchy; Louis XVI accepts new constitution • In France, Jews are given civil liberties, clergy are placed under civil organisation, titles are abolished and sweeping administrative reforms are introduced • Leopold II becomes Holy Roman Emperor • Russia gains part of Finland from Sweden, and Russian-Swedish war ends • Austrians suppress independence movement in Belgium • Philosopher Immanuel Kant (Ger): *Critique of Judgment*

1 January Haydn docks at Dover. The next day he arrives in London where he is immediately the centre of media attention. He is wined and dined by London's elite, but has to implement strict measures to safeguard both his health and work: 'Except for the nobility, I admit no callers until 2 o'clock.'

21 February Composer, pianist and teacher **Carl Czerny** is born in Vienna.

4 March Mozart premières his lyrical Piano Concerto No. 27 in B flat major (K. 595), in Vienna. It has been three years since the composer's last piano concerto; his former theatrical mood has given way to reflection and nostalgia.

11 March Salomon's three-month series of weekly concerts begin at the Hanover Square Rooms in London. Works by **Haydn** take pride of place, with the rousing Symphony No. 96 in D major premièred on the opening evening.

June Cimarosa leaves the court of Catherine II in St Petersburg after four years of service. He arrives in Vienna three months later and is immediately appointed to the post of *Kapellmeister* by Leopold II.

Summer Mozart is commissioned to write a Requiem for a patron who wishes to remain anonymous. This is in fact Count Walsegg-Stuppach, whose wife died earlier this year. The Count is an amateur musician and desires to pass off the Requiem as his own work.

8 July Haydn is awarded an honorary doctorate by Oxford University. While there he conducts his Symphony No. 92 (1789), thereafter nicknamed *Oxford*.

5 September Composer **Jakob Liebmann Meyer Beer** (later **Giacomo Meyerbeer)** is born in Vogelsdorf, near Berlin.

6 September Mozart's *La clemenza di Tito* (The Clemency of Titus) receives a luke-warm reception in Prague when it is introduced as part of the coronation celebrations of Leopold II. Mozart has had less than one month to write the opera, which he has done with the help of his pupil **Franz Süssmayr**. The Empress has two words for it: 'German rubbish.'

30 September Mozart directs *Die Zauberflöte* (The Magic Flute) at the Theater auf der Wieden in Vienna. Composed to a libretto by the theatre's owner, **Emanuel Schikaneder**, the opera allegories Freemasonry in a quasi-Egyptian land at an unspecified time. It becomes a huge success and the talk of Vienna; over the next ten years Schikaneder will present *Die Zauberflöte* more than 200 times.

October Mozart completes his Clarinet Concerto in A major. The following month he falls ill, possibly with rheumatic fever, but manages to continue composing his Requiem with the help of **Süssmayr**.

November Dussek, in London, publishes his charming Harp Concerto in E flat major (Op. 15), a work likely inspired by his future wife, the harpist **Sophia Corri**.

5 December Mozart, aged 35, dies shortly before 1 a.m., having entrusted **Süssmayr** with the completion of his Requiem. Two days later he is buried in an unmarked communal grave, in accordance with current Viennese custom.

1791 President Washington selects site on Potomac River for new US capital • Upper and Lower Canada, with separate legislative assemblies, are created by Britain's Canada Constitution Act • In French Revolution, King Louis XVI and royal family are stopped trying to escape from France; French National Assembly adopts constitutional monarchy, then dissolves • Britain declares neutrality over French revolution • Berlin's Brandenburg Gate is completed • George Morland (Eng) paints *The Stable* • James Boswell (Scot): *The Life of Samuel Johnson* • Marquis de Sade (Fr): novel *Justine* • British-born journalist Thomas Paine (US): *The Rights of Man*, Part I

14-year old **Johann Nepomuk Hummel**, temporary resident of London with his father, brings out his Piano Sonata No. 1 in C major, together with a Trio and an accompanied Sonata (Op. 2a).

7 February Cimarosa achieves a resounding success with his comic opera *Il matrimonio segreto* (The Secret Marriage), premièred in Vienna. Emperor Leopold II attends the second performance and is completely transfixed. He orders supper for the cast, and thereafter a repeat performance of the entire opera.

29 February Italian opera composer **Gioachino Antonio Rossini** is born in Pesaro.

March Pleyel (recently arrived from Strasbourg) begins a series of concerts in London with violinist and entrepreneur **Wilhelm Cramer**. The media encourages rivalry between Pleyel and **Haydn**, although the two composers remain completely civil towards each other.

23 March Haydn presents his *Surprise* Symphony, No. 94, in London. He will later explain (to his biographer, Griesinger) the Andante's arresting kettledrum outburst: 'my intention was to surprise the public with something new, and also to première in a brilliant manner, so not to be outshone by my pupil **Pleyel**.'

24 March Pianist **John Field**, aged nine, gives his début performance at the Rotunda Assembly Rooms in Dublin.

6 April Süssmayr completes the rondo-finale of Mozart's Horn Concerto in D major, K. 412.

24 April Claude-Joseph Rouget de Lisle writes both words and music to the *Chant de guerre pour l'armée du Rhin*, later called *La Marseillaise* after the Marseilles Volunteer Battalion.

3 May Haydn directs a wonderfully successful concert for his own benefit in London. Included in the programme is the première of his Symphony No. 97 in C major.

16 May The rebuilt Teatro La Fenice in Venice is inaugurated by **Paisiello**'s *I giuochi d'Agrigento* (The Games of Agrigento). The famous castrato **Gasparo Pacchierotti** leads the cast.

14 June Haydn attends the races at Ascot. Shortly afterwards he leaves London for Vienna.

July Viotti flees France and its revolutionary wars for London.

30 September Gossec's *L'offrande à la liberté* (The Offering to Liberty) is staged at the Paris Opéra. The work depicts French revolutionary conflict with foreign powers, and climaxes with a setting of Rouget de Lisle's *La Marseillaise*. Gossec scores an instant hit, with 143 performances over the next five years.

Thomas Hardy's portrait of Joseph Haydn, 1792.

November Beethoven leaves Bonn for Vienna. His father dies the following month.

4 November Paisiello and librettist **Calzabigi** launch the opera season in Naples with their tragedy *Elfrida*, staged at the Teatro San Carlo.

1792 French Revolution continues: Swiss guards are massacred in Paris; royal family is imprisoned; France is proclaimed a republic; trial of Louis XVI begins • The first guillotine is erected in Paris (Fr) • Austria and Prussia form an alliance against France, which declares war on them and Sardinia • Franz II (Aus) becomes last Holy Roman Emperor • Denmark abolishes the slave trade • Gas lighting is introduced in England • The dollar becomes the official US currency unit • British-born Thomas Paine (US): *The Rights of Man*, Part II; Britain accuses Paine of treason • Mary Wollstonecraft (Eng): *Vindication of the Rights of Women*

Haydn, back in Vienna, pens his imposing Symphony No. 99 in E flat major, beginning his second set of *London* symphonies. He also completes his String Quartets Op. 71 and Op. 74, with the intention of presenting them in London the following year.

Haydn introduces his pupil **Beethoven** to the cream of Viennese society. Beethoven struggles to make musical progress with Haydn, so he takes extra counterpoint lessons from **Johann Schenk** in secret.

27 January Gossec, quintessential composer of the revolution, presents *Le triomphe de la République* at the Paris Opéra. The *divertissement-lyrique* celebrates the recent French victory at the battle of Valmy.

5 March Méhul's ballet *Le jugement de Paris* is first performed at the Paris Opéra. The production includes music by Gluck, **Haydn** and **Pleyel**.

23 November 'Beethoven will in time fill the position of one of Europe's greatest composers, and I shall be proud to be able to speak of myself as his teacher.' **Haydn** writing to Beethoven's patron, the Elector of Cologne.

Execution of Louis XVI, 21 January.

Having struggled to make musical progress under **Haydn**, **Beethoven** takes counterpoint lessons with **Johann Albrechtsberger** and studies Italian text setting with **Salieri**.

Piccinni is placed under house arrest in Naples, implicated in his daughter's marriage to a French Jacobin. In fact, Piccinni has had nothing to do with the union. He is unable to leave Naples for the next four years.

19 January Haydn departs Vienna for a second visit to England, where he will stay until the following year. A new series of concerts in London, again organised by the impresario Johann Salomon, is a rousing success, with his Symphony No. 100 (*Military*) the crowning glory of the spring season.

22 January Haydn's musically apathetic patron, Prince Anton Esterházy (see 1790), dies after just over three years of reign.

6 May Méhul's *Mélidore et Phrosine* is warmly received at the Opéra-Comique (formerly the Comédie-Italienne) in Paris. Despite early success, the opera does not survive long in the repertory due to its rather uncomfortable theme of unrequited incestuous love.

23 May Composer and pianist **Ignaz Moscheles** is born in Prague.

31 May The 11-year-old violinist **Nicolò Paganini** gives his début performance in Genoa.

19 September The prolific **Grétry** presents *Callias, ou Nature et patrie* (Callias, or Nature and Homeland), his fourth one-act opera in as many months, at the Opéra Comique, Paris.

1793 French Revolution continues: King Louis XVI and Queen Marie Antoinette are executed; Maximilien Robespierre rises to power; Reign of Terror • USA declares its neutrality • France declares war on Britain and Netherlands, which join coalition with Austria, Prussia, Spain and Sardinia • Eli Whitney (US) invents the cotton gin

1794 Jay's Treaty between USA and Britain stabilises trade relations • French Revolution continues; Danton and Robespierre are executed; Reign of Terror ends; Paris Commune is abolished • Britain, Russia and Austria form alliance against France • Thomas Paine (now a US citizen): *The Age of Reason* • William Blake (Eng) paints *The Ancient of Days*

Haydn signs up to **Viotti**'s Opera Concerts in London, as Salomon has cancelled his own concert season due to a lack of first-rate singers from abroad. The escalating French Revolutionary Wars have made continental travel often perilous.

The Paris Conservatoire is founded. Staff members include **Gossec**, **Méhul**, **Grétry**, **Cherubini** and **Le Sueur**.

I. J. Pleyel settles in Paris, where he soon establishes the publishing house Maison Pleyel.

Martín y Soler (left) collaborates with **Da Ponte** in London, having arrived from St Petersburg the previous year. They gain success with the opera *La scuola dei maritati* (The School for the Married), but fall out during the production of the poorly received *L'isola del piacere* (The Island of Pleasure).

1 February The Prince of Wales arranges a soirée for **Haydn**, with George III and the queen in attendance. Haydn enjoys considerable royal endorsement throughout the concert season, and is offered residence at Windsor Castle over the summer.

29 March Beethoven makes his Vienna début at the Burgtheater, introducing his Piano Concerto in B flat major (No. 2).

4 May Haydn directs the last and arguably greatest of his 12 *London* symphonies, No. 104 in D major, during his own benefit concert at the King's Theatre. The concert season has also introduced his Symphony No. 102 in B flat major (composed the previous year) and Symphony No. 103 in E flat major (*Drumroll*).

July Beethoven's Opus 1—three piano trios in E flat, G, and C—is published in Vienna and dedicated to Prince Lichnowsky. The third trio of the set proves the most popular, dispelling **Haydn**'s concerns that it would be too modern for Vienna.

15 August Haydn leaves England for the last time. He has enjoyed the happiest years of his life there, having savoured unremitting success and widespread fame during his two visits. Once back in Austria he resumes nominal duties as *Kapellmeister* to Prince Nikolaus Esterházy II.

16 August German opera composer **Heinrich August Marschner** is born in Zittau.

31 August François-André Danican Philidor, composer and one of the greatest chess players of the century, dies in London, aged 68.

6 November Bohemian composer **Georg Benda** dies in Köstritz, Gotha, aged 73.

21 November Joseph Wölfl's heroic-comic *Der Höllenberg*, on a libretto by **Schikaneder**, is well received in Vienna. This is Wölff's first attempt at opera; at the age of 22 he is already a renowned keyboard virtuoso.

18 December Beethoven performs the première of his Piano Concerto No. 1 in C major (later revised) at a concert organised by Haydn, in Vienna.

Emanuel Schikaneder: librettist, impresario, actor, singer and composer.

1795 French occupy the Netherlands and create Batavian Republic • France and Prussia conclude Peace Treaty of Basel • Britain acquires Ceylon (Sri Lanka) from the Dutch • Bread riots in Paris • Britain occupies Cape of Good Hope on behalf of Willem V of Orange • Troops under General Napoleon Bonaparte put down royalist insurrection in Paris • Belgium is absorbed by France • Russia and Austria partition Poland for the third time • Spain and the USA establish boundaries between Florida and USA • Scotsman Mungo Park explores the Niger River • Inventor Joseph Bramah (Eng) patents his hydraulic press • Francisco Goya (Sp) paints *The Duchess of Alba*

Active again as Esterházy *Kapellmeister*, **Haydn** is requested to compose a mass each year for the name day of Princess Maria Esterházy. This adds to a significant concentration of sacred works in Haydn's output at this time. The *Missa Sancti Bernardi von Offida* and the *Missa in tempore belli* (Mass in Time of War) are completed this year.

Haydn composes his popular Trumpet Concerto in E flat major for **Anton Weidinger** (currently a member of the Vienna Court Opera), exploiting the groundbreaking chromatic facility of Weidinger's keyed instrument.

Martín y Soler leaves London for St Petersburg, where he will remain for the rest of his life.

Around this time **Viotti** completes his Violin Concerto No. 22 in A minor, in London. Later admired by Brahms, it is widely regarded as the best of his 29 violin concertos.

21 January Cherubini directs a concert in Paris celebrating the third anniversary of the beheading of Louis XVI. (See also 1817.)

26 January Simon Mayr establishes his credentials with his second opera, *La Lodoiska*, introduced with great success in Venice.

February Beethoven begins a European concert tour. Planned at six weeks, it lasts six months.

26 March Haydn's oratorio arrangement of his orchestral work *Seven Last Words* (1787) is first heard at the Schwarzenberg Palace, Vienna.

23 July Swedish composer and violinist **Franz Berwald** is born in Stockholm.

Beethoven composes his Piano Sonata No. 4 in E flat major (Op. 7, published this year) and the Piano Trio in B flat major ('Gassenhauer'), Op. 11.

Clementi publishes his popular Six Sonatinas for piano Op. 36, in London.

31 January Franz Schubert is born in Vienna. He is the 12th of 14 children, only five of whom survive infancy.

12 February Haydn's Emperor's Hymn, *Gott erhalte Franz den Kaiser*, is performed at various Habsburg theatres in celebration of the emperor's birthday. Count Joseph Franz Saurau has commissioned the work in the hope that Austria will gain its own equivalent of England's *God Save the King*. Germany will later borrow the tune for their national anthem, *Das Lied der Deutschen*, and later still, the Nazis for the song *Deutschland über alles*.

13 March Cherubini's *Médée* (Medea) is premièred with reasonable success at the Théâtre Feydeau in Paris (left). One of the composer's outstanding achievements, the Greek legend opera is better received in Germany, and productions continue there throughout the next century.

Autumn Haydn completes his Six String Quartets Op. 76. The collection includes the *Emperor* Quartet (No. 3 in C major), incorporating the *Emperor's Hymn* (see above) as a basis for the second movement variations.

29 November Italian composer **Gaetano Donizetti** is born into poverty in Bergamo.

1796 Savoy and Nice are ceded to France • Britain captures the island of Elba • France and Spain form an alliance against Britain • Britain captures West Indian islands, including Grenada and St Lucia • Britain opens negotiations for peace with France • Physician Edward Jenner (Eng) introduces vaccination against smallpox

1797 John Adams assumes office as second President of the USA • French forces cross the Alps into Austria • France proclaims the Cisalpine Republic, comprising most of northern Italy • Napoleon is appointed to command a French invasion of Britain • Samuel Taylor Coleridge (Eng): poem *Rime of the Ancient Mariner*

Beethoven completes his *Pathétique* piano sonata (Op. 13) and begins composing his Op. 18 string quartets, commissioned by Prince Lobkowitz. This year sees the publication of the Three String Trios Op. 9 and Three Piano Sonatas Op. 10, in Vienna.

Clementi establishes his publishing and instrument-making firm Clementi & Co, in London.

20 January Influential German composer **Christian Cannabich**, author of more than 70 symphonies, dies in Frankfurt, aged 66.

19 February Composer **Pierre Gaveaux** and librettist **Jean-Nicolas Bouilly** create the original *Léonore, ou L'amour conjugal* (Leonora, or Conjugal Love) at the Opéra-Comique, Paris.

March The British authorities order **Viotti** to leave the country, accusing him of revolutionary agitation. The composer writes to *The Times* protesting his innocence, but to no avail.

29–30 April **Haydn**'s *The Creation* débuts before a select audience at the Schwarzenberg Palace, Vienna. Funded by aristocratic subscription, the oratorio is the first work to be written in two languages simultaneously—English and German. Haydn will tell his biographer Griesinger 'I was never so devout as when I wrote *The Creation*. Every morning I knelt and prayed to God to give me strength for a happy completion of the work.' (See also 1799.)

Summer **Haydn** composes his dramatic *Missa in Angustiis*. (See also 1800.)

18 October **Mayr**'s opera *Che originali* opens in Venice. It is the fourth of six new stage works produced this year by Mayr for the city's theatres.

November **Beethoven**'s Romance for violin and orchestra (No. 2) in F Major is likely introduced around this time, in Vienna.

Beethoven composes his Septet in E flat major (Op. 20) and his Symphony No. 1 (Op. 21). This year he piano-duels **Joseph Wölfl**; accounts suggest that Wölfl has the edge in technical skill.

J. L. Dussek flees to Hamburg as his London publishing business, co-owned with his father-in-law, Domenico Corri, runs into massive debt. With creditors unpaid, Corri ends up in jail. Dussek leaves his wife and daughter behind, very possibly never to see them again.

Haydn composes his Two String Quartets Op. 77, dedicating them to Prince Joseph Franz Lobkowitz. He also begins to write the oratorio *The Seasons*, although with his advancing years he finds the strain of the process enormous.

The Duke of Brunswick appoints 15-year-old **Louis Spohr** as court chamber musician.

19 March Box office records are smashed at Vienna's Burgtheater with the first public performance of **Haydn**'s *The Creation* (1798). The oratorio soon becomes a Europe-wide sensation and the greatest success of the composer's career.

19 May In the short-lived Republic of Naples, **Cimarosa**'s *Inno patriottico* (Patriotic Hymn), to words by Luigi Rossi, accompanies the ceremonial burning of the royal flag. (See also December.)

11 October **Méhul**'s *Ariodant* is introduced at the Opéra-Comique, Paris.

24 October Prolific Austrian composer **Karl Ditters von Dittersdorf** dies in Neuhof, Bohemia, aged 59.

December **Cimarosa** and the poet Luigi Rossi are imprisoned and condemned to death in Naples for openly supporting the French and the formation of a 'Parthenopean Republic' (see 19 May). Rossi is beheaded, but the composer's sentence is later reduced to one of banishment from the kingdom.

1798 French government proclaims a Helvetian Republic in Switzerland • French forces occupy Rome and proclaim a Roman Republic • Pope Pius VI moves to Valence, France • Napoleon begins Egyptian campaign • British defeat French in Battle of the Nile • English poets William Wordsworth and Samuel Taylor Coleridge publish *Lyrical Ballads*

1799 French army is expelled from Italy; the Parthenopean and Roman Republics are ended • Russia leaves coalition against France • Napoleon returns to Paris and establishes the Consulate with himself as first consul and virtual dictator of France • In Egypt, French uncover the Rosetta Stone, advancing understanding of hieroglyphics

1800–1849

1800–1849

T HE SHOCKWAVES of the French Revolution (1789) and the Revolutionary and Napoleonic Wars (1792–1815) were felt all over Europe and beyond. So too was the impact of the Industrial Revolution, the technological and economic phenomenon that transformed society, and musical life also, throughout the 1800s. During the early decades of the century the weight of musical patronage passed decisively from the royal courts and aristocracy to the financially empowered bourgeoisie. They flocked to the opera houses and newly-established concert halls, and demanded increasing quantities of sheet music for domestic use.

The role of the musical artist, both creative and performing, changed as a result of these influences, and the achievement of one man in particular proved a recurring and enduring inspiration: Ludwig van Beethoven. No composer after him could be unaware of the standards he set in technique and expressive range. Beethoven spearheaded the musical transition from the Classical to Romantic style, emphasising the personal viewpoint of the creative artist. The Romantic composer was a visionary, often a cultural hero, but most importantly of all, a free agent.

◀ *Liszt at the Piano*, an idealised scene of famous literary and musical residents of Paris, by Joseph Danhauser, 1840. Heads are turned towards the bust of Beethoven—the painter alluding to the composer's towering status among the Romantics.

The Classical–Romantic transition

The Classical era in music extended into the third decade of the 19th century, but by 1800 the Romantic movement had already found expression in literature. A quarter of a century had passed since the publication of Johann von Goethe's seminal novel *The Sorrows of Young Werther* (1774), the story of a young man driven to suicide by unrequited love. It had caused a Europe-wide sensation; men had identified with the character—some dressed like him, some, it seems, took their own lives. Werther epitomised the character type so beloved by the Romantics: a desperate dreamer; sensitive, passionate, irrational and intractable. In Britain, Gothic novels by Horace Walpole and Ann Radcliffe had become very popular during the 1780s and 90s, but the nation's literary Romantic movement was conclusively launched in 1798 with the publication of *Lyrical Ballads* by Wordsworth and Coleridge. Opening the collection was Coleridge's *Rhyme of the Ancient Mariner*, a story of an epic physical and emotional voyage, wherein natural and supernatural worlds collide.

Among the first to join the literary revolution were William Blake, Lord Byron and Walter Scott in Britain, François-René de Chateaubriand in France, and Ludwig Tieck and Heinrich von Kleist in Germany. They banished Classical reason and restraint to unleash their emotions and imagination; cue magic and myth, passion and excess. Favourite subject

▶ The poet Samuel Taylor Coleridge, co-founder of the English Romantic movement.

matter included rustic life, folklore and medieval tales, horror and the supernatural. Yearning and unrequited love were central themes of tragedy, while the emotionally raw dramas of Shakespeare became hallowed ground.

The Romantic composer was a child of the Revolution and averse to aristocratic control. Beethoven was a figurehead in this respect, and it is also clear that his audiences recognised something revolutionary in his art. 'Beethoven's music,' wrote the poet and composer E. T. A. Hoffmann (1776–1822), 'sets in motion the lever of fear, of awe, of horror, of suffering, and awakens that infinite longing which is the essence of Romanticism.' How true this is; yet at the same time Beethoven was a grounded disciple of the Enlightenment and not prone to Romantic fantasy. His discipline was rooted in the Classical language, forms and genres championed by Haydn and Mozart. What propelled Beethoven's music forward towards the Romantic era was the subjectivity he injected into each and every musical genre. The emotional journey of the Fifth Symphony to the noble vision of *Fidelio*; from the brotherhood of all mankind in the epic Ninth Symphony to the intimacy of his late string quartets: these were all Beethoven's feelings, pains, moral codes and ideals.

▼ *Fantasy Based on Goethe's 'Faust'*, by the British painter Theodore von Holst, 1834. Holst was a renowned illustrator of German Romantic literature but often considered too risqué and macabre for polite society. He was the great-uncle of the composer Gustav Theodore Holst.

Romantic themes invaded opera early in the century, evident in Spohr's *Faust* (1816), Weber's rustic and magical *Der Freischütz* (The Freeshooter, 1821) and Marschner's *Der Vampyr* (1828). In response to such themes as the supernatural, insanity and unrequited passions, composers widened their harmonic vocabulary in search of new expressive intensity, with emphasis on chromaticism, sensuous chords and unorthodox harmonic progressions. More intimately, the Romantic 'language of the emotions' encouraged the proliferation of expressive and supple miniatures, such as the *lied, nocturne, étude, intermezzo* and *polonaise*, fashionable genres that responded to a rising demand for music in the home.

A new vogue for programmatic music took hold, drawing on Romantic narratives from literature or freely invented. This approach reflected the Romantic composer's wider interest in the arts. Some composers even turned their hand to literary pursuits, for instance Schumann and Berlioz, who both secured extra income through music criticism. Schumann launched his own music journal, the *Neue Zeitschrift für Musik*, which reviewed music past and present, attacked musical philistinism (mindless virtuosity included), and promoted aspiring composers. Berlioz wrote one of the most entertaining autobiographies of the century. Wagner's literary interests inspired him to write several musical manifestos, an autobiography, and more importantly his own opera libretti.

Instruments benefited from the technological advances of the age. The piano, especially, gained enormous expressive potential, enabling Liszt to exploit the lucrative opportunities available to the 'heroic virtuoso'. Within the orchestra, woodwind intonation improved, while trumpets and horns gained chromatic capabilities with the introduction of valves. The composer's orchestral palette widened considerably, and as large-scale works moved from the aristocratic salons into the new concert halls, the orchestras expanded accordingly, in some cases tripling the size of their Classical counterpart.

The symphony and concert overture

Beethoven

The symphony had become the most prestigious of all musical genres by the end of the 18th century, thanks most of all to Haydn. Keenly aware of the fact, Beethoven approached the genre only after completing many solo piano pieces (including ten numbered sonatas), a variety of chamber works, two full-scale cantatas and two piano concertos. With each symphony Beethoven made a personal statement: they were written first and foremost on artistic impulse, not on the whim of a patron. Moreover, his pioneering examples established the wider significance of the symphony—the most public of all genres—as a medium that in some way reflected the *zeitgeist*, the preoccupations, ideals and aspirations of contemporary society. With his Ninth (*Choral*) Symphony Beethoven presaged Mahler's oft-quoted edict: 'the symphony must be like the world'.

Beethoven's First and Second symphonies date from 1800 and 1802 and correspond to his 'first period'. They owe a debt to Haydn, apparent from the outset with their slow introductions, but an individual style is unmistakable. In the First Symphony Beethoven opens with harmonic ambiguity; he also gives ample space to wind instruments, polarises his themes and enlarges the outer movement codas. This was a composer bent on making his mark, not proving himself a mere disciple of either Mozart or Haydn. His inclusion of a Scherzo (literally 'joke') third movement in the Second Symphony, as an alternative to the traditional minuet, was a first for the genre, although the minuet in the First Symphony is a scherzo in all but name.

Following the Second Symphony, Beethoven plunged into a suicidal mood, crushed by the reality of his deteriorating hearing. He wrote of his despair in the famous 'Heiligenstadt Testament', in which he confessed,

▶ The 45-year-old Ludwig van Beethoven by Joseph Willibrord Mahler (1815).

I would have been at the point of ending my life. The only thing that held me back was my art. It seemed impossible to leave the world until I had produced all the works that I felt the urge to compose.

Symphony No. 3 in E flat (*Eroica*)

Emerging with renewed purpose he wrote a groundbreaking tour-de-force, the Symphony No. 3 *Eroica* (1803). Napoleon's name was originally included in the title of the work, but Beethoven furiously scrubbed it out in 1804 after the French military leader proclaimed himself Emperor. For posterity's sake, this was happily serendipitous, for the work reveals much more about Beethoven himself. Napoleon, who in the mind of Beethoven formerly personified Revolutionary ideals, certainly provided inspiration, and the prevailing fashion for heroic subject matter is reflected also; but where we sense nobleness, resistance, confrontation, renewal and triumph, we sense also Beethoven's values, predicaments and conquering perseverance.

Beethoven unleashed the *Eroica* on a public totally unprepared for a symphonic marathon. 'The work appears to lose itself in anarchy', wrote one critic. Modern day audiences are able to recognise the music's Classical structures and clarity of vision, but those of the day were challenged by the length of Beethoven's Third—twice as long as the average Classical symphony—and baffled by the content. Of the first movement this is especially true, with its complex development section climaxing in powerful syncopated dissonances, and a coda almost equal in length to the recapitulation. The colossal 'Funeral March' second movement will have tested audience stamina too, besides adding mystery to the direction of the symphony as a whole. But then the mood changes with an exciting six-minute Scherzo, which brings a sense of rebirth in the light of the preceding movement. In the finale Beethoven sets in motion a sequence of variations based on a theme he had used three times before, most tellingly in the *Prometheus* ballet music (1801). The movement thus echoes heroism and apotheosis, with discord, dynamics and expansive orchestration fully exploited to create some epic moments. The theme turns magnificently hymnal three-quarters of the way through, and a *presto* coda brings crushing victory. Beethoven, at the start of the century, had created a Classical masterpiece of veritable Romantic scale and scope.

Each Beethoven symphony is distinctive. After the 'first period' symphonies, the Fourth (1806) and Eighth (1812) perhaps remain closest to the Classical ideal, while the Seventh (1812) is marked by its development of rhythmic figures, culminating in a restless finale full of climaxes. Of the 'middle period' symphonies, No. 5 in C minor and No. 6 in F major, both completed in 1808, are the most popular. It is easy to regard the Fifth as Beethoven's most personal symphonic statement, a work in which he seems to battle with the constraints of his deafness. In the first movement, the severe, obstinately memorable four-note rhythmic gesture conflicts with a relaxed and lyrical major-key second subject; Beethoven wrestles to find resolution, but the minor-key close refutes victory. In the slow movement noble lyricism meets with proud hymnal declamation, while the third movement echoes the fate and defiance of the first movement with clear allusions to its rhythmic motto. Out of this the finale emerges via a mighty crescendo. Trombones add weight to the orchestral *tutti*, generating a tremendous momentum that sweeps all before it in a blaze of triumph, asserting the composer's strength and vision with its imagery of triumph over fate. This emotional architecture had a considerable influence upon the Romantic composers, for whom the finale became the goal and justification for the symphonic journey.

Symphony No. 5 in C minor

In the Sixth, the *Pastoral*, Beethoven wanted to create a very different composition, one loosely programmatic that conveyed his heartfelt love of nature. 'I love a tree more than a man', he once said (only furthering his reputation as a misanthrope). It is not surprising that within this five-movement symphony Beethoven downplays 'tonal conflict', the very structural element that provides enormous tension in so many other works. The delightfully tuneful first and second movements are both constructed in sonata form, but harmonic polarity fuels only the momentum of ideas—it does not serve to heighten conflicting emotions, as there are none. The fourth movement delivers thunderous discords, but for the sole reason that it depicts a storm. Beethoven chose to conclude with a folk-inspired song of thanksgiving, the only time he was to end a symphony on a note of tranquility.

Symphony No. 6 in F major 'Pastoral'

Beethoven crafted his most impressive overtures, *Coriolan* (1807) and *Egmont* (1810), on less explicit programmes. In *Egmont* he once again turned to an heroic subject, Goethe's noble Count Egmont who battles against Spanish tyranny in pursuit of freedom for his fellow Netherlanders. The overture sets out in an oppressive F minor mood, leading to what some see as rebellion in the main Allegro. The major-key climax arrives to dispel once and for all the earlier tensions, and the full force of the orchestra is deployed to proclaim a victorious moment in the fight for liberty.

Egmont Overture

In subsequent years Beethoven's artistic activities were hamstrung by a series of events that took the composer on an emotional roller-coaster. Forlorn affairs of the heart with an unnamed 'immortal beloved', together with financial hardship and worsening hearing, led to depression and a possible suicide attempt in 1813. Substantial career breaks then presented themselves with the end of the Napoleonic wars and the Congress of Vienna (1814–15). However, to seize commercial opportunities he had to write *pièces d'occasions* quickly, and discounting the revival of *Fidelio* (1814),

Personal life and the Congress of Vienna (1814–15)

his two largest works from this time are both third-rate: *Wellington's Victory* (or the *Battle Symphony*, 1813) and *The Glorious Moment* Cantata (1814). Beethoven composed his heavily programmatic *Wellington's Victory* in response to Wellington's defeat of the French at Vittoria, Spain (21 June 1813). Makeshift and full of gimmicks, the work made such a spectacular impression that one reviewer pronounced the Seventh Symphony, jointly premièred on 8 December 1813, its 'companion piece'. During the Congress period Beethoven's music was frequently performed; the financial success of his concerts and the revival of *Fidelio* benefited both himself and charity, and public acclamation had never been so high. Fêted by royalty, state leaders and dignitaries, Beethoven briefly attained a lifetime stature unmatched by any other composer in history.

Beethoven fell into his deepest creative nadir in the years following the Congress. His emotional energies were consumed by legal battles with his bereaved and mistrusted sister-in-law (Johanna) over the guardianship of her son, Karl. Beethoven eventually won custody, but his domineering attitude towards Karl resulted in a fractious relationship. It was also around this time that Beethoven began using conversation books, rather than rely on ear trumpets. He usually replied orally, but this deepening world of silence demanded profound psychological adjustment, diminishing for a while his creative resources.

Symphony No. 9 in D minor   Twelve years separate the Eighth Symphony from the Ninth (1824), which alongside the Fifth has had the biggest impact upon composers and the public. By the 1820s Beethoven had largely withdrawn from public life. It is ironic that his boldest statement of Enlightenment and revolutionary values came at a point when he seemed to want little to do with mankind. He will have excused himself on account of his deafness; but then he had always manifested a dual nature, constantly struggling to live up to his own ideals, except in the realm of music. 'O God! Give me strength to conquer myself', reads one of his diary entries. His methods of composition involved sketching ideas, grappling with them, shaping and honing—music was the only realm in which Beethoven could subjugate material and spiritual weakness.

The journey of the Ninth echoes that of the Fifth, though with even more weight thrown at the finale. Emerging out of dark fragments and building to a massive unison, the symphony quickly reveals its epic intentions. The first movement's power struggle culminates in a huge coda, akin to a second development, which brings an implacable minor-key lamentation. The second movement is an explosive motivic Scherzo, the third a lyrical foil that presents a double theme with extended variations. It is only then that Beethoven gives voice to a profound notion: the brotherhood of all mankind. Schiller's *Ode to Joy* is excitedly declaimed in a sequence of variations on Beethoven's commanding hymnal theme. The over-arching structure of the movement is inventive, from the searching thematic quotations of the opening bars, onto secondary themes, a fugal interlude for orchestra, a third theme (Andante maestoso), a second fugal section with choir, and finally a fast, triumphant coda. This hour-long, pioneering symphony made a forceful impression at its première in 1824, but a repeat performance was poorly attended. In subsequent years the work divided composers: Louis Spohr rated it lower than all other Beethoven symphonies; Berlioz, Schumann and Wagner revered it as a towering, sacred monument. Not one was able to escape its impact.

In the shadow of Beethoven

There are very few symphonic works contemporaneous with the Beethovenian canon that attract any real interest today. Rarely heard are Étienne Méhul's four Viennese-influenced symphonies (1808–10), or the two youthful symphonies of Weber, both composed in 1807. On the other hand, Weber's operatic overtures—conspicuously *Der Freishütz* (1821), *Euryanthe* (1823) and *Oberon* (1826)—have become concert hall fixtures, independent of the stage works. The symphonies of Louis Spohr (1784–1859) were revered only during his lifetime. He produced ten essays over a period of some 40 years from 1811; Nos. 4–9 date from 1832–50 and demonstrate an approach typical of the new age, with literary and pictorial influences, virtuoso orchestration, a strong lyrical impulse and chromatic harmonies.

The Romantic symphony

Beethoven changed the symphony forever. He himself had grown up in an era when a composer of fewer than 20 symphonies could barely be called a symphonist at all. Now the symphony was a pedestal genre, a medium for the composer's most profound, visionary thoughts. It was a work to be listened to, not talked through. And anyone who wrote more than eight numbered symphonies could start making funeral arrangements. 'Nine' became an almost mystical number: Schubert, Spohr, Dvořák, Bruckner and Mahler all made it to nine, more or less. Some of them attempted a tenth, like Beethoven, but either ran out of steam or died trying.

Franz Schubert

The 1820s brought what is widely regarded as the last great Classical symphony and the first Romantic symphony. They were authored by the same composer, and not in the order one might expect. The orchestral music of Franz Schubert (1797–1828) gained recognition only posthumously, since it was largely unperformed during his lifetime. The public enjoyed briefly his overture and incidental music to *Rosamunde, Queen of Cyprus* (1823), but they rejected Helmina von Chezy's play outright, which managed just two performances. Schubert successfully emulated the model of Mozart in his first six symphonies, composed between 1813 and 1818 while he worked as a schoolteacher. The finest of these is the pleasingly tuneful Fifth in B flat major (1816), one of the most remarkable symphonies ever written by a teenager. The Seventh, begun in 1821, failed to survive beyond the sketch pad, but the Eighth (1822) and Ninth (1826) are magnificent and distinctive contributions to symphonic literature.

Symphony No. 8 *Unfinished*

Schubert broke off from the third movement of Symphony No. 8, the famous *Unfinished* Symphony, and never returned to it. The Romantic temperament of this work is immediately revealed in the dark and brooding string theme of the opening bars. It is an ominous prelude to the wintry isolation and mounting tension of the principal subject, forged by oboe and clarinet over restless semiquaver movement in the violins. While the idyllic, *ländler*-like second subject evokes a more Classical idiom, Schubert does not follow conventional key schemes, and the movement maintains emotional unrest through to its end. Romanticism in the second (final) movement finds expression through impassioned minor-key eruptions, which destabilise an otherwise gallant mood. There is an accidental Romantic flavour afforded by the symphony's two-movement structure, particularly as the emotional turbulence of the work is hardly resolved according to Classical norms. Perhaps Schubert left his Eighth unfinished because he was unable to decide where his journey should lead. Or did he believe it to be too progressive for the Viennese? We will probably never know.

Symphony No. 9

In his Symphony No. 9, distinctive from the outset with its noble horn theme, Schubert returned to more established ideals of language and expression. While it represents the culmination point of the Classical tradition, its length and grandeur, adventurous harmonic schemes and rich orchestral colours all betoken the Romantic age. The majestic *pianissimo* trombone theme in the first movement's exposition is just one of many strokes of genius. An edited version of the symphony was premièred posthumously at Leipzig under Mendelssohn in 1839. Schumann praised the 'splendid romantic introduction' and 'heavenly length', although the orchestra found it extremely difficult to play.

Hector Berlioz: *Symphonie fantastique*

The composer who unequivocally announced the symphonic Romantic dawn was not one of Austro-German extraction, but a passionate, headstrong Frenchman: Hector Berlioz (1803–69). His astonishing *Symphonie fantastique* (1830), subtitled *Episode in the Life of an Artist*, was completed within three years of Beethoven's death and resulted from emotional turmoil—his obsession with the Anglo-Irish actress Harriet Smithson, whom he was eventually to marry. The published programme admits the inspiration:

A young musician of morbid disposition and powerful imagination poisons himself with opium in an attack of despairing passion. The dose of the drug, too weak to kill him, plunges him into a deep sleep accompanied by strange dreams in which sensations, feelings and memories are transformed in his sick brain into musical images and ideas. The beloved herself appears to him as a melody, like an idée fixe, an obsessive idea that he keeps hearing wherever he goes.

One can scarcely imagine such a programme inspiring a Classical symphony, and the door is flung wide open for a thoroughly subjective musical approach. With the opening sections of the symphony, 'Rêveries–Passions', Berlioz immerses the listener in sensuous 'waves of passion and melancholy', beginning what is in effect a five-movement symphonic poem. He insisted that the audience have a copy of the programme at hand for a full understanding of the work. His descriptions were explicit; 'Passions', for example, explores a state of 'frenzied passion, with its gestures of fury, of jealousy, its return of tenderness, tears and religious consolation'. In formal design the symphony departs from Classical convention; statements and transformations of the *idée fixe* displace some of the traditional processes of thematic development, and tonal contrast is not so fundamental to the struc-

ture; nor is there a standard recapitulation. The *idée fixe* brings thematic unity to the entire work, appearing in different guises in each subsequent movement: 'A Ball', 'Scene in the Country', 'March to the Scaffold', and 'Dream of a Witches' Sabbath'. Berlioz employed an orchestra of unprecedented colouristic range, with forces expanded by a cor anglais, an E flat clarinet, four bassoons (as opposed to the usual two), two harps, two ophicleides (precursor of the euphonium) and a large percussion complement. His orchestration of the 'Witches' Sabbath' finale was outstandingly original, with tremolandi for muted strings, *col legno* strings (using the wood of the bow), woodwind glissandi, and tolling bells in a parody of the Dies Irae.

◄ Caricature of Hector Berlioz and his shockingly loud super-orchestra. The composer was among the first generation of baton conductors.

While Berlioz took inspiration from his own life in his first symphony, its themes also reflect those common to contemporary Romantic literature, unrequited love and the supernatural especially. *Harold en Italie* (1834), a blend of symphony and viola concerto, likewise engages personal and literary sources. Berlioz sets 'impressions recollected from wanderings in the Abruzzi mountains', while his viola part represents 'a melancholy dreamer in the style of Byron's *Childe Harold*'. His 'Harold theme' serves an important programmatic function; it reappears in each of the four movements, but unlike the *idée fixe* of the *Symphonie fantastique*, it preserves its character. Berlioz's *Romeo and Juliet* followed in 1839, a programmatic 'dramatic symphony' that presents a variety of vocal and instrumental movements adapted to the outline of Shakespeare's play. The fleet and delicate 'Queen Mab Scherzo' is perhaps its most remarkable movement, with light orchestration that flickers with brilliant colours in strings and woodwinds. In the large-scale finale the two families reconcile in a rousing choral peroration, completing a work that is a full concert in itself.

A year later Berlioz completed his Fourth Symphony, the *Symphonie Funèbre et Triomphale*, a sizeable *pièce d'occasion* celebrating the tenth anniversary of the July Revolution of 1830. Originally conceived for wind band alone, this three-movement work departs from traditional key schemes, with a progression from F minor in the first movement to B flat major in the third. Berlioz also composed concert overtures, such as *Le roi Lear* (1831) and *Le carnaval romain* (1844), which are masterly examples of the most vivid orchestral imagination of the age.

The upper-middle-class German composer Felix Mendelssohn (1809–47), not one prone to Romantic indulgence, composed orchestral pieces of a more conservative nature. His creative apprenticeship included 13 sinfonias for string orchestra, completed by the age of 14, before his skilfully-written Symphony No. 1 in C minor for full orchestra (1824). At the age of 17 he wrote a concert overture sensation, *Midsummer Night's Dream* (1826), a Classically-organised realisation of Shakespeare's fairy world which reaches into the Romantic realm with magically descriptive material and imaginative orchestration. It is an unsurpassed example of precocious musical genius. Mendelssohn continued to compose programmatic concert overtures, equivalent in scale to operatic overtures but independent, therefore precursors of the symphonic poem. Among these we find the evocative *Hebrides* (*Fingal's Cave*), begun during his visit to Scotland in 1829 and completed by 1832, and the *Fair Melusine* (1833).

Mendelssohn's mature symphonies flank his busy years as musical director at Düsseldorf (1833–35) and his first period as conductor of Leipzig's Gewandhaus concerts (1835–40). The numbering of these works is confusing. Symphony No. 2 is the *Lobgesang* (1840), essentially a sacred symphony (see *Sacred Music*), while No. 5, the *Reformation* (1830), is a quasi-religious work Mendelssohn composed to mark the tercentenary of the Augsburg Confession. His most admired symphony, the *Italian*, No. 4 in A major (1833), was conceived during an extended tour of 1830–31. The result is highly festive, inspired by 'the ruins, the landscapes, the glories of nature'. The first movement is youthful, joyful and striking, boasting one

Harold en Italie

Romeo and Juliet

Felix Mendelssohn

Symphonies Nos. 2–5

of the most memorable of all symphonic opening themes. This major-key work also stands out for its unusual minor-mode conclusion. Symphony No. 3, the *Scottish*, was begun in 1829 during a visit to the ruined chapel of Holyrood Castle in Edinburgh. Mendelssohn eventually completed the work in 1842 and conducted its première at the Leipzig Gewandhaus in March of that year. Scottish folk-idioms are transparent in the joyous second movement Scherzo, expressed through its principal rustic melody and a recurring *Scotch-snap* rhythm (an accented short note followed by an unaccented long note). More important to Mendelssohn was the symphony's overall form and passage, its expanded canvass, and the unity he forged through inter-related materials among the movements, which themselves follow one another without breaks.

Robert Schumann (1810–56) completed his first symphony at the age of 30, following some abortive attempts at the genre. Like Mendelssohn, he sought to build on Beethoven's symphonic legacy, but his progressive and introspective tendencies took him beyond his compatriot's semi-Classical idiom and deeper into Romanticism. Schumann, like Berlioz, wrote music more adventurous in harmony, structure and emotional range, even if his orchestration at times lacks finesse. His Symphony No. 1 *Spring*, sketched in just four days, was completed in early 1841 and gained a happy reception under Mendelssohn's direction in Leipzig. The music is fresh, ebullient, occasionally bucolic, although the symphony's moniker appears to have been an afterthought. Writing about the work to Spohr, Schumann stated, 'I did not attempt to depict and describe anything in it; but I do believe that the season … influenced its structure and made it what it is.' The year 1841 also witnessed the first version of the Symphony No. 4 in D minor. Schumann revised it ten years later, creating a passionate and tightly unified piece, with themes reappearing across four continuous movements. Cyclical themes also appear in the less effusive Symphony No. 2 in C major (1846), a work deeply indebted to Bach and composed amid bouts of depression and illness—likely attributable to the syphilitic condition that was to cut his life tragically short.

The five-movement *Rhenish*, No. 3 (1850), crowns Schumann's symphonies. It was begun soon after his appointment as musical director at Düsseldorf, and the rousing first movement reflects (short-lived) high spirits. The noble fourth movement is the heart of the symphony, rich in polyphony and subtitled *In the style of an accompaniment to a solemn ceremony*, probably inspired by Archbishop von Geissel's elevation to cardinal at the magnificent cathedral of Cologne. Beyond the symphony, Schumann indulged his love of Byron in the *Manfred* Overture (1849), in which the hero's inner turmoil finds expression through angular melodies and chromatic harmony—a style that anticipates the 'New German School'. Schumann was probably the most widely read composer of the early Romantics; in fact in his teens he aspired to be a writer, first and foremost. But his love of literature did not turn him towards the programmatic literalism of Berlioz; *Manfred*, indeed, is barely programmatic. Schumann's orchestral output, anchored to the tradition of Beethoven and Schubert, thus looks forward to the non-programmatic, muscular style of Brahms. It is the body of work through which German orchestral Romanticism truly came of age.

Robert
Schumann

The piano and the Romantic miniature

Piano
evolution

At the outset of the 1800s, piano manufacturers such as Broadwood and Clementi in London, Érard and Pleyel in Paris, and Graf and Streicher in Vienna (to mention only a few), were competing to produce ever more powerful and expressive instruments. Wooden frames were strengthened and enlarged to facilitate the piano's widening compass and dynamic range; metal bracing began to appear around the 1820s and 30s to cope with increasing string tension (thicker double-course wires, or triple stringing, yielding greater power), leading to the iron framed, seven-octave instrument of the later century. These changes responded to the demands of both composers and performers. Beethoven was particularly keen to encourage such progress; an anecdote by his friend Anton Reicha illustrates the issue:

> He asked me to turn pages for him. However, I was mostly occupied in wrenching the strings of the pianoforte that snapped, while the hammers stuck amongst the broken strings. Beethoven insisted on finishing the concerto, and so back and forth I jumped, jerking out a string, disentangling a hammer, turning a page, and I worked harder than Beethoven.

This account dates from 1795, and Beethoven was actually playing a Mozart piano concerto at the time! It certainly reveals much about Beethoven's longing for an instrument equal to his needs. He pestered the Viennese manufacturers Streicher for a more powerful and sonorous piano, and they, recognising the composer's growing celebrity, responded enthusiastically.

Beethoven's
piano sonatas

Beethoven's early piano sonatas already demonstrate his concern for dynamic range and subtlety, as well as sustaining power. His *Moonlight* Sonata (Op. 27, No. 2) dates from 1801 and begins in radical fashion, swapping the customary Allegro for a romantic Adagio sostenuto. In this renowned slow movement Beethoven sets long note values at *pianissimo*, capitalising on the advanced resonating tone of his instrument. Two years later he received a gift of an Érard piano with an above-average compass of just over five and a half octaves, which he exploited to the full. In scale and expression the *Waldstein* Sonata, Op. 53 (1804), ventures into new territory. All three movements begin *pianissimo*, confirming the importance of dynamic range in his developing style. This is found also in the *Appassionata* Sonata, Op. 57 (1805), in which the music is built from the strongest contrasts. The sudden changes of direction, the pauses followed by torrents of sound, represented a new intensity for piano music.

Beethoven's last five piano sonatas, from the A major Op. 101 (1816) to No. 32 in C minor, Op. 111 (1822), correspond to a yet more powerful instrument. Beethoven prized his new six-octave Broadwood piano, sent by the London firm as a gift in 1818, though the Viennese 'Hammerklavier' inspired him more. Each of the late sonatas pursues wide-ranging sonorities, but this breadth is felt above all in the notoriously demanding *Hammerklavier* Sonata, Op. 106 (1818). Its structural and expressive dimensions are vast, from the bold first-movement conflicts to the imaginative and ambitious fugal finale, creating music strikingly symphonic in scope. Beethoven's last substantial piano work was the resourceful *Diabelli Variations* (1823), a monumental composition four years in the making, featuring 33 variations (or 'transformations', as he called them) on a short waltz by the publisher-composer Anton Diabelli (1781–1858). A final set of *Bagatelles* (Op. 126) appeared the following year, short 'trifles' that contributed to the growing popularity of the piano miniature.

There were a number of composer-pianists of international renown during the Beethovenian era. One was the London resident Muzio Clementi (see also *Chapter 4*), who expended a great deal of energy in creating one of England's most important music publishing and piano-making firms. He had by now retired from public performance, but he still found time to compose, concluding his piano output with the three sonatas of Op. 50 (published 1821), and the 100 études of his three-volume *Gradus ad Parnassum* (1817–26). His revered status was confirmed by his burial in Westminster Abbey and an epitaph that read 'The father of modern piano-forte playing'. Piano pieces by Johann Cramer (1771–1858), Johann Hummel (1778–1837) and Weber were likewise esteemed in their day and are still performed now, but only the mature works of Schubert survive comparison with those of Beethoven.

Muzio Clementi

Schubert was inspired by Beethoven's sonatas, but not overwhelmed by them. While his teenage examples do not match the maturity of his songs of the same period, his late sonatas offer a distinctive voice. One of his earliest piano masterpieces is the *Fantasia in C* (1822), a sonata-like work that quotes from his song *The Wanderer* and betrays his partiality to thematic transformation. The distinctly solemn mood of the sonata that followed, the A minor (D. 784, 1823), seems to reflect Schubert's sudden deterioration of health; but it is also inspired, and it set in motion a sequence of sonatas that culminated in the composer's finest offerings: the C minor (D. 958), A major (D. 959) and B flat major (D. 960). Schubert composed these sonatas in the autumn of 1828 around the same time that he wrote his String Quintet in C major. He planned them on a spacious scale with compelling themes, wide emotional range and innovative tonal design. With a performing time of between 30 and 40 minutes, they emphasised the connoisseur value of the sonata genre.

Schubert

Schubert wrote more manageable pieces as miniatures, like the *Moments Musicaux* and the two sets of *Impromptus*. These succeed both as stand-alone compositions, and as a larger collection, equivalent to a sonata. The *Impromptus* (D. 899 and D. 935, both 1827) are mostly organised in ternary form with sharp contrasts between the sections. Masterly Romantic mood-pieces, they responded to the expanding market for miniatures, spurred by the music of Clementi's one-time piano-selling apprentice, the Irishman John Field (1782–1837). Field had been cultivating his celebrated *Nocturnes* from around 1812. Cantabile melodies, arpeggiated accompaniments and considerable use of the sustaining pedal gave his music a dreamy and often melancholic quality. Importantly, his Nocturnes emphasised mood and feeling without recourse to formal procedures of development or variation. As such they were well ahead of their time and proved a major inspiration to the first generation of Romantic pianist-composers.

John Field & the rise of the miniature

1800–1849

The popularity of the lithe and poetic miniature overwhelmed that of the piano sonata during the early Romantic period. Its ascendancy was tied in part to the demands of an educated middle class with cultural ambitions. Amateur piano playing was on the rise, but comparatively few could tackle the weighty sonatas of Beethoven and Schubert. While some miniatures accommodated music to challenge the most gifted of pianists, others were graded alongside accessible variations and duets as player-friendly music for the parlour. Mendelssohn, who wrote some fine sonatas and variations, contributed to the trend with his eight collections of *Songs without Words*, six of which appeared in print during his lifetime. As the generic title suggests, these are lyrical pieces built very closely on song structures. The first appeared in the early 1830s and represented something quite new for the time; they certainly delighted the public as unpretentious, clear-cut compositions, even if their emotional scope was limited.

Most of Schumann's miniatures were assembled into larger suites and carry extra-musical associations, as in the light, nostalgic pieces of *Kinderszenen* (Scenes of Childhood, 1838) and the virtuosic *Kreisleriana* (1838), inspired by an E. T. A. Hoffmann character. Another technically-demanding collection had a particularly idiosyncratic genesis. During the 1830s, Schumann's iconoclastic journal, the *Neue Zeitschrift für Musik*, created the idea of the 'Davidsbund', a group of musicians fighting the artistic philistines. In the *Davidsbündlertänze* (Dances of the Band of David, 1837) the 18 pieces derive from a motto composed by Clara Wieck, his wife-to-be. The differing outlooks—pensive and extrovert—relate to the fictitious personae of Florestan and Eusebius, Schumann's alter-egos who 'express contrasting points of view about art'.

The Polish composer Frédéric Chopin (1810–49) took very little interest

Mendelssohn

Schumann

Frédéric Chopin

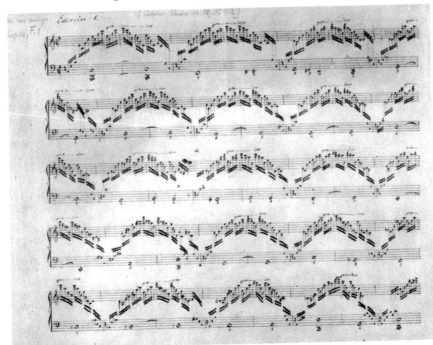

▶ Frederic Chopin: hand written manuscript of Etude No. 1 in C, Op. 10.

in the cross-fertilisation of the arts—notwithstanding his relationship with the writer Amandine Dudevant, better known as George Sand. Resident in Paris from 1831, he built upon the elegant style of Hummel and Field, and exploited both the miniature and the piano's *cantabile* capabilities above any other composer. Chopin preferred the intimate surroundings of the salon to the public spectacle of the concert hall, and this priority is reflected in his music, though there is no lack of virtuoso technique. Schumann summed him up as 'the boldest, most proud poet of these times'.

Chopin composed sonata masterpieces that respected the classical tradition, notably No. 2 in B flat minor (1837) and No. 3 in B minor (1844). But it was his single-movement compositions like the *Polonaises*, *Scherzos* and *Nocturnes* that overtly acknowledged the spirit of Romanticism, fusing Bellini's *bel-canto* style with rich, sensuous harmonies and sliding chromaticism. His *Études*, written between 1830 and 1837, raised the bar for the 'study' genre, exploring aspects of technique while being characterful compositions in their own right. The *Mazurkas* and *Polonaises* acknowledged Chopin's proud sense of homeland, particularly in their use of Polish folk rhythms.

The four *Ballades* (the last completed in 1843) are larger-scale, single-movement pieces that rank among Chopin's greatest achievements. The first, in G minor (*c.*1835), is cast in a structure not dissimilar to sonata form. It sets the indicative dramatic style with the conflict of various moods: the supplication found at the outset, the rejection expressed in the *agitato* fast music, the tenderness when the triplet figure from the introduction makes its insinuating reappearance. The results are many and varied, and sometimes stormy, until in the final *presto con fuoco* the conflicts are unequivocally put to rest.

> Ballade in G minor

Chopin studied Bach's *48 Preludes and Fugues* before composing the 24 pieces he gathered together as his *Préludes* Op. 28 (1839). Chopin's title is misleading, since the pieces are in truth miniature tone poems, each occupying one of the major or minor keys and painting a single emotion or mood. He began writing them in 1838 while in miserable health, and downcast sentiments are pervasive. His later works include the *Barcarolle* (1845), similar in length to the *Ballades* and a supreme example of pianistic lyricism. Its lilting rhythm fuses with an outpouring of melody, while harmonies enhanced by the sustaining pedal create impressionistic textures. The extensive *Polonaise-Fantaisie* (1846) dismantles the strong outlines of the earlier polonaises and contains complex motivic relationships. Chopin's entire output was based around the piano and nearly all of it made an enduring mark; there are few pieces by him not performed nowadays.

Mendelssohn, Chopin, Schumann and Liszt were all born between 1809 and 1811, but only one of them lived beyond his 40s. Hungarian by birth, Franz Liszt (1811–86) based himself in Paris and came under the influence of Paganini, Berlioz and Chopin. In 1833 he took inspiration from Paganini's showmanship and began to cultivate his own reputation as a heroic virtuoso. He gave concerts around Europe, from Russia to England to Portugal, and invented the 'piano recital' along the way. His years of travelling ended in 1848, when he took the post of *Kapellmeister* at Weimar. There he completed and edited many of his earlier projects, including the magnificent

> Franz Liszt

Études d'execution transcendante and the first two books of *Années de Pèlerinages* (see *Chapter 6*). He also championed other composers' music in the form of piano transcriptions, including Berlioz's *Symphonie fantastique* (first version 1833), and operatic paraphrases, for example of works by Verdi, Wagner and Meyerbeer.

In his touring days Liszt transfixed audiences with his unique combination of charisma, dashing looks and Herculean pianistic skill. He exploited the part to the full and sent the ladies wild: they wrestled each other to get close to the stage, some fought tooth and nail over discarded gloves or cigar stubs, others simply fainted (or pretended to, at least). The poet Heinrich Heine dubbed this phenomenon 'Lisztomania'. Listening to the rampaging symphonic gestures of *Mazeppa* (1840) or the fireworks of the *Paganini Études* (1840), one can easily imagine the frenzied emotions of the audience, prefiguring the hysteria surrounding rock & roll by well over a century.

The concerto: the artist as hero

Two contrasting forms of concerto emerged in the 19th century: one was sophisticated in design, reflecting the integrity of the symphony; the other was the virtuoso concerto, primarily conceived by the composer-performer as a showpiece. The composers who sought to combine elements of both usually weighted their apporach towards the symphonic style. Other related genres took their place within these extremes, from the single-movement *romance* and *concertino* to the multi-movement programme concerto.

In the realm of the concerto the increasingly powerful piano reigned supreme, although the violin was not far behind, its profile raised by the 29 essays of Giovanni Viotti (1755–1824) and 15 of Spohr. Many wonderful concertos were written for the clarinet, even if they barely extend into the Romantic period. Among these we find two by Weber, as well as his

Concertino (all composed 1811), four by Spohr, the last written in 1828, and three by the Swedish-Finnish composer Bernard Crusell (1775–1838), the finest of which is the remarkably tuneful No. 1 in E flat (*c*.1808). The trumpet concerto, on the other hand, had already become unfashionable; the excellent examples by Haydn (1796) and Hummel (1803) were written for the newly-invented keyed trumpet (a precursor of the valved variety), but the solo instrument was not sensual enough for the Romantics. Hummel, together with Weber and John Field, composed some admired and even influential piano concertos, generally ensuring that Classical refinement held sway over Romantic excess.

Beethoven wrote his concertos before the advent of the true virtuoso model. His output is represented by five for piano (see also *Chapter 4*), one for violin (1806) and one *concertante* work for piano, violin and cello (the Triple Concerto, 1807). Standing just outside the concerto genre are such works as the two Romances for violin and orchestra (1798, 1802), and the speedily-written, quasi-improvisatory *Choral Fantasia* (1808), a single-movement work for piano, orchestra and chorus, whose choral finale anticipates that of the Ninth Symphony. While Beethoven's concertos prioritise substance over style and effect, they also present great challenges for the performer. In form they recall the models of Mozart, though in scope they are more symphonic, and Mozart's operatic atmosphere has all but evaporated. The soloist is heard not as it were 'in the theatre', but 'in the world'. The relationship between soloist and orchestra becomes representative of that between the individual and society, and here we begin to wave goodbye to the Classical era.

Beethoven

The Violin Concerto in D major (1806) is markedly symphonic in style. Its opening gesture, a five-note rhythmic cell on timpani answered by *legato* woodwinds, anticipates the work's wide palette of orchestral colour. The violin part is technically demanding and there are moments of display, but it is the musical motifs and themes that drive this concerto. Its structural dimensions further assert a symphonic manner: this is the longest concerto that Beethoven ever wrote. The first movement's performing time of around 24 minutes is extraordinary; Viotti's Violin Concerto in A minor, No. 28, and Spohr's Violin Concerto No. 5 are contemporaneous works that only just exceed this length in their entirety. Beethoven's concerto was not immediately influential, however, as it gained a central repertory position only around the mid century, thanks to the advocacy of the great Austro-Hungarian violinist Joseph Joachim (1831–1907).

Violin Concerto in D major

Beethoven's modifications to the genre continued in his Fourth Piano Concerto in G major (*c*.1807), whose introduction by solo piano alone immediately demolishes any sense of 'operatic' prelude. When the orchestra takes over, it does so not in G major, but in B major, and the dynamic drops from *piano* to *pianissimo*. A Classical concerto had never begun with such subtlety. Beethoven provided plenty of opportunity for dazzling passage work, though such periods are held in check. The Fifth Piano Concerto (1809), closer to the Third (1803) in character, projects the soloist as a heroic protagonist in the explosive cadenzas that launch the work, another procedure that breaks ties with convention. The first movement presents

Piano Concertos Nos. 4 & 5

Beethoven in full duality mode, with the delicate second subject far removed from the opening thunderous gestures. The slow movement, set in the remote key of B major, fuses grace with nobility in a beguiling reverie. The heroics return in final movement and remind us why the concerto is thoroughly deserving of J. B. Cramer's epithet *Emperor*.

While Beethoven conveyed heroism primarily through commanding themes and gestures, the Italian composer-violinist Niccolo Paganini (1782–1840) cultivated heroism through virtuosity. Paganini's violin concertos suggest the sense of an individual battling against the throng and obliterating all with super-human prowess. Paganini toured exten-sively—first in Italy, then Europe-wide—and the concerto genre raised his status as a phenomenon. He dressed in dark clothing, and his skeletal, aquiline figure added to the great mystery and spectacle of his performances. Audiences were spellbound; the pianist and composer Fanny Mendelssohn—sister of Felix—wrote in her diary (March, 1829) of this 'miraculous, incredible talent … [Paganini] has the appearance of an insane murderer and the movements of a monkey. A supernatural, wild genius, extremely exciting and provoca-tive.' Paganini did nothing to dispel rumours that he was in league with the Devil, since it proved a good marketing tool.

Paganini's first two of six violin concertos join his astounding and influential *24 Caprices* for solo violin (published 1820) as his best-known compositions. The Violin Concerto No. 1 in D, originally cast in E flat with the violin tuned up a semitone, set the standard for the 19th-century virtuoso concerto. Its theatrical tone is established by the orchestral exposition, a virtual overture with a profusion of tunes and a distinctly Rossinian flavour. The soloist then enters in *maestoso* style, and across a mere eight bars practically the whole compass of the instrument is exploited, from its low G to the E nearly two octaves above the stave. Throughout the concerto techniques of playing abound, with arpeggios, triple and quadruple stopping, left-hand *pizzicato*, ricochet bowing and light harmonics. Paganini also explores the lyrical qualities of the violin, both with the *dolce* second subject, and his slow movement lament.

The 19th-century composer-virtuoso was truly born with Paganini. He inspired a younger generation of violinist-composers, including Charles-August de Bériot (1802–70), Heinrich Ernst (1814–65) and Henry Vieuxtemps (1820–81). It was the very image of 'Paganini the phenomenon' that motivated Liszt to tour and conquer Europe as the world's foremost pianist. But Paganini was much more than a violin-playing

Niccolò Paganini

Violin Concerto No. 1 in D

THE MODERN ORPHEUS.
Opera House - June 3ª 1831
Sketches of the Musical World N°. to be continued

demigod. The rich substance of his music, the unaccompanied *Caprices* especially, was acknowledged by leading composers of his day and later generations. Liszt and Schumann transcribed a number of the Caprices for piano, while Chopin forged his *Études* in their image. The renowned Caprice No. 24 alone stimulated variations by a diverse range of composers, most famously Brahms (1863) and Rachmaninov (1934), also Szymanowski (1918), Lutosławski (1941) and Boris Blacher (1947).

Programme concerto: Weber, Berlioz

While Paganini was flaunting his first concerto around Italy, Weber was exploring alternative possibilities for the concerto in his *Konzertstück* for piano and orchestra. He wrote it in 1821, alongside his groundbreaking Singspiel *Der Freischütz*. This single-movement 'concert piece' is based on a narrative, telling of a chatelaine who awaits the return of her husband, a Crusader knight. Weber laid out his ideas in four distinct sections, creating in effect a medieval-themed tone-poem. Berlioz, as noted earlier, developed a semi-autobiographical programme in his expansive viola concerto, *Harold en Italie* (1834), an extreme example of the symphonic approach to concerto writing. It is, more accurately, a 'Symphony with Viola obbligato'. Paganini, who commissioned *Harold*, refused to play it, objecting most of all to the rests in the solo part. When he finally heard the music in concert he was so impressed that he gave Berlioz a gift of 20,000 francs.

Chopin

Chopin's interest in concerto form derived from the models of Hummel and Field, who had themselves built upon the legacy of Mozart. He wrote his two piano concertos—No. 1 in E minor and No. 2 in F minor—back to back and premièred them on separate occasions in Warsaw, shortly before leaving Poland in November 1830. He was just emerging from his teens at this time, but despite a perfunctory orchestral technique, his piano style was already mature. The minor-key settings invite stormy Romantic passion, but poetic intimacy and lyrical emotion predominate. The slow movement of No. 1, for instance, anticipates the dreamy world of the *Nocturnes*. These pieces demand a virtuoso to do them justice, though substance is placed well before style. Chopin, averse to public performance, composed only one more piece for piano and orchestra, the *Grande polonaise brillante* (Op. 22), which he introduced himself in Paris at the Société des Concerts du Conservatoire in 1835.

Mendelssohn

Mendelssohn wrote two fine piano concertos (No. 1 in G minor, 1831, No. 2 in D minor, 1837), though it is his Violin Concerto in E minor of 1844 that crowns his achievements in the genre. It is a superb example of the symphonic style embellished with virtuoso elements. Mendelssohn was innovative in his approach to first-movement form, discarding the orchestral exposition and instead having the violinist instigate the expansive principal theme from the outset. The cadenza provides another break with convention, placed as it is at the end of the development section where it becomes an integrated structural element. All three movements are linked: a held note in the bassoon part leads into the slow movement where Mendelssohn offers up one of his most beautiful instrumental arias. The effervescent finale follows in E major, presenting multiple themes in a sonata structure adorned with brilliant passagework.

Schumann

Schumann completed his glorious Piano Concerto in A minor the following year, 1845. He had envisaged writing a concerto for his wife Clara soon after their marriage in 1840, first producing a single-movement *Fantasia* for piano and orchestra (1841), which he later developed into the first movement of the concerto. Schumann referred to his creation as 'something between symphony, concerto, and grand sonata', affirming not only the close integration of soloist and orchestra, but also his anti-virtuoso stance. Clara Schumann, who premièred the piece at Leipzig on New Year's Day, 1846, developed a similar antagonism towards showmanship, despite being one of the supreme virtuosos of the era.

Schumann's other major contribution to the genre was the Cello Concerto in A minor (Op. 129), composed in two weeks at Düsseldorf in 1850. Having played the cello as a child, Schumann returned to the instrument in 1832 after crippling his right hand with some disastrous finger strengthening exercises, which put an end to his pianistic ambitions. The concerto, neither virtuosic nor symphonic in style, is intimate and lyrical, and tightly organised in three movements linked by transitional passages. Premièred posthumously in 1860, it was not immediately recognised as the first important cello concerto of the Romantic era.

Chamber music

Beethoven and the string quartet

Beethoven's chamber music bestrides epochs, extending from the popular Op. 1 Piano Trios (1795) to the complex and introspective string quartets of the 1820s, pieces so ahead of their time that many who heard them considered Beethoven quite mad. His first set of string quartets, Op. 18 (1800), together with the Septet in E for strings and winds (1800) and the *Spring* Violin Sonata (1801), crown his 'first period' chamber output. The Septet became one of Beethoven's best-loved works during his lifetime, so often played that he himself tired of it. The Classically-organised Op. 18 quartets were written under the influence of Haydn, but their thematic character and expressive individuality pointed towards Beethoven's mature style.

The *Kreutzer* Violin Sonata of 1803 was one of the first chamber pieces Beethoven completed after resolving to fight the constraints of his deafness. Embodying apposite determination, power and scope, it is technically demanding and in places not unlike a concerto. The first string quartets of his 'middle period' were the three extraordinary *Razumovsky* Quartets, Op. 59. The eminent violinist Felix Radicati did not regard them as 'music', and told Beethoven as much; he received the immortal response: 'They are not for you, but for a later age.' The remark of a veritable Romantic! Composed for the violin-playing Russian Ambassador, Count Razumovsky, the collection appropriately incorporates Russian folk tunes, appearing in the finale of No. 1 in F major and in the *trio* of No. 2 in E minor. Beethoven planned these pieces on a wide scale, extending them well beyond the length of most Classical counterparts with extensive development sections and codas. He also blurred the internal structural divisions of the movements, to the frustration of traditionalists.

Razumovsky *Quartets*

The Op. 59 quartets gave Beethoven a renewed focus in chamber music. Among the pieces that followed were the Cello Sonata in A (Op. 69) and the *Ghost* Piano Trio (both 1808), and the *Archduke* Piano Trio in B flat and the *Serioso* Quartet in F minor (both 1810–11). During the distractions of 1813–18 his pace and artistry suffered (see *The Symphony and concert overture: Beethoven*), though in 1815 he produced two fine cello sonatas, in C and D (Op. 102), which look forward to the more intimate chamber music of his late period.

Beethoven found deeper spiritual depth in the silent isolation of his final decade, and he turned to the string quartet as a vehicle for his most challenging and intimate musical thoughts. In his last quartets—Opp. 127, 130, 131, 132 and 135—he achieved a level of emotional intensity that at times verges on the mystical. Typical 'late period' features abound, including fugal textures and variation form. The final movement of Op. 130 in B flat was originally conceived as a monumental fugue, but was so vast that Beethoven's friends and publisher persuaded him to replace it. The extracted movement became a work in its own right: the *Grosse Fuge*, Op. 133 (1826).

Beethoven's introspection encouraged a return to the kind of structural ambiguities explored in the *Razumovsky* Quartets. And distancing himself yet further from Classical convention, he cast Opp. 130 (B flat major) and 131 (C sharp minor) in six and seven movements respectively. In both of these quartets, elegiac slow movements unfold transcendentally. That of Op. 130, the *Cavatina*, was forged in deep sorrow, and Beethoven prized it as one of his most profound musical statements. The seven linked movements of the C-sharp minor Quartet, Op. 131 (1826), open with an Adagio fugal fantasia in place of the usual sonata Allegro. The contrast with the 'middle period' heroism could not be greater, since this is no short prelude

The late quartets

to a larger, vigorous fast movement. Beethoven instead sets a spiritual tone of searching intensity, followed with a triple-time Allegro second movement, without heroics, half the length of the first. His powers of invention excel above all in the Andante fourth movement, with its sequence of seven wide-ranging variations.

With their inimitable material and treatment, the late quartets are Beethoven's most timeless pieces. They stand at the threshold of a new era, yet whilst studied by the likes of Mendelssohn and Schumann, neither they nor the later Romantics were able to advance the string quartet beyond Beethoven's expressive soundworld.

Schubert and the early Romantic chamber repertory

Beethoven took chamber music beyond the capabilities of typical amateurs and into the realm of professionals. But he was not the only one to do so. We can trace rising performing demands in the output of Hummel, comparing for example his popular Piano Quintet in E flat of 1802 with the longer, more virtuosic Septet in D minor (Op. 74), composed around 1816. Hummel almost always featured the piano in his chamber music and would typically give it the most difficult (and interesting) material—a natural proclivity for one of Europe's leading piano virtuosos. Louis Spohr, a violin maestro second only to Paganini, was even more biased in his string *Quatuors brillants*, in which the first violin takes a soloistic role, creating a virtual concerto texture in the process. The *Quatuor brillant in D minor* (Op. 11) of 1806 was the first of six such compositions.

Schubert

In his earlier years Schubert composed some player-accessible music for his circle of family and friends, including the String Trio in B flat major (1817) and the famous Piano Quintet in A major, *Trout* (1819). But in full maturity he switched towards the professional sphere and elevated his chamber style at the same time. The turning point was his single-movement *Quartettsätz* in C minor (1820), one of the most satisfying and enjoyable pieces of the quartet repertory. The string writing is brilliantly idiomatic, facilitating rapid mood shifts from restlessness to lyrical charm, into torment followed by sorrow—and that's just the exposition. The form is Classical, but the sensibility is irresistibly Romantic.

Schubert continued in this vein in more minor-key quartets: the *Rosamunde* in A minor and *Death and the Maiden* in D minor (both 1824), the latter making its entrance with one of the most aggressive themes of quartet literature. Like *The Trout*, the Quartet in D minor owes its appellation to one of Schubert's songs, providing the material for variations of spiralling intensity in the second movement. Another composition from 1824 was the hour-long Octet in F major, modelled closely on Beethoven's shorter Septet. Expansive chamber music was now the norm for Schubert, and in masterpieces such as the String Quartet in G major (1826) and the two piano trios, in B flat and E flat (1827), he pursued similarly ambitious scales.

String Quintet in C

It is tantalising to think what Schubert might have achieved had he lived beyond his 31 years. His final chamber piece was his crowning achievement: the String Quintet in C (1828), scored with extra cello.

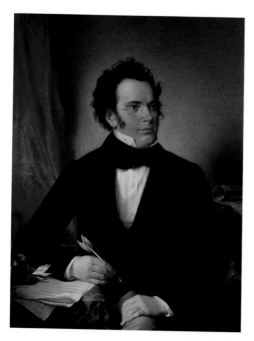

Typical of his mature style, the first movement oscillates around major and minor tonal centres from the start. The first theme, motivic and unsettled, flits between C minor and major, while the intensely lyrical second subject appears almost out of nowhere in the unprepared tonality of E flat major. The latter's effect is spectacular, as the cellos, in harmony, sing together with great beauty of tone. The slow movement is the most revered of the four, and its opening section represents one of the moving, elegiac creations ever set in a major key. Throughout the quintet the cellos rarely play together; more often one is allowed to soar upwards while the other supplies a bass foundation. The richness of thematic and textural invention is nothing short of miraculous.

Those who followed in Beethoven's wake struggled to find new paths in chamber music; as in the symphony and piano sonata, Beethoven's legacy was overwhelming. Of the top-rank early Romantics following Schubert, only Mendelssohn and Schumann managed to create a significant, enduring chamber output. Mendelssohn, like Schubert, wrote masterpieces in his teens, works of greater maturity than those of the teenage Mozart. The Octet for Strings (Op. 20, 1825), which he composed aged 16, is a prime example, boasting an exhilarating first movement of quasi-orchestral textures, a Scherzo of pure fairy music and a finale abounding in lively counterpoint. He never wrote a more effective chamber piece.

Mendelssohn

Mendelssohn composed his string quartets under the influence of Beethoven. His Quartet in A minor Op. 13 (1827) is inventive and strongly characterised by its opening Adagio, introducing a three-note motif that in various guises pervades the entire work. Aspects of cyclical treatment appear again among the three quartets of Op. 44 (1837–38), specifically in the E minor and E flat major quartets, which are both Romantic in spirit. The agitation and disturbing dissonances of Mendelssohn's final quartet, the F minor Op. 80 (1847), were likely stimulated by his state of shock and mourning following the death of his pianist-composer sister, Fanny Mendelssohn (1805–47). The F minor is in many respects his most engaging quartet. Other chamber highlights include the piano trios in D minor Op. 49 (1839) and C minor Op. 66 (1845), and the Cello Sonata No. 2 in D (1843). Schumann hailed Op. 49 as 'the master-Trio of the age'. It is certainly the best known, and exhibits wonderful breadth in its opening theme. The second movement is reminiscent of the *Songs Without Words*, while a playful Scherzo leads to a Rondo-finale that takes on a Schubertian flavour in both theme and harmonic design.

It was with Mendelssohn's encouragement that Schumann turned to

Schumann

chamber music. He had enjoyed a spectacularly creative year with lieder in 1840, and found symphonic inspiration in 1841, but then depression set in. Disappointed by the reception of his Symphony in D minor (No. 4, first version) at Leipzig in December 1841, he suffered feelings of insecurity and rejection while his wife, Clara, enjoyed the limelight as one of Europe's finest pianists. No one seemed much interested in Robert Schumann at the start of 1842. But he managed to crawl out of his hole of self-pity with a surge of chamber music, most significantly the three string quartets (Op. 41), the Piano Quartet, Op. 47, and the Piano Quintet, Op. 44. The magnificent Piano Quintet in E flat is full of romantic ardour, combining extremes of serenity and wildness in a perfectly controlled structure. It easily ranks among his best compositions. Subsequent years saw occasional activities in chamber music, including the two piano trios (D minor and F major) of 1847. Schumann's loyalty to the piano was reflected in all of his chamber music save the string quartets.

Vocal music

Sacred music

Demand and supply

The comparative neglect of sacred music during the first half of the 19th century reflected the continuing decline of church and royal patronage. The bottom line, for the increasingly emancipated composer, was that sacred music now rarely paid the bills. But while church attendance had diminished during the Enlightenment, the Napoleonic Wars fuelled disillusionment with Enlightenment-based rationalism. The early century thus welcomed a variety of revivalist Christian movements and an increased drive to bring religion back into political life. Church music still had its place. Moreover, Handel had demonstrated over half a century earlier that religious subject matter presented in the secular arena could be at once reverent, exhilarating and profitable. Sacred music written for the concert platform was far more malleable in expression, form and scope. Little surprise, then, that many enduring sacred pieces of the Romantic era were cultivated through a marriage of religious and secular endeavour.

Haydn, Hummel, Cherubini

At the outset of the century sacred music still had important support from the courts. Haydn, aged 70, produced his final mass in 1802 for the wife of his patron Prince Nicholas Esterházy II. The so-called *Harmoniemesse* was his sixth 'name-day' mass written in honour of Princess Maria Hermenegild. Following Haydn's full retirement, Hummel secured the position of *Konzertmeister* to the Esterházys and took over the responsibilities of composing sacred works for special occasions. He produced five well-crafted masses between 1804 and 1808, which are indebted to Haydn and his former teacher, Mozart. Following the termination of his contract in 1811, Hummel all but abandoned sacred music. Meanwhile in Paris, Luigi Cherubini (1760–1842) embarked on a busy period of sacred music composition as co-superintendent of the royal chapel, a position he secured following the reinstatement of Louis XVIII in 1815. In this capacity he produced his Requiem in C minor (1816), a work admired by Beethoven and the early Romantics.

Beethoven, who in Vienna never held court or church position, wrote only a few sacred works. His personal faith incorporated a significant dose of pantheism, though it embraced the biblical view of an eternal, omnipotent God. It is not certain whether he viewed Christ as divine, but themes of purity and suffering inspired his first substantial sacred piece, the oratorio *Christ on the Mount of Olives* (1803). This was a commercial venture following the Handelian precedent, which Haydn had so successfully revived with *The Creation* (1798) and its secular successor, *The Seasons* (1801).

Beethoven wrote two masses, both for high nobility. The first was the Mass in C (1807), commissioned by Prince Esterházy. Unfortunately the prince did not appreciate it, to the relief and delight of *Konzertmeister* Hummel. The second, the great *Missa Solemnis* in D (1823), was intended for the grand installation of Beethoven's friend and patron Archduke Rudolph as Archbishop of Olmütz. Beethoven began the work in 1819, but missed the 1820 deadline by three years.

The *Missa Solemnis* is far more than sacred music designed for a liturgical context. It became a deeply personal statement, and one that Beethoven prepared for by a committed study of the Roman (Latin) Mass and the Renaissance choral style. At the same time the Mass lost none of its grand aspirations—witness the dramatic sweep of the opening 'Kyrie', where solo voices answer the gigantic symphonic-choral throng, pleading for God's mercy. The 'Gloria' follows with the enthusiasm and excitement of an operatic finale, and integrates vivid word-painting throughout. Beethoven enriched the musical language of his Mass by incorporating church modes, as in the Dorian-mode 'Et incarnatus est', a movement suitably infused with mystery, reflecting that of the incarnation. The intimate, solo violin part of the 'Benedictus', soaring high among the heavenly hosts, offers another fascinating dimension. Writing this Mass, Beethoven broke away from rigid Classical structures, particularly in melodic line, presenting a subjective vision that extended deep into the heart of Romanticism.

Missa Solemnis

Schubert, probably desirous of a secure church or court chapel appointment, produced a late concentration of sacred music. By nature a pantheist, he will have probably composed his religious works—including six masses—to a 'God in all things'. His greatest sacred opus was one of his last, the Mass in E flat (No. 6, 1828), a large piece dominated by the chorus. The grandeur of the liturgy meets Schubert's subjective response, and both the 'Gloria' and 'Agnus Dei' conclude with magnificent fugues.

Schubert

Schubert's Mass in E flat was premièred posthumously in Vienna in 1829. That same year the 20-year-old Mendelssohn directed a Berlin performance of Bach's *St Matthew Passion*. In so doing he returned the masterpiece to the repertory and single-handedly launched a Bach revival. Jewish by birth but baptised into the Christian faith, Mendelssohn became prominent in sacred music. Like Beethoven, he drew on earlier music in his choral works, including Palestrina and Lassus, but Bach's contrapuntal style inspired him most. The chorale cantatas (1827–32) clearly betray this influence.

Mendelssohn

Mendelssohn noted irony in the fact that he, Jewish by birth, seemed to be the one composer most keen to champion the Christian musical tradition. How fitting, then, was the subject matter of his first oratorio:

St Paul

St Paul (1836), accounting the apostle's conversion from Jew (Saul) to Christian (Paul). Fusing the models of Bach's Passions and Handel's oratorios, he scored a narrator's role and the traditional assortment of recitatives, arias and choruses. His reverent use of the chorale is in homage to Bach, and the whole oratorio exhibits contrapuntal mastery. Romantic subjectivism is unmistakable in the scoring of Christ's voice ('Saul, Saul, why do you persecute me?') for woodwinds and women's choir, at once veering from any 'literal' representation of God, while emphasising the mysterious, ascendant Christ. *St Paul* gained rapid and widespread success, securing performances across Europe and in the United States before the end of the decade.

▶ Felix Mendelssohn. Portrait by the composer's brother-in-law, painter Wilhelm Hensel, husband of the pianist and composer Fanny Mendelssohn.

Elijah

Mendelssohn's second oratorio, *Elijah* (1846), was commissioned by England's Birmingham Festival. Like *St Paul*, it responds to the power of the story (from *1* and *2 Kings*), the impressive opening setting the tone as Elijah's recitative prophesies drought. This uses a descending interval as a 'curse motif', which recurs as an agent of expressive unity. There are many contrasts, from the angelic charm of 'Lift thine eyes to the mountains' to the passionate and stormy intensity of 'And then shall your light break forth'. Vividly dramatic, *Elijah* created a sensation and eventually surpassed *St Paul* as a regular concert fixture.

Lobgesang

In between the oratorios Mendelssohn composed his Symphony No. 2 *Hymn of Praise* (*Lobgesang*, 1840), a symphony-cantata hybrid that enjoyed immediate popularity. It broadly observes the model of Beethoven's Ninth, with a three-movement Sinfonia followed by an extended choral finale. Mendelssohn chose Biblical verses and harmonised the hymn 'Nun danket alle Gott' ('Now thank we all our God') to generate an anthology of praise, set in solos, duets and choruses. On the score he quoted Luther: 'I would happily see all the arts, especially music, in the service of Him who has given and created them.'

Berlioz: Requiem & Te Deum

Berlioz lacked Mendelssohn's resolute convictions of faith but still composed sacred masterpieces, the first being the *Grande Messe des Morts* (1837). This is his Requiem, sometimes refined and lyrical, sometimes powerful and monumental. The orchestral deployment is typically indulgent, with four brass ensembles around the auditorium and no fewer than 16 timpani, plus other resources to match. The full forces of the Requiem make their explosive entry at the 'Tuba Mirum', but the sixth of the ten movements, the 'Lacrymosa', forms the heart of the work. Berlioz likewise conceived his Te Deum (1849) with a spacious auditorium in mind, emphasising the majesty of God and the insignificance of man. The gentle and intimate music makes the splendour of the climaxes all the more magnificent. The score calls for solo tenor, triple chorus, orchestra and organ. Berlioz explained that organ and orchestra should be 'like Pope and Emperor, speaking from opposite ends of the nave'.

Romantic song: Lied and Mélodie

During the early 1800s writing *lieder* was principally an amateur pursuit. Professional, 'successful' composers regarded it no more than a diversion from other, more prestigious activities. Schubert was a fluent and prolific composer, but his lack of material success in Vienna encouraged a devotion to the more intimate genres, and lieder, in particular, fascinated him. His 600 songs established a repertoire and a point of reference that later composers built upon and sought to emulate. He regularly performed his songs (alongside piano and chamber music) for the benefit of friends— gatherings that became known as 'Schubertiads'. Among the attendees were Johann Mayrhofer and Franz von Schober, whose poetry Schubert set.

Schubert

As a teenager Schubert excelled in lieder and his sensitivity to poetry brought penetrating results. Songs such as his exalted Goethe settings *Gretchen am Spinnrade* (Gretchen at the Spinning Wheel) and *Erlkönig* (Erlking), composed 1814–15, set a new expressive intensity for the genre. In both pieces the piano assumes a role of equal importance to the voice: cyclical rhythmic patterns suggest the turning of Gretchen's spinning wheel, while pounding triplets in the *Erlking* evoke the desperate riding rhythm of a father carrying his dying son on horseback. Fusing musical realism with folklore and the supernatural, Schubert transported the art-song into the Romantic era.

Gretchen am Spinnrade; Erlkönig

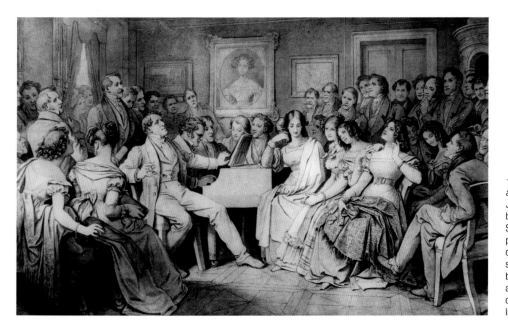

◀ A 'Schubertiad' at the home of Joseph von Spaun by Moritz von Schwind. Schubert's progressive musical outlook was stimulated above all by his intimate love and understanding of Romantic literature.

Die schöne Müllerin; Winterreise

Beethoven, not Schubert, set the very first song cycle with *An die ferne Geliebte* (To the Distant Beloved, 1816), his finest achievement in solo vocal music. Schubert followed the example with *Die schöne Müllerin* (The Fair Maid of the Mill, 1823) and *Winterreise* (Winter Journey, 1827), both based on the poetry of Wilhelm Müller. Nine of the 20 *Müllerin* songs are set strophically, while the others are through-composed. The musical imagery is spontaneous, even startling, the tension mounting inexorably from song to song until the lovelorn miller accepts the cool embrace of the stream when life has lost its charms. In *Winterreise*, poetry and music were at one with Schubert's psychological state. The protagonist is a poet, burdened by unrequited love, who trudges through an inhospitable wintry landscape. At length he meets a beggar, and against the drone of the hurdy-gurdy they disappear into the snow and the darkness. They will wander forever, like Byron's Manfred, in search of consolation.

Schumann

Carl Loewe (1796–1869) contributed some notable romantic *ballads* into the German song repertory, including his own setting of *Erlkönig*, published in 1824. But it was Schumann, with more than 200 songs to his credit, who inherited Schubert's mantle. He wrote over half of his songs in a single year, 1840, including the famous *Dichterliebe* (Poet's love), based on texts by Heinrich Heine. In this cycle there is an affinity between poet and composer, full of deep feeling, reflecting the individual's inner emotional world. In his piano writing Schumann observed even greater detail of tone-painting than Schubert. The piano part of 'Hör' ich das Liedchen klagen', for example, provides both vocal accompaniment and its own textual interpretation, describing the 'savage affliction' and 'dark longing' of past love. At the end of the cycle Schumann adds a piano postlude that seems to reflect his own personal response to Heine's narrative. No composer better exemplified the Romantic spirit than Schumann, whose own expressive yearnings and enthusiasm for literature found passionate release in song.

French Romantic song began with Berlioz. Best known by far is his song-cycle *Les nuits d'été* (1841), on poems by Théophile Gautier. This is not a narrative cycle, more a collection of six love songs that traverse joy, longing and grief. It is introduced by the idyllic 'Villanelle' and concludes with the teasing *barcarolle* 'L'île inconnue', but songs of sorrow and yearning, such as 'Sur les lagunes' and 'Absence', set the pervasive mood. Berlioz orchestrated *Les nuits d'été* in 1856, and thereby created the first orchestral song-cycle. If Berlioz began the transformation of the Classical *romance* into the Romantic *mélodie*, Charles-François Gounod (1818–93) completed the process. He wrote more than 200 songs, with his first important examples dating from the 1840s. These include *Le vallon* and *Le Soir* (both 1842), settings of poetry by Alphonse de Lamartine.

Berlioz: Les nuits d'été

Centres of opera

Italy

The cultural position of native Italian opera became ever stronger during the 19th century. Rossini brought to a climax the high Classical tradition, while Bellini, Donizetti and Verdi moulded the genre to Romantic tastes. Opera ultimately became so dominant that most of the region's leading composers gave little attention to instrumental music. The international appetite for Italian opera was phenomenal, with works by Rossini, Bellini, Donizetti and Verdi produced not only across Europe, but also in North and South America, even in the Far East.

The Bavarian Johann Simon Mayr (1763–1845) enjoyed prominence in Italy during the early years of the century, particularly since both Cherubini and Spontini were busy making their names in France (see next section). Mayr was influential as a composer of both comic and serious opera, and as a music academic. Mayr's tragic operas include his masterpiece, *Medea in Corinto* (Naples, 1813), written 'in the French manner' and using the orchestra throughout, without *secco* recitatives. He would have enjoyed much more success had it not been for the fast-rising star of Gioacchino Rossini (1792–1868), who composed 39 operas in 19 years before abandoning operatic composition at the age of 37.

Gioacchino Rossini

Rossini was 18 when he produced his first staged opera, the one-act farce *La cambiale di matrimonio* (1810), a commission from Venice's Teatro San Moisè secured through family connections. The success of the production launched Rossini into a busy opera-writing schedule. Eight operas later, in 1813, his career took flight with two masterworks, the serious *Tancredi* and the comic *L'italiana in Algeri*. Both premièred in Venice with huge success, they made the 21-year-old famous across Europe. Rossini's gift for melody and musical spontaneity gave his operas enormous vitality.

He developed a style in arias known as the *Code Rossini*, characterised by an expressive, slow opening followed by a fast and brilliant *cabaletta*. The cabaletta traditionally allowed singers freedom to display their vocal skills through improvised embellishments in repeated stanzas. Rossini was uncomfortable with this artistic concession, so from the time of *Elisabetta, Regina d'Inghilterra* (1815) he chose to write out his vocal decorations. In other respects he was prepared to cut corners and make compromises, since he usually composed in a hurry. He had, for instance, used the overture to *Elisabetta* two years earlier in Aureliano in Palmira, and he used it yet again for his comic masterpiece *Il barbiere di Siviglia* (The Barber of Seville, 1816). Rossini was in fact an unashamed self-borrower and would often lift music from one opera to another. That his music is so interchangeable—even from serious opera to comedy—reveals much about his pre-Romantic style. But there is no doubting his dramatic flair: Figaro's famed aria 'Largo al factotum' features the most compelling operatic entrance before Verdi's *Otello*, not least because it begins offstage.

Il barbiere got off to a shaky start, suffering a nearly disastrous première (owing to an anti-Rossini cabal), and was not initially among the composer's best-loved operas. The year 1817 brought better success with the Cinderella-inspired comedy *La Cenerentola* and also *La gazza ladra* (The Thieving Magpie), the composer's finest *semiseria* opera. Rossini then created something quite different in the biblical epic *Mosè in Egitto* (Moses in Egypt, 1818), which opens not with an overture but with thunderous chords and a fretful chorus of disorientated Egyptians in a 'pall of darkness'. Devised as a musical drama suitable for Lent, the opera is nevertheless embellished with a love story. Ancient times also provided the setting for Rossini's last opera for Italy, the vocally-challenging tragedy *Semiramide* (1823). Set in Babylon during the eighth century B.C., it failed to please unanimously at its Venice première, which in turn incited Rossini to accept lucrative offers beyond Italy.

Rossini was the most popular composer in Europe when he arrived in Paris to manage the Théâtre Italien. There he produced French-language versions of existing operas, as well as the one-act comic opera *Il viaggio a Reims* (The Journey to Rheims) for the coronation celebrations of Charles X in 1825. Only two new full operas date from this time, and both were written for the Paris Opéra: the two-act comedy *Le Comte Ory* (1828), which adapts music from *Il viaggio*, and Rossini's operatic swansong, *Guillaume Tell* (1829, see *France*, p. 341). Rossini retired from opera at the height of his powers, having enriched the genre with his superb dramatic timing, outstandingly catchy tunes and opulent orchestration. Meanwhile, younger Italian composers were attempting to yoke his theatrical flamboyance and *bel canto* vocal style with the evolving Romantic movement.

The career of Vincenzo Bellini (1801–35) lasted only a decade, with ten operas mostly written with the librettist Felice Romani (1788–1865). Their first collaboration, *Il pirata* (The Pirate), was produced with outstanding success for La Scala, Milan, in 1827. For this Bellini composed an essentially Classical score, but he was already observing a depth of textual nuance and melodic expressivity that ventured beyond Rossini. The opera itself tells of a count-turned-pirate, Gualtiero, and his illicit love for a woman who has become the wife of his enemy, the Duke of Caldora. The tormented Gualtiero kills the duke, but is condemned to death; his former lover, crushed with emotion, goes insane. Exploring unrequited love and irrational behaviour, *Il pirata* is a prime example of how the Romantic flavour of 1820s Italian opera was articulated first and foremost through the scenario.

Bellini's fame grew rapidly and more operatic commissions soon followed, including *I Capuleti e I Montecchi* (1830) for Venice, based on Shakespeare's *Romeo and Juliet*. He set a new standard in his synthesis of melody and text, and built up expansive melodic lines that became a feature of his style. Bellini thrived on gripping, emotionally-wrought drama. 'Mad scenes', for example, create pathos and transfixing vocal opportunities for the heroines of *La sonnambula* (The Sleepwalker, 1831) and *I puritani* (1835). His greatest opera is *Norma* (1831), a tragic tale of a Druid priestess who, torn between duty and love, breaks her religious vows. Describing opera as 'the difficult art of drawing tears by means of song', Bellini made great demands of his singers. His departure from the Rossinian vocal model may be noted in the renowned 'Casta diva', whose flowing melisma forms part of the musical line, reaching far beyond mere decoration. Of this aria Verdi claimed: 'No-one has written anything more beautiful or celestial.' There is no finer example of the *bel canto* style.

Gaetano Donizetti (1797–1848), a pupil of Mayr, emerged under Rossini's spell. More conservative in style than Bellini, he was extremely prolific, composing over 70 operas among which several still hold the stage. The comic *L'elisir d'amore* (1832) is sentimental, lively and wonderfully tuneful, while the tragic, melodramatic style of *Lucrezia Borgia* (1833) looks forward to Verdi. Donizetti created his magnum opus in *Lucia di Lammermoor* (1835), one of the many Romantic operas inspired by the writing of Walter Scott. The Scottish story was adapted by the librettist Salvadore Cammarano, who was later to collaborate with Verdi on *Il trovatore*. Donizetti is at his dramatic best in the sextet that concludes Act 2, with its complex amalgam of character emotions, all swept up with the chorus into a powerful climax. The music reaches its expressive heights in the spellbinding 'mad scene' of Act 3, including Lucia's aria 'Ardon gl'incensi' and her bravura cabaletta 'Spargi d'amaro'. The success of *Lucia* was truly global, with performances as far afield as Cuba and Indonesia within ten years.

Donizetti wanted recognition from Paris, so he moved there in 1838 while continuing to fulfil commissions from Italy and Vienna. His French

Vincenzo Bellini

Gaetano Donizetti

▲ Europe's most prestigious opera house, La Scala (Milan), early 19th century.

productions included *La Fille du régiment* (1840) for the Opéra-Comique, and his final *buffa* masterpiece, *Don Pasquale* (1843), for the Théâtre Italien. Of the composer, the poet Heinrich Heine remarked, 'This Italian has great talent, but even greater is his fecundity, in which he is exceeded only by rabbits.' Donizetti's final years were unpleasant: like several prominent Romantic composers (including Schubert, Schumann, Smetana and Wolf) he was plagued by syphilis, and he ended his life confined to an asylum.

Giovanni Pacini (1796–1867) and Saverio Mercadante (1795–1870), two lesser names of Italian opera, were both prolific. Following his own *Il giuramento* (The Oath, 1837) Mercadante wrote: 'I began a revolution here: forms varied, trivial cabalettas banished, vocal lines simplified, fewer repeats … emphasis on the drama, orchestra rich but not swamping the voices, no long solos in ensembles, not much bass drum and a lot less brass band.' No wonder Verdi admired him.

Giuseppe Verdi

When Giuseppe Verdi (1813–1901) completed his first opera, *Oberto* (1839), listeners would have noted the presence of the prevailing style. The publisher Giovanni Ricordi bought the rights to the score, and La Scala offered a contract for three more operas. Verdi was then struck by family tragedy, with the death of his son and daughter, and then wife, which created the worst possible conditions for his second operatic attempt, the comedy *Un giorno di regno* (King for a Day). He was obliged to complete the work, which failed at its première in 1840. It was half a century before he attempted comedy again.

Verdi had wanted to give up composition completely, but soon inspiration got the better of him. His third opera was *Nabucco* (1842). With its celebrated 'Chorus of Hebrew Slaves' (or 'Va, pensiero'), this biblical epic proved an outright triumph and Verdi became a national celebrity, in demand at every Italian theatre. He responded with an astonishing flow of creativity in his 'anni di galera' (years in the galleys), with a further 12 operas before 1850. During this time the nationalist movement, the Risorgimento, latched on to Verdi as a high-profile sympathiser and adopted his 'Va, pensiero' as a patriotic hymn. The Risorgimento did not achieve an independent unified state until the 1860s, so much of Verdi's career was spent in an era of foreign domination. He received close attention from the censor, since his operas contained nationalist ideas, such as the line 'You may have the universe but leave Italy to me' in *Attila* (1846) and the chorus of exiles in *Macbeth* (1847).

Verdi forged his career by building upon the established foundations of strong vocal writing and melodic line, clear construction and robust orchestration. He read widely, selecting from historical epics and political dramas. With psychological insights into the motivations and actions of his characters, the conflict between love and duty featured frequently. A good example is *Ernani* (1844), in which three men love the same woman, but are so obsessed with their own codes of honour that none achieves happiness. This opera is typical: a series of vivid numbers and ensembles, driven with dramatic pace.

During this decade *Macbeth* and *Luisa Miller* (1849) were the operas that advanced Verdi's development with the closest fusion of drama and music. Of the role of Lady Macbeth he wrote: 'I would rather that Lady's voice were rough, hollow and stifled.' Verdi considered vocal acting much more important than beautiful singing to develop character and dramatic truth. This is vividly illustrated by the sleepwalking scene of Act 4, where Lady Macbeth dreams about the murders she and her husband have committed. Her free-form mix of recitative and *arioso* presents great challenges for the singer, with awkward melodic intervals and a wide, expressive vocal range yielding chilling declamation.

With vision and creative genius, Verdi had gained the attention of the world. His operas were now playing from Portugal to Russia, from Sweden to Algeria, even in Argentina and Chile. Verdi, not yet 40, was poised to enter the most remarkable stage of his career.

France

Paris became the musical capital of Europe during the early 19th century. Foreign composers flocked to the city, some taking up short- or long-term residency to fulfil operatic ambitions, such as Cherubini, Spontini, Rossini, Donizetti, Bellini, Meyerbeer and Wagner, or exploit opportunities in the salon and concert hall, notably Chopin (almost solely in the salon), Liszt and Paganini. Berlioz was the greatest among the nationals, who included the stage composers Adrien Boieldieu, Daniel Auber, Adolphe Adam and the librettist Eugène Scribe.

French opera was broadly divided into two categories during this time. One was the continuing tradition of *opéra comique*, a light form of opera

Genres

performed with small casts and simple staging, typically mixing spoken dialogue with arias, ensembles and orchestral interludes. Then there was *grand opéra*, which became Paris's most spectacular form of entertainment. It was 'grand' in every dimension, presented in five acts with huge vocal and instrumental forces, lavish sets, complex staging (with machinery and lighting effects) and elaborate costumes. Narratives usually took historical settings and would attempt to make some sort of social or moral statement. Grand opéra had a profound influence on the broader European operatic scene; Glinka, Verdi and Wagner all took direct inspiration from its characteristic forms and structures.

Rescue opera
At the turn of the century, with the republican spirit fomenting, the 'rescue' theme was very much alive in opera. Luigi Cherubini's opéra comique *Les Deux Journées* (1800) was a distinctive example, with its story of deliverance from injustice. The wider political overtones of rescue opera were obvious: Europe was in need of rescuing from monarchical tyranny. Self-proclaimed as emperor in 1804, Napoleon recognised the propaganda value of opera, and in preparation for his Spanish campaign he requested such a work on the Mexican Conquest of 1521. The result, *Fernand Cortez* (1809), featured music by another Paris-based Italian, Gasparo Spontini (1774–1851). The opera did not enjoy the success of the same composer's *La vestale* (1807), but its vast scale, impressive sets, 17 live horses and the spectacle of an on-stage cavalry charge all served Napoleon's purposes. Its extravagant treatment of an historical narrative set a path towards *grand opéra*.

Opéra comique
Opéra comique was now embracing both light and serious subject matter. Adrien Boieldieu (1775–1834) made his name with the genre, his breakthrough coming with the one-act comedy *Le calife de Bagdad* (1800). His most lasting opéra comique was *La dame blanche* (1825), a Gothic, supernatural tale inspired by the novels of Walter Scott. Adolphe Adam (1803–56) followed on the heals of Boieldieu, enjoying popular success with *Le Chalet* (1834) and *Le postillon de Lonjumeau* (The Coachman of Lonjumeau, 1836), though it is his delightful ballet *Giselle* (1841) that sustains his reputation today. Donizetti, as noted in the previous section, added to the opéra comique repertory in 1840 with his witty *La Fille du régiment* (The Daughter of the Regiment).

Daniel Auber & grand opera
Daniel Auber (1782–1871) composed 47 operas, 38 of which used libretti by Eugène Scribe (1791–1861), whose vast output provoked talk of 'the Scribe factory'. Auber's one enduring opera is an opéra comique, *Fra Diavolo* (Brother Devil, 1830), but of greater historical importance is his five-act *La muette de Portici* (The Mute Girl of Portici, 1828). This work, more than any other, set the definitive style for French grand opera, with its through-composed style, historical setting (a Neapolitan uprising against the Spanish in 1647) and opulent production, incorporating magnificent sets, large crowd scenes with dances and choruses, and a climactic finale featuring the eruption of Vesuvius.

Rossini: *Guillaume Tell*
Rossini adopted this grand manner when he composed his four-act *Guillaume Tell* (William Tell, 1829) for the Paris Opéra. Based on Schiller's play about the Swiss patriot, it is one of his masterpieces, from galloping

◀ The first Belgian performance of Auber's *The Mute Girl of Portici*, 25th August 1830. The scene shows the politically-charged opera stirring up revolutionary fervour within the audience. The opera-goers subsequently took to the streets in protest and initiated the Belgian revolution.

overture to incandescent finale. A Romantic spirit runs through *Tell*, not just in its heroic narrative and pastoral setting, but also in the music's unprepared modulations, adventurous harmonic schemes and expansive structural architecture. According to Donizetti, who later saw a three-act abridgement of the opera, 'The first and last acts were written by Rossini, but the second was written by God'. *Tell* is the first masterpiece of the grand opera tradition, although with it Rossini ended his career as an opera composer.

The Paris Opéra institutionalised grand opera, which became a permanent fixture by the early 1830s. The German composer Giacomo Meyerbeer (1791–1864), resident in Paris from 1826, collaborated with Scribe on several grand operas, the most influential stage works of their kind between those of Rossini and Wagner. Their first was the morality tale of *Robert le diable* (Robert the Devil), which received a spectacular production in 1831 and propelled Meyerbeer to international stardom. Five years later he and Scribe created another sensation with *Les Huguenots*. Berlioz believed *Les Huguenots* 'contained enough material for ten operas', and there are no fewer than seven key roles. Fromental Halévy (1799–1862) also collaborated with Scribe on his finest grand opera, *La Juive* (The Jewess, 1835), a tragedy set during a period of persecution in the 15th century. It was admired by many of the Romantics, including Wagner.

Hector Berlioz may have been the supreme French composer of the age, but he experienced frustrations with his operatic projects from the outset (see also *Chapter 6*). *Benvenuto Cellini* (1838), a two-act *opéra semiseria*, taxed the performers and terminated his working relationship with the Opéra. His next dramatic project, *La damnation de Faust*, reflected his admiration for Goethe. However, he designated it a 'dramatic legend', and organised the mammoth work for two (very disappointing) concert performances in 1846. Twenty scenes are divided into four parts, in what is

Giacomo Meyerbeer

Berlioz

▶ Mikhail
Ivanovich Glinka

a fusion of opera, cantata and symphony. Even so, the colourful score includes theatrical directions, and nowadays it is not uncommon to find staged performances.

Russia

Until the early 19th century Russian musical life was divided into two extremes: traditional folk music on the one hand, and the imported Western classical idiom on the other. It was the bringing together of these traditions in the early 19th century that led to the establishment of a truly Russian classical music style.

Mikhail
Glinka

Mikhail Glinka (1804–57) developed his talent for music through domestic and provincial music making. As a young teenager he took some lessons with John Field, but it was his three years of study in Italy, from 1830 to 1833, that proved most formative. There he immersed himself in the youthful music of Bellini and Donizetti, whose lyricism left an indelible mark on his own style. Back in Russia, Glinka embarked on his first opera,

A Life for
the Tsar

A Life for the Tsar (1836). In terms of structure and expression the work does little to hide Western influences, presented as it is in the grand French manner with Italianate arias and Germanic harmonies. In other respects the opera represented a significant departure. Set in 1613, the story concerns a peasant, Ivan Susanin, who valiantly and sacrificially thwarts the efforts of an invading Polish army bent on assassinating the first Romanov tsar. The heavily patriotic subject matter inspired Glinka to draw Russian folk melodies and rhythms into the heart of the music. He also broke new ground by moulding his recitatives to the patterns of the Russian language, and even anticipated Wagner in the use of recurring character motifs. Premièred at St Petersburg in December 1836, *A Life* was a resounding triumph and changed Russian music forever.

In 1842 Glinka set the fantastical tale of *Ruslan and Lyudmila*, integrating national colour into an imaginative score enriched by exotic harmonies and magical whole-tone melodies. As in *A Life for the Tsar*, the orchestration is remarkably vibrant and exceptional in the manner it frequently transcends mere accompaniment. Glinka's quest to institute a Russian classical idiom took him beyond the opera house and into the concert hall. His seminal composition was *Kamarinskaya* (1848), a short, unpretentious orchestral fantasia based on two Russian folk melodies, one a wedding song, the other a dance tune. When Tchaikovsky later considered the source of the Russian symphonic school, he wrote 'It is all in *Kamarinskaya*, just as the whole oak is in the acorn'. Both on and off the stage, Glinka was the indisputable father of Russian musical nationalism.

Austro-German lands

German opera was struggling to expunge Italian and French influences at the start of the 19th century. The national genre was the Singspiel, which had evolved to combine spoken dialogue with recitative, arias, ensembles and choruses, as in Mozart's two singspiel masterpieces, *Die Entführung aus dem Serail* (The Abduction from the Harem, 1782) and *Die Zauberflöte* (The Magic Flute, 1791).

Beethoven, a progressive in so many ways, created a relatively conservative work in his Singspiel *Fidelio*, which cost him more effort than practically any other composition. Based on J. N. Bouilly's libretto *Léonore, ou L'amour conjugal*, the noble story concerns a wife who in disguise rescues her wrongly-imprisoned husband. Beethoven looked to Cherubini's rescue opera *Les Deux Journées* (The Two Days, 1800) and Mozart's *The Magic Flute* in preparation for the work. First produced in 1805 then revised in 1806, the opera found definitive form in 1814, its revival prompted by the celebratory atmosphere anticipating the Congress of Vienna. In *Fidelio* we observe Beethoven's vision of promoting mankind to a better world. This is plainly articulated through the contrast between the beginning of Act II, the dark F minor of Florestan's dungeon, and the bright C major celebrations of freedom of the opera's final chorus. Beethoven's one opera was the last great essay in the Classical 'rescue' tradition.

Louis Spohr was the orchestral leader at the Theater an der Wien when he completed his Singspiel *Faust* (1813), drawing principally from 16th-century stories rather than from Goethe's poem of 1808. Faust sells his soul to the devil in return for knowledge and power; though he attempts to do good, power corrupts him and he is finally dragged off to Hell by Mephistopheles. Magic, Satan, the duality of good and evil, love and lust: these quintessential Romantic ingredients inspired some of the composer's most daring chromatic harmonies. Spohr also explored the use of recurring signifying motifs. When Weber conducted the première of *Faust* in Prague (1816), he admired how 'a few melodies, carefully devised, weave their way through the work like delicate threads, holding its structure together'. Spohr's greatest triumph followed with the Indian tale of *Jessonda* (1823), whose through-composed style, leading motifs, emphasis on scenes, choruses and ballet, made it a seminal work of German grand opera.

Soon after launching Spohr's *Faust*, Carl Maria von Weber (1786–1826) left his director's post at the Prague Opera and moved to Dresden. As Royal Saxon *Kapellmeister* he was encouraged to advance a distinctly German brand of opera to counter the pervasive Italian style. He began work on *Der Freischütz* (The Freeshooter) and completed the opera four years later, in 1821. Weber's Singspiel, sometimes translated as *The Marksman with Magic Bullets*, unites a pastoral love story with a Faustian blend of Satanism. Much of Weber's score is Classical, though with a colourful infusion of folk music in the choruses of the huntsmen and bridesmaids. It also incorporates 'reminiscence' motifs (undoubtedly influenced by Spohr), anticipating the methods of Wagner. It is in the sinister and atmospheric 'Wolf's Glen Scene', however, that both the story and music

Beethoven: *Fidelio*

Louis Spohr: *Faust*

Carl Maria von Weber: *Der Freischütz*

plunge headlong into Romanticism. Here the misguided forester Max, desperate to win the hand of Agatha by means of a shooting contest, procures magic bullets from the demonic Samiel. Scene-painting the moonlit forested glen, the spells and apparitions, Weber's music is remarkably free in form, mixing soft eerie textures with sudden ghoulish outbursts from an offstage chorus of demons; Samiel's evil presence is reflected by a mysterious, shimmering diminished seventh chord. The imaginative orchestration and wild, sensuous scoring set a new standard for descriptive music. Weber had translated dark Romantic horror, all the rage in contemporary literature, into powerful musical form.

Few German operas have matched the immediate and widespread success of *Der Freischütz*, and Weber's subsequent efforts were failures by comparison. In 1823 he produced a through-composed opera, *Euryanthe*, which despite containing some excellent music, suffered as an artistic whole due to a poor libretto. He then travelled to London for the 1826 première of *Oberon*. The opera was initially well received, but it is memorable only in moments, for example its splendid overture and the fairy music of Act I. While in London, Weber died of tuberculosis. Eighteen years later his body was transported back to Germany with due ceremony.

Heinrich Marschner

Following Weber, Heinrich Marschner (1795–1861) became a leading light of German Romantic opera. He melded the Singspiel tradition with a more musically unified operatic style, while employing increased chromaticism (including remote modulations) to amplify a sense of mystery within his chosen narratives. In *Der Vampyr* (1828) he responded to the model of *Der Freischütz* and to the vampire obsession in literature and theatre. His greatest success was *Hans Heiling* (Berlin, 1833), which tells of an underworld spirit king who seeks the love of a mortal woman—a scenario reminiscent of E. T. A. Hoffmann's opera *Undine* (1813). Both operas explore the confrontation between human and supernatural worlds so favoured by the Romantics. Albert Lortzing (1801–51) also found fame in the second quarter of the century as the leading representative of German comic opera. He authored both the music and text for popular Singspiels such as *Zar und Zimmermann* (Tsar and Carpenter, 1837) and the farcical *Der Wildschütz* (The Poacher, 1842).

Richard Wagner

During the 1830s a new figure emerged who would dwarf his predecessors in German opera. Richard Wagner (1813–83) worked in the theatre from the outset of his career and his understanding of contemporary trends shaped his creative development. His first opera, *Die Feen* (1834, premièred 1888) was influenced by Weber and Marschner, whereas his second, *Das Liebesverbot* (1836), owes more to Donizetti in its melodious treatment of

Shakespeare's *Measure for Measure*. Wagner never lacked self-belief, and he determined that recognition in Paris would benefit both himself and the world at large. When this did not materialise he never forgave the French, but his third opera, *Rienzi* (1840, premièred Dresden 1842), responded to Parisian grand opera and marked a real advance. He resolved to rescue opera from tired traditions, 'not only to imitate but to surpass all that had gone before'.

Wagner introduced *Der fliegende Holländer* (The Flying Dutchman) at Dresden in January 1843, shortly before taking up a court appointment there as second *Kapellmeister*. This opera was Wagner's first to explore the theme of redemption through selfless love. His next two operas took inspiration from Germanic legend to examine conflicts between spiritual and carnal desires: *Tannhäuser* (1845) and *Lohengrin* (1848, premièred Weimar, 1850). Wagner possessed a literary gift and wrote his own libretti, first of all in prose, then in verse, in order to manage a close relationship between music and text.

In his developing style he sought to break down the divisions that existed within conventional opera—divisions in formal structure, in vocal and instrumental roles, and even in the exigencies of staging. *Lohengrin* went some way towards achieving this ambition, with narrative cohesion enhanced by fluid transitions between recitative, aria, duets and chorus, creating an effect that harked back to early 17th-century opera. With bold and assured orchestration, Wagner wields enormous power in his climaxes, as in the spectacular close of Act I, where the victorious unnamed Knight of the Grail (Lohengrin, Parsifal's son) spares the life of the defeated Telramund. It is in the subtleties of texture, however, that the composer's musical imagination takes flight. The best example is the music of the prelude, which opens with the violins split into four parts, supported by oboes and flutes, above which harmonics produced by four solo violins complete a delicate, glistening texture, representative of an angelic host bearing the Holy Grail. Celestial harmony has never been bettered. Compositionally the prelude is remarkable for the fact that there is no recurring melodic theme and no strict repetition; the musical material undergoes constant development. This process reflects an organic unity that pervades the entire opera.

Lohengrin

Following precedents laid down by Spohr and Weber, among others, Wagner's operas of the 1840s revealed a growing preoccupation with the recurring signifying theme, or 'leitmotif', which was to become a defining feature of his style (see *Chapter 6*). In the meantime, the composer's career at Dresden came to an abrupt halt when he became embroiled in the Revolutionary fervour that swept Europe in 1848. Siding with the insurrectionists and with a price on his head, he was compelled to flee in 1849. Reaching Switzerland on a fake passport, Wagner began 11 years of exile.

Chronology
1800–1849

Beethoven composes his Violin Sonatas in A minor Op. 23 and F major (*Spring*) Op. 24.

Carl Czerny, aged nine, makes his public début with Mozart's Piano Concerto in C minor (K. 491), at the Augarten hall, Vienna.

16 January
Cherubini's *Les deux journées* (The Two Days) is first staged at the Théâtre Feydeau in Paris. Set in 1647 at the time of the Fronde, the opera alludes to a heroic rescue story from the recent Reign of Terror. Cherubini (left) receives enormous praise for the work—**Beethoven** regards him as the greatest opera composer of the day.

February Haydn publishes his oratorio *The Creation*, selling it by subscription across Europe. The initial list of 400 names includes the Austrian Empress Maria Theresa, King George III and the Prince of Wales.

2 April Beethoven presents a concert for his own benefit at Vienna's Burgtheater, with reasonable success. The programme includes a revised version of the Piano Concerto No. 1 in C major (1795) and the premières of his First Symphony and the Septet (Op. 20). Works by **Mozart** and **Haydn** are also performed.

Late spring Beethoven tackles the virtuoso **Daniel Steibelt** in a piano improvisation duel at the palace of Prince Lobkowitz in Vienna. Steibelt goes first, performing thunderous bass passages and dazzling the audience with his exemplary technique. Next up, Beethoven grabs the cello part of a chamber composition by Steibelt as he makes his way to the piano. Turning it upside down, he bangs out the first four notes from the end of the piece. He proceeds to improvise on the theme, overtly mocking and trouncing his opponent in the process. Steibelt storms out of the room, never to set foot in Vienna again.

7 May Prolific Italian composer **Niccolò Piccinni** dies in Passy, outside Paris, aged 72.

September A Te Deum by **Haydn**, dedicated to Empress Maria Theresa, is performed in honour of Admiral Nelson (below) and Lady Hamilton who are visiting Prince Esterházy in Eisenstadt. Also performed is his *Missa in angustiis* (1798), which later gains the sobriquet *Nelson Mass*.

16 September **F-A Boieldieu** achieves his first major operatic success with the one-act *Le calife de Bagdad*, staged at the Opéra-Comique in Paris.

23 October Nicolas-Marie Dalayrac's most popular opera, *Maison à vendre*, is premièred at the Opéra-Comique in Paris.

24 November
The opera *Das Waldmädchen* (The Forest Maiden) by the 14-year-old **Carl Maria Weber** is introduced in Freiburg, Saxony. Virtually all of the music is lost (see 1802).

1800 US government moves to the new capital, Washington, D.C., and John Adams moves into the White House • Adams is defeated in US presidential elections; Thomas Jefferson (Republican) wins Presidency after a tied vote with Aaron Burr • British parliament passes an Act of Union creating the United Kingdom of Great Britain and Ireland • Napoleon re-conquers Italy: an Austrian army is defeated at Hohenlinden; French troops advance on Vienna • Eli Whitney (US) designs muskets with inter-changeable parts • Composer turned astronomer William Herschel (Ger/UK) discovers infra-red solar rays • Alessandro Volta (It) invents the electric battery • British Royal College of Surgeons is founded • Maria Edgeworth (Ire): novel *Castle Rackrent*

Beethoven's Six String Quartets Op. 18 and Piano Concerto No. 1 are published in Vienna, while his First Symphony and Piano Concerto No. 2 are published in Leipzig. This year Beethoven pens his most famous piano piece, the *Moonlight* Sonata, Op. 27 No. 2, dedicated to his pupil Countess Guicciardi.

The 19-year-old Irish composer **John Field**, apprentice to Clementi & Co. in London, publishes his three Piano Sonatas Op. 1 through his employer's firm.

Rodolphe Kreutzer publishes his first two (of 19) violin concertos, in Paris.

Viotti returns to London around this time (see 1798). He remains largely aloof from musical life and instead develops a career as a wine merchant.

11 January Domenico Cimarosa dies in Venice, aged 51. Rumours abound that he has been poisoned at the behest of Queen Marie Caroline of Naples. Three months later the Venetian government issues an official verdict stating that he died from an internal ailment.

17 February Méhul enjoys instant and durable success with his Italianate comedy *L'irato* (The Angry Man), a so-called 'comédie-parade', at the Opéra-Comique, Paris.

28 March With incidental music by **Beethoven**, the ballet *Die Geschöpfe des Prometheus* (The Creatures of Prometheus) receives the first of 22 performances at the Burgtheater in Vienna. Beethoven will recycle thematic material from the finale in his Piano Variations Op. 35 (1802) and in the finale of the *Eroica* Symphony (1803).

24 April Haydn's oratorio *The Seasons* (completed 1800), on words by **Baron Gottfried van Swieten** after a poem by James Thomson, is given a successful private première at the Schwarzenberg Palace. Public interest in the work is modest, with less than a full house at its launch the following month. Haydn later remarks that *The Seasons* lacked the inspiration of *The Creation* due to its earthly subject matter. In time it nevertheless becomes one of his most popular pieces.

Title page of Haydn's oratorio *Die Jahreszeiten* (The Seasons)

I have been avoiding all social functions simply because I feel unable to tell people: I am deaf. If I belonged to any other profession, it would not be so bad.

29 June Beethoven, aged 30, writes for the first time about his deafness, to his friend Franz Wegler.

13 September Haydn directs his *Schöpfungsmesse* (Creation Mass) at Eisenstadt.

23 October German stage composer **Albert Lortzing** is born in Berlin.

26 October Clementi publishes his *Introduction to the Art of Playing on the piano forte*, in London.

3 November Italian opera composer **Vincenzo Bellini** is born in Catania, Sicily.

9 November German instrumental composer **Carl Stamitz** dies in Jena, aged 56.

1801 Thomas Jefferson is inaugurated as 3rd President of the USA • Austria and France sign the Peace of Luneville; France gains large territories including much of Italy • Concordat is signed between France and the Pope, Pius VII • Tsar Paul I of Russia is assassinated and succeeded by his son Aleksandr I • Chemist John Dalton (Eng) formulates his law of gas • Astronomer Giuseppe Piazzi (It) discovers Ceres, the first known asteroid • Napoleon founds the Bank of France • Henry Fuseli (Switz/UK) paints *Silence* • J. M. W. Turner (Eng) paints *Calais Pier* • Jacques-Louis David (Fr) paints *Napoleon at the Saint-Bernard Pass*

The Singakademie is founded in Leipzig.

Beethoven completes his Second Symphony and the Three Violin Sonatas, Op. 30.

Clementi tours Europe with his pupil **John Field** to advertise and demonstrate his new 'Clementi' pianos, and obtain publishing rights of new works.

Musician and musicologist **J. N. Forkel** publishes his influential biography of J. S. Bach.

Czech composer **Franz Krommer** writes his Concerto for Two Clarinets in E flat major (Op. 35). He currently serves as *Kapellmeister* to Duke Ignaz Fuchs in Vienna.

Pleyel begins the publication of the first pocket scores, issuing **Haydn** symphonies and string quartets.

Around this time the 16-year-old **Weber** destroys most of his adolescent compositions, so to restart his career with a clean sheet.

April Paisiello moves to Paris at the behest of Napoleon. Three months later he is instated as Napoleon's private *maître de chapelle*, a position he will hold for just under two years.

14 April Méhul (left) presents his mass *Domine, salvum fac Rempublicam* (O Lord make safe the Republic), for two choirs and two orchestras, in Paris.

Commissioned by Napoleon Bonaparte, the work follows the signing of the Concordat (1801), which has re-established Catholicism as the state religion in France.

8 September Haydn directs the first performance of his final large-scale work, the *Harmoniemesse*, at Eisenstadt. Afterwards he dines at Prince Esterházy's table, receiving a toast for his work and service. Haydn, aged 70, now officially retires, stepping down from his duties as *Kapellmeister*.

October While staying in the town of Heiligenstadt, **Beethoven** writes his famous 'Heiligenstadt Testament' (left), a letter and will to his brothers (together with the rest of humanity) about the despair and suicidal thoughts he experiences with the loss of his hearing. The document will be found 25 years later, shortly after Beethoven's death.

... I would have been at the point of ending my life. The only thing that held me back was my art. It seemed impossible to leave the world until I had produced all the works that I felt the urge to compose.

Extract from **Beethoven**'s *Heiligenstadt Testament*.

End of year Beethoven begins work on the oratorio *Christ on the Mount of Olives* Op. 85. The narrative of the work—Christ's undeserved suffering, his inner turmoil over his impending sacrifice and his subsequent ascendancy—resonates with Beethoven as he works on his first major composition post-*Heiligenstadt*.

1802 The Treaty of Amiens between Britain and France brings temporary peace to Europe • Napoleon makes himself First Consul of France for life, with the right to appoint his successor • A new French constitution reduces the powers of legislative bodies • Napoleon creates the Legion of Honour • Health and Morals of Apprentices Act in Britain aims at improving standards for young factory workers • Johann Ritter (Ger) builds first electrochemical cell • William Cobbett (Eng) founds *The Political Register* weekly paper • François Gérard (Fr) paints *Madame Récamier* • Madame de Staël (Fr): first novel, *Delphine* • William Paley (Eng): *Natural Theology*

Boieldieu moves from Paris to St Petersburg, working for the next eight years as director of French Opera at the court of Alexander I of Russia.

The American composer **Samuel Holyoke** publishes his *Columbian Repository of Sacred Harmony* in Exeter, New Hampshire.

Bohemian-born composer **Anton Reicha** issues his *36 Fugues for piano*, in Vienna. This folk-inspired collection, exploring polyrhythms and unconventional tonal organisation, is dedicated to **Haydn**.

Nineteen-year-old **Louis Spohr** completes his Violin Concerto No. 1, published this year as his Op. 1. He will write 14 further violin concertos over the next 40 years.

March In Augsburg the 16-year-old **Weber** introduces his two-act opera *Peter Schmoll*, composed under the supervision of his teacher, **Michael Haydn**.

29 March Paisiello's *Proserpine* struggles at the Paris Opéra.

5 April Beethoven premières his Second Symphony, Third Piano Concerto and the oratorio *Christ on the Mount of Olives* (see also 1802) at the Theater an der Wien. The First Symphony is also included in the programme.

24 May Beethoven introduces his commanding Violin Sonata No. 9 in A major (Op. 47) with the West Indian-Polish violinist **George Bridgetower** (right). In time the two men fall out and Beethoven dedicates the piece instead to **Rodolphe Kreutzer**. The French violinist will never play the *Kreutzer* Sonata in public as he deems it 'outrageously unintelligible'.

Summer Beethoven begins work on his Third Symphony (*Eroica*), which he plans to dedicate to Napoleon. Unprecedented in scale, the symphony will explore the universal qualities of heroism in the face of adversity. It will also embody Beethoven's determination to battle on despite the crushing reality of his encroaching deafness.

24 July French stage composer **Adolphe Adam** is born in Paris.

September Weber begins studies with **Georg Vogler** in Vienna. Vogler exploits the teenager, insisting that he prepares a vocal score of his current operatic commission, *Samori*, before he receives any composition tuition—a process that occupies Weber for the next nine months.

17 September Remembered primarily for his role in completing Mozart's Requiem, **Franz X. Süssmayr** dies in Vienna, aged about 37.

4 October Michael Haydn's *St Francis Mass* is likely first performed on this day, in Vienna.

8 December Hummel completes his popular Trumpet Concerto in E major for **Anton Weidinger**, now a member of the Esterházy orchestra (see also 1796). Hummel's unusual choice of key (for the trumpet) has been inspired by the chromatic capability of Weidinger's keyed instrument, although publishers later issue the concerto in the easier key of E flat.

11 December French composer **Hector Berlioz** is born in La Côte-Saint-André, Isère.

1803 The Louisiana Purchase: USA buys Louisiana Territory, including New Orleans, from France for 80 million francs • Napoleon gives Switzerland a new constitution and establishes a federal republic of 19 cantons • Britain embargoes French and Dutch ships in British ports • War is renewed between Britain and France over French interference in Switzerland and Italy • Britain captures the West Indian islands of St Lucia and Tobago, and Dutch Guiana • Irish nationalist Robert Emmet leads an abortive rebellion against British rule in Ireland; is captured and hanged • Benjamin West (US) paints *Christ Healing the Sick* • Jean Baptiste Say (Fr): *Treatise on Political Economy*

Beethoven (below) completes one of his greatest piano works, the *Waldstein* Sonata (dedicated to his patron Count Waldstein), and also the Triple Concerto for Violin, Cello and Piano.

The 12-year-old **Gioachino Rossini** completes some of his first compositions with six *Sonate a quattro* for string ensemble.

March Composer-pianist **John Field**, aged 21, gives his first public performance at the St Petersburg Philharmonic Society. Field, a Russian resident since late 1802, will remain based in the country for nearly 30 years.

14 March Composer **Johann Strauss** (**the Elder**) is born in Vienna.

1 April Hummel becomes *Konzertmeister* to Prince Nikolaus Esterházy. In effect he assumes the full responsibilities of *Kapellmeister*, although the retired **Haydn** still holds the title.

May In a turnaround of republican ideals, Napoleon proclaims himself Emperor of France. **Beethoven**, on hearing this news, flies into a rage and scratches out the name 'Bonaparte' on the title page of his Third Symphony. Napoleon is crowned in December.

1 June Russian composer **Mikhail Ivanovich Glinka** is born in Novospasskoye (later renamed Glinka) in the Smolensk district.

11 June Weber arrives in Breslau to take up the post of theatre conductor, secured thanks to a

recommendation from his teacher, **Vogler**. The 17-year-old immediately instigates bold reforms, changing the orchestra's seating plan (bringing the strings to the front), sacking useless players and throwing out unworthy operas. He will hold the position in the Silesian town for two years in the face of stiff opposition.

10 July Jean-François Le Sueur, Napoleon's newly-appointed *maître de chapelle*, triumphs with his new opera *Ossian, ou Les bardes* at the Paris Opéra.

August Beethoven's Third Symphony (*Eroica*) is premièred privately at the palace of Prince Lobkowitz in Vienna. Ironically, the symphony is now dedicated to the prince himself, having previously been dedicated to Napoleon who had, until May of this year, personified the republican spirit and rejection of the *ancien régime*. (See also 1805.)

Summer Paisiello departs Paris (and the service of Napoleon) for Naples.

18 September Muzio Clementi, aged 52, marries Caroline Lehmann, daughter of the director of the Berlin Opera, aged 19. He loses her following childbirth a year later.

3 October Ferdinando Paer's opera *Leonora, ossia L'amore conjugale* (Leonora, or Conjugal Love) generates great excitement at the Dresden Hoftheater.

10 November Salieri's final opera, *Die Neger* (The Negroes), fails to arouse much interest at the Theater An der Wien (Vienna).

1804 US statesman Alexander Hamilton is killed in a pistol duel with Vice-President Aaron Burr • Holy Roman Emperor Franz II assumes the title of Austrian Emperor • Spain declares war on Britain • Austria and Russia support Ottoman Empire against France • The French Empire is proclaimed; Napoleon crowns himself emperor at a ceremony conducted by Pope Pius VII • Richard Trevithick (Eng) launches the world's first load-hauling, steam railway locomotive • Chemist Friedrich Sertürner (Ger) isolates morphine from opium poppy resin • The British and Foreign Bible Society is founded • William Blake (Eng): poem *Jerusalem* • Friedrich Schiller (Ger): *William Tell*

The Concert Spirituel is revived in Paris, 15 years after its initial closure.

Beethoven completes his capricious and impassioned Piano Sonata No. 23 in F minor, Op. 57. Some 30 years later the Hamburg publisher Cranz will give the piece the fitting appellation *Appassionata*.

Cherubini composes *Chant sur la mort de Haydn* for soprano, two tenors and orchestra, having heard that the most famous composer of the age has just died. **Haydn** survives the work by four years.

Paganini, aged 22, performs and teaches at court in Lucca, serving Napoleon's sister, Elisa, and her husband, Prince Felice Baciocchi. Around this time he begins writing his 24 Caprices, Op. 1. High in compositional merit, the influential collection of studies represents Paganini's exhaustive treasury of violin technique. He is very likely the only violinist alive who can play it as intended.

Gaspare Spontini (left) becomes *compositeur particulier de la chambre* to Empress Josephine in Paris. By the end of the year he completes the first draft of what will be his most successful opera: *La vestale*.

7 April Beethoven conducts the public première of his groundbreaking Third Symphony, *Eroica*, at the Theater an der Wien. Twice as long as the average symphony of the period, the work even challenges Beethoven's ardent admirers. Its reception irritates the composer:

The audience and Herr van Beethoven, who himself conducted, were not happy with each other on that evening. The audience thought the symphony too weighty, too long, and Beethoven himself too rude, as he did not give even a nod to acknowledge the applauding part of the audience. Beethoven, however, felt that the applause was far from sufficient.

Der Freimüthige, on **Beethoven**'s Symphony No. 3, Berlin, 26 April.

May Joseph Wölfl arrives in England where he will remain until his death in 1812. During this time he builds on his continental reputation as a virtuoso pianist and composer, becoming very popular with the London public.

28 May Composer and cellist **Luigi Boccherini** dies of tuberculosis in Madrid, aged 62. He is remembered chiefly for his string quintets (with second cello)—the minuet from Op. 11 No. 5 especially.

26 July Mayr and librettist **Gaetano Rossi** enjoy success with *L'amour conjugal* (Conjugal Love) at Padua's Teatro Nuovo. Their one-act opera is based on **J. N. Bouilly**'s libretto *Léonore, ou L'amour conjugal*.

20 November Following the success of **Paer** (1804) and **Mayr** (above), **Beethoven** introduces the first version of his three-act rescue opera *Fidelio, or Conjugal Love*, after **J. N. Bouilly**'s popular libretto (1798). The production unhappily coincides with the early stages of the first French occupation of Vienna. The response is unenthusiastic, from an audience largely consisting of soldiers in a half-empty Theater an der Wien.

1805 US war (since 1801) with Barbary States ends • The Third Coalition of Britain and Russia against France is formed; Austria joins later • Napoleon is crowned King of Italy • At Battle of Trafalgar a British fleet under Horatio Nelson destroys French and Spanish fleets; Nelson is killed in action • Battle of Austerlitz: French win decisive victory against Austro-Russian forces • Ottoman commander Muhammad Ali becomes governor of Egypt • British Royal Navy officer Francis Beaufort devises his Beaufort scale of wind speed • Francisco Goya (Sp) paints *Doña Isabel Cobos de Porcal* • William Wordsworth (Eng): poem *Ode to Duty* • Walter Scott (Scot): poem *Lay of the Last Minstrel*

Beethoven completes his three ambitious *Razumovsky* String Quartets (Op. 59), dedicated to the Russian ambassador to Vienna. The violinist Felix Radicati, offering advice on fingering, tells Beethoven that the pieces are unmusical, but the composer rejoins: 'They are not for you, but for a later age.' This year Beethoven composes his Fourth Symphony and Fourth Piano Concerto.

Gaetano Donizetti, aged eight, is among the first pupils of the Lezioni Caritatevoli di Musica, a music school in Bergamo founded by the opera composer **Simon Mayr**.

Weber, aged 19, accidentally drinks engraving acid from a wine bottle. He is ill for two months and ruins his singing voice for life. When he returns to work at the theatre in Breslau he finds that many of his recent reforms have been revoked. He resigns immediately.

27 January Prodigious Spanish composer **Juan Cristostomo Arriaga** is born in Bilbao.

29 March A revised and shortened two-act version of **Beethoven**'s opera *Fidelio* is staged with a new overture, *Leonore No. 3*, at the Theater an der Wien. The opera fairs better than the production of the previous year, but Beethoven soon withdraws it, having fallen out with the theatre director (Baron von Braun) over box-office shares.

April Rossini, aged 14, begins studies at the Liceo Musicale in Bologna where he is tutored in singing, piano, cello and counterpoint.

17 May Scored without violins, **Méhul**'s opera *Uthal* premières at the Opéra-Comique, Paris.

10 August Composer **Michael Haydn**, younger brother of **Joseph**, dies in Salzburg aged 68.

Autumn–Winter Weber sojourns with Duke Eugen of Württemberg-Öls as his honorary *Musik-Intendant*. During his stay he begins work on his two symphonies, both in C major, for the duke's court orchestra, which he completes early the following year.

10 October Prince Louis Ferdinand of Prussia is killed at the battle of Saalfeld (below). **Dussek**

later writes the piano sonata *Elégie harmonique sur la mort du Prince Louis Ferdinand de Prusse*, having served the prince as *Kapellmeister* for the last two years.

23 December Franz Clement, orchestral leader at the Theater an der Wien, gives the first performance of **Beethoven**'s epic Violin Concerto in D major, completed only a few hours beforehand. The concert interval falls between the first and second movements of the concerto, at which point Clement performs solo variations with his violin turned upside down. The entertainment value of the event wins over the public, although the concerto suffers due to lack of rehearsal time.

1806 British Prime Minister William Pitt dies • Napoleon makes his brothers kings: Joseph rules Naples and Louis rules Holland • Britain declares war on Prussia • Napoleon dominates most of Germany • Prussia declares war on France • Emperor Franz II formally ends the Holy Roman Empire • Napoleon's troops defeat the Prussians at Jena and Auerstadt, and occupy Berlin • Napoleon launches the Continental System; blocking all continental European ports to British shipping • Scientist Humphry Davy (Eng) demonstrates the existence of potassium, sodium and chlorine • Ernst Moritz Arndt (Ger): poem *Spirit of the Age*

Paganini composes his *Napoléon* sonata, scored for violin and orchestra, for the Emperor's name day. The entire violin part is written for the G string alone, tuned up a minor third.

Bohemian composer **Václav Tomášek** writes his first Six Piano Eclogues, Op. 35, important piano miniatures in the evolution of the Romantic character-piece.

17 February Méhul's biblical opera *Joseph* is performed for the first time at the Opéra-Comique, Paris. It becomes one of his most respected stage works.

March Beethoven conducts the private premières of his Fourth Symphony and the *Coriolan* Overture at the palace of Prince Lobkowitz. It is possible that the programme also includes the first performance of his Fourth Piano Concerto.

April Beethoven agrees to sell to **Clementi** the British copyright of several recent works: his Fourth Symphony, String Quartets Op. 59, *Coriolan* Overture, Piano Concerto No. 4 and Violin Concerto, all for £200.

August Weber is appointed general secretary to Duke Ludwig Friedrich Alexander in Stuttgart. Although his musical duties are minimal—simply teaching the duke's children—he will strike up a stimulating friendship with **Franz Danzi**, *Kapellmeister* to the King of Württemberg.

Opening bars of Beethoven's 5th Symphony

September Dussek moves to Paris where he becomes *maître du chapelle* to Talleyrand, the French foreign minister.

13 September Beethoven's Mass in C, commissioned by Prince Esterházy, is first performed at Eisenstadt. Unfortunately the prince is less than happy with the work, allegedly remarking to the composer: 'But, my dear Beethoven, what is this that you have done?' Overhearing, *Konzertmeister* **Hummel** breaks into a titter. Beethoven storms out of the room in a huff.

Autumn Beethoven resumes work on his Fifth Symphony, begun some three years previously. Anton Schindler will famously relate of the opening motif: *'Thus fate knocks at the door.'* **Czerny**, on the other hand, thinks that the opening notes derive from the chirping of a yellowhammer. Posterity favours Schindler. Beethoven's written assertion that he 'will seize fate by the throat' (in relation to his deteriorating hearing) is cathartically explored in the work: torment and struggle meet with hope and transcendence, culminating in final triumph.

15 December Spontini's opera *La vestale* (The Vestal Virgin) triumphs at the Paris Opéra. The three-act *tragédie lyrique* becomes the composer's greatest success, remaining in the Opéra's repertory for many years and enjoying popularity across Europe.

1807 Napoleon's troops defeat the Russians and Prussians at Friedland • Treaty of Tilsit: Russia recognises French conquests and agrees to back France against Britain if the British do not make peace; the size of Prussia is reduced by nearly one-half • The kingdom of Westphalia is created, ruled by Napoleon's brother Jerome • French forces invade Portugal; Portugal's royal family flees to Brazil • Britain abolishes the slave trade in its colonies; now illegal to ferry slaves on British ships • Jacques-Louis David (Fr) paints *The Coronation of Napoleon* • Lord Byron (Eng): *Hours of Idleness* • William Wordsworth (Eng): *Ode on Intimations of Immortality*

Napoleon's son-in-law, Eugène de Beauharnais, establishes the Milan Conservatory, while in the same city Giovanni Ricordi sets up the Ricordi publishing firm.

Beethoven composes his lyrical Cello Sonata No. 3 in A major, Op. 69. It bears the enigmatic title 'Amid Tears and Sorrow'.

Méhul composes his Symphony No. 1 in G minor. This and three subsequent symphonies composed over the next two years will establish Méhul as the leading French symphonist of the day.

The first of **Thomas Moore**'s *Irish Melodies* are published in London.

In Vienna **Schubert**, aged 11, secures a place in the Hofkapelle choir and begins his studies at the Imperial City College.

Catalan composer and guitarist **Fernando Sor** fights against the invading French and boosts troop morale with his patriotic songs *Venid, vencedores* and *Vivir en cadenas*. Two years later he will be an administrator for the occupying French; five years later he will follow the retreating French army to

Paris, compelled to leave Spain as a collaborator, never to return.

27 March Confined to a chair, **Haydn** is greeted with trumpets and applause as he is carried into Vienna's university hall for a 76th birthday celebration concert (below). He sits beside the Austrian Empress, as **Salieri** conducts *The Creation* before an audience of friends, admirers and nobility. During the interval, **Beethoven** joins other prominent Viennese to pay their respects to the great maestro. The excitement of the event proves too much for Haydn, who makes his leave before the second half, blessing the audience on his way out. It is the composer's final public appearance.

Summer Beethoven composes his *Pastoral* (Sixth) Symphony while staying in Heiligenstadt. Following soon after the Herculean Fifth Symphony, the Sixth is his reverent hymn to nature. The idyllic moods within the loosely programmatic work perhaps justify his later claim, 'No one can love the country as I do', and even, 'I love a tree more than a man'. Beethoven dedicates the work, along with the Fifth Symphony, to two of his most important patrons, Prince Lobkowitz and Count Razumovsky.

22 December Beethoven stages a mammoth four-hour long concert in freezing conditions at the Theater an der Wien, premièring his Fifth and Sixth Symphonies, and the Choral Fantasia. The programme also includes three movements from the Mass in C, the aria 'Ah perfido!', piano improvisations, and the first public performance of the Fourth Piano Concerto.

1808 Pope Pius VII refuses to recognise the kingdom of Naples • French troops occupy Rome and Madrid: popular revolt forces abdication of Charles IV of Spain; Napoleon forces abdication of Charles's successor, his son Ferdinand VII • Joseph Bonaparte is made King of Spain • The Spaniards begin a general resistance against Napoleon; British troops under Arthur Wellesley land in Portugal; the Peninsular War begins • The French withdraw troops from Portugal • Russia conquers Finland • Secretary of state James Madison is elected president of the USA • Jean Auguste Ingres (Fr) paints *La Grande baigneuse* • Johann Wolfgang Goethe (Ger): *Faust*, Part I

Beethoven accepts an offer of 4,000 florins per annum from Archduke Rudolph, Prince Lobkowitz and Prince Kinsky on the simple condition that he stays in Vienna. This comes as a counter-offer to the post of *Kapellmeister* to King Jérôme Bonaparte (Napoleon's brother) in Kassel.

Rossini completes his first opera, *Demetrio e Polibio*, around this time.

Beethoven composes his Fifth Piano Concerto (later published as the *Emperor*) amidst the second French invasion of Vienna. He also begins to write the Piano Sonata No. 26, *Das Lebewohl*, for his departing (fleeing) pupil and patron Archduke Rudolph.

3 February Composer **Felix Mendelssohn** (later **Felix Jakob Ludwig Mendelssohn-Bartholdy**) is born in Hamburg.

7 March **Johann Albrechtsberger** dies in Vienna aged 73. A respected composer and organist, he is remembered chiefly as a composition teacher to **Beethoven**, whom he regarded as an unpromising pupil.

10/11 May **Haydn** and **Beethoven** remain in Vienna in the face of the French bombardment (right). Haydn calms his servants, 'Don't be afraid, children; where Haydn is, no harm can reach you!' Beethoven, less optimistically (or possibly unable to make it to Haydn's house), finds refuge in his brother Caspar's cellar, covering his ears with pillows so to protect what is left of his hearing.

31 May **Joseph Haydn** dies in Vienna aged 77. Mozart's Requiem is performed at a memorial service in Vienna's Schottenkirche the following month.

Summer **Beethoven** completes his String Quartet Op. 74 (*Harp*).

Autumn Georg Griesinger serialises his biographical notes on the life of Joseph Haydn in the *Allgemeine musikalishce Zeitung*. They are published in book form the following year.

18 September The Covent Garden Theatre re-opens, having burnt down the previous year. The exorbitant costs of rebuilding result in a ticket hike from six to seven shillings. Incensed members of the public riot in protest, and the theatre management responds by hiring bouncers. Two months later the management backs down, issuing an apology and reducing its prices.

28 November **Spontini** points the way towards *grand opéra* with *Fernand Cortez*, premièred at the Paris Opéra. Napoleon has commissioned the opera for propaganda purposes, hoping that his countrymen will identify his invasion of Spain with Cortez's conquest of Mexico. An immense cast, live horses and a thrilling on-stage cavalry charge arouse great excitement.

1809 Non-Intercourse Act in USA bans commerce with France and Britain • British troops land in north-west Spain but retreat to Corunna • British forces defeat the French at Oporto and Talavera • French forces overrun Andalusia, Spain • Austria declares war on France; the French take Vienna and defeat the Austrians at Wagram • By the Peace of Schönbrunn, Austria loses territories and joins Napoleon's Continental System • Emperor Napoleon I (Fr) is excommunicated for annexing Papal States and seizing Pope Pius VII • John Constable (Eng) paints *Malvern Hall* • Lord Byron (Eng): *English Bards and Scotch Reviewers*

Johann Baptist Cramer publishes his second set of enduring *Studio per il pianoforte*.

The German writer and composer **E. T. A. Hoffmann** reviews **Beethoven**'s Fifth Symphony in Leipzig's *Allgemeine musikalische Zeitung* (General Music Journal), combining detailed analytical observations, philosophical considerations and his own personal response. It is a watershed in music criticism.

Méhul composes his Symphony No. 4 in E major. It is his final and most innovative symphony, with bold exposed scoring for the cellos in the second (Andante) movement, and thematic development between the third and fourth movements. Plans for two further symphonies never materialise.

9 February Weber and his father are arrested for embezzling royal funds and evading military service. They are further charged, without any proof, of stealing. Weber is imprisoned for several days, although the charges of theft are quickly dropped. During this time he manages to complete his opera *Silvana*. On release the Webers are banished from Württemberg for life; for a short while they relocate to Mannheim.

22 February Maltese-French composer **Nicolas Isouard** triumphs with the fairy-tale opera *Cendrillon* (Cinderella) at the Opéra-Comique in Paris.

1 March Polish composer and pianist **Frédéric Chopin** is born in Żelazowa Wola, near Warsaw.

E. T. A. Hoffmann: self portrait

27 April Beethoven signs off on his bagatelle 'WoO. 59' with the dedication 'Für Therese'. Years later, the publisher Ludwig Nohl misreads this and issues the piece as *Für Elise*. The 'Therese' in question is probably Therese Malfatti, to whom Beethoven proposes marriage, unsuccessfully.

8 June Robert Schumann, son of a bookseller and publisher, is born in Zwickau, Saxony.

15 June Beethoven's overture and incidental music to **Goethe**'s play *Egmont* is first heard at Vienna's Burgtheater.

22 June Virtuoso clarinettist **Simon Hermstedt** premières **Spohr**'s festive Clarinet Concerto No. 2 in E flat, in Frankenhausen.

16 September Weber's opera *Silvana* premières in Frankfurt without much success. This year also marks the composer's Piano Concerto No. 1 in C major.

October Beethoven composes the String Quartet in F minor (*Quartet Serioso*), Op. 95. Anticipating that audiences will find the work too taxing, he writes in a letter, 'The quartet is written for a small circle of connoisseurs and is never to be performed in public'. His wishes are observed for four years.

3 November Aged 18, **Rossini** witnesses his first staged opera, *La cambiale di matrimonio* (The Matrimonial Market), successfully introduced at the San Moisè Theatre in Venice.

1810 Spain's South American colonies move towards independence: Simón Bolívar emerges as leader in Venezuelan uprising; revolts follow in Mexico, New Granada and Chile • In Portugal, the French take Ciudad Rodrigo, but British troops hold the Line of Torres Vedras, forcing the French army to withdraw • British forces occupy the French colonies of Mauritius, Seychelles and Guadaloupe • Napoleon I orders the sale of all seized US vessels • Napoleon annexes the Netherlands • Francisco Goya (Sp) paints *Majas on a balcony* • William Blake (Eng) completes his *Great Red Dragon* paintings • Goethe (Ger): *Theory of Colour* • Walter Scott (Scot): poem *Lady of the Lake*

1811

Swedish-Finnish composer **Bernhard Crusell** has his strikingly melodious Clarinet Concerto No. 1 in E flat published in Leipzig. Inspired throughout, the work is one of the finest Classical-era pieces of its kind.

Stepan Degtyaryov composes the first Russian patriotic oratorio, *Minin and Pozharsky, or The Liberation of Moscow*, based on the revolt against the Poles in the early 17th century.

Musician **Vincent Novello** establishes the publishing house Novello & Co., in London.

Spohr brings out his conservative Symphony No. 1 in E flat major (Op. 20).

March Beethoven completes his finest piano trio, the *Archduke* Piano Trio in B-flat major (Op. 97), dedicated to his patron Archduke Rudolph (right).

March The Austrian national currency is massively devalued by a Finanz-Patent, owing to economic turmoil from the Napoleonic wars. The value of **Beethoven**'s 4,000 florin annuity (see 1809) is reduced to around 1,600 florins. Archduke Rudolph partially compensates for this loss through redemption bonds.

30 March Aged 14, **Schubert** composes his earliest surviving string quartets and earliest surviving song, *Hagars Klage*.

24 April Teaching begins at the Prague Conservatory.

May Hummel's contract with the Esterházy court as *Konzertmeister* is terminated. The composer returns to Vienna.

13 June Weber's dramatic Clarinet Concerto No. 1 in F minor is premièred in Munich. This year also sees the composition and first performance of his Clarinet Concerto No. 2 in E flat major, again in Munich. Both works have been composed for the virtuoso **Heinrich J. Baermann**.

Summer Beethoven composes incidental music to *König Stephan* (Op. 117) and *Die Ruinen von Athen* (Op. 113) while convalescing at the spa at Teplitz on doctor's orders. Returning to Vienna, he begins work on his Seventh Symphony.

6 July Having lost his first wife in childbirth, the 59-year-old **Clementi** marries Emma Gisborne (some 30 years his junior), in London. They will have four children together.

September Prince Lobkowitz, one of **Beethoven**'s annuity benefactors, is declared bankrupt.

22 October Composer, pianist and conductor **Franz Liszt** is born in Raiding, Hungary

26 October Rossini, aged 19, stages his two-act comic opera *L'equivoco stravagante* (The Curious Misunderstanding) at the Teatro del Corso in Bologna. Local censors deem the libretto offensive and demand the swift withdrawal of the work. Rossini follows up with the one-act melodrama *L'inganno felice* (The Happy Deception), which arouses excitement at the Teatro San Moisè in Venice, early next year.

28 November Friedrich Schneider gives the first performance of **Beethoven**'s monumental Fifth Piano Concerto (*Emperor*), at the Gewandhaus in Leipzig. It is the first time the composer has not premièred his own piano concerto, now too deaf to gauge dynamic subtleties or keep time with the orchestra. To ensure that his ideas are carried out to the letter, Beethoven has written out the piano part in full, with cadenza.

1811 In Britain, King George III's insanity results in the passing of a Regency Act: the Prince of Wales is made Prince Regent • In Portugal, British troops led by Lord Wellington defeat the French at Fuentes d'Onoro and Albuhera • Russian forces take Belgrade and defeat the Turks • Egyptian Viceroy Mehemet Ali has Mamelukes, the ruling dynasty, massacred

• Venezuela and Paraguay declare their independence from Spain • President James Madison (US) threatens war over Britain's maritime trade policy • Jane Austen (Eng): first novel, *Sense and Sensibility* • Goethe (Ger) begins writing *My Life, Poetry and Truth* • Friedrich de la Motte Fouqué (Ger): *Undine*

11 February Czerny gives the Vienna première of **Beethoven**'s Fifth Piano Concerto (see also 1811).

14 March Rossini's new two-act biblical opera *Ciro in Babilonia* (Cyrus in Babylon) struggles at the Teatro Comunale in Ferrara. For the audience its redeeming feature is the *aria del sorbetto*, notable because the entire piece is sung on one note: B flat. Rossini has written it so as it is the only note that the soprano Anna Saivelli can sing to his satisfaction. He later records, 'The piece gave much pleasure and was applauded, and my unitone singer was extremely delighted with her triumph'.

20 March Jan Ladislav Dussek, aged 52, dies of gout in Paris while in the service of Talleyrand. He is credited as the first pianist to play to the audience side on, instead of facing the orchestra.

21 April William Crotch's oratorio *Palestine*, his most successful work, is first performed in London.

May Beethoven completes his Seventh Symphony. He begins his Eighth Symphony in the autumn.

9 May Rossini's one-act farce *La scala di seta* (The Silken Ladder) is premièred at the Teatro San Moisè, Venice.

June Schubert begins counterpoint lessons with **Salieri**.

6 July In Teplitz **Beethoven** writes for the first time to his 'Immortal Beloved', an unnamed woman, but possibly the married aristocrat Antonie Brentano. In this and two subsequent letters he passionately laments the impossibility of their union. The letters are never sent.

19 July Beethoven and **Goethe** (below) meet at Teplitz. While both men have great admiration for each other, their personalities are somewhat at odds:

He is an utterly untamed personality. He may not be entirely wrong in thinking the world odious, but that attitude does not make it any more pleasant for himself or for others.

Goethe on Beethoven.

He enjoys the courtly air too much, more than is proper for a poet.

Beethoven on Goethe.

26 September Rossini triumphs with *La pietra del paragone* (The Touchstone) at La Scala, Milan. The comic opera enjoys 53 performances this season.

November The first Nocturnes by **John Field** (Nos. 1–3) are published in St Petersburg.

17 December Weber premières his Piano Concerto No. 2 in E flat major, in Gotha. In design his dazzling work betrays a clear debt to Beethoven's *Emperor* Piano Concerto (No. 5 in E flat major).

29 December Archduke Rudolph and **Pierre Rode** give the first performance of **Beethoven**'s contemplative Violin Sonata in G major, Op. 96, in Vienna.

1812 USA declares war on Britain • In Spain, British general Viscount Wellington's forces take Ciudad Rodrigo and Badajoz, defeat French at Salamanca, and enter Madrid • Emperor Napoleon I (Fr) leads an invasion of Russia: wins victory at Borodino, and enters Moscow, which is burned by Russians; French army meets disaster crossing Beresina River and begins a punishing retreat in bitter conditions • A conspiracy to overthrow Napoleon fails: he returns hurriedly to Paris • John Blenkinsop (Eng) constructs first commercially successful locomotive, Salamanca • Goya (Sp) paints *Lord Wellington* • The Grimm Brothers (Ger): *Fairy Tales* • Johann Wyss (Switz): *The Swiss Family Robinson*

The Philharmonic Society is founded in London for the promotion of contemporary music. **Clementi** is appointed to the board of directors.

Schubert, aged 16, composes his First Symphony (D. 82, in D). He drops his studies at the Imperial City College and attends a teacher training college instead.

Ludwig Spohr (right) becomes orchestral leader at the Theater an der Wien (Vienna) and composes his Nonet in F major and Singspiel *Faust*.

January Weber, while promoting his Piano Concerto No. 2 (1812) in Prague, accepts an impromptu offer of the position of opera director at the Estates Theatre. He remains there for three years.

6 February Rossini's *Tancredi* is staged at the Teatro La Fenice, Venice. With libretto by **Gaetano Rossi** after Voltaire's tragedy (revised with a happy ending), the *opera seria* triumphs and soon makes Rossini, 21 this month, famous throughout Europe.

14 February Russian composer **Alexander Dargomïzhsky** is born in Troitskoye, Tula province. He will not learn to speak until he is five.

22 May German opera composer **Wilhelm Richard Wagner** is born in Leipzig. His father, a police registrar, dies six months later.

22 May Rossini's two-act comic opera *L'italiana in Algeri* (The Italian Woman in Algiers) is premièred with great success at the Teatro San Benedetto, Venice.

Summer Johann Mälzel, inventor of the metronome, convinces **Beethoven** to compose *Wellington's Victory* for his panharmonicon: a brass-bellowing, wind-whistling, string-scraping musical machine. The piece is based on Wellington's recent victory over the French at Vittoria, Spain. Beethoven scores out a full orchestral version for a concert later this year.

20 August Author of some 100 quartets and more than 70 symphonies, **Johann Baptist Vanhal** dies in Vienna, aged 74.

24 September French composer **André Grétry** dies outside Montmorency, Seine-et-Oise, aged 72.

9/10 October Italian opera composer **Giuseppe Fortunino Francesco Verdi** is born in the village of Le Roncole, near Parma.

29 October Paganini, aged 31, transfixes his audience with mind-bending violin virtuosity as he makes his La Scala début in Milan.

28 November Mayr and the librettist **Felice Romani** captivate Naples with their tragic opera *Medea in Corinto*, presented at the Teatro San Carlo. The Spanish soprano **Isabella Colbran** (later Rossini's wife) creates the title role.

8 December Beethoven launches his Seventh Symphony, together with his bombastic *Wellington's Victory*, at a benefit concert for Austrian and Bavarian Soldiers wounded at the battle of Hanau. **Salieri**, **Hummel**, **Spohr**, **Meyerbeer**, **Moscheles** and **Dragonetti** are among the orchestral players, all giving their services for free. Enormously successful, the charity event is repeated four days later, and again on 2 January next year.

1813 War between Britain and USA continues • Prussia declares war on France • Russians occupy Hamburg and Dresden • British forces under Marquess of Wellington (UK) defeat French at Vittoria (Sp) and drive King Joseph from Spain; British troops enter France and besiege Bayonne • Napoleon is defeated by allied armies at Leipzig (Ger) • Confederation of the Rhine is dissolved • Popular risings drive French from Netherlands • Austrians invade France by way of Switzerland • Simón Bolivar becomes virtual dictator of independent Venezuela • J. M. W. Turner (Eng) paints *Frosty Morning* • Jane Austen (Eng): *Pride and Prejudice*

The Stalybridge Old Band, the world's first brass band, is formed in Lancashire.

Beethoven and **Mälzel** fall out over rights to *Wellington's Victory*, the inventor claiming paternity over the original conception and structure of the work. Beethoven files a lawsuit.

Spohr composes his Octet in E major.

27 February Beethoven's uplifting Eighth Symphony (1812) is premièred in a concert also featuring his now immensely popular *Wellington's Victory* and Seventh Symphony. The Eighth receives only polite applause.

11 April Beethoven introduces his *Archduke* Piano Trio (completed 1811). The Viennese audience probably does not appreciate the exceptional quality of the work, as the piano is out of tune and Beethoven is too deaf to notice.

6 May German teacher and composer **Georg Vogler** dies from a stroke in Darmstadt, aged 64.

23 May Beethoven revives *Fidelio* as Vienna prepares to host its momentous Congress. The revised rescue opera is now perceived less as a work stimulated by revolutionary idealism, as one that celebrates recent liberation from French occupation. First staged in 1805, *Fidelio* now triumphs, with 19 further performances throughout the year.

14 August Rossini's comic opera *Il turco in Italia* opens at La Scala, Milan.

14 September Francis Scott Key is inspired to write *The Star-Spangled Banner* whilst detained aboard a British frigate in Baltimore harbour, having seen the American flag flying over Fort McHenry following a British bombardment. Ironically, he adapts the tune from *To Anacreon in Heaven* by the English composer **John Stafford Smith**. It will become the national anthem of the United States in 1931.

19 October The 17-year-old **Schubert** completes his song-setting of Goethe's *Gretchen am Spinnrade* (Gretchen at the Spinning Wheel), one of the most advanced works ever composed by a teenager. This same month his Mass in F major is sung at the Lichtental parish church. Therese Grob, purportedly the one love of Schubert's life, sings the soprano part.

29 November Beethoven presents his topical and celebratory cantata *Der Glorreiche Augenblick* (The Glorious Moment) at a concert in the Redoutensaal, nearly two months into the Congress of Vienna. The programme includes *Wellington's Victory* and the Seventh Symphony—the latter referred to as 'a companion piece' by a reviewer at the *Wiener Zeitung*. The concert is repeated three days later.

The Congress of Vienna (1814–15). Attended by state representatives from across Europe, the Congress is convened to negotiate a peace settlement following the Napoleonic wars and resolve territorial disputes.

1814 Anglo-American War (of 1812): British land at Chesapeake Bay, defeat Americans at Bladensburg, occupy Washington and burn the Capitol; a British force is repulsed at Baltimore; Treaty of Ghent ends the war • French forces are defeated at Bar-sur-Aube and Laon; the British take Bordeaux; Allies enter Paris; Napoleon I abdicates and is exiled to Elba • Louis XVIII, brother of Louis XVI, becomes King of France • Congress of Vienna convened • Engineer George Stephenson (Eng) builds the first successful steam locomotive • Goya (Sp) paints *The Charge of the Mamelukes* and *3 May 1808* • Antonio Canova (It) sculpts *The Three Graces* • Jane Austen (Eng): *Mansfield Park*

Beethoven composes the piano Polonaise Op. 89 for the Empress of Russia, and his last two Cello Sonatas—C major and D major—Op. 102. This year also marks his final public performance, accompanying the tenor **Franz Wild**.

April–May Cherubini, in London, introduces the Overture in G and his one and only symphony (D major), both works commissioned by the Philharmonic Society.

Hummel (above) returns to public performance amid the celebratory atmosphere of the Congress of Vienna. He is quickly recognised as the city's leading piano virtuoso.

Ignaz Moscheles, aged 21, excites Vienna with his piano showpiece *La marche d'Alexandre*.

Schubert, now an 18-year-old schoolteacher, produces an early masterpiece with the brilliantly descriptive *Der Erlkönig* (The Erlking), for male voice and piano. Throughout this year he is remarkably prolific, composing over 140 songs, four *Singspiele* operas, two masses and the String Quartet in G minor. He also completes his Second Symphony (begun in December 1814) and composes his Third Symphony.

19 February Spohr introduces his Violin Concerto No. 7 in Vienna to great acclaim. This year he resigns as orchestral leader at the Theater an der Wien and begins a two-year tour of Europe.

6 May Paganini is imprisoned in Genoa, accused of abducting and impregnating Angiolina Cavanna (aged 17), with whom he had eloped the previous year but since deserted. The violin virtuoso is released nine days later, having agreed in writing to pay Angiolina's father 1,200 lire. It is a bluff—he has no intention of paying.

20 May Paganini issues Sig. Cavanna (see above) with a counter-suit, charging him with extortion. The composer gains credibility in the case the following month: Angiolina's baby is stillborn and evidence suggests that Paganini is not the father. He will be fined later, however, for breaching the terms of his signed agreement.

9 June As the Congress of Vienna comes to an official close, so does an 18-month period representing the height of **Beethoven**'s fame and success.

4 October Recently engaged to write for the theatres in Naples, **Rossini** presents his opera *Elisabetta, regina d'Inghilterra* at the Teatro San Carlo. Its overture, lifted from his opera *Aureliano in Palmira* (1813), will be used again for *The Barber of Seville*.

15 November Beethoven's brother Caspar dies of tuberculosis. His wife, Johanna, becomes joint guardian of her son Karl with Beethoven. Distrustful of Johanna, Beethoven begins a legal battle for sole guardianship of his nephew.

15 December Rossini is contracted to compose *The Barber of Seville* for a production in Rome. **Paisiello** gets wind of the commission and, fearing that his own *Barber* (1782) will be eclipsed, writes to a friend in Rome to ensure that the opera fails (see 1816).

1815 The Hundred Days: Napoleon I returns from Elba to France; Louis XVIII flees to Ghent; Britain, Austria, Russia and Prussia form a new alliance • Congress of Vienna brought to a close, having decided on future map of Europe • Napoleon's troops rout Prussians at Ligny, but are decisively defeated by Wellington's army at Waterloo; Napoleon abdicates again and is exiled to St Helena • Louis XVIII returns to throne of France • British Corn Law prohibits import of wheat below fixed price • Scientist Humphry Davy (Eng) invents miners' safety lamp • Tambora Volcano on Sumbawa Island (Indon) produces largest eruption in recorded history; tens of thousands die; world-wide weather patterns disrupted

Beethoven writes the first song cycle, *An die ferne Geliebte* (To the Distant Beloved), and the Piano Sonata in A major, Op. 101. His health, physical and emotional, is at low ebb and will remain so for several years, restricting his compositional output considerably.

Cherubini joins **Le Sueur** as joint superintendent of the royal chapel following the return of King Louis XVIII (1815). Controversially, Le Sueur had been serving Napoleon in this same post.

Hummel publishes his spirited Septet in D minor (Op. 74), nearly 40-minutes in duration and widely considered his greatest chamber achievement.

Paganini composes his spectacular Violin Concerto No. 1, Op. 6, promoting conquering virtuosity and the Romantic notion of the 'heroic soloist'.

Schubert and friends begin the first of the 'Schubertiad' musical gatherings. This year the composer completes his Fourth Symphony (*Tragic*) and writes his sprightly Fifth Symphony and song *Der Wanderer*.

19 January Beethoven is legally appointed sole guardian of his nephew Karl, whom he swiftly packs off to boarding school. Karl's mother will appeal against the court's decision (see 1818).

20 February Paisiello supporters severely mar the première of **Rossini**'s *Almaviva*—renamed *Il barbiere di Siviglia* (The Barber of Seville) later this year—at the Teatro Argentina in Rome. Despite the disruptions, instigated by Paisiello himself (see 1815), the comical masterpiece gains overwhelming support with

successive performances. Whilst not the most popular of Rossini's operas in its day, *The Barber* eventually becomes the most widely-loved *opera buffa* of all time.

21 March Abraham Mendelssohn has his children baptised into the Christian faith under the name **Mendelssohn-Bartholdy**.

5 June Giovanni Paisiello, Napoleon's favourite opera composer, dies in Naples, aged 76.

3 August Human and supernatural worlds collide in **E. T. A. Hoffmann**'s opera *Undine* (1814), first staged in Berlin.

1 September Spohr, on tour in Italy, is unable to attend the première of his Singspiel *Faust* (1813), introduced under **Weber**'s direction in Prague. The opera makes effective use of the 'reminiscence motif', which will later influence Weber in his writing of *Der Freischütz*. The libretto, by Joseph Carl Bernard, is based on the early Faust legends rather than Goethe's recent publication.

27 September Spohr 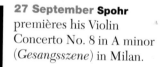 premières his Violin Concerto No. 8 in A minor (*Gesangsszene*) in Milan.

7 October Having resigned as director of the Estates Theatre, **Weber** leaves Prague and travels to Berlin. There he composes the *Grand duo concertant* (Op. 48) for clarinet and piano.

4 December *Otello* (Othello), an *opera seria* by **Rossini** (left), opens with considerable success at at the Teatro del Fondo in Naples.

1816 US administration introduces tariffs as a protection against dumping of British goods • Maria I of Portugal dies; is succeeded by her son, João VI, who prefers to remain in Brazil, which becomes an empire • United Provinces of Rio de la Plata (Arg) declare independence • Demands for parliamentary reform are made in Britain: violent demonstrations in London • James Monroe is elected President of the USA • Britain restores Java to the Netherlands • Réné Laennec (Fr) invents the stethoscope • Jane Austen (Eng): *Emma* • Walter Scott (Scot): *The Antiquary* and *Old Mortality* • Samuel Taylor Coleridge (Eng): poem *Kubla Khan*

The first publication by **Chopin,** a Polonaise in G minor, is issued in Warsaw. In aristocratic circles the seven-year-old is exalted as a 'second Mozart'.

Clementi publishes the first volume of his pedagogical piano anthology *Gradus ad Parnassum* (Steps to Parnassus).

Mendelssohn, aged eight, begins composition lessons with **Carl Zelter**.

The publisher Breitkopf and Härtel rejects **Franz P. Schubert**'s manuscript of the *Erlkönig* (1815) and return it to the only Franz Schubert they know: **Franz Anton Schubert**, from Dresden. The Dresden Schubert writes back to the publishers complaining that he feels insulted by them to think that he would write 'that sort of rubbish'.

(**F. P.**) **Schubert** composes his classic songs *An die Musik* (To Music), *Der Tod und das Mädchen* (Death and the Maiden) and *Die Forelle* (The Trout).

12 January The Teatro San Carlo in Naples (below), destroyed by fire the previous year, reopens with **Mayr**'s new melodrama *Il sogno di Partenope*.

13 January Weber arrives in Dresden where he has been appointed Royal Saxon *Kapellmeister*, with the specific task of promoting German-language opera. This year he begins work on his pioneering opera *Der Freischütz* (The Freeshooter).

21 January Ever the opportunist, **Cherubini** directs his Requiem in C minor for the memorial service of Louis XVI. (21 years earlier he had directed a third anniversary concert celebrating the beheading of the same king.) The work is admired by Beethoven, and later Berlioz, Mendelssohn and Schumann.

25 January Rossini's comic opera *La Cenerentola* (Cinderella) is first performed at the Teatro Valle in Rome. Its popularity is far-reaching: within a few years it will have been staged across Europe and beyond, with New York and Buenos Aires mounting productions in 1826. It will also be the first opera to be performed in Australia, in 1844.

31 May Falsely accused of stealing, the servant girl Ninetta faces the gallows in **Rossini**'s semi-serious opera *La gazza ladra* (The Thieving Magpie), which premières and triumphs at La Scala, Milan.

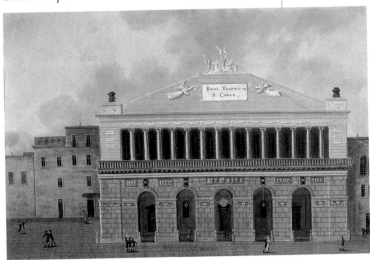

Autumn Beethoven, having written very little all year, begins work on his *Hammerklavier* Sonata, Op. 106.

18 October Étienne-Nicolas Méhul, one of France's leading composers, dies in Paris, aged 54.

11 November Rossini's lavishly staged opera *Armida* fails to ignite much enthusiasm at the Teatro San Carlo in Naples. Many regard it as a little too German for Neapolitan taste.

1817 James Monroe is inaugurated as 5th President of the USA • Quadruple alliance powers (Austria, Britain, Prussia, Russia) begin reducing their army of occupation in France • War against Seminole Indians in Florida begins • Spain agrees to end Slave Trade • Quaker philanthropist Elizabeth Fry (Eng) forms association for improved treatment of women in prison • Construction of Erie Canal begins • John Constable (Eng) paints *Flatford Mill* • Lord Byron (Eng): poem *Manfred* • George William Freidrich Hegel (Ger): *Encyclopaedia of Philosophical Sciences* • Economist David Ricardo (Eng): *Principles of Political Economy and Taxation* • Thomas Moore (Ire): poem *Lalla Rookh*

With ever worsening hearing, **Beethoven** begins using conversation books with friends and visitors.

February Schubert completes his Sixth Symphony. The following month his music is heard in public for the first time—one of his Italian overtures is performed in a Vienna inn. At the end of the year the 21-year-old effectively gives up teaching for good.

February Beethoven writes a letter of thanks to the English firm Broadwood in anticipation of their gift of a new piano (below): 'I shall regard it as an altar upon which I will give up the most beautiful offerings of my mind to the divine Apollo.' By the end of the summer Beethoven has completed his colossal *Hammerklavier* Sonata, op.106. Dedicated to his pupil and patron Archduke Rudolph, it is one of the most demanding piano sonatas ever written.

24 February Chopin, aged seven, gives his first major public performance with a concerto by **Adalbert Gyrowetz** at the Radziwiłł Palace in Antonin, Poland.

5 March Rossini's *Mosè in Egitto* (Moses in Egypt), a staged oratorio acceptable for Lenten performance, premières at the Teatro San Carlo,

Naples. The librettist, **Andrea Tottola**, has spiced up the story with a love affair between Pharaoh's son (Osiride) and an Israelite girl (Elcia).

17 June Composer **Charles-François Gounod** is born in Paris.

30 June The opera *Le petit chaperon rouge*, an adult version of *Little Red Riding Hood* with music by **Adrien Boieldieu** (right), opens at the Opéra-Comique, Paris.

28 October The nine-year-old **Mendelssohn** makes his public début as a pianist in a chamber music concert in Berlin.

November Hummel resigns as *Hofkapellmeister* in Stuttgart, unhappy in his work and unpopular with the theatre management.

14 November Gaetano Donizetti, 21 this month, presents his début opera, *Enrico di Borgogna* (Henry of Burgundy), with reasonable success at the Teatro di San Luca in Venice.

December Beethoven's sister-in-law, Johanna, legally contests the composer's guardianship of her son, Karl. During the hearings at the Landrechte—the court of the nobility—Beethoven lets it slip that he is not of noble birth, having previously fostered the fallacy that the 'van' in his name is the Dutch equivalent of the aristocratic 'von'. The case is transferred to the commoners' court, where the embarrassed composer loses custody of his nephew. (See also 1820.)

24 December The priest Joseph Mohr asks **Franz Xaver Gruber** to set his text *Stille Nacht* (Silent Night) for choir and guitar. The carol is sung that same evening during Midnight Mass, at St Nicholas Church, Oberndorf, near Salzburg.

1818 Britain and USA agree to 49th Parallel boundary between USA and Canada: Oregon is left to joint occupation • In Britain, attempts at parliamentary reform are defeated • Conference of the Quadruple alliance at Aix-la-Chapelle (Aachen): Allies agree to remove occupation troops from France • France is invited to join the Concert of Europe, an informal alliance of European powers • Chile and Venezuela become independent • *Northanger Abbey* and *Persuasion* by Jane Austen (Eng) are both published posthumously • Walter Scott (Scot): *Heart of Midlothian* and *Rob Roy* • Mary Wollstonecraft Shelley (Eng): *Frankenstein* • Lord Byron (Eng): poem *Don Juan*

The one-act opera *Los Esclavos Felices* by the 13-year-old **Juan Arriaga** is first performed in Bilbao, Spain.

Anton Diabelli, publisher and composer, sends a waltz he has penned to 50 composers, including **Beethoven**, **Hummel**, **Václav Tomášek**, **Schubert** and the child **Liszt**, inviting them to send back a piano variation on it that he will publish in a combined anthology. Beethoven, according to his (unreliable) biographer Anton Schindler, is at first dismissive of the waltz, but soon begins writing his celebrated 33 variations, completed four years later.

Krommer, imperial court composer at Vienna, issues his first two quartets for clarinet and strings (Op. 21).

Reicha issues his Six Wind Quintets, Op. 99, his third set of such works in two years, in Paris.

Schubert pens his Piano Quintet in A major, *Die Forelle* (The Trout), while on holiday in Stayr with the renowned singer **Johann Vogl**. Commissioned by Vogl's friend Silvester Baumgartner, the work features variations on the composer's own song *Die Forelle* in its fourth movement.

Weber's programmatic piano rondo *Aufforderung zum Tanz* (Invitation to the Dance) introduces compositional sophistication into the waltz.

5 January Hummel signs his contract for the post of grand-ducal *Kapellmeister* at Weimar. The conditions of his employment are extremely favourable, allowing him three months' annual leave for concert tours. He will remain at Weimar for the rest of his life, joining Goethe as one of the city's most famous citizens.

Late spring Beethoven begins composing his *Missa solemnis*. He plans to complete the mass by March the following year, ready for the installation ceremony of his pupil and patron Archduke Rudolph as the Archbishop of Olmütz. Beethoven will miss the deadline by nearly three years.

20 June French operetta composer **Jacques Offenbach** is born in Cologne.

26 June Giacomo Meyerbeer scores his first significant success with the heroic melodrama *Emma di Resburgo*, introduced at the Teatro San Benedetto, Venice. The opening run notches up 74 performances.

19 August Italian composer **Saverio Mercadante**, aged 23, establishes his reputation with his first mature opera, *L'apoteosi d'Ercole* (The Apotheosis of Hercules), staged at the Teatro San Carlo, Naples.

13 September German pianist and composer **Clara Wieck** (later **Schumann**) is born in Leipzig.

24 October Rossini premières *La donna del lago* (The Lady of the Lake) at the Teatro S Carlo, Naples. Based on Sir Walter Scott's poem of the same name (1810), the opera is too protracted for most. The composer's next stage-work, the melodrama *Bianca e Falliero, ossia Il consiglio dei tre*, encounters a similarly cool response in Milan at the end of the year.

1 November Following the failure of his wine business in London, **Viotti** (left) becomes director of the Paris Opéra. (See also February 1820).

1819 Spain cedes Florida to the USA • US Supreme Court decision (McCulloch vs Maryland) strengthens power of federal authority over states • Britain establishes a settlement in Singapore • 'Peterloo' massacre in Manchester, England: 11 people are killed when troops disperse demonstrators seeking parliamentary reform and repeal of Corn Laws • Repressive Carlsbad Decrees are passed by Diet of the German Confederation • Hans Christian Oersted (Den) discovers electromagnetism • Théodore Géricault (Fr) paints *The Raft of the Medusa* • John Keats (Eng): *Hyperion* • Johan Wolfgang Goethe (Ger): *The West-Eastern Divan* • Philosopher Arthur Schopenhauer (Ger): *The World as Will and Idea*

Spohr is engaged for a season with the Philharmonic Society Orchestra in London. While there he introduces the English to the conductor's baton (for rehearsals only) and composes his Second Symphony.

1 February Spontini is appointed director of the Berlin Court Opera.

13 February Viotti's directorship of the Paris Opéra takes a blow as the Duke of Berry is

assassinated by a Bonapartist as he leaves the building (above). Patronage of the Opéra falls into decline and Viotti quits the following year.

16 March Steibelt performs his Eighth Piano Concerto in St Petersburg, concluding the work with a choral finale.

April Beethoven breaks off work on his *Missa Solemnis* to write some piano works for the publisher Friedrich Starke. He begins the piano sonata Op. 109 and also a series of bagatelles. The Bagatelles Op. 119 Nos. 7–11 are supplied to Starke and published the following year.

8 April After many months of legal wrangling, **Beethoven** finally wins back the guardianship of his nephew, Karl, from the boy's mother, Johanna.

May Beethoven commits to composing three piano sonatas—Nos. 30 to 32, the last three he will write—for the Berlin publisher Adolf Schlesinger, to be delivered in three months. Only No. 30 in E major (Op. 109) is completed this year.

14 June Schubert's first theatrical commission, the one-act farce *Die Zwillingsbrüder* (The Twin Brothers), fails to impress at the Kärntnertortheater in Vienna.

19 August Schubert's three-act melodrama *Die Zauberharfe* (The Magic Harp), commissioned by the Theater an der Wien, receives the first of eight performances.

December Schubert composes his most advanced and harmonically intense chamber work to date, the Quartettsatz in C minor (D. 703). The one-movement work is a marvel of compositional virtuosity, with fiery surges of passion mixing with some of the most beautiful, idiomatic phrases ever conceived for the quartet medium. Schubert abandons a second movement. The piece will not be heard in public until 1867.

3 December Rossini's opera *Maometto II* (Mahomet II) opens at the Teatro San Carlo in Naples. The audience struggles with what is the composer's most audacious music to date. Rossini twice revises the work, the second time for Paris as *le siège de Corinthe* (1826).

26 December Mayr introduces *Fedra*, a two-act *melodramma serio* (after Racine's play *Phèdre*), at La Scala, Milan.

1820 Under the Missouri compromise, Missouri is to be admitted without restriction on slavery • Revolution in Spain: Fernando VII gives way, restores liberal Constitution of 1812 abolishing the Inquisition • Britain's King George III dies, and is succeeded by the prince regent as George IV • US President James Monroe is unopposed for a second term

• André Ampére (Fr) develops his law of electromagnetism • John Constable (Eng) paints *Dedham Mill* • William Blake (Eng) paints *Ghost of a Flea* • Walter Scott (Scot): *Ivanhoe* • Percy Bysshe Shelley (Eng): play *Prometheus Unbound* • John Keats (Eng): *The Eve of St Agnes and Other Poems* • Washington Irving (US): *Sketchbook of Geoffrey Crayon, Gent*

1821

The Paris Opéra relocates to a new theatre in the Rue Le Peletier, following the assassination of the Duke of Berry (1820). The old building has since been pulled down.

3 February Felix Mendelssohn, on his 12th birthday, stages his one-act Singspiel *Die Soldatenliebschaft* (The Soldier's Love Affair) in the hall of the family home with musicians from the royal *Kapelle* in Berlin.

7 March Johann Vogl introduces **Schubert**'s *Erlkönig* to the public for the first time during a concert of songs and chamber music at Vienna's Kärntnertortheater. *Der Erlkönig* and *Gretchen am Spinnrade* are published as Schubert's Opp. 1 and 2 this spring.

11 June Piano virtuoso **Ignaz Moscheles** enjoys a very successful London début with the Philharmonic Society Orchestra.

18 June Weber's *Der Freischütz* (The Freeshooter) (below)

Der Freischütz costumes for Samiel and Caspar

triumphs at the Schauspielhaus in Berlin. Weber has taken four years to conceive and produce this pioneering work of German Romantic opera, interrupted by tuberculosis and various duties as *Kapellmeister* in Dresden. Combining German folk legend with the supernatural, the Singspiel becomes an international phenomenon, with productions in ten languages by the end of the decade.

August Schubert sketches his Symphony No. 7 in E major, but never finishes it.

30 September Having lost his father at six months of age, **Wagner**, now eight, loses his step-father, Ludwig Geyer. It is later speculated that Geyer was in fact Wagner's biological father.

November Passionate about music, **Berlioz** instead studies medicine in Paris having gained his bachelor's degree at Grenoble. His interest in medicine is non-existent, but his father's wishes are binding.

November Carl Zelter introduces the 12-year-old **Mendelssohn** to the 73-year-old **Goethe** in Weimar. The prodigy and polymath become friends.

11 November Domenico Barbaia requests a new opera from **Weber** for the Kärntnertortheater in Vienna. Hoping for a *Der Freischütz*-style opera, he will eventually receive *Euryanthe*. (See 1823.)

25 December Following a year beset with illness, **Beethoven** finally completes his Piano Sonata in A flat major Op. 110, the second of his three piano sonatas promised to the Berlin publisher Adolf Schlesinger. The work ends with an intricate fugue, a typically concentrated procedure of Beethoven's late style.

1821 Greek war of independence against Turkey begins • Revolt at Piedmont: Austria intervenes • Peru, Mexico, Guate-mala, Panama, and San Domingo declare independence from Spain • Britain's Queen Caroline dies • British West Africa, comprising Gambia, Gold Coast and Sierra Leone, is formed • Portuguese king João VI agrees to leave Brazil and return to Portugal • Egyptian Hieroglyphics are deciphered by Jean-François Champollion (Fr) • Thomas Johann Seebeck (Estonia-Ger) invents the thermocouple • Michael Faraday (Eng) develops the electric motor • John Constable (Eng) paints *The Hay Wain* • Walter Scott (Scot): *Kenilworth* • Thomas de Quincey (Eng): *Confessions of an English Opium Eater*

Cherubini becomes director of the Paris Conservatoire. **Le Sueur**, who has been teaching there since 1818, accepts the 19-year-old **Berlioz** into his composition class this same year.

The Paris Opéra begin using gas lighting, introduced with **Nicolas Isouard**'s *Aladin, ou La lampe merveilleuse*.

Schubert begins to make an income from publishing deals, primarily with his lieder. By the end of the year he has contracted syphilis.

13 January Beethoven completes his final piano sonata, No. 32 in C minor (Op. 111), exercising 'late-period' fugal textures (first movement) and variation form (second, final movement). Beethoven's historic 32 piano sonatas (1795–1822) have substantially expanded the expressive, dynamic and compositional range of the genre and encouraged crucial innovations in pianoforte manufacture.

16 February Rossini presents his final opera for Naples, *Zelmira*, which is well received. The following month the composer, aged 30, marries the Spanish soprano **Isabella Colbran** (right), aged 37.

13 April Impresario Domenico Barbaia, **Rossini**'s Neapolitan business partner, launches a resoundingly successful three-month season of the composer's operas in Vienna.

12 May Donizetti enjoys success with *La Zingara* (The Gypsy Girl), his first opera for Naples, staged at the Teatro Nuovo.

25 June Influential author, composer and music critic **E. T. A. Hoffmann** dies from syphilis and alcohol abuse in Berlin, aged 46.

Summer Mendelssohn meets **Spohr** in Cassel, where the latter has recently become *Kapellmeister*. Mendelssohn begins to compose the Piano Quartet in C minor, which is published as his Op. 1 the following year.

Autumn With the *Missa Solemnis* virtually complete, **Beethoven** begins work on his Ninth Symphony.

September Schubert completes his Mass in A flat major (No. 5), begun three years earlier. There are no records of a performance during the composer's lifetime.

October Schubert breaks off from the third movement of his B minor Symphony, never to return to it. (Sudden inspiration for a new piano piece, the *Wanderer* Fantasy, may be to blame.) Not performed until 1865, the *Unfinished* Eighth is widely considered the first Romantic symphony. The notion that Schubert regarded the two movements as a complete work is unlikely, not least due to the Allegro–Andante structure and irregularity of key scheme, beginning in B minor and ending in E major.

3 October The drama *Die Weihe des Hauses* (The Consecration of the House), with an overture by **Beethoven**, reopens Vienna's Josephstadt Theatre.

1 December Liszt, aged 11, gives his first public concert, in Vienna.

10 December Composer **César Franck** is born in Liège, Belgium.

1822 Greeks declare independence from Turkey; Turks massacre inhabitants of the island of Chios • Mexican nationalist Augustin de Iturbide is proclaimed emperor of newly independent Mexico • Brazil is formally declared independent of Portugal; Dom Pedro, eldest son of King João of Portugal, is proclaimed emperor • American Colonialisation Society founds Liberia as a colony for freed American slaves • Orangemen attack the viceroy of Ireland in Dublin • New Corn Laws reduce price at which wheat may be imported into Britain • Eugène Delacroix (Fr) paints *The Bark of Dante* • Washington Irving (US): *Bracebridge Hall* • Walter Scott (Scot): *The Fortunes of Nigel*

1823

German-Danish composer **Friedrich Kuhlau** has his Piano Quartet No. 2 (Op. 50) his three Flute Quintets Op. 51 published in Bonn. Two sets of piano sonatas, Opp. 46 & 52, are published in Hamburg.

Schubert writes his influential song cycle *Die schöne Müllerin* (The Fair Maid of the Mill). Composed on a poem by Wilhelm Müller, the songs tell the tender story of a young miller who falls in love with another miller's daughter. She begins to return his affection, but then discards him for a huntsman. The young miller drowns himself in despair.

Spohr writes his Double Quartet No. 1 in D minor, creating distinct roles for the two quartet groups. He will produce three further works in the genre.

27 January French composer **Édouard Lalo** is born in Lille.

3 February Rossini and librettist **Gaetano Rossi** try to recapture the success of *Tancredi* (1813) with another Voltaire adaptation, *Semiramide*, at the Teatro La Fenice, Venice. Most Venetians consider Rossini's last opera for Italy rather heavy going. At the end of the year the composer and his wife, **Isabella Colbran**, visit England (via Paris) and gain an audience with King George IV in Brighton.

19 March Beethoven finally delivers his majestic yet deeply personal *Missa Solemnis* to his patron Archduke Rudolph (see 1819).

23 March The Royal Academy of Music opens its doors in London's Hanover Square, with **William Crotch** as its first principal.

3 May English composer **Henry Bishop** collaborates with American playwright **John Howard Payne** on the operetta *Clari, or The Maid of Milan*, at Covent Garden. The production is a hit, thanks largely to the song *Home, Sweet Home*.

12 May French composer **Ferdinand Hérold** enjoys success with the one-act *Le muletier* (The Mule Driver) at the Opéra-Comique (Théâtre Feydeau) in Paris.

We present here to the world Variations of no ordinary type, but a great and important masterpiece worthy to be ranked with the imperishable creations of the old Classics—such a work as Beethoven, the greatest living representative of true art, and only Beethoven can produce.

June The publisher **Diabelli** announces, without hyperbole, the publication of **Beethoven**'s *33 Variations on a waltz by Anton Diabelli* (Op. 120), the composer's last major piano composition.

28 July Spohr's exotic *Jessonda* opens and triumphs at Kassel. Set in India, the opera tells of a rajah's widow who is rescued from her husband's funeral pyre by her former love, a Portuguese general. With its through-composed style, choruses and ballet, *Jessonda* becomes a leading example of German opera.

25 October Weber's grand heroic opera *Euryanthe* achieves only moderate success at the Kärntnertortheater in Vienna. The opera is let down by its weak libretto, authored by the inexperienced **Helmina von Chezy**.

7 December Felix Mendelssohn, aged 14, performs his Double Piano Concerto in E major with his sister, **Fanny**, in Berlin.

20 December Schubert's overture and incidental music to **Helmina von Chezy**'s *Rosamunde, Queen of Cyprus* is first heard at the Theater an der Wien (Vienna). The music is well appreciated, but Chezy's play is a disaster and survives only two performances.

1823 Mexican emperor Augustin Iturbide abdicates under pressure; Mexico becomes a republic • French forces invade Spain • British move towards free trade with Warehousing of Goods Act • Rising in Portugal, partly over loss of Brazil: João VI dismisses the Cortés (parliament) • Costa Rica, Guatemala, Honduras, Nicaragua and San Salvador form the Confederation of United Provinces of Central America • Pope Pius VII dies; is succeeded by Leo XII • Charles Macintosh (Scot) patents a waterproof fabric • Jean Ingres (Fr) paints *La Source* • J. M. W. Turner (Eng) paints *The Storm* (*Shipwreck*) • James Fenimore Cooper (US): *The Pioneers* • Stendhal (Marie Henri Beyle; Fr): *Racine and Shakespeare*

Liszt's first published piece appears in *Vaterländischer Künstlerverein*, one of the 50 variations on a Diabelli waltz submitted by prominent central European composers. This year the 12-year-old prodigy makes his English début, including a performance before George IV at Windsor Castle.

The **Rossini** season at London's King's Theatre fails to deliver its much promised excitement. Matters are not helped when Rossini's wife, **Isabella Colbran**, quits the stage after a dire performance as the eponymous *Zelmira*, due to her weakening voice. (See also 26 July.)

Weber's recently revised Bassoon Concerto in F major (original version 1811) is published in Berlin as his Op. 75. It is one of the major pieces of the bassoon repertory.

February–March Amid chronic ill-health, **Schubert**'s genius continues unabated with his six-movement Octet in F major (D. 803), the A minor Quartet (D. 804), the D minor Quartet (*Death and the Maiden*, D. 810) and *Arpeggione* Sonata (D. 821).

2 March Czech composer **Bedřich Smetana** in born in Litomyšl.

3 March Italian composer and violinist **Giovanni Viotti** dies in London, aged 68.

7 March Meyerbeer's heroic opera *Il crociato in Egitto* (The Crusader in Egypt) captivates its audience at the Teatro La Fenice, Venice. It is the last major opera to incorporate a castrato role.

31 March Tortured by syphilis, **Schubert** writes, 'I am the unhappiest, most wretched creature in the world ... every night I go to bed hoping I shall not wake again; each morning only brings back the grief of the day before'.

31 March Mendelssohn, aged 15, has his accomplished First Symphony introduced in Berlin.

7 April Prince Golitsïn instigates the first full performance of **Beethoven**'s *Missa solemnis*, in St Petersburg.

7 May Beethoven premières his monumental Ninth (*Choral*) Symphony in D minor at a packed Kärnthnertortheater in Vienna. *Kapellmeister* **Michael Umlauf** stands with Beethoven on stage to help direct the work (in fact he has told the orchestra and choir to ignore the stone-deaf composer). After the symphony has ended with its tumultuous *Ode to Joy* finale, Beethoven, with his back to the audience, stands still over his score. The contralto **Caroline Unger** (left) tugs his sleeve, pointing behind him. The maestro turns to see the audience cheering and applauding wildly.

26 July Rossini and his wife leave England having pocketed £7,000, mostly from private teaching engagements and soirée performances. They travel to Paris where the 32-year-old composer takes up the post of musical director at the *Théâtre Italien*.

4 September Austrian composer **Anton Bruckner** is born in Ansfelden, near Linz.

29 September Prolific opera composer **Giovanni Pacini** raises his profile with the success of *Alessandro nelle Indie* (Alexander in India), his first opera for Naples.

1824 War between Britain and Burma: British capture Rangoon • King Louis XVIII of France dies; is succeeded by his brother Charles X • South American patriot Simón Bolívar defeats Spanish armies in Peru and is proclaimed president • US presidential election ends with no-one having a clear majority; House of Representatives chooses John Quincy Adams as President • Repeal of the Combination Act in Britain legalises trade unions • Thomas Lawrence (Eng) paints *Portrait of Master Lambton* • Walter Scott (Scot): *Red Gauntlet* • Walter Savage Landor (Eng): first two volumes of *Imaginary Conversations* • Johan Freidrich Herbert (Ger): *Psychology as a Science*

Beethoven completes three of his incomparable 'late' quartets: Op. 127 in E flat major, Op. 132 in A minor and Op. 130 in B flat major, commissioned by Prince Golitsïn two years previously. The Schuppanzigh Quartet gives the premières of the E flat major and A minor quartets this year.

Moscheles marries Charlotte Embden in Hamburg. The newlyweds settle in London where Moscheles becomes one of the piano tutors at the recently formed Royal Academy of Music.

February Vincenzo Bellini's first opera, *Adelson e Salvini*, is introduced in Naples.

March Mendelssohn, visiting Paris with his father, impresses the hard-to-please **Cherubini** with his piano quartets. The teenage Mendelssohn writes of the older maestro, 'Cherubini is an extinct volcano that occasionally spews forth ash'.

April Schubert (right), enjoying a respite from the agony of his syphilitic condition, composes the third of his Walter Scott songs, *Ellens dritter Gesang*, commonly known as *Ave Maria*. This year sees the publication of his Mass in C major (D. 452).

7 May Antonio Salieri, having categorically denied to **Moscheles** that he poisoned Mozart, dies in Vienna, aged 74.

2 June Chopin's Piano Rondo in C minor is published as his Op. 1.

19 June Rossini introduces his one-act comic opera *Il viaggio a Reims* (The Journey to Rheims), a *pièce d'occasion* for the coronation celebrations of Charles X, at the Théâtre Italien, Paris.

Summer Schubert composes his 'Great' C major Symphony (No. 9, D. 944) while on holiday in the lakeside town of Gmunden, Upper Austria. The crowning work of Schubert's orchestral oeuvre will be 'discovered' by **Schumann** and premièred by **Mendelssohn** in 1839.

10 July Berlioz's *Messe solennelle*, one of his earliest extant works, is first performed at the Church of St Roch in Paris.

23 July Paganini and his lover Antonia Bianchi have a son, Achille. The pair will separate three years later, with the composer taking charge of his only child.

15 October Mendelssohn, aged 16, completes his first masterpiece: the String Octet in E flat major, Op. 20.

25 October Johann Strauss II is born in Vienna. At this time his father, **Johann Strauss I**, is director of a chamber ensemble in partnership with **Joseph Lanner**.

10 December Boieldieu and librettist **Eugène Scribe** introduce their Walter Scott-inspired opera *La dame blanche* at the Opéra-Comique in Paris. The success of the work is phenomenal, with more than 1,000 performances by the company alone over the next 40 years.

1825 John Quincy Adams is inaugurated as 6th President of the USA • Japanese revolt against the Dutch • Portugal recognises independence of Brazil • Bolivia declares independence from Peru • Tsar Alexander I of Russia dies; is succeeded by his brother, Nikolai I • In England, the world's first passenger railroad, from Stockton to Darlington, begins to operate • Chemist Hans Christian Oersted (Den) produces aluminium • In North America the Erie Canal is opened to shipping • *Diary* of Samuel Pepys (Eng, 1633–1703) is deciphered for the first time • William Hazlitt (Eng): *The Spirit of the Age* • Walter Scott (Scot): *The Talisman*

Berlioz, aged 22, enrols as a full-time student at the Paris Conservatoire.

Chopin, aged 16, enrols at the Warsaw Conservatoire.

Paganini composes his Violin Concerto No. 2 in B minor, which becomes immensely popular thanks to its third movement Rondo, 'La Campanella'.

Mid January Promising Spanish composer **Juan Arriaga** dies in Paris, shortly before his 20th birthday. The cause is probably exhaustion combined with a pulmonary infection.

5 March Weber (right) arrives in England to present his commissioned opera *Oberon* at Covent Garden. He has agreed to a lump sum of £500 for the score and British publication rights, together with £255 to conduct the first 12 performances. He will also make a further income from other concert engagements. His primary concern is to provide for his family, gravely aware that he may soon die from his chronic illness.

12 April Weber directs a spectacular première of *Oberon* at Covent Garden, London. In spite of early success, the opera never quite makes core repertory.

4 June Carl Maria von Weber dies from tuberculosis at the home of George Smart in Great Portland Street, London, aged 39. His funeral takes place later this month at St Mary Moorfields, accompanied by extracts of Mozart's *Requiem*. **Wagner** will assist with the relocation of Weber's coffin to Dresden in 1844.

Late June Schubert composes his String Quartet in G major (Op. 161), his final essay in the genre.

August Beethoven sends his publisher, Schott, what he regards as his greatest quartet, the seven-movement String Quartet in C sharp minor, Op. 131. He pens a note on the MS: 'Put together from pilferings from one thing and another.' Schott panics. Beethoven has to reassure the firm that he was only joking.

August The 17-year-old **Mendelssohn** completes his miraculously mature concert overture *A Midsummer Night's Dream*.

6 August 'Tormented' by his uncle and in the depths of despair, Karl Beethoven shoots himself in the head with two pistols. Neither bullet penetrates his skull. **Beethoven** is mortified by his nephew's attempted suicide.

Autumn Beethoven composes the String Quartet Op. 135 in F major, the last of his 'late' quartets. He also composes a new finale to his Op. 130 quartet at the request of his publisher; the original finale will be published separately as the *Grosse Fuge*, Op. 133.

9 October Rossini's first French opera, *Le siège de Corinthe* (The Siege of Corinth), is received enthusiastically at the Paris Opéra. The *tragédie lyrique* is a revised and downsized version of his *Maometto II*.

December Beethoven suffers from jaundice and dropsy. Doctors tap off the fluid from his massively swollen abdomen.

1826 King João VI of Portugal dies; succeeded by his son Pedro, emperor of Brazil; Pedro refuses to leave Brazil and cedes the Portuguese throne to his seven-year-old daughter Maria, with his brother Dom Miguel as regent • Britain's war with Burma ends • Russia declares war on Persia • The Panama congress, planned by patriot leader Simón Bolivar to produce unity among republics, is ineffective • Jesuits are permitted to return to France • London Zoological society is founded • Benjamin Disraeli (Eng): *Vivian Grey* • *Memoirs* of Giovanni Casanova's (It) published posthumously • Alfred de Vigny (Fr): *Cinq Mars* • James Fenimore Cooper (US): *The Last of the Mohicans*

1827

The London piano manufacturers Broadwood & Sons patent iron bracing, introduced into their instruments to provide greater tuning stability.

Schubert explores loneliness in his desolate song-cycle *Die Winterreise* (The Winter Journey), a setting of Wilhelm Müller's 24 poems. This year also sees the composition of his two piano trios, B flat major (D. 898) and E flat major (D. 929), and the two sets of Impromptus for Piano (D. 899 and D. 935).

Collaborators **Strauss I** and **Lanner** part company. Strauss sets up his own orchestra.

1 February Mendelssohn's First Symphony (introduced privately in 1824) receives its public première at the Gewandhaus in Leipzig.

19 March Schubert visits the bed-ridden **Beethoven**. It is their first and last meeting, despite having both lived in the same city for the last 30 years.

26 March Rossini directs his *Moïse et Pharaon* (Moses and Pharaoh)—a French adaptation of *Mosè in Egitto*—at the Paris Opéra.

Beethoven on his deathbed

26 March Ludwig van Beethoven dies from cirrhosis of the liver in Vienna, aged 56. He leaves everything he owns to his nephew, Karl.

29 March In Vienna a crowd of around 10,000 attends Beethoven's funeral ceremony. **Hummel** and the ailing **Schubert** are among the 40 torchbearers. In his graveside eulogy the poet Franz Grillparzer reflects: 'He withdrew from mankind after he had given them his all and received nothing in return … Thus he was, thus he died, thus he will live to the end of time.'

3 April Pope Leo XII makes **Paganini** a Knight of the Golden Spur.

26 April The Royal Academy of Music sacks the composer **Nicholas Bochsa**, professor of harp and general secretary, displeased with his record of forgery, bankruptcy and alleged bigamy.

29 April Mendelssohn's Singspiel *Die Hochzeit des Camacho* (Camacho's Wedding) is first performed at the Schauspielhaus in Berlin.

12 June Spontini's final opera, *Agnes von Hohenstaufen*, is premièred in Berlin.

28 August Liszt's father dies from typhoid in Boulogne-sur-Mer. Liszt, aged 15, moves to Paris where he is later joined by his mother.

11 September Berlioz is captivated by Shakespeare and the actress Harriet Smithson, who he sees playing Ophelia in *Hamlet*.

27 October Vincenzo Bellini and librettist **Felice Romani** enjoy great success with their first operatic collaboration, *Il pirata* (The Pirate), at La Scala, Milan.

1827 Britain sends troops to Portugal to support Queen Maria but withdraws them after Regent Miguel undertakes to support the constitution • Turks capture Athens and occupy the Acropolis; by the Treaty of London, Russia, France and Britain recognise Greek autonomy, but Turkey rejects their proposal for truce with Greece; in naval Battle of Navarino, Turkish and Egyptian fleets are destroyed by the Allies; Count Capo d'Istria is elected president of Greece • Joseph N. Niepce (Fr) makes a crude photograph on sensitised metal plate • George Simon Ohm (Ger) formulates mathematical law for electrical currents • Victor Hugo (Fr): *Cromwell* • Alessandro Manzoni (It): *I Promessi Sposi*

1828

Berlioz self-publishes his *Eight scenes of Faust*, Op. 1. He later withdraws the choral work and incorporates its material into *La damnation de Faust* (1846).

29 February Daniel Auber and librettist **Eugène Scribe** give birth to *grand opéra* with the five-act epic *La muette de Portici* (The Mute Girl of Portici), premièred at the Opéra, Paris. (See also 1830.)

26 March In Vienna **Schubert** gives his first public concert devoted entirely to his own works. The evening of chamber music is performed to a packed house, but then quickly forgotten as public attention turns towards the visiting virtuoso **Paganini**.

29 March Heinrich Marschner attempts to capitalise on the current vampire craze in both literature and drama with his opera *Der Vampyr*, staged at Leipzig's Stadttheater. Heavily influenced by Weber's *Der Freischütz*, the opera has been inspired by John Polidori's story *The Vampyre*, itself an adaptation of Byron's *Fragment of a Novel*.

31 March The 17-year-old law student **Robert Schumann** observes his future wife, the eight-year-old **Clara Wieck**, performing at a soirée in Leipzig. He soon starts piano lessons with her father, Friedrich.

Der Vampyr: Act 1, Scene 6

July Schubert completes his Mass (No. 6) in E flat major, one of several liturgical works of this year, possibly written to increase his employment opportunities within the Church.

24 July Paganini gives the première performance of his Violin Concerto No. 3 (1826), at the Redoutensaal (Hofburg Palace) in Vienna.

20 August Rossini adapts parts of his opera *Il viaggio a Reims* (1825) into the Crusades-era French comedy *Le Comte Ory*, first staged at the Paris Opéra.

8 September Mendelssohn's Goethe-inspired overture *Meeresstille und glückliche Fahrt* (Calm Sea and a Prosperous Voyage) is introduced in Berlin.

September–October In a final flurry of inspired genius, **Schubert** completes his 14 *Schwanengesang* (D. 957) and composes three remarkable piano sonatas: C minor (D. 958), A major (D. 959), B flat major (D. 960). He also pens one of the crown jewels of chamber music, his String Quintet in C major (D. 956).

4 November Schubert—though the greatest composer alive and suffering rapidly deteriorating health—feels compelled to take a counterpoint lesson from the teacher and composer **Simon Sechter**.

6 November Friedrich Kuhlau achieves his greatest success with his incidental music to Heiberg's *Elverhøj* (The Elf Hill), first staged in Copenhagen.

19 November Franz Schubert, having eaten virtually nothing all month, dies in Vienna, aged 31. The cause of death may be typhoid or syphilis. Leaving an estate worth just 63 florins, he is buried next to Beethoven in Währing cemetery.

1828 US congress passes the 'Tariff of Abominations' controlling the import of foreign goods • The Duke of Wellington (Tory) becomes Britain's Prime Minister • Pedro IV abdicates throne of Portugal: a *coup d'état* makes his brother Miguel king • Russia declares war on Turkey and occupies Varna • Britain, France and Russia guarantee Greek independence after the withdrawal of Turkish and Egyptian forces • Uruguay becomes independent of Brazil • Chemist Friedrich Wohler (Ger) founds the science of organic chemistry • John Constable (Eng) paints *Salisbury Cathedral from the Meadows* • Aleksandr Pushkin (Russ): poem *Poltava* • Noah Webster (US): *American Dictionary of the English Language*

Berlioz starts work on the most famous piece of music he will ever write, the ground-breaking *Symphonie fantastique*. Berlioz's passion for literature (particularly Shakespeare), Beethoven and the Anglo-Irish actress Harriet Smithson will inspire one of the great early Romantic symphonies.

Cherubini produces his String Quartet No. 2 in C major, a revision and transformation of his Symphony in D (1815).

Chopin, aged 19, composes his Piano Concerto in F minor (No. 2).

January Paganini begins the German leg of his European tour, meeting with **Spohr**, **Hummel** and **Goethe** along the way. During this time he composes his Violin Concerto No. 4 in D minor.

14 February Bellini and the librettist **Felice Romani** triumph in Milan with the two-act melodrama *La Straniera* (The Stranger).

16 February Paris-based Netherlander **François-Joseph Gossec** dies in Passy, aged 95.

11 March In Berlin the 20-year-old **Mendelssohn** (right) conducts a centenary performance of Bach's *St Matthew Passion*, the first revival of the work since Bach's death. Its success is phenomenal. *Kapellmeister* **Spontini**, possibly jealous of Mendelssohn, fails to prevent a repeat performance ten days later—on Bach's birthday. The concerts spark a Bach revival.

8 May American pianist-composer **Louis Moreau Gottschalk** is born in New Orleans.

16 May Bellini and **Romani** inaugurate the Teatro Ducale in Parma with their unimpressive opera *Zaira*.

25 May Mendelssohn makes his English public début, conducting his Symphony No. 1 in C minor Op. 11 at a concert of the Philharmonic Society. Other concerts follow, with the English premières of *A Midsummer Night's Dream* overture and the Double Piano Concerto in E major, performed with **Moscheles**. Audiences are, as one critic writes, 'spellbound' by the young composer, conductor and performer.

Mid summer Mendelssohn visits Scotland with his friend Karl Klingemann. While there he is inspired to write the introductory bars to both his Scottish Symphony (completed 1842) and the *Hebrides* overture, completed in its first version the following year. The friends also visit Wales, where Mendelssohn is affronted by 'atrocious, vulgar, out-of-tune rubbish': his reaction to Welsh ditties performed by local pub harpists.

3 August Rossini presents his 36th opera, the four-act *Guillaume Tell* (William Tell), at the Paris Opéra. Henceforward the 37-year-old retires from writing opera, though he creates a three-act abridgement of *Tell* in 1831. Rossini composes only a small handful of works during the rest of his life.

28 November Composer **Anton Rubinstein** is born in Vikhvatintsï, Ukraine.

22 December Marschner's *Der Templer und die Jüdin* (The Templar and the Jewess) is first staged in Leipzig. With libretto by **Wilhelm Wohlbrück** based on Walter Scott's *Ivanhoe*, the opera is the most highly regarded of Marschner's career.

1829 Andrew Jackson is inaugurated as 7th President of the USA • The Treaty of Andrianople ends Russo-Turkish War: Russia gains navigation rights in Dardanelles and Bosphorus • Western Australia is colonised by British settlers • Pope Leo XII dies; is succeeded by Pius VIII • Joseph Henry (US) devises an electro-magnetic motor • James Nielson (Scot) invents a high-temperature blast furnace • Robert Stephenson (Eng) designs the *Rocket*, an advanced steam locomotive with a multi-tubular boiler • Louis Braille (Fr) publishes a raised alphabet for the blind • Honoré de Balzac (Fr): *The Human Comedy* • Alfred de Musset (Fr): *Stories of Spain and Italy*

Schumann composes the *Abegg Variations* for piano, his first mature work.

28 January Auber and librettist **Eugène Scribe** enjoy great success with their opera *Fra Diavolo* (Brother Devil), introduced at the Opéra-Comique in Paris.

11 March Bellini's opera *I Capuleti e i Montecchi* (The Capulets and Montagues), composed in around six weeks, enjoys a successful première in Venice.

17 March Chopin, aged 20, makes his official Warsaw début with the first public performance of his Piano Concerto in F minor (No. 2).

May Glinka leaves Russia for Italy, where he stays for three years. During this formative time he will meet **Donizetti**, **Bellini**, **Berlioz** and **Mendelssohn**.

12 May Mendelssohn completes his Symphony No. 5 (*Reformation*), celebrating the tercentenary of the Augsburg Confession.

29 July Berlioz completes his Prix de Rome entry, the cantata *La Mort de Sardanapale*, and then joins the revolutionary mobs in the streets of Paris, musket in hand, singing the *Marseillaise*. To his annoyance the fighting is already over.

19 August Berlioz, with his fourth attempt, wins the Prix de Rome. In his private life he has shifted his affections towards the pianist Camille Moke, having been ignored by the Anglo-Irish actress Harriet Smithson. By the end of the year, he and Moke are engaged.

25 August As Belgian resentment against Dutch rule reaches breaking point, **Auber**'s *La Muette*

de Portici (1828) is performed in Brussels. Depicting a Neapolitan rebellion against Spanish rule in 1647, the opera taps into the political unrest, galvanising revolutionary fervour at the Theatre de la Monnaie (below). The audience pours out onto the street, shouting revolutionary slogans. Rallying further support they attack and ransack government buildings; the city dissolves into anarchy and the Belgian revolution begins.

11 October Chopin premières his Piano Concerto in E minor (No. 1) in Warsaw. The following month he sets out for Vienna, never to see his homeland again.

5 December Berlioz's revolutionary *Symphonie fantastique* excites Paris. Its published programme fires the imagination of the audience, beginning: *A young musician of morbid disposition and powerful imagination poisons himself with opium in an attack of despairing passion.* **Liszt** and **Spontini** are awestruck by the daring novelty of the symphony, while the *Figaro* declares the work 'monstrous' in a spirit of praise.

26 December Donizetti launches his international career with the opera *Anna Bolena*, to a libretto by **Romani**, first staged in Milan.

1830 George IV of Britain dies; succeeded by William IV • Citizens of Paris revolt, King Charles X abdicates; Louis Philippe appointed king • New French constitution provides for an elected monarchy • French forces invade Algeria and capture Algiers • Belgians revolt against Dutch rule (see above); a provisional Belgian government declares independence • Venezuela becomes independent • Ecuador becomes independent • Greece recognised as independent • First railroad in USA (Baltimore and Ohio) opens • Liverpool to Manchester railroad opens in England • Joseph Smith (US): *Book of Mormon* • Stendhal (Fr): *Scarlet and Black* • Alfred Tennyson (Eng): *Poems, Chiefly Lyrical*

6 March Bellini and the librettist **Romani** present *La Sonnambula* at the Teatro Carcano in Milan. The success of the opera is instantaneous, with productions following this same year in London and Paris.

8 March Berlioz arrives in Rome to take up temporary residence at the Villa Medici, as dictated by the rules of the *Prix de Rome*. However, the following month he begins a return journey to Paris, having heard nothing from his fiancée, Camille Moke, since his departure three months earlier.

9 March The 48-year-old **Paganini** (below) gives his first Paris concert, enjoying a packed house despite the doubling of ticket prices. His intimidating appearance and stupefying virtuosity encourage rumours that he is in league with the devil. Débuts in England, Ireland and Scotland follow in the summer.

THE MODERN ORPHEUS.
Opera House - June 5.th 1851.
Sketches of the Musical World N.to be continued

14 April Berlioz, still in Italy, receives crushing news from his fiancée's mother that the love of his life, Camille Moke (right), has decided to marry instead a rich piano manufacturer—Camille Joseph Pleyel. Fuming, Berlioz hatches a plan to murder both mother and faithless daughter. He buys a chambermaid's outfit for his disguise, together with guns and poison (the latter to end his own life), and sets off for Paris. On the way he attempts suicide by jumping into the sea, but he is quickly rescued. By the time he reaches Nice, his anger has dissipated and he sees the folly of his intentions. He returns to Rome.

27 September Chopin arrives in Paris (from Vienna), having recently completed his Opp. 6 and 7 mazurkas.

17 October Mendelssohn gives the first performance of his Piano Concerto No. 1 in G minor, in Munich.

November Schumann's piano cycle *Papillons* is published as his Op. 2.

14 November Ignace Pleyel, composer, publisher and piano manufacturer, dies in Paris aged 74. His son, Camille (see 14 April), takes full control of the piano firm.

21 November Meyerbeer's Gothic grand opera *Robert le diable* (Robert the Devil) is lavishly premièred at the Opéra in Paris.

26 December Bellini's greatest opera, *Norma*, on a libretto by **Romani**, opens at La Scala, Milan. The tragedy of the Druid priestess—one of the most demanding *bel canto* roles of the repertory—takes its time to win over the Milanese public, but the opera triumphs at Bergamo the following year.

1831 Russia quashes Polish Cadet Revolution • Leopold I of Saxe-Coburg is declared first king of the Belgians; Dutch troops invade Belgium but withdraw when French forces go to the Belgian's aid • President Capo d'Istria of Greece is assassinated • Emperor Pedro I of Brazil abdicates and returns to Portugal to aid his daughter Maria against the regent, his brother Miguel • British explorer James Clark Ross reaches the magnetic North Pole • Naturalist Charles Darwin (Eng) begins his scientific voyage on HMS Beagle • Pope Pius VIII dies; succeeded by Gregory XVI • Victor Hugo (Fr): *Notre-Dame de Paris* (Eng: *The Hunchback of Notre Dame*) • Aleksandr Pushkin (Russ): *Boris Godunov*

Theobald Boehm devises the interlinking mechanism for his ring-key flute.

Mendelssohn publishes *Original Melodies for the Pianoforte* in London. The collection of lyrical piano miniatures is issued in Bonn the following year as *Lieder ohne Worte* (Songs without Words).

Rossini, suffering ill health, completes only half of his commissioned *Stabat Mater*; his friend Giovanni Tadolini supplies additional movements. Nine years later Rossini replaces Tadolini's movements with his own, ready for publication.

To strengthen a lazy digit, **Schumann** contrives a mechanical device that instead renders the fourth finger on his right hand completely useless. A Dresden doctor suggests the remedy of an 'animal bath', and Schumann optimistically inserts his partially-crippled hand into the abdomen of a freshly slaughtered cow. The procedure proves futile and the 22-year-old gives up his dreams of becoming a piano virtuoso.

26 February Chopin makes his widely acclaimed Paris début at the Salle Pleyel, three days before his 22nd birthday.

10 March Italian composer, publisher and piano manufacturer **Muzio Clementi** dies in Evesham, Worcestershire, aged 80. He is buried at Westminster Abbey.

12 March Marie Taglioni makes ballet history by donning a white tutu and dancing *sur les pointes*

Gaetano Donizetti

(on the tips of the toes) in *La Sylphide*. Her father, Philippe Taglioni, choreographs the ballet, with music provided by **Jean Schneitzhöffer**.

12 May Donizetti's pastoral peasant-boy-wins-rich-girl romance *L'elisir d'amore* (The Elixir of Love) triumphs in Milan. The libretto by **Romani**, reworking **Scribe**'s *Le Philtre* (1831), inspires some of Donizetti's finest music, including the celebrated 'Adina Credimi' (from Act I) and 'Una furtiva lagrima' (from Act II).

14/25 May In London **Mendelssohn** premières his evocative *The Isles of Fingal* (later *Hebrides Overture* or *Fingal's Cave*), then his *Capriccio brillant* for piano and orchestra. Mendelssohn returns home to Berlin the following month, having completed a two-year tour of Austria, Italy, France and England.

June Verdi, aged 18, is denied a place at the Milan Conservatory due to his advanced years, lack of spaces, living in the wrong place and possessing a 'mediocre' talent.

15 December Hérold enjoys outstanding success with *Le pré aux clercs* at the Opéra-Comique. It becomes one of the most popular operas in Paris for decades to come, but the composer is unable to reap its rewards: he dies on the 19th of the following month from tuberculosis, aged 42.

25 December Field gives the first complete performance of his final piano concerto, No. 7 in C, at the Salle du Conservatoire in Paris.

1832 South Carolina challenges the US Tariff Act, and declares it void in the state; Vice-President John C. Calhoun resigns in support of South Carolina • Andrew Jackson is re-elected President of the USA • British parliament passes a Reform Bill, extending franchise to many new voters, including many reforms on electoral system • Tsar Nikolai I (Russ) abolishes Polish constitution • Turkey declares war on Egypt • In Portugal ex-king Pedro defeats Regent Miguel's forces and takes Oporto • Honoré de Balzac (Fr): *Contes drôlatiques* • Alfred Tennyson (Eng): poem *The Lady of Shallot* • Johann Wolfgang Goethe (Ger): *Faust*, Part II • Victor Hugo (Fr): *Le Roi s'amuse*

Chopin injects poetic flair into the study piece with his influential 12 Etudes Op. 10 (below), dedicated to the 21-year-old **Liszt** and published in Paris, Leipzig and London. At this time most of Chopin's income derives from lucrative teaching engagements.

François-Joseph Fétis, famous for his music criticism, is appointed director of the recently-established Brussels Conservatory. He also secures the post of *maître de chapelle* to Léopold I.

Liszt, greatly inspired by the music of his friend **Berlioz**, writes a piano transcription of the Frenchman's *Symphonie fantastique*. The work is published the following year, predating the publication of Berlioz's symphony by 11 years.

Wagner, aged 20, begins writing his first complete opera, *Die Feen* (The Fairies), to his own libretto. Completed the following year, the opera will not be heard in public until 1888, five years after the composer's death.

27 February **Auber**'s grand opera *Gustave III*, based on the assassination of the King of Sweden, is first performed at the Paris Opéra.

16 March **Bellini**'s opera *Beatrice di Tenda* fails to excite in the first of six performances at the Teatro La Fenice, Venice. The hurriedly written libretto by the overworked **Romani** is largely to blame, thereafter bringing about the end of the Bellini-Romani partnership.

7 May German composer **Johannes Brahms** is born in Hamburg.

13 May **Mendelssohn** premières his youthful Fourth Symphony in A major (*Italian*) at a Philharmonic Society concert in London. Having been inspired by 'the ruins, the landscapes, the glories of nature', Mendelssohn is less than happy with the work and withholds it from publication during his lifetime. The *Italian* proves an instant hit with the English and will in time become his most popular symphony.

24 May **Marschner** and the librettist **Eduard Devrient** bring together natural and supernatural worlds in the rustic fable *Hans Heiling*, which opens with spectacular success in Berlin.

22 July **Cherubini**'s final opera, *Ali Baba*, is staged at the Paris Opéra. **Berlioz** attends the première, but only to shout out rude remarks.

1 October **Mendelssohn** begins a two-year tenure as music director in Düsseldorf.

3 October **Berlioz** marries the actress Harriet Smithson in the chapel of the British Embassy in Paris. **Liszt** witnesses the event. The marriage becomes increasingly volatile and separation follows around seven years later.

12 November Russian composer **Alexander Porfir'yevich Borodin**, illegitimate son of Prince Luka Stepanovich Gedianov, is born in St Petersburg.

26 December **Donizetti**'s tragic opera *Lucrezia Borgia*, with libretto by **Romani** after Victor Hugo's play, is launched with immediate success at La Scala, Milan.

1833 US Congress passes the Force Act, authorising the collection of revenues from South Carolina by force if necessary • Britain acquires the Falkland Islands as a Crown colony • Netherlands and Belgium declare an armistice • King Fernando of Spain dies and is succeeded by his three-year-old daughter Isabel II • Journalist William Lloyd Garrison (US) forms the Anti-slavery Society • A General Trades Union is formed in New York • The British Education Grant Act provides state aid for education • Slavery is declared abolished in the British Empire • Katsushika Hokusai (Jap) completes his *36 Views of Mount Fuji* prints • Nikolai Gogol (Russ): *The Government Inspector*

Berlioz begins composing a concerto for viola and orchestra at the request of **Paganini**. On inspection of early sketches, the virtuoso, keen to display both his talent and a Stradivari viola, dismisses the work as inadequate. Berlioz presses on and completes *Harold in Italy*, a 'Symphony with Viola obbligato' based on 'impressions recollected from wanderings in the Abruzzi Mountains'. (See below and also 1838.)

Chopin composes his Fantasy Impromptu in C sharp minor, Op. 66. His publications this year include the Four Mazurkas, Op. 17, composed 1832–33, issued in Leipzig.

29 January Mendelssohn, currently musical director in Düsseldorf, completes his *Rondo brillant* (Op. 29) for piano and orchestra. He premières the one-movement piece in London, in May.

April Mendelssohn on **Berlioz**, in a letter to **Moscheles**: 'His orchestration is so frightfully muddy, such a confused mess, that you want to wash your hands after handling one of his scores.'

April Bellini sets to work on his final opera, *I Puritani* (The Puritans), in collaboration with the librettist **Carlo Pepoli**.

3 April The first issue of the *Neue Zeitschrift für Musik* (New Music Magazine) (right) is published in Leipzig. **Schumann**, one of the co-founders of the enterprise, takes ownership of the periodical at the end of the year.

Neue Leipziger Zeitschrift für Musik. Herausgegeben durch einen Verein von Künstlern und Kunstfreunden. Erster Jahrgang. № 1. Den 3. April 1834.

28 April Paganini introduces his orchestral work *Sonata per la grand viola* at the Hanover Square Rooms in London. He has composed the work following his disappointment with Berlioz's viola concerto. The critics would rather he returned to the violin.

21 July Edward Loder attempts to revitalise home-grown English opera with *Nourjahad* at the English Opera House (Lyceum Theatre), London. **John Barnett**'s more popular *The Mountain Sylph* follows in August.

Late summer Schumann and Ernestine von Fricken become engaged.

25 September Adolphe Adam secures his first operatic triumph with the one-act *Le chalet*, premièred in Paris. Based on Goethe's Singspiel *Jery und Bätely*, Adam's *opéra-comique* clocks up over 1,000 performances during the next 40 years.

8 October French opera composer **François-Adrien Boieldieu** dies in Jarcy, Seine et Oise, aged 58.

23 November Berlioz's symphonic concerto *Harold in Italy* for viola and orchestra is given a shaky but generally well received first performance, at the Paris Conservatoire. The viola part represents 'a melancholy dreamer in the style of Byron's *Childe Harold*'.

25 December Piano virtuosos **Chopin**, aged 24, and **Liszt**, aged 23, duet at a Christmas charity event for a local music school, in Paris.

1834 Tolpuddle Martyrs: six Dorset agricultural labourers are transported to Australia for attempting to form a union; all are released within three years • Ex-king Pedro IV of Portugal dies; his 15-year-old daughter Maria II, Queen since 1826, is declared of age to rule • Civil war starts in Spain with a claim to the throne by Don Carlos; is opposed by an alliance of England, France and Portugal with the established Spanish government • Civil war erupts in Ecuador • The South Australia Association receives a charter to found a British colony • Sir Robert Peel succeeds Lord Melbourne as UK Prime Minister • Cyrus McCormick (US) patents a harvesting machine

Liszt elopes with Countess Marie d'Agoult, separated wife of Count Charles d'Agoult and mother of two. Fleeing the scandal in Paris, they arrive in Geneva where Marie gives birth to their first daughter, Blandine.

Back in Genoa after six years abroad, **Paganini** composes 60 Variations on *Barucabà* for violin and guitar.

Schumann completes *Carnaval* (Op. 9), a cycle of piano pieces based around the letters of his fiancée's birthplace, Asch, translating A flat, C and B natural in German musical notation. Also completed this year is the *Etudes symphoniques* (Op. 13), a piano work based on a theme by his prospective (but never to be) father-in-law, Captain von Fricken.

18 January Russian composer and critic **Cesar Cui** is born in Vilnius.

24 January Bellini presents his final opera, *I Puritani* (The Puritans), at the Théâtre-Italien. Set in 17th-century England during the civil war, the opera storms Paris, as it does London in May.

23 February Halévy (right) and his librettist, **Scribe**, enjoy a sensational première of *La Juive* (The Jewess), lavishly staged at the Paris Opéra. The epic five-act grand opera impresses **Berlioz** and **Wagner** profoundly. Halévy makes colourful use of valve trumpets and valve horns, both very new to the orchestra.

12 March Donizetti's opera *Marino Faliero*, commissioned by **Rossini**, opens at the Théâtre-Italien, Paris.

26 April Chopin introduces his *Grand Polonaise* Op. 22 for piano and orchestra, in Paris. Works for solo piano this year include his Polonaises Op. 26, and the Scherzo in B minor Op. 20.

August Mendelssohn swaps his Düsseldorf contract of 600 thaler with three months annual leave for a Leipzig contract of 1,000 thaler with six months annual leave. He will serve as director of the Gewandhaus orchestra for the next 12 years. In the autumn Mendelssohn pens his most famous song, *Auf Flügeln des Gesanges* (On the Wings of Song).

23 September Vincenzo Bellini dies from amoebic dysentery at Puteaux, near Paris, aged 33. **Rossini**, **Paer** and **Cherubini** are among the pall-bearers at his funeral nine days later.

26 September Donizetti's greatest opera, *Lucia di Lammermoor*, is premièred in Naples. Based on Walter Scott's *The Bride of Lammermoor* (1819), its success is rapid throughout Europe and beyond, with productions mounted in Cuba, Mexico, Trinidad, the United States and Indonesia within ten years.

9 October Composer **Camille Saint-Saëns** is born in Paris.

November Schumann, aged 25, has fallen in love with the 16-year-old **Clara Wieck**. He breaks off his engagement with Ernestine von Fricken at the start of the following year.

30 December Donizetti's opera *Maria Stuarda*, to a libretto by Giuseppe Bardari, gets off to a shaky start at La Scala, Milan, with star singer Maria Malibran performing while ill. The composer describes the opening night as 'painful'.

1835 Emperor Franz I of Austria dies and is succeeded by his son Ferdinand I • French republicans try to shoot King Louis Philippe of France; the King escapes but 18 people die; strict laws are introduced in France to curb the Press and to expedite the trial of insurgents • The city of Melbourne, Australia, is founded • In Argentina, politician Juan de Rosas imposes a dictatorship • The Municipal Reform Act provides for locally elected councils in Britain • Samuel Colt (US) patents his revolver • Nikolai Gogol (Russ): *Dead Souls* • William Wordsworth (Eng): poem *Yarrow Revisited* • Honoré de Balzac (Fr): *Le Père Goriot*

1836

English composer **William Sterndale Bennett** composes his *Naiads* overture.

Chopin's Ballade in G minor for piano (Op. 23), the first work of his own invented genre, is published in Leipzig, Paris and London.

Rossini separates from his wife **Isabella Colbran**. The retired soprano will live with Rossini's father until her death in 1845. Towards the end of the year Rossini leaves Paris, returning to Italy where he remains for the next 19 years.

21 February French opera composer **Léo Clément Philibert Delibes** is born in St Germain du Val.

29 February **Meyerbeer**'s five-act epic *Les Huguenots*, on a libretto by **Scribe** and **Emile Deschamps**, premières at the Paris Opéra with resounding success. **Berlioz** is awestruck by Meyerbeer's conducting and musical imagination. Depicting Catholic fanaticism in the 16th century, *Les Huguenots* becomes one of the most frequently performed operas of the 19th century.

29 March The world-renowned Spanish mezzo soprano **Maria Malibran** (above), aged 28, marries the Belgian composer-violinist **Charles-Auguste de Bériot**. During the summer she is thrown from her horse while riding in London's Regents Park. Bériot loses both his wife and unborn child on 23 September.

22 May Mendelssohn breathes life into the abeyant form of the oratorio with

St Paul, first performed in Düsseldorf with the composer conducting.

13 October Adam's comic opera *Le postillon de Longjumeau* is premièred in Paris. It soon enjoys considerable international success.

18 November Librettist **William Schwenck Gilbert** is born in The Strand, London.

24 November Wagner begins a turbulent marriage with the actress Minna Planer. Just months later, in a fit of despair, Minna runs off with a rich merchant. (See also 1837.)

9 December Glinka, aged 32, lays the foundation stone of Russian opera with *A Life for the Tsar*, staged at the Bol'shoy Theatre in St Petersburg. The co-authored libretto is heavily influenced by the nationalistic literary movement, while the music successfully integrates Russian folk rhythms and folksong. 'What an opera you can make out of our national tunes!' writes Nikolai Gogol, 'Glinka's opera is only a beautiful beginning'.

12 December Venice's Teatro La Fenice (Phoenix Theatre) is destroyed by fire. It re-emerges from the ashes the following year.

A Life for the Tsar: stage design for Act V (Epilogue): Red Square, Moscow

1836 Texas declares independence from Mexico: 150 Americans are killed at the Siege of Alamo: defeat of the Mexicans at San Jacinto wins Texas Freedom as a republic • In South Africa, many Boers move northwards from Cape Colony in the 'Great Trek' and found the Orange Free State • Adelaide is founded as the capital of South Australia • Peru and Bolivia form a federation • John Ericsson (Swed) patents a screw propeller for ships • Edmund Davy (Eng) discovers acetylene gas • Charles Darwin (Eng) returns to Britain aboard the HMS Beagle • Charles Dickens (Eng): *The Pickwick Papers* and *Sketches by Boz* • Nikolai Gogol (Russ): *The Inspector-General*

1837

Chopin issues his second set of 12 Etudes, Op. 25.

Schumann enriches his piano music output with two sets of character pieces: the *Davidsbündler Dances*, Op. 6, and *Fantasiestücke*, Op. 12.

Clara Wieck has her Piano Concerto in A minor published in Leipzig. She completed the work two years previously, aged 16.

2 January Composer **Mily Alekseyevich Balakirev** is born in Nizhniy Novgorod.

23 January Influential Dublin-born composer and pianist composer **John Field**, inventor of the nocturne and champion of the cantabile style, dies aged 54 in Moscow.

28 March Mendelssohn marries Cécile Jeanrenaud in Frankfurt.

31 March Liszt (right) makes a return visit to Paris to contest **Sigismond Thalberg**'s status as the city's leading piano virtuoso. After criticising his compositions in the *Revue et gazette musicale*, Liszt goes head-to-head with Thalberg in a piano duel at the home of Princess Cristina Belgiojoso in Paris. Both composers perform fantasies on operatic themes—Thalberg on **Rossini**'s *Mosè in Egitto*, Liszt on **Pacini**'s *Niobe*. Afterwards the hostess adjudicates tactfully: 'Thalberg is the premier pianist of the world. Liszt is unique.'

Early–mid July Chopin, accompanied by the piano manufacturer Camille Pleyel, visits England for the first time. He attends to business affairs in London with the publisher Wessel, but otherwise keeps a low profile and departs after 11 days.

21 August Wagner arrives in Riga to take up the post of musical director to the town's theatre. His tiny apartment is soon shared with his repentant wife (see 1836), his sister-in-law and a pet wolf cub. After a few weeks they decide the wolf has to go.

September Schumann, eager to marry **Clara Wieck**, is grilled by her father. In no uncertain terms he is told that marriage is out of the question, as are any sort of private meetings; only very public encounters are permissible. Schumann writes of the meeting to Clara: 'Such coldness, such malice … he thrusts the knife into the heart, right up to the hilt.'

21 September Mendelssohn gives a very successful première of his Piano Concerto No. 2 in D minor at the Birmingham Music Festival.

17 October Composer and pianist **Johann Hummel** dies in Weimar, aged 58.

5 December Berlioz's Requiem (*Grande Messe des Morts*), commissioned by the French government, triumphs at the church of Les Invalides in Paris. In addition to a 300-strong orchestra and choir, Berlioz incorporates four antiphonal brass sections and an array of percussionists to create an epic representation of the last judgement in the *Dies Irae*.

22 December Albert Lortzing writes the libretto, composes the music and sings the part of Peter Ivanov in his opera *Zar und Zimmermann* (Tsar and Carpenter), premièred in Leipzig. Lortzing is now recognised as Germany's leading composer of comic opera.

24 December Cosima Liszt is born to Countess Marie d'Agoult and **Franz Liszt** in Como, Italy.

1837 Martin van Buren is inaugurated as 8th President of the USA • Financial panic in USA is caused by wave of speculation • William IV of England dies; is succeeded by Queen Victoria as ruler of England and by the Duke of Cumberland, as King Ernst August of Hanover • A rebellion in Lower Canada is defeated after initial success • Boers begin occupying Zulu-land and Natal in South Africa • Henry Craufurd (Eng) patents galvanised Iron • Nathanial Hawthorne (US): *Twice-Told Tales* • Isaac Pitman (Eng) publishes *Stenographic Soundhand*, developing shorthand • Thomas Carlyle (Scot): *The French Revolution* • Charles Dickens (Eng): *Oliver Twist*

The Promenade Concerts begin in London. **Liszt** begins composing the first of his *Années de pèlerinage* piano pieces, and also the *Etudes d'exécution transcendante d'après Paganini*, dedicated to the young virtuoso **Clara Wieck**.

The first two volumes of **A. B. Marx**'s influential treatise *Die Lehre von der musikalischen Komposition* (The School of Musical Composition) are published in Leipzig.

Mendelssohn composes his Violin Sonata in F major and the Cello Sonata No. 1 in B flat major.

Schumann composes piano character pieces in his popular *Kinderszenen* (Scenes from Childhood) and the monumental *Kreisleriana* suite.

6 January German composer **Max Christian Friedrich Bruch** is born in Cologne.

30 January Donizetti's *Maria de Rudenz* falls flat at the Teatro La Fenice, Venice. With libretto by **Salvadore Cammarano**, the opera folds after two performances.

Spring While in Venice, **Liszt** hears news of a devastating flood in Pest that has destroyed neighbourhoods and farmland, creating a humanitarian crisis. He travels to Vienna where he gives ten charity concerts, raising 24,000 gulden for the flood victims.

7 March In Stockholm the Swedish soprano **Jenny Lind** makes her operatic début as Agathe in *Der Freischütz*.

15 March Clara Wieck, aged 18, is named Royal and Imperial Chamber Virtuosa by the Emperor of Austria.

12 April Johann Strauss (**I**) and his band begin a British tour, performing at public concerts, private balls and soirées at Buckingham Palace. Cashing in on the coronation celebrations of Queen Victoria, Strauss has written the waltz *Hommage à la reine de la Grand Bretagne*, Op. 102.

Summer Chopin begins a relationship with the French novelist and pipe-smoker George Sand, née Amandine Aurore Dupin (left), of whom just the previous year he had commented, 'What an unattractive person La Sand is. Is she really a woman? I am inclined to doubt it.' They spend the winter months in Majorca, residing in a cold monastery where Chopin's health deteriorates severely.

17 August For the past 33 years a US resident, legendary Classical-era librettist **Lorenzo da Ponte** dies in New York, aged 89.

10 September Berlioz's opera *Benvenuto Cellini* flops at the Paris Opéra, primarily due to an inept libretto.

October Donizetti leaves Naples to make his name in Paris. He finds accommodation in the same building as stage composer **Adolphe Adam**.

25 October French opera composer **Georges Alexandre César Léopold Bizet** is born in Paris.

16 December In Paris **Paganini** attends a concert given by **Berlioz** and hears for the first time the work he himself rejected: *Harold in Italy* (1834). The symphony for solo viola and orchestra so impresses Paganini that he sends Berlioz a gift of 20,000 francs two days later. (See also 1839.)

1838 Rebellion in Upper Canada is suppressed • Chartist movement: a People's Charter, demanding parliamentary and social reform, is published in Britain • Boers defeat forces of Zulu chief Dingaan at Blood River • The British Military Mission at Herat, Persia, is besieged • Samuel Morse (US) sends his first telegraph message • An 'underground railroad' is organised for escaping slaves in USA • A regular transatlantic steamship service starts • The National Gallery opens in London, England • Edgar Allan Poe (US): *Arthur Gordon Pym* • Karl Immerman (Ger): *Münchhausen* • Charles Dickens (Eng): *Nicholas Nickleby* • Victor Hugo (Fr): play *Ruy Blas*

Czerny's *Complete Theoretical and Practical Pianoforte School*, Op. 500, is published in Vienna.

The two-year-old **W. S. Gilbert** is kidnapped by brigands while on a family holiday in Naples. He is held to ransom and later released to his father on payment of £25. The incident will later inspire Gilbert in his writing of *The Gondoliers*.

Mendelssohn composes his Piano Trio in D minor, Op. 49.

Schumann publishes his much lauded *Fantasie in C major* for piano (Op. 17), composed three years earlier but recently revised.

1 January Schumann visits Ferdinand Schubert, brother of Franz Schubert (d. 1828), to examine the composer's unpublished scores. He finds Schubert's Ninth (*Great*) Symphony in C major, which he sends to **Mendelssohn**. (See below.)

17 January Mendelssohn conducts the first performance of **Sterndale Bennett**'s Piano Concerto No. 4 in F minor, at the Gewandhaus in Leipzig.

21 March Composer **Modest Petrovich Mussorgsky** is born in Karevo, in the Pskov district of Russia.

21 March Mendelssohn conducts the première of Schubert's Ninth Symphony in Leipzig. Despite some editing, the technical difficulties of the music challenge the orchestra, which accounts for the slow acceptance of the symphony into the repertory.

3 May Italian composer **Ferdinando Paer** dies in Paris, aged 68.

9 May A third child, Daniel, is born to **Liszt** and Marie d'Agoult (right), but their relationship will break down by the autumn. 1839 sees the composition of the *Dante* Sonata.

10 July Fondly remembered for his guitar music, **Fernando Sor** dies in Paris, aged 61. Towards the end of his life the composer had become deeply frustrated with public demand for facile music. One of his later guitar publications, Op. 45, is introduced as 'Six short and easy pieces … dedicated to the person with the least patience.'

Summer With heavy debts and impounded passports, **Wagner** and his wife, Minna, together with their dog, Robber, quietly exit Riga and sneak across the boarder at nightfall, evading armed Cossack guards. They are smuggled aboard a merchant vessel in Pillau, Prussia, and endure a perilous voyage to London, taking shelter in a Norwegian fjord during a violent storm. Their journey ends in Paris, where for the next two years Wagner will scrape together an existence as an arranger and music critic.

Summer-autumn Chopin, now enjoying good health at Nohant, completes a number of piano works begun in previous years, including his Mazurkas Op. 41, the Sonata in B flat minor Op. 35 (including the famous Funeral March), and the 24 Preludes, Op. 28.

17 November Verdi's first opera, *Oberto*, to a libretto by **Temistocle Solera** and possibly absorbing an earlier effort entitled *Rocester*, opens with reasonable success at La Scala in Milan.

24 November Berlioz's Third Symphony, *Romeo and Juliet*, scored for solo voices, chorus and orchestra, triumphs in Paris. The composition of the 'dramatic symphony' has been facilitated by **Paganini**'s gift of 20,000 francs from the previous year. Berlioz dedicates the work to the violin maestro.

1839 Chartists' petition is rejected by Britain's parliament and riots follow • First Anglo-Afghan War begins • First Opium War between Britain and China begins • The Peru-Bolivian Federation is dissolved after Chilean victory at Yungay • Uruguay at war with Argentina • French forces withdraw from Mexico • Belgium's independence is recognised by the Netherlands

• Luxembourg becomes an independent Grand Duchy • Charles Goodyear (US) discovers vulcanisation of rubber • William Fox Talbot (Eng) reveals his invention of photographic paper • J. M. W. Turner (Eng) paints *The Fighting Téméraire* • Henry Wadsworth Longfellow (US): poem *Voices of the Night* • Stendhal (Fr): *The Charterhouse of Parma*

4 January Liszt is presented with a jewel-encrusted sabre in Pest in recognition of his outstanding achievements and service that have brought honour to Hungary.

February Schumann, up to now rather dismissive of lieder, begins what he will later refer to as his *Liederjahr* (Year of Song). Over the next 11 months he composes around 128 songs, including the celebrated *Dichterliebe* cycle, Op. 48.

11 February Donizetti scores an instant hit with his comic opera *La fille du regiment* (The Daughter of the Regiment) in Paris.

7 May Russian composer **Pyotr Il'yich Tchaikovsky**, second son of a mining engineer, is born in Kamsko-Votkinsk, Vyatka province.

27 May Having spent his last years dealing in fine stringed instruments, **Nicolò Paganini** dies in Nice, aged 57. He is denied a Catholic burial on the grounds that he refused the 'last rites', a decision he took believing he was not about to die.

9 June Liszt introduces the term 'recital' to musical performance, advertising his solo concert at London's Hanover Square Rooms.

18 June Verdi loses his wife, Margherita, to encephalitis, shortly after the death of his two children. In a profound state of grief he has to complete the comic opera *Un giorno di regno* (A day of reign). Staged later this year, it fails miserably and Verdi vows to abandon composition.

25 June Mendelssohn conducts the première of his Second Symphony (*Lobgesang*) in Leipzig. His 'symphony-cantata after words of the Holy Bible' has been commissioned for a festival celebrating the quadricentenary of Gutenberg's Leipzig printing press. Comprising a three-movement orchestral sinfonia followed by a nine-movement cantata, this ambitious work enjoys immense popularity during Mendelssohn's lifetime.

28 July Berlioz's *Grande symphonie funèbre et triomphale* premières in Paris, marking the tenth anniversary of the July Revolution.

12 September Schumann marries **Clara Wieck** following a court battle with her father who has attempted to prevent their union. The ceremony takes place in Schönefeld, near Leipzig.

> *We wonder how [George Sand] can be content to wanton away her dreamlike existence with an artistic nonentity like Chopin.*
> **October** From the *Musical World*, London.

Late October Wagner is imprisoned for debt, in Paris. He has just completed his opera *Rienzi*.

Joseph Danhauser's painting, from this year, depicting Liszt at the piano surrounded by famous literary and musical figures of the Paris scene. Left to right: Dumas, Hugo, George Sand (Amandine Dudevant), Paganini, Rossini and Liszt. To the right of Liszt sits his mistress, Marie d'Agoult.

1840 Upper and Lower Canada are united by Canadian Act of Union • An uprising in France led by Louis Napoleon, nephew of Napoleon I, fails • Russia, Britain, Austria and Prussia unite in a war against Egypt • New Zealand becomes a British colony and the city of Auckland is founded • The penny post is introduced in Britain, together with the first adhesive postage stamps • Eugène Delacroix (Fr) paints *The Justice of Trajan* • Jean Louis Agassiz (Switz): *Study of Glaciers* • Edgar Allan Poe (US): *Tales of the Grotesque and Arabesque* • Charles Dickens (Eng): *The Old Curiosity Shop* • Charles Darwin (Eng): *Zoology of the Voyage of the Beagle*

1841

Berlioz composes his *Rêverie et caprice* romance for violin and orchestra. He also completes his sensuous *Nuits d'été*, setting six poems by his firend **Théophile Gautier**. Scored for solo voice and piano, the songs are orchestrated by Berlioz 15 years later.

Chopin composes the F sharp minor Polonaise Op. 44, the two nocturnes of Op. 48, and the F minor Fantasy Op. 49.

Adolphe Sax invents the saxophone, which he patents five years later.

18 January French composer **Emmanuel Chabrier** is born in Ambert, Puy-de-Dôme.

31 March Schumann's First Symphony *Spring* suggests the season's arrival through to its farewell, at Leipzig's Gewandhaus. **Mendelssohn** conducts the successful première and Schumann's confidence is bolstered considerably.

26 April Chopin, under pressure from friends, gives a rare public concert at the Salle Pleyel in Paris. Nearly 400 attend the evening's performance, from which the composer-pianist pockets around 6,000 Francs. The sale of his printed works subsequently rockets.

28 June Believing herself jilted, a beautiful peasant girl dies with a broken heart and turns into a dancing spirit (a 'Wili') in the ballet *Giselle*, premièred with spectacular success at the Paris Opéra. **Adolphe Adam** (right) brings to musical life a scenario by **Théophile**

Gautier and **Vernoy Saint-Georges**. The original idea derives from a poem in Heinrich Heine's *De l'Allemagne* (1835).

July Spontini is accused of *lèse majesté*—offending the crown—with some ill-judged remarks made in Berlin. He is sacked from his job as music director of the Royal Opera House and sentenced to nine months' imprisonment. **Meyerbeer** takes up the vacant post. Spontini is eventually saved from jail by a royal pardon.

1 August Mendelssohn arrives in Berlin to take up a one-year appointment as *Kapellmeister* to Friedrich August II, King of Prussia. The composer has recently completed his *Variations sérieuses* in D minor (Op. 54) for piano.

8 September Composer **Antonín Leopold Dvořák** is born in Nelahozeves, 25 miles north of Prague.

Autumn Verdi completes his opera *Nabucco* despite his resolution to give up professional composition. (See 1840.)

6 December Schumann's *Overture, Scherzo and Finale* and his Symphony in D minor, both composed this year, make little impression at the Gewandhaus in Leipzig. (Schumann will revise the symphony ten years later as his Fourth Symphony.) The disappointment of the concert triggers several months of depression.

26 December La Scala, Milan, mounts the first production of **Donizetti**'s opera *Maria Padilla*.

1841 William Henry Harrison, inaugurated as the 9th President of the USA, dies a month later: Vice-President John Tyler becomes 10th President • The Pre-Emption Distribution Act controls land settlement in the USA • The Straits Convention closes Dardanelles and Bosphorus to all but Turkey's warships • New Zealand becomes a British colony

• Thomas Cook (Eng) starts his travel agency • David Livingstone (Scot) starts his missionary work in South Africa • James Russell Lowell (US): first volume of poems • Edgar Allan Poe publishes one of the first detective classics: *The Murders in the Rue Morgue* • Humourous and satirical magazine *Punch* makes its first appearance in England

Schumann composes his Piano Quintet in E flat major (Op. 44), one of his most popular and enduring works. Other chamber compositions this year include the Piano Quartet in E flat major (Op. 47) and the *Phantasiestücke* for piano trio (Op. 88).

3 March **Mendelssohn** conducts the première of his recently completed *Scottish* Symphony, in Leipzig.

3 March **Liszt** is driven ceremoniously to the Brandenburg Gate in a coach drawn by six white horses after a sensational series of 21 concerts in Berlin. Admirers follow in scores of carriages and private coaches, with cheering fans lining the streets. The poet Heinrich Heine has dubbed the craze surrounding the composer 'Lisztomania'.

9 March **Verdi** establishes his international reputation with *Nabucco*, his third opera, premièred with enormous success at La Scala, Milan. With the popularity of the 'Chorus of the Hebrew Slaves'—or 'Va, pensiero'—Verdi becomes associated with the Risorgimento, a movement campaigning for Italian unity and independence.

15 March French citizen **Luigi Cherubini**, Italian-born composer and teacher, dies in Paris, aged 81.

28 March In Vienna **Otto Nicolai** conducts the inaugural concert of the Philharmonic Academy, later renamed the Vienna Philharmonic.

16 April Tsar Nicholas I meets **Liszt**, in Russia:

'We are almost compatriots, Monsieur Liszt.'
'Sire?'
'You are Hungarian, are you not?'
'Yes, Your Majesty.'
'Well, I have a regiment in Hungary.'

Late April **Liszt** performs at the Nobles' Assembly Hall, St Petersburg before an audience of 3,000.

12 May French Composer **Jules Emile Frédéric Massenet** is born in Montaud.

13 May Composer **Arthur Seymour Sullivan** is born in Lambeth, London.

19 May **Donizetti**'s opera *Linda di Chamounix* triumphs at the Kärntnertortheater in Vienna. This year Emperor Ferdinand I makes Donizetti his court composer and *Hofkapellmeister* to the Habsburg court.

Summer In Nohant **Chopin** composes an inspired series of keyboard masterpieces, including the Ballade in F minor Op. 52, the Polonaise in A flat (*Heroic*) Op. 53, and the Scherzo in E major Op. 54. At the end of the summer Chopin and George Sand relocate to Square d'Orléans in Paris.

June–July **Mendelssohn** twice enjoys the company of Queen Victoria and Prince Albert. The queen sings songs by Mendelssohn and his sister, **Fanny**.

20 October **Wagner** achieves his first major operatic success with a lavish, six-hour production of *Rienzi, der Letzte der Tribunen* (Rienzi, the Last of the Tribunes), in Dresden. Composed to his own libretto after an English novel by Edward Bulwer-Lytton, the five-act grand opera follows in the heroic tradition of Auber and Meyerbeer.

2 November **Liszt** becomes *Kapellmeister* at Weimar, but does take up residence until 1848.

9 December **Glinka**'s magical *Russlan and Ludmilla* is introduced in St Petersburg. Based on a narrative poem by Pushkin, the composer's second opera fails to match the popularity of *A Life for the Tsar* (1836).

31 December **Lortzing**'s new comic opera *Der Wildschütz* (The Poacher) delights Leipzig.

1842 Webster-Ashburton Treaty settles boundary disputes over the frontier between USA and Canada • British forces withdraw from Afghanistan; the First Afghan War ends • Britain's war with China ends • Hong Kong becomes British • Industrial unrest in Britain is marked by Chartist risings • The Second Seminole war ends • Christian Döppler (Aus) describes the effect of velocity on sound and light waves • Income tax is reintroduced into Britain • Alfred Tennyson (Eng): *Morte d'Arthur and Other Idylls* • Edgar Allan Poe (US): *The Masque of the Red Death* • Henry Wadsworth Longfellow (US): *Poems of Slavery* • Nikolai Gogol (Russ): *Dead Souls*, an 'epic poem in prose'

Schumann organises the publication of **Robert Franz**'s first song collection, *Zwölf Gesänge*, without the composer's knowledge.

2 January Wagner conducts the first of only four performances of *Der Fliegende Holländer* (The Flying Dutchman) in Dresden. The opera concerns a Dutch sea captain who seeks release from purgatory through the unconditional love of a woman. Wagner later states that a perilous sea crossing he undertook with his wife and dog from Prussia to England directly inspired the work (see 1839).

3 January Donizetti's hugely popular *Don Pasquale* is first staged in Paris. Productions of the comic opera follow in Milan, Vienna and London over the next six months.

8 January Schumann's Piano Quintet (See 1842) is premièred at the Gewandhaus in Leipzig. At the piano is **Clara Schumann**, to whom the quintet is dedicated.

11 February Thunderous applause greets **Verdi**'s new opera *I Lombardi alla prima crociata* (The Lombards on the First Crusade) at La Scala, Milan. The libretto is by **Temistocle Solera**, Verdi's collaborator on *Oberto* (1839) and *Nabucco* (1842).

2 March Danish composer **Niels Gade** has his First Symphony successfully introduced under **Mendelssohn** in Leipzig.

15 March Halévy's grand opera *Charles VI* is warmly received in Paris.

3 April The Leipzig Conservatory opens under the directorship of **Mendelssohn**, with staff members including **Schumann** and **Ferdinand David**.

14 April Dance music maestro **Josef Lanner** dies of typhus near Vienna, aged 42.

May Berlioz ends a six-month concert tour of predominantly German towns and cities. This year his *Grand traité d'instrumentation et d'orchestration modernes* is published in Paris.

15 June Composer **Edvard Hagerup Grieg** is born in Bergen, Norway.

August Violinist **Joseph Joachim**, aged 12, makes his public début at the Gewandhaus in Leipzig.

14 October Mendelssohn's incidental music to *A Midsummer Night's Dream* is first played in its entirety for a Ludwig Tieck production at the Potsdam court. This year Mendelssohn composes his Cello Sonata No. 2 in D, Op. 58.

13 November The première of **Donizetti**'s final opera, the five-act *Dom Sébastien*, encounters a luke-warm reception in Paris. The composer will struggle with worsening physical and mental health over the next five years.

27 November The Irish composer **Michael Balfe** (right) introduces *The Bohemian Girl* at London's Drury Lane Theatre. His grand opera wins over the public and soon gains popularity abroad.

2 December Franz Berwald's First Symphony, *Sinfonie sérieuse*, is premièred in Stockholm. It is the only one of his four symphonies performed during his lifetime. The critics are disparaging.

4 December Schumann enjoys success with his mythical oratorio *Das Paradies und die Peri* (Paradise and the Peri) in Leipzig. Adapted from Thomas Moore's poem *Lalla Rookh*, the work tells the tale of Peri, a Persian spirit, who finds passage into paradise by understanding the eternal significance of a repentant sinner.

1843 British troops led by General Charles Napier conquer the Sind region of India • Gambia in West Africa becomes a separate British Crown Colony • Greeks rise against King Otto I • Natal in South Africa is declared a British Crown Colony • Basutoland (modern Botswana) is put under British protection • A Treaty with China gives Britain most-favoured-nation status • First Maori War begins in New Zealand • James Prescott Joule (Eng) establishes the relation of heat to energy • The Mormon Church recognises polygamy • The United Free Church of Scotland is formed • William Wordsworth is appointed Britain's Poet Laureate • Charles Dickens (Eng): *A Christmas Carol*

Fétis publishes his *Biographie universelle des musiciens* and *Traité de l'harmonie* in Brussels.

Mendelssohn's compositions this year include the English anthem *Hear my Prayer* to a text by his friend William Bartholomew, and his Violin Concerto in E minor, written for the virtuoso **Ferdinand David**.

25 January The **Schumanns** embark on a four-month tour of Russia. The trip does much to promote Clara's reputation as a celebrated pianist, but does little for Robert's career. Meanwhile the composer's physical and mental health deteriorates.

3 February Berlioz directs the first performance of his *Roman Carnival* overture (above). This year he also composes the *Corsaire* overture, and conducts more than 1,000 performers at a concert of the Grand Festival de l'Industrie in Paris.

21 February Composer and organist **Charles-Marie-Jean-Albert Widor** is born in Lyon.

9 March Verdi's fifth opera, *Ernani*, based on Victor Hugo's *Hernani*, premières with great success at the Teatro la Fenice, Venice. It is Verdi's first collaboration with the librettist **Francesco Piave**.

18 March Russian composer **Nikolay Andreyevich Rimsky-Korsakov** is born at Tikhvin, in the province of Novgorod.

May Mendelssohn arrives in London with the 12-year-old violinist **Joachim** who stuns the public with a performance of Beethoven's violin concerto. Mendelssohn conducts several concerts at the Philharmonic society and performs Bach's Triple Concerto in D minor with **Moscheles** and **Thalberg**.

Summer Schumann suffers a nervous breakdown.

15 October As composer and conductor, **Johann Strauss II** makes his public début at Dommayer's Garden Restaurant, Vienna. He closes the concert with his waltz *Sinngedichte*, which the audience seems to enjoy. They encore it 19 times.

8 December Clara Schumann takes part in the first performance of her husband **Robert**'s Piano Quartet at a farewell party for the composer and his wife in Leipzig. Five days later they depart for Dresden.

LE DÉSERT.

FÉLICIEN DAVID

8 December Félicien David presents his exotic symphonic ode *Le désert* (left) in Paris, scored in three movements for speaker, soloists, male-voice chorus and orchestra. This and other works by David inspired by the Near East will influence the next generation of French composers, including Bizet, Delibes and Saint-Saëns.

30 December Flotow's melodious three-act opera *Alessandro Stradella*, based on the amorous antics of the 17th century composer and singer, premières with success in Hamburg.

1844 Daniel O'Connell, Irishman who advocates repealing the Act of Union with Britain, is sentenced for sedition, but the verdict is not upheld by the House of Lords • The Treaty of Wanghsia between USA and China protects US citizens • James Knox Polk is elected 11th President of the USA • Samuel Morse's telegraph is first used to transmit a news message in the US • Horace Wells (US) introduces nitrous oxide ('laughing gas') to dentistry • J. M. W. Turner (Eng) paints *Rain, Steam and Speed* • Alexandre Dumas (Fr): *The Three Musketeers* • Charles Dickens (Eng): *Martin Chuzzlewit* • Economist John Stuart Mill (Eng): *Unsettled Questions of Political Economy*

Berwald composes his Symphony No. 3 in C major (*Symphonie singulière*) and Symphony No. 4 in E flat major.

Mendelssohn (right) composes his Piano Trio in C minor, Op. 66, dedicated to **Louis Spohr**.

Schumann is suffering from depression, exhaustion and insomnia, as well as a host of additional bodily complaints. His doctor advises him to abandon composition, as it seems to exacerbate his condition.

13 March Mendelssohn combines symphonic and virtuoso concerto styles in his renowned Violin Concerto in E minor (1844), premièred with the soloist **Ferdinand David** and the Gewandhaus Orchestra, in Leipzig. **Niels Gade** conducts, as Mendelssohn is struggling with poor health.

March–April In Paris **Berlioz** organises two concerts of **Glinka**'s music, including extracts from the operas *A Life for the Tsar* (1836) and *Ruslan* (1842). Glinka, almost at the end of a 10-month sojourn in the French capital, departs for Spain in May.

21 April Lortzing's 'romantic magic opera' *Undine* is first performed in Magdeburg.

12 May French composer **Gabriel Urbain Fauré** is born in Pamiers, Ariège.

4 June William Fry's *Leonora* premières in Philadelphia. It is considered to be the first publicly-staged opera written by an American-born composer.

Summer Schumann adds a slow movement and rondo to his *Phantasie* in A minor for piano and orchestra (1841), creating his immensely popular Piano Concerto Op. 54. **Clara Schumann** will champion the work in her concert tours.

10 August The Beethoven monument is unveiled in Bonn. **Liszt** attends the ceremony, having helped raise crucial funds for the memorial through charity concerts.

11 August Donizetti writes to his brother-in-law about his nervous breakdown. The doctors have advised no composition for two years, regular footbaths, 'decoctions four times a day', and '12 leeches on the anus'.

Autumn Inspired by Spanish folk music, **Glinka**, in Madrid, composes the overture *Capriccio brillante on the Jota aragonesa*.

19 October Wagner combines the legends of a Venus-worshiping knight and a song contest at Wartburg in *Tannhäuser*, first staged at the Hoftheater in Dresden. The reception is mixed, although the opera is accepted into the German repertory over the next ten years. Wagner's repeated revisions will result in four versions of the opera, none of which are to his complete satisfaction.

2 December German composer (**Johann**) **Simon Mayr**, admired for his music for stage and church, dies in Bergamo, aged 82.

25 December Wilhelm Friedrich Ernst Bach (son of J. C. F. Bach) brings to an end the illustrious Bach musical dynasty, dying in Berlin aged 86.

1845 Florida becomes the 27th state of the USA • Texas is annexed and becomes 28th State of the USA • Seven Swiss Roman Catholic cantons unite to form the Sonderbund • The USA and Mexico disagree over frontiers • British are victorious in war with Sikhs in India; annexes the Punjab • The Great Famine begins in Ireland as Potato crops fail • Building of London's Trafalgar Square completed • Gustave Courbet (Fr) paints *The Desperate Man* (Self-portrait) • Alexandre Dumas (Fr): *The Count of Monte Cristo* • Honoré de Balzac (Fr): *Les Paysons* • Edgar Allan Poe (US): *Tales of Mystery and Imagination* • Benjamin Disraeli (Eng): *Sybil* • Friedrich Engels (Ger): *Condition of the Working Classes in England*

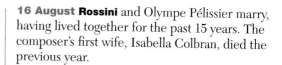

Chopin completes his Cello Sonata in G minor, Op. 65, and the Barcarolle in F sharp major, Op. 60 and composes the Polonaise-Fantasy, Op. 61. During this year his relationship with George Sand deteriorates and next year they separate.

Composer **Fanny Mendelssohn**, previously discouraged from publishing by her brother, **Felix**, finally goes to print, issuing six Lieder and four Piano Lieder as her Opp. 1 & 2. This year marks the composition of her Piano Trio.

Moscheles, aged 52, leaves London for Leipzig where he will become principal professor of piano at the city's conservatory.

1 January Clara Schumann, nine months pregnant, premières **Robert**'s richly melodic Piano Concerto in A minor under **Mendelssohn**'s direction at the Leipzig Gewandhaus.

1 February Suffering paralysis and dementia due to syphilis, **Donizetti** is institutionalised at a sanatorium in Ivry, outside Paris.

17 March Verdi's *Attila* meets with little acclaim at the Teatro La Fenice, Venice. The opera will enjoy a short period of success during the 1850s.

16 April Once the highest paid orchestral player in England, Italian composer and double-bassist **Domenico Dragonetti** (right) dies in London, aged 83.

6 May Saint-Saëns, aged ten, makes his début at the Salle Pleyel in Paris. He performs from memory a programme that includes Mozart's Piano Concerto in B flat, K. 450 (with his own cadenza), and Beethoven's Piano Concerto No. 3 in C minor.

16 August Rossini and Olympe Pélissier marry, having lived together for the past 15 years. The composer's first wife, Isabella Colbran, died the previous year.

26 August Mendelssohn conducts the first performance of his oratorio *Elijah* in Birmingham. The monumental work creates a sensation: 'The last note of *Elijah* was drowned in a long-continued unanimous volley of plaudits, vociferous and deafening', reports *The Times*, 'never was there a more complete triumph'.

Summer–autumn Liszt begins writing the first of his *Hungarian Rhapsodies* for piano, having been inspired by folk and gypsy music while touring Hungary.

5 November Schumann's Second Symphony receives its première at the Leipzig Gewandhaus under **Mendelssohn**. Progressing from turmoil and struggle in the first movement to celebration and victory in the last, the work reflects Schumann's physical health during the compositional process.

10 November Influential Italian opera composer **Saverio Mercadante** recounts ancient Roman legend in *Orazi e Curiazi* (The Horatii and the Curiatii), introduced with great success at the Teatro San Carlo in Naples.

24 November Robert and **Clara Schumann** begin a concert tour of Vienna, Brno and Prague.

6 December Berlioz's ambitious *La Damnation de Faust*, his self-termed *Légende dramatique*, is given the first of two concert performances at the Opéra-Comique (Salle Favart) in Paris. Having financed the copyists, performers and theatre-hire, Berlioz is mortified at the poor turn out. Freezing weather plus general apathy equals financial disaster.

1846 War breaks out between USA and Mexico: Americans capture Sante Fe: New Mexico is annexed • Oregon Treaty with Britain extends 49th Parallel as boundary between USA and Canada to Pacific Coast • In India, British war against the Sikhs ends and British possessions are expanded • Elias Howe (US) patents a sewing machine • Mormons begin the migration which ends at the Great Salt Lake • Pope Gregory XVI is succeeded by Pius IX • British parliament repeals corn laws • The Irish potato crop again fails and famine spreads • Astronomer Johann Galle (Ger) observes the planet Neptune • Fyodor Dostoyevsky (Russ): first novel, *Poor Folk*

10 January The renowned soprano **Jenny Lind** appears in a sell-out concert with **Clara Schumann** in Vienna. Three concerts of **Robert Schumann**'s music over the past month have been otherwise disappointing, poorly-attended affairs.

14 February Hoping to make amends for the financial failure of *Faust* (see 1846), **Berlioz** sets out for a Russian tour, leaving Paris by train and arriving by horse-drawn sledge in St Petersburg two weeks later.

14 March The first version of **Verdi**'s *Macbeth* is introduced at the Teatro della Pergola, Florence. With text by **Piave** after Shakespeare's tragedy, the opera enjoys immediate success. Verdi will revise the work in 1865.

15 March In St Petersburg **Berlioz** kicks off his Russian concert tour with a programme including the first two acts of *The Damnation of Faust* and the *Roman Carnival*. Halfway through the concert he is summoned before the Empress who flatters him with praise. Berlioz pockets 12,000 francs from the evening, with another concert ten days later producing similar results.

12 April Mendelssohn arrives in England for a short tour of London, Manchester and Birmingham. He brings with him a revised version of his oratorio *Elijah*.

14 May Fanny Mendelssohn (right), pianist and composer of many lieder and piano works, dies from a stroke in Berlin, aged 41. Her devastated brother, **Felix**, composes his anguished String Quartet

in F minor (Op. 80) two months later. (See also below.)

22 July Queen Victoria attends the successful première of **Verdi**'s *I Masnadieri* (The Bandits) at Her Majesty's Theatre, London. The soprano **Jenny Lind** heads up the cast of what is one of Verdi's more forgettable operas. The queen later records in her diary, 'the music is very shoddy and banal'.

September Liszt, aged 35, gives up professional concert giving, never again taking a fee for a public performance. This year marks the composition of his Hungarian Rhapsody No. 2—the most famous of the collection.

4 November Berlioz arrives in London where he has been appointed conductor of the Grand English Opera at the Drury Lane Theatre. The company will survive only one season.

4 November Mendelssohn dies in Leipzig, aged 38, after a series of strokes. His funeral is held three days later, with **Schumann** and **Moscheles** among the pall-bearers and thousands in attendance. The coffin is conveyed to Berlin and buried beside the grave of the composer's sister, Fanny, at Trinity Church.

25 November German composer **Friedrich Flotow** triumphs in Vienna with his opera *Martha, oder Der Markt zu Richmond* (Martha, or The Richmond Market), set in 18th-century England at the time of Queen Anne. The romantic comedy becomes a global hit by the end of the 1850s.

1847 The Mexican-US war continues: American forces led by General Winfred Scott capture Mexico City • Liberia becomes an independent republic • Civil war in Switzerland: Sonderbund union of Roman Catholic cantons defeated and Lucern is captured: the Sonderbund is dissolved • Gold is discovered in California • Physician James Simpson (Scot) pioneers the use of chloroform as an anaesthetic • Delacroix (Fr) paints *St George and the Dragon* • Charlotte Brontë (Eng): *Jane Eyre* • Emily Brontë (Eng): *Wuthering Heights* • William Makepeace Thackeray (Eng): *Vanity Fair* • Henry Wadsworth Longfellow (US): poem *Evangeline* • Karl Marx (Ger): *The Poverty of Philosophy*

Valentin Alkan's *Grande sonate: Les quatre âges* and the *Douze études* (in all major keys) are published in Paris.

American composer **Stephen Foster** issues his infectious song *Oh! Susanna*.

Drawing on Russian folk melodies, **Glinka** pioneers a nationalistic brand of instrumental music with the orchestral fantasia *Kamarinskaya*, composed in Warsaw.

Liszt, at Weimar (see below), composes the first versions of his symphonic poems *Ce qu'on entend sur la montagne* and *Les preludes*. With these one-movement programmatic works (and others that soon follow) he modifies sonata form and cultivates the process of thematic transformation to create a sense of unfolding narrative.

Nicolai becomes *Kapellmeister* at the Berlin Opera and director of the Berlin Cathedral choir.

Amid the turmoil of the 'Year of Revolutions', **Strauss I** (right) composes his imperialist *Radetzky-Marsch*, but also hedges his bets with the revolution-friendly *Marsch der Studenten-Legion* and *Freiheits-Marsch*.

Tchaikovsky's life is disrupted with the departure of his beloved governess, two home moves and the start of boarding school. The highly sensitive eight-year-old also suffers a prolonged attack of the measles.

February To fulfil his duties as *Kapellmeister*, **Liszt** moves to Weimar where in time he expands the court orchestra and improves the working conditions of its members. He is joined by Princess Carolyne, the separated wife of Prince Nicholas von Sayn-Wittgenstein, with whom he had begun a relationship the previous year.

16 February Chopin, in spite of ill-health, gives his first concert in six years, performing at the Salle Pleyel in Paris.

26 March The revolution in Paris forces **Adolphe Adam**'s Opéra-National to close down only four months after its opening. Adam will take four years to pay off 70,000 francs of debt.

8 April Italian opera composer **Gaetano Donizetti** dies in the care of family and friends in Bergamo, aged 50. The autopsy diagnoses 'cerebro-spinal syphilis'.

20 April While revolutions rage across Europe, **Chopin** escapes to London at the invitation of Jane Stirling and her sister, Mrs Erskine. His hopes for a quiet sojourn are dashed however, with 'endless rounds of visits, dinners and soirées'. A performance in the presence of Queen Victoria fails to gain him any special royal attention.

29 June Berlioz impresses the public and critics alike with a concert of his music at the Hanover Square Rooms in London. He returns to post-revolution Paris the following month.

October Child prodigies **Bizet** and **Saint-Saëns** enrol at the Paris Conservatoire.

23 November Chopin's health deteriorates further as he departs London for Paris.

1848 War between the USA and Mexico ends; Mexico abandons its claim to Texas, and cedes California and New Mexico to USA • 'Year of Revolutions' in Europe: uprisings in Berlin, Budapest, Milan, Naples, Rome, Prague, Venice, Vienna and Warsaw • Pope Pius IX flees from Rome • In France, Louis Napoleon Bonaparte is elected president of the Second Republic • New constitutions are adopted in Austria, Switzerland and Germany • In South Africa, Britain annexes Orange Free State • Pre-Raphaelite Brotherhood of painters is founded in Britain • Karl Marx (Ger) and Freidrich Engels (Ger) publish their *Communist Manifesto* • John Stuart Mill (Eng): *Principles of Political Economy*

1849

Composer **Sterndale Bennett** forms the Bach Society in England.

Louise Farrenc, the only female professor at the Paris Conservatoire, composes her Nonet in E flat major (Op. 38).

14 March Bruckner, aged 24, completes his first significant work, the Requiem in D minor, in memory of his friend Franz Sailer who has bequeathed him a Bösendorfer piano.

16 April Meyerbeer's grand opera *Le Prophète* goes down a storm at the Paris Opéra. It includes a roller-skating ballet (simulating skaters on ice) and uses electricity to power 50 elements of a carbon arc, creating the effect of a rising sun.

Early May As Prussian troops gain control of Dresden, an arrest warrant is issued for **Wagner** who has been identified as a revolutionary activist. With like-minded friends receiving death sentences or life imprisonment, Wagner escapes to Switzerland on a false passport, aided by **Liszt**. Once safely in Zurich he writes his polemical treatise 'Die Kunst und die Revolution' (Art and Revolution). Wagner remains in exile for the next 11 years.

Early May The **Schumanns** escape the revolution in Dresden, fleeing to Kreischa. This year sees the completion of the composer's Byron-inspired *Manfred* overture and incidental music, as well as his *Album for the Young* piano collection.

11 May Composer and conductor **Otto Nicolai** dies

from a stroke in Berlin aged 38, just two months after the triumphant première of his opera *Die lustigen Weiber von Windsor* (The Merry Wives of Windsor).

28 August Liszt presents the first version of his symphonic poem *Tasso: Lamento e Trionfo* (Tasso: Lament and Triumph) in Weimar.

25 September Johann Strauss I dies from scarlet fever in Vienna, aged 45. Two days later around 100,000 Viennese line the streets as his coffin is conveyed to St Stephen's Cathedral. He is laid to rest at Döbling cemetery, next to Josef Lanner.

October Johann Strauss II takes over the directorship of his father's orchestra.

17 October Frédéric Chopin (below) dies in Paris from consumption, aged 39. His heart is removed in accordance with his dying request, the composer having feared being buried alive. The organ is sent in an urn to the Church of the Holy Cross in Warsaw.

30 October Around 3,000 mourners attend Chopin's funeral at the Church of the Madeleine in Paris, with **Meyerbeer** and Delacroix among the pall-bearers. Mozart's Requiem is performed, together with an orchestral arrangement of Chopin's Funeral March from the B flat minor Sonata.

8 December Verdi's tragic opera *Luisa Miller*, with libretto by **Salvadore Cammarano**, is successfully introduced at the Teatro San Carlo in Naples.

1849 Zachary Taylor is inaugurated as 12th President of the USA • In Italy, the patriot Giuseppe Garibaldi fails in an attempt to prevent French troops entering Rome • The French restore Pope Pius IX to Rome • Austrian forces defeat the Piedmontese • King Carlo Alberto of Sardinia and Piedmont abdicates in favour of Vittorio Emmanuele II • The siege of Venice ends uprising in Italy • Denmark adopts a democratic constitution • Walter Hunt (US) patents the safety pin • Pope Pius IX condemns socialism and communism • The California Gold Rush is at its height • Ivan Aivazovsky (Russ-Arm) paints *Stormy Sea at Night* • Charles Dickens (Eng): *David Copperfield* • Theodor Storm (Ger): *Immensee*

1850–1899

1850–1899

MUSICAL ROMANTICISM continued to flourish against the backdrop of European industrialisation and colonisation. The richest nations of Europe grew ever stronger as they supplied cutting-edge machinery and technologies to the rest of the world, while also pursuing expansionist policies. Prosperity had dramatically swelled the middle classes, who were themselves the governing patrons of music. Some composers still sought Church appointments, a tiny minority were supported by royalty, but most survived by commissions, publishing deals, teaching and concert giving.

As Romantic individualism instigated an ever-greater diversity of style, the schism between the conservatives and progressives widened deeply, fuelling the so-called 'War of the Romantics'. Brahms became the figure-head of a musical approach that extended classical ideals of form and expression, while Liszt and Wagner championed a more chromatically-enhanced musical language and the overhaul of classical forms. Yet for the Romantic-Classicists and the New German School alike, inspiration was to come as often from looking backwards as from advancing trends. Folk traditions, Renaissance choral music, Baroque oratorios and, of course, the legacy of Beethoven, were each assimilated by both sides. Folk traditions also played a vital part within a rising national consciousness, as composers in Eastern Europe and Scandinavia searched out musical idioms that reflected a proud sense of homeland.

'Programme' versus 'absolute' music?

Symphonic works of the later 19th century are often divided into two oppositional categories: 'programme music', in which a composer draws upon some form of extra-musical source for inspiration, and 'absolute music', which is devoid of all external connections. Narrative and pictorial instrumental music had been in existence since the 17th century, but it was Franz Liszt (see also *Chapter 5*) who coined the term 'programme music'. He believed that the programmatic inspiration behind a work should be made explicit, so as to 'guard the listener against a wrong poetical interpretation'. By contrast, 'absolute music' implied a total absence of specific meaning. Indeed, the Viennese critic Eduard Hanslick, a staunch supporter of the absolute music of Johannes Brahms (1833–97), produced a monograph entitled *The Beautiful in Music* (1854) in which he categorically denied that a piece of music could have any meaning at all outside of itself. He described music as simply 'moving forms in sound', and dismissed Liszt's programmatic music as trite and poorly conceived.

◀ *The Opera Orchestra*, by Edgar Degas, *c.*1869.

Brahms himself wrote disdainfully of Liszt's programmatic approach to Clara Schumann in January 1860:

I expect that he [Liszt] will produce yet another symphonic poem before this winter is over. This plague spreads increasingly, and surely lengthens and ruins the ass's ears of the public and young composers alike.

Although a number of composers refused to embrace the programmatic model, many who are generally considered to be of the 'absolute' school wrote overtures or other orchestral pieces that reflect extra-musical sources of inspiration. Such was the close connection between music and the other arts during this period that most compositions were to some extent written, or interpreted, with extra-musical content in mind.

Programmatic orchestral music

Franz Liszt's years as director of music to the court of Weimar—1848 to 1861—were extraordinarily rich and fruitful. As a conductor he premièred new music, including Wagner's opera *Lohengrin* in 1850, and organised Berlioz and Wagner festivals to promote these progressives to a wider public.

Franz Liszt: 'symphonic poem'

As a composer, he forged the revolutionary genre he named the 'symphonic poem' (*symphonische Dichtung*), based on the earlier form of the concert overture. Liszt completed 13 such single-movement works, all but one at Weimar, attempting to revitalise and evolve traditional symphonic form by way of extra-musical stimuli. His subjects extended from historical narratives to literature, artwork, philosophy and mythology, each with its own level of connection, greater or lesser, to the music itself. Thus while *Tasso* (1854) and *Mazeppa* (1854) incorporate full-flown narratives, the high-spirited *Festklänge* (Festive Sounds, 1861) suggests extra-musical elements only by its title.

The principle behind the symphonic poem was to create a musically unified, single-movement form based on an extra-musical source, such as literature, poetry or painting. On a fundamental level, specific musical ideas were imbued with particular meaning; in *Tasso*, for example, two highly-contrasting themes depict the eponymous hero's oscillation between extreme states of mind. To reinforce a framework of interconnected themes, Liszt drew heavily on sonata form and other classical structures. Yet the procedure of musical repetition, traditionally employed to maintain formal stability, stood at odds with the forward thrust

▶ An early photograph of Franz Liszt, dating from his period as musical director to the court of Weimar.

of narrative development. Resolving this problem was the key to the evolution of the symphonic poem. Liszt re-modelled sonata form by extending thematic development—or more accurately, 'the metamorphosis of themes'—to the recapitulation and coda sections, and by integrating other formal elements, such as variation and ternary organisation, to produce quasi-cyclical structures.

It is a measure of the flexibility of this genre that Liszt's best-known symphonic poem, *Les Préludes* (1855), began life as an overture to a choral piece, completely devoid of associations with its eventual programme. It was only later, during the process of revision, that he drew a connection between the music and Lamartine's *Méditations poètiques*. Themes of love, nature, war (metaphoric or otherwise) and victory seem to be drawn together in this movement, though whether Liszt accurately depicts the imagery of the original poem is open to question. The musical themes are linked organically and set in a sonata-like structure; when they reappear later they are transformed in various ways, to mark the development of the narrative, such as it is.

Of course, the programmatic approach was not restricted to single-movement compositions. Following the example of Berlioz's *Symphonie Fantastique*, Liszt himself wrote the *Faust* and *Dante* symphonies. The *Faust-Symphonie* (1857, 1861) presents character sketches of the three central protagonists: the first movement Faust, the second Gretchen and the third Mephistopheles. According to Goethe, Mephistopheles could not create, but only twist and destroy; his themes are therefore all distortions of Faust's own music. Liszt later added a short fourth movement, which introduces a male chorus to symbolise Faust's salvation. It appropriately draws on themes from Gretchen's movement, since she is the redeeming figure of the narrative.

Faust-Symphonie

Liszt's programmatic essays—the symphonic poems especially—proved a major influence on music in the late century and paved the way for the 'tone poems' of Richard Strauss. In Liszt's immediate sphere of influence was Joachim Raff (1822–82), who in the early Weimar years acted as advisor to Liszt in the art of orchestration. A talented composer in his own right, Raff went on to write a number of symphonic works, including one of the best (if little-known) programme symphonies of the period, Symphony No. 5 *Lénor* (1872). Composers in Bohemia and Russia saw the symphonic poem as a means of presenting narratives from their own country, from historical events to aspects of legend and folklore. Some sought to expand the genre, notably Bedřich Smetana (1824–84) with the 'symphonic cycle' *Má vlast* (1879) and Rimsky-Korsakov with the hybrid 'symphonic suite' *Sheherazade* (1888).

Liszt's influence

Pyotr Il'yich Tchaikovsky (1840–93) was largely content to juggle programmatic and absolute approaches. His professional education and early career were nurtured in the fledgling Russian conservatories (St Petersburg and Moscow), but it was his contact with the 'Mighty Handful' nationalist composers that galvanised his interest in programmatic music. The leader of the group, Mily Balakirev, provided him with a programme for the exciting 'fantasy overture' *Romeo and Juliet*, the first version of which

Pyotr Il'yich Tchaikovsky

Tchaikovsky completed in 1869. Balakirev suggested some modifications, but still thought it Tchaikovsky's best work to date. Another programmatic work instigated by Balakirev was the *Manfred* 'symphony' (1885), which is in essence a four-movement symphonic poem. Tchaikovsky found the prescribed programme stifling: 'I am very discontented', he wrote to a friend, 'It is a thousand times more agreeable to compose without a programme'. On completion, Tchaikovsky rightly thought *Manfred* to be one of his finest orchestral pieces. By this time he had also written the 'symphonic fantasia' *Francesca da Rimini* (1876), based on a story in Dante's *Divine Comedy*, as well as his explosive *1812 Festival Overture* (1880), commemorating Russia's victory over Napoleon.

▲ Pyotr Il'yich Tchaikovsky. His melodic flair, command of form and masterly orchestration made him the supreme composer of 19th century Russia. In private he was deeply troubled by his life-long neuroses, hypochondria and closet homosexuality.

In his numbered symphonies Tchaikovsky chose a more abstract, 'absolute' approach, with just occasional narrative (usually autobiographical) references. The first three symphonies each bear brief subtitles, but none is truly programmatic. The First Symphony is sub-headed 'Winter Daydreams' (a designation never fully explained by the composer) and the Second Symphony, 'Little Russian' for its use of Ukrainian folk melodies. The nickname of the Third Symphony, 'Polish', did not originate from Tchaikovsky, but derives from the 'Polacca' (polonaise) tempo designation and rhythms of the final movement.

Conversely, whilst none of his remaining three symphonies bears an explicit programmatic title, the Fourth (1878) is confessedly programmatic, employing a descending 'Fate' motif that shapes and directs the course of the entire work. The Fifth Symphony (1888) employs a similar motto device, although here its exact meaning is less clear—Tchaikovsky had certainly considered extra-musical stimuli in its creation, but chose not to reveal their significance. With the Sixth Symphony in B minor, *Pathétique* (1893), he tantalisingly alluded to 'a programme that will remain a mystery [to all]'. Attempts to uncover this mystery have yielded a variety of often contradictory conclusions, tying in, or not, with the composer's homosexuality and possible suicidal intentions. Certainly the *Pathétique* seems to chart an epic emotional journey, progressing from the stormy opening movement, by turns agitated and intensely lyrical, into a lighter waltz-like movement in 5/4, on to a proud militaristic march, followed by an anguished *adagio lamentoso* that fades away into silence. The symphony was premièred on 28 October 1893, and prompted mixed reactions. Tchaikovsky, possibly suffering post-choleric complications, took his secretive programme to the grave just nine days later.

Sixth
Symphony
Pathétique

'Absolute' orchestral music

Among the most representative composers of 'absolute' orchestral music were Anton Bruckner (1824–96), Brahms and, specifically in his numbered symphonies, Dvořák. Despite the fact that Bruckner and Brahms shared some common ground, each disagreed wholeheartedly with the approach of the other: Bruckner puzzled over Brahms's refusal to incorporate Wagnerian chromaticism, and Brahms openly criticised Bruckner's 'symphonic boa constrictors'.

In 1853, the 20-year-old Brahms was introduced to Robert and Clara Schumann, who were to become close friends and mentors. Robert wrote an enthusiastic article pronouncing the young composer a musical genius and prophesying that he would achieve great things. Brahms was both encouraged and burdened by the expectations placed upon him. He saw enormous potential in traditional genres such as the symphony and the string quartet, but was adamant that he should take more time to study and prepare. Combined with the overwhelming legacy of Beethoven, this turned the symphony, in particular, into a seemingly insurmountable problem for Brahms. 'I'll never compose a symphony', he wrote despairingly to the conductor Hermann Levi, 'You have no idea of how it feels to hear the footsteps of such a giant marching behind you.'

Johannes Brahms

Such pressure, imposed and self-imposed, accounts for both his modest symphonic output and its late placing within his career—post-dating his two serenades (1858 and 1859), First Piano Concerto (1859) and the *Variations on a Theme of Haydn* (1873). It is hardly surprising that Brahms's four symphonies are openly indebted to Beethoven. We may also note the influence of Mozart and Schubert, as well as references to folk music, art-song and even Baroque idioms. Brahms's aesthetic legacy was a rejuvenation and re-invention of Classical forms.

In his musical language Brahms was fundamentally diatonic and cautiously chromatic. Though he seldom strayed from the tonal boundaries established by Beethoven and Schubert, he often used chromaticism to generate surging emotional intensity. This is demonstrated in the stirring opening of the First Symphony in C minor (completed 1876), where chromatically descending winds and violas build dramatic tension against rising violins and cellos, while a low C pedal, energised by pounding timpani, provides a firm harmonic foundation. The Third Symphony (1884) also opens powerfully with chromatic passion, only here the tonic key (F major) is undermined by foreign chords and 'false relations' to create instant drama. Whilst this destabilises the harmonic foundations of the section, Brahms avoids prolonged tonal uncertainty.

Style and language

Another characteristic of Brahms's music is the formal technique of 'developing variation', as Schoenberg was later to describe it. Brahms creates an initial kernel of melodic or harmonic material that is organically extended, elaborated and developed over a single movement or even an entire symphony. The Second Symphony (1877) offers an excellent example, presenting in its opening eight bars a handful of simple motivic ideas that feed and nurture the symphony's four movements. The technique also pervades the Fourth Symphony (1885), whose fourth movement is based on the Baroque structure of variations over a ground bass. This itself is a classic example of how Brahms enriched the traditional symphonic format through the assimilation of non-traditional devices.

Bruckner worked with a very different palette of influences, though he too derived inspiration from much earlier sources. His eleven symphonies (counting the early Study Symphony '00' and his self-rejected Symphony in D minor '0') reveal not only his admiration of late Beethoven and Wagner, but also a deeply religious personality. Bruckner had served the Church from the age of 13, first as a chorister, then as a choirmaster, organist and composer. His sacred output was considerable and he made constant reference to church music in his symphonies by incorporating chorales and Palestrinian polyphonic textures. There is a cathedral quality to the shape and expanse of Bruckner's music, and his orchestration is not infrequently organesque.

In spite of his progressive tendencies, Bruckner did not reject Classical structural forms: all his symphonies adopt a four-movement plan and the sonata principle remains the basis of almost all of the outer movements. The form is extended and given new dramatic weight by his 'breakthrough' technique, where new material—for example, the chorale theme in the finale of the Fifth Symphony (1878)—bursts into the musical texture and gradually integrates itself into the whole. Bruckner's harmonic schemes are complex and vast: themes embark on epic tonal journeys with resolution delayed as long as possible to heighten tension and impact. This process is typically extended beyond the recapitulation and only fully realised in an expansive coda.

While Bruckner's symphonies are often cited as examples of 'absolute' composition, it is difficult not to sense a recurring programme of 'spiritual quest', with uncertainty, soul-searching and trials culminating in final triumph. And an extra-musical element certainly shaped the second movement of the Seventh Symphony (1883), written as a kind of hypothetical funeral march for Wagner, still alive at the time. Bruckner wrote to his student Felix Mottl: 'One day I came home and felt very sad. The thought had crossed my mind that before long the Master would die, and then the C sharp minor theme of the Adagio came to me.' The movement was sketched in late January 1883, and less than a month later Wagner was dead. The news stimulated the deeply emotional dirge for Wagner tubas (a hybrid of horn and tuba) that brings the movement to its heartfelt conclusion. Premièred in December 1884, the Seventh rewarded Bruckner with his greatest popular and critical success.

Following this, Bruckner faced bitter disappointment when his Eighth Symphony was rejected by one of his staunchest supporters, the conductor Hermann Levi (1839–1900), who declared the work impenetrable. Bruckner set about revising and recomposing the symphony between 1887 and 1890, while simultaneously revising sections of his First, Third and Fourth symphonies. (It is very difficult to identify the 'composer's version' of a number of Bruckner's symphonies, given his

motivations behind the revision process.) Bruckner also began work on the Ninth Symphony in 1887, but due to exhaustion and prolonged illness,

◀ The opening bars of Bruckner's Adagio from the Ninth Symphony.

he completed only the first three movements. The symphony's vast third-movement Adagio actually serves as a wholly satisfying conclusion. It is, after all, the composer's self-described 'Farewell to Life', a movement approaching half an hour in length marked by distress in the opening bars, a solemn chorale intoned by Wagner tubas, some dramatic climaxes, and serene acceptance to finish. Regardless of questions this raises about Bruckner's programmatic intentions, it is not how he wanted to end the symphony. He managed to write a great deal of the finale, enough for modern scholars to complete a convincing performing edition. According to Bruckner's housemaid, he was busy attempting to finish the symphony on the day of his death, 11 October 1896.

Antonín Dvořák's international reputation was sealed in 1878 with the help of Brahms, who encouraged his own publisher, Simrock, to issue the *Slavonic Dances* in both piano duet and orchestral editions. Although the collection made Dvořák tremendously popular, he was aware that overtly nationalist music represented a 'political statement' and was thus not always greeted favourably in western and central Europe. So in approaching the symphony—the most public of genres—Dvořák was cautious in his use of Czech folk idioms. Only the Eighth Symphony (1889), which draws heavily on folk music, can be regarded as meaningfully nationalistic. Like those of Brahms, Dvořák's symphonies are concerned with the models of Beethoven and Schubert, as well as being heavily indebted to Brahms's own musical style.

Dvořák's nine symphonies are all in essence 'absolute' compositions. This is true even of the First Symphony, *The Bells of Zlonice* (1865), which was given its title purely for identification purposes in a competition. The Ninth Symphony, subtitled *From the New World* (1893), is more ambiguous, including as it does musical allusions to American folk music, African-American Spirituals and Amerindian melodies. Nevertheless, there is no explicit narrative and it is not intended as a depiction of American life (see also *United States*). In between these career milestones comes what is widely regarded as Dvořák's greatest symphony: No. 7 in D minor (1885). It was commissioned by England's Philharmonic Society following the composer's triumphant first visit to the country in 1884. Thoroughly Classical in its organisation, this symphony is striking for its clarity of vision,

Antonín Dvořák

Seventh Symphony

dramatic pacing and deep emotional intensity. Dvořák had been profoundly moved by Brahms's Third Symphony, and was determined to create music of equivalent beauty and gravitas. This might explain the shades of melancholy and struggle that pervade much of the work. If there is respite, it comes in the form of the third movement Scherzo, itself based on the rhythm of a Czech folk dance, the furiant. Perhaps Dvořák could not resist reminding the English that his was a Czech, not German, symphony.

Fin de siècle: Strauss and Mahler

The final decades of the 19th century saw the emergence of two new orchestral composers on the German musical scene: Richard Strauss (1864–1949) and the Austrian Gustav Mahler (1860–1911). Both were professional conductors, both possessed exceptional expertise in orchestration, and both championed the progressive tendencies of the New German School. In Strauss, programmatic orchestral music found some of its most vibrant representation, while in Mahler the Romantic symphony expanded to breaking point.

Over the course of his musical career Strauss experimented with almost every aspect of programmatic and absolute music. He composed two traditional symphonies in the early 1880s while learning the art of conducting from the great Hans von Bülow, director of the Meiningen Orchestra. Aged 22, he took up the post of third conductor at Munich, where he completed his first programmatic piece, *Aus Italien* (1886), a 'symphonic fantasy' that betrays a collective debt to Liszt, Wagner and Brahms. By the time of *Don Juan* (1889) Strauss had invented a new designation altogether: the tone poem (*Tondichtung*), a term that acknowledged its Lisztian forerunner, though neatly severed the nominal connection to the symphony. His subsequent tone poems—*Tod und Verklärung* (1889), *Macbeth* (revised version 1891), *Also sprach Zarathustra* (1896), *Ein Heldenleben* (1898) and *Symphonia domestica* (1903)—accommodated literary, philosophical and autobiographical subject matter.

Richard Strauss: Tone poems

In his vividly pictorial approach to composition Strauss ventured beyond Liszt, whose symphonic poems were often only vaguely descriptive. Strauss's tone-poems, for the most part, achieve their narrative flow through a remoulding of sonata-form. A good example is *Don Juan*, organised with cavorting opening statements (representing Don Juan) and a sensual love scene in the dominant key. In subsequent sections description is prioritised above development. A recapitulation of sorts begins with another strident Juan statement in the tonic-key, occurring unusually late for a sonata-form structure. Strauss creates tonal resolution while working towards his frenzied climax—the sword duel and killing of Don Juan—and a subdued, unsentimental coda shudders to a close.

Don Juan

Strauss designated his best-known programmatic piece a 'Rondeau Form for Large Orchestra', although the traditional rondo plan was only loosely applied. *Till Eulenspiegels lustige Streiche* (Till Eulenspiegel's Merry Pranks, 1895) presents thematic material signifying Till as the rondo itself (notably the famous horn theme), which reappears in various guises to portray the sequence of his exploits. A similar technique is

A MALÉR-SZYFÓNIA.

(A Filharmóniai konczerten.)

REKLÁM

Hatás !

found in *Don Quixote* for solo cello and orchestra (1897), subtitled 'Fantastic Variations on a Knightly Theme'. Here the central character's thoughts, feelings and actions find an equivalent in the development of his musical theme.

Strauss, like Mahler, marshalled some of the largest forces ever to appear on the concert platform. The indulgent *Ein Heldenleben* (A Hero's Life) demands quadruple winds, an enlarged brass and percussion section, two harpists and 64 strings, totalling over 100 players. Dramatic flair in conjunction with superlative orchestration enabled Strauss to transfigure ideas and images into high musical definition—qualities that were to give him a leading edge in the early 20th-century world of opera.

Gustav Mahler was more highly regarded as a conductor than a composer in his own lifetime. Conducting professional operetta at the age of 20, he rapidly progressed to the more serious fare of Mozart, Weber and Verdi as he moved into increasingly important posts: Kassel, Prague, Leipzig, and then Budapest by 1888. That year saw the completion of his first major orchestral composition, a five-movement symphonic poem (organised in two parts), later entitled *Titan* after the novel by Jean-Paul Richter. Its 1889 première in Budapest was unfortunately a miserable failure.

Gustav Mahler

Following his move to Hamburg's Stadttheater in 1891, Mahler revised *Titan* as his First Symphony (1893). Even this early work demonstrates the characteristics that Mahler later proclaimed were key to the genre: 'the symphony must be like the world. It must embrace everything.' Mahler's eclecticism—pulling songs, marches, band music, dances and chorus into the symphonic form—accounts for the highly individual and epic nature

First Symphony

409

of his symphonies. The First Symphony contains direct (instrumental) quotations from the composer's own *Lieder eines fahrenden Gesellen* (Songs of a Wayfarer, 1885), as well as a satirical funeral march (third movement), folk references, and an epic Wagnerian finale.

Second Symphony Resurrection

Mahler opened his gigantic Second Symphony, *Resurrection* (first version 1894), with another funeral march, continuing with a nostalgic Andante (a *ländler* with Beethovenian flavours) and a brilliant, multifaceted scherzo built on one of his settings of folk poetry from *Des Knaben Wunderhorn* (The Boy's Magic Horn). The fourth movement features a mezzo-soprano solo quoting another *Wunderhorn* song, 'Urlicht', and the fifth a full chorus singing lines from Klopstock's poem *Aufersteh'n* (Resurrection), as well as Mahler's own added text. The symphonic journey is vaguely programmatic, concerning the purpose and passage of man, not Christ. Hugely ambitious in scope and vision, the work seems to have moved and stunned the composer just as much as his audience. 'The whole thing sounds as though it came to us from some other world', he wrote after the first complete performance in 1895, 'and I think nobody can resist it. One is battered to the ground and then raised on angels' wings to the highest heights.'

Third Symphony

Only the first two symphonies received their complete premières in the 1890s, and Mahler continued to revise these works into the early 20th century. The Third Symphony (first version 1896) 'begins with lifeless Nature', according to Mahler, 'and ascends to Divine Life'. Once more he summoned vocal forces—a contralto soloist, and boys' and women's chorus—and derived material from a *Wunderhorn* setting. Other text comes in the form of the 'Midnight Song' of the haunting fourth movement, taken from Nietzsche's novel *Also sprach Zarathustra*. At six movements and lasting just over one-and-a-half hours, the Third is the longest symphony of the standard repertory. Mahler's symphonic corpus, extending to his final year, was to mark the culmination of the Austro-German Romantic tradition, the ultimate expansion of the concert medium before its collapse into the sparse writing of the Expressionists.

Chamber music as a public medium

As with symphonic music, those wishing to compose chamber pieces in the late 19th century were faced with the monumental legacy of Beethoven: in particular the string quartets, piano trios and accompanied sonatas. The technical skills that both he and subsequent generations of composers demanded of their musicians pushed these genres way beyond the capabilities of the average amateur and into the realm of the professional, even virtuoso, performer. As the professional-amateur gap widened, chamber music became something quite different. Whilst it retained its identity as music for small ensemble, it was increasingly tailored for a public forum. In other words, it left the chamber far behind, and the 'public chamber music concert' was born.

Chamber music post-1850 is represented in the outputs of a relatively small number of major composers. The most important exponent was

Brahms, whose 24 instrumental chamber works express his love of—and debt to—Beethoven, Schubert and Schumann. Directed principally at the professional, his output comprises string quartets, quintets and sextets, piano trios and quartets, a single piano quintet, a horn trio, sonatas for violin and for cello, and the four clarinet-centred chamber pieces of his final decade. Brahms made clear his respect of traditional forms, as in his symphonic writing, while enriching sonata and rondo structures with subtle elaborations and developing variation. Representative in this respect is the muscular Piano Quintet in F minor (Op. 34, 1865), as well as the two string sextets written relatively early in his career. A number of pieces, such as the piano quartets in G minor and A major (both 1861) and the String Quintet No. 2 in G major (1890), feature movements coloured by the rhythms and melodies of Hungarian gypsy music, of which Brahms was particularly fond. (His collections of *Hungarian Dances* for piano duet, as well as the *Gypsy Songs* for vocal quartet, display this preoccupation vividly.) The clarinet chamber pieces were all stimulated by, and written for, the renowned clarinettist Richard Mühlfeld (1856–1907), a member of Hans von Bülow's Meiningen Orchestra. Surely the best-loved of these pieces is the Clarinet Quintet in B minor (Op. 115, 1891), modelled on Mozart's Clarinet Quintet in A, K. 581 (1789). In Brahms, themes unfold organically and find interrelationship across the movements; melancholy is more pervasive, and we savour just a hint of Hungarian flavour in the beautiful second-movement Adagio.

Brahms

It was in chamber music that Smetana displayed his earliest artistic maturity. The Piano Trio in G minor (1855), variously agitated, disturbing and mournful, is a work he composed in response to the painful tragedy of the death of his eldest (4-year-old) daughter. His two string quartets were also driven by personal concerns. The most widely-played is the String Quartet No. 1 (1876), subtitled *From my Life*, which begins with youthful passions such as art, dancing and romance, and famously concludes with a reference to the onset of the composer's deafness.

Smetana

Dvořák

Smetana's great compatriot Dvořák composed a large body of chamber music centred on piano trios and string quartets. His most popular trio is the *Dumky* (1891), with its six vividly contrasting sections of Ukrainian national dances and songs. His finest string quartet was his 12th essay in the genre, the so-called *American* Quartet, Op. 96 (1893). Written during the composer's stay in the prairie town of Spillville, Iowa, the piece is partially indebted to the clarity and concision of Haydn's string quartets. It draws together aspects of African-American Spirituals, Amerindian and Czech folk music, all of which share some rhythmic elements and particular harmonic colours. The Scherzo is said to contain a motive based upon the call of the Scarlet Tanger, a bird indigenous to the US eastern interior, which Dvořák heard singing in a wood near to the town. The String Quintet in E flat, Op. 97, completed the same year, stands alongside the Op. 96 at the pinnacle of Dvořák's American-period chamber music.

France and Gabriel Fauré

In France, the founding of the Société Nationale de Musique in 1871 created a vital platform for the promotion of home-spun chamber music. It was through this institution that Saint-Saëns's pupil Gabriel Fauré (1845–1924) launched his chamber music career with the critically acclaimed Violin Sonata No. 1 in A major (1877). Buoyed by its reception, Fauré went on to complete the piano quartets in C minor (1879) and G minor (1886), and a number of popular pieces for accompanied cello, including *Elégie* (1880), *Papillon* (1884) and *Romance* (1894), which paved the way for his more complex cello sonatas of the next century. Fauré's great achievement was to develop and enrich established forms through new structural techniques and harmonic (especially modal) developments. In places he anticipates the language of Debussy, whose one completed String Quartet, premièred at the Société Nationale in 1893, ranks among the finest works of the French chamber repertory.

Tchaikovsky

In Russia the situation was rather different. When Tchaikovsky wrote his String Quartet No. 1 (1871)—made popular by its tuneful 'Andante cantabile' second movement—a Russian chamber tradition did not exist. And nor would it for many years. Tchaikovsky never developed a passion for the medium, in spite of notable achievements like his Second String Quartet (1874) and the Piano Trio in A minor (1882). Meanwhile, the nationalist members of the so-called 'Mighty Handful' were far more interested in vocal or programmatic forms; neither Balakirev nor Mussorgsky wrote any mature instrumental chamber music. Only Borodin demonstrated an affinity for chamber writing, and his String Quartet No. 2 (1881), dedicated to his wife, is a beautiful and accomplished work.

Edvard Grieg

The chamber output of Norway's Edvard Grieg (1843–1907) was relatively modest, largely because he lacked interest in large-scale Classical forms. However, his String Quartet in G minor (1878), deriving in part from his song *Spillemaend* (Fiddlers, 1876), is particularly notable for its chromatic dissonances and colouristic use of harmony. His final chamber compositions, the Cello Sonata (1883) and Violin Sonata No. 3 (1886), are highly concentrated in musical form and in places further explore a proto-Impressionist approach to 'non-functional' harmony.

German and French song: the Lied and the Mélodie

While the first half of the century had seen the progressive commercialisation of music and the rise of domestic music making, the second was swamped by the fruits of such pursuits, including a 'song flood' (*Liederflut*) of epic proportions. Song held a unique position in the public imagination, uniting the worlds of the amateur (the parlour song) and the professional (the concert aria). It embraced a diversity of texts, from the light-hearted to the political, and incorporated melodies of all kinds, from folk style through to finely-crafted high art music.

The most significant composers of Lieder in the late-century were Brahms and the Austrian Hugo Wolf (1860–1903). Brahms, who wrote Lieder consistently throughout his life, began composing vocal music at a time when folk traditions were central strands in both literature and music. His works extend from straightforward folk song treatments (he arranged and edited over 130 folk melodies for publication) to intricately elaborated strophic structures, such as *Feldeinsamkeit* (Alone in the Fields, *c*.1882) and *Sapphische Ode* (*c*.1884). He also effected sophisticated integrations of these two approaches. A good example is *Geistliches Wiegenlied* (Sacred Lullaby, 1864), the second of two songs for alto, viola and piano, in which a traditional folk melody in the viola part is used to form a melodic foil to the vocal line. Brahms's poetic sources are rich and varied, from anonymous folk texts to the great writers of German literature, including Goethe and Heine, and lesser figures whose names are still known thanks largely to his music.

Brahms

Hugo Wolf worked in various genres, but he was prolific only in Lieder. He composed most of his 300 songs between 1888 and 1897, after which his life was blighted by the final stages of syphilis—derangement leading to incarceration, then death in 1903. In his Lieder, Wolf retained certain elements of the folk style that so inspired Brahms, but his extended chromaticisms and minutely incisive approach to text setting placed him in an oppositional stylistic camp. Wolf's loyalties ultimately lay with Wagner.

Hugo Wolf

Wolf achieved an extraordinary synthesis of music and poetry. He made his breakthrough in 1888 while setting verse by Eduard Mörike, traversing vigorous declamation and fertile lyricism in songs of piercing psychological insight. Much of Wolf's ability to reflect mood and subtle textual nuance resided in his varied and intricate piano accompaniments. He was so impressed with his own efforts that he wrote of *Erstes Liebeslied eines Mädchens* (The First Lovesong of a Young Girl): 'the music is so striking in character and of such intensity that it would

◀ Hugo Wolf, composer of some of the finest Romantic lieder.

lacerate the nervous system of a block of marble.' There are 53 songs in his *Gedichte von Eduard Mörike* (1889), a collection variously sombre, metaphysical, witty and not infrequently erotic. Next came his 20 *Eichendorff-Lieder* (1889) and 51 *Goethe-Lieder* (1890), the latter containing his celebrated 'Mignon' songs. He produced what are probably his most well-known collections with the *Spanisches Liederbuch* (1890) and the two volumes of the *Italienisches Liederbuch* to text translations by Paul Heyse (1891 and 1896). Both sets feature songs for male and female voices, with certain songs addressed from one character to the other, although curiously, the two never sing together.

Strauss

Richard Strauss was the third great Lieder champion of the late century. One of his defining characteristics, at least from the time of his Op. 27 songs (1894), lies in his predilection for orchestral-style piano accompaniments. The impassioned *Cäcilie* (1894) demonstrates this tendency conspicuously with its powerful chords and striding progressions. Another piece from the same set, the beloved *Morgen*, savours a delicate pianistic approach, introducing itself with a voiceless prelude. These were among the first short, intimate Lieder that Strauss orchestrated and projected into the wider public arena. In so doing he was following a path prepared by composers such as Berlioz (the song cycle *Les nuits d'été*, 1841, orchestrated 1856) and Wagner.

Wagner, Mahler

Wagner's small song output is crowned by the *Wesendonck Lieder* (1858), five pieces originally written for voice and piano. The author of the text, Mathilde Wesendonck, was for a time Wagner's neighbour and close friend—to the distress of Minna, the composer's first wife. Wagner's relationship with Mathilde, which he maintained was not of a sexual nature, inspired his writing of *Tristan und Isolde* (1859), and material from two *Wesendonck* songs were integrated into its composition. Mahler, similarly, wove his own Lieder into larger, more public genres. By transferring themes from his *Lieder eines fahrenden Gesellen* (songs based on his own love poetry) to instrumental form in his First Symphony, he effectively elevated an intimate, solo confession to a universal voice representing humanity. The *Wunderhorn* folk-song settings that enrich his symphonies Nos. 2–4 (see above and *Chapter 7*) present another dimension of this genre cross-fertilisation. The Lied, consequently, carried with it a history so powerful that Schoenberg, Webern and Berg, initially at least, could not conceive of a musical landscape without it.

France and the Mélodie

The French song tradition was hampered by its own idiosyncrasies: specifically the issue of setting traditional French poetry to music, where accentuation and pronunciation differs so much from spoken language. French song was difficult to export, but the national appetite was sufficient to attract the major composers. Gounod was prolific, writing over 100 secular French songs, in addition to his settings of English and Italian texts for the British market. It is no small irony that his now most famous song is neither in French, nor truly by him—namely the Latin-set *Ave Maria* (1859), based on Bach's C major Prelude from Book I of the *Well-Tempered Clavier*.

A truly national style for the *Mélodie* was defined by the following generation of song composers: Fauré, Debussy, Henri Duparc (1848–1933) and Ernest Chausson (1855–99). Here, the writings of Symbolist poets were realised in a vibrant harmonic palette of modality, post-Wagnerian chromaticism and the first hints of neo-classicism. Fauré's *La bonne chanson* (1894), one of the most praised French song cycles, is striking for its unusual harmonic schemes. The nine selected poems form an unfolding narrative of a young couple in love, while musical unity is provided by recurring motifs, all brought together in the final song, 'L'hiver a cesse' (Winter has Ended). Other representative works from this time include Chausson's *Serres chaudes* (Hothouses, 1896) to texts by Maeterlinck, and Debussy's *Cinq poèmes de Baudelaire* (1890). This was song-writing with an authentic French accent, and a style ripe for the 20th century.

The piano as orchestra

Industrial developments of the early 1800s had facilitated the mass-production of the piano, an instrument which, by mid-century, was to be found in almost every middle-class home. The upright piano had now superseded the wider and deeper (horizontally-strung) square piano as the drawing-room essential. The technological advances benefiting the concert grand piano included the perfection of the double-escapement action—enabling the rapid repetition of a single note—and the introduction of the full iron-frame, bringing increased range, depth of tone and volume. Both as a tool of performance and a compositional medium, the piano became powerful enough to truly compete with the orchestra. It was now unrivalled as the pre-eminent instrument of the concerto at a time when public concert life was rapidly expanding across Europe and America.

During this period, virtuosos continued to flourish, with composers daring to make ever greater demands upon their skill. Liszt's two piano concertos (final versions 1856 and 1861), Brahms's *Variations on a Theme by Paganini* (1863) and Sergei Rachmaninov's youthful Piano Concerto No. 1 (1891, revised 1917) are all prominent examples of this fearsome virtuosity. The French composer Charles-Valentin Alkan (1813–88) exploited the piano's expressive potential to the extreme in his 'Symphony for Piano Solo' (1857), one of a series of titanic and quasi-orchestral compositions accessible to only the most talented of pianists. Its three movements form part of the composer's 12 *Études* for solo piano, which also includes a three-movement concerto and an overture.

Charles-Valentin Alkan

In concertos and related genres, composers began to redress the balance between the piano and the orchestra. The concertos of Liszt, Brahms, Tchaikovsky and Saint-Saëns present a more thoroughly symphonic approach to the medium: the orchestra is no longer required to be silent or *pianissimo* for the soloist, and the respective roles of piano and orchestra become more interchangeable. Thus in Saint-Saëns's Piano Concerto No. 2 (1868) the successive sections of its first movement are presented with great fluidity of material between soloist and orchestra. The piano provides not only principal melodies, but also underpins much of the connecting material that would previously have been the role of the orchestra alone. The famous opening passage of Tchaikovsky's Piano

Concerto No. 1 (1875) also requires an instrument of considerable power, with the soloist's rising octaves, hammered out *fortissimo*, serving as the predominant accompaniment to the strings' commanding first melody.

In terms of the concerto style itself, both 'virtuoso' and 'symphonic' approaches persisted. Two of the most celebrated examples from this time display the divergent characteristics. Edvard Grieg's Piano Concerto in A minor (1868) is essentially set in an early Romantic, bravura mould. Grieg announces the soloist as hero from the outset with pounding chords and cascading octaves, while the most dazzling and daring virtuosity is saved for the cadenza and rapid progressions of the finale. In between comes the gentle, folk-inflected Adagio where it is the soloist's lyricism and melodic shaping that is put to the test. By contrast, Brahms's Piano Concerto No. 2 in B flat major (1881) is clearly in the symphonic mould. Cast in four movements rather than three, this work demands a very different kind of virtuosity, one less overt and showy than Grieg, with much of the piano's material designed to work with the orchestra, rather than in contrast or relief from it. Brahms strives for greater invention in the presentation of themes, such as we find in the third movement Andante, whose principal lyrical melody, introduced and recalled by a solo cello, remains outside the domain of the piano. It is certainly fair to say that Grieg offers the soloist greater reward for less effort than Brahms—and indeed, Grieg's Concerto enjoyed tremendous public acclaim and launched his international career. Liszt marvelled at the young Grieg, but he also admired Brahms, judging the Concerto No. 2 an illustrious work of art, with its noble harmony of 'thought and feeling', a creation that to his mind deserved and rewarded repeated listening.

Virtuoso vs symphonic style: Grieg and Brahms

▶ Piano Concerto performance at Jullien's Concerts, Covent Garden Theatre, London. Louis Jullien was a French-born conductor and composer who found fame in England, specialising in concert spectaculars during the 1840s and 50s.

Liszt and the solo piano

With his days as a touring virtuoso now over (see *Chapter 5*), Liszt was able to devote time to the revision and completion of an existing body of solo piano works, such as the lyrical *Consolations* (1850) and the *Grandes études de Paganini* (1851). He also set about rejuvenating traditional forms through new compositional techniques. The most important example of this is the

Sonata in B minor (1853), which comprises four continuous movements set in an over-arching sonata form structure. The construction is rooted in a series of short thematic cells that are subsequently developed and metamorphosed as the piece advances—the same method used in his symphonic poems.

As the greatest pianist of his day, Liszt infused established genres such as the sonata or study with a dazzling virtuosic edge, as in the *Études d'exécution transcendante* (1851). He also pursued an increasingly sophisticated manipulation of tonality and dissonance, often for illustrative purposes. The second book of the three-volume *Années de pèlerinage* (Years of Pilgrimage) ends with the extended *Après une lecture du Dante, fantasia quasi sonata* (1861), in which Liszt presents musical representations of heaven and hell as two polarised themes. The music of hell is, in its barest form, a tritone (a so-called *diabolus in musica*, 'devil in music'), and it is a string of tritones that opens the piece, providing no clue as to the tonality of the music ahead. Such progressive harmonic language seemed to fascinate Liszt, as is evident from later pieces such as *Trübe Wolken* (also known as *Nuages gris*, 'Grey Clouds', 1881) and the astonishing *Bagatelle ohne Tonart* (Bagatelle without Tonality, 1885). The impressionism of his late compositions, with their drifting (or, as in the *Bagatelle ohne Tonart*, absent) tonality, acted as a defining influence upon French and German composers alike.

From the late 1860s Liszt divided his time between Weimar, Budapest and Rome. It was in Weimar that he seems to have invented the 'masterclass', giving individual tuition to pianists before a student group. This naturally facilitated group learning, but also created a stimulating and testing environment for aspiring concert pianists. Liszt's masterclasses were free; his methods were seldom academic and he was little interested in teaching technique. His major concern was interpretation, and he would make pictorial suggestions to his pupils so that they might execute passages with convincing drama or sensitivity. His close circle included the German composer-pianists Sophie Menter (1846–1918) and Eugen d'Albert (1864–1932), and the Polish pianist Moriz Rosenthal (1862–1946).

The masterclass

A new age for the string concerto

By the early 19th century instrumental advances had brought the violin, viola and cello to a state roughly resembling that of their modern relatives, and subsequent developments in string and bow manufacture allowed for a new power and clarity of sound. Nicolò Paganini's technical explorations had pushed the violin well and truly into the spotlight as an instrument of tremendous expressive and virtuosic potential. During the late century, violinists, cellists and even violists demanded from composers an increasingly broad and testing repertory.

As with the equivalent body of piano music, string concertos can be loosely divided into symphonic and virtuosic works (see also *Chapter 5*). Influencing the repertory was a cluster of virtuoso performers, who either composed themselves or else advised composers who were not adept string players. The virtuoso violin concertos are almost solely the creations of

Violin concerto

▶ Johann Brahms (seated) with the Hungarian virtuoso Joseph Joachim.

violinists (following the Paganini mould), including Bériot, Vieux-temps and Henryk Wieniawski (1835–80). Many of the great symphonic pieces, however, can be linked to a single performer: the Austro-Hungarian Joseph Joachim (1831–1907). A close friend of Schumann and Brahms, Joachim was the dedicatee of Schumann's Violin Concerto (1853, although not publicly performed until 1937), Bruch's instantly popular Violin Concerto No. 1 in G minor (1868), Dvořák's Violin Concerto (1879), and Brahms's richly symph-onic Violin Concerto (1878) and Double Concerto (1887, written for Joachim and the cellist Robert Hausmann). Later in the century concerto finales were commonly coloured and energised by folk-like melodies and rhythms; both the Brahms and Bruch violin concertos conclude with dazzling Hungarian folk-inspired finales, all the more appropriate considering Joachim's heritage. Joachim wrote violin concertos of his own, the best known entitled *Konzert in ungarischer Weise* (Concerto in the Hungarian Style, 1861) and featuring virtuosic elaborations and developments of Hungarian folk melodies.

Max Bruch was a central figure in the development of the wider solo string repertory. In addition to three violin concertos he wrote many shorter compositions for violin, cello and viola soloists with orchestra, some based upon Scottish, Hebrew, Russian and Swedish folk melodies. Most often heard are *Kol Nidrei* (1880) for cello and orchestra, and the *Schottische Fantasie* (1880) for violin and orchestra. The latter is sometimes compared to Eduard Lalo's *Symphonie espagnole* (1874), a five-movement suite for violin and orchestra with a similarly strong regional accent. Lalo's piece had a major impact on Tchaikovsky, who in response composed his Violin Concerto in D (1878). Tchaikovsky's concerto is both optimistic and epic, balancing lyrical passion with fiendish virtuosity, served up with character-istic orchestral brilliance. It is perhaps hard to understand why the work was once rejected by the public, but its status as core repertory was more or less assured before the composer's death, demonstrating continuing Romantic appetite for the 'soloist as hero'.

Cello concerto

Following a period of neglect during the late Classical and early Romantic periods, the cello concerto was now truly reborn. Schumann completed the first great Romantic cello concerto in 1850 (see also

Chapter 5), although it was not premièred until 1860, four years after his death. Its reception was mixed, but Clara Schumann's earliest impression of the concerto is one that is now shared by many: 'The romantic quality, the flight, the freshness and the humour, and also the fascinating interweaving of cello and orchestra are, to be sure, wholly ravishing.' The most famous relations of Schumann's concerto are considerably younger: the two of Saint-Saëns (1872 and 1902) and that of Dvořák (1895). It was while serving as director of America's National Conservatory of Music, in New York, that Dvořák composed his dramatic Cello Concerto in B minor. Like the symphonies, it looks to Classical structural models without falling prey to tired conventions. Brahms was impressed by the concerto's profusion of melodies, expressive range and masterful balance of resources: he confessed that had he known such things were possible in a cello concerto, he would have written one long before.

Several composers produced symphonic works featuring *concertante* string parts: Tchaikovsky's *Variations on a Rococo Theme* (1876) and Strauss's tone poem *Don Quixote* (1897) both make use of a solo cello. Saint-Saëns's novelty piece *Carnival of the Animals* (1887) showcases a number of solo instruments for comic pictorial effect, including the graceful cello solo of 'The Swan' and the lumbering double-bass line of 'The Elephant'.

Sacred music: old and new

Choral music is an important, if neglected, medium of the late 19th century. This period saw the rise of amateur choral singing in countries with established traditions—England, Germany, France—and the foundation of choral societies in countries such as Spain and the USA. As the market for choral music expanded, the central works of the repertory (those of Handel especially) became ever more widely known. In turn, a new generation of composers were suitably inspired to search out new ways to match or exceed the choral achievements of the previous century.

A number of composers sought to preserve the distinctions of the sacred and secular performance arenas—the church and the concert hall—while others attempted to dissolve them altogether. In France, a strong church music tradition lived on in the music of Gounod, Saint-Saëns, Franck and Fauré, and the focus remained largely in the cathedral. Gounod was especially committed to sacred music, writing 21 stylistically-diverse masses as well as cantatas and motets. However, his oratorios *La Rédemption* (1882) and *Mors et Vita* (1885) were introduced to great acclaim at the Birmingham Festival in the town hall. It was from this 'secular' achievement that Gounod gained a reputation among the English as Mendelssohn's worthy successor. The vitality of the English choral tradition encouraged large-scale festival pieces from locals such as William Sterndale Bennett (1816–75), Hubert Parry (1848–1918) and the Irishman Charles Villiers Stanford (1852–1924). Stanford and John Stainer (1840–1901) were also leading figures in Anglican liturgical music.

In Germany the 'Cecilian movement' (after St Cecilia, the patron saint of music) saw a revival of interest in the music of Palestrina and traditional

Church traditions

1850–1899

sacred music composition. This was something that interested Bruckner and found representation in his masses and motets. But Germany's musical position was at once traditional and innovative: those same Bruckner motets also feature strong influences of Wagnerian harmonic construction. Then there was the progressively-minded Liszt, an 'honorary German', who became ever more absorbed in religion as he grew older. His substantial but little known sacred output includes the oratorios *Die Legende von der heiligen Elisabeth* (1862) and *Christus* (1872), and organ pieces such as the variations on 'Weinen, Klagen, Sorgen, Zagen', (*c.*1863) and the *Requiem for Organ* (1883).

In the secular arena Sacred music certainly gained for itself a greater concert-hall temperament during the late-century. This went beyond the theatrical oratorio tradition, such as we find in Berlioz's dramatic *L'enfance du Christ* (1854), the score of which includes stage directions to explain the action as it unfolds. Giuseppe Verdi openly employed a range of operatic techniques in his monumental Requiem Mass (1874), even adapting a discarded duet from *Don Carlos* for the 'Lacrymosa'. Premièred at St Mark's Cathedral in Milan, the Requiem was denounced by some as a distasteful operatic setting of a liturgical text. Tellingly, its second performance took place in an opera house, Milan's La Scala, after which Verdi toured his masterpiece around Europe. Similarly, Fauré's Requiem was first presented with formal reverence, liturgically with chamber forces, at the Madeleine church in Paris in 1888. Twelve years later, in full orchestral attire, it was relaunched at the grand Palais du Trocadéro amid the secular excitement of the Paris Exposition Universelle. Dvořák, conversely, composed his Requiem (1890) specifically for the concert hall, the work having been commissioned by the Birmingham Festival.

The Requiems of Verdi and Fauré epitomise a Romantic, subjective response to liturgical text setting. Fauré, for instance, gave little emphasis to the darkest passages of the requiem text, such as the 'Dies irae' (Day of Wrath), because he wanted to convey death 'as a joyful deliverance, an aspiration towards happiness beyond the grave, rather than as a painful experience'. Beyond this, the secularisation of sacred music occasionally fostered a proclamation not so much of religious faith, but of a coming together of humanity. Brahms, an agnostic, created the title *Ein Deutsches Requiem* (A German Requiem, 1868) to stress the universal significance of the work beyond the bounds of religious belief. He maintained that he could have happily changed 'German' to 'Human', and he omitted liturgical references to specific belief in God's Son. This trend would later lead to such pieces as Frederick Delius's *A Mass of Life* (1905), a thoroughly atheistic response to the sacred genre.

Music on the stage

Wagner and the 'total artwork' (*Gesamtkunstwerk*)

Wagner's eight mature 'music dramas' begin with *Lohengrin* (see *Chapter 5*), premièred under Liszt at Weimar in 1850, and culminate with *Parsifal* (1882). Owing to his part in the Dresden Insurrection of 1849, Wagner was exiled from German lands for 11 years, and throughout this time he was heavily dependent upon the generosity of Liszt (his future father-in-law) both for financial support and musical advocacy. It was not until the intervention of Ludwig II of Bavaria in 1863 that he could return to his homeland and construct his opera house at Bayreuth. During his years of exile, he finished the full text for all four operas of *Der Ring* (self-published in 1853): *Das Rheingold*, *Die Walküre*, *Siegfried* and *Götterdämmerung*. The first two operas of the cycle were fully completed in 1854 and 1856. The complex and darkly erotic love story *Tristan und Isolde* followed in 1859. This was a milestone opera, whose drifting chromatic harmonies began a journey towards the breakdown of functional tonality. Wagner then set about the semi-comic *Die Meistersinger von Nürnberg*, finished back on German soil in 1867.

The early years of exile also saw Wagner's attempt to codify his new theories of the music drama in a series of three articles: 'Art and Revolution' (1849), 'The Artwork of the Future' (1849) and 'Opera and Drama' (1851). In these essays Wagner held up Greek tragedy as a model of the unified artwork, bringing together music, dance and poetry. He proposed an 'artwork of the future' in which all the arts, including architecture, sculpture and painting, might be brought together in a single musical form representing the achievements of the *Volk*—the people, in a nationalist

Aesthetic concerns

◀ Richard Wagner and his second wife, Cosima, in 1872, two years into their marriage. Following Wagner's death, Cosima took control of the Bayreuth Festival, presiding as artistic director for 22 years. Her son, Siegfried Wagner, took over the position in 1906.

sense. This *Gesamtkunstwerk* (total artwork) would include a new approach to verse-setting, in which the musical line would grow directly from the text. To this end he formulated a thorough system of *leitmotifs* (guiding motifs) to attach objects, feelings, characters and events to particular musical themes. Furthermore, he did not want the orchestra to be subordinated to the role of mere accompanist. He extended the integrated practices of Marschner so that themes and melodies could pass seamlessly from singer to orchestra and back again. His aim was to unify the orchestra within the 'total artwork' to the point where the audience would become unaware of its existence as an individual entity. As Wagner himself explained:

> … *the most elevated language of the orchestra is manifested with the artistic objective of not being noticed, so to speak, of not being heard at all: that is, not heard in its mechanical role, but only in its organic capacity, wherein it is One with the Drama.*

Der Ring des Nibelungen

The four music dramas that make up *Der Ring des Nibelungen* were the richest realisation of Wagner's artistic credo. *Das Rheingold* sets the scene for the epic tale. The story, in its barest outline, revolves around a ring fashioned from gold stolen from the Rhinemaidens, which can bestow terrific power on any owner who rejects both divine and human love. Having seized the ring from the evil dwarf Alberich, the chief god Wotan exchanges it for the release of Freia, goddess of youth and beauty. The three ensuing operas trace the efforts of Wotan to retrieve the ring through the help of his eldest daughter, Brünnhilde (a Valkyrie warrior), and Siegfried, Wotan's human grandson. In the third opera, *Siegfried* (1871), Siegfried gains possession of the ring and marries Brünnhilde, naturally against Wotan's wishes. Finally, in *Götterdämmerung* (1874), Alberich's son Hagen tricks Siegfried and Brünnhilde into betraying each other; Hagen slays Siegfried and Brünnhilde's subsequent suicide brings about the downfall of the gods. The Rhinemaidens recover their lost gold.

The first complete performance of the 16-hour *Ring* cycle took place in Wagner's purpose-built Festspielhaus in Bayreuth, in August 1876. The mystical-mythological libretto was inspired by a mixture of Norse and German legends, notably a medieval German epic poem, the *Nibelungenlied* (The Song of the Nibelungs). In a complex world of gods, monsters and heroes, characters are drawn much larger than life to represent universal symbols and elemental forces. Wagner desired to offer something close to a religious experience through his operas: in the *Ring* he preached on the epic struggle between love and power.

Wagner loathed the idea of packaging emotions in tightly organised forms. He therefore abandoned the sectionalising principles of early Romantic opera and created extended musical structures to channel progression and development. Rarely do arias stand out; more often, in hybrid forms, they emerge and sink back seamlessly within the composer's so-called 'endless melody'—an *arioso* style sitting between recitative and the aria. Binding the fabric of the operas, his diverse array of leitmotifs are transformed, developed and elaborately woven to create intricate

associations and dramatic relationships. Some leitmotifs share meaningful similarities, such those representing Alberich's ring and Valhalla (home of the gods), which in turn implies a symbolic link between Alberich and Wotan. Orchestral timbre and texture play a crucial role in motivic tone painting, as revealed in the string arpeggios of the Rhine in *Das Rheingold*, and the sombre trombone octaves representing Wotan's spear, reoccurring throughout the four-part drama. Wagner used the term 'melodic moments', rather than 'leitmotifs' when describing his 'labyrinthine-building of the drama'. Spohr, Marschner, Verdi and Glinka had all experimented with this method, but Wagner raised it to a new level entirely.

Wagner's grandeur often emerges from intimate moments, such as the intense, climactic passion of Brünnhilde's awakening in *Siegfried*. With the most adventurous chromatic harmony of the day Wagner plumbed new psychological depths; the essence of his own complex, often ambiguous philosophy finds its musical realisation in amorphous, unfurling passages of restless emotion. Such language tested audiences, as did Wagner's narrative pace, deliberately measured in order to draw out vivid symbols and deeper meaning from unfolding events. Wagner's 'total artwork' generated a hitherto unchallenged, integrated presentation of both the history and psychology of the world on-stage.

Italian opera

Italian opera had enjoyed extraordinary international success during the first half of the century. However, by 1850 both Bellini and Donizetti were dead, and Rossini was well into his retirement. The 37-year-old Verdi was now the pre-eminent composer of Italian opera and he was to remain so until Puccini's ascension to fame in the 1890s.

Verdi had been writing operas since the 1830s, yet of those 16 works completed between 1839 and 1850, only *Nabucco* (1842) and *Macbeth* (1847; revised 1865) have remained within standard repertory (see *Chapter 5*). The early 1850s saw the creation of three major operas: the dark tales of *Rigoletto* (1851) and *Il trovatore* (1853), and the tragic *La traviata* (1853).

Verdi

SIGNOR ARRIGO BOITO
The Author of the Libretto

SIGNOR RICORDI
Verdi's Agent and Publisher

SIGNOR GIUSEPPE VERDI
The Composer

THE PRODUCTION OF VERDI'S NEW OPERA "FALSTAFF" AT LA SCALA MILAN
PORTRAITS FROM SKETCHES TAKEN FROM LIFE BY OUR SPECIAL ARTIST

▲ The partnership of librettist Arrigo Boito, the publisher Giulio Ricordi and composer Giuseppe Verdi.

Verdi caused an immediate sensation with both *Rigoletto* and *Il trovatore*, but not so with *La traviata*. In fact he forecast its initial failure at La Fenice, Venice, knowing that most of his cast were not up to the job. Recast and relaunched in 1854, the masterpiece was drawing crowds in a dozen countries across Europe and the Americas within just two years. Meanwhile, Verdi's pace barely slackened: *Les vêpres sicilliennes*, *Simon Boccanegra*, *Aroldo* and *Un ballo in maschera* all appeared before 1860. Thereafter operas for both Italian and foreign venues appeared at greater intervals: *La forza del destino* and *Don Carlos* in the 1860s, and *Aida*, a substantially revised *Simon Boccanegra*, *Otello* and *Falstaff* as the operas of his final three decades.

Evolving style

At the half-century Verdi's operatic style underwent profound change. *La traviata*, in particular, is worthy of being considered the first truly 'modern' Italian opera, since Verdi's musical language was so directly and intimately connected with Francesco Maria Piave's scenario. We can note, by way of comparison, the lack of integration between musical style and subject matter in such operas as Bellini's *Norma* and even Verdi's own *Nabucco*. Like Wagner, Verdi disliked the short, formulaic musical structures employed by earlier opera composers. This led him to manipulate, extend and eventually replace some traditional forms, even if he stopped short of Wagner's 'endless melody'. One convention that increasingly bothered Verdi was the three-part grand aria form of slow cantabile–'tempo di mezzo'–fast cabaletta. He recrafted this sequence in an attempt to bind the sections more intimately to the drama and emotional state of the characters. Parts were cut, the lengths of each section varied considerably, and the divisions between solo and dialogue sections were broken down. Just as lyrical melody could enliven recitative, declamation could now bring expressive flexibility to the aria. Formal fluidity, descriptive melody, recurring motivic fragments and an increasingly symphonic

sound-world: these were the tools with which Verdi transformed the static set-piece into a dynamic narrative.

In later life Verdi may have produced fewer operas but his music displayed a new dramatic potency and concentration. *Aida* was commissioned by the Khedive of Egypt to both inaugurate a new opera house in Cairo and to mark the opening of the Suez Canal. Verdi missed his 1869 deadline (*Rigoletto* was staged instead) and only just made the rescheduled date of 24 December 1871. The ancient Egyptian love-and-honour story invited moments of great spectacle, such as the exotic dances and the famous triumphal march 'Gloria all'Egito'; but Verdi also concerned himself with the psychological depth of his characters, moving beyond the one-dimensional figures common to the epic genre. This is especially true of his female protagonists, Amneris and her slave-girl, Aida.

Aida

The Shakespeare-inspired *Otello* (1887) and *Falstaff* (1893), along with the 1881 revision of *Simon Boccanegra*, were all collaborations undertaken with the librettist Arrigo Boito (1842–1918). The partnership was a truly equal one, as Verdi bowed to Boito's judgement on some critical aspects of narrative and pace. This was unusual for Verdi, who was typically a ruthless autocrat when it came to shaping and supervising his operas. As a comedy, *Falstaff* was all the more remarkable because over 50 years had passed since Verdi's previous comedic effort, *Un giorno di regno* (King for a Day, 1840), which was a resounding failure. Verdi wrote *Falstaff* simply for his own pleasure, not even knowing whether he would finish it. In the end he created a comic tour-de-force that exhibited some of the most diverse and harmonically progressive music he ever wrote.

Arrigo Boito

Verdi's Indian summer coincided with a new fashion in Italian opera, inspired by the Realism and Naturalism movements that had occupied literature and painting since the mid-century. Following much in the manner of Flaubert and Zola, Italian *verismo* presented true-to-life drama featuring

Verismo

gritty and flawed lower-class protagonists. Pietro Mascagni's *Cavalleria Rusticana* (1890) and Ruggero Leoncavallo's *Pagliacci* (1892) were among the first operatic realisations of this school, and both deal with infidelity, revenge and violence. The tautness, brevity and emotional intensity of *verismo* had a profound effect upon Italian composers at the end of the century. The notables include Umberto Giordano (1867–1948) with *Andrea Chénier* (1896), and the remarkable Giacomo Puccini (1858–1924).

The emergence of Puccini

Puccini was born with music in his blood: four generations of Puccinis had worked as composers and musicians in his home city of Lucca. Giacomo gained a scholarship to study at the Milan Conservatoire in 1880, and four years later produced his first opera, *Le villi* (The Willis or The Fairies). The publisher Ricordi, recognising promising talent, signed him up. Puccini launched his international career with *Manon Lescaut* (1893), a bold choice of subject given the popularity of Jules Massenet's opera on the same story, written ten years earlier. This was followed by *La bohème* (1896), based on the mid-century novel *Scènes de la vie de bohème* by Frenchman Henri Murger. The story resonated with *verismo* insofar as it concerned young, penniless Bohemians and the love interest of one of these with Mimi, a consumptive seamstress. The narrative passes from optimism and humour into intense romantic passion and on to tragedy. *La bohème* confirmed Puccini's unsurpassed gift for passionate lyricism and subtle characterisation. His symphonic compositional approach was at times Wagnerian, and there were few in Europe who could combine vocal and instrumental forces with such effortless melodic fluency. Towering above his peers, Puccini became the new standard-bearer of Italy's hallowed operatic tradition.

France: repertory and influence

Opera

The predominance of grand opera in Paris was almost at an end by the mid-century, yet its influence extended not only to the next generations of French composers, but also to those in Germany (including Wagner) and Italy. The year 1864 brought the première of Meyerbeer's final grand opera, *L'Africaine*, and also the passing of new legislation that broke the traditional boundaries of 'high' and 'low' drama. The various opera houses, which had each operated under specific rules of musical style, were now allowed complete freedom. This naturally had a significant impact upon the topics and structuring of French stage works in the later part of the century.

Berlioz

The 1850s and 60s saw the meeting of old and new generations in Parisian opera houses. A mature, deeply embittered Berlioz struggled to get his monumental opera *Les Troyens* staged, a process that took over five years and necessitated him cutting the opera into two parts for performance purposes. The second part, *Les Troyens à Carthage*, was well received in 1863, but Berlioz only ever heard a single extract of the first part performed during his lifetime. His final stage work, the light comedy *Béatrice et Bénédict*, rewarded him with immediate success at Baden-Baden in 1862. Meanwhile, the young Charles Gounod followed up the success of *Sapho* (1851) and *La nonne sanglante* (The Bleeding Nun, 1854) with

Gounod

Der Krieg Deutschlands gegen Frankreich.

◀ The Siege of Paris, during the Franco-Prussian War, 1870–71. With the capital surrounded, balloons and carrier pigeons were the only means of communication between Parisians and the outside world. Bizet, Saint-Saëns, Massenet, Fauré, Duparc and D'Indy all fought with the National Guard or other regiments. Most of them escaped Paris before the subsequent civil revolt, which culminated in a bloodthirsty assault by government on the Communards in May 1871.

Faust (1859), the opera that was to make him famous across Europe for his music, and infamous in German-speaking lands for his apparent defamation of Goethe's play. Gounod's subsequent stage-works, including *Mireille* (1864), brought mixed fortunes, but he managed another sensation with the five-act *Roméo et Juliette* in 1867. Especially powerful are the stunning love duets, culminating in the lovers' final expressions of devotion and consolation in the tomb scene of Act 5.

One of the most interesting figures on the Paris scene was Georges Bizet (1838–75), who barely enjoyed any success in his own lifetime. He had a spectacular gift for lyrical melody and orchestration, and was additionally a top-rank pianist with a formidable musical memory. His second-best known work, *Les pêcheurs de perles* (The Pearl Fishers, 1863), was, like Gounod's *Faust*, originally conceived as a semi-sung *opéra comique*. Not long before its première, Bizet turned it into an all-sung *opéra*, in which form it managed a reasonable run of 18 performances at Paris's Théâtre Lyrique. The critics had been hostile—only Berlioz seemed to respond favourably.

Bizet

Had Bizet lived past his 36 years, *Carmen* (1875) would have changed his fortunes. It was his own idea to set Prosper Mérimée's novel, and in many ways he and the librettists Henri Meilhac and Ludovic Halévy, in their pursuit of contemporary realism, anticipated the Italian *verismo* movement. The opera certainly fascinated Parisian audiences as much for its low-life violence and sexual passion as for Bizet's vibrant music. The press penned some scandalised responses, but in spite of stiff opposition, *Carmen* fared reasonably well on its initial run. The death of the 36-year-old Bizet, three

Carmen

months after the première, aroused the curiosity of many, and followers of the opera gradually grew. What began as a minor scandal became one of the most overwhelmingly successful operas of the century. And no wonder: there are few vocal works more popular than the habanera 'L'amour est un oiseau rebelle' (Love is a rebellious bird), nor more infectious than 'Votre toast', better known as the 'Toreador Song'.

Opera, in its various forms, was fundamental to French music both at home and abroad throughout the late century. In terms of narrative and style there was no specific formula for success, witness other highlights such as Offenbach's farcical *Orphée aux enfers* (an opéra bouffe, see *Operetta*), Delibes's exotic *Lakmé* (a three-act tragic opera) and Massenet's impulsive *Manon* (a five-act tragic opéra comique). Emmanuel Chabrier's loosely-historical *Le roi malgré lui*, a comical opéra comique, may have enjoyed more than modest success had its opening run not been upset by fire at the Salle Favart. Saint-Saëns's full opera *Samson et Dalila*, premièred under Liszt at Weimar in 1877, had to wait until the 1890s for French favour, having taken an initial battering by the critics when it appeared in a concert version in 1875.

Operetta

In the early 1800s, the preferred antidote to the gravity of grand opera and Italian tragedy had been semi-sung *opéra comique*, all-sung *opera buffa* and vaudeville productions. The ambiguous position of *opéra comique* (a genre that could be either comic or deeply tragic) together with the diminished popularity of *opera buffa*, resulted in a gap in the market for musical satire and farce.

Jacques Offenbach   In 1855 Jacques Offenbach (1819–80) opened his Théâtre des Bouffes-Parisiens and began staging short satirical sketches with occasional musical items. Offenbach himself contributed to his theatre's repertory, as did Adolphe Adam and Léo Delibes. Their productions became extraordinarily popular, and when new regulations in 1858 allowed for the increase of players on stage, Offenbach mounted his first full-length *opéra bouffe*: *Orphée aux enfers* (Orpheus in the Underworld). The farce introduced his infectious *can-can* and secured his international reputation. He produced new works as fast as he could to meet public demand, averaging two new shows every year between 1856 and 1869. Offenbach was, above all others, responsible for both defining and propagating the genre of operetta: a world of witty, satirical and utterly implausible plots and light-hearted, energetic musical numbers.

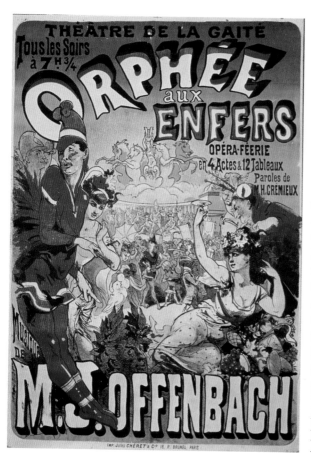

◀ Poster for Jacques Offenbach's *Orphée aux enfers* (Orpheus in the Underworld), at the Théâtre de la Gaîté, Paris.

The formula was soon taken up elsewhere in Europe. In Vienna, Franz von Suppé (1819–95) began writing operettas in the 1860s and continued to do so through to his final years. In the same city Johann Strauss II (1825–99) produced a striking assimilation of *opéra bouffe* and the Viennese waltz in *Die Fledermaus* (1874), by far the best known of his 12 contributions to the genre. In England, it was as a direct result of witnessing one of Offenbach's *opéra bouffes* that Arthur Sullivan (1842–1900) composed his first operetta, *Cox and Box*, in 1866. His 25-year collaboration with the librettist W. S. Gilbert (1836–1911), beginning in 1871, resulted in 14 operettas that parodied everything from literature and government to the British armed forces. The most successful of these, *The Mikado* (1885), enjoyed an opening run of 672 performances—a taster of the remarkable success of the operetta's offspring in more recent times: the musical.

Gilbert and Sullivan

Ballet

It is hardly surprising that the modern stand-alone genre of ballet burst forth from the most ardent dance-loving nation of Europe. Whilst France's *ballet de cour* tradition was long dead, dance productions had survived in the form of 'pantomime ballets' and integrated parts of opera. Such practices were not exclusive to France, but customs there were so strong that throughout much of the 1800s the Paris Opéra *insisted* that its productions contain a divertissement of some kind for the dancers—hence Verdi's revised 'Parisian' versions of many of his operas. When Wagner deviated from this convention in the Paris version of *Tannhäuser* in 1861, his hugely expensive production was booed off stage and out of Paris completely, albeit by an aristocratic minority.

It was the Romantic interpretation of danced narrative that launched the modern ballet repertory. The milestone work was *La Sylphide*, premièred at the Paris Opéra in 1832 with choreography by Filippo Taglioni and music by Jean-Madeleine Schneitzhoeffer. The ballerina Marie Taglioni, Filippo's daughter, brought a new poetic elegance to ballet, performing graceful

▶ Pelagia
Karpakova,
who danced as
Odette/Odile in the
first production of
Swan Lake in 1877.

leaps and pirouettes, and dancing *en pointe* (on the tips of toes) to conjure ethereal lightness. She was costumed in white, her bell-shaped skirt falling just below her knees to allow the audience to marvel at her exquisite footwork. It was from this time that ballet began to exploit fantasy, creating the illusion of weight-lessness, suspension and flight. Male dancers, who had enjoyed pre-eminent roles for centuries, now played second fiddle to the prima ballerina until the early 20th century.

Our present-day ballet repertory is thus rooted in France, with Adolphe Adam's *Giselle* (1841), and Delibes's *Coppélia* (1870) and *Sylvia* (1876) among the represen-tative examples. Delibes's light, witty, elegant ballet music, echoing the charm and humour of his operettas, made

Russia: Tchaikovsky

a deep impression on Tchaikovsky, whose three ballet scores are all major symphonic compositions in their own right. The first, *Swan Lake* (1876), was not a success in the composer's lifetime (some found his harmonies too Wagnerian), though it now stands as his earliest enduring stage-work. His two subsequent ballets, *The Sleeping Beauty* (1889) and *The Nutcracker* (1892), were immediate triumphs. The memorable melodies and often delicate orchestration contribute to the magical quality of his scores, but the initial success of these later ballets owed much to the French choreographer Marius Petipa, ballet-master of the Russian Imperial Ballet, and his assistant Lev Ivanov. Carefully worked-out dramatic scenarios, exotic set pieces and spectacular presentation assured their triumph. Ivanov was also responsible for choreographing the well-known 'Polovtsian Dances' in the first production of Borodin's *Prince Igor* in 1890. Petipa's legacy provided the foundations for the great balletic impresario of the early 20th century, Sergey Diaghilev.

French orchestral music and new impressions

In contrast with the longevity of France's late-century stage music, its contemporaneous symphonic tradition is now largely forgotten. Modern audiences are unfamiliar with the symphonies of Gounod, Vincent d'Indy (1851–1931), Edouard Lalo and Chausson. Popular within the French orchestral repertory are pieces that eschew traditional format or at least exhibit some sort of novelty, such as Saint-Saëns's *Danse macabre* (1874) and Third ('Organ') Symphony (1886), Lalo's *Symphonie Espagnole*, Chabrier's *España* (1883), Paul Dukas's *L'apprenti sorcier* (1897) and Chausson's *Poème* for violin and orchestra (1898).

One of the most influential musical figures in Paris was César Franck (1822–90), a Belgian-born composer, organist and teacher. He had already demonstrated a precocious talent for piano and harmony by the time his parents brought him to Paris as a 12-year-old. His first publication was a set of Piano Trios (1843), a product of his teenage years at the Paris Conservatoire and one that caught the interest of several leading composers, including Liszt, Chopin and Meyerbeer. Franck went on to create some of the most heavily chromatic works of the French school. He was an ardent admirer of Wagner (he quotes the famous 'Tristan' chord in several of his major compositions) and is now best known for his Symphony in D minor (1888) and the fantasia-like *Variations symphoniques* for piano and orchestra (1885). His smaller works include an important body of organ music, the *Prélude, choral et fugue* for piano (1884), Violin Sonata (1886) and String Quartet (1889). Accordingly, he championed harmonic progressivism within the context of Classical form, an approach similar to Bruckner's. Franck was a renowned teacher and received reverential respect from many pupil-disciples, notably Duparc, d'Indy and Dukas.

Two progressive and influential composers emerged on the Paris scene towards the end of the century: Erik Satie (1866–1925) and Claude Debussy (1862–1918). Satie pursued a new aesthetic of sparse clarity in an attempt to distance himself from the excessive passion (as he saw it) of 19th-century music. His most famous creations are the three *Gymnopédies* (1888) and the *Gnossiennes* (six in total, composed 1889–97) for piano solo. These strange and beautiful compositions draw together elements of extreme chromaticism, modal writing, and a fusion of Western, Oriental and ancient worlds. Debussy described Satie in 1892 as 'a gentle medieval musician lost in this century'.

Steeped in the ideas of Baudelaire and Mallarmé, Debussy made a conscious effort to look both beyond Wagnerism and before it. Having been 'through the mill' (as he himself put it) at the Paris Conservatoire, he fought hard to free himself of the shackles of academic tradition. His experience of Javanese gamelan in 1889 at the Paris Universal Exhibition was formative, encouraging his

César Franck

Erik Satie and Claude Debussy

◀ Achille-Claude Debussy, aged about 22.

exploration of whole-tone and pentatonic scales. Among Debussy's most interesting early compositions are the pianistic essays of *Suite Bergamasque* (*c.*1890, revised 1905), which includes the beautiful *Clair de lune*. He reached compositional maturity with the String Quartet in G minor (1893) and two landmark orchestral pieces: *Prélude à l'après-midi d'un faune* (1894) and the three orchestral *Nocturnes* (1899). In response to the encored première of Debussy's *Prélude*, the symbolist poet Stéphane Mallarmé wrote, 'This music extends the emotion of my poem and sets the scene more vividly than colour could have done'. Debussy had found his voice. The floating chromaticism, parallel chord movement and modally-inflected harmony broke down tonal traditions and propelled French music forward into a new century, and fresh international renown.

Nationalist movements

Nationalism was one of the most potent and vital forces of the Romantic movement. Motivated by conditions both personal and political, the phenomenon manifested itself in different ways across the entire landscape of Western classical music. Chopin's mature mazurkas and polonaises (1830s and 40s), mostly written in Paris, were lightly nationalistic as nostalgic references to the Polish composer's homeland. By contrast, a confrontational brand of nationalism arose in western and southern Europe via references to nationhood. This is apparent in 'Va, pensiero', the so-called 'Chorus of Hebrew Slaves' from Verdi's opera *Nabucco* (Milan, 1842), whose themes of oppression and loss of homeland became allied to the Risorgimento's campaign for Italian independence and unification. A more explicit example of national pride is found in the final chorus of Wagner's *Die Meistersinger von Nürnberg*, proclaiming that the people should honour their German masters and pay homage to 'Holy German Art'. The opera was premièred at Munich in 1868, when the movement in support of German unification was at its height.

In Eastern Europe and Scandinavia musical nationalism had an even more crucial political agenda. It sought independence from the mainstream musical inheritance by developing a broad awareness of the mother country's culture and traditions. National literary stories, legends and history provided the basis for compositions, while traditional folk songs and dances influenced musical style. Russia's Mikhail Glinka had pioneered the approach in his opera *A Life for the Tsar* (see *Chapter 5*), but during the second half of the century the practice extended to programmatic orchestral music, choral works, songs and piano pieces. The patriotic composers involved were not merely celebrating their homeland, they were giving national identity back to the people.

Russia

It seems fitting that 1848, a year of tremendous political and social upheaval in Europe, was also the year that Glinka wrote the orchestral piece *Kamarinskaya*. Following his nationalistic operas *A Life for the Tsar* and *Ruslan and Lyudmila*, this new work paved the way for an independently Russian style of orchestral music. The potency of *Kamarinskaya* lay in the simplicity of its concept: a short orchestral composition in which two Russian folk melodies are developed and combined through varied repetition, thus uniting a new means for symphonic development with a genuinely Russian style.

Following Glinka's death in 1857, the most prominent figures in Russian musical life were Alexander Dargomïzhsky (1813–69) and Anton Rubinstein (1829–94). A formidable pianist, Rubinstein co-founded the Russian Musical Society in 1859, and the St Petersburg Conservatory in 1862. His brother, the pianist and conductor Nikolay Rubinstein (1835–81), then founded the Moscow Conservatory, with Anton's help. Although Anton was ideally placed to advance a nationalist approach to composition, he was more concerned with cultivating academic rigour; in fact, he viewed the absorption of folk idioms into art music as amateurish, believing that it tended to curb formal design and thematic development.

Instead, the so-called 'Mighty Handful' or 'The Five'—Mily Balakirev, Alexander Borodin, Modest Mussorgsky, Nikolay Rimsky-Korsakov and César Cui—took up Glinka's mantle. Encouraged by the influential critic Vladimir Stasov (1824–1906), they were a diverse band of brothers, respectively a mathematician, chemist, army officer, naval officer, and an army engineer. Balakirev, the only formally-trained musician among them, worked diligently to nurture the skills of the group, promoting them as the new vanguard of Russian music. Their most decisive statements were made in opera, including Mussorgsky's *Boris Godunov* (St Petersburg, 1874) and Borodin's *Prince Igor* (1890, completed by Rimsky-Korsakov and Glazunov). Programmatic orchestral music also provided a platform for transparent nationalism, as found in Borodin's *In the Steppes of Central Asia* (1880), Balakirev's *Russia* (1884), and Rimsky-Korsakov's *Russian Easter Festival Overture* (1888). The piano proved an inspirational medium for both virtuosic and lengthy essays, most famously Balakirev's 'Oriental Fantasy' *Islamey* (1869) and Mussorgsky's *Pictures at an Exhibition* (1874).

'Mighty Handful'

◄ *Slav composers*, an idealised gathering by Ilya Repin. In the foreground Mikhail Glinka talks with Mikhail Balakirev, the music critic Prince Vladimir Odoyevsky and Nikolai Rimsky-Korsakov. Other featured composers include Bedřich Smetana (seated left with manuscript) and the Rubinstein brothers, Anton and Nikolai, at the piano.

Balakirev's activities as a pedagogue extended to the setting up of St Petersburg's Free School of Music in 1862. But despite his stature and influence, Balakirev himself produced only a handful of enduring pieces. Cui, who became a prominent music critic, left an even smaller legacy.

Borodin

Borodin's musical achievements, however, were remarkable for a full-time chemist who also found time to establish Russia's first medical school for women. Composing mostly at weekends, he was denounced by Tchaikovsky as someone who could not 'write a line without outside help'. Yet Borodin was the only one of The Five to gain lasting success in the genres of the symphony and quartet. His thematically rich Symphony No. 2 (1876) is a loosely programmatic, nationalistic work that found definitive form under revision in 1879. Best known is his lyrical Nocturne for string orchestra (1885), an arrangement of the same-named slow movement of his String Quartet No. 2. *Prince Igor* remains an important opera of the Russian repertory, even if elsewhere it is famous only for its vibrant 'Polovtsian Dances'.

Mussorgsky

Modest Mussorgsky (1839–81) was the least technically accomplished composer of 'The Five', but he was arguably the most imaginative and progressive. Few pieces by the group are better known than his brilliantly descriptive *Pictures at an Exhibition*. Later orchestrated by Ravel (among others), the *Pictures* piano suite was composed in response to a memorial exhibition of paintings and drawings by Mussorgsky's friend Victor Hartmann, who died in 1873. The eclectic mix of Hartmann's pictures gives the suite wide colouristic range, extending from the bulky gestures of 'Bydlo' (a large Polish cart) and madcap unruliness of 'Hut on Fowl's Legs' to the light-hearted depictions of the Paris 'Tuileries' and 'Limoges, Market Place'. Meanwhile in his vocal works, Mussorgsky pursued what he termed 'the melody of life', meticulously moulding the melodic line to the rhythms and intonations of the Russian language. This is most apparent in the short opera *The Marriage* (1868) and song-cycles *Sunless* (1874) and *Songs and Dances of Death* (1877). The technique is present though less concentrated in his operatic masterpiece, *Boris Godunov*, and in the unfinished *Khovanshchina*.

Rimsky-Korsakov

Thanks to Nikolay Rimsky-Korsakov (1844–1908) we have a completed version of Mussorgsky's *Khovanshchina* and a full orchestral version of the same composer's orchestral fantasy *St John's Night on Bald Mountain* (1867). As a young naval officer Rimsky-Korsakov developed his musical gifts under the influence of Balakirev. A three-year tour-of-duty (1862–65) on the warship *Almaz* took him as far as Rio de Janeiro, during which time he studied Beethoven and Mendelssohn, pored over Berlioz's manual on orchestration, and wrote most of his First Symphony. Subsequent years were more settled, but Rimsky-Korsakov gave up his naval career in 1871, aged 27, when he was invited to become Professor of Harmony and Composition at the St Petersburg Conservatoire. This appointment met with derision within his predominantly anti-establishment artistic circle.

Chiefly an opera composer, Rimsky-Korsakov was particularly skilled in creating exotic music to enhance colourful evocations of fairy-tale and Eastern worlds. Among his 15 operas are the mythical epics *The Snow Maiden* (1881), *Sadko* (1897) and *The Legend of the Invisible City of Kitezh*

(1905). Each one of these features striking orientalisms, such as the popular 'Song of the Indian Guest' from *Sadko* (also known as the 'Hindu song'). The decision to look East rather than West was a sure way of making Russian music independent of mainstream German influence. The symphonic suite *Scheherazade* (1888), based on *The Thousand and One Nights*, was the supreme concert-hall expression of Russian orientalism. It would be wrong, however, to view Rimsky-Korsakov as a composer solely concerned with nationalistic trends. In terms of technique he became the most sophisticated and Westernised of The Five, and he even kept a framed photograph of Wagner above his desk.

To the wider world it was Tchaikovsky who carried the flame for Russian music (see also earlier sections), yet he held great allegiance to the Western musical tradition. Russian themes are explored on the stage, as in the Pushkin-inspired operas *Eugene Onegin* (Moscow, 1879) and *Queen of Spades* (1890), and in the concert hall, with surcharged patriotism in the *Slavonic March* (1878), more subtly in the folksong-based finales of his First and Second symphonies (1868, 1880). His famous *Ceremonial Overture '1812'* was commissioned to celebrate the Silver Jubilee of Tsar Nicholas I in 1882. It was introduced at the All-Russian Art and Industrial Exhibition in Moscow, an event timed to coincide with the completion of the Cathedral of the Redeemer, built in commemoration of the 'Patriotic War' of 1812. Tchaikovsky's later (and greater) instrumental compositions took a more cosmopolitan approach, combining Western and Russian elements of style, harmony and structure in unique combination. The sublimation of East into West became subtle to the point where his music ceased to have any obvious nationalist connotations.

Tchaikovsky's nationalism

Bohemia

Nowhere was the expression of cultural nationalism more significant than in the Czech province of Bohemia, a region that had long desired independence from Habsburg rule. Heavily influenced by German culture, it had been producing composers of international stature for well over a century: Jan D. Zelenka, Johann Stamitz, Jan L. Dussek, Johann Vanhal (1739–1813) and Václav Tomášek (1774–1850), to name just a few. Their success owed much to the standard of German musical education in Bohemia, and it was occupationally judicious for these composers to remain allied to German (and Italian) trends.

During the late-century the Czech crusade for national identity grew ever stronger. One important milestone was the building of Prague's Provisional Theatre, in 1862, for the promotion of Czech-language drama and opera. A Bohemian aristocrat, Count Jan Harrach, had already publicised a competition to advance the fledgling Czech operatic repertory, and it was in response that Bedřich Smetana composed his first opera, *The Brandenburgers in Bohemia*, a historical tale based on a Czech libretto by Karel Sabina. Smetana had only recently begun to read and write Czech; as a member of the educated middle-classes he had been raised speaking German, Bohemia's 'official' language. Submitting the score in 1863, he had to wait three years for the indecisive judges to declare it the winning entry. In

Bedřich Smetana

The Bartered Bride

musical style *The Brandenburgers* looked mainly to German models, but in narrative and language it was distinctly Czech. The opera found instant success.

Smetana collaborated with Sabina again on his second opera, *The Bartered Bride*. When the semi-sung two-act comedy struggled to please in 1866, Smetana immediately began revising his score. The opera was presented many times in different versions, but its definitive three-act form came in 1870, with recitatives replacing the spoken dialogue. Smetana furnished this humorous and warm-hearted tale of Bohemian village life with music rich in Czech folk idioms: dances such as the *polka* and *furiant* create a rustic atmosphere, while the Czech language shapes the metre and articulation of the text. The scent of folk melody is ever-present, and folk-loric economy clearly influenced the lucid musical style. By the 1880s, *The Bartered Bride* was being lauded as the archetypal Czech opera.

Smetana was the principal conductor of the Provisional Theatre from 1866 to 1874, during which time he introduced his epic but unappreciated historical opera *Dalibor* (1868) and promoted works by other Czech composers. Beyond the opera house he depicted the greatness of the Czech nation in the mighty symphonic cycle *Má vlast*, a work all the more extraordinary for having been written after he was struck by total hearing loss. Completed in 1879, the cycle of six symphonic poems presents a succession of musical portraits of Bohemian heroes, landscapes (most famously the river Vltava), settlements and people. Smetana's music acted as a powerful catalyst for the development of a distinctly national style, and in turn encouraged similar patriotism from younger composers including Antonín Dvořák, Zdeněk Fibich (1850–1900) and Leoš Janáček (1854–1928).

Dvořák came under Smetana's direct influence while serving as violist in the orchestra of the Provisional Theatre. When he resigned from his position, aged 30, he had every intention of becoming a major composer of Czech-language opera. He wrote some appealing operas in the light comic vein of Smetana's *Bartered Bride*, such as *The Stubborn Lovers* (1874) and *The Cunning Peasant* (1877), and also enjoyed some success in (serious) grand opera, notably with the historical *Dimitrij* (1882). His most enduring stage-work, the fairy-tale opera *Rusalka* (1900), owes its greatest debt not to Slavic traditions but to Fouqué's *Undine* and Hans Andersen's *Little Mermaid*.

Away from the stage, Dvořák's music was by turns proudly nationalist and more subtly abstract. It was a patriotic choral piece that brought his first real taste of success in Prague: *The Heirs of the White Mountain* (1872), which entreated the Czech people to love their native land. Six years later the *Slavonic Dances*, with their folk-like tunes and Slavic rhythms, launched Dvořák's international career. Lightly nationalistic are his four symphonic poems inspired by Czech fairy tales: *The Water Goblin*, *The Noon Witch*, *The Golden Spinning-Wheel* and *The Wild Dove* (all 1896). In his symphonies Dvořák generally avoided explicit nationalism (see *'Absolute' Orchestral Music*), although allusions to Czech dance rhythms and folk tunes appear regularly across his entire oeuvre.

Dvořák's nationalism

Scandinavia

Norway's nationalist movement began in the early 1800s. Under Danish rule for nearly 300 years, the country tasted just a few months of independence in 1814, but then entered into a political union with Sweden that was to last until 1905. Thanks to the efforts of musicians such as the violin virtuoso Ole Bull (1810–80), Norwegian culture was not completely unknown beyond the country's borders. But it was not until the second half of the century, with the emergence of composers such as Halfdan Kjerulf (1815–68), Johan Svendsen (1840–1911), Rikard Nordraak (1842–66) and, above all, Edvard Grieg, that Norwegian classical music found a truly national voice.

Edvard Grieg

Born in Bergen, Grieg was musically home-schooled until he was 15. Encouraged by Ole Bull, he then left Norway to study music at the Leipzig Conservatory, as Kjerulf and Svendsen had done before him. Grieg did not relish the experience, but there he took instruction from Moscheles and Carl Reinecke, and became intimately familiar with the music of Schumann. Following a further period of study under Niels Gade at Copenhagen (1863–64), Grieg met Rikard Nordraak, the composer of the Norwegian national anthem. Nordraak, whose life was to be cut short by tuberculosis, awakened Grieg's passion for Norwegian folk music. Grieg made piano transcriptions of the music of the Hardanger fiddle (a Norwegian folk violin) and composed many *Romancer*, art-songs based on Norwegian texts, shaped by folk-like melodies. His best-loved solo piano music was equally inspired by the melodies, modes and dance rhythms of his country's indigenous music, including the *Humoresques* (1865), ten sets of *Lyric Pieces* (1867–1901) and the *Ballade* in G minor (1875).

Grieg claimed that his artistic aim was to 'create a national form of music, which could give an identity to the Norwegian people'. This priority drew him to some

◀ The celebrated Norwegian folk musician Myllarguten playing the hardanger fiddle. The instrument's characteristic sound derives largely from its sympathetic (drone) understrings.

of Norway's leading literary figures. His vocal compositions with the poet Bjørnstjerne Bjørnson include *Before a Southern Convent* for female voices and orchestra, and the melodrama *Bergliot* (both 1871). His greatest life-time success derived from the music he provided to Heinrich Ibsen's play *Peer Gynt*, which was performed for the first time at Christiania in 1876. Grieg split his incidental music into two colourful orchestral suites, whose international popularity surpassed that of his acclaimed Piano Concerto in A minor (see *The piano as orchestra*, p. 415). Grieg created another enduring concert work in *Fra Holbergs tid* (From Holberg's Time, 1884), conceived as a piano suite to mark the bicentenary of Holberg's birth. Arranged for strings in 1885, it draws on Baroque forms dating from the Bergen-born poet's own lifetime.

Carl Nielsen and Jean Sibelius

Among the emerging generation of Scandinavian composers were Carl Nielsen (1865–1931) and Jean Sibelius (1865–1957). Denmark's Carl Nielsen forged his musical identity largely through a personalisation of the central European vernacular, looking to Brahms and Dvořák especially. He rejected the conservative approach of his distinguished teacher Niels Gade (1817–90) and went on to explore new tonal structures and progressive harmonies in his First Symphony (1892). Boasting colourful combinations of diatonic and modal progressions, his was the first Classically-organised symphony to begin in one key and end in another. Jean Sibelius, on the other hand, launched his career with politically-sensitive pieces at a time when Russian governance of Finland was becoming increasingly oppressive. His inspiration derived from Finland's landscapes and folk traditions, including the epic folk poetry of the *Kalevala*. Among his early nationalistic works are the symphonic poem *Kullervo* (1892), a biographical colossus for soloists, chorus and orchestra, and the *Karelia Suite* (1893). Sibelius produced his melodically fertile First Symphony in 1899, and the same year completed the first version of his most famous symphonic poem, *Finlandia*. Originally entitled *Finland Awakens*, it was particularly provocative for its narrative of suppression, awakening, conflict and liberation.

Other national awakenings

Spain

The Napoleonic wars, political unrest and civil war had blighted Spain's cultural life in the early decades of the century. Fernando Sor (1778–1839) and Juan Arriaga (1806–26) were just two of the many Spanish composers who left the country to advance their careers elsewhere, adapting to the musical mainstream in the process. The Spanish appetite for Italian music, for years mimicked and imported, held fast until nationalist resentment began to boil around the half-century.

A rising national consciousness was reflected in music theatre as the home-grown zarzuela experienced a revival. The semi-sung zarzuela was an equivalent of the German singspiel and the English ballad opera. While its music tended to be Italianate in style, the genre brought together popular Spanish elements and often presented narratives relating to the lives of ordinary people. Francisco Barbieri (1823–94) composed

◄ Spanish violinist and composer Pablo Sarasate.

more than 60 zarzuelas, some identified with the aptly named Teatro de la Zarzuela in Madrid (the first theatre dedicated to the genre), which opened in 1857. During the final decade of the century around 1,500 zarzuelas were presented in the capital's 11 designated theatres.

Few worked as hard as Felipe Pedrell (1841–1922) to encourage pride in Spain's musical heritage. A composer of zarzuelas and ambitious operas, Pedrell published influential journals and periodicals featuring unknown Spanish music and his own musicological research. He created important collections of Spanish sacred music, and also taught and inspired two major figures of the next generation: Isaac Albéniz (1860–1909) and Enrique Granados (1867–1916). It was as composers of piano music that these younger men excelled. Among their earlier compositions, Albéniz's *Suite española* (mostly completed by 1886) and Granados's *Danzas españolas* (1890) demonstrate how specific locations and folk dances could stimulate music undeniably Spanish in character (see also *Chapter 7*).

Felipe Pedrell, Isaac Albéniz and Enrique Granados

Francisco Tárrega (1852–1909) was the first to popularise the music of Albéniz and Granados in guitar transcription. Indeed, compositions such as Albéniz's 'Sevilla' and 'Asturias' (from *Suite española*) are arguably more compelling as guitar pieces, since much of the original inspiration derives from Spanish folk guitar styles. Tárrega's idiomatic transcriptions and compositions, including his own captivating *Recuerdos de la Alhambra*, provided the foundation for the modern guitar repertory. Tárrega toured throughout Western Europe and was lauded as the 'Sarasate of the guitar'. The virtuoso violinist Pablo Sarasate (1844–1908), whose celebrity was global, likewise promoted himself as a performer-composer. His nationalist music includes four books of *Spanische Tänze* (1878–82), although it is the spectacular *Zigeunerweisen* (1878), taking inspiration from Hungarian gypsy music, that has done most to secure his lasting fame.

Francisco Tárrega and Pablo Sarasate

United States and England

Throughout the early 19th century, the musical life of the United States was almost entirely dependent upon European imports. However, by the 1850s a national musical voice was beginning to emerge as native composers like Stephen Foster (1826–64) began writing music reflective of American life. A number of his 200 songs are still well known today, such as *Oh, Susannah* and *Camptown Races*. Composers wishing to identify their music as truly American seized upon such songs. By far the best-known of the mid-century generation is Louis Moreau Gottschalk (1829–69), a prolific composer and concert pianist whose vast piano output draws upon Foster's melodies, the French salon style, Italian *bel canto* and the songs and dances of South

Louis Moreau Gottschalk

America, where he spent considerable time. His piano caprice *Pasquinade* (*c*.1863) even seems to pre-empt Ragtime, some 36 years before Scott Joplin's *Maple Leaf Rag* (1899).

Edward MacDowell

Later in the century, Edward MacDowell (1860–1908) sought to combine European models with Amerindian melodies and rhythms; his Suite No. 2 *Indian* (1895) is a much-loved example. In other works he made reference to his homeland through depictions of the American landscape, as in the *Woodland Sketches* for solo piano (1896), which begins with the pretty miniature *To a Wild Rose*. Amy Beach (1867–1944), America's leading female concert composer, chose a different vernacular for her First Symphony (1896) by looking to the Gaelic tradition, identified as part of her country's musical inheritance. More commercially-minded was the bandmaster John Philip Sousa (1854–1932), a composer of operettas and some 135 marches, including *The Washington Post* (1889) and the nation's favourite, *The Stars and Stripes Forever* (1897). Brilliantly crafted, his marches gained phenomenal popularity because brass band culture was rife throughout the United States—virtually every town had its own brass band. Sousa also made his name in Europe, which he first toured in 1900. By that time he was his country's most famous musician, his optimistic marches synonymous with American patriotism.

John Philip Sousa

Dvořák in America

The importance of Dvořák should not be underestimated in the quest for an American idiom. 'The future music of this country must be founded on what are called Negro melodies,' Dvořák declared upon his arrival in America. His sojourn to the United States (1892–95) saw the creation of several significant compositions, such as the *American* String Quartet (1893, see *Chamber music*) and the Symphony No. 9, *From the New World* (1893). In this, his final symphony, Dvořák incorporated pentatonicism, drones, ostinato rhythms and pronounced syncopation that were to varying degrees reminiscent of Native American and African American folk music. It has been pointed out that he had already used such musical devices in Europe, and there are also doubts as to whether the beautiful English horn tune of the second movement was in fact, as previously thought, inspired by the African-American spiritual. But Dvořák's intention to compose 'original themes' influenced by American folk traditions cannot be refuted.

England, Elgar

Meanwhile across the Atlantic, Hubert Parry (1848–1918), Charles Stanford (1852–1924) and Edward Elgar (1857–1934) were puzzling over problems of national style in English music. All three drew heavily upon the German tradition, the music of Mendelssohn especially. Since the folk music movement did not really take effect in England until the early 20th century, any sense of 'Englishness' was to be found more generally within the chosen musical forms and harmonic palette. The continued importance of organised religion gave the choral and organ repertory a major role in musical life. In addition, non-liturgical choral commissions were being offered for festivals held in London, Birmingham and Manchester. Stanford and Parry united a Brahmsian approach to form and harmonic language with a distinctly English hymnal style. Examples include Stanford's set of Three Motets (*c*.1890) and Requiem (Birmingham, 1897), and Parry's anthem *I Was Glad*, written for the coronation of Edward VII in 1902.

Elgar achieved early popularity with his charming *Salut d'amour* for violin and piano, composed in 1888. The following year he married Caroline Alice Roberts, who became his muse, as well as the author of a number of texts he set to music. Mature pieces followed, including the *Froissart* Overture (1890), the cantata *Scenes from the Saga of King Olaf* (1896), and *Chanson de nuit* and *Chanson de matin* for violin and piano (1897–99, orchestrated 1899). With such pieces Elgar attained critical recognition, but the impact of his superbly orchestrated 'Variations on an Original Theme' (1899) was something else altogether. In these so-called *Enigma* Variations, Elgar forged a new path by combining elements of motivic variation and character-piece writing. First performed under Hans Richter in London on 19 June 1899, it at once raised the bar for English orchestral music and thrust Elgar fully into the public eye. Bolstered by his new-found fame, he set to work on a commission for the 1900 Birmingham Festival that would prove to be his choral masterpiece: *The Dream of Gerontius*.

▲ London's Royal Albert Hall, built in memory of Queen Victoria's late husband and opened in 1871. Its cavernous design yielded a substantial echo, a problem not fully solved until 1969 when fibreglass discs were suspended from the ceiling to aid sound diffusion.

Chronology
1850–1899

American songwriter **Stephen Foster** writes his popular *Camptown Races*.

Wagner begins to sketch *Siegfrieds Tod* (Siegfried's Death), which will later become *Götterdämmerung* (The Twilight of the Gods), the final opera of the *Ring* cycle.

2 January To awaken national pride, founder **Ole Bull** opens the Norwegian National Theatre in Bergen with an orchestral concert followed by a production of Holberg's play *Den Vægelsindede* (The Waverer).

11 January Louis Moreau Gottschalk performs his exotic piano piece *Le bananier* (The Banana Tree) in Paris. Forming part of his four-piece *Louisiana Quartet* collection, the Afro-Caribbean-inspired miniature will make the American pianist-composer famous throughout Europe.

19 February Berlioz conducts the first concert of his Société Philharmonique in Paris. He has established the institution primarily to promote his own works, but also to rival the Concerts du Conservatoire.

25 June Schumann premières his opera *Genoveva* (completed 1848) at the Stadttheater, Leipzig. Reasonably successful at the time, the composer's first and last opera soon disappears from the German repertory.

28 August Following 46 rehearsals, **Liszt** conducts the first performance of **Wagner**'s *Lohengrin*, in Weimar. The three-act opera (completed 1848) is well received, although Wagner, currently exiled in Switzerland, will not hear it for another 11 years. The constantly developing music of the prelude is perhaps his most imaginative to date. Excerpts from the opera become very popular, none more so than the *Bridal Chorus*.

1 September Soprano **Jenny Lind** arrives in America (below), greeted by around 30,000 admirers and spectators in New York Harbour. Dubbed 'The Swedish Nightingale', she will tour the country for two years, performing around 150 recitals at $1,000 a time. Her tour manager, Phineas T. Barnum, pockets even more.

JENNY LIND AND THE AMERICANS.
From our own Reporters.

CORONATION OF JENNY THE FIRST—QUEEN OF THE AMERICANS.

2 September Schumann arrives with his family in Düsseldorf to take up the post of music director. The following month he completes his Cello Concerto in A minor (Op. 129), and before the end of the year his *Rhenish* Symphony in E flat major (No. 3, Op. 97).

3/6 September The pseudonymous K. Freigedank (Free-thought) criticises and belittles the likes of **Meyerbeer** and the late Mendelssohn in his anti-Semitic essay 'Das Judenthum in der Musik', published in two parts in the *Neue Zeitschrift für Musik*. It quickly transpires that the author is **Wagner**.

October Joachim, aged 19, becomes leader of the Weimar orchestra, under the directorship of **Liszt**.

16 November Verdi's opera *Stiffelio* premières at the Teatro Grande in Trieste. The production runs into problems with the censors due to sensitivities over its religious subject matter. Verdi and his librettist, **Piave**, will rework material of the opera into *Aroldo* (1857).

1850 US President Zachary Taylor dies; Vice-President Millard Fillmore becomes 13th President • California becomes the 31st state of the USA • Creation of the future states of New Mexico and Utah is agreed • South Australia, Victoria and Tasmania obtain representative government • British engineer John Brett establishes telegraphic communication with continental Europe by submarine cable • Physicist Rudolf Clausius (Ger) states the second law of thermodynamics • Britain gets its first public libraries • Alfred Tennyson (Eng) publishes *In Memoriam* and becomes Poet Laureate in succession to Wordsworth • Nathaniel Hawthorne (US): *The Scarlet Letter*

Breitkopf & Härtel begin to publish the first complete Bach edition (completed 1899).

In Paris the Hungarian composer **Stephen Heller** writes his contemplative *Spaziergänge eines Einsamen*, a suite of six progressive character pieces for piano.

Liszt's *Etudes d'exécution transcendante d'après Paganini* is revised and republished as *Grandes études de Paganini*.

Anton Rubinstein, aged 21, composes the first version of his Symphony No. 2 (*Ocean*). He will later revise and expand the work, from four to six then seven movements (1880).

Bedřich Smetana's piano collection *Six morceaux caractéristiques*, Op. 1, is published in Leipzig, with the help of **Liszt**.

Henry Vieuxtemps (right) completes his Violin Concerto No. 4 in D minor, in St Petersburg. It becomes his favourite, and **Berlioz** declares it 'a magnificent symphony for orchestra with principal violin'. No. 4 is now probably the most popular of Vieuxtemps's seven violin concertos.

10 January Wagner finishes his essay *Oper und Drama*. This year he begins work on *Der junge Siegfried* (Young Siegfried), later *Siegfried*, the third opera of the *Ring* cycle.

20 January Albert Lortzing's opera *Die Opernprobe* (The Opera Rehearsal) opens in Frankfurt. The next day, in Berlin, the composer dies from a stroke, aged 49.

24 January Composer **Gaspare Spontini** dies in Maiolati, aged 76. The town, situated in the Italian province of Ancona, will be renamed Maiolati Spontini in 1939.

6 February Schumann conducts a very successful first performance of his Third (*Rhenish*) Symphony in Düsseldorf.

11 March Verdi's *Rigoletto*, introduced at the Teatro La Fenice, creates a sensation in Venice. The libretto by **Piave**, after a play by Victor Hugo, has been slightly modified in response to the Venetian censors who had initially banned the opera for its 'abhorrent immorality and obscene triviality'.

27 March Composer **Vincent d'Indy** is born into a wealthy aristocratic family, in Paris.

16 April Gounod, aged 32, presents his first opera, *Sapho*, at the Paris Opéra. Some critics respond favourably, but the opera fails to excite the public.

May Berlioz's Société Philharmonique folds due to poor funding.

September Gottschalk, aged 22, begins a 14-month concert tour of Spain. The American pianist-composer gains wide popularity and secures the patronage of Queen Isabella II.

Autumn Schumann completes his Violin Sonata No. 1 in A minor (Op. 105), the Piano Trio in G minor (Op. 110) and the Violin Sonata No. 2 in D minor (Op. 121).

1851 Louis Napoleon, President of the French Republic, organises a *coup d'état* leading to a new constitution • British Foreign Secretary Lord Palmerston is forced to resign for supporting Louis Napoleon's actions • Victoria, Australia, becomes a separate British colony • Britain's window tax (introduced 1696) is repealed • Isaac Singer (US) makes a practical sewing machine • Discovery of gold in Australia • The Great Exhibition is held in Hyde Park, London (UK) • Physicist Hermann Helmholtz (Ger) invents the ophthalmoscope • *The New York Times* is founded • Gustave Courbet (Fr) paints *Young Women from the Village* • Herman Melville (US): *Moby Dick*

Balakirev, aged 15, demonstrates early nationalistic pride in his *Grande Fantaisie on Russian Folksongs*, scored for piano and orchestra.

The celebrated Norwegian violinist **Ole Bull** buys over 11,000 acres in Potter County, Pennsylvania, to help establish a New Norway colony. Immigrant farmers soon arrive, only to find the musician's plot unsuitable for farming. The scheme collapses and Bull sells back the land.

Joachim, aged 21, steps down as orchestral leader at Weimar. The following year the virtuoso becomes principal violinist at the Court of Hanover.

Liszt composes his *Fantasia on Hungarian Folk Melodies* for piano and orchestra. Publications this year include the first 15 of his *Hungarian Rhapsodies*, and a revised *Douze Grandes études*, issued under the title *Etudes d'exécution transcendante* (Transcendental Studies).

Wagner completes the poems of *Das Rheingold* and *Die Walküre*.

5 February Schumann (right) introduces his fairytale oratorio *Der Rose Pilgerfahrt* (The Pilgrimage of the Rose) in Düsseldorf. During the spring he begins to suffer nervous attacks, which persist until the autumn.

24 March German-born composer **Fredrik Pacius** launches Finland's first opera, the three-act Singspiel *Kung Karls jakt* (King Charles' Hunt), premièred in Helsinki.

24 March Berlioz, on his third visit to England, conducts the first of six concerts of the New Philharmonic Society before an audience of almost 1,500 at London's Exeter Hall. The programme includes Mozart's Symphony No. 41, Beethoven's Triple Concerto and Part I of Berlioz's own 'dramatic symphony' *Roméo et Juliette*. Berlioz laps up wide critical praise.

13 June Schumann has his overture and incidental music to *Manfred* (1849) performed complete for the first time, under **Liszt** in Weimar. The overture is one of Schumann's most inspired orchestral pieces, fuelled by his deep passion and empathy for Byron's tormented hero.

18 June In Vienna **Strauss II** introduces his waltz *Liebes-Lieder*, Op. 114, and with it gains acclamation from Eduard Hanslick in the *Wiener Zeitung*. With regular performances of his work in the city, the young Strauss has by now established his reputation outside the shadow of his father.

4 September Adam enjoys instant success with *Si j'étais roi* (If I Were King), lavishly staged at the Théâtre Lyrique in Paris. The three-act opera notches up more than 60 performances by the end of the year.

November Liszt organises a 'Berlioz Week' in Weimar, attended by **Berlioz** himself. Works performed include a revised three-act version of the opera *Benvenuto Cellini*.

November Brahms, aged 19, completes his rousing Piano Sonata No. 2 in F sharp minor.

11 December Niels Gade's Symphony No. 5 is performed for the first time, in Copenhagen.

12 December Bizet receives the *premier prix* for piano at the Paris Conservatoire. The young teenager begins composition classes with **Halévy** the following year.

30 December In Düsseldorf **Schumann** conducts his revised, tightly wrought Symphony in D minor, now renumbered as his Fourth Symphony.

1852 The Second French Empire is proclaimed after a plebiscite: Louis Napoleon becomes Emperor as Napoleon III (to 1870) • A new constitution in New Zealand gives the colony representative government • Britain recognises the independence of Transvaal, South Africa • The Second Burmese War begins; Britain annexes Lower Burma • Taiping revolution breaks out in China • Victoria and Albert Museum is opened in London • Scottish missionary David Livingstone begins exploration of the Zambesi River • John Everett Millais (Eng) paints *Ophelia* • Publication of *Uncle Tom's Cabin* by Harriet Beecher Stowe (US) causes storm over slavery • Charles Dickens (Eng): *Bleak House*

Brahms completes his Piano Sonata No. 1 in C major (i.e. after No. 2, 1852) and composes his Piano Sonata No. 3 in F minor.

Heinrich E. Steinweg establishes Steinway & Sons in New York.

Wagner takes a step on a slippery slope, composing the Piano Sonata in A flat (Op. 85) for his neighbour, Mrs Mathilde Wesendonck. This year he publishes the complete text of his *Ring* cycle: *Das Rheingold*, *Die Walküre*, *Siegfried* and *Götterdämmerung*.

10 January Famous in Europe, **Gottschalk** arrives back in his native America where he begins touring extensively.

19 January Verdi's *Il trovatore* (The Troubadour) provokes enormous excitement at the Teatro Apollo in Rome. Despite a convoluted libretto by **Salvadore Cammarano** after Antonio Gutiérrez's play, the opera is a vehicle for some of Verdi's most stunning arias and ensembles, making it one of his most popular works.

February Liszt completes his Piano Sonata in B minor, one of the most celebrated keyboard pieces of the Romantic repertory. Composed in one movement, the sonata assimilates four movements moulded around a sonata form structure (exposition, development, development/return and recapitulation/coda). The progressive work remains little appreciated until the 20th century.

The soprano Rosina Penco, creator of Leonore in *Il Trovatore*

6 March Verdi's *La traviata* (The Fallen Woman) begins a short run at the Teatro La Fenice, Venice. Composed at a furious speed to a libretto by **Piave**, the opera fails, largely due to ill-cast performers. (Fanny Salvini-Donatelli, playing the heroine who wastes away at the end of Act 3, was apparently obese.) Verdi later writes, '*La traviata* was a grand fiasco, and what is worse, they laughed'. (See also 1854.)

30 September The 20-year-old **Brahms**, with a letter of introduction from **Joachim**, visits the **Schumanns** in Düsseldorf. Robert Schumann immediately recognises Brahms's genius, writing soon afterwards in the *Neue Zeitschrift für Musik*, 'Even outwardly he bore the marks proclaiming: "This is a chosen one"'.

October Schumann completes his Violin Concerto in D minor (WoO. 23) for **Joachim**. The young violinist harbours doubts about the work's artistic merit following the composer's attempted suicide a few months later (see February 1854). It will not be performed in public until 1937.

27 October Virtuoso **Henryk Wieniawski**, aged 18, premières his Violin Concerto No. 1 in F sharp minor, in Leipzig.

10 November Schumann fails to turn up to direct a subscription concert in Düsseldorf following criticisms of his ability to conduct the works of other composers. He follows up his boycott with a stiffly-worded letter to the Musikverein committee, effectively resigning.

1853 Franklin Pierce is inaugurated as 14th President of the USA • The Gadsden Purchase confirms southern New Mexico and southern Arizona as parts of USA • Turkey rejects Russia's claim to protect Christians in the Ottoman Empire: Russian troops invade Moldavia and Wallachia • British and French fleets gather at the Dardanelles • Britain embarks on a Free Trade policy • Britain annexes Nagpur in India • France annexes New Caledonia • Alexander Wood (Scot) introduces the hypodermic syringe • The first railroad between New York and Chicago is opened • Nathaniel Hawthorne (US): *Tanglewood Tales* • Elizabeth Gaskell (Eng): *Cranford* • Charlotte Brontë (Eng): *Villette*

Brahms publishes his *Sechs Gesänge* Op. 7, six love songs each set in a minor key. This year sees the completion of the Piano Trio No. 1 in B major (first version, Op. 8).

Hanslick considers musical form and expression in his influential treatise *Vom Musikalisch-Schönen*, published in Leipzig. He argues that music is autonomous, incapable of representing anything outside of itself.

Liszt presents five of his symphonic poems during the year at Weimar: the newly-composed *Orpheus* and *Festklänge*, and revised versions of *Les Préludes*, *Mazeppa* and *Tasso*.

The Nibelung dwarf Alberich steals gold from the Rhinemaidens to make an all-powerful ring in *Das Rheingold*. **Wagner** completes the composition of his first *Ring* cycle opera.

16 February Meyerbeer presents *L'étoile du nord* (The North Star), with libretto by **Scribe**, at the Opéra-Comique, Paris. The opera is a phenomenal success, with productions following across Europe and the Americas.

27 February Schumann attempts suicide by throwing himself off a bridge into the Rhine. Rescued by fishermen, he is confined to a private asylum within the week. **Clara**, pregnant with their eighth child, is advised not to visit him. They will not see each other for over two years, and then just two days before the composer's death.

3 March Harriet Smithson, the separated wife of **Berlioz**, dies, having suffered several years of severe paralysis. Berlioz marries his mistress, Marie Recio, later this year.

6 May Verdi's tragedy *La traviata* is revived at the Teatro San Benedetto, Venice. Following a disappointing first run (see 1853), Verdi has recast the singers and revised parts of the score. With its poignant characterisation of the hapless heroine,

Violetta, and irrepressible flow of infectious melodies, the opera is an uncontested triumph.

25 June Tchaikovsky loses his mother to cholera. This year the 14-year-old begins his life-long passions of composing and smoking.

3 July Czech composer **Leoš Janáček** is born in Hukvaldy, Moravia.

'I sat near him so that I could see both his hands and face. For the first time in my life I beheld real inspiration…'
Late summer Mary Ann Evans (George Eliot) makes **Liszt**'s acquaintance in Weimar.

1 September German composer **Engelbert Humperdinck** is born in Siegburg.

Autumn Otto Wesendonck bails **Wagner** out of debt to the tune of nearly 10,000 francs. Wagner agrees to repay his friend through future box office receipts.

October Liszt completes his *Faust* Symphony, whose opening bars introduce a theme that encompasses all 12 notes of the chromatic scale. A new ending to the work, featuring solo tenor and male chorus is added three years later, shortly before its première.

18 October Gounod's second opera, the five-act *La nonne sanglante* (The Bleeding Nun), opens at the Paris Opéra. With libretto by **Scribe**, the Gothic tale struggles and folds after 11 performances.

6 November American composer and bandmaster **John Philip Sousa** is born in Washington, DC.

10 December Berlioz premières his magnificent oratorio *L'Enfance du Christ* (The Childhood of Christ) with great success at the Salle Herz in Paris. The concert is repeated on Christmas Eve.

1854 The Crimean War begins: Britain and France join Turkey against Russia • USA makes a commercial treaty with Japan • The US Republican Party is formed • The USA proposes taking Cuba by force if Spain refuses to sell the island • In South Africa, the Orange Free State declares its independence • The Immaculate Conception of the Virgin Mary is proclaimed as dogma by Pope Pius IX • Florence Nightingale (Eng) pioneers modern nursing in the Crimea • Holman Hunt (Eng) paints *The Light of the World* • Charles Dickens (Eng): *Hard Times* • Alfred Tennyson (Eng): poem *The Charge of the Light Brigade*

Bizet, aged 17, composes his Symphony in C major, and then more or less discards it. 80 years later the derivative but engaging work will receive its première in Basel, having been discovered in the archives of the Paris Conservatoire.

20 January Composer **Ernest Chausson** is born in Paris.

4 February Gounod's First Symphony is premièred in Paris. This year also sees the composition of the Second Symphony and the first performance of the *Messe solennelle de Sainte Cécile*.

17 February Liszt gives the first performance his Piano Concerto No. 1 in E flat under the baton of **Berlioz**, during a 'Berlioz Week' in Weimar. Combining virtuoso and symphonic approaches in the concerto, Liszt asserts unity by way of recurring themes and interlinked movements. Unfortunately the prominent triangle part in the *Allegretto vivace* receives much criticism; Liszt's arch-critic Eduard Hanslick dubs the work the 'Triangle Concerto'.

Spring Rossini, physically ailing and depressed in mind, decides to leave Italy (his home for the last 19 years) and return to Paris with his wife, Olympe. They rent lodgings in the rue de la Chaussée d'Antin and life suddenly becomes exciting again. Rossini's physical and mental health is restored and he even returns to composition.

March–June Wagner has a miserable time in England at the hands of the press while conducting concerts for the Philharmonic Society. To make matters worse, the weather is appalling, he is unable to speak English, and he finds the musical tastes of Londoners insuperably unrefined.

For our part, we should prefer a state of perpetual coma to a lively apprehension of Herr Wagner, his doctrines and his music.

Extract from *The Musical World*.

30 April Berlioz conducts the first performance of his dramatic Te Deum (composed 1849, uncommissioned) at the church of Saint Eustache (below) during the celebrations surrounding the Paris Exhibition. A children's choir of several hundred orphans joins a 150-strong orchestra and a similar-sized double choir for the one complete performance in Berlioz's lifetime.

13 June Verdi's grand opera *Les Vêpres siciliennes* (The Sicilian Vespers), on a French libretto by **Scribe**, is introduced at the Paris Opéra. Initially well appreciated, the opera achieves only short-lived success.

5 July Offenbach opens his modest Bouffes Parisiens theatre in the Champs Elysées. His company enjoys instant popularity, presenting operetta and *opéra bouffe*.

18 October Liszt directs the first performance of his symphonic poem *Prometheus* (a revision of his overture of 1850), in Brunswick.

1855 Tsar Nikolai I of Russia dies: is succeeded by his son Aleksandr II • In Britain the ministry of Lord Aberdeen fails: Lord Palmerston becomes Prime Minister • Sweden enters an anti-Russian alliance with Britain, France and Turkey • Uprisings in Yunnan and Kweichow, China • The Taiping rebellion virtually ends • Austria threatens war against Russia • Alexander Parkes (Eng) invents celluloid • Chemist Robert Bunsen (Ger) invents his burner • Gustave Courbet (Fr) paints *The Artist's Studio* • Alfred Tennyson (Eng): *Maud and Other Poems* • Anthony Trollope (Eng): *The Warden* • Charles Kingsley (Eng): *Westward Ho!* • Walt Whitman (US): *Leaves of Grass* • John L. Motley (US): *The Rise of the Dutch Republic*

23 January Adam's ballet *Le Corsaire* is first danced at the Paris Opéra.

25 January Bruckner beats off opposition to secure the post of organist of Linz Cathedral.

5 March Fire destroys London's Covent Garden Theatre. The building of a new, larger opera house begins the following year and is completed within six months.

23 March Wagner completes the score of his opera *Die Walküre*, soon afterwards declaring it 'more beautiful than anything I have ever written'. The second instalment of the *Ring* cycle will have to wait 14 years to make the stage.

April Borodin is posted to the Second Military Land Forces Hospital in St Petersburg as a junior medic. There he meets **Mussorgsky**, a recently commissioned army officer.

April Berlioz begins writing his most ambitious work, the opera *Les Troyens* (The Trojans), based on Virgil's *Aeneid*.

3 May French stage composer **Adolphe Adam** dies in his sleep in Paris, aged 52.

16 May The opera *Rusalka*, with music and libretto by **Alexander Dargomïzhsky** (right), encounters a lukewarm reception at the Circus Theatre in St Petersburg. A revival nine years later launches it into the Russian repertory.

July Liszt completes his *Dante* Symphony.

27 July Clara Schumann is allowed to visit her husband at the private asylum in Endenich. Although he is unable to speak, severely delusional, barely conscious and suffering from pneumonia, **Schumann** manages to recognise his wife.

'I saw him yesterday … I did receive a few tender looks and I shall carry them with me to the end of my life!'

28 July Clara Schumann writing to **Joachim** about her first meeting with her husband in over two years.

29 July Robert Schumann dies outside Bonn, aged 46. All his symptoms point to syphilis, possibly contracted some 25 years previously.

31 August Liszt conducts the first performance of his *Missa solemnis* in Esztergom, Hungary. He premières his symphonic poem *Hungaria* in Pest, nine days later.

September Wagner begins to compose *Siegfried*. By the end of the year he will have also begun sketching *Tristan and Isolde*.

16 October Smetana, aged 32, arrives in Sweden to take up a teaching post in Göteborg. In a letter written to his parents at the end of the year he states, 'Prague did not want to acknowledge me, so I left it'.

December Mussorgsky begins taking composition lessons from **Balakirev**.

1856 Abolitionists led by John Brown murder five pro-slavers at Pottawatomie Creek, Kansas, in 'Bleeding Kansas' war over slavery • Treaty of Paris ends Crimean War; the Black Sea is neutralised; the Danube River is reopened to international shipping • Britain declares war on China after Chinese sailors board a British ship; the city of Canton is shelled • Natal in South Africa becomes a separate British Crown colony • Skull of early man (Neanderthal) is discovered in Neander Gorge, Germany • 'Big Ben' largest bell of London's Houses of Parliament clock, is cast • William Holman Hunt (Eng) paints *The Scapegoat* • Gustave Flaubert (Fr): *Madame Bovary*

1857

Alkan completes his monumental *12 études* in all the minor keys for solo piano, Op. 39. The format of the etudes includes a 'symphony' in four movements and an hour-long 'concerto' in three movements. The complete set is published in two books but is rarely performed due to its length and fiendish difficulty.

Charles Hallé founds the Hallé Orchestra in Manchester.

7 January Liszt conducts the first performance of his Second Piano Concerto in Weimar, with his pupil **Hans von Bronsart** as soloist. **Hans von Bülow** premières Liszt's Piano Sonata in B minor (see also 1853) in Berlin, later this month.

15 February Mikhail Glinka, the father of Russian classical music, dies in Berlin aged 52.

12 March Verdi's *Simon Boccanegra* opens with modest success at the Teatro La Fenice, Venice.

April Wagner and his wife Minna move to a lodge outside Zürich, owned by the Wesendoncks. Wagner names the retreat *Asyl* (Refuge). While there his friendship with Otto Wesendonck's wife, Mathilde, intensifies. She provides inspiration for *Tristan and Isolde* as well as the *Wesendonck Lieder*. (See also 23 December and 1858).

9 April Bizet's *Le Docteur Miracle* opens in Paris, having won joint first prize (shared with **Charles Lecocq**) in a one-act operetta competition organised by **Offenbach**'s Bouffes-Parisiens company.

2 June British composer **Edward William Elgar** is born in Broadheath, near Worcester.

4 July At the Paris conservatoire the 19-year-old **Bizet** wins joint first prize with Charles Colin in the Prix de Rome. At the end of the year he leaves for his residency at the Villa Medici in Rome.

15 July Austrian composer, pianist and teacher **Carl Czerny**, remembered chiefly for his extensive piano studies, dies in Vienna aged 66.

18 August Hans von Bülow (left) marries **Liszt**'s daughter Cosima. During their honeymoon they visit their future marriage-breaker, **Wagner**, in Zurich.

5 September Liszt marks the unveiling of the Goethe-Schiller monument in Weimar with the first performances of his *Faust* Symphony and the symphonic poem *Die Ideale*.

7 November Liszt introduces his *Dante* Symphony in Dresden. The performance is a failure due to (self-acknowledged) sloppy conducting and inaccurately copied orchestral parts. A performance in Prague the following year meets with success.

December Saint-Saëns becomes organist at the Madeleine Church in Paris.

23 December Wagner presents *Träume*, the fifth song of the *Wesendonck Lieder*, to Mathilde Wesendonck on her birthday. He conducts an arrangement of the piece, for violin and chamber orchestra, in front of her house in Zurich.

1857 James Buchanan becomes 15th President of the USA • Financial panic in USA follows over-expansion and speculation • The US Supreme Court rules that the Missouri Compromise of 1820 was unconstitutional • The India Mutiny (Sepoy Rebellion) breaks out • British destroy Chinese fleet and take Canton • Giuseppe Garibaldi (It) forms the Italian National Association • Transvaal state is formally proclaimed as the South African Republic • Divorce courts are set up in Britain • Jean-François Millet (Fr) paints *The Gleaners* • Charles Dickens (Eng): *Little Dorrit* • Thomas Hughes (Eng): *Tom Brown's School Days* • Charles Baudelaire (Fr): *Les Fleurs du mal*

Berlioz, as composer and librettist, completes his vast grand opera *Les Troyens*. He will never witness the work in its entirety (see 1863).

Brahms, aged 25, completes his first orchestral composition, the Serenade No. 1, and his first two accompanied choral pieces: *Ave Maria* and *Begräbnisgesang*. He more or less finishes his symphonic Piano Concerto No. 1 (begun 1854), whose second movement represents a 'gentle portrait' of the recently bereaved **Clara Schumann**. The concerto is introduced with appalling results the following year (see January 1859).

The famous Norwegian violinist **Ole Bull** persuades **Edvard Grieg**'s parents to send their musically gifted 15-year-old son to study at the Leipzig Conservatory.

César Franck, aged 35, is appointed organist at Ste-Clotilde in Paris. He becomes renowned for his after-service improvisations.

Wagner completes his *Wesendonck Lieder*, five song-settings of poetry by Mathilde Wesendonck scored for voice and piano.

1 January The final version of **Stanisław Moniuszko**'s opera *Halka* is given its first fully staged outing in Warsaw. Instantly popular, it will become the most enduring of all Polish operas.

April Minna Wagner intercepts a letter from her husband to Mathilde Wesendonck, which suggests they are in an intimate relationship. **Wagner** pleads innocence. Minna retreats to Brestenberg for three months on account of a weak heart, while Wagner heads off to Venice.

7 April Publisher and composer **Anton Diabelli** dies in Vienna, aged 76.

22 April Composer **Ethel Smyth** is born in London.

15 May Borodin gains a doctorate in chemistry with his dissertation *On the Analogy of Arsenic with Phosphoric Acid in Chemical and Toxicological Behaviour*.

17 June Mussorgsky resigns from his post in the Russian Imperial Guard to commit himself full time to music.

21 October Offenbach (left) stages his Greek myth satire *Orphée aux enfers* (Orpheus in the Underworld) at his Bouffes-Parisiens theatre. The two-act opera, particularly famous for its *Galop infernal* (better known as the 'Can-can'), gets off to a slow start but picks up to enjoy an opening run of 228 performances. The cast is then given a few weeks' rest to prepare for a second run.

15 December Peter Cornelius's opera *The Barber of Baghdad* opens under the direction of **Liszt** in Weimar. The première is marred by angry protests against Liszt, whose musical progressiveness has landed him out of favour with the royal court, press and theatre staff. He subsequently resigns from his post as *Kapellmeister*.

18 December Rossini and his wife host the first of their *Samedi Soirs* at their home in Paris. The Saturday evening musical gatherings become renowned within the musical world.

22 December Italian opera composer **Giacomo Antonio Domenico Michele Secondo Maria Puccini** is born in Lucca. Representing the fifth generation of musical Puccinis, he loses his father, the composer and teacher **Michele Puccini**, shortly after his fifth birthday.

1858 British Columbia is made a colony • Ottawa is named as the capital city of Canada • The Indian Mutiny is suppressed: the East India Company's powers are removed and the British Crown rules India • Britain's war with China ends with the Treaty of Tientsin: the opium trade is legalised and Chinese ports are opened to British and French trade •

Under the Compact of Plombières, Emperor Napoleon III of France and Italian statesman Camillo Cavour plan the unification of Italy • The Suez Canal Company is formed • William P. Frith (Eng) paints *Derby Day* • Oliver Wendell Holmes (US): *The Autocrat of the Breakfast Table*

1859

2 January **Balakirev**, on his 22nd birthday, introduces his *Overture on Three Russian Themes* at St Petersburg University.

22-27 January **Brahms** performs his Piano Concerto No. 1 for the first time, in Hanover and then Leipzig. The première, conducted by **Joachim**, receives a luke-warm reception. The Leipzig performance fares far worse, as recounted by Brahms: 'At the end, three pairs of hands attempted to fall slowly one upon the other, at which point a clear hissing from all sides forbade it.'

17 February **Verdi**'s opera *Un ballo in maschera* (A Masked Ball) triumphs at the Teatro Apollo in Rome. While in the city, Verdi notices graffiti reading VIVA VERDI (below). Italian nationalists have latched onto his name partly as he himself is a famous sympathiser, but also because it serves

as an acronym for 'Vittorio Emanuele, Re D'Italia' (Victor Emmanuel, King of Italy). It is under Vittorio Emanuele's rule that nationalists envisage a united Italy.

March **Wagner** leaves Venice ahead of imminent conflict between the Austrian army and Italian nationalists. He travels to Lucerne, via Milan.

19 March **Gounod**'s *Faust* opens as an *opera-comique* at the Théâtre-Lyrique, Paris, managing an initial run of 57 performances. Gounod revises his opera the following year, replacing the spoken dialogue with recitative. The opera proves especially popular in Germany.

June Tens of thousands flock to a series of three concerts at the Crystal Palace in commemoration of the centenary of Handel's death. **Michael Costa** conducts a choir and orchestra of over 3,000 performers, with renditions of *Messiah*, a so-called 'Grand Selection', and *Israel in Egypt*.

15 June **Tchaikovsky**, aged 19, takes a clerical job with the Ministry of Justice.

26 July **Jules Massenet**, aged 17, wins the *premier prix* for piano at the Paris Conservatoire.

6 August **Wagner** completes the composition of *Tristan and Isolde* in Lucerne. A story of lovers united only in death, the opera has been inspired in part by the composer's recent relationship with Mathilde Wesendonck. Wagner's abstruse chromatic harmonies pave the way towards the breakdown of 'functional tonality'. (See also 1860, 1865.)

29 August **Verdi** marries his second wife, the retired singer **Giuseppina Strepponi**—his partner for the past 12 years.

22 October German composer, violinist and conductor **Louis Spohr** dies in Kassel, aged 75.

November **Wagner** is joined by his wife, Minna, in Paris, where they attempt reconciliation following the Mathilde Wesendonck revelations of the previous year.

1859 Anti-slaver John Brown leads an abortive attack on a US arsenal at Harper's Ferry, now in West Virginia; Brown is executed • Piedmont-Sardinia and France at war with Austria over the move towards the unification of Italy; ends with Treaty of Zurich • Queensland becomes a separate Australian colony • The Steamroller is invented in France •

Jean-Augustine Ingres (Fr) paints *The Turkish Bath* • Jean François Millet (Fr) paints *The Angelus* • Edouard Manet (Fr) paints *The Absinthe Drinker* • Karl Marx (Ger): *Criticism of Political Economy* • Charles Dickens (Eng): *A Tale of Two Cities* • British naturalist Charles Darwin: *The Origin of the Species by Natural Selection*

Brahms publishes his 'Manifesto' against the aesthetic principles of Liszt and the New German School. **Joachim** is among the co-signatories.

Liszt composes his *Two Episodes from Lenau's 'Faust'* for solo piano, which includes the popular *Mephisto Waltz No. 1*. He orchestrates the work the following year.

Henryk Wieniawski (right) composes *Légende* for violin and orchestra, dedicating it to his English fiancée, Isabella Hampton, whom he marries this year. Encouraged by **Anton Rubinstein**, the itinerant Polish violinist-composer settles with his wife in St Petersburg where he becomes an influential figure in Russian musical life.

25 January Wagner conducts the first of three concerts programmed with extracts of his operas at the Théâtre Italien, Paris. The event is financial failure, but the music is well received by the public—all except the Prelude from *Tristan*, which confounds many with its nebulous chromatic harmony. Even the progressively-minded **Berlioz** is hostile: 'I found it a painful experience … the diminished sevenths, dissonances and violent modulations threw me into a fever; I hate that style of music.'

10 February Offenbach pokes fun at **Wagner** in his satire *Le carnaval des revues*, staged at the Bouffes-Parisiens.

18 February Gounod's opera *Philémon et Baucis* opens at the Théâtre Lyrique, Paris.

13 March Austrian composer **Hugo Wolf** is born in Windischgraz, Styria (now in Slovenia).

25 March Saint-Saëns, aged 24, hears his Symphony No. 2 in A minor introduced at the Salle Pleyel in Paris. The audience encores the second movement.

6 May Brahms and **Joachim** lead an attack on the aesthetics of **Wagner** and the New German School, published in the *Berliner Musikzeitung Echo*.

29 May Composer and pianist **Isaac Albéniz** is born in Camprodón, northern Spain.

25 June French composer **Gustave Charpentier** is born in Dieuze, Moselle.

7 July Austrian composer and conductor **Gustav Mahler** is born in Kalischt, Bohemia. His family soon relocates to a German-speaking Jewish community in Iglau, Moravia.

12 August Wagner, former revolutionary agitator (see 1849), sets foot on German soil for the first time in 11 years.

20 October Brahms's String Sextet No. 1 in B flat major is first heard in Hanover.

18 November Composer **Ignacy Jan Paderewski** is born in Kursk, Poland

24 November Viennese operetta is established by **Franz Suppé**'s *Das Pensionat* at the Theater an der Wien.

November–December Offenbach achieves success beyond his Bouffes-Parisiens theatre, with the ballet *Le papillon* at the Paris Opéra, and the three-act *Barkouf* at the Opéra-Comique.

1860 Sardinian king Vittorio Emmanuele (It) invades the Papal States; Giuseppe Garibaldi leads attack on Naples and Sicily • The Russian port of Vladivostok is founded • Britain and France are at war with China which ends with the Treaty of Peking • Republican Abraham Lincoln is elected President of the USA; South Carolina secedes from the Union in protest

• The first international conference of chemistry is held at Karlsruhe • Edgar Degas (Fr) paints *Spartan Boys and Girls Exercising* • Edouard Manet (Fr) paints *The Guitarist* (sometimes known as *The Spanish Singer*) • Charles Dickens (Eng): *Great Expectations* • George Eliot (Eng): *The Mill on the Floss* • Ivan Turgenev (Russ): *On the Eve*

The first publication of *Hymns Ancient and Modern* appears in London.

Brahms composes his *Variations and Fugue on a Theme by Handel* for piano solo, and his first two Piano Quartets (in G minor and A major) Opp. 25 and 26.

German composer **Joachim Raff**, former orchestration consultant to **Liszt**, composes the first of his 11 numbered symphonies, entitled *To the Fatherland*.

18 February Having been elected as the representative for Busseto, **Verdi** attends the opening of Italy's first parliament, in Turin.

9 March **Ferenc Erkel** taps into his country's rich heritage of folk music in the opera *Bánk bán*, premièred with great success at the Pest National Theatre, Hungary.

13 March Rowdy aristocratic members of the Jockey Club de Paris wreck **Wagner**'s revised *Tannhäuser* (1845) at the Paris Opéra. Outraged at Wagner's rebuff of French operatic convention (omitting a ballet entrée to the second act), they also harbour political enmity towards Princess Pauline Metternich, who has aided the production. Having underwritten over 160 rehearsals, the management are keen to persist with the opera. Two more performances follow, both equally blighted by the same cabal. *Tannhäuser* is withdrawn and Wagner leaves Paris.

24 May **Halévy** hosts a dinner in Paris with **Liszt** and the 22-year-old **Bizet** (top right) among the guests. Afterwards, Liszt performs one of his new, fiendishly difficult piano pieces, declaring that just two pianists in Europe can play it accurately at his desired tempo: himself and **Hans von Bülow**. With encouragement from Halévy, Bizet takes his place at the piano and blazes through one of the most difficult passages of the work by memory. He then plays the whole piece by sight, flawlessly. Liszt

promptly admits Bizet as a third member of his select group, adding that 'the youngest of the three is perhaps the boldest and most brilliant'.

August Visiting London **Tchaikovsky** reports that the city 'makes a bleak impression on the soul. You never see the sun and it rains at every step.'

21 October On the eve of their wedding night in Rome, the marriage between **Liszt** and Princess Carolyne zu Sayne-Wittgenstein is suddenly called off. The Princess's expected annulment from her existing marriage has failed to materialise. The composer and princess apparently continue a platonic relationship.

14 December **Heinrich Marschner**, one of Germany's leading opera composers, dies in Hanover, aged 66.

18 December Composer **Edward MacDowell** is born in New York.

- -

1861 Abraham Lincoln becomes 16th President of the USA • Ten Southern States join South Carolina in seceding from the Union, and form the Confederate States of America; Jefferson Davis becomes Confederate President • Confederate capture of Fort Sumter, SC, starts American Civil War • Gold is discovered in New Zealand • Russian troops occupy Tsushima in Japan • Vittorio Emmanuele II proclaimed King of Italy by the country's new Parliament • Moldavia and Wallachia unite as Romania • Wilhelm I becomes King of Prussia (until 1888) • Tsar Aleksandr II abolishes serfdom in Russia • George Elliot (Eng): *Silas Marner* • Fyodor Dostoyevsky (Russ): *House of the Dead*

1862

Eminent composers from four leading European nations are commissioned to write a piece for the Great London Exhibition (below). **Sterndale Bennett** is chosen for England, **Auber** for France, **Meyerbeer** for Prussia and **Rossini** for Italy. Rossini declines on account of age and the commission passes to **Verdi**, who composes a cantata in collaboration with the 20-year-old poet **Arrigo Boito**. Verdi's piece is rejected by the disobliging Italian-born musical director, **Michael Costa**, who was expecting a rousing march.

Ludwig von Köchel publishes his catalogue of Mozart's works.

Anton Rubinstein and the Grand Duchess Yelena Pavlovna establish the St Petersburg Conservatory. **Wieniawski** joins the staff and **Tchaikovsky**, aged 22, becomes one of the first students, although he continues in his job at the Ministry of Justice.

29 January Composer **Frederick Theodore Albert Delius** is born of German parentage in Bradford, Yorkshire.

30 March St Petersburg's Free School of Music, the brainchild of **Balakirev**, opens its doors. The aim of the institution is to provide free tuition for poor students, prepare singers for the Orthodox Church and promote the music of both Russian and pioneering Western composers, such as Liszt and Berlioz.

May Having completed his studies at the Leipzig Conservatory, **Grieg** gives his first public concert in Bergen, performing his Four Piano Pieces, Op. 1.

12 May David's exotic opera *Lalla-Roukh*, based on Thomas Moore's oriental romance, opens at the Opéra-Comique, Paris. It becomes his most celebrated work.

9 August Berlioz conducts the first performance of *Beatrice et Bénédict* in Baden-Baden. The cheery two-act opera, based on his own libretto after Shakespeare's *Much Ado*, is well received but will never become regular repertory.

22 August French composer **Achille-Claude Debussy** is born to china-shop owners in Saint Germain-en-Laye.

10 November Verdi attends the première of his opera *La forza del destino* at the Imperial Theatre in St Petersburg. Commissioned by the theatre, the opera is a success but does not please unanimously due to the growing nationalistic preference for Russian music.

23 November Wagner organises a reading of his poem *Die Meistersinger von Nuremberg* (The Mastersingers of Nuremberg), completed early this year. The critic Eduard Hanslick, perceiving himself caricatured in the narrow-minded character of Beckmesser, storms out in anger.

27 November Wieniawski introduces his Violin Concerto No. 2 in D minor under the baton of **Nikolay Rubinstein** in St Petersburg.

29 November Brahms charms both the public and critics with his Piano Quartet No. 2 in A major, first performed in Vienna. This year marks the compositional beginnings of his Symphony No. 1 in C minor, completed 14 years later.

1862 American Civil War continues • France annexes Cochin China • In Italy the patriot Giuseppe Garibaldi is captured at Aspromonte by Italian government troops • Otto von Bismarck becomes prime minister of Prussia • Richard Gattling (US) patents his machine-gun • Chemist Friedrich Wöhler (Ger) discovers the gas acetylene • Édouard Manet (Fr) paints *Music in the Tuileries* • John Ruskin (Eng) attacks capitalism in *Unto This Last* • Victor Hugo (Fr): *Les Misérables* • Ivan Turgenev (Russ): *Fathers and Sons* • Henrik Ibsen (Nor): *Love's Comedy* • Elizabeth Barrett Browning (Eng): *Last Poems*, published posthumously • Christina Rossetti (Eng): poem *Goblin Market*

Brahms is appointed conductor of the Vienna Singakademie. This year he completes his *28 Paganini Variations*, Op. 35.

Gottschalk, around this time, composes his playful *Pasquinade* for piano. This year the touring virtuoso struggles with concert fixtures due to ill-health, but continues to provide happy diversions to audiences amid the ongoing American Civil War.

Saint-Saëns composes his Piano Trio No. 1 and the programmatic overture *Spartacus*.

Smetana composes *The Brandenburgers in Bohemia*, his first opera. He enters it anonymously into a competition devised by Count Jan Harrach to promote original Czech opera. Three years later he is declared the winner.

May Tchaikovsky resigns from the civil service. He continues to study under **Anton Rubinstein** at the St Petersburg Conservatory.

20 June Liszt begins a two-year monastic existence at the Madonna del Rosario, a monastery at Monte Mario, outside Rome. He occupies a spartan cell with a small upright piano and minimal furniture.

22 June In Strasbourg **Berlioz** (right) conducts a 500-strong orchestra and choir in a performance of his oratorio *L'Enfance du Christ* (premièred 1854). Mounted during the Lower Rhine Festival, the concert draws an audience of 6,000.

Summer Rossini, in Paris, begins composing his last significant work, the *Petite Messe solennelle*.

11 July Offenbach enjoys a successful summer in operetta, beginning with *Il signor Fagotto*, followed ten days later by *Lischen et Fritzchen*. Both works are introduced at Bad Ems (Germany) before receiving Paris premières at the Théâtre des Bouffes Parisiens.

11 July Pope Pius IX calls in on **Liszt** at the Madonna del Rosario monastery outside Rome (see 20 June). Liszt performs at the piano and the Pope sings a Bellini aria.

3 August Jules Massenet, aged 21, wins the Prix de Rome with his cantata *David Rizzio*.

30 September Bizet, aged 24, presents his opera *The Pearl Fishers* at the Théâtre-Lyrique in Paris. The ancient Ceylonese tale is well appreciated by the public, but critics (all except **Berlioz**) condemn the opera. 'There were neither fishermen in the libretto nor pearls in the music,' grumbles *Le Figaro*. The opera manages an initial run of 18 performances but is not staged again during Bizet's lifetime.

4 November Unable to mount a complete performance of *Les Troyens* on account of its length, **Berlioz** premières the second part of the opera, *Les Troyens à Carthage*, at the Théâtre-Lyrique, Paris. The production is repeated 20 times, but with various cuts made at the insistence of the theatre directors. Artistic frustrations aside, Berlioz reaps substantial royalties, enabling him to retire from his now tedious sideline job as music critic for the *Journal des débats*.

7 December Italian composer **Pietro Mascagni** is born in Livorno.

1863 In American Civil War, Union army gains victory over Confederacy at Battle of Gettysburg; Lincoln delivers his famous Address • Denmark annexes the Duchy of Schleswig, German forces enter neighbouring Holstein • French troops occupy New Mexico • Japan attempts to expel foreigners; British ships bombard the Japanese port of Kagoshima •

Edouard Manet (Fr) paints *Luncheon on the Grass* • James Whistler (US), paints *Symphony in White* • Eugène Boudin (Fr) paints *The Beach at Trouville* • Charles Kingsley (Eng): *The Water Babies* • Edward Everett Hale (US): *The Man Without a Country* • Henry Wadsworth Longfellow (US): *Tales of a Wayside Inn*

456

Borodin is promoted to professor of chemistry at the Medical-Surgical Academy in St Petersburg.

Wagner and Cosima von Bülow (née Liszt) begin an affair.

10 January Collapsing from a fever, American songwriter **Stephen Foster** hits his head on a stone wash-basin, resulting in concussion and cuts to his neck and face. Admitted to hospital, he is found to be also suffering from an untreated burn. He dies three days later, aged 37.

March Wagner flees Vienna to escape debt collectors and jail. The 18-year-old King Ludwig II of Bavaria (below) comes to his aid, settling 4,000 gulden worth of debts, providing him with housing and granting him a yearly stipend of 4,000 gulden.

The king also pays Wagner 30,000 gulden to gain a copyright stake in the *Ring* cycle.

14 March Rossini's *Petite Messe solennelle*, for 12 voices, two pianos and harmonium, inaugurates the private chapel of Countess Pillet-Will, in Paris. On the final page of the score the 72-year-old composer has written: 'Dear God. Here it is finished, this poor little Mass. Have I composed sacred music [*musique sacrée*] or damned music [*sacrée musique*]? I was born for *opera buffa*, as you well know! … Glory be to God, and grant me a place in Paradise.'

19 March Gounod presents his five-act opera *Mireille* at the Théâtre-Lyrique in Paris. Poorly received in both Paris and London this year, the opera will struggle for some time. An edited three-act version will finally succeed some 25 years later at the Opéra-Comique.

17 April Brahms's Sonata for Two Pianos in F minor is first performed in Vienna. This year the composer writes his String Sextet No. 2.

2 May German composer **Giacomo Meyerbeer** dies in Paris aged 72, having just completed his grand opera *L'Africaine* (The African Maid). He was the most famous and often performed opera composer of his generation.

11 June German composer and conductor **Richard Strauss** is born in Munich.

20 November Bruckner's Mass No. 1 in D minor is first sung in Linz Cathedral.

17 December Following on from the success of *Orphée aux enfers* (1858) **Offenbach** stages another Greek myth *opéra bouffe* with *La Belle Hélène* (The Fair Helen) at the Théâtre des Variétés, Paris. Initially meeting with indifference, the classical satire wins over the public with its catchy tunes and provocative spirit, becoming one of the composer's most popular works.

1864 Prussia and Austria seize duchies of Schleswig-Holstein from Denmark • Archduke Maximilian of Austria, backed by France, becomes Emperor of Mexico • American Civil War continues; Abraham Lincoln is re-elected President of the USA • Louis Pasteur (Fr) invents pasteurisation and saves France's wine industry • The International Red Cross is founded in Geneva, Switzerland • Philosopher Herbert Spencer (Eng) coins phrase 'survival of the fittest' in *Principles of Biology* • Arnold Böcklin (Switz) paints *Villa at the Sea* • Charles Dickens (Eng): *Our Mutual Friend* • Alfred Tennyson (Eng): poem *Enoch Arden* • Henrik Ibsen (Nor): play *The Pretenders* • Leo Tolstoy (Russ): *War and Peace*

Brahms (below) completes his Piano Quintet in F minor, Op. 34. The masterpiece contains some of his most arresting melodies, above all the richly expressive subjects of the opening movement and the feisty theme of its Scherzo. Echoes of Schubert and Schumann are heard throughout.

Grieg publishes his *Humoresker* for piano Op. 6, dedicating it to **Rikard Nordraak** who has done much to inspire his new direction of nationalism.

1 January 'I can die now without anger or bitterness.' **Berlioz**, aged 61, ends his memoirs. 1,200 copies are printed, most of which Berlioz stores for release after his death.

24 March Dvořák, aged 23, completes his Symphony No. 1 in C minor (*The Bells of Zlonice*), although it will not be performed during his lifetime. At the end of the year he completes his Symphony No. 2 in B flat major.

10 April The affair between **Wagner** and Cosima von Bülow produces a first child, Isolde.

15 April Liszt's *Totentanz* (Dance of Death) for piano and orchestra is premièred in The Hague, with the composer's son-in-law, **Bülow**, as soloist.

25 April Liszt receives the tonsure, taking minor orders in the Catholic Church. For just over one year Abbé Liszt resides in the Vatican.

9 June Composer **Carl Nielsen** is born of musical peasant stock on the Island of Funen, Denmark.

10 June Wagner's momentous *Tristan and Isolde* (1859) is premièred under **Bülow**'s direction at Munich. Initially conceived as an accessible work suitable for provincial theatres, the four-and-a-half-hour opera represents a landmark in music. Each act is restricted to one major dramatic event, with otherwise minimum action on stage. Wagner pushes the boundaries of chromatic melody and harmony to convey the heightened passion, yearning and neurosis of the two lovers. Reaction to the opera is mixed, ranging from loathing to adoration.

10 August Composer **Alexander Glazunov** is born in St Petersburg.

6 December King Ludwig II succumbs to pressure from his court and family to banish **Wagner** from Bavaria. The composer's affair with Cosima von Bülow, together with his political meddling and excessive exploitation of Ludwig's resources, has resulted in the loss of both official and public support.

8 December Composer **Johan** (later **Jean**) **Christian Julius Sibelius** is born into a middle-class family in Hämeenlinna, Finland.

17 December Johann von Herbeck conducts the first performance of Schubert's Symphony No. 8 in B minor, 'Unfinished' (1822), in Vienna.

31 December Balakirev conducts the première of **Rimsky-Korsakov**'s First Symphony (in its original key of E flat minor) in St Petersburg. The composer and his close circle regard it as the first true Russian symphony.

1865 General Robert E. Lee surrenders the Confederate armies to the Union General: the American Civil War ends • President Abraham Lincoln is assassinated: is succeeded by Vice President Andrew Johnson • Slavery is ended in the USA • The Convention of Gastein gives Holstein to Austria and Schleswig to Prussia • Louis Pasteur (Fr) discovers a cure for silkworm disease • A transatlantic telegraph cable is successfully laid • Evangelist William Booth starts the Christian Mission (Salvation Army) in London • Edouard Manet (Fr) paints *Olympia* • James Whistler (US) paints *Old Battersea Bridge* • Charles Dodgson (Lewis Carroll; Eng): *Alice's Adventures in Wonderland*

William Sterndale Bennett becomes Principal of the Royal Academy of Music.

Bruckner, 42 this year, completes his Symphony No. 1 in C minor and composes his Mass No. 2 in E minor.

Niels Gade becomes one of the directors of the newly-established Copenhagen Conservatory. He has recently completed his Seventh Symphony.

25 January Wagner's estranged wife, Minna, dies in Dresden.

27 January Mozart's two-act singspiel *Zaide* (completed 1780) is premièred in Frankfurt on the 110th anniversary of the composer's birth.

20 March Rikard Nordraak, close friend of **Grieg** and composer of the Norwegian national anthem—*Ja, vi elsker dette landet* (Yes, we Love this Land)—dies of tuberculosis in Berlin, aged 23.

1 April Ferruccio Dante Michelangelo Benvenuto Busoni is born in Empoli, Tuscany. With middle names corresponding to three Tuscan greats, his parents seem to harbour high hopes, albeit outside of musical spheres.

17 May Composer **Erik Satie** is born in Honfleur to a French father and Scottish mother.

30 May Smetana turns to a provincial love story for his second opera, *The Bartered Bride*, premièred without much success at Prague's Provisional Theatre. He will revise the comic opera several times, replacing the spoken dialogue with recitative in 1870. By the 1890s this new definitive version will be a regular fixture in the repertory and lauded by nationals as the archetypal Czech opera.

1 September Tchaikovsky, aged 26, begins teaching at the Moscow Conservatory, recently founded by **Nikolay Rubinstein**. Later this year he completes the first version of his Symphony No.1 in G minor, subtitled *Winter Daydreams*.

15 September Smetana (left, with his second wife, Bettina) is appointed conductor of the Provisional Theatre in Prague.

15 October Grieg organises a concert in the Norwegian capital, Christiania (now Oslo), where he has recently set up home. Consisting primarily of songs and piano works by himself and the late Rikard Nordraak, the event promotes Grieg as a young champion of Norwegian music. Over the next three months he secures the conductorship of the Philharmonic Society and co-founds the Norwegian Academy of Music with the critic Otto Winter-Hjelm.

17 November Ambroise Thomas's most successful opera, *Mignon*, is staged for the first time, at the Opéra Comique, Paris.

20 November Brahms's String Sextet No. 2 in G major is first played in Zurich. This year has also seen the first performance of the composer's Piano Quintet in F minor (see also 1865), in Leipzig.

December Borodin informs **Balakirev** of the completion of his Symphony No. 1 in E-flat, although he will tweak the work throughout the following year.

1866 The 14th Amendment to the US Constitution ensures that no person is deprived of 'life, liberty or property without due process of law' • Prussia and Austria war over Schleswig-Holstein: Germany annexes Holstein: Austria are defeated at Sadowa; many German principalities and Schleswig-Holstein are incorporated with Prussia • Robert Whitehead (US) develops the torpedo • Riots break out in London after new Reform Bill fails in parliament • Dr Thomas Barnardo (Ire) opens his first home for orphans in London's East End • Claude Monet (Fr) paints *Camille* • Fyodor Dostoyevsky (Russ): *Crime and Punishment* • Victor Hugo (Fr): *Toilers of the Sea* • Henrik Ibsen (Nor): play *Brand*

15 February **Strauss II**'s *Blue Danube* waltz is introduced at a Carnival ball hosted by the Vienna Men's Choral Association. Scored for orchestra and chorus, the work is not well received. Strauss discards the vocal parts and re-orchestrates the waltz for a successful performance at the Paris Exhibition this same year.

17 February A second daughter, Eva, is born to **Wagner** and Cosima von Bülow. Later this year Cosima's father, **Liszt**, challenges the adulterous pair in Lucerne, but to no avail. The two composers break off contact with each other for the next five years.

11 March **Verdi** premières *Don Carlos* at the Paris Opéra in the presence of Napoleon III and the Empress. In spite of an initial run of 43 performances, the five-act opera struggles to maintain a foothold in the repertory.

25 March Conductor **Arturo Toscanini** is born in Parma, Italy.

27 April **Gounod** presents his five-act *Roméo et Juliette* at the Theatre Lyrique in Paris. *Faust* librettists **Jules Barbier** and **Michel Carré** have edited Shakespeare's narrative to provide Gounod ample room for stunning love duets. The work enthrals the French public and becomes the most successful opera based on the bard's great tragedy.

May Norway's **Johan Svendsen**, aged 26, leaves the Leipzig Conservatory having completed his Symphony No. 1 in D major.

Caricature of Verdi and Napoleon III after first premiere of *Don Carlos* in Paris

8 May **Bruckner** is confined to the sanatorium at Bad Kreuzen for three months having suffered a nervous breakdown. Conspicuous among his symptoms is a number fixation, counting such trivia as windows in buildings, dots upon clothes, and leaves on trees. Against doctors orders he begins composing again in the autumn, working on his Mass in F minor.

24 May **Balakirev** conducts and premières his *Overture on Czech Themes* and **Rimsky-Korsakov**'s *Fantasia on Serbian Themes* in Moscow. Reviewing the concert, the critic Vladimir Stasov coins the term 'Mighty Handful' (*Moguchaya kuchka*) for the new nationalistic school of Russian composers. In time the *kuchka* will be recognised as Balakirev, **Borodin**, **Cui**, **Mussorgsky** and Rimsky-Korsakov.

8 June **Liszt**'s Hungarian Coronation Mass is first performed in Budapest for the coronation ceremony of King Franz Josef and Queen Elisabeth. Later the same day Liszt is spotted in the street and spontaneously applauded by a crowd of 100,000 who have gathered to witness the coronation procession.

11 June **Grieg** marries his cousin, Nina Hagerup. This year he composes his first *Lyric Pieces* for piano (Op. 12) and his Violin Sonata No. 2 in G major.

November **Berlioz** travels to Russia to mount a series of concerts in St Petersburg and Moscow. Although successful, the three-month tour severely exhausts him.

1867 USA buys Alaska from Russia for $7,200,000 • The Dominion of Canada, consisting of New Brunswick, Nova Scotia, Quebec and Ontario, is created by the British North American Act • French troops leave Mexico; Emperor Maximilian is executed • The Italian revolutionary Giuseppe Garibaldi again marches on Rome, but is captured by French and Papal troops at Mentana • The Irish Fenian Brotherhood organises terrorist activities in Britain and Australia • Second Reform Act passed in UK • Joseph Lister (Eng) introduces antiseptic surgery • Alfred Noble (Swe) invents dynamite • Henrik Ibsen (Nor): play *Peer Gynt* • Karl Marx (Ger): *Das Kapital*, first volume

Max Bruch (below) completes his Violin Concerto No. 1 in G minor. The work's phenomenal popularity overshadows everything else he composes, much to his annoyance.

Tchaikovsky comes to the defence of **Rimsky-Korsakov**, whose *Fantasia on Serbian Themes* is criticised by a reviewer. This comradeship brings him into contact with the new school of nationalistic Russian composers, most of whom he regards as gifted but conceited amateurs.

10 February Rossini's grand opera *William Tell* (1829) achieves its 500th performance at the Paris Opéra.

5 March Boito's *Mefistofele*, composed to his own libretto after Goethe's *Faust*, flops at La Scala, Milan. The vast work, comprising a prologue, five acts and an epilogue, is later cut and revised by the composer-librettist for a successful performance in Bologna seven years later.

9 March Ambroise Thomas's grand opera *Hamlet* triumphs at the Paris Opéra.

3 April Franz Berwald, the foremost Scandinavian composer of the early 19th century, dies in Stockholm aged 71.

10 April The first four movements of **Brahms**'s *German Requiem* (fully completed later this year) are introduced to great acclaim at Bremen Cathedral.

9 May Bruckner conducts the first performance of his Symphony No. 1 in C minor, in Linz. The following month he settles in Vienna where he becomes professor of harmony and organ at the Conservatory.

13 May Saint-Saëns's Piano concerto No. 2 in G minor is introduced in Paris under the baton of **Anton Rubinstein** with the composer at the piano. **Liszt** witnesses the event and is full of praise.

21 June Wagner's *Die Meistersinger von Nürnberg* (The Mastersingers of Nuremberg) is premièred under **Bülow** at the Court Theatre in Munich. The critic Eduard Hanslick (who is himself caricatured in the opera) is dismissive, although others react with great enthusiasm. Wagner commits a major faux pas by taking a bow from the royal box.

Summer Grieg composes his celebrated Piano Concerto in A minor, in Søllerød, Denmark.

6 October Mussorgsky's *Zhenit'ba* (The Marriage), after Gogol's comedy, receives a private première in St Petersburg. Scored without key signatures and entirely in recitative, his so-called *opéra dialogué* attempts to explore new boundaries of speech imitation, following natural conversational rhythms and avoiding lyrical melodic intervals. The work has to wait 40 years for a public performance.

13 November Rossini dies at his villa in Passy, near Paris, aged 76. His funeral takes place eight days later at the Eglise de la Trinité, drawing a crowd of over 4,000. His body will find its final resting place at the Church of Santa Croce, Florence, in 1887.

16 November Cosima von Bülow finally leaves her husband to live with **Wagner**. She is already pregnant with Wagner's third child and will gain custody of her two daughters by **Bülow** the following year.

1868 British troops invade Ethiopia to rescue an imprisoned consul, capture Magdala, release other prisoners and withdraw • After a Liberal revolution in Spain, Queen Isabel II is deposed • In Japan, Emperor Mutsuhito takes control of the government, replacing the Shogun (military dictator): the Meiji (Enlightened Rule) Period begins • The first Trades Union Congress meets in Manchester, England • Edgar Degas (Fr) paints *The Orchestra* • Pierre Renoir (Fr) paints *The Skaters* • Louisa M. Alcott (US): *Little Women* • Fyodor Dostoyevsky (Russ): *The Idiot* • Wilkie Collins (Eng): *The Moonstone* • William Morris (Eng): poem *The Earthly Paradise* • Robert Browning (Eng): poem *The Ring and the Book*

1869

Balakirev completes his challenging oriental fantasy *Islamey* for piano.

Grieg composes his *Norwegian Folksongs and dances* (Op. 17), comprising 25 delectable piano miniatures.

Wagner and the 24-year-old Nietzsche strike up a friendship, although they disagree about the merits of vegetarianism. The philosopher argues that it is morally wrong to eat meat. The composer maintains that life is about compromise, and in order to do good things one requires meaty sustenance. Nietzsche soon gives up vegetarianism. This year sees the reprint of Wagner's bigoted, anti-Semitic essay *Das Judenthum in der Musik* (1850).

16 January Borodin's First Symphony, introduced under the baton of **Balakirev**, wins public approval in St Petersburg. Later this year Borodin begins writing his opera *Prince Igor*, based on his own libretto after a scenario by Vladimir Stasov.

17 January Aleksandr Dargomïzhsky dies in St Petersburg, aged 55. He leaves unfinished an opera, *The Stone Guest*, which will be completed by **César Cui** and orchestrated by **Rimsky-Korsakov**.

18 February Brahms attempts to comfort the living in his vernacular *German Requiem*, first fully performed under **Carl Reinecke** in Leipzig. This year also sees the publication of Brahms's *Magelone Lieder* Nos. 7–15 (Op. 33) and the first two collections of *Hungarian Dances* for piano duet.

8 March Hector Berlioz dies in Paris, aged 65, after a year of chronic exhaustion. He is buried three days later in the Cimetière Montmartre. **Ambroise Thomas**, **Gounod** and **Auber** are among the pallbearers, while **Sax** directs the National Guard in a trumpet salute.

22 March Rimsky-Korsakov's Second Symphony (*Antar*) is introduced in St Petersburg.

3 April Grieg's Piano Concerto in A minor is premièred in Copenhagen. Unable to attend, Grieg misses the work's sensational reception.

5 April French composer **Albert Roussel** is born in Tourcoing.

Summer Strauss II composes the *Pizzicato Polka* with his brother, **Josef**.

6 June As **Wagner** continues to compose *Siegfried* (the third opera of the *Ring* cycle), Cosima gives birth to their first son, Siegfried.

22 September At King Ludwig's behest and to **Wagner**'s dismay, *Das Rheingold* (the first opera of the *Ring*) opens in Munich under the baton of a local conductor, **Franz Wüllner**. Having waited 15 years for the event, Wagner boycotts his own première.

1 November Verdi's *Rigoletto* (1851) inaugurates the Royal Cairo Opera House. Italian architects have designed the building, made mostly of wood.

18 December American pianist-composer **Louis Moreau Gottschalk** (left), on a concert tour of South America, dies from yellow fever in Rio de Janeiro, Brazil, aged 40.

1869 General Ulysses S. Grant becomes the 18th President of the USA • In Wyoming, women are given the vote • Canada purchases Northwest Territory from Hudson's Bay Company • Emperor Napoleon III introduces parliamentary system of government in France • Britain, France and Italy assume control of Tunis in North Africa • Dmitri Mendeleev (Russ) devises a periodic table classifying the chemical elements • The Suez Canal is opened to shipping • Francis Galton (Eng): *Hereditary Genius, its Laws and Consequences*, founds the science of genetics • Claude Monet (Fr) paints *The Balcony* • R. D. Blackmore (Eng): *Lorna Doone* • Jules Verne (Fr): *20,000 Leagues under the Sea*

Bruch's Symphony No. 1 in E flat major (1868) and his Symphony No. 2 in F minor are premièred this year in Bremen and Berlin respectively.

Grieg enjoys encouraging meetings with **Liszt** in Rome. The older maestro sightreads his compositions and is bowled over by the brilliance of the Piano Concerto in A minor. He urges him, 'You carry on, my friend—you're made of the real stuff. And let no one frighten you off!'

Composer **Ivan Zajc** takes charge of the Croatian Opera and the Croatian Institute of Music. He becomes the figurehead of his country's classical music tradition.

January Charles-Marie Widor, aged 25, is appointed organist at St Sulpice in Paris. He will hold the post for the next 64 years.

3 March Pauline Viardot sings the lead in the first performance of **Brahms**'s heartfelt *Alto Rhapsody* Op. 53, scored for alto, male voice choir and orchestra.

10 March Ignaz Moscheles dies in Leipzig, aged 75, having served his later years as professor of piano at the city's conservatory.

16 March Nikolai Rubinstein conducts the first performance of **Tchaikovsky**'s fantasy-overture *Romeo and Juliet*, in Moscow. Poorly received, the work is revised by the composer following advice from **Balakirev**.

2 May Delibes's music to the magical ballet *Coppélia* is heard for the first time at the Paris Opéra. With its attractive melodies, Eastern-European influences and rich orchestration, the score secures major success for Delibes. This year he resigns from his post as organist at the Opéra to devote himself exclusively to composition.

Late May Verdi begins work on *Aida*, with an ancient Egyptian scenario provided by leading Egyptologist François Auguste Mariette.

26 June Wagner's *Die Walküre* (The Valkyries) makes a powerful entrance in Munich, but fails to captivate its audience throughout. Wagner is unhappy with the production, which, like *Das Rheingold* before it (see 1869), has been ordered by his patron, King Ludwig. *Die Walküre* is the second opera of the *Ring* cycle.

25 August Wagner and Cosima are married in a Protestant church in Lucerne, following the dissolution of Cosima's marriage to **Hans von Bülow** the previous month.

13 September Gounod (left) and his family arrive in England to escape the Franco-Prussian War. With his house in Paris soon afterwards destroyed, Gounod remains in England for the next five years.

25 September The definitive version of **Smetana's** comic opera *The Bartered Bride* opens at the Provisional theater in Prague. (See also 1866.)

24 December Cosima Wagner awakens early in the morning to the première of the *Siegfried Idyll*—a birthday present from her husband, performed by a chamber orchestra positioned up the staircase of their house in Tribschen, Switzerland. At the end of the piece she cries, 'Now let me die'.

1870 Franco-Prussian War: Napoleon III defeated and Prussians besiege Paris • A new French government declares France a republic (Third French Republic) • French forces withdraw from Rome, which becomes Italy's capital • The 15th Amendment to the US Constitution ensures voting rights for slaves • Papal infallibility is proclaimed by the Vatican Council • Austria revokes its Concordat with the Papacy • The Standard Oil company is founded by John D. Rockefeller (US) • Compulsory education for all begins in Britain • Jean Corot (Fr) paints *Woman with a Pearl* • Charles Dickens (Eng) dies, leaving *The Mystery of Edwin Drood* unfinished

Grieg sets Bjørnstjerne Bjørnson's poem *Before a Southern Convent* for soprano, alto, female chorus and orchestra.

Wagner completes the composition of *Siegfried*.

February Mussorgsky begins to revise his opera *Boris Godunov* following its rejection by the Mariinsky Theatre on the grounds that it lacks an important female role. He creates the role of Maryna Mniszech and completes further (unrequested) revisions by the end of the year.

25 February Saint-Saëns and Romain Bussine establish the Société Nationale de Musique in Paris. Members of its committee include **César Franck** and **Gabriel Fauré**.

29 March Queen Victoria opens the Royal Albert Hall (below) in memory of her husband, who died ten years previously. The echoing acoustics of the huge venue inspires the witty observation that it is the one place in Britain where a composer is guaranteed a repeat performance.

12 May French opera composer **Daniel Auber** dies in Paris, aged 89.

April The **Wagners** visit Bayreuth where they hope to stage the first complete *Ring* cycle. Finding no suitable venue, they boldly decide to build a new opera house. The town council grants them a free site later in the year.

Summer Rimsky-Korsakov accepts a teaching post at the St Petersburg Conservatory to the dismay of various members of his anti-establishment circle, **Mussorgsky** in particular.

18 October Brahms considers the lot of mankind in *Schicksalslied* (Song of Destiny) for chorus and orchestra, after a poem by Friedrich Hölderlin, first performed in Karlsruhe.

1 November *Lohengrin* (premièred 1850) becomes the first **Wagner** opera to be performed in Italy. Successfully staged in Bologna, it is not initially to **Verdi**'s taste: 'The action moves slowly, as do the words; hence boredom.'

25 November Olga Janina, unhinged piano pupil and perhaps short-term lover of **Liszt**, bursts into the composer's Pest apartment and holds him at gunpoint. She gives him two options: commit himself to her, or drink a vial of poison. After several hours of madness she drinks the poison herself and collapses. In fact, the potion does little harm at all. She flees to Paris to escape legal repercussions. (See also 1873.)

24 December Verdi's opera *Aida*, originally commissioned to inaugurate the new opera house in Cairo, receives a sensational première there two years after the building's completion. Verdi, not present for the occasion (partly due to a fear of sea travel), is infuriated by reports of its extravagant presentation, which appear to have overshadowed artistic considerations.

1871 King Wilhelm I of Prussia is proclaimed Kaiser (Emperor) of a united Germany • Otto von Bismarck becomes German Chancellor • Paris capitulates to the Prussians: France cedes Alsace-Lorraine to Germany • A radical group, the Commune, is set up in Paris, but is suppressed by troops in 'Bloody week' • Louis A. Thiers becomes President of France's Third Republic • Charles Taze Russell (US) founds the Jehovah's Witnesses • The Mont Cenis Tunnel through the Swiss Alps is opened • British Trade Unions are legalised by Act of Parliament • J. Whistler (US) paints *Whistler's Mother* • Lewis Carroll (Eng): *Through the Looking Glass, and What Alice Found There*

Mussorgsky begins composing his opera *Khovanshchina* (The Khovansky Affair), which he will never finish.

Joachim Raff composes his programmatic Symphony No. 5 *Lenore*, his most popular work.

Anton Rubinstein completes the definitive version of his Piano Concerto No. 4 (originally composed 1864).

Johan Svendsen composes his *Carnival in Paris*, an 'episode for orchestra'. His friend **Wagner** hums through the score and responds, 'It looks amusing!'

6 January Composer **Alexander Scriabin** is born in Moscow.

8 February *Aida*, first performed in Cairo (1871), receives its European première at La Scala, Milan. Having rigorously supervised the preparations for the event, **Verdi** enjoys a glittering triumph.

April The **Wagners** relocate their family to Bayreuth. The following month the foundation stone of the Bayreuth opera house is laid.

June Flanked by a string of assistant conductors, **Strauss II** (right) directs his *Blue Danube* waltz (1867) with an orchestra of 1,000, and a choir of 20,000, at the Peace Jubilee concert in Boston. 'Despite rehearsals,' Strauss later recollects, 'there was no possibility of an artistic performance … and there broke out an unholy racket such as I will never forget.' Nevertheless, 14 American concerts organised by the impresario Patrick S. Gilmore

prove massively lucrative, with 'The Waltz King' bagging $100,000 in fees.

18 July **Balakirev** takes a clerical job with the Warsaw railway company, disillusioned with the struggles and financial hardships of musical life.

September **Bruckner** completes his Second Symphony. The Vienna Philharmonic Orchestra rehearses the work, but then rejects it due to length. (See also 1873.)

Autumn **Liszt** begins to reconcile himself to the union of his daughter Cosima and his new son-in-law, **Wagner** (see 1867). The couple visit him in Weimar, and Liszt visits Bayreuth.

12 October Composer **Ralph Vaughan Williams** is born in Down Ampney, Gloucestershire.

22 October **Debussy**, aged ten, begins studying at the Paris Conservatoire, having had no previous formal schooling.

November **Brahms** begins a three-year tenure as conductor of the Vienna Gesellschaft der Musikfreunde.

10 November **Bizet** presents his orchestral suite *L'Arlésienne* (The Maid of Arles) in Paris. Extracted from his incidental music to Alphonse Daudet's play—itself premièred with little success the previous month—the suite gains a tremendous reception and achieves enduring popularity.

Strauss enjoys an enormous female fan-base at this time. So many American women desire a lock of his hair that he has to resort to snippets taken from his Newfoundland dog.

1872 Carlist War in Spain: Don Carlos claims throne by succession through the female line • The Emperors of Germany, Austria and Russia form an alliance • Rebellion against Spanish rule breaks out in the Philippines • Britain introduces the secret ballot • France and Japan adopt conscription • Ulysses S. Grant is re-elected President of the USA • New York's Brooklyn Bridge is opened • Edgar Degas (Fr) paints *Dance Foyer at the Opera* • Camille Pissarro (Fr) paints *The Wash House* • Thomas Hardy (Eng): *Under the Greenwood Tree* • Alphonse Daudet (Fr): *Tartarin of Tarascon* • Jules Verne (Fr): *Around the World in Eighty Days*

Borodin completes the piano score of his Second Symphony, and publishes his final scientific research paper on aldehydes.

Adopting pseudonyms, Olga Janina (above) begins writing a series of books sensationalising her relationship with **Liszt** (see 1871). Although names are changed, the 'Cossack Countess' leaves little doubt as to the identities of the real-life protagonists. The first book, *Souvenirs d'une Cosaque*, enjoys five reprints in Paris within its first year and causes Liszt much embarrassment.

13 January Rimsky-Korsakov's first opera, *Pskovityanka* (The Maid of Pskov), premières in St Petersburg. The composer will twice revise the work, also known as *Ivan the Terrible*.

19 January Saint-Saëns's superbly crafted Cello Concerto No. 1 in A minor is first performed at the Paris Conservatoire.

7 February Tchaikovsky's Symphony No. 2 in C minor is introduced with enormous success

in Moscow. The work's extensive incorporation of Russian folk melody encourages one critic to nickname it *Little Russian*.

9 March Dvořák presents his patriotic male-voice cantata *Hymn: the Heirs of the White Mountain* in Prague, delighting the public and raising his profile considerably. This year the 32-year-old writes his Third Symphony.

19 March German composer and conductor **Maximilian Reger** is born in Brand, outside Bayreuth.

1 April Composer and pianist **Sergei Rachmaninov** is born in Semyonovo, north-west Russia.

1 April Verdi's String Quartet in E minor is premièred before friends at the Hotel delle Crocelle in Naples. It is his one and only instrumental chamber work.

29 May Liszt conducts the first complete performance of his oratorio *Christus* at the Herder Church in Weimar. **Wagner** attends with his wife, Cosima.

Summer Brahms completes his first two string quartets—in C minor and A minor, Op. 51— having destroyed around 20 previous efforts.

26 October Bruckner directs the first performance of his Second Symphony in Vienna, to mixed audience response. By the end of the year he completes his Third Symphony, which he dedicates to **Wagner**.

29 October The Salle Le Peletier, home of the Paris Opéra, is destroyed by fire.

2 November Brahms's *Variations on a theme by Haydn* is introduced in Vienna with great success. The theme unlikely belongs to Haydn, more probably emanating from an old hymn, the *St Anthony Chorale*.

1873 Marshal Prince McMahon is elected President of France on the resignation of Louis Thiers • France completes paying reparations for the Franco-Prussian War, and the German occupation ends • Carlist (rival monarchist) risings are followed by the declaration of a Spanish republic • Ashanti tribesmen fight British troops in West Africa • Japan adopts Gregorian calendar; embarks on a policy of religious toleration • Business panic in Europe and the USA; beginning of the Long Depression • London's Alexandra Palace, eight years in the making, destroyed by fire 16 days after opening • Berthe Morisot (Fr) paints *The Cradle* • Claude Monet (Fr) paints *The Poppy Field*

Edouard Lalo composes his popular *Symphonie espagnole* for violin and orchestra. The work makes a strong impression on **Tchaikovsky**.

January The Norwegian playwright **Henrik Ibsen** asks **Grieg** (right) to provide incidental music for *Peer Gynt* in the hope that it will make his play more accessible. The composer completes his score by the summer of next year. (See also 1876).

8 February Mussorgsky's opera *Boris Godunov* is performed for the first time, at the Mariinsky Theatre in St Petersburg. Overwhelmed by the composer's vivid pictures of Russian nationalism, the audience finds it impossible to stop clapping. Mussorgsky takes 30 curtain calls. In stark contrast, critics loathe it, variously describing it as 'chaotic', 'incoherent' and 'a cacophony in five acts'.

27 March Smetana conducts the first performance of his opera *The Two Widows* in Prague.

5 April Strauss II's tuneful operetta *Die Fledermaus* (The Bat) opens at the Theater an der Wien (Vienna). By the end of the year the comedy of mistaken identities has swept across Germany, with a production also mounted in New York.

28 April The Wagners moves into their new villa at Bayreuth, built with funds provided by King Ludwig. **Wagner** names the house *Wahnfried* (Peace from Illusion).

22 May Verdi's dramatic Requiem, written in memory of the poet Alessandro Manzoni, is first performed under the direction of the composer at the Church of San Marco in Milan. Applause is banned in the church. Public reaction is not fully gauged until three days later when a performance at La Scala is greeted with wild enthusiasm. Verdi subsequently takes the Requiem on a European tour, which includes a performance next year with a 1,000-strong choir at London's Royal Albert Hall.

August Mussorgsky completes *Pictures at an Exhibition*, a piano suite laced with Russian folk references, based on a series of paintings by his late friend Victor Hartmann. This year also sees the composition of his song cycle *Sunless*.

13 September Revolutionary Austro-Hungarian composer **Arnold Franz Walter Schoenberg** is born in Vienna.

21 September Composer **Gustav Holst** is born of Swedish and Irish descent, in Cheltenham, England.

October Smetana loses his hearing completely, having suffered four months of worsening tinnitus. With his creative spirit remaining strong, the 50-year-old begins composing his most famous work, the symphonic cycle *Má Vlast* (My Fatherland).

20 October Progressive American composer **Charles Edward Ives** is born in Danbury, Connecticut.

21 November Wagner completes the score of *Götterdämmerung* (conceived 26 years previously as *Siegfrieds Tod*) and with it the final opera of the *Ring* cycle.

22 November Bruckner completes the first version of his Fourth Symphony.

1874 Conservative Benjamin Disraeli becomes Britain's Prime Minister • The Ashanti War in Africa ends in British victory • Iceland obtains self-government from Denmark • The Spanish Republic ends; Queen Isabel's son is proclaimed King Alfonso XII • G. Annauer Hansen (Nor) discovers the bacillus of leprosy • Joseph Glidden (US) patents barbed wire • Pierre Renoir (Fr) paints *The Box at the Opera* • Alfred Sisley (Eng) paints *Foggy Morning, Voisins* • Claude Monet (Fr) paints *Impression Sunrise* (giving name to Impressionists); first Impressionist exhibition in Paris • Thomas Hardy (Eng): *Far from the Madding Crowd* • George Eliot (Eng): *Middlemarch*, Vol. I published

1875

5 January Tchaikovsky plays through his Piano Concerto in B flat minor to its dedicatee, **Nikolay Rubinstein**, who angrily dismisses the work as 'worthless', 'clumsy' and 'vulgar'. He says he will only play it with a complete rewrite. Tchaikovsky changes nothing and offers it to instead to **Hans von Bülow** (see 25 October).

5 January The new Paris Opéra, designed by Charles Garnier, opens.

24 January Saint-Saëns's *Danse Macabre* is premièred in Paris. Its novel orchestration, featuring xylophone and castanets, induces a hostile reception, but the symphonic poem ultimately defies the conservatives and gains the composer international fame. This year he writes his Piano Concerto No. 4 in C minor.

1 February Sir William Sterndale-Bennett, England's musical figurehead, dies in London, aged 58.

3 March Bizet's final masterpiece, *Carmen*, is premièred at the Opéra-Comique in Paris. Many critics condemn the opera, some disturbed by Carmen's sexual bewitchery, others denouncing the musical style as Wagnerian. Bizet begins to suffer ill health, exacerbated by melancholia. He will not live to witness the imminent triumph of *Carmen* as a worldwide phenomenon.

Galli-Marié as Carmen

7 March French composer **Maurice Joseph Ravel** is born in Ciboure, Basses-Pyrénées.

10 March Karl Goldmark's opera *Die Königin von Saba* (The Queen of Sheba) enjoys a jubilant opening night in Vienna.

25 March Gilbert and **Sullivan**'s short one-act operetta *Trial by Jury* opens at Richard D'Oyly Carte's Royalty Theatre, London.

March–April *Vyšehrad* and *Vltava*, the first two symphonic poems from **Smetana**'s *Má Vlast*, are performed to great acclaim on separate occasions in Prague. Although present the composer hears not one note, as he is now stone deaf.

May Isaac Albéniz and his father, a government official, set off for the Carribean. In Puerto Rico and Cuba the 15-year-old pianist gives recitals, drawing newspaper reviews with his party stunt of playing with his back to the piano.

3 June Shortly after the 33rd performance of Carmen, and following two heart attacks, **Georges Bizet** dies in Bougival, near Paris, aged 36.

15 August Composer **Samuel Coleridge-Taylor** is born to Sierra Leonese and English parents in Croydon, London.

September Gustav Mahler and **Hugo Wolf**, both aged 15, begin studying at the Vienna Conservatory. During the second academic year, Wolf is expelled for 'breach of discipline'.

25 October Bülow performs the première of **Tchaikovsky**'s Piano Concerto No. 1 before an eager audience in Boston. **N. Rubinstein**, having rejected the concerto, will later reconsider his judgement and become an important advocate of the work.

19 November N. Rubinstein directs the première of **Tchaikovsky**'s Symphony No. 3 in Moscow.

1875 Britain buys 176,602 Suez Canal shares from the Khedive (ruler) of Egypt, gaining virtual control of the shortest route to India and the Far East • US Congress passes an anti-discrimination Civil Rights Act; eight years later US Supreme Court declares it unconstitutional • Rebellion breaks out in Cuba • Japan secures a treaty with Korea, establishing Korean independence from China • Richard M. Hoe of New York City invents a rotary printing press • The Universal Postal Union is founded in Berne, Switzerland • Claude Monet (Fr) paints *Woman with a Parasol* and *Argenteuil* • Edgar Degas (Fr) paints *Place de la Concorde*

Smetana completes his String Quartet No. 1 in E minor, subtitled *From my Life*. Youthful and nationalistic passions come to an abrupt halt in the coda of the final movement, where he charts the sad demise of his hearing. The section is introduced with a high E harmonic, suggestive of his tinnitus.

24 February **Ibsen**'s drama *Peer Gynt* is staged in Christiania (now Oslo) with incidental music by **Grieg**. The production is a great success, running for 37 performances until a fire destroys the theatre. This same year Grieg completes his Ballade in G minor (Op. 24) for piano.

April **Tchaikovsky** completes his ballet *Swan Lake*. Other compositions this year include the *Variations on a Rococo Theme* for cello and orchestra, the symphonic poem *Francesca da Rimini* and his Third String Quartet.

8 April **Amilcare Ponchielli**'s one lasting success, the opera *La gioconda*, opens at La Scala, Milan.

10 May **Wagner**'s *Grosser Festmarsch*, celebrating the centenary of American Independence, is first performed in Philadelphia. The whopping $5,000 commission does not inspire him to produce his best work: 'Unless the subject absorbs me completely, I cannot produce twenty bars worth listening to.'

14 June **Delibes**'s *Sylvia* is first danced at the Paris Opéra. Based on Tasso's pastoral poem *Aminta*, the ballet soon disappears from the repertory but will resurface with great success during the 1950s.

13–17 August **Wagner**'s epic *Der Ring des Nibelungen* (The Ring of the Nibelung) begins its first complete performance under **Hans Richter** in the purpose-built Festspielhaus in Bayreuth (right). Among the impressive list of attendees are Kaiser Wilhelm, King Ludwig II, Nietzsche, **Liszt**, **Tchaikovsky**, **Bruckner** and **Grieg**. Although a huge artistic success, the four-opera cycle is a financial failure. It will be several years before the *Ring* festival becomes a profitable enterprise.

4 November **Brahms**'s First Symphony, some 14 years in the making, is premièred to great acclaim under **Otto Dessoff** in Karlsruhe. Many regard it as the most accomplished symphonic début of any composer. The work explores the struggles and ultimate triumph of the human spirit, paying homage to Beethoven's *Ode to Joy* in the final movement.

7 November The première of **Smetana**'s second most popular opera, *The Kiss*, is a major triumph at Prague's Provisional Theatre.

23 November Spanish composer **Manuel de Falla** is born in Cádiz.

December The wealthy widow Nadezhda von Meck becomes benefactress to **Tchaikovsky**. The relationship is conducted through letter alone—they will never meet.

10 December **Dvořák**'s *Serenade for Strings* (Op. 22) makes its charming début in Prague.

1876 Colorado becomes the 38th State of the USA • A Little Big Horne, Mont, Lieutenant Colonel George Custer and his men are massacred by Sioux Indians • Bulgarians rebel against Turkish misrule; massacre by Turkish troops arouses widespread anger; Serbia and Montenegro declare war on Turkey; Russia, too, threatens war • Scottish-born scientist Alexander Graham Bell patents the telephone in the USA • Nicolas-August Otto (Ger) invents an internal combustion engine • Pierre-Auguste Renoir (Fr) paints *Le Moulin de la Galette* • Winslow Homer (US) paints *The Cotton-Pickers* • Mark Twain (US): *The Adventures of Tom Sawyer* • Lewis Carroll (Eng): poem *The Hunting of the Snark*

1877

Thomas Edison invents the cylinder phonograph. (See also 1888.)

Goldmark composes his Violin Concerto in A minor and the symphonic poem *Rustic Wedding*.

Lalo completes his Cello Concerto in D minor.

Mussorgsky takes a break from writing *Khovanshchina*, beginning work on the opera *Sorochintsï Fair* and completing his song cycle *Songs and Dances of Death*.

27 January Fauré and the violinist **Marie Tayau** give the first performance of the composer's Violin Sonata No. 1 at the Société Nationale de Musique in Paris. Later this year Fauré starts work on his richly melodic Requiem, undertaken 'for the pleasure of it'.

4 February The Imperial Ballet dance to the music of **Ludwig Minkus** in the first performance of *La Bayadère*, in St Petersburg.

4 March Tchaikovsky's fairytale tragedy *Swan Lake* is danced for the first time at the Bolshoi Theatre in Moscow. Many critics respond unfavourably, dismissing the music as too complex, even 'Wagnerian'. An immensely successful production in 1895, two years after Tchaikovsky's death, launches the masterpiece into the repertory.

10 March Borodin's Second Symphony in B minor is introduced with only modest success by the Russian Musical Society. Revised two years later, it becomes the most famous symphony produced by any member of 'The Five'.

18 July Tchaikovsky begins a short, chaotic marriage with Antonina Milyukova, who is infatuated with the composer. Three months later, having suffered a nervous breakdown and attempted suicide, Tchaikovsky separates from his wife.

August Liszt completes his third book of *Années de pèlerinage* for piano, including the impressionistic *Les jeux d'eaux à la Villa d'Este*.

2 December Dvořák's Symphonic Variations are first heard in Prague. Other compositions this year include his Stabat Mater (see also 1880) and Romance in F minor for violin and orchestra.

2 December Saint-Saëns's *Samson et Dalila* (Samson and Delilah), turned down by several French theatres, is staged with the help of **Liszt** in Weimar. The Martinique-born **Ferdinand Lemaire** supplies the libretto for the composer's one enduring opera.

16 December Bruckner steps up at the 11th hour as a replacement conductor in the first performance of his revised Third (*Wagner*) Symphony in Vienna. The result is catastrophic: the orchestra play unwillingly and audience members walk out in droves during the performance.

30 December Brahms's Second Symphony is successfully premièred by the Vienna Philharmonic Orchestra under **Hans Richter**. In contrast to his First Symphony, written over a period of around 14 years, his second essay in the genre has taken less than a year to complete.

Tchaikovsky with Antonina Milyukova

Dvořák (below) draws on Bohemian folk music in his eight *Slavonic Dances*, scored for piano duet (Op. 46) and soon after orchestrated.

Commissioned by the Berlin publisher Simrock, the collection proves exceptionally popular and establishes Dvořák's international profile. This year also sees the composition of the *Three Slavonic Rhapsodies*, Op. 45.

Sarasate's impassioned *Zigeunerweisen* (Gypsy Airs) for violin (virtuoso) and piano is published in Leipzig. Also published this year is his first book of *Spanische Tänze* (Spanish Dances).

January Tchaikovsky completes his opera *Eugene Onegin*, and the orchestral score of the Fourth Symphony in F minor—his first symphony to find a permanent place in the repertory. This year he resigns from his teaching post at the Moscow Conservatory thanks to the provision of

a 6,000-rouble annuity from his patron, Mme von Meck, to whom the symphony is dedicated.

27 January The Czech-language comic opera *The Cunning Peasant* rewards **Dvořák** with success at the Provisional Theatre in Prague.

24 March Dvořák's Piano Concerto in G minor (1876) is premièred in Prague.

April Tchaikovsky completes his optimistic Violin Concerto in D major. A performance of the work is delayed as the original dedicatee of the work, **Leopold Auer**, finds it too awkward to play. The challenging honour will pass to **Adolf Brodsky** three years later in Vienna.

25 May Gilbert and **Sullivan** consolidate their creative partnership with *HMS Pinafore*, produced by the impresario D'Oyly Carte in London. Satirising naval discipline and the English way of life, the operetta enjoys massive success in England and soon afterwards in the USA. Many American productions are unauthorised, but all three men make considerable profits from English performances. Gilbert buys himself a yacht with the proceeds.

28 May Saint-Saëns and his young wife, Marie-Laure, lose their two-year-old son, who falls to his death out of a fourth-floor window of their home in Paris. Their second son dies six weeks later from an illness, aged six months. The composer holds his wife responsible and deserts her three years later.

Summer Brahms composes his Violin Concerto in D major in consultation with his friend **Joachim**. Material from a discarded Scherzo will later resurface in the composer's Second Piano Concerto (1881).

1 October Massenet is appointed composition and counterpoint professor at the Paris Conservatoire.

1878 Russians defeat Turks at Shipka Pass, Bulgaria, and take Andrianople (Edirne) in European Turkey • Britain sends troops to Constantinople • The treaties of San Stefano and Berlin reshape the Balkans; Romania, Montenegro and Serbia gain independence; Russia acquires Bassarabia, south west of Ukraine; Cyprus goes to Britain • Pope Pius IX dies; is succeeded by Leo XIII • Eadweard Muybridge (Eng) creates an early motion picture, *Sallie Gardner at a Gallop*, using multiple cameras to capture a racehorse in motion • First weekly weather reports published in UK • Pierre Renoir (Fr) paints *Madame Charpentier and her Children* • Thomas Hardy (Eng): *The Return of the Native*

Albéniz, aged 19, completes his studies at the Brussels Conservatoire. He returns to Spain to continue his career as a piano virtuoso.

Dvořák composes his Violin Concerto in A minor for **Joachim**. The great virtuoso rehearses the work but seems to lose interest, never playing it in public. (See also 1883.)

César Franck completes his finest religious work, the oratorio *Les Béatitudes*.

George Grove publishes the first volume (A to Impromptu) of *A Dictionary of Music and Musicians*. Three further volumes appear over the next ten years.

1 January Brahms welcomes the New Year by conducting the première of his Violin Concerto, with **Joachim** (below) as soloist, at the Gewandhaus in Leipzig. Classical in form,

the symphonic concerto is a vehicle for great lyricism and poetic reflection, while boasting an invigorating final movement flavoured by Hungarian folk music. However, the public reception is lukewarm and **Bülow**, normally supportive of Brahms, asserts that he has written a 'concerto against the violin'. Most critics are equally unconvinced.

1 February Suppé's operetta *Boccaccio* opens and enjoys overwhelming success in Vienna.

29 March N. Rubinstein directs students of the Moscow Conservatory in the first performance of **Tchaikovsky**'s *Eugene Onegin* (1878). As Pushkin's story offers few dramatic opportunities, the opera meets with a muted response. Only in the second half of the 20th century will audiences begin to embrace the opera's intimate moods and emotions.

29 April Conductor **Thomas Beecham**, heir to the Beecham's Pills empire, is born in St Helen's, Lancashire.

9 July Italian composer **Ottorino Respighi** is born in Bologna.

19 October Widor premières his Organ Symphony No. 5, furnished with the adored toccata, at the Trocadéro in Paris.

9 November Distinguished by its strong Czech flavours, **Dvořák**'s String Sextet is performed for the first time, in Berlin. This year also marks the completion of the String Quartet No. 10 in E flat.

31 December *The Pirates of Penzance*, **Gilbert** and **Sullivan**'s follow-up operetta to the hugely successful *HMS Pinafore*, is staged at the Fifth Avenue Theatre, New York. Sullivan has only just met the deadline, composing the overture in the early hours of the morning. Instantly popular, the production follows an incomplete amateur British première the day before at the humble Royal Bijou Theatre in Paignton, South Devon.

1879 British fight Zulus in South Africa; Zulu leader Cetawayo captured and war ends • By agreement, Britain occupies the Khyber Pass between India and Afghanistan • Britain invades Afghanistan after the British Legion at Kabul is massacred; Emir Ya'qub abdicates • Britain and France resume joint control of Egypt • Irish Land League formed to help tenant farmers • Thomas Edison (US) invents an incandescent electric lamp • David Hughes (US) invents the spark-gap transmitter, a pioneering step towards radio • Auguste Rodin (Fr) sculpts *St John the Baptist Preaching* • Henrik Ibsen (Nor): play *A Doll's House* • George Meredith (Eng): *The Egoist* • Fyodor Dostoyevsky (Russ): *The Brothers Karamazov*

Bruch takes up the conductorship of the Liverpool Philharmonic Society, holding the post for the next three years. This year he composes his folk-tune inspired *Scottish Fantasy* for violin and orchestra.

Bülow becomes director of the Meiningen orchestra. He implements bold reforms, requiring players to perform standing up and from memory.

Tchaikovsky composes his *Serenade for Strings* and *Capriccio Italien*. This year also sees the commission of his programmatic *1812 (Festival) Overture*. On completion he confesses that he has 'written it without affection or enthusiasm, so it will probably have little artistic merit'.

17 January Franck's heartfelt Piano Quintet is successfully introduced at the Société Nationale, Paris. Performing at the piano is **Saint-Saëns**, who refuses the kind dedication of the piece because he dislikes it too much.

11 February Fauré combines elegance and passion in his Piano Quartet No. 1 in C minor, premièred with the composer at the piano at the Société Nationale, Paris.

10 March John Knowles Paine's Second Symphony is first performed in Cambridge, Massachusetts. It is widely regarded as the most important symphony by a native composer up to this time.

20 April 'Out of the silence of the sandy steppes of central Asia come the sounds of a peaceful Russian song': *In the Steppes of Central Asia*, an 'Orchestral picture' by **Alexander Borodin** (right), makes its evocative entrance under **Rimsky-Korsakov** in St Petersburg.

3 May Brahms introduces his third and fourth books of *Hungarian Dances* for piano four hands with **Clara Schumann**, in Mehlem, near Bonn. This year also marks the composition of his *Academic Festival Overture* (Op. 80) and *Tragic Overture* (Op. 81).

July Lying about his age, the 17-year-old **Debussy** secures a summer job teaching piano to the children of the widowed Nadezhda von Meck, **Tchaikovsky**'s unseen benefactress.

24 July Composer **Ernest Bloch**, son of a clock-maker, is born in Geneva.

25 July Wagner, aged 67, completes his autobiography, *Mein Leben* (My Life).

17 August Norwegian violinist **Ole Bull** dies in Bergen, aged 70.

5 October Stage composer **Jacques Offenbach** dies in Paris from a gout-related illness, aged 61.

15 October Sullivan conducts his oratorio *The Martyr of Antioch* at the Leeds Festival. With text by **Gilbert**, the pair's one 'serious' work divides critics.

23 December Dvořák's monumental Stabat Mater (1877), scored for four soloists, chorus and orchestra, premières in Prague. The 90-minute work was stimulated by the death of the composer's baby daughter Josefa in 1875 and completed following the death of two more of his children, leaving him childless.

31 December Sullivan calculates his net takings 'earned by my profession' to be a fraction shy of £10,000 for the year.

1880 In Ireland, Charles Stewart Parnell, allied with the land league, leads a drive for Home Rule • Transvaal (South Africa) declares independence from Britain and proclaims itself a republic under the Boer leader Paul Kruger • Chile defeats Bolivia and Peru in the War of the Pacific; Chile gains valuable nitrate territory while Bolivia loses access to the Sea •

The first cricket test match between England and Australia is played at Melbourne • Camille Pissarro (Fr) paints *Washerwoman* • Dante Gabriel Rossetti (Eng) paints *The Day Dream* • Emile Zola (Fr): *Nana* • Louis Wallace (US): *Ben Hur*; becomes the best-selling US novel of the century

1881

Borodin composes his String Quartet No. 2 in D major, famous above all for its infectiously melodic third movement 'Notturno'.

Chabrier completes his *10 pièces pittoresques* for piano.

Henry Lee Higginson establishes the Boston Symphony Orchestra, with **Georg Henschel** as its musical director.

10 February Offenbach's *The Tales of Hoffmann* is premièred four months after the composer's death, in Paris. Incorporating the figure of E. T. A. Hoffmann as a character within the writer's own stories, the 'serious' *opéra fantastique* is an immediate sensation, topping 100 performances at the Opéra-Comique by the end of the year. (See also 8 December.)

20 February **Richter** conducts a hugely successful first performance of **Bruckner**'s Fourth Symphony (second version, 1880) in Vienna. It is the composer's first triumph. Later this year Bruckner completes his Sixth Symphony and immediately begins his Seventh.

25 February **Tchaikovsky**'s opera *The Maid of Orléans* is first performed in St Petersburg. It manages only short-lived success, largely owing to some savage criticism led by **César Cui**.

24 March **Verdi**'s much revised *Simon Boccanegra* (1857) opens at La Scala, Milan.

25 March Composer **Bela Bartók** is born in Nagyszentmiklós, southern Hungary (now Sînnicolau Mare, Romania).

28 March Composer **Modest Mussorgsky** (below), having battled with alcoholism for many years, dies in a St Petersburg hospital, aged 42.

9 May **Liszt**'s orchestrated *Second Mephisto Waltz* premières in Budapest. New works this year include his loosely tonal, impressionistic *Trübe Wolken/Nuages gris* (Gloomy Clouds) for piano.

13 July **Leoš Janáček**, aged 27, marries his piano pupil Zdenka Schulzová, aged 15.

20 October **Bruch** draws on sacred Jewish chant in *Kol Nidrei*, *Adagio on Hebrew Melodies* for cello and orchestra, premièred in Leipzig. Bruch is currently the director of the Liverpool Philharmonic.

30 October **Svendsen**'s Violin Romance, Op. 26, is introduced at Kristiania, Norway.

9 November **Brahms** gives the first performance of his symphonic four-movement Second Piano Concerto in Budapest.

4 December **Tchaikovsky**'s melodious Violin Concerto in D major is premièred with the soloist **Adolph Brodsky** in Vienna. The critic Eduard Hanslick offers his verdict: 'Tchaikovsky's violin concerto poses for the first time the ghastly notion that music can stink to the ear.'

8 December A second run of Offenbach's *The Tales of Hoffmann* at Vienna's Ring Theatre ends abruptly with a fire that kills 384 members of the audience. The opera, regarded by some as jinxed, disappears from the Vienna repertory for many years.

1881 James A. Garfield, 20th President of the USA is assassinated four months after taking office; Vice-President Chester A. Arthur becomes the 21st President • Treaty of Pretoria; Transvaal's independence is recognised by Britain • Tunis becomes a French protectorate • Tsar Aleksandr II of Russia is assassinated; his son, Aleksandr III, succeeds him

• Louis Pasteur (Fr) develops an anthrax vaccine • Construction of Canadian Pacific Railway is started • Louis Pasteur (Fr) develops anthrax vaccine • Claude Monet (Fr) paints *Sunshine and Snow* • Henrik Ibsen (Nor): play *Ghosts* • Anatole France (Fr): *The Crime of Sylvestre Bonnard* • Henry James (US): *Portrait of a lady*

The Berlin Philharmonic Orchestra is founded.

Edward MacDowell composes his First Piano Concerto. The 21-year-old American is currently a piano teacher at Darmstadt's Academy for Musical Arts.

German composer **Carl Reinecke** conjures a female water-nymph in his limpid Flute Sonata in E minor (*Undine*).

13 January Wagner completes *Parsifal*, his final opera. It has been arranged that **Hermann Levi**, the son of a Rabbi, will conduct the 'sacred festival drama'. Wagner is unsuccessful in his attempt to persuade his friend to undergo Christian baptism before the première. (See 26 July.)

15 January Auguste Renoir visits **Wagner** in Palermo, Sicily, and paints his portrait (above) in less than an hour.

10 February Rimsky-Korsakov's opera *Snegurochka* (The Snow Maiden), based on an old Russian folk tale, is first staged in St Petersburg. The critics give it a cool reception.

29 March The 16-year-old **Alexander Glazunov** has his First Symphony introduced with great success under **Balakirev** in St Petersburg.

18 April Conductor **Leopold Stokowski** is born in London.

17 June Composer **Igor Fyodorovich Stravinsky** is born in Oranienbaum, near St Petersburg.

26 July Wagner's *Parsifal* receives the first of 16 performances at the Bayreuth festival. The story of knights and the Holy Grail breaks the mould of Wagner's previous operas, with redemption gained not through love but through suffering, denial and forgiveness. Wagner's festival, for the first time, achieves financial success.

20 August Tchaikovsky's programmatic *1812 Overture*, climaxing in canon fire and pealing bells, entertains the public for the first time at the Moscow Arts and Industrial Exhibition.

30 August Gounod conducts his commissioned 'sacred trilogy', *La Rédemption*, at the Birmingham Festival, England.

31 August Parry's Symphony No. 1 is premièred at the Birmingham Festival.

5 November The six symphonic poems of **Smetana**'s *Má Vlast* (My Fatherland) are heard together for the first time, in Prague.

25 November Gilbert and **Sullivan**'s *Iolanthe* opens before an eager audience at the Savoy Theatre, London. Sullivan, conducting the operetta, has just received the news that his brokers have gone bankrupt, losing virtually all of his savings—around £7,000. *Iolanthe* restores his fortunes, with very profitable runs in both England and America.

16 December Composer **Zoltán Kodály** is born in Kecskemét, Hungary.

1882 Germany, Austria and Italy form Triple Alliance (ends 1914) • The USA issues the Chinese Exclusion Act, banning immigration of Chinese into the USA for an intended period of ten years; the ban lasts until 1943 • British forces occupy Cairo and Sudan after defeating rebel forces at Tel-el-Kebir • Italy makes Eritrea a colony • Jews suffer repressive regulations in Russia • Robert Koch (Ger) discovers the bacillus of tuberculosis • Edouard Manet (Fr) paints *The Bar at the Folies-Bergères* • Edgar Degas (Fr) paints *The Laudresses* • Henrik Ibsen (Nor): play *An Enemy of the People* • Thomas Edison switches on the first commercial electrical power station, serving customers in Lower Manhattan •

Grieg completes his Cello Sonata, (Op. 36) the *Walzer-Capricen* for piano duet (Op. 37) and a second book of *Lyric Pieces* for piano solo (Op. 38). A second piano concerto, begun this year, is never completed.

The 71-year-old **Liszt** completes his solo piano pieces *Valse de concert*, *Mephisto-Polka* and the *Mephisto Waltz No. 3*.

11 February The second and third movements of **Bruckner**'s Sixth Symphony are introduced and well appreciated in Vienna.

13 February In Venice the 69-year-old **Wagner** has a blazing row with his wife, Cosima, who is suspicious about a pending visit from the singer Carrie Pringle. Wagner retreats to a study, where a few hours later he suffers a fatal heart attack. On discovering her husband, Cosima remains clenched to his corpse for 25 hours. The body is transported back to their home, Wahnfried in Bayreuth, and buried in a private ceremony.

8 March Fauré's oratorio *La Naissance de Vénus* is first performed in Paris.

14 April Delibes (right) exploits fashionable orientalism in *Lakmé*, premièred at the Opéra-Comique, Paris. Set in India and inspired by Pierre Loti's exotic tale *Rarahu*, the three-act tragic opera enjoys immediate success. Highlights include 'Où va la jeune Hindoue' and 'Dôme épais', better known as the 'Bell Song' and the 'Flower Duet'.

May The Royal College of Music opens under the directorship of **George Grove**.

22 May Arthur Sullivan receives a knighthood from Queen Victoria.

3 October Polish composer **Karol Szymanowski** is born in Tymoszówka, outside Kiev.

14 October Dvořák's Violin Concerto in A minor is first performed by **František Ondříček** in Prague. A rhapsodic tendency is apparent in both the first and second movements, while the joyous third immerses itself in Slavonic folk influences. Extremely popular in its day, the work never quite matches the repertory status of the **Bruch** (No. 1 in G minor), **Brahms** and **Tchaikovsky** violin concertos.

22 October Gounod's *Faust* (premièred 1859) inaugurates the Metropolitan Opera House in New York.

4 November Chabrier's popular orchestral rhapsody *España*, inspired by the composer's recent trip to the country, premières in Paris. His *Trois Valses Romantiques* for two pianos is first performed in the same city a month later.

2 December Brahms's Third Symphony is successfully introduced under **Hans Richter** in Vienna. The heroism and dramatic urgency of the opening movement (noting the also the numbering of the symphony) prompts Richter to subtitle the work Brahms's *Eroica*.

3 December Composer **Anton Webern** is born in Vienna.

22 December Composer **Edgard Varèse** is born in Paris.

1883 Germany founds settlements in south-west Africa • Paul Kruger becomes President of the Boer South African Republic • France begins to colonise west Africa and gains control of Tunisia in north Africa • In Egypt, Muhammad Ahmad al Mahdi organises the defeat of Egyptian troops at El Obeid and obtains control of most of Sudan • John Carbutt (US) introduces a coated celluloid film for photography • Edwin Klebs (Ger) identifies the diphtheria germ • Pierre Renoir (Fr) paints *Children at the Beach at Guernsey* • Ilya Repin (Russ) paints *Easter Procession* • Robert Louis Stevenson (Scot): *Treasure Island* • Friedrich Nietzsche (Ger): philosophical novel *Thus Spake Zarathustra*

7 January The opera *Sigurd* by the French composer **Ernest Reyer** premières in Brussels.

10 January **Verdi**'s revised *Don Carlos* (1867), now in four acts with an Italian libretto, is staged for the first time at La Scala, Milan.

19 January **Massenet**'s five-act *Manon*, based on Prévost's novel *L'histoire du chevalier des Grieux et de Manon Lescaut* (1731), opens at the Opéra-Comique, Paris. The composer's skilful portrayal of innocence corrupted launches the opera into the repertory.

15 February **Tchaikovsky**'s nationalistic opera *Mazeppa*, based on Pushkin's historical poem *Poltava*, is respectfully received at the Bolshoi Theatre, Moscow. The next day the composer's Orchestral Suite No. 2 débuts in the same city with immense critical success.

March **Frederick Delius**, aged 22, leaves England to run an orange plantation in Florida.

March **Dvořák** visits England for the first time, conducting tried and tested works including his *Stabat mater* (1877) at the Albert Hall and his Sixth Symphony (1880) at St James's Hall. A third concert at the Crystal Palace programmes his *Scherzo capriccioso* (1883) and the Nocturne in B major for string orchestra (1875). Enjoying effusive praise from the London press, Dvořák receives a commission for a new symphony (No. 7) from the Philharmonic Society.

Anton Bruckner

28 March **Zdeněk Fibich**'s tragic opera *The Bride of Messina* is first performed in Prague.

12 May **Bedřich Smetana**, having suffered rapidly deteriorating mental health, dies in an asylum in Prague, aged 59.

31 May **Puccini**'s début opera, the one-act *Le Villi*, is presented at the Teatro Dal Verme in Milan. Revised for a two-act production in Turin at the end of the year, it rewards the composer with an early taste of success.

5 August **Debussy**, aged 22, wins the *Prix de Rome* for his cantata *L'enfant prodigue*. He will spend the next two years in Rome, as required of all prize-winners, residing at the Villa Medici.

3 December **Grieg**'s solo piano work *From Holberg's Time* is introduced in Bergen to mark the bicentennial celebrations of Holberg's birth. Grieg will arrange the suite for string orchestra the following year, creating one of his best-loved compositions.

30 December **Bruckner**'s Seventh Symphony (completed 1883) enjoys a glorious première under **Arthur Nikisch** in Leipzig. The measured pace and searching depth of the first movement leads to the composer's most sublime Adagio—hymnal, poignant and grief-stricken, apparently inspired by imagining the death of the composer he called 'The Master': Wagner. Coincidentally, Wagner died (February 1883) shortly after Bruckner had sketched the movement.

1884 European colonisation in Africa continues: the Berlin Conference establishes an independent State of the Congo • Germany establishes protectorates over Togoland and Cameroons • Britain sends General Gordon to direct Egyptian withdrawal from Sudan • Charles Parsons (Eng/Ire) devises a practical steam-turbine engine • Boston and New York City are connected by telephone • Third Reform Act extends voting rights in UK; women and many working-class men still not allowed to vote • France presents the Statue of Liberty to the USA • In Chicago, the first skyscraper is built • Georges Seurat (Fr) paints *Bathers at Asnières* • Mark Twain (US): *The Adventures of Huckleberry Finn*

Franck composes his *Symphonic Variations* for piano and orchestra.

Liszt composes his progressive *Bagatelle ohne Tonart* (Bagatelle without tonality). Opening with a motif distinguished by a tritione, the short, heavily chromatic piano piece never settles in any particular key, thereby breaking down the traditions of 'functional tonality' and anticipating 20th-century trends.

Mahler completes the first version of his song cycle *Lieder eines fahrenden Gesellen* (Songs of a Wayfarer).

Saint-Saëns composes his Violin Sonata No. 1 in D minor.

Hugo Wolf completes his symphonic poem *Penthesilea*.

9 February Austrian composer **Alban Maria Johannes Berg** is born in Vienna.

4 March Richard Strauss looks to the earlier Romantics in his Horn Concerto No. 1 in E flat major (1883, written at the age of 18), premièred in Meiningen. The composer's familiarity with the horn derives from his father, Franz, who is the Principal Horn of the Munich Court Orchestra.

14 March *The Mikado* (right) begins a run of 672 performances at the Savoy Theatre in London. Regarded by most as **Gilbert** and **Sullivan**'s finest operetta, it enjoys phenomenal popularity on both sides of

the Atlantic and becomes the pair's first major success beyond the English-speaking world.

22 April Dvořák conducts the first performance of his Seventh Symphony in D minor (Op. 70), in London. While the severity of the work takes some by surprise, it will in time become recognised as one of the greatest of all Romantic symphonies. During this second English visit, Dvořák also conducts his cantata *The Spectre's Bride* (1884).

26 August Gounod's final oratorio, *Mors et vita*, premières at the Birmingham Festival. The composer is unable to attend, having just lost a libel case with his former landlady and business associate Mrs Georgina Weldon, who has sued him on grounds of unpaid debts and defamatory remarks. Gounod faces immediate arrest if he sets foot on English soil.

4 October Tchaikovsky completes his Manfred Symphony, based on Byron's dramatic poem. As with his fantasy-overture *Romeo and Juliet*, the initial idea for the work has come from **Balakirev**.

24 October Strauss II delights Vienna with his new operetta *The Gypsy Baron*, staged at the Theater an der Wien.

25 October Brahms conducts the first performance of his Symphony No. 4 in E minor (Op. 98), in Meiningen. Audiences are generally slow to embrace what is arguably the composer's greatest essay in the genre.

30 November Massenet's opera *Le Cid*, based on Corneille's drama of 1637, opens at the Paris Opéra.

The Two Very Fanny Japs at the Savoy.

1885 General Gordon Killed at Khartoum; Muhammad Ahmad dies five months later but Dervishes maintain control of Sudan under khalifa Abdullah • Belgium establishes Congo colony • Germany makes a protectorate of north New Guinea, and annexes Tanganyika and Zanzibar • British establish protectorates in Nigeria, north Bechuanaland and south New Guinea • British at war with Burmese • Gottlieb Daimler (Ger) develops an internal-combustion gasoline engine; with Wilhelm Maybach he builds the first motorcycle: Daimler Reitwagen. • Karl Benz (Ger) produces a three-wheel automobile • Louis Pasteur (Fr) successfully vaccinates a child against rabies • Emile Zola (Fr): *Germinal*

Albéniz draws on regional folk idioms in his *Suite española* for solo piano. 'Sevilla' and (the later added) 'Asturias' are among the principal crowd-pleasers, especially in subsequent guitar transcriptions.

Fauré completes his Piano Quartet No. 2 in G minor (Op. 45).

D'Indy completes *Symphonie sur un chant montagnard français* (Symphony on a French Mountaineer's Song), his most popular work.

Richard Strauss, aged 22, composes his symphonic fantasy *Aus Italien*. This same year he takes the post of third conductor at the Munich Court Opera.

10 January Hans Richter directs the first public performance of **Bruckner**'s Te Deum (1884), in Vienna. The work is enthusiastically received.

9 March Saint-Saëns's chamber work *Le carnaval des animaux* (The Carnival of the Animals) is premièred in Paris. Apart from one movement, 'The Swan', he will not allow the work to be performed again in his lifetime, concerned that its triviality will damage his reputation.

April Liszt (left) visits England for the first time in over 40 years. There the 74-year-old is coaxed into performing before students at the Royal Academy of Music, and also Queen Victoria at Windsor castle. The queen records in her diary that Liszt is now 'a quiet, benevolent looking old priest, with long white hair and scarcely any teeth'.

1 May Tchaikovsky's fantasy overture *Romeo and Juliet*, in its third and final version, is performed for the first time, in Tbilisi.

19 May Saint-Saëns's Symphony No. 3 in C minor (*Organ Symphony*), commissioned by the London Philharmonic Society, is introduced under the composer's direction at St James's Hall. Employing the (Lisztian) technique of thematic transformation, Saint-Saëns repeatedly draws on his principal subject. The celebrated *Maestoso* section introduces the symphony's most famous thematic transformation, featuring divided strings and glistening four-hand piano accompaniment, followed by full-throttle organ and triumphant brass.

13 June King Ludwig II of Bavaria, Wagner's former patron, drowns suspiciously in Lake Starnberg with his physician, just three days after being deposed by the government on grounds of insanity.

31 July Following several busy months of touring and concert giving, **Liszt** dies at Bayreuth, aged 74. His funeral is held there three days later, with **Bruckner** among the mourners.

August Delius arrives in Leipzig to enrol at the Conservatory. He has spent the last two years managing an orange grove in Florida.

> *'Played Brahms, the scoundrel. What a talentless bastard! It annoys me that this presumptuous mediocrity should be considered a genius.'*

9 October Tchaikovsky, diary entry.

24 November Brahms presents his Cello Sonata No. 2 in F major at the Kleiner Musikvereinssaal in Vienna, and eight days later at the same venue his Violin Sonata No. 2 in A major.

1886 In Britain, the Irish Home Rule Bill is defeated in the House of Commons • Britain annexes Upper Burma • Britain and Germany agree on the borders of Togoland and Gold Coast • Carl von Welsbach (Aus) invents an incandescent gas mantle • Gold is discovered in South Africa • The American Federation of Labour is formed • The Statue of Liberty is dedicated in New York • Georges Seurat (Fr) paints *Sunday Afternoon on the Island of La Grande Jatte* • John Singer Sargent (US) paints *Carnation, Lily, Lily, Rose* • Robert Louis Stevenson (Scot): *Doctor Jekyll and Mr Hyde* • H. Rider Haggard (Eng): *King Solomon's Mines* • Henry James (US): *The Bostonians*

Delius completes his *Florida Suite* while studying at the Leipzig Conservatory.

Rimsky-Korsakov latches onto the vogue for Spanish exoticism in his effervescent *Spanish capriccio* for orchestra.

Widor's Organ Symphonies Nos. 5–8 are published in Paris as his Op. 42.

January Dvořák completes his second set of *Slavonic Dances* (Op. 72), in part to induce his publisher, Simrock, to pay him properly for his Seventh Symphony.

22 January Gilbert and **Sullivan**'s *Ruddigore* opens at the Savoy Theatre, London. Following a string of hits, their new operetta achieves only modest success.

5 February Verdi's first new opera in over 15 years, *Otello*, (right) with libretto by **Boito** after Shakespeare's play, causes a sensation at La Scala, Milan. The première has attracted an international body of media and public emotion ranges from excited to hysterical. After the performance, mobbing fans detach Verdi's carriage from the horses and draw it themselves, conveying Boito, Verdi and his wife back to their hotel. A crowd remains outside the hotel throughout most of the night, cheering and playing music.

24 February John Stainer's most enduring large-scale work, the oratorio *The Crucifixion*, is first performed at St Marylebone Parish Church,

London. The English composer and organist will later dismiss all his music as 'rubbish'.

27 February Composer **Alexander Borodin** drops down dead from heart failure at a Medical-Surgical Academy ball in St Petersburg, aged 53.

5 March Brazilian composer **Heitor Villa-Lobos** is born in Rio de Janeiro.

18 May Chabrier's *Le roi malgré lui* (King, in Spite of Himself) makes little impact at the Opéra-Comique, Paris. The opera house itself burns down later this month.

10 August Bruckner completes the first version of his Eighth Symphony, only to have the conductor **Hermann Levi** reject the work as incomprehensible. He immediately starts revisions, and at the same time begins work on his Ninth Symphony.

15 August The 61-year-old **Strauss II** marries his third wife, the 30-year-old Adèle Deutsch. Born a Catholic and a Jew respectively, both parties have converted to Lutheran Protestantism to gain permission to wed.

18 October Brahms conducts the première of his Double Concerto for violin and cello, in Cologne. It is performed by its dedicatees, **Joachim** and **Robert Hausmann**.

31 December Franck's Violin Sonata in A major is introduced by **Eugène Ysaÿe** at the Société Nationale in Paris.

1887 The Dawes Act authorises the end of Indian tribal government and division of Indian land in the USA • German Chancellor Otto von Bismarck calls for a larger German army • Germany, Austria and Italy renew their Triple Alliance • France creates a Union of Indo-China, consisting of Annam, Cambodia, Cochin-China and Tonkin • Yellow River flood in China claims around 900,000 lives • Gottlieb Daimler (Ger) produces first successful automobile • Heinrich Hertz (Ger) produces electromagnetic waves • Vincent van Gogh (Neth) paints *Bridges across the Seine at Asnieres* and three self-portraits • Arthur Conan Doyle (Scot): first Sherlock Holmes story, *A Study in Scarlet*

Nietzsche publishes *Der Fall Wagner* (The Case of Wagner) in which he greatly revises his youthful admiration for the composer. He attacks Wagner's self-importance and condemns his art as 'sick'; he instead exalts Bizet's *Carmen* as the epitome of operatic perfection.

Rimsky-Korsakov composes the *Russian Easter Festival* overture and the exotic symphonic suite *Sheherazade*.

Erik Satie completes his three modal *Gymnopédies* (Nude Gymnasts) for solo piano. At the age of 22 he has already produced his most enduring and popular work.

Richard Strauss completes his tone poems *Macbeth* (first version) and *Don Juan*.

February Wolf begins a marathon song-writing spree that will continue well into the following year. During this time he completes his collections of *Mörike-Lieder*, *Eichendorff-Lieder* and *Goethe-Lieder*. Overcome by his own brilliance, he informs friends of '*Fussreise*' (A Morning Walk): 'When you have heard this song you can have only one wish—to die.'

March Mahler completes a two-part tone poem, later entitled *Titan* and effectively the first version of his Symphony No. 1 in D major. This year he takes up the directorship of the Budapest Opera.

29 March Composer **Charles-Valentin Alkan** dies in Paris, aged 74.

7 May Lalo's *Le roi d'Ys* (The King of Ys) is staged at the Opéra-Comique, Paris. The three-act opera triumphs and becomes the composer's most famous work in France.

13 July Tchaikovsky writes in his diary: 'I have never encountered anything more false and foolish than the effort to get truth into opera. In opera everything is based upon the untrue.'

14 July Jesse H. Lippincott forms the North American Phonograph Company. As owner of the first record company, the Pittsburgh businessman fails to see any potential in the product beyond that of an office dictating machine.

3 October Gilbert and **Sullivan**'s *The Yeoman of the Guard* opens at the Savoy Theatre, London.

5 October Sullivan records a message on a phonograph for its inventor, Thomas Edison:

'… *I can only say that I am … astonished at the wonderful power you have developed, and terrified at the thought that so much hideous and bad music will be put on records forever.*'

Thomas Alva Edison with his cylinder phonograph

17 November Tchaikovsky introduces his Fifth Symphony in St Petersburg. It is the most tightly wrought of all the composer's symphonies, marked above all by a 'fate' motif appearing in each of the four movements.

1888 Wilhelm II becomes (last) German emperor (to 1918) • Britain establishes protectorates in Sarawak, Brunei and north Borneo • Serfdom is ended in Brazil • The Suez Canal is declared open to all ships at all times by the convention of Constantinople • 'Jack the Ripper' murders occur in London • John Boyd Dunlop (Scot) invents pneumatic bicycle tyres

• George Eastman (US) introduces the Kodak box camera • Georges Seurat (Fr) paints *La Parade du Cirque* • Vincent van Gogh (Neth) paints *Sunflowers* • Rudyard Kipling (Eng): *Plain Tales from the Hills* • Thomas Hardy (Eng): *Wessex Tales* • Edward Bellamy (US): *Looking Backward*

Brahms reworks his Piano Trio No. 1 in B major (Op. 8), originally written at the age of 20.

Debussy is captivated by Javanese gamelan music at the Paris Exposition Universelle.

Satie composes his first three unbarred, modal *Gnossiennes* for solo piano.

Verdi and **Boito** begin work on their final collaboration (and Verdi's last opera), *Falstaff*.

17 February Franck's Symphony in D minor (completed 1888) is premièred with just modest success by the Société des Concerts du Conservatoire in Paris. **Gounod** judges the work as 'the affirmation of incompetence pushed to dogmatic lengths'. History refutes him: it is one of the few late Romantic French symphonies to survive into the modern repertory.

14 May Massenet's four-act medieval fantasy *Esclarmonde* opens at the Opéra-Comique in Paris.

15 June John Philip Sousa (right) introduces his march *The Washington Post* at the newspaper's essay awards ceremony. The piece is so phenomenally successful that it significantly enhances the newspaper's reputation.

8 September Richard Strauss takes up his appointment as *Kapellmeister* to the Grand Duke of Saxe-Weimar-Eisenach.

21 October Strauss II's *Kaiser-Walzer* (Op. 437) is performed for the first time in Berlin.

8 November Dvořák completes his Eighth Symphony.

11 November Richard Strauss conducts the first performance of his tone poem *Don Juan* in Weimar. The success of the work advances his reputation as one of the leading German

composers of the day. This same year sees the composition of the tone poem *Tod und Verklärung* (Death and Transfiguration).

11 November Elgar's *Salut d'amour*, composed the previous year for violin and piano, is introduced in its orchestral version at the Crystal Palace, London. It is the composer's first enduring work.

20 November Mahler conducts *Titan* in Budapest. Conceived in five movements and billed as a 'Symphonic Poem in Two Parts', the work is both applauded and booed. 'My friends shunned me in terror … I wandered about like a leper', Mahler later recollects.

7 December Gilbert and **Sullivan**'s two-act operetta *The Gondoliers*—their last major success—opens at London's Savoy Theatre. The story, concerning the infant heir to the throne of Barataria, stolen by the Grand Inquisitor, has been inspired in part by Gilbert's own kidnapping, aged two, in Naples (see 1839).

1889 Benjamin Harrison becomes 23rd President of the USA • Japan forms a parliament with upper and lower houses, but Emperor Mutsuhito retains wide powers • Italy claims Ethiopia as an Italian protectorate; Menelik II becomes King of Ethiopia • Construction of the Panama Canal is halted by lack of funds • Pedro II of Brazil abdicates, and Brazil becomes a republic • The Eiffel Tower in Paris is completed • George Eastman (US) produces film roll for cameras • Vincent van Gogh (Neth) paints *Starry Night* • Auguste Rodin (Fr) completes sculpture of *The Burghers of Calais* • Jerome K. Jerome (Eng): *Three Men in a Boat* • George Bernard Shaw (Ire): *Fabian Essays*

Albéniz moves his family to London, where they live for the next three years.

Enrique Granados completes his 12 *Danzas españolas* for piano.

Nadezhda von Meck suddenly terminates **Tchaikovsky**'s annuity and breaks off all communications. It is speculated that she had learned of the composer's homosexuality, although financial embarrassment coupled with ill-health may have motivated her decision. Tchaikovsky is confused and devastated, having confided in her for many years.

15 January Tchaikovsky's enchanting ballet *The Sleeping Beauty* receives its first performance at the Mariinsky Theatre in St Petersburg. Its reception is lukewarm.

2 February Dvořák conducts the first performance of his Eighth Symphony in Prague, with great success. The influence of Bohemian folk melody is felt throughout much of the work, resonating deeply with the Czech nationalistic spirit.

17 May Pietro Mascagni (right), aged 26, makes his indelible mark on the operatic world with *Cavalleria rusticana* (Rustic Chivalry), the winning work of a one-act opera competition in Rome. Telling of an unfaithful soldier, a jealous girlfriend, an adulterous wife and her revengeful husband, the opera typifies Italian *verismo*—a true-to-life style featuring common people in contemporary, regional settings. By the end of the year Mascagni's one

enduring opus has played throughout Europe and North America.

10 September Elgar conducts the first performance of his *Froissart Overture* at the Worcester Public Hall during the Three Choirs Festival.

4 November Borodin's *Prince Igor*, completed by **Rimsky-Korsakov** and **Glazunov**, premières with reasonable success at the Mariinsky Theatre in St Petersburg, three years after the composer's death. The opera becomes one of the most important of the Russian repertory.

8 November César Franck dies in Paris, aged 67. Two days later, **Fauré**, **Widor**, **Lalo**, **Chabrier** and **Delibes** all attend his funeral.

8 December Czech composer **Bohuslav Martinů** is born in Polička, Bohemia. For the first 11 years of his life he lives with his family in a church tower.

19 December Tchaikovsky's tragic opera *The Queen of Spades* opens at the Mariinsky Theatre in St Petersburg. With libretto by the composer's brother, **Modest**, adapted from a short story by Pushkin, the opera wins immediate admiration from critics and public alike. Over the next 20 years it will secure its place in the international repertory.

21 December The final version of **Bruckner**'s Third Symphony is premièred by **Richter** in Vienna. Audience reaction is mixed but the event is considered a success. (See also 16 December 1877.)

1890 The Force Bill, protecting Black voters' rights, is rejected by the Senate (USA) • Kaiser Wilhelm II dismisses Otto von Bismarck as German Chancellor • Britain gives Heligoland to Germany in return for Zanzibar and Pemba • Britain annexes Uganda • Cecil Rhodes (Eng/SA) becomes Premier of Cape Colony • German East Africa (Tanganyika) becomes a German colony • Luxembourg becomes independent of the Netherlands • Journalist Nellie Bly (US) completes her circumnavigation of the globe in '72 days, six hours, 11 minutes and 14 seconds' • Vincent van Gogh (Neth) paints two versions of *Portrait of Dr Gachet* • Sir John Millais (Eng) paints *Dew-Drenched Furze*

Dvořák composes his concert overture triptych *Nature, Life and Love*. He later renames each overture to emphasise its individual identity: *In Nature's Realm, Carnival* and *Othello* (Opp. 91–93).

Rimsky-Korsakov begins work on the definitive version of his orchestral fantasia *Sadko* (first version 1867), completed the following year.

Wolf completes his *Spanisches Liederbuch* (Spanish Song Book), begun two years previously. The two-volume set comprises 44 translated settings of Spanish poetry from the 16th and 17th centuries. The following year Wolf will complete the first volume of his *Italienisches Liederbuch* (Italian Song Book).

10 January Austrian composer **Carl Zeller** secures his greatest success with the operetta *Der Vogelhändler* (The Bird Seller), first performed at the Theater an der Wien (Vienna).

16 January Stage composer **Léo Delibes** dies in Paris, aged 54.

March Mahler takes up his new appointment as conductor of the Hamburg Opera.

11 April Dvořák's *Dumky* Piano Trio (Op. 90) is heard for the first time, in Prague.

23 April Composer **Sergey Prokofiev** is born in Sontsovka, Ukraine.

26 April Tchaikovsky arrives in New York. In a letter to a Russian friend he writes: 'I am convinced that I am ten times more famous in America than in Europe. Several of my works … unknown even in Moscow, are frequently played here.'

5 May Walter Damrosch and **Tchaikovsky** conduct the inaugural concert of New York's Carnegie Hall (below).

15 June Tchaikovsky requests his publisher to buy him a recent musical invention by Auguste Mustel: the celesta. The instrument is sent secretly to St Petersburg, as Tchaikovsky is worried that Rimsky-Korsakov and Glazunov might get hold of one before him. He uses it later this year in his symphonic poem *Voyevoda*, but more famously the following year in the 'Dance of the Sugar-Plum Fairy' from his ballet *The Nutcracker*.

Summer Rachmaninov, aged 18, completes his First Piano Concerto, begun while studying at the Moscow Conservatory. He will revise it in 1917.

2 August Composer **Arthur Bliss** is born in Barnes, London.

9 October Dvořák's Requiem (1890) premières and delights the public at the Birmingham Music Festival. While in England the composer is awarded an honorary doctorate from Cambridge University.

10 October Delius achieves his first public performance with the Ibsen-inspired symphonic poem *Paa Vidderne* (On the Heights), introduced in Christiania.

12 December Brahms's Clarinet Trio in A minor (Op. 114) and Clarinet Quintet in B minor (Op. 115) are premièred in Berlin with the clarinettist **Richard Mühlfeld**, dedicatee of the two works.

1891 Germany, Austria and Italy renew their Triple Alliance; Kaiser Wilhelm II of Germany fails to persuade Britain to join • Nyasaland (now Malawi) becomes a British protectorate • Britain and Italy agree spheres of influence in East Africa • Building of the Trans Siberian Railroad is begun • Physicist Johnstone Stoney (Ire) coins the word 'electron' • Anthropologist Eugène Dubois (Neth) discovers bones of *Pithecanthropus erectus* (Java Man) • Paul Gauguin (Fr) paints *Women on the Beach* • Thomas Hardy (Eng): *Tess of The D'Urbervilles* • Rudyard Kipling (Eng): *The Light that Failed* • Oscar Wilde (Ire): *The Picture of Dorian Gray*

Ernest Chausson completes his *Poème de l'amour et de la mer* (Poem of love and the sea), scored for voice and orchestra.

Rachmaninov, aged 19, composes his stately and sombre Prelude in C sharp minor for piano. It forms part of his *Morceaux de Fantaisie*, Op. 3, and becomes a repertory essential—so much so that the composer will tire of it.

John Philip Sousa forms his 100-strong military Sousa Band to tour the United States.

16 January Massenet's opera *Werther*, based on Goethe's novel *The Sorrows of Young Werther*, opens in Vienna. It will ultimately vie with *Manon* as the composer's best-loved creation, although initially it claims little success.

February As **Richard Strauss** struggles to conduct a rehearsal of his tone poem *Macbeth* in Berlin, he receives crucial advice from **Bülow**: 'You should have the score in your head, not your head in the score!'

10 March French composer **Arthur Honegger** is born in Le Havre.

19 March Tchaikovsky presents *The Nutcracker* suite in St Petersburg, with music taken from his forthcoming ballet. (See 18 December.)

22 April French composer **Edouard Lalo** dies in Paris, aged 69.

28 April In Helsinki **Sibelius** establishes himself as a leading voice of Finnish music with *Kullervo*, a symphonic epic for soprano,

baritone, male chorus and orchestra, inspired by the poetry of the Kalevala. This year also marks the composition of his tone poem *En saga*.

21 May Ruggero Leoncavallo (below) triumphs with the raw emotions of *Pagliacci* (Clowns, or Strolling Players), staged at the Teatro Dal Verme, Milan, and conducted by **Toscanini**. Set in a prologue and two acts to the composer's own libretto, the opera adopts the *verismo* (social realism) style, popularised by **Mascagni**'s *Cavalleria Rusticana* (1890).

4 September French Composer **Darius Milhaud** is born in Aix-en-Provence.

26 September Dvořák, accompanied by his wife and two of his children, arrives in New York with a Te Deum (Op. 103) composed for the 400th anniversary of Columbus's discovery of America. The following month Dvořák takes up the directorship of the New York National Conservatory of Music with a promised salary of $15,000.

18 December Tchaikovsky presents the double-bill premières of his one-act opera *Iolanthe* and the ballet *The Nutcracker* (based on a story by E. T. A. Hoffmann) at the Mariinsky Theatre in St Petersburg. The ballet, commissioned as a companion piece to the opera, encounters a muted response.

18 December An epic journey from darkness to light, **Bruckner**'s revised Eighth Symphony is introduced under **Richter** in Vienna.

1892 The People's Party, founded in St Louis, Mo, urges financial reforms • Corruption in Panama Canal dealings causes scandal in France • In Egypt, Abbas Hilmi II (pro French, anti-British) succeeds Tewfik Pasha as khedive (ruler) • Russia suffers famine • The marriage age for girls in Italy is raised to 12 years • English physicist Oliver Heavside discovers the ionosphere • Pierre-Auguste Renoir (Fr) paints *Girls at the Piano* • Toulouse-Lautrec (Fr) paints *At the Moulin Rouge* • Paul Cézanne (Fr) paints *The Cardplayers* • Oscar Wilde (Ire): play *Lady Windermere's Fan* • Henrik Ibsen (Nor): play *The Master Butler* • Emile Zola (Fr): *The Debacle*

Cui publishes *Kaleidoscope* for violin and piano—24 miniatures all more or less forgotten except the popular encore piece *Orientale* (No. 9).

Dvořák's American compositions this year include his Ninth Symphony (see below) and two of his greatest chamber pieces, the String Quartet No. 12 in F major and String Quintet in E flat major.

Erik Satie composes his minimalist *Vexations* for piano, a short piece of music to be played 840 times. Avoiding tonal structures, the work deliberately creates forgettable material; played precisely it lasts 14 hours. The challenge is not met publicly until 1963.

1 February Puccini scores resounding success at Turin's Teatro Regio with *Manon Lescaut* despite several years of turmoil over the libretto, with contributions from no less than five authors. Unanimously praised, the opera soon establishes Puccini's reputation outside of Italy.

9 February Verdi's final opera, *Falstaff*, with libretto by **Boito**, opens at La Scala, Milan. Inspired by Shakespeare's plays *The Merry Wives of Windsor* and *King Henry IV*, the comic opera delights a loyal and reverent public. The composer turns 80 this year.

18 October French composer **Charles Gounod** dies in Saint-Cloud, aged 75.

Librettist Arrigo Boito with Giuseppe Verdi

28 October Tchaikovsky conducts the first performance of his Sixth Symphony in St Petersburg. The slow final movement of the work, ending in a mood of despair, confounds many in the audience. Tchaikovsky's brother, Modest, nicknames the symphony *Pathétique*.

6 November Tchaikovsky dies in St Petersburg, aged 53, having possibly contracted cholera by drinking un-boiled water. Rumours will surface about Tchaikovsky taking his own life to avoid a very public homosexual scandal.

13 November Sibelius introduces his patriotic *Karelia Suite* in Helsinki. Most of the audience talk through the performance.

16 December Premièred by the New York Philharmonic, **Dvořák**'s Ninth Symphony (*From the New World*) causes a sensation at the Carnegie Hall. Dvořák reports back to his publisher, 'The newspapers say no composer has ever before had such a triumph'.

23 December Humperdinck's *Hänsel und Gretel*, conducted by **R. Strauss**, opens at the Weimar Hoftheater. The composer's skilful melding of simple melody with Wagnerian harmonic colour gives the fairytale opera immediate appeal to audiences across Europe.

29 December Debussy's String Quartet in G minor is introduced by the Ysaÿe Quartet in Paris. Its impressionistic gestures and textures confuse most of the audience.

1893 The Independent Labour Party is founded in Britain • Financial panic in USA follows British investors' sales of US stock • Ivory Coast and Guinea become French colonies, and Dahomey becomes a French protectorate • Uganda becomes a British colony • In southern Africa, British troops suppress a rising by Matabele tribesmen • Anarchist outrages in France include a bomb explosion in the Chamber of Deputies • Laos becomes a French protectorate • Women are given the vote in New Zealand • Paul Gauguin (Fr) paints *Tahitian Landscape* • Edvard Munch (Nor) paints first version of *The Scream* • Oscar Wilde (Ire): *A Woman of No Importance*

1894

Fauré completes his song cycle *La bonne chanson*, inspired by his love for the singer Emma Bardac, who later becomes **Debussy**'s second wife.

12 February Conductor, pianist and composer **Hans von Bülow** dies in Cairo, aged 64. His body is shipped back to Berlin.

14 March Carl Nielsen's Symphony No. 1 in G minor (1892) enjoys a successful royal première under the baton of the Norwegian composer-conductor **Johan Svendsen** at the Concert Palace in Copenhagen. The symphony is pioneering in its use of progressive tonality, beginning in one key and ending in another.

16 March Massenet's *Thaïs* opens at the Paris Opéra. The opera will never attain the popularity of *Manon* or *Werther*, although it includes one of the most famous pieces of the violin repertory, *Méditation*, which serves as an entr'acte between Acts 2 and 3.

8 April Bruckner's commanding Fifth Symphony (revised version completed 1878) is first performed under **Franz Schalk** in Graz. Bruckner, too ill to attend, will never hear a performance of the work.

10 May In Weimar **Richard Strauss** introduces his first opera, *Guntram*, which manages only short-lived success (see 1895). On this same day he announces his engagement to **Pauline de Ahna**, the opera's lead soprano.

June Mahler completes his Second Symphony, *Resurrection*. The inspiration for its huge final choral movement has come from Klopstock's *Resurrection Ode*, a setting of which moved Mahler profoundly at the funeral of Hans von Bülow earlier this year.

13 September Composer **Emmanuel Chabrier** dies from the effects of syphilis, aged 53, in Paris. His collection of Impressionist paintings, pastels and etchings, including eight Monets, six Renoirs, eleven Manets (including *A Bar at the Folies-Bergère*, left), two Sisleys and one Cézanne, is sold off at auction two years later.

October Dvořák returns from his holiday in Bohemia to the National Conservatory of Music in New York, despite shortfalls in his salary. This year has seen the first performances of his String Quartet No. 12 and String Quintet (Op. 97), in Boston and New York respectively.

16 November Tenor **Enrico Caruso**, aged 21, makes his operatic début in **Mario Morelli**'s *L'amico francesco* in Naples.

20 November Russian composer, pianist and conductor **Anton Rubinstein** dies in Peterhof, outside St Petersburg, aged 64.

23 December Debussy's *Prélude à l'après-midi d'un faune* (Prelude to the Afternoon of a Faun) is premièred at a Société Nationale concert in Paris. Inspired by Stéphane Mallarmé's poem, the evocative orchestral piece presents, in the composer's own words, 'a series of scenes against which the dreams and desires of the Faun stir in the afternoon heat'. It captivates the audience, who immediately demand an encore. The critics respond unfavourably.

1894 French President Sadi Carnot is assassinated • Japan at war with China over Korea (until 1895) • Tsar Alexandr III of Russia dies; is succeeded by his son, Nikolai II • In France, army officer Alfred Dreyfus sentenced to life imprisonment for spying; evidence against him has been faked, and soon causes a public outcry • Italian forces invade Ethiopia • Inventor Hiram Maxim (US) experiments with a heavier-than-air flying machine • Bacteriologist Shibasaburo Kitasoto (Jap) isolates the bubonic plague germ • An inheritance tax is introduced in Britain • Monet (Fr) paints *Rouen Cathedral* • Rudyard Kipling (Eng): *The Jungle Book* • George Bernard Shaw (Ire): play *Arms and the Man*

Delius contracts syphilis while in Paris. It will later cause him paralysis and blindness.

Zdeněk Fibich completes his Op. 44 set of *Moods, Impressions and Reminiscences* for piano.

Greig composes his *Haugtussa* song cycle on poems by Arne Garborg.

Ernest Hogan publishes the earliest ragtime songs in America. He is accused of betraying his own race by imprudently issuing *All Coons Look Alike to Me*. It sells more than one million copies and initiates a wave of racist songs. This same year the songwriter **Ben Harney** publishes his early ragtime hit *You've Been a Good Old Wagon, But You've Done Broke Down*.

Richard Strauss completes *Till Eulenspiegels lustige Streiche* (Till Eulenspiegel's Merry Pranks). The tone poem is not universally appreciated, with some unimpressed by the earthy subject matter

of Till's adventures. Others are bemused by the music itself, including **Debussy**: 'An hour of music in an asylum … You do not know whether to roar with laughter or with pain.'

February Dvořák completes his masterful Cello Concerto in B minor amid deepening dissatisfaction with his job at the National Conservatory in America. Homesick, with little time to compose and inconsistent wages, he returns with his wife to Bohemia during the spring.

4 May The opera *Der Evangelimann* by the Austrian composer **Wilhelm Kienzl** enjoys instant success in Berlin.

10 July Composer **Carl Orff** is born in Munich.

10 August Robert Newman and **Henry Wood** establish the Summer Promenade Concerts at the Queen's Hall.

September Rachmaninov completes his Symphony No. 1 in D minor (see 1897).

16 November Richard Strauss stages his opera *Guntram* (premièred 1894) in Munich. What had been accepted provincially is now completely rejected, mainly due to Strauss's weak libretto.

16 November Composer **Paul Hindemith** is born in Hanau, near Frankfurt.

10 December Rimsky-Korsakov's opera *Christmas Eve*, a so-called 'Carol come-to-life' after a story by Gogol, débuts in St Petersburg.

13 December Gustav Mahler (left) conducts the first complete performance of his Second Symphony, *Resurrection*, in Berlin. Organised at the composer's own expense, the concert proves an overwhelming triumph with the public. Most critics dismiss what will become Mahler's greatest lifetime success.

1895 Armenians in Turkey form a revolutionary movement; Turks massacre many Armenians • Italian invaders are defeated by Ethiopians at Amba Alagi • Territories claimed by British South Africa Company named Rhodesia, after Cecil Rhodes • USA protests against brutal Spanish suppression of a Cuban uprising • Wilhelm Konrad Röntgen (Ger) detects X-rays • The Lumière brothers (Fr) begin motion picture screenings • Sir Frederick Leighton (Eng) paints *Flaming June* • Vasily Surikov (Russ) paints *The Conquest of Siberia by Yermak* • H. G. Wells (Eng): *The Time Machine* • Oscar Wilde (Ire): *The Importance of Being Ernest* • Henryk Sienkiewicz (Pol): *Quo Vadis*

Dvořák composes four symphonic poems inspired by the Czech poet K. J. Erben: *The Water Goblin*, *The Noon Witch*, *The Golden Spinning-Wheel* and *The Wild Dove* (Opp. 107–110).

Mahler composes his Third Symphony and completes the revisions to *Lieder eines fahrenden Gesellen* (Songs of a Wayfarer).

Alexander Scriabin composes his Piano Concerto in F-sharp minor.

23 January MacDowell's *Indian Suite*, based on Native American music, enthrals its first audience at the Metropolitan Opera House in New York. His Piano Concerto No. 1 (1882) also shares the programme. Later this year MacDowell becomes the first appointed professor of music at Columbia University.

1 February Puccini's opera *La bohème*, based on a story by Henry Murger, is introduced under **Toscanini** at the Teatro Regio, Turin. The critics are unenthusiastic, but their reviews have no impact: premières follow in no less than 20 countries over the next two years, including Argentina, Mexico and Egypt.

7 March Gilbert and **Sullivan**'s final comic operetta, *The Grand Duke*, makes little impression at the Savoy Theatre, London.

19 March Dvořák conducts the first performance of his Cello Concerto in B minor, in London. The critical reception is mixed. *The Musical Times* accuses the composer of mishandling the balance between cello and orchestra, and surrendering the more interesting material to the latter. 'We are by no

means sure that, as a violoncello concerto, this work will become a favourite', it adjudicates. History proves otherwise: it is the most popular cello concerto ever written.

28 March Umberto Giordano's historical *verismo* opera *Andrea Chénier* opens to wild applause at La Scala, Milan.

20 May Virtuoso pianist and composer **Clara Schumann** dies in Frankfurt, aged 76.

7 June Wolf's opera *Der Corregidor* (The Magistrate) is first staged in Mannheim.

11 October Anton Bruckner dies in Vienna, aged 72, leaving the finale of his Ninth Symphony unfinished. Thousands join his funeral procession three days later.

31 October American composer and pianist **Amy Beach**, aged 29, witnesses her *Gaelic* Symphony triumph at its official première in Boston.

27 November Richard Strauss conducts the first performance of his tone poem *Also sprach Zarathustra* (Thus Spake Zarathustra) in Frankfurt. He later writes: 'I did not intend to write philosophical music or to portray Nietzsche's great work in music. I wished to convey by musical means an idea of the development of the human race from its origins, through the various phases of its development, religious and scientific, up to Nietzsche's idea of the superman.'

27 December Inspired by a short story by Turgenev, **Chausson**'s *Poème* for violin and orchestra premières in Nancy, France.

1896 Italy renounces its protectorate over Ethiopia • Turks accept self-government for Crete • British forces begin the re-conquest of Sudan • France annexes the island of Madagascar • Scientist Alfred Nobel (Swed) dies; Nobel prizes instituted • The Olympic Games are revived in Athens • Henry Ford (US) makes his first automobile • Antoine Henri Becquerel (Fr) detects radiation from uranium • Akseli Gallen-Kallela (Fin) paints *Defense of the Sampo* • Paul Cézanne (Fr) paints *Annecy Lake* • Anton Chekhov (Russ): play *The Seagull* • Theodor Herzl (Aus): *The Jewish State*, advocating the founding of a Jewish state in Palestine

1897

Debussy's lover, Gabrielle Dupont, discovers evidence of the composer's affair with Rosalie Texier. Heartbroken, she shoots herself, non-fatally. (See also 1904.)

Sousa composes his march *Stars and Stripes Forever*. It will earn him more than $300,000 during his lifetime.

23 January Humperdinck introduces 'Sprechgesang' (speech-song) in the melodrama *Königskinder* (The King's Children), which enjoys a rapturous reception in Munich. The composer transforms the work into a fully sung opera for a New York première in 1910.

23 February Mahler converts from from Judaism to Roman Catholicism in order to qualify for the post of director at the Vienna Opera.

12 March D'Indy's opera *Fervaal* is staged for the first time at the Théâtre de la Monnaie in Brussels.

27 March Rachmaninov witnesses his First Symphony (1895) introduced disastrously under **Glazunov** in St Petersburg. Reviewing the première **César Cui** (right) writes: 'If there existed a conservatory in Hell and one of its students was ordered to write a programmatic symphony on the Ten Plagues of Egypt, were he to compose one like Mr Rachmaninov's, he would have succeeded brilliantly.' Rachmaninov's confidence is shattered and over the next two years he suffers severe depression. The symphony is not performed again until 1945, a year after the composer's death.

3 April Johannes Brahms dies in Vienna, aged 63. His funeral is held three days later, with **Dvořák** and **Busoni** among the mourners. He is laid to rest in the Zentralfriedhof, close to the graves of Beethoven and Schubert.

6 May Leoncavallo's *La bohème* is first performed at the Teatro Fenice in Venice. Failing to match the cohesion and emotional intensity of **Puccini**'s version (1896), his opera struggles for recognition from the outset.

18 May Dukas conducts the first performance of his symphonic poem *L'apprenti sorcier* (The Sorcerer's Apprentice) at the Société Nationale, Paris. The magical evocation of the apprentice and unruly broomstick wins Dukas concert-hall immortality.

29 May Austrian composer **Erich Wolfgang Korngold** is born in Brno.

September Mahler takes up the post of *Kapellmeister* at the Vienna Opera. **Hugo Wolf**, suffering bouts of syphilis-related derangement, insists that it is he who holds the post, having sacked Mahler. Wolf is ushered off to a lunatic asylum.

13 November Delius's fantasy overture *Over the Hills and Far Away* is performed for the first time in Elberfeld, Germany.

1898

Will Marion Cook's *Clorindy, or The Origin of the Cake Walk* makes history as the first musical written, produced and performed by African-Americans.

Grieg draws on Norwegian folk themes in his four *Symphonic Dances*.

Charles Ives, aged 23, works on his First Symphony while studying under the composer **Horatio Parker** at Yale University. Ives graduates this year.

MacDowell composes his *Sea Pieces* for piano.

Richard Strauss completes his tone poem *Ein Heldenleben* (A Hero's Life). Controversially, the hero of the work's programme seems to be Strauss himself; the hero's wife thus Pauline Strauss (represented by solo violin), and the hero's adversaries, we infer, Strauss's critics. He later remarks, 'I do not see why I should not compose a symphony about myself. I find myself quite as interesting as Napoleon or Alexander.'

Joseph Suk marries **Dvořák**'s daughter, Otilka.

7 January Rimsky-Korsakov's opera *Sadko*, based on an epic folk tale about a wandering minstrel, opens in Moscow.

8 March Richard Strauss's tone poem *Don Quixote* (1897), subtitled *Fantastic Variations on a Theme of Knightly Character*, premières in Cologne.

24 May British composer **Ethel Smyth** has her first opera, *Fantasio*, introduced at Weimar.

26 September Composer **George Gershwin** is born to Russian Jewish immigrant parents in Brooklyn.

October Elgar, extemporising at the piano, passes over a tune that instantly catches his wife's attention. At her request, he repeats what he had just played and then begins to vary the idea, conjuring up musical portraits of their friends: 'Powell would have done this ... Nevinson would have looked at it like this ... Who does this remind you of...?' So begins the *Enigma* Variations: 'Commenced in a spirit of humour and continued in deep seriousness,' according to the composer.

November Delius buys Gauguin's Tahitian nude *Nevermore* for 500 francs.

11 November Samuel Coleridge-Taylor (below) has his cantata *Hiawatha's Wedding Feast* premièred under the baton of **Charles Stanford** at the Royal College of Music. Its immediate appeal establishes the composer's reputation in England and America.

7 December Rimsky-Korsakov's 'dialogue opera' *Mozart and Salieri*, based on Pushkin's romanticised tragedy, is first staged in Moscow. **Rachmaninov** plays the piano behind the scenes.

10 December André Messager, newly-appointed musical director of the Opéra-Comique, stages his operetta *Véronique*.

1898 USA declares war on Spain over the Cuban rebellion; ends with Treaty of Paris: Cuba gains independence and Spain cedes Puerto Rico, Guam and the Philippines to the USA • The US annexes Hawaii • Emile Zola writes an open letter, 'J'Accuse', to the French president in the case of officer Alfred Dreyfus; Zola is sentenced for libel, but flees to England • Scientists Marie and Pierre Curie (Fr) discover radium • Auguste Rodin (Fr) sculpts *The Kiss* • Henri Matisse (Fr) paints *Maisons à Fenouillet* • Henry James (US): *The Turn of the Screw* • H. G. Wells (Eng): *The War of the Worlds*

Francis Barraud paints a picture of his late dog, Nipper, listening to a phonograph. Finally settling on the title *His Master's Voice*, he sells it to the Gramophone Company for £100.

Ives begins work on his Second Symphony, whilst still trying to complete his first. Both works are completed by 1902, but later revised. The composer (and soon to be full-time insurance broker) will have to wait half a century for their complete performance.

Scott Joplin composes his *Maple Leaf Rag*. He shrewdly acquires a one-cent royalty on each copy sold through the publishers John Stark & Son. Sales are slow at first, but will pass the half-million mark within ten years. (See also 13 September.)

Ravel, aged 24, composes his *Pavane pour une infante défunte* (Pavane for a Dead Princess) for solo piano. He will orchestrate the work in 1910.

7 January French composer **Francis Poulenc** is born in Paris.

15 February French composer **Georges Auric** is born in Lodève, near Montpellier.

26 February Bruckner's complete Sixth Symphony is premièred posthumously in Vienna.

3 March Richard Strauss introduces his sixth tone poem, *Ein Heldenleben* (A Hero's Life), in Frankfurt. Many critics frown on what they regard as Strauss's pseudo-autobiographical ego-trip. (See also 1898.)

26 April Sibelius explores Finnish national consciousness in his Symphony No. 1 in E minor, first performed in Helsinki. Aged 33, Sibelius is now composing full time thanks to the award of a state pension.

3 June Austrian composer **Johann Strauss II**, the 'Waltz King', dies in Vienna, aged 73.

10 June Composer **Ernest Chausson** (right), cycling with his children in Limary, Seine-et-Oise, crashes into a wall and dies from his injuries, aged 44.

19 June Elgar's *Variations on an Original Theme* (*Enigma*) is introduced under **Hans Richter** at St James's Hall, London. The 42-year-old's first piece for large orchestra is a resounding success and marks a career turning point. (See also October 1898.)

September Schoenberg, aged 25, composes his atmospheric string sextet *Verklärte Nacht* (Transfigured Night). Musically indebted to Wagner, the work is inspired by the poem *Weib und die Welt* (Woman and World) by Symbolist Richard Dehmel.

> *A wave of vulgar, filthy and suggestive music has inundated the land. Nothing but ragtime prevails, and the cakewalk with its obscene posturings, its lewd gestures. It is artistically and morally depressing, and should be suppressed by press and pulpit.*

13 September From the *Musical Courier*.

19 October Debussy marries Rosalie (Lily) Texier. This year also sees the completion of his three *Nocturnes* for orchestra: *Nuages, Fêtes, Sirènes*.

2 November Grieg's beautiful song cycle *Haugtussa* is introduced in Kristiania, Norway.

1899 In South Africa, war begins between British and Boers • The USA faces insurrection of the Philippines • Britain acquires Tonga and Savage islands • A Geneva conference establishes a permanent international Court of Arbitration at The Hague, Netherlands • Motor omnibuses are introduced in London, England • Monet (Fr) paints *Bridge over a Pond of Water Lilies* • Paul Gauguin (Fr) paints *Maternity* • Peder S. Krøyer (Nor/Den) paints *Summer Evening on Skagen's Beach* • Leo Tolstoy (Russ): *The Resurrection* • Joseph Conrad (Pol/UK): *Heart of Darkness* (first published in *Blackwood's Magazine*) • Zoologist Ernst Heinrich Haeckel (Ger): *The Riddle of the Universe*

1900–1949

1900–1949

N EVER IN the history of the world has there been such a turbulent half-century. Two world wars ravaged the social landscape, the second the most devastating conflict in the history of mankind. In between, economies and empires crumbled, and Stalin and Hitler began unprecedented genocidal campaigns that would see innocent civilians slaughtered in their tens of millions.

In spite of man's inhumanity to man, great advances were made. The discovery of penicillin and manufacture of insulin saved countless lives; quantum mechanics opened up the paradoxes of the sub-atomic world, while Einstein's General Theory of Relativity explained the complex interaction of gravity, space and time. In many countries across the globe women finally obtained full voting rights. Transportation evolved rapidly: motorcars and buses replaced horses, railway networks increased, and passenger air travel took off in the 1920s. The entertainment and information industries were revolutionised by records, film, radio and early television.

The musical world responded with its own age of innovation and discovery, confronting tradition with a bold challenge to tonal logic. Following the First World War, Romanticism finally gave way to new 'objective' approaches to composition, consolidated primarily in the movements of neo-classicism and serialism. Popular idioms such as ragtime, jazz, blues and cabaret infiltrated 'high art' music, which itself struggled increasingly to maintain wide cultural relevance.

The musical landscape at the start of the century

Romanticism remained the dominant force in music until the First World War. Until that time, shifting musical values, provoked by such trends as Symbolism, Expressionism, Primitivism and Cubism, as well as the analytical pursuits of ethnomusicology, challenged but did not overpower established traditions. Leading composers effectively perpetuating the Romantic spirit included Mahler, Strauss, Grieg, Rimsky-Korsakov, Massenet and Fauré; and among the slightly fresher faces, Puccini, Elgar, Sibelius, Albéniz, Suk, Ravel, Rachmaninov and the American Amy Beach —to mention a cosmopolitan mix. If some were beginning to undermine the conventions of tonality (Mahler and Strauss, for example), their harmonic language did not itself define a radically new era, as it remained rooted in the Romantic 'language of feeling'.

Even Debussy's symbolism-impressionism and Schoenberg's expressionism perpetuated a subjective compositional approach. Schoenberg's

◀ *Girl with a Mandolin* by Pablo Picasso, Paris, 1910. Picasso provided costumes and scenery to several important ballets in the early century, including Satie's *Parade* (1917), Falla's *El sombrero de tres picos* (1919) and Stravinsky's *Pulcinella* (1919/20).

transition from the tonal *Verklärte Nacht* (1899) to the atonal monodrama *Erwartung* (1909) was one that involved increasing chromaticism to the point where key centres evaporate; yet this remained, as the composer himself insisted, *heartfelt* music. Schoenberg was reaching into the unconscious mind with a musical language that carried no overt cultural codes, his work resonating with the internal worlds of Freudian psychoanalysis and Kandinsky's abstract art.

That both Debussy and Schoenberg were reacting against the Romantic order is, at the same time, undeniable. Debussy's idiom is often impersonal and he rejected Romantic excess; so too did Schoenberg in his expressionist atonal pieces, which also renounced sentimentalism. And here we find a connection to a more widespread revolution, that of the variously named 'back-to-Mozart' or 'back-to-Bach' movement. Max Reger (1873–1916) and Ermanno Wolf-Ferrari (1876–1948) were leaders in this field, controlling late-Romantic chromaticism within tightly organised 18th-century forms to produce 20th-century variants of Baroque suites and Classical opera. Their approach may have been anticipated in places by Brahms, even by Tchaikovsky and Grieg, but this broader musical objectivity laid crucial foundations for the detached, unsentimental manner of neo-classicism. Such diverse composers as Strauss, Busoni, Nielsen, Elgar, Satie and Debussy were directly affected by this mindset in the first decade of the century.

Back-
to-Bach
movement

Béla Bartók's unsentimental and analytical approach to Hungarian folk music was another manifestation of artistic objectivity. And while Igor Stravinsky made no academic study of Russian folk music, he too pursued a nationalist aesthetic of increasing emotional detachment. The most important pre-war musical upheaval, therefore, was not so much the attack on tonality, rather the rebuff of the subjective spirit that lies at the very heart of Romanticism.

Late Romanticism

On the stage: Puccini and Strauss

Giacomo
Puccini

Giacomo Puccini (1858–1924) and Richard Strauss (1864–1949) dominated early 20th century opera. By 1900 both composers were famous: Puccini for the operas *Manon Lescaut* and *La bohème*, Strauss as a conductor and the creator of tone poems (see *Chapter 6*).

With *La bohème* Puccini had approached the realm of *verismo* opera, a style that allowed him to explore the sordid emotions of the character Scarpia in *Tosca* (1900). Critics denounced *Tosca* for its offensive mix of religion, sadistic depravity, murderous revenge and suicide; the public, however, were captivated, and within three years the opera had been produced in nearly 30 countries worldwide. In both *Tosca* and *Madama Butterfly* (1904) Puccini created operas that do not require the audience's close comprehension of the sung word itself. He demanded simplified narratives so that intention and drama might be self-evident from actions, sets, costumes, lighting, direction and, of course, musical language. In a sense this was Puccini's re-imagination of Wagner's 'total artwork', with all the integral parts of opera working together in magical synergy. Wagnerian

depth it lacked, but such immediacy gave his music the widest popular appeal. Puccini proclaimed that his priority was 'to make people weep'.

Puccini thrived on diverse styles and influences, the exotic especially. In *Madama Butterfly* pentatonicism and authentic Japanese melodies convey native colour, and serving a similar function are the American folk idioms of *La fanciulla del West* (The Girl of the Golden West, 1910). The unfinished *Turandot* (1924) brought an altogether more sophisticated integration of 'world' music. In Carlo Gozzi's tale of a vindictive Chinese princess, Puccini drew orientalisms into the very soul of emotional expression, as in the pentatonicism of Liù's imploring aria 'Signore ascolta' from Act I. The opera revealed the composer at his most progressive, its musical language coloured by whole-tone, modal and bitonal harmonies, while at the same time maintaining remarkable melodic appeal.

Melody was Puccini's trump card; it flowed effortlessly from his pen, leaving younger compatriots like Umberto Giordano (1867–1948) and Italo Montemezzi (1875–1952) competing for second-best recognition. From the wide-ranging intensity of 'O soave fanciulla' (*La bohème*) and intimate delicacy of 'O mio babbino caro' (*Il trittico: Gianni Schicchi*, 1918), to the climactic power of 'Nessun dorma' (*Turandot*), Puccini's melodic fertility and technical command secured his fame and fortune. The great tradition of Italian opera, predominant on the international stage since the 17th century, fell into sudden decline following Puccini's death in 1924.

In Germany, Engelbert Humperdinck (1854–1921), famous for his opera *Hänsel und Gretel* (1893), found his rank usurped by Richard Strauss, who established himself as the nation's leading opera composer with a work even more controversial than Puccini's *Tosca*. This was his third opera, the explosive one-act 'stage tone-poem' *Salome* (1905), based on Oscar Wilde's narrative. The theatrical presentation of biblical characters was still controversial at this time, so by fashioning shocking entertainment out of a biblical tale of depravity, the opera provoked a huge outcry, as had Wilde's play. Strauss revelled in the story's uncompromising eroticism, wickedness and butchery, creating a leitmotivic score that climaxes in frenzied dissonance following the execution of John the Baptist. The shock factor is ramped up with a time-honoured 'mad-scene', where eerie textures and restless harmonies paint the moon-lit madness of Salome, who fondles and kisses the decapitated head of the prophet. Herod, outraged, orders

Richard Strauss

her death and a terrifying orchestral pounding impels the soldiers' heavy shields as they crush Salome to death.

Strauss's next opera, the one-act *Elektra* (1909), launched a 20-year collaborative partnership with the librettist Hugo von Hofmannsthal (1874–1929). In this Greek tale of revenge Strauss again adapted his methods of leitmotivic tone-poem writing and ventured periodically into atonality. *Elektra* epitomised modernity, and its brutal harmonies and rhythms challenged audiences. Fearing the logical evolution of his musical language, as well as the detrimental effect on his wallet, Strauss subsequently back-peddled, reverting to 'safer' harmonies in *Der Rosenkavalier* (The Knight of the Rose, 1910). Set in mid-18th-century Vienna, the work tapped into the popular re-interpretation of *opera buffa*, following the lead of Ermanno Wolf-Ferrari in *I quatro rusteghi* (The Four Curmudgeons, 1906) and *Il segreto di Susanna* (Susanna's Secret, 1909). Strauss filled his own modern-day take on Mozart–da Ponte opera with abundant lyricism and a colourful array of Viennese waltzes *alla* Lanner and Johann Strauss II. The three-act comedy received thunderous applause at Dresden in 1911 and enjoyed spectacular success across Europe.

Strauss and Hofmannsthal never came close to repeating the triumph of *Der Rosenkavalier*. Their satirical chamber opera *Ariadne auf Naxos*, presenting an 'opera within an opera', gained just modest success (upon revision) in 1916, and the fairy-tale *Die Frau ohne Schatten* (The Woman Without a Shadow, 1917) fared no better when it made the stage in 1919. Set in both spirit and mortal worlds, *Die Frau* is a heavily symbolic study of motherhood and human values, most importantly compassion, selflessness and love. Hofmannsthal's libretto baffled audiences and critics (and still does), but the music, frequently lush and Romantic, has given this opera longevity—indeed some regard this as Strauss's finest score. Barak's spirit-world aria 'Mir Anvertraut' (Entrusted to me), leading into the reconciliation duet with his wife, is just one of many highlights. Strauss composed 15 operas in all, including *Arabella* (1932), his last with Hofmannsthal, and culminating with the one-act 'conversation piece' on the subject of opera itself, *Capriccio* (1941).

In the concert hall

During the early years of the century, Elgar and Delius drew international attention to England's musical renaissance, Albéniz and Granados in Spain melded impressionism with the Romantic absorption of folk idioms, and

Sibelius in Finland and Nielsen in Denmark wrought post-Romantic tonal styles out of the 19th-century symphonic tradition (see later sections). In Paris, a respected vanguard preserved the Romantic spirit at the same time that Satie, Ravel and Debussy were inventing modernist alternatives. Gustave Charpentier responded to the *verismo* movement with his opera *Louise* (1900), while Saint-Saëns penned his Cello Concerto No. 2 in D minor (1902) and created one of the first original film scores, for *L'assassinat du duc de Guise* (1908). Jules Massenet maintained his reputation as France's foremost opera composer with important revivals and the occasional new success, such as *Don Quichotte* (1910). Fauré was writing some of his most beloved chamber pieces at this time, including the Piano Quintet No. 1 (1905) and song cycle *La chanson d'Eve* (1910). Never prolific, Fauré was director of the Paris Conservatoire from 1905 to 1920 and found little time to compose. Even so, as a deaf septuagenarian he wrote several repertory classics: the Violin Sonata No. 2 (1917), two cello sonatas (1917/21), the Piano Quintet No.2 (1921) and his one and only String Quartet (1924). His late style could be markedly severe and chromatic, although the music is equally characterised by heartfelt lyricism and Romantic ardour.

Fauré

Gustav Mahler, one of the world's most famous conductors, pursued a busy and demanding schedule that did much to exacerbate his failing health towards the end of his life. Following ten years as director of the Vienna Opera (1897–1907) he was diagnosed with a serious heart problem, yet he summoned the energy to make several trips to the USA to conduct seasons with the Metropolitan Opera and the New York Philharmonic. Composing was work on the side for Mahler, but it was he who brought to a climax the Austro-German Romantic symphonic tradition (see also *Chapter 6*).

Mahler

As Romantic works, Mahler's symphonies reflect the world through the subjective perspective of their creator. A child-like playfulness defines much of the Fourth (1900), which draws on the song 'Das Himmlische Leben' (from the composer's *Des Knaben Wunderhorn*) in its final movement to describe a child's notion of heaven. In the Fifth Symphony (1902), a work renowned for its captivating Adagietto, he returned to a purely instrumental and apparently non-programmatic form. Its evolving, angular themes, unexpected mood shifts and complex contrapuntalism did not go down well with either the critics or public. In fact, Mahler endured a series of disappointing premières. The dark and personal Sixth (1904; revised

◀ Gustav Mahler, 1907. Under his direction the Vienna Opera flourished, though he was impossibly demanding and frequently worked his musicians to exhaustion. As a symphonic composer he drew on uncommonly wide frames of reference in an attempt to make sense of life and meaning.

1906), with Classically-organised movements culminating in a gargantuan, tragic finale, was marred by Mahler's own nervous conducting on the night. Perhaps he feared he was tempting ill fortune, assailing and ultimately killing off the 'hero' (himself?) in the finale with three 'hammer-blows of fate'. The Seventh (1905), which like the Second, Fourth and Fifth is constructed with progressive tonality (beginning and ending in different keys), 'was scarcely understood by the public', as Mahler's wife Alma recalled.

Symphony of a Thousand

The Eighth (1907), premièred at Munich in September 1910, rewarded Mahler with a first-night triumph. In the year of its completion Mahler made his famous proclamation to Sibelius: 'the symphony must be like the world; it must embrace everything'. The *Symphony of a Thousand*—so called for its colossal vocal and instrumental forces—was his most complete fulfilment of this edict. Structured in two parts, the first is based on a Medieval Latin text, *Veni, Creator Spiritus* (Come, Creative Spirit), a 'hymn' to the Holy Spirit; the second is a dramatic realisation of the final scene from Goethe's *Faust*, part II, where Faust receives salvation. The end product is not dissimilar to a life-affirming oratorio. Mahler couldn't help but enthuse about his creation: 'Just imagine,' he wrote to the conductor William Mengelberg, 'that the universe is beginning to sound and ring. It is no longer human voices, but circling planets and suns.'

Das Lied von der Erde

The year 1907 brought Mahler professional trauma and emotional crises, with an acrimonious end to his directorship of the Vienna Opera, the loss of his daughter Maria to diphtheria, and the discovery of his own critical heart condition. (It was hard for the Mahlers not to make a supernatural connection between these events and the fate-themed Sixth Symphony.) He consequently sank into the gloom and despair of the symphonic song cycle *Das Lied von der Erde* (The Song of the Earth, 1908) and the Ninth Symphony (1909), neither of which he lived to hear performed. The contrast with the optimism of the Eighth symphony could hardly be greater. Based on six ancient Chinese poems, *Das Lied* is pantheistic and bleak, contemplating life in all its transient beauty while burdened with a sense of emptiness and desolation. Its music plumbs astonishing metaphysical, dualistic depths and in no other work did Mahler bring to pass such uninterrupted genius. In his Ninth Symphony he continued to bid the world a bitter farewell, and yet perhaps with a message of peace and acceptance in the sublime final movement. Mahler left his Tenth Symphony unfinished when he died in Vienna on 18 May 1911, aged 50.

Sergei Rachmaninov

The pre-war period witnessed the ascendancy of Sergei Rachmaninov (1873–1943), successor to Tchaikovsky and the last of the Romantic heroic virtuosos. Following his studies at the Moscow Conservatory, Rachmaninov gained early fame with the brooding Prelude in C sharp minor (1892) and critical commendation for his opera *Aleko*, introduced at the Bolshoi in 1893. However, his ambitious First Symphony (1895) brought only humiliation at its première in 1897, perhaps due in part to some poor conducting by Glazunov. Rachmaninov's confidence was shattered, so he decided to seek creative revitalisation through hypnotherapy. It seemed to work. He returned to the concert platform in 1901 with his voluptuous Piano Concerto No. 2 and launched one of the most popular pieces of the 20th century.

◀ Sergei Rachmaninov in 1934, the year he wrote and premièred *Rhapsody on a Theme of Paganini.*

When Rachmaninov embarked on his first tour of the USA in 1909 he took with him his recently completed Piano Concerto No. 3, a work more technically demanding than No. 2, less obviously tuneful and structurally more complex. He introduced it in November of that year under the direction of Walter Damrosch in New York, and then returned to the city two months later to play it under Mahler. Subsequent European tours served to increase Rachmaninov's popularity and promote his wider output, one characterised by a pervasive melancholy (he adored the minor mode), formal conservatism, powerful themes and a distinctive Russian flavour. This includes his Second Symphony (1907), the symphonic poem *Isle of the Dead* (1909), the *Vespers* (1915) and many outstanding pieces for solo piano, such as the Preludes of Op. 23 (1903) and Op. 32 (1910). Most of his 80 songs were composed before the war, a number of which retain an important place in the Russian repertory.

Following the 1917 Revolution Rachmaninov moved his family out of Russia and took up residency in the USA. Based in New York, he undertook fatiguing touring schedules with frequent visits to Europe, allowing him little time for composition. His post-war output is therefore slight, but includes the ever-popular *Rhapsody on a Theme of Paganini* (1934) and the bracing Third Symphony (1936), both pieces written at the composer's Swiss summer villa at Lake Lucerne. In the symphony especially, Rachmaninov acknowledged the more objective world of twentieth-century modernism. Shortly before the outbreak of WWII he returned to the USA where he wrote his final composition, the *Symphonic Dances* (1940), and created the definitive version of his Fourth Piano Concerto (1926/41).

Debussy and Ravel: Impressionism, Symbolism and Exoticism

One of the most important innovators in the history of music, Claude Debussy (1862–1918) was the earliest composer to offer a convincing challenge to the centuries-old tonal tradition. He enjoyed a truly idiosyncratic mastery of rhythm, harmony and texture, and claimed that 'the primary aim of French music is to give pleasure'. Multi-layered, exotic, richly colouristic, his music broadly pursued a Romantic 'language of feeling', while abjuring extravagance and sentimentalism.

Debussy was strongly influenced by the symbolist movement. While he was creating his breakthrough orchestral piece *Prélude à laprès midi d'un faune* in response to Mallarmé's symbolist poetry (see *Chapter 6*), he was at the same time converting Maurice Maeterlinck's symbolist play *Pelléas and Mélisande* (1892) into his first—and last—opera. The music was mostly completed by 1895, with orchestration, a few amendments and some extra interludes following in 1901/2. In this subtle opera of ill-fated love, action surrenders to atmosphere and emotion: the allegorical world-on-stage is dream-like and the characters elusive. Debussy seized on Wagner's leitmotif principle, but took this further into the psychological realm to suggest states of mind and poetic impressions. His syllabic recitative achieved a new intensity in its minute reflection of the patterns of spoken French, while melody was all but banished for its limited expressivity. Debussy created a characteristically equivocal sound-world, with unsettled whole-tone and modal harmonies adding apposite mystery, especially to the more fatalistic elements of the narrative. *Pelléas and Mélisande* was recognised by the *Grove* dictionary in 1911 as 'the most important of recent musical events in Paris'.

Pelléas and Mélisande (1902)

La mer

In 1905 Debussy completed his first piano collection of *Images* and the three symphonic sketches of *La mer* (The Sea), the closest thing to a symphony he ever wrote. He described his sound-world as one of 'colours and rhythmicised time', while his contemporaries began to label his music 'impressionist', suggesting a parallel with the painting style of Monet and Manet. Debussy was irritated

▶ Claude Debussy and company at Eragny, 1902. Left to right: Paul Poujaud (friend and lawyer), Debussy, Pierre Lalo, Lilly Debussy (the composer's first wife) and Paul Dukas.

◀ *The Celestial Art*, lithograph by the French symbolist artist Odilon Redon, mid 1890s. 'My drawings inspire and are not to be defined. They determine nothing. They place us, as does music, in the ambiguous realm of the undetermined.' The aesthetics of symbolism shaped the development of Debussy's mature style.

by the term (partly because critics used it too loosely, he felt), yet its application has persisted. In *La mer* he conveyed his subjective response to the sea, creating colouristic impressions by exploiting the expressive potential of musical materials beyond traditional tonal organisation and thematic development. Pentatonic, octatonic (alternating tones and semitones), whole-tone and chromatic elements are absorbed into multi-layered textures to suggest fleeting eddies, violent surges, the play of sunlight and gusts of wind. This wonderfully atmospheric work might well bring to the listener's mind the seascapes of J. M. W. Turner, whose proto-Impressionist painting Debussy adored.

Debussy's final orchestral concert pieces were the three *Images* (1905–12), including the popular *Ibéria*. He then pushed his language to expressive (at times atonal) extremes in the orchestral ballet *Jeux* (1913), a single movement of seemingly disconnected themes, knocked about with gestures loosely reminiscent of a game of tennis. Vaslav Nijinsky choreographed and danced at the première, which enjoyed little success. What impression the ballet did make was swept away just days later by the première of another progressive ballet, Stravinsky's *The Rite of Spring*.

Piano music

At the core of Debussy's output is the piano music, including *Estampes* (1903), *Children's Corner* (1908), a second collection of *Images* (1907), two sets of *Préludes* (1910, 1913) and the *Etudes* (1915). It is easy to associate the *Estampes*, *Préludes* and *Images* with 'impressionism'. Many pieces convey wistful moods and vague description; textural contrast is common, but directional development is avoided. Several are exotic, such as 'Pagodes' (from *Estampes*) and 'Et la lune descend sur le temple qui fut' (from *Images II*), mesmerising pieces characterised by pentatonicism and static harmonic fields. Debussy's last works, including the Cello Sonata (1915) and the Violin Sonata (1917), reflected the 'absolute' world of the *Etudes*, avoiding extra-musical associations and treading a more objective, anti-Romantic path.

Maurice Ravel

Maurice Ravel (1875–1937) was similarly labelled an impressionist. A pupil of Fauré at the Paris Conservatoire, he matured quickly and shared Debussy's appreciation of 'world music', Spanish culture in particular. The *Shéhérazade* song-cycle (1903), *Rapsodie espagnole* (1907) and the comic opera *L'heure espagnole* (1909), as well as later compositions such as *Tzigane* (1924) and the famous *Boléro* (1928), at once testify to Ravel's exquisite manipulation of orchestral colour and his infatuation with the exotic. His pre-war music, while emotionally controlled, maintained a strong link to the Romantic tradition. He was less daring than Debussy, so while we find extended chords (commonly 9ths and 11ths), and modal and whole-tone harmonies, they are couched more firmly within tonal structures. The magical orchestral-choral ballet *Daphnis et Chloé* (1912), arguably his finest achievement, features all the tools of his trade: modes (notably the Dorian), a comprehensive tonal system, lyrical melodies, sensuous harmonies and vivid orchestration.

Piano music   Ravel's importance to the piano repertory begins with the renowned *Pavane pour une infante défunte*, composed in 1899. Two years later, in his shimmering *Jeux d'eau* (Water Games), he created a milestone example of musical impressionism. Seeking to capture 'the sprays of water, the cascades and the brooks', he collapsed the boundaries between melody and harmony with rapid passages of broken 7th and 9th chords, major-second chordal arpeggiations, bitonal harmonies and sliding chromaticism. With this piece Ravel began to emerge from Debussy's shadow. Other popular piano works include *Miroirs* (1905), the children's suite *Mother Goose* for four hands (1910) and *Valses nobles et sentimentales* (1911). In the suite *Le Tombeau de Couperin* (1917), Ravel again showed his fondness for dance forms and images from the past, looking to 18th-century France. This is a suite of Baroque forms—prelude, fugue, minuet, toccata, etc.—although the musical language belongs to the 20th century. The composer dedicated each move- ment to the memory of a friend who had died in the Great War.

1920s–30s   In later years Ravel maintained his obsession with timbral and textural detail while becoming ever more eclectic. The turbulent 'choreographic poem' *La valse* (1920), the fairy-tale theatre piece *L'enfant et les sortilèges* (1925), the ever-climaxing *Boléro* and the impulsive *Piano Concerto for the Left Hand* (1931) each offer unique sound-worlds. One of the most striking stylistic developments of Ravel's career was his assimilation of jazz and blues. He completed his Sonata for Violin and Piano (1927) shortly before his first American tour, anticipating the locals would enjoy its breezy slow movement, subtitled 'Blues'. The glittering Piano Concerto in G major (1931) occasionally brings to mind Gershwin's bluesy Piano Concerto in F (1925), although similarities are superficial; Ravel was the superior craftsman and one of the greatest orchestrators of all time.

Second Viennese School

Schoenberg and the 'emancipation of the dissonance'

More than any other composer, the Austro-Hungarian Arnold Schoenberg (1874–1951) is seen as the revolutionary architect of 20th-century art music. Atonality, the abandonment of tonality in its traditional sense, which Schoenberg embraced around 1908 and later systematised in his 12-note serial method, is perhaps the most divisive aesthetic in the history of music.

Despite the revolutionary aura of Schoenberg's techniques, his gradual dismantling of the tonal framework was a logical extension of the free use of chromatic harmony, already present in the late Romantic style of Wagner and Liszt. Schoenberg's early compositions display an intense

Romanticism, notably the string sextet *Verklärte Nacht* (Transfigured Night, 1899) and the cantata *Gurrelieder* (1901). The symphonic poem *Pelléas und Mélisande* (1903) was also born of this tradition, although in language and form it confounded many listeners. As Schoenberg continued his journey away from tonality in the First Chamber Symphony (1906) and the String Quartet No. 2 (1908), he alienated himself from the public even further. In the final movement of the quartet, scored with soprano, he introduced the world to pure atonality; the world, or at least those present at the Vienna première of December 1908, mocked and laughed. Schoenberg persisted with his vision, completing his first entirely atonal works the following year: the *Three Piano Pieces*, Op. 11, and the *Five Orchestral Pieces*, Op. 16.

Towards atonality

Eschewing traditional building blocks of music—even recurring ideas and development—Schoenberg struggled to forge large-scale works. His early atonal instrumental pieces are consequently marked by extreme intimacy and concision. With sharp juxtapositions of both timbral and harmonic colours, they compare to the vibrant, expressionist paintings of Wassily Kandinsky, an artist with whom the composer enjoyed close correspondence. Both these revolutionaries were discarding rules and systems to explore the turbulence of inner states, the realm of the subconscious.

Text setting, conversely, enabled Schoenberg to create extended structures, as in the song cycles *Das Buch der Hängenden Gärten* (The Book of the Hanging Gardens, 1909) and *Pierrot Lunaire* (Pierrot in the Moonlight, 1912). The public knew of Schoenberg's atonal style through a small handful of works, since the composer was hardly prolific (his income derived mainly from teaching) and what he did produce was difficult to programme. Some pieces had to wait many years for a performance, such as the monodrama *Erwartung*, composed in 1909 but not premièred until 1924. However, the melodrama *Pierrot Lunaire*, scored for speaker and five instrumentalists, was unusual in that it was performed in Berlin soon after completion; and on that occasion applause drowned out the booing. Setting 21 poems by Albert Giraud, Schoenberg exploited the technique of *Sprechstimme*—'speech-voice', spoken but pitched—as used in *Gurrelieder* and by Humperdinck before that in the first version of his *Königskinder* (the King's Children, 1897). Schoenberg's otherworldly music translates Pierrot's irrational feelings under the spell of the moon, expressing love, subversion

Pierrot Lunaire

and nostalgia with a new enigmatic fusion of poetry and music. While the musical language was atonal and uncompromising, the declaimed text gave audiences insight into Schoenberg's artistic objectives, a feature that clearly contributed to the work's wider appeal.

Schoenberg silenced a few more critics with *Harmonielehre* (1911), a book of music theory that demonstrated his profound knowledge of traditional techniques. There were even brief moments of critical and public adulation, which left Schoenberg wondering whether he was writing anything of worth. But, as he himself recorded, 'this was a time when everybody made believe he understood Einstein's theories and Schoenberg's music'. In 1918, he instituted a new society for the private performance of works by himself and his pupils. Critics were excluded and applause prohibited.

12-note technique

The year 1921 marked Schoenberg's breakthrough '12-note system of composition'. This revolutionary method begins with a note-row, presenting all 12 notes of the chromatic scale in a particular order. Adjacent intervals of thirds and sixths are usually avoided to ensure maximum distance from tonal implications. The series may also be used in its inverted state (upside down), in retrograde (backwards), or in inverted retrograde. One note row can thus generate 48 rows through transposition. The sequence of notes sustains both melody and harmony, and should always be used in its set order to ensure grammatical consistency. 'Serial' organisation offered the composer a cohesive musical language and seemingly limitless creative potential.

Schoenberg combined his serial method with classical structures, as found in the Suite for Seven Instruments (1926), Third String Quartet (1927) and Variations for Orchestra (1928). Within such forms as variation, sonata (of a kind) or rondo, rhythm, texture and timbre served an important part in the development and transformation of material. Such was the extent of Schoenberg's own neo-classicism. On the stage his greatest project was

Moses und Aron

unfinished, the opera *Moses und Aron*. Its two completed acts, composed on the permutations of one 12-note row, represent Schoenberg's most ambitious exploration of serial technique. The contrasting characters of Moses and Aaron are musically conveyed through baritone 'speech-song' and tenor *arioso* respectively. The chorus is dominant throughout, representing the voice of the Israelites as well as God Himself. Schoenberg abandoned the opera in 1932, unsure how to score the third, final act.

Jewish by birth, Schoenberg was persecuted by the Nazis. In 1933 he was effectively expelled from his composition post at the Berlin Academy of Arts, in accordance with a new Reichstag directive to remove all Jews from public office. A Lutheran since 1898, he now felt compelled to readopt the Jewish faith; he emigrated to America and settled in Hollywood. The relief to enjoy religious freedom in a land of (comparative) artistic tolerance was enormous: 'I was driven into paradise', he publicly exclaimed in 1934. Schoenberg became a professor at the University of California in 1936 and in the same year completed his Violin Concerto and Fourth String Quartet. Among his last pieces is the one-movement Piano Concerto (1942), variously Romantic and neo-classical in outlook, and the short but moving cantata *A Survivor from Warsaw* (1947), stimulated by harrowing stories of Nazi brutality.

Berg and Webern

Schoenberg began teaching Alban Berg (1885–1935) and Anton Webern (1883–1945) in 1904, and together these three composers formed the historic triumvirate of the so-called 'Second Viennese School'.

Alban Berg

Berg was strongly influenced by the music of both Mahler and Schoenberg. He assumed full maturity with the concise *Altenberger Lieder* (Op. 4, 1912), five orchestral songs wide in harmonic vocabulary, based on texts by his friend Peter Altenberg. Berg developed a prodigious formal thoroughness which he put to good use as a dramatist. In *Wozzeck*, begun during the war and completed in 1922, he created a predominantly atonal opera and a milestone of Western art-music. Based on Georg Büchner's play, the story is bleak: Wozzeck, a mistreated and exploited soldier, learns that his lover, Marie, is having an affair with a drum major. Wozzeck kills her and in turn unwittingly drowns himself. The opera ends with his young orphaned son failing to understand what has happened. *Wozzeck* investigates various levels of social oppression and may be interpreted as fatalistic or deterministic, controversially implying that Wozzeck is innocent of his crimes because of his circumstances. Berg's expressionistic score is leitmotivic and founded on traditional forms and styles—such as variation, rondo and sonata; march, fugue and lullaby—so as to present each scene with a self-contained musical structure. Such organisation, while often extremely subtle, is pivotal to the intensifying drama. The influence of Schoenberg is naturally strong, especially in moments of speech-song melodrama, as in Marie's bible-reading scene at the beginning of Act 3. With its powerful and superbly-paced narrative, *Wozzeck* is one of the most accessible of all (near) atonal stage works.

Wozzeck

Following *Wozzeck*, Berg experimented with 12-note composition. He was never comfortable with rigid serialism, and in pieces such as his Chamber Concerto (1925) and *Lyric Suite* for string quartet (1926) he allowed room for free atonality. Berg liked to temper his musical language with occasional tonal allusions, so he often impregnated his note-rows with intervals that suggested major or minor chords. This idiom characterises his final compositions, the Violin Concerto (1935) and the unfinished opera *Lulu*. The concerto, which interrupted work on the opera, was inspired by a tragic event—the death of Manon Gropius, 18-year-old daughter of Mahler's widow, Alma, and her second husband, the architect Walter Gropius (founder of the Bauhaus School). The first two movements form a portrait of Manon;

Violin
Concerto

◀ Alban Berg and Anton Webern in 1912.

the third represents death, the fourth, lamentation and transfiguration. Shortly after completing the work, Berg himself died of blood poisoning from an infected insect bite.

Anton Webern was more experimental than Berg. As he began to write atonally, following his studies with Schoenberg, he entered what has become known as his 'aphoristic' phase, beginning 1908/9 with the songs of Opp. 3 & 4 on texts by Stefan George. The first collection includes 'Im Windesweben', whose angular vocal line and rippling, pointillistic accompaniment build to a single climax in around 30 seconds. Similarly succinct are the *Five Pieces for Orchestra* (1913). Each piece employs diaphanous, soloistic orchestration; the fourth comprises only 28 notes and is static in the extreme. With these and other miniatures, Webern cultivated the art of Schoenberg's *klang-farbenmelodie*, the organisation and development of 'tone-colour-melody', functioning in a manner analogous to harmonic progression.

When Webern fully adopted 12-note methods in the String Trio of 1927, he was able to embrace traditional forms, which in turn allowed his music to achieve concise structural purity. His serial language, in contrast to Berg's, features a propensity for semitone intervals (often appearing successively in a note-row), angular melody, and sparse, pointillistic textures built of polyphonic lines, punctuated by rests. Webern also enjoyed canonic techniques and would build various symmetries into his note-rows and broader musical

structures. The two-movement *Symphony* (1928) is an exemplar of his style. It is based on a palindromic note-row, in which the intervallic sequence of the first six notes corresponds to that of the last six notes read backwards. Its musical lines are distributed pointillistically note-by-note among different instruments and the whole piece lasts only around ten minutes. Other major serial pieces include the Concerto for Nine Instruments (1935) and the String Quartet (1938), the latter deriving all its material from permutations of B–A–C–H (German notation of B flat–A–C–B natural). His final composition was his largest, the Cantata No. 2 (1943) for soprano, bass, chorus and orchestra, based on the poetry of Hildegard Jone.

Webern's logic and concision represented the very heart of modernism and betokened a future freed from 'flawed' subjectivity. He himself would have continued on this journey had he not been shot dead by a reckless American soldier, on 15 September 1945, while enjoying an after-meal cigar.

The dissemination of serialism

The serial aesthetic was slow to attract composers beyond the Second Viennese School. The Austrian Ernst Krenek (1900–91), famous for his jazzy neo-classical opera *Jonny spielt auf* (Jonny Strikes Up, Leipzig, 1927), turned to serial techniques in the 1930s, adopting a style that was by that time effectively proscribed by the Nazis. Krenek emigrated to the USA after Hitler's annexation of Austria in 1938. Another convert was Italy's leading modernist composer, Luigi Dallapiccola (1904–75), who created his first fully 12-note composition with *Cinque frammenti di Saffo* (Five Fragments from Sappho) in 1942. He had remained in Italy despite the oppressive artistic conditions wrought by Mussolini's fascist regime.

Following the Second World War serial techniques gained wider currency. The French composer Pierre Boulez (b.1925) incorporated quarter-tone serialism in his cantata Le visage nuptial (1946), while in America, Milton Babbitt (1916–2011) applied serial procedures to non-pitch parameters in his *Three Compositions for Piano* (1947) and *Composition for Four Instruments* (1948). Babbit's forays into what would become termed 'integral' or 'total' serialism were groundbreaking, though the most influential essays were to be written in Europe.

The religiously-devout ornithologist Olivier Messiaen (1908–92) was in many respects an unlikely figure to spearhead the evolution of serialism, as he was never a card-carrying serialist. However, he always had a fondness for systematic structures, as found in his *Quartet for the End of Time* (1940), a remarkable, esoteric piece he composed and premièred with fellow inmates in a German prisoner-of-war camp. Scored for clarinet, violin, cello and piano, the eight-movement quartet incorporates an additive and subtractive approach to rhythmic values, along with 'symmetrical' modes that can only be transposed a few times before the note sequences repeat themselves. He used similar techniques again in the exhilarating *Turangalîla Symphony* (1948), which moved further towards 12-note methods with its inclusion of pitch and rhythmic series. Then in the milestone piano piece *Mode de valeurs et d'intensités* of 1949, Messiaen rigorously systematised several different musical parameters: pitch, duration, timbre (or 'attack') and dynamics. Unlike Schoenberg's system, each note has a fixed duration, dynamic and attack for the entire piece, and the notes are freely placed—they are not fixed in the order of the original row.

Messiaen's serial experiments were short-lived, yet his *Mode de valeurs* did much to galvanise the European expansion of serialism in the second half of the century. For his students at Darmstadt's Summer Courses for New Music, including Pierre Boulez, Karlheinz Stockhausen and Luigi Nono, the piece represented 'the first complete and methodical exploration of the universe of sound'.

Olivier Messiaen

Neo-classical trends

In music the term 'neo-classical' denotes a relationship with the past, from the medieval to early Romantic eras, yet more often than not with the eighteenth century. It involves a modernist approach to (usually tonal) harmony and rhythm, and implies an objective compositional process; the resulting music is not necessarily without sentiment, but rather without sentimentalism. Such an anti-Romantic aesthetic encouraged a preference for the dry timbres of woodwinds, brass and percussion—piano included. French neo-classicism developed a penchant for irony and wit, whereas Austro-German brands were generally more earnest in style.

Stravinsky: ballet and the journey into neo-classicism
Igor Stravinsky (1882–1971) contends with Schoenberg as the most influential composer of the 20th century. He was born in Russia and tutored by Rimsky-Korsakov, but his career took off in Paris with a series of ballets

commissioned by the Russian impresario Sergey Diaghilev. The world can thank Diaghilev and the 'Ballets Russes' for *The Firebird* (1910), *Petrushka* (1911) and *The Rite of Spring* (1913), as well as Ravel's *Daphnis et Chloé* (1912), Debussy's *Jeux* (1913) and Falla's *El sombrero de tres picos* (1919), to name a few.

Stravinsky emerged under the spell of Russian nationalism. His dazzling evocation of the Russian *Firebird* legend, indebted to the techniques of Rimsky-Korsakov, rewarded him with overnight fame. Stravinsky's strengths appeared to reside in thrilling orchestral effects and atmospheres. But next came *Petrushka*, stylistically progressive with polyrhythms and prominent bitonal harmonies, thematically stronger and structurally more original. Telling the tale of the hapless fairground puppet, the ballet abandoned the opulent style of *The Firebird* and divulged Stravinsky's post-Romantic tendencies. The character of Petrushka demands our sympathy, yet there is scarcely any musical sentimentality to tug at our heartstrings.

The Rite of Spring

With *The Rite of Spring*, Stravinsky seemed to turn the musical world upside down. The ballet's barbaric scenario, largely devised by the Primitivist painter and anthropologist Nicholas Roerich, depicts an ancient Russian springtime ritual, beginning with the 'Adoration of the Earth' and climaxing with the self-sacrifice of a virgin, who dances herself to death. Compared to Strauss's opera *Salome*, the *Rite* was only moderately risqué, but some of those present at the Paris première of 1913 were restless from the opening prelude, no doubt reacting to the music's dissonant, twittering climax of woodwind polyrhythms. As the curtain rose, female adolescents broke into provocative, primitive stomping impelled by music of startling violence—bitonal, near-cluster sonorities, hammered out in asymmetrical rhythms. Nijinsky's anti-traditional choreography aroused as much displeasure as the music; the public dissolved into a frenzy of protest and continued to shout throughout the performance, at times overpowering one of the largest orchestras ever placed in a pit. But then Paris loved to remonstrate. In fact, the riot served Stravinsky well: the ballet became the talk of the town and subsequent performances went without incident.

The Rite of Spring owes its watershed status to a combination of non-developmental schemes and dynamic belligerence, and also to its supple rhythmic organisation. This is nowhere better illustrated than in the carnal 'Danse sacrale', which convulses with bar-by-bar shifts of time signature. The ballet is located within a period of 'Primitivism', represented by such works as Bartók's *Allegro barbaro* (1911), Holst's 'Mars' (1914) from *The Planets* (completed 1917), and Prokofiev's *Scythian Suite* (1915). Yet Stravinsky, despite his *succès de scandale*, subsequently abandoned musical savagery and the super-orchestra. This change of direction is evident in the sparse Primitivist ballet-cantata *Les Noces* (The Wedding), begun in 1914, which exploits hypnotic driving rhythms with the aid of four pianos and assorted percussion. Both the financial constraints brought by war and a growing anti-Romantic sentiment in Europe encouraged Stravinsky's preference for smaller forces. Moreover, his increasingly impersonal, lucid and neutral musical aesthetic was one that seemed to resonate with the new dawn of scientific analysis and discovery. 'Art,' wrote Jean Cocteau in 1918, 'is science made flesh.'

Exempted from military service, Stravinsky spent the war years in Switzerland and worked on several major projects, including the opera-ballet *Renard* (1916) and the work-in-progress *Les noces*, not fully completed until 1923. In between came his influential *The Soldier's Tale* (1918). Scored for three actors, a dancer and a seven-piece chamber group, this modest piece of music theatre was likewise conducive to the restrictive political and economic climate. Packing a Russian Faustian narrative, it prefigured many aspects of the French neo-classical manner: cool detachment, irony, popular styles (including tango and ragtime), wind/brass-orientated instrumentation and lucid textures. Stravinsky developed the work's 'Ragtime' section into *Ragtime* for 11 instruments and followed this in 1919 with *Piano-Rag Music*. His sudden interest in ragtime and jazz was entirely informed through sheet music—he had never heard a note of it in performance.

The Soldier's Tale

Also formative to Stravinsky's middle period was *Pulcinella* (1920), a ballet with song requested by Diaghilev and staged with designs by Pablo Picasso. The music is entirely based on little-known pre-classical pieces (erroneously all thought to be Pergolesi's), re-moulded with twentieth-century twists of harmony, rhythm and instrumentation. *Pulcinella* was Stravinsky's first true foray into neo-classicism; he described it as 'my discovery of the past, the epiphany through which the whole of my late work became possible'.

Pulcinella

Returning to France, his 'second Motherland' as he called it, Stravinsky completed the *Symphonies of Wind Instruments* (1921) and dedicated it to the memory of Debussy. Of this piece he later wrote:

It would be futile to look in it for any passionate impulse or dynamic brilliance … This music is not meant to 'please' an audience or to rouse its passions. I had hoped, however, that it would appeal to those in whom a purely musical receptivity outweighed the desire to satisfy emotional cravings.

Such commentary would serve nearly all of Stravinsky's neo-classical compositions, though the *Symphonies* does not itself draw on 18th-century forms. A more decisive neo-classical statement was made with the dispassionate *Octet* for winds and brass (1923), whose dry textures and quirky tunes find composure within Classical forms. Cocteau regarded the piece as 'magnificent instrumental arithmetic'.

Most of Stravinsky's neo-classical pieces draw from the 18th and early 19th centuries. The Baroque concerto is the mainspring for the *Concerto for Piano and Winds* (1924), *Dumbarton Oaks* Concerto for Chamber Orchestra (1938) and the jazzy *Ebony Concerto* (1945). High Classicism (Beethoven especially) is suggested in the Symphony in C (1940), while the *Capriccio* for piano and orchestra (1929) and the *Symphony in Three Movements* (1945) absorb both Classical and Romantic idioms. In vocal music, the statuesque Latin opera-oratorio *Oedipus Rex* (1927) acknowledges Handelian oratorio, and the opera *The Rake's Progress* (1951) models Mozart; the Mass (1948) reaches back further, conjuring medievalisms with its male voices and dry reedy textures. These are generalisations to be sure—pieces often contain multiple historical references.

Stravinsky gained his first American commission in 1928 with the ballet *Apollon Musagètes*, which made its début at the Library of Congress in Washington, DC. The composer's fame in the USA was bolstered by three tours between the wars, encouraging further commissions such as the *Symphony of Psalms* (1930), the ballet *The Card Game* (1936) and the *Dumbarton Oaks* Concerto. Leaving Europe just after the outbreak of war, Stravinsky settled in Hollywood. Over the next ten years he produced a mixed assortment of music, some of which, like the conservative *Four Norwegian Moods* (1942), emanated from abandoned film projects. The most unusual commission of this period was a polka for a circus company: 50 elephants and as many ballerinas 'danced' the triumphant première of Stravinsky's *Circus Polka* at New York's Madison Square Garden on 9 April 1942.

The Rake's Progress

Stravinsky brought his neo-classical period to a close with the satirical opera *The Rake's Progress*, composed between 1947 and 1951 in collaboration with the poets W. H. Auden and Chester Kallman. Based on Hogarth's famous paintings, the three-act work traces a man's self-destruction through selfishness and vice. Stravinsky looked squarely to the Mozartian operatic model, though his stylistic references extended from Venetian Baroque through to *Bel canto* Romanticism and beyond. *The Rake's Progress* successfully weathered accusations of 'tired pastiche' and was to become one of the most often performed operas of the 20th century. But commercial and popular success was bitter-sweet for Stravinsky: he knew well his own historical importance, so he was perturbed to find young composers dismissing his latest ideas as anachronistic. Poised to enter his eighth decade, he was now to succumb to the influence of serialism.

Satie and Les Six

Eric Satie (1866–1925) rejected the grand gestures of high Romanticism from the very start of his career. His modal *Sarabandes* and *Gymnopédies* (1887/8; see *Chapter 6*) set his style, throwing out traditional means of

▲ Picasso's
curtain décor for
Erik Satie's ballet
Parade, 1917.

motivic development, climax and form in general, with no imperative to resolve dissonant harmonies. Satie was both an experimentalist and a musical humourist. His chordal *Vexations* (1893) for piano demands 840 repetitions of its near-atonal material for a complete performance, while the very titles of some later pieces openly betray an anti-establishment stance, such as the *Three Pear-Shaped Pieces* (1903) and *Dessicated Embryos* (1913), again for piano. He wrote his entertaining and occasionally surrealist *Memoirs of an Amnesiac* in 1912.

Satie exerted some influence in Paris, but elsewhere he was virtually ignored. Only in the last ten years of his life did he gain more recognition from the wider musical community. For the ballet *Parade* (1917) he evoked light popular styles, including ragtime, in a clownish collaboration with Cocteau (scenario), Picasso (costumes and set design) and Leonid Massine (choreography), all welded together under Diaghilev's supervision. Bizarre and irreverent, the work prompted the poet Guillaume Apollinaire to coin the term 'surrealism'. Satie's greatest achievement was the classically-refined *Socrate* (1918), a serious 'symphonic drama' featuring extracts of Plato's dialogues for soloists and chamber orchestra, without a hint of irony or popular pastiche.

Described as an 'icon of nonconformist chic', Satie was inspirational to a group that the French critic Henri Collet branded 'Les Six': Georges Auric, Louis Durey, Arthur Honegger, Darius Milhaud, Francis Poulenc and Germaine Tailleferre. Les Six were a mixture of talents and personalities that came to light in Paris after the First World War.

Les Six

▶ Members of 'Les Six' at the Eiffel Tower, 1921. Left to right: Germaine Tailleferre, Francis Poulenc, Arthur Honegger, Darius Milhaud, the writer/dramatist Jean Cocteau, and Georges Auric. Louis Durey is absent from the picture.

Their common purpose—until the 1920s at least—was articulated, and arguably initiated, by Jean Cocteau in *Le coq et l'arlequin* (The Cockerel and Harlequin, 1918). This artistic manifesto built upon Satie's rejection of Romanticism, decrying also impressionism and influences outside French music, above all Wagner. Les Six aligned themselves to the neo-classical movement, Stravinsky's aesthetics especially, and most of them shared Satie's whimsicality and irony. They accordingly looked back to Baroque forms, but also sideways to the music hall, modern dance, ragtime and jazz.

Francis
Poulenc

Of the six 'members', only Poulenc, Milhaud and Honegger are now performed with any regularity. The Paris-born Francis Poulenc (1899–1963), the best-known composer of the group, set out under the influence of Satie's quirky manner with such pieces as the *Trois mouvements perpétuels* for piano (1918). His musical language never strayed far from tonal-modal frameworks; and irony, lightness and charm became finger-prints of his compositional style. For Diaghilev he created the playful ballet score *Les biches* (1923), and for the keyboard player Wanda Landowska, the charming *Concert champêtre* for harpsichord and orchestra (1928). The Concerto for Two Pianos (1932) is one of his most famous concert pieces, a thrilling and ironic composition that pulls together the worlds of Balinese gamelan, Mozart, music-hall and circus slapstick.

Poulenc's finest writing is for the voice, and he is a central figure in the canon of French art song. His songs are as varied as his whole output, from the nostalgic 'Montparnasse', written in wartime, to the irreverent trifles of his song-cycle *Chansons gaillardes* (1926). The song-cycle *Tel jour, telle nuit* (As is the Day, So is the Night, 1937) is one of his career highlights, composed on texts by the surrealist Paul Éluard, his favourite poet.

Having renewed his Catholicism in the mid 1930s, Poulenc created some superbly-crafted church music, including *Litanies a la vierge noire* (1936) for women's choir and organ, the Mass in G major (1937), Stabat Mater (1950) and Gloria (1960). His sacred music is by no means strictly correlated with his more serious aesthetic, containing some idiosyncratic word stresses and lighthearted themes and gestures. Religious conviction also inspired his *Dialogues des Carmélites* (1956), an opera that sets faith against fear in a story of martyred Carmelite nuns. Poulenc's final stage work was *La voix humaine* (The Human Voice, 1958), a monodrama consisting of a 40-minute telephone call.

The Swiss-French composer Arthur Honegger (1892–1955) was the most stylistically earnest of the six. In fact much of his music has little to do with the aesthetic ideals of the group, usually avoiding neo-classical economy and irony; 'I have no taste for the fairground, nor for the music hall', he declared. He might thus be compared more closely with other French composers on the fringe of neo-classicism, such as Albert Roussel (1869–1937), best known for his Third Symphony (1930) and ballet *Bacchus et Ariane* (1931). Honegger sealed his reputation with *Le roi David* (1921), a powerful and austere oratorio based on the Handelian model. The same genre also provided the platform for his crowning achievement: *Jeanne d'Arc au bûcher* (Joan of Arc at the Stake, 1935).

Honegger's passion for steam trains inspired his most famous composition, the tone poem *Pacific 231* (1923), in which locomotive gestures intensify from slow chugging through to full flight, unleashing a brutal mechanistic force. Orchestral music became central to Honegger's output during and after World War II, with four symphonies (Nos. 2–5) that in their various ways reflect his thoughts and feelings through troubled times.

Darius Milhaud (1892–1974) developed an eclectic style early in his career and became the first European composer to extensively explore polytonality (the use of several keys at once). Particularly formative were the years 1917–19 spent as a French cultural attaché in Brazil, where he fell in love with the country's dance music and popular song styles. The experience inspired his most famous composition, *Le boeuf sur le toit* (The Ox on the Roof), which assembles Latin melodies and rhythms—including tango, maxixe, samba and Portuguese fado—in rondo form to produce a vibrant polytonal 'fantasia'. The music was originally intended as an accompaniment to a Charlie Chaplin film, but Jean Cocteau snapped it up instead for an absurdist pantomime-ballet, produced in Paris in 1920. In his score to another ballet, *La création du monde* (1923), Milhaud drew on jazz idioms he heard first-hand during a visit to Harlem. The work is largely polytonal, and a jazzy ambience is pervasive in some of its more energetic moments, which include a jazz-inspired fugue for double bass, trombone, saxophone and trumpet.

Milhaud's Jewish heritage also inspired his creativity. He set many Jewish songs and liturgical texts, including the *Service Sacré* in Hebrew, and was commissioned by the Koussevitsky Foundation to compose the opera *David* (1953). Wearing yet another stylistic hat, Milhaud produced the two-piano suite *Scaramouche* (1937), an important addition to lighter music. His

Arthur Honegger

Darius Milhaud

prodigious output includes 12 symphonies for full orchestra, nine full-length operas, 18 string quartets, over 30 concertos and many film scores.

Germany and the 'New objectivity'

Historians divide Germany's inter-war years into two contrasting periods. The first is that of the Weimar Republic, 1919–33, during which artists of all kinds enjoyed great freedom of expression. With the Third Reich, established in 1933, Hitler commandeered the arts to bring them in line with Nazi ideology, resulting not only in musical conservativism but also in a mass exodus of Jewish and 'degenerate' progressive musicians, otherwise known as 'cultural Bolsheviks'.

An artistic movement promoting 'New Objectivity' (*Neue Sachlichkeit*) was dominant throughout the Weimar period. In music, this was effectively the German answer to French neo-classicism, and similarly had its roots in the wider 'back-to-Bach' mindset. Max Reger and Ferruccio Busoni (1866–1924) provided significant impulse to this trend with their advocacy of a more impersonal, objective musical style. Busoni called for 'the casting off of what is sensuous and the renunciation of subjectivity'.

Having survived trench warfare, the composer and viola player Paul Hindemith (1895–1963) began to distance himself from his youthful Romanticism. He gained public attention with music ranging from the chromatic expressionism of the opera *Sancta Susanna* (1921) to the dry 'new objectivity' of the Third String Quartet (1920) and *Kammermusik No. 1* (1922). The soloistic scoring that dominates the first *Kammermusik* developed further in the six subsequent *Kammermusiken* (1924–27), each

Paul Hindemith: early maturity

▶ Adolf Hitler about to experience some of Wagner's 'Holy German Art' at the Bayreuth Festival, 1936. Much of Hitler's favourite music was rooted in 19th century German nationalism. The Nazis sought to supress 'elitist' modernism and Weimar decadence (jazz included to a point), movements considered subversive and opposed to the true German spirit. All 'Jewish' classical music was banned, melodious or not, even that of Mendelssohn.

one a dispassionate, Baroque-style chamber concerto. With pithy themes, pervasive counterpoint, motoric rhythms and tonal orientation, they sound like a re-imagining of Bach's *Brandenburg* concertos. Hindemith's sober musical language found effective application for the dry wit of *Neues vom Tage* (News of the Day, 1929), an operatic satire on contemporary mores and tabloid journalism. Hitler was apparently shocked by the opera's nude bathtub scene, which contributed to later Nazi hostilities towards the composer. Meanwhile, Hindemith was emerging as a major advocate of 'utility' music—written for a specific purpose, not simply as artistic expression. He became one of the most important European composers active in music for children and amateurs.

The most famous and successful musical product of the Weimar Republic was *Die Dreigroschenoper* (The Threepenny Opera, 1928), with music by Kurt Weill (1900–50) and libretto by Bertolt Brecht and Elisabeth Hauptmann. Based on John Gay's *Beggars' Opera*, it is similarly a satirical 'number opera' that places miscreants centre-stage with the aim of attacking hypocrisy and bourgeois values. Weill's score employs the kind of popular music associated with liberalism and subversion. The well-known opening number, 'Mack the Knife', is delivered in cabaret style and appears to celebrate the debauched antics of the eponymous thief-murderer-rapist. Irony was common to neo-classicism, and the accessibility of Weill's musical language placed the work comfortably within the spirit of Weimar 'New Objectivity'. It was a smash hit, with well over 100 different productions (in translation) around the world within five years. Weill and Brecht took socio-political critique into conventional opera with *The Rise and Fall of the City of Mahagonny* (1930), a reworking of their short 'songspiel' *Mahagonny* (1927). Examining a community built on greed and vice, it was a no-holds-barred satire on capitalism that sent shockwaves through polite society.

At the end of the 1920s, the ever-strengthening Nazi party began their crusade against the liberal values of the Weimar Republic. Free-spirited modernists active in Germany, including Hindemith, Weill, Schoenberg and Ernst Krenek, found themselves increasingly censored and one by one these composers relocated to the USA. Weill, a Jew, left Germany for Paris in 1933 and two years later emigrated to America. There he wrote film scores and several Broadway musicals, including *Lady in the Dark*, produced in 1941 in collaboration with lyricist Ira Gershwin, and *Street Scene* (1946).

Hindemith remained longer in Germany, hoping that he might be given some latitude. That never materialised, but he still managed to complete his finest opera, *Mathis der Maler* (Mathis the Painter, 1935), together with its associated symphony. The Nazis banned the opera, so its première took place at Zürich, with notable success, in May 1938. Hindemith made his way from Switzerland to the USA in 1940 and joined the Yale School of Music faculty, where he taught for 13 years. His war-time compositions included the piano studies of *Ludus Tonalis* (1942), a response to Bach's *Well Tempered Clavier*, and the *Symphonic Metamorphoses on Themes by Carl Maria von Weber* (1943).

Strauss, Carl Orff (1895–1982) and Karl Amadeus Hartmann (1905–63) were among the composers who remained in Germany and answerable

Kurt Weill:
*Die Dreigro-
schenoper*

Strauss and
Carl Orff

517

to the Nazi authorities. Hartmann was deeply troubled by Nazism and so withdrew from public life. Strauss and Orff both came into close contact, and at times conflict, with the Party, although both considered music as an autonomous medium that existed outside, or rather 'above', politics. This was at best a morally negligent, conscience-easing viewpoint. But Orff, a prominent educationalist who secured immortal fame with *Carmina Burana* (1936), harboured no sympathy for Nazi ideology. The same was true of Strauss, who lost his job as president of the Reichsmusikkammer in 1935 for criticising the Nazi regime. If Strauss still courted Nazi officials, it was not simply to limit their interference with his music, but also to secure protection for his Jewish daughter-in-law and grandsons. Charged with Nazi collaboration after the war, Strauss was cleared in 1948.

National styles and nationalism

Scandinavia

Jean Sibelius

Jean Sibelius established his reputation amid Finland's growing unrest under Russian domination. His explicit nationalistic statements, effectively begun with *Kullervo* (1892), had largely been made by 1900 (see *Chapter 6*). His First Symphony (1899) was a pivotal work, both the summation of the nationalist influences of previous years and the beginning of a more individual style. But Sibelius's patriotism ran deep, and even towards the end of his composing career, in a fully independent Finland, his music retained a sense of national identity.

In his Symphony No. 2 (1902), the haunting *Valse triste* (1904) and the Violin Concerto in D minor (1904, revised 1905), Sibelius largely perpetuated the Romantic tradition. By moving into a more objective manner, as in the symphonic fantasy *Pohjola's Daughter* (1906) and the Third Symphony (1907), he released himself from traditional constraints, developing a new candour with organic themes and a more concise approach to form. Pastoral moods are common, but they are rarely idyllic, since his point of reference was the Finnish landscape in both its beauty and bleakness. He typically avoided big thematic contrasts, preferring a sense of interconnection within movements and even across entire works. Such conci-

Symphony No. 4

sion of thought is reflected in the dark and severe Fourth Symphony (1911), a harmonically elusive composition that germinates from

▶ Finland's foremost composer, Jean Sibelius, in 1915.

a tonally-unstable tritone. This tour-de-force left contemporary listeners deeply puzzled; it was neither Romantic, nationalist, epic nor uplifting. Sibelius saw no value in becoming an ivory-tower composer and was determined to reconnect with his public. So to mark his 50th birthday—an occasion of national celebration—he composed the more tonally secure Fifth Symphony (1915), a climactic four-movement work that appealed for optimism in the midst of worldwide conflict. The symphony was better received but it cost Sibelius much effort; he revised it twice, reaching the definitive three-movement version in 1919.

Symphony No. 5

In the more restrained Sixth and stirring single-movement Seventh symphonies (1923/4) Sibelius remained rooted in his idiomatic style, arousing the Nordic spirit in musical panoramas shaped by Romantic and post-Romantic impulses. His final orchestral masterpiece was the tone poem *Tapiola* (1926), which recalls the stark textures of the Fourth Symphony to evoke the harsh yet magical forested realm of the mythic Finnish god Tapio. Sibelius abandoned composition not long afterwards. His ongoing battle with alcoholism may have played a part in this as he felt unable to achieve the standards he set himself. He was also disillusioned with the direction of modernism. Internationally famous, he had increasingly divided critical opinion and endured some savage reviews. But then, as he once stated, 'no one ever put up a statue to a critic'.

Last major works

The other major presence among Scandinavian composers was Carl Nielsen, who had already found fame by the end of the 1890s (see *Chapter 6*). Though he became the figurehead of Danish music, Nielsen gave rare attention to musical nationalism, unlike Sibelius or the Swedish composer Hugo Alfvén (1872–1960). Nielsen's most important creations are his six symphonies, works marked by progressive tonality and a virile musical language divested of vanity and emotionalism. Among them is the turbulent Symphony No. 3 *Sinfonia espansiva* (1911), one of his greatest lifetime successes, and the wartime Symphony No. 4, *The Inextinguishable* (1916), dealing with conflict and awarding resounding victory to the 'inextinguishable' human spirit. The two-movement Symphony No. 5 (1922) likewise explores conflict, fundamentally that between good and evil. Various musical elements are set in opposition, such as consonance and dissonance, order and anarchy. A belligerent snare drum plays a central role, representing one of the corrupting, destructive forces, and at one point the player is asked 'to improvise, as if at all costs trying to prevent the continuation of the music'. The Fifth is widely recognised as Nielsen's masterpiece.

Carl Nielsen

Symphony No.5

Bartók and the internalisation of folk idioms

Born in the southern Hungarian province of Torontál, Béla Bartók (1881–1945) was one of the first to undertake analytical musical research into Magyar folk traditions. Predominantly vocal, the music itself reflected the deep-rooted customs of Hungarian peasant communities, thus representing something distinct from the richly ornamented Hungarian gypsy music beloved by Liszt and other Romantics. Bartók was sometimes joined by his compatriot Zoltán Kodály (1882–1967) as he toured remote villages and settlements in the early years of the century, recording numerous

▶ Béla Bartók, aged around 27, recording folk songs with an Edison phonograph in Transylvania, *c.*1908. Bartók began field work in 1906 and went on to collect thousands of folk songs (and several hundred fiddle tunes) from Eastern Europe and North Africa.

folk songs in notebooks and on wax cylinders. He endeavoured to understand folk music in its cultural context and soon extended his research into Slovakia and Romania, then Bulgaria, Turkey and North Africa. This activity represented pioneering ethnomusicology and proved invaluable to the development of Bartók's own musical style.

Folk-infused language

Bartók absorbed the language and rhythms of Magyar folk music to the point where it became an instinctive element within his own compositional style. He rejected the sentimental Romantic distillation of folk idioms and instead sought to preserve the raw expressive power of 'peasant music'. He conceived and coloured his harmonies using the characteristic intervals of folk melodies, maintaining that 'the simpler the melody, the more complex and strange may be its suitable harmonisations and accompaniments'. Thus his language extends from simple triadic forms through to complex bitonality, polymodality and even atonality.

Only in his very earliest pieces did Bartók express clear nationalistic interests, as in the tone poem *Kossuth* (1903), based on the figure of Lajos Kossuth, leader of the abortive Hungarian revolution of 1848. For its form and style Bartók looked to Strauss, whose influence is also conspicuous in the intensely chromatic String Quartet No. 1 (1907). In his one opera, *Bluebeard's Castle* (1911), Bartók created the Hungarian answer to Debussy's *Pelléas and Méllisande*, likewise employing modes and musical symbolism, joined with a syllabic, declamatory treatment of the Hungarian language. And with a penchant for the primitive rhythmic qualities of Eastern European folk music, reflected in the piano piece *Allegro barbaro* (1911), Bartók was also drawn to the music of Stravinsky.

Bartók was deemed physically unfit for military service, so during the war years he, along with Kodály, continued to research and promote in arrangements of Hungarian and Romanian folk music. Bartók's assimilation of folk idioms and modernist trends brought considerable diversity to his music style, as revealed in the melodic accessibility of the *Romanian Folk Dances* (1917), the expressionistic language of the String Quartet No. 2 (1917), the enchanting pastoral euphony of the ballet *The Wooden Prince* (1917) and the primitivism of the pantomime *The Miraculous Mandarin* (1919, revised 1926).

During the 1920s Bartók embarked on a more concentrated path of folk-inspired expressionism. This is articulated in the folk-inflected, twisting harmonies of Sonata No. 2 for Violin and Piano (1922), a two-movement work that sets out in an arcane, quasi-improvisatory style and finds its way towards excitable dance rhythms and pronounced lyricism—a reflection, it has been suggested, of the evolution of peasant music itself. The single-movement String Quartet No. 3 (1927) is also spontaneous, feeding folk-like themes into a dissonant, often fiercely percussive musical discourse, enlivened by wild glissandi and snapping 'Bartók pizzicatos'. The music of the 1920s commonly broached atonality and challenged convention. Yet Bartók was hardly an ivory-tower composer, as witnessed by the accessible *Dance Suite* (1923), composed in celebration of the 50th anniversary of the formation of the Hungarian capital, Budapest, and the impassioned Rhapsodies for violin and piano (1928).

Bartók toured widely (including the USA) and performed much of his own piano music, including his first two piano concertos (1926 and 1931). The First Piano Concerto, introduced at Frankfurt in 1927 under Wilhelm Furtwängler (1886–1954), has pounding ostinatos, tone clusters and complex harmonic schemes. The Second Piano Concerto, first performed in January 1933, again in Frankfurt, marked Bartók's final concert performance in Germany. His revulsion of Hitler and fascism prompted him to ban performances of his music, including radio broadcasts, in both Germany and Italy.

Bartók's exploration of polytonality led to what he described as 'poly-modal chromaticism', created by the simultaneous use of different modes (often Lydian and Phrygian), built from the same tonic note. The technique is employed in the first-movement fugue of the renowned *Music for Strings, Percussion and Celesta* (1936) and also in sections of the Second Violin Concerto (1938). The last pieces Bartók wrote in Europe include the highly virtuosic *Rhapsody* (later *Contrasts*) for clarinet, violin and piano (1938), commissioned by the clarinet phenomenon Benny Goodman (1909–86); also the *Divertimento* for string orchestra and String Quartet No. 6, both completed in 1939. For their quality of invention and technical brilliance, Bartók's six string quartets are collectively the most important since those of Beethoven.

In October 1940, following the death of his mother and at odds with his country's pro-Nazi regime, Bartók emigrated to the USA. There he arranged his *Sonata for Two Pianos and Percussion* (1937) into a concerto to thrust both himself and his pianist wife, Ditta, into the spotlight; but the plan failed to arouse much interest. However, his five-movement *Concerto for Orchestra* (1943), commissioned by Serge Koussevitzky, was a major success. The enduring popularity of the music rests on many intriguing

Post-war music

To the USA

ingredients: its emotional journey, the *concerto grosso* organisation, prominent themes, folk-based material, and a brief quotation from Shostakovich's Seventh Symphony (the significance of which is debated) in the fourth movement. While working on the concerto, Bartók was already suffering from leukaemia. He finished only two more masterworks: the Sonata for Solo Violin—complete with quarter tones—for Yehudi Menuhin in 1944, and the Piano Concerto No. 3 in 1945. Bartók's Viola Concerto, left in sketch form, was completed by his pupil and friend Tibor Serly.

Kodály

Bartók's pedagogical concerns are represented by his vast instructional piano collection *Mikrokosmos* (1926–39), six books for children containing 153 study pieces addressing technique and 20th-century style, many of them drawing on eastern European folk music. Here again he shares interests with Kodály, who himself wrote an entire music course for schools in Hungary, one that has since been adopted by institutions around the world. As a composer Kodály is chiefly remembered for his orchestral *Dances of Galánta* (1933), together with the oratorio *Psalmus Hungaricus* (1923) and the extracted orchestral suite from the folk Singspiel *Háry János* (1927). His importance to the musical life of Hungary exceeds that of Bartók, who himself wrote, in 1928, 'If I were to name the composer whose works are the most perfect embodiment of the Hungarian spirit, I would answer Kodály.'

Other European national traditions

The modernist 'internalisation' of folk music, as practised by Bartók, found wide currency. It was a natural progression from late 19th-century nationalism, which had seen folk music moulded and sublimated into the western tonal aesthetic.

Leoš Janáček

The Czech composer Leoš Janáček (1854–1928) began studying native Moravian folk song well before Bartók took to the field. His first collection appeared in 1890 and within ten years he had transcribed over 1,000 folk songs. However, most of Janáček's representative pieces do not quote folk melodies. Rather, his identification with Czech culture stems largely from his extensive study of the rhythms and cadences of the Moravian dialect, and his rigorous application of these to his vocal music. The result is a kind of 'speech melody', similar to that of Mussorgsky, bringing naturalistic characterisation to his operas from the time of *Jenůfa* (1903). Janáček's musical importance derives almost entirely from his late-career output, dating from the revised version of *Jenůfa* (1916) and the Gogol-inspired orchestral rhapsody *Taras Bulba* (1918). After the war, in the newly formed state of Czechoslovakia, he achieved astonishing productivity with his two string quartets (1923, 1928), the *Sinfonietta* (1926), the *Glagolitic Mass* (1927), and four important operas, including the tuneful cycle-of-life tale *The Cunning Little Vixen* (1924).

The chief inspiration behind Janáček's Indian summer came from his unrequited infatuation with a young married woman, Kamila Stösslová. He wrote hundreds of letters to her and transformed her into the heroines of three operas, most transparently the lovelorn, doomed figure of *Kát'a Kabanová* (1921). Four years later, writing *The Makropulos Case*, he was identifying her with the heartless Emilia Marty, a character whose youth

has been greatly prolonged by an elixir, but who cannot love because life has lost its meaning. His preoccupation with Kamila influenced instrumental works also, famously the emotional Second String Quartet, subtitled *Intimate Letters*.

There is no reference to Kamila in Janáček's final operatic masterpiece, *From the House of the Dead* (1928). In setting Dostoevsky's Siberian prison drama Janáček was able to draw on distinctive elements of his own style. His penchant for extremes of texture—muddy lows and piercing highs—found correspondence with the opera's masculine characters and bleak Siberian atmosphere. The austerity of the music is also realised in sparse, expressionistic passages and some of Janáček's most dissonant music. The score as he left it at the time of death was incorrectly perceived as unfinished, due to its extreme textural economy and bleak ending. Two of Janáček's pupils revised it ready for a posthumous première at Brno's National Theatre in 1930. Only in the second half of the century was the error recognised, and the opera returned to the composer's original performing edition.

From the House of the Dead

The nationalist interests of Bohuslav Martinů (1890–1959), the leading Czech composer of the next generation, diminished over the years. Most of his professional life was spent in Paris and the USA, where he developed his own serious, full-bodied brand of neo-classicism, one sometimes Romantic and worlds away from the neutral manner of Stravinsky. Much of Martinů's renown rests on his six symphonies, the first five of which he composed in America in quick succession between 1942 and 1946. Some of his most important patriotic compositions were written in response to Nazi aggression, such as the rousing *Double Concerto* for two string orchestras, piano and timpani (1938), whose clamorous rhythms and gesticulations represented a confrontational response to Germany's invasion

Bohuslav Martinů

of Czechoslovakia's Sudetenland. Martinů dedicated his Second Symphony to his fellow countrymen resident in Cleveland; its premiere by the Cleveland Orchestra, on 28 October 1943, commemorated the 25th anniversary of the founding of Czechoslovakia. The composer's *Memorial to Lidice* was introduced in New York the same day. Whereas the symphony is upbeat and indomitable in spirit, the instrumental *Memorial* adopts a meditative tone to reflect on the horrific Nazi massacre of Czechs at the village of Lidice, 10 June 1942.

Romania: George Enescu

The compositional output of Romania's George Enescu (1881–1955) was restricted by his busy conducting and performing schedules. A formidable violin virtuoso, Enescu latched on to the rhapsodical treatment of folk tunes from an early age. A well-known example is his *Romanian Rhapsodies* for orchestra (1901), whose popularity did much to inhibit public recognition of his later and greater output. In maturity and stimulated by a profound love of homeland he moved towards a more folk-inflected style, as found in his Violin Sonata No. 3 (1926), the Third Piano Sonata (1935) and the nostalgic *Impressions d'enfance* for violin and piano (1940). The Romanian influence can be strong, as it is in the violin sonata with some remarkable quasi-improvisatory, tecnique-laden folkish melody, inspired by the country's fiddler tradition. There is often 'dreaming and melancholy' in Enescu, characteristics he regarded as innate to Romanian music.

Poland: Karol Szymanowski

One of the many contemporaries Enescu generously promoted in his violin recitals was Poland's Karol Szymanowski (1882–1937), a composer sometimes referred to as Chopin's true heir. Szymanowski's nationalist interests developed only after his country regained its independence following WWI. Up until that time he had been cultivating an impressionist-Straussian blend in such acclaimed works as the Violin Concerto No.1 and Symphony No. 3, both completed in 1916, and in the Nietzschean opera *King Roger* (1924). Szymanowski's nationalism was less rooted in patriotism than his love of the ancient and exotic, his desire to distance himself from Germanic influences, and a timely introduction to the folk music of Poland's Tatra Highlands. In his late period he focused on 'crystallising elements of tribal heritage', as he put it, in a more lucid musical style. There are few better examples than the beautifully lyrical Stabat Mater (1926), an emotionally restrained sacred piece that displays rustic and ancient qualities in simple triadic harmony, chant, and modal and folk-inflected melodies. Even though Szymanowski absorbed folk materials in a 20th century manner, he was reluctant to fully banish his Romantic tendencies, as we can hear in the richly expressive Second Violin Concerto of 1933. In this respect he shares similarities with Martinů and Enescu.

Italy: Malipiero, Casella, Respighi

The preoccupations of Italian composers were entirely different to those of Eastern Europe and Scandinavia. Italy, after all, had been a dominant force in music since Renaissance times, and fully united and independent since 1870. However, many Italian composers saw a vital need to revive the country's interests in instrumental music, which had been suffocated by operatic fanaticism in the previous century. This was something that concerned Gian Francesco Malipiero (1882–1973) and Alfredo Casella (1883–1947), two leading Italian 'revivalists' of the early century. Malipiero composed numerous concertos and 11 symphonies (1933–69) in addition to some 40 stage works, while Casella found popular success with lightly nationalistic pieces such as the *Italia* orchestral rhapsody (1909) and the neo-classical *Scarlattiana* for piano and small orchestra (1926). By the end of the 1920s, Malipiero, Casella, Ottorino Respighi (1879–1936) and Ildebrando Pizzetti (1880–1968) had all achieved international recognition for their concert music. Respighi was the most widely known, thanks above all to his indulgently nationalistic, brilliantly orchestrated Roman tone-poems: *The Fountains of Rome* (1916), *The Pines of Rome* (1924) and *Roman Festivals* (1928). His representative orchestral works include *Church Windows* (1926), *A Botticelli Triptych* (1927) and *The Birds* (1928), which had their respective premières in Boston (USA), Vienna and São Paulo (Brazil).

In Respighi we find a combination of ancient, Romantic and modern idioms. So too in the music of the Swiss-American composer Ernest Bloch (1880–1959), whose best known pieces derive inspiration from his Jewish heritage. The lyrically expressive *Schelomo* (Solomon, 1916), a 'Hebrew Rhapsody' for cello and orchestra, is probably Bloch's most popular 'Jewish Cycle' composition, completed the year he moved to the USA. Other important works include the *Israel Symphony* for voices and orchestra (1916), *Baal-Shem* for violin and piano (1923) and the *Sacred Service* for baritone, chorus and orchestra (1933). In step with many other composers exploring folk traditions, Bloch rarely attempted to quote authentic Hebraic melodies. Jewish qualities emerge in often meditative atmospheres through modal accents (the distinctive Hedjaz mode especially) and melodic quarter-tones, occasional allusions to religious chant, and even mimicry of the shofar.

In Spain (see also *Chapter 6*), the composer and piano virtuoso Isaac Albéniz combined the passion of provincial songs and dances with impressionistic textures in his *Iberia* collection for solo piano (1906–09). Enrique Granados followed Albéniz into a 20th-century Spanish style with his *Goyescas* piano pieces (1909/11) and the opera *Goyescas* (1915), both inspired by the paintings of Francisco Goya. Among the next generation, Joaquín Turina (1882–1949) achieved popularity with folk-flavoured compositions such as the vibrant *Danzas fantásticas* for orchestra (1920). But it was in the music of Manuel de Falla (1876–1946) that Spain's vernacular traditions merged most tellingly with 20th-century modernism.

Falla was an experienced composer when he left Spain for Paris in 1907. His finest work to date was his unperformed *La vida breve* (Life is Short, 1905), a *verismo* opera set in Granada, southern Spain, that displayed national colour in its Spanish dances and use of *cante jondo*, an Andalusian flamenco vocal style. Falla composed little during the seven years he spent in France, but he absorbed the colouristic approach of Debussy and Ravel, and gained significant encouragement from Dukas. Having witnessed the success of *La vida breve* in Nice (1913) and Paris (1914), Falla was forced back to Spain at the outbreak of war. His impressionistic *Nights in the Gardens of Spain* for piano and orchestra, completed on his return, was almost as French in mood as it was Spanish. Subsequently Falla found a more personal voice with a deeper-rooted national style.

Ernest Bloch

Spain

Manuel de Falla

The transition is evident in the sung ballet *El amor brujo* (Love, the Magician, 1915), whose raw gypsy passion is now commonly conveyed in orchestral suite form. Falla's celebrated Diaghilev ballet *El sombrero de tres picos* (The Three Cornered Hat) followed in 1919, a comical folk-laden feast of Spanish dance, enriched by Massine's choreography and Picasso's sets and costumes. Ernest Ansermet (1883–1969) conducted the première in London and Falla's international reputation was sealed.

Falla's post-war compositions responded to the influence of Stravinsky and the neo-classical preoccupation with classical forms. A prime example is the Concerto for Harpsichord (1926), in effect a concerto for multiple instruments, which looks back to the music of Domenico Scarlatti while treating folk idioms in a stylised manner. Declining in health, Falla produced very little after the concerto. He spent his final years in Argentina (from 1939), enticed by a conducting appointment with the Institución Cultural Española in Buenos Aires. His scenic cantata *Atlántida*, begun in 1926, was completed posthumously by his pupil Ernesto Halffter.

Latin America

Latin America's interests in the European musical tradition had been nurtured by generations of 'creoles' throughout the colonial period. By the second half of the 19th century there was enough local interest and talent to warrant the institution of national conservatories in Mexico, Brazil and Argentina. The rise of political nationalism, in various countries across Latin America, in turn stirred an indigenous awakening in the imported Western musical idiom. This trend found vigorous expression in the early decades of the 20th century.

Mexico:
Carlos
Chávez

Mexico's musical nationalism was fired up in the wake of the country's 1910–20 revolution by Manuel Ponce (1882–1948), with an output concentrated around songs and solo pieces for piano and guitar. He was joined in this quest by Silvestre Revueltas (1899–1940) and Carlos Chávez (1899–1978). Chávez became Mexico's pre-eminent musical figure of the early 20th century, brandishing a fusion of modern styles, particularly primitivism and neo-classicism, though he could equally indulge epic moods and flights of passion. He achieved a national flavour by drawing on ancient indigenous melodies both real (*Sinfonía india*, 1936) and imagined (*Xochipilli* for winds and percussion, 1940). The Piano Concerto (1940) suggests an undercurrent of national consciousness in its use of folk rhythms, although in many later pieces, including his last three symphonies (Nos. 4–6, 1953–63), Chávez aspired to a more universal aesthetic, making little attempt to evoke Mexican colour.

Alberto Williams (1862–1952), founder of the Buenos Aires Conservatory of Music (1893), was the first significant figure of Argentine nationalism. His stylisation of Gaucho (cowboy) songs and dances set a trend that extended to the output of Alberto Ginastera (1916–83), one of Argentina's most prominent modernist composers. Ginastera's early characteristic works include the piano pieces *Three Argentinian Dances* (1937) and *Malambo* (1940), the ballet *Panambí* (1937) and the spirited *Estancia* orchestral suite (1941). In the second half of the century he became a committed advocate of serialism. *(Argentina)*

The most representative Latin American composer of the period was Brazil's Heitor Villa-Lobos (1887–1959), who drew many local resources into colourful fusion. Both folk and modern popular styles suffuse his highly idiosyncratic nationalist idiom, one variously Romantic, impressionist, primitivist and neo-classical. His most quintessential nationalist pieces are the 14 *Chôros*, composed between 1920 and 1929. The appeal of the 'chôro'—itself a modern, urban instrumental style—was its malleability. Just as the *chôro* embraces any number and combination of instruments, so Villa-Lobos's pieces engage a wide variety of musical forces, from solo guitar (No. 1) up to full chorus and orchestra (Nos. 10 and 14). Considered 'serenades' by the composer, they evoke the full exotic experience of Brazil, from the dynamic passion of modern Carnival (No. 8) out to the wild Amazonian waterways and rainforest (No. 10). Another major collection is the *Bachianas brasileiras* (1930–45), a suite of nine pieces, again diversely scored, of which No. 5 for solo voice and eight cellos is the most famous. Like Chávez and several prominent US composers of the period, Villa-Lobos was committed to classical forms, writing five piano concertos, 12 symphonies and no fewer than 17 string quartets. His music for guitar remains central to the 20th-century repertory, in particular the 12 Études (1929) and the Guitar Concerto (1951), the latter composed for the legendary Spanish guitarist Andrés Segovia (1893–1987). *(Brazil: Heitor Villa-Lobos)*

Britain

Elgar to Vaughan Williams

England's musical renaissance, begun around the 1880s, was initiated not only by Parry, Stanford and Elgar, but also by new institutions that nurtured musical culture. In 1883 George Grove established The Royal College of Music; Stanford joined the composition staff and Parry assumed the directorship in 1895. During the 1890s Stanford taught nearly every significant composer of the 'renaissance' generation: Ralph Vaughan Williams (1872–1958), Gustav Holst (1874–1934), Samuel Coleridge-Taylor (1875–1912), Frank Bridge (1879–1941) and John Ireland (1879–1962). Another key development was the London Promenade Concert series, launched in 1895 by Henry Wood and Robert Newman at the newly-opened

Elgar

Queen's Hall. Ticketed at one shilling, the first concerts were programmed with accessible music to pull in the general public who could smoke, eat and drink during performances. Works by the Scotsman Alexander Mackenzie (1847–1935)—principal of the Royal Academy of Music from 1888—and Elgar soon found popular appeal. After the Great War the Proms became a major platform for the more progressive works of younger British composers.

Following his *Enigma Variations* (1899, see *Chapter 6*), Elgar created what he himself regarded as his greatest achievement, the oratorio *The Dream of Gerontius* (1900). Based on Cardinal Newman's poem, the work owed an enormous debt to European influences—Wagner especially, not only in the use of leitmotifs,

but also in the close rhythmic integration of text and musical line. Strauss at once recognised it as a masterpiece. The following year Elgar composed the first two of his ceremonial *Pomp and Circumstance* marches as well as the *Cockaigne* concert overture (*In London Town*). To the public, who double-encored the première of March No. 1 at the Proms in 1901, Elgar epitomised the English spirit. To the composer's detriment, the marches overshadowed the more serious essays that followed, such as the superb concerto-grosso style *Introduction and Allegro* (1905), scored for string quartet and string orchestra.

Within Elgar's impressive body of instrumental music are two symphonies (1908, 1911), the Violin Concerto (1910), the 'symphonic study' *Falstaff* (1913) and the Cello Concerto (1919). The First Symphony, announced with the composer's commanding *nobilmente* style, is a work wide in emotional scope and, according to Elgar, 'written out of a full life experience'. It gained around 100 performances during its first year alone and proved a veritable springboard for the English symphonic tradition. The Second Symphony is a more restive and complex composition, which finds unity through a cyclical 'spirit of delight' theme. Elgar dedicated the symphony to the late king, Edward VII, whose passing is reflected in the funereal second movement Larghetto. The symphony concludes with a thoughtful valediction, a far cry from the triumphant close of the First Symphony.

The lyrical Cello Concerto in E minor is bathed in an even deeper meditative spirit. Standing close in stature to Dvořák's masterly Cello Concerto in B minor, it is popularly considered a lament for the millions of lives lost during World War I. Elgar wrote it while at the height of his creative powers, but following the death of his beloved wife and muse in

1920, he virtually abandoned composition. He now felt out of touch with the arts and simply detested the new directions of modernism. Nevertheless, in between his rounds of golf and visits to the horse racing track he continued to play his part in England's music life. He became Master of the King's Music in 1924, and made the inaugural recording of the Abbey Road studios in 1931, recording his *Pomp and Circumstance* March, No. 1 with the London Symphony Orchestra.

Born in Bradford to German parents, Frederick Delius (1862–1934) was never much interested in joining the family wool business. He travelled from a young age, and his formative years included exposure to African-American music during the 1880s while managing an orange plantation in Florida. Committed to a musical career, he enrolled for conservatory training at Leipzig (1886–88), which coincided with a pivotal meeting with Grieg. Delius subsequently took up residency in Paris, the musical capital of Europe, though he gained his earliest success in Norway and, more importantly, Germany. Like Elgar, he drew heavily on Germanic influences, Wagner especially, but at the turn of the century he found marked stylistic individuality with his fourth opera, *A Village Romeo and Juliet* (1901). More individual still was his cantata *Sea Drift* (1904), a poignant fable of tragedy and loss inspired by the poetry of Walt Whitman. It is a work remarkable for its majestic fusion of text and music, wrought by supple wind-swept rhythms and formal fluidity. The première at Essen, Germany, in 1906, was one of the composer's early triumphs.

Delius was not famous in England until the conductor Thomas Beecham began to promote his music, around 1908, introducing such works as *A Mass of Life* (1905) and *Songs of Sunset* (1907). Occasionally impressionistic, Delius sealed his popular fame with evocative orchestral tone poems like *Brigg Fair: An English Rhapsody* (1907), *In a Summer Garden* (1908) and *On Hearing the First Cuckoo in Spring* (1912), works whose pastoral lyricism and charm held enormous appeal for the English. After the war, Delius's output declined with the advance of syphilis, though Beecham continued to raise his profile. Compositions from the last six years of his life include the orchestral pieces *A Song of Summer* (1930) and *Irmelin* Prelude (1931), completed with the help of Eric Fenby (1906–97), the composer's devoted amanuensis.

While Elgar and, to a point, Delius created music in some way reminiscent of English sensibilities, it was Ralph Vaughan Williams who, for the first time in centuries, established a musical style based on England's musical heritage. Vaughan Williams was not cut off from Europe by any means, studying abroad with Bruch and Ravel, but the germinating seeds of his style were domestic, rooted in his activities editing the music of Purcell and the English Hymnal (pub. 1906), and his transcriptions of English folk songs. Politically, Vaughan Williams regarded himself as an internationalist, but he steadfastly believed in cultural patriotism. It was a creed he expressed into old age: 'What we have to offer must derive essentially from our own life. It must not be a bad imitation of what other nations already do better.'

Vaughan Williams was in his mid-30s by the time he began to find his distinctive musical voice, his watershed compositions including the song

Frederick Delius

Ralph Vaughan Williams

cycle *On Wenlock Edge* (1909), the *Sea Symphony* (1910) and the *Fantasia on a Theme of Thomas Tallis* for double string orchestra (1910). In treating Tallis's Phrygian hymn tune, Vaughan Williams found new applications for chordal harmonies, quite different to those used by the tonal composers of previous centuries. While the rest of Europe was exploring the inflation of dissonance, Vaughan Williams gave new life to basic triads through modal harmonic sequences and novel juxtapositions. Fingerprints of his style include 'false relationships' between adjacent chords (contrasting chords from different keys), parallel harmonies and intense homophonic climaxes.

Vaughan Williams only occasionally quoted folksong. Examples are found in the *London* Symphony (1913), the *English Folksong Suite* (1923) and most famously in the *Fantasia on Greensleeves* (1934), which first appeared in his Falstaff opera *Sir John in Love*, in 1928. More often he simply absorbed folk idioms, creating modal or pentatonic themes that convey simplicity, spontaneity and nostalgia. The rhapsodic 'romance' *The Lark Ascending* for violin and orchestra (1914, revised 1920), interpreting a poem by George Meredith, is a well-known example, though the connection in some way extends to nearly everything Vaughan Williams wrote.

In his nine symphonies Vaughan Williams created his most expansive, universal music. Among these we find the largely meditative, bitonal Third (the *Pastoral*, 1921), his 'war requiem' featuring a wordless soprano solo in its final movement, and the astringent Fourth (1934), the most dissonant of the symphonies. His Sixth (1947), which concludes with an entire movement (Epilogue) played *pianissimo*, is commonly thought to reflect the bleak aftermath of war. Vaughan Williams viewed himself as a composer for the people, and in this capacity he felt drawn to religious themes despite his own agnosticism. It goes some way to explaining how the 'masque for dancing' *Job* (1930) and the opera (or 'morality') *The Pilgrim's Progress* (1951) inspired some of his finest music.

Gustav Holst
& *The Planets*

Vaughan Williams's close friend Gustav Holst combined interests of English folksong and Hindu philosophy early on in his career, producing such innovative compositions as the chamber opera *Sāvitri* (1908). Wide public recognition came shortly after the war with the first performances of his magnum opus: *The Planets* (completed 1917). Its seven movements—no Earth; and Pluto, disregarding its questionable status, was as yet undiscovered—portray the supposed effect on the human psyche of each planet from an astrological perspective. 'Mars,' subtitled 'Bringer of War', features a rhythmic ostinato in 5/4 time which grows from a threatening murmur to a belligerent climax, amplified by strong bitonal dissonances. (Appropriately, the movement was completed in 1914, shortly before the outbreak of World War I.) 'Jupiter' contains the most famous of all Holst's melodies, one later adapted for the nationalistic hymn 'I Vow to Thee My Country'. 'Neptune' (The Mystic) suggests the influence of Debussy in its impressionistic textures and concludes the sequence of movements with a mystical off-stage female chorus, fading away into the infinity of time and space. The success of *The Planets* has tended to obscure Holst's wider oeuvre, one that includes the *St Paul's Suite* for strings (1913), *The Hymn of Jesus* for choir and orchestra (1917) and *A Choral Fantasia* (1930).

The English folksong revival led to a flowering of art song. One of the most committed folk enthusiasts was the Australian Percy Grainger (1882–1961), who made field recordings of English folk song on wax cylinders between 1905 and 1909. His most famous arrangements include 'Country Gardens' and 'Shepherd's Hey'. Of the native composers, Peter Warlock (1894–1930), George Butterworth (1885–1916) and Gerald Finzi (1901–56) each made major contributions to a canon of largely syllabic, tonal settings of English texts that spanned a wide gamut of lyric expressivity.

Elsewhere, Arnold Bax (1883–1953) looked to Irish culture (particularly the poetry of Yeats), Celtic folklore and Scottish landscapes in the creation of a diverse oeuvre that includes seven symphonies and the enduring tone poems *The Garden of Fand* (1916) and *Tintagel* (1919). Arthur Bliss (1891–1975) married an English Romantic impulse with 20th-century European influences in such pieces as the *Colour Symphony* (1922, revised 1932), the Clarinet Quintet (1932) and the Piano Concerto (1939), while Edmund Rubbra (1901–86) struck a similarly tonal path in 11 symphonies (1937–79) that largely shun modernist aesthetics.

English song

Arnold Bax, Arthur Bliss

Walton, Tippett and Britten

Next to Vaughan Williams, England's most significant composer of the inter-war years was William Walton (1902–83). He wrote much of his best music in response to European influences, which he successfully absorbed into his own musical style. Setting abstract poetry by Edith Sitwell, Walton launched his career with *Façade* (1923), a satirical piece for narrator and small ensemble that tapped into the Parisian neo-classical vein with wind-orientated textures, jazzy inflections and dance styles.

William Walton

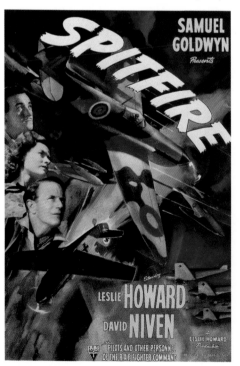

Walton turned more serious in the *Sinfonia Concertante* for piano and orchestra (1927) and the superb Viola Concerto (1929). In his festival cantata *Belshazzar's Feast* (1931) he made the English musical renaissance self-referential: the Babylonian homage to the 'god of gold' can be regarded as a parody of Elgar's *Pomp and Circumstance* marches. But throughout the work—in essence an oratorio—decadent and explosive moods discharge a compelling dramatic style. Walton's Symphony No. 1, first performed complete in 1935, assured his status as a composer of international standing. In patriotic mode he took genuine inspiration from Elgar for his 1937 march *Crown Imperial*, and this same 'noble' aesthetic found its way into his morale-boosting wartime film scores, notably *The First of the Few* (1942) and Laurence Olivier's adaptation of *Henry V* (1944).

◄ *Spitfire* (a.k.a. *The First of the Few*, UK), US theatrical poster, 1942. William Walton extracted music from his film score to create the concert piece *Spitfire Prelude and Fugue*.

531

If Walton released the oratorio from its Victorian sensibilities, Michael Tippett (1905–98), the pacifist intellectual, gave it a new purpose. *A Child of Our Time* (1941) is a work of protest against injustice, based on events in the build-up to the Second World War. In shaping his work Tippett followed both the three-part macrostructure of Handel's *Messiah* and the smaller-scale formal structures of Bach's Passions. But whereas Bach employed Lutheran chorales, Tippett chose African-American Spirituals to imbue his oratorio with a universal message; his concern was to give voice to the marginalised, whoever they were. The result is a lyrical, multi-layered, unique oratorio that seeks a reconciliation of the dichotomies that mark the human condition.

The 'struggle of the individual' was a theme also close to the heart of Tippett's friend Benjamin Britten (1913–76), the leading light of the generation that succeeded Vaughan Williams. Britten achieved principal importance as an opera composer; indeed he was the most significant English figure in this field since Henry Purcell. It was his first large-scale opera, *Peter Grimes* (1945), that effectively launched the revival of English opera. The story of a violent yet downtrodden fisherman, *Grimes* is in many ways a traditional work in its reliance on recitatives, arias, choruses and ensembles. It even incorporates tried-and-tested dramatic formats, such as the background use of liturgical music, a storm scene and a 'mad scene'. The emotional force of the opera is felt in Britten's deft musical characterisation and penetration of psychological states, revealed through lyrical arias, belligerent recitative and chilling choruses. Scenes are connected by evocative orchestral 'sea inter-

ludes', essentially miniature tone poems, whose rhythms and textures extend into the scenes themselves, simultaneously reflecting the turbulent mind of Grimes. The opera's social criticism and tragedy echoes that of *Wozzeck* (see *Berg and Webern*), which was itself a significant source of Britten's inspiration.

Britten, like Tippet a pacifist homosexual, was to return to the deeply felt theme of alienation and victimisation in the opera *Billy Budd* (1951), based on Herman Melville's novella. In between came his chamber operas *The Rape of Lucretia* (1946) and *Albert Herring* (1947), only the second of which secured repertory status. Beyond opera, the voice remained central to Britten's output, confirmed by fine pieces like the Serenade for tenor, horn and strings (1943), the song

▶ An angry mob in search of Grimes: scene from the US première of Britten's opera *Peter Grimes*, Berkshire Music Festival, 1946.

cycle *Holy Sonnets of John Donne* (1945) and the choral *Spring* Symphony (1949). His instrumental music from this time includes the ever-popular *Young Person's Guide to the Orchestra* (1946), taking melodic inspiration from the composer whose death, 250 years previously, it commemorates: Henry Purcell.

United States of America

The early 20th century saw the flowering of art music in the USA. The search for an authentic national style was an important mission for many US-born composers (see also *Chapter 6*), though the influence of European trends, past and present, was inescapable. Many young American composers flocked to Europe, Paris especially, to expand their musical horizons, while leading European musicians increasingly populated America's land of plenty. Between the beginning of the First World War and end of the Second, the composers Bloch, Varèse, Rachmaninov, Schoenberg, Korngold, Weill, Krenek, Stravinsky, Hindemith, Bartók and Martinů all became long-term residents. European conductors attracted to the USA included Arturo Toscanini (1867–1957), Sergey Koussevitzky (1874–1951) and Leopold Stokowski (1882–1977); each of them made critical contributions to American musical life, with Koussevitzky and Stokowski standing out as major supporters of Modernism.

During this time, the US musical scene became almost as heterogeneous as that of Europe. In one camp were the avant-gardists, whose concerns tended to transcend nationalistic priorities (Charles Ives was unusual in this respect); the other major groups comprised late-Romantics and neo-classical modernists, and out of the latter emerged the most committed exponents of US nationalism.

The avant-garde: Ives to Cage

The son of a versatile bandmaster, Charles Ives (1874–1954) studied music at Yale but opted for a lucrative career as an insurance entrepreneur. Because he never relied on music for income, he could afford to be experimental. Indeed, in pioneering spirit he anticipated many 20th-century techniques, including bitonality, polytonality, micro-tonality, pitch series, collage and indeterminacy. Ives is rightly regarded as a father figure of modern American music, though much of his output was unknown to the public until the mid-century.

Ives's early works betrayed his innovative curiosity, such as the polytonal *Song for Harvest Season* (1894), but also his grounding in late Romanticism and, most importantly, his search for an authentic American musical style. In his Second Symphony (first version 1902) he prefigured the Americana sound-world of Copland and Roy Harris, drawing heavily upon popular hymns and tunes, including Stephen Foster's *Camptown Races* for the final movement. By no means forsaking his nationalist concerns, Ives found his mature style with disparate, super-imposed sound layers in conjunction with spatial performance techniques. The polytonal orchestral pieces *The Unanswered Question* (1906) and *Central Park in the Dark* (1906)

Charles Ives

▶ The visionary American composer and businessman Charles Ives. His unconventional musical perspective was encouraged in childhood by his father, a bandmaster and teacher, who would instruct him to sing folk tunes in one key while he accompanied him in another.

both feature multiple layers of material, the second with a collage of sounds representing nature, a fire engine, a casino, a runaway cab horse, street musicians (etc.), all imaginatively superimposed to raucous climax.

Ives's music, at once nostalgic, multifaceted and progressive, distilled the rich and diverse life he breathed and observed. Like Beethoven and Bruckner, he was rarely content with his first efforts and so he repeatedly revised his compositions. Most of them were conceived before 1920, including his Third Symphony (*The Camp Meeting*, *c.*1911), String Quartet No. 2 (*c.*1913), *A Symphony: New England Holidays* (*c.*1919) and the Piano Sonata No. 2: *Concord, Mass., 1840–60* (*c.*1919). Each of these pieces quotes popular or classical themes (sometimes both), and nearly all had to wait until the 1940s or later for their first public performance. Ives only heard individual

Fourth Symphony

movements of his Fourth Symphony (completed *c.*1925) played during his lifetime, and then never its fourth, final movement. Premièred complete in 1965, it is a summation of his stylistic concerns and the most ambitious piece he ever wrote. Dense, multi-layered, abounding in quotation and collage techniques, the symphony demands the separation of instrumental groups and three conductors to manage multiple layers of contrasting metre and tempo. Also central to Ives's output are nearly 200 songs, most of which were self-published in the collection *114 Songs*, in 1921. They express the full gamut of Ives's musical personality, from whimsical, hymnal and patriotic pieces to songs that are, by Ives's reckoning, so complex, they 'cannot be sung'.

Edgard Varèse

During the 1920s, while Ives was still a virtual unknown, the French émigré Edgard Varèse (1883–1965) was the most important composer on the American avant-garde musical scene. His seemingly chaotic assemblage of sounds in *Hyperprism* provoked nothing short of revulsion among the critics at its New York première in 1923. Scored for nine wind and brass, and seven percussionists on 16 instruments (including a siren), the atonal, gestural work introduced the composer's vision of 'organised sound'. The chamber pieces *Octandre* (1923) and *Intégrales* (1925) followed, inciting reviews as savage as the music itself. But not everyone was baffled by Varèse. The eminent conductor Leopold Stokowski recognised the composer's logic and premièred his first large-scale orchestral compositions: *Amériques* (1921) in 1926, and *Arcana* the following year. Percussion is central to nearly all of Varèse's sonic landscapes and exploited to the extreme in *Ionisation* (1931). Formed of constantly evolving rhythmic cells, the six-minute work is scored almost exclusively for unpitched and pitched percussion. It is effectively the first stand-alone percussion piece by a major Western classical composer (see also *Chapter 8*).

Henry Cowell (1897–1965) was another composer who embraced alter-native sound-worlds. As early as 1913, aged 16, he began to methodically explore 'tone-clusters', requiring the pianist to use palm or forearm across adjacent notes to produce dense sound-masses. Bartók later asked Cowell's permission to use the cluster technique; and in fact many of the paths Cowell explored during the 1920s and 30s were revisited by avant-gardists in the latter half of the century. In *The Banshee* (1925) the pianist plays the entire piece inside the instrument, plucking, scraping and sweeping along the strings. The score incorporates various symbols and graphics to indicate the techniques involved. His experiments in improvisation and 'indeterminacy' also began in the 1920s. *Ensemble* (1924) asks string players to improvise most of the music from a few provided bars, while the *Mosaic Quartet* (1935) allows the performers to determine the order and repetition of movements.

Henry Cowell

Cowell was a tireless student of world music. He incorporated non-Western instruments and exotic rhythms into his work from the 1930s, as in *Ostinato Pianissimo* (1934), scored for a percussion ensemble that includes rice bowls and bongos. By drawing West and East into musical fusion, Cowell was acknowledging his country's growing ethnic diversity. Harry Partch (1901–74) similarly produced music reflective of a cross-cultural communal spirit. His innovations extended to the adaptation and creation of diverse instruments—Western and exotic—to facilitate a musical language based on a 43-note microtonal scale.

Other important contributors to early American modernism included Carl Ruggles (1876–1971), now best known for his orchestral work *Sun Treader* (1933), and Ruth Crawford Seeger (1901–53), one of America's leading experts in American folk music. Both these composers had close professional contact with Cowell, as did John Cage (1912–92), who also came under the influence of Schoenberg in Los Angeles. Cage's innate experimentalism found an outlet in contemporary dance and other forms of accompaniment music. From Cowell he developed a fascination with exotic instruments, but he also desired to harness the musical potential of diverse, unconventional media, including electronics. His percussive inci-dental music *Imaginary Landscape No. 1* (1939) broke new ground with its incorporation of two variable-speed turntables playing frequency recordings. His pithy *Imaginary Landscape No. 3* (1942) went further with its frequency oscillators, tin cans, muted gong, variable-speed turntables, a buzzer and an amplified coil of wire. Around the same time Cage had the idea of wedging screws, bolts, rubber and felt between the strings of a piano to create an extended percussion battery for the dance piece *Bacchanale* (1940). He produced more so-called 'prepared piano' compositions throughout the 1940s while immersing himself in Eastern philosophy. By the half-century Cage was the very epitome of the progressive American spirit.

John Cage

Prepared piano

Neo-classicism and Nationalism

A number of American composers gained first-hand experience of the European modernist scene. Roger Sessions (1896–1985) and George Antheil (1900–59) both established their careers in Europe, while others simply visited for extended study periods. Many of them shared a common teacher: Nadia Boulanger (1887–1979). Also a composer and conductor, the Paris-based Boulanger counted among her students Aaron Copland, David Diamond, Roy Harris, Walter Piston, Virgil Thomson and Elliott Carter. Virgil Thomson (1896–1989), who sealed his reputation with the opera *Four Saints in Three Acts* (premièred 1934), later joked that Boulanger was a 'one-woman graduate school so powerful and so permeating that legend credits every U.S. town with two things: a five-and-dime and a Boulanger pupil'.

Aaron Copland

Aaron Copland (1900–90) assimilated jazz into his musical style before he went to France as a 21-year-old to study with Boulanger. His secure neo-classical grounding was evident on his return to the USA with such jazz-inflected works as *Music for the Theatre* (1925), commissioned by Koussevitzky, and the Piano Concerto (1926). Thereafter he considered alternative modernist approaches, even experimenting with serial configuration in the *Piano Variations* (1930). But by this time America's economy was plunging and unemployment was soaring: the public wanted relief from the Great Depression and plenty of American composers thought serialism and atonality would simply add to the misery. Copland responded by forging a new folk-based tonal idiom and found popular appeal. First came the evocative *El Salón México* (1936), an orchestral piece inspired by Mexican folk traditions and his own fond impressions of the country. He then introduced the cowboy song to ballet in *Billy the Kid* (1938) and *Rodeo* (1942); these pieces established Copland's quintessential musical Americana, a rhythmically forceful rustic-style cast with widely-spaced tonal harmonies. Overtly nostalgic, the style reached its apotheosis in a ballet about American pioneer settlers, *Appalachian Spring* (1944). This masterpiece is now popular in its full orchestral attire, but Copland's craft is best appreciated in the original chamber setting for 13 instruments, where timbral colours, harmonic diversity and rhythmic vibrancy are at their most exposed.

Copland's 'imposed simplicity', as he called it, provided the language for his heroic war-time morale booster, *Fanfare for the common man* (1942), whose quartal sonorities found their way into the closing movement of his lyrical Symphony No. 3 (1946). Copland's expansive oeuvre includes the film scores *Of Mice and Men* (1939), the Piano Sonata (1941), the song cycle

12 Poems of Emily Dickinson (1950) and the opera *The Tender Land* (1954). His post-war music lurched back towards a more modernist aesthetic and some of it succumbed to serial influences (see *Chapter 8*). A dedicated and high-profile advocate of modern American music, Copland gained numerous awards and plaudits, including a Pulitzer Prize for *Appalachian Spring*, an Oscar for his score to the film *The Heiress* (1949), a Presidential Medal of Freedom (1964) and a string of honorary doctorates.

▲ 'The Card Game' from Copland's ballet *Billy the Kid* (première, 1938).

The symphonic tradition was critical to the development of American music. Like Copland, Roy Harris (1898–1979) tapped into a nationalistic vein with folk-derived themes and translucent harmonies in his powerful single-movement Third Symphony (1937). Walter Piston (1894–1976) was less inclined to quote folk music but nonetheless inculcated older colloquial styles into his appealing Second and Fourth symphonies (1943, 1950). Among the other high-profile American symphonists of the period were Howard Hanson (1896–1981) and William Schuman (1910–92). Thanks to the advocacy of Koussevitzky, Schuman made an enormous impact with his intensely contrapuntal Third Symphony (1941). A triumvirate of symphonic 'thirds'—by Schuman, Harris and Copland—represent the cream of the American symphonic tradition. Most high-profile American symphonists of this time shared a predilection for strong tonal organisation and richly expressive, often boldly dramatic orchestral styles.

American symphonists

Samuel Barber (1910–81) was one of the leading American composers not swept along by the neo-classical movement. Instead he fostered a lyrical, Straussian style that allowed him to experiment with modern dissonance within a tonal framework. His most celebrated music includes the Violin Concerto (1939), the *Second Essay for Orchestra* (1942) and many songs, most famously *Knoxville: Summer of 1915* for high voice and orchestra (1947). While active in just about every genre, including ballet and opera, Barber is best known as the composer of the *Adagio for Strings*, an arrangement of the second movement of his String Quartet (1936). The work bears testament to his irrepressible Romanticism and creative treatment of extended melody.

Samuel Barber

A number of American-born concert composers, including Copland and George Antheil, were active in film music, but it was the Austrian

Erich
Wolfgang
Korngold

Erich Wolfgang Korngold (1897–1957) who revolutionised the genre by creating the symphonic, leitmotivic film score. Arriving in Hollywood in 1934 he gave full voice to his Romantic urges, scoring around 20 films including the Errol Flynn classics *Captain Blood* (1935), *The Adventures of Robin Hood* (1938) and *The Sea Hawk* (1940). Korngold's concert compositions are similarly characterised by a lyrical Romantic manner and include the Violin Concerto (1937), Cello Concerto (1946) and Symphony in F sharp (1952). Out of fashion post-war, his chamber and orchestral music experienced a great surge of interest from major performers and conductors at the end of the 20th century.

George
Gershwin

George Gershwin (1898–1937) was the first popular music composer to make a direct, historic impression on the history of American classical music. Born to Russian parents in Brooklyn, New York, Gershwin graduated from song-plugging on Tin Pan Alley to songwriting for Broadway before he was 20. He wrote his first full Broadway musical, *La La Lucille*, in 1919, and a year later saw his fame rocket after Al Jolson recorded his song *Swanee*. His legendary partnership with his lyricist brother Ira Gershwin (1896–1983) was launched in 1924 by the hit musical *Lady, Be Good*, starring Fred and Adele Astaire. That was the watershed year in which George took his giant leap into the classical world with *Rhapsody in Blue*, written for the Paul Whiteman Band.

Rhapsody in Blue

Orchestrated by Ferde Grofé, *Rhapsody in Blue* was pioneering in its spectacular fusion of jazz/blues and classical idioms. This was Gershwin's 'vivid panorama of American life … its feverishness, its vulgarity, its welter of love, marriage and divorce, and its basic solidity in the character of the people'. Gershwin played the piano part in the première at New York's Aeolian Hall, the piece programmed with many others as *An Experiment in Modern Music*. His 'experiment' polarised critics but created a public sensation, later landing his picture on the cover of *Time* magazine. Gershwin now pursued dual ambitions as a 'popular' and 'art music' composer. The Piano Concerto in F (1925), the tone poem *An American in Paris* (1928) and his opera *Porgy and Bess* (1935), are all infused with the fresh jazz-blues vernacular that he did so much to formalise. The musical significance

Porgy and Bess

▶ Gershwin and (left) the director Rouben Mamoulian with cast of *Porgy and Bess*, opening night curtain call at the Alvin Theatre, New York, 10 October 1935.

of *Porgy and Bess*, beyond classic songs such as 'Summertime' and 'It Ain't Necessarily So', resided in its blend of forms—integrating African-American folk music into an opera with a traditional, leitmotivic structure. Featuring lyrics by Ira Gershwin, *Porgy* struggled for recognition for many years. Success for the original version, scored with recitative, barely arrived in Ira's long lifetime, let alone George's.

The music of the most famous US composers of this period—Copland and Gershwin—demonstrates how the evolving North American classical idiom found its greatest identity through the absorption of vernacular folk and jazz styles. This testifies to a mindset that did not recognise the depth of division between 'high' and 'low' art that existed in Europe, where folk elements and (imported) jazz were commonly integrated in more subtle ways. It is not surprising, therefore, that in the second half of the century the USA would become fertile ground for pop/rock-influenced minimalism, pluralism and postmodernism.

Russia

Scriabin and early Prokofiev

Russian musical life largely followed that of western Europe until the early 1930s, when Communist artistic policy began to severely restrict modernist practices. Rimsky-Korsakov survived eight years into the new century, continuing the Romantic tradition in the operas *The Invisible City of Kitezh* (1905) and *The Golden Cockerel* (1907). His pupils Alexander Glazunov (1865–1936) and Reinhold Glière (1875–1956) took up his mantle, alongside the itinerant Sergei Rachmaninov. Reacting against the Romantic mindset were Alexander Scriabin (1872–1915), Stravinsky and Sergey Prokofiev (1891–1953). Scriabin evolved a post-Romantic mystical manner, while Stravinsky and Prokofiev journeyed into neo-classical objectivism.

Alexander Scriabin

Alexander Scriabin's mystical aura was encouraged by two events outside his control: his Christmas-day birth (Russian calendar; otherwise 6 January) and his death from septicaemia around Easter time, 1915. The mystical basis of his artistic journey resided partly in his fascination with theosophy—encompassing the belief that true knowledge of God can only be attained through spiritual ecstasy. Scriabin's transition from Romanticism to neo-tonal mysticism is well illustrated by his ten piano sonatas, composed between 1892 and 1913, and the five Preludes of 1914. The early sonatas are written in a Chopin-inspired idiom, but the last five carry no key signatures and occasionally countenance atonality, with the late Preludes, Op. 74, representing his most extreme departure. Scriabin escaped fixed tonality by sustaining whole movements from dominant sonorities, resulting in a restless, impressionistic musical style.

When Scriabin wrote the extended orchestral-choral work *Prometheus*, between 1908 and 1910, he was experiencing delusions, even believing himself to be a Messiah. Yet there is little to identify mental imbalance in his music. For *Prometheus* he used a dominant-inflected pitch-set—the so-called 'mystic' chord—as almost the sole basis for harmonic and melodic material. Starting on C, the degrees of the chord continue F sharp, B flat,

E, A and D. It appears in various inversions and spacings, and is freely transposed, modified and looted for its constituent parts. This quasi-serialist, quartal harmony pervades nearly all of Scriabin's mature works. If his harmonic resources were economic, they were offset by a refined timbral sensibility (he was a famous synaesthete) and a polyphonic rigour, instilled in him as a pupil of the composer Sergey Taneyev (1856–1915).

Sergey Prokofiev

While Scriabin was planning his eschatological, mixed-media *Mysterium* to bring about humankind's spiritual transcendence (a work he left unfinished), Prokofiev was establishing his reputation as an 'ultra modernist', or at least so-called by critics. He composed his First Piano Concerto in 1912, as a student aged 20, announcing himself in pseudo-Romantic spirit, only to suffocate the sentimental impulse under quirky chromaticisms and mordant moods. The Second Piano Concerto, produced the following year, was similarly anti-emotional, with sensuous moments confronted by strident counter gestures amid pianism of stunning virtuosity. Prokofiev's music reflected his personality—matter-of-fact, sardonic, sometimes cutting. The public and critics puzzled over his style, but Prokofiev carried on regardless, as a composer must. His wartime music included the primitivist *Scythian* Suite (1915), inspired by Stravinsky's *Rite of Spring*, and the opera *The Gambler*, completed in 1917. That same historic year he finished his Violin Concerto No. 1 and *Classical Symphony*, the latter a delectable re-interpretation of the Haydn symphonic style with unusual twists of harmony and phrasing. It was a milestone in the development of neo-classicism, pre-dating Stravinsky's *Pulcinella* by two years.

Shortly after the Russian Revolution of 1917, Prokofiev followed Rachmaninov into self-imposed exile. He struggled to make his name in the USA, although while there he managed to produce two of his most characteristic

▶ Soldiers and workers of Petrograd during the October Revolution of 1917, which saw the Russian Provisional Government overthrown and power transferred to the Bolsheviks.

works: the Third Piano Concerto (1921) and the opera *The Love of Three Oranges* (1921). Prokofiev's years abroad were mainly spent in Paris, where his fortunes were mixed. During this time he made several visits back to the Soviet Union to promote his music. As a result, some of his Paris compositions had Russian premières, such as the Sinfonietta (1929), while other pieces, including *The Love of Three Oranges*, became standard repertory.

Socialist Realism: Shostakovich and Prokofiev

Under Lenin, and then for a few years under Stalin (from 1924), Communist Russia allowed all brands of modernism, even if the Russian Association of Proletarian Musicians was advocating more accessible music. The Association for Contemporary Music promoted works by the Second Viennese School, Stravinsky and Hindemith, and encouraged Soviet composers to develop along similar lines. The young Dmitry Shostakovich (1906–75), drawing inspiration from Tchaikovsky, Mahler and Stravinsky, was therefore allowed to write brash irony into his First Symphony (1926) and percolate highly dissonant textures in the satirical opera *The Nose* (1930).

Dmitry Shostakovich

In 1932 the Union of Soviet Composers was established to promote Soviet artistic policy. The official line was one of 'Socialist Realism', an ideology that in music demanded simplicity, clear tonality, lyricism and optimism. It was the duty of art to inspire pride and joy among the masses, celebrating Marxist truth and the benefits of communist life. In contrast, Western modernism, the atonal aesthetic especially, was decried as 'degenerate', 'bourgeois' and 'undemocratic' (the latter, because most people did not like it).

In just a few years this new official artistic policy effected major changes in Soviet music. Shostakovich's opera *Lady Macbeth of Mtsensk District*, extolled as a 'masterpiece' by critics after its première in 1934, received a damning appraisal two years later in the government newspaper, *Pravda*. Stalin had finally witnessed the work and found both its lurid subject matter and musical language repugnant. 'Muddle instead of Music' ran the headline. *Lady Macbeth*, enjoying success worldwide, was banned from the Soviet stage.

Lady Macbeth of Mtsensk District

As the most renowned composer living in Russia, Shostakovich was an obvious target for official rebuke. He was judged a good candidate for rehabilitation, since he had previously produced pieces that toed the Party line—notably his scores to government propaganda films. *Pravda*, to dispel any sense of ambiguity, sent an official warning to the composer, that unless he changed his ways, 'things … may end very badly'. In Stalin's Soviet Union, political undesirables were commonly excised, whether by labour-camp imprisonment or execution. Many of Shostakovich's family and friends disappeared in this way and he therefore decided not to call Stalin's bluff.

Shostakovich buried his weighty, ultimately pessimistic Fourth Symphony (1936) in a drawer and began work on what he called 'a Soviet artist's response to just criticism': the Fifth Symphony (1937). Was he being sarcastic? The symphony certainly carries a more accessible, positive tone, climaxing with a tour-de-force finale, but elements of possible satire and

Shostakovich: Fifth Symphony

mockery—the circus-like militaristic march in the first movement, for example—confuse the issue. Looking beyond music into his private life, a similar question of political conformity arises. An unnatural repetition of positive adjectives in his letters (which were liable to be intercepted) seems to reduce the sincerity of his message: it is as though this method serves as a 'reverse code'. There also seems to be a flavour of irony and sarcasm in his fawning yet formal statements of official apology or allegiance. In neither case, of course, could any bureaucrat indict the composer.

Prokofiev's return

Before Prokofiev returned to the Soviet Union for good, in 1936, he recognised his homeland as totalitarian, but he also noted its receptivity to his 'new simplicity'. In recent years he had retreated from chromatically-dense pieces like the 'iron and steel' Second Symphony (1925), and turned towards a clearer tonal manner, as in the romping Fifth Piano Concerto (1932) and expressive, even Romantic, Violin Concerto No. 2 (1935). His Russian film scores, unsurprisingly, were even more tonally assured, such as *Lieutenant Kijé* (1933), whose infectious music he adapted into a popular orchestral suite.

Prokofiev wrote *Romeo and Juliet* (1936) in the hope it would happily proclaim his return to the Soviet fold. Despite its lyrical melodies and strong tonal design, the ballet struggled from the outset, rejected by the Bolshoi as too complicated to choreograph. It was instead premièred in Brno, Czechoslovakia, in 1938. Even the symphonic fairytale *Peter and the Wolf*, written as accessible and educational music for children, failed to make an impression at its 1936 première. Prokofiev's greatest pre-war Russian success was his score to Sergey Eisenstein's patriotic film *Alexander Nevsky* (1938), which he converted into a hugely popular cantata in 1939. The next Eisenstein-Prokofiev collaboration, *Ivan the Terrible*, was split into two films. The first, unashamedly patriotic, was released in 1944. The second, which portrayed the brutal side of the 16th-century tsar, was banned until after Stalin's death.

War years

Prokofiev and Shostakovich, together with Aram Khachaturian (1903–78) and Nikolay Myaskovsky (1881–1950), wrote some dynamic patriotic music during World War II, much of which quickly faded from view. Among the lasting exceptions is Shostakovich's Seventh Symphony *Leningrad* (1941), undeniably a morale-boosting work, though one clouded with moments of characteristic ambiguity. 'It's not about Leningrad under siege,' Shostakovich later insisted, 'it's about the Leningrad that Stalin destroyed and Hitler merely finished off.' The score was microfilmed and smuggled out to the West, where the symphony became an artistic monument to resistance against Nazism. The war also galvanised Prokofiev's ambitious opera *War and Peace* (1942), begun just after the German invasion of the Soviet Union in 1941. Tolstoy's account of the 1812 Russian expulsion of Napoleon's armies could not fail to instil hope in the Soviet people. Divided into two parts, the opera was given a concert première in 1944. Prokofiev only ever saw Part I staged in his lifetime, in 1946, and it proved one of his outstanding successes.

Russian music written during and immediately after the war owed its diversity of style to a temporary relaxation of the restrictions of 'socialist realism'. Some works were squarely in the tonal-melodious-optimistic mould, like Prokofiev's ballet *Cinderella* (1944) and also his Fifth Symphony, triumphantly introduced in 1945. Others pieces strayed far from the narrow path, like the same composer's gruff Piano Sonata No. 6 (1940) and tragic Sixth Symphony (1947), and Shostakovich's desolate Eighth Symphony (1943) and the 'ideologically weak' Ninth Symphony (1945). Creative 'aberrations', common to all the arts including film, were in due course severely punished. In 1948 the Soviet Central Committee, led by the Minister of Culture, Andrei Zhdanov, issued a decree denouncing virtually all front-line Soviet composers, including Shostakovich and Prokofiev, but also conservatives like Khachaturian and Myaskovsky. They were all found guilty of marketing 'formalist perversions and anti-democratic tendencies … alien to the Soviet people and their artistic tastes'. Lists of banned pieces were published for each composer.

1948: Andrei Zhdanov

Prokofiev obediently relented to political pressure, stating in agreement that 'the formalistic movement, which leads to the impoverishment and decline of music, is alien to the Soviet people'. He promised to write more tuneful music in the future. Shostakovich followed suit, and in 1949 was personally encouraged by Stalin to join his country's delegation at the Cultural and Scientific Conference for World Peace in New York. The composer politely pointed out to the Soviet leader that his position was compromised, given that so many works by himself and his comrades were blacklisted. Stalin revoked the oppressive decree just before Shostakovich left for America. There the composer testified to 'reasonable' artistic constrictions in the Soviet Union.

Returning home, Shostakovich found himself back in favour with Party officials. He consolidated his advantage with the compliant oratorio *Song of the Forests* (1949), praising Stalin's reforestation programme. But given the political sensitivities surrounding high-profile compositions, Shostakovich began making a deeper commitment to the more private world of chamber music. The 1940s marked several major pieces in this field, notably the Piano Trio No. 2, the Piano Quintet and the Third String Quartet.

Prokofiev, reeling from the blow of 1948 and physically in poor health, struggled to maintain his creative powers. His Symphony-Concerto for cello and orchestra (1951) is one of the best offerings from his last five years. He drew his final breath the very same day as his chief oppressor, Joseph Stalin, on 5 March 1953.

◀ Dmitri Shostakovich at the Cultural and Scientific Conference for World Peace, New York, March 1949.

Chronology 1900–1949

14 January Puccini's emotionally tempestuous opera *Tosca* premières at the Teatro Costanzi, Rome, amid feverish expectations and a bomb scare. The public are enraptured, demanding footlight appearances of the composer throughout. In his eponymous heroine, Puccini has created one of the repertory's most engaging female roles.

22 January Rachmaninov visits Tolstoy. Still depressed over the bitter fiasco of his First Symphony (1897), the composer plays the writer some of his music. Tolstoy retorts, 'Tell me, does anybody need music like that?' Rachmaninov takes the reaction with a pinch of salt, as Tolstoy then declares Beethoven to be 'nonsense'.

January–April Rachmaninov meets regularly with Dr Nikolay Dahl, an eminent psychologist, who attempts to restore his self-confidence through auto-suggestion. During the summer the composer begins work on his Second Piano Concerto.

2 February Gustave Charpentier's *Louise*, a tale of a humble working woman in search of self-fulfilment and love, opens at the Opéra Comique, Paris. Many decry the opera as licentious and improper, yet it proves such a success that the composer, using his profits, establishes the Conservatoire Populaire de Mimi Pinson, offering working-class girls free musical education.

2 March Stage composer **Kurt Weill** is born in Dessau, Germany.

2 July Sibelius supports Finland's right to self-rule with his symphonic poem *Finlandia* (1899, revised 1900), premièred in Helsinki. Performances of the work are usually advertised under the title 'Impromptu', so to avoid drawing attention from Russian authorities.

12 July The full orchestral version of **Fauré**'s Requiem (possibly orchestrated by his pupil Jean Roger-Ducasse) is introduced at the Trocadéro in Paris. This year the composer adapts his incidental music to *Pelléas et Mélisande* (1898) to make a popular four-movement orchestral suite.

23 August Austrian composer and writer **Ernst Křenek** is born in Vienna.

3 October Inadequate rehearsal time hampers **Elgar**'s oratorio *The Dream of Gerontius*, introduced under **Hans Richter** in Birmingham. An acclaimed performance takes place the following year in Dusseldorf.

3 November Rimsky-Korsakov's opera *The Tale of Tsar Saltan* is staged for the first time, in Moscow. Its third act introduces what will later become an instrumental showpiece—*Flight of the Bumblebee*.

14 November Composer **Aaron Copland** is born in Brooklyn, New York.

22 November Sir Arthur Sullivan dies in London, aged 58. *The Times* declares: 'The death of Sir Arthur Sullivan may be said without hyperbole to have plunged the whole empire in gloom.'

1900 Hawaii becomes a territory of the USA • Britain annexes Orange Free State and Transvaal; guerrilla warfare follows • Boxer Rebellion: European legations in Peking are besieged by Chinese Nationalists; an international coalition relieves them • The Commonwealth of Australia becomes an independent British Dominion • Physicist Max Planck (Ger) develops the quantum theory of light • Walter Reed (US) discovers the transmission of yellow fever by mosquitoes • Paul Signac (Fr) paints *The Papal Palace, Avignon* • Childe Hassam (US) paints *New York, Late Afternoon, Winter* • Sigmund Freud (Aus): *The Interpretation of Dreams* • Anton Checkov (Russ): *Uncle Vanya*

1901

Grieg completes his tenth and final collection of *Lyric Pieces* for piano (Op. 71).

Rachmaninov composes his Cello Sonata, Op. 19.

Ravel composes his impressionistic piano piece *Jeux d'eau* (Water Games), inspired by Liszt's *Jeux d'eau a la Villa d'Este*.

17 January Mascagni's opera *Le Maschere* (The Masks) opens to high expectations in six Italian opera houses simultaneously. Five out of the six productions are dismal failures, with the Genoa performance booed off the stage before the finish.

27 January Following a stroke, **Giuseppe Verdi** dies in Milan, aged 87. One month after burial his coffin is exhumed, together with that of his wife, and conveyed past tens of thousands of mourners lining the streets of Milan to the Casa di Riposo, a retirement home for musicians founded by Verdi. **Toscannini** conducts a choir of 800 singing 'Va, pensiero' (from *Nabucco*) during the ceremony.

31 March Dvořák's lyric fairytale *Rusalka*, completed the previous year, opens at the National Theatre in Prague. It becomes the composer's most popular opera.

April Schoenberg completes the short score of his *Gurrelieder* cantata. The full score (1911) will incorporate a narrator, five solo voices, three male choirs, an eight-part mixed choir and a 140-piece orchestra. (See also 1913.)

1 June Universal Edition is founded in Vienna.

20 June Elgar introduces his *Cockaigne (In London Town)*

Overture at the Queen's Hall in London. This year also marks the première of his orchestrated *Chanson de nuit* and *Chanson de matin*, written for violin and piano in 1899.

19 October Elgar presents the first two of his five *Pomp and Circumstance* military marches in Liverpool. March No. 1, with its anthem-like trio section, becomes an instant hit—even more so when the following year it gains the word setting of *Land of Hope and Glory* by A. C. Benson, prompted in part by King Edward VII.

9 November Rachmaninov (below) premières his symphonic Piano Concerto No. 2 to great acclaim in Moscow. The work is dedicated to the psychologist Dr Nikolay Dahl, who revitalised Rachmaninov's creativity in the wake of the catastrophic First Symphony première (see 1897). Passionate, dreamy, effervescent, it becomes the most popular concerto of the 20th century.

21 November Richard Strauss's one-act opera *Feuersnot* (Fire Famine) is premièred in Dresden.

22 November Spanish composer **Joaquin Rodrigo** is born in Sagunto, Valencia. He loses his sight at the age of three after contracting diphtheria.

25 November Mahler's Fourth Symphony (1900) is heard for the first time, in Munich. Based on his song 'Das himmlische Leben' (Heavenly Life), the work is a journey of innocence, culminating with a direct quotation of the song (sung by solo soprano) in the final movement.

Carl Nielsen completes his Second Symphony, *De fire temperamenter* (The Four Temperaments). His collection of symphonic portraits has been inspired by a woodcut depicting the four medieval 'humours': choleric, phlegmatic, melancholic and sanguine.

8 March Sibelius conducts the first performance of his Second Symphony, in Helsinki. Whilst not an explicitly nationalistic work, its stirring heroic outer movements resonate with the oppressed Finns, who continue to exist under the cloud of Russian oppression.

9 March Mahler, aged 41, marries Alma Schindler, an amateur composer nearly 20 years his junior.

29 March Composer **William Turner Walton** is born in Oldham, Lancashire.

9 April Ethel Smyth's opera *Der Wald* opens in Berlin. The following year it becomes the first opera by a woman to be staged at New York's Metropolitan Opera.

11 April In a Milan hotel the tenor **Enrico Caruso** earns himself £100 recording ten arias for Fred Gaisberg, a talent-scout of the Gramophone Company. They are released on the Victor *Red Seal* label the following year and fast-track Caruso to international stardom. He is the first great artist of the record industry.

30 April Based on Maeterlinck's play, the symbolist opera *Pelléas et Mélisande* by **Debussy** (right) premières under

André Messager at the Opéra-Comique, Paris. Maeterlinck, disgruntled that his mistress has not been granted the lead part, writes in the *Figaro*: 'I am compelled to wish that it fails resoundingly and instantly.' Critical reaction is mixed, but the Parisian public demonstrate sufficient interest to launch the opera into the repertory.

9 June Mahler triumphs with the first complete performance of his Third Symphony, in Krefeld. During the summer he completes his Fifth Symphony, whose beguiling fourth-movement Adagietto will become his most famous piece of music.

9 August Three new works are heard during the coronation of Edward VII: **Elgar**'s hymn *O Mightiest of the Mighty*, **Parry**'s anthem *I Was Glad*, and **Saint-Saëns**'s Coronation March (Op. 117). The Frenchman is later appointed a Commander of the Victorian Order for his services.

2 October Elgar's setting of *Land of Hope and Glory* is heard for the first time in the finale of the *Coronation Ode* for King Edward VII. The tune has been taken from his *Pomp and Circumstance* March No. 1, and will subsequently return there with vocal parts attached.

6 November The début of **Francesco Cilea**'s opera *Adriana Lecouvreur* rouses great excitement at Milan's Teatro Lirico. Tenor **Enrico Caruso** sings the part of Maurizio, Count of Saxony.

1902 The Boer War ends with Treaty of Vereeniging; the Boers recognise British sovereignty • Germany, Italy and Austria renew their Triple Alliance • President Theodore Roosevelt is empowered to purchase French shares in the Panama Canal and so gain control of the Canal Zone for the USA • Russia agrees with China to evacuate Manchuria •

Egypt's Aswan Dam is completed • Gustav Klimt (Aus) paints *Buchenhain* • Camille Pissarro paints *Le Pont-Neuf* • Arthur Conan Doyle (Scot): *The Hound of the Baskervilles* • Rudyard Kipling (Eng): *Just So Stories* • Beatrix Potter (Eng) writes and illustrates *Peter Rabbit* • Henry James (US): *Wings of the Dove*

Sweden's **Hugo Alfvén** charms national folk tunes into his Swedish Rhapsody No. 1 (*Midsummer Vigil*) for orchestra.

Debussy composes his evocative *Estampes* (Engravings) for piano, comprising *Pagodes* (Pagodas), *Soirée dans Grenade* (Evening in Granada) and *Jardin sous la pluie* (Gardens in the rain).

HMV records the first complete opera, Verdi's *Ernani*, issued on 40 single-sided discs.

Rachmaninov completes his ten Preludes, Op. 23, for solo piano. The set includes the popular No. 5 in G minor ('Alla Marcia'), whose opening percussive theme is blissfully contrasted with the Russian languor of the work's central section.

Ravel dabbles in orientalism in the song cycle *Shéhérazade* for mezzo soprano and orchestra. This year also sees the completion of his String Quartet in F major.

Satie completes his *Trois morceaux en forme de poire* (Three Pieces in the Shape of a Pear) for piano duet.

11 February Bruckner's unfinished Ninth Symphony ('Dedicated to my dear God—if He accepts it') is posthumously premièred under **Ferdinand Löwe** in Vienna. Löwe is also responsible for the performing edition of the symphony, but has taken considerable liberties with the score. The public will not hear the composer's version until 1932.

22 February Hugo Wolf dies syphilitically insane at an asylum in Vienna, aged 42. Melanie Köchert, his mistress, slips into depression, berating herself in the belief that she had failed him as a partner. Three years later she commits suicide by jumping from a fourth-floor window of her home in Vienna.

8 March George Enescu (left), aged 21, secures his status as a leading voice in Romanian music with his two orchestral *Rhapsodies roumaines* (1901), premièred in Bucharest.

6 June Armenian composer and conductor **Aram Khachaturian** is born in Tbilisi, Georgia.

17 June Victor Herbert's operetta *Babes in Toyland* opens in Chicago. It begins a run of theatrical hits for the Dublin-born composer, making him one of the most famous names in American music.

Summer Stravinsky begins regular composition lessons with **Rimsky-Korsakov**.

8 October The sun rises and sets over the Aegean Sea in **Nielsen**'s *Helios Overture*, first performed in Copenhagen.

14 October Elgar's oratorio *The Apostles* premières before an appreciative audience at Birmingham's Town Hall.

15 November Eugen D'Albert's opera *Tiefland* (The Lowlands) opens in Prague.

30 November Chausson's opera *Le Roi Arthus*, musically inspired by Wagner, premières posthumously at La Monnaie in Brussels.

1903 Serbia's Alexander I and Queen Draga are assassinated • USA secures control of the Panama Canal Zone • Canada and the USA agree Alaska's frontier • The Russian Social Democratic Party divides into Mensheviks and Bolsheviks • Pope Leo XIII dies; succeeded by Pope Pius X (until 1914) • Emmeline Pankhurst founds the Women's Social and Political Union, beginning Britain's suffragette movement • First flights by Orville and Wilber Wright (US); Wilber manages continuous flight for nearly one minute • Claude Monet (Fr) paints *Waterloo Bridge* • Joaquín Sorolla (Sp) paints *Children on the Seashore* • Jack London (US): *Call of the Wild*

1904

The London Symphony Orchestra is founded.

Debussy leaves his first wife, Rosalie (neé Texier), for the married singer Emma Bardac. Like Debussy's shunned lover before her, Rosalie shoots herself, non-fatally. (See also 1897.)

Glazunov writes his Violin Concerto in A minor, dedicated to the Hungarian violinist **Leopold Auer**.

Ives completes his Third Symphony.

Scriabin leaves Russia for five years, abandoning his wife and four children for a younger woman. Based in central Europe (principally Switzerland), he becomes fascinated with theosophy.

21 January Janáček's domestic tragedy *Jenůfa* is staged for the first time, in Brno. The 50-year-old composer will later revise the opera substantially. (See also 1916.)

8 February Sibelius conducts a disappointing première of his Violin Concerto in D minor in Helsinki. A revised version, given in Berlin the following year under **Strauss**, also creates little stir. The concerto's status is elevated some 30 years later in the hands of Jascha Heifetz.

17 February Puccini's *Madama Butterfly* opens and flops at La Scala, Milan. The raucous audience, shouting, whistling and laughing, mauls the production and Puccini is accused of plagiarism. He immediately withdraws the opera for revision, despite believing

that rivals initiated the debacle. The new version, staged three months later in Brescia, is a resounding triumph.

21 March In New York **Richard Strauss** introduces his *Sinfonia domestica* (completed 1903), depicting a 24-hour period of his family life.

30 March Delius's opera *Koanga*, with a German libretto, premières in Elberfeld.

25 April Sibelius conducts his haunting *Valse Triste* in Helsinki. The one-movement work has been lifted from incidental music composed the previous year to the play *Kuolema* (Death), written by his brother-in-law, Arvid Järnefelt.

1 May Leading Czech composer **Antonín Dvořák** dies (possibly from a heart attack) in Prague, aged 62. Four days later his body is laid to rest at the Vyšehrad cemetery.

Summer Mahler completes his Sixth Symphony (which he will revise several times) and begins his Seventh. This year also sees the completion of his orchestral song cycle *Kindertotenlieder* (Songs on the Deaths of Children).

18 October Mahler introduces his Fifth Symphony in Cologne. With the return to purely orchestral (and apparently non-programmatic) symphonic form, he explores a more complex contrapuntal style, employing angular themes and unexpected shifts in mood. Both the critics and public react unfavourably.

10 November Ferruccio Busoni performs as soloist in the first performance of his monumental Piano Concerto, complete with choral finale, in Berlin.

11 December Giuseppe Martucci, aged 48, conducts the première of his Symphony No. 2, one of his greatest achievements, in Milan.

1904 Russia and Japan war over rival interests in China; Russian warships on the way to Japan fire on British trawlers in the North Sea • An *Entente Cordiale* between Britain and France settles their differences over Egypt; Britain recognises the Suez Canal Convention • Tibet's independence is established by a treaty with Britain • France's possessions in west Africa are reorganised as French West Africa, with Dakar as the capital • Herero tribesmen revolt against German rule in south-west Africa • Ilya Repin (Russ) paints *State Council* • James M. Barrie (Scot): play *Peter Pan* • Anton Chekov (Russ): *The Cherry Orchard*

1905

Bartók and **Kodály** begin independent research into Hungarian folk music. They produce their first joint publication the following year.

Ravel, now an established composer, fails for the fifth (and final) time to win the Prix de Rome at the Paris Conservatoire. The press takes notice of the situation, also reporting on the shameful revelation that all the finalists of the Prix are pupils of Lenepveu, a jury member. Dubois, the director of the Conservatoire, resigns and is replaced by **Fauré**.

2 January Composer **Michael Tippett** is born in London.

26 January **Schoenberg**'s tone poem *Pelléas und Melisande* (completed 1903) is performed for the first time, meeting with hostility in Vienna.

8 March **Elgar** conducts the first performance of his *Introduction and Allegro* for string quartet and double string orchestra, in London.

21 March Professor **Rimsky-Korsakov** is sacked from the St Petersburg Conservatory having expressed anti-Tsarist views following the massacre of protesters at the Tsar's Winter Palace earlier this year. Other professors tend their resignations in support of the composer. Within a few months the authorities are forced to reinstate Rimsky-Korsakov.

28 June **Elgar** receives an honourary doctorate at Yale University. In obeisance to the composer, his *Pomp and Circumstance* March No. 1 is performed at the end of the ceremony. It subsequently becomes an American graduation standard.

The chorus from *The Merry Widow*

July **Debussy** finishes his first book of *Images* for piano while staying at the Grand Hotel in Eastbourne.

15 October **Debussy**'s three-movement symphonic poem *La Mer* (The Sea) premières in Paris. Powerfully colouristic, the seascape 'sketches' do not receive critical approval. The music's break with functional tonality is only in part the cause—critics are still outraged at the composer's infidelities with Emma Bardac.

30 October The adulterous **Claude Debussy** and Emma Bardac have a daughter together: Claude-Emma.

9 December **Strauss**'s controversial *Salome* takes Dresden by storm, with the audience demanding 38 curtain calls on the opening night. The erotic one-act production establishes Strauss as a leading composer of opera.

30 December **Franz Lehár**'s *Die Lustige Witwe* (The Merry Widow) premières sensationally at the Theater an der Wien (Vienna). It becomes one of the most successful operettas of the 20th century.

1905 Russo-Japanese War continues • Revolution in Russia: sailors mutiny on the warship Potemkin; a general strike is called; Tsar Nikolai II agrees to an elected parliament • Union of Sweden and Norway dissolved • Moroccan crisis: secret agreements by Britain, France and Spain to divide Morocco upset by visit of Kaiser Wilhelm II to Tangier, where he declares support for the Moroccans • Bengal partitioned • Albert Einstein (Ger) publishes his special theory of relativity, with mass-energy formula $E = mc^2$ • Bertrand Russell (Wal): essay 'On Denoting' • Paul Cézanne (Fr) paints *The Bathers* • Gustav Klimt (Aus) paints *The Three Ages of Woman* • Baroness Orczy (Hung/UK): *The Scarlet Pimpernel*

Ives composes the first version of his progressive tone poem *Central Park in the Dark*. Disparate musical ideas are superimposed to conjure up a 'picture in sounds' of a summer's night in New York's Central Park, with an appropriately cacophonous climax. Revised twice afterwards, the one-movement work is not performed publicly until 1946.

Suk completes his *Asrael* Symphony, a heartfelt response to the deaths of his beloved wife, Otilka, and father-in-law, Dvořák.

Vaughan Williams completes his revisions and cataloguing of the *English Hymnal*. In addition to resetting a number of hymns with folk tunes, he and other composers have contributed new compositions. These include his own *For All the Saints* and *Come Down O Love Divine*, and **Gustave Holst**'s setting of *In the Bleak Midwinter*.

6 January Ravel's piano suite *Miroirs* is introduced by **Ricardo Viñes** at the Salle Erard in Paris.

19 March Wolf-Ferrari's comic opera *I Quatro rusteghi* (The Four Curmudgeons) premières at the Hoftheater in Munich. Based on Carlo Goldini's play *I rusteghi* (1760), the work adds popularity to the post-Romantic 'back to Mozart' movement.

24 May One of **Delius**'s greatest compositions, *Sea Drift*, scored for baritone, chorus and orchestra to words by Walt Whitman, is first performed in Essen.

Late May Mahler rehearses his Sixth Symphony in Essen.

The composer is overwhelmed by his own work, as his wife Alma later recalls: 'When it was over, Mahler walked up and down in the artists' room, sobbing, wringing his hands, unable to control himself.' Anxiety gets the better of him as he conducts the première on the 27th, resulting in a poor performance.

July Schoenberg completes his Chamber Symphony No. 1, moving ever further away from tonality.

23 August Vaughan-Williams's folk-tune inspired *Norfolk Rhapsody No. 1* is performed for the first time, at the Promenade Concerts in London.

25 September Composer **Dmitri Shostakovich** is born in St Petersburg.

3 October Elgar's oratorio *The Kingdom*, sequel to *The Apostles* (1903), premières in Birmingham.

November Rachmaninov leaves St Petersburg and relocates with his family in Dresden. He begins work on his Second Symphony.

11 November Carl Nielsen introduces his comic opera *Maskarade* to a receptive audience at the Royal Theatre in Copenhagen.

11 November The opera *The Wreckers*, by British composer **Ethel Smyth** (left), premières in Leipzig.

24 December In Brant Rock, Massachusetts, Reginald Aubrey Fessenden transmits the first radio programme, featuring poetry, song and a violin solo.

1906 Germany plans to build a fleet of battleships • The Liberal Party led by Henry Campbell-Bannerman obtains a large majority in British elections; it proceeds to introduce a series of social reforms • The Russian Duma (parliament) meets, but is quickly dissolved because its members criticise the government of Tsar Nikolai II • Transvaal and Orange Free State win self-government from Britain • British navy launches HMS *Dreadnought*, the most advanced warship of the day • Frederick Hopkins (Eng) discovers the existence of vitamins • John Galsworthy (Eng) begins the 'Forsyte Saga' with *The Man of Property*

Caruso (below) records the first million-selling disc, singing **Leoncavallo**'s 'Vesti la giubba' from the opera from *Pagliacci*.

Debussy completes his second book of *Images* for Piano.

Mahler finishes the orchestration of his mammoth Eighth Symphony, scored for quadruple woodwinds, two brass sections (the second off-stage), two harps, two mandolins, piano, celesta, harmonium and organ, eight solo voices, three choirs, a large battery of percussion, and strings. He regards it as his greatest work to date.

Rachmaninov completes his Second Symphony and composes his First Piano Sonata.

Rimsky-Korsakov completes *The Golden Cockerel*. Anti-Tsarist undertones in the opera delay its performance for two years.

Caruso as Canio in *Pagliacci*

Scriabin completes his symphonic *Poem of Ecstasy* (Symphony No. 4), which struggles at its New York première the following year.

January Bartók becomes professor of piano at the Budapest Academy.

5 February Schoenberg's String Quartet No. 1 in D minor (1905), exploring extended tonality, provokes a frosty reaction at its première in Vienna. Three days later the 32-year-old's Chamber Symphony No. 1 in E major (1906) is played for the first time, also in Vienna, and fairs no better.

21 February Delius's opera *A Village Romeo and Juliet*, indebted to Wagner, opens in Berlin. This year also sees the composition of his orchestral rhapsody *Brigg Fair*.

5 March In New York, Rossini's *William Tell* overture becomes the first orchestral music to be transmitted by wireless waves.

10 May Dukas's *Ariane et Barbe-Bleue* (Ariane and Bluebeard), based on a play by Maeterlinck, opens at the Opéra-Comique, Paris.

5 July Mahler loses his eldest daughter, four-year-old Maria Anna, to diphtheria. He soon afterwards learns of his own serious heart defect.

15 August Violin maestro **Joseph Joachim** dies in Berlin, aged 76.

4 September Leading Norwegian composer **Edvard Grieg** dies in Bergen, aged 64. A crowd of 50,000 gather to watch his funeral procession five days later.

25 September Sibelius conducts the première of his Symphony No. 3 in C major in Helsinki. A national hero, he can observe his portrait hanging in many of the city's shop windows.

October Mahler steps down from the Vienna Opera amid strained relationships both within the opera house itself and with a largely anti-Semitic press. Though suffering poor health, he has accepted a lucrative offer to conduct at the Metropolitan Opera in New York.

1907 Second Hague Peace Conference; Germany opposes arms limitations • Russia's second Duma (parliament) is dissolved after disagreement; a third Duma embarks on the repression of revolutionary activities • Britain and Russia form an Entente • The Triple Alliance of Germany, Italy and Austria is renewed • The Korean Emperor Kojong abdicates; Korea becomes a Japanese protectorate • British soldier Robert Baden-Powell founds the Boy Scout movement • Women obtain the vote in Norway • Pablo Picasso (Sp) paints *The Young Ladies of Avignon* • Gustav Klimt (Aus) paints *Portrait of Adele Bloch-Bauer I* • First exhibition of Cubism in Paris • G-B Shaw (Ire): play *Major Barbara*

Debussy completes his piano suite *Children's Corner*, dedicated to 'Chou-Chou', his beloved daughter, Claude-Emma.

Ives completes his chamber work *The Unanswered Question*. This same year he marries a nurse, Harmony Twitchell. He will later write (in *Memos*): 'If I have done anything good in music, it was first, because of my father, and second, because of my wife.'

Saint-Saëns produces one of the first original film scores with his music to Henri Lavédan's film *L'assassinat du duc de Guise* (The Assassination of the Duke of Guise).

Two of **Schoenberg**'s pupils complete their opus ones: **Anton Webern**, the Passacaglia for orchestra, and **Alban Berg**, the single movement Piano Sonata.

January Vaughan Williams begins a three-month stay in Paris, studying with **Ravel**.

2 January The third book of **Albéniz**'s piano suite *Iberia* is introduced at the salon of Princess de Polignac in Paris. The composer completes the fourth and final book this year.

18 January Delius's *An English Rhapsody* is premièred in Liverpool.

23 January American composer **Edward MacDowell** dies in New York, aged 47.

4 February Stravinsky's Symphony in E flat (Op. 1) is given its first complete performance, in St Petersburg. This year the composer also writes the orchestral scherzo *Fireworks*, composed as a

wedding present for **Rimsky-Korsakov**'s daughter, Nadezhda.

8 February Rachmaninov conducts the first performance of his Second Symphony to great acclaim in St Petersburg.

15 March The first performance of **Ravel**'s symphonic suite *Rapsodie espagnole* is warmly applauded in Paris.

21 June Composer **Rimsky-Korsakov** dies outside St Petersburg, aged 64.

19 September Mahler premières his Seventh Symphony (completed 1905) with only modest success in Prague. This year also marks the completion of his orchestral song cycle *Das Lied von der Erde* (The Song of the Earth).

Edward Elgar (right) with organist George Sinclair and conductor Hans Richter (seated)

3 December Elgar's Symphony No. 1 is introduced under **Hans Richter** in Manchester. It is the first significant symphony by an English composer.

10 December French composer **Olivier Messiaen** is born in Avignon.

11 December Composer **Elliot Carter** is born in New York.

21 December The Rosé Quartet première **Schoenberg**'s highly dissonant Second String Quartet with the soprano **Marie Gutheil-Schoder** in Vienna. The audience begins to laugh during the second movement, followed up with some stronger reactions as the final movement introduces pure atonality. The groundbreaking work suffers, in Schoenberg's words, 'tumultuous rejection'.

- -

1908 Portugal's King Carlos and Crown Prince Luis are assassinated • Herbert H. Asquith takes over as leader of the Liberals and Prime Minister of UK • Bulgaria declares its independence from Turkey; Prince Ferdinand is made Tsar • Austria annexes the Balkan states of Bosnia and Herzegovina • Germany continues to build large warships, creating tense relationship with Britain • Congo (now Zaire) becomes a Belgian colony • Émile Cohl (Fr) releases the first animated cartoon on film: *Fantasmagorie* • Bruno Liljefors (Swe) paints *Winter Hare* • Gustav Klimt (Aus) paints *The Kiss* • E. M. Forster (Eng): *A Room with a View* • Kenneth Graham (Scot): *The Wind in the Willows*

Kodály captures Hungarian folk melody in his String Quartet No. 1.

Schoenberg completes *Three Piano Pieces*, Op. 11, and the *Five Orchestral Pieces*, Op. 16. They are the composer's first completely atonal works.

Vaughan Williams, aged 38, completes his first symphonic work, *A Sea Symphony*, scored for orchestra and voices throughout.

Webern composes his *Five Movements for String Quartet*, Op. 5, and *Six Pieces for Orchestra*, Op. 6. The 12-minute orchestral suite, inspired by Schoenberg's *Five Orchestral Pieces*, points to Webern's mature style with its predominantly sparse, fragmentary atonal textures.

25 January Strauss's potent one-act opera *Elektra* (below), completed the previous year to a libretto

by **Hugo von Hofmannsthal**, is performed for the first time, in Dresden. The opera incorporates some of Strauss's most harmonically daring passages, flirting at times with atonality.

March Schoenberg completes the song cycle *Das Buch der hängenden Gärten* (Book of the Hanging Gardens).

18 May Spanish composer and pianist **Isaac Albéniz** dies in Cambô-les-Bains (French Pyrenees), aged 48, having suffered from Bright's disease for several years.

2 June The ballet *Les Sylphides*, with Chopin's music orchestrated by **Glazunov**, is first danced in St Petersburg.

7 June Thomas Beecham premières **Delius**'s *A Mass of Life* (1905) at the Queen's Hall, London. True to his anti-religious disposition, Delius has drawn his text from Nietzsche's *Also sprach Zarathustra*.

Summer Mahler, suffering from a weakening heart, senses the looming presence of death as he works on his Ninth Symphony.

7 October Rimsky-Korsakov's final opera, *The Golden Cockerel*, is posthumously premièred in Moscow.

16 November Bartók, aged 28, marries his piano pupil Marta Ziegler, aged 16. This year has seen the completion of his String Quartet No. 1.

28 November Rachmaninov, touring America for the first time, introduces his perilously demanding Piano Concerto No. 3 under **Walter Damrosch** in New York. This year has also seen the composition of his symphonic poem *The Isle of the Dead*.

4 December Wolf-Ferrari's one-act intermezzo *Il Segreto di Susanna* (Susanna's Secret) opens in Munich.

1909 William Howard Taft (Rep) takes office as President of the USA • Young Turks depose Sultan Abdul Hamid; Muhamad V succeeds him as ruler of Turkey • The conditions of Russian peasants are improved by Land Laws • Old-age pensions are introduced in Britain • Henry Ford (US) begins assembly-line production of 'affordable' Ford Model T cars •

Louis Blériot (Fr) makes first powered air crossing of English Channel • Leo H. Baekeland (US) introduces Bakelite plastic • Explorer Robert E. Peary (US) possibly reaches the North Pole • The first motion-picture newsreels are shown in N. America and Europe • Futurist Manifesto by poet Filippo Tommaso Marinetti (It) is published in Italian and French newspapers

1910

Berg composes his String Quartet, Op. 3.

Rachmaninov composes his 13 Preludes for piano, Op. 32.

Scriabin completes his mystical Fifth Symphony, *Prometheus: the Poem of Fire*. Scored for orchestra, piano, organ and choir, he has created the work utilising his condition of synesthesia, perceiving sounds as colours.

5 January Debussy completes his first book of Préludes for piano.

7 March Wilhelm Stenhammar's String Quartet No. 4 is first played in Gothenburg, Sweden.

9 March Composer **Samuel Barber** is born in West Chester, Pennsylvania.

20 April Jeanne Leleu and **Genevieve Durony**, aged 11 and 14, introduce **Ravel**'s suite *Ma mère l'oye* (Mother Goose) for piano duet at the inaugural concert of the Société Musicale Indépendente in Paris. The programme also features the first performances of **Fauré**'s song cycle *Chanson d'Eve* (Song of Eve) and **Debussy**'s *D'un cahier d'esquisses* (From a Sketchbook) for piano solo, performed by Ravel.

29 May Composer and conductor **Mily Balakirev**, the original style guru of 'The Five' dies in St Petersburg, aged 73.

25 June Diaghilev stages **Stravinsky**'s first ballet, *The Firebird*, at the Paris Opéra. Influenced by Rimsky-Korsakov's *Le Coq d'or* (premièred 1909), the colourfully descriptive music brings together Russian high Romanticism, bursts of primitivism, melodic exoticism and vivid orchestration. Stravinsky becomes famous overnight.

26 August With an ailing heart and fears for his marriage, **Mahler** undergoes psychoanalysis with Sigmund Freud.

6 September Vaughan Williams conducts the first performance of his *Fantasia on a Theme by Thomas Tallis* for string orchestra, at Gloucester Cathedral. He will twice revise the work, producing its definitive version in 1919.

12 September Mahler triumphs with the première of his Eighth Symphony (1907) in Munich. The colossal forces involved—a chorus of 850 and an orchestra of 171—gives the work its sobriquet: *Symphony of a Thousand*.

4 October The 13-year-old **Erich Korngold** beguiles a Viennese audience at the Hofoper with his ballet *Der Schneemann* (The Snowman).

10 November Elgar's Violin Concerto is premièred by **Fritz Kreisler** at the Queen's Hall in London. Elgar conducts and enjoys ecstatic applause.

Tamara Karsavina as the Firebird

10 December New York's Metropolitan Opera stages its first première: **Puccini**'s *La fanciulla del West* (The Girl of the Golden West). **Toscanini** conducts **Enrico Caruso** and **Emmy Destinn**, and the audience lap it up; by the end of the performance the composer, conductor and cast have received over 50 curtain calls between them.

15 December Max Reger's Piano Concerto in F minor is introduced in Leipzig.

1910 Britain's King Edward dies; is succeeded by his son George V • Liberals win a second general election in UK under Herbert H. Asquith • Cape Colony, Natal, Transvaal and Orange Free State unite to form the Union of South Africa • Revolution breaks out in Portugal, and a republic is declared • Japan annexes Korea • Thomas Edison (US) demonstrates the first talking motion picture • Henri Matisse (Fr) paints *The Dance* • Pablo Picasso (Sp) paints *Girl with a Mandolin* • Wassily Kandinsky (Russ) begins abstract *Composition* series • British philosopher-mathematicians Bertrand Russell and A. N. Whitehead: *Principia Mathematica*, Vol. I • E. M. Forster (Eng): *Howard's End*

Bartók submits his one-act opera *Bluebeard's Castle* for an opera competition in Budapest, only to have it rejected as 'unperformable'. This same year he composes his short Primitivist piano piece *Allegro barbaro*, very likely in response to a comment made by a critic referring to himself and **Kodály** as 'young barbarians'.

Irving Berlin writes *Alexander's Ragtime Band*, his first hit song.

Ethel Smyth composes her suffrage battle song *The March of the Women*. The following year she conducts the work with a toothbrush at Holloway prison, incarcerated with other suffragettes for acts of vandalism.

Webern begins his concise *Six Bagatelles for String Quartet* (Op. 9) and *Five Pieces* (for chamber orchestra, Op. 10). Completed in 1913, both works feature atonal, pointillistic textures, with motifs broken up into fragments and dispersed among the instruments. Some movements are surprisingly brief, lasting around 30 seconds.

26 January Strauss retreats from the progressive harmonies of *Elektra* in his new opera *Der Rosenkavalier* (The Knight of the Rose), first staged in Dresden. Librettist **Hofmannsthal** sets the scene in 18th-century Vienna and both he and Strauss enjoy the greatest triumph of their careers.

15 March Scriabin (right) has his mystical *Prometheus: the Poem of Fire* introduced under **Koussevitzky** in Moscow. An American première in New York four years later will incorporate the composer's *Tastiera per Luce*, 'keyboard of

lights', which projects colours onto a screen during the course of the symphony.

3 April In Helsinki **Sibelius** conducts the first performance of his reflective and austere Fourth Symphony. The public are mostly unappreciative.

18 May Gustav Mahler, suffering from fatigue and a chronic heart infection, dies in Vienna, aged 50. He leaves a Tenth Symphony unfinished.

19 May Ravel's one-act opera *L'Heure espagnole* (The Spanish Hour) opens at the Opéra-Comique in Paris.

24 May Elgar's Symphony No. 2 leaves the public unimpressed at London's Queen's Hall.

29 May Librettist and dramatist **Sir William S. Gilbert**, aged 74, dies from a heart attack while trying to save a young woman from drowning in a lake, in the grounds of his home at Harrow Weald, Middlesex.

13 June Stravinsky's allegorical ballet *Petrushka*, staged by Diaghilev's Ballets Russes with Nijinsky in the lead role, triumphs at the Théâtre du Châtelet, Paris.

7 July Composer **Gian Carlo Menotti** is born in Cadegliano, northern Italy.

20 November Mahler's masterly *Das Lied von der Erde* (The Song of the Earth, 1908) is premièred posthumously under **Bruno Walter** in Munich. Based on Hans Bethge's adaptations of ancient Chinese poetry, the six-movement orchestral song cycle begins and ends in pessimism, reflecting Mahler's state of mind in his final troubled years.

1911 The Anglo-Japanese treaty is renewed • Britain's House of Lords passes a Parliament Act curbing its own powers • Italy declares war on Turkey; annexes Tripoli and Cyrenaica in north Africa • International tension is caused by the arrival of the German warship, *Panther*, at Agadir, Morocco • France is given virtual control over Morocco • Qing dynasty under threat as China is torn by revolution • Roald Amundsen (Nor) beats Robert F. Scott (UK) to the South Pole by five weeks • Wassily Kandinsky (Russ) and Franz Marc (Ger) found the 'Blue Rider' artists' group in Munich • Gaston Leroux (Fr): novel *Phantom of the Opera*

Berg composes his Five Orchestral Songs (Op. 4) based on short poetic texts by Peter Altenberg. It is the first work that Berg completes without any advice from Schoenberg.

Delius composes his evocative orchestral tone poem *On Hearing the First Cuckoo in Spring*.

William Christopher Handy's *The Memphis Blues* is published in Memphis and becomes one of the first 12-bar blues hits. **Hart Wand**'s *Dallas Blues* and **'Baby' F. Seals**'s *Baby Seals Blues* are also published this year.

29 January Ravel's ballet *Ma mère l'oye* (Mother Goose), an orchestrated and expanded version of his suite for piano duet (1910), is first staged in Paris.

28 February Nielsen conducts the first performance of his Violin Concerto in Copenhagen. Also on the programme is his popular Symphony No. 3 *Sinfonia espansiva* (1911).

8 June Ravel's ballet *Daphnis et Chloé* is introduced by the Ballets Russes at the Théâtre du Châtelet, Paris. It is not unanimously appreciated.

26 June Bruno Walter conducts the posthumous première of Mahler's harmonically progressive Ninth Symphony in Vienna. A restless contemplation of life and death, the work seems to find resolution and peace in its transcendent fourth movement Adagio.

7 August Prokofiev, aged 21, performs as soloist introducing his Piano Concerto No. 1 in Moscow. Most critics hate it, one declaring the work 'primitive cacophony'.

13 August French opera composer **Jules Massenet** dies in Paris, aged 70.

1 September Composer **Samuel Coleridge-Taylor** dies of pneumonia in Croydon, aged 37.

3 September Sir Henry Wood (left) conducts the première of **Schoenberg**'s atonal *Five Orchestral Pieces* at a London Promenade concert. Audience reaction is divided—some hiss and laugh while others applaud. The critic Ernest Newman later writes, 'Schoenberg is not the mere fool or madman that he is generally supposed to be … May it not be that the new composer sees a logic in certain tonal relations that to the rest of us seem merely chaotic at present, but the coherence of which may be clear enough to us all some day?'

5 September Musical innovator **John Cage** is born in Los Angeles.

16 October Following 40 rehearsals, **Schoenberg**'s expressionist chamber song cycle *Pierrot lunaire* is introduced in Berlin.

25 October The first version of **Strauss**'s opera *Ariadne auf Naxos* (Ariadne on Naxos) is presented in Stuttgart as a third act to a production of the play *Le Bourgeois Gentilhomme*. Strauss writes a prologue four years later to take the place of the first two acts.

17 November 'Today … with unbearable toothache, I finished the music of the *The Rite*.' **Stravinsky**, Châtelard Hotel, Clarens.

1912 New Mexico becomes the 47th State of the USA • President Theodore Roosevelt (US) is wounded in an assassination attempt • End of Quing Dynasty in China; republic formed • In the Balkans, war breaks out between Turkey and an alliance of Bulgaria, Serbia, Montenegro and Greece • Albania becomes independent • Germany continues to increase its naval strength • The British Liner *Titanic* sinks on its maiden voyage; 1,500 people are drowned • Albert Berry (US) makes the first parachute jump from an aeroplane • Marcel Duchamp (Fr) paints *Nude Descending a Staircase, No. 2* • August Macke (Ger) paints *Coloured Composition* • Rabindranath Tagore (Ind): poems *Gitanjali*

Holst completes his *St Paul's Suite* for the string orchestra of St Paul's Girls' School in London, where he serves as Director of Music.

Rachmaninov composes *The Bells*, a choral symphony based on the poem by Edgar Allen Poe. He later refers to it as his favourite composition. This year also sees the completion of his Second Piano Sonata (first version).

Satie pens his three *Desiccated Embryos* for piano.

25 January Polish composer **Witold Lutosławski** is born in Warsaw.

26 January Debussy's *Images* for orchestra, comprising *Gigues*, *Ibéria* and *Rondes de printemps*, is performed in full for the first time, in Paris.

23 February Schoenberg's cantata *Gurrelieder* (1901) is premièred with great success in Vienna. At the end the composer refuses to acknowledge the audience's enthusiastic applause: 'For years those people who cheered me tonight refused to recognise me. Why should I thank them for appreciating me now?'

31 March Schoenberg conducts a performance of his Chamber Symphony No. 1 (1906) and the première of **Webern**'s atonal *Six Pieces for Orchestra* in Vienna. He also programmes two of **Berg**'s *Five Orchestral Songs* (Op. 4). The nerves of half the audience are shredded: shouting, whistling and fist-fights mar the evening's performances.

1 April Manuel De Falla's first opera, *La Vida breve* (The Short Life), opens successfully in Nice.

10 April Italo Montemezzi creates a *verismo* sensation with the opera *L'amore dei tre re* (The Love of Three Kings), introduced at La Scala, Milan.

15 May Nijinsky dances to **Debussy**'s colouristic music in the ballet *Jeux*, premièred with disappointing results in Paris. It is the composer's last completed orchestral work.

29 May Stravinsky's ballet *The Rite of Spring*, depicting a frenzied pagan ritual, creates mayhem at the Théâtre des Champs-Elysées, Paris. Discordant, rhythmically aggressive music combined with Nijinsky's unconventional choreography offends ballet purists who are looking for a fight: 'People shouted insults, howled and whistled, drowning out the music; there was slapping and even punching,' recalls the artist Valentine Gross. Subsequent performances go without incident.

5 July With her cantata *Faust et Hélène*, **Lili Boulanger** becomes the first woman to win the Prix de Rome.

5 September Prokofiev, aged 22, introduces his Piano Concerto No. 2 in Pavlovsk. Audience members boo and shout out rude remarks: 'My cat can play like that!' Prokofiev ignores them and performs an encore.

1 October Elgar conducts the première of his tone poem *Falstaff* at the Leeds Festival.

22 November Composer **Benjamin Britten**, son of a dentist, is born in Lowestoft, Suffolk.

A Schoenberg concert, caricatured in *Die Zeit*

1913 Woodrow Wilson (Dem) becomes 28th President of the USA • King George of Greece is assassinated • Greece, Serbia Romania and Turkey defeat Bulgaria in Second Balkan War • Albania declares independence • Ireland poised for civil war following House of Lords rejection of Third Home Rule Bill • In China, revolutionary forces capture Nanking; Yuan Shih-Kai is elected President of the Chinese Republic • The newly-completed Panama Canal opens to shipping • In India, British authorities arrest nationalist leader Mahatma Ghandi • British suffragettes demand the Vote • Charlie Chaplin (Eng) makes his film début • Thomas Mann (Ger): *Death in Venice* • G-B Shaw (Ire): *Pygmalion*

1914

The British Performing Right Society (PRS) and the American Society of Composers, Authors and Publishers (ASCAP) are established.

As conflict looms across Europe, **Holst** completes 'Mars, the Bringer of War'—the first movement of *The Planets*.

Reger composes his *Variations and Fugue on a Theme of Mozart*. At the outbreak of war he tries to enlist in the German army, but is refused on grounds of poor health.

5 March The 16-year-old **Henry Cowell** introduces his pioneering tone clusters in *Adventures in Harmony* for solo piano, performed in San Francisco. Cowell becomes the first to systematically explore the use of clusters beyond sound effects.

27 March Vaughan Williams's London Symphony premières under **Geoffrey Toye** at the Queen's Hall in London. This year the composer writes his immensely popular *The Lark Ascending* for violin and orchestra, inspired by English folk music and the poetry of George Meredith.

26 May Stravinsky's opera *The Nightingale*, based on the story by Hans Christian Andersen, is first staged by Diaghilev in Paris.

4 June Sibelius premières his tone poem *The Oceanides* to great acclaim at the Norfolk Music Festival in Connecticut. The $1,000-commission facilitates a very successful concert tour around the east of America. Later this month the Finnish composer receives an honorary doctorate from Yale University.

Early July Stravinsky pays a brief visit to Ustilug and Kiev. Upon the outbreak of war he returns to Switzerland; he does not set foot on Russian soil again until 1962.

Poets ought to be permitted to stay at home. There is plenty of cannon fodder available: critics, opinionated stage producers, Molière actors, etc. I am convinced there will be no world war; the little altercation with Serbia will soon be over and I will receive the third act of my Frau ohne Schatten. May the devil take the damned Serbs.

31 July Strauss vents his frustration on hearing that his librettist (**Hofmannsthal**) has enlisted in the Austrian Army.

August Ravel completes his Piano Trio. Keen to join the war effort, he attempts to enlist in the French air force, but is turned down on grounds of poor health.

August Elgar, aged 57, does his bit for king and country by enlisting in the Hampstead Police Division as a special constable. During the war, *Land of Hope and Glory* (1901/2) becomes Britain's 'second' national anthem.

The only thing that wrings my heart and soul is the thought of the horses—oh! My beloved animals— the men and women can go to hell—but my horses—I walk round & round this room cursing God for allowing dumb brutes to be tortured.

25 August Elgar writes to his friend Frank Schuster.

24 September Polish composer and conductor **Andrzej Panufnik** is born in Warsaw.

1914 The assassination in Serbia of Austria's Archduke Franz Ferdinand precipitates World War I • Austria attacks Serbia • Germany declares war on Russia and France, and invades Belgium • Britain declares war on Germany • Italy and the USA declare neutrality • German troops occupy Brussels • Turkey joins the war on Germany's side • Britain annexes Cyprus • Zeppelins carry out first air-raids on Britain • An Irish Home Rule Bill is passed by Britain's House of Commons despite opposition by Ulster Unionists, but is suspended for the duration of war • Amedeo Modigliani (It) paints *Frank Burty Haviland* • Edgar Rice Burroughs (US): *Tarzan of the Apes*

Bartók composes his Sonatina and the *Romanian Folk Dances* for piano.

Berg finishes his Three Orchestral Pieces, Op. 6.

Ives completes his String Quartet No. 2 'for 4 men—who converse, discuss, argue … fight, shake hands, shut up—then walk up the mountainside to view the firmament!' The public will not hear it until 1946.

Prokofiev completes his Primitivist *Scythian Suite*. Inspired by mythical tales and Stravinsky's *Rite of Spring*, the music is a reworking of the ballet *Ala and Lolli* (1914), requested and subsequently rejected by Diaghilev. (See also 1916.)

Swedish composer **Wilhelm Stenhammar** completes his Symphony No. 2.

Stravinsky begins composing *Renard* (The Fox), scored for four male singers and chamber orchestra. The dance-theatre work is completed the following year, but not performed publicly until 1922.

19 March John Alden Carpenter gains critical attention with his *Adventures in a Perambulator*, introduced in Chicago. This charming orchestral suite gives a toddler's-eye perspective on a day out in his pram.

23 March Rachmaninov's *All-Night Vigil* (or *Vespers*) for unaccompanied choir is first sung in Moscow.

15 April Falla's ballet *El Amor Brujo* (Love, the

Magician) is premièred in Madrid with little success. Falla adapts a vocal-orchestral suite from the ballet (completed 1916), resulting in one of his most popular concert works.

27 April Alexander Scriabin dies of a blood infection in Moscow, aged 43.

Summer Debussy rents a villa in the coastal town of Pourville, near Dieppe. There he is inspired to compose his Cello Sonata, the *Douze Etudes* for piano, and the Sonata for flute, viola and harp. His health deteriorates towards the end of the year due to rectal cancer.

11 July 'Blues is Jazz and Jazz is Blues.' The *Chicago Daily Tribune* attempts to define a new music.

28 October Strauss conducts the first performance of *Eine Alpensinfonie* (An Alpine Symphony) in Berlin. Effectively a tone poem, the one-movement work depicts a day's hiking in the Bavarian Alps, inspired by Strauss's own experiences as a 14-year-old.

8 December Sibelius (left) turns 50 and Finland celebrates. An evening concert is held in Helsinki where the composer introduces his Fifth Symphony—a searching, four-movement work that throws its weight at a climactic finale, inspired by the sighting of 16 migrating swans. Sibelius will twice revise the work, reordering and refining his material into the definitive three-movement version in 1919.

1915 World War I continues; Italy joins the Allies (France and Britain) • German troops use poison gas and flamethrowers on the Western Front • Allied soldiers land at Salonika, Greece, and Gallipoli, Turkey • British forces take Mesopotamia • Serbia is overrun by the Central Powers (Germany and Austria) • German armies enter Warsaw and capture Brest-Litovsk • German submarines inflict heavy losses on Allies' merchant ships • A German fleet is defeated by the British navy at Dogger Bank • US forces occupy Cuba • Pablo Picasso (Sp) paints *Harlequin* • Albert Einstein (Ger) expounds his general theory of relativity • John Buchan (Scot): *The Thirty-Nine Steps*

1916

Bartók composes his Piano Suite, Op. 14.

Henry Cowell, aged 19, composes *Dynamic Motion* for piano, his first important work incorporating tone-clusters.

In between teaching commitments at St Paul's School for Girls, **Holst** completes *The Planets*. (See also 1920.)

Parry composes his choral setting of William Blake's poem *Jerusalem*.

Szymanowski completes his Third Symphony (*The Song of the Night*) and his Violin Concerto No. 1.

4 January Debussy records his irritation: 'I have just seen **Stravinsky**. He says "my Firebird, my Sacre," just as a child would say, "my top, my hoop," and that's just what he is: a spoilt child who wears loud cravats and kisses a lady's hand while stepping on her feet.'

29 January Prokofiev conducts the first performance of his *Scythian Suite* in St Petersburg. The press responds scathingly to the wild and restive orchestral work, much in the manner of the critic Leonid Sabaneyev who has—by accident—already published his damning verdict prior to the evening's première, not having heard or seen a note of the music.

1 February Nielsen's Fourth Symphony, *The Inextinguishable*, is premièred with great success in Copenhagen. Conceived while most of Europe is embroiled in war, the symphony is published with the message: 'Music is life and, like it, inextinguishable.'

March Ravel is given a job as a driver in the motor transport corps.

24 March Two months after the première of **Granados**'s opera *Goyescas* in New York, the Spanish composer (aged 48) and his wife drown in the English Channel when their homebound ship is torpedoed by a German submarine.

9 April Falla's *Nights in the Garden of Spain*, a symphonic impression for piano and orchestra, is performed for the first time, in Madrid.

11 May Max Reger dies from a heart attack in Leipzig, aged 43. The influential composer is the author of one of the most famous responses to a hostile critic: 'I am sitting in the smallest room in my house. I have your review before me. Soon, it will be behind me.'

26 May Janáček presents a revised version of his opera *Jenůfa* (1903) at the Prague National Opera. Also produced in German two years later in Vienna, the opera establishes Janáček's international reputation.

5 August 31-year-old **George Butterworth**, best known for his orchestral rhapsody *A Shropshire Lad* (1912), is killed by sniper fire shortly after capturing a German trench during the Battle of the Somme (left).

October Schoenberg is discharged from the Austro-Hungarian army on grounds of ill health.

1916 World War I continues: the Battle of Verdun rages for ten months; Romania enters the war against the Germans, who take Bucharest; British and German fleets fight indecisive Battle of Jutland • Britain's war minister Lord Kitchener is drowned when the *Hampshire* is sunk • Battle of the Somme: British tanks used for first time; over one million British, French and German soldiers killed or wounded • Sinn Fein's 'Easter Rising' in Dublin is suppressed by British troops • US troops quell disorders in the Dominican Republic • Gustav Klimt (Aus) paints *Friederike Maria Beer* • James Joyce (Ire): *Portrait of the Artist as a Young Man*

Czech composer **Alois Hába**, aged 23, uses quarter-tones for the first time in his Suite for String Orchestra.

John Ireland completes his Violin Sonata No. 2.

Russian composer **Nikolai Medtner** completes two sets of *skazki* (Tales) for piano, Opp. 34 and 35.

Prokofiev completes his Classical Symphony (see 1918), First Violin Concerto and the opera *The Gambler*, based on the novel by Dostoevsky.

Suk completes his autobiographical symphonic poem *Zrání* (Ripening), inspired by a poem of the same name by Antonín Sova.

11 March Ottorino Respighi, aged 37, has his orchestral *Fontane di Roma* (Fountains of Rome) introduced in Rome. His pupil and future wife, Elsa Sangiacomo, records: 'Rather cold reception with some hissing at the end of the work.' The tone poem triumphs the following year under **Toscanini** in Milan.

27 March The neutral ground of Monte Carlo plays host to the première of **Puccini**'s opera *La Rondine* (The Swallow). Not among the composer's masterworks, it manages only modest success.

1 April Ragtime composer **Scott Joplin** dies from syphilis in New York, aged 49.

Pablo Picasso's cubist costume design for 'The Manager in His Tailcoats', from *Parade*.

3 May Ernest Bloch's *Israel Symphony* and *Schelomo* (Solomon) for cello and orchestra, both completed the previous year, are first performed in New York.

5 May Debussy performs in public for the last time, introducing his Violin Sonata No. 3 with the violinist **Gaston Poulet**, in Paris.

18 May The ballet *Parade*, featuring music by **Satie**, provokes a storm in Paris. With scenario by **Jean Cocteau**, choreography by Massine and set and costumes by Picasso, the frivolous work is slated by the press. Heated exchanges follow and Satie ends up in court for libellous comments made against an arch-critic. Cocteau hinders the proceedings by shouting down the critic's lawyer with obscenities. Satie narrowly escapes jail, incurring a suspended sentence and fine.

12 June Hans Pfitzner's opera *Palestrina* is first performed under the direction of **Bruno Walter** in Munich. The composer's own libretto is based on the apocryphal story that Palestrina (d. 1594) deterred the Council of Trent from banning polyphony by composing his wondrous *Papae Marcelli* Mass.

22–25 September W. C. Handy's Memphis Orchestra records its first blues, jazz and ragtime tracks.

December Following the revolution, **Rachmaninov** and his family leave Russia for Stockholm (and later the USA), never to return.

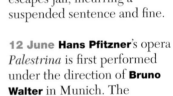

1917 USA declares war on Germany; US troops arrive in Europe • Revolution in Russia; Nicholas II abdicates; Allies Eastern Front collapses and German-Russian armistice is signed • German submarine warfare intensifies • In the Middle East, the Allies win the Battle of Gaza and capture Jerusalem from the Turks • Britain's Foreign Secretary Arthur Balfour announces that the British favour a national home for Jews in Palestine • Bolshevik party, led by Vladimir Lenin, overthrows Provisional Russian Government and seizes power • Finland declares its independence from Russia • Marcel Duchamp (Fr/Amer) anticipates conceptual art with *Fountain* (a urinal) • Paul Valéry (Fr): poem *La Jeune Parque*

Janáček composes his Russian orchestral rhapsody *Taras Bulba*, based on the historical novel by Nikolai Gogol.

Satie completes his most important work, *Socrate*, a 'symphonic drama' for four voices and chamber orchestra based on Plato's *Dialogues*. Serious and sensitive, it extends Satie's reputation beyond that of a mere musical humourist.

19 January Fauré's Cello Sonata No. 1 is first played in Paris.

3 March Bartók's three-movement String Quartet No. 2 débuts in Budapest. Its second movement, featuring driving ostinatos and percussive gestures, takes inspiration from North African folk music.

25 March Claude Debussy dies of cancer aged 55, amid a German bombardment of Paris.

26 March Composer and critic **César Cui**, the last surviving member of 'The Five', dies aged 83. He joins his former comrades in the grounds of the Aleksandr-Nevsky monastery in St Petersburg.

21 April Inspired by the music of Haydn, **Prokofiev**'s Classical Symphony (No. 1) is first performed in St Petersburg. Classical forms and themes are treated with humour and parody, resulting in the first major work of neo-classicism.

24 May Bartók and librettist **Béla Balázs** present their one-act *Bluebeard's Castle* (right) in Budapest. This minimal-action opera, completed in 1911 but since revised, shares double billing with their ballet *The Wooden Prince*, premièred the previous year.

27 July The 61-year-old **Gustav Kobbé**, author of the *Complete Opera Book*, dies when a US Navy seaplane strikes his sailing boat off Long Island.

25 August Composer and conductor **Leonard Bernstein** is born in Lawrence, Massachusetts.

September Prokofiev arrives in New York, escaping (temporarily) an uncertain future in Russia in the wake of revolutionary events.

28 September Ernest Ansermet directs the first performance of **Stravinsky**'s Faustian ballet *L'Histoire du soldat* (The Soldier's Tale) in Lausanne. The short music theatre piece incorporates just three actors/dancers, a narrator and seven instrumentalists, so to facilitate modest productions in uncertain times. With clear textures, dance parodies and dry musical wit, Stravinsky edges towards neo-classicism.

24 October Sibelius's patriotic cantata *Oma maa* (Our Native Land) is first performed in Helsinki.

10 November Rachmaninov docks with his wife in New York. He quickly secures an agent and the following month embarks on a four-month concert tour of America.

14 December Puccini presents three one-act operas under the title *Il trittico* (The Triptych) at the Metropolitan Opera, New York. The collection comprises *Il tabarro* (The Cloak), *Suor Angelica* (Sister Angelica), and the comedy *Gianni Schicchi*, famous above all for its beautiful aria 'O mio babbino caro'.

1918 World War I ends after Allied victories; Kaiser Wilhelm abdicates and a so-called 'Popular' government assumes power • The Austrian emperor Karl abdicates; Austria becomes a republic • Lithuania and Latvia proclaim their independence from Russia • Poland is declared a republic • Turkey and Austria-Hungary surrender • Yugoslavia and Czechoslovakia become independent • Iceland becomes a sovereign state • Tsar Nicholas II and his family are executed in Russia • Women over 30 get the vote in Britain • Artist Paul Nash (Eng) brings back his paintings of the Western Front • First Tarzan film: *Tarzan of the Apes* (US) • Egon Schiele (Austria) paints *Portrait of Albert Paris von Gütersloh*

Alfvén completes his single-movement Fourth Symphony (*From the Outermost Skerries*), scored with wordless soprano and tenor.

Ives completes his ambitious Piano Sonata No. 2 (subtitled *Concord, Mass., 1840–60*).

Ravel orchestrates his piano suite *Le tombeau de Couperin* (1917) and begins work on the symphonic poem *La valse*.

Stravinsky adapts early to mid 18th-century works in his first neo-classical composition, the ballet *Pulcinella*.

January Arnold Bax completes his tone poem *Tintagel*, his most popular orchestral composition.

11 January Delius's tone poem *Eventyr* (Once Upon a Time) is first performed under the baton of **Henry Wood** in London.

17 January Composer-pianist **Ignacy Jan Paderewski** (below) becomes Prime Minister of Poland. Like many after him, he holds the office for less than a year.

1 March Strauss's appointment as co-director of the Vienna State Opera is officially announced. Almost all of the 800 employees sign a petition in protest over the composer's huge salary, given the severe economic climate in Austria.

10 April Revising earlier works, **Fauré** provides incidental music for René Fauchois's *Masques et bergamasques*, a choreographic *divertissement* staged in Monte Carlo. A suite adapted from the score becomes one of his few enduring orchestral works.

2 June Hindemith, aged 24, organises a concert of his own music in Frankfurt, including performances of his String Quartet No. 2 and a Sonata for Viola and Piano (from Op. 11). The event proves a great success and leads to a lifelong partnership with Schott Publishers.

22 July Falla's satirical *El sombrero de tres picos* (The Three Cornered Hat) gains a rapturous reception under **Ernest Ansermet** in London. Produced by Diaghilev, the Spanish ballet is a reworking of Falla's pantomime *El corregidor y la molinera* (1917) and features choreography by Massine, with sets and costumes by Picasso. Falla extracts two orchestral suites.

9 August Composer **Ruggero Leoncavallo** dies in Montecatini, Italy, aged 62.

10 October Strauss's *Die Frau ohne Schatten* (The Woman without a Shadow) opens to little acclaim at the Vienna State Opera. Successful only in the second half of the century, the opera will ultimately rank among the composer's finest.

27 October Elgar conducts **Felix Salmond** and the London Symphony Orchestra in the première of his Cello Concerto at London's Queen's Hall. Sadly under-rehearsed, the performance of the composer's final masterpiece is poor.

1919 The Treaty of Versailles imposes reparations and demilitarisation on Germany • The USA begins period of isolationism • The National Socialist (Nazi) Party is formed in Germany • Start of Irish war of Independence (until 1921) • Anti-British demonstrations occur in India: at Amritsar, troops fire on a mob, killing 379 people • Amendment 18 to the US constitution is ratified; it prohibits the manufacture or sale of alcoholic liquor • Theo van Doesburg (Neth) paints *Composition in gray (Rag-time)* • Walter Gropius (Ger) founds the Bauhaus design school in Weimar • Vicente Ibanez (Sp): *The Four Horsemen of the Apocalypse* • Felix the Cat becomes the first popular cartoon film star

Joseph Hauer composes *Nomos* for piano in which he employs a 12-note technique: all 12 notes are sounded before any are repeated. While the work pre-dates Schoenberg's system, it does not adhere to a strict serial sequence of notes.

The non-conformist **Ravel** rejects the Légion d'Honneur. **Satie** gibes: 'M. Ravel refuses the Legion of Honour, but all his music accepts it.'

Spanish composer **Joaquín Turina** completes an orchestral arrangement of his *Danzas fantásticas* (written initially for piano) and composes the *Sinfonía sevillana*.

16 January Writing an article in *Comoedia*, the critic Henri Collet confers the title of 'Les Six' on a new generation of French composers: **Georges Auric**, **Louis Durey**, **Arthur Honegger**, **Darius Milhaud**, **Francis Poulenc** and **Germaine Tailleferre**.

21 February **Darius Milhaud** and **Jean Cocteau** (right) present their pantomime *Le Boeuf sur le Toit* (The Bull on the Roof) at the Comédie des Champs-Elysées, Paris. Inspired by the popular music of Brazil, Milhaud's score had been originally conceived as an accompaniment to a Charlie Chaplin film.

8 March **Satie** invents 'muzak' with his *Musique d'ameublement* (Furniture music) at the Galeries Barbazange, Paris. Designed specifically as background music not to be listened to, the plan backfires when everyone stops talking to pay attention to it. 'Satie had

not bargained for the charm of his own music', notes **Milhaud**.

23 April **Janáček** opera *The Excursions of Mr Brouček* opens at Prague's National Theatre.

15 May **Ansermet** conducts the first performance of **Stravinsky**'s neo-classical ballet *Pulcinella* (1919), in Paris. Diaghilev's Ballets Russes production includes choreography by Massine and set and costumes by Picasso.

August **Strauss** embarks on a four-month opera and concert tour of South America with the Vienna Philharmonic.

2 October German composer **Max Bruch** dies in Berlin, aged 82.

15 November **Holst** has his epic orchestral suite *The Planets* (1916) premièred at the Queen's Hall, London. In the programme notes he writes, 'These pieces were suggested by the astrological significance of the planets; there is no programme music in them, neither have they any connection with the deities of classical mythology bearing the same names.'

4 December **Korngold**'s opera *Die tote Stadt* (The Dead City) opens simultaneously in Hamburg and Cologne.

12 December **Ravel**'s choreographic poem *La valse*—commissioned but subsequently dismissed by Diaghilev as being inappropriate music for ballet—débuts under **Camille Chevillard** in Paris.

1920 The League of Nations, brainchild of Woodrow Wilson, comes into being, but the US Senate votes against joining • Estonia becomes independent of Russia • Russia goes to war with Poland • Britain annexes Kenya • The International Court of Justice is established at The Hague, Netherlands • Prohibition (of alcoholic liquor) comes into force in USA •

Public radio broadcasting begins in Britain • Film: *The Mark of Zorro*, starring Douglas Fairbanks • Stanisław Witkiewicz (Pol) paints *Laughing boy* • F. Scott Fitzgerald (US): *This Side of Paradise* • Edith Wharton (US): *Age of Innocence* • Agatha Christie (Eng) introduces Hercule Poirot in *The Mysterious Affair at Styles*

1921

Milhaud combines Brazilian rhythms and polytonality in his vibrant piano suite *Saudades do Brasil*. The work has been inspired by the country where he served as French attaché for wartime propaganda, 1917–18. Milhaud also creates an orchestral version of the suite.

Schoenberg (right) works on his *Serenade* (Op. 24, begun the previous year) the fourth movement of which contains his first serial 12-note music. He tells his pupil, Josef Rufer, 'I have made a discovery which will ensure the supremacy of German music for the next 100 years'.

In the US **Edgard Varèse** co-founds the International Composers' Guild to promote progressive contemporary music. This year sees the completion of his orchestral piece *Amériques* (Americas).

17 May In France for the summer, **Prokofiev** conducts the première of his Diaghilev-commissioned ballet *Chout* (also known as *The Tale of the Buffoon*), in Paris.

21 May Fauré's Piano Quintet No. 2 is introduced in Paris.

10 June Sergey Koussevitzsky conducts the first performance of **Stravinsky**'s *Symphonies of Wind Instruments*, in London. Dedicated to the memory of Debussy, the piece leaves the critic Ernest Newman unimpressed: 'I had no idea Stravinsky disliked Debussy so much as this.'

11 June Honegger's incidental music to René Morax's drama *Le roi David* (King David) is first heard in Mézières, Switzerland. The success of the production launches Honegger's international career. A concert version, for enlarged forces, is completed the following year.

26 June Aaron Copland, aged 20, enrols at the Conservatoire Américain in Fontainebleau where he will study with **Nadia Boulanger**.

1 August Tenor **Enrico Caruso** dies of a lung ailment in Naples, aged 48.

27 September Composer **Engelbert Humperdinck** dies in Neustrelitz, aged 67.

21 October English composer **Malcolm Arnold** is born in Northampton.

23 November Janáček's opera *Kát'a Kabanová* opens in Brno. The music has been inspired by Janáček's muse, the (married) 25-year-old Kamila Stösslová. His love for her is unrequited.

16 December Camille Saint-Saëns dies in Algiers, aged 86. His body is transported to Paris for a state funeral at La Madeleine.

16 December Prokofiev, back in the US, premières his resourceful Third Piano Concerto, in Chicago.

30 December Prokofiev conducts the first performance of his satirical fairy tale opera *The Love for Three Oranges*, in Chicago. He has written the libretto himself, based on a scenario by the 18th-century playwright Carlo Gozzi. Prokofiev returns to Europe next year, unhappy with his reception in the USA.

1921 The Immigration Act limits entry into the USA • US, France, Japan and Britain sign Pacific Treaty • The League of Nations settles a dispute between Poland and Germany • Rebellion in Ireland ends with a treaty dividing the country: 26 southern counties become Irish Free State with dominion status; six northern counties remain part of the UK • Greece declares war on Turkey • Germany suffers a financial crisis as the Mark falls in value • Film: *The Sheik*, starring Rudolph Valentino • Pablo Picasso (Sp) paints two versions of *Three Musicians* • Surrealist Max Ernst (Ger) paints *The Elephant Celebes* • D. H. Lawrence (Eng): *Women in Love*

Hindemith completes his *Kammermusik* (Chamber Music) No. 1 for small orchestra, and the Suite *1922*, for piano.

Jacques Ibert stirs up atmospheric impressions of Rome-Palermo, Tunis-Nefta and Valencia in his orchestral suite *Escales* (Ports of Call).

Conductor **Koussevitsky** pays **Ravel** 10,000 francs to orchestrate Mussorgsky's *Pictures at an Exhibition* (1874).

24 January Nielsen conducts his masterful Fifth Symphony (completed just nine days earlier) in Copenhagen. He acknowledges (to Ludvig Dolleris) that the great confrontations within the symphony are representative of the 'division of dark and light, the battle between evil and good'.

26 January Vaughan Williams's contemplative Third (*Pastoral*) Symphony is introduced under **Adrian Boult** in London.

5 February Respighi's *Gregorian Concerto for Violin and Orchestra* is performed for the first time, in Rome.

17 March Ernst Krenek, aged 21, has his Symphony No. 1 introduced with great success in Berlin. This year he composes his Symphony No. 2.

26 March Hindemith's one-act opera *Sancta Susanna*, after August Stramm's play (1913), premières in Frankfurt. The volatile mixture of nuns and sexual temptation causes a scandal.

23 April Varèse's surrealist *Offrandes* (Offerings) for soprano and small orchestra is premièred and appreciated at the Greenwich Village Theater in New York.

One of the BBC's earliest broadcast performances: Olive Sturgess and John Huntingdon, accompanied by Stanton Jefferies, at Marconi House.

13 May The Société National de Musique introduces **Fauré**'s song cycle *L'horizon chimérique* and Cello Sonata No. 2, in Paris.

29 May Architect-composer **Iannis Xenakis** is born of Greek parentage in Braïla, Romania.

2 June Stravinsky's neo-classical one-act opera *Mavra* opens at the Paris Opéra but fails dismally.

7 September Arthur Bliss conducts the first performance of his *Colour* Symphony, which is well appreciated at the Three Choirs Festival in Gloucester. The work explores the heraldic connotations of purple, red, blue and green.

18 October Marconi and other prominent wireless manufacturers form the British Broadcasting Corporation. Radio broadcasts follow in November (below).

1 November Karol Szymanowski's avian Violin Concerto No. 1 (1916) is premièred in Warsaw. The impressionistic work takes inspiration from the poem *May Night* by Tadeusz Micinski.

1922 Egypt wins independence from British rule • Irish Free State proclaimed; Northern Ireland votes against inclusion • Fascist chief Benito Mussolini takes over Italian government • Independence leader Mohandas Gandhi is imprisoned by British authorities in India • Greece defeated in war with Turkey • Joseph Stalin becomes Secretary General of the Communist Party in Russia • Pharoah Tutankhamun's tomb discovered at Luxor, Egypt • Pope Benedict XV dies; succeeded by Pius XI • Canadians Frederick Banting and Charles Best develop insulin treatment for diabetes • The British Broadcasting Company Ltd is established • James Joyce (Ire): *Ulysses* • T. S. Eliot (US/Eng): poem *The Waste Land*

French composer and folk-song collector **Joseph Canteloube** begins publishing his *Chants d'Auvergne*—30 dialect folk songs arranged for voice and orchestra, issued in five volumes over the next 32 years.

Hindemith composes *Kleine Kammermusik* (Little Chamber Music) for wind quintet and completes the song cycle *Das Marienleben*.

Schoenberg completes three works containing his first experiments in serialism: the *Five Piano Pieces*, Op. 23, the *Serenade*, Op. 24, and the entirely serialist *Suite for Piano*, Op. 25.

Alexander von Zemlinsky completes his impassioned *Lyrische Symphonie* for soprano, baritone and orchestra. Reminiscent of Mahler's *The Song of the Earth*, the work is based on seven poems by Rabindranath Tagore.

8 January The BBC broadcast the first complete opera—*The Magic Flute*—from Covent Garden.

15 January Danish composer **Rued Langgaard** premières his apocalyptic Symphony No. 6 (*The Heaven Rending*) in Karlsruhe.

19 February Temperate moods permeate **Sibelius**'s Sixth Symphony, introduced under the composer's direction in Helsinki.

4 March The gesturing 'organised sound' of **Varèse**'s *Hyperprism*, created with percussion battery and winds, is first heard in New York. Critics respond scathingly.

12 May Fauré's Piano Trio (Op. 120) is first performed on his 78th birthday at the Société Nationale de Musique in Paris. This year the now deaf composer begins his String Quartet in E minor (Op. 121), his final composition.

28 May Hungarian composer **György Ligeti** is born in Transylvania.

12 June *Façade* (1922), by the 21-year-old **William Walton** on texts by **Edith Sitwell**, receives its public première in London. Scored for speaker and six instruments, the piece engages Sitwell herself reciting poetry behind a painted curtain featuring a huge mouth in the form of a megaphone. Most of the audience hate it.

13 June Stravinsky's unremitting *Les Noces*, a symbolic portrayal of a rustic Russian wedding, opens under the Ballets Russes in Paris. Completed in 1917 as a dance cantata, the (revised) work is scored for four solo voices and chorus, and a vast array of non-pitched and pitched percussion, including four pianos.

18 October Schoenberg's wife, Mathilde, dies. The composer marries the 27-year-old Gertrud Kolisch, sister of one of his pupils, shortly before his 50th birthday the following year.

18 October Stravinsky consolidates his new direction of neo-classicism with his Octet for wind instruments, premièred at the Paris Opéra. The evening's programme includes the first performance of **Prokofiev**'s Violin Concerto No. 1.

25 October Drawing on African folk mythology, **Milhaud**'s jazz-infused ballet *La Creation du Monde* is first staged at the Théâtre des Champs-Elysées, Paris.

11 November Employing quarter tones in a tonal framework, **Bloch**'s Piano Quintet No. 1, variously tender and wild, is first performed by **Harold Bauer** and the Lenox Quartet at the inaugural concert of the League of Composers in New York.

19 November Ernő Dohnányi conducts a concert celebrating the 50th anniversary of the formation of the Hungarian capital, Budapest. Commissions for the event include **Bartók**'s *Dance Suite*, **Kodály**'s choral masterwork *Psalmus Hungaricus* and Dohnányi's own *Festival Overture*.

- -

1923 US President Warren G. Harding dies; is succeeded by Vice-President Calvin Coolidge (Rep) as 30th President • Russia becomes the Union of Soviet Socialist Republics • Gustav Stresemann becomes Chancellor of Germany • Nazi leader Adolf Hitler fails in an attempted *coup d'etat* in Munich; in prison he begins *Mein Kampf* (My Struggle) • Indepen-dent Transjordan (later Jordan) is proclaimed • Miguel Primo de Rivera becomes dictator in Spain • George II of Greece is deposed • Mustafa Kemal Atatürk becomes president of the new Turkish Republic • In Japan, around 140,000 people die in Kantō earthquake • Theo van Doesburg (Neth) paints *Composition XXI*

Bloch composes *From Jewish Life*, three plaintive movements for cello and piano.

Austrian composer **Ernst Toch** traverses irony, wit and heartfelt introspection in his Cello Concerto, scored with chamber forces.

6 January **Poulenc**'s new ballet *Les biches* (The Does), commissioned by Diaghilev, delights the public and critics alike in Monte Carlo.

12 February **George Gershwin** (right) electrifies New York's Aeolian Hall with his one-movement jazz concerto *Rhapsody in Blue*. Famous for hit songs such as the million-selling *Swanee* (1920), the composer-pianist has completed his first orchestral work with help from **Ferde Grofé**. Renowned musicians including **Rachmaninov**, **Bloch**, **Sousa** and **Stokowski** witness the event that certifies the language of jazz as worthy of the concert hall.

24 March **Sibelius** conducts the first performance of his single-movement Seventh Symphony, in Stockholm.

26 April Violinist **Jelly d'Arányi** introduces **Ravel**'s *Tzigane* (Gypsy) in London.

8 May **Honegger**'s steam-engine inspired tone poem *Pacific 231* (1923) is launched sensationally under **Koussevitzky** in Paris. The composer reveals, 'I have always loved locomotives passionately … as others love women or horses.'

22 May **Stravinsky** takes the solo part in the first performance of his neo-classical Concerto for Piano and Wind Orchestra, in Paris. The conductor, **Koussevitzky**, has to remind him how to begin the second movement.

6 June Composer **Alexander Zemlinsky** conducts the première of **Schoenberg**'s 1909 monodrama *Erwartung* (Expectation) in Prague.

27 July Composer and pianist **Ferruccio Busoni** dies in Berlin, aged 58.

14 October **Schoenberg**'s short music drama *Die glückliche Hand* (The Lucky Hand, 1913) receives its first performance in Vienna.

4 November 'I did what I could. Now let God be my judge.' **Gabriel Fauré** dies in Paris, aged 79.

4 November **Strauss** capitalises on his recent marital difficulties in *Intermezzo* (completed 1923), first staged in Dresden. The two-act opera presents a sequence of short scenes from his volatile family life.

6 November **Janáček**'s popular opera *The Cunning Little Vixen*, based on a cartoon strip from a local paper, opens at the National Theatre in Brno. This year also marks the first performance of his String Quartet No. 1 (1923).

29 November Following an operation for throat cancer, **Puccini** dies in Brussels, aged 65. A funeral service is held four days later at Milan Cathedral, with much of the city at a standstill. His opera *Turandot* remains unfinished.

14 December **Respighi**'s *Pines of Rome* enthrals the public at its première in Rome. Featuring a phonograph of a singing nightingale, it is the first orchestral work to incorporate recorded sound.

1924 Britain's first Labour government, under J. Ramsey Macdonald, lasts only nine months; following an election victory, the Conservatives under Stanley Baldwin take over • The Kuomintang (Nationalist Party) in China admits Communists • Giacomo Matteotti, socialist opponent of Benito Mussolini, is murdered • Albania becomes a republic • The USA bans Japanese immigrants • First Winter Olympics (in Chamonix, France) • English Physicist Arthur Eddington interprets Albert Einstein's theory of relativity in *The Mathematical Theory of Relativity* • E. M. Forster (Eng): *A Passage to India* • A. A. Milne (Eng) introduces Winnie-the-Pooh in *When We were Very Young*

Henry Cowell creates *The Banshee*, an unworldly soundscape produced by the plucking and scraping of strings inside a grand piano.

11 January Copland's Symphony for Organ and Orchestra is premièred in New York. This year marks the composer's *Music for the Theatre* chamber suite.

1 March Stokowski conducts **Varèse**'s *Intégrales* for wind and percussion, in New York. Few can fathom the work, least of all the critic Ernest Newman: 'It sounded a good deal like a combination of early morning in the Mott Haven freight yards, feeding time at the zoo, and a Sixth Avenue trolley rounding a curve, with an intoxicated woodpecker thrown in for good measure.'

21 March Ravel enjoys high praise in Monte Carlo for his one-act fairytale opera *L'Enfant et les sortilèges* (The Child and the Spells).

26 March Composer and conductor **Pierre Boulez** is born in Montbrison, France.

21 May Busoni's opera *Doktor Faust*, completed by **Philipp Jarnach**, is posthumously premièred in Dresden.

1 June Bloch blends 20th-century harmony with Baroque idioms in his *Concerto Grosso No. 1* for piano and string orchestra, introduced in Cleveland.

6 June Prokofiev's 'iron and steel' Second Symphony débuts but disappoints in Paris.

1 July For years a heavy drinker, **Erik Satie** dies from cirrhosis of the liver aged 59, in Paris.

13 September Schoenberg turns 51. Among his birthday presents is a *Kammerkonzert* (Chamber Concerto) by his pupil **Berg** (left), scored for piano, violin and 13 wind instruments. Berg's semi-serialist work acknowledges by way of musical anagram the triune membership (including **Webern**) of the Second Viennese School.

24 October Composer **Luciano Berio** is born in Oneglia, Italy.

3 December Gershwin's jazzy Piano Concerto in F is performed by the composer under **Walter Damrosch** in New York. Written in a more classical vein than his sensational *Rhapsody in Blue* (1924), the concerto receives mixed reviews, with some accusing the composer of poor technique. The work's fecund melodies and kinteic energy wins over the public, regardless.

11 December Nielsen divides the public with his Sixth Symphony (*Sinfonia Semplice*), first performed in Copenhagen. It is his final work in the genre.

14 December Following 137 rehearsals, **Berg**'s deeply psychological *Wozzeck* (1922) premières under **Erich Kleiber** in Berlin. The atonal tragic opera, based on Georg Büchner's play, provokes extreme reactions both in praise and in protest. Productions in Prague and Leningrad follow, consolidating Berg's international reputation.

1925 President Sun Yat-sen of China dies • Paul von Hindenburg becomes German President on the death of Friedrich Ebert • The Locarno Treaties provide a system of guarantees for European frontiers • French occupation troops evacuate the Rhineland; British occupation troops leave Köln • The League of Nations settles a dispute between Greece and Bulgaria • Arabs revolt against the French in Syria; Damascus is bombarded • Reza Khan Pahlevi seizes Persian throne • Film: Charlie Chaplin's *The Gold Rush* • Paul Klee (Switz) paints *Fish Magic* • Jacob Epstein (US/UK) sculpts *Rima* for W. H. Hudson memorial • F. Scott Fitzgerald (US): *The Great Gatsby* • Franz Kafka (Czech): *The Trial*

Bartók, in a flurry of piano compositions, writes *Out of Doors* (suite), *Nine Little Pieces*, the Piano Sonata and the Piano Concerto, and the first works of his compilation *Mikrokosmos*.

Peter Warlock (otherwise known as **Philip Heseltine**) composes the *Capriol Suite* for string orchestra, his best known work.

12 January Composer **Morton Feldman** is born in New York.

9 April **Stokowski** throws his weight behind the avant-garde **Varèse**, conducting the Philadelphia Orchestra in the first performance of the composer's complex *Ameriques*.

25 April Puccini's unfinished opera *Turandot* is introduced posthumously under **Toscanini** at La Scala, Milan. Completed by Franco Alfano, the audience only hears the music of Puccini: after the death of the slave girl Liù in Act 3, Toscanini lays down his baton and proclaims, 'Here, at this point, Puccini broke off his work'.

12 May **Shostakovich**, aged 19, witnesses his Symphony No. 1 premièred and wildly applauded in Leningrad. The success catapults him onto the international stage as renowned conductors— **Toscanini** and **Stokowski** among them—take up his music.

June **Webern**'s pithy and pointillistic *Five Pieces for Orchestra* (Op. 10, 1913) is introduced at Zurich's ISCM (International Society for Contemporary Music) Festival.

19 June Resident in Paris, the 25-year-old composer **George Antheil** unleashes his *Ballet mécanique*, whose machine-age sound-world is realised with an amplified pianola, wooden and metal propellers, electric bells and a siren.

26 June **Janáček**'s vibrant *Sinfonietta* (1925) is premièred in Prague. The brass-heavy

orchestration derives from the work's original conception as a collection of military-band fanfares, which themselves maintain a powerful presence throughout. Each of the five movements depicts an aspect of Janáček's adopted city, Brno.

1 July German composer **Hans Werner Henze** is born in Gütersloh, Westphalia.

16 October **Kodály**'s opera *Háry János* opens with great success in Budapest.

5 November **Falla** conducts the first performance of his neo-classical Concerto for Harpsichord, Flute, Oboe, Clarinet, Violin and Cello—one of his last and finest pieces—in Barcelona. At the keyboard is the renowned harpsichordist **Wanda Landowska**, who has suggested and commissioned the work.

9 November Dresden Staatsoper débuts **Hindemith**'s opera *Cardillac*.

11 November **Villa-Lobos** melds popular Brazilian song, rainforest evocations and contemporary classical harmonies in his *Chôros No. 10*, colourfully scored for chorus and orchestra, premièred in Rio de Janerio.

28 November **Bartók**'s pantomime *The Miraculous Mandarin* (piano score 1919), a tale of a prostitute and her depraved coterie, opens in Cologne. The production survives only one performance due to grievances led by the city's mayor over the ballet's sordid subject matter.

18 December **Janáček**'s opera *The Makropulos Case* (1925) opens successfully in Brno. Compositions this year have included the sacred masterpiece *Glagolitic Mass*.

26 December **Sibelius** summons the Finnish god of the forests in the symphonic poem *Tapiola*, his last major work, introduced in New York.

1926 Hejaz becomes the Kingdom of Saudi Arabia • Germany is admitted to the League of Nations • The Riff rebels, led by Abd-el-Krim, are defeated in Morocco by the French • Lebanon becomes a republic • The Russian revolutionary leader Lev Trotsky is expelled from the Soviet Politburo • General Strike (first and last) across Britain lasts ten days • The British Broadcasting Corporation (BBC) is formed with a royal charter • John Logie Baird (Scot) demonstrates television in London • British economist John Keynes: *The End of Laisez-Faire* • T. E. Lawrence ('of Arabia'): autobiographical *The Seven Pillars of Wisdom* • Ernest Hemingway (US) *The Sun Also Rises*

Duke Ellington and his band, The Washingtonians, secure residency at Harlem's Cotton Club (below). With regular live radio broadcasts, 'From the Cotton Club', the jazz composer-performer becomes a household name.

British composer Constant Lambert writes his exuberant *The Rio Grande* for chorus and orchestra.

Respighi composes *Trittico Botticelliano* (Three Botticelli Pictures) for chamber orchestra.

8 January The Kolisch String Quartet gives the first performance of Berg's serialist *Lyric Suite*, in Vienna. The work derives important musical material from the notes A, B flat, B, F, the notated initials of Alban Berg and his (married) lover, Hanna Fuchs-Robettin.

21 January Koussevitzky conducts Roussel's neo-classical Suite in F major, written for the Boston Symphony Orchestra.

28 January Copland introduces his Piano Concerto in Boston.

10 February Ernst Krenek's opera *Jonny spielt auf* (Jonny Strikes Up, 1925) premières in Leipzig. Infused with jazz and contemporary dance styles, it creates a sensation in Germany and abroad. Productions in more than 100 towns and cities follow by the end of the decade.

18 March Rachmaninov's Fourth Piano Concerto (1926) meets with disapproval at its première in Philadelphia. The composer withdraws the work for revision.

8 April Varèse's colouristic *Arcana* is first performed under Stokowski with the Philadelphia Orchestra. Now regarded as one of Varèse's more accessible pieces, the symphonic poem receives a pummelling by critics. This year the French composer becomes an American citizen.

30 May In Paris Ravel introduces his Sonata for Violin and Piano with the composer-violinist George Enescu, who has memorised the piece after just one rehearsal session. The influence of popular music is apparent in the work's second movement, subtitled *Blues*.

30 May Stravinsky's opera-oratorio *Oedipus Rex*, with text by Jean Cocteau after Sophocles, is presented at the Théâtre Sarah Bernhardt in Paris. The first staged production is mounted the following year in Vienna.

14 June Reinhold Glière captures communist values in his melodious ballet *The Red Poppy*, first staged at the Bolshoi Theatre.

1 July Bartók punches and glides through his formidable First Piano Concerto (1926), premièred under Furtwängler in Frankfurt. The reception is generally unfavourable. This year marks the completion of the composer's single-movement String Quartet No. 3.

19 September Schoenberg's String Quartet No. 3 is first performed in Vienna.

6 October The filmed musical *The Jazz Singer*, starring Al Jolson, opens in New York. It is the first feature-length film to incorporate synchronised speech and music.

5 November Shostakovich's Second Symphony—a one-movement oratorio-symphony subtitled *To October*—premières in St Petersburg.

1927 Allied military control ends in Germany and Hungary • Josef Stalin secures political control in the Soviet Union; Lev Trotsky is expelled from the Russian Communist Party • Chinese Nationalist leader Chiang Kai-Shek purges communists from the Kuomintang • The German economy collapses and the Mark becomes worthless •

German scientists Fritz London and Walter Heitler introduce concept of quantum chemistry • Charles Lindbergh (US) makes first solo transatlantic flight • Universum Film AG (Ger) release Fritz Lang's pioneering science-fiction film *Metropolis* • L. S. Lowry (Eng) paints *Peel Park, Salford* • Virginia Woolf (Eng): *To the Lighthouse*

Respighi composes the tone poem *Feste romane* (Roman Festivals) and draws on themes by Baroque composers (including Pasquini and Rameau) in *Gli uccelli* (The Birds) for small orchestra. These works attest to Respighi's rank as one of the world's greatest orchestrators.

Frank Bridge completes his orchestral impression *There is a Willow Grows Aslant a Brook*; he also takes on a promising composition pupil: **Benjamin Britten**.

5 January Walton's *Sinfonia concertante* is introduced under **Ansermet** in London.

16 January Webern's first fully serialist composition, the String Trio, is first performed in Vienna. This year sees the completion of his *Symphony* for chamber orchestra.

2 April Nikolay Myaskovsky's one-movement Symphony No. 10 makes its irrepressible entrance in Moscow. The composer's four-movement Symphony No. 9 is premièred later this month.

27 April Stravinsky's ballet *Apollon musagète* (Apollo Father of the Muses), scored for strings only, is first danced in Washington. **Diaghilev** organises a European première for June, in Paris.

6 June *Die ägyptische Helena* (The Egyptian Helen), the final completed collaboration between **Strauss** and **Hofmannsthal**, opens in Dresden.

9 August At the Hollywood Bowl **Percy Grainger** premières *To a Nordic Princess*, dedicated to the

Macheath at the gallows (moments before his reprieve) in the final scene of *The Threepenny Opera*.

love of his life, the Swedish artist and poet Ella Viola Ström. At the end of the concert, before a crowd of over 15,000, he marries her.

12 August Composer **Leos Janáček** dies from pneumonia in Ostrava, Czechoslovakia, aged 74. He had recently completed the opera *From the House of the Dead*.

22 August Visionary German composer **Karlheinz Stockhausen** is born in Burg Mödrath, near Cologne.

31 August Weill and **Brecht** present their milestone of musical theatre, *The Threepenny Opera*, in Berlin. Set in London's Soho during the Victorian age, the edgy updated version of John Gay's *The Beggars' Opera* (first performed 200 years previously) enthrals the city and soon the rest of Europe.

22 November Ida Rubinstein dances **Ravel**'s unremitting *Boléro* for the first time at the Paris Opéra. **Toscanini** launches it as a concert hall standard the following year, in New York, but Ravel soon tires of his best-known work, deriding it as 'a piece for orchestra without music'.

2 December Schoenberg's *Variations for Orchestra*, the composer's first serial essay for large forces, premières.

13 December Damrosch conducts the first performance of **Gershwin**'s tone poem *An American in Paris*, in New York. Reviews range from 'buoyant' and 'engaging' down to 'nauseous claptrap'.

1928 Albania becomes a kingdom, with King Zog as monarch • The Fascist Grand Council extends its political power in Italy • Newly-elected president Alvato Obregón of Mexico is assassinated • The Soviet Union launches its first five-year Economic Plan • The Economy of Brazil collapses • Islam ceases to be the state religion of Turkey • Alexander Fleming (Scot) discovers penicillin • Voting rights for women over 21 in Britain • First Mickey Mouse cartoons are released, including *Steamboat Willie*—first cartoon with synchronised sound • John Logie Baird (Scot) demonstrates early colour television • René Magritte (Belg) paints *The Empty Mask* • Evelyn Waugh (Eng): *Decline and Fall*

22 February BBC Radio broadcast the première of **Bartók**'s String Quartet No. 4.

28 February Toscanini introduces **Ildebrando Pizzetti**'s *Concerto dell'estate* in New York.

21 March Vaughan Williams's *Sir John in Love* is staged for the first time at the Royal College of Music in London. Based on Shakespeare's *The Merry Wives of Windsor*, the opera introduces the composer's *Fantasia on Greensleeves*.

12 April The 12-year-old violin prodigy **Yehudi Menuhin** performs concertos by Bach, Beethoven and Brahms under **Bruno Walter** (below with Menuhin), with the Berlin Philharmonic.

> *Now I know there is a God in Heaven!*
>
> **12 April** Albert Einstein expresses his amazement while embracing the young **Menuhin** after his Berlin concert

29 April Prokofiev's Dostoyevskian opera *The Gambler* opens at the Théâtre Royal de la Monnaie in Brussels.

3 May Poulenc's *Concert Champêtre* (1928) for harpsichord and orchestra is performed for the first time, in Paris. This year also marks the 30-year-old's 'choreographic concerto' *Aubade*, a blend of chamber ballet and piano concerto.

17 May Prokofiev's Third Symphony makes its explosive entrance in Paris. The dramatic work draws a great deal of its material from the opera *The Fiery Angel* (first version completed 1923).

15 July Hugo von Hofmannsthal dies from a stroke in Vienna, aged 55. **Strauss**, having collaborated with the librettist for the past 23 years, is too distraught to attend the funeral.

18 July Noel Coward enjoys great success with his operetta *Bitter-Sweet*, first performed in London.

19 August Impresario Sergey Diaghilev dies in Venice, aged 57.

3 October Hindemith gives the first performance of **Walton**'s Viola Concerto to great acclaim in London. The German composer and violist was not Walton's first choice: the distinguished English violist **Lionel Tertis** had already turned the work down, considering it incomprehensible.

10 October Lehár's operetta *Das Land des Lächelns* (The Land of Smiles) opens and triumphs at the Metropoltheater in Berlin.

6 December Stravinsky performs as soloist in his *Capriccio* for piano and small orchestra, introduced in Paris.

18 December Webern's Symphony, commissioned by the American League of Composers, premières in New York. Scored for chamber forces, it stands as a key work of the serialist school and its influence will be far reaching. Critics are scathingly dismissive; Olin Downes entitles the work 'The Ultimate Significance of Nothing'.

1929 Herbert Hoover becomes 31st President of the USA • A world economic crises begins with the collapse of the US Stock Exchange • Fascists monopolise Italian parliament • An experimental public TV service begins in Britain; regular TV broadcasts begin in Germany • Italian government recognises Vatican City as an independent state • Popeye the Sailor makes his comic strip début • Paul Klee (Switz) paints *Monument in Fertile Country* • Salvador Dalí (Sp) paints *Enigma* and gives his first solo exhibition, in Paris • Ernest Hemingway (US): *A Farewell to Arms* • D. H. Lawrence (Eng): *Lady Chatterley's Lover* • Erich Remarque (Ger): *All Quiet on the Western Front*

Ferde Grofé composes his *Grand Canyon Suite*.

Paris-based **Prokofiev** composes his Fourth Symphony, commissioned by the Boston Symphony Orchestra in celebration of its 50th anniversary. He also accepts a $1,000 commission from the Library of Congress for his String Quartet No. 1.

Villa-Lobos blends Baroque and Brazilian styles in his *Bachianas brasileiras No. 1*, scored for eight (or more) cellos.

18 January Shostakovich's opera *The Nose*, based on the story by Gogol, is first staged in Leningrad. Critics slate the work. This same month sees the première of the composer's one-movement Symphony No. 3 (*May Day*), also in Leningrad.

1 February Schoenberg explores love and art in his serialist comic opera *Von Heute auf Morgen* (From One Day to the Next, 1929), premièred in Frankfurt.

9 March In Leipzig **Weill** and **Brecht** present shocking capitalist satire with the opera *Rise and Fall of the City of Mahagonny*, an expanded version of their 'songspiel' *Mahagonny* of 1927.

1 April Cosima Wagner dies in Bayreuth, aged 92. She has survived her second husband by 47 years.

12 April The posthumous première of Janáček's prison opera *From the House of the Dead* (1928) takes place in Brno.

5 May Milhaud's first large-scale opera, *Christophe Colomb*, premières with great success in Berlin. With libretto by **Paul Claudel**, the production combines four principal characters, narrator and chorus, a large pit orchestra and off-stage ensemble. Pantomime, ballet and film projection are incorporated to reflect events on different levels of consciousness.

4 June Berg's concert aria *Der Wein* (Wine), scored for soprano and orchestra, is first performed in Königsberg.

8 October Composer **Tōru Takemitsu** is born in Tokyo.

24 October Roussel hears his Symphony No. 3 introduced under **Koussevitzky** in Boston.

28 November Kodaly's *Dances of Marosszék* for orchestra is first given in Dresden.

The German baritone Theodor Scheidl in the title role of *Christophe Colomb*

13 December Stravinsky's reverential *Symphony of Psalms*, composed 'to the glory of God', receives its first performance under **Ansermet** in Brussels. Initially conceived to commemorate the 50th anniversary of the Boston Symphony Orchestra, the work receives its delayed American première six days later.

17 December Chiefly remembered as a song composer, **Peter Warlock** (**Philip Heseltine**) dies from gas poisoning at his Chelsea flat in London, aged 36. The coroner records an open verdict, unable to establish whether the death is a result of accident or suicide.

1930 In the USA, the Great Depression worsens and unemployment grows • Indian 'Salt March': Mohandas Gandhi leads a civil disobedience campaign seeking independence from British rule; he and thousands of protestors are arrested and jailed • Haille Selassie (statesman Ras Tafari) becomes Emperor of Ethiopia • The Allied occupation of Germany (since World War I) ends • The National Socialists (Nazis) win one third of the seats in the German Reichstag • The Empire State Building is built in New York (USA) • Clyde Tombaugh (US) discovers the planet Pluto • Uruguay wins the first World Cup football final • Grant Wood (US) paints *American Gothic* • Noël Coward (Eng): play *Private Lives*

As personal incomes nose-dive during the Great Depression, **George** and **Ira Gershwin** pocket a tidy $100,000 for the score to the filmed musical *Delicious*. George adapts the theme *Manhattan Rhapsody* from the score into his Second Rhapsody for Piano and Orchestra.

Prokofiev composes his Piano Concerto No. 4 for the left hand for the one-armed war veteran and pianist **Paul Wittgenstein**. Unfortunately, Wittgenstein (brother of the philosopher, Ludwig) does not care for the piece and refuses to play it. The composer hides away his score, never to hear it performed.

Varèse completes *Ionisation*, probably the first stand-alone piece of Western classical music scored for percussion ensemble.

10 January **Ives**'s *Three Places in New England* for chamber orchestra is introduced in Boston. The work taxes the skills of **Nicolas Slonimsky**, who at one point has to conduct different beats with his right and left hand simultaneously to direct the orchestra through conflicting rhythms and tempi.

May The 64-year-old **Toscanini** is harassed and physically abused by a mob in Bologna for refusing to conduct the Fascist anthem *Giovinezza*. The (Fascist) authorities side with the mob: they confiscate the conductor's passport and place him under house arrest.

17 September **Delius**'s tone poem *A Song of Summer* is introduced at a Promenade Concert in London. Now blind and paralysed from the late stages of syphilis, Delius has completed the work with the help of his amanuensis, **Eric Fenby**. The composer, at home in France, hears the première broadcast by radio.

3 October Leading Danish composer **Carl Nielsen** dies from angina in Copenhagen, aged 66.

10 October **Walton**'s oratorio *Belshazzar's Feast*, commissioned by the Leeds Festival, is first performed there under **Malcolm Sargent**. It is an indisputable triumph with both the public and critics.

23 October Violinist **Samuel Dushkin** premières **Stravinsky**'s Violin Concerto under the composer's baton with the Berlin Radio Orchestra.

28 October **William Grant Still** (left) has his *Afro-American Symphony* (1930) premièred under **Howard Hanson** with New York's Rochester Philharmonic. The opening movement features infectious 12-bar blues, while the third draws on ragtime and jazz (complete with banjo part). This is the first time a major orchestra has performed a symphony by a black American.

12 November **Elgar** and the London Symphony Orchestra inaugurate Abbey Road Studios, recording the popular *Pomp and Circumstance March, No. 1*.

2 December Composer **Vincent d'Indy** dies in Paris, aged 80.

26 December **George** and **Ira Gershwin**'s musical *Of Thee I Sing* opens on Broadway. The following year it becomes the first musical to win a Pulitzer Prize for drama.

1931 Mohandas Gandhi is released from jail • By the Statute of Westminster, Dominions of the British Empire are recognised as sovereign states • Japan invades Manchuria, beginning a Sino-Japanese war • Revolution flares in Spain: King Alphonso XIII leaves the country and a republic is proclaimed • Collapse of Austria's largest bank, Credit Ansalt, precipitates a financial crisis in Europe • New York's Empire State Building completed • Physicist August Piccard (Switz) ascends by balloon into the stratosphere • Rio de Janeiro's *Christ the Redeemer* statue completed • Films: *Dracula* (with Béla Lugosi); *Frankenstein* (with Boris Karloff) • Salvador Dalí (Sp) paints *The Persistence of Memory*

Poulenc (below) composes his comic secular cantata *Le Bal masque* for voice and chamber ensemble, setting four poems by Max Jacob.

He also begins composing his 15 Improvisations for piano, the last completed in 1959.

Schoenberg breaks off from his opera *Moses und Aron*, never to compose the third act.

Stravinsky, following a successful tour of his Violin Concerto (1931) with Samuel Dushkin, composes the *Duo concertant* for violin and piano, to add to their concert-giving repertoire.

5 January Paul Wittgenstein performs the première of Ravel's dramatic *Piano Concerto for the Left Hand* (1930) in Vienna. The pianist has commissioned this and other works for left hand only, having lost his right arm during World War I.

14 January Ravel conducts Marguerite Long in the first performance of his Piano Concerto in G major, in Paris.

25 February Carl Ruggles's orchestral *Sun-Treader* is introduced under Slonimsky in Paris. The American composer will not hear the work performed in his own country until 1966, shortly before his 90th birthday.

6 March Composer and bandmaster John Philip Sousa dies in Reading, Pennsylvania, aged 77.

24 March Randall Thompson captures critical attention with his Second Symphony, first performed in New York.

16 August Albert Coates conducts the première of Gershwin's *Cuban Overture* (originally entitled *Rumba*) at Lewisohn Stadium.

5 September Poulenc performs his Concerto for Two Pianos in D minor with Jacques Fevrier in Venice. Commissioned by Princess de Polignac, the neo-classical concerto overflows with irony and humour. Wild and capricious in its first movement, the second overtly parodies Mozart's piano concerto slow movements—notably that of K. 466 in D minor. The third returns to cavorting mood and wraps up Poulenc's enduring crowd-pleaser.

7 October Sir Thomas Beecham conducts the inaugural concert of his London Philharmonic Orchestra at the Queen's Hall.

9 October Szymanowski takes the solo part in his *Symphonie Concertante* for piano and orchestra, introduced in Poznan, Poland. Also designated 'Symphony No. 4', the three-movement work boasts powerful textural and thematic contrasts, culminating in an enthralling, barbarous climax. The audience encore the final movement.

31 October Prokofiev gives the first performance of his Fifth Piano Concerto with the Berlin Philharmonic under Furtwängler. The composer's final essay of the genre generates little interest.

1932 Japan establishes a puppet state of Manchukuo in Manchuria, China • A World Disarmament Conference (in which the USA and USSR join) opens in Geneva • The National Socialists (Nazis) become the largest party in the German Reichstag (parliament) • War between Bolivia and Paraguay breaks out over the ownership of the Gran Chaco region • British Physicist James Chadwick discovers the neutron and US physicist Carl D. Anderson discovers the Positron • Sydney Harbour Bridge is opened in Australia • Shirley Temple, aged three, makes her film début • Ernest Hemingway (US): *Death in the Afternoon* • Aldous Huxley (Eng): *Brave New World*

1933

Benjamin Britten, aged 19, begins composing his *Simple Symphony*, incorporating themes composed prior to his teens. He completes the work the following year.

Schoenberg loses his teaching post at the Prussian Academy of Arts in Berlin as Nazis begin ejecting Jews from public office. Anticipating worsening oppression, he leaves the country, reconverts to Judaism (in Paris) and emigrates to America.

23 January Bartók performs as soloist in the première of his acclaimed Second Piano Concerto (1931) in Frankfurt. This is one of the composer's final appearances in Germany: after Hitler's rise to power, he shuns the country and forbids his works to be performed there.

2 March The film *King Kong* (below) opens in New York with a seminal score by Austrian-American composer **Max Steiner**, godson of **Richard Strauss** and former piano pupil of Brahms. It marks the beginning of the fully-scored 'talkies'.

12 April Jascha Heifetz gives the first performance of **Mario Castelnuovo-Tedesco**'s Violin Concerto No. 2 (*The Prophets*), with **Toscanini** conducting the New York Philharmonic.

20 May Howard Hanson's opera *Merry Mount* is introduced in concert version in Michigan. The following year it receives its first staging at the Metropolitan Opera in New York.

June Italy's **Goffredo Petrassi**, aged 18, gains international attention with his neo-classical *Partita* for orchestra, introduced at the ISCM Festival in Amsterdam.

1 July At times sentimental operetta, **Strauss**'s *Arabella* opens in Dresden.

The composer muses to the writer Stefan Zweig, 'Must one become seventy to recognise that one's greatest strength lies in creating kitsch?'

6 October Pawel Kochánski gives the first performance of **Szymanowski**'s folk-influenced Violin Concerto No. 2 in Warsaw. Kochánski, advisor to the composer on both his violin concertos, provides the cadenza.

15 October In Leningrad the 27-year-old **Shostakovich** performs the première of his energetic (and in places Romantic) Piano Concerto No. 1, scored with solo trumpet and strings. This year also sees the completion of his 24 Preludes for piano.

23 October Kodály's *Dances of Galánta* for orchestra and **Bartók**'s *Five Hungarian Folksongs* for voice and orchestra both début in Budapest.

17 November Alfredo Casella's Concerto for piano, violin, cello and orchestra makes its compelling, brassy entrance in Berlin.

23 November Composer **Krzysztof Penderecki** is born in Dębica, Poland.

1933 Franklin D. Roosevelt (Dem) becomes 32nd President of the USA, and announces a 'New Deal' to cure the Depression • Nazi leader Adolf Hitler becomes Chancellor of Germany; under his rule, open persecution of Jews begins, and trade unions are suppressed • Germany withdraws from the international disarmament conference and leaves the League of Nations • Japan also leaves the League • The USA and Canada abandon the gold standard • The 21st Amendment to the US Constitution repeals prohibition • James Hilton (Eng) introduces Shangri-La in *Lost Horizon* • H. G. Wells (Eng): *The Shape of Things to Come*

Glazunov, now living in Paris, composes his Saxophone Concerto (Op. 109).

Hindemith completes his symphony *Mathis der Maler* (Mathias the Painter), while continuing to work on an opera of the same name.

Prokofiev creates his much loved *Suite from Lieutenant Kijé*, adapting his 1933 film score.

Django Reinhardt and **Stephane Grappelli** form the *Quintette du Hot Club de France* (below).

22 January Shostakovich's second opera, *Lady Macbeth of the Mtsensk District* (completed 1932), premières in Leningrad. Critics declare it a masterpiece, but then radically change their minds two years later (see 1936). This year also sees the first performance of the 27-year-old's *Suite for Jazz Orchestra No. 1*.

26 January Koussevitzky introduces **Roy Harris**'s Symphony *1933* (No. 1) with the Boston Symphony Orchestra. It will become the first American symphony to be commercially recorded.

8 February Virgil Thomson's opera *Four Saints in Three Acts*, with libretto by **Gertrude Stein**, opens in Hartford, Connecticut. Featuring an all-black cast, the production triumphs and transfers to Broadway later this month.

23 February Sir Edward Elgar, England's musical figurehead, dies in London, aged 76.

2 April Italian composer **Gian Francesco Malipiero** has his First Symphony premièred at the ISCM Festival in Florence. He will write eleven symphonies in total.

25 May Following an operation to remove an ulcer, English composer **Gustav Holst** dies from heart failure in London, aged 59.

10 June Bradford-born **Frederick Delius** dies at Grez-sur-Loing, aged 72.

15 July Composer **Harrison Birtwistle** is born in Accrington, Lancashire.

8 September Composer **Peter Maxwell Davies** is born in Salford, Greater Manchester.

7 November Rachmaninov performs his *Rhapsody on a Theme of Paganini* under the baton of **Stokowski** in Baltimore. The work combines 24 variations on Paganini's Caprice No. 24 into a three-movement form, with occasional references to the liturgical plainchant melody *Dies Irae*. Of the famously tuneful Variation No. 18 (based on an inversion of the original theme) the composer remarks, 'this one is for my agent'.

30 November Berg's *Lulu Suite*, comprising five pieces adapted from his unfinished opera, is introduced under **Erich Kleiber** in Berlin. Kleiber resigns his directorship of the Berlin Staatsoper the following month in protest against artistic censorship imposed by the Nazi regime.

1934 Austrian Chancellor Engelbert Dollfuss is killed by Nazis; Justice Minister Kurt von Schuschnigg succeeds him • President Paul von Hindenburg of Germany dies; Chancellor Adolf Hitler is given dictatorial powers as Führer (leader) • King Alexander of Yugoslavia and French Foreign Minister, Jean Barthou, are assassinated in Marseilles (Fr) • A Balkan Entente is formed by Greece, Romania, Yugoslavia and Turkey • The USSR joins the League of Nations • F. Scott Fitzgerald (US): *Tender is the Night* • Mikhail Sholokhov (Russ) *And Quiet Flows the Don* • Robert Graves (Eng): *I Claudius* • Agatha Christie (Eng): *Murder on the Orient Express*

8 February *The New York Times* runs a confession by **Fritz Kreisler**, in which the violinist-composer admits he has been deceiving the public for years: many pieces of his repertoire attributed to 18th-century composers—Tartini, Stamitz, Vivaldi and others—are in fact by himself. Kreisler offers his excuse: 'I found it impudent and tactless to repeat my name endlessly on the programmes.'

8 April **Bartók**'s Fifth String Quartet is premièred in Washington D.C. by the Kolisch Quartet.

10 April **Adrian Boult** directs the first performance of **Vaughan Williams**'s Fourth Symphony, in London. Despite its daring dissonances and angular melodies—untypical of the composer—the work is warmly received. 'I wrote as I felt,' the composer remarks.

17 May French composer and critic **Paul Dukas** dies in Paris, aged 69.

29 May Czech composer **Joseph Suk** dies in Benešov, near Prague, aged 61.

24 June **Strauss**'s comic opera *Die Schweigsame Frau* (The Silent Woman), based on Ben Jonson's play *Epicoene*, opens in Dresden. The production achieves just four performances before Nazi authorities ban the work, displeased with the involvement of the Jewish librettist **Stefan Zweig**.

13 July By order of Goebbels, **Strauss** 'resigns' as president of the Reichsmusikkammer following the interception of a letter from the composer to **Stefan Zweig** criticising the Nazi regime.

6 September **Manuel Ponce**'s *Suite en estilo antiguo* for orchestra is premièred under **Ansermet** in Mexico City.

30 September **George** and **Ira Gershwin**'s African-American cast folk-opera *Porgy and Bess* opens in Boston. Infectious songs such as 'Summertime', 'It Ain't Necessarily So' and 'Oh, I Got Plenty

of Nuthin'' are not enough to seduce the critics unanimously, some finding the work lacking depth. Despite a 124-performance run, the production is not profitable. Commercial success follows six years later when dialogue replaces the recitative.

6 November **Walton**'s Symphony No. 1 receives its first complete performance in London. It seals the reputation of the 33-year-old composer.

21 November **Bax**'s Symphony No. 6, generally considered the composer's magnum opus, débuts in London under **Sir Hamilton Harty**.

1 December French violinist **Robert Soëtans** premières **Prokofiev**'s lyrical Violin Concerto No. 2 in Madrid.

11 December **Cowell** explores indeterminate form in his *Mosaic Quartet*, introduced in New York.

24 December **Alban Berg**, aged 50, dies from blood poisoning caused by an infected insect bite (or sting). He leaves his opera *Lulu* unfinished.

Soprano Anne Brown, creator of the role of Bess

1935 Germany rejects the disarmament clauses of the Versailles Treaty (which ended World War I) and introduces conscription • In a plebiscite, the Saarland votes to return to Germany • Britain signs a naval treaty with Germany • German Jews are deprived of citizen's rights by the Nuremberg Laws • Abyssinian War: Italian troops invade Ethiopia • Kurt von Schuschnigg tries to curb growing Nazi strength in Austria • Stresa Conference: Britain, France and Italy denounce unilateral repudiation of treaties • Persia changes its name to Iran • Physicist Robert Watson Watt (Scot) devises radar • T. S. Elliot (US/Eng): play *Murder in the Cathedral* • Dorothy L. Sayers (Eng): *Gaudy Night*

Prokofiev completes his ballet *Romeo and Juliet* and extracts from it the first of three orchestral suites. This year he returns with his family to live in the Soviet Union.

21 January On the day following the death of King George V of England, **Hindemith** composes *Trauermusik* (Funeral music) for viola and string orchestra, completed in just over five hours. BBC radio broadcasts the poignant eight-minute work the next day, with Hindemith performing the solo viola part.

23 January Mexican composer **Carlos Chávez** conducts the radio première of his Symphony No. 2 (*Sinfonia India*) in New York.

28 January Almost certainly on Stalin's orders, *Pravda* newspaper publishes a hostile attack on **Shostakovich**'s opera *Lady Macbeth* (1932), accusing the composer of writing degenerate, 'formalist' music, contrary to the true spirit of the Russian people. The paper warns that unless the composer changes his ways, 'things … may end very badly'. Shostakovich withdraws his Fourth Symphony before its première, fearing disastrous consequences. It remains unperformed for 25 years.

16 February Varèse's *Densité 21.5* for solo platinum flute is first performed at the Carnegie Hall, New York. The title derives from the density of platinum: 21.5 grammes per cubic centimetre.

21 March Russian composer **Alexander Glazunov** dies in Paris, aged 70.

18 April Composer **Ottorino Respighi** dies from a heart infection in Rome, aged 56.

19 April Louis Krasner performs the posthumous première of Berg's Violin Concerto (1935)—'To the memory of an Angel'—in Barcelona. Berg's last completed and most popular work represents his heartfelt response to the death of Manon Gropius, 18-year-old daughter of Mahler's widow, Alma, and her second husband, the renowned architect Walter Gropius.

2 May Prokofiev's didactic symphonic fairytale *Peter and the Wolf*, written for orchestra and narrator, is introduced at a children's concert in Moscow. Prokofiev finds its reception disappointing.

1 August Strauss conducts his commissioned *Olympic Hymn*, for orchestra and chorus, at the opening of the Berlin Olympics (left). The 72-year-old composer has found his involvement ironic: 'I, of all people, who hate and despise sports!'

3 October Minimalist composer **Stephen (Steve) Reich** is born in New York.

6 November Rachmaninov's Symphony No. 3, completed almost 30 years after No. 2, receives its first performance under **Stokowski** with the Philadelphia Orchestra.

13 December Samuel Barber's muscular Symphony No. 1 is premièred in Rome. The 26-year-old composer is currently fulfilling his residency as winner of the American Prix de Rome.

1936 King George of Britain dies; is succeeded by his eldest son, Edward VIII, Edward soon abdicates and is succeeded by his brother, George VI • Italy annexes Ethiopia • In Spain, the left-wing Popular Front wins elections; a right-wing army revolt led by Emilio Mola and Francisco Franco starts a bloody civil war • Dictators Adolf Hitler (Ger) and Benito Mussolini (It) proclaim a Berlin-Rome 'Axis' (alliance) • A regular public television service begins in Britain • Track and field athlete Jesse Owens (US) wins four gold medals at the Berlin Olympics • Georgia O'Keeffe (US) paints *Summer Days* • Margaret Mitchell (US): *Gone With the Wind* • Dylan Thomas (Wal): *Twenty-Five Poems*

21 January Bartók's Music for Strings, Percussion and Celesta is premièred under **Paul Sacher** in Basel. Commissioned by Sacher and the Basel Chamber Ensemble, it will become one of the most often studied works of the 20th century.

31 January Composer **Philip Glass** is born in Baltimore.

March Hindemith resigns from the Berlin Hochschule, a decision made following a Nazi ban on all his music. He has been labelled, variously, a 'cultural Bolshevist', a 'spiritual non-Aryan' and an 'atonal noisemaker'. This same month he makes his first trip to America.

12 March Composer and organist **Charles Widor** dies in Paris, aged 93.

29 March Tuberculosis and heavy smoking send Polish composer **Karol Szymanowski** to the grave in Lausanne, aged 54.

2 June Berg's unfinished opera *Lulu* is posthumously premièred at the Municipal Theater in Zürich. The complete opera will not be performed until 1979 owing to an embargo implemented by Berg's widow on the incomplete third act.

8 June Based on a collection of 13th-century poems of unknown authorship, **Carl Orff**'s *Carmina Burana* (Songs of Buren) is introduced in Frankfurt. It is the first work in a trilogy of 'scenic cantatas' entitled *Trionfi* (Triumphs) and will make Orff internationally famous.

16 June Marc Blitzstein's left-wing 'play in music' *The Cradle Will Rock* is premièred in an ad-hoc concert version (with piano accompaniment only) at the Venice Theater in New York. It follows the withdrawal of government support for Orson Welles's theatre production.

11 July America loses its most famous composer: **George Gershwin** dies from a brain tumour in Hollywood, aged 38.

23 August Composer **Albert Roussel** dies in Royan, France, aged 68.

27 August Benjamin Britten rises to international prominence with his *Variations on a Theme of Frank Bridge*, first performed at the Salzburg Festival. Ironically, the orchestral work becomes more famous than any by **Bridge** himself.

27 August Copland draws on native colours in *El Salón México* for orchestra, introduced in Mexico City under the country's leading composer, **Carlos Chávez**.

12 September Milhaud premières his orchestral *Suite Provençale* in Venice. This year also sees the composition of the *Scaramouche* suite for two pianos—later adapted for saxophone and orchestra.

21 November Shostakovich (left) presents his Fifth Symphony in Leningrad. Its composition follows harsh criticisms made by the Soviet propaganda paper *Pravda* against his opera *Lady Macbeth*. The symphony triumphs, with one critic hailing it as 'a work of extraordinary profundity, by a mature artist who has successfully overcome the childish disease of leftism'.

28 December Following brain surgery, **Maurice Ravel** dies in Paris, aged 62.

1937 In the Spanish Civil War, Germany and Italy give open military support to forces led by General Franco; the City of Guernica is bombed; Almeria is shelled; the Spanish Republic government withdraws to Barcelona • France and Britain adopt a policy of appeasement towards Axis powers (Germany and Italy) • Japanese invade China, beginning an eight-year war • The film *Snow White and the Seven Dwarfs* (Walt Disney) is released • Salvador Dalí (Sp) paints *Sleep* • Pablo Picasso (Sp) paints *Guernica* • Ernest Hemingway (US): *To Have and Have Not* • John Steinbeck (US): *Of Mice and Men* • George Orwell (Eng): *The Road to Wigan Pier*

1938

Music philosopher **Theodor W. Adorno** publishes his *Glosse über Sibelius*, trashing the Finnish composer as anachronistic, second-rate, and popular only with an ignorant public.

Prokofiev scores Eisenstein's film *Alexander Nevsky*. He will adapt and expand the music the following year to produce his acclaimed *Alexander Nevsky* Cantata (Op. 78).

Mexican composer **Silvestre Revueltas** creates the full orchestral version of his celebrated tone poem *Sensemayá*.

Shostakovich composes his String Quartet No. 1 and the *Suite for Jazz Orchestra No. 2*.

16 January Bela Bartók and his (second) wife, **Ditta** (below), make their first concert appearance together, performing the piano parts of the composer's *Sonata for Two Pianos and Percussion*, premièred in Basel.

8 May Stravinsky pays homage to Bach's Brandenburg Concertos in his *Dumbarton Oaks* (Concerto in E flat major), introduced under **Nadia Boulanger** at Dumbarton Oaks, Washington, D.C. The eponymous location is the estate of Mr and Mrs Robert Woods Bliss, who commissioned the concerto for their 30th wedding anniversary. (Six years later the venue famously hosts the wartime strategising for the United Nations.)

12 May Honegger's opera-oratorio *Jeanne d'Arc au bûcher* (Joan of Arc at the Stake, 1935), to words of **Paul Claudel**, premières to great acclaim in Basel. This same year the composer and poet create the dramatic oratorio *La Danse des Morts* (The Dance of the Dead).

28 May Hindemith's opera *Mathis der Maler* (Mathis the Painter) opens in Zürich. Owing to a Nazi ban on all of Hindemith's music (see also 1937), the opera will not be staged in Germany until after the war.

18 August Britten, aged 24, débuts his Piano Concerto under **Sir Henry Wood** in London.

22 September Webern's String Quartet is performed for the first time, in Pittsfield, Massachusetts.

5 October In London **Vaughan Williams**'s *Serenade to Music*, scored for 16 voices and orchestra, celebrates **Sir Henry Wood**'s 50th anniversary as a conductor.

16 October Copland incorporates cowboy songs in his short ballet *Billy the Kid*, first performed in a two-piano version in Chicago. An orchestral suite drawn from the ballet makes its concert hall appearance two years later.

5 November Toscanini conducts the premières of **Barber**'s *Adagio for Strings* and *First Essay for Orchestra*, in New York. The *Adagio*, which will become Barber's most popular work, is a transcription of the slow movement of his String Quartet Op. 11 (1936).

30 December Prokofiev's ballet *Romeo and Juliet*, rejected by the Bolshoi for being impossible to choreograph, is first staged in Brno, Czechoslovakia. A revised version is presented by the Kirov ballet in Leningrad, just over one year later.

1938 German Führer (leader) Adolf Hitler assumes command of Germany's armed forces • Germany invades Austria • Demands for autonomy by Germans in Sudentenland causes a crisis in Czechoslovakia • Munich Pact: Germany, Britain, France and Italy agree, without consulting the Czechs, to a German occupation of the Sudetenland; Czech President Edouard Beneś resigns • Czechs cede Teschen to Poland and southern Slovakia to Hungary • *Kristallnacht*: Nazi anti-Jewish pogrom • Georg Biro (Hung) introduces the ball-point pen • Superman comic strip introduced in the USA • Salvador Dalí (Sp) paints *España* • Graham Greene (Eng): *Brighton Rock*

Milhaud composes his Symphony No. 1. This year also sees the first performance of his opera *Médée* (1938), in Antwerp.

Blind Spanish composer **Joaquín Rodrigo** writes the world's most famous guitar concerto: *Concierto de Aranjuez.*

Villa Lobos composes *New York Skyline* for piano. The melody of the piece reflects the topography of New York rooftops, traced from a photograph.

9 January Endre Petri (piano), **Benny Goodman** (clarinet) and **Josef Szigeti** (violin) introduce **Bartók**'s energetic, two-movement *Rhapsody* in New York. The composer subsequently adds a middle movement and rechristens the piece. *Contrasts* is recorded by Bartók, Goodman and Szigeti the following year.

23 March Zoltán Székely gives the first performance of **Bartók**'s Second Violin Concerto, in Amsterdam.

24 March John Cage's ethereal *Imaginary Landscape No. 1* accompanies a production of Cocteau's play *The Eiffel Tower Wedding Party* (1921) in Seattle. Scored for muted piano, Chinese cymbal, and two variable-speed turntables (playing frequency recordings), it represents one of the earliest electro-acoustic compositions.

April Britten and the tenor **Peter Pears** leave England for North America. While staying in Quebec, Canada, Britten will compose his Violin Concerto, Op. 15, and the song cycle *Les Illuminations* for high voice and string orchestra.

21 June Poulenc's Concerto for Organ, Strings and Timpani (1938) makes its striking entrance in Paris. The work has been commissioned by the prominent arts patron Princess Edmond de Polignac.

Summer With war looming, **Rachmaninov** leaves Europe and returns to America.

3 November Roy Harris (below) draws inspiration from American folk music in his Symphony No. 3 (1938), performed complete for the first time under **Koussevitzky** in Boston. The organic one-movement piece rewards Harris with spectacular success. This same year he writes his Symphony No. 4 (*Folk Song*) for chorus and orchestra.

21 November Shostakovich's Sixth Symphony is premièred in Leningrad. Whilst the finale is encored, the work does not meet audience expectations following the triumphant Fifth Symphony (1937).

23 November Kodály's *Variations on a Hungarian Folksong* (or *Peacock Variations*) is first performed in Amsterdam. The city's Concertgebouw Orchestra has commissioned the work in celebration of its 50th anniversary.

7 December Jascha Heifetz introduces **Walton**'s Violin Concerto in Cleveland.

21 December Celebrating the 60th birthday of Stalin, **Prokofiev**'s cantata *Zdravitsa* (A Toast) is dutifully performed in Moscow.

1939 The Spanish Civil War ends with victory for Francisco Franco • Spain leaves the League of Nations • German troops complete their occupation of Czechoslovakia • The USSR and Germany sign a non-aggression pact • German troops invade Poland; Britain and France declare war on Germany • Soviet forces invade Poland which is divided between Germany and the USSR • Russian armies invade Finland • Physicists Otto Hahn (Ger) and Fritz Strassmann (Ger) achieve nuclear fission • Film: *Gone With the Wind* • Frida Kahlo (Mex) paints *The Two Fridas* • DC Comics (US) introduce Batman • John Steinbeck (US): *The Grapes of Wrath* • James Joyce (Ire): *Finnegans Wake*

Britten, currently living in America, composes the *Sinfonia da Requiem*, commissioned for the 2,600th anniversary of the Japanese empire. Written following the death of his father, the three movements of the symphony adopt titles associated with the Roman Catholic Mass for the Dead. The 'Christian' work is rejected as an insult to the Japanese Emperor.

John Cage creates his first work for prepared piano, *Bacchanale*, to accompany a performance by the dancer Syvilla Fort. Written over three days, the percussive piece requires the wedging of objects such as screws, bolts, rubber and felt between the strings of the piano. Cage demonstrates his multi-timbral invention to the composer **Lou Harrison** who laments, 'Oh dammit! I wish I'd thought of that!'

26 January Gerald Finzi's Cantata *Dies Natalis* for soprano (or tenor) and strings is introduced at London's Wigmore Hall.

9 February Bohuslav Martinů's highly-charged Double Concerto for two string orchestras, piano and timpani (1938) premières in Basel. 'Composed under terrible circumstances,' writes Martinů in reference to post-Munich Pact Czechoslavakia, 'the emotions it voices are not those of despair but rather of revolt, courage and unshakable faith in the future'.

9 March Stravinsky marries his second wife, Vera de Bossett, a year on from the death of his first wife, Catherine. Later this year he celebrates 50 years of the Chicago Symphony Orchestra with his Symphony in C.

14 March Hindemith's Violin Concerto (1939) premières in Amsterdam. Now living in the USA, the composer writes his Cello Concerto, the Theme and Variations: *The Four Temperaments* and the Symphony in E flat. He begins teaching at Yale University next year.

28 March Spanish violinist **Antonio Brosa** gives the first performance of **Britten**'s Violin Concerto, conducted by **John Barbirolli** with the New York Philharmonic at Carnegie Hall.

21 April Michael Tippett conducts the première of his finest work to date, the Concerto for Double String Orchestra (1939), in London.

16 May New York's Museum of Modern Art hosts the first performance of **Chávez**'s imagined Aztec music *Xochipilli*, scored for percussion ensemble (including indigenous instruments) and winds. The work compliments an exhibition of 20 centuries of Mexican art.

11 June Paul Sacher and the Basel Chamber Orchestra introduce **Bartók**'s *Divertimento* for string orchestra (1939). The composer and his wife immigrate to the USA later this year.

20 June Messiaen, composer and infantryman, is captured by the Germans. He is later imprisoned at Stalag VIII-A in Görlitz, Silesia. (See also 1941.)

24 October Frederick Stock conducts the first performance of **Carpenter**'s Symphony No. 1, commissioned for the 50th anniversary of the Chicago Symphony Orchestra.

16 November David Oistrakh gives the first performance of **Khachaturian**'s Violin Concerto in Moscow. Also introduced is **Myaskovsky**'s 15-minute Symphony No. 21.

23 November Shostakovich's Piano Quintet is first heard in Moscow. It later wins the composer a Stalin Prize of 100,000 roubles.

6 December Stokowski premières **Schoenberg**'s Violin Concerto in Philadelphia, with **Louis Krasner** as soloist. Completed in 1936, the work is fiendishly difficult to play, as Schoenberg gleefully acknowledges: 'I am delighted to add another unplayable work to the repertoire.'

1940 World War II continues: Germany invades Norway and Denmark • N. Chamberlain resigns as British Prime Minister; succeeded by Winston Churchill • German armies over-run Belgium, the Netherlands and Luxembourg, and invade France • British forces evacuated form Dunkirk • Italy enters the war on Germany's side • French conclude an armistice with Germany; the southern part of France, ruled from Vichy, remains independent; Germans occupy the rest • 'The Battle of Britain': major British air-victory thwarts German plans for invasion • Italy invades Greece • The Russo-Finnish War ends with Soviet victory • Film: Disney's *Fantasia* • E. Hemingway (US): *For Whom the Bell Tolls*

Britten, in America, composes the *Scottish Ballad* for two pianos and orchestra, and his First String Quartet (Op. 25). He is also awarded the Library of Congress Medal for services to chamber music. Next year he returns to England.

Honegger, in Nazi-occupied Paris, composes his Symphony No. 2 for string orchestra.

3 January Rachmaninov's *Symphonic Dances* is introduced under **Eugene Ormandy** in Philadelphia.

15 January Messiaen and three fellow inmates première his *Quartet for the End of Time* in Hut 27B, Stalag VIII-A, Görlitz. Scored for clarinet, violin, cello and piano, the eight-movement work is performed in freezing conditions before an audience of guards and several hundred prisoners. The composer is released a few weeks later.

20 January The Kolisch Quartet gives the first performance of **Bartók**'s String Quartet No. 6 (1939), in New York.

28 January Copland's orchestral arrangement of *Quiet City*, originally conceived as incidental music to Irwin Shaw's play (1939), is first heard in New York. This same year the composer writes his Piano Sonata No. 1.

7 February Violinist **Albert Spalding** performs the public première of **Barber**'s Violin Concerto (1939) under **Ormandy** with the Philadelphia Orchestra.

3 April In Chicago **Frederick Stock** conducts **Walton**'s *Scapino* overture, composed for the 50th anniversary of the city's Symphony Orchestra.

27 June The BBC begin broadcasting the letter V in Morse code… followed by the four-note opening of Beethoven's Fifth symphony as part of their V for Victory campaign. Nazi propaganda minister Josef Goebbels (right) attempts to sabotage the idea by adopting the same ploy—

even though 'victory' in German is translated as 'sieg'. The BBC's 'Colonel Britton' responds, 'The Germans will not drown out the knocking of fate, however loud they beat. For when they tap out the V they are merely signalling their own impending doom.'

29 June Ignacy Jan Paderewski, composer, pianist and former Polish Prime Minister, dies in New York, aged 80.

17 October William Schuman achieves his first major success with his richly textured Symphony No. 3, introduced under **Koussevitzky** in Boston.

December As the Nazis sweep across western Russia, **Shostakovich** completes his patriotic Seventh Symphony for his besieged home city of Leningrad (formerly St Petersburg). The composer will later declare that the work 'is not about Leningrad under siege—it's about the Leningrad that Stalin destroyed and Hitler merely finished off.' (See also March 1942.)

1941 World War II continues: British troops drive Italian forces out of Egypt and into Libya • British forces liberate Ethiopia from the Italians • British navy sinks Germany's *Bismarck* • Operation Barbarossa: German armies (with Axis coalition, including Romania, Hungary, Italy and Finland) invade the USSR; Siege of Leningrad; Russian armies mount a counter-offensive • Japan begins a campaign of conquest: Japanese planes bomb Pearl Harbour, Hawaii, inflicting heavy damage on the US fleet; USA declares war on Axis Powers • Japanese forces capture the Philippines and Hong Kong • Bertolt Brecht (Ger): play *Mother Courage and Her Children* first staged, in Zürich • Film: *Citizen Kane* (Orson Welles)

Khatchaturian composes his Symphony No. 2 in response to the German invasion of the Soviet Union.

Prokofiev completes his Piano Sonata No. 7 during the Red Army's defence of Stalingrad (right). It becomes the most celebrated of his 'War Sonatas' (Nos. 6–8) and wins him a Stalin Prize (second class) the following year.

1 January Chávez has his percussive Piano Concerto No. 1 premièred by the pianist **Eugene List** with the New York Philharmonic.

1 March Cage's three-minute *Imaginary Landscape No. 3* is first performed at the Arts Club of Chicago. Scored for six players, instruments include an assortment of frequency oscillators, tin cans, muted gong, variable-speed turntables (playing frequency recordings), a buzzer, an amplified marimbula and an amplified coil of wire. Cage's *Imaginary Landscape No. 2*, for percussion quintet, is premièred just over two months later in San Francisco.

5 March Shostakovich's Seventh Symphony, *Leningrad*, is premièred in Kuybïshev, becoming a symbol of resistance to the German invasion. A secret microfilm of the score is smuggled out to the West, with performances following in London and America this same year.

9 April 50 elephants and 50 ballerinas dance the sensational première of **Stravinsky**'s *Circus Polka* at Madison Square Garden, New York. This year also marks the first performance of *Danses Concertantes* for chamber orchestra, and the composition of *Four Norwegian Moods* for orchestra.

16 April Bruno Walter introduces **Barber**'s discursive *Second Essay for Orchestra* with the New York Philharmonic.

29 May Bing Crosby records **Irving Berlin**'s *White Christmas* for Decca records. Released 30 July this year, it becomes the best-selling song of all time.

14 August British composer **Edmund Rubbra**, in battle dress, conducts the première of his Fourth Symphony at the London Proms.

16 October Copland's ballet *Rodeo* (or *The Courting at Burnt Ranch*), commissioned and danced by the Ballet Russe de Monte Carlo, is performed for the first time, in New York.

28 October Strauss's one-act *Capriccio* premières in Munich. Set in a château outside Paris in 1775, the work presents an allegorical consideration of whether words or music are more important in opera; there is neither action nor characterisation. The composer's so-called 'conversation piece' is his 15th and final opera.

13 November Martinů, aged 51, has his Symphony No. 1 introduced by **Koussevitzky** and the Boston Symphony Orchestra, to great acclaim.

9 December Khatchaturian's ballet *Gayane* is danced for the first time in Molotov. The *Sabre Dance* of the final act becomes a widely-performed concert piece.

1942 World War II continues; Japanese forces invade Dutch East Indies and Burma, and Singapore surrenders • US troops block Japanese drive in naval battles of the Coral Sea and Midway • German troops drive the British out of Libya and back into Egypt • Germans besiege Stalingrad (modern St Petersburg) and are trapped in a Russian counter-offensive • El Alamein: Germans under Rommel are defeated by Allies in Egypt • Nazis begin major period of mass-murder (mainly Jews, but also gypsies, homosexuals, religious and political opponents, the disabled and POWs) by gas chamber • US-led Manhattan Project begun to develop atomic bomb • Anne Frank (Ger), aged 13, begins her diary

Poulenc composes his cantata *Figure humaine* for unaccompanied choir. Written in occupied Paris to texts by Paul Éluard, the moving work closes with the poet's *Liberté*—a poem leaflet-dropped by the RAF all over France.

American composer **William Schuman** is the first winner of the newly created Pulitzer Prize for Music with his Secular Cantata No. 2: *A Free Song* (1942).

21 January Bartók and his wife, Ditta, appear as piano soloists at the première of the composer's Concerto for Two Pianos, Percussion and Orchestra with the New York Philharmonic Orchestra. The work is an arrangement and augmentation of the Sonata for Two Pianos and Percussion (1937).

26 February Roy Harris's Fifth Symphony, dedicated to 'the heroic and freedom-loving people of our great ally, the USSR', is premièred in Boston and broadcast via short-wave radio to the Soviet Union.

3 March Webern's *Variations for Orchestra* (1940), one of the composer's more dynamic essays, receives its première in Winterthur, Switzerland. This year Webern completes his Cantata No. 2 for soprano, bass, chorus and orchestra.

12 March Copland's wartime morale booster *Fanfare for the Common Man*, scored for brass and percussion, is first heard in Cincinnati.

28 March Sergei Rachmaninov, the last great Romantic virtuoso, dies from cancer in Los Angeles, aged 69.

10 May Messiaen and **Yvonne Loriod** (later the composer's second wife) introduce *Visions de l'Amen* for two pianos, in occupied Paris.

21 June Tippett, ardent pacifist and determined composer, begins a three-month jail sentence for non-compliance with the conditions of exemption from military service as a conscientious objector. He is released after two months.

24 June Vaughan Williams offers respite from the horrors of war in his largely serene Fifth Symphony, premièred in London.

Summer Koussevitzky visits the ailing **Bartók** in hospital and commissions a new orchestral work. The *Concerto for Orchestra* is completed eight weeks later.

8 October Koussevitzky (right) introduces **Stravinsky**'s *Ode* for orchestra in Boston, composed in memory of the conductor's late wife, Natalie.

28 October Martinů's Symphony No. 2—celebrating the 25th anniversary of the founding of the Czechoslovak Republic—premières in Cleveland. Meanwhile in New York the composer's *Memorial to Lidice* responds to the sickening Nazi genocide of Czechs at the small town of Lidice, outside Prague (June 1942).

4 November Shostakovich's Eighth Symphony is introduced in Moscow.

14 November Leonard Bernstein steps in at the last minute as replacement conductor of the New York Philharmonic in a programme that includes **Strauss**'s *Don Quixote*. Broadcast nationally, the concert is a resounding success and makes Bernstein famous overnight.

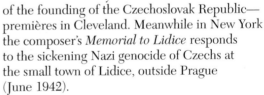

1943 World War II continues: America begins heavy air raids against Germany • Germans at Stalingrad surrender to the Russians, who then recapture considerable territory throughout the year • Valiant Jewish resistance in the Warsaw Ghetto Uprising crushed by Nazis • German/Italian forces are defeated in North Africa and surrender • US and British troops invade Italian mainland; Italians depose Mussolini • Italy surrenders unconditionally and joins the war against Germany • In Yugoslavia, Communist resistance forces led by Josip Broz ('Tito') open an offensive against the Germans • A US fleet defeats a Japanese fleet in the Battle of the Bismarck Sea

Messiaen composes the monumental piano cycle *Vingt regards sur L'Enfant-Jésus* (Twenty Contemplations of the Child Jesus).

Prokofiev completes his ballet *Cinderella* and his *War* Sonata No. 8. New compositions this year include his popular Fifth Symphony and the score to Eisenstein's film *Ivan the Terrible* (Part I).

5 January William Grant Still's *In Memoriam: The Colored Soldiers Who Died for Democracy* is premièred by the New York Philharmonic under **Artur Rodzinsky**.

20 January Hindemith's *Symphonic Metamorphoses of Themes by Carl Maria von Weber* is welcomed in New York. The following month his fugal *Ludus Tonalis* for piano is first played at the University of Chicago.

28 January Composer **John Kenneth Tavener** is born in London.

6 February Eduard Steuermann gives the first performance of **Schoenberg**'s Piano Concerto (Op. 42), under **Stokowski** in New York. This year also sees the première of the composer's non-serialist *Theme and Variations* for orchestra, in Boston.

19 March *A Child of Our Time* (1941), by **Michael Tippett** (right), premières in London. The oratorio examines the consequences of a young man's desire for justice through violent means—a scenario motivated by the shooting of a German diplomat by a young Jew in 1938, which precipitated Nazi pogroms. Promoting unity in the face of tyranny, the work attains a wide collective significance with its inclusion of African-American spirituals. Tippet's *Child* becomes recognised as one of the foremost choral works of the century.

18 April Leonard Bernstein premières his first ballet, *Fancy Free*, with huge success in New York. This same year he adapts the work into his first musical comedy, *On the Town*.

May Howard Hanson becomes the second winner of the Pulitzer Prize for Music with his Symphony No. 4 (1943).

8 May Composer **Dame Ethel Smyth** dies in Woking, England, aged 86.

17 June David Oistrakh performs **Prokofiev**'s Violin Sonata No. 2 in Moscow. The composer has adapted the work from his Flute Sonata of the previous year.

18 October Nazis execute German-Czech composer **Viktor Ullmann** at Auschwitz. (See also 1975.)

30 October Copland's one-act ballet *Appalachian Spring* opens to great acclaim in Washington, D.C. Martha Graham choreographs and dances the tale of 19th-century American pioneers. (See also 1945.)

14 November Shostakovich's String Quartet No. 2 is first performed in Leningrad.

26 November In New York the 28-year-old **Yehudi Menuhin** introduces **Bartók**'s Sonata for Solo Violin, having commissioned the piece himself.

1 December Bartók's *Concerto for Orchestra* (1943) is introduced to tremendous acclaim in Boston. The composer is at this time struggling with leukaemia.

1944 World War II continues: US, British and allied forces land in Normandy; they liberate Antwerp, Brussels and Paris • French leader Charles de Gaulle sets up a provisional government in Paris • Allied forces land in southern France • Russians enter Romania, Bulgaria, Yugoslavia and Hungary • An attempt by German officers to assassinate Hitler fails • Germans launch rocket-bomb (V-1 and V-2) attacks on Britain • Britain begins re-conquest of Burma • Dumbarton Oaks Conference (Washington D.C.): US, British and Russian delegates agree to set up the United Nations • Salvador Dalí (Sp) paints *Dream Caused by the Flight of a Bee* • T. S. Elliot (US/UK): poems *Four Quarters*

Britten composes *The Young Person's Guide to the Orchestra: Variations and Fugue on a Theme of Henry Purcell* for a BBC documentary film, commissioned by the Ministry of Education. The work marks the 250th anniversary of Purcell's death.

The Italian musicologist **Remo Giazotto** reconstructs a movement from a fragment of a trio sonata purportedly by Albinoni (d.1751), discovered in the bombed-out ruins of the Dresden State Library. The Baroque phoenix is re-born as Albinoni's Adagio in G minor for string orchestra and organ.

Messiaen composes his song cycle *Harawi* (A Song of Love and Death) for soprano and piano, inspired by the *Tristan and Isolde* legend.

1 January Iannis Xenakis, aged 22, suffers a broken jaw and the loss of an eye while fighting the British in Athens. Abandoned for dead, he is rescued by his father.

13 January Prokofiev introduces his Fifth Symphony in Moscow: 'a song of praise of free and happy man: his strength, his generosity, and the purity of his soul.' It enjoys the stamp of approval by the Soviet authorities and becomes one of the composer's most popular works.

May Copland is awarded a Pulitzer Prize for *Appalachian Spring* (1944). This year he arranges the music of the ballet into a suite for orchestra, creating one of his most popular concert works.

7 June Britten revives British opera with *Peter Grimes* at Sadler's Wells Theatre, London. The tale of an ill-mannered but victimised fisherman triumphs instantly, with productions following in translation across Europe. **Bernstein** conducts the American première in Lenox, Massachusetts, the following year.

2 August Composer **Pietro Mascagni**, unpopular with many in the musical community for supporting Mussolini, dies in Rome aged 81.

15 September The 61-year-old **Anton von Webern**, while enjoying an after-meal cigar, is accidentally shot and killed by an American soldier in Mittersill, outside Salzburg.

26 September Béla Bartók, Hungary's leading composer, dies in New York from leukaemia, aged 64.

3 November Shostakovich's Ninth Symphony is first performed in Leningrad. Well received at first, it is denounced by Soviet authorities the following year for failing to 'reflect the true spirit of the people of the Soviet Union'.

4 November Malipiero's Third Symphony is performed through to its closing lament, in Florence.

21 November Prokofiev's *Cinderella* is first danced by the Bolshoi in Moscow. The composer extracts three orchestral suites (Opp. 107–109) from the ballet the following year.

Peter Grimes; Tenor Peter Pears in the title role.

1945 World War II: Allies bomb Dresden • US, British and allied troops cross the Rhine River; Russian forces capture Warsaw, Cracow, Tilsit and Berlin • Mussolini assassinated by Italian partisans • Adolf Hitler commits suicide in the ruins of Berlin • Germany surrenders unconditionally; 8 May is declared VE (Victory in Europe) day • US drop atomic bombs on Hiroshima and Nagasaki, Japan • Japan surrenders; World War II ends • Harry S. Truman takes up as 33rd US President following death of Franklin D. Roosevelt • Clement Attlee replaces Winston Churchill as UK prime minister • The United Nations Organisation comes into formal existence • George Orwell (Eng): *Animal Farm*

590

Honegger responds to the horrors of war in his Symphony No. 3 (*Symphonie liturgique*). This year also marks his lighter Symphony No. 4.

Leading Turkish composer **Ahmed Saygun** writes *Yunus Emre*, an oratorio setting of texts by the (eponymous) 13-century Turkish poet.

24 January Stravinsky introduces his *Symphony in Three Movements* in New York.

25 January Sacher conducts the first performance of **Strauss**'s sombre *Metamorphosen*, scored for 23 solo strings, in Zürich. The 81-year-old composer's Oboe Concerto is premièred in the same city the following month.

8 February Bartók's Third Piano Concerto, completed by **Tibor Serly**, is posthumously premièred in Philadelphia.

25 March Stravinsky's *Ebony Concerto* (1945)

for clarinet and jazz band is performed for the first time, in New York. The composer describes it as 'a jazz concerto grosso with a blues slow movement'.

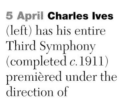

5 April Charles Ives (left) has his entire Third Symphony (completed *c.*1911) premièred under the direction of **Lou Harrison** in New York. Subtitled *The Camp Meeting*, the piece wins Ives a Pulitzer Prize the following year,

though the septuagenarian gives the prize money away, declaring, 'prizes are for boys, and I'm all grown up'.

8 May The opera *The Medium*, with music and words by **Gian Carlo Menotti**, opens with great success at Columbia University. It transfers to Broadway in 1947 with more than 200 performances that year.

14 May Hindemith's *When lilacs last in the dooryard bloom'd*, a 'Requiem for those we love', based on the poem by Walt Whitman, is introduced in New York. This year the composer takes American citizenship.

16 May Berlin's musical *Annie Get Your Gun* opens on Broadway.

17 May Frank Martin's neo-classical *Petite symphonie concertante* is introduced under **Paul Sacher** in Zürich. It becomes the Swiss composer's most popular work.

12 June Part I of **Prokofiev**'s operatic epic *War and Peace* (1942), based on Tolstoy's novel, is introduced in Leningrad. Part II, scheduled the following year, fails to progress beyond its dress rehearsal. Prokofiev will make continued revisions to his sixth and final opera over the next six years.

12 July Britten's opera *The Rape of Lucretia* is premièred with only modest success at Glyndebourne under **Ansermet**. **Kathleen Ferrier** makes her operatic début as Lucretia.

2 August Schoenberg suffers a near-fatal heart attack. Convalescing, he begins his thematically unstable String Trio, reflecting on his ordeal.

18 October Copland's admired Symphony No. 3 premières in Boston. His *Fanfare for the Common Man* (1943) theme opens the final movement.

14 November Spanish composer **Manuel de Falla** dies in Alta Gracia, Argentina, aged 69.

16 December Shostakovich's String Quartet No. 3 is first heard in Moscow.

1946 The League of Nations is wound up • The United Nations establish permanent headquarters in New York; Trygve Lie (Nor) is elected secretary-general • Albania, Bulgaria, Yugoslavia and Czechoslovakia adopt Communist governments • King Vittorio Emanuele III of Italy abdicates; is succeeded by his son, Umberto II, who leaves Italy after a referendum favouring a republic • Republic of Hungary proclaimed • Jordan becomes independent • Juan Perón becomes president of Argentina • The Philippines becomes an independent republic • US Supreme Court declares racial segregation on interstate buses unconstitutional • Marc Chagall (Russ/Fr) paints *Cow with Sunshade*

American composer **Milton Babbit** steers towards integral serialism in *Three Compositions for Piano*, with structural ordering of pitch and rhythm.

Boulez, aged 22, completes the first version of *Le Visage Nuptial*, a cantata for soprano, alto, two ondes martenot, piano and percussion.

Maurice Duruflé completes his stirring Requiem, combining Gregorian chant, modal polyphony and sensuous 20th-century French harmony.

German composer **Karl A. Hartmann** completes his Fourth Symphony, scored for string orchestra.

9 January Weill's 'American opera' *Street Scene* (premièred Philadelphia, 1946) begins a 148-performance run at the Adelphi Theatre in New York. Mixing opera and Broadway musical, the work eventually closes due to crippling production costs.

27 January Sacher premières **Stravinsky**'s Concerto in D for string orchestra, celebrating 20 years of the Basel Chamber Orchestra.

15 February Composer **John Coolidge Adams** is born in Worcester, Massachusetts.

15 February Jascha Heifetz gives the first performance of **Korngold**'s Violin Concerto in D major, rapturously received in St Louis.

27 February Peter Mennin, aged 23, receives critical attention for his Symphony No. 3, introduced by the New York Philharmonic.

4 April Barber completes *Knoxville Summer of 1915* for soprano and orchestra, inspired by the writing of James Agee.

7 May Virgil Thomson's suffrage opera *The Mother of Us All* is first staged at Columbia University, New York. The libretto is by Gertrude Stein, who died the previous year.

3 June Poulenc's surrealist opera *Les Mamelles de Tirésias* (The Breasts of Tiresias), based on the play by Guillaume Apollinaire, opens at the Opéra-Comique in Paris. This year also marks the composer's optimistic Sinfonietta.

20 June Britten's chamber opera *Albert Herring* premières at Glyndebourne with a live BBC radio broadcast. The audience responds warmly.

> *Mr Britten is still pursuing his old problem of seeing how much indigestible material he can dissolve in music*
>
> Frank Howes of *The Times*, reviewing *Albert Herring*.

Summer Milhaud composes his Symphony No. 4: *1848* during an Atlantic crossing.

6 August Austrian composer **Gottfried von Einem** receives international attention with his political opera *Dantons Tod* (Danton's Death), premièred in Salzburg.

Autumn A political dissident, **Xenakis** flees Greece on a false passport. Reaching Paris, he finds work at Le Corbusier's architectural firm.

11 October Prokofiev's Sixth Symphony is premièred in Leningrad. Though containing many light moments and lyrical ideas, it is criticised the following year by Soviet authorities for being too highbrow.

14 November Violinist **Louis Krasner** performs the official première of **Roger Session**'s Violin Concerto (completed 1935), with the Minneapolis Symphony Orchestra under **Dimitri Mitropoulos**.

27 November German composer **Boris Blacher** establishes his international reputation with his *Orchestral Variations on a theme by Paganini*, first performed in Leipzig.

1947 UN approves a partition of Palestine with an internationalised Jerusalem against strong Arab opposition • Independence of India creates separate dominions of India and Pakistan; riots follow • Burma becomes an independent republic • Ceylon (later Sri Lanka) gains independence as a dominion • General Agreement on Tariffs and Trades is signed by 23 countries • US Marshall Plan for European recovery is established • The Dead Sea Scrolls are discovered at Qumran, Jordan • Jackson Pollock pours paint on to canvas in what becomes known as his 'drip period' • Tennessee Williams (US): *A Streetcar Named Desire* • Yasunari Kawabata (Jap): *Snow Country*

Inspired by Hindu philosophy, **Cage** completes his 70-minute *Sonatas and Interludes* for prepared piano. The meticulous preparation of the instrument with materials such as screws, bolts, rubber and plastic, takes two to three hours.

British composer **Elizabeth Maconchy** writes her acclaimed String Quartet No. 5.

Milhaud, suffering severe rheumatoid arthritis, is confined to a wheelchair.

Shostakovich completes his First Violin Concerto. He withholds the work from performance fearing a backlash from the CCCP (see below).

Strauss composes the *Four Last Songs* for soprano and orchestra, his final work. This year a court in Munich clears him of all charges of Nazi collaboration.

10 February The Central Committee of the Communist Party of the Soviet Union issues a damning condemnation of **Shostakovich**, **Prokofiev**, **Khatchaturian**, **Myaskovsky** and others, for their 'formalist perversions and anti-democratic tendencies … which are alien to the Soviet people and their artistic tastes'. The Committee outlaws any music it deems complex, modernist or pessimistic.

Andrei Zhdanov (with Stalin, right), Second Secretary of Soviet Communist Party and chief architect of artistic purges

16 February Having previously protested, 'formalism is the name given to music not understood on first hearing', **Prokofiev** capitulates under pressure in a letter to the Union of Composers: 'No matter how painful it may be … I welcome the resolution of the Central Committee, which establishes the conditions for the recovery of the entire organism of Soviet music … The formalistic movement, which leads to the impoverishment and decline of music, is alien to the Soviet people.'

20 February Lina Prokofieva, **Prokofiev**'s abandoned first wife, is arrested in Moscow on spurious charges of spying. She is incarcerated for the next eight years in a Siberian labour camp.

21 April **Vaughan Williams**'s Symphony No. 6 is introduced with enormous success under **Sir Adrian Boult** in London.

16 May American composer **Wallingford Riegger** wins extensive public and critical approval with his hybrid 12-note Symphony No. 3, first performed in New York.

15 June **Weill**'s folk-opera *Down in the Valley* (1947) opens in Bloomington, Indiana. It becomes his second most popular stage-work, after *The Threepenny Opera*.

August **Lennox Berkeley**'s Piano Concerto (1947) is introduced at the London Proms.

5 October Electro-acoustic engineer **Pierre Schaeffer** broadcasts his *Études de Bruits* (Noise Studies) on French National Radio. The *Étude aux Chemins de Fer* (Railroad Study), comprising a sequence of recorded steam-engine sounds, represents the earliest example of his self-termed 'musique concrète'.

27 October **Ansermet** directs the first performance of **Stravinsky**'s *Mass*, in Milan.

29 October **Dmitri Kabalevsky**'s Violin Concerto receives a simultaneous première in Leningrad and Moscow.

1948 Indian religious leader Mohandas K. Gandhi is assassinated • The 'Cold War' intensifies; Russians begin a blockade of West Berlin; Western Powers start a successful airlift in reply • British mandate in Palestine ends: Jews proclaim the State of Israel, which is immediately recognised by the USA; an Arab-Israeli war begins • Republic of Korea is established with Seoul as its capital; Communist North Korea is established as a rival republic • South Africa adopts Apartheid as official policy • John Bardeen, Walter Brattain and William Shockley (US) unveil the transistor • Jackson Pollock (US) paints *Number One* • Ezra Pound (US): *The Pisan Cantos* • Evelyn Waugh (Eng): *The Loved One*

Prolific Danish composer **Vagn Holmboe** completes the first three of his 20 numbered string quartets.

Messiaen (right) experiments with pitch and rhythmic orders in his piano piece *Cantéyodjayâ*. In the influential *Mode de valeurs et d'intensités*, again for piano, he employs a structural approach to pitch, rhythm, dynamics and attack.

Schoenberg composes *Phantasy* for violin and piano, and the unaccompanied choral work *Dreimal tausend Jahre* (Three Times a Thousand Years).

Late March Pressured by Stalin, **Shostakovich** attends the Cultural and Scientific Conference for World Peace in New York, where he testifies to the 'reasonable' constrictions imposed on composers by the Soviet Central Committee. (The composer's compliance has induced Stalin to officially revoke the CCCP's directive of 1948, but governmental control over artistic expression continues.)

8 April Bernstein takes the solo part in his Symphony No. 2: *The Age of Anxiety* for piano and orchestra, performed under **Koussevitzky** in Boston. The work is inspired by W. H. Auden's recent poem *The Age of Anxiety: A Baroque Eclogue*.

14 July Britten's choral *Spring* Symphony is introduced in Amsterdam.

10 August Milhaud's String Quartet No. 14 and String Quartet No. 15 are first performed at Mills College, Oakland, California. Introduced one after the other, they are then played together simultaneously as an octet for strings.

8 September German composer **Richard Strauss** dies in Garmisch, Bavaria, aged 85.

4 November Schoenberg's cantata *A Survivor from Warsaw* (1947) is first performed in Albuquerque. The work explores the resilience of Jewish faith amidst Nazi brutality. It is one of his most powerful and emotive serialist creations.

20 November Rudolf Firkušný gives the first performance of **Martinů**'s Piano Concerto No. 3, in Dallas, Texas.

26 November Shostakovich's environmentally-friendly oratorio *Song of the Forests* triumphs in Leningrad. Praising the Soviet Union's reforestation programme, the work delights his erstwhile adversaries of the Central Committee of the Communist Party.

2 December Messiaen's monumental *Turangalîla-symphonie* (1948), scored for ondes martenot, piano, extensive percussion and large orchestra, is premièred by the Boston Symphony Orchestra under **Bernstein**. Messiaen has devised the title from the Sanskrit words *turanga* and *lîla*, giving the expansive ten-movement work connotations of 'a song of love; a hymn to the superhuman joy that transcends everything.'

2 December William Primrose performs Bartók's Viola Concerto, introduced posthumously under the baton of **Antal Dorati** in Minneapolis. Only sketched out by Bartók, the composition has been completed and orchestrated by **Tibor Serly**.

1949 Communist forces under Mao Tse-tung seize power in China • Belgium, Britain, Canada, Denmark, France, Iceland, Italy, Luxembourg, the Netherlands, Norway, Portugal and the USA pledge mutual assistance in the North Atlantic Treaty • The Council of Europe is established in Strasbourg • West Germany becomes the German Federal Republic •

The USSR ends its blockade of Berlin • The East German Democratic Republic is created • India becomes a republic within the British Commonwealth • The USA withdraws its occupying forces from South Korea • Russians test their first atomic bomb • Henry Moore (Eng) sculpts *Family Group* • George Orwell (Eng): *1984*

1950–2000

1950–2000

I N THE aftermath of World War II, new brands of modernism emerged to release music from a tonal past, flying the flag of innovation and freedom during the Cold War era. The Soviet Union and Eastern-bloc countries denounced the atonal avant-gardists as degenerate and continued to enforce artistic controls until the fall of the Iron Curtain. Though the age of neo-classicism was over, prominent composers in Britain and the USA were hesitant to abandon tonality.

Increasingly dependent on state sponsorship, contemporary classical music experienced wide diversification, notably integral serialism, indeterminacy, *musique concrète*, electronic music, textural music; then also minimalism, pluralism, postmodernism, neo-Romanticism, new complexity and spectralism. On the fringe or outside these 'schools' completely were many older established composers, as well as younger generations who offered yet more aesthetic alternatives within the rapidly shifting musical landscape.

At the same time, the world of modern art music was facing the charge of elitism, having lost much of its traditional cultural significance after World War I. The void it left had profited jazz, blues and dance music, fashionable styles that paved the way for the advent of pop music in the 1950s. While broadcast and record media proved invaluable to the dissemination of all kinds of music, a classical repertory of ages past found surging popularity, presenting enormous challenges to an unprecedented number of composers competing for recognition.

The tonal vanguard in Britain, the USA and the Soviet Union

Any musician who has not experienced … the necessity of dodecaphonic language is useless. His whole work is irrelevant to the needs of his epoch.

Pierre Boulez

The fervent avant-gardist Pierre Boulez discharged his youthful scorn of modern tonal composers in 1952. Tonal compositions of the following year included Shostakovich's Tenth Symphony, Tippett's *Fantasia Concertante on a Theme of Corelli* and Martinů's Sixth Symphony. More 'irrelevant' pieces followed, such as Douglas Moore's operatic sensation *The Ballad of Baby Doe* and Walton's Cello Concerto, both in 1956. Poulenc, noting a wind of discontent, saw fit to 'apologise' for one of his greatest works, the opera *Dialogues des Carmelites* (1957): 'It seems that my Carmelites can only sing tonal music. You must forgive them.'

◀ *The silent music* by Eduardo Chillida, 1955.

Fierce polemics from the staunch advocates of atonalism served to widen the rift with the tonal vanguard. By emphasising the links between Nazism and the Romantic-nationalist tradition, the atonalists claimed to hold the moral high ground: to compose tonal music was at best weak-minded, at worst, fascist. Moreover, atonalism had been effectively outlawed by the Nazi and communist regimes; it therefore signified democracy and freedom of speech. Indeed the very language of atonality was deemed democratic, with its absence of governing key centres. Tonality, on the other hand, was the enforced aesthetic of Soviet 'Socialist Realism' (see *Chapter 7*), and was by nature a 'hierarchical' language.

Tonal music, or at least music that incorporated aspects of tonality, remained especially important in Britain, the USA and the Soviet Union, albeit for different reasons. Both Britain and the USA had only recently established their musical identities, and in both cases this had found very successful expressions through a fusion of indigenous folk idioms, modal-tonal styles and neo-classical influences. Another factor was that neither country felt quite the same need as central Europe to move on from a troubled past, whether that be associated with the humiliation of Nazi occupation and oppression, or the shameful perpetration of Nazism itself. The incentive to produce the kind of music that the Nazis hated most was simply not as strong. Yet another determining factor resides in the stature of the leading British and US composers at the half-century, most of whom were tonalists. By contrast, many famous German, French and Italian tonal composers had recently faded from view, died or emigrated to the USA. Karl Amadeus Hartmann in Germany, Poulenc in France, and Pizzetti and Malipiero in Italy were among the few exceptions.

Britain   In Britain at the mid-century, none of the leading composers—Vaughan Williams, Walton, Tippett and Britten—gave up tonality completely. Benjamin Britten, who re-launched English opera with *Peter Grimes* (1945, see *Chapter 7*), represented the third generation of British 'renaissance' composers. In developing his musical style he had distanced himself from the folk idioms of the Pastoralists and instead looked to the assorted influences of Purcell, the English choral tradition, the cosmopolitan, chromatic style of his teacher Frank Bridge, and Stravinskyan neo-classicism.

Britten valued tonality as fundamental bedrock. Even in his chilling chamber opera *The Turn of the Screw* (1954), where serialist methods generate the rotating 'screw theme', the larger organisational structures revolve around tonal centres. His brilliantly atmospheric *A Midsummer Night's Dream* (1960) vaguely indulges 12-note procedures, though the opera harnesses the lyrical, expressive style for which Britten was best loved. It speaks accessibly in multiple languages, weaving in and out of 'extended tonality'—using recognisable chords in unconventional ways, and non-tonal elements within a broader tonal framework. An emphasis on the supernatural elements of Shakespeare's play brings with it the kind of ethereal (sometimes sensual) dissonance that modern audiences generally find easy to abide.

There was a shift towards asceticism in Britten's style thereafter. This may be felt in the renowned *War Requiem* of 1962, one of Britten's greatest

commercial successes, and even more so in the three one-act *Church Parables* (1964–68), forged with a texturally simplified, often austere, musical language. This he found suited to the most intimate of mediums, as in the three unaccompanied, Baroque-style cello suites (1964–71), written for the Russian maestro Mstislav Rostropovich (1927–2007). But Britten maintained his distance from the avant-garde and strict atonality, famously stating: 'I want my music to be of use to people, to please them … I do not write for posterity.' By the time of his last opera, *Death in Venice* (1973), he was again freely employing 12-note techniques. If this late work is more 'difficult' than *The Turn of the Screw*, it is due to its amorphous expressionism and recitative-heavy score. Nonetheless, the intense chromatic language does not obscure an entrenched tonal idiom.

Britten's friend Michael Tippett (see also *Chapter 7*) negotiated greater atonal extremes in the operas *King Priam* (1962) and *The Knot Garden* (1970), as he explored themes of relationship psychology, love and self-fulfilment. However, even at his most harmonically daring, he saw no reason to banish tonality entirely. The one-movement Second Piano Sonata (1962), fragmented in structure and striking in textural contrasts, presents a colourful fusion of his wide-ranging mid-career aesthetics. Tippett's reverence for the classical tradition is demonstrated by five string quartets, four concertos and four symphonies. Prominent mid-century British composers rooted in more avowedly tonal styles included Arthur Bliss, Edmund Rubbra and Malcolm Arnold (1921–2006), each a master of orchestral technique.

In the USA, home to avant-gardists and conservatives alike, the long-lived composers Howard Hanson (1896–1981), Roy Harris (1898–1979), William Schuman (1910–92) and David Diamond (1915–2005) were among those who, like many British composers, exploited tonality often beyond traditional, 'functional' means (see also *Chapter 7*). At the mid-century these composers were all leading lights of their country's symphonic tradition. Hanson had a strong traditional bias, evident in works like the *Song of Democracy* (1957) for chorus and orchestra, and the Romantic Fifth Symphony (1955). Diamond was also traditional, often Romantic, in his treatment of both form and language. Schuman, like Harris, could write tonal music identifiably American, as in the popular *New England Triptych* (1956), though he was much more adventurous in some of his last symphonies, such as the Eighth (1962), which advances from ascetic dissonance in its first two movements to lively fragmented jazzy gestures in the last.

USA

Copland and Barber, standard-bearers of accessible American tonal music, both experimented with serialism in the 1950s and 60s. Barber attempted to steer serial technique into his Romantic-cum-neo-classical style, but achieved greater success without it, as in his critically acclaimed Piano Concerto (1962). Copland produced a succession of quasi-serialist pieces, including the ambitious *Piano Fantasy* (1957) and the orchestral *Connotations* (1962). If Leonard Bernstein (1918–90) flirted briefly with serial procedures, it served only to convince him of the universal significance of tonal anchoring. Bernstein's opinions on the matter were influential: he was an impeccably gifted communicator and conductor, and by the end of the 1950s the most famous figure in American classical music.

Soviet Union

After Stalin's death in 1953, the Soviet Union began to relax the tight controls over musical style that had existed under 'socialist realism'. However, the leading Soviet composers of the 1950s and 60s—Shostakovich, Khachaturian and Dmitry Kabalevsky (1904–87)—all remained committed tonalists, not least because excessively dissonant music still procured no official favour. This largely explains the conservativism of Khachaturian's ballet *Spartacus* (1954) and Kabalevsky's Cello Concerto No. 2 (1964), both of which manifest a Romantic spirit. Even Shostakovich, the most progressive of the three, could evoke Romantic nostalgia, as in the slow movement of his Second Piano Concerto (1957).

Shostakovich carefully managed his adventurous tendencies throughout the 1950s. Circumstances changed in 1962 when he and the poet-librettist Yevgeny Yevtushenko angered the authorities by criticising Soviet anti-semitism in the choral Symphony No. 13 *Babi Yar*. Tonal yet forbidding, the work had to be withdrawn and the text re-written. The following year Khrushchev reminded composers of their duty to the Soviet people by making a formal pronouncement on 'dodecaphony': 'We flatly reject this cacophonous music,' he ranted, 'our people can't use this rubbish as a

▼ Aram Khachaturian's melodious ballet *Spartacus* (Act III), Kirov ballet, Leningrad, 1956.

tool of their ideology.' Nevertheless, Shostakovich wrote some extremely dissonant music towards the end of his career. A life-threatening heart condition brought introspection and pessimism in his Symphony No. 14 (1969), which adapts serial methods in its 11-movement meditation on death. The bleak six-movement String Quartet No. 15 (1974) is another composition that allies depression and death with extreme dissonance. At the same time, it is a work built around tonal centres—indeed it firmly begins and ends in the key of E flat minor. The Symphony No. 15 in A major (1972) and Viola Sonata in C major (1975) further confirm that Shostakovich's sound-world remained fundamentally tonal to the last. (See also *Statements of Belief*.)

Integral serialism and beyond

Anton Webern (1883–1945), the least celebrated member of the Second Viennese School during his lifetime, emerged as the father figure to a new generation of European avant-garde composers. His refined and deeply rationalised brand of serialism, laid bare in sparse atonal textures, offered appealing logic and cohesion to the compositional process. Influential too was Messiaen's piano piece *Mode de valeurs et d'intensités* (1949). Although not a fully 12-note composition, its methodical organisation of pitch, duration, dynamic and modes of attack demonstrated new possibilities for serial technique. Many young composers were introduced to the work at the progressive Darmstadt Summer School, an institution that counted among its students Karlheinz Stockhausen, Luigi Nono and Hans Werner Henze. It is worth emphasising that serialism itself was an attractive aesthetic for post-war composers since the Nazis loathed it; to produce a music utterly divorced from anything deemed 'good' by that evil regime had to be very positive indeed.

The path of what became known as 'integral' or 'total' serialism came to something of an impasse in the early 1950s. Paris-based Boulez, a pupil of Messiaen, realised his clearest vision of integral serialism in *Structures I* for two pianos, in 1952. The 'pre-composition' of the work entailed not only the organisation of note rows (derived from Messiaen's *Mode de valeurs*), but also 12-set series of durations, dynamics and attack. The first part of the work, *Structures Ia*, contained the most rigorous application of the technique. Each note embodied a defined quality, its musical properties exposed through a pointillistic texture reminiscent of Webern, but even more fragmentary. However, for all its logic and cohesion, such 'pure' serial music was liable to sound random and directionless. This was a problem that confronted the Belgian composer Karel Goeyvaerts (1923–93) in his *Opus 2 for thirteen instruments* (1951), Karlheinz Stockhausen (1928–2007) in *Kreuzspiel* (1951) and Jean Barraqué (1928–73) in his 40-minute, single-movement Piano Sonata (1952). These young integral-serialists soon realised that compositional flexibility was necessary to provide character and direction.

Boulez relaxed his serial processes in *Le marteau sans maître* (The Hammer Without a Master, 1954), scored for alto voice and small ensemble, comprising alto flute, viola, guitar, vibraphone, xylorimba and assorted

Pierre Boulez

Le marteau sans maître

▶ The young progressives Luigi Nono, Pierre Boulez and Karlheinz Stockhausen at Donaueschingen, *c.*1950. The Donaueschingen Festival was revitalised during the 1950s as the first festival devoted exclusively to contemporary music.

percussion, including bongos and maracas. The cycle features settings of poetry by René Char in four of its nine movements, while the five instrumental movements relate to, or 'comment on', the vocal movements by way of re-interpretation (a characteristic device of Boulez's style). While serially organised structures remain, the music largely avoids the pointillistic textures of *Structures I*. Premièred in 1955 at the ISCM Festival in Baden-Baden, *Le marteau* received enormous critical praise: it seemed to do for the composer what *Pierrot* did for Schoenberg, since its sung (surrealist) text offered a window into Boulez's otherwise inscrutably complex sound-world.

Stockhausen: *Kontra-Punkte*

Stockhausen met Boulez in 1952 when he arrived in Paris to study under Messiaen. Persisting with integral serialism, he tackled issues of form and direction in *Kontra-Punkte* (Counter-Points, 1953), scored for ten-piece ensemble. Its diverse material is introduced in a pointillistic manner, seemingly chaotically at first, with notes distributed among the instruments; slowly this material integrates, to the point where it coalesces at a unified dynamic (*pianissimo*) in the piano part alone. In this and subsequent serial works Stockhausen cultivated what he termed 'group form', creating sub-structures based on properties such as timbre, textural density and register. *Gruppen* (Groups, 1957) provides the most famous example, scored for three spatially-separated orchestras, each with its own conductor. Positioned on three sides of the audience, the orchestras perform independent musical sequences, or groups, that range from pointillistic textures through to dense walls of sound. The groups are heard at various points individually, overlapping, and occasionally in unified combination. Contrasting tempos, rhythms, dynamics and textures collide or fuse in a multitude of ways, sending sonorities and gestures flying around the concert hall.

Gruppen

The socialist Italian composer Luigi Nono (1924–90), another major figure of the 1950s musical avant-garde, adopted integral serialism in *Il canto sospeso* (The Suspended Song, 1956). This cantata for solo voices, choir and orchestra incorporates moving last words written by condemned prisoners of war, which are set in carefully chosen serial parameters. Musical expression is given broad range in response to the various texts (expressing grief though to defiance), which are themselves broken up into fragments— including fragments of words—and dispersed into pointillistic textures. The sung text is for the most part unintelligible and yet vital to the work's emotional intensity.

Luigi Nono: Il canto sospeso

During the 1950s most of the leading young composers experimented with serialism in one form or another. In America, Milton Babbitt developed the extended serial techniques he had begun exploring in *Three Compositions for Piano* (1947) in such works as the song cycle *Du* (1951), String Quartet No. 2 (1954) and *All Set* for jazz ensemble (1957). The German composer Hans Werner Henze (1926–2012) chose serialism to launch his operatic career (*Boulevard Solitude*, premièred 1952), and the style shaped the early works of Italy's Luciano Berio (1925–2003) and Britain's Alexander Goehr (b.1932). So dominant was the serial aesthetic that even Stravinsky felt compelled to acknowledge it. His stylistic transition from neo-classicism to serialism was gradual: the Septet (1953), *In Memoriam Dylan Thomas* (1954), *Canticum sacrum* (1956) and the ballet *Agon* (1957) all incorporate aspects of 12-note technique. Only then did he employ full serialism, beginning with *Threni* (1958) and *Movements for Piano and Orchestra* (1959). During the 1960s, entering his ninth decade, Stravinsky was the most prominent exponent of the technique.

Stravinsky

By the time Stravinsky wrote his *Requiem Canticles* in 1966, general enthusiasm for strict serialism was in decline, even if Milton Babbitt and the Argentinian composer Alberto Ginastera (1916–83) felt there was significant mileage left in the method. The organisational strategies of serialism, however, continued to inspire a wide range of composers, bringing cogency and form to typically atonal musical languages. It is a legacy that has shaped the music of such notables as the American modernists George Perle (1915–2009) and Charles Wuorinen (b.1938), Finland's Einojuhani Rautavaara (b.1928), Germany's York Höller (b.1944), and Britain's Peter Maxwell Davies (b.1934) and Oliver Knussen (b.1952).

Indeterminacy

Concurrent with integral serialism was a musical approach that may be considered its very antithesis: indeterminacy. However the idea of introducing undetermined compositional elements to classical music was not completely new. The early 20th century had seen notation from Charles Ives that was impossible to render exactly (thus demanding interpretation), and Henry Cowell had invited performer choice over musical structure in his String Quartet No. 3 *Mosaic* (1935) and other works. But it was John Cage who, during the 1950s, brought indeterminacy or 'aleatory' processes firmly into the sphere of art music.

John Cage

Fascinated with Eastern philosophy, Zen Buddhism especially, Cage was attracted to the idea of music created through non-intention. His *Music of Changes* (1951), a work for solo piano inspired by the *I Ching* (the Chinese book of changes), relies on the tossing of a coin to determine such parameters as musical order, dynamic and duration. Cage toyed with 'non-intention' again that same year with his *Imaginary Landscape No. 4* for 12 radios, where each individually tuned 'instrument' pipes out whatever happens to be broadcast at the time.

4'33"

In 1952 Cage conceived his most famous work, *4'33"*. A pianist (or other performer) is instructed to sit without playing a note. The unpredictable sounds of coughs, creaking chairs, ventilation systems, extraneous noises outside the concert hall—even public remonstrations—all become the 'music'. 'Premièred' by Cage's close collaborator David Tudor (1926–96), the amorphous, uncomposed work forced its audience to re-evaluate their conceptions of music. As Cage later commented, 'it leads out of the world of art into the whole of life'.

Morton
Feldman &
Earle Brown

Other American composers further expanded the horizons of indeterminacy. Morton Feldman (1926–87) was one of the first to apply graphic notation, beginning with *Projection 2* for chamber ensemble (1951). Given deliberately imprecise notation, the musicians are forced to interpret the score and inevitably the result is never the same from one performance to the next. Earle Brown (1926–2002) joined Feldman in graphic notation with his *December 1952*, written for 'one or more instruments and/or sound-producing media' as part of his seven-piece *Folio* (1953). The same year he composed the 'open-form' piano work *Twenty-five Pages*, presented in an unbound score so that the performer(s) could begin on any page and play the music in any sequence they chose. This flexible approach to structure, enabling a piece of music to be perceived from different 'perspectives', was the first method of indeterminacy that found appeal in Europe, specifically in the works of Stockhausen and Boulez.

Stockhausen pipped Boulez to the post in what he termed 'mobile form' with *Klavierstück XI* (1956). Here the pianist is directed to choose at will the playing order of 19 groups of material; at the end of each group are directions indicating the dynamic, speed and attack of the next section of choice. Boulez desired to work within tighter parameters of control, but similarly presented mobile material in his Third Piano Sonata (1957, first version) and in *Pli selon pli* (Fold Upon Fold) for soprano and orchestra (1962, first version). While Boulez had little respect for the 'chance' works of the Americans, Stockhausen soon embraced their approach, incorporating graphic notation and variable form in *Zyklus* for solo percussionist (1959). A spiral-bound score allows the performer to begin on any page; thereafter all the pages of the score are played through in order—whether forwards, backwards or even upside down—ending with the first percussive stroke on the starting page.

During the 1960s Stockhausen experimented with ever more radical indeterminate methods, reaching extremes in 15 'intuitive' text compositions collectively entitled *Aus den sieben Tagen* (From the Seven Days, 1968). The music is improvised and prompted by prose instruction alone. Extreme among these is *Goldstaub* (Gold Dust), requiring four performers to fast in solitary confinement for four days, sleeping and thinking as little as possible, before meeting together to improvise on single sounds.

The Polish composer Witold Lutosławski (1913–94) was also among the early European exponents of aleatoric techniques. In compositions ranging from *Jeux vénitiens* (Venetian Games, 1961) for chamber orchestra to late works such as *Chain 2* for violin and orchestra (1985), he adopted elements of chance and performer choice 'for the purpose of rhythmic and expressive enrichment of the music', without losing control over the formal design. Lutosławski's initial inspiration had come from Cage, yet his philosophy bore closer resemblance to that of Boulez.

Stockhausen & Boulez

1960s onwards

Witold Lutosławski

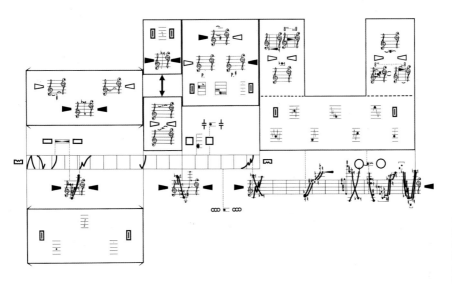

◀ Notational suggestion from Stockhausen's *Zyklus* for solo percussionist (1959).

Henri
Pousseur

Cage:
'Europeras'

Helmut
Lachenmann

The Belgian composer Henri Pousseur (1929–2009) took chance into opera with *Votre Faust* (Milan, 1969) by allowing the audience to vote on narrative direction. His indeterministic methods resonated with the 'Fluxus' mindset, whose aims—inspired by Cage—were anti-commercial, anti-rational, chance-orientated, conceptual, and artistically eclectic. Cage himself pursued this ideology on the stage: his series of five postmodern 'Europeras', begun in the late 80s, contain no music by himself, but instead randomly assembled fragments of operas from the 18th and 19th century. In all five operas the singers are allowed perform standard operatic arias of their own choice. The first two operas of the series, premièred in 1987, are the most complex and adventurous, with indeterminacy extended to plot lines, lighting schemes, set design, costumes and stage directions.

The hey-day of indeterminacy was well over by the 1980s, but aspects of the approach remained at the end of the century. Helmut Lachenmann (b.1935) provides a good example in *Nun* (1999), a double concerto (featuring extended instrumental techniques) for flute and trombone, eight male voices and orchestra. The climax of the work is part-improvisatory, both for the soloists, who improvise around given material, and for the conductor, who brings in and silences orchestral sections at will.

The electronic age

The early landmarks of electronic music include Respighi's incorporation of a singing nightingale on gramophone record in *The Pines of Rome* (1924), Varèse's first use of the electronic ondes martenot (1929; Messiaen from 1937), and John Cage's manipulation of variable speed turntables in his *Imaginary Landscape No. 1* (1939, see *Chapter 7*). Of greater significance were the electronic experiments conducted at the studios of Radiodiffusion Francaise (or French National Radio). It was here, in 1948, that the electro-acoustic engineer Pierre Schaeffer (1910–95) created an organised composition of steam-engine sounds entitled *Étude aux Chemins de Fer* (Railroad Study). In so doing he pioneered audio 'sampling' and a new musical style: *musique concrète*.

Schaeffer's initial recording medium was the gramophone record, but from around 1950 he began experimenting with magnetic tape, which was becoming a widely available media. Acoustic manipulation with tape was much easier, as sounds could be captured and cut up into fragments of any length, then rearranged or electronically processed and re-recorded. Schaeffer collaborated with Pierre Henry (b.1927) to compose the first substantial piece of 'concrete music', *Symphonie pour un homme seul* (Symphony for a Man Alone, 1950). The work's 12 movements present a provocative collage of processed vocal fragments, breathing, laughing and footsteps, with some strumming, banging and prepared piano chopped in. The conservatoire-trained Henry subsequently spearheaded developments in musique concrète and caught the attention of other young progressives. Stockhausen was at the front of the queue, producing his first work for tape, *Konkrete Etüde*, at Radiodiffusion's Paris studio in 1951.

*Musique
concrète*

While the early European tape experiments were preoccupied with environmental sounds, the Americans were more interested in the manipulation of performed music. In 1952 Cage premièred his *Imaginary Landscape No.5*, a short work for tape consisting of random musical extracts taken from 42 selected records. Later that same year the electronic music faculty of New York's Columbia University mounted the first concert of 'Music for Tape', featuring transformed piano and flute sounds in compositions by Vladimir Ussachevsky (1911–90) and Otto Luening (1900–96).

The next evolutionary step for electronic music was made at the newly-created Electronic Music Studios of West German Radio in Cologne—a city still recovering from its near-obliteration during WWII. Stockhausen was lured there to research sound synthesis and he worked tenaciously with a sine-wave generator until his ears hurt. Within a few months he had created his *Elektronische Studien I* (1953), the first piece of music composed of pure electronic sound.

Because the range of electronic sounds available through existing technology was limited in scope, Stockhausen soon began to mix recorded and electronically-generated sounds, as in his renowned *Gesang der Jünglinge* (Song of the Youths, 1956). Combining a transformed recording of a boy singing with electronic synthesis, it was further enhanced by its spatial design, played through a surround-sound configuration of five speakers. Two years later Edgard Varèse (see also *Chapter 7*) adopted this style of musical 'spatialisation' in collaboration with the architect Le Corbusier and composer-architect Iannis Xenakis (1922–2001), producing the ground-breaking *Poème Électronique*. Commissioned for the Philips Pavilion at the 1958 Brussels World Fair, the work drew together recorded and electronic sounds on three-track tape, channelled through 400 speakers around and above the standing audience. Similarly, one of Xenakis's most important tape pieces, *La légende d'Eer*, was conceived for a specially-created acoustic space—'Le Diatope', a temporary curvilinear building that Xenakis himself designed for the opening of Paris's Centre Georges Pompidou in 1977.

Music for tape was to play an important role in the genesis of minimalism, particularly influencing the work of Steve Reich (see *Minimalism*). However, many composers were reluctant to dismiss the live performance element altogether, so virtually from the outset musicians and electronic elements were brought together in combination. Early works of this category include Varèse's *Déserts* (1954), which alternates sections for

◀ The Phillips Pavilion, built for the 1958 Brussels World Fair. In addition to Varèse's *Poème électronique*, visitors also heard *Concrèt PH* by the Pavilion's co-designer Iannis Xenakis, his piece a manipulation of sounds of burning charcoal.

Stockhausen

Edgard Varèse and Iannis Xenakis

▶ Composition with the RCA Mark II synthesiser. Picture courtesy of Columbia University.

live wind and percussion with sections for tape alone, and Berio's *Différences* (1959) for five-piece ensemble and tape.

RCA Mark II Synthesiser

By the end of the 1950s the kind of electronic devices Stockhausen had painstakingly manipulated in the Cologne studios had been brought together in the 'synthesiser'. The first successful model was the RCA Mark II, built in the mid-50s at the Sarnoff Research Center in New Jersey, and like the earliest computers, the instrument required the space of an entire room. For Milton Babbitt, a composer intrigued by rigorous formal processes, it held tremendous potential since it allowed him precise control over all musical parameters. His *Composition for Synthesiser* (1961) was the first influential work created for the instrument. The RCA Mk II was a mass of knobs and switches, and operated via a type-writer style keyboard with punched paper tape. Synthesisers with piano-style keyboards and of much smaller dimensions soon followed, made possible by the integration of transistor technology. Prominent among them was the Moog synthesiser, invented by Robert Moog in 1964. By the end of the decade the instrument had been popularised by Wendy Carlos (born Walter Carlos, 1939) in the album *Switched-On Bach* (1968), and had attracted interest from bands such as The Doors and The Rolling Stones.

Electronics in art music was further aided by the increasing availability of computers. Computer-generated sound was developed in New Jersey at the Bell Laboratories in 1957, but composer interest was minimal for some time, despite the development of more advanced programmes in subsequent years. Computers, after all, were the instruments of nuclear physicists and engineers, and the complexities of computer language presented obvious barriers. Xenakis, a trained mathematician, was one of the few composers who initially utilised the computer as an aid to the compositional process, rather than a tool for sound synthesis. However, in 1977 the world of electronic music, and computer-aided music especially, received an enormous boost with the creation of IRCAM: Institut de Recherche et Coordination Acoustique/Musique. Located

IRCAM

underground next to the Centre Georges Pompidou in Paris, this cutting-edge facility for musical technology was the brainchild of Boulez. He was himself its first director, bringing together acoustic engineers and musicians worldwide to probe unchartered musical territories. Boulez's first IRCAM composition was *Répons* (first version 1981), incorporating computerised sound synthesis and the real-time electronic processing of live performance. Among those who have sampled IRCAM's creative potential are Berio, the English composer Jonathan Harvey (1939–2012), the French composers Gérard Grisey (1946–98) and Tristan Murail (b.1947), and the Finnish composers Kaija Saariaho (b.1952) and Magnus Lindberg (b.1958).

Towards the end of the century composers sought diverse ways of manipulating technology for their needs (see also Murail, next section). Grisey's dynamic *Le noir de l'étoile* (Black of the Star, 1990) incorporates real-time pulsar signals from outer space in combination with live percussion, while Stockhausen's *Helicopter String Quartet* (1995) requires live audio transmission and video link-up for the players who perform their parts from separate circling helicopters. Back on earth, Lindberg used IRCAM technology to implement sound morphing in *Related Rocks* (1997), in which sampled sounds of percussive instruments are very gradually transformed into sounds of vastly contrasting timbre and texture.

Music of timbres and textures

Though serialism attracted composers in eastern and south-eastern Europe, a number of leading figures of the region rejected the style as too restrictive. Some hailed from countries that had only recently sought distance from Germanic traditions in the search for a national musical identity. The general cultural mindset was therefore conducive to alternative musical ideas that fell outside central European modernism. And so it was that the most compelling, revolutionary approaches to musical texture found expression in the diverse art of a Greek, a Pole and a Jewish Hungarian.

The early life of the composer and architect Iannis Xenakis (see also *The electronic age*) was perilous. In wartime Greece he joined the communist-led resistance (EAM), demonstrating against the Nazis. At the outset of 1945, street fighting against the invading British, he suffered severe shrapnel wounds, including the loss of an eye. During the Greek Civil War (1946–49), Xenakis opposed the right-wing Greek government and was arrested. He managed to escape and made it to Paris on a false passport in 1947; meanwhile he was condemned to death *in absentia*.

Iannis Xenakis

In Paris Xenakis found engineering and design work under Le Corbusier while pursuing musical interests with Messiaen. Composing was a spare-time activity for Xenakis during much of the 1950s. Attempting to create music that translated geometric principles, his methods of composition were complex—arguably more so than those of integral serialism, although the music was intended to have a much more immediate effect on the listener. Often reflecting the turbulent environment of his youth, his compositions could be experienced viscerally in a way that integral serialism could not. This is generally true of all 'textural music'.

In 1955 Xenakis sent shockwaves through the musical community with his otherworldly *Metastasis* for 61 instruments and percussion. Allocating an independent part for each player, he generated utterly new, massive textures with chromatic clusters diverging in waves of string glissandi. This was the composer's first major piece of 'stochastic music', in which mathematical laws and probability theory are applied to parameters of pitch, timbre and timing. The stochastic process is a type of organised indeterminacy, where individual indeterminate musical events are gathered up into large, stable, goal-orientated structures. Early stochastic orchestral works included *Pithoprakta* (1956), the Greek word itself meaning 'actions by probability'.

Xenakis worked with computer programmes to facilitate his acoustic stochastic processes. He also took his textural transformations into electronic music, his interests galvanised by the tape experiments of Varèse and a five-year working period (1957–62) at Schaeffer's studios in Paris. Music for percussion figured significantly in his output too, including such accessible pieces as *Pléïades* (1979) for six percussionists and *Rebonds* (1988) for solo percussionist. His later ensemble and orchestral music revealed remarkably diverse sound-worlds. *Jonchaies* (1977) announces itself with characteristic string glissandi, but finds direction through a busy combination of motivic interplay and exciting, primitivist rhythmic propulsion. The violin concerto *Dox-Orkh* (1991) combines neo-classical rhythms, glissandi gestures and complex microtonal dialogues between soloist and orchestra, while his string sextet *Ittidra* (1996) unleashes abrasive, industrial sonorities.

Krzysztof Penderecki

The Polish composer Krzysztof Penderecki (b.1933) established his reputation with music of clusters, glissandi, quarter-tones and radically new performance methods. He devised new forms of notation to indicate such techniques as playing the highest note possible, repeating a note as fast as possible, playing behind the bridge, and hitting the sound-board of

Dem Südwestfunk-Orchester gewidmet

FLUORESCENCES

Krzysztof Penderecki
1961 - 62

▶ *Fluorescences,* page from score. In this and other contemporaneous pieces, Penderecki sought to 'destroy' the conventional orchestra.

a stringed instrument with fingertips. To aid his processes of organic transformation he mapped out his scores with indications of time periods in seconds, rather than using metrical notation. *Anaklasis* (1960) for percussion and 42 solo strings (each string player with a separate part) introduced these methods and won Penderecki international acclaim. His most famous work immediately followed: *Threnody for the Victims of Hiroshima* (1960). Scored for 52 solo strings, the music is violent, agitated and anguished. Tone clusters enter with high-pitched, harrowing intensity, gradually subsiding in volume before a barrage of instrument beatings and textural contortions break out in a frenzied melange. Penderecki's exclusively textural period ended with the First Symphony in 1973, his acknowledged summation 'of avant-garde, radical pursuits'.

The Hungarian-Jewish composer György Ligeti (1923–2006) fled his homeland during the revolution of 1956 and, following a period in Cologne, based himself in Vienna. His very earliest music had followed in the tradition of Bartók and Kodály, but he found his own identity in amorphous, texturally-complex music. With the sense-assaulting *Apparitions* for orchestra (1959) he introduced an assorted array of extended performance techniques and his first mass clusters, all of which provoked huge interest at the 1960 ISCM Festival in Cologne. In *Atmosphères* (1961) he focused exclusively on the gradual transformation of chromatic orchestral clusters, produced both by sustained tones and dense quasi-canonic effects that he termed 'micropolyphony'. He used the technique in parts of his disquieting *Requiem* (1965) and again in the orchestral work *Lontano* (1967).

Beyond his swarming micropolyphony, Ligeti concurrently created a semi-satirical musical style full of absurdities and exaggerated gestures, both instrumental and vocal. This 'nonsense' aesthetic, allied to the anti-establishment Fluxus movement, first appeared in his theatrical chamber work *Aventures* (1962). Scored for three voices and seven instruments, it invokes five emotional states with the aid of snorting, whispering, shrieking and clicking of teeth; one character blows into a paper bag and pops it. Audience members may well (and should) smile, but they are also invited to consider the complexities of language and communication.

In 1968 Ligeti's fame increased significantly owing to the (unauthorised) use of his music in Stanley Kubrick's film *2001: A Space Odyssey*. The pieces 'borrowed' included *Atmosphères* and the single-movement *Lux Aeterna* (1966), whose ethereal micropolyphonic textures are formed by 16 solo voices gliding slowly in canon. Ligeti wrote the acclaimed apocalyptic

György Ligeti

opera *Le grand macabre* between 1974 and 1977, after which he scaled down his composing activities, chiefly due to health problems. Many of his later pieces draw on folk music, both from Hungary and around the world, and employ a wide harmonic palette that steers somewhat towards tonality. The sound-world of Bartók is evoked in the Horn Trio (1982), while the Violin Concerto (1992) reveals Ligeti's late-style preoccupations with world music, polyrhythms, alternative tunings, microtones and harmonic spectra.

During the 1970s, around the time that Ligeti and Penderecki were considering alternative stylistic directions, a new textural aesthetic of 'spectralism' emerged in France. Exemplified in the oeuvres of Gérard Grisey and Tristan Murail, spectral music exploits the overtone series, the fundamental harmonic property of acoustic sound. While recurring pitch centres sometimes come into play, super-imposed harmonic layers result in very dissonant (yet often accessible) sound masses. Bell-like timbres feature prominently in many spectral compositions.

Among the early masterpieces of spectralism is Murail's orchestral work *Gondwana* (1980), whose textural transformations are experienced in the form of slowly shifting waves through to violent eruptions, echoing the geological metamorphoses of continental drift. The same composer's *Bois flotté* (1996) is among the many spectral works that incorporate live electronics. Composed for trombone, string trio, piano and synthesised sounds (triggered by on-stage MIDI keyboard), its material derives from the spectral analysis of sea sounds—breaking waves, swells and undertow. Murail had used an advanced computer programme to access the inner structures of complex natural sounds, and another to translate them into a unique musical language. At the end of the century, acoustic and electronic media were attaining a new, remarkable fusion.

Minimalism and its tributaries

North America

Reacting against modernist complexity, minimalism sought to scrutinise the fundamental components of music in refreshingly simplified terms. It took root on American soil in the early 1960s and drew from diverse sources. All the pioneers of the movement—La Monte Young, Terry Riley, Steve Reich and Philip Glass—had active interests in 'world' music, above all that of the East. Their music, initially at least, was similarly contemplative and harmonically static. Another source of inspiration came from the lively rhythms and narrow harmonic focus of bebop jazz and rock'n'roll, and in keeping with the world of popular music each of the above named composers formed a band (more appropriately, 'ensemble') to promote his own music. Classical music traditions were nevertheless absorbed, but whereas Young found stimulation in the disciplined serialism of Webern, others looked to Stravinsky and music of the 18th century. For some time the music establishment rejected minimalism, so much so that concerts were held in art galleries and museums.

La Monte Young (b.1935) first experimented with minimalism in his String Trio (1958), where three sustained notes provide the entire substance

Tristan Murail

La Monte Young

◀ La Monte Young performing with his Theater of Eternal Music in 1965. His seminal minimalist pieces include *The Four Dreams of China* (1962), which combines long sustained notes with improvisation and potentially 'lasts forever by virtue of including silences of indeterminate length'.

for the work's first five minutes. His *Compositions 1960* revealed him to be a 'concept art' visionary and a driving force behind the Fluxus movement, along with his friend Yoko Ono. In *Composition #2* he asks the performer to 'build a fire in front of the audience'; and in #5 to 'turn a butterfly (or any number of butterflies) loose in the performance area'. However, Young's interests were primarily musical, and by the time of The Tortoise, his Dreams and Journeys (1964), scored for voices, acoustic instruments and an amplified aquarium motor, the sustained tone had become his minimalist hallmark. This set his music apart from the rhythmic brands of Riley and others who immediately followed.

Terry Riley (b.1935) rubbed shoulders with Young as a fellow student at the University of California, Berkeley, and began producing works for tape in the early 60s. In 1964 he created his most celebrated composition: *In C*—indeed, the first famous work of minimalism. 53 motifs, all based around a pulsating C tonic, are performed and repeated at will by any number of performers for any amount of time, using any instruments. Introduced at the San Francisco Tape Music Centre, Riley's classical-jazz-pop jamboree set the pulse racing for minimalism.

Steve Reich (b.1936) was among those who performed at the première of *In C*. A year later at the same venue he presented *It's gonna rain* for two tape loops. Two identical copies of the spoken phrase 'It's gonna rain' (delivered by an impassioned Pentecostal preacher) are played on tape machines positioned left and right, with one running slightly faster than the other, slowly shifting the words out of sync. The work thereby executes every conceivable permutation of set rhythm and pitch, and ends with the phrase back in sync. Reich transferred his so-called 'phasing' technique to the acoustic medium with *Piano Phase* and *Violin Phase* (both 1967). His early artistic manifesto became 'Music as a Gradual Process': the creation of clear musical transformation, perceptible even to the untrained. Representative

Terry Riley

Steve Reich

works include *Four Organs* (1970), incorporating the gradual lengthening of a single dominant 11th chord, and *Drumming* (1971), composed after studying African drumming styles in Ghana.

Reich enriched his musical language during the 1970s, rejecting much of his 60s compositional creed. His milestone *Music for 18 Musicians* (1976) included trademark pulsations and motivic repetitions, but also a cyclical chord structure with timbral and textural variety. Reich's interest in his Jewish heritage then marked a new career phase, beginning with the Hebrew-language Psalm settings of *Tehillim* (1981). In the remarkable *Different Trains* for quartet and tape (1988) he incorporated recorded extracts from interviews with Holocaust survivors, using their vocal pitches and rhythmic patterns to shape the work's instrumental melodies and rhythms. The recorded interview is also a central component of *The Cave* (1993), a theatrical multi-media collaboration with Reich's wife, the video artist Beryl Korot, which discloses reactions of Jews, Muslims and Americans (Christians included) to Old Testament characters.

Philip Glass

Philip Glass (b.1937) studied with Vincent Persichetti (1915–87) and Milhaud in the USA, and for two years with Nadia Boulanger in Paris, but he found his greatest inspiration in Indian music. Drawn to cyclical structures and un-accentuated rhythmic pulses, Glass developed an 'additive/subtractive' compositional process, by which melodic units are systematically augmented or diminished note by note, or cell by cell. He applied this procedure in his first major compositions, including *Music in Similar Motion*, *Music in Contrary Motion* and *Music in Fifths*, all composed in 1969.

Like Reich, Glass eventually found himself too restricted by the harmonic and textural stasis of his early work. His departure is apparent in the marathon *Music in Twelve Parts* (1974), written for his own ensemble of keyboards, amplified winds and soprano, and combining additive compositional processes, modulation and dense polyphony. In collaboration with the director Robert Wilson, Glass then pioneered minimalist opera with the plotless, nearly five-hour *Einstein on the Beach*. In this watershed stage-work Glass scored various episodes relating to the life of Albert Einstein with repetitive music generally unrelated to the on-stage action. The concept was to present a unique visual and aural experience through metaphor, allusion and cultural reference. The opera was premièred in 1976 at Avignon, France, without any intermission, and the public were invited to come and go at will. Produced later that same year at the Metropolitan Opera in New York, *Einstein* provoked controversy but thrust Glass into the limelight.

Glass was later to describe the opera as a 'portrait' of Einstein—the man and his legacy. He went on to complete a 'portrait opera' trilogy, with *Satyagraha* (Truth-force, 1979) and *Akhnaten* (1984), based on the lives of Ghandi and the Egyptian pharaoh. Glass was also writing music for film at this time, with scores for the wordless eco-documentary *Koyanisqaatsi* (1981) and Paul Schrader's *Mishima* (1984) taking him ever further towards the popular mainstream. With a steady supply of lucrative opera and film score commissions, Glass saw little reason to abandon his formula—to the frustration of many music critics.

Born in Worcester, Massachusetts, John Adams (b.1947) is now probably the most performed living composer. He rose to prominence with works such as *Harmonium* for chorus and orchestra (1981) and *Harmonielehre* for orchestra (1985), but it was the opera *Nixon in China* that secured his international reputation. Premièred at the Houston Grand Opera on 22 October 1987, *Nixon* gave fresh impulse to both 'post-minimalism' and contemporary American opera. The music may have been reminiscent of Glass, strongly triadic and rhythmically repetitive, but it was compositionally directional and tightly harnessed to Alice Goodman's libretto. On the concert platform Adams has enjoyed considerable success with his motoric *A Short Ride in a Fast Machine* (1986) and classically-organised Violin Concerto (1993). The latter is an unremitting lyrical piece, whose virtuosity, modal character, polyphony and dense textures are indicative of the stylistic shift Adams made in the 1990s. The opera *The Death of Klinghoffer* (1991), *Slonimsky's Earbox* for orchestra (1996) and the symphonic *Naïve and Sentimental Music* (1998) reveal a broadening, expressive (sometimes neo-Romantic) language that extends well beyond the meaningful boundaries of minimalism, even if attributes of the style remain embedded within.

John Adams

◀ The American composer John Adams. Photograph courtesy of Margaretta Mitchell.

Other American composers have written music that may be in some ways classified as minimalist, even if they themselves have not been associated with the movement. Morton Feldman's *The Viola in My Life* series (1970/71), with its sparse materials, textural transparency and narrow dynamic range, is compositionally restricted in order to address some fundamental concerns. Feldman's style has been compared to the contemplative abstract paintings of his friend Mark Rothko, who inspired the composer with his rectangular colour fields. Rothko's desire to envelop the viewer in his large-scale forms finds its counterpart in Feldman's glacial String Quartet No. 2 (1983), which requires around six hours for a full performance. Typically unhurried, dissonant, quiet and fragmentary, Feldman's late-period sound-world was thus far removed from kinetic, triadic minimalism.

Morton Feldman

Europe

Minimalism in Europe encompassed divergent styles. The Dutch composer Louis Andriessen (b.1939) aroused international interest with *De Staat* (The State, 1976), a choral-instrumental work that owes much to American minimalists like Reich, but embraces edgy dynamics and a great deal more dissonance. His *De Tijd* (Time, 1981), in contrast, is a sustained textural

Louis Andriessen

Michael
Nyman

piece (closer to La Monte Young's aesthetic) interspersed with disquieting percussive chimes. In England, Michael Nyman (b.1944) sought to develop a more lyrical minimalist style, one he popularised through many years of collaboration with the filmmaker Peter Greenaway. Successful album releases of *The Draughtsman's Contract* (1982) and *Drowning by Numbers* (1988), together with the multi-platinum soundtrack to Jane Campion's film *The Piano* (1993), have greatly overshadowed his concert and stage music, which includes the chamber opera *The Man Who Mistook His Wife for a Hat* (1986).

John
Tavener

Nyman's exact contemporary John Tavener (1944–2013) achieved popular recognition when John Lennon organised the release of his dramatic cantata *The Whale* (premièred 1968) on the Beatles' Apple record label. Among his outstanding early compositions is *Ultimos ritos* (1972), a commanding meditation for vocal soloists, four choirs, large orchestra, organ and tape, on the words of Christ and the 16th-century Spanish mystic St John of the Cross. Static harmony and non-developmental form—as contained within the work's third movement—became increasingly important to Tavener after he was received into the Orthodox Church, in 1977. Vocal compositions form the heart of his output, which ranges from the intimacy of *The Lamb* for *a cappella* choir (1982) through to the large choral-orchestral *Akathist of Thanksgiving* (1987) and *The Apocalypse* (1993). However, it was the affecting *Protecting Veil* (1988), scored for cello and strings, that brought him his most widespread success.

Tavener's music is sometimes described as 'sacred minimalism', as is that of the Polish composer Henryk Górecki (1933–2010), whose mesmerising Symphony No. 3 (1976) created a global sensation on its recorded release in 1992, selling more than one million copies. The music of the enigmatic

Arvo Pärt

Estonian composer Arvo Pärt (b.1935) perhaps best typifies this category. Having first composed in neo-classical and serialist styles, Pärt developed a simple, translucent triadic musical language that he called 'tintinnabuli', from the Latin word for 'bells'. This largely consonant style was inspired not by American minimalism but by his keen interest in plainchant and early music, especially that of Guillaume Machaut (*c.*1300–77). Pärt's watershed 'tintinnabuli' year was 1977, introducing *Cantus in memoriam Benjamin Britten* for strings and bell, *Tabula Rasa*, a double concerto for two violins, strings and prepared piano, and *Fratres* for chamber ensemble. After leaving the Soviet Union in 1980 he was able to openly proclaim his Christian faith in larger choral works, such as *Passio* (1982), *Miserere* (1989) and *Litany* (1994). In such music we hear a reflective asceticism that renounces the relentlessness and throw-away philosophy of modern society. Pärt offers the listener spiritual respite and breathing space, even if the *Miserere* demonstrates his ability to summon disturbing apocalyptic thunder.

Minimalism of the late century was accordingly represented by diverse music, just some of which bore a 60s birthmark. Terms such as 'post-minimalism' and 'maximalism' have been employed to describe some of this evolved style. While the movement had begun by exploring concepts chiefly concerned with their own 'being', it now represented a something multidimensional, equally preoccupied with expression, meaning and purpose.

Developments in opera and music theatre

Established composers were working with the stage at a time when most emerging avant-gardists were busy in studios and concert halls. In fact, the 1950s proved a ripe decade for stage-music. In Britain, the revival of national opera was consolidated with Benjamin Britten's *Billy Budd* (1951) and *The Turn of the Screw*. Walton made his operatic début with *Troilus and Cressida* in 1954 and Tippett the following year with *The Midsummer Marriage*. On mainland Europe, Dallapiccola's finest opera, *Il prigioniero* (The Prisoner, 1948), received its première at Florence in 1950, Schoenberg's unfinished masterwork *Moses und Aron* finally made the stage posthumously at Zürich in 1957, and Poulenc's *Dialogues des Carmélites* opened in Milan the same year. In the USA, Gian Menotti introduced his remarkably successful opera *The Consul* in 1950, and the following year Stravinsky, an American resident since 1939, presented his final neo-classical masterpiece, *The Rake's Progress* (see *Chapter 7*). Prominent among the US-born composers were Copland with *The Tender Land* (1954), Carlisle Floyd (b.1926) with *Susannah* (1954), Douglas Moore (1893–1969) with *The Ballad of Baby Doe* (1956) and Samuel Barber with *Vanessa* (1958). In lighter genres Leonard Bernstein created two of the most vibrant stage works of the century, with the Voltaire-inspired operetta *Candide* (1956) and the Shakespeare-inspired musical *West Side Story* (1957).

Hans Werner Henze was one of the few younger Europeans to write and succeed in opera during the 1950s. His breakthrough came in 1952 with the serial *Boulevard Solitude*, a one-act adaptation of the *Manon Lescaut* story, musically influenced by Stravinsky and Berg. Despite public approbation, Henze felt ill at ease in the new conservative Germany; he was after all a left-wing homosexual and the memories of the Holocaust were

Hans Werner Henze

◀ Hans Werner Henze's opera *Der Junge Lord* (The Young Lord), after an early 19th-century story by Wilhelm Hauff. Production by the Cologne Opera Ensemble, 1969.

deeply unsettling. He chose exile and relocated to Italy. There he indulged his neo-Romantic passions, distancing himself ever further from the avant-garde: he virtually abandoned serialism in the lush fairytale opera *König Hirsch* (The Stag King, 1956), and looked squarely to the model of Italian Romantic opera in *Der Prinz von Homburg* (1958).

Henze wrote three acclaimed operas during the 1960s: *Elegy for Young Lovers* (1961), *Der junge Lord* (The Young Lord, 1965) and *The Bassarids* (1966). Attacking hypocrisy and the class system, *Der junge Lord* is a comedy of manners in which Lord Barrat, a stranger in town, reveals himself to be nothing more than a costumed ape. The breezy orchestrations, the ensembles, the gestures and turns of phrase, are all expertly based on the *buffa* style of Mozart and Rossini. *The Bassarids*, after Euripides' *The Bacchae*, is a neo-Romantic *opera seria* and in various respects a counterpart to *Der junge Lord*. This one-act tragedy sets the rational world of Pentheus, King of Thebes, against the emotional hedonism of Dionysus to bring comment on cultural codes and the human condition. The work is structured as a four-movement symphony with intermezzo (inserted between the third and fourth movements) and creates a heady mix with its combustive energy and powerful choruses.

Music-theatre 1960s &70s: alternative forms

With his commitment to Marxism deepening, Henze temporarily abandoned opera after *The Bassarids*, a decision that reflected the growing desire among younger composers to search out less exclusive varieties of music theatre. One popular approach was to meld theatre and concert music traditions, as in Schoenberg's *Pierrot lunaire* and Stravinsky's *The Soldier's Tale*. This hybrid style appealed to composers because not only did it bypass the complications of an expensive, 'bourgeois' opera production, it also allowed enormous scope in the presentation of ideas. A famous example

Peter Maxwell Davies: Eight Songs

is *Eight Songs for a Mad King* (1969) by Britain's Peter Maxwell Davies. Based on the intensifying insanity of King George III, this frenzied chamber song-cycle entails interaction between the costumed mad king (baritone), his captive birds (string and woodwind players, ideally placed in giant cages) and his keeper (percussionist). The lead role demands bizarre gestures of movement and challenging vocal gymnastics. In a similar psychological vein, Berio's *Recital I* (1972) is a 'monodrama' about a recital, thus a piece about itself, and charts a female character's mental disintegration. Other compositions were exhibiting dramatic dimensions without suggesting plots of any kind. Ligeti's *Aventures* (see p.611), with its phonetic language and theatrical noise-making, deliberately avoids any narrative coherence. And the American composer George Crumb (b.1929) offers nothing more than provocative visual stimulus by using masked musicians to perform his atmospheric chamber pieces *Lux aeterna* and *Vox balaenae* (both 1971).

Mauricio Kagel: Staatstheater

If the above-named composers were seeking to broaden the scope of music-theatre, the Argentine-German composer Mauricio Kagel (1931–2008) went out on a limb to subvert tradition in his postmodern *Staatstheater* (Hamburg, 1971). Although designated an opera, the work turns operatic convention upside down: the characters' actions are nonsensical and events appear to have no narrative meaning; chorus members are given solos, soloists sing as a chorus, minor percussive instruments feature prominently, and untrained dancers perform ballet. The bizarre content and the manner of presentation combine to celebrate nonconformity.

Anti-establishment sentiment in the West, symptomatic of left-wing fervour, was abating by the late 1970s. Henze returned to the opera house with his massive split-stage production *We Come to the River* (Covent Garden, 1976), though its attack on class and capitalism acknowledged the composer's continuing commitment to grass-roots socialism. Ligeti produced his first opera in 1978 at Stockholm with the satirical *Le grand macabre*, and Berio entered the opera house (Milan's La Scala) for the first time with *La vera storia* (The True Story, 1982). Non-traditional music theatre nonetheless maintained a strong presence. Berio, uninterested in conventional narrative, designated his subsequent stage works azione *musicale* (musical action): *Un re in ascolto* (A Listening King, 1984), *Outis* (Nobody, 1996) and *Cronaca del luogo* (Chronicle of the Place, 1999). Nono also remained drawn to the non-literal, evinced by his meditations on the Prometheus legend, *Prometeo* (1984), designated 'a tragedy for listening'.

In 1977 Stockhausen began work on what is probably the most ambitious musical project ever undertaken by one composer. *Licht* (Light, 1977–2003) is a cycle of seven operas, each named after a day of the week, which relate mankind's spiritual journey towards a higher state of consciousness. The operas revolve around three principal characters—Michael, Eve and Lucifer—and draw inspiration from the Judeo-Christian tradition and the mystical concepts propounded in the Urantia Book. Modular structures enabled parts of *Licht* to be presented independently prior to the completion of each opera. All seven operas have now been staged, with the concluding opera of the series, *Sonntag* (Sunday), at Cologne in 2011, and *Mittwoch* (Wednesday), at Birmingham, England, in 2012.

Others in the final quarter-century upheld the more traditional approach to opera. The German composer Aribert Reimann (b.1936) cast the famous baritone Dietrich Fischer-Dieskau in his expressionistic *Lear* (1978), a dark, unsettling opera that stems from the sound-world of Berg. Reimann's compatriot Wolfgang Rihm (b.1952) also looked to Berg in his breakthrough chamber opera *Jakob Lenz* (1978). Rihm's dynamic expressionist manner—gestural, virtuosic, sometimes featuring historical allusion—pervades a prolific output that includes the operas *Oedipus* (1987) and *Die Eroberung von Mexico* (1991). The mid 1970s also witnessed Joonas Kokkonen (1921–96) and Aulis Sallinen (b.1935) creating Finnish opera of international standing. Kokkonen's *The Last Temptations* (1975), and Sallinen's *The Horsemen* (1974), *The Red Line* (1978) and *Kullervo* (1988), are for the most part tonal operas, each rooted in a national consciousness.

Britten and Tippett (see *Tonal Vanguard*) maintained their commitment to the British stage during the 1960s and 70s, writing operas that achieved recognition abroad. This period also saw the first stage works by the 'Manchester Group' of composers: Alexander Goehr, Maxwell Davies and Harrison Birtwistle (b.1934). The last named cultivated a modernist style of raw, often violent power, intended to engage both the senses and intellect. Birtwistle made his bold music-theatre début in 1968 with *Punch and Judy*, a vicious chamber opera that may be fairly described as an 'immorality play'.

Stockhausen: *Licht*

British opera: Harrison Birtwistle

▶ Harrison Birtwistle's *Mask of Orpheus*, premièred by the English National Opera, 1986. The protagonists of the story are each represented in three forms – by singer (as human), by mime (as hero) and by puppet (as myth). The narrative is non-linear; and different, sometimes contradictory, versions of events are portrayed on stage concurrently and repeated from alternative perspectives.

Benjamin Britten's Aldeburgh Festival hosted the first production, but the musical statesman himself apparently walked out in disgust.

Birtwistle was musical director at London's National Theatre from 1975 to 1983, during which time he wrote incidental music for a dozen plays and consolidated his concert-hall reputation. A career turning point came in 1986 when the English National Opera staged *The Mask of Orpheus* to immense critical acclaim. Awards and honours (including a knighthood) followed, inciting Birtwistle to devote more of his time to music theatre. Complex, multi-layered and fiercely atonal, Birtwistle's operas include *Gawain* (1991), *The Second Mrs Kong* (1994) and *The Minotaur* (2008). Common to each are themes of myth and ritual, which provide a symbolic environment for the examination of human nature and experience. Beyond Birtwistle, British opera was being enlivened by less esoteric fare from a younger generation of composers. These included Judith Weir (b.1954) with *A Night at the Chinese Opera* (1987), Mark-Anthony Turnage (b.1960) with *Greek* (1988) and *The Silver Tassie* (2000), and Thomas Adès (b.1971) with *Powder Her Face* (1995).

USA Like most other countries, the USA struggled to produce new opera that attracted any real foreign interest; moreover, national successes were few in number and opera commissions were in decline during the 1960s and 70s. It is revealing that while Philip Glass almost single-handedly revitalised American contemporary opera, beginning with his non-traditionalist *Einstein on the Beach* (1976, see *Minimalism*), none of his early operas were American commissions. His achievements nonetheless inspired and prepared the way for fellow minimalist John Adams (*Nixon* and *Klinghoffer*), and also piqued public interest in a wide range of other new operas, prominent among them Anthony Davis's largely atonal *X: the Life and Times of Malcolm X* (New York City Opera, 1986), Libby Larsen's cinematic *Frankenstein: The Modern Prometheus* (Minnesota Opera, 1990), John Corigliano's 'grand opera buffa' *The Ghosts of Versailles* (New York Met, 1991) and John Harbison's melodious and jazzy *The Great Gatsby* (New York Met, 1999).

Statements of belief

Faith and religion

Despite declining church patronage and increasing secularisation, personal expressions of faith remained important to many free-world composers, their devotional works often emanating from secular commissions. Behind the Iron Curtain religious oppression was widespread. With communist regimes seeking to stamp out religious belief, a proclamation of faith within a public musical work was effectively proselytising and a direct challenge to the authority of the state.

The Russian composer Sofia Gubaidulina (b.1931) had to downplay or even conceal the religious nature of her music until Mikhail Gorbachev ushered in the glasnost era in the late 1980s, and with it greater freedoms of expression. Until that time she disclosed her inspiration principally through allusive religious titles, such as *Introitus* (piano concerto, 1978) and *In Croce* (for cello and organ, 1979). Branded both religious and avant-garde, Gubaidulina struggled for public recognition. Her fortunes changed in the mid-80s when another subtly religious piece brought her international attention, the violin concerto *Offertorium* (1980), which uses treatments of Bach's *Musical Offering* to metaphorically imply the sacrifice of Christ. Once free to express her faith she produced openly Christian pieces, such as *Alleluia* for boy soprano, chorus and orchestra (1990), but religious symbols continued to stimulate her instrumental music. A fine example is *Two Paths* for two solo violas and orchestra (1999), inspired by the contrasting perspectives of the New Testament figures Mary and Martha (represented by the soloists) in their love towards Christ.

Sofia
Gubaidulina

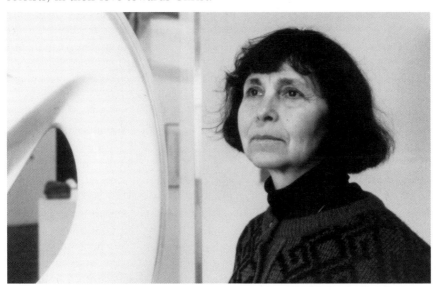

◀ The Russian composer Sofia Gubaidulina

Galina
Ustvolskaya

Galina Ustvolskaya (1919–2006), declared a 'phenomenon' by Shostakovich (whose offer of marriage she turned down), was another Russian composer drawn to expressions of spiritual devotion. Many of her works bear Christian subtitles, none more provocative to the authorities than that of her Third Symphony: *Jesus, Messiah, Save us!* (1983). While her musical language is dissonant and often violent, she insisted that her works 'are infused with a religious spirit and … best suited to performance in a church'. She was blacklisted for much of her career, though primarily

Arvo Pärt

on aesthetic grounds. The Estonian composer Arvo Pärt, before his radical simplification of musical style (see *Minimalism*), came under political scrutiny with *Credo* (1968), which opens with the proclamation 'I believe in Jesus Christ'. Combining deep religious commitment with avant-garde musical expression, it was precisely the type of work the communist party hated most. Pärt endured intermittent blacklisting and censorship until 1980, when he and his wife of Jewish descent were permitted to leave the Soviet Union.

Belief in the
free world

The most conspicuous Christian composer in post-war Western Europe was Olivier Messiaen. As an organ music composer of such substantial collections as the *Livre d'orgue* (1951) and the 80-minute *Méditations sur le mystère de la Sainte Trinité* (1969), he was the most important of the century. He claimed that the chief purpose of his music was to express 'the religious sentiments exalted by the theology and the truths of [the] Catholic faith'. His commitment to this creed only increased from the 1960s. He targeted the secular arena with some gigantic sacred works, including the oratorio *La Transfiguration de notre Seigneur Jésus Christ* (1969) and his contemplative opera *Saint François d'Assise* (1983). The subject of a bird-loving saint was an obvious choice for the composer-ornithologist. For Messiaen birdsong was a very natural expression of God's love and creation: both at home and abroad he made meticulous birdsong transcriptions and employed them as fundamental strands within many compositions. There are nearly 90 bird species represented in *La Transfiguration* alone.

James
MacMillan

In Britain, John Tavener (see *Minimalism*) and the Scottish Catholic James MacMillan (b.1959) brought spiritual concerns to bear on their divergent styles. In his music MacMillan addresses not only personal faith but also issues of religious injustice and persecution. He gained prominence through the London Promenade concerts, introducing the orchestral piece *The Confession of Isobel Gowdie* (1990) and the percussion concerto *Veni, veni Emmanuel* (1992), the latter written for fellow Scot Evelyn Glennie (b.1965). MacMillan has explained that his musical language assimilates strident modernist harmonies because 'religious faith is rooted in the mess of real life, and my music has to be true to that experience'.

Buddhism and Eastern philosophy has shaped the musical outlook of composers as diverse as Cage and Glass (see earlier sections). Cage's beliefs were radically realised: the supression of the ego finds expression in his indeterminate compositions that relinquish the composer's control

Stockhausen

entirely. Stockhausen stood at the opposite end of the spectrum with an ego of Romantic proportions. In his faith he personified an eclectic mix: he claimed to be a 'child of God' and a believer in reincarnation, but also an alien on earth, light-years from his homeland—a planet orbiting the star Sirius. From the late 70s he regarded his music as a guiding medium by which listeners could advance their own spiritual journey (not so unlike Wagner). Other composers, alternatively, simply acknowledged religious tradition. Leonard Bernstein and Steve Reich, for instance, have drawn from their Jewish heritage without making bold statements of personal faith.

Politics

Expressions of political solidarity or protest were particularly apparent during the third quarter of the 20th century. The concerns were largely rooted in communism and the rise of socialist ideology, whether enforced or freely articulated.

Scholars will debate endlessly the political mind of Shostakovich, pre- and post-Stalin (see also *Chapter 7*). With his masterful Symphony No. 10 (1953) he may have condemned the Stalin years and he certainly caused a rift at the Composers' Union. His Symphony No. 11 (1957), ostensibly a memorial to the abortive anti-Tsarist Revolution of 1905, was later claimed to be inspired by the (anti-Soviet) Hungarian Revolution of 1956. In Symphony No. 12: *The Year 1917* (1961) Shostakovich towed the propaganda line, having recently joined the Communist Party, but artistically he fell short. The next year he attacked Soviet history in his Symphony No. 13 *Babi Yar*, and thereafter opposed values of 'socialist realism' with the morose Symphony No. 14 (see *Tonal Vanguard*). His final symphony, No. 15 (1972), was provocative only in terms of its syntactic enigmas, quoting material by himself, Rossini and Wagner. The post-Stalin activity reveals Shostakovich as a composer increasingly inclined to challenge the State, explicitly or implicitly. But because high-profile works attracted the greatest political scrutiny, the 15 intimate string quartets, the first written in 1938, the deeply pessimistic last in 1974, offer a more consistent view of the composer's artistic outlook.

There is an irony in that a composer such as Luigi Nono, an Italian Communist Party member, could express himself in complex, dissonant musical languages that in the communist Soviet Union would have been labelled 'formalist' and 'bourgeois', and effectively banned. But then Nono's ideology had little in common with that of Kruschev or Brezhnev. Lenin, however, had advocated progressivism in music, while insisting that that art 'must be understood and loved' by the working classes. Nono valued this edict and sometimes mounted concerts in factories, meeting with an audience who would otherwise never had heard his work. He condemned exploitation and intolerance in his 'scenic action' *Intolleranza 1960* (1960), highlighted the impact of harsh noise on factory workers in the electro-acoustic *La fabbrica illuminata* (The Illuminated Factory, 1964), and incorporated a recording of Fidel Castro reading a letter from Che Guevara in *Y entonces comprendió* (1970). Nono preferred subtle political references to bold explicit statements: texts are typically overlaid or fragmented, often beyond immediate recognition. His concentrated political phase ended around the time of another 'scenic action' piece, *Al gran sole carico d'amore* (In the Bright Sunshine, Charged with Love, premièred 1975), examining

Shostakovich

Luigi Nono

100 years of communist history from the time of the Paris Commune, 1871, and including quotes from Marx, Lenin, Bertolt Brecht and Castro.

Cornelius Cardew

The communist philosophy of the English composer Cornelius Cardew (1936–81) manifested a very different musical approach. A pupil of Stockhausen, Cardew famously co-established the Scratch Orchestra in 1969, comprising skilled and unskilled musicians from all walks of life. For this ensemble he wrote *The Great Learning* (1970), whose score combines graphic notation, prose instructions and conventional notation. With a full performance lasting over seven hours, it was hardly music for the masses. Cardew's deepening Maoist sympathies led him to a dramatic volte-face in the early 70s: he denounced the avant-garde as elitist, published a collection of essays under the title *Stockhausen Serves Imperialism* (1974), and turned to tonality and folk song to create a musical aesthetic closer to what he saw as the Marxist-Lennist ideal.

Henze

Henze was galvanised by Marxism around the time left-wing sentiment was feeding social unrest throughout Europe and beyond. *Essay on Pigs* (1968) for baritone and orchestra was written in support of protesting students in Berlin, while the texts of *El Cimarrón* and the Sixth Symphony (both 1969) express solidarity with Castro's Cuba. His oratorio *Das Floss der Medusa* (The Raft of Medusa), dedicated to the memory of Che Guevara, caused a riot at what was to be its 1968 première in Hamburg, when chorus and orchestra members refused to perform behind a red flag fixed to Henze's podium. As noted earlier, Henze also took his political message into the opera house with *We Come to the River*, in 1976. In collaboration with the librettist Edward Bond, Henze must have savoured the moment as his bloody morality tale of class struggle spoke to the moneyed classes at London's Covent Garden.

Issues of race

The waning popularity of hard-line socialism encouraged a shift of focus in the political works of the 1980s and 90s. A number of these addressed sensitive issues of race. John Adams focused on Arab-Israeli tensions in *The Death of Klinghoffer* (1991), which concerns the 1985 hijacking of the cruise liner Achille Lauro by Palestinian terrorists and subsequent killing of a disabled American Jew. It proved controversial, receiving criticism (primarily in America) for being soft on terrorism. On somewhat safer ground, Anthony Davis (b.1951) drew wide attention with his operas *X: the Life and Times of Malcolm X* and *Amistad* (1997), both exploring themes of human rights and black cultural history.

Other late-20th-century musical styles

Some modernist alternatives

Musical modernism in the late 20th-century expressed itself through diverse languages, but in essence it remained rational and forward thinking, often serious, intellectual and resistant to emotionalism. Such is the music of the American composer Elliott Carter (1908–2012). Tutored by Ives, Piston, Holst and Nadia Boulanger, he set his early style on the bearings of European neo-classicism, but it was not until the mid-century that he found his true voice. The String Quartet No. 1 (1951) was his watershed composition, with its largely atonal language, complex polyrhythms and minute details of sonority. Carter's signature rhythmic device became 'tempo modulation', the fluid transformation of metre through the subdivision of a set pulse. Mid-career activities saw extremely cerebral, rhythmically-layered pieces like the Pulitzer Prize-winning Second and Third String Quartets (1960, 1973), and also the Double Concerto for harpsichord and piano (1961), an effervescent, exquisitely balanced work that gained considerable commendation from Stravinsky. The later works, including the Oboe Concerto (1987) and the opera *What Next?* (1999), are more accessible in terms of their expressive immediacy and lucid textures and forms. Carter can confidently be described as the oldest front-rank composer who ever lived.

Elliott Carter

The American-born Conlon Nancarrow (1912–97) was another modernist who specialised in metre and tempo, but in his case with the aid of a mechanical piano player. A Communist Party member, Nancarrow rejected life in the USA and in 1940 settled in Mexico. His music was largely unknown to the public until the 1970s, when 41 piano player studies, begun in the late 40s, were released on record. His compositions are simple in melody and (often tonal) harmony, but extremely advanced in rhythm, incorporating polyrhythmic 'tempo canons' produced by a combination of mathematically-proportioned tempos and rapid changes of metre.

Conlon Nancarrow

Messiaen was fascinated by palindromic rhythms, or what he preferred to call 'non-retrogradable rhythms', which on paper read the same forwards as backwards. Musical symmetries are central to Messiaen's style

Messiaen

◀ Olivier Messiaen, 1973.

and commonly expressed through 'modes of limited transposition'. These modes are heterogeneous: one mode is the whole-tone scale, another the octatonic scale (alternating semitones and tones); others are more idiosyncratic, but each mode is symmetrical in shape and can be transposed only a few times before it repeats itself. The manipulation of transcribed bird-song, as noted earlier (*Statements of Belief*), was another central feature of the composer's style. A more subtle influence derived from his sensitivity to sound-colour. Whilst Messiaen did not claim to have a true condition of synaesthesia, he certainly undertook to transmit his 'intellectual' synaesthetic perceptions, controlling his music in terms of specific shifting colours. The first explicit compositions of this category were *Sept haïkaï* (1962) and *Couleurs de la cité céleste* (1963), both focusing on winds and percussion, although the aesthetic no doubt fortifies the multi-coloured *Turangalîla Symphony* of 1948.

Messiaen manipulated his orchestral forces with astonishing virtuosity. Occasionally he built elaborate textures from high-definition 12-note chords, a technique more thoroughly explored by Lutosławski, Poland's leading composer of the late-century (see also *Indeterminacy*). Lutosławski first experimented with 12-note chords in his *Five Songs* for voice and orchestra (1958), while still under the spell of Bartók. In full artistic maturity he became more texturally-minded, bringing together 12-note chords, 'aleatory counterpoint', extreme contrasts and refrain-episode design. Early highlights include the Second String Quartet (1964) and Second Symphony (1967), both two-movement, goal-orientated pieces that progress from uncertainty to an implacable climax.

In later life Lutosławski tempered his modernist language with greater transparency and melodic warmth. His many-times recorded Third Symphony (1983) is a wonderful example, with its structural organisation around pitch and limited application of aleatory (improvisatory) technique. The work emphatically begins and ends on a pounding E tonic, is episodic in design and contains both textural and lyrical ideas. In some of his last pieces Lutosławski combined light aleatory processes with 'chain technique'—the overlapping and interlocking of different thematic and textural strands. Three compositions during the 1980s carried his formal designation, beginning with *Chain I* for 14 players (1983), written for the London Sinfonietta. Chain technique also occurs in the final movement of his melodic Piano Concerto (1988), which exploits dazzling concerto conventions to the full.

Lutosławski

In Britain a 'new complexity' modernist trend emerged through the music of Brian Ferneyhough (b.1943) and Michael Finnissy (b.1946). Ferneyhough's *Time and Motion Study* trilogy (1974–77) and *Unity Capsule* (1976) for solo flute are among the early representative works, saturated in complex rhythms and dense atonal textures, testing 'the extremes of what a player might reasonably be expected to perform'. Within this process the composer is also investigating the communicative capacity of staff notation: scores are meticulously prepared with detailed regard to microtones, timbres, dynamics, intricate polyrhythms and 'extended techniques'. The demands on the performer are unquestionably both intellectual and practical. Composers interested in this aesthetic include James Dillon (b.1950) and Richard Barrett (b.1959), although the movement has itself influenced a diverse range of composers worldwide.

New complexity: Brian Ferneyhough

Postmodernism and pluralism

The term 'postmodernism' has been applied to everything from architecture to philosophy, categorising an array of cultural reactions to conventional norms. In the arts, postmodernism rejected any sense of definitive order, embracing instead the juxtaposition of disparate forms and ideas, often with irony or humour. In music this has involved the use of stylistic collage and borrowed material. Such music represents an affront to modernism on two levels: first, it tends to use collage and quotation in a manner that creates stylistic disunity, and second, it almost invariably draws on the very musical language—tonality—that post-war modernism rejected as irrelevant. However, to label all music that employs collage and/or quotation as 'postmodern' could be misleading, given that individual composers have exploited these musical combinations with vastly different agendas.

Collage and quotation

The ambitious opera *Die Soldaten* (1960, revised 1964), by the German composer Bernd Alois Zimmermann (1918–70), affords an early example of collage and quotation. The work presents separate self-contained areas of action on a split-level stage, showing past, present and future events. Complementing the multi-layered dramaturgy is serially-organised music (influenced by Berg) that incorporates Bach, Gregorian chant and jazz, calling on the widest possibly array of instrumentation: pit orchestra, electronic music, concrete music, jazz ensemble and percussion group. This was Zimmermann's greatest attempt 'to form the phenomenon of pluralistic opera', transcending the restrictions of time and place.

One of the first monuments of postmodernism, the Portland Building (Oregon), designed by Michael Graves and completed in 1982. The design rejects uniformity and incorporates historical allusion, such as the giant, stylised pilasters and garlands.

Berio:
Sinfonia

Berio employed quotation even more directly in his fascinating *Sinfonia* (1968) for eight voices and orchestra. The third movement is dominated by the Scherzo of Mahler's Second Symphony, over and around which a myriad of contrasting quotations make fleeting appearances, from Monteverdi, Bach and Beethoven, through to contemporary composers such as Boulez, Stockhausen and Berio himself. Texts quoted throughout are from diverse sources too, most importantly from Samuel Beckett's *The Unnamable*, but also Claude Levi-Strauss, James Joyce and student protest graffiti. On one important level, *Sinfonia* considers the artist's historical position in relationship to the past and the future. If not postmodern in ideology, the work certainly resonated with a postmodern soundworld.

George
Rochberg

The American composer George Rochberg (1918–2005) is a more representative exponent of musical postmodernism. Initially an advocate of serialism, he reacted against the style following the death of his son from a brain tumour in 1964, since it provided no outlet for his grief. Rochberg's new path led him to quotation—for example the music of Mozart in *Music for the Magic Theatre* (1965)—and then into pluralist composition, as in his String Quartet No. 3 (1972), which juxtaposes Beethovenian and Mahlerian styles with harsh dissonance. His Violin Concerto (1974) again touches on a Romantic sound-world, along with burlesque neo-classicism and lyrical expressionism. In the face of critical opposition, Rochberg espoused 'maximum variety of gesture and texture, and the broadest possible spectrum' for the rest of his creative life.

Alfred
Schnittke

First
Symphony

The Russian composer Alfred Schnittke (1934–98) abandoned serialism in the mid-60s to experiment with compositional pluralism, or 'polystylism', as he called it. The quotation of disparate 'musics' is common to many of his works, deriving from his interest in the eclectic styles of Mahler, Ives, Berg and Shostakovich, and from his experience as a film composer. His First Symphony (1972) considers the place of music in culture and history in a dramatically different way to Berio's *Sinfonia*. It begins with the orchestra tuning up, draws upon the music of a wide range of composers, including Beethoven, Chopin and Grieg, and incorporates improvised jazz and a semi-theatrical reference to Haydn's *Farewell* symphony, with the whole orchestra leaving the stage—only to then return. With its ingredients of eclecticism, humour and irony, it is a classic example of musical postmodernism. Schnittke finally grabbed the attention of the West with his *Concerto Grosso No. 1* for two violins, harpsichord, prepared piano and strings (1977), a thoroughly engaging composition that signalled his move towards less theatrical polystylism. The pan-epoch dialogue remained a constant presence in his music, which includes nine symphonies, six concerti grossi, four violin concertos (the last written in 1984) and two cello concertos (1986, 1990).

Helmut
Lachenmann

Helmut Lachenmann is another important European figure who has drawn on past music, such as Beethoven's Ninth Symphony in the orchestral work *Staub* (1987), and Mahler in the opera *The Little Match Girl* (1996). He is also a pioneer of what he calls 'musique concrète instrumentale', which seeks to create new aural experiences by means of unconventional

◀ Three Russian legends, left to right: violist (violinist and conductor) Yuri Bashmet, cellist and conductor Mstislav Rostropovich and composer Alfred Schnittke.

performance techniques. Lachenmann, like Penderecki before him, has developed new methods of notation to realise his alternative soundworld.

Crossover music

The cross-fertilisation of contemporary musical styles demonstrates another face of pluralism. Classical composers had been drawing on the riches of ragtime and jazz since the 1910s, emphasising their relevance to modern culture, but the 1950s saw a more thorough integration of style, from both classical and jazz perspectives. In 1957 the American composer Gunther Schuller (b.1925) coined the term 'Third Stream' for this type of music, in which improvisation often played a central role. Early representative works include Charlie Mingus's *Jazzical Moods* (1954) and Schuller's own Concertino for jazz quartet and orchestra (1959).

    Though the African-American composer William Grant Still (1895–1978) engaged 12-bar blues in his *Afro-American* Symphony as far back as 1930, pop/rock music made little impact on classical trends until the advent of minimalism (noted earlier). Even then it was more the spirit of popular music, rather than its specific formulas, that inspired the minimalists. Bernstein edged closer to authentic pop/rock styles in *Mass* (1971), which strays at times into rock-musical territory. Indeed various parts of the score, such as the bluesy confession 'I don't know', may seem contrived unless staged. Bernstein's compatriot William Bolcom (b.1938) took a more cautious approach in his song-cycle *Songs of Innocence and Experience* (1982). Combining modern classical idioms with jazz, folk song and wide-ranging popular music, he set the poetry of William Blake in a work that remains rooted in its classical comfort zone. England's Michael Tippett, who famously drew African-American spirituals into

Third Stream

Blues, pop & rock influences

Tippett

his oratorio *A Child of Our Time* (1941), returned to popular influences throughout his career. The blues, for example, finds its way into the opera *The Knot Garden* (1970) and the lauded Third Symphony (1972). Tippett was largely intent on acknowledging popular music rather than seeking a synthesis of styles. Aged 84, he even incorporated stylised rap and break-dance into his esoteric opera *New Year* (1989).

A deepening concern to connect with wider culture broke down further divisions between 'high' and 'low' art towards the end of the century. Inspired by the music of David Bowie and Brian Eno, Philip Glass composed his *Low Symphony* (1993), sublimating themes from Bowie's adventurous album *Low* (1977) into a minimalist orchestral soundworld, although with no attempt to replicate the rock aesthetic. John Adams, conversely, enlisted seven singers and an eight-piece pop band for his 'songplay' *I Was Looking at the Ceiling and Then I Saw the Sky* (1995), a study of American cultural diversity with styles ranging from Broadway to blues and rock. Other composers demonstrating a convincing affinity with pop and rock include Christopher Rouse (b.1949) and John Zorn (b.1953) in the USA, and Mark-Anthony Turnage and Steve Martland (1959–2013) in Britain. While Rouse and Turnage are classical in orientation, choosing to subsume the raw power of rock music, Zorn and Martland have pursued crossover aesthetics, often blurring the viewpoint of musical style.

Glass & Adams

On the other side of the 'divide', pop/rock songwriters have of course incorporated classical idioms, though many have merely plundered the classical repertory for catchy tunes. Deeper interest came from the British progressive rock bands of the 1970s—notably Pink Floyd, King Crimson, Yes, Genesis and Emerson, Lake & Palmer—who rejected the limitations of the three-minute pop song to accommodate more complex harmonies and chord progressions in extended song structures. Among the solo artists, America's Laurie Anderson (b.1947), France's Jean-Michel Jarre (b.1948) and Britain's Mike Oldfield (b.1953) each absorbed classical influences with popular success. The most versatile figure in this category was the American performer-composer Frank Zappa (1940–93). His interest in contemporary classical music was given free rein in his first solo album, *Lumpy Gravy* (1967/68), a postmodern mix of spoken dialogue, pop, rock, musique concrète, and both tonal and atonal orchestral writing. Another crossover album of Zappa's, *The Perfect Stranger* (1984), included three tracks featuring the Ensemble InterContemperain, conducted by Pierre Boulez and recorded at the studios of IRCAM. His final album, *The Yellow Shark*

Frank Zappa

► Frank Zappa with Pierre Boulez, in conversation at UCLA's Schoenberg Hall, 1989.

(1993), was recorded with the Ensemble Modern and counts among its tracks 'Dog Breath Variations'. Zappa seemed determined to attack elitism and superficial pop culture simultaneously.

World influences

Ethnic influences in classical music can be comfortably traced back to Domenico Scarlatti's assimilation of Spanish folk idioms in his keyboard sonatas of the 1730s–50s. Like the late-18th-century 'Turkish craze', or 19th-century orientalism, such musical exoticism (as opposed to nationalism) commonly sought only the excitement of foreign colour and mystery. During the 20th century the absorption of 'world music', such as gamelan, began to take on deeper significance. This phenomenon, noted earlier in reference to John Cage and minimalism, became largely symptomatic of the artist's desire to recognise and celebrate the new multi-cultural social order.

The prolific American composer Henry Cowell (1897–1965) was among the first to unite disparate musical worlds (see *Chapter 7*). He stated that composers should 'draw on those materials common to the music of all the peoples of the world, to build a new music particularly related to our own century'. Cowell was conspicuously true to his beliefs in some of his late works, looking to India in his Symphony No. 13 *Madras* (1958), to Japan in his *Concerto for Koto* (1962), and to Iceland in his Symphony No. 16 (1962). Lou Harrison (1917–2003) is another American who drew extensively on world music, principally that of China, Korea and Indonesia.

Henry Cowell

Tōru Takemitsu (1930–96), in ironic contrast, turned to his Japanese heritage only after experiencing Cage's enthusiasm for Eastern culture. In his remarkable *November Steps* for biwa, shakuhachi and orchestra (1967), a commission from the New York Philharmonic, Takemitsu brought together Japanese tradition and a Western modernist idiom—dense, textural, and saturated with chromatic clusters. The work creates a concerto-like dialogue between East and West, but largely avoids a synthesis or reconciliation of soundworlds. Takemitsu's most well-known compositions include *Quatrain* for clarinet, violin, cello, piano and orchestra (1975), and *A Flock Descends into the Pentagonal Garden* for orchestra (1977). Neither piece incorporates traditional instruments, but formal aspects of both derive from Japanese influences: 'emaki' scroll painting in the first, the Japanese garden in the second. The composer's long-standing involvement in film music resulted in around 100 scores, a number of which, like that for Kurosawa's *Ran* (1987), exploit East-West fusions and modernist idioms.

Tōru Takemitsu

◀ A performance of Takemitsu's *November Steps*, for biwa, shakuhachi and orchestra, at the Hibiya City Hall, Tokyo, with the Toho Gakuen School of Music orchestra.

Cross-culturalism has also inspired the prolific Australian composer

Peter Sculthorpe (b.1929), who has looked to Aboriginal chant and didjeridu music, and more widely to music of the Pacific Rim, gamelan included. Like Sibelius, he is spellbound by landscapes and his music at times possesses a similar ruggedness and melancholic beauty. Among his most popular pieces is *Kakadu* (1988), taking its name from Australia's Kakadu National Park. Other composers have explored their non-western cultural heritage including the South African Kevin Volans (b.1949) and

the Chinese-American Tan Dun (b.1957). Sofia Gubaidulina, born in Russia's Tatar Republic, found herself mid-way between East and West, and throughout her career she has blended diverse instruments and traditions. Her *Seven Words* (1982) is essentially a concerto for bayan (a Russian accordion), cello and string orchestra in which wild textures and mounting tension are created with an imaginative sonic fusion of the two contrasting solo instruments. A sense of unity within diversity bestows profound significance on a piece laced with Christian symbolism. Gubaidulina's polyculturalism extends also to the far east, as in her microtonal work *In the Shadow of the Tree* (1998), scored for koto, bass koto, (Chinese) zheng and orchestra.

The resuscitation of tonality

There were many outstanding young composers of the early post-war era who never bought wholesale into the atonal aesthetic. Some of these have been already mentioned—Bernstein and Malcolm Arnold, for example—and the long list would include Sweden's Allan Pettersson (1911–80), France's Henri Dutilleux (1916–2013), America's Peter Mennin (1923–83), Greece's Mikis Theodorakis (b.1925) and Scotland's Thea Musgrave (b.1928).

Once the minimalist and postmodern movements were established, 'tonality' in avant-garde circles was no longer a dirty word. Moreover, 1970s was a time when many progressives found themselves frustrated by the expressive limitations of strict atonalism. Maxwell Davies, Takemitsu, Penderecki and Ligeti were just some of the major figures who acclimatised their style to accommodate tonal elements. Among

these composers, Penderecki took the most dramatic departure, claiming that he had nothing further to explore with his textural style. Freely expressive neo-Romanticism in a variety of concertos and symphonies confirmed his objective to 'gain inspiration from the past and look back on my heritage'. Within this new period are also some politically-charged religious pieces, such as the *Lacrimosa*, written in 1980 for Poland's Solidarity trade union, and the *Polish Requiem* (1984, revised 1993).

Maxwell Davies found his outlook changed dramatically when he relocated to the wild, windswept Orkney Island of Hoy in 1971. Approaching middle age and amid quiet solitude (for several years with no electricity and running water), he had no urge to revisit the kind of dark, violent, often wacky language of the music-theatre pieces *Revelation and Fall* (1966) and *Eight songs*. What he retained was a close affinity with medieval music— its material and techniques—and a fondness for unfolding moods, unbridled emotions and strident harmonies. He began writing symphonies under the spell of Sibelius in the mid 70s, applying transformation processes

(as opposed to traditional development) to material that he could steer with non-functional tonality. His ten assorted *Strathclyde Concertos* (1987–96) further confirmed a broadening lyrical outlook, while serving to introduce Strathclyde's schoolchildren to orchestral instruments and compositional techniques. Davies later remarked that he desired to 'bridge gulfs between antagonistic parties': atonal versus tonal, minimalism versus new complexity, and so on. It is a viewpoint that summed up much of the *fin de siècle* mindset.

Einojuhani Rautavaara, Ellen Taaffe Zwilich

Finland's Einojuhani Rautavaara and America's Ellen Taaffe Zwilich (b.1939) turned even more emphatically towards tonality. Rautavaara established his reputation with such pieces as the imposing Third Symphony (1960), which marries serial methods to the climactic style of Bruckner. His international breakthrough came much later with his Seventh Symphony: *Angel of Light* (1994). Reminiscent of Sibelius, this intensely expressive work combines serial strategies with tonality, luxuriant 'false relationships' and chromatic harmonies, all of which has helped give the work wide appeal. Within his varied, virtuosic, predominantly neo-Romantic oeuvre are three piano concertos (1969, 1989, 1999), the *Cantus Arcticus* concerto for taped birdsong and orchestra (1972) and the already four-times recorded Eighth Symphony: *The Journey* (1999).

Zwilich likewise made her mark within the broad ambit of neo-Romanticism. She started out under the guidance of Sessions and Carter, but after the death of her husband in 1979 she abandoned modernist thinking. With her Symphony No. 1 (1982) she became the first woman to win a Pulitzer Prize for music. Organic in form and loosely tonal, the symphony was something of a transitional work, inasmuch as Zwilich's subsequent concertos, symphonies and quartets took an increasingly diatonic complexion. By the end of the century she was one of America's most performed living composers.

We might note the utterly disparate character of musical styles that share some kind of tonal concern: the dissonant languages of late-period Maxwell Davies and Ligeti are a world away from Zwilich; and Schnittke's postmodernism has little in common with Steve Reich's minimalism, which is in turn at variance with Rautavaara's neo-Romanticism. It is also important to stress that a wide range of modern composers (including 'tonalists') concur that atonal soundworlds reflect and enrich different aspects of our culture. But the 1970s–90s tonal shift signalled something constructive: the world of art music evidently saw fit to dismantle some of its ivory-towers and take much more seriously the values, and the needs, of the wider public.

Chronology
1950–2000

Copland completes the song cycle *Twelve Poems of Emily Dickinson* for voice and piano, and wins an Oscar for his music to the film *The Heiress*. His serialist Piano Quartet is also completed and premièred this year.

Holmboe composes his Symphony No. 7.

6 January Poulenc performs his Piano Concerto under **Charles Munch** in Boston. This year marks the composition of his Stabat Mater.

1 March *The Consul*, by **Gian Carlo Menotti** (right), opens in Philadelphia. In a tragic tale of misery under tyranny, a wife attempts to flee a police state to join her exiled husband. Powerfully topical, the (tonal) opera transfers to Broadway later this month and subsequently wins the Pulitzer Prize for Music and the Drama Critics' Circle Award. Productions in translation follow throughout Europe.

18 March *Symphonie pour un homme seul* (Symphony for a Man Alone) by **Pierre Schaeffer** and **Pierre Henry** is presented at the École Normale de Musique de Paris. It is the first major work of 'musique concrète', based on noises created by the human body.

3 April German stage composer **Kurt Weill** dies of heart failure in New York, aged 50.

12 May Milhaud's opera *Bolivar*, completed in 1943, premières at the Paris Opéra.

20 May Luigi Dallapiccola's 12-note opera *Il prigioniero* (The Prisoner, 1948) receives its first public performance, in Florence. Accounting a prisoner's emotional torture under the Spanish Inquisition, the story symbolises something of the composer's own suffering under Fascism, having married a Jew and been forced into hiding during World War II.

22 May Furtwängler conducts the posthumous première of Strauss's exquisite *Four Last Songs*, sung by the soprano **Kirsten Flagstad** in London.

23 June Webern's Cantata No. 2 (1943) is posthumously premièred in Brussels.

June–July Schoenberg composes his *De profundis* (Psalm 130) for unaccompanied choir.

18 July Boulez's *Le soleil des eaux* for three voices and chamber orchestra, based on words by French surrealist René Char, premières in Paris. This year the 25-year-old composer sees the publication of his Second Piano Sonata (1948), which soon gains him critical attention outside of France.

7 September British composer **Herbert Howells** conducts the première of his *Hymnus paradisi* (A Hymn to Paradise) in Gloucester Cathedral. He wrote the deeply moving choral work 12 years previously to find 'release and comfort' after losing his nine-year-old son to polio.

6 November Benny Goodman introduces **Copland**'s Clarinet Concerto under **Fritz Reiner** in New York. Commissioned by Goodman, the tuneful two-movement work incorporates elements of popular music from North and South America.

1950 The USSR announces it has the atomic bomb • The McCarthy Committee begins a 'witch-hunt' of Communists in the USA • The German Federal Republic becomes a member of the Council of Europe • The Korean War (until 1953) begins when North Korean troops invade South Korea; UN sends troops to aid South Korea; Chinese forces come to the aid of the North Koreans • Albert Giacometti (Switz) sculpts *Seven Figures and a Head* • Jackson Pollock (US) paints *Autumn Rhythm (No. 30)* • Mark Rothko (Latvia/US) paints rectangular *No. 10* • Belfast-born C. S. Lewis launches his *Narnia Chronicles* with *The Lion, the Witch and the Wardrobe*

Cage experiments with what he terms 'chance operations' in *Sixteen Dances* for chamber ensemble and percussion, and in the fitful *Music of Changes* for solo piano. Further aspects of chance are explored in his *Imaginary Landscape No. 4* for 12 radios (playing whatever happens to be broadcast at the time), and the Concerto for prepared piano and chamber orchestra.

Morton Feldman incorporates indeterminacy in *Intersection 1*, for orchestra, piano and cello, and in *Projection 2* for flute, trumpet, violin, cello and piano. *Projection 2* is one of the earliest works to include graphic notation.

Belgian composer **Karel Goeyvaerts** completes the most refined example of integral serialism to date with his *Opus 2 for 13 instruments*.

Messiaen composes his *Livre d'orgue* (Organ Book).

22 February Bernstein conducts the public première of **Ives**'s Second Symphony (revised version, 1909) in New York.

26 April Vaughan Williams's 'morality' *The Pilgrim's Progress* is first staged at Covent Garden.

Igor Stravinsky (right) with Robert Craft

7 May The tenor **Peter Pears** introduces **Tippett**'s song cycle *The Heart's Assurance* at the Wigmore Hall in London. **Britten** accompanies on the piano.

4 June Russian-born **Serge Koussevitzky**, American conductor and commissioner of numerous 20th-century classics, dies in Boston aged 76.

7 June French composer **Henri Dutilleux**, aged 35, draws critical attention with his Symphony No. 1, introduced with a subtly jazzy 'Passacaille' in Paris.

17 June English composer **Alan Rawsthorne** enjoys success in London with his Second Piano Concerto, introduced under **Malcolm Sargent** with **Clifford Curzon** as soloist.

13 July Arnold Schoenberg, the inventor of serialism, dies in Los Angeles, aged 76.

11 September Stravinsky directs the eagerly awaited première of his chamber opera *The Rake's Progress* (1950) at the Teatro La Fenice, Venice. Dismissed as archaic by some, Stravinsky's final neo-classical work becomes one of the most often performed operas of the 20th century.

6 October Boulez pushes the boundaries of serialism at the Donaueschingen festival with his prickling, twisting *Polyphonie X* for 18 solo instruments. Not satisfied with his creation, he withdraws the work.

1 December Britten returns to themes of alienation and the sea in his psychological opera *Billy Budd*, introduced under his own baton at Covent Garden. The libretto, based on Herman Melville's tale, has been co-authored by **E. M. Forster** and **Eric Crozier**. Revisions bring the four-act opera into its final two-act form in 1960.

24 December NBC TV broadcasts **Menotti**'s *Amahl and the Night Visitors*, the first opera written for television.

1951 The Korean War continues: UN forces supporting South Korea establish a front north of the border; truce talks begin • Winston Churchill is re-elected as British Prime Minister • Egypt rejects Anglo-Egyptian agreement on Suez Canal • King Abdullah of Jordan is assassinated in Jerusalem • India-Pakistan dispute over Kashmir continues; Prime Minister Ali Khan of Pakistan is assassinated • Electricity is produced by atomic energy in the USA • The Comet, first jet airliner, is developed in Britain • Pablo Picasso (Sp) paints *Massacre in Korea* • Hannah Arendt (Ger/US): *The Origins of Totalitarianism* • J. D. Salinger (US): *The Catcher in the Rye*

Georges Auric composes the music to John Huston's film *Moulin Rouge*.

Jean Barraqué explores integral serialism in his 40-minute, single movement Piano Sonata.

Boulez completes his *Structures book 1* for two pianos. His pointillistic *Structures Ia* is one of the most pure examples of integral serialism ever written, with serial technique rigorously applied to pitch, duration, dynamics and attack.

Holmboe, Denmark's leading composer, completes his Symphony No. 8 (*Sinfonia boreale*). Tonal, frequently vigorous and strident, it becomes the best known of his 13 symphonies.

Karlheinz Stockhausen, currently studying with **Messiaen** in Paris, produces his first work for tape, *Konkrete Etüde*.

24 January Hilding Rosenberg's Symphony No. 6 is first heard in Gävle, Sweden. The composer's Violin Concerto No. 2 is also premièred this year, in Stockholm.

17 February Hans Werner Henze, aged 25, sees his serially constructed one-act *Boulevard Solitude* introduced at the Hanover Opera. Henze's first opera, a modern adaptation of the *Manon Lescaut* story, attracts wide international attention.

18 February Cellist and dedicatee **Mstislav Rostropovich** introduces **Prokofiev**'s Symphony-Concerto for cello and orchestra, in Moscow.

10 April Prokofiev delights the Soviet authorities with his nostalgic Symphony No. 7, premièred in Moscow. Outside of Russia, critics are disparaging.

This year also sees the completion of Prokofiev's opera *War and Peace* in its final version.

29 August John Cage (below) forces his audience to re-evaluate their conceptions of music with *4'33"* at the aptly named Maverick Concert Hall in Woodstock (NY). **David Tudor**, with a score and stopwatch, sits at a piano and closes the lid. Soon he opens it; he closes it; he opens it; he closes it … all the while turning the pages of the score. He raises the lid one last time, and leaves. Some of the audience have done so already.

28 October America's first public concert of music for tape is given by the electronic music faculty of Columbia University at New York's Museum of Modern Art. Among the works premièred are **Vladimir Ussachevsky**'s *Sonic Contours* for taped piano and **Otto Luening**'s *Fantasy in Space, Invention in Twelve Tones* and *Low Speed*, all for taped flute.

11 November In Los Angeles **Stravinsky** conducts the first performance of his Cantata, scored for soprano, tenor, female chorus and instrumental ensemble. At this time he has also begun work on his Septet: both works incorporate his first experiments with serial techniques.

25 November Henry Cowell looks to his American-Irish roots in his Symphony No. 7 for small orchestra, first performed in Baltimore.

29 November American composer and pianist **Vincent Persichetti** premières his virtuosic *Concerto for Piano Four Hands* with his wife, Dorothea, at the Pittsburgh International Contemporary Music Festival.

1952 Britain's King George VI dies and is succeeded by Elizabeth II • Vincent Massey becomes the first Canadian governor-general of Canada • Jawaharlal Nehru becomes first elected prime minister of India • *Coup d'etat* in Egypt: constitution of 1923 is abolished • Former president Fulgencio Batista of Cuba returns to power and establishes a brutal dictatorship • Mau Mau uprising against British rule in Kenya (until 1960) • Greece and Turkey join NATO • Willem de Kooning (Neth/US) paints *Woman I* • Lucian Freud (Ger/UK) paints *Francis Bacon* portrait • Ernest Hemingway (US): *The Old Man and the Sea* • Samuel Beckett (Ire): *Waiting for Godot*

1953

Israeli composer **Paul Ben-Haim** writes his most celebrated work, *The Sweet Psalmist of Israel*, scored for harpsichord, harp and orchestra.

Earle Brown completes *Folio*, exploring indeterminacy and alternative notation. The seven-piece collection includes *December 1952* (below), one of the first works scored entirely graphically.

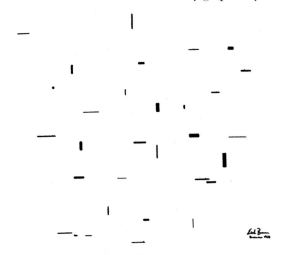

This year also marks Brown's *Twenty-five Pages*, presented on 25 unbound pages, playable in any order and combination by one to 25 musicians.

Exiled Catalan composer **Roberto Gerhard**, now living in England, completes his Symphony No. 1.

Stockhausen composes *Elektronische Studien I*, the first composition of pure electronic music. His second study follows in 1954.

14 January Sir John Barbirolli conducts the first performance of **Vaughan Williams**'s Symphony No. 7 (*Sinfonia Antartica*), in Manchester. Scored for wordless soprano, chorus and orchestra, the work derives from the composer's film score to *Scott of the Antarctic* (1948).

26 February Elliot Carter draws attention with his String Quartet No. 1, introduced in New York.

5 March Sergey Prokofiev dies of a brain haemorrhage near Moscow, aged 61. In the days following, no flowers are available for the composer's coffin; all the florists have sold out for the funeral of his chief persecutor, Joseph Stalin, who died the same day.

16 April Half a century after its conception, **Ives**'s Symphony No. 1 is given its first performance, in Washington, D.C.

26 May Copland appears in a closed hearing before McCarthy's Congressional subcommittee, accused of communist activities. He successfully defends himself against the charges.

8 June Britten's opera *Gloriana*, celebrating the coronation of Queen Elizabeth II, is presented with appropriate pageantry at Covent Garden, London. The production fails to impress.

29 August Tippett introduces his *Fantasia Concertante on a Theme of Corelli* for string orchestra in Edinburgh.

11 October Messiaen's *Réveil des oiseaux* (Awakening of the Birds), a dawn chorus for piano and orchestra, meets with general confusion at Donaueschingen.

17 October German composer **Boris Blacher** rejects comprehensible words and narrative in his jazz-infused *Abstrakte Oper No. 1*, staged publicly for the first time, in Mannheim.

17 December Shostakovich's Tenth Symphony gains an enthusiastic public reception in Leningrad. The composer later writes: 'The second [movement] is a musical portrait of Stalin … Of course there are many other things in it, but that is the basis.' The third movement introduces his self-referencing D-S-C-H theme, alluding to his name via German notation: D, E flat, C and B.

1953 Dwight D. Eisenhower becomes 34th President of the USA • Egypt becomes a republic • In the USSR, death of Stalin leads to a struggle for power: Georgy Malenkov becomes Premier (until 1955); Nikita Khrushchev becomes First Secretary • Korean War ends • Josip Tito becomes first president of Yugoslavia • Francis Crick (Eng) and James Watson (US) discover the structure of DNA • Edmund Hillary (NZ) and Tenzing Norgay (Nep/Ind) make the first successful ascent of Mount Everest • Francis Bacon (Ire) paints *Study after Velázquez's Portrait of Pope Innocent X* • Mark Rothko (Latvia/US) paints *Homage to Matisse* • Arthur Miller (US): play *The Crucible*

English composer **Malcolm Arnold** pens three concertos (Opp. 45–47) back to back: the Flute Concerto No. 1, the Harmonica Concerto and the Concerto for Organ, two Trumpets and Strings.

Havergal Brian, aged 78, hears one of his ten symphonies played for the first time—the Eighth, conducted by **Sir Adrian Boult**. Inspired by the performance, the Englishman notches up an additional 22 symphonies over the next 14 years.

Eric Coates composes an uncommissioned, Elgar-style March. Just days later it is snapped up by producers for a new WWII film: *The Dam Busters*.

French composer and former atonalist **André Jolivet** writes his playful, unabashedly tonal Trumpet Concerto No. 2.

Rodrigo conjures Spanish antiquity in his attractive *Fantasía para un gentilhombre*, dedicated to **Andres Segovia**. The dance suite for guitar and orchestra borrows from the music of Baroque Spanish composer-guitarist Gaspar Sanz.

Austrian composer **Ernst Toch**, a US resident for nearly 20 years, completes his Symphony No. 3 in California. The work later wins him a Pulitzer prize.

12 March Schoenberg's serialist opera *Moses und Aron* (1932) is given a posthumous concert première in Hamburg.

19 May Charles Ives, the father of American art music, dies in New York, aged 79.

6 June Joseph Haydn's skull, purloined from his coffin two days after his funeral (for

pseudo-scientific purposes), is reunited with his body after 145 years' separation.

13 June Vaughan Williams's Tuba Concerto makes its merry entrance in London.

July Andrzej Panufnik, during a visit to Zürich, defects to the West. His music is immediately banned in his native Poland.

5 July Elvis Presley, aged 21, makes his first commercial recordings: *That's All Right* and *Blue Moon of Kentucky*.

14 September Britten conducts the first performance of his ghostly chamber opera *The Turn of the Screw* at the Teatro La Fenice, Venice. With libretto by **Myfanwy Piper** after Henry James's novella, the semi-serialist work gains a favourable reception.

25 November Prokofiev's opera *The Fiery Angel* is posthumously premièred in Paris.

26 November Witold Lutosławski looks to Polish folk music and the legacy of Bartók in his popular Concerto for Orchestra, first performed in Warsaw.

2 December Varèse (left) employs pre-recorded sound for the first time in his colouristic *Déserts* for woodwind, percussion and tape, premièred at the Théâtre des Champs-Elysées, Paris. French radio broadcasts the concert live, in stereo.

3 December Walton's opera *Troilus and Cressida* opens at Covent Garden to mixed reviews.

1954 The Western European Union is formed • Colonel Gamel Abdul Nasser becomes premier of Egypt • France recognises independence of Laos, Cambodia, and Vietnam; the Communists and French agree to evacuate South Vietnam and North Vietnam respectively • French government sends 20,000 troops to Algeria to quell nationalist revolt • US Supreme Court declares racial segregation unconstitutional • Medical student Roger Bannister (Eng) runs the first under-four-minute mile • Film: *The Seven Samurai* (Akira Kurosawa; Jap) • Dylan Thomas (Wal): *Under Milk Wood* radio play • William Golding (Eng): *Lord of the Flies* • J. R. R. Tolkien (Eng): *The Fellowship of the Ring*

1955

Following studies with **Nadia Boulanger**, Argentinian composer **Astor Piazzolla** launches Nuevo Tango, remodelling the dance form with improvisation, virtuosity and modernist harmonies.

7 January Charles Münch introduces **Martinů**'s commanding *Fantaisies Symphoniques* (Symphony No. 6) during a 75th anniversary concert of the Boston Symphony Orchestra. This year the composer completes *Les fresques de Piero della Francesca* for orchestra, and the Oboe Concerto for small orchestra.

27 January Tippett's first opera, *The Midsummer Marriage*, struggles to impress at its première in Covent Garden. It will be some 20 years before it is accepted as one of the composer's masterworks.

18 February Howard Hanson's Romantic Symphony No. 5 (*Sinfonia Sacra*) is first heard in Philadelphia.

24 February Carlisle Floyd creates an American repertory favourite with his opera *Susannah*, premièred in Tallahassee, Florida.

25 March The film *Blackboard Jungle* introduces a mass audience to a version of *Rock around the Clock* (1954) by **Bill Haley and His Comets**. The song goes on to sell over 20 million copies and, more than any other, marks the advent of rock'n'roll.

4 May George Enescu dies in Paris, aged 73. A composer, conductor, teacher and violin virtuoso, the Romanian maestro was also renowned for his formidable musical memory. He could recall, note-for-note, every Beethoven symphony, quartet and trio, the *Missa Solemnis* and *Fidelio*. He also memorised

Wagner's entire *Ring* cycle. Just two rehearsals of any violin work were often enough for him to dispense with the written score.

18 June Boulez's *Le marteau sans maître* (The Hammer Without a Master) for contralto, alto flute, xylorimba, vibraphone, percussion, guitar and viola, is first performed in Baden-Baden. Based on three poems by René Char, the serial chamber work gains high critical praise and affirms the composer's international reputation as a leading figure of the musical avant-garde.

8 August Luigi Nono, aged 31, marries Schoenberg's daughter, Nuria, in Venice.

16 October Xenakis, aged 33, introduces his glissandi masses in *Metastasis* (Transformations) for orchestra, composed utilising probability theory, serialist techniques and the Fibonacci series. The groundbreaking textural piece receives a mix of boos and cheers at Donaueschingen, Baden-Württemberg.

29 October Shostakovich's Violin Concerto No. 1 is introduced in Leningrad. **David Oistrakh** (left), for whom the work has been written, performs as soloist.

4 November William Schuman's orchestral work *Credendum* (Article of Faith) is premièred in Cincinnati in honour of UNESCO. It is the first ever commission by a US government agency.

27 November Composer **Arthur Honegger** dies from a heart attack in Paris, aged 63.

13 December Master of the Queen's Music, **Sir Arthur Bliss** has his orchestral masterpiece *Meditations on a Theme by John Blow* premièred in Birmingham.

1955 British prime minister Winston Churchill resigns; succeeded by Anthony Eden • West Germany becomes a member of NATO • The USSR creates the Warsaw Pact organisation as rival to NATO • In Algeria, independence fighters protesting against French rule carry out sabotage and killings • Violence breaks out in Cyprus over union with Greece • South Vietnam is proclaimed a republic • An uprising in Argentina results in the resignation and exile of President Juan Perón • Bandung Conference: First major conference between African and Asian states held in Indonesia • Lynn Chadwick (Eng) sculpts *Winged Figures* • Tennessee Williams (US): play *Cat on a Hot Tin Roof*

Stockhausen composes his 'open form' *Klavierstück XI* (Piano Piece XI), and *Zeitmasse* (Tempos) for five wind instruments, both incorporating aleatory (indeterminate) elements.

2 March Villa-Lobos (above) introduces his energetic Symphony No. 11 with the Boston Symphony Orchestra. This year also sees the first performance of his Guitar Concerto with **Andres Segovia** in Houston, and the completion of his Harmonica Concerto.

10 March Messiaen's *Oiseaux exotiques* (Exotic Birds) for piano, winds and percussion débuts at the Petit Theatre Marigny in Paris.

4 April Paul Creston's Symphony No. 5 is introduced in Washington, D.C.

2 May Barbirolli conducts the first performance of **Vaughan Williams**'s Eighth Symphony in Manchester.

30 May Cologne Radio broadcasts **Stockhausen**'s *Gesang der Jünglinge* (Song of the Youths), scored for recorded boy soprano and electronic sounds. Taking its text from the book of Daniel, the work is groundbreaking in its vocal processing techniques, creating an inscrutable fusion of recorded and electronic sound.

7 July Douglas Moore's folk opera *The Ballad of Baby Doe* opens in Colorado. A story of the misfortunes of love and wealth set in Colorado during the gold-rush, the opera is unashamedly melodic and captures the public's imagination. It is the composer's greatest triumph.

13 September Stravinsky's semi-serialist *Canticum sacrum* is introduced at St Mark's Basilica, Venice. *Time* magazine publishes its review under the title 'Murder in the Cathedral'.

23 September Berlin State Opera introduces **Henze**'s neo-Romantic opera *König Hirsch* (The Stag King), based on the fable by Carlo Gozzi.

24 October Nono's *Il canto sospeso* (The Suspended Song), scored for solo voices, choir and orchestra, premières in Cologne. Employing integral serialism, the work quotes from ten letters written by condemned boys, men and women of the European Resistance, shortly before their executions. Six countries are represented: Bulgaria, Greece, Poland, Soviet Union, Italy and Germany. Each letter is a farewell, some of brave defiance, others of moving lament.

13 November Musical wit **Malcolm Arnold** assembles three vacuum cleaners, one floor polisher and four rifles to add to organ and orchestra for the première of *A Grand Grand Overture*, held at London's Royal Festival Hall.

1 December Bernstein's *Candide*, opens on Broadway. Later hugely popular, the operetta meets mixed reactions and folds after two months.

Early December Composer **György Ligeti** and his wife escape Soviet-occupied Hungary, hiding on a train under mailbags and crossing the border into Austria by foot under the cover of night.

26 December Khachaturian's melodious Romantic ballet *Spartacus* is first staged at the Kirov Theatre in Leningrad.

1956 Egypt seizes the Suez canal, Britain and France refer the question to the United Nations; the USSR vetoes a compromise solution • Israeli troops invade Egypt; Anglo-French forces invade Egypt to protect the canal • An international force is sent to Egypt to enforce ceasefire; British and French troops withdraw • Revolution breaks out in Hungary; Communist rule is restored and 150,000 refugees escape to the West • Japan is admitted to the UN • France grants independence to Tunisia and Morocco • Jøern Utzon (Den) designs the Sydney Opera House • Elvis releases *Heartbreak Hotel* and *Hound Dog* • Winston Churchill (Eng): *A History of the English Speaking Peoples*

The *Illiac Suite for String Quartet* is composed by a computer, programmed with the rules of Fux's counterpoint and the techniques of serialism.

Malcolm Arnold writes his popular *Four Scottish Dances* and, in just ten days, the Oscar-winning score to David Lean's film *The Bridge on the River Kwai*, starring Alec Guinness (below).

The Brazillian Ministry of Education and Culture announce a 'Villa-Lobos year' in honour of the composer who turns 70 in March.

1 January Covent Garden premières **Britten**'s exotic *Prince of the Pagodas*, the first full-length ballet written by a major English composer.

16 January Conductor **Arturo Toscanini** dies in New York, aged 89.

25 January **Walton**'s melodious Cello Concerto is first performed in Boston. This year also sees the composition of his Partita for orchestra.

26 January **Poulenc**'s *Dialogues des Carmélites* triumphs at La Scala, Milan. Set during the French revolution and subsequent Reign of Terror, the composer's greatest opera tells of the martyrdom of 16 Carmelite nuns. Productions in Paris, Cologne and San Francisco follow this same year.

12 April **Wallingford Riegger**'s Symphony No. 4 is first performed at the University of Illinois Contemporary Music Festival.

May American composer **Norman Dello Joio** is awarded a Pulitzer Prize for his *Meditations on Ecclesiastes* for string orchestra (1956).

10 May **Shostakovich**'s Second Piano Concerto makes its jocular entry in Moscow. The composer's son, **Maxim** (celebrating his 19th birthday), performs as soloist.

6 June The two completed acts of *Moses and Aron* by Schoenberg (d. 1951) finally make the stage, in Zürich.

17 June **Stravinsky** begins tonally and ends serially in the ballet *Agon* (Contest), choreographed by George Balanchine and premièred in Los Angeles.

3 August Renowned cellist **Pablo Casals**, aged 80, marries his pupil **Marta Montañez**, 60 years his junior.

11 August **Hindemith** considers the life of Johannes Kepler in *Die Harmonie der Welt* (The Harmony of the World, 1950), first staged in Munich. Reaction to the opera is unenthusiastic.

19 August The musical *West Side Story*, a resetting of *Romeo and Juliet* with music by **Bernstein** and lyrics by **Stephen Sondheim**, opens in Washington, D.C. The production transfers to New York the following month where it begins a healthy 734-performance run. A filmed version follows in 1961, bringing much wider success.

20 September Finland loses a national hero: **Jean Sibelius** dies in Järvenpää, aged 91.

30 October **Shostakovich** appears to pay homage to the unsuccessful Russian Revolution of 1905 in his Symphony No. 11, premièred in Moscow.

29 November Austrian composer **Erich Korngold** dies in Hollywood, aged 60.

1958

Luciano Berio composes *Sequenza* (*I*) for solo flute, the first of many *Sequenzas* he writes for solo performers.

Messiaen completes his *Catalogue d'oiseaux* (Catalogue of Birds) for piano, based on his transcriptions of birdsong.

15 January Barber's first opera, *Vanessa*, with libretto by **Menotti**, opens to wide acclaim at the Metropolitan Opera, New York.

February Babbitt is outraged on finding out that his article 'The Composer as Specialist' in *High Fidelity* magazine has been changed to 'Who Cares if you Listen?'

5 February In London, the première of **Tippett**'s Second Symphony, broadcast live, dissolves into confusion, grinding to a standstill barely after it has begun. Conductor **Sir Adrian Boult** turns to the audience and apologises, 'Sorry, entirely my fault', and begins again.

24 March Boulez, **Bruno Maderna** and **Stockhausen** conduct the first performance of Stockhausen's *Gruppen* (Groups, 1957) for three orchestras, in Cologne. A major serial work of the decade, it explores complex layers of tempi and spatial dimensions as the orchestras, surrounding the audience, perform at various times independently, together and antiphonally.

26 March Lutosławski's *Musique funèbre* (Funeral Music), composed in memory of Bartók, is first performed in Katowice, Poland.

2 April The 85-year-old **Vaughan Williams** has his Ninth Symphony premièred under **Sir Malcolm Sargent** at London's Royal Albert Hall.

2 May Varèse's *Poème électronique* for voices, electronic sounds, machine noises and percussion, is first conveyed on three-track tape in the Philips Pavilion through 425 loud speakers. The building

itself (above), a temporary structure of the Brussels World's Fair, has been designed by Le Corbusier and the composer-architect **Iannis Xenakis**.

15 May Cage's *Concert for Piano and Orchestra* is first performed in New York. Employing electronic sounds and indeterminacy, the work may be performed 'in whole or part, any duration … as a solo, chamber ensemble, symphony, concerto for piano and orchestra, aria, etc.'.

30 May In Basel **Hans-Heinz Schneeberger** premières Bartok's Violin Concerto No. 1 (1908), written for (and rejected by) the violinist Steffi Geyer, with whom the composer had been in love.

26 August Composer **Ralph Vaughan Williams** dies in London, aged 85.

23 September Stravinsky's *Threni* (Tears), based on the Lamentations of Jeremiah, is first performed at the International Festival of Contemporary Music in Venice. It is the composer's first completely serial composition.

5 December Charles Munch introduces **Alexander Tcherepnin**'s Fourth Symphony (1957) in Boston. The Russian-born composer has this year become an American citizen.

1958 Continuing war in Algeria leads to crisis in France; Charles de Gaulle becomes Prime Minister • Egypt and Syria unite to form the United Arab Republic; Yemen later joins the UAR • In USSR, First Secretary Nikita Krushchev also becomes Premier of the Soviet Union • The USA launches Earth satellite *Explorer 1*; The USSR launches *Sputnik 3*

• Pope Pius XII dies; succeeded by John XXIII • Stereophonic phonograph recording is developed in Britain • First motorway in Britain is opened, the Preston Bypass (M6) • Truman Capote (US): *Breakfast at Tiffany's* • Harold Pinter (Eng): *The Birthday Party* • Ian Fleming (Eng): *Dr No*, the sixth James Bond novel

American jazz saxophonist and composer **Ornette Coleman** pioneers avant-garde free-style jazz in *The Shape of Jazz to Come*. His album *Free Jazz* for double jazz quartet follows a year later.

Feldman considers texture and colour in *Atlantis*, graphically scored for large chamber ensemble.

Giacinto Scelsi explores microtones, overtones and timbres in his transfixing *Quattro pezzi, su una nota sola* (Four pieces, each on a single note), for orchestra.

6 February Poulenc's one-act *La voix humaine* (The Human Voice), a tale of a relationship break-up, opens at the Opéra-Comique, Paris. With libretto by **Cocteau** (based on his own play), the opera is scored for just one soprano and orchestra, with most of the drama played out in the form of a telephone call.

31 May Swedish composer **Karl-Birger Blomdahl** launches space-age opera with *Aniara* (below), based on an epic poem by Harry Martinson. Staged at the Royal Opera of Stockholm, the atonal allegory concerns nuclear holocaust survivors on a Mars-bound spaceship thrown off course. Purpose, chance and fate are considered as the passengers realise they are doomed to meet death in the emptiness of space.

15 July Swiss-born American composer **Ernest Bloch** dies in Portland, Oregon, aged 78.

28 August Czech composer **Bohuslav Martinů** dies of cancer in Liestal, Switzerland, aged 68.

23 September Herbert von Karajan attempts to conduct by memory **Messiaen**'s *Réveil des oiseaux* (premièred 1953), resulting in disaster. Afterwards the dispirited composer finds the conductor in a remarkably buoyant mood: 'Thank you! At last, thanks to you, my first scandal!'

2 October Stockhausen's *Refrain*, scored principally for piano, celesta and vibraphone, is first performed in Berlin. The work incorporates 'variable form' by the use of a circular transparency, bearing the notated 'refrain', which can be rotated to different positions over semi-circular systems within the score.

4 October Shostakovich's Cello Concerto No. 1 is introduced in Leningrad with **Mstislav Rostropovich** as soloist.

16 November Rodgers and **Hammerstein** present *The Sound of Music* on Broadway.

17 November Heitor Villa-Lobos, leading 20th-century Brazilian composer, dies in Rio de Janeiro, aged 72.

11 December Dutilleux's Second Symphony: *Le Double*, scored for large orchestra and chamber orchestra, is premièred in Boston.

18 December Two days after his 77th birthday, **Kodály** marries his 19-year-old pupil Sarolta Péczely.

1959 In Cuba, Batista government ousted by Communists; Fidel Castro becomes premier • General Charles de Gaulle is proclaimed President of France's 5th Republic • UK grants Cyprus independence • Anti-Belgian riots in the Belgian Congo • Russian spaceship *Lunik II* reaches the Moon; *Lunik III* photographs the far side of the Moon • Americans Robert Noyce and Jack Kilby both invent the 'microchip' • Film: *Ben Hur* (US); *Some Like it Hot* (with Marilyn Monroe; US) • Jasper Johns (US) paints *False Start* • William S. Burroughs (US): *Naked Lunch* • Laurie Lee (Eng): *Cider With Rosie*

Berio explores the semantic properties of poems by E. E. Cummings in *Circles* for female voice, harp and two percussionists. The five-movement, partially serialist work is dedicated to his wife, the singer **Cathy Berberian**.

Cage considers music, Zen philosophy and mushrooms in his book *Silence*.

Poulenc completes his *Gloria* for soprano, chorus and orchestra, commissioned by the Koussevitsky Foundation.

10 January Stravinsky conducts the première of his serial *Movements* for piano and orchestra in New York.

25 March Carter's discursive String Quartet No. 2 is introduced by the Juilliard Quartet in New York. It gains the composer his first Pulitzer Prize later this year.

14 May Virgil Thomson conducts the first performance of his *Missa Pro Defunctis* for double chorus and orchestra, in New York.

22 May Henze's opera *Der Prinz Von Homburg*, musically inspired by the Italian Romantic tradition, enjoys great success at its opening in Hamburg.

11 June Britten's magical opera *A Midsummer Night's Dream* is staged for the first time, at Aldeburgh. In adapting the libretto from Shakespeare's play, the composer and **Peter Pears** have cut half of the text and added just one new line.

19 June György Ligeti grabs critical attention with his

sonic extravaganza *Apparitions* for orchestra, premièred with great success at the ISCM Festival in Cologne.

2 September Walton's Symphony No. 2 is introduced at the Edinburgh Festival. The inclusion of intense chromaticism in the final movement is not enough to deflect accusations of anachronism. Towards the end of the century this tonal symphony gains wider critical recognition.

14 September Shostakovich feels obliged to join the Communist Party of the USSR, to the dismay of many friends. This year brings the first performance of his harrowing String Quartet No. 8 in C minor, 'dedicated to the victims of fascism and war'.

16 October Penderecki's *Anaklasis* for strings and percussion débuts at the Donaueschingen Festival. The short textural work gains an encore and establishes the composer's international reputation. The concert concludes with the première of **Messiaen**'s *Chronochromie* (Colour of Time) for large orchestra.

Jennifer Vyvyan as Titania and Owen Brannigan as Bottom in *A Midsummer Night's Dream*

21 October American composer **Lukas Foss** performs at the piano in the première of his part-improvisatory *Time Cycle* for soprano and orchestra, in New York.

28 October Stockhausen surrounds the audience with his serial, 'moment form' *Carré* (Square) for four choirs and four orchestras, premièred with four conductors in Hamburg.

1960 Seventeen African countries become independent • Sharpeville Massacre, South Africa: Anti-apartheid demonstrations lead to shooting of 69 Africans • Civil war in newly-independent Congo: Katanga province attempts to break away under Moise Tshombe • France tests nuclear bombs in the Sahara • Sirima Bandaranaike (Ceylon) becomes the world's first female Prime Minister • American scientists develop laser beams • Brasilia, largely the architectural brainchild of Oscar Niemeyer, is inaugurated as Brazil's capital city • M. C. Escher (Neth) draws *Ascending and Descending* (optical illusion) • Harper Lee (US): *To Kill a Mockingbird* • Robert Bolt (Eng): play *A Man for All Seasons*

13 April Attacking capitalism, fascism and exploitation of the working classes, **Nono**'s stage work *Intolleranza* premières in Venice. The performers—the pit orchestra especially—suffer the displeasure of neo-fascists who pelt them with stink-bombs. The conductor-composer **Bruno Maderna** valiantly guides the production through to the end.

24 April Lutosławski fails to meet his deadline for the première of his part-aleatory *Venetian Games*—performed incomplete at the Teatro La Fenice, Venice. Lutosławski will increasingly avoid committing to deadlines.

30 April Alberto Ginastera's *Cantata para America Magica* (1960) for soprano and large percussion ensemble is introduced with great success at the Inter-American Music Festival in Washington.

9 May Programmed with the room-size RCA Mark II synthesiser (shown in part below), **Babbitt**'s *Composition for Synthesiser* is first played at Columbia University.

20 May Henze's opera *Elegy for Young Lovers* opens in Schwetzingen, Germany.

31 May Penderecki's *Threnody: To the Victims of Hiroshima* (1960) is given a broadcast première by Warsaw Radio. The composer's most famous creation draws tone-clusters, microtonal glissandi and strident percussive sounds from 52 strings in a formidable textural depiction of suffering.

5 June BBC Radio broadcasts Piotr Zak's *Mobile for Tape and Percussion*. The composer is fictitious—the work is a spoof composition of random noises by Hans Keller and Susan Graham. No one spots the hoax. 'That fake music can be indistinguishable from the genuine is a reflection on certain trends in present-day composition', remarks Graham.

3 July Malcolm Arnold conducts the Hallé Orchestra in the first performance of his Symphony No. 5, in Cheltenham.

6 September Carter's Double Concerto, for harpsichord, piano and two chamber orchestras, is first performed in New York. **Stravinsky** (in a polemical mood) hails it as the first American masterpiece.

15 October Shostakovich celebrates the October Revolution (again—see 1927) in his Symphony No. 12 (*The Year 1917*), introduced in Moscow.

22 October Ligeti continues his exploration of orchestral clusters in *Atmosphères*, introduced at the Donaueschingen Festival. The work gains an encore and consolidates the composer's international reputation. **Berio**'s *Epifanie* for mezzo soprano and orchestra is premièred at the same concert.

26 October Robert Ward's opera *The Crucible*, based on Arthur Miller's play, opens to huge acclaim in New York.

30 December Shostakovich finally dares to première his colossal Fourth Symphony (1936) in Moscow. (See also 1936.)

1961 John F. Kennedy becomes 35th President of the USA • US-supported invasion of Cuba by Cuban exiles at the 'Bay of Pigs' fails • South Africa becomes a republic • East Germans build the Berlin Wall • UN troops occupy breakaway Congo province of Katanga, and its secession ends • Tanganyika and Sierra Leone become independent • Latin American Free Trade Association (LAFTA) formed • The USSR sends the first man (Yuri Gagarin) into space in the spaceship *Vostock*; the USA follows with Alan B. Shepard • Alberto Giacometti (Switz) sculpts *The Walking Man I* • Joseph Heller (US): *Catch-22* • Muriel Spark (Scot): *The Prime of Miss Jean Brodie*

Auric is appointed director of both the Paris Opéra and the Opéra-Comique.

Boulez completes *Pli selon pli* (Fold by Fold) for soprano and orchestra, incorporating material from his two *Improvisations sur Mallarmé* (1957).

Earle Brown completes his *Available Forms II* for divided orchestra and two conductors.

Hartmann, in his penultimate year, completes his Eighth Symphony.

Ligeti creates a musical language of exaggeration and gesticulation in his semi-theatrical *Aventures*, scored for three singers and seven instrumentalists.

Poulenc composes his popular Clarinet Sonata for **Benny Goodman**.

6 May Mauricio Kagel's *Sur Scène* (1960), a disparate one-act theatrical work for speaker, mime, singer and three instruments, opens in Bremen, Germany.

29 May Tippett's *King Priam* opens with a blaze of trumpets at the Coventry Festival, itself organised for the consecration of the rebuilt Cathedral. Based on Homer's *Iliad*, Tippett's second opera examines the emotional and moral conflicts inherent in war.

30 May Britten's *War Requiem* premières in the rebuilt Coventry Cathedral. Interspersing the text of the Latin Requiem Mass with poetry by Wilfred Owen, the work proclaims the futility of war. An apposite British-German-Russian line-up with the soloists **Peter Pears**, **Dietrich Fischer-Dieskau** and **Galina Vishnevskaya** is unfortunately confounded as the Soviet government refuses the soprano permission to take part. **Heather Harper** takes her place and the première proves one of Britten's major triumphs.

21 September The 80-year-old **Stravinsky** lands in Moscow, accompanied by his wife and Robert Craft. It is the first time the composer has set foot on Russian soil in 48 years. During his visit he conducts concerts of his own music, all necessarily programmed with non-religious works.

23 September Copland turns to serial methods of composition in the orchestral work *Connotations*, first performed under **Bernstein** at the inauguration of the Lincoln Center's Philharmonic Hall, New York.

Aaron Copland with UN Secretary-General U. Thant at the opening of the Lincoln Center's Philharmonic Hall

24 September Barber's dramatic and demanding Piano Concerto is first played by **John Browning** at the Lincoln Center, New York. The work wins the composer his second Pulitzer Prize.

5 October The Beatles release their first record, *Love Me Do*.

18 December Shostakovich's Symphony No. 13, scored for bass soloist, chorus and orchestra, premières in Moscow. Soviet authorities promptly ban the work for its inclusion of **Yevgeny Yevtushenko**'s poem *Babi Yar*, which criticises Soviet anti-semitism. Yevtushenko is forced to rewrite his text, and the revised symphony is reintroduced two months later.

1962 Jamaica and Trinidad and Tobago become independent • Uganda becomes independent • The USA establishes a military command in South Vietnam • Cuban Missile Crisis: US announces that the Russians have built missile bases in Cuba; US warships blockade Cuba; USSR agrees to dismantle its bases • US agrees to supply Britain with Polaris atomic missiles • Ferhat Abbas becomes president of the newly-independent Algeria • The USA puts three astronauts into orbit around the Earth • Andy Warhol (US) paints *Marilyn Diptych* following the death of Marilyn Monroe • Doris Lessing (UK): *The Golden Notebook* • Ken Kesey (US): *One Flew Over the Cuckoo's Nest*

30 January Composer **Francis Poulenc** dies from a heart attack in Paris, aged 64.

9 February Kabalevsky's *Requiem*, dedicated to the fallen Soviet heroes of World War II, is first performed in Moscow.

3 March NBC-TV broadcasts **Menotti**'s television opera *Labyrinth*. Other premières for the composer this year include the dramatic cantata *The Death of Bishop Brindisi* in Cincinnati, and the opera *L'ultimo selvaggio* (The Last Savage) in Paris.

Dmitri Kabalevsky (left) with the conductor Melik Pashayev

8 March Walton conducts the first performance of his *Variations on a Theme of Hindemith* in London.

9 May Lutosławski demonstrates 'aleatory counterpoint' in *Trois poèmes d'Henri Michaux*, premièred in Zagreb. Expansive in atonal textures, the three-movement work demands two conductors to direct the chorus and orchestra separately.

16 May Bernstein conducts the first performance of **Henze**'s Fifth Symphony, in New York. Henze's Fourth Symphony also receives its première this year, in Berlin.

28 August Tippett's Concerto for Orchestra, dedicated to **Britten**, is introduced in Edinburgh.

9 September John Cage leads a performance of Erik Satie's *Vexations* at the Pocket Theatre, New York. Probably a world première, nine other pianists participate to render the required 840 repetitions of the piece, which lasts 18 hours 40 minutes. Purists point out that the work was meant for one performer only.

13 September In Hilversum, Dutch Television rolls up at City Hall where the town mayor, the Spanish ambassador and other prominent guests have gathered for the concluding civic reception of Gaudeamus Music Week. With high expectations of **Ligeti**'s majestically titled *Poème symphonique*, jaws drop as ten assistants whip off the covers of 100 clockwork metronomes to unleash a mass clatter of tick-tocking. With each set to a different speed, the instruments run down—very slowly— one by one. 'The last tick was followed by oppressive silence. Then there were menacing cries of protest'. Ligeti later recalls. Dutch TV is not allowed to broadcast the event.

11 October Jean Cocteau, aged 74, and **Edith Piaf**, aged 47, die this same day in France.

23 October Alan Hovhaness's *Symphony for Metal Orchestra* (Symphony No. 17) premières in Cleveland. The work has been inspired by the composer's study of Gagaku music in the Far East.

30 October Messiaen, recently returned from a trip to Japan, presents his *Sept Haïkaï* (Seven Haiku, 1962) for piano, percussion, winds and violins, in Paris.

10 December Bernstein introduces his *Kaddish* Symphony (No. 3) in Tel Aviv, Israel. Dedicated to the memory of John F. Kennedy, the work is scored for female narrator, soprano, boys' chorus, mixed chorus and orchestra.

28 December Composer **Paul Hindemith** dies in Frankfurt from acute pancreatitis, aged 68.

1963 Federation of Malaya is formed • Martial law in South Vietnam follows the assassination of President Ngo Dinh Diem • US President John F. Kennedy is assassinated; he is succeeded by Vice President Lyndon B. Johnson as 36th President of the USA • Fighting breaks out between Greeks and Turks in Cyprus; British troops establish a neutral zone between the factions • Russian cosmonaut Valentina Tereshkova becomes first woman in space • Pope John XXIII dies; succeeded by Paul VI • Andy Warhol (US) paints *Eight Elvises* • A 'Pop Art' exhibition is held at the Guggenheim Museum, New York City; includes work by Roy Lichtenstein and Andy Warhol

10 January Boulez introduces his *Figures–Doubles–Prismes* for orchestra (an expansion of his *Doubles*, 1958) in Basel.

22 January American composer **Marc Blitzstein**, beaten up the previous day by three sailors in a Martinique bar, dies from his injuries, aged 59.

12 March Rostropovich is the soloist in **Britten**'s Symphony for Cello and Orchestra, premièred under the composer's direction in Moscow.

7 May Chávez's Symphony No. 6 is introduced under **Bernstein** in New York. This year also marks the Mexican composer's *Resonances* for orchestra.

12 June Inspired by Japanese noh theatre, the first of **Britten**'s 'church parables', *Curlew River*, is performed at Orford Church in Suffolk.

24 July Ginastera combines grand opera, instrumental forms and 12-note technique in his historical *Don Rodrigo*, introduced at the Teatro Colón in Buenos Aires. Requiring sizeable orchestral forces and a chorus of 100 singers, the composer's first opera receives critical praise, though a muted public response. A North American première two years later, featuring **Plácido Domingo** in the title role, is an uncontested triumph.

12 August Panufnik's *Sinfonia Sacre* (Symphony No. 3) is first performed in Monte Carlo. The work commemorates 1,000 years of Polish Christianity.

17 October Messiaen's *Couleurs de la Cité Céleste* (Colours of the Celestial City) for piano, three clarinets, ten brass, tuned and non-pitched percussion, is introduced under **Boulez** at the Donaueschingen Festival.

31 October The centenary birthday anniversary of Elizabeth Sprague Coolidge (1864–1953) is celebrated at the Library of Congress in Washington with four new chamber pieces:

Schuman's *Amaryllis Variations* for string trio, **Hanson**'s *Four Psalms* for baritone and string sextet, **Walter Piston**'s String Sextet and **Milhaud**'s String Septet. Coolidge is remembered as one of the most important patrons of 20th-century chamber music.

1 November Terry Riley's sparkling and undeviating *In C*, the first famous work of minimalism, is premièred in San Francisco with **Steve Reich** among the performers.

20 November Shostakovich's String Quartets Nos. 9 and 10 are introduced in Moscow.

9 December Stockhausen (below) presents his *Mikrophonie I* in Brussels. The work demands six participants, four to create sounds on a single tam-tam, two more to manipulate the sound electronically. The composer's wife, Doris, is surprised to discover her missing kitchen items amongst the implements used to strike the gong.

1964 Greeks and Turks renew fighting in Cyprus • Guerrilla warfare by Communist Vietcong movement in South Vietnam intensifies; US aircraft attack bases in North Vietnam • In the USSR; Leonid Brezhnev succeeds deposed Nikita Khrushchev as First Secretary of the Communist Party • Harold Wilson (Labour) becomes Prime Minister of Britain • Northern Rhodesia becomes the independent Republic of Zambia • Drilling for oil and natural gas begins in the North Sea • The Beatles (Eng) pop group becomes a global phenomenon • Roald Dahl (UK): *Charlie and the Chocolate Factory* • Philip Larkin (Eng): poems *The Whitsun Weddings* • Jean Paul Satre (Fr): *Les Mots*

27 January Steve Reich presents the first performance of his tape piece *It's gonna rain* at the San Francisco Tape Music Center. The work introduces the composer's phasing technique, using two tape machines (positioned left and right) playing loops of identical spoken phrases, one running slightly faster than the other to gradually shift the parts out of, then back in to, synchronisation.

15 February Bernd Alois Zimmermann (above) triumphs with his social critique *Die Soldaten* in Cologne. The opera tells of a young, ambitious woman degraded and ruined by affairs with unscrupulous soldiers. A pioneering example of pluralism, the work presents separate dramatic episodes simultaneously on a divided stage. It also employs musical quotation—from Bach to standard jazz motifs—and diverse instrumental groups including 'concrete' music (on tape), pit orchestra, jazz ensemble and an on-stage percussion ensemble.

24 February Richard Rodney Bennett's opera *The Mines of Sulphur* opens at Sadler's Wells, London.

12 March Witold Lutosławski's String Quartet, commissioned by Swedish Radio, is first performed in Stockholm.

14 March Ligeti's *Requiem* for soprano, mezzo, chorus and orchestra, is premièred to wide critical acclaim in Stockholm. Unearthly sonic tapestries meet zany vocal histrionics in a thoroughly alternative response to death and the afterlife.

26 March Celebrating his 40th birthday, **Boulez** conducts the first performance of his *Éclat* for 15 instruments in Los Angeles.

7 April Henze's *buffa* style opera *Der Junge Lord* (The Young Lord) opens at the Deutsche Oper Berlin.

17 April Stravinsky's *Variations for Orchestra*, composed in memory of Aldous Huxley, is first performed in Chicago.

26 April Ives's Fourth Symphony (completed around 1925), considering the metaphysical questions of 'What' and 'Why', has its first full (posthumous) performance in New York. **Stokowski** has to be assisted by two extra conductors to manage the vast forces involved—including spatially separated choral and percussive groups—and to cope with complex combinations of multiple rhythms.

5 July Maria Callas, aged 41, quits the stage after singing *Tosca* at Covent Garden.

15 July Bernstein introduces his *Chichester Psalms* in New York. Variously rousing and serene, the choral work has been commissioned by Walter Hussey, Dean of Chichester Cathedral (England), and receives its British première on 31 July.

30 September The first of **Peter Sculthorpe**'s *Sun Music* orchestral pieces is premièred in London.

6 November Edgard Varèse, French composer of 'organised sound', dies in New York, aged 81.

10 December Composer **Henry Cowell** dies in New York, aged 68.

1965 US involvement in the Vietnam War increases; regular bombing raids on North Vietnam; the first US marines arrive in South Vietnam • Singapore secedes from the Federation of Malaya • Rhodesian Premier Ian Smith issues a Unilateral Declaration of Independence; Britain declares the new regime illegal and imposes trade restrictions • India and Pakistan fight the Second Kashmir War • The death penalty is abolished in Britain • Soviet and American astronauts float and 'walk' in space • France launches its first satellite, *Asterix-1* • Film: *Doctor Zhivago* • Pablo Picasso (Sp) paints *The Seated Man* (Self Portrait) • Bob Dylan (US): song *Like a Rolling Stone*

Barraqué composes *Chant après chant* for soprano, piano and percussion. It is the third and final work of his *La mort de Virgile*, inspired by Hermann Broch's novel.

Penderecki completes his *St Luke Passion*, inspired by the Passions of Bach.

Scelsi continues to explore sustained sonorities and overtones in *Ohoi* (*The Creative Principles*) for 16 solo strings. Almost static in harmony, his music stands apart from other textural pieces of the period.

19 January Tippett interprets religious experience in his complex cantata *The Vision of St Augustine* for baritone, chorus and orchestra, premièred under his own direction in London. The composer receives a knighthood this year.

20 January The Chicago Symphony Orchestra celebrates its 75th anniversary with **Gunther Schuller**'s Concerto for Orchestra No.1 (Gala Music).

3 April An 88-piece orchestra, all seated among the audience, introduces *Terrêtektorh* by **Xenakis**, in Royan, France.

28 April American composer **David Diamond** has his Symphony No. 5 (1964) and Piano Concerto (1950) premièred under **Bernstein** with the New York Philharmonic.

28 May Shostakovich's Eleventh String Quartet is first performed in Leningrad. At the same concert the 59-year-old composer performs in public for the last time—already in poor health, he suffers a non-fatal heart attack shortly afterwards.

9 June Britten's presents his second 'church parable', *The Burning Fiery Furnace*, at Aldeburgh.

6 August Henze's opera *The Bassarids*, after Euripides, is first staged in Salzburg.

16 September Barber's *Anthony and Cleopatra* inaugurates the new $46m Metropolitan Opera House in New York. **Franco Zeffirelli** supplies the libretto and an opulent production to match the occasion. 'Artifice masquerading with great flourish as art,' complains Harold Schonberg in the *New York Times*.

25 September Shostakovich's Second Cello Concerto is premièred in Moscow.

30 October Sir Adrian Boult celebrates the 90th birthday of **Havergal Brian** (left) with the first professional performance of the composer's *Gothic Symphony* (1927), at the Royal Albert Hall in London. The orchestra, nearly 200-strong, includes four separate brass bands placed around the concert hall, each with its own set of timpani; four solo vocalists, two double choruses and a boys' chorus augment numbers to around 800. The work's four-movements plan, recalling that of Beethoven's Ninth with a choral finale, lasts around one and three-quarter hours. All dimensions considered, it is the largest symphony ever written.

8 October Robert Craft conducts **Stravinsky**'s last major work, the serial *Requiem Canticles*, in Princeton, USA.

2 November Ligeti's otherworldly *Lux Aeterna* (Eternal Light) for 16 mixed voices is first performed in Stuttgart. The work ends with 30 seconds of scored silence.

1966 France announces its withdrawal of troops from NATO • UN votes sanctions against Rhodesia • Mrs Indira Ghandi becomes Prime Minister of India • The Tashkent Declaration restores friendly relations with India and Pakistan • China denounces Soviet collaboration with the West • Vietnam War continues, interrupted only by a 48-hour truce at Christmas • The USA's first black senator, Edward Brooke (Rep, Mass) is elected; meanwhile, race riots rage in American cities • Marc Chagall (Fr) paints mural *The Triumph of Music* for the Met Opera, New York City

Reich composes his first significant pieces of notated minimalism: *Piano Phase* for two pianos and *Violin Phase* for four violins.

26 January Pierre Fournier is the soloist in the first performance of **Frank Martin**'s Cello Concerto, in Basel.

5 March Hamburg's Staatsoper introduces *Arden muss sterben* (Arden must Die), the first opera by the British composer **Alexander Goehr**.

6 March Hungary's **Zoltán Kodály**, a national hero, dies in Budapest, aged 84. Thousands attend his funeral five days later.

20 April Rodion Shchedrin's *pasticcio* ballet *Carmen, after Bizet* premières in Moscow, only then to be banned as an affront to Bizet's opera. **Shostakovich** intervenes, pulling strings at the Ministry of Culture, and assists the ballet into the repertory.

19 May Ginastera's opera *Bomarzo* opens in Washington, Accounting sordid episodes of the life of the eponymous anti-hero, the work is banned in the composer's native Argentina for its preoccupation with sex and violence.

21 May The **Stockhausen** Ensemble performs the composer's *Prozession* for acoustic instruments and electronics, in Helsinki. The notation of the work includes *plus*, *minus* and *equals* signs to indicate *more*, *less*, *the same* in application to pitch, dynamic, duration and complexity. The music itself is drawn from any previously composed pieces by Stockhausen that the players can recall by memory.

26 May *Echoes of Time and the River* by **George Crumb** is first heard at the Mandel Hall in Chicago. The orchestral piece gains the American composer a Pulitzer Prize the following year.

1 June The Beatles' landmark album *Sgt Pepper's Lonely Hearts Club Band* is released in the UK, and the following day in the US.

3 June The Aldeburgh Festival mounts the first production of **Walton**'s 45-minute opera *The Bear*, based on a story by Chekov.

17 June In West Berlin, Korean composer **Isang Yun** (left) and his wife are abducted by South Korean agents and taken to Seoul, where they are accused of espionage. Both are tortured and imprisoned, the composer sentenced for life. International pressure from diplomats and artists (led by **Stravinsky**) prompts the Yuns' release in 1969.

26 September David Oistrakh gives the first official performance of **Shostakovich**'s soul-searching Second Violin Concerto in Moscow.

22 October Ligeti's *Lontano* for orchestra and **Penderecki**'s *Capriccio* for Violin and Orchestra are both premièred at Donaueschingen.

9 November Tōru Takemitsu juxtaposes Eastern and Western mindsets in *November Steps* for biwa, shakuhachi and orchestra, introduced in New York. The work has been composed to mark the 125th anniversary of the New York Philharmonic.

1967 Right-wing military coup in Greece • The 'Six Day War': fearing attack from the Arab countries, the Israeli's strike first, and inflict a humiliating defeat on the Arab forces; Israeli troops occupy the Sinai Peninsula and the Gaza strip (Egyptian), the Golan Heights (Syrian), and all Jordanian territory west of the Jordan River, including eastern Jerusalem • Civil war breaks out in Nigeria (to 1970) • Christiaan Barnard (S. Afr) performs the world's first heart transplant operation • Film: Disney's *The Jungle Book* • David Hockney (Eng) paints *A Bigger Splash* • V. S. Naipaul (Trin/UK): *A Flag on the Island* • Gabriel García Márquez (Colomb): *One Hundred Years of Solitude*

The Prix de Rome, held annually since 1803, is abolished.

Bennett composes his Piano Concerto No. 1 and *Capriccio* for piano duet.

Stanley Kubrick's *2001: A Space Odyssey* introduces an international audience to **Ligeti**'s music, including *Atmosphères* (1961) and *Lux aeterna* (1966). Neither Kubrick nor MGM have sought the composer's permission.

24 January John Tavener's dramatic cantata *The Whale* (1966), commissioned by the newly-formed London Sinfonietta, enjoys a sensational première at the ensemble's inaugural concert in London. Impressed by Tavener's music, **John Lennon** helps secure the work's release on the Beatles' Apple record label.

8 February Roy Harris's Symphony No. 11 is first performed in celebration of the 125th anniversary of the New York Philharmonic.

8 June Harrison Birtwistle's violent chamber opera *Punch and Judy* premières at the Aldeburgh Festival. With libretto by **Stephen Pruslin**, the work features characters and scenarios from Punch and Judy plays within structures derived from Greek tragedy, Baroque opera and oratorio. **Benjamin Britten** finds the whole thing unbearable and walks out.

10 June Britten introduces *The Prodigal Son*, the third of his 'church parables', in Orford, Suffolk.

14 September Shostakovich's Twelfth String Quartet is first performed in Leningrad.

10 October Berio (right) grabs international attention with his *Sinfonia*, introduced under his own direction in New York. Scored for eight amplified voices and orchestra, the work considers the place of music in cultural history by quoting disparate musical and literary materials.

In the third movement, fragments by numerous composers past to present make brief appearances in parallel with the Scherzo from Mahler's Second Symphony. Quoted texts include extracts from Samuel Becket's novel *The Unnamable*.

10 October (**Gustaf**) **Allen Pettersson** has his Seventh Symphony introduced under **Antal Dorati** with outstanding success in Stockholm. The Swedish composer is afterwards housebound by crippling arthritis, in which condition he will compose his next nine symphonies.

9 December The planned Hamburg première of **Henze**'s political oratorio *Das Floss der Medusa* (The Raft of Medusa), dedicated to the late Che Guevara, is abandoned when members of the orchestra and chorus refuse to perform under a red flag that students have fixed onto Henze's podium. The police intervene, fights break out and seven arrests are made.

9 December Stockhausen paves the way for 'spectral' composition with *Stimmung* in Paris. Lasting over an hour, six amplified performers sit cross-legged in a circle, vocalising overtones based on low B flat.

1968 In USA, Civil Rights leader Dr. Martin Luther King Junior is assassinated; Senator Robert L. Kennedy assassinated • The Vietnam War continues to escalate: more than 500,000 US troops are now involved • The USA, USSR, Britain and 58 other countries sign a treaty on the non-proliferation of nuclear weapons • Mass student protests (anti- war and injustice; pro-civil liberties) around Europe and the Americas • USSR invades Czechoslovakia to reverse a new liberal reform programme • Apollo 8, crewed by three US astronauts, makes the first orbit of the Moon • Max Perutz (Austria/UK) establishes the structure of the haemoglobin molecule • Alexander Solzhenitsyn (USSR): *The First Circle*

1969

Lennox Berkeley composes his semi-serialist one-movement Symphony No. 3.

A throw of dice begins **Cage**'s chance and choice work *HPSCHD*, for one to seven harpsichords and up to 51 tapes.

English avant-garde composer **Cornelius Cardew** forms his experimentalist Scratch Orchestra. The following year he completes his seven-hour choral work *The Great Learning*, for skilled and unskilled musicians.

Minimalist **Philip Glass** forms the Philip Glass Ensemble. Compositions this year include *Music in Contrary Motion*, *Music in Similar Motion*, *Music in Fifths* and *Music in Eight Parts*.

Messiaen completes his oratorio *La Transfiguration de Notre Seigneur Jésus-Christ* and composes the organ work *Méditations sur le mystère de la Sainte Trinité*.

American composer **David Del Tredici** veers from modernism with his Lewis Carroll-inspired *An Alice Symphony* (revised 1976), scored for soprano, folk group and orchestra.

9 January Harry Partch's *Delusion of the Fury: a Ritual of Dream and Delusion* (1966) is premièred in Los Angeles. The music-theatre piece draws on folk tales from Japan and Africa, and uses the composer's own tuning system, based on a 43-microtonal scale. The ensemble instruments have been adapted or invented by Partch (over many years) for his individual requirements.

15 January Henri Pousseur allows the audience to make narrative decisions in *Votre Faust*, a 'Fantasy in the manner of an opera', at the Piccola Scala in Milan.

14 February Henze's *Essay on Pigs* for baritone and orchestra is first performed in London. The work focuses on the reactions of left-wing students in Berlin following the attempted assassination of their key spokesperson, Rudi Dutschke, in 1968.

22 April Peter Maxwell Davies (left) presents his milestone *Eight Songs for a Mad King* in London. King George III (baritone) jabbers with his birds (caged musicians) in a disturbing music-theatre work that summons diverse musical sources, including Handel, foxtrots and The Beatles. This year also sees the première of his orchestral *Worldes Blis* at the London Proms, which causes many to flee the concert hall. It is now recognised as one of his finest achievements.

20 June Penderecki's opera *The Devils of Loudun* triumphs in Hamburg.

29 September Shostakovich meditates on death in his austere Fourteenth Symphony, first heard in Leningrad. Scored for soprano and bass soloists, strings and percussion, the composer's penultimate symphony is dedicated to **Benjamin Britten**.

24 November A temporary resident of Cuba, **Henze** co-conducts the first performance of his Symphony No. 6 for two chamber orchestras, in Havana. Henze incorporates material from revolutionary songs and refers to the piece as his 'expression of solidarity with the modern Cuba that I love so much'.

21 December The Hamburg Staatsoper mounts the first production of **Menotti**'s children's opera *Help, Help, the Globolinks!*

1969 Richard M. Nixon takes office as 37th President of the USA • The Vietnam War continues • IRA (Irish Republican Army) terrorist activities grow; troops from mainland Britain move in to restore order • French President Charles de Gaulle resigns; succeeded by Georges Pompidou • US astronauts Neil Armstrong and Edwin Aldrin become the first men to set foot on the Moon • The supersonic Anglo-French airliner Concorde makes its first flight from Toulon (Fr) • The US Supreme Court rules that segregation in schools must end immediately • Voting age is reduced from 21 to 18 in Britain • Film: *2001: A Space Odyssey* (Stanley Kubrick) • Mario Puzo (US): *The Godfather*

Feldman composes the first three pieces of *The Viola in My Life* for chamber-sized forces. An orchestral work completes the series the following year.

Milhaud, 78 this year, composes his opera-oratorio *Saint Louis, roi de France*.

Reich gradually lengthens a dominant eleventh chord in *Four Organs*, scored for four electric organs and maracas. This year Reich undertakes a five-week course in drumming at the University of Ghana in Accra, and then begins work on *Drumming*. (See also 1971.)

Roger Sessions, aged 73, completes his Rhapsody for Orchestra and his celebrated cantata *When Lilacs Last in the Dooryard Bloom'd*.

5 February Carter's *Concerto for Orchestra*, featuring four orchestral groups organised by register, is first performed in New York.

13 April After nearly two years' house arrest and imprisonment by the Greek right-wing military government, dissident composer **Mikis Theodorakis** is released and flown to France for urgent medical treatment. He remains in exile for four years, while his family are detained in Greece.

24 May Stokowski premières **Panufnik**'s cantata *Universal Prayer* in New York.

June Britten conducts the first performance of **Bliss**'s Concerto for Cello and Orchestra, with dedicatee **Rostropovich** as soloist, at the Aldeburgh Festival.

22 June Henze's *El Cimarrón* (The Runaway Slave), scored for baritone, flute, guitar and percussion, débuts at the Aldeburgh Festival. Written during Henze's residency in Cuba, the piece features the Cuban composer-guitarist **Leo Brouwer** among its performers.

25 July Rostropovich performs as soloist in the première of **Dutilleux**'s Cello Concerto, in Aix-en-Provence. This year Rostropovich incurs the wrath of the Soviet authorities for having defended in writing the Nobel Prize-winning dissident Alexander Solzhenitsyn. His movements are severely restricted over the next four years.

19 August Mario Davidovsky introduces his *Synchronisms No. 6* for piano and tape at Tanglewood, Lenox, Massachusetts. The piece gains the Argentine-American composer a Pulitzer Prize the following year.

13 September Shostakovich continues in the sombre vein of his Fourteenth Symphony in his one-movement Thirteenth String Quartet, introduced in Leningrad.

1 October Ligeti's Chamber Concerto for 13 instruments is given its first complete performance, in Berlin.

23 October *Black Angels* for amplified string quartet, by **George Crumb** (left), makes its spine-tingling entrance in Ann Arbor, Michigan. The work's 'Thirteen Images from a Dark Land' have been stimulated by the horrors of the Vietnam War.

2 December Drawing on Shakespeare's *The Tempest*, **Tippett** explores relationship psychology in his intimate opera *The Knot Garden*, premièred at Covent Garden, London.

1970 The Vietnam War continues: US and South Vietnamese forces briefly enter Cambodia, President Richard M. Nixon announces that 150,000 US troops will be withdrawn from Vietnam • Communist leader Salvador Allende becomes President of Chile • Violence continues in Northern Ireland • The civil war in Nigeria ends with the collapse of the breakaway province of Biafra • Middle East tension increases when Palestinian guerrillas hijack and blow up four airliners; Civil war between Jordanian army and Palestinian guerrillas ensues • The Aswan High Dam in Egypt is completed • Henri Charrière (Fr): *Papillon* • Richard Bach (US): *Jonathan Livingston Seagull* • Ted Hughes (Eng): poems *Crow*

Boulez becomes principal conductor of both the BBC Symphony Orchestra and the New York Philharmonic Orchestra.

Exiled composer **Mikis Theodorakis** decries the Greek junta in the song-cycle *Tragoudia tou agona* (Songs of the Struggle), completed in France.

5 March Vincent Persichetti has his Symphony No. 9 (*Sinfonia: Janiculum*) introduced under **Ormandy** in Philadelphia.

6 April Igor Stravinsky dies in New York, aged 88. A funeral ceremony is held there three days later, after which his body is flown to Venice. He is interred on the island of San Michele, close to the grave of Diaghilev.

25 April Kagel (below) presents *Staatstheater* at the Hamburg Staatsoper. The plotless work turns operatic convention on its head: chorus members sing solos, while soloists are required to sing as a chorus; minor percussive instruments are given prominent parts and non-dancers perform a ballet.

The composer describes the work as 'not just a negation of opera, but of the whole tradition of music theatre'.

27 April William Bolcom mixes serious and popular styles in *Whisper Moon*, introduced by the Aeolian Chamber Players in New York. The composer dedicates the work to his teacher, **Milhaud**.

16 May The BBC broadcasts the first performance of **Britten**'s television-opera *Owen Wingrave*.

23 May Gottfried Von Einem's opera *Der Besuch der alten Dame* (The Old Lady's Visit), a setting of the play by Friedrich Dürrenmatt, opens with great success in Vienna.

8 September Bernstein integrates stylised rock, blues, folk and brass band music into his non-liturgical *Mass*, first performed for the inauguration of the Kennedy Center in Washington. Examining a crisis of faith in the 20th century, the music-theatre piece receives some harsh criticism, with conservatives denouncing the libretto as profane and critics unconvinced by Bernstein's melding of styles.

10 September Ginastera's third (and last completed) opera, *Beatrix Cenci*, is staged for the first time, in Washington.

28 October Cairo's historic Royal Opera House is burned to the ground, probably caused by an electrical malfunction.

3 December Wild applause greets **Reich**'s minimalist *Drumming* at the Museum of Modern Art in New York. Scored for nine percussionists, two female voices and piccolo, the 90-minute work explores permutations of one rhythmic pattern.

10 December The intricate, glistening polyphony of **Ligeti**'s orchestral piece *Melodien* is heard for the first time, in Nuremberg.

1971 East Pakistan breaks from West Pakistan and declares itself independent as Bangladesh • The Vietnam War continues • The UN finally admits Communist China as a member state; Taiwan leaves the UN • Northern Ireland: internment of IRA members; violent protests with fatalities follow • *Coup d'état* in Uganda: General Idi Amin ousts Pres-ident Milton Obote and seizes power • *Apollo 15* (US) lands on the Moon and two astronauts drive a lunar vehicle on the Moon's surface • Intel invent the microprocessor • John Lennon (Eng) song *Imagine* • David Hockney (Eng) paints *Mr and Mrs Clark and Percy* • Frederick Forsyth (Eng): *The Day of the Jackal*

Finnish composer **Einojuhani Rautavaara** writes his 'Concerto for Birds and Orchestra', *Cantus Arcticus*, featuring recordings of birdsong from Northern Finland.

Tavener completes *Ultimos ritos* (Last Rites), scored for soloists, five small choirs, orchestra and tape. The 50-minute oratorio derives its material from the Crucifixus of Bach's B minor Mass (clearly apparent only in the final movement) and honours the 16th-century mystic St John of the Cross. The composer states that the work is about 'dying to oneself'.

8 January Shostakovich considers past and present in his Symphony No. 15, successfully introduced in Moscow. His final symphony quotes Rossini's *William Tell* overture, as well as material from Wagner's *Ring* cycle and *Tristan und Isolde*.

16 January Crumb's *Lux aeterna* for soprano, bass flute/recorder, sitar and two percussionists is premièred by masked musicians in Richmond, Virginia. This year also sees the first performance of *Vox balaenae* (Voice of the Whale) for amplified flute, cello and piano, introduced in New York.

9 April Feldman's tender *Rothko Chapel* for soprano, alto, mixed choir, percussion and viola, is first performed in Houston, Texas. This deeply reflective work commemorates the composer's friend, the artist Mark Rothko, who committed suicide two years earlier.

15 May George Rochberg steers into a recreated sound-world of Beethoven and Mahler in his postmodern String Quartet No. 3, premièred in New York.

Rothko Chapel, Houston

1 June Birtwistle takes inspiration from the 16th-century Flemish artist Pieter Bruegel in his funereal orchestral piece *The Triumph of Time*, introduced in London. It is one of the composer's most acclaimed and accessible concert works.

22 June Beethoven and the blues stimulate **Tippett** in his two-part Third Symphony, premièred in London under **Colin Davies** with the soprano **Heather Harper** and the London Symphony Orchestra. The work's design and emotional journey look to Beethoven's Ninth Symphony—Tippett repeatedly quotes the thunderous passage that announces the Ninth's finale, as if to reinforce the point.

12 July Maxwell Davies's opera *Taverner* (1968) débuts under **Edward Downes** at Covent Garden, London. This same year marks the first performance of Davies's *Hymn to St Magnus* for mezzo soprano and ensemble, inspired by his new found home in the Orkney Islands.

20 August Stockhausen and three fellow musicians create *Goldstaub* (Gold Dust), following a four-day preparation period of fasting in silence and solitary confinement. Drawn from the composer's 15 'intuitive' text compositions collectively entitled *Aus den sieben Tagen* (From the Seven Days, 1968), the work is an improvisation on single sounds for performers of heightened awareness. It is recorded for posterity at Stockhausen's home in Kürten.

5 September Tcherepnin's Sixth Piano Concerto (1965), his last of the genre, has its première in Lucerne, Switzerland.

12 October Lutosławski's *Preludes and Fugue* for 13 solo strings is first heard in Graz, Austria.

1972 Northern Ireland: Bloody Sunday; British fire on protestors killing 14, wounding 13 • US president Richard Nixon (reelected this year) visits the USSR and China • The USA and USSR agree a treaty to halt nuclear arms race • Pakistan withdraws from the British Commonwealth and SEATO • The Vietnam War continues: North Vietnamese forces advance into South Vietnam; US aircraft bomb Hanoi and Haiphong • Arab terrorists kidnap and kill 11 members of the Israeli team at the Olympic Games in Munich (Ger) • First digital-display watch marketed • Dame Barbara Hepworth sculpture: *Conversation with Magic Stones* • Film: *The Godfather* (Francis Ford Coppola)

23 January Carter's String Quartet No. 3 (1971) is introduced in New York. The work gains the composer his second Pulitzer Prize.

8 February Crumb explores extended piano-playing techniques in the first of his captivating *Makrokosmos* collections (Vol. I) for amplified piano, first played (and whistled and vocalised) by **David Burge** in Colorado Springs.

17 April The chamber opera *Infidelio* (1954) by English composer **Elisabeth Lutyens** finally sees the light of day at London's Sadler's Wells Theatre. Later this year the composer's cantata *De amore* (1957) premières at the London Proms.

4 May Frank Martin, aged 83, directs the first performance of his *Requiem*, in Lausanne.

16 May Reich's *Six Pianos* and the gamelan-influenced *Music for Mallet Instruments, Voices and Organ* are premièred in New York.

16 June Restrained yet intense, **Britten**'s semi-serialist *Death in Venice* opens at Aldeburgh with **Peter Pears** as the troubled writer Aschenbach. The composer's final opera, to a libretto by **Myfanwy Piper** based on Thomas Mann's novel, comes just two years after Luchino Visconti's cinematic adaptation, famously featuring the music of Mahler. Britten is largely inactive at this time, having recently undergone surgery to replace a failing heart valve.

19 July Commissioned by Perkins Engines Ltd. of Peterborough, **Penderecki**'s textural Symphony No. 1 premières under the composer's direction at Peterborough Cathedral, Northamptonshire. Of this piece he later states, 'I made an attempt to summarise the twenty years of my music experience, of avant-garde, radical pursuits'.

20 August Karajan conducts the first performance of the opera *De Temporum Fine Comoedia*, **Carl Orff**'s last major work.

15 October Ligeti's *Clocks and Clouds* for 12-part female chorus and orchestra makes its spellbinding minimalist entrance in Graz, Austria. The inspiration of the piece derives from an essay by philosopher Karl Raimund Popper ('Clouds and Clocks', 1966), which addresses issues of determinism and free will.

20 October Queen Elizabeth II opens the Sydney Opera House (below). Originally a five-year project with a A$7 million budget, the building of

the venue has taken 15 years, with costs escalating to over A$100 million.

12 November Shostakovich's Fourteenth String Quartet premières in Leningrad.

13 November Italian composer and conductor **Bruno Maderna** dies in Darmstadt, aged 53. His part-indeterminate collage opera *Satyricon* was premièred earlier this year (16 March) at the Holland Festival in Scheveningen.

1973 The Watergate Scandal: seven men accused of burgling and trying to bug Democratic Party headquarters in Watergate building, Washington D.C.; and of trying to 'bug' it; rumours of White house involvement • Military coup d'état in Chile • Yom Kippur War: Egyptian and Syrian troops invade Israel; ceasefire imposed after three weeks of fighting • Arab countries double the price of their oil, causing an energy crisis in Western countries • Relays of American astronauts dock their vehicles with the Skylab space station • USSR launches four probes to Mars • Drought in Ethiopia leaves more than 50,000 dead • Aleksandr Solzhenitsyn (Russ): *The Gulag Archipelago* • Richard Adams (Eng): *Watership Down*

Marxist-Leninist composer **Cornelius Cardew** publishes 'Stockhausen Serves Imperialism', attacking the avant-garde movement and rejecting much of his own earlier music in the process.

Lou Harrison employs his own custom-built percussion in his melodious *Suite for Violin and American Gamelan*.

Rostropovich and his wife, the soprano **Galina Vishnevskaya**, are allowed to leave the Soviet Union (see 1970). They eventually settle in the United States.

Xenakis creates the wild and arresting compositions *Erikhthon* (for piano and orchestra) and *Noomena* (for orchestra) using arborescent graphic notation.

9 February Quoting and transforming the music of Haydn, Beethoven, Chopin and others, **Alfred Schnittke**'s postmodern Symphony No. 1 premières in Gorky.

1 June Glass, with his Philip Glass Ensemble, presents his minimalist marathon *Music in Twelve Parts* at New York's Town Hall. The total performing time for the work is in excess of four hours, so they break in the middle for supper.

22 June French composer **Darius Milhaud** dies in Geneva, aged 81.

20 October Henze's ambitious *Tristan*, scored for piano, orchestra and tape, pays homage to Wagner in London. Conductor **Colin Davis** tries to coordinate with the tape without using a stopwatch, resulting in all round confusion.

15 November Shostakovich's sombre and introspective Fifteenth String Quartet is introduced by the Taneyev Quartet in Leningrad.

20 November Messiaen's *Des canyons aux étoiles*, for piano, percussion and small orchestra, is premières in New York.

Danish composer **Per Nørgård** completes his Symphony No. 3 for orchestra and chorus. Premièred under **Herbert Blomstedt** the following year, it combines textural styles with the composer's quasi-tonal 'infinity series'.

19 February Modernist composer **Luigi Dallapiccola** dies in Florence, aged 71.

27 March Sir Arthur Bliss, Master of the Queen's Music, dies in London, aged 83.

4 April Nono explores communist history through the activities of women—fighters and mothers—in his 'scenic action' *Al gran sole carico d'amore* (In the Bright Sunshine, Charged with Love), premièred at La Scala, Milan.

17 July 40-year-old Finnish composer **Aulis Sallinen** gains critical favour for his first opera, *Ratsumies* (The Horseman), premièred at the Savonlinna Festival in Finland.

9 August Dmitry Shostakovich dies from lung cancer in Moscow, aged 68. Thousands pay their respects five days later, filing past the composer's body as it rests in state at the Moscow Conservatory.

1 September Takemitsu's *Quatrain* for clarinet, violin, cello, piano and orchestra, is first given in Tokyo.

2 September Finnish National Opera introduce *The Last Temptations* by **Joonas Kokkonen**, in Helsinki. The neo-Romantic work soon achieves international renown.

16 December *Der Kaiser von Atlantis* (The Emperor of Atlantis), composed by Viktor Ullmann at Terezín concentration camp in 1944, receives its posthumous première in Amsterdam. Both Ullmann and his librettist, Petr Kien, were executed at Auschwitz shortly after completing the opera.

1974 The Watergate scandal escalates; President Richard Nixon resigns; he is succeeded by Vice-President Gerald R. Ford • Army officers in Ethiopia depose Emperor Haille Selassie • Inflation hits all parts of the world • Arab states lift embargo on oil supplies to the USA • Alexander Calder (US): *Flamingo* sculpture unveiled in Chicago's Federal Plaza

1975 The Vietnam War ends as South Vietnamese resistance collapses; a Communist provisional revolutionary government is established • Mozambique and Angola become independent • Spanish dictator Francisco Franco dies; the monarchy is restored with Prince Juan Carlos as king • CN Tower in Toronto (Can) is completed

English composer **Brian Ferneyhough** explores the boundaries of virtuosity in *Unity Capsule* for solo flute and *Time and Motion Study II* for cello and live electronics.

Henryk Górecki sets Polish folk themes and impassioned religious texts in his searching Symphony No. 3, *The Symphony of Sorrowful Songs*. During the 1990s a recording of the work catapults Górecki into the popular limelight with over one million copies sold.

7 February Frederic Rzewski's *The People United Will Never Be Defeated!*, 36 piano variations on a Chilean protest song, is first performed at the Kennedy Center, Washington.

24 February Carter marks the United States bicentennial with *A Mirror on which to Dwell* for soprano and chamber orchestra, first performed in New York.

25 March Isang Yun explores spiritual and physical incarceration in his Cello Concerto, introduced at the Royan Festival, France. Yun's piece is autobiographical (with the cello part representing himself), motivated by his period of imprisonment in South Korea, 1967–69. (See 1967.)

24 April Steve Reich and Musicians give the first performance of the composer's *Music for 18 Musicians* at New York's Town Hall. Reich gains long-awaited critical acceptance.

4 May Bernstein's White House musical *1600 Pennsylvania Avenue*, a collaboration with the writer **Alan Jay Lerner**, flops on Broadway with just seven performances.

2 June Feldman's *Oboe and Orchestra* is introduced at the Holland Festival in Rotterdam.

2 July Queen Elizabeth II makes **Britten** a life peer, the composer becoming Baron Britten of Aldeburgh in the County of Suffolk.

12 July Henze's class-struggle opera *We Come to the River* opens at London's Royal Opera House. Accounting the moral awakening of a brutal general, the so-called 'actions for music' involves the division of a featureless stage into three separate performance areas, each with its own instrumental ensemble.

25 July Glass and Robert Wilson (left) present *Einstein on the Beach* at the Avignon Festival in France. Lasting close on five hours, the minimalist and plotless opera runs without intermission, although the audience are free to come and go as they choose. The American première takes place at the Metropolitan Opera in November this year. Whilst dividing audiences, *Einstein* brings Glass international fame.

28 November Louis Andriessen launches his international career with *De Staat* (The Republic) for four female voices and large ensemble, first performed in Amsterdam. Heavily influenced by the American minimalist aesthetic, the work incorporates passages by Plato to explore 'the relation of music to politics'.

4 December Benjamin Britten, England's leading composer, dies in Aldeburgh of heart failure, aged 63.

1976 China's Chairman Mao Tse-tung dies • British Prime Minister Harold Wilson resigns; succeeded by Chancellor of the Exchequer James Callaghan • Civil war in Lebanon ends • Civil war in Angola ends with victory for the Communist M.P.L.A. • In South Africa, racial riots break out in Soweto and other black townships: 400 die • Vietnam is reunited under North Vietnamese control • Terrorism continues in Northern Ireland as attempts to establish a new government fail • Massive earthquake centred on Tangshan, China, claims around 240,000 lives • Anglo-French supersonic Concorde goes into service • British evolutionary biologist Richard Dawkins publishes *The Selfish Gene*

1977

Nasa launches two Voyager space probes. The payload includes a 'Golden Record' that consists of music taken from diverse cultures, so to offer intelligent alien life-forms a taste of Earth's musical treasures. Anthony Holborne (*c.*1545–1602), Bach, Mozart, Beethoven and Stravinsky have been chosen to represent the Western classical music tradition.

Boulez becomes the first director of IRCAM, the Institut de Recherche et de Co-ordination Acoustique/Musique (right), in Paris. The cutting-edge institute for music technology, created at the request of Boulez, has been aided by expertise and equipment developed at Stanford University, USA.

Austrian composer **Heinz Karl Gruber**, aged 34, creates *Frankenstein!!* for baritone reciter and orchestra.

Schnittke raises his international profile with his polystylistic *Concerto Grosso No. 1.*

17 February Boulez premières **Carter**'s *Symphony of Three Orchestras* in New York.

27 April Dedicatee **Isaac Stern** gives the first performance of **Penderecki**'s dramatic Violin Concerto No. 1 in Basel. Penderecki has now abandoned concentrated textural composition, cultivating instead his individual brand of neo-Romanticism.

1 May Arvo Pärt's *Cantus in memoriam Benjamin Britten* for strings and bell is first performed in Tallinn. This year also marks the composition of the double concerto *Tabula Rasa* for two violins, strings and prepared piano, and the first of his *Fratres*, for chamber ensemble. These represent the first significant works of a style he terms 'Tintinnabuli' (from the Latin word for 'bells').

5 May Boulez and three further conductors introduce **Crumb**'s ambitious, spatially organised oratorio *Star-Child* at New York's Avery Fisher Hall.

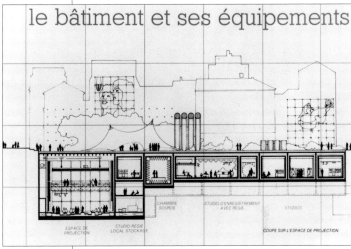

le bâtiment et ses équipements

7 July Tippett's opera *The Ice Break* opens at Covent Garden. This year also sees the première of the composer's Symphony No. 4 in Chicago

8 August Stockhausen's inter-planetary semi-drama *Sirius* is performed complete for the first time, in Aix-en-Provence. The composer will later write, 'It is an inner revelation that has come several times to me, that I have been educated on Sirius, that I come from Sirius.'

13 September British-born conductor **Leopold Stokowski** dies in Nether Wallop, Hampshire, aged 95.

30 November Takemitsu takes inspiration from Japanese tradition in his orchestral work *A Flock Descends into the Pentagonal Garden*, premièred in San Francisco.

21 December The Orchestre National de France introduces *Jonchaies* by **Xenakis**, in Paris. This year also marks the composer's *Akanthos* for soprano and octet.

1977 James Earl Carter takes office as 39th President of the USA • Spain holds its first free parliamentary elections for 41 years • 81-year-old Morarji Desai of the Janata coalition succeeds Mrs Indira Gandhi as Indian Prime Minister • In an unexpected peace move, President Sadat of Egypt visits Israel and addresses the Knesset • South Africa clamps down on opposition to its apartheid policies, detaining many black leaders and banning *The World Newspaper* • Nasa launches the Voyager spacecraft program • Film: *Annie Hall* (Woody Allen); *Star Wars* (George Lucas) • Dennis Potter (Eng): play *Brimstone and Treacle* • John Ashbery (US): poems *Houseboat Days*

1978

Pärt continues his 'tintinnabuli' style in *Spiegel im Spiegel* for piano and violin. It will become his best known composition.

11 February Xenakis introduces his ear-splitting textural tape work *La Légende d'Eer* complete with laser display in 'Le Diatope', a temporary building of his own design, erected for the opening of the Centre Georges Pompidou in Paris.

12 April Ligeti satirises 1960s hedonism in his opera *Le grand macabre* (right), introduced with great success at the Royal Opera in Stockholm. A prelude for 12 car horns introduces a sequence of events concerning sexual desire, politics, excessive drinking and death.

1 May Composer **Aram Khachaturian** dies in Moscow, aged 74.

17 May Philips unveils the musical medium of the future: the Compact Disc, invented by James T. Russell.

9 July Aribert Reimann's brutish opera *Lear*, with **Dietrich Fischer-Dieskau** in the lead role, opens in Munich.

30 November Sallinen attracts international attention with his opera *Punainen viiva* (The Red Line), first staged in Helsinki.

8 December John Adams conducts his minimalist *Shaker Loops* for seven strings at Hellman Hall in San Francisco.

10 December Carter's setting of John Ashbery's *Syringa*, scored for two voices and chamber orchestra, is first performed in New York.

1979

Pettersson finishes his last (completed) symphony, No. 16, scored for alto saxophone and orchestra.

20 January George Rochberg seeks a naturalistic blend of harmonic languages in his *Concord* String Quartets, Nos. 4–6, premièred at the University of Pennsylvania, Philadelphia.

24 February Boulez conducts the first complete performance of Berg's opera *Lulu*, in Paris. The Austrian composer and conductor **Friedrich Cerha** has completed Act 3, working from the composer's sketches.

1 March Sondheim's *Sweeney Todd, the Demon Barber of Fleet Street* is introduced at the Uris Theatre, New York.

8 March The 26-year-old **Wolfgang Rihm** charts a playwright's descent into madness in his chamber opera *Jakob Lenz* (after Georg Büchner's *Lenz*), premièred with great success in Hamburg.

6 September Oliver Knussen's Symphony No. 3, commissioned by the BBC, is first performed under **Michael Tilson Thomas** at the Royal Albert Hall during the London Proms season.

22 September Finding order from disparate fragments, **Robin Holloway**'s Second Concerto for Orchestra premières in Glasgow.

20 October Cage's *Roaratorio: an Irish circus on Finnegans Wake*, based on James Joyce's final novel, is performed for the first time in Donaueschingen. The work incorporates recordings of both sounds and traditional music at locations around Ireland, referred to by Joyce.

22 October World-renowned music instructor **Nadia Boulanger** dies in Paris, aged 92.

1978 Pieter Willem Botha becomes Prime Minister of South Africa • Vietnam invades Cambodia • Polish cardinal Karol Wojtyla elected pope (John Paul II): first non-Italian pope in over four centuries • First 'test tube' baby is born, in Britain • Space Invaders becomes the world's first arcade game • Iris Murdoch (Ire/UK): *The Sea, the Sea*

1979 Exiled Religious leader Ayotollah Komeini returns to Iran • Margaret Thatcher becomes Britain's first woman Prime Minister • Landmark Israel-Egypt peace treaty is signed in Washington, D.C. • Military dictator Idi Amin flees Uganda • Lord Mountbatten assassinated by IRA • Mother Teresa awarded Nobel Peace Prize

3 January **Lutosławski**'s *Epitaph for oboe and piano* is performed for the first time, at London's Wigmore Hall.

17 January **Sessions**, aged 83, has his Symphony No. 9 (1978) premièred in Syracuse, New York.

2 March Commissioned by Polish Radio, **Górecki**'s motoric Concerto for Harpsichord and String Orchestra débuts in Katowice, Poland

5 March **George Benjamin**, aged 20, introduces his diaphanous *Ringed by the Flat Horizon* for chamber orchestra, in Cambridge, England. A London première follows at a BBC Promenade concert in August.

7 April Georgian composer **Giya Kancheli** presents his Sixth Symphony in Tbilisi.

8 April **Robert Simpson** reflects the emergence and development of life, applying thematic metamorphoses in his Symphony No. 6, introduced in London under **Sir Charles Groves**.

23 April **Schnittke**'s Second Symphony (*St Florian*), a setting of the mass for soloists, chorus and orchestra, premières in London. This year the Russian composer writes his Third Symphony.

18 May **Von Einem** and his librettist-wife **Lotte Ingrisch** create a national scandal in Vienna with their mystery opera *Jesu Hochzeit* (Jesus' Wedding). Sexually-charged moments involving Christ with a female representation of death lead to severe criticism from the Catholic Church. The work is withdrawn.

24 May **Takemitsu** creates his self-described 'sea of tonality' with *Far Calls, Coming, far!* for violin and orchestra, premièred in Tokyo.

2 June **Nono** considers the metaphysical question of 'being' in his string quartet *Fragmente–Stille, an Diotima*, first given in Bonn.

18 June **Barenboim** conducts the first performance of **Boulez**'s *Notations I–IV* for orchestra, in Paris.

21 July *Gondwana*, by the French composer **Tristan Murail**, is introduced at the Darmstadt Festival. One of the early masterpieces of spectralism, its textural waves and eruptions evoke the geological upheaval of continental drift.

22 August **Tippett**'s Triple Concerto for Violin, Viola and Cello is introduced at the London Proms under **Colin Davies**.

24 August **Paul Sacher** directs the première of **Lutosławski**'s Double Concerto for oboe, harp and chamber orchestra at the Lucerne Festival. Taking part are the oboist and composer **Heinz Holliger** and his wife, harpist **Ursula Holliger**.

2 September The one-act chamber opera *The Lighthouse*, with music and libretto by **Maxwell Davies**, opens in Edinburgh. Three keepers are taunted by ghosts from their past in a story based on the mysterious desertion of the Flannan Isles lighthouse (Outer Hebrides) in 1900.

5 September **Glass**, having been asked by Netherlands Opera for a 'real opera', turns to the early political life of Gandhi in *Satyagraha*. Staged in Rotterdam, the minimalist opera creates a universal relevance to Gandhi's ideology of 'passive resistance' by invoking the sympathetic figures of Tolstoy (with whom Gandhi corresponded), the writer and philosopher Rabindranath Tagore, and Martin Luther King.

8 October **Galina Ustvolskaya**'s Second Symphony *True and Eternal Bliss*, for boy speaker and small orchestra, débuts in Leningrad.

30 October **Edison Denisov**'s non-religious *Requiem* for soprano, tenor, chorus and orchestra premières in Moscow.

1980 Robert Mugabe becomes Prime Minister of newly-independent Zimbabwe (formerly Rhodesia) • Earthquake in Algeria kills 20,000 • Long-standing Yugoslavian President Josip Broz Tito dies • Lech Walesa becomes chairman of the Polish Solidarity Free Trade Union • Iraq invades Iran beginning the Iran-Iraq War (until 1988) • General Kenan Evren leads a military coup in Turkey • Reinhold Messner (It) makes first solo ascent of Mount Everest, achieved without supplementary oxygen • Ex-Beatle John Lennon assassinated • Helen Frankenthaler (US) paints *Cameo* • Salman Rushdie (Ind/UK): *Midnight's Children* • Umberto Eco (It): *The Name of the Rose* • Carl Sagan: *Cosmos* (TV series/book)

Andriessen completes his sonorous and textrual *De Tijd* (Time), scored for female chorus and large ensemble.

14 January György Kurtág (left) seals his international reputation with *Messages of the Late Miss R.V. Troussova* for soprano and chamber ensemble, introduced at IRCAM, in Paris.

23 January Composer **Samuel Barber** dies from cancer in New York, aged 70.

15 March Stockhausen premières *Donnerstag* (Thursday) at La Scala, Milan. Launching his projected seven-part operatic *Licht* (Light) cycle, the work explores the childhood and musical awakening of archangel Michael, son of Eve and Lucifer, and his desire to become incarnate as a human being. *Donnerstag* concludes with five trumpeters performing a 'Thursday Farewell' from nearby rooftops and balconies as the audience leaves the building.

15 April Adams's first large-scale mature work, *Harmonium* for chorus and orchestra, is first performed in San Francisco.

20 September Reich introduces *Tehillim* for voices and chamber ensemble, in New York. Featuring Hebrew settings of verses from four psalms, the work reflects Reich's growing interest in his Jewish heritage.

18 October Boulez conducts the first version of his IRCAM project *Répons* in Donaueschingen, scored for two pianos, orchestra and electronics.

29 November Colin Matthews has his Oboe Quartet No. 1 premiered in Nottingham.

William Bolcom completes his magnum opus, the three-hour *Songs of Innocence and Experience*.

Conlon Nancarrow, renowned for his rhythmically complex Player Piano studies, becomes the first composer to receive a maximum 'genius' award of $300,000 from the American MacArthur Foundation.

Pärt composes his *St John Passion*.

26 February Adams conducts the première of his *Grand Pianola Music* for orchestra before a 'befuddled audience' (according to the composer), in San Francisco.

29 March Composer and influential music educator **Carl Orff** dies in Munich, aged 86.

5 May Ellen Taaffe Zwilich (right) has her Symphony No. 1 premièred under **Gunther Schuller** in New York. The following year Zwilich gains a Pulitzer Prize for the work, becoming the first female recipient of the award.

20 October Sofia Gubaidulina's *Seven Last Words* for cello, bayan (a Russian accordion) and strings is introduced at the Moscow Conservatory under the title *Partita*. Soviet authorities have censored the Christian title of the work.

11 November The draft copy of Stravinsky's *The Rite of Spring* is auctioned off at Southeby's for £330,000 to the Paul Sacher Collection in Basel.

3 December Jonathan Harvey's *Bhakti*, for 15 players and tape, premières at IRCAM in Paris.

1981 Ronald Reagan becomes 40th president of the USA • France abolishes the death penalty (and with it, the guillotine) • Egyptian President Anwar Sadat assassinated • Space Shuttle 'Colombia' launched • Britain's last American mainland colony, Belize, gains independence • AIDS virus identified • Britain's Prince Charles marries Lady Diana Spencer

1982 Falklands War: Argentina invades the Falkland Islands; Britain sends task force and gains swift victory • Death of President Brezhnev (USSR); Yuri Andropov succeeds him • Israel invades Lebanon, beginning First Lebanon War • First artificial human heart implanted, in Utah • Film: *Blade Runner* • Michael Jackson (US) releases album *Thriller*

American modernist composer **Charles Wuorinen** contributes to the virtuoso concerto repertory with his breathtaking Piano Concerto No. 3.

11 January Penderecki's Cello Concerto No. 2 is introduced in Berlin with **Rostropovich** as soloist.

8 March Composer **Sir William Walton** dies on the island of Ischia, aged 80.

17 June Bernstein's *A Quiet Place*, his last opera, opens in Houston. It has been jointly commissioned by the Kennedy Center, the Houston Grand Opera and La Scala.

23 July 'Les Six' composer **Georges Auric** dies in Paris, aged 84.

29 September Lutosławski (right) has his Symphony No. 3 introduced under **Sir Georg Solti** with the Chicago Symphony Orchestra. It becomes one of the most popular symphonies composed in the final quarter of the century.

7 November Germaine Tailleferre, the last surviving member of 'Les Six', dies in Paris, aged 91.

28 November Messiaen's first and last opera, *Saint François d'Assise*, premières at the Paris Opéra. Composed over a period of eight years to his own libretto, the four-and-a-half-hour work divides critics, though audience reaction during the 11-performance run is extremely favourable.

4 December The Kronos Quartet gives **Feldman**'s sparse String Quartet No. 2 a four-hour première in Toronto. The full version of the work, which runs as continuous music, lasts around six hours.

Polish-Russian composer **Moisey Weinberg** completes his Symphony No. 18 'War, there is no word more cruel'.

17 March Reich takes a rare break from ensemble-sized forces in *The Desert Music*, scored for chorus and orchestra. The cantata is broadcast live from Cologne.

24 March Glass explores ancient Egyptian themes in *Akhnaten*, staged for the first time in Stuttgart. The opera completes his historical triptych of 'religion, orthodoxy and reaction'. (See also *Einstein*, 1976 and *Satyagraha*, 1980.)

5 April Tippett's *The Mask of Time* for solo voices, chorus and orchestra, is premièred in Boston. The composer states that the work 'deals with those fundamental matters that bear upon man, his relationship with time, his place in the world as we know it and in the mysterious universe at large'.

25 May *Samstag* (Saturday), the second opera of **Stockhausen**'s *Licht* (Light) cycle, premières in Milan.

7 August Berio recasts Shakespeare's Prospero in his 'musical action' *Un re in ascolto* (A Listening King), first staged in Salzburg.

25 September Claudio Abbado directs the première of **Nono**'s *Prometeo* in Venice. The so-called 'tragedy of listening' requires four chamber orchestras, vocal and instrumental soloists, choir, and live electronics with surround-sound design.

28 September Penderecki writes from the heart to his suffering compatriots in the *Polish Requiem*, introduced under **Rostropovich** in Stuttgart.

1983 Soviets shoot down a Korean Airlines flight for invasion of air space; 269 passengers killed, including 81 South Koreans and 61 Americans • President Regan announces defensive 'Star Wars' program • Christo (Bulg/US) and Jeanne-Claude (Fr/US) unveil *Surrounded Islands* in Miami's Biscayne Bay, using 6.5 million sq ft of floating pink fabric

1984 Ethiopian famine claims around one million lives • Indian PM Indira Ghandi assassinated by her Sikh bodyguards, shortly after ordering a raid on a temple in Amritsar • IRA bomb Conservative Party conference: five die, 34 injured • Apple computers launch the Macintosh • Milan Kundera (Czech) publishes *The Unbearable Lightness of Being*

Dutilleux completes his Violin Concerto, *L'arbre des songes* (Tree of Dreams), composed for **Isaac Stern**.

French spectralist **Gérard Grisey** completes his magnum opus: *Les espaces acoustiques*, a cycle of six pieces incorporating ever-increasing forces, evolving from *Prologue* (1976), a movement for solo viola, through to *Epilogue* for full orchestra.

Schnittke writes his Viola Concerto for **Yuri Bashmet**. During the summer the composer suffers his first stroke.

18 January Lutosławski's *Partita* for violin and piano is first given in St Paul, Minnesota. The composer's *Chain 2*, a 'dialogue' for violin and orchestra, is completed this year.

19 April Goehr's opera *Behold the Sun* is first staged in Duisburg, Germany.

1 June Akira Kurosawa's epic film *Ran* is released in Japan, with music by **Takemitsu**.

13 July Singer-songwriters **Bob Geldof** and **Midge Ure** launch *Live Aid* to raise funds for millions starving in Ethiopia. Staged chiefly in London and Philadelphia, the so-billed 'Global Jukebox' is the largest music event in history, watched by an audience of around 1.5 billion and raising more than $100m.

9 September An oratorio on the life of Bach in the manner of Bach's own Passions, **Kagel**'s *Sankt-Bach-Passion* is first performed in Berlin.

13 October British composer **John Rutter** introduces his Requiem at the United Methodist Church, Dallas, Texas.

Malcolm Arnold completes his ninth and final symphony.

American composer **Joan Tower** composes her dynamic *Silver Ladders* for orchestra, a work that will later gain her a $150,000 Grawemeyer award. She also writes her *Fanfare for the Uncommon Woman* (No. 1) for brass and percussion.

21 May *The Mask of Orpheus* (1984), by **Birtwistle** (left), opens at the London Coliseum. The complex atonal opera receives immense critical praise and proves a turning point in the composer's career. This year also sees the first performance of his 'mechanical pastoral' *Yan Tan Tethera* and the completion of *Earth Dances* for orchestra.

13 June Adams's exhilarating orchestral miniature *Short Ride in a Fast Machine* is first performed in Mansfield, Massachusetts.

28 September Anthony Davis's first opera, *X: the Life and Times of Malcolm X*, receives its official première in New York.

9 October Andrew Lloyd Webber's *Phantom of the Opera* opens at Her Majesty's Theatre in London. The musical begins its run on Broadway 15 months later, with other productions following worldwide. It becomes the most financially successful musical work of all time.

27 October Michael Nyman presents his chamber opera *The Man Who Mistook His Wife for a Hat* at the Institute of Contemporary Arts, London. The libretto, by **Christopher Rawlence**, is based on an actual neurological case study.

1985 Mikhail Gorbachev becomes Soviet leader • Mexico City earthquake claims around 10,000 lives; leaves tens of thousands homeless • British scientist Dr Joe Farman identifies ozone hole over Antarctica • Boris Becker (Ger), aged 17, becomes youngest ever men's Wimbledon champion • Gabriel García Márquez (Colomb): *Love in the Time of Cholera*

1986 A nuclear reactor explodes at Chernobyl, Ukraine; Soviet authorities deny any cause for concern • Space Shuttle Challenger explodes 73 seconds after lift-off, killing its seven crew members • Corporal punishment is abolished in British schools • Film: *Jean de Florette* and *Manon des Sources* (Fr) • Mark Tansey (US) paints *Forward Retreat*

1987

8 July *A Night at the Chinese Opera*, the first full-length opera by the Scottish composer **Judith Weir**, opens at the Everyman Theatre in Cheltenham.

10 August **Nicholas Maw**'s orchestral *Odyssey*, running in excess of 90 minutes without a break, is first performed at the London Proms.

3 September Modernist composer **Morton Feldman** dies from cancer in Buffalo, New York, aged 61.

17 September **Isang Yun**'s 5th symphony is premièred in Berlin with baritone **Dietrich Fischer-Dieskau** and the Berlin Philharmonic.

4 October **Rihm**'s opera *Oedipus*, based on his own libretto and drawing from Sophocles, Nietzsche and Heiner Müller, opens in Berlin.

7 October **Reich**'s *The Four Sections* is first performed by the San Francisco Symphony Orchestra.

22 October **John Adams** (left) and librettist **Alice Goodman** scrutinise Richard Nixon's 1972 meeting with Mao Zedong in *Nixon in China*, premièred in Houston. Though the opera does not garner critical favour, it is soon recognised as one of the most significant American stage works of recent times.

12 December **Cage**'s *Europera 1* and *Europera 2* are introduced by the Frankfurt Opera Company. They are the first two of five planned 'Europeras' in which indeterminacy is applied to music and stage production, including set design, lighting and costumes. Public response is mostly negative.

1988

Butterflies, dung beetles and grasshoppers are among the featured species of the *Insect Symphony*, the seventh symphony by Finnish composer **Kalevi Aho**.

14 January *Drill* for two pianos, by British composer **Steve Martland**, premières in Rotterdam, Holland.

29 February **Ligeti** draws on jazz-blues, Bartók and the complex textures of Nancarrow in his Piano Concerto, first performed in Vienna.

7 May **Stockhausen** celebrates Eve in his opera *Montag* (Monday), the third day of his *Licht* cycle, at La Scala, Milan.

17 June **Mark-Anthony Turnage** gains international acclaim with *Greek*, premièred at the Carl Orff Saal in Munich. Based on the play by Steven Berkoff, the two-act opera transposes the ancient Oedipus tale to London's East End.

24 July **Peter Sculthorpe** derives inspiration from Aboriginal chant in his ecological orchestral piece *Kakadu*, premièred in Colorado.

23 September **Jonathan Harvey**'s *Timepieces* for two conductors and orchestra premières in Saarbrucken, Germany.

2 November **Reich**'s *Different Trains* for string quartet and tape is introduced by the Kronos Quartet in London. The work contrasts the American train journeys made by the composer as a child with those made at the same time by condemned Jews in Nazi-occupied Europe. Reich incorporates 'sampled' testimonials—of his governess, a retired porter, and three holocaust survivors—to generate melodic and rhythmic subject matter.

21 November **Tavener**'s *Akathist of Thanksgiving*, for solo voices, chorus and orchestra, gives glory to God at Westminster Abbey, London.

· ·

1987 World population exceeds five billion • Soviet leader Gorbachev and President Reagan sign historic treaty to reduce nuclear arsenals • British Prime Minister Margaret Thatcher wins a third term • Black Monday: Dow Jones share index nose-dives initiating a global stock market crash • Toni Morrison (US): *Beloved*

1988 Benazir Bhutto becomes Prime Minister of Pakistan: first woman leader of a Muslim country • Islamic terrorists blow up a Pan Am 747 commercial jet over Lockerbie, Scotland; 270 people killed • Armenian earthquake claims over 25,000 lives • End of Iran-Iraq war • Physicist Stephen Hawking (Eng): *A Brief History of Time*

Finnish composer **Magnus Lindberg** pens *Kinetics*, the first work of an orchestral trilogy completed the following year with *Marea* and *Joy*.

Nancarrow composes his Concerto for Player Piano and Orchestra.

17 January Rihm incorporates light touches of music-theatre in his nervous Eighth String Quartet, first played by the Arditti Quartet in Milan. The players appear to revise the score by correcting, erasing and rewriting passages. The prolific German composer enjoys several other premières this year, including *Schwebende Begegnung* (Floating Encounter) for orchestra (Ludwigshafen) and *Frau/Stimme* (Woman/Voice) for 'soprano and orchestra with second soprano' (Donaueschingen).

2 February Zwilich's Tenor Trombone Concerto débuts under the direction of **Sir Georg Solti** in Chicago. This year marks the composition of her concertos for bass trombone and for flute.

20 May German composer **York Höller** allegorises 1930s Stalinism in the opera *Der Meister und Margarita* (The Master and Margarita), which is received enthusiastically at the Paris Opéra. The score features collage technique and combines live orchestra and tape.

16 July Conductor **Herbert von Karajan** dies in Anif, Austria, aged 81.

4 September Knussen conducts cellist **Steven Isserlis** and the BBC Symphony Orchestra in the première of **Tavener**'s *The Protecting Veil* during the London Proms. The cello part represents the Mother of God, whose songful presence is continuous throughout. Tavener's meditative 'lyrical ikon' becomes his most famous composition.

22 September Irving Berlin, Russian-born songwriter of such classics as *White Christmas, There's No Business Like Show Business, Cheek To*

Cheek and *Let's Face The Music And Dance*, dies in New York, aged 101.

5 October Carter's orchestral tryptich *Three Occasions* is premièred under **Knussen** with the BBC Symphony Orchestra at London's Royal Festival Hall.

27 October Tippett's fifth and final opera, *New Year*, opens at the Grand Opera in Houston. Determined to connect with contemporary culture, the 84-year-old English knight of the realm has infused his creation with stylised popular music, including rap.

23 December Bernstein directs a performance of Beethoven's Ninth Symphony at the Kaiser Wilhelm Kirche in West Berlin, in celebration of the fall of the Berlin Wall (below). On Christmas day the concert is repeated at the Schauspielhaus in East Berlin. Bernstein has made one significant change to the text: 'Freude' (joy) has become 'Freiheit' (freedom). A live television broadcast of the event reaches tens of millions around the world.

1989 George H. W. Bush takes office as 41st president of the USA • Soviet forces pull out of Afghanistan following nine-year occupation • Berlin Wall demolished • Playwright Václav Havel becomes President of Czechoslovakia following peaceful Velvet Revolution • F. W. de Klerk becomes State President of South Africa • Iranian leader Ayatollah Khomeini offers $3m reward to any Iranian who assassinates Salman Rushdie, author of *The Satanic Verses* • 96 Liverpool Football Club supporters crushed to death at Hillsborough Stadium British computer scientist Tim Berners-Lee invents the World Wide Web

1990

1 February The 75-year-old **Panufnik** builds his Symphony No. 10 to an abrasive brassy climax and concludes in devotional mood. Introduced under his own direction in Chicago, his final symphony has been commissioned for the centenary celebrations of the city's symphony orchestra.

15 March John Corigliano's Symphony No. 1, a heartfelt memorial to friends lost to AIDS, débuts under **Daniel Barenboim** with the Chicago Symphony Orchestra.

8 May Italian modernist composer **Luigi Nono** dies in Venice, aged 66.

17 May Antiquarian music specialists Otto Haas acquire the autographed manuscript of the first movement of Beethoven's Cello Sonata in A major (Op. 69) for £480,000, at Sotheby's.

27 May Schnittke's impassioned and demanding Cello Concerto No. 2 is premièred with **Rostropovich** as soloist in Evian, France.

22 August Scotsman **James MacMillan** wins critical acclaim with *The Confession of Isobel Gowdie*, introduced at the Royal Albert Hall during the London Proms season.

11 September *Alleluia* for boy soprano, chorus, organ and orchestra, by **Gubaidulina**, premières in the recently unified German city of Berlin.

14 October Leonard Bernstein dies in New York, aged 72. His extraordinary success both as a composer and conductor made him the most famous American in classical music.

19 October Ozawa directs the first performance of **Takemitsu**'s *From me flows what you call Time* for five percussionists and orchestra, in New York.

2 December Influential composer and conductor **Aaron Copland** dies in New York, aged 90.

1991

Terry Riley composes *June Buddhas* (based on Kerouac's poem *Mexico City Blues*) for chorus and orchestra, commissioned by the Koussevitzky foundation. This year also brings *The Sands*, a concerto for string quartet and orchestra, commissioned by the Salzburg Festival.

February Houston Grand Opera début *Atlas*, a metaphysical odyssey by **Meredith Monk**.

19 March Adams's second opera, *The Death of Klinghoffer*, based on the PLO hijacking of the *Achille Lauro* cruise ship in 1986, opens in Brussels. Accusations of anti-Semitism dog productions over ensuing years.

30 May Birtwistle's densely threaded Arthurian opera *Gawain* opens at Covent Garden, London. Some of the audience boo, but most applaud.

31 October Finnish composer **Kaija Saariaho** manipulates acoustic instruments and electronics in the ballet *Maa* (Earth), first danced in Helsinki.

21 November Ralph Shapey conducts the Chicago Symphony Orchestra in the first performance of his *Concerto Fantastique*. The work wins the vote of the Pulitzer Prize jury the following year, yet is denied by the board for lacking popular appeal.

19 December Corigliano and librettist **William M. Hoffman** create an opera within an opera in their Beaumarchais adaptation *The Ghosts of Versailles* (1987), premièred with tremendous success by New York's Metropolitan Opera (right). The Met originally commissioned the work for its 1983 centenary celebrations.

Prolific American composer **Alan Hovhaness** composes his final two symphonies, Nos. 66 and 67, both scored for strings, harp, timpani and percussion.

9 February Rihm's multi-layered tableaux opera *Die Eroberung von Mexico* (The Conquest of Mexico) opens in Hamburg.

25 February Sallinen's richly expressive opera *Kullervo* (1988) premières in Los Angeles.

28 April Influential composer **Olivier Messiaen** dies in Paris, aged 83. He had recently completed his hour-long, Revelation-inspired *Eclairs sur l'Au-delà* (Illuminations on the Beyond…) for 128-piece orchestra.

10 August *Veni, veni Emmanuel*, a Concerto for Percussion and Orchestra by **MacMillan**, is first performed with soloist **Evelyn Glennie** and the Scottish Chamber Orchestra at the Royal Albert Hall, London.

12 August Pioneering American composer **John Cage** dies in New York, aged 79.

8 October Ligeti (right) presents a late-career masterpiece with his Violin Concerto, introduced by its dedicatee, **Saschko Gawriloff**, in Cologne. Gawriloff creates a final movement cadenza from the concerto's discarded material.

12 October Glass's opera *Voyage* premières at the Metropolitan Opera House, New York. Commissioned by the Met in commemoration of the 500th anniversary of Columbus's arrival in the New World, it entertains the public far more than the critics.

5 February Lutosławski, aged 80, conducts the Los Angeles Philharmonic in the first performance of his Fourth Symphony.

24 February Henze's *Requiem* is given its first complete performance in Cologne.

16 May Reich and his wife, the video-artist **Beryl Korot**, present their 'documentary video opera' *The Cave*, in Vienna. Featuring video images, recorded interviews and a live ensemble, the work reflects the attitudes and feelings of Jews, Palestinian Muslims and a cross-section of Americans (including Christians) towards the biblical story of Abraham Sarah, Hagar, Ishmael and Isaac.

28 May Stockhausen's *Dienstag* (Tuesday) receives its first staged performance at the Leipzig Opernhaus. Depicting the day of war between Michael and Lucifer, it is the fourth opera of the composer's *Licht* (Light) cycle.

3 July Michael Berkeley draws on the childhood of Rudyard Kipling in *Baa Baa Black Sheep*, premièred by Opera North in Cheltenham.

8 September Composer-conductor **George Benjamin** premières **Unsuk Chin**'s fairy-tale inspired *Akrostichon-Wortspiel* (Acrostic Wordplay) for soprano and ensemble, complete for the first time, in London.

26 September Kathryn Stott is the soloist in **Nyman**'s *The Piano Concerto*, introduced at the Festival de Lille. The music derives from Nyman's popular film score to *The Piano* (1993).

2 December Gunther Schuller's *Of Reminiscences and Reflections* for large orchestra is welcomed in Louisville. A Pulitzer Prize-winner of 1994, it is a memorial to Schuller's wife, who died the previous year.

1992 War in former Yugoslavia continues; 'ethnic cleansing' carried out by Serbs, but atrocities committed on all sides • Conservatives win general election, returning John Major as Prime Minister • Maastricht (Neth) Treaty signed, establishing the European Union • El Salvador's 12-year civil war ends • Jeff Koons (US) creates 12-metre-high floral sculpture *Puppy*

1993 Czechoslovakia divides into independent Czech Republic and Slovakia • William J. Clinton takes office as 42nd president of the USA • Nelson Mandela and F. W. de Klerk receive Nobel Peace Prize • Israel and Palestine sign peace accord: Palestinians given limited autonomy in Gaza Strip and West Bank • Sebastian Faulks (Eng): *Birdsong*

Holmboe completes his Symphony No. 13, his final work in the genre.

January Superman comics and film music inspire **Michael Daugherty**'s thrilling *Metropolis* Symphony for Orchestra, premièred in Baltimore.

19 January Adams's modal Violin Concerto, scored with orchestra and two keyboard samplers, is introduced at the Ordway Music Theater, St Paul, Minnesota. Set in a traditional three-movement format with cadenza, the fantasia-like work enjoys widespread success.

9 February Polish composer **Witold Lutosławski** dies in Warsaw, aged 81.

10 February Schnittke's Symphony No. 7 makes its lyrical entrance in New York. The composer suffers a (third) stroke in the early summer, from which he will not fully recover. His Symphony No. 8 is introduced in Stockholm in November of this year.

20 April Judith Weir's chamber opera *Blond Eckbert*, based on a story by Ludwig Tieck, opens at London's Coliseum.

9 June Xenakis's earth-shattering orchestral piece *Dämmerschein* (Rays of Twilight) makes its entrance in Lisbon.

24 June Pärt's *Litany* for soloists, choir and orchestra premières at the Oregon Bach Festival. The composer's first American commission sets 24 short prayers by St John Chrysostom.

9 August Maxwell Davies derives inspiration from Sibelius in his Fifth Symphony, introduced under his own direction at the London Proms.

14 December Claudio Abbado conducts the first performance of **Kurtág**'s funereal *Stele* with the Berlin Philharmonic. Kurtág is at this time the orchestra's composer-in-residence.

20 January Thea Musgrave's opera *Simón Bolívar* opens in Norfolk, Virginia.

19 February Virtuosic in style and substance, **Wuorinen**'s modernist Piano Quintet is first played by **Ursula Oppens** and the Arditti String Quartet, in Chicago.

7 March The Ensemble InterContemperain premières **Reich**'s *City Life* for 18 musicians (with sampled city sounds and speech), in Metz, France.

23 April Rautavaara's popular Seventh Symphony (*Angel of Light*) débuts in Bloomington, Indiana.

24 June Dedicatee **Anne-Sophie Mutter** performs as soloist in **Penderecki**'s Violin Concerto No. 2, introduced in Leipzig.

26 June Four helicopters circle over Amsterdam, each with a member of the Arditti Quartet and a sound engineer, in the première of **Stockhausen**'s dream-inspired *Helicopter String Quartet*. Sounds from the helicopters, together with the performed parts (coordinated by click tracks), are transmitted down to the Westergasfabriek Theatre, together with live video links. The work forms part of *Mittwoch* (Wednesday) from his *Licht* opera cycle.

1 July British composer **Thomas Adès** draws considerable critical attention with his first opera, *Powder Her Face*, introduced at the Everyman Theatre in Cheltenham.

3 July Purcell meets jazz meets minimalism in **Martland**'s lively chamber work *Beat the Retreat*, first performed in Cheltenham to mark the tercentenary of Purcell's death.

16 September Birtwistle's atonal *Panic*, for saxophone, percussion and orchestra, is unleashed at the televised Last Night of the Proms in London. Thousands of affronted traditionalists do as the title suggests, jamming the BBC phone lines with complaints.

1994 Zapatista rebellion in Chiapas, Mexico • Civil war breaks out in Rwanda between Tutsis and Hutus • Nelson Mandela elected first black President of South Africa • Russia mounts attacks in breakaway republic of Chechnya, beginning a 20-month war • The Channel Tunnel opens • Church of England ordains its first woman priests

1995 World Trade Organisation established • Israeli Prime Minister Yitzhak Rabin assassinated by Jewish student • Jaques Chirac elected French President • Nick Leeson bankrupts Barings Bank • Damien Hirst wins the Turner Prize for *Mother and Child Divided* (cow and calf cut in two, preserved in formaldehyde)

20 February Japanese composer **Tōru Takemitsu** dies from cancer, aged 65, in Tokyo.

15 March Peter Eötvös's *Shadows*, a quasi-concerto for flute, clarinet (both amplified) and spatially displaced chamber orchestra, débuts in Ludwigshafen, Baden-Baden. This year the Hungarian composer begins work on his opera *Three Sisters*, commissioned by Opera National de Lyon.

28 April Birtwistle's *Pulse Shadows* for soprano, string quartet and ensemble gains critical praise in Witten, Germany.

7 May Tan Dun (right) fuses Eastern and Western musical traditions in his opera *Marco Polo*, premièred with great success in Munich. The libretto is by the music critic and writer **Paul Griffiths**.

18 May Glass presents *Les enfants terribles* in Zug, Switzerland. It is the last of his three dance operas to films by Cocteau, following *Orphée*, 1993, and *La belle et la bête*, 1994.

12 September Eve is tempted by Lucifer in **Stockhausen**'s opera *Freitag* (Friday—from his ongoing *Licht* cycle), first staged at the Leipzig Opernhaus.

15 September American composer **Michael Torke**, aged 34, draws inspiration from his country's musical idioms in the *Book of Proverbs* for soloists, chorus and orchestra, premièred in Utrecht, Holland.

2 October Berio questions human identity and morality in the music theatre work *Outis* (Nobody), inspired by Homer's Odyssey, first staged at La Scala, Milan.

11 January Henze's opera *Venus und Adonis* (1995) opens to critical acclaim at the Munich Staatsoper. This year also sees the première of his choral Ninth Symphony.

26 January Helmut Lachenmann's 'music with images' *Das Mädchen mit den Schwefelhölzern*, based on Hans Christian Andersen's *The Little Match Girl*, is introduced at the Hamburg Staatsoper. The work requires extended performance techniques, where instruments are manipulated in highly unconventional ways. The process itself is central to the visceral experience of the drama.

6 June South Korean composer **Unsuk Chin** has her Piano Concerto premièred at St David's Hall in Cardiff.

12 June Andriessen's *Trilogy of The Last Day*, scored for voices and chamber orchestra, receives its first performance in Cologne, under **Sian Edwards**.

1 July Tan Dun's *Symphony 1997: Heaven Earth Mankind* celebrates the reunification of Hong Kong with China. Premièred in the former British colony, the work is scored for solo cello, an array of Chinese instruments (including recently unearthed 2,400-year-old *bianzhong* bells), children's choir and orchestra.

1 October *Asyla* by **Adès** is first performed under **Simon Rattle** with the City of Birmingham Symphony Orchestra. The 26-year-old's first major orchestral piece wins a $200,000 Grawemeyer Award three years later.

9 October Seiji Ozawa introduces the variegated timbres and textures of **Dutilleux**'s *The Shadows of Time* with the Boston Symphony Orchestra.

1996 Taliban takes control of Afghanistan • Prince Charles and Princess Diana divorce • Dunblane (Scot) school shooting: 16 children and their teacher massacred by former Scout leader • Scientists successfully clone an animal: Dolly the sheep • Completion of Niterói Contemporary Art Museum, Rio de Janeiro, designed by Oscar Niemeyer (Braz)

1997 Bill Clinton begins second term as US President • 'New Labour' leader Tony Blair becomes Prime Minister of UK, ending 18 years of Conservative government • Hong Kong returns to China • Princess Diana dies in Paris car crash • NASA's 'Pathfinder' probe lands on Mars • J. K. Rowling (Eng): *Harry Potter and the Philosopher's Stone*

Glass's premières this year include *Days and Nights of Rochina* for orchestra (Vienna) and the opera *White Raven* (Lisbon).

8 January Composer **Sir Michael Tippett** dies in London, aged 93.

10 January The Lark Quartet introduces **Aaron Jay Kernis**'s String Quartet No. 2 in New York City.

22 January **Ned Rorem**'s 90-minute song cycle *Evidence of Things Not Seen*, for four singers and piano, is first performed in New York.

9 February St Francis of Assisi inspires **Sofia Gubaidulina** (right) in her optimistic *Canticle for the Sun* for cello, chamber choir and percussion, premièred in Frankfurt. The work is dedicated to the soloist, **Rostropovich**.

15 February Elgar's 'Sketches for Symphony No. 3 [1932–3], elaborated by **Anthony Payne**' premières with great success in London.

12 March **Esa-Pekka Salonen** conducts the first performance of **Lindberg**'s *Fresco*, in Los Angeles.

19 May Italy's **Salvatore Sciarrino** draws on the music of Claude Le Jeune in his sparsely scored opera *Luci mie traditrici* (My Treacherous Sight), premièred in Schwetzingen, Germany. The 70-minute chamber work is loosely based on the murderous antics of the Renaissance composer Prince Gesualdo, and demands a colourful array of extended instrumental techniques.

3 August Russian composer **Alfred Schnittke**, having recently suffered his fifth stroke, dies in Hamburg aged 63.

14 January **Weir**'s *Natural History* for soprano and orchestra, inspired by the Taoist writings of Chuang-Tzu, premières in Boston.

19 February **Adams**'s symphonic *Naïve and Sentimental Music* triumphs in Los Angeles under the direction of **Esa-Pekka Salonen**.

6 July Spanish composer **Joaquín Rodrigo** dies in Madrid, aged 97.

29 July *Aerial*, a trumpet concerto by **HK Gruber**, delights both the public and critics at the London Proms.

16 September Estonian composer **Erkki-Sven Tüür** mixes modernism and minimalism in his Violin Concerto, introduced in Frankfurt, Germany, with **Isabelle van Keulen** as soloist.

16 September *What Next?*, the first opera by the 90-year-old **Elliot Carter**, enjoys critical acclaim at the Staatsoper in Berlin. With libretto by **Paul Griffiths**, the short one-act work focuses on six characters as they emerge from the wreckage of a car crash.

20 October **Lachenmann** employs improvisation and extended instrumental techniques in *Nun*, a double concerto for flute and trombone, eight male voices and orchestra, premièred in Cologne.

1 December The Royal Opera House in Covent Garden reopens following a £218m revamp.

20 December **John Harbison**'s opera *The Great Gatsby* opens at the Metropolitan Opera, New York, to mixed reviews.

1998 Good Friday Agreement establishes a devolved Northern Irish assembly • Omagh bombing by 'Real IRA' in Northern Ireland kills 29 • Famine in Southern Sudan claims around 100,000 lives • The 'City of Arts and Sciences' opens in Valencia, Spain • Sculpture *Angel of the North* by Anthony Gormley (Eng) is unveiled in Gateshead

1999 World population reaches six billion • Super-cyclone in India kills over 10,000 and leaves 1.5 million homeless • Boris Yeltsin resigns as Russian president • Britain introduces minimum wage • Two students gun down 13 at Columbine High School, Co (US), before committing suicide • John M. Coetzee (SA/Australia) publishes *Disgrace*

The unstoppable nonagenarian **Elliot Carter** composes his Cello Concerto for **Yo-Yo Ma** and the Chicago Symphony Orchestra.

Henze completes his Tenth Symphony.

1 January Tan Dun's *2000 Today: a World Symphony for the Millennium* is broadcast worldwide by around 55 television networks.

4 January Tavener (right) considers creation, sin, redemption and hope in *Fall and Resurrection*, inspired by Byzantine chant and scored for soloists, chorus, ancient instruments and orchestra. Written in anticipation of the new millennium, the hour-long cantata receives a broadcast première at St Paul's Cathedral, London. Tavener is knighted later this year.

16 February Turnage's anti-war opera *The Silver Tassie*, with libretto by **Amanda Holden**, opens at London's Coliseum to wide critical acclaim.

17 February Contrasting scrambling virtuosity with lyrical beauty, the violin concerto *Contes de Fées* (Fairy Tales), by American composer **John Zorn**, is first played in New York.

6 March Poul Ruders's opera *The Handmaid's Tale*, based on the dystopian novel by Margaret Atwood, opens in Copenhagen.

18 April Berlin's Staatsoper mount the first performance of **Birtwistle**'s 'dramatic tableaux' *The Last Supper*.

7 June Penderecki's two-movement Sextet is introduced in Vienna with **Rostropovich** (cello) and **Yuri Bashmet** (viola) among the performers.

15 August Kaija Saariaho sets a story of idealised love in *L'amour de loin* (Love from Afar), her first opera, introduced with great success at the Salzburg Festival.

7 November Greek President Stephanopoulos presents to the composer and political activist **Mikis Theodorakis** the Alexander Onassis Foundation award of $250,000.

11 November Murail's textural *Winter Fragments*, scored for chamber ensemble with computer-generated sounds, premières in the picturesque town of Annecy, France. The work is dedicated to the memory of his friend and fellow 'spectral' composer Gérard Grisey, who died two years previously.

30 November Corigliano's Symphony No. 2 for string orchestra is first performed under **Ozawa** with the Boston Symphony Orchestra. It gains the composer a Pulitzer Prize the following year.

15 December John Adams suggests a spiritual storm in his nativity oratorio *El Niño*, introduced at the Théâtre du Châtelet, Paris, under **Kent Nagano**, with **Dawn Upshaw**, **Lorraine Hunt Lieberson** and **Willard White** in principal roles. A silent film by **Peter Sellars** (co-librettist with Adams) accompanies the performance.

2000 Vladimir Putin is elected Russian president • Vicente Fox Quesada of the National Action Party becomes Mexican president; ends 71 years of PRI government • George W. Bush wins the US presidential election • India's population passes one billion • America Online announces decision to buy Time Warner: the completed $162 acquisition (2001) is the largest in corporate history • Global stock markets go into freefall as the 'dot-com bubble' bursts • Air France Concorde Flight 4590 crashes, killing all 109 on board and four on the ground • Tate Modern art gallery opens in London • Zadie Smith (Eng): *White Teeth* • Margaret Atwood (Can): *The Blind Assassin*

Postlude

The contemporary composer

THE CONTEMPORARY classical music composer no longer enjoys the ecclesiastical importance of a Palestrina or Bach, nor the cultural significance of a Beethoven, Verdi or Sibelius. After World War I, when objective approaches to music displaced the subjective Romantic mindset, contemporary composers *en masse* began to alienate the wider public, and subsequently the 'museum' concert programme flourished. One critic, writing for *The Times* in 1935, summed up the *zeitgeist*: '… taste seems to have changed comparatively little in these last 25 years, for though new composers, native and foreign, have arisen … the general orchestral repertory remains very much today what [it was] before the War.' The principal difference, he noted, was that 'Bach, Handel, Mozart and Haydn take a larger place in the programmes than they did in days when Strauss, Debussy, Elgar, Delius and others were fascinating everyone'. While some composers strived to reach out to the general public—Vaughan Williams and Walton in Britain, for example—others rejected popular opinion, even insisting that they would be acclaimed by a 'later age'. Of his own music Anton Webern declared: 'In 50 years one will find it obvious, children will understand it and sing it.' More than 50 years on, most *adults* do not understand it, let alone sing it. One reason for this is that the grammar of atonal music typically changes from one piece to the next. There is, furthermore, a disorientating multiplicity of contemporary musical styles. Little surprise, then, that the latter half of the 20th century witnessed an insatiable public appetite for dead composers.

Even if we do not agree with Sir John Barbirolli's estimation of modern music—'Three farts and a raspberry, orchestrated'—we might be concerned with the present-day scene. If countless composers are speaking in different musical languages then we get a Babel effect, and the chance of intelligible communication becomes ever more remote. On one level, this reflects our fragmented society, the 'me' culture, and a tendency towards moral relativism. Postmodern aesthetics that encourage stylistic free-for-alls only seem to reinforce the point. On the other hand, we can see that the contemporary musical scene at once reflects personal expression, freedom of speech and multi-culturalism. It is at the same time combatting the charge of elitism, as styles merge, subjectivity and tonality

◀ The Music Center's Walt Disney Concert Hall in Los Angeles. Designed by Frank Gehry, the venue opened in 2003 and is now home of the Los Angeles Philharmonic Orchestra.

◀ Thomas Adès conducting his *Piano Concerto with Moving Image: 'In Seven Days'*, composed 2008.

Postlude

▲ The South Korean-born composer Unsuk Chin. A pupil of Ligeti, she has demonstrated an astonishing sensitivity to sonority and texture in a range of expressive pieces that draw on Eastern/Western aesthetics and past epochs.

return to 'serious' music, and popular influences from around the world become assimilated.

So we could, in fact, view the state of contemporary classical music very positively. Musical pluralism often celebrates differences and synthesises resources, encouraging an inspiring view of social and ethnic diversity. Tan Dun's remarkably wide-ranging *Symphony 1997 (Heaven Earth Mankind)*, composed in celebration of the reunification of Hong Kong with China, is one of the more prominent examples of East-West fusion. Purpose and meaning preoccupy such diverse composers as Sofia Gubaidulina, Arvo Pärt and James MacMillan, who offer spiritual themes and reflections that resonate even with a non-church-going public. Peter Maxwell Davies, Australia's Brett Dean and America's John Luther Adams have brought attention to ecological issues, while socio-political concerns are familiar to the music of John Adams (recently in his salutary opera *Dr Atomic*, 2005), Anthony Davis, Aaron Jay Kernis and the Danish composer Poul Ruders. Women composers are increasingly acknowledged: Gubaidulina, Ellen Zwilich, Kaija Saariaho, Judith Weir and Unsuk Chin rank among the most significant figures of contemporary music. As for the very boundaries of style and language, innovators of both sexes, including York Höller, Tristan Murail, Magnus Lindberg, Saariaho and Chin, have demonstrated that analytical approaches to acoustic and electronic music remain a foremost concern at the outset of the third millennium. (It is a fascinating study to see how many techniques in pop music, from synthesising and sampling to looping and sound morphing, have their origins in the experiments of classical composers.) And of course virtually all composers continue to write music for entertainment—whether this corresponds to the richly complex works of Brian Ferneyhough and James Dillon, the contemporary modernism of Charles Wuorinen and Australia's Liza Lim, the avant-gardism of Peter Eötvös, Austria's Olga Neuwirth and Germany's Jörg Widmann, or the more intuitive and capricious styles of Wolfgang Rihm, Thomas Adès and Erkki-Sven Tüür.

Ideally, the process of composition is emotionally or intellectually cathartic. Beyond this, the contemporary composer may seek to be, in any combination, a commentator, activist, comforter, motivator, facilitator, mystic, evangelist, therapist, educator, innovator and entertainer. There are more composers now than there have ever been: the competition for performances and recognition is daunting. This state of affairs is made all the more challenging by the prevalence of museum pieces in radio schedules, in opera houses and concert halls. Moreover, state-sponsorship—the critical form of modern patronage—appears in many countries to be facing perennial cuts. If art-music is to continue to survive without making saccharine commercial compromises it obviously needs our support. And support it we should, because masterpieces are still being written for those prepared to listen.

Glossary of musical terms

absolute music Music composed without reference to literature, images or any other extra-musical stimuli (in contrast to *programmatic music*).

a capella Vocal music sung without instrumental *accompaniment*.

accompaniment Any complementary part to the voices or instrument bearing the principal part (or parts) in a musical composition. It is *ad libitum* when the piece can be performed without it, and *obbligato* when it is necessary to the piece.

acoustics The science of sound and perception; encompasses matters of sound sources, space (room/environment) and hearing.

adagio Slow, leisurely; a slow *movement*. *A. assai*, *a. molto*, very slow; *a. non molto* or *non tanto*, not too slow.

ad libitum 'At will'. A direction signifying that:
(1) performers may choose their own tempo or expression; or
(2) a vocal or instrumental part may be left out.

aeolian mode The mode corresponding to the *scale* from A to A on the white keys of the piano.

Agnus Dei See *Mass ordinary*.

air or **ayre** Melody, tune; also, a song. *Airs detaches*, single numbers taken from operas, etc.

aleatory music From the Latin *alea*, 'dice'. Music fashioned to some extent by chance procedures. A score created with aleatory techniques may or may not include *indeterminacy* in performance. Also called 'chance music'.

allegro Lively, brisk, rapid. An allegro (*movement*) is not quite as fast as a *presto*. *Allegro assai*, *a. di molto*, very fast (usually faster than the foregoing movement); *a. ma non troppo*, fast, but not too fast.

allemande 1. A German dance in moderate *duple time*.
2. A stylised dance of the Baroque *suite*, appearing either first or following the *prelude*.

alto 1. The deeper of the two main divisions of women's or boys' voices, the *soprano* being the higher. Also called *contralto*. Ordinary *compass* from g to f2; in voices of great range, down to d and up to c2, or even higher.
2. An instrument of similar compass; as the alt-horn.
3. The *countertenor* voice.
4. The viola.

antecedent An unresolved *phrase* that is 'answered' by a *consequent*, which typically brings about harmonic balance. See also *periodic phrasing*.

anthem A piece of *liturgical* (sacred) vocal music usually based on biblical words, with or without instrumental *accompaniment*.

Glossary

antiphon Originally, a responsive system of plainsong by two choirs (or divided choir), an early feature of Christian worship; later applied to responsive or alternated singing, *chanting* or *intonation* in general, as practiced in the Greek, Roman, Anglican and Lutheran churches. Also, a short sentence, generally from Holy Scripture, sung before and after the psalm or canticle in the Latin service.

aria An *air*, song, melody. The *grand* or *da-capo aria* is in three divisions:
(1) *Theme*, fully developed;
(2) a more tranquil and richly harmonised second section; and
(3) a repetition *da capo* of the first, with more florid *ornamentation*.

arioso In vocal music, a style between *recitative* and the *aria*.

arpeggio Notes of *broken chords* played in succession.

atonal [**atonality**] The absence of *tonality*. Music in which traditional *tonal* structures are abandoned completely.

augmentation Doubling or generally increasing the time value of the notes of a *theme* or *motive*, often in imitative *counterpoint*.

ballad 1. A medieval dance-song (i.e. a song intended for a dance accompaniment)
2. A simple narrative poem, generally meant to be sung.
3. A simple, popular song.

ballade 1. A popular type of medieval French song (*chanson*), characterised by fixed-form refrain poetry and often relating to courtly love.
2. A composition in narrative style. Chopin first applied the term, to four of his lyrical and dramatic piano pieces.

ballad opera An opera chiefly made up of *ballads* and folk songs.

bar 1. A vertical line dividing *measures* on the *staff*, indicating (unless otherwise noted) that the strong beat falls on the note just after it.
2. Popular name for the measure.

baritone The male voice between *bass* and *tenor*.

bass 1. The lowest *tone* in a *chord*, or the lowest part in a composition.
2. The lowest male voice; ordinary *compass* from F to e1 (or d).

bass [**instrument**] (a) an old bowed instrument between the violoncello and double bass, with five or six strings; (b) the same as 'Kontrabass' (double bass)

basso continuo 1. An Italian invention of the early Baroque, presenting a written out bass line with harmonies (chords) indicated only by numerals and accidentals. The harmonies are commonly 'realised' on lute or keyboard instruments. (See *figured bass*.)
2. The instrument or instrumental group that provides the bass line and chordal accompaniment of a figured bass composition.

bel canto (It.) Beautiful singing, marked by vocal agility and beauty of *tone*, and clarity of melodic line. Exemplified in much nineteenth-century Italian opera.

binary form A form comprising two distinct sections (A–B), both of which are normally repeated.

bitonality The simultaneous use of two different keys (*tonalities*), such as C major and F sharp major.

bolero 1. A Spanish national dance in *triple time* and lively *tempo* (allegretto), the dancer accompanying his or her steps with castanets.
2. A composition in bolero style.

bourée A dance probably of French origin in rapid *tempo*, having two sections of eight *measures* each in *duple time*. The stylised variant sometimes found in the Baroque *suite* has a moderate to fast tempo.

branle An old French group dance in *duple time* featuring side-steps. Men and women in pairs form a circle or line, join hands, and take the lead in turn. Eng., *brawl*.

brass [**instruments**] Metal instruments with a cup-shaped or conical mouth piece and flared bell. Standard orchestral brass: French horn, trumpet, trombone, tuba.

breve A note equal to two *semibreves*, or *whole notes*; the longest used in modern notation.

broken chords *Chords* whose notes are sounded in succession, not together. See *arpeggio*.

burden Principally, a *chorus* or refrain, repeated after each stanza of a song or hymn. English term in common usage during 15th and 16th centuries.

cabaletta In Italian Romantic opera, the concluding section of an *aria*, forming a showy summary marked by repeated rhythms in rapid tempo.

cadence The close or ending of a *phrase* or section. *Authentic* or *perfect c.*, a cadence in which the penultimate *chord* is the *dominant*, and the final chord is the *tonic* (also *full c.*); *half* or *imperfect c.*, a cadence coming to rest on the dominant (also *half close*); *plagal c.*, the *subdominant* chord followed by the tonic; *avoided, broken, deceptive, evaded,* or *false c.*, a cadence that settles on an unexpected chord.

cadenza 1. In a vocal *solo*, a brilliant passage, often performed near the end.
2. In a *concerto*, a virtuosic passage or fantasia near the end of the first or last *movement*, played by the soloist.

canon The strictest form of musical *imitation*, in which two or more parts take up, in succession, the given subject note for note. See also *fugue*.

cantata A vocal work with instrumental *accompaniment*, consisting of *choruses* and *solos*, *recitatives*, duets, etc.; may be sacred or secular.

cantor The leading singer in German Protestant church services or in Jewish synagogues.

cantus firmus A fixed or given melody (such as a *plainsong* tune), often set in long note values, providing the structural basis for a *polyphonic* composition. Popular in Renaissance music.

canzona (It., 'song') Most commonly, an instrumental piece (*solo* or *ensemble*) modeled on a vocal form. Popular during the 16th and early 17th century, but superseded by the *sonata*.

canzonetta A light air or song; a short *part-song* marked by dance rhythms.

caprice or **capriccio** An instrumental piece free in form, distinguished by originality in harmony and rhythm. *A capriccio*, at pleasure.

cassation An 18th-century instrumental *suite*, similar to the divertimento and serenade.

castrato (pl., **castrati**) Male singer castrated before puberty to preserve his *alto* or *soprano* vocal range. Popular in mid-to late-Baroque opera.

Glossary

catch A *round* or *canon* for three or more voices, each singer having to 'catch' or take up his part at the right instant. Catches are generally humorous (e.g. 'Three Blind Mice').

cavatina A song; particularly, a short *aria* without a second section or *da capo*.

celesta Percussion instrument invented by Mustel in Paris, 1886, consisting of tuned steel bars connected to a keyboard. Tchaikovsky's 'Dance of the Sugar Plum Fairies' from his *Nutcracker Suite* is one of the best-known works featuring this instrument.

chaconne 1. A lively dance originating in Latin America during the 16th century.
2. An instrumental piece consisting of a series of *variations* above a *ground bass*, in slow *triple time* (17th and 18th centuries).

chamber music Vocal or instrumental music suitable for performance in a room or small hall; especially, *trios*, *quartets* and similar *concerted* pieces for solo instruments.

chamber opera An *opera* suitable for performance in a small venue, using a limited number of on-stage performers and a small orchestra (or *ensemble*).

chanson Fr., song.

chant A short, sacred song, usually unharmonised and characterised by a free, unmetred melody. See also *Gregorian chant* and *plainsong*.

character piece A musical work depicting a definite mood, impression, scene or event.

chittarone The largest member of the lute family.

chorale A hymn tune of the German Protestant Church, or one similar in style.

chorale prelude An instrumental (frequently organ) composition based on a *chorale*, often played before the sung chorale.

chord 1. A *harmony* of notes (usually three or more).
2. *Flat c.*, or *solid* c., a chord whose notes are produced simultaneously (see also *broken chord*).
3. A string.

choreography The dancing scenario in a stage work.

chorus 1. A company of singers
2. A composition, often in four parts, each sung by several or many singers; a double chorus has eight parts.
3. The refrain or *burden* of a song.

chromatic Relating to notes foreign to a given *key* (scale); as opposed to *diatonic*. *Chromatic scale*: step-wise sequence of *semitones*.

clef A character set at the head of the *staff* to fix the pitch or position of one note, and thus of the rest.

cluster See *tone cluster*.

coda A 'tail'; hence, a passage ending a *movement*.

collage The unexpected or jarring juxtaposition of musical ideas, often using *quotation* and referencing earlier styles.

coloratura Vocal runs, passages, trills, etc., enhancing the brilliance of a composition and displaying the skill of the singer (esp. soprano).

colour [tonal colour] Instrumental timbre; the contrast and blending thereof.

comédie-ballet A French play featuring spoken dialogue, songs and dance interludes. Devised by Molière during the 1660s.

commedia dell'arte Semi-improvised comic drama, popular in Italy during 16th and 17th centuries. Features stock scenes and characters with masks.

compass The pitch range of a voice or instrument.

concerted music Music written in parts for several instruments and/or voices.

concertino The group of soloists in a *concerto grosso*.

concertmaster The leader of the first violin section in the orchestra.

concerto An extended composition for solo instrument(s) and orchestra, frequently in three *movements*.

concerto grosso An instrumental composition in several *movements*, featuring passages for a small group of soloists (*concertino*) in alternation with a larger *ensemble*, or full orchestra (*ripieno* or *concerto grosso*).

conductus A medieval vocal work (12th–13th centuries), usually set in 2 to 3 parts to a sacred Latin text. Superseded by the motet.

consequent The melodic *phrase* that answers and compliments the *antecedent*.

conservatory A public or private institution for providing practical and theoretical instruction in music.

consonance A combination of two or more notes, harmonious and pleasing in itself, and requiring no further progression. *Consonant intervals*, consonances of two notes; *imperfect consonances*, the *major* and *minor* thirds and sixths; *perfect consonances*, the octave, fifth and fourth.

consort An old English term for an instrumental *ensemble*.

continuo See *basso continuo*.

counterpoint 1. The art of *polyphonic* composition.
2. Composition with two or more simultaneous melodies.

countersubject [or **countertheme**] A *fugal theme* following the subject in the same part.

countertenor A male singer, usually a falsettist, able to sing music of unusually high tessitura; a male alto.

courante A French dance in triple *metre*; a standard *movement* of the Baroque *suite*.

Credo See *Mass ordinary*.

crotchet A quarter note.

cue A short vocal or instrumental passage occurring near the end of a long pause in another part, and inserted in small notes in the latter to serve as a guide in timing its reentrance.

cyclical form A structure that repeats musical material (often a principal *theme*) across separate *movements*.

da capo From the beginning.

declamation In vocal music, clear and emphatic enunciation of the words.

degree The position of a note in a *major*, *minor* or *modal* scale, counted upwards from the *tonic*.

development 1. The procedure of changing and extending thematic material by melodic, harmonic and rhythmic elaboration, *variation*, etc.
2. A section of a piece where such procedures take place.

diatonic Relating to the notes of the standard *major* or *minor* scale.

Glossary

dirge A funeral hymn, or vocal or instrumental composition written in commemoration of the dead.

discord See *dissonance*.

dissonance A jarring combination of two or more notes. *Dissonant interval*, two notes forming a dissonance, i.e., the second, seventh, and diminished and augmented intervals; *dissonant chord*, one containing one or more dissonant intervals.

divertimento (It.) **divertissement** (Fr.) 1. A light and easy piece of instrumental music.

2. An instrumental composition in six or seven *movements*, like a *serenade*.

3. An *entr'acte* in an *opera*, in the form of a short ballet, etc.

dodecaphony 'Twelve-note', from the Greek words *dodeca* 'twelve' and *phone*, 'sound'. See *Twelve-note* music.

dominant The fifth note (*degree*) of a *major* or *minor scale*. *Dominant seventh chord*, one built on the fifth note of a major or minor scale, consisting of a major *triad* with an added minor seventh. Normally resolves onto the tonic chord.

dorian mode The mode corresponding to the *scale* from D to D on the white keys of the piano.

duet or duo 1. A composition for two voices or instruments.

2. A composition for two performers on one instrument (e.g. the piano).

3. A composition for the organ, in two parts, each to be played on a separate manual.

duple time Metrical pattern of two beats to a *measure*.

duplum In late medieval music, the second voice (above the tenor) of a *polyphonic* composition.

dynamics The varying and contrasting degrees of intensity or volume of sound.

elegy A vocal or instrumental composition of a melancholy cast, having no fixed form.

empfindsamer Stil The 'sensitive' style, exemplified in the mid-18th century output of C. P. E. Bach. Less courtly and more spontaneous than typical *galant* music.

English horn (Cor Anglais in F) A tenor instrument of the oboe family; sounds a perfect fifth below the written note.

enharmonic notes Notes similar in *pitch* but different in name; e.g. E-flat and D-sharp. Where pitch is fixed, as on a piano, the notes are identical. On instruments capable of pitch modification (voice, violin, clarinet, trombone, etc) there can be a slight difference in pitch, according to *key*. The term 'enharmonic' may be applied to *intervals*, *chords* and keys also.

ensemble 1. Any combination of two or more musicians.

2. In *opera*, a set piece for two or more soloists.

entr'acte 'Interval between acts'; hence, a light instrumental composition or short ballet, for performance between the acts of a large stage work.

entrée A term common to 17th- and 18th-century stage music:

1. An instrumental piece in a ballet or *opera*, during which characters make their entrance on stage.

2. A self-contained scene or act in a ballet or opera.

3. A subdivision of an act in ballet.

étude A study, especially one affording practice in some particular technical difficulty.

extended technique The manipulation of an instrument (voice included) to produce unorthodox and unusual sounds.

false relation The *chromatic* contradiction of a note in one part by another (e.g. F natural and F sharp), either in a single *chord* or consecutive chords.

fantasia, **fantasy** 1. An improvisation.

2. An instrumental piece in free *imitation* (16th to 18th centuries).

3. A composition free in form and improvisatory in character.

figured bass A shorthand notational method, conventional in Baroque music, presenting a bass line annotated with numbers and accidentals (flat, sharp and natural signs) signifying *harmonies* to be played, typically on a keyboard or lute-family instrument. See *basso continuo*.

Fluxus Art movement of the early 1960s, inspired by the experimental work of John Cage, which gave birth to highly original, mostly theatrical and often humorous mixed media works, frequently involving novel uses of sound.

form The structural organisation of musical materials in a composition.

forte Loud, strong (abbreviated *f*). *Fortissimo*, very loud (*ff* or *fff*).

fugue The most highly developed form of contrapuntal *imitation*, where a subject (theme) introduced by one part is taken up successively by all participating parts, thus bringing each in turn into special prominence. The subject may be 'answered' in the *dominant* in exact transposition (a 'real answer') or modified in some way (a 'tonal answer'). See also *countersubject*.

galant A term connoting pleasure, elegance and accessibility. Galant music, which rose to prominence during the early 18th century, favoured *periodic phrasing* and light, chordal accompaniment. Oppositional to the Baroque *contrapuntal* church style.

galliard A 16th/17th-century dance for two dancers, in *triple time*, merry and spirited, but not rapid. Often paired (second) with a *pavan*.

gamelan An Indonesian orchestra, variously comprising tuned gongs, chimes, metallophones, chordophones, xylophones, flutes, drums and small cymbals.

gavotte A moderately paced French dance in strongly marked *duple time*, beginning on the upbeat. An optional *movement* in the late Baroque *suite*.

gigue (**giga**) A jig; a *movement* commonly placed last in the Baroque *suite*.

glissando 1. To slide from one note to another (as in *portamento*).

2. The effect obtained by sliding a finger across the keys of a piano or the strings of a harp.

3. In some passages for strings, the rapid performance of a chromatic *scale* with one finger sliding up or down the fingerboard.

glockenspiel A set of tuned steel bars, arranged like a keyboard, struck with small hammers.

Gloria See *Mass ordinary*.

Glossary

gradual 1. An Antiphon (responsorial chant) following the Epistle.

2. A liturgical book of *chants* of the Roman Catholic *Mass*.

grand opera A style of 19th-century *opera*, usually in five acts, treating a historical (sometimes legendary or mythical) subject, sumptuously staged and featuring large *choruses* and ballet.

graphic notation A deliberately vague type of musical notation using shapes and patterns, which the performer interprets freely. Developed during early 1950s in the USA. See also *indeterminate music*.

Gregorian chant Liturgical melodies attributed to (but not necessarily authored by) Pope Gregory I (d.604). See *plainsong*.

ground bass A continually repeated bass pattern, normally of four or eight *measures*.

harmonic series A natural series of overtones, starting an octave above the fundamental note, then a fifth higher than that, a fourth higher, a major third higher, a minor third higher, etc. The first six notes, counting the fundamental, form the harmony of the major chord.

harmony 1. Any combination of musical notes.

2. (a) *Diatonic h.*, harmony containing notes of the established *key*; (b) *Chromatic h.*, harmony containing chromatic notes, foreign to the established key.

hexachord 1. The six notes *ut, re, mi, fa, sol, la* in *solmisation*.

2. A set of six different pitch classes, usually the first (or last) six of a twelve-note set. (See *twelve-note serialism*.)

homophonic Sounding together; chordal. In application to sections of music, or entire pieces: a style in which one melodic part is largely supported by sequences of chords (as opposed to *polyphonic*).

imitation The repetition of a *motive*, *phrase* or *theme* in a different part from the original, with or without modification.

impromptu A short composition, often found in ternary (A–B–A) or *variation* form, occasionally improvisatory in character. The best known are piano pieces by Schubert and Chopin.

improvise To make up spontaneously; extemporise.

incidental music Music supplementary to a spoken drama, such as an overture or interludes.

indeterminate music [indeterminacy] Music whose substance is to some degree undetermined by the composer, allowing for performer and/or conductor (in rare cases, audience) choice. See also *aleatory music* and *graphic notation*.

intermezzo 1. A light musical entertainment alternating with the acts of the early Italian tragedies.

2. *Incidental music* in modern dramas.

3. A short 19th-century instrumental composition.

interval The difference in *pitch* between two notes. Intervals are regularly measured from the lower note to the higher. *Augmented interval*, wider by a chromatic semitone than major or perfect; *compound i.*, wider than an octave.

intonation 1. The production of *tone*, either vocal or instrumental; the accuracy of *pitch*.

2. The opening *phrase* of a *plainsong* melody, sung solo before the entry of other voices.

inversion 1. The repositioning of the notes of an *interval* or *chord*. A chord is inverted when its lowest note is not the *root*. A *major* or *minor triad* thus has two possible inversions.

2. The rewriting of a melody 'upside down': ascending intervals are changed to descend by the same degree, and vice versa.

ionian mode The mode corresponding to the *scale* from C to C on the white keys of the piano; identical to the *major* scale.

jongleur A wandering medieval *minstrel* employed by royalty and aristocracy to provide light entertainment, musical and otherwise; the word itself corresponds to the English 'juggler'.

Kapellmeister (Ger., 'chapel master') Originally, a musician in charge of a court chapel. Later, a director of court music. Modern usage: a musical director of an orchestra or choir.

key 1. The tonality of music, at any given point, defined by the prevailing *diatonic scale*. *Parallel k.*, a *minor* key with the same tonic (keynote) as the given *major* key, or vice versa; *relative k.*, major and minor keys that share the same *key signature*.

2. A finger lever in the keyboard of a piano or organ.

3. A flat padded disk attached to a lever worked by the finger or thumb, closing the soundholes of various wind instruments.

key signature The sharps or flats at the head of the *staff*.

Kyrie 'Lord'. The opening division of the *Mass*. (See *Mass ordinary*.)

Ländler A German/Austrian folkdance in 3/4 time.

largo Large, broad. Slow and stately with ample breadth of style.

legato Bound, slurred; a direction to perform the passage in a smooth and connected manner.

legno, col A direction to a string player to play notes with the back (the stick) of the bow.

libretto The words of an *opera*, *oratorio*, etc. Authored by a librettist.

Lied (pl., **Lieder**) 1. Originally, any song in the German vernacular, as opposed to religious (Latin) texts.

2. In the 19th century, a song expressing deep emotion, lyrically and musically, suitable for concert (recital) performance.

3. An art song.

liturgy The written, formal religious service of the Christian Church.

lydian mode The mode corresponding to the *scale* from F to F on the white keys of the piano.

madrigal The most important secular vocal form of the late Renaissance; a short lyric love poem setting in three to eight parts (frequently four or five), *contrapuntal*, and usually for unaccompanied voices. *Solo madrigal*, popular during early Baroque (early 17th-century), commonly scored with a small *continuo ensemble*.

maestro di cappella (It., 'chapel master') Choirmaster; musical director. Equivalent of German *Kapellmeister*.

Glossary

Magnificat 'Magnificat anima mea dominum' (My soul doth magnify the Lord). Canticle of the Virgin Mary (Luke 1, 46–55), sung at Evensong or as part of the Office of Vespers in the Roman Catholic Church.

major 'Greater'; opposed to minor, or 'lesser'. To define a *key*, as in A major, or a *triad* (*chord*), or a *scale*. The major scale includes *intervals* of a major third and major sixth from the root.

march (**marcia**, It.) A composition of strongly marked *rhythm*, suitable for timing the steps of a body of persons proceeding at a walking pace. *March form* is in *duple* (2/4), compound duple (6/8), or quadruple (4/4) time, with reprises of four, eight, or sixteen *measures*, followed by a trio section, and ending with a repetition of the march. *Alla marcia*, in march style.

marimba A hammered *percussion* instrument of African origin, a larger and more mellow version of the xylophone. Commonly four octaves in range (from one octave below middle C) and constructed with large metal resonators beneath tuned wooden blocks.

masque A ceremonial entertainment, popular in 16th and 17th century England; a spectacular courtly play featuring spoken monologue and dialogue, songs, dance and instrumental music.

Mass In the Roman Catholic Church, the celebration of the Eucharist (Holy communion): 'High Mass', one celebrated with much ceremony, music and incense; 'Low Mass', a read mass, normally without hymns.

Mass ordinary [**Ordinary of the mass**] The fixed sequence of five congregational passages, set with *chorus* and sometimes instruments: (1) Kyrie (2) Gloria (3) Credo (4) Sanctus and Benedictus, (5) Agnus Dei. From the 18th century onwards, composers would often subdivide the text to create further *movements*; thus the Gloria yields several, including 'Laudamus te' and 'Qui tollis'.

Mass proper [**Proper of the mass**] The variable sequence of *plainsong* passages (Introit, Gradual, Alleluia, Sequence, Offertory and Communion), set according to the Church calendar.

matins The music sung at morning prayer; the first of the Canonical Hours.

mazurka A Polish national dance in *triple time* and moderate *tempo*.

measure The notes and rests between two bar lines; the metrical unit in a composition, with regular accentuation, familiarly called a *bar*.

mediant The third *degree* of the *scale*.

melodrama Stage declamation with a musical *accompaniment*. May refer to an entire stage work, or a section within.

melody The ordered progression of single notes.

metre [**meter**], The grouping of beats into recurring *rhythms* (partitioned, on the page, by bar lines). The *time signature* at the beginning of a piece ($\frac{3}{4}$, $\frac{4}{4}$, $\frac{6}{8}$, etc) normally indicates the prevailing metre.

microtones Intervallic divisions smaller than the *semitone* (or half tone).

minim A note equal to two *crotchets*.

Minnesingers German aristocratic poet-musicians of the 12th–14th centuries.

minor 'Smaller', used in music in two different senses:

1. To indicate a smaller *interval* of a kind, as in minor second, minor third, etc.

2. To define a *key*, as in A minor, or a *scale*, as in the A minor scale, or *triad*. Both minor scales (harmonic and melodic) feature a semitone interval between the second and third degree.

minstrel In the Middle Ages, professional musicians who sang or declaimed poems, often of their own composition, sometimes to a simple instrumental accompaniment.

minuet A French dance form, in *triple time*; usually set in A–B–A form with B-section *trio* (the trio being another minuet, traditionally more lightly textured). Popular as a third *movement* of a Classical *symphony*.

mixolydian mode The mode corresponding to the *scale* from G to G on the white keys of the piano.

modal harmony The type of harmony derived from church, exotic or invented modes, as distinct from *tonal* harmony.

modulate To pass from one key or mode into another.

monodrama A dramatic or musical presentation, with a single performer.

monody *Recitative*-like accompanied song style, originating in Italy at the end of the 16th century.

monophonic 'One sound'.
1. Music for a single part, as in unaccompanied song; an instrument capable of single sounds only.
2. Early form of one-channel recording and playback of sound.

monophony Unaccompanied *melody*; as contrasted with polyphony.

motet Medieval era: a secular *polyphonic* vocal piece for three voices with mixed texts. Renaissance: a sacred polyphonic composition for several voices, without instrumental accompaniment. Baroque and later: a sacred vocal work for one or more voices with instrumental accompaniment. (Pieces in *anthem* style are sometimes called motets.)

motive [or **motif**] A short (usually reccurring) musical figure; the smallest subdivision of a *phrase* or *subject*.

movement 1. *Tempo*.
2. A principal division or section of a composition.

multiphonics A modern method of sound production resulting in two or more sounds being produced simultaneously by one performer on a normally monophonic instrument, brass or woodwind.

musique concrète 'Concrete music'; a practice developed by French Radio engineers in 1948, in which all kinds of environmental sounds and natural noises are recorded and ordered (sometimes electronically manipulated) to form a musical work.

neo-classical [**neo-classicism**] A revival in 20th-century composition of 18th-century (or earlier) musical idioms, exemplified in many of the post-World War I works of Stravinsky and Les Six.

nocturne A piece dreamily romantic or sentimental in character, without fixed form.

notation The art of representing musical notes, and their modifications, by means of written characters.

note row [**tone row**] The fundamental musical idea in a *serial* composition, laying out all twelve notes of the chromatic *scale* in any chosen order. See *twelve-note serialism*.

Glossary

number opera An *opera* consisting of self-contained musical 'numbers'— *arias*, *ensembles* and *choruses*—and *recitative* or spoken dialogue. Term used in conjunction with much Classical opera.

obbligato Required, indispensable. An obbligato part is a concerted, essential instrumental part.

octatonic scale An eight-note *scale*, most commonly constructed from alternating *tones* and *semitones*.

octet A composition for eight voices or instruments.

ode 1. A chorus in ancient Greek plays.

2. A secular musical work of praise.

ondes martenot A monophonic electronic instrument that produces sounds with the aid of an oscillator. Invented by Maurice Martenot, *c*.1928.

opera A dramatic work, of Italian origin, in which vocal music is predominant throughout. Includes *recitatives*, *arias*, *ensembles*, *choruses* with instrumental *accompaniment*. Originally inspired by the example of classical Greek drama.

opéra-ballet A French courtly entertainment of the late 17th and 18th centuries featuring music, drama and dance.

opéra bouffe A type of 19th-century French *opera*, comical and satirical.

opera buffa Italian comic *opera* of the 18th and early 19th centuries.

opéra comique French *opera* incorporating spoken dialogue (equivalent of German *Singspiel*); not necessarily comical.

opera seria Serious (grand, heroic, tragic) *opera*.

operetta A 'little opera'; comic, mock-pathetic, parodistic, or anything but serious vein; music is light and lively, often interrupted by dialogue.

opus A musical work. Often written *Op.* or *op.* and followed by a numeral (e.g. Op. 1); traditional method for cataloguing published works.

oratorio A dramatic but unstaged composition for vocal soloists and *chorus*, with accompaniment by orchestra and/or organ.

orchestration The art of writing music for performance by an orchestra; the science of combining, in an effective manner, the instruments constituting the orchestra.

organum The first documented polyphonic music, featuring a line of plainchant with added part(s). The earliest form is *parallel organum*, where two parts progress in parallel fifths and fourths.

overture A musical introduction to an *opera*, *oratorio*, etc. A concert overture is an independent composition, frequently in *sonata form*.

panharmonicon An early 19th-century barrel organ, invented by J. N. Maezel (inventor of the metronome); very elaborate and capable of playing orchestral music.

parameter A term associated with *serialism* relating to a variable musical element, typically *timbre*, *pitch*, *rhythm*, volume.

parody mass A type of late Renaissance Mass (Ordinary), whose polyphonic materials have been lifted from another, often secular, composition.

part-song A song typically written for several voices, with melody in the highest part, others in *accompaniment*.

partita 1. A set of *variations* (16th and 17th century).

2. A *suite* (late 17th century).

3. A multi-*movement* work, similar to a *sonata* or suite (18th century).

passion A musical setting descriptive of Christ's sufferings and death, as recorded in the four gospels.

pastoral [**pastorale**] 1. A scenic *cantata* representing pastoral life; a pastoral *opera*.

2. An instrumental piece imitating in style and instrumentation rural and idyllic scenes.

pavan[**e**] A stately dance, probably of Italian origin, in *duple time* and slow *tempo*. Popular during the 16th and 17th centuries, the pavan was often paired with a faster triple-metre dance, typically a *galliard*, which might share the same theme.

pedal note A sustained or extensively repeated note.

pentatonic scale A five-note *scale*, usually that which avoids semitonic steps by skipping the fourth and seventh degrees in the *major*, and the second and sixth in the *minor*.

percussion The instrument group whose sounds are made by the striking of one body against another; includes the drum, tambourine, cymbal, bell, triangle, as well as pitched instruments such as the dulcimer, vibraphone and pianoforte.

periodic phrasing A two-part *phrase*, consisting of an *antecedent* and *consequent* (or 'question' and 'answer').

phrase Any short figure or passage unbroken in continuity, typically longer than a *motive*, shorter than a *subject*.

phrygian mode The mode corresponding to the *scale* from E to E on the white keys of the piano.

piano 1. Soft, quiet (*p*). *Pianissimo*, very quiet (*pp* or *ppp*).

2. Familiar contraction of pianoforte.

pitch The position of a note in the musical *scale*. Pitch is either relative or absolute. The relative pitch of a note is its position (higher or lower) as compared with another note. Its absolute pitch is its fixed position in the entire range of musical notes. The number of vibrations per second made by a note establishes its absolute pitch; the standard concert pitch for A directly above middle C is 440 double vibrations per second.

plainsong [**plainchant**] The unmeasured, *monophonic* vocal music of the Christian Church, probably dating from the first centuries of the Christian era. The style remains obligatory in the Roman Catholic ritual.

pluralism The use of disparate styles within a composition, sometimes simultaneously. Common to postmodern music.

polonaise A dance of Polish origin in triple *metre* and moderate *tempo*, often stately.

polychoral The combination of two or more distinct choral groups

polyphonic 1. Consisting of two or more independently treated *melodies*; *contrapuntal*.

2. Capable of producing two or more notes simultaneously, like the piano, harp or organ.

polyrhythm The combination of multiple rhythmic patterns.

polytonality The simultaneous use of two or more *keys*, common to 20th-century music. (See also *bitonality*.)

Glossary

pointillism Emphasis on single notes (commonly widely dispersed) in a serially-organised composition; a style cultivated by Webern.

portamento Smooth gliding from one note to another; used to describe a continuous glide between *pitches* (as obtainable with the voice, violin, trombone, etc.), rather than the effect of a harp or piano *glissando*.

prelude 1. A musical introduction to an instrumental composition or drama. 2. An independent composition for solo piano.

preparation (of a dissonance) In part writing, the preparation of a dissonance requires a consonant note of a chord to be sustained or repeated in the chord following, where it becomes a dissonance (a non-harmonic note).

prepared piano A modernistic practice initiated by the American composer John Cage, in which the *timbre* of a piano is altered by systematically placing such objects as screws, bolts and rubber under its strings.

presto Fast, rapid; faster than *allegro*.

prima donna A leading lady in an *opera*.

programme music A class of instrumental music (commonly orchestral) that expresses an extra-musical idea, sourced from literature, painting, nature, history, etc. Dating from the high Baroque, the approach was popularised by Liszt in the mid 19th century. (See also *symphonic poem*.)

quarter tone Half a *semitone*; an interval common to modern *microtonal* compositions, also used in some non-Western music.

quartet 1. A *concerted* instrumental composition for four performers. 2. A composition, *movement*, or number, either vocal or instrumental, in four parts. 3. The (four) performers as a group.

quaver A note half the value of a *crotchet*. An eighth note.

quintet 1. A *concerted* instrumental composition for five performers. 2. A composition, *movement*, or number, vocal or instrumental, in five parts. 3. The (five) performers as a group.

quotation The incorporation of pre-existing music, usually short fragments, in a composition.

rag or **ragtime** A *syncopated* American music of black origins, popular from the 1890s to *c*.1918. During this period the term included vocal and instrumental music, and dance styles associated with the music. As an instrumental genre, it existed as both a popular ballroom style and as the earliest form of jazz. In today's usage, the term usually refers to *solo* works in 'ragtime style' for piano.

recitative A supple style of singing, free in rhythm and tempo, that closely matches the natural rhythms and inflections of speech. Common to *opera* and *oratorio*.

relative key A term referring to *major* and *minor* keys that share the same *key signature*. The *tonic* of a major key lies a minor third above that of its relative minor. Thus the *relative minor* of C major is A minor; the *relative major* of A minor is C major.

requiem The first word in the *Mass* for the dead; hence, the title of the musical setting of that Mass.

retrograde Reverse; a *melody* performed backwards.

retrograde inversion In 12-note composition, a version of a note-row played backwards and upside-down (falling intervals rising, and vice versa).

rhapsody Generally an instrumental *fantasia* on folk songs or on *motives* taken from primitive national music.

rhythm The effect produced by the systematic grouping of notes in time, and characterised by the regularity and sequence of accentuation.

ricercar[e] Instrumental composition of the 16th and 17th centuries generally characterised by *imitative* thematic treatment.

ripieno The full *ensemble* or orchestra in a *concerto grosso*, as opposed to the *concertino* (solo group).

ritornello 1. A repeat; a return.

2. In early Baroque operatic *arias*, an instrumental prelude, interlude, or postlude.

3. In a Baroque *concerto*, the *tutti* (orchestral) refrain.

rondo An instrumental piece in which the leading *theme* (A) is repeated in its original *key*, alternating with other sections. A typical pattern, with letters representing thematic sections, would be: A–B–A–C–A–B–A.

root The note from which a chord takes its name. The chord of C major thus has a root of C.

round A type of vocal *canon* at the unison, without *coda*; sometimes with harmonic support or accompaniment, the 'pes'.

saltarello A lively *triple time* Italian dance featuring jumping movements.

Sanctus See *Mass ordinary*.

sarabande A stately, triple-*metre* dance of Spanish of Latin American origin; a standard *movement* of the Baroque *suite*.

scale A schematic series of notes in ascending or descending order. A particular scale will be defined by the notes within an octave from its root.

scena An accompanied dramatic *solo* consisting of *arioso* and *recitative* passages, and often ending with an *aria*.

scherzo A joke, jest.

1. An instrumental piece of a light, piquant, humorous character.

2. A vivacious middle *movement* in the *symphony*, with strongly marked *rhythm* and sharp and unexpected contrasts.

scordatura A change in the ordinary tuning of a stringed instrument to achieve new sonorities, effects, or easier execution.

score A systematic arrangement of the vocal and/or instrumental parts of a composition on separate *staves*. *Full* or *orchestral s.*, one in which each vocal and instrumental part has a separate staff; *Short s.*, any abridged arrangement or skeleton transcript—includes *Vocal s.*, displaying vocal parts and piano reduction of orchestral parts.

secco Dry, simple; not dwelt upon. *Recitativo secco*, recitative with a simple *figured-bass* accompaniment.

semibreve A note twice the value of a *minim*. Same as *whole note* (U.S.).

semitone Half a *tone*; a minor second.

septet 1. A *concerted* composition for seven voices or instruments.

2. The (seven) performers as a group.

sequence 1. The repetition, at different *pitch* levels and more than twice in succession, of a musical passage; may be melodic or chordal. In a *tonal*

Glossary

s., the intervals between notes are altered; in a *real s.*, the intervals remain the same.

2. In church music, a type of hymn that follows the Gradual and Alleluia.

serenade 1. An 'evening song'; especially a song sung by a lover before his lady's window.

2. An instrumental composition imitating the above in style. Ger., *Nacht-musik* (Night music).

serenata 1. A species of dramatic *cantata* in vogue during the 18th century.

2. An instrumental composition midway between a *suite* and a *symphony*, but freer in form than either, having five or more *movements*, and in chamber music style. Similar to *divertimento*.

serialism See *twelve-note music* and *total serialism*.

sextet 1. A *concerted* composition for six voices or instruments.

2. The (six) performers as a group.

shawm A medieval high-pitched wind instrument, with a double reed; an ancestor of the oboe.

sinfonia 1. A *symphony*.

2. An *overture* to an *opera*.

Singspiel (Ger., 'songplay') A type of light German *opera* featuring spoken dialogue; established during the 18th century.

solmisation A method of teaching the *scales* and *intervals* by syllables, ascribed to Guido d'Arezzo. It was based on the *hexachord*, or six-note scale; the first six notes of the major scale, *c d e f g a*, were named *ut, re, mi, fa, sol, la*. The seventh syllable *si* [later *te*], for the leading note *b*, was added during the 17th century; around the same time the name *ut* for *C* was changed to *do*, except in France.

solo Alone. A piece or passage for a single voice or instrument, or one in which one voice or instrument predominates. In orchestral scores, 'solo' marks a passage where one instrument takes a leading part.

sonata An instrumental composition in three or four extended *movements* contrasted in theme, *tempo*, and mood; usually for *solo* instrument up to chamber *ensemble*.

sonata da camera A Baroque ensemble piece suitable for chamber performance; typically a set of stylised dances.

sonata da chiesa A Baroque ensemble piece suitable for church performance; commonly set in four *movements* (slow–fast–slow–fast).

sonata form A structural procedure common to the first *movement* of a Classical *symphony, concerto, chamber* work, or *solo* or *accompanied sonata*. An organisation of conflicting tonal centres, resolving with the opening *key* (or 'home tonic'). Typically presented in a tripartite form: exposition, *development*, recapitulation.

sonatina A short *sonata* in two or three (rarely four) *movements*, the first being in abbreviated *sonata form*.

song cycle A sequence of songs unified by text or musical *theme*.

soprano The highest class of the human voice; the female soprano, or *treble*, has a normal *compass* from *c1* to *a2*; solo voices often reach above *c3*.

Stabat Mater A Latin text on the sorrow of Christ's mother as she stands at the foot of the Cross; sung in the Roman Catholic liturgy.

staff or **stave** The five parallel lines used in modern *notation* (pl., *staves*).

strophic A song structure in which the same music is used for each verse.

subdominant The fourth note (degree) of a *major* or *minor scale*; a chord (triad) built upon the fourth degree.

subject A musical idea, combining *motives* and/or *phrases*, upon which a composition or *movement* is founded; a principal *theme*. *Sonata-form* movements often feature two subjects.

suite A set or series of pieces in various sylised dance forms. The earlier suites have four chief divisions: *Allemande, Courante, Saraband* and *Gigue*; other forms introduced at will include the Bourree, Branle, Gavotte, Minuet, Musette, Passepied and *Pavane*, often before the concluding Gigue. Also referred to as Baroque Suite or Classical Suite; the modern orchestral suite is more like a *divertimento*.

suspension A *dissonance* created by suspending (holding back) a note or notes of a *chord* while the other notes change harmony; stepwise resolution follows, usually downwards.

symphonic poem A one-*movement* orchestral composition which often follows in its development the thread of a story or the ideas of a poem, repeating and interweaving its themes appropriately; it has no fixed form. Championed by Liszt in the mid 1800s.

symphony An orchestral composition containing three to five distinct *movements* or divisions, each with its own *theme(s)* and its own *development*. Typical Classical/Romantic plan: I. Allegro (often *sonata form*, sometimes with a slow introduction); II. Adagio; III. *Minuet* or *Scherzo*; IV. Allegro or Presto (often *rondo* form).

syncopation Shifting the accent in a *bar* to a weak beat or off-beat, upsetting the regular *metre* and creating rhythmic tension.

tablature 1. Early musical notation for the lute, viol, and organ. 2. A method of showing the finger-positions on stringed instruments, especially popular for teaching guitar and banjo.

Te Deum A Latin hymn of praise. ('Te Deum laudamus': Thee, O God, we praise).

temperament A system of tuning in which notes of very nearly the same *pitch*, such as C sharp and D flat, are made to sound alike by slightly 'tempering' them (that is, raising or lowering them). When applied to all the notes of an instrument (as on the modern piano), this system is called *equal temperament*. By contrast, *unequal temperament*, used formerly, gives greater tuning accuracy to some *keys* to the detriment of others.

tempo 1. Rate of speed, movement. 2. Time, *measure*. *A tempo*, return to the preceding pace.

tenor The high natural male voice, with a range from *c* to *b1*. 2. A prefix to the names of instruments of similar *compass*, such as *tenor* trombone. 3. Old English name for the viola.

textural music Music that prioritises *timbre* and atmospheric sound masses.

theme A musical *subject*; an extended and rounded off *melody* or *phrase*, proposed as the basis for *variations* or *development*.

through bass or **thorough bass** Same as *basso continuo*.

Glossary

through composed 1. Applied to a song: featuring different music for each stanza (as opposed to *strophic*).

2. Applied to a theatrical work: music scored from beginning to end.

timbre *Tone* colour or quality.

time signature A sign or number appearing at the beginning of a composition, or within it, to indicate *metre*. $\frac{3}{4}$ indicates that there are three 'quarter notes' (*crotchets*) to the bar; $\frac{6}{8}$ indicates that there are six 'eighth notes' (*quavers*) to the bar, etc.

toccata (It., from *toccare*, 'to touch') A composition for keyboard instrument, free and bold in style, consisting of runs and elaborate passages alternating with *contrapuntal* work; flowing, animated and rapid in movement.

tonality, **tonal** See *key*.

tone 1. Quality of sound.

2. An interval of a major second (also *whole tone*); *half t.*, an interval of a minor or *chromatic* second.

3. American usage for musical 'note'.

4. In acoustics, the pure note, above which upper partials sound.

5. Any one of eight liturgical *plainsong* melodies used in the Roman Catholic Church (as in 'Gregorian tone').

tone cluster Several consecutive notes, or notes lying close together, played simultaneously in a cluster. Pioneered by the US composer Henry Cowell.

tone poem Richard Strauss's preferred term for the *symphonic poem*.

tonic 1. The first note of any given *scale*.

2. The *triad* on the keynote (*tonic chord*).

3. The prevailing *key*.

total serialism [or **integral serialism**] A rigorous expansion of the *twelve-note* method into the domain of note values, dynamics, and instrumental timbres. A style associated with the 1950s–60s avant-garde.

transcription 1. A music copying process where the presentation, but not the substance, of the music is changed.

2. The writing down of music perceived by ear.

triad A *chord* of three notes: the root, third and fifth, in any inversion. *Major t.*, one comprising a major third and a minor third from the root; *minor t.*, one comprising a minor third and major third from the root; *diminished t.*, one comprising two minor thirds from the root; *augmented t.*, one comprising two major thirds from the root.

trill or **shake** The even and rapid alteration of two notes close together; the lower note is the *principal*, the higher note the *auxiliary*.

trio 1. A piece for three voices or instruments.

2. A piece set in three parts (such as a *trio sonata*).

3. In *minuets*, *marches*, etc., the *trio* or *alternative* is a second dance or march, after which the first is repeated.

trio sonata A type of Baroque chamber music written in three parts, the upper two supported by *continuo*.

triple time Metrical pattern of three beats to a *measure*, as in $\frac{3}{4}$ or $\frac{3}{8}$.

tritone An interval of three *tones* (*whole notes*); i.e. the augmented fourth (C to F sharp), or diminished fifth (C to G flat).

troubadours A class of poet-musicians, many of noble birth, originating in

Provence and flourishing from the end of the 11th century toward the close of the 13th. Their language was *langue d'oc* and they sang principally of courtly or idealised love.

trouvères A class of poet-musicians, similar to the *troubadours*, originating in the north of France; flourished from the 12th century toward the close of the 13th; their language was *langue d'oil*.

tutti The full *ensemble* or orchestra.

twelve-note serialism [twelve-note composition] Non-hierarchical method of musical organisation, most profoundly developed by Schoenberg, wherein all twelve notes of the *chromatic scale* are ordered into a *note-row* and treated on an equal basis. The term is generally interchangeable with *dodecaphony*, the result normally *atonal*.

variation One of a set or series of transformations of a theme by means of harmonic, rhythmic and melodic changes and embellishments.

verismo A type of *opera* that emerged in Italy in the 1890s, featuring mainly commoner protagonists in gritty, true-to-life situations. Stories taken from contemporary fiction or real life events.

verset In church music a short interlude for organ, taking the place of a sung part of the *liturgy*.

versicle In Church worship a short verse and response; for example:
Vers. O Lord, save Thy people,
Resp. And bless Thine inheritance.

vespers Evensong (or Evening Prayer).

vibraphone A *percussion* instrument consisting of suspended metal bars in keyboard arrangement, which, when struck with mallets, produce notes that are amplified by resonator tubes below the bars. A motor-driven mechanism causes the *vibrato* that gives the instrument its name.

vibrato A wavering or tremulous effect, typically applied to enhance expression and beauty of *tone*.

viola da gamba 'Leg viol'; a bowed stringed instrument of the 16th, 17th and early 18th centuries, typically held between the knees.

virginal A small type of harpsichord.

virtuoso A highly proficient instrumentalist or vocalist.

Wagner tuba A brass instrument introduced by Wagner for his *Ring* cycle; derived from the horn but more suited to solemn music. Made in two sizes, tenor and bass, often played by horn players.

waltz A dance in *triple time*, varying in *tempo* from slow to moderately fast.

whole note American term for the *semibreve*; in common ($\frac{4}{4}$) time a note held for four beats.

whole-tone scale A *scale* consisting only of whole-tone *intervals*; much used by Debussy.

wind quintet A quintet for five wind instruments, commonly flute, oboe, clarinet, bassoon and horn.

woodwind The group of orchestral instruments that comprises flutes and reed instruments (oboes, clarinets, bassoons, and their like). Also includes recorders and saxophones.

xylophone A *percussion* instrument consisting of a row of tuned wooden blocks, suspended on a wooden frame, and struck with mallets.

Further reading
(From a selective bibliography)

General histories

Anderson, Neil. *Baroque Music*. London: Thames and Hudson, 1994

Brown, Howard M. *Music in the Renaissance*. Englewood Cliffs (N.J.): Prentice Hall, 1976

Burney, Charles (Scholes P., ed.). *Dr. Burney's Musical Tours in Europe (1776–89)*. Oxford University Press, 1959

Carter, Tim. *Music in Late Renaissance and Early Baroque Italy*. London: B. T. Batsford Ltd, 1992

Griffiths, Paul. *Modern Music: The avant garde since 1945*. London: J. M. Dent, 1986

Griffiths, Paul. *The String Quartet: A History*. London: Thames & Hudson, 1985

Grout, Donald; Burkholder, Peter; Palisca, Claude. *A History of Western Music*. New York: Norton & Co., 2005

Heartz, Daniel. *Music in European Capitals. The Galant Style, 1720–1780*. New York: Norton & Co., 2003

Hoppin, Richard H. *Medieval Music*. New York: Norton & Co., 1978

Kimbell, David. *Italian Opera*. Cambridge University Press, 1991

Lewis, Anthony; Fortune, Nigel. *Opera and Church Music 1630–1750*. London: Oxford University Press, 1975

Morgan, Robert P. *Twentieth Century Music*. New York: Norton & Co., 1991

Nicholls, David (ed.). *The Cambridge History of American Music*. Cambridge University Press, 1998

Palisca, Claude. *Baroque Music*. Englewood Cliffs: Prentice Hall, 1991

Peyser, Joan. *To Boulez and Beyond: Music in Europe Since the Rite of Spring*. New York: Billboard Books, 1999

Price, Curtis (ed.) *The Early Baroque Era*. Basingstoke: Macmillan Press, 1993

Ringer, Alexander (ed.). *The Early Romantic Era*. London: Macmillan, 1990

Roche, Jerome. *The Madrigal*. London: Hutchinson University Library, 1972

Ross, Alex. *The Rest is Noise: Listening to the Twentieth Century*. New York: Farrar, Straus and Giroux, 2007

Sadie, Stanley, and Tyrrell, John (eds.). *The New Grove Dictionary of Music and Musicians*. London: Macmillan, 2001 (Also website: oxfordmusiconline.com)

Samson, Jim (ed.). *The Cambridge History of Nineteenth Century Music*. Cambridge University Press, 2001

Samson, Jim. (ed.). *The Late Romantic Era. From the mid-19th Century to World War I*. London: Macmillan, 1991

Schonberg, Harold C. *The Lives of the Great Composers*. London: Abacus, 1992

Schwarz, K. Robert. *Minimalists*. London: Phaidon Press Ltd, 1996

Swan, Alfred J. *Russian Music and its Sources in Chant and Folksong*. London: John Baker, 1973

Taruskin, Richard. *Music from the Earliest Notations to the Sixteenth Century*. Oxford University Press, 2010

Wollenberg, Susan, and Simon McVeigh. *Concert life in Eighteenth-Century Britain*. Aldershot: Ashgate, 2004

Young, Percy M. *A History of British Music*. London: Ernest Benn Ltd, 1967

Zaslaw, Neal (ed.). *The Classical Era*. London: Macmillan, 1989

Composers and their works

Adams, Martin. *Henry Purcell: The Origins and Development of His Musical Style*. Cambridge University Press, 2009

Arnold, Denis. *Monteverdi* (Master Musicians Series). Oxford University Press, 2000

Further reading

Ashbrook, William. *Donizetti and his Operas*.
Cambridge University Press, 1982

Blaukopf, Kurt and Herta (ed.). *Mahler: His Life, Work and World*.
London: Thames and Hudson, 1991

Borchmeyer, Dieter (Ellis, D., trans.). *Drama and the World of Richard Wagner*. Princeton & Oxford: Princeton University Press, 2003

Bowen, Meirion. *Michael Tippett*. London: Robson Books Ltd. 1997

Boyd, Malcolm. *J.S. Bach* (Oxford Composer Companions).
Oxford University Press, 1999

Braunbehrens, Volkmar. *Mozart in Vienna*. London: Andre Deutsch, 1990

Brown, David. *Tchaikovsky: A Biographical and Critical Study* (3 vols).
London: Victor Gollancz, 1978–91.

Budden, Julian. *Verdi*. London: Dent, 1985

Cairns, David. *Mozart and His Operas*. London: Allen Lane, 2006

Carpenter, Humphrey. *Benjamin Britten: A Biography*.
Faber and Faber, 1992

Chissell, Joan. *Schumann*. London: Dent, 1977

Clapham, John. *Antonín Dvořák. Musician and Craftsman*. London:
Faber & Faber, 1966

Cooper, Barry. *Beethoven*. London: Oxford University Press, 2000

Cross, Jonathan (ed.). *The Cambridge Companion to Stravinsky*
(Cambridge Companions to Music). Cambridge University Press, 2003

Del Mar, Norman. *Richard Strauss. A Critical Commentary on His Life and Works*. London: Barrie & Rockliff, 1978

DeNora, Tia. *Beethoven and the Construction of Genius*.
University of California Press, 1995

Einstein, Alfred. *Mozart*. London: Granada, 1977

Frisch Walter (ed.). *Schoenberg and His World*.
Princeton University Press, 1999

Gibbs, Christopher. *The Cambridge Companion to Schubert*. Cambridge University Press, 1997.

Griffiths, Paul; Neighbour, Oliver; Perle, George. *Second Viennese School* (New Grove Composer Biography) London: Macmillan, 1983

Hill, Peter; Simeone, Nigel. *Messiaen*. Yale University Press, 2005

Keates, Jonathan. *Handel: The Man & His Music*. London: Pimlico, 2009

Kirkpatrick, Ralph. *Domenico Scarlatti*. Princeton University Press (Rev edition), 1983

Kolneder, Walter (Searle, H., trans.). *Anton Webern: An Introduction to His Works*. London: Faber and Faber, 1968

Kurtz, Michael (Toop R., trans.) *Stockhausen: A Biography*. London: Faber and Faber, 1994

Landon, Howard C. Robbins. *The Mozart Compendium*. London: Thames & Hudson, 1990

Landon, H.C. Robbins; Wyn Jones, David. *Haydn: His Life and Music*. London: Thames & Hudson, 1988

Lockspeiser, Edward. *Debussy: His Life and Mind* (2 vols). London: Cassel, 1962 & 1965

Lockwood, Lewis. *Beethoven: the music and the Life*. New York: Norton & Co., 2003

Macdonald, Hugh. *Berlioz*. London: Dent, 1982

Moore, Jerrold Northrop. *Edward Elgar: A Creative Life*. Oxford University Press, 1984

Musgrave, Micheal. *The Music of Brahms*. Oxford: Clarendon, 1994

Nectoux, Jean-Michel (Nichols, R., trans.). *Gabriel Fauré. A Musical Life*. Cambridge University Press, 1991

Newbould, Brian. *Schubert: The Music and the Man*. Berkeley: University of California Press, 1997

Nicholls, David. *The Cambridge Companion to John Cage*. Cambridge University Press, 2002

Orledge, Robert. *Satie the Composer*. Cambridge University Press, 1990

Further reading

Osborne, Charles, *The Complete Operas of Wagner*. London: Gollancz, 1992

Osborne, Richard. *Rossini*. London: Dent, 1986

Rosen, Charles. *The Classical Style: Haydn, Mozart, Beethoven*. London: Faber and Faber, 1977

Siepman, Jeremy. *Chopin: The Reluctant Romantic*. London: Victor Gollancz, 1995

Steinitz, Richard. *György Ligeti: Music of the Imagination*. London: Faber and Faber, 2003

Stevens, Halsey. *The Life and Music of Béla Bartók*. (Revised ed. 1964.) Oxford University Press, 1972

Talbot, Michael. *Vivaldi*. Master Musicians. London: J. M. Dent, 1993

Todd, R. Larry. *Mendelssohn: A Life in Music*. London: Oxford University Press, 2003

Walker, Alan. *Franz Liszt* (3 vols). London: Faber and Faber, 1983–96

Warrack, John. *Carl Maria von Weber*. Cambridge University Press, 1976

Westrup, Jack. *Schubert Chamber Music*. London: Ariel, 1986

Williamson, John (ed.). *The Cambridge Companion to Bruckner*. Cambridge University Press, 2004

Wolff, Christoph. *Johann Sebastian Bach: The Learned Musician*. New York: Oxford University Press, 2001

Autobiographies, published letters, journals, etc.

Adams, John. *Hallelujah Junction: Composing an American Life*. London: Faber and Faber, 2008

Beethoven, Ludwig van (Hamburger, Michael, trans., ed.). *Letters, Journals and Conversations*. London: Thames & Hudson Ltd, 1984

Berlioz, Hector (Cairns, David, trans., ed.). *The Memoirs of Berlioz*. London: Panther, 1971

Blom, Eric (ed.). *Mozart's Letters*. London: Penguin, 1961

Hensel, Fanny Mendelssohn. *Letters of Fanny Hensel to Felix Mendelssohn*. New York: Pendragon Press, 1986

Henze, Hans Werner. *Bohemian Fifths: An Autobiography*. Princeton University Press, 1999

Litzmann, Berthold (ed.). *Letters of Clara Schumann and Johannes Brahms, 1853–1896* (2 vols). New York: Vienna House, 1973

Shostakovich, Dmitri (Volkov, S., ed.). *Testimony: The Memoirs of Dmitri Shostakovich*. London: Faber and Faber, 1987

Stravinsky, Igor. *Igor Stravinsky: An Autobiography*. New York: Norton & Co, 1962

Wagner, Richard (Gray, A., trans.). *My Life*. Cambridge University Press, 1987

Musical aesthetics, collected essays and writings, etc.

Bacharach, Alfred L., and Pearce John R. (eds.). *The Musical Companion*. London: Victor Gollancz, 1977

Barzun, Jacques (ed.). *Pleasures of Music*. London: Cassell and Co., 1977

Hanslick, Eduard (Payzant, G., trans.). *On the Musically Beautiful* (1854). Indianapolis: Hackett Publishing, 1986

Schoenberg, Arnold (Black, L., trans.). *Style and Idea*. London: Faber and Faber, 1984

Schumann, Robert. *On Music and Musicians*. London: Dobson, 1956

Vaughan Williams, Ralph. *National Music and Other Essays*. Oxford University Press, 1987

Picture credits

Picture credits

Index

Index

A

Index

Index

Index

Index

Index

Index

Index

Index

Index

Index

Index

Index

Index

Index

Index

Index

Index

S

Index

Index

Index

Index

Index

W

Index

About the authors

Jon Paxman is a freelance writer on music and the principal author and editor of this volume. He has worked regularly with the Music Sales Group since 2001, notably for Wise Publications and Omnibus Press. Between 1999 and 2010 Jon was also active as a music arranger in television and film, and contributed to the informative anthology *European Film Music* (Ashgate, 2006).

Terry Barfoot is a much in demand lecturer and widely-published writer on music. He is Publications Consultant to the Bournemouth Symphony Orchestra and Vice President of the Arthur Bliss Society. With his own company, Arts in Residence, Terry hosts musical events at agreeable locations throughout Britain and Europe.

Dr Katy Hamilton lectures on Performance History at the Royal College of Music. An active scholar and pianist, she is a specialist in the vocal music of Johannes Brahms and his contemporaries. She is a contributor and co-editor on the forthcoming volume *Brahms in the Home* published by Cambridge University Press.

Thomas Lydon is a freelance writer, editor and composer. He is currently editor of *Music Teacher* magazine and is a regular arranger for the Novello Choral Pops series. He also writes for *Classical Music* and *Opera Now* magazines and has contributed articles on opera and early music to Universal Music's online resource sinfinimusic.com

Dr Robert Rawson is a musicologist and performer who specialises in music before *c*.1800. He is published in leading journals including *Early Music*, *Eighteenth Century Music* and *Early Music Performer*. He has also contributed to The New Grove Dictionary of Music and Musicians and is the author of *Bohemian Baroque—Czech Musical Culture and Style 1600–1750* (Boydell & Brewer, 2013).